Handbook of
THE PSYCHOLOGY OF AGING

THE HANDBOOKS OF AGING

Consisting of Three Volumes:

Critical comprehensive reviews of
research knowledge, theories,
concepts, and issues

Editor-in-Chief: **James E. Birren**

Handbook of the Biology of Aging

Edited by Caleb E. Finch and Leonard Hayflick

Handbook of the Psychology of Aging

Edited by James E. Birren and K. Warner Schaie

Handbook of Aging and the Social Sciences

Edited by Robert H. Binstock and Ethel Shanas

Editorial Committee

Vern L. Bengtson • Robert H. Binstock • James E. Birren • Jack Botwinick • Harold Brody • Sheila Chown • Carl Eisdorfer • Caleb E. Finch • Leonard Hayflick • George L. Maddox • Isadore Rossman • K. Warner Schaie • Ethel Shanas • F. Marott Sinex • Dorothy Wedderburn

Handbook of
THE PSYCHOLOGY OF AGING

Editors
James E. Birren
K. Warner Schaie

With the assistance of Associate Editors
Jack Botwinick
Sheila Chown
Carl Eisdorfer

VAN NOSTRAND REINHOLD COMPANY
NEW YORK   CINCINNATI   ATLANTA   DALLAS   SAN FRANCISCO
LONDON   TORONTO   MELBOURNE

Van Nostrand Reinhold Company Regional Offices:
New York   Cincinnati   Atlanta   Dallas   San Francisco

Van Nostrand Reinhold Company International Offices:
London   Toronto   Melbourne

Manufactured in the United States of America

Published by Van Nostrand Reinhold Company
135 West 50th Street, New York. N. Y. 10020

Published simultaneously in Canada by Van Nostrand Reinhold Ltd.

15 14 13 12 11 10 9 8 7

Library of Congress Cataloging in Publication Data

Main entry under title:

Handbook of the psychology of aging.

   (The Handbooks of aging)
   Includes bibliographies.
   1. Aged—Psychology—Addresses, essays, lectures.
I. Birren, James E.   II. Schaie, Klaus Warner, 1928–
III. Series.   [DNLM: 1. Aging.   2. Psychology. WT150
H236]
BF724.8.H36   155.67   76-40900
ISBN 0-442-20797-2

CONTRIBUTORS

David Arenberg, Ph.D.
Chief, Learning and Problem Solving Section, Gerontology Research Center, National Institute on Aging, National Institutes of Health, Baltimore, Maryland

Paul B. Baltes, Ph.D.
Professor of Human Development, College of Human Development, Division of Individual & Family Studies, The Pennsylvania State University, University Park, Pennsylvania

Benjamin Bell, M.D.
Formerly Director, Normative Aging Study, Veterans Administration Outpatient Clinic, Boston; Boston University School of Medicine, Boston, Massachusetts

Vern L. Bengtson, Ph.D.
Laboratory Chief, Laboratory for Social Organization and Behavior, Andrus Gerontology Center; Associate Professor of Sociology, University of Southern California, Los Angeles, California

James E. Birren, Ph.D.
Executive Director, Andrus Gerontology Center; Dean, Leonard Davis School of Gerontology; Professor, Department of Psychology, University of Southern California, Los Angeles, California

William Bondareff, M.D., Ph.D.
Professor and Chairman, Department of Anatomy, Northwestern University Medical School, Chicago, Illinois

Jack Botwinick, Ph.D.
Director, Aging and Development Program; Professor, Department of Psychology, Washington University, St. Louis, Missouri

Sheila M. Chown, Ph.D.
Department of Psychology, Bedford College, University of London, London, England

John F. Corso, Ph.D.
Distinguished Professor of Psychology and Chairman, Department of Psychology, State University of New York, Cortland, New York; Visiting Research Scientist, Department of Otolaryngology and Communication Sciences, State University of New York Upstate Medical Center, Syracuse, New York

Fergus I. M. Craik, Ph.D.
Professor, Department of Psychology, Erindale College, University of Toronto, Mississauga, Ontario, Canada

Carl Eisdorfer, Ph.D., M.D.
Professor and Chairman, Department of Psychiatry and Behavioral Sciences, University of Washington, Seattle, Washington

Merrill F. Elias, Ph.D.
Associate Director for Research, All-University Gerontology Center, Associate Professor, Department of Psychology, Syracuse University, Syracuse, New York

Penelope Kelly Elias, Ph.D.
NIA Postdoctoral Fellow, Department of Psychology, Syracuse University, Syracuse, New York

Trygg Engen, Ph.D.
Professor of Psychology, Walter S. Hunter Laboratory of Psychology, Brown University, Providence, Rhode Island

James L. Fozard, Ph.D.
Co-Director for Psychosocial Activities, Geriatric Research, Education and Clinical Center, Veterans Administration Outpatient Clinic, Boston, Massachusetts; Assistant Clinical Professor of Psychiatry, Department of Psychiatry, Harvard Medical School, Boston, Massachusetts

Vladimir V. Frolkis, D.M.S.
Professor, Chief, Laboratory of Psyciology and Experimental Department, Institute of Gerontology AMS USSR, Kiev, USSR

David Gutmann, Ph.D.
Professor, Department of Psychology, University of Michigan, Ann Arbor, Michigan

Patricia L. Kasschau, Ph.D.
Research Associate, Andrus Gerontology Center; Assistant Professor, Department of Sociology, University of Southern California, Los Angeles, California

Dan R. Kenshalo, Ph.D.
Professor of Psychology, Florida State University, Tallahassee, Florida

M. Powell Lawton, Ph.D.
Director, Behavioral Research, Philadelphia Geriatric Center; Adjunct Professor of Human Development, The Pennsylvania State University

Marjorie Fiske Lowenthal
Professor and Director, Human Development Program, Department of Psychiatry, University of California, San Francisco, California

Ross A. McFarland, Ph.D.
Guggenheim Professor of Aerospace Health and Safety, Emeritus, Harvard School of Public Health, Boston, Massachusetts

Gail R. Marsh, Ph.D.
Associate Professor of Medical Psychology, Senior Fellow, Center for the Study of Aging and Human Development, Lecturer, Department of Psychology, Duke University, Durham, North Carolina

John R. Nesselroade, Ph.D.
Professor of Human Development, College of Human Development, Division of Individual and Family Studies, The Pennsylvania State University, University Park, Pennsylvania

Bernice L. Neugarten, Ph.D.
Professor, Committee on Human Development, Department of Behavioral Sciences, University of Chicago, Chicago, Illinois

Gilbert S. Omenn, M.D., Ph.D.
Associate Professor, Department of Medicine, Division of Medical Genetics, University of Washington, Seattle, Washington

Eric Pfeiffer, M.D.
Professor of Psychiatry, Duke University School of Medicine; Associate Director for Programs, Center for the Study of Aging and Human Development, Duke University, Durham, North Carolina

Stephen Podolsky, M.D., F.A.C.P.
Chief, Endocrinology and Metabolism Section, Boston Veterans Administration Outpatient Clinic; Assistant Professor of Medicine, Boston University School of Medicine, Boston, Massachusetts

Patrick Rabbitt, Ph.D.
Fellow, The Queen's College Oxford; Lecturer in Psychology, University of Oxford, Oxford, England

Pauline K. Ragan, Ph.D.
Research Associate, Andrus Gerontology Center; Assistant Professor, Department of Sociology, University of Southern California, Los Angeles, California

V. Jayne Renner, Ph.D. (candidate)
University of Adelaide; Research Assistant, Andrus Gerontology Center, University of Southern California, Los Angeles, California

Klaus F. Riegel, Ph.D.
Professor, Department of Psychology, University of Michigan, Ann Arbor, Michigan

Elizabeth Robertson-Tchabo
Gerontology Research Center, National Institute of Aging, National Institutes of Health, Baltimore, Maryland

Joyce P. Schaie, Ph.D.
Post-Doctoral Fellow, Department of Psychology, University of California at Los Angeles, Los Angeles, California

K. Warner Schaie, Ph.D.
Director, Gerontology Research Institute, Andrus Gerontology Center; Professor, Department of Psychology, University of Southern California, Los Angeles, California

Nathan W. Shock, Ph.D.
Chief, Gerontology Research Center, National Institute on Aging, National Institutes of Health, Bethesda, Maryland; Baltimore City Hospitals, Baltimore, Maryland

Bernard A. Stotsky, M.D., Ph.D.
Associate Director of Psychiatric Education at St. Elizabeth's Hospital of Boston; Professor of Psychiatry and Behavioral Sciences, University of Washington, Seattle, Washington; Professor of Psychology, Boston State College; Associate Professor of Psychiatry, Tufts University School of Medicine

Larry W. Thompson, Ph.D.
Professor and Area Head, Developmental/Aging Program, Department of Psychology; Chief, Developmental Psychology Research Laboratory, Andrus Gerontology Center, University of Southern California, Los Angeles, California

A. T. Welford, Sc.D.
Professor, Department of Psychology, The University of Adelaide, Adelaide, South Australia

Frances Wilkie, M.A.
Department of Psychiatry and Behavioral Sciences, School of Medicine, University of Washington, Seattle, Washington

Sherry L. Willis, Ph.D.
Assistant Professor of Human Development, Division of Individual and Family Studies, College of Human Development, The Pennsylvania State University, University Park, Pennsylvania

Ernst Wolf, Ph.D.
Senior Scientist, Retina Foundation, Boston, Massachusetts; Lecturer in Opthamology, Harvard Medical School, Boston, Massachusetts

FOREWORD

This volume is one of three handbooks of aging: the *Handbook of the Biology of Aging*; the *Handbook of the Psychology of Aging*; and the *Handbook of Aging and the Social Sciences*. Because of the increase in literature about the many facets of aging, there has been an increasing need to collate and interpret existing information and to make it readily available in systematic form, providing groundwork for the more efficient pursuit of research. The phenomena and issues of aging cut across many scientific disciplines and professions, and a review of research necessarily involves many experts. A decision was made, therefore, to develop a multidisciplinary project, the purpose of which was to organize, evaluate, and interpret research data, concepts, theories, and issues on the biological, psychological, and social aspects of aging.

It is expected that investigators will use these books as the basic systematic reference works on aging, resulting in the stimulation and planning of needed research. Professional personnel, policy-makers, practitioners, and others interested in research, education, and services to the aged will undoubtedly find the volumes useful. The new handbooks will also provide a compendium of information for students entering and pursuing the field of gerontology and will, we hope, also stimulate the organization of new courses of instruction on aging.

The Editorial Committees generated the final outline of each volume, suggested contributors, and discussed sources of information and other matters pertinent to the development of the work. Committee recommendations were reviewed by the Advisory Board and the Editor-in-Chief.

Project Advisory Board

Vern L. Bengtson
Robert H. Binstock
James E. Birren
Sheila M. Chown
Caleb E. Finch
Leonard Hayflick
K. Warner Schaie
Ethel Shanas
Nathan W. Shock
F. Marott Sinex

James E. Birren, *Editor-in-Chief*

Editorial Committees

Handbook of the Biology of Aging

Harold Brody
Caleb E. Finch (Co-Editor)
Leonard Hayflick (Co-Editor)
Isadore Rossman
F. Marott Sinex

Handbook of the Psychology of Aging

James E. Birren (Co-Editor)
Jack Botwinick
Sheila M. Chown
Carl Eisdorfer
K. Warner Schaie (Co-Editor)

Handbook of Aging and the Social Sciences

Vern L. Bengtson
Robert H. Binstock (Co-Editor)

George L. Maddox
Ethel Shanas (Co-Editor)
Dorothy Wedderburn

There are many individuals who contributed to the successful completion of this publication project: Phoebe S. Liebig, Project Coordinator; Julie L. Moore, Research Bibliographer; Project Assistants Barbara H. Johnson, Aelred R. Rosser, Rochelle Smalewitz, and Robert D. Nall; Editorial Assistant V. Jayne Renner; Copy Editors Robert D. Nall and Judy Aklonis (social sciences), James Gollub (psychology), and Peggy Wilson and Carolyn Croissant (biology); Julie L. Moore, Indexing; and Library Assistance, Emily H. Miller and Jean E. Mueller. It is impossible to give the details of their many and varied contributions to the total effort, but they reflect the best traditions of respect for scholarship.

The preparation of the handbooks has been a nonprofit venture; no royalties are paid to any individual or institution. The intent was to give the books a wide circulation on an international level and to reduce publication costs.

The project was supported by a grant from the Administration on Aging under the title "Integration of Information on Aging: Handbook Project," Grant Number 93-P-75181/9, to the University of Southern California, with James E. Birren as the principal investigator. The Editor and his associates wish to thank Dr. Marvin Taves, who encouraged the development of the project as a staff member of the Administration on Aging, and also the agency itself, which perceived the value of such work and provided the grant for its support.

JAMES E. BIRREN

PREFACE

The purpose of preparing this *Handbook of the Psychology of Aging* is to provide an authoritative review and reference source of the scientific and professional literature on the psychological and behavioral aspects of aging. While most of the volume is devoted to the behavioral aspects of human aging, there is material on infrahuman species as well. The development of this reference work was thought to be essential in bringing together a widely scattered research literature. Since the publication of the first handbook on the behavioral aspects of aging in 1959 (*Handbook of Aging and the Individual*. Chicago: University of Chicago Press), the growth of the published literature has been dramatic.

Primarily, the book is intended for use by graduate students, researchers and professionals who require a definitive reference work. The present *Handbook* shows a broad concern for all behavioral processes from primary sensory phenomena to personality and behavior deviation. In the various chapters, the authors attempt to explain change in behavior and capacities which occur with advancing age and also generational differences or the differences between age groups. Such age-related phenomena are examined in terms of both biological and social determinants.

While the Editors and the Advisory Committee sought to develop a definitive and comprehensive work, the individual chapters could not include all the references on any particular topic. This is becoming increasingly difficult as the volume of literature is growing. Rather than attempt an exhaustive citation, the choice was to present systematic treatments in terms of basic principles, theories, and issues. While no great attention was given to practical problems of individuals, the book clearly provides the scientific basis which gives justification and directions for many practical services to older adults.

The Editorial Committee for this volume consisted of Drs. James E. Birren, Jack Botwinick, Sheila M. Chown, Carl Eisdorfer and K. Warner Schaie. This committee met to discuss possible outlines of the book and to discuss potential contributors. Their dedication to the task of identifying the right topic and the right persons to do the chapters was admirable. It was a pleasure to be associated with colleagues who were so well informed, cooperative, and so generous with their time. About five years elapsed from the time the original project was discussed to the time of publication, with the earlier years mostly involved in planning the total project.

The scope of this book is but one expression of the dramatic increase of interest in the subject matter of human aging. In few other areas do psychologists have as much to contribute in terms of research which has implications for the well-being of millions of people and for the health of our society. It is expected that the publication of this volume will facilitate the organization of research and courses in the psychology of aging and research seminars.

It has been a pleasure to have the support of the Administration on Aging of the Department of Health, Education and Welfare and to have the opportunity of working with scientific and professional colleagues and a dedicated staff in producing this book.

James E. Birren
K. Warner Schaie

CONTENTS

PART THREE

Environmental and Health Influences on Aging and Behavior 249

PART FOUR
Behavioral Processes

PART 1 BACKGROUND

1
RESEARCH ON THE PSYCHOLOGY OF AGING:
Principles and Experimentation

James E. Birren

and

V. Jayne Renner

University of Southern California

The purpose of this chapter is to provide a perspective on research in the psychology of aging. A large increase in the number of scientific and professional publications on aging, perhaps a doubling of the total volume of literature, has occurred in the last 15 years. In the 1959 *Handbook* (Birren, 1959b), there was one chapter on principles of research on aging. The subject matter has expanded sufficiently for the current volume to include several chapters in order that adequate coverage be given to research design, methods and theory.

This chapter introduces some of the elements of research on the psychology of aging and will orient the reader to the chapters that follow. This includes definitions, concepts and different contemporary perspectives on aging with a particular focus on experimental studies. Psychology is a biological, behavioristic and social science. Nowhere is this more apparent than in considerations of aging. It seems desirable at the outset to contrast some definitions and concepts which influence the directions of research into aging.

DEFINITIONS OF AGING

In common practice, developmental psychology usually refers to the differentiation of the organism up to the age of physical maturity, and aging refers to the changes or differentiation after the age of physical maturity. While adult behavior can have antecedents in childhood and distinctions between development and aging may be somewhat arbitrary, if not undesirable, development does appear to be characterized by increases in size, form, and function of the organism in a somewhat parallel fashion with age. In contrast, after physical maturity is reached, there may be selective reductions in function or reorganization in functions and structures. However, there are some processes, like the storage of information, which increase with adult age so that after physical maturity is reached there is not a simple reduction in psychological capacities. One might say that the basic scientific question for general psychology is: How *is* behavior in the adult organized? Similarly, it can be said that the basic question for developmental psychology is: How does behavior *become* organized? The latter seems to be the more dynamic and relevant question.

Few psychologists have defined aging. In contrast, more biologists are willing to limit the topic of discourse with a definition. One of the earlier influences on the study of aging was the activity of the Josiah Macy Jr. Foundation which led to the publication of E. V. Cowdry's, *Problems of Ageing*, published in 1939. Cowdry did not offer a formal definition but he did make a statement that is an equivalent, "Since almost all living organisms pass through a sequence of changes, characterized by growth, development, maturation, and finally senescence, ageing presents a broad biological problem" (Cowdry, 1942, p. XV). He distinguished two main points of view that are similar to those found today in psychology. "Two conflicting views are held today by students of ageing in man. One considers ageing as an involutionary process which operates cumulatively with the passage of time and is revealed in different organ systems as inevitable modifications of cells, tissues, and fluids. The other view interprets the changes found in aged organs as structural alterations due to infections, toxins, traumas, and nutritional disturbances or inadequacies giving rise to what are called degenerative changes and impairments" (Cowdry, 1942, p. XVI). Here one finds that an endogenous (genetic) causality is contrasted with an exogenous (environmental) causality as in the early nature versus nurture viewpoints in developmental psychology.

Later biologists preferred a narrower definition of aging than that stated by Cowdry. Thus, Comfort defined it this way: "Senescence is a change in the behavior of the organism with age, which leads to a decreased power of survival and adjustment" (Comfort, 1956, p. 190). He used the term *senescence* in place of *aging* to avoid some of the everyday implications of the use of the term aging. As yet, however, the term *senescence* has not replaced aging in either scientific discourse or daily speech when a narrower biological causality is implied.

A still more specific definition of aging was offered by Handler, "Aging is the deterioration of a mature organism resulting from time-dependent, essentially irreversible changes intrinsic to all members of a species, such that,

with the passage of time, they become increasingly unable to cope with the stresses of the environment, thereby increasing the probability of death" (Handler, 1960, p. 200). Such definitions, while precise, are probably too restrictive to psychologists who are not only interested in aging in the sense of behavior that relates to life limiting phenomena, or to the probability of dying, but also in incremental processes or differentiation of behavior that may occur concurrently with an increasing probability of dying.

The authors offer the following definition of aging for the behavioral sciences, since it does not imply an exclusively biological, environmental, or social causality, and keeps the door open for the study of the incremental as well as decremental changes in functions which occur over the life span. *Aging refers to the regular changes that occur in mature genetically representative organisms living under representative environmental conditions as they advance in chronological age.* To further restrict the definition, one can insert the word *behavioral* to modify the term, changes. By restricting consideration to genetically representative organisms, we avoid the rare or unusual which is not typical of most members of a species. Similarly, by restricting the definition to organisms living under representative conditions (i.e., conditions under which the organisms evolved or are commonly found) keeps the definition coordinate with what most people have in mind when they discuss aging. (For a fuller discussion of representativeness see Birren, 1959a, pp. 26–30.) One should be aware, however, that investigators can become overly concerned with definitions, a tendency that is more likely to appear in the absence of data. Refined definitions of aging sharpen our discourse but cannot substitute for clarification resulting from research information.

TYPES OF AGE

Since investigators frequently consider different dependent variables in their research on aging, it is useful to differentiate three aspects of human age and aging. The *biological age* of an individual can be defined as an estimate of the individual's present position with respect to his potential life span. Presumably, the measurement of biological age would encompass measurements of the functional capacities of the vital life-limiting organ systems. Such an assessment leads to a prediction as to whether the individual is older or younger than other persons of the same chronological age and hence whether the individual has a longer or shorter life expectancy than other persons of his average age. Thus, a person with a young biological age has a long life expectancy with regard to the species potential for life span.

Psychological age can, by definition, refer to the adaptive capacities of individuals, that is, how well they can adapt to changing environmental demands in comparison with the average. Clearly, psychological age is influenced by the state of key organ systems like the brain and the cardiovascular system, but it also goes considerably beyond this and involves the study of memory, learning, intelligence, skills, feeling, motivation, and emotions. The concept of *functional age* is closely related to psychological age. Functional age is an individual's level of capacities relative to others of his age for functioning in a given human society. The concept of functional age needs refinement as a construct, and as an applied and experimental tool before its usefulness is fully realized.

Social age refers to the roles and social habits of an individual with respect to other members of a society. Compared with the expectations of his group and society, does an individual behave younger or older than one would expect from his chronological age? Since the basis of age-graded, expected behavior is a product of one's culture, both biological and psychological characteristics of individuals enter the societal norms and the values of society.

CONCEPTS AND THEORY

At the time Cowdry edited his second edition of *Problems of Ageing*, he wrote: "A general theory of ageing is very difficult, if not impossible to formulate at the present time since the rate and expression of ageing vary widely in different organisms: some plants, protozoa and insects, for example, do not exhibit the usual sequence of changes nor undergo what is called senescence," (Cowdry, 1942, p. XV). There is still no general theory of aging and the few that

have been proposed are quite narrow or specific in character. Thus, the psychology of aging is predominantly a problem and data oriented area of research as the chapters in this *Handbook* by Shock (Chapter 5), Lowenthal (Chapter 6), and Baltes (Chapter 7) indicate. Largely, the psychology of aging appears to be a collection of concepts and hypotheses proposed to explain or predict limited aspects of behavior. There has been no pressure on the field to produce a unifying theory to explain how behavior becomes organized over time, and there is great diversity in the subject matter.

Simplistically, there are four points of view represented in this chapter in which the independent variables are: (a) biological, (b) behavioral, (c) social, or (d) the results of interactions between these three. Biologically oriented research tends to use length of life, susceptibility to disease, or life-limiting functions related to survival as the dependent variable. Because psychological research has often examined those behavioral processes or functions that relate to longevity, or susceptibility to disease, it has sometimes been characterized erroneously as reflecting a "biodecrement model" of aging. While it appears true that biologically oriented psychologists have examined decrements in function, their experimental manipulations are often designed to perturb the organism or its environment so that the decremental relationships can be understood and thereby modified or prevented. Behavioral and socially oriented research often is more interested in what the individual does in either an inter- or intrapersonal sense without consideration of length of life. Since psychologists are rarely trained as both biological and social investigators, one does not find much research that explores the results of bio-social interactions. Presumably, we will see more research of an interactive nature as investigators acquire the background and interest to form multidisciplinary teams.

THE NATURE OF TIME

The topic of aging encompasses both our objective and subjective approaches to time. Some experimental scientists object to the use of the term *aging*, since they believe that time cannot cause anything, and one cannot have a science based on the organization of events in time. This proposition, however, does not seem to be a constructive one. For example, it can be pointed out that the origins of astronomy as a science depended upon observations of recurrent patterns that occurred in the positions of the planets and stars. Subsequently, the periodicities in the movements of these bodies began to be explained in terms of other variables. Extracting time from astronomy would have prevented the development of astronomy as a science. Similarly, it would seem to unduly hobble or restrict scientific inquiry by blind adherence to a belief that since time doesn't cause anything there cannot be a science of aging. The reader is referred to the *Handbook of Aging and the Individual* in which there is an extensive review on the position of time and aging in the natural sciences (Reichenbach and Mathers, 1959, pp. 43–80). Perhaps behavioral scientists are less exposed to time dependent processes than are biologists and are more frustrated in attempts to explain phenomena of aging that are partially time dependent.

To be a cause of something, the cause must occur before the consequence, and the ordering of events in time is crucial to understanding the development of mankind. Concepts of the Stone Age, Bronze Age, and Iron Age require that we be able to determine or measure sequence. Indeed, much effort is spent in anthropology in dating bits of pottery, carvings, and skeletal remains, to test an explanation of the development of culture. How the North American continent was settled, by whom, and when, requires detailed measurements of the age of objects. In this sense the social scientist only uses time as an index. However, the measurement of the age of an object can take advantage of time dependent processes within it. For example, the shift in amino acid composition in bone with time can be utilized in dating a skull.

In some inorganic systems, the regularity of a molecular change is so great that it can be used as a measure of time and as a standard for other time determinations. A somewhat similar relation may exist in survival of life forms phylogenetically lower than man in which the survival curve is exponential in character (Landahl, 1959, p. 86). Thus, the ratio of animals alive, to those born at some initial time is a decreasing

exponential function of age. The probability of dying in such living systems does not change; unlike human populations which show an increasing probability of dying after the approximate age of 10 years. It is possible that there may be relationships between time and molecular changes within cells or cell assemblies that impart a strong biochronicity to the organism. In such instances, the relationships with age are so intimate (as in the exponential survival curve) that time or age may be alternately used as the dependent or the independent variable.

Reichenbach and Mathers (1959) point out that in a large system, time direction can be different for its subsystems. By analogy, the human organism may have a subsystem which is growing "older" concurrent with another subsystem which is growing "younger." Thus one might attempt to describe an individual in terms of the biological age of the organs, e.g., nervous system, heart, skin, etc. Many cells of the body regenerate (e.g., liver) and during a period of regeneration the average age of the cells of an organ might be younger than at some prior interval. As a consequence, the functional capacity of the organ might also be greater at a later date.

Failure of a critical subsystem of the organism would limit the survival of the whole organism. Thus, knowing the average age of the subsystem or organ system does not necessarily permit a valid prediction of organism survival since a failure of only one subsystem could limit the life of the whole organism. Among the life-limiting subsystems or organs, the ones that are potentially more important are those that are primarily composed of cells fixed at their present level of differentiation, and which may no longer contain primitive precursor cells in the tissues. Such fixed, postmitotic cells include the neuron and heart muscle cells. These cells have lost their capacity for further mitotic division and remain with the individual "from birth to death" unless as an individual cell it dies earlier than the others. (In the instance of the nervous system, loss of neurons can occur during the life span of the individual.) Aging may also be due to a failure in the mechanisms of the cell as has been proposed by recent models in the study of immunology and cancer; these will be examined for their implications in the processes of aging.

Since the nervous system is not only essential to the organization of behavior but also to the regulation of vital vegetative functions, it is one of the key organ systems within which to study aging. Its aging presumably will not only be reflected in changes in behavior but also in a changing probability of survival. It is possible that the nervous system (along with the immune system) becomes one of the critical life-limiting organ systems in those individuals surviving both infectious diseases of early life and middle age diseases such as arteriosclerosis and diabetes.

The quality of life is limited by the integrity of the aging nervous system. Thus for the behavioral scientist, aging has an important dual aspect in which the cellular changes of the nervous system may determine behavioral capacities, and in which behavior patterns may influence the rate and mode of aging of cells of the nervous system. As the prime integrative organ system of the body, the nervous system plays an even more crucial role as initiator and disseminator of influences to other organs. An example of this is the control that the central nervous system exercises over the endocrine glands via the hypothalamus and pituitary. Although many regard menopause as a primary phenomenon of ovarian aging, in fact, the ovary may retain many ova that never reach maturity due to lack of stimulation (Krohn, 1966). Thus, menopause is primarily a phenomenon of the central nervous system with the peripheral changes being secondary or tertiary to central nervous system activity (Finch, 1976). If indeed menopause should be looked upon as a manifestation of the aging of the central nervous system, the question may be posed as to why this organ system should lose capability for timing. Many other biological rhythms are known to exist in man and lower organisms, yet they are not often examined in the context of failing control or regulation with age.

TIME DEPENDENT PROCESSES

The menstrual cycle illustrates a rhythm of the organism, which is primarily disrupted due to the inability of the nervous system to maintain its periodic stimulation of the endocrine system. Dampening of psychological and physiological rhythmic processes may underlie the mechanisms of aging (see Berger, 1975, p. 101). If such rhythms continue, after the environmental variations have been controlled, (e.g., light-dark cycles) they are called circadian rhythms, a term coined by Halberg in 1959 (see Brown, 1972). These rhythms can involve body temperature, enzyme activity, neural firing, and other physiological phenomena varying in 24-hour phases even under stable environmental conditions (Winfree, 1975). With regard to the locus of the control of rhythms, Winfree suggests that we search for "a mechanism of spontaneous oscillation within the organism" (Winfree, 1975, p. 315). The nervous and neuroendocrinological systems are likely loci of these oscillatory mechanisms. Sampson and Jenner (1975) reaffirm the importance of circadian rhythms in the regulation of biological organisms and review how desynchronization states can reduce mental efficiency to the extent of causing pathological conditions. That circadian rhythms alter with age, even in the absence of diseased states, has been demonstrated in a small number of studies to be discussed later in this section. Such studies have been reported concurrently with exciting research into the physiology and biochemistry of these rhythms. A brief summary of the direction of this research is presented here to provide the reader with a biological framework in which to assess the more psychologically oriented experiments.

Circadian rhythms are thought to be dependent on the relative concentration of the biogenic amines present in the neurons of the upper brain stem and hypothalamus (Sampson and Jenner, 1975, p. 4). Clocklike changes in the concentration of these amines in the pineal gland have also been discovered, and it is possible that these rhythmic changes in concentration alter with age. In his review on the pineal gland, Axelrod (1974) summarizes the relevant experimental data which show that there are circadian rhythms in serotonin, N-acetylserotonin and the end product of such pineal cell synthesis, melatonin, which is known to exert an inhibitory effect on the gonads. Especially important from the viewpoint of regulation is the discovery that the enzyme, N-acetyltransferase, which converts serotonin to N-acetylserotonin also undergoes these circadian rhythms. The CNS center for regulating this rhythm appears to be in or near the suprachiasmatic nucleus in the hypothalamus.

Studies on the age and sex differences in behaviors mediated by the ventromedial hypothalamus have been well documented in the rat and the results of such experiments support the well known observations that there is a decline in activity level with age in humans. Nisbett, Braver, Jusela, and Kesur (1975), in examining the change in circadian rhythms with age in 56 Wistar rats, found that in both sexes there was a highly significant deterioration in a behavior pattern related to such rhythms, namely the total food intake which decreased in a linear fashion with age.

In humans, experimental psychological studies of biological clocks have been mainly confined to those that have examined the alteration in sleep patterns with age. Such studies however, do illustrate how these changing physiological processes manifest themselves in changing behavioral patterns. For instance, a decline in activity patterns with age is accompanied by less sleeping time. Berger (1975) points out that disruptions in sleep, wakefulness and activity rhythms of the body and brain have a dampening or detrimental effect on both psychological and physiological functions such as impairments of mood and performance and reduced metabolic rates. He further suggests that such disruptions in circadian rhythms may also underlie many of the processes of aging. Further quantitative analysis in this relatively unexplored area will enable psychologists to gain further insights into the mechanisms which underlie changes in the adaptive capacities of individuals over the life span.

The above considerations lead us to question whether the changes with aging in rhythms of sleep, wakefulness and activity are adaptive to reduced energy demands or are representative of a change in the capacity of the older nervous system to maintain rhythms. The view of Winfree (1975) concerning the control of rhythms is that the organism should be viewed as a "clock shop" rather than as a simple clock. Experiments are possible in which one perturbs,

by environmental manipulation, the circadian rhythms of organisms of varying age and observes the consequences on the amplitude and phasing of the rhythm. Experimental desynchronization of circadian rhythms would appear to offer a useful way of assessing the effectiveness of nervous system control with age. It is not plausible at this stage to suggest that changes in rhythmic activity are themselves the cause of the major phenomena of aging. Rather, phase disruption in circadian rhythms over a wide age range seems to offer a methodological advance in experimental studies.

Winfree's point that there may be many oscillators in the body reemphasizes the importance of time in biological processes. Perhaps multicellular organisms keep time, not by a single clock ". . . but by averaging many independent circadian oscillators" (Winfree, 1975, p. 315). In his earlier review on biological periodicities and aging, Landahl pointed out that most biological processes are associated with a characteristic time (Landahl, 1959, p. 81). He states that, "Time is inseparable from aging; it may therefore be useful in organizing our thoughts about aging to consider the role of time in some biological processes. Many processes are clock-like in their rhythmicity, while others have a characteristic duration. It might be said that most biological processes are appreciably modified by aging no matter in what sense the word is used" (Landahl, 1959, p. 81). The hypothesis of a declining effectiveness of the aging nervous system in timing regulatory functions is an important one, though perhaps psychologists have not given it serious attention because it appears to deal with the hardware of the organism to the exclusion of the software of experience and learning. It is however, precisely because such a hypothesis encourages study of both the hardware and environmental conditions that future experiments on nervous system control over rhythmic activity are so attractive.

EVOLUTION OF AGING

There are two general approaches to the psychology of aging. One approach is to look for what the processes of aging of mankind have in common with other species. This utilizes a comparative method based upon the thought that if aging is a determinate process, other species, particularly those close to mankind phylogenetically, should show similar morphological, biochemical, and behavioral changes with age. Individual differences within the species can be looked upon as variations of the species' potential. Perhaps more common in psychology is the second approach which looks at individual differences within the species. For example, individual variations in intelligence with age are studied with regard to unique heredity or life circumstances of the individuals, e.g., educational opportunities and diseases. The essential point is to remind ourselves that such studies look for the commonalities among individual variation within the species. There is another more extreme approach to the study of individual differences in which the unique pattern of aging of one individual is studied in great detail. From this point of view, investigators might see great value in studying a few cases of progeria as a kind of accelerated aging or caricature of normal aging. However, the interpretation of data obtained from single individuals does presume a great amount of normative data (see Schaie and Schaie, Chapter 29 in this volume).

One of the basic questions a comparative approach to aging might answer is how much diversity exists in late life phenomena since there may be greater phylogenetic similarity in mechanisms of development than of aging. An early symposium sponsored by the Ciba Foundation, was devoted to the methodology of the study of aging (Wolstenholme and O'Connor, 1957). Two contributors to that volume, Bourlière and Muhlbock, pointed to the usefulness of a comparative approach in aging studies. Muhlbock stated, "It can be presumed that animals do not differ from man in the basic principles of the process of ageing, so that valid conclusions can be reached" (1957, p. 115). However, caution in such statements must be exercised, for although, within the phylum of mammals, patterns of aging changes between different species are under genetic regulation and share similar mechanisms, there are nevertheless, some species differences (Finch, 1976).

Previously, Birren (1964) pointed out that theories about aging could generally be divided into three groups; accident or wear and tear, genetic, or counterpart theories. In the latter, favored by the authors, age changes in the mature organism are regarded as counterparts of processes of earlier development. If the postreproductive characteristics of a species can not be directly selected for, despite evidence for genetic control, then the counterpart theory advocates that these regularly appearing features must be a consequence of traits that were selected for at the time of fertilization. "The counterpart theory does not require that all characteristics of the postreproductive animal be controlled as a counterpart of some developmental characteristic. It describes a pathway through which order could have been introduced into the changes in the old, or postreproductive animal. Obviously, beyond the order implied by a counterpart theory, events occur that superimpose their consequences on organisms that in the above view have some long-term programming" (Birren, 1964, p. 74).

The theory that aging is a counterpart of early development emphasizes that aging cannot necessarily be viewed as a mirror-image of early life processes. Thus, a late life disability might in fact be a consequence of selection for some early favorable trait. Smith made this point rather well, "A high blood pressure may contribute to death from cardiac disease in old age, but cannot have consistently adverse effects on fitness, since if a high blood pressure were uniformly disadvantageous, natural selection would reduce the mean level in the population. It is, therefore, probable that the deleterious effects of high blood pressure in old age are counter-balanced by advantages, perhaps earlier in life, natural selection maintaining the mean arterial pressure in the population at an optimal value" (Smith, 1957, p. 121).

Although programming of late life characteristics, including that of longevity, could emerge on the basis of counterpart selection including behavioral selection, how much organization of late life change is genetically programmed is open to question. Genetic programming of aging may not be as well organized as that of development. Indeed, there appears to be a biological procession of favorable survival traits appearing early in life and disadvantageous traits appearing late. A variety of genetic diseases of late life would fit such a view in which the longer one lives the more likely there will appear some deleterious disease.

Given the emergence of chronic diseases of late life, some changes in behavior may arise secondary to damage to the nervous system. Whether there is a genetically programmed constellation of primary age changes in behavior and the nervous system is a question that can only be answered through research. Stress is one of the general environmental factors influencing the manner in which we age (see Eisdorfer and Wilkie, Chapter 12 in this volume) and the cumulative effects of stress over many years may initially seem to be a genetically programmed sequence of changes.

A very different form of ordering of late life events could arise via natural selection of longer-lived and intelligent persons. That is, while individual differences in longevity don't appear until after reproduction has been completed, offspring whose parents survive a long time are themselves more favored to survive in the environment. In fact, the reasoning might be extended further to the pre-industrial societies, in which those who lived a long time and were therefore more likely to accumulate wealth could have provided more favorable conditions, e.g., food, for the survival of their offspring. In this manner, genetic selection for longevity could result in favorable late life behavioral traits. In a related manner, those individuals who show great capability for learning, retention of information and wisdom in late life would be more likely to provide favorable environmental circumstances for their tribe and offspring.

The probability of survival of a tribe might be higher if its elders or leaders showed the quality of wisdom. In contrast, the accumulation of large numbers of debilitated old persons in competition for food with warlike groups would be unfavorable for survival of a group. It is impossible to sketch the various circumstances that might lead to selective pressures for long lived individuals who would show characteristics favorable to the survival of the family and tribe. However, natural selection for longevity may be based on this association with late life behavioral characteristics.

The capacity of complex organisms for effective behavior governs their survival in wild or natural environments. In this sense, behavior has determined genetics. But since the process of selection took place in particular environments, the exposure of animals, including humans, to new and unfamiliar environments may result in characteristics never seen before. Not all of these responses to the new environment are predictable and genetic-environmental interactions can be profound. For example, Henry, Meehan, and Stephens (1967) demonstrated that inbred mice will or will not show a rise in blood pressure with age depending upon the social structure and interaction of the mice in the colony. Perhaps the often observed rise in blood pressure in aging humans is less an expression of a genetic characteristic than it is a manifestation of the expression of genetic predispositions as they interact with a particular environment. Omenn, in Chapter 10 of this volume, discusses environmental interactions in relation to behavioral genetics. He believes that there is significant interaction between genetic and environmental factors and that genetic factors set the action range within which environmental influences have effect.

Within the evolution of complex animals there is a loss of general characteristics in favor of specialization. Thus, the interaction between our genetic and environmental backgrounds may lead to specialization, disuse and loss of function. Such selective differentiation has led, for example, to the Kiwi bird of New Zealand being unable to fly. The environment may also force individuals through social pressure, and perhaps by biological factors, to narrow their range of activity at an early age leading to a reduction in their capacity for adaptability late in life. Health problems characteristic of the late years may reflect interactions between genetic predispositions and interactions with a particular environment. In human populations, the simultaneous interactions of genetic background and the environment allow for large variations; they are important for survival and performance, but very difficult to study.

METHODOLOGY

The previously cited Ciba Foundation Symposium on methodology was a systematic attempt to examine alternative approaches to the study of aging. Subsequent to the Ciba Symposium, the West Virginia Conference series on life-span developmental psychology contributed to the increasing methodological sophistication of research (Goulet and Baltes, 1970; Baltes and Schaie, 1973a; Nesselroade and Reese, 1973). For a further discussion on paradigms used in experimental-developmental research and the major methodological problems which may be encountered see Wohlwill (1973).

There are many age differences and age changes in behavior that have been identified (see Birren, 1959b), but Welford (1957), Comfort (1957), and others have pointed out the difficulties in identifying the mechanisms that underlie the data (see also Wolstenholme and O'Connor, 1957).

One of the most efficient tools elucidating mechanisms or causes is the experimental method. A shortcoming of the experimental method is that its precision may lull the investigator into a premature exploration of a mechanism before the context of the phenomenon has been described adequately. Thus, the investigator may find himself employing elegant methods for a trivial problem, i.e., trivial in that it is a problem which when solved leads to a generalization of limited scope. Given the myriad of details about aging and the apparently inexhaustible opportunities for studying its dynamics, there are many opportunities for clever guesses as to the most productive vantage points. The structured approach to experimentation is, of course, most efficient, nevertheless the unstructured approach remains highly desirable since there are so many important phenomena of aging yet undetermined. An exclusive partisanship for one method of research design seems, at present, undesirable. If, in any area of science, reflection and unfettered imagination are called for, it is in those sciences that propose to study aging. A high tolerance for ambiguity and humility would also seem helpful to the investigator before leaping into the public media with a theory and "cure" of aging.

Psychologists still tend to favor the study of the young organism in preference to the study of change in the adult. In part, this emphasis on early developmental research results from social-cultural values which scientists share with the rest of the population. There is also the fact that it is easier to study children since change occurs more rapidly. In aging research, as in the development of child psychology, there seems to be a progression from descriptive studies, to studies based on associative hypotheses, and finally to studies of an experimental nature with causal hypotheses.

Transition from unstructured to structured observation represents a progression in the development of science. Early fixation upon a particular method of gathering data or an experimental design can limit our approach to the psychology of aging at this point in its history. Possibly we suffer, still, from an overreaction to the divorce of psychology from philosophy. That is, we have cultivated a compulsion on the part of psychologists to use existing methods and experimentation rather than to develop a broadly scientific orientation. Perhaps in the immediate future, progress in our understanding of aging will be effected as much by conceptual contributions as by experimental contributions. Piaget observed and talked to children in such a way as to lead to scientific generalizations (see Piaget, 1973; Flavell, 1963; Maier, 1969). The authors' opinion is that there are many important and complex areas of adult development and aging that await exploration, e.g., mood, love, creativity, and wisdom (see Birren, 1976). Generally there is an orderly progression of steps in the development of a topic, by thinking, reading, talking to experts and nonexperts, observation, and experimentation; and this progression is more rapid the smaller the topic. This has promoted an avoidance of the more complex and important areas of adult behavior and favors narrow topics.

If there is an orderly progression in the development of a topic, including conceptual breakthroughs, such a progression is not likely to be simple in aging research. At some point however, the investigator is likely to reach the stage where he can attempt to manipulate that variable which he believes to be the cause of the pattern of age-associated changes under study. Literally, the research attempts to replace chronological age or time with other variables. In other words, an experiment on the psychology of aging attempts to reproduce those changes in individuals that are associated with chronological age by manipulation of the suspected causal variables. There are many studies that experimentally manipulate variables that are not experimental studies of aging in the sense that they do not replace age with the independent variable, but manipulate associated or correlated variables.

Given an opportunity to study a change in behavior associated with aging, one may be able to produce the behavior in young adults and to reverse it in older adults by manipulation of the same variable. For example, numerous studies have indicated that with advancing age, there is a slowing of reaction time very likely reflecting a general reduction in speed of information processing. If one purports to understand the process by which this occurs, it should be possible to produce a slowing of the reaction time in young adults, and to produce a quickening of reaction time in older adults by manipulation of the same variable. This, however, is based on the assumption that the change is a reversible one, although this is not always a valid assumption. This topic will be developed in more detail later in this section.

Research in the psychology of aging is controlled inquiry into the differences in behavior between young and old organisms or into the changes which occur within individuals with age. The research may be nonmanipulative in its controls, and therefore essentially descriptive based upon either no hypotheses, or associative hypotheses. In contrast it may be based on hypotheses, be manipulative in its controls and be truly experimental.

A common pathway to research is the *naturalistic* one in which the investigator begins with an observation of some behavioral characteristic of organisms that shows a relationship to age. He then describes this phenomenon and perhaps later attempts to replicate the finding in subsequent descriptive studies which may employ sophisticated multivariant designs involving associated variables. At this stage, he wishes to know the magnitude of the generational differences, ontogenetic changes, or time of measurement phenomena. The naturalistic sequence may often conform to the following pattern: (a) describing a trait that shows an association with age, (b) finding and describing other variables that appear to be associated with the age-related phenomenon or trait, (c) planning and conducting studies that are based upon associative hypotheses, i.e., that one will find other predicted variables associated with the main phenomenon or trait, (d) planning and conducting sequential longitudinal studies to give a precise estimate of the magnitudes of the association with age and with the other variables identified, (e) conducting experimental studies in which attempts are made to manipulate the hypothesized independent variable causing the dependent variable to change, and (f) carrying out experimental studies based upon quantitative predictions as reasoned from theory.

At stage (e), the investigator may conduct further experiments in which the irreversibility of the phenomenon is considered. Not all phenomena associated with aging are reversible since loss of some types of cells, whether due to disease or some inherent genetic program, may not be reversed. Thus, if the experimenter has indeed identified the causal variable, he may expose young organisms to it in order to see if he can reproduce the phenomenon as seen in naturally aging organisms. He may attempt to remove the phenomenon from appearance in old organisms and cause the phenomenon to appear in young organisms.

In the naturalistic progression from unstructured to structured experimental testing of hypotheses, investigators develop a depth of experience with a phenomenon of aging and with the conditions under which it appears. Conceptual refinement tends to accompany the progression of research, whereas if one moves prematurely to structured research or moves from structured to unstructured research, inefficiency enters. Early movement toward structured research brings with it the use of methods designed for other purposes and the control of variables which may have little to do with the phenomenon to be studied. Experimental investigators must become sensitive as to what to look for and what to look out for; a sensitivity that most often comes from a considerable amount of observation and thought before experimentation.

Often experiments related to aging are generated from theories or observations in other aspects of psychology and are not true experiments in the sense that there is a hypothesized independent variable or cause that is manipulated to produce the aging effect. Such experiments often manipulate variables that have no plausible relevance to the causal factor in the age relationship. For example, an investigator may raise the level of illumination under which young and old adults are to perceive small differences in objects. Old subjects will gain more than young adults from raising the level of illumination. But, reducing the age difference in perception by increasing the level of illumination does not in itself tell us why the visual process is different in older adults. Reducing the age difference is useful in some ways, and it may lead to experiments that can contribute to the understanding of the principal effect. In this illustration, raising the level of illumination is an *intervention* (in some current terminology) since it may obviate some problems of visual functioning with age; the manipulation is not designed to tell us much about the mechanisms involved in the relationship of age and vision. Experimentation on aging is designed not only to see an end product but also to *understand* the process as a result of the manipulation. The goal of the research is to predict, on the basis of reasoning, what should occur with a particular manipulation.

Since this chapter is primarily focused on psychological processes it is worthwhile to consider how large areas of human capacity are interrelated with advancing age, particularly if one includes not only measures of behavioral processes but also biological and social variables. Questions are beginning to be raised about the pathways of aging, that is, how change is organized within individuals such that aging patterns may be identified. Among the more interesting attempts at such investigations are the work of Jalavisto, Lindquist, and Makkonen (1964), who attempted to operationalize the measurement of a "familial longevity factor," and the work on functional age (Heron and Chown, 1967; Dirken, 1972).

FAMILIAL LONGEVITY FACTOR

In the early work on human life expectancy, an association was found between the life spans of individuals and the length of life of their im-

mediate ancestors (Pearl, 1934). Although at the present time, this does not account for even the major individual differences in life span, the association is a significant one and has been presumed to reflect differences in heredity. In a second phase of descriptive research design, Jalavisto *et al.*, attempted to operationalize biological age by linking it with familial longevity. They expand the concept of biological age to embrace the idea of survival vigor and they created a battery of measurements that would reflect this concept. Familial and parental longevity were therefore chosen as criteria for biological vigor. It was thought that if in analysis a factor of familial longevity appeared, "those tests which load on that factor would more likely be related to biological vigor than tests which do not" (Jalavisto, Lindquist, and Makkonen, 1964, p. 3).

They measured blood pressure, coordination, reaction time, hearing loss, memory, abstracting ability and related intellectual functions, and respiratory functions in a group of 130 women aged 44 to 93 years. The study resulted in the isolation of six factors, one of which was the parental longevity factor, which the authors regarded as a reflection of potential longevity based upon biological vigor. Of significance was the finding that the parental longevity factor was related to intellectual abilities which have been shown to be related to survival in other research. The fact that there was a significant positive relationship between abstracting ability and parental longevity gives some credence to the point made earlier in this chapter, that longevity and wisdom may vary, and be jointly subjected to selective pressures in survival. A significant "aging factor" was identified in this study that accounted for most of the variance since most of the sensory, perceptual, and intellectual tests showed high loadings on this factor. This rather pervasive aging factor was not related to the parental longevity factor which might have been expected. The results lend some support for the separation of the concepts of biological vigor and aging. For example, two test results, which were intimately related to the aging factor, were those of slower reaction time and decreased vital capacity, neither of which showed a correlation with the parental longevity factor.

Since only women were studied, there is uncertainty that the same parental longevity factor would appear as clearly in males. Also, it must be mentioned that this was not a longitudinal study and generational differences are mixed with ontogenetic changes, though this contamination was likely more important for the aging factor than for the parental longevity factor. Given an improvement in the standard of living for large populations and a reduction in adventitious events that shorten life, the parental longevity or biological vigor factor may in future studies account for a greater part of the individual differences with age.

Ironically the study of Jalavisto, Lindquist, and Makkonen (1964) while using females as subjects did not raise the question of the relationship between biological vigor and sex differences in mortality. Women live significantly longer than men, a difference in life expectancy of about eight years at birth in the United States. Even at the older ages, there is a greater life expectancy for women than men. If longevity is a product of biological vigor, then presumably women have more of the factor than men and should show more favorable psychological measurements on functions that reflect biological vigor. Indeed, if a factor of biological vigor exists, it should pervade behavioral characteristics. The study of sex differences and aging offers the opportunity of testing the relative independence of the factors of disuse-disease and familial longevity or biological vigor.

In the present context, there remains the question of how to extend these and other lines of research to the point where the basic hypotheses underlying the work might be subject to experimental study. At the present time, the hypotheses are ones of association, that is, advancing age is associated with lower scores in a wide range of physiological and psychological tests, and also with parental longevity. The next phase of such research might reasonably be a cross-sequential, longitudinal study to formulate a more precise idea of how the differences between generations contribute to the data. Also, increasing the range of psychological and physiological measurements would help to sharpen the identification of the functions that are negatively associated with advancing age and those that are positively related to biological vigor. Comparative descriptive studies might also be undertaken using rats or mice for example, in which parental longevity is related to longevity of offspring in highly inbred and outbred lines. The performance of the animals on a variety of memory, learning, and motor tasks could be related to age and to the parental longevity factor.

One element of the Jalavisto, Lindquist, and Makkonen (1964) study, that lends itself to the design of a "true" experiment, would be a test of the hypothesis that the significant loading of vital capacity on the aging factor reflects a disuse atrophy with increasing age as well as with consequences of diseases. The fact that vital capacity of the lungs was related to sensory, motor, and cognitive processes is an important finding. "Particularly striking was the intercorrelation of vital capacity and neural tests even when the age dimension was eliminated by partialling it out" (Jalavisto, Lindquist, and Makkonen, 1964, p. 17). They offered two interpretations: the first, that a large vital capacity reflected strong muscular effort and motivation, and the second, that reduced vital capacity is an indication of mild hypoxia in the brain which in turn may be related to impaired neural function.

In support of these claims, Retzlaff and Fontaine (1965) reported an experiment with rats undergoing forced exercise. Twice a day for 10 minutes each, the rats ran in a revolving drum exerciser for 155 meters. The old exercised rats showed histological staining characteristics of spinal motor neurons similar to those of younger animals. The investigators did not study respiratory function, though the result clearly links the state of neurons with exercise. One could now proceed with the design of an experiment to test the hypothesis that physical activity is a large contributor to the decline in respiratory function and nervous system integrity with age, by linking the results of these two investigations.

Given a society that provides maximum health care, which eliminates nutritional deficiencies of a qualitative or quantitative nature, and which provides opportunities for relaxation and hygienic exercise, it is possible that individuals might show a smaller *aging factor* as in the Jalavisto *et al.* study. Thus, as the environmental conditions improve, variance would be reduced in what we now would be tempted to identify as the aging factor, and individual differences in genetic background related to parental longevity would be more apparent. This is to say, that as we control deleterious environmental factors, genetic factors will become more significant in man's well-being and longevity. It seems to the writers that it is useful to relate the aging factor to the heritable aspects of our longevity and its associated behavior, to be consistent with the comparative approach of the biologist. It would, in fact, be extremely valuable if psychologists' definition of human aging was equivalent to that of the cellular and molecular biologists since it should promote easier discourse between these disciplines.

The fact that the main factor of the Jalavisto *et al.* study (termed by them "aging") is in this discussion called the "disuse-disease" factor should not discourage experimental studies. Individual differences in the heritable part of our life span and aging are probably not the largest factors in our population statistics at the present time, a point that Jones (1959) made earlier. How much the impressive disuse-disease factor represents the accumulation of consequences of independent processes is not clear. However, there are many opportunities for associative descriptive, associative experimental and experimental studies to be carried out for purposes of gaining an understanding of and a control over the deleterious accompaniments of growing old. Such studies may eventually permit an alteration of the rate of aging or senescence.

It is appropriate to mention that Botwinick (Chapter 24 in this volume) points out that aged individuals who perform poorly on psychological tests tend not to survive in comparison with those who test well. There is therefore a selective survival variable expressing some poorly understood etiological factors in human aging. One promising approach for delineation of individual differences in longevity and performance involves conceptualization, establishment of criteria and measurement of functional age.

FUNCTIONAL AGE

How one performs on a variety of tests can be used as an index of functional age. The use of performance itself on tests *per se* as the criterion for judgment of functional age has become widespread (Fozard, 1972; Dirken, 1972; Gribbin, Schaie, and Parham, 1974). Fozard employed a variety of ability tests and a personality questionnaire, and used the results to predict chronological age. The most important predictors of age were performances on three of his ability tests. When personality and ability measures were combined to predict age, personality was found to contribute only about 5 percent of the variance. This also confirms other studies, in which personality measures were found not to be highly related to age (Heron and Chown, 1967).

Dirken and his colleagues (1972) carried out a large study of the measurement of functional age in industrial workers in Holland. Their study population consisted of 316 male industrial workers, about 8 individuals for each year between 30 and 70 years. From the literature, 150 variables of a personal background or functional character were identified as being relevant. In the case of physiological and psychological functions, they chose to measure those that they thought were subject to deterioration after the age of 30, and which were presumably important for functioning in society, particularly in industrial work. Many of the measurements were the same as those of the Jalavisto, Lindquist, and Makkonen (1964) study (e.g., hearing, reaction time, vital capacity, and blood pressure), but there were many others as well. Since the investigators were interested in assessing functional age, they correlated each variable with age and finally reduced the number of functional variables to 28, which they then intercorrelated and subjected to cluster analysis.

The results of this study are startlingly similar to those of Jalavisto, Lindquist, and Makkonen (1964). Using eight variables as an index of functional age, Dirken (1972) identified a battery of tests that would require about an hour and a quarter for each person. These measurements showed a regression coefficient with chronological age of about 0.87. In this battery of measurements were: auditory pitch-ceiling, figure comprehension, reaction time to multiple choice, accuracy in semantic categorization, maximum breathing frequency, maximum systolic tension, aerobic capacity, and forced expiratory volume. The investigators could have used vital capacity in their composite group of factors, since like the measure of one-second maximum expiratory volume, it had high correlations with chronological age.

The investigators' intention in this study was to develop a composite index of functional age to replace chronological age as an indicator of the likely functional capacities of workers. "The term functional is a twofold indication of: measurable characteristics in the individual, on the one hand, and of his functioning in a physically, socially or otherwise determined environment on the other" (Dirken, 1972, p. 5). It is of interest that Dirken and his colleagues only chose those measurements that were presumed to decline with age in order to build their composite index of functional age. This approach is characteristic of most of the studies of functional age in that they assume a "... decrement model of aging and consequently may be inappropriate for many psychological variables over the major portion of the adult life-span" (Schaie and Gribbin, 1975, p. 70). One might, by contrast, build an index of functions that rise over much of the adult life span. However, it is not clear what criteria one would use to decide whether incremental or decremental factors were the most relevant for judging functional capacity in individuals over a wide age range, working in any specified occupation. If the previous reasoning about the Jalavisto study is correct, then the Dirken study concentrated on measurements that are closely related to disuse and to consequences of disease rather than to aging in the sense of an individual's likely remaining length of life. Nuttall (1972, p. 149) suggests taking the number of years remaining in an individual's life as a criterion of functional age, rather than the number of years since birth, since he believes nearness to death is a function of the individual's bodily processes.

Remarkably similar results were reported by Heron and Chown (1967) on age and function. Their study was based upon results from 540 men and women, 50 men and 40 women in each decade of life from the twenties to the seventies. Of dramatic similarity is the loading of 0.73 of the one-second forced expiratory volume on the age factor. In the Dirken study, the loading was 0.75. Apparently we have remarkable convergence in three major studies, that psychological and physiological variables cluster together in their relationship with age. While these studies may have used laboratory techniques that appear to be experimental in character, the designs of the studies were not experimental but associative-descriptive. The great value of the work lies in its potential for encouraging research designed to provide insight as to why the clusters of psychological and physiological variables vary with age. In addition, manipulative or experimental studies can arise from these descriptive studies. The status of functional age as a concept, and as an index, is still uncertain, and until predictive studies are undertaken (using an index based upon a composite of psychological and physiological measurements) it is difficult to know the usefulness of such an index. For one thing criteria or variables of predictive significance have to be agreed upon. Birren (1969, p. 214) suggested several criteria that could be used. These include survival, the presence of disease, functional recovery following illness and re-adaptation. Work output and training capacity could be used to indicate an individual's adaptability to environmental change. Other criteria Birren recommended were accident-proneness, motivation, drive, and self concept of age. Heron and Chown (1967, p. 215) advised against using a global index in determining an estimate of functional age because low intercorrelations between their measures were found, and because of the diversity in functions demanded in different occupations. They proposed using a functional age profile which would allow for more differentiation of information. Using such a profile however, does not eliminate the problem of establishing a criterion, for one must still compare different profiles with measures that will indicate validity.

Dirken (1972, p. 11) in computing a functional age score primarily used measurements that were negatively related to age, since one of his basic assumptions was that biological and psychological functions as selected for this study deteriorated with age. In this vein, the earlier parts of this section dealt with decremental factors that would lead to an increasing probability of death with time, e.g., disuse-disease and parental longevity. Such constellations of changes were related to the central nervous system both as causes and as consequences. There remains the possibility that parallel to the biological changes which decrease our probability of survival with age, there are simultaneous incremental changes in behavior mediated by the central nervous system. Thus, concurrent with a body that is less able to survive due to somatic changes, there may occur an increase in some behavioral capacity, e.g., the growth of wisdom in an old person.

The capacity for memory gives healthy older organisms an advantage in that they accumulate more knowledge. Memory gives the organism direction in time; events are sorted out as to whether they occur before or after another event. It is conceivable that memory could provide an irreversible property to organisms, like the ratchet and cog wheel in a watch, which permit movement in one direction only. An irreversible property of memory would not imply in any way, that the events registered were regularly ordered in time. The accumulation of events could in fact be randomly distributed in time, though the consequences of the events would continue to rise with such accumulation.

While the mechanisms of memory may in themselves become somewhat less efficient with age (see Craik, Chapter 17 in this volume) the accumulation of information will still be greater with time. Consequently, at least one incremental process may coexist with decremental processes and it should be incorporated into a set of criteria to assess the validity of a measurement of functional age.

EXPERIMENTAL GERONTOLOGY

Some new points of attack concerning biological and behavioral interactions promise to become increasingly important for students of behavioral phenomena. To understand issues that will be raised later on, it is necessary to embed the concerns of psychologists within a more general context of experimental gerontology, a biological science which includes physiology, biochemistry, physics and morphology as well as experimental psychology (see Verzar, 1963, pp. 4-5). This will be done by considering the special issues of the immunological system and of cancer as they relate to behavioral studies of age.

Immune System

There would appear to be important relationships between the immune system, the nervous system, and behavior with age. In order for the psychological studies, cited later, to be meaningful to the reader, a brief introduction to the principles of the functioning of the immune system is given.

Along with the nervous system, the immune system has a memory. It remembers organisms and molecules to which it has previously been exposed and which may be deleterious to the organism. Having recognized that it has met a foreign body before, it mobilizes antibodies and cells to destroy it. Time is required to build up the immune defenses of the body as is shown by the high susceptibility of the newborn to infectious diseases. Late in life, the organism is again susceptible to disease; such susceptibility may involve mechanisms that can influence the central nervous system and thereby behavior. That this process may be related to the immune system is emphasized by Burnet (1970a, b) who claims that aging is largely influenced by a progressive weakening of immunological surveillance mediated by autoimmune processes.

The cells that respond specifically to antigenic challenge defending the body against infection and tumor growth are the lymphocytes. Immunologists distinguish between two distinct classes of lymphocytes: T cells which are responsible for *cell-mediated immunity* and B cells which provide *humoral (antibody) immune responses*. These cells become specific for certain antigens; this commitment being expressed by a display of antigen-specific receptors on the cell surface. When an antigen enters the body, the receptors on the selected lymphocytes become activated, leading to an antigen-lymphocyte receptor interaction, while the resting lymphocytes proliferate and/or differentiate into effector cells which will attack the antigenic substance (see Raff, 1974). The immune response mediated by these lymphocytes may either (a) allow the organism to become tolerant so that the system will not react when the same antigenic substance represents itself to the body tissues, or (b) induce the development of *functional* effector cells which direct the development of antibodies. These together with non-specific factors and cells (for example, macrophages) allow the body to reject the foreign substance. These normal immunological functions, either in terms of tolerance or in changes in the regulatory activity of the antigen-antibody response, decline with age. There is also an age-related increase in the incidence of infection, autoimmune disease and cancer. It is unlikely that the relationship between these two biological phenomena is coincidental. (For an excellent review on immunity and aging the reader is referred to Makinodan, Chapter 15 of the *Handbook of the Biology of Aging*.)

That these changes in the organism may also display themselves in behavioral phenomena is suggested in two longitudinal studies of aging of a large number of healthy subjects aged 45 years and older. A significant inverse relationship in both samples was observed between an increase in serum immunoglobulin concentrations and a decrease in intelligence measures with age (Roseman and Buckley, 1975). These investigators were unable from their data to identify the precise mechanism underlying their results, but did suggest that one possible testable explanation was that antibodies which react against the CNS increase with age and may play a role in effecting cognitive decline. This hypothesis would appear promising especially in view of a recent study by Nandy (1975). In this study, it was demonstrated that brain-reactive or anti-neuron antibodies are present in the serum of old mice but not of young mice. However, his experiments showed that the loss or damage of nerve cells, known to occur in aging mammals, is not the primary reason for the formation of these neuron-reactive antibodies, for when these antibodies were presented to damaged neurons of the sciatic nerve in young and old mice no antigen-antibody reaction was established. Rather, "it appears more likely that the brain-reactive antibodies are formed by an alteration in the immune system in old age and these in turn are capable of reacting in equal fashion with healthy nerve cells in the brains of young and old mice" (Nandy, 1975, p. 415). Nandy also investigated the migration of ^{125}I-labeled globulins across the blood-brain barrier and his results indicated that the blood-brain barrier normally prevents these antibodies from invading brain tissue. However, since the radioactive globulins migrated slowly across the blood-brain barrier in his experiments, he hypothesized that such a slow rate of migration across this barrier could account for the "scattered loss of nerve cells in the brain of old animals" (Nandy, 1975, p. 416).

This line of research suggests again that there are significant links between behavior and underlying biological systems however complex the relationship. The immune system is a relatively new and important area for the psychobiologist to consider when studying aging organisms. The relationship between such biological and psychological activities is not simple, but this complexity should not deter the investigator from formulating new hypotheses and designing appropriate experiments in this area.

As indicated previously, it is possible that there is a relationship between the declining ability of the immune system and the increased susceptibility of the organism to disease such as cancer. In addition to explaining this susceptibility in terms of a less effective immune system, recent evidence suggests explanation at a genetic level, a topic discussed in the next section.

Cancer and Age

The links between cancer and behavior are not as well delineated experimentally as those in the immune system. However, some of the more significant findings are cited later in this section, after a brief introduction to recent models of tumorigenesis.

One of the fundamental facts awaiting explanation is why the incidence of cancer increases with age. The increase in susceptibility to cancer with age would suggest there is a tendency toward biological instability which makes cancer as well as other late life diseases more likely to develop in the adult organism. Here, as elsewhere in this chapter, it has been noted that perhaps the central nervous system shares with other organ systems a tendency toward a decline in its regulatory capacity with age. Strong (1968) in his book on *Biological Aspects of Cancer and Aging*, discussed the resistance that a mouse host will show to a transplanted tumor as a function of its age. ". . . many of the specific characteristics of the individual are gradually acquired during adolescence, remain at a fairly constant level or plateau during adult life and are gradually lost during senescence." In Strong's view, the mature male or female organism shows, ". . . perfect or, at least, partial biological equilibrium where all organs and systems are functioning properly and in balance with each other in an organized whole" (Strong, 1968, p. 3).

One of the interesting experimental studies that Strong carried out was to vary maternal age to determine its effect on offspring longevity. To perform this research, he took one mouse and mated it to several females of a different strain. He then went through many generations of inbreeding by selection of maternal age. Selective breeding according to maternal age produces some important results: (a) the selection toward young mothers leads to later birth of first litters; (b) female offspring of mothers in their "prime of life" outlived mice born to younger and to older mothers; and (c) the age when tumors appeared also varied in offspring as a function of maternal age. Whether these studies on mice have direct implications for human populations is by no means certain

but they do show that at least in one other mammal there appears to be some form of biological equilibrium that changes with age and is accompanied by a change in susceptibility to cancer. Strong did not make any observations on the behavior of his mice inbred by maternal age, but it is possible that if he had, he would have found differences between the short-lived and long-lived lines. This is a line of research that can approach the question of the extent to which the behavioral manifestations of aging are part of biological changes with age.

A disturbance in the cell's normal homeostatic replication mechanisms occurs during the initiation of neoplastic growths. Results, emerging from biological experiments during the last decade, have shown that there are normal or mutational host cell genes, some of which have been identified as being of critical importance in the etiology of spontaneous and induced cancers (Huebner and Gilden, 1971). The discovery of an RNA-dependent DNA polymerase (called reverse transcriptase) in all RNA tumor viruses is attributed to Temin and his colleagues (Temin, 1970, 1971, 1972; Temin and Kang, 1974). This enzyme permits a DNA copy of the viral RNA to be made after its integration into the host DNA which serves as the template. Integration of the viral RNA into the host genome means that the experimenter adds genes to (and alters the sequence of) the host DNA. More startling is the discovery that the viral RNA is present in a latent form in the cells of embryos of many different species including mammals (see for example Huebner and Gilden, 1971; Todaro, 1974). At some later point in development, these otherwise latent RNA viruses may become active, inducing the formation of tumors possibly through the activation of the enzyme, reverse transcriptase.

The viral oncogene theory of Huebner (see Huebner and Todaro, 1969) suggests that we inherit structural and regulatory genes which serve as determinants of neoplastic expression. These genes may lead to the induction of a tumor by the derepression or turning-on of the endogenous tumor-inducing RNA viral oncogenes. This process may be determined by either external or internal stimuli. Todaro (1974) puts forward an interesting hypothesis as to why the cells of organisms should inherit a potentially lethal system. "The virus or certain viral components would serve some normal function during development either of the embryo or of the trophoblast. It need only perform this essential function for a brief time during development or perhaps only in a specific organ for the system to be preserved. Developing cells grow rapidly, and cells such as trophoblast cells can be highly invasive, having many of the properties associated with tumor cells. Expression of the virus-related oncogenic information, though inappropriate in the adult, may be part of the normal developmental process" (Todaro, 1974, p. 155).

The link between the development of tumors, the central nervous system, and behavior lies in the fact that stress may encourage the proliferation of cancer cells. Stress alters the process of interpreting the environment and results in sustained and altered regulatory activity of many organ systems.

The possibility that stress and associated psychological factors might influence the development of neoplastic growth is a small and relatively untested hypothesis. Such factors most likely act in the form of a releasing or triggering agent, since we have seen from the biological evidence that the potentiality of cancer may rest in the cells in latent form from an early embryonic stage and be activated by either exogenous or endogenous stimuli. That psychological factors and emotional states may affect the onset and growth of cancer is still highly speculative; conclusions rest on largely anecdotal or descriptive investigations. That the onset of cancer is associated with some form of long-term psychological stress, such as the loss of a loved one, depression, or repression of emotions (particularly those to do with hostility) has been concluded by many investigators (see Greene, 1954; LeShan and Worthington, 1955, 1956; Schmale and Iker, 1966; Kissen, 1963, 1969). It should be emphasized that these findings are tentative. There are fundamental problems in most of the research done in this area, which involve serious methodological inadequacies, such as lack of adequate control groups and the indiscriminate use of multiple statistical tests. In an earlier section of this chapter, it was suggested that much research has its birth in relatively unstructured contexts. It is the task for investigators in the future to take these suggestive hypotheses relating psychological factors to the process of carcinogenesis and create structured controlled experimental programs.

PSYCHOLOGY OF AGING AND ACTION RESEARCH

While psychology is clearly part of a broader area of study, gerontology, it has some of its own requirements, limitations and traditions. The transition from descriptive study to experimentation may be slower in psychology than in biology, since investigators cannot manipulate many of the variables thought to be important in the development and aging of man, for moral and ethical reasons. Experimenters are not privileged to tamper with those characteristics that may produce permanent or semipermanent deleterious effects (Birren, 1970, p. 124). Thus a mild dietary deficiency over many years might produce effects on the central nervous system and behavior that are not reversible by resumption of an adequate diet.

While it is often possible to use animals as substitutions for humans in studies, some of the more complex forms of human behavior that may change with age, e.g., speech, are not found in animals. It then becomes necessary to make studies of changes with age on humans themselves, while still mindful of our moral obligations as to what variables can be manipulated. The volume produced by the National Institute of Child Health and Human Development (U.S., D.H.E.W., 1968) on *Perspectives on Human Deprivation*, listed many influences of biological, psychological, and social deprivation on mental development, personality, and skills, and proposed a number of strategies for improvement of the environment to maximize man's potential for development and maintenance of competence. In addition, the authors of that book suggest that those variables, which for ethical reasons cannot be manipulated in the laboratory, be studied in the natural environment. They refer to such studies as "natural experiments over time" (U.S., D.H.E.W., 1968, p. 161). Such "natural experiments" are longitudinal in nature. They follow individuals over time and do not involve manipulation of the suspected causes of the phenomena. Such investigations are not experiments, as the term is usually understood, but should rather be called experiments of nature or action research. Such research may involve environmental manipulation or intervention, such as medical care, in an effort to improve the living conditions. The introduction of environmental manipulation is not necessarily experimentation in the usual sense of the word even though it may require control groups of individuals unexposed to the improved conditions for evaluation of the expected beneficial effects.

Other differences between experimentation and action research designed to improve conditions for disadvantaged populations arise from the fact that action research is not inherently interested in the mechanisms or the pathways through which the effects are brought about. There is a presumption in such research that one already knows the causes and that it may be a matter of social injustice to some members of the population if they are not given the advantages of, for example, education. Fundamental research and experimental social-psychological research can be undertaken on questions of how public policies are formed which at present lead to deprivation of individuals.

To reiterate a fundamental point, such research does not have as its intent the uncovering of information about the mechanisms of deprivation and its effects on early development, as this would lead to disadvantaged adults who might show early signs of aging. However, there are opportunities for research that would find correlates of deprivation and which would lead to subsequent research of an experimental character that would reveal the pathways or mechanisms by which deprivation leads to limitations or deficits in individuals. The report on deprivation (U.S., D.H.E.W., 1968) stated the issues in this way:

"Perhaps the most urgent need in the study of the effects of psychosocial deprivation is to analyze and identify the elements and patterns of environmental input into the complex inter-action between the individual and his stimulus surround." And further, ". . . these efforts should be encouraged to extend considerably beyond the usual population studies, that is up to age 22, the usual school leaving age for more favored members of society. The environment of the young adult, the middle-aged adult, and the older adult must be characterized in more detail and in such a way that it can be incorporated into a psychological theory of human development" (p. 161). "Institutional barriers to investigators' research must be reduced in order to increase opportunities for relating social class differences to health services and outcomes for development of productive maturity and aging. In particular, psychological functioning in the adult years is significantly related to health status, which in turn, appears to vary with economic level. Cause and effect relationships must be established here in order to improve the quality of life for adults" (p. 162).

INTERVENTION

One of the current terms used to designate therapeutic manipulations of behavior without regard to underlying causes is *intervention*. Thus rearing of potentially disadvantaged children in an enriched environment from birth is a way of intervening to prevent limitations in the behavior of the developing child. Similarly, attempts have been made to modify the characteristics of institutions for the aged, with either physical changes or changes in routines along the lines of operant conditioning. Before and after measurement on individuals exposed to such improved environments will indicate the extent of the effect, though they may tell us nothing about the circumstances that led to the original limitation in function. Without a long history of descriptive work preceding experimental design, interventions can produce harmful effects because not enough is known about the context of the behavior and the underlying processes. In discussing interventions, the U.S., D.H.E.W. publication cautioned, "When action programs and interventions are undertaken, they should be undertaken with an awareness of the possibilities of latent, unintended and perhaps, harmful effects. To judge unintended effects, widely spaced dependent variables should be included in evaluative research which will monitor unintended consequences" (U.S., D.H.E.W., 1968, p. 285).

One of the proponents of intervention in behavior of older adults is W. J. Hoyer. In particular, he advises the application of operant techniques to the modification of the behavior of the older adult. "Current reinforcement contingencies are seen as an important determinant of behavioral deficits associated with aging. The use of operant techniques which focus on the design of new reinforcement contingencies is suggested as a promising intervention strategy" (Hoyer, Kafer, Simpson, and Hoyer, 1974, p. 18). If behavior patterns seen in older adults are a result of selective reinforcement, then reinforcement strategies can bring about results that may lead to amelioration of the behavioral deficits seen in the older adult. They may also contribute to the understanding of the causes of a particular behavior pattern. In so far as the basic phenomenon or deficit is not the result of reinforcement contingencies, the intervention will not contribute to insight, e.g., use of reinforcements to relieve depression in an older person when the causal variable may be an endogenous change in the concentration levels of catecholamines (Finch, 1973). Intervention does not emphasize historical events in the alteration of behavior. Operant conditioning gives emphasis to those elements in the present environment which are most effective in leading to the control of the behavior. Of less importance are the developmental processes which led to the particular behavior or behavior deficit (Baltes and Labouvie, 1971).

One of the limitations of the operant conditioning approach to intervention is that it disregards the origins of the behavior that is modified. Indeed, emphasis on intervention can delay experimentation that could lead to the understanding of the pathways to the disorder and thereby increase the number of alternative interventions. Clearly in the present context, intervention is taken to mean the elimination or modification of undesired behavior by methods that have no known relationship to the pathways by which the behavior originally appeared.

Intervention does have a relationship to experimentation, as does description. It is perhaps possible that its use with a particular target behavior can build up a body of knowledge that would help lead to a rational *understanding* of that behavior, in the natural science sense of the term. When operant conditioning is used to check a hypothesis or a theory, then it becomes part of the experimental tradition, and the term intervention should be dropped in case it comes to be used exhortatively with the implicit assumption that it is better than something else.

Simulation

In recent years, simulation models have been proposed to explain the phenomena of development and aging. The major proponents of this approach, as it applies to developmental psychology, its rationale, assumptions, methodology, and limitations, are well summarized in Wohlwill (1973), to which the reader is referred. In the field of aging, some of the more avid proponents have been Baer (1973), Baltes and Goulet (1971), and Baltes and Nesselroade (1973). Reference to their work will be made later in this section. First it is necessary, however, to briefly assess whether the term *simulation model* makes a useful and worthwhile contribution to the field of gerontology.

To simulate is to mimic or feign some original event or thing. Although a *simulation* may, but not necessarily, produce equivalent effects, there is no guarantee that the processes entailed are identical. By contrast, a *model* is an attempt to reproduce more exactly an event or a process. The basic prerequisite for a successful model, if it is to explain something, is that a partial understanding of the process and product of the behavior under examination, be achieved before the model is produced. For this, experimentation is required, and then, for the results of such experiments to become meaningful, a theoretical framework is necessary. In the sense that experiments may precede or result from a model (or theory which underlies the model), there is to some extent a simulation of a system or phenomenon. From this viewpoint, therefore, the use of the term *simulation model* becomes an unjustified exercise in semantics. Like the contributions of intervention or operant conditioning, simulation is useful only when it becomes part of the experimental tradition, and not when an attempt is made to incorporate it into the area of theoretical paradigms or models.

Even the present models that are available to the psychology of aging are still inadequate. It is beyond present expectations that our models can account for most of the variance among individuals as they age. There are in fact few mathematical models that lead to quantitative predictions and perhaps none that introduce quantification of parameters on the basis of assumptions and data transformed into rational equations to express the lawfulness of the relationships. One exception might be the Gompertz function that is used to describe the mortality rate of man as a function of age. While the Gompertz function (Curtis, 1966) is associated with the concept of the force of mortality, it should be looked upon as a descriptive equation. It is not a rational equation, and therefore not a model of "aging" to be used in planning simulation experiments in the sense of testing its correspondence to observed data.

Another approach to the simulation of aging that has been attempted, is exposing animals to radiation damage in an effort to accelerate aging. Arising from the reasoning that there is a correlation between the production of mutations or chromosome aberrations and aging, it was thought that one could accelerate aging experimentally by exposing animals to radiation (see Lindop and Sacher, 1966, and Curtis, 1966). The fact that radiation damage has a life-shortening effect as a result of genetic damage to the cell is proof of the validity of the simulation. If radiation damage were to mimic the processes of normal aging, then it should reproduce the pattern of changes seen in animals and humans. Unfortunately, from the point of view of the experimental scientist, radiation damage seems to affect the most rapidly dividing cells such as the crypt cells of the gastrointestinal tract which, since they must divide so often, have little time to repair the radiation damage to the chromosomes. Neurons as fixed, postmitotic cells no longer divide and can absorb large doses of radiation. Were the effects of radiation greater on the

fixed, postmitotic cells rather than the rapidly dividing cells then one would have had an experimental·tool to manipulate aging. Instead, we know that while radiation accelerates mutations and accelerates the death rates of whole animals, it does not resemble aging in some essential features, particularly with regard to changes in the central nervous system.

At the other extreme from the radiation approach, simulation investigators have examined the organism in an exclusively behavioristic context. Baltes and Nesselroade (1973) posed a multivariate approach for the study of the environment and environmental change. On the one hand, their approach is a call for more information about the environments in which individuals live during their life spans, and on the other hand, a call for the greater use of multivariate techniques of data analysis. In so far as this will lead to further descriptive information and delineation of aging phenomena it will be useful. However, it is less likely that it will lead to the development of rational models that can be evaluated experimentally. No mention is made by Baltes and Nesselroade that the human organism is a biological system that shows properties independent of a great range of environmental variation, e.g., persistent diurnal cycles independent of environmental light-dark cycles. The basic assumption of Baltes and Goulet in a related paper is, ". . . it is possible to produce behavioral changes in a short period of time that are indicative of and/or identical with long-term ontogenetic changes as they occur in nature" (Baltes and Goulet, 1971, p. 154). They wish to look at changes with age under "*time-compressed* (accelerated) conditions" (Baltes and Goulet, 1971, p. 154). Yet one of the fundamental features of living organisms is the dimension of time (see Omenn, Chapter 10). Omenn stresses the need to assess phenotypes of processes involved in aging over time, and to look at the interaction of genetic and environmental factors also over a period of time. For example, it is not reasonable to expect that simulation research could produce cognitive changes in the newborn while myelinization has not been completed, or to simulate in a brief period of time in the young organism, the behavioral consequences of a mid-life presenile dementia which is certainly an ontogenetic phenomenon. Their approach appears to be neo-behavioristic and while it may hold some advantage for programs designed to modify undesirable behavior, it does seriously neglect the fundamental biological nature of the organism. Moreover it neglects essential processes that make up the product, behavior. This can be seen in their statement that, "If seen in its most extreme form, a basic assumption here is that age functions (at least theoretically) can be modified to approximate *any* criterion age function if *all* developmental antecedents are known *and* are under the control of the experimenter" (Baltes and Goulet, 1971, p. 153). While the qualification that the investigator must know all of the developmental antecedents and have control of them all softens the argument, the assumption that "age functions" can be modified almost without limit seems more a statement that might be made by an enthusiast of the operant conditioning school working with the age constant organism than by a developmental psychologist. There is a strong possibility that biological and health variables become more important the older we get, making it imperative that we develop bio-behavioral models.

An even more extreme operant conditioning position has been taken by Baer (1973) who argues that research into developmental psychology should adopt the strategies of behavior modification. He asserts that many, and possibly all of the behavior changes that are considered to be developmentally significant can be subjected to the techniques used in experimental behavior modification which he claims to be "mechanism rich" contrasting with the approach of developmental psychology which he claims "has often been a mechanism-free concept" (Baer, 1973, p. 190). Baer advocates acceleration of development throughout the life span arguing that waiting along the "time course" which has characterized developmental research is not valuable. In his words, "The philosophy of behavior modification is, in effect, 'why not?'" (Baer, 1973, pp. 186-187). In addition, he questions the irreversibility of developmental patterns. On both these issues he would seem to be denying that biological processes are of significant consequence in the aging of the organism, that time even in the guise of experience has considerable value and that some aspects of irreversibility may be desirable not only for the survival of the species but for the quality of life for each individual. To reiterate, the simulation approach has serious weaknesses because it neglects the fundamental biological character of the human organism; *it may ignore essential processes which make up the product, behavior*; and it reduces the significance of time and experience as important variables.

MECHANISM AND POPULATION REPRESENTATION

Experimental studies of aging lead to the identification of causes or mechanisms. They do not in themselves indicate the extent to which the cause is distributed in the population. Thus, a study of disuse and experimental exercise can lead to the understanding of the contribution of low physical activity or disuse to some operational definition of aging, e.g., survival, susceptibility to disease or sensori-motor capability. The identification of such a pathway in humans or in experimental animals does not lead to a grasp of how many persons in the population show the phenomenon and to what extent. There is in fact a tradition in the experimental biological sciences of excluding individual differences from research by using inbred animals and constant environmental conditions. Many psychologists and social scientists, on the other hand, use individual differences within a population as a variable. Thus, individuals in a population might be arrayed along a dimension of physical activity and measures of behavior studied in association with it. In populations where there is a small range of individual differences, it is difficult to observe any association since every member of the population shows the trait in a constant amount. Such would also be the case if all members of a population had the same genetic characteristics for a trait.

Given the possibility of a disuse factor in the population that is homogeneous for this characteristic, e.g., all adults in the population engage in little physical activity upon reaching maturity, there will be little individual difference within the culture to analyze and one will not be able to isolate its contribution to "aging." Recourse might be had to the study of two different cultures, one showing high physical activity and the other low, in an effort to test the associative hypothesis. But there are many concurrent variables that could contribute to the characteristics of two populations other than activity *per se* and it would be tenuous to conclude from one cross-cultural study that a difference in behavior with age was due to the difference between the cultures in physical activity levels. Several pairs of cultures might be compared to reduce the possibilities of error.

Since aging is a result of many causes, there can be a drift over generations in the contribution of these various causes to the phenomena of aging. Therefore, one has to be on guard against making assumptions from the apparent clarity of a particular experimental demonstration, about its representation in the population, or the stability of its importance over time. In fact, population studies should show us, after decades of study, the magnitudes in the shifts of those important etiological factors which contribute to aging. For example, the shifting magnitude in sex differences in mortality indicates that women are living disproportionately longer in recent decades than men. Understanding the sex-associated mechanisms of aging, as may be discovered in experimental studies, doesn't lead directly to an estimate or an understanding of the increasing importance of sex-associated phenomena of aging in the population.

Race or ethnicity is another aspect of a population that can be studied to secure information that can lead to identification of mechanisms and concepts of aging. For example, blacks in the United States show a greater rise in the incidence of hypertension with age than do whites. Blacks also show a less favorable mortality rate in the middle years than do whites (U.S. Public Health Service, 1970). For this reason it can be hypothesized that a population study using blacks compared with whites should show a much larger "aging factor" in

blacks (as in the Dirken study) that can be ascribed to disease than to the parental longevity factor (of Jalavisto *et al.*). After blacks reach the sixth decade, they tend to have equal or better life expectancies than do whites. This would lead to the further hypothesis that with age in the later years of life, e.g., over the age of 55, the parental longevity or biological vigor factor will appear increasingly in both blacks and whites, but that blacks will show greater loading or saturation on the factor than whites.

By contrast to the parental longevity factor, if blacks and whites are studied in the middle years of life, then the age-associated disease factor should explain more of the variance in blacks than in whites. Since there has been recent improvement in life expectancy for blacks, it might be assumed that the aging-disease factor will show less saturation in the black population in future decades and perhaps there will be no difference in the phenomena of aging in the middle years for blacks and whites.

Since Chicanos and American Indians have lower life expectancies at present than blacks (U.S. Public Health Service, 1970), presumably due to mortality from early and mid-life diseases, these groups have little opportunity to express their potential for longevity as based upon inheritance. Such a factor of individual differences in longevity or potential for senescence can be seen in rodents. Rats, for example, rarely survive in the wild state before they complete growth or arrive at full maturity since predators kill them. However, under the favorable conditions of the laboratory colony, rats will live two to three times longer than they would live in their natural or wild habitat (see Birren, 1964). The important feature about this phenomenon is that a species will show a potential for senescence if given a favorable environment. It would appear that this potential is inherent in the species and is a determinate process of aging—one that may arise by counterpart of early life selection as was suggested previously. In the context of the present discussion, the important feature is that a mechanism of aging may exist in the population which will show a shift in its expression with a change in the environment. The human potential for senescence and our individual differences in the parental longevity (or biological vigor) factor can be expected to appear more clearly in the populations of developed countries in future years. Hence, there is clearly a complementarity between experimental studies of aging mechanisms and descriptive-associative studies of populations. Each has its strengths in answering particular questions.

Many of the "variables" used in population studies are themselves indices, such as socioeconomic status, ethnicity, or length of education. These indices stand for constellations of variables, and are not in themselves "causes" in experimental research. Their use in research is like that of tracking a nutritional deficiency in which one finds a relationship between a deficiency syndrome and the amount of food eaten. As the research becomes refined, one discovers the particular dietary element that may have led to the health and behavioral problems, e.g., vitamin B_1-deficiency. The amount of food eaten would be equivalent to the use of socioeconomic status as an index, whereas identification of the vitamin would be the isolation of the necessary and sufficient condition for the consequences to appear.

Communication between the mechanists of the experimental tradition and those utilizing individual differences or societies in cross-cultural studies is not great. The traditions of training and research skills make it almost prohibitive that investigators conduct both types of research in pursuit of the understanding of a particular phenomenon. The increase in efficiency of science may lie in communications of the sort encouraged by this volume and its companion volumes.

EXPERIMENTAL PSYCHOLOGY OF AGING

As pointed out earlier in this chapter, an experimental study of aging is one which attempts to replace age by a variable that is believed to be the cause of the phenomenon of aging. Since most students of aging believe it to be the result of many causes with a wide range of manifestations, unless one limits oneself to length of life, there are a variety of experiments that can be undertaken. Age is probably the most powerful index we have for biological and psychological

phenomena, but as an index, one cannot presume that there are similar causes among the wide range of changes that show an association with age. In a rigorously experimental sense, age must be approached in research as a variable that ultimately must be eliminated. That is, so long as age is used as the independent variable to array data, research remains at the descriptive state, despite the refined or experimental character of the data gathering process. Approaches to the formulation of research paradigms, other than those of the authors, are given by Baltes and Schaie (1973b, pp. 365–395). These include unbiased description, explanation and predictive analysis, and modification, prevention or optimization under the framework of a modified stimulus and response model. For a comprehensive view of methodological issues associated with these life span models see Schaie and Gribbin (1975).

One of the difficulties in using the term *experimental psychology of aging* is the fact that the term *experimental psychology* tends to be used both in the classical sense of experimentation and also as regards content or area. Thus, research on perception, learning and memory tends to be identified as being experimental psychology, whether or not the research employs an experimental design. In the book, edited by Eisdorfer and Lawton (1973), *The Psychology of Adult Development and Aging*, a section consisting of four chapters was called "Experimental Psychology." The chapters included studies on cognitive processes, animal behavior, and psychophysiology. In the chapters, numerous studies were described which were not experimental studies in the classical sense. The term, experimental psychology, was therefore used to define implicitly a content area rather than to focus on the logic of experimentation on aging *per se*.

Experimental, in the present chapter, is not meant to define a content, e.g., experimental as contrasted with social. Unfortunately, psychology has a legacy of using the term *experimental psychology* to distinguish it from an earlier stage of philosophical psychology. Now most persons will assume that psychology, like biology, can be experimental if the problem studied requires it, but it can also be descriptive. In other areas of psychology it seems unproductive to separate the descriptive from the experimental studies on particular topics, since their information is complementary in character. Given the fundamental task of discovering how behavior becomes organized or disorganized with age, one might be alternately clinical or social, experimental or descriptive, or use a variety of other approaches in the pursuit of understanding.

Much of the experimental study of aging begins with the fact that under a wide variety of laboratory conditions, older adults tend not to perform as well as younger adults on measurements of memory, learning, perception, reaction time, and other functions mediated by the central nervous system. Such studies can be the departure for experiments on aging but the original observations were not experiments, since there was no intent to explain age differences by manipulating the circumstances of measurement. Several examples of experimental studies will now be given to illustrate some of the essential features of this type of research.

SOCIAL CONFORMITY

Klein (1972) investigated the tendency for individuals to be swayed by group opinions so that they would agree with the group rather than hold to their previously preferred position. Klein postulated that older individuals in comparison with young adults would be more susceptible to informational social influence in making perceptual judgments. He justified this hypothesis in part by previous research which showed that older adults tend to be more cautious and would therefore be more likely swayed by the opinions of others. His study consisted of exposing subjects to the task of making perceptual judgments (judging which of two circular disks was the smaller) under conditions in which they received false information to create social pressure to make erroneous judgments. Results showed older adults to be more conforming with a greater increase in conformity as the difficulty of the perceptual judgments was increased. This first study, while an experimental social psychological experi-

ment, was not an experimental study of aging, since it posed and found a relationship of social conformity with age, but did not manipulate that which was purported to be the cause of the age association.

The second set of studies undertaken by Klein was designed to find out how the tendency toward increased conformity generalized with age. There are, in such instances, two questions of universality: how many persons in a given population show the phenomenon, and how generalized is the phenomenon in an individual? If aging is assumed to be a universal process, all individuals should show its manifestations, if at different rates. If our susceptibility to social conformity is universal, then all of us will show an increase with age; and we will show a generalization across all our behaviors, such that if we are conforming in one situation we are likely to be conforming in others. Klein designed his second set of experiments to look at the degree of generality of the phenomenon of conformity across tasks, i.e., the extent to which it is shown under all types of conditions and tasks. For this purpose he exposed young and old subjects to conditions of social pressures for conforming on five different tasks: (1) visual perceptual judgments, (2) auditory perceptual judgments, (3) auditory signal detection, (4) arithmetic problem solving, and (5) social attitudes involving statements of nationalism. It was impossible to have all subjects exposed to all five conditions, given the nature of the false information, and the requirements that individuals be told of the true nature of the experiments after their exposure to the false conforming information. It is essential in the experiments that the subjects be naive in order to secure valid results.

The five parallel studies did show older adults to be more conforming under all the conditions. Since all five conditions produced similar results using different groups of subjects, it is highly probable that social conformity is a generalized tendency on the part of older adults. The tendency toward social conformity might be thought of as a trait most characteristic of older individuals. In this research, the origin of the tendency was not subjected to manipulation. It should be noted that Klein avoided the tendency of some investigators to assume he had identified a general trait before demonstrating it.

Having established the fact that, within a high probability, he was dealing with a general trait of older adults to conform, Klein turned to the task of attempting to unravel the causes of this conformity. One possibility was that conformity in older adults was not a recent change but they had been conforming since young adulthood because of generational differences in values and experience. An alternative, which he adopted, was that older adults were more conforming resulting from uncertainty because they perceived themselves as being of low competence. In his study, he manipulated the situation in such a way as to increase the older subjects' self-perception of competence. Under the conditions of increased self-perceived competence, the conformity of older adults diminished. The particular results in the present context are not as important as are the principles of the research in which a true experimental study of aging was carried out by manipulating that which was purported to be the cause.

Given a hypothetical universal characteristic of aging that all persons show if they live long enough, one should be able to produce the phenomenon in young adults as well as reduce the phenomenon in older adults. It does not automatically follow that because older adults are more conforming as a result of a low self-perception of competence, attempts to increase their self-appraisal will reverse their tendency to be socially conforming. The easiest condition for the psychologist to deal with is a trait that is reversible. Had the manipulation study of Klein failed, it would not have proven that self-perception of competence was not the causal element since its consequences might not have been reversible.

SPEED OF RESPONSE

One of the most clearly established phenomena of aging is the tendency toward slowness of perceptual, motor, and cognitive processes (see Birren, 1965; Botwinick, 1973; and Welford, Chapter 19 in this volume). The history of the observation of age-related behavioral slowness goes well back into the last century. Early psychologists tended to characterize this evidence of slowing primarily as a peripheral sensorimotor phenomenon, which thus held minimal implications in the capacity of the nervous system to deal with more complex behavior. The early studies were purely descriptive in nature, but the replication of the main findings of a slowing with age were important, and led to subsequent descriptive research that showed that reaction times for complex decision making were disproportionately slow compared with reaction times for a simple choice. The evidence was contrary to the view that the slowing was more peripheral than central in character, since presumably, complex choices involved higher levels of the nervous system which should have shown minimal slowing if the peripheral sensorimotor structures were primarily involved.

A series of studies was conducted by Birren and Botwinick, *et al.* (see Birren, 1964, pp. 111–132) which clearly pointed to the fact that this slowing was a major feature of the central nervous system. These were experimental studies designed to localize the phenomenon. They were not experimental studies in the sense that the presumed causes of the slowing were manipulated. Again this distinction is useful since every bit of research on aging that appears to be experimental is not always so in its logic.

Once the phenomenon of age-related behavioral slowing was identified as characteristic of the central nervous system rather than of peripheral structures, then new possibilities of research arose. Birren, Riegel, and Morrison (1962) reported results that indicated that slowing of response speed with age was a general trait of older adults. Slowing with age was shown to manifest itself in all forms of behavior mediated by the central nervous system (Birren, 1974).

Parallel with the above line of research, descriptive evidence was gathered showing that with advancing age, human subjects showed a slowing in the EEG. Particularly the alpha frequency showed a tendency to decline or to move toward a slower modal frequency. Surwillo obtained EEG data from healthy community volunteers between the ages of 28 and 99 years of age and reported an increase in the alpha period of 4 milliseconds per decade (Surwillo, 1963). Similar information was reported by others on EEG and other bioelectric changes in the brain with age (see Marsh and Thompson, Chapter 11 in this volume). However, on the basis of descriptive studies, Surwillo reported an association between the slowing of alpha frequency with age and reaction time. On the basis of his findings, Surwillo formulated the hypothesis that the alpha frequency of the EEG was the master timing mechanism in behavior and that the slowing in reaction time was due to the slowing of the alpha frequency. This is one of the few causal hypotheses to be proposed in the psychology of aging, i.e., that the slowing of the alpha frequency with age is the causal factor that may underlie the diffuse slowing in information processing. Note that this causal hypothesis results from careful prior descriptive and descriptive-associative research. The direct testing of the hypothesis awaited an attempt to manipulate the alpha frequency since changing it would presumably change reaction time (changing reaction time would not necessarily lead to a change in alpha frequency unless a condition was used which jointly influenced the processes, e.g., a drug).

Woodruff (1972) put the Surwillo EEG-reaction time causal hypothesis to test in a classical experimental design by utilizing a modern manipulation, biofeedback. One should be able to make either a young or an old adult younger or older than the norm of his age group or better still younger or older than his average or basal level of performance (if the phenomenon is reversible). In the design of Woodruff, subjects were trained via biofeedback to increase or decrease their mean alpha frequency. Young and old subjects were randomly assigned to the increased or the decreased frequency condition, i.e., about 2 Hertz above or below their basal level. After training toward the altered frequency range, the subjects' reaction times were measured. The brain wave frequency for each reaction time was computed for each subject. In addition to the feature of using the subjects as their own

controls, a dummy feedback control group was also used in which young and old subjects were treated exactly as the experimental subjects but their brain wave frequency did not control the feedback.

The results of this experimental study showed that reaction time was faster in the fast alpha wave condition than in the slow alpha wave condition. To some extent, the results showed a verification of the causal hypothesis, though the age changes in EEG appeared to be unable to account for the magnitude of the increase in reaction time variability with age. Thus, it would appear that, in addition to alpha frequency or some other correlate of electrical activity of the brain, there are other determinants of the slowing of reaction time with age.

This classical experimental design was planned with the assumption that brain wave frequencies were modifiable. A causal relationship between age, alpha frequency and reaction time might exist without the possibility that the older nervous system could be modified. Also, alpha frequency might potentially be modified by lowering the basal level but not by increasing it. In biological systems, there is often an upper limit of function which in this study was not explored. Had the age groups responded differently to the manipulation of the alpha frequency, then further experimental analysis could have been undertaken to test the irreversible nature of the phenomenon.

One of the more significant aspects of this area of research is the fact that slowing of the EEG frequency seems to be related to survival. Muller, Grad, and Engelsmann (1975) reported on the characteristics of survivors and non-survivors of a group of 206 geriatric subjects followed over a five-year period. Slow waves were more marked in subjects who died within five years than in survivors. These findings when placed side by side with the experimental work of Woodruff raise some fundamental questions about EEG, reaction time and survival. Since Woodruff showed that the EEG could be modified in frequency, does this suggest that one can improve survival by altering EEG frequency? Woodruff's subjects were healthy and it is possible that she would not have had success in modifying brain wave frequencies in senile subjects as studied by Muller, Grad, and Engelsmann (1975). Reports have linked EEG slowing to basal ganglia atrophy in late life dementia (Leroy, Brion, and Soubrier, 1966). It is also of direct relevance that in a review by Hicks and Birren (1970), they linked the basal ganglia with speed of initiation and execution of movements, and they proposed that damage to or dysfunction of the basal ganglia may be involved in the slowness of behavior noted in older humans and animals. Thus the experimental, clinical, and descriptive literature appears to converge on a tentative anatomical location for both slowness in behavior with age, and slowing of the EEG, the latter related to survival. What is not clear is the extent to which the slowness of behavior and the EEG is a consequence of disease, or of a phylogenetic pattern to some extent modifiable by experimental manipulation.

PERCEPTUAL MASKING

Another approach for assessment of the extent of slowing with age in information processing as well as identification of additional contributing factors is the use of perceptual masking methods. Kline and Szafran (1975) employed visual masking to determine whether the timing of events in the nervous system is slower with age. In their study, they presented a visual figure followed, after a variable interval, by a visual masking stimulus known to "erase" the perception of the figure. Under these conditions older subjects require a longer interval after a stimulus in order to resist or escape masking. This suggests a longer duration of an after-effect to stimulation in the nervous system. One of the questions that has arisen in this area of research is whether the locus of the time change is "central" or "peripheral" in the sense of being in the visual cortex or in the eye (Kline and Birren, 1975).

Walsh and Till (in press) carried out a study designed to separate target energy and target duration in old and young subjects. They reported differences in peripheral processing time between age groups, i.e., the older peripheral

visual system operates more slowly. Walsh (in press) also reports data on age changes in central processing time with a 24 percent longer interval being required to escape masking between about the ages of 20 and 65 years.

These experiments are important contributions to the understanding of the slowing with age in information processing. They have been more concerned with where the slowing is localized conceptually and anatomically than with the causes of the slowing. To that extent, they should be classified as experimental descriptive studies, even though they will very likely lead to experiments which attempt to manipulate the causes of the slowing in information processing.

REACTION TIME AND PRACTICE

Other research has been carried out on reaction time and age, testing different hypotheses. Murrell, for example, thought that older adults might improve their reaction time with practice and his results do indicate that long-term practice appears to speed up reaction time, (Murrell, 1970). His hypothesis was essentially a disuse hypothesis but, if true, increasing practice should change the subjects' alpha frequency if one is dealing with a system of causal relationships. Both disuse and slowing of alpha cannot be the proximal causes of the slower reaction time. One can hardly reason that slowing of alpha can cause lack of practice, but one can reason that possible lack of practice of fast responses might change the basal alpha frequency. Thus it is when dealing with results from classical experimental studies that crucial, mutually exclusive hypotheses can emerge and be tested.

A more recent study of reaction time in active sports enthusiasts was carried out with an examination of the inevitability of the age change toward slowness in reaction time with age (Spirduso, 1975). Apparently, older active individuals show less slowness of response than do inactive persons. A difficulty of attempting to test such a hypothesis using different groups is the fact that older sports enthusiasts may in fact have been different at an early age; thus they may not have resisted aging so much as they had very fast reaction times at an early age. Yet another problem with complex behavior, like reaction time, is that practice may result in compensatory changes that obviate a deficit in one of the components.

There is an important distinction, made earlier, between a causal hypothesis and experimental studies and an attempt at intervention. One may, by intervention, bring a performance of a subject back to the high level he had previously. The nature of the intervention, however, may have nothing to do with the original deficit or indeed shed any light on its causation. Intervention may thus be regarded as bringing about a behavioral prosthesis without regard to understanding the original process. For example, increasing the brightness level of a room and providing older adults with correct lenses for the eye may relieve most if not all of the problems resulting in the inability to perceive material clearly as a result of accommodation. Demonstrating that older adults have a relatively greater increase in vision under high brightness does not tell us anything about the poorer accommodation resulting from a greater rigidity in the older lenses. One of the closest associations of function with age that has been identified has been that of the accommodation power of the eye (Weiss, 1959). Intervention and the obviation of the problem by compensatory lenses in no way leads to an understanding of the close association of accommodation of the eye with age.

The future of experimental psychology of aging is bright in the sense that there are many important relationships between age and functions to be explained. Many of the chapters in this volume identify such important problems. At the present time the lack of a theoretical framework gives a heavy empirical cast to the subject matter which will require, as time goes by, a dynamic structure in which to place the bricks of knowledge. Improved research design and multivariate methods of data analysis will not in themselves resolve this need. There may be a tendency to revert to a stimulus and response type of psychology or "neobehaviorism" to avoid the prospect of facing large masses of data that await systematic explanation. Hopefully, the developmental psychology of aging

and related experimental studies will not go through the painful processes that learning theory went through on its way to sophistication, a process that was marked by scholastic provincialism.

RESEARCH EVALUATION

Often researchers, teachers, and students are asked to give a critique of a research report or a proposed study. The content of a research proposal or published article can resist dissection, and it has proven useful to have an outline that poses questions for the reader to consider in arriving at an evaluation. The outline that follows has been adapted from a previous one (Birren, 1959a, pp. 38-40). It covers many aspects of research from the initial question to the conclusions drawn from the results. The components of research studies and their published reports are, characteristically, not uniformly strong in quality. It helps to consider each aspect in arriving at an evaluation of a dissertation or research proposal, or in determining whether a published article represents a significant addition to knowledge. Although intuitive thinking is part of the process that accompanies the weighing of the strengths and weaknesses of a study, the following evaluation outline is given in the hope that a more logical approach will also guide those of us who find it necessary to make judgments about research.

A. PROBLEM

1. What is the purpose of the research?
2. Is the problem clearly and concisely stated so that it can be researched or solved?
3. Does the research problem have a conceptual framework?
4. Is it clear whether this is a descriptive or normative study, a survey or a study to test a hypothesis?
5. Is the context of the problem described in such a way that it is readily apparent; what is included and excluded from consideration?
6. Are the essential concepts that are necessary to understand the problem defined?
7. Are the terms well defined? Is there

confusion in the definition of terms? Do they have arbitrary or multiple meanings?

8. Are assumptions stated and are they tenable in the light of existing knowledge?
9. Is the literature of previous studies adequately reviewed or taken into account?
10. Does the author attempt to make a contribution to systematizing previous information?
11. Are the hypotheses and objectives stated in the context of the research problem?
12. If a hypothesis is tested, is the theory from which it is derived sufficiently stated so that the hypothesis can be evaluated?
13. Are the independent and dependent variables clearly identified and defined?
14. Are the consequences of possible findings pointed out?
15. Is the scope of the problem too large for the resources available and the methods which can be used?

B. Experience of the Investigators

1. Are the investigators trained in the particular methods and procedures used?
2. Do the investigators have experience with the particular population studied?
3. If the study is large in scope has the investigator the skills or experience to manage it?

C. Design

1. Was the design of the study planned and evaluated beforehand?
2. Is the design applicable to, oversimplified, or unnecessarily complicated for the problem? Can it answer the questions posed?
3. Does the design take into account all the pertinent aspects of the study: subjects and materials, environments, manipulated variables or stimuli, measurements and observations and statistical methods?
4. Were alternative designs considered and the basis for their rejection given?
5. Are the compromises made with an ideal design described?
6. Is the design succinctly presented, as in a diagram, so that it can be readily understood?
7. Is the design an efficient one to solve the problem in terms of money, subjects and time?
8. Are the statistical methods to be used determined before the experiment starts?

9. Was the level of significance with respect to accepting or rejecting the null hypothesis determined and discussed before the study was undertaken?
10. Is the methodology appropriate for the design selected?
11. Has it been described clearly how the independent and dependent variables are to be manipulated?
12. Are there sufficient criteria set up against which the predictive and explanatory value of the test instruments and the experimental results can be measured?
13. Are there sufficient criteria established against which the internal and external validity of the experiment can be measured?

D. Sampling of Subjects or Materials

1. Was the sample adequately described?
2. Of what population was the sample representative?
3. Was the population sampled or were subgroups of the population sampled?
4. Was the sample an appropriate one for the purposes of the study?
5. Was the sample collected for the purposes of this study or for some other purpose?
6. Was there any possibility of the introduction of a sampling bias?
7. Were the subjects selected according to the design of the study and with regard to the statistical methods to be used?
8. Was the sampling adequate to result in a small enough standard error for the purposes of the study?
9. If animals were used, have the conditions of the colony been evaluated and described?
10. Has the health of the subjects been evaluated and described?
11. Were the subjects taking medications? If so, how may this affect the results?
12. Was there any loss of subjects or mortality in the sample and if so, is there a discussion of its possible effect on the results?
13. If replacement procedures for missing subjects were used, were such procedures adequate and were they sufficiently described?
14. Were the methods of sampling described?
    a. Simple random
    b. Systematic

c. Multistage random
d. Stratified
    i. proportional allocation
    ii. optimum allocation
    iii. disproportionate allocation
e. Cluster
f. Stratified cluster
g. Biased
h. Purposive
i. Incidental
j. Repetitive
k. Judgment, quota

E. CONTROLS

1. What controls were exercised through sampling (e.g., twins, littermates, and matching)?
2. What controls were exercised by selection of setting or natural habitats?
3. If relevant, were blind or double blind controls used in the gathering, evaluating and interpretation of the data?
4. Were placebo effects controlled?
5. What controls were exercised by experimental manipulation? Are the controlled variables adequately described?
6. Were the conditions the same for all subjects or were adjustments made or a treatment given?
7. If controls were changed, were results analyzed with respect to the altered conditions?
8. Were any important controls absent that are usually found in a study of this type, and, if so, was the absence justified?
9. Could any additional controls have been included which would have increased the efficiency of the study?

F. MEASUREMENTS AND DATA COLLECTION

1. Were the techniques of measurements or observations adequately described?
2. Was a pilot study conducted, particularly if the materials used were constructed for the present experiment?
3. If standardized tests were used, was there reference to normative data?
4. Were all variables of the study categorized and quantified sufficiently?
5. Were the data collected accurately and objectively? What checks were made to guard against possible error in collecting and tabulating data?

6. If several measures were taken, was a reasonable and predetermined time schedule followed?
7. Have reliability coefficients been calculated between observers or examiners concerning their scoring of tests or evaluation of their subjects? Were possible examiner biases measured?
8. Were the methods and measurements suitable for the problem, for testing the hypotheses and meeting the objectives of the research?
9. Were calibrations of instruments, observer differences and other aspects of the techniques described? From the information presented could the measurements be repeated by another investigator?
10. Were the measurements or observations known to be sufficiently reliable for the study or, if new, were reliability coefficients reported?
11. Was the validity of the measurements used established? Has the construct validity of the tests or measures been reported?

G. DATA TREATMENT

1. Were the methods of recording and the treatment of data described?
2. Were the statistical procedures clearly described?
3. Were the statistical procedures used appropriate for the research problem and the data?
4. If several different statistical analyses were made, is it clear how they are related? What contribution did each analysis make to the results?
5. Were the underlying assumptions of the statistical tests used violated due to the methods, sampling, or the data?
6. Were the tests of significance described and are they suitable?

H. RESULTS

1. Were the results or data adequately presented so that the reader may verify the author's statements about them?
2. Were the results clearly reported in tables and graphs so that others may use the data or reproduce the results?
3. Have the essential relationships posed by the problem been analyzed and tested for significance?

4. Are the results a logical product of the procedures and analyses, and are the results relevant to the problem as originally outlined? Do the results reflect the investigation of the present problem(s) or has the experimenter attempted to solve problems which may be nonexistent due to the fact that he misunderstood the nature of the real problem?
5. Have the statistical limitations of the study been appreciated and explained?
6. Are estimates of error provided and are sources of error identified and quantified?
7. If several related variables were examined are the results consistent?
8. Are the results consistent within themselves?
9. Has the experiment high external and internal validity?
10. What is the predictive validity of the study?
11. What is the explanatory power of the study?
12. Are results established that are not contained in the data and are the results confused with conjecture by the researcher?
13. Can the results be attributed to a treatment, spontaneous recovery or other effect?

I. CONCLUSIONS

1. Does the author draw conclusions about the major problem posed in the study?
2. Are the conclusions clearly supported by the data? Are there inconsistencies between the results and conclusions? Are conjectures clearly separated from the researched facts?
3. Are limitations of the study clearly stated?
4. Are the results generalized to the population at large? What rationale is provided and is the generalization valid?
5. Have unexpected results been rejected merely because they do not agree with the researcher's expectations or because they appear to conflict with common sense?
6. Are statistically non-significant tests evaluated or are they interpreted to be meaningless and unimportant?
7. Are important reservations or qualifications pointed out? Are possible artifacts or spurious relations pointed out?
8. Has the author overlooked important aspects of the results?

9. Can additional questions or new hypotheses be generated from the study and are they stated?
10. Can the study be replicated and cross-validated in terms of A, B, C, D, E, F, and G?
11. Are the results interpreted in relation to other published information and is their significance for related fields pointed out?
12. Are the methods used in the study critically reviewed in the light of the obtained results?
13. Are the interpretations, implications for future research, and the development of new methods appropriate for the scope of the present study, or do they reflect an overestimation or underestimation of the significance of the study?
14. What is the potential importance of the study and what scientific or practical advances will result?
15. Are necessary modifications of theory, current interpretations of data, or practice pointed out?
16. What contributions have been made to the theory of the subject?

EPILOGUE

The stance of this chapter has been to urge experimental research on aging since it has usually been accompanied by fewer errors and is more efficient than descriptive research or descriptive-associative research. However, lawful relations have been arrived at by purely descriptive research in many natural sciences. For this reason, investigators are urged to be flexible, and be descriptive or experimental in relation to the problem studied and not avoid large issues that must at present be studied with descriptive approaches. Sometimes this seems to present us with ". . . the dilemma of either working elegantly on the trivial, or inelegantly on great issues. Rather, it would seem we should encourage a descriptive and analytical psychology of aging while striving toward experimental control of the major causes of aging" (Birren, 1970, p. 135).

Pursuit of research on aging has three values—cultural, scientific, and practical. A culture which does not encourage speculation or research on perhaps mankind's greatest dilemma, his aging and mortality, would seem to be sterile. However difficult acquisition of generalizations about aging will be, when we gain them they are likely to be some of the most profound that mankind could possess. In the long-term pursuit of such knowledge, the trained, intelligent, curious mind is the most fundamental ingredient.

While there is much to be optimistic about our advancement in understanding the processes of aging, the chapters on theory in this handbook indicate how little there is in the way of systematic theory to help us organize the information that exists. Without a strong conceptual base, the organization of research and information is highly data oriented in the sense of being directed toward narrow, specific problems. Research sectarianism is another impediment to research on aging that has perhaps blocked theoretical formulations that take into account the fundamental biological as well as social nature of mankind.

Aging seems ubiquitous among living things and it seems pervasive as a force(s) in the history and future evolution of man as a species. The evolution of aging is of itself a puzzle, for it would seem reasonable that mankind shares some processes of aging with earlier evolved species. What are the biochemical changes in non-vertebrate forms that have rudimentary or no nervous systems that lead to their lower survival with age? Which of these have we in common? If mankind shares processes of aging with lower animals, then much experimentation can be conducted using those creatures showing more rapid aging. On the other hand, as highly differentiated organisms we may have special forms of aging not displayed by lower animals. Thus the nervous system, so crucial to complex behavior, may show a pattern of aging unique among the vertebrates since it is a lately evolved structure with highly specialized functions. Questions about wisdom, creativity, mood, and love in relation to age hardly seem appropriately studied by considerations of aging of flatworms or parabiosed rats, though some elementary processes run through the animal kingdom. Perhaps there is a hierarchical nature to the way we age: phylogenetic, unique individual heredity (parental longevity), disease, disuse, and progressive experience leading to further psychological differentiation.

We can look at the aging of mankind as a a species, or look at the aging of individuals. In the latter case, one may study the strategies of an aging individual whereby his failing body may house a mind expanding in wisdom. Survival of such a person must be the result of a balance between the somatic vulnerabilities and the capacity of the nervous system for executive management of behavioral choices as well as maximization of the declining functions of the body through an integrative role over vegetative processes.

At this point, it is perhaps appropriate to reflect upon the different obligations we have as members of a species hopeful of survival, and our obligations to survive as individuals. It would seem that natural selection has favored reproduction during young adulthood when there is the least risk in terms of the possibility of defective offspring. Conceiving at an age when we are neither too young nor too old would seem to provide the circumstance under which an optimum germ cell would develop. If aging provides an advantage to the species by decreasing the probability of conception by old parents and thereby of defective offspring, it leaves to the individual an uncertain struggle for biological and psychological survival. Under optimal conditions of a changing body and changing environment, the older person would seem to seek to maintain maximum adaptive capacity, and to establish an equilibrium or homeostasis with the biological, psychological, and social forces upon him. This implies that the executive portion of the nervous system that is consciously involved with voluntary activity, is directing behavior toward achievement of a balance that is congruent with a lifetime of experience, a unique set of values and personality. The effort to establish a personal equilibrium among the forces that surround us results in some of us becoming wise as we grow old, more valuable to ourselves, to others, and to the broader flow of events that comprise a history of human destiny.

REFERENCES

Axelrod, J. 1974. The pineal gland: a neurochemical transducer. *Science*, 184, 1341–1348.

Baer, D. M. 1973. The control of developmental processes: Why wait? *In*, J. R. Nesselroade and H. W. Reese (eds.), *Life-Span Developmental Psychology*, pp. 187–193. New York: Academic Press.

Baltes, P. B., and Goulet, L. R. 1971. Exploration of

developmental variables by manipulation and simulation of age differences in behavior. *Hum. Develop.*, **14**, 149–170.

Baltes, P. B., and Labouvie, G. V. 1971. Adult development of intellectual performance: description, explanation, modification. *In*, C. Eisdorfer and M. P. Lawton (eds.), *The Psychology of Adult Development and Aging*, pp. 157–219. Washington, D.C.: American Psychological Association.

Baltes, P. B., and Nesselroade, J. R. 1973. The developmental analysis of individual differences on multiple measures. *In*, J. R. Nesselroade and H. W. Reese (eds.), *Life-Span Developmental Psychology*, pp. 219–251. New York: Academic Press.

Baltes, P. B., and Schaie, K. W. (eds.) 1973. *Life Span Developmental Psychology: Personality and Socialization.* New York: Academic Press.

Baltes, P. B., and Schaie, K. W. (eds.) 1973a. *Life Span developmental research paradigms: retrospects and prospects. In*, P. B. Baltes and K. W. Schaie (eds.), *Life Span Developmental Psychology: Personality and Socialization.* New York: Academic Press.

Berger, R. J. 1975. Bioenergetic functions of sleep and activity rhythms and their possible relevance to aging. *Federation Proc.*, **34**, 97–102.

Birren, J. E. 1959a. Principles of research on aging. *In*, J. E. Birren (ed.), *Handbook of Aging and the Individual*, pp. 3–42. Chicago: University of Chicago Press.

Birren, J. E. (ed.) 1959b. *Handbook of Aging and the Individual.* Chicago: University of Chicago Press.

Birren, J. E. 1964. *The Psychology of Aging.* Englewood Cliffs, New Jersey: Prentice-Hall.

Birren, J. E. 1965. Age changes in speed of behavior: its central nature and physiological correlates. *In*, A. T. Welford and J. E. Birren (eds.), *Behavior, Aging, and the Nervous System*, pp. 191–216. Springfield, Illinois: Charles C. Thomas.

Birren, J. E. 1969. The concept of functional age, theoretical background. *Hum. Develop.*, **12**, 214–215.

Birren, J. E. 1970. Toward an experimental psychology of aging. *American Psychologist*, **25**, 124–135.

Birren, J. E. 1974. Psychophysiology and speed of response. *American Psychologist*, **29**, 808–815.

Birren, J. E. 1976. New aspects of transitions in adult development. Proceedings Conference on, Transitional Phases in Human Development. International Society for the Study of Behavioral Development. In press.

Birren, J. E., Riegel, K. F., and Morrison, D. F. 1962. Age differences in response speed as a function of controlled variations of stimulus conditions. *Gerontologia*, **6**, 1–18.

Botwinick, J. 1973. *Aging and Behavior.* New York: Springer.

Brown, F. A., Jr. 1972. The "clocks" timing biological rhythms. *Amer. Scient.*, **60**, 756–766.

Burnet, F. M. 1970a. *Immunological Surveillance*, pp. 224–257. New York: Pergamon Press.

Burnet, F. M. 1970b. An immunological approach to aging. *Lancet*, **2**, 358–360.

Comfort, A. 1956. *The Biology of Senescence.* London: Routledge and Kegan Paul.

Comfort, A. 1957. The biological approach in the comparative study of ageing. *In*, G. E. W. Wolstenholme and C. M. O'Connor (eds.), *Methodology of the Study of Ageing*, pp. 2–19. London: J. and A. Churchill.

Cowdry, E. V. 1942. *Problems of Ageing.* Baltimore: Williams & Wilkins.

Curtis, H. J. 1966. *Biological Mechanisms of Aging.* Springfield, Illinois: Charles C. Thomas.

Dirken, J. M. (ed.) 1972. *Functional Age of Industrial Workers.* Groningen, Netherlands: Wolters-Noordhoff.

Eisdorfer, C., and Lawton, M. P. (eds.) 1973. *The Psychology of Adult Development and Aging.* Washington, D.C.: American Psychological Association.

Finch, C. E. 1973. Catecholamine metabolism in the brains of ageing male mice. *Brain Res.*, **52**, 261–276.

Finch, C. E. 1976. The regulation of physiological changes during mammalian aging. *Quart. Rev. Biol.* In press.

Flavell, J. H. 1963. *The Developmental Psychology of Jean Piaget.* New York: Van Nostrand Reinhold.

Fozard, J. L. 1972. Predicting age in the adult years from psychological assessments of abilities and personality. *Hum. Develop.*, **3**, 175–182.

Goulet, L. R., and Baltes, P. B. (eds.) 1970. *Life-Span Developmental Psychology Research and Theory.* New York: Academic Press.

Greene, W. 1954. Psychological factors in reticuloendothelial disease. *Psychosomat. Med.*, **16**, 220–230.

Gribbin, K. J., Schaie, K. W., and Parham, I. A. 1974. A longitudinal study of functional age. Program, Meeting of the Gerontological Society, 1974, p. 4, abstract.

Handler, P. 1960. Radiation and aging. *In*, N. W. Shock (ed.), *Aging*, pp. 199–223. Washington, D.C.: American Association for the Advancement of Science.

Henry, J. P., Meehan, J. P., and Stephens, P. M. 1967. The use of psychosocial stimuli to induce prolonged systolic hypertension in mice. *Psychosomat. Med.*, **29**, 408–432.

Heron, A., and Chown, S. 1967 *Age and Function.* London: J. and A. Churchill.

Hicks, L. H., and Birren, J. E. 1970. Aging, brain damage, and psychomotor slowing. *Psychol. Bull.*, **74**, 377–396.

Hoyer, W. J., Kafer, R. A., Simpson, S. C., and Hoyer, F. W. 1974. *Gerontologist*, **14**, 149–152.

Huebner, R. J., and Gilden, R. V. 1971. Inherited RNA viral genomes (virogenes and oncogenes) in the etiology of cancer. *In*, P. Emmelot and P. Bentvelzen (eds.), *RNA Viruses and Host Genome in Oncogenesis*, pp. 197–219. Amsterdam: North Holland Publishing.

Huebner, R., and Todaro, G. J. 1969. Oncogenes of RNA tumor viruses as determinants of cancer. *Proc. Nat. Acad. Sci.*, **64**, 1087-1094.

Jalavisto, E., Lindquist, C., and Makkonen, T. 1964. Assessment of biological age III: mental and neural factors in longevity. *Annales Academiae Scientiarum Fennicae*, **106**, 3-20.

Jones, H. B. 1959. The relation of human health to age, place, and time. *In*, J. E. Birren (ed.), *Handbook of Aging and the Individual*, pp. 336-363. Chicago: University of Chicago Press.

Kissen, D. 1963. Personality characteristics in males conducive to lung cancer. *Brit. J. Med. Psychol.*, **36**, 27.

Kissen, D. 1969. The present status of psychosomatic cancer research. *Geriatrics*, **24**, 129-137.

Klein, R. L. 1972. Age, sex and task difficulty as predictors of social conformity. *J. Gerontol.*, **27**, 229-236.

Klein, R. L., and Birren, J. E. 1973. Age, perceived self-competence and conformity. Proceedings, 81st annual convention, American Psychological Association, pp. 779-780.

Kline, D. W., and Birren, J. E. 1975. Age differences in backward dichoptic masking. *Exper. Aging Res.*, **1**, 17-25.

Kline, D. W., and Szafran, J. 1975. Age differences in backward monoptic visual noise masking, *J. Gerontol.*, **30**, 307-311.

Krohn, P. L. (ed.) 1966. *Topics in the Biology of Aging*. New York: John Wiley.

Landahl, H. D. 1959. Biological periodicities, mathematical biology, and aging. *In*, J. E. Birren (ed.), *Handbook of Aging and the Individual*, pp. 81-115. Chicago: University of Chicago Press.

Leroy, C., Brion, S., and Soubrier, J. P. 1966. Correlation between anatomical lesions and the alpha rhythm in senile dementia. *Electroencephalo. and Clin. Neurophysiol.*, **20**, 532.

LeShan, L., and Worthington, R. E. 1955. Some psychologic correlates of neoplastic disease—A preliminary report. *J. Clin. and Exper. Psychopath.*, **16**, 281-288.

LeShan, L., and Worthington, R. E. 1956. Loss of cathexis as a common psychodynamic characteristic of cancer patients—an attempt at statistical validation of a clinical hypothesis. *Psych. Reports*, **2**, 183-193.

Lindop, P. J., and Sacher, G. A. (ed.) 1966. *Radiation and Ageing. Proceedings of a Colloquium held in Semmering, Austria*. London: Taylor and Francis.

Maier, H. W. 1969. *Three Theories of Child Development*. Revised Edition. New York: Harper & Row.

Muhlbock, O. 1957. The use of inbred strains of animals in experimental gerontology. *In*, G. E. W. Wolstenholme and C. M. O'Connor (eds.), *Methodology of the Study of Ageing*, pp. 115-125. London: J. and A. Churchill.

Muller, H. F., Grad, B., and Engelsmann, F. 1975. Biological and psychological predictors of survival in a psychogeriatric population. *J. Gerontol.*, **30**, 47-52.

Murrell, F. H. 1970. The effect of extensive practice on age differences in reaction time. *J. Gerontol.*, **25**, 268-274.

Nandy, K. 1975. Significance of brain-reactive antibodies in serum of aged mice. *J. Gerontol.*, **30**, 412-416.

Nesselroade, J. R., and Reese, H. W. (eds.) 1973. *Life-Span Developmental Psychology: Methodological Issues*. New York: Academic Press.

Nisbett, R. E., Braver, A., Jusela, G., and Kesur, D. 1975. Age and sex differences in behaviors mediated by the ventromedial hypothalamus. *J. Comp. Physiol. Psychol.*, **88**, 735-746.

Nuttall, R. L. 1972. The strategy of functional age research. *Aging and Human Develop.*, **3**, 149-152.

Pearl, R. 1934. *The Ancestry of the Long-lived*. Baltimore: Johns Hopkins University Press.

Piaget, J. 1973. *The Child's Conception of the World*. St. Albans, England: Granada Publishing.

Raff, M. C. 1974. Development and differentiation of lymphocytes. *In*, T. J. King (ed.), *Developmental Aspects of Carcinogenesis and Immunity*. New York: Academic Press.

Reichenbach, M., and Mathers, R. A. 1959. The place of time and aging in the natural sciences and scientific philosophy. *In*, J. E. Birren (ed.), *Handbook of Aging and the Individual*, pp. 43-80. Chicago: University of Chicago Press.

Retzlaff, E., and Fontaine, J. 1965. Functional and structural changes in motor neurons with age. *In*, A. T. Welford and J. E. Birren (eds.), *Behavior, Aging and the Nervous System*, pp. 340-352. Springfield, Illinois: Charles C. Thomas.

Roseman, J. M., and Buckley, C. E. 1975. Inverse relationship between serum IgG concentrations and measures of intelligence in elderly persons. *Nature*, **254**, 55-56.

Sampson, G. A., and Jenner, F. E. 1975. Circadian rhythms and mental illness. *Psychol. Med.*, **5**, 4-8.

Schaie, K. W., and Gribbin, K. J. 1975. Adult development and aging. *Annual Review of Psychology*, **26**, 65-96.

Schmale, A., and Iker, H. 1966. The psychological setting of uterine cervical cancer. *New York Academy of Science Annals*, **125**, 807.

Smith, J. M. 1957. Genetic variations in ageing. *In*, W. B. Yapp and G. H. Bourne (eds.), *The Biology of Ageing*, pp. 115-122. London: Institute of Biology.

Spirduso, W. W. 1975. Reaction and movement time as a function of age and physical activity level. *J. Gerontol.*, **30**, 435-440.

Strong, L. C. 1968. *Biological Aspects of Cancer and Aging*. London: Pergamon Press.

Surwillo, W. W. 1963. The relation of simple response time to brain wave frequency and the effects of age. *Electroencephalo. Clin. Neurophysiol.*, **15**, 105-114.

Temin, H. M. 1970. Malignant transformation of cells by viruses. *Perspectives Biol. Med.*, **14**, 11-26.

Temin, H. M. 1971. The protovirus hypothesis. *J. Nat. Cancer Inst.*, **46**, III–VIII.

Temin, H. M. 1972. The protovirus hypothesis and cancer. *In*, P. Emmelot and P. Bentuelzen (eds.), *RNA Viruses and Host Genome in Oncogenesis*. Amsterdam-London: North-Holland Publishing.

Temin, H. M., and Kang, C.-Y. 1974. RNA-directed DNA polymerase activity in uninfected cells. *In*, T. J. King (ed.), *Developmental Aspects of Carcinogenesis and Immunity*. New York: Academic Press.

Todaro, G. J. 1974. Endogenous viruses in normal and transformed cells. *In*, T. J. King (ed.), *Developmental Aspects of Carcinogenesis and Immunity*. New York: Academic Press.

U.S., D.H.E.W., National Institute of Child Health and Human Development. 1968. *Perspectives on Human Deprivation: Biological, Psychological, and Sociological*. Washington, D.C.: Public Health Service.

U.S., Public Health Service. 1970. *Vital Statistics of the United States*. Volume II, Section 5, Life tables. Washington, D.C.: Government Printing Office.

Verzar, F. 1963. *Lectures in Experimental Gerontology*. Springfield, Illinois: Charles C. Thomas.

Walsh, D. A. 1976. Age differences in central perceptual processing: a dichoptic backward masking investigation. *J. Gerontol.*, **31**, 178–185.

Walsh, D. A., and Till, R. E. (In press). Age differences in peripheral perceptual processing: a monoptic backward masking investigation.

Weiss, A. D. 1959. Sensory functions *In*, J. E. Birren, (ed.), *Handbook of Aging and the Individual*, pp. 503–542. Chicago: University of Chicago Press.

Welford, A. T. 1957. Methodological problems in the study of changes in human performance with age. *In*, G. E. W. Wolstenholme and C. M. O'Connor (eds.), *Methodology of the Study of Ageing*, pp. 149–169. London: J. and A. Churchill.

Winfree, A. T. 1975. Unclocklike behavior of biological clocks. *Nature*, **253**, 315–319.

Wohlwill, J. E. 1973. *The Study of Behavioral Development*. New York: Academic Press.

Wolstenholme, G. E. W., and O'Connor, C. M. (eds.) 1957. *Methodology of the Study of Ageing*. London: J. and A. Churchill.

Woodruff, D. S. 1972. Biofeedback control of the EEG alpha rhythm and its effect on reaction time in the young and old. Dissertation. University of Southern California.

2
QUASI-EXPERIMENTAL RESEARCH DESIGNS IN THE PSYCHOLOGY OF AGING*

K. Warner Schaie
University of Southern California

INTRODUCTION

Whenever age is to be treated as the independent variable, it becomes impracticable to utilize the more precise experimental paradigms. Of course age may be treated as the dependent variable or substituted for by other parameters such as performance. Otherwise recourse need be taken to the quasi-experimental approaches to be discussed in this chapter.

Moreover, there is a need for parametric studies of variables of interest to the psychologist which by their nature require assessment in field situations where statistical rather than experimental controls must be utilized. Quasi-experimental designs refer to situations where random assignment of subjects to treatment or experiential conditions is impossible. Instead, comparison is made of individuals under circumstances where they are found in different conditions, but other than being a member of the class subject to that condition, are thought to be randomly selected from the general population of interest.

*Several of the components of this chapter have previously been discussed in more extensive form or different context in Schaie (1965, 1972b, 1973) and Schaie and Gribbin (1975).

Most commonly investigators have compared samples of individuals at different ages (cross-sectional method) and have concluded that any difference found on the dependent variable could be attributed to chronological age, assuming that their samples were somehow equivalent in all other aspects which might relate to the dependent variable under study (also see Schaie and Gribbin, 1975). Critics of the cross-sectional method have suggested that descriptive data on age changes in populations must properly be obtained by the longitudinal study of the same individuals. But such studies are plagued by their impracticable time line if one is interested in the entire adult age span, as well as with problems of attrition and sociocultural change during the course of a given study. Either method is simplistic unless specific assumptions about aging and change over time are introduced and incorporated into the requisite experimental design.

It is the purpose of this section to examine the types of quasi-experimental designs most frequently used in aging studies and to explicate some of the more serious threats to their internal and external validity (cf. Campbell and Stanley, 1963). Such an examination will have to concern itself with common implicit assumptions made by researchers about the direction and slope of the aging process as well as change in behavior over time. We will next have to differentiate the three processes so frequently confused in aging studies: ontogenetic change, cohort differences and sociocultural change. Then, we will discover that for work on aging the notion of a representative sample is an unattainable ideal, but that there may be more or less undesirable ways of departing from the ideal. Finally, we will consider the embarrassing fact that measurement instruments age just as people do and that techniques are not generally comparable across wide age ranges.

ASSUMPTIONS ABOUT AGING AND CHANGE OVER TIME

Since we know that two groups of subjects who differ in age generally also differ on many other parameters, it is no longer permissible to offer for publication results of a study comparing young and old organisms unless the underlying model which would permit such an approach is clearly specified. Given such specification, it is possible to capitalize upon experiments of nature which may permit testing of one's model, or alternatively program one's sample selection in such a way as to permit derivation of quasi-experimental hypothesis-testing designs.

In order to permit explication of threats to the internal and external validity of a given empirical study, it is necessary to understand both the particular dimension of development which is to be investigated and the function which is presumed to underlie the developmental gradient to be studied (Baltes and Schaie, 1973). On the former issue, most aging researchers implicitly wish to generalize in regard to maturational events (age changes). Such generalizations, however, explicitly require time series measurement, even though such series might be composed of segments for which data are obtained simultaneously during a brief time period.

But many policy-relevant research studies merely consider age as an index for different maturational levels to be compared at one point in time (age differences). In this instance it is much preferred to talk about cohort analysis

(Riley, 1973) rather than age differentiation, and non-equivalent control group designs may suffice. Where theory testing regarding the appearance of certain phenomena at a given age is required, or where treatment effects which influence developmental phenomena independently of maturation are to be examined (time-lag), separate sample pretest-posttest designs of various levels of complexity may be required.

Models of Aging

The design of experiments involving age as an independent variable will inevitably be influenced by the basic assumptions accepted by the investigator as characterizing the nature of adult age changes. Most empirical investigations have assumed one of three basic models: irreversible decrement, stability, and decrement with compensation.

The most common model, particularly in the areas of intelligence, creativity and achievement, assumes that a maximal level of functioning is reached at some point in adulthood and that the characteristic age function thereafter involves linear (or linearly accelerating) and irreversible decrement. An implicit assumption of the model is that the effects of pathology are either uncorrelated with the variables of interest or that the investigator's sample contains at each age level a representative selection of pathology characteristic of the general population. The irreversible decrement model is most appropriate for those variables where performance may be dominated by the level of efficiency of the peripheral sensory functions and by psychomotor speed. The model implicitly specifies that age changes will occur as a function of maturational events, regardless of environmental input. But level and peak of performance may still shift as a consequence of events occurring to the species or any of its subgroups over long periods of time. The latter generational or cohort effects must be differentiated from within generation effects under such circumstances and a cohort-sequential design will usually be required (e.g., Riegel, Riegel, and Meyer, 1967a).

A less popular model, one which is often implicitly subsumed in personality studies, postulates that once maturity is reached adult behavior remains stable. Since irreversible changes are incompatible with this model, it is necessary to specify that performance on the variables of interest is uncorrelated with pathology, or that the investigator's interest is restricted to pathology-free populations. The model allows for cyclical change about an optimal level (cf. also Schaie, 1973; Goulet, Hay, and Barclay, 1974) occurring as a function of both external and internal events. The stability model, in addition to personality dimensions, may also fit measures of crystallized intelligence and those biologically mediated behaviors whose base remains relatively stable from maturity until the terminal drop (Riegel and Riegel, 1972) occurring just before death. But if we accept the stability model, concern then shifts from within generation age functions or age differences, since we postulate the age effect to be trivial. Instead we would now be concerned with such questions as the determination of generational shifts in asymptotic levels attained at maturity and the pattern of transient cyclical events related to time specific inputs. In other words, we would now require cross-sequential designs to differentiate generational differences from time of measurement effects (e.g., Schaie and Labouvie-Vief, 1974).

A third model, whose plausibility is implicitly assumed by the gerontological behavior modifier, expects age decrement past maturity, but also allows that significant environmental remediation may compensate for the maturationally programmed deficit. In this model the presence or absence of age-related pathology is not critical, since if pathology mediated by biological decrement events is indeed age-related, such pathology would also be considered subject to remediation via environmental inputs. The model may in particular fit variables such as fluid intelligence and other psychological variables where speed of response is involved. In general this model fits wherever age changes during the adult period must be expected due to their correlation with biological events, and where long-term shifts over generations appear unlikely but where environmental inputs should have important moderating effects. For such variables it would seem important to differen-

tiate maturational variance from transient environmental input, with the time-sequential strategy being most appropriate (e.g., Schaie, 1970).

Just as we have specified different age functions for the irreversible decrement model, there are similar alternatives available for both stability and decrement with compensation assumptions. These models have been specified elsewhere (Schaie, 1973).

Utilization of "Experiments of Nature" in the Psychology of Aging

Since age, or cohort membership, or time of occurrence of a developmental event are not assignable variables, it is generally necessary to maximize the availability of suitable experimental controls which arise from fortuitous combinations of environmental events. Rather than taking advantage of such naturalistic quasi-experiments, many aging researchers in the past have taken one of two equally disastrous courses of action. Some investigators have assumed that if individuals are classified by age, they will be randomly distributed with respect to any other demographic classification related to the dependent variables of interest, and that they can therefore conclude that any differences found in the dependent variable can be causally related to the effects of aging—an assumption too strong for any empirical investigation in the behavioral domain. Alternately, researchers have attempted to control for variables such as education, presence or absence of pathology, institutionalization, income level, etc. It is often not recognized that such controls, if used without careful planning, will lead to the comparison of sub-populations which for different ages and cohorts differ in their representativeness of the total population from which they have been drawn, severely impairing the external validity of the study. For example, requiring a twelfth grade education would lead to the selection of the top decile of 70-year-olds while providing a 95 percent sample of 20-year-olds.

The proper quasi-experiment would maximize the facts that sociocultural change occurs at different rates in similar cultures and in sub-groups of the population, that certain kinds of pathology appear at differential rates in various population sub-groups, and that social roles shift at markedly varied rates within the complexities of a pluralistic society. In other words, the role of age as a carrier (cf. Wohlwill, 1970) rather than a true independent variable makes it incumbent upon us to identify populations offering naturalistic controls for explanatory alternatives to the age difference hypothesis. For example, a study of disengagement as a function of age ought to consider comparing the personality patterns of young adults who have been forced out of active societal participation (say as a consequence of chronic disease) with adults disengaging as a function of retirement. Or as another example a study of creativity across different adult age groups might handle the obvious cohort differences in intellectual function by examining special populations such as high school teachers where the level of required education as well as social class membership has remained relatively constant. Attempts at controlling for environmental events might capitalize on such fortuitous occurrences as the change in voting age or differences in mandatory retirement ages in different jurisdictions.

Derivation of Quasi-Experimental Hypothesis-Testing Designs

Campbell and Stanley (1963) list ten types of quasi-experimental designs, all of which may be applicable in certain situations faced by the student of adult development and which are therefore recommended for careful attention. However, some of the proposed designs are less attractive than others, in that they are either vulnerable to those sources of internal and external invalidity which are particularly troublesome in developmental investigations or control for the effect of maturation which is our typically assumed "treatment."

It may be useful to review briefly the implications of these threats to validity as they apply to the design of aging studies. Let us consider the typical pretest-posttest paradigm, where the "treatment" is assumed to be the aging of the organism. That is, we compare the behavior of a sample of individuals at two points in time (T1 and T2) and infer that a change in the dependent variable has occurred as a function of the treatment.

Eight threats to the internal validity of this design are suggested by Campbell and Stanley (1963):

1. *History*. Environmental events occurring between T1 and T2 may account for the behavior change. This particular problem has led us to conclude that the single cohort longitudinal study may rarely be useful for testing hypotheses about age changes in behavioral studies (cf. Schaie, 1972a; Nesselroade and Baltes, 1974).

2. *Maturation*. If the intent is to measure the effect of aging, then this variable is no threat to validity, but we must worry about designs which implicitly control for maturation, since we should not design away the very variable of interest.

3. *Testing*. The pretest may have an effect upon performance at T2, particularly on tests of ability and achievement. Such an effect, more generally known as practice effect, is particularly serious over short time periods, but probably needs to be controlled also in studies covering extended periods of time (see Schaie and Parham, 1974).

4. *Instrumentation*. This refers to changes in the measurement instrument or process from T1 to T2. In addition to the obvious changes in procedures or observers we need to worry about shifts in the genotypic structure of the specific measurement operations which may be pertinent even though the phenotypic measurement is rigorously maintained over time. The latter issue will be more thoroughly discussed later on.

5. *Statistical regression*. Unless our measurement instrument has perfect reliability, high mean scores at T1 will go down at T2 and low scores at T1 will go up. Such regression effects may serve to enhance or obscure true maturational change (cf. Baltes, Nesselroade, Schaie, and Labouvie, 1972; Furby, 1973).

6. *Mortality*. A further threat to internal validity occurs when not all subjects tested at T1 are available for retest at T2. In aging studies mortality includes death, disappearance and failure to cooperate for the second test (cf. Baltes, Schaie, and Nardi, 1971; Riegel, Riegel, and Meyer, 1967b; Schaie, Labouvie, and Barrett, 1973). Finally, in all cross-sectional and sequential studies there is the problem of comparability across samples.

TABLE 1. CLASSIFICATION OF QUASI-EXPERIMENTAL DESIGNS[a] IN TERMS OF FAMILIAR DEVELOPMENTAL PARADIGMS.

Quasi-experimental Design	Equivalent Developmental Paradigm	Applicability
1. Time series	Single cohort longitudinal	Limited to species universals
2. Equivalent time samples	None	Not applicable
3. Equivalent materials samples	Single cohort longitudinal with alternate forms for each measurement	Same as 1
4. Non-equivalent control group design	Time-sequential	Differentiates age and secular trends
5. Counterbalanced designs	None	Not applicable
6. Separate-sample	Cross-sectional	Most suitable for identifying generation differences
a) Controlled for history	Cohort-sequential with independent samples	Differentiates age and cohort differences, controlling for history, testing and reactivity
b) Controlled for secular trends	Cross-sequential with repeated measurement	Differentiates cohort and secular trends
7. Separate sample pretest-posttest control group design	Cross-sequential with independent samples	Differentiates cohort and secular trends controlled for testing and reactivity
8. Multiple time series design	Cohort-sequential with repeated measurements	Differentiates age and cohort effects controlled for history
9. Institutional cycle design	Time-lag or time-sequential	Assesses secular trends and/or differentiates age trends
10. Regression discontinuity	Functional age analysis	Developmental criteria other than age

[a]According to Campbell and Stanley (1963).

7. *Selection.* It is frequently well-nigh impossible to rule out the possibility that differences across groups may be a function of differential recruitment, particularly in volunteer panel studies (Schaie, 1959).

8. *Selection-maturation interaction.* Although one would not control for maturation in an aging study, it is important to note when maturation interacts with selection, because in the latter instance the occurrence of an aging effect might erroneously be accepted even though they might occur only given certain selection conditions but not others.

Threats to the external validity of an experiment are represented by the interaction of each of the above with the treatment effect (in our case age). Campbell and Stanley (1963) examine possible designs to control for the effects of treatment interacting with testing, selection and reactive arrangement. Of these, the interaction with testing (or reactivity) is of particular importance to aging research, but in addition interactions with history and experimental mortality are of direct concern and should be controlled whenever possible.

Since developmental psychologists have typically couched their quasi-experimental designs in a different language than do experimenters not interested in developmental issues, it may be well to provide some translation. Table 1 examines the ten experimental plans proposed by Campbell and Stanley, indicates which ones appear appropriate for aging research, and identifies the more familiar developmental terminology. The latter designs will next be examined in more detail.

DESIGNS FOR THE STUDY OF ADULT DEVELOPMENT

Here we will outline some of the specific designs which have been found most useful in studies of aging. Later we will consider ways to control for the effects of testing and experimental mortality. Throughout we will use the ANOVA model, because we differ from Wohlwill (1973) in viewing the applicability of the analysis of variable model to developmental questions. We consider that once we treat a differential model as a quasi-experimental one, and as long as we

are concerned with population parameters rather than individual growth curves, the assumptions of the analysis of variance model are met, provided we regard levels of age, time of measurement and cohort membership as fixed constants, and do not pretend that we can generalize beyond the levels of those dimensions for which data have been accumulated. With that caveat in mind it becomes inconsequential that we cannot assign subjects at random to the parameters of interest. We will in turn examine designs bearing upon the description of ontogenetic change, cohort differences and sociocultural change. No attention can be given here to the implications of developmental designs for the assessment of heritability, the relative contribution of nature and nurture to behavior change over time (for a discussion of that issue see Schaie, 1975).

Throughout this discussion we will refer to

TABLE 2. SAMPLING PLAN AND GENERALIZED ANALYSIS OF VARIANCE MODEL FOR THE COHORT-SEQUENTIAL METHOD WITH REPEATED MEASUREMENT.
(Multiple Time Series)

A. Sampling Plan for 2 × 2 Minimum Design (Two Samples Observed Twice)

		Time of Birth (Cohort)	
		Oldest	Youngest
Time of Test	First	$C_1 S_1 A_1$	–
	Second	$C_1 S_1 A_2$	$C_2 S_1 A_1$
	Third	–	$C_2 S_1 A_2$

B. Generalized Analysis of Variance Model[a]

Source of variation	Degrees of freedom
Between subjects	$\frac{N}{A} - 1$
Between Cohorts (C)	$C - 1$
Residual between subjects	$\frac{N}{A} - C$
Within subjects	$N - \frac{N}{A}$
Between ages (A)	$A - 1$
Cohort × age interaction	$(C - 1)(A - 1)$
Residual within subjects	$N - \left(\frac{N}{A}\right) - C(A - 1)$
Total variation	$N - 1$

[a]The residual between subjects mean square is used to test the cohort effect, while the residual within subjects mean square is the proper error term for age and the cohort by age interaction.

age (A) as the number of years from birth to the point at which the organism is observed or measured. Cohort (C) will denote a group of individuals entering the environment at the same point of time, and time of measurement (T) will indicate the temporal occasion on which a given individual or group of individuals is observed or measured. Sample (S) will indicate the particular random entry into the same cohort for a given cell of a design. N represents the total number of observations made. It should be obvious also that sex should always be carried as an additional main effect in all of the proposed designs whenever both men and women are included in a given study.

Description of Ontogenetic Change (age changes)

The basic paradigm in aging research asks the question whether change in a dependent variable can be explained as a function of age. As already indicated above, the traditional longitudinal study of a single sample over two or more points in time is essentially a pretest-posttest time series design where age is considered to be the treatment variable. Unless experimental isolation is possible, or where it can be shown that the dependent variable is not influenced by external events, it must be concluded that the single cohort longitudinal design is very weak and should be avoided (Labouvie, Bartsch, Nesselroade, and Baltes, 1974; Schaie, 1972b).

The traditional longitudinal design can be much strengthened, however, by converting to a multiple time series or cohort-sequential method. In this approach we control for the effects of history by carrying two or more cohorts over the equivalent age range, occurring over different time ranges. (See Table 2.) We can then conclude that the absence of cohort differences and presence of age changes (if found) would suggest the identification of an age-related behavior, or if we found a significant age by cohort interaction we would have to consider that the variable of interest showed cohort specific age trends.

This design assumes the absence of secular trends and can therefore be recommended only if we assume that the irreversible decrement model for aging is tenable. The design does not control for testing and/or reactivity. If the latter are deemed to be important we would then

TABLE 3. SAMPLING PLAN AND GENERALIZED ANALYSIS OF VARIANCE MODEL FOR THE COHORT-SEQUENTIAL METHOD WITH INDEPENDENT MEASUREMENT.
(Separate-sample Pretest-Posttest Controlled for History)

A. Sampling Plan for 2 × 2 Minimum Design (Two Independent Samples from Each of Two Cohorts)

		Time of Birth (Cohort)	
		Oldest	Youngest
Time of Test	First	$C_1 S_1 A_1$	–
	Second	$C_1 S_2 A_2$	$C_2 S_1 A_1$
	Third	–	$C_2 S_2 A_2$

B. Generalized Analysis of Variance Model[a]

Source of variation	Degrees of freedom
Between cohorts (C)	$C - 1$
Between ages (A)	$A - 1$
Cohort × age interaction	$(C - 1)(A - 1)$
Error (within cells)	$N - (C)(A)$
Total variation	$N - 1$

[a]The within cell error mean square is used to test all effects.

suggest a separate samples variation of the cohort-sequential design. In that case we draw random samples from two or more samples, each of which is tested only at one age and at no other. (See Table 3 and Schaie, 1972b.)

The effects of treatments, intervention and/or practice can, of course, also be investigated by randomly splitting each age/cohort sample into groups assigned to different treatment or practice conditions (see Baltes and Goulet, 1971). Table 4 provides the recommended extension of the cohort-sequential separate samples design which examines the effect of different levels of practice.

It should be pointed out once again that the cross-sectional method is not appropriate for the study of age changes, unless there is strong independent evidence for the absence of cohort differences and then only if samples differing in age are controlled for on other demographic variables which could be related to the independent variable of interest. But before we dismiss the cross-sectional approach entirely, we must call attention to the fact that a design which repeats cross-sectional studies at regular time intervals covering a given age range of interest is a most feasible approach to the study of age change parameters when used in conjunction with the cross-sectional separate samples design.

TABLE 4. SAMPLING PLAN AND GENERALIZED ANALYSIS OF VARIANCE MODEL FOR THE COHORT-SEQUENTIAL METHOD WITH INDEPENDENT MEASUREMENTS.
(Controlled for the Effects of Practice)

A. Sampling Plan for $2 \times 2 \times 2$ Minimum Design (Two Samples for Each of Two Cohorts Under Each of Two Conditions of Practice)

		Time of Birth (Cohort)	
		Oldest	Youngest
Time of Test	First	$C_1 S_1 A_0 *$	–
	Second	$C_1 S_1 A_1$ $C_1 S_2 A_1$ $C_1 S_3 A_1 *$	$C_2 S_1 A_0 *$
	Third	$C_1 S_3 A_2$ $C_1 S_4 A_2$	$C_2 S_1 A_1$ $C_2 S_2 A_1$ $C_2 S_3 A_1 *$
	Fourth	–	$C_2 S_3 A_2$ $C_2 S_4 A_2$

*Data from starred samples do not enter analysis. Testing of these samples, however, is required to establish differential levels of practice.

B. Generalized Analysis of Variance Model[a]

Source of variation	Degrees of freedom
Between cohorts (C)	$C - 1$
Between ages (A)	$A - 1$
Between practice levels (P)	$P - 1$
Cohort $\times$ age	$(C - 1)(A - 1)$
Cohort $\times$ practice	$(C - 1)(P - 1)$
Age $\times$ practice	$(A - 1)(P - 1)$
Cohort $\times$ age $\times$ practice	$(C - 1)(A - 1)(P - 1)$
Error (within cells)	$N - (C)(A)(P)$
Total variance	$N - 1$

[a]The within cell error mean square is used to test all effects.

TABLE 5. SAMPLING PLAN AND GENERALIZED ANALYSIS OF VARIANCE MODEL FOR THE TIME-SEQUENTIAL METHOD.
(Non-equivalent control group design)

A. Sampling Plan for 2 × 2 Minimum Design (Two Ages Sampled at Two Times of Measurement)

		Time of Birth (Cohort)		
		Oldest	Second	Youngest
Time of Test	First	$C_1 S_1 A_2$	$C_2 S_1 A_1$	–
	Second	–	$C_2 S_2 A_2$	$C_3 S_1 A_1$

B. Generalized Analysis of Variance Model[a]

Source of variation	Degrees of freedom
Between times (T)	$T - 1$
Between ages (A)	$A - 1$
Time × age interaction	$(T - 1)(A - 1)$
Error (within cells)	$N - (T)(A)$
Total variation	$N - 1$

[a]The within cells error mean square is used to test all effects.

TABLE 6. SAMPLING PLAN AND GENERALIZED ANALYSIS OF VARIANCE MODEL FOR THE TIME-SEQUENTIAL METHOD CONTROLLED FOR THE EFFECT OF PRACTICE.

A. Sampling Plan for 2 × 2 × 2 Minimum Design (Two Ages Sampled at Two Times of Measurement Each Under Two Conditions of Practice)

		Time of Birth (Cohort)		
		Oldest	Second	Youngest
Time of Test	First	$C_1 S_1 A_1{}^*$	$C_2 S_1 A_0{}^*$	–
	Second	$C_1 S_1 A_2$ $C_1 S_2 A_2$	$C_2 S_1 A_1$ $C_2 S_2 A_1$ $C_2 S_3 A_1{}^*$	$C_3 S_1 A_0{}^*$
	Third	–	$C_2 S_3 A_2$ $C_2 S_4 A_2$	$C_3 S_1 A_1$ $C_3 S_2 A_1$

*Data from starred samples do not enter analysis. Testing of these samples, however, is required to establish differential levels of practice.

B. Generalized Analysis of Variance Model[a]

Source of variation	Degrees of freedom
Between times (T)	$T - 1$
Between ages (A)	$A - 1$
Between practice levels (P)	$P - 1$
Time × age	$(T - 1)(A - 1)$
Time × practice	$(T - 1)(P - 1)$
Age × practice	$(A - 1)(P - 1)$
Time × age × practice	$(T - 1)(A - 1)(P - 1)$
Error (within cells)	$N - (T)(A)(P)$
Total variance	$N - 1$

[a]The within cells error mean square is used to test all effects.

The recommended alternate approach, the time-sequential method, is essentially a non-equivalent control group design. It controls for cohort differences by replicating each age observation for two or more cohorts by assessing the same age range at two or more times of measurement. This design is efficient in differentiating age changes from secular trends, given the decrement with compensation model and assuming that cohort differences are either uniform or trivial. Table 5 gives the appropriate ANOVA design and Table 6 provides the extension of this design to examine the effects of practice and/or reactivity (for empirical examples see Schaie and Parham, 1974).

Description of Cohort Differences (age differences)

Although cross-sectional studies cannot yield acceptable age functions, they are well suited for the investigation of inter-generational differences, provided that such differences remain stable over time. Since the latter assumption may be hazardous for many variables which we suspect to be affected by sociocultural impact, we would prefer a third sequential design, the cross-sequential method, which is essentially a separate sample pretest-posttest design controlled for secular trends.

The most simple version of the cross-sequential design carries a minimum of two samples over the same time interval, testing each member of the sample twice. This is essentially a follow-up design, where individuals at all ages are retested after a constant time interval. However, since all members of the initial samples age at the same rate, the effects due to aging and time of measurement will be confounded. Nevertheless, if we can assume that individuals do not age or age at a uniform rate it is then possible to differentiate cohort from secular trends. Table 7 provides the design for the cross-sequential ANOVA with repeated measurement; Table 8 gives the alternate separate samples design required if effects of practice or reactivity are to be controlled, and Table 9 indicates the modification of the latter design to examine the effects of practice. Empirical examples of these designs are provided by Schaie, Labouvie, and Buech (1973) and by Schaie and Labouvie-Vief (1974).

The researcher interested in inter-generational differences may either elect a relatively short-term study if he feels that generation differences tend to remain stable over time, i.e., sample as many generations as available for two points in time; or he may wish to study differences between two generations at many points in time, which would raise serious issues of sample maintenance which will be discussed later.

Description of Sociocultural Change (time lag)

In addition to the problem of differentiating between aging and cohort differences, there is the problem of attending to the matter of secular trends possibly affecting individuals at all ages at a given point in time. In a developmental context we might assess this problem by means of a time-lag design which compares, for example, 65-year-olds, at several successive 5-year intervals. The time-lag method, however, confounds cohort differences and secular trends while controlling for age. For age ranges where little or no maturational change is expected, we would therefore again recommend use of the cross-sequential method (Tables 7-9) which would permit differentiation of the effects of secular trend from those of cohort specific generation differences.

Recommendation for an "All Purpose" Design

In many discussions with researchers interested in aging it becomes clear that most investigators wish to ask questions with respect to age (although being sensitive to the issue of generational differences) but do not wish to follow their subjects over these subjects' life course. We consequently would like to reiterate a compromise scheme which was first suggested some time ago (Schaie, 1965). The recommended "all purpose" design consists of a data collection scheme permitting analysis via the cross-sequential and time-sequential methods as follows:

1. Draw a random sample from each cohort over the age range to be investigated, and measure at Time 1. (Score 11.)
2. Get a second measurement on all subjects tested at Time 1 and Time 2. (Score 12.)

TABLE 7. SAMPLING PLAN AND GENERALIZED ANALYSIS OF VARIANCE MODEL FOR THE CROSS-SEQUENTIAL METHOD WITH REPEATED MEASUREMENT.
(Separate Sample Pretest-Posttest Controlled for Secular Trends)

A. Sampling Plan for 2 × 2 Minimum Design (Two Samples Each Tested Twice)

		Time of Birth (Cohort)	
		Oldest	Youngest
Time of Test	First	$C_1 S_1 A_2$	$C_2 S_1 A_1$
	Second	$C_1 S_1 A_3$	$C_2 S_1 A_2$

B. Generalized Analysis of Variance Model[a]

Source of variation	Degrees of freedom
Between subjects	$\frac{N}{T} - 1$
Between cohorts (C)	$C - 1$
Residual between subjects	$\frac{N}{T} - C$
Within subjects	$N - \frac{N}{T}$
Between times (T)	$T - 1$
Cohort × time interaction	$(C - 1)(T - 1)$
Residual within subjects	$N - \left(\frac{N}{T}\right) - C(T - 1)$
Total variation	$N - 1$

[a] The residual between subjects mean square is used to test the cohort effect, while the residual within subjects mean square is the proper error term for times of measurement and the age by time interaction.

TABLE 8. SAMPLING PLAN AND GENERALIZED ANALYSIS OF VARIANCE MODEL FOR THE CROSS-SEQUENTIAL METHOD WITH INDEPENDENT MEASUREMENTS.
(Separate Sample Pretest-Posttest)

A. Sampling plan for 2 × 2 Minimum Design (Two Cohorts Sampled Independently at Two times of Measurement)

		Time of Birth (Cohort)	
		Oldest	Youngest
Time of Test	First	$C_1 S_1 A_2$	$C_2 S_1 A_1$
	Second	$C_1 S_2 A_3$	$C_2 S_2 A_2$

B. Generalized Analysis of Variance Model[a]

Source of variation	Degrees of freedom
Between cohorts (C)	$C - 1$
Between times (T)	$T - 1$
Cohort × time interaction	$(C - 1)(T - 1)$
Error (within cells)	$N - (C)(T)$
Total variation	$N - 1$

[a] The within cells error mean square is used to test all effects.

TABLE 9. SAMPLING PLAN AND GENERALIZED ANALYSIS OF VARIANCE MODEL FOR THE CROSS-SEQUENTIAL METHOD CONTROLLED FOR EFFECTS OF PRACTICE.

A. Sampling Plan for $2 \times 2 \times 2$ Minimum Design (Two Cohorts Sampled Independently at Two Times of Measurement Each Under Two Conditions of Practice)

		Time of Birth (Cohort)	
		Oldest	Youngest
Time of Test	First	$C_1 S_1 A_1$*	$C_2 S_1 A_0$*
	Second	$C_1 S_1 A_2$ $C_1 S_2 A_2$ $C_1 S_3 A_2$*	$C_2 S_1 A_1$ $C_2 S_2 A_1$ $C_2 S_3 A_1$*
	Third	$C_1 S_3 A_3$ $C_1 S_4 A_3$	$C_2 S_3 A_2$ $C_2 S_4 A_2$

*Data from starred samples do not enter analysis. Testing of these samples, however, is required to establish differential levels of practice.

B. Generalized Analysis of Variance Model[a]

Source of variation	Degrees of freedom
Between cohorts (C)	$C - 1$
Between times (T)	$T - 1$
Between practice levels (P)	$P - 1$
Cohort × time	$(C - 1)(T - 1)$
Cohort × practice	$(C - 1)(P - 1)$
Time × practice	$(T - 1)(P - 1)$
Cohort × time × practice	$(C - 1)(T - 1)(P - 1)$
Error (within cells)	$N - (C)(T)(P)$
Total variance	$N - 1$

[a] The within cells error mean square is used to test all effects.

3. Draw a new random sample from each cohort in the range tested at Time 1 plus a sample from the next younger cohort below the range and measure at Time 2. (Score 22.)

Given such data collection it is then possible to implement the following plans of analysis: (a) Cross-sequential method (Scores 11 and 12) for all cohorts tested twice (see Table 7); (b) Time-sequential method (Scores 11 and 22) for samples matched by age (see Table 5); (c) Cross-sequential method with separate samples (Scores 11 and 22) for samples matched by cohort (see Table 8). In addition, of course, two cross-sectional studies and several longitudinal slices are available.

If both cross-sequential and time-sequential analyses can be conducted it is then possible to differentiate the presence of cohort and/or age differences by logical analysis as follows: If both cohort and time-of-measurement effects are detected at an acceptable level of confidence in the cohort-sequential analysis, and the assumption of no age change is violated, we would expect spurious increase in the F ratios for both age and cohort main effects. Upon time-sequential analysis this should lead the time-of-measurement effect to decrease and the age effect to be larger than the cohort effect in the cross-sequential study. If neither shift occurs we can then accept the appropriateness of our initial assumptions and disregard the results of the time-sequential analysis. If the time-sequential analysis detects a time-of-measurement effect not found in the cross-sequential analysis, we would assume this to be further evidence of the violation of the assumption of no cohort differences (also see Schaie, 1972b).

Much increased flexibility of analysis becomes possible if a Time 3 testing occasion can be programmed. In that instance we would add the following data collections:

4. Get a third measurement on all subjects tested at Time 1 and 2 (Score 13) at Time 3.
5. Get a second measurement on all subjects tested only at Time 2 (Score 23) at Time 3.
6. Draw a third random sample from each cohort in the range tested at Time 2 plus a sample from the next younger cohort below the range, measured at Time 3 (Score 33).

In addition to the analyses suggested above it is now possible to add: (d) Cohort-sequential method for each set of two cohorts (Scores 11, 12, 22 and 23), (see Table 1); (e) Cohort-sequential method with separate samples for each set of two cohorts (Scores 11, 22 and 33), (see Table 2); (f) Cross-sequential method controlled for practice (Scores 12, 22, 23 and 33), (see Table 6); and (g) Time-sequential method controlled for practice (Scores 12, 22, 23 and 33), (see Table 9). Of course, both cross- and time-sequential methods are also applicable to the 3 X *n* designs.

SAMPLING AND GENERALIZABILITY

At least three different options are available for the selection of subject populations in aging investigations. These options arise out of the inescapable fact that there are few truly "captive" adult populations, purposive or random removal from which can readily be prevented by the experimenter. Since pathology and mortality increase in frequency with age, attrition for these reasons is also unavoidable. In volunteer populations additional attrition may be caused by a *faux pas* in public relations or changes in attitudes towards participation in research studies. As a consequence it is not feasible to plan a design which assumes the absence of attrition, but the manner in which the relation between sample and parent population changes can be selected. First, it is possible to select a sample at the inception of a study such that the sample is representative of the population to which the investigator wishes to generalize, a strategy suitable for one point in time investigations. Second, he might consider data only for those subjects who remain in a longitudinal study until the study's conclusion. Third, the investigator might specify a sample which is appropriate to the variable to be studied, but which does not pretend to represent any identifiable population group.

Representation of Populations at One Point in Time

The issues to be discussed here apply equally to sample selection for a traditional cross-sectional study and to the first data collection for any of the sequential designs, particularly for any of the sequential strategies employing separate samples for each time-of-measurement.

It is theoretically possible in a cross-sectional study to obtain a sample representative of whatever population one wishes to generalize to by using appropriate census-type sampling methods. However, no age-cohort sub-sample will be representative of the cohort from which it has been drawn. Because of differential mortality and prevalence of pathology by age and cohort, it is unlikely that any samples from two cohorts (unless cohort boundaries are very narrowly defined) will be equally representative of the total cohort. Where this information is known, one might therefore wish to oversample the cohorts more affected by preselection effects of mortality and pathology. Nevertheless, we are faced with the problem that samples representative of any given cohort at birth will successively become less representative of that cohort at successive ages, and in a manner which does not necessarily follow the changes in any other cohort with which it is being compared. Thus, a cross-sectional sample of a population obtained at one point in time cannot have generality, because rates of cumulative trauma and other factors involving cohort attrition will not be uniform from one generation to the next.

It does not help to argue that one should carefully equate samples of different ages on a variety of demographic parameters. For example, equating samples by educational level would surely result in highly selected samples for the old given average education of young adults as the matching variable. Similar issues arise across levels of income, health status, etc. On the other hand, there might be some merit in matching samples in terms of relative status with respect to the cohort mean on such demographic variables, an approach which to our knowledge has yet to be attempted.

Perhaps we must simply accept the fact that cross-age matching of populations is quite difficult if not impossible, and rely more heavily on careful descriptions and measurement of possible covariates which could be used for the statistical control of those factors which are thought to confound analysis of age-related differences in the variables of interest (cf. Schaie, 1959).

Representation Over Time: The Problem of Attrition

Obtaining a representative sample in a longitudinal, cohort- or cross-sequential study is much simpler because we can readily obtain representative samples from the specific cohorts which are to be followed over time. Other problems, however, compel our attention in this instance. Note, for example, that the representative nature of our sample will only hold for the first time-of-measurement, and not at any other occasion, because attrition whether due to natural causes or artifacts introduced by the experimenter will rarely be random.

We must note further that in any repeated measurement study a sample will cease to be representative of its parent population as soon as it has been examined because of the practice/reactivity problem. That is, the measurement has changed the sample in ways in which the parent population has not changed. But even if our sample remained intact, we would have to consider the possibility that the characteristics of the parent population might change, say due to the various reasons for population mobility.

Two collateral types of investigations are consequently needed if we wish to generalize from the results of studies conducted over a period of time. First, if the investigator is interested in estimating population parameters, it is suggested that repeated measurement studies of intact panels be supplemented by separate sample designs which would give us information on successive changes in the parent population to which data obtained on our panel is to be generalized. Requisite designs are provided by Tables 3, 5 and 8. Second, it is necessary to conduct collateral studies which examine the effect of non-random attrition.

The effects of attrition, or experimental mortality (Campbell and Stanley, 1963), may be of two types. The first, over which the experimenter could exert some control, involves factors such as lack of interest, active refusal, change of residence, or disappearance. Such sources of attrition may affect performance on the dependent variable but need not be related specifically to age, cohort membership or time of measurement. But the second type of experimental mortality, over which the experimenter has no influence, involves age-related aspects due to biological causes, including physical trauma and individual differences in longevity.

All of the above sources of attrition can seriously affect findings on ontogenetic changes. Reported findings suggest that in studies of cognitive variables, panel survivors tend to be brighter (Baltes, Schaie, and Nardi, 1971; Blum, Jarvik, and Clark, 1970; Schaie, Labouvie, and Barrett, 1973), have more positive attributes with respect to interest and attitudes (Riegel, Riegel, and Meyer, 1968; Streib, 1966) and have higher social and educational levels (Rose, 1965).

Research designs protecting against the effect of experimental mortality require one more time of measurement than would be minimally needed for any design without such protection, since we cannot classify performance of our subjects as to attrition until the attrition has actually occurred. Table 10 provides a plan for the time-sequential method with a test for the effect of experimental mortality. This analysis can be conducted with the data collected under our three occasion "all purpose" plan described on page 48. Extension to the other sequential designs can readily be effected by referring to Tables 3 or 8.

TABLE 10. SAMPLING PLAN AND GENERALIZED ANALYSIS OF VARIANCE MODEL FOR THE TIME-SEQUENTIAL METHOD CONTROLLED FOR EFFECTS OF EXPERIMENTAL MORTALITY.

A. Sampling Plan for 2 × 2 × 2 Minimum Design (Two Ages Sampled at Two Times of Measurement at Two Levels of Participation)

		Time of Birth (Cohort)		
		Oldest	Second	Youngest
Time of Test	First	$C_1 S_1 A_2 (P + D)$	$C_2 S_1 A_1 (P + D)$	–
	Second	$C_1 S_1 A_3 (P)$*	$C_2 S_1 A_2 (P)$* $C_2 S_2 A_2 (P + D)$	$C_3 S_1 A_1 (P + D)$
	Third	–	$C_2 S_2 A_3 (P)$*	$C_3 S_1 A_2 (P)$*

*Data from the starred samples (re-test scores) do not enter analysis. Testing of these samples is necessary, however, to classify members of each sample at first test into participants (P) and dropouts (D).

B. Generalized Analysis of Variance Model[a]

Source of variation	Degrees of freedom
Between times (T)	$T - 1$
Between ages (A)	$A - 1$
Between participants/dropouts (D)	$(D - 1)(A - 1)$
Time × age interaction	$(T - 1)(D - 1)$
Time × dropout interaction	$(A - 1)(D - 1)$
Time × age × dropout interaction	$(T - 1)(A - 1)(D - 1)$
Error (within cells)	$N - (T)(A)(D)$
Total variation	$N - 1$

[a]The within cells error mean square is used to test all effects.

A further complication arises, however, when performance in the same individuals is to be considered, or the independent random sampling designs are not feasible. In the latter instance it would be necessary to distinguish also between the effects of practice and of experimental mortality. The required sampling plan for the cross-sequential method is presented in Table 11. A similar plan can be derived for the cohort-sequential method by reference to Tables 1 and 4, and for the time-sequential method by referring to Tables 5 and 6.

Limits of Functioning: When Not to Seek Representative Samples

Because of the severe problems in maintaining the representative characteristics of any panel, and in the design and logistic problems involved in controls for experimental mortality, most investigators should ask themselves whether they are in fact interested in estimating population parameters. Perhaps the major purpose of their research question is to study how a given behavior is expressed at different developmental stages under conditions which may be idealized or extreme. If this is the case, a strong argument can then be made for the desirability of obtaining a biased but homogeneous sample. We have argued before, for example, that if one wants to gather data on optimal intellectual function in old age for such purposes as developing programs, it might be useful to work with samples of the active well-functioning and intelligent aged (cf. Schaie and Strother, 1968). On the other hand it may be quite useful to study the institutionalized aged if we either wish to define minimum levels of survival or if we wish to examine change over time as rapidly as possible (cf. Eisner and Schaie, 1971, for a one-year sequential study).

Studies of the kind proposed here are often

exploratory in nature, but they should conform to all the caveats expressed above, if they are to give us any leads at all. In other words, exploratory studies may utilize non-representative samples conducted under unusual conditions, but they must still conform to conventional design requirements. Some additional cautions are in order. For example, if favorable extremes are studied, procedures must be designed to discourage all but the most motivated volunteers. If lower limits are to be considered, design of instrumentation must carefully consider problems of detecting behavior differences at such base levels, as well as protect against excluding potential subjects who appear to be difficult to examine.

The experimenter again faces the question of whether he should randomly sample from his

TABLE 11. SAMPLING PLAN AND GENERALIZED ANALYSIS OF VARIANCE MODEL FOR THE CROSS-SEQUENTIAL METHOD CONTROLLED FOR EFFECTS OF PRACTICE AND EXPERIMENTAL MORTALITY.

A. Sampling Plan for $2 \times 2 \times 2 \times 2$ Minimum Design (Two Cohorts Sampled at Two Times of Measurement for Two levels of Practice Each at Two Levels of Participation)

		Time of Birth (Cohort)	
		Oldest	Youngest
Time of Test	First	$C_1 S_1 A_1 (Pp + Pd + Dd)*$	$C_2 S_1 A_0 (Pp + Pd + Dd)*$
	Second	$C_1 S_1 A_2 (Pp + Pd)$ $C_1 S_2 A_2 (Pp) + (Pd)* + (Dd)$ $C_1 S_3 A_2 (Pp + Pd + Dd)*$	$C_2 S_1 A_1 (Pp + Pd)$ $C_2 S_2 A_1 (Pp) + (Pd)* + (Dd)$ $C_2 S_3 A_1 (Pp + Pd + Dd)*$
	Third	$C_1 S_1 A_3 (Pp)*$ $C_1 S_2 A_3 (Pp + Pd)*$ $C_1 S_3 A_3 (Pp + Pd)$ $C_1 S_4 A_3 (Pp) + (Pd)* + (Dd)$	$C_2 S_1 A_2 (Pp)*$ $C_2 S_2 A_2 (Pp + Pd)*$ $C_2 S_3 A_2 (Pp + Pd)$ $C_2 S_4 A_2 (Pp) + (Pd)* + (Dd)$
	Fourth	$C_1 S_2 A_4 (Pp)*$ $C_1 S_3 A_4 (Pp)*$ $C_1 S_4 A_4 (Pp + Pd)*$	$C_2 S_2 A_3 (Pp)*$ $C_2 S_3 A_3 (Pp)*$ $C_2 S_4 A_3 (Pp + Pd)*$
	Fifth	$C_1 S_4 A_5 (Pp)*$	$C_2 S_4 A_4 (Pp)*$

*Data from starred samples do not enter analysis. Testing of these samples is required, however, to establish differential levels of participation for each level of practice: participants who remain in the study after the second test (Pp); participants who drop out after the second test (Pd); and participants who drop out after the initial test (Dd).

B. Samples Entering Analysis in the Minimum Design

		Level of Participation			
		Participants		Dropouts	
		No prior practice	Prior practice	No prior practice	Prior practice
Oldest Cohort	Time 2	$C_1 S_2 A_2 (Pp)$	$C_1 S_1 A_2 (Pp)$	$C_1 S_2 A_2 (Dd)$	$C_1 S_1 A_2 (Pd)$
	Time 3	$C_1 S_4 A_3 (Pp)$	$C_1 S_3 A_3 (Pp)$	$C_1 S_4 A_3 (Dd)$	$C_1 S_3 A_3 (Pd)$
Youngest Cohort	Time 2	$C_2 S_2 A_1 (Pp)$	$C_2 S_1 A_1 (Pp)$	$C_2 S_2 A_1 (Dd)$	$C_2 S_1 A_1 (Pd)$
	Time 3	$C_2 S_4 A_2 (Pp)$	$C_2 S_3 A_2 (Pp)$	$C_2 S_4 A_2 (Dd)$	$C_2 S_3 A_2 (Pd)$

TABLE 11 (*Continued*).

C. Generalized Analysis of Variance Model[a]

Source of variation	Degrees of freedom
Cohorts (*C*)	$C - 1$
Time (*T*)	$T - 1$
Participants/dropouts (*D*)	$D - 1$
Practice levels (*P*)	$P - 1$
Cohort × time interaction	$(C - 1)(T - 1)$
Cohort × dropout interaction	$(C - 1)(D - 1)$
Time × dropout interaction	$(T - 1)(D - 1)$
Time × practice interaction	$(T - 1)(P - 1)$
Dropout × practice interaction	$(D - 1)(P - 1)$
Cohort × time × dropout interaction	$(C - 1)(T - 1)(D - 1)$
Cohort × practice interaction	$(C - 1)(P - 1)$
Cohort × time × practice interaction	$(C - 1)(T - 1)(P - 1)$
Cohort × dropout × practice interaction	$(C - 1)(D - 1)(P - 1)$
Time × dropout × practice interaction	$(T - 1)(D - 1)(P - 1)$
Cohort × time × dropout × practice interaction	$(C - 1)(T - 1)(D - 1)(P - 1)$
Error (within cells)	$N - (C)(T)(D)(P)$
Total variation	$N - 1$

[a] The within cells error mean square is used to test all effects.

class of extreme subjects or whether he should define the class in such a way that it becomes possible to conduct an exhaustive study of the entire class. It should be noted here that in a finite study one would compare measures of change only upon the survivors, since a finite population can only be defined in terms of the members of the class available at the final time of measurement. Comparisons of random samples of a class, conversely, would need to be based on the total class membership available at each measurement point.

Even though we do not directly raise the question of generalizability when studying extreme samples, it is still important to know the relation of our unusual sample to its parent population. Such issues as the base rate of the extreme subjects to be investigated and the manner in which those subjects are likely to differ from the population average may become important later on if subsequent parametric studies on the entire range of the behavior of interest are to be contemplated.

Control or Description of Psychopathology

Some attention should be given to the question of whether the dependent variable of interest is to be examined in a population which has been screened for the presence of pathology or whether the frequently observed increase in the incidence of pathology with increasing age is simply taken for granted. The common specification that subjects are to be excluded who suffer from physical disabilities or who are under psychiatric care may lead to peculiar sampling problems in aging studies. We would expect to find that certain arbitrary exclusions would ensure differential representation by cohort in cross-sectional studies and differential attrition by age in longitudinal studies. If certain decremental developmental changes are exaggerated by physical or emotional problems, then the changes in samples screened for pathology will be serious underestimates of similar changes in population at age levels where high prevalence of pathology is the rule.

Since cumulative effects of pathology can be noted in all aging individuals it is probably futile to attempt the identification of behavior change in pathology-free processes, except in such instances where one can demonstrate the lack of correlation between a given pathology and chronological age. In the latter case, experimental or statistical control of the extent of pathology is mandatory and/or exclusion criteria may be reasonable. But otherwise we should be content to begin to understand the relationship of prevalent pathology at given ages to our variable of interest.

SUITABILITY OF TEST INSTRUMENTS

This final section concerns itself with the embarrassing problem that our methods of measurement are also liable to "age," that most techniques for measuring human behavior were originally invented for use with children or young adults and that there is no good reassurance that behavioral phenotypes are indeed related to the same genotypes at different stages of human development. It will be taken for granted that the threats to internal validity attributable to instrumentation, of course, also interact with selection. That is, all our instrumentation problems may differentially affect samples who are not comparable with respect to pathology or major demographic characteristics.

Cohort and Age Appropriate Measurement Instruments

Just as was the case with our other components of developmental change, problems in the area of test instruments may be of three different types. First, a test may be inappropriate for the entire age range to be investigated. That is, a test developed and standardized upon behavior facets sampled in young adults, may be inappropriate to test similar facets in older individuals, either in terms of content or instructional set.

Second, if there are cohort differences in the factor structure of a test, it may be appropriate for the entire age range to be examined, but only within a particular cohort, assuming there are no age cohort interactions. Thus, the first version of the Wechsler-Bellevue might be a more appropriate technique for the aged today than is the WAIS, because the former test was developed with the aid of a group of subjects who are now entering old age. The cohort inappropriateness of test material is particularly noticeable in verbal intelligence tests, and, of course, in questionnaire material testing attitudinal and personality concepts, where changes in semantic fashion may be all important in producing spurious differences.

Finally, tests may be both cohort and age appropriate over the range of interest but may suffer from obsolescence because of time-of-measurement effects. Most noteworthy effects of the latter variety are changes in the ceiling level of tests due to general increments in information level, loss of sensitivity of unobtrusive test items due to wide publicity regarding the relation between such items and the dimensions assessed, and finally shifts in the social desirability value of attitude or personality test items.

The above problems have been known for a long time and account for the publication of alternate test forms for different age levels for both ability and personality tests for children but the writer is not aware of any serious attempts up to this time (but see Demming and Pressey, 1957) to construct alternate test forms for different adult age levels. The issue of time-of-measurement effects has, of course, been addressed by the restandardization studies for some of the major psychological tests and questionnaires (e.g., Matarazzo, 1972). But the design of the comparison studies used makes it difficult to relate the observed changes to developmental issues. Here is clearly a fruitful field for much additional effort.

Comparability of Psychological Constructs Across the Adult Life Span

Even if we assume that our design has controlled for most validity threats, we must still be concerned with possible changes in meaning of the true component of any observed score. What is at issue then is whether the phenotypes observed across time and age do indeed reflect similar genotypes.

The problem has three different aspects. These include attempts to determine whether or not factor structures remain invariant across developmental dimensions, the description of developmental functions for factorially distinct dimensions, and the separation of ontogenetic and cohort variation on factorially stable dimensions. But these matters are best approached by multivariate methods and are therefore treated in Chapter 3 of this *Handbook*.

REFERENCES

Baltes, P. B., and Goulet, L. R. 1971. Exploration of developmental variables by manipulation and simulation of age differences in behavior, *Hum. Develop.*, 14, 149–170.

Baltes, P. B., Nesselroade, J. R., Schaie, K. W., and Labouvie, E. W. 1972. On the dilemma of regression effects in examining ability-level related differentials in ontogenetic patterns of intelligence. *Developmental Psychology*, 6, 78–84.

Baltes, P. B., and Schaie, K. W. 1973. On life-span developmental research paradigms: Retrospects and prospects. *In*, P. B. Baltes and K. W. Schaie (eds.), *Life-Span Developmental Psychology: Personality and Socialization*, pp. 365–395. New York: Academic Press.

Baltes, P. B., Schaie, K. W., and Nardi, A. H. 1971. Age and experimental mortality in a seven year longitudinal study of cognitive behavior. *Developmental Psychology*, 5, 18–26.

Blum, J. E., Jarvik, L. F., and Clark, E. T. 1970. Rate of change on selective tests of intelligence: A twenty-year longitudinal study of aging. *J. Gerontol.*, 25, 171–176.

Campbell, D. T., and Stanley, J. C. 1963. Experimental and quasi-experimental designs for research on teaching. *In*, N. L. Gage (ed.), *Handbook of Research on Teaching*, pp. 171–246. Chicago: Rand McNally.

Demming, J. A., and Pressey, S. L. 1957. Tests indigenous to the adult and older years. *J. Consult. Psychol.*, 4, 144–148.

Eisner, D. A., and Schaie, K. W. 1971. Age change in response to visual illusions from middle to old age. *J. Gerontol.*, 26, 146–150.

Furby, L. 1973. Interpreting regression toward the mean in developmental research. *Developmental Psychology*, 8, 172–179.

Goulet, L. R., Hay, C. M., and Barclay, C. R. 1974. Sequential analysis and developmental research methods: Descriptions of cyclical phenomena. *Psychol. Bull.*, 81, 517–521.

Labouvie, E. W., Bartsch, T. W., Nesselroade, J. R., and Baltes, P. B. 1974. On the internal and external validity of simple longitudinal designs. *Child Development*, 45, 282–290.

Matarazzo, J. D. 1972. *Wechsler's Measurement and Appraisal of Adult Intelligence*. 5th Edition. Baltimore: Williams & Wilkins.

Nesselroade, J. R., and Baltes, P. B. 1974. Adolescent personality development and historical change: 1970–1972. *Monographs of the Society for Research in Child Development.*, 39 (1, Whole No. 154), 1–80.

Riegel, K. F., and Riegel, R. M. 1972. Development, drop and death. *Developmental Psychology*, 6, 306–319.

Riegel, K. F., Riegel, R. M., and Meyer, G. 1967a. Socio-psychological factors of aging: A cohort-sequential analysis. *Hum. Develop.*, 10, 27–56.

Riegel, K. F., Riegel, R. M., and Meyer, G. 1967b. A study of the dropout rates of longitudinal research on aging and the prediction of death. *J. Pers. Soc. Psychol.*, 5, 342–348.

Riegel, K. F., Riegel, R. M., and Meyer, G. 1968. The prediction of retest resisters in research on aging. *J. Gerontol.*, 23, 370–374.

Riley, M. W. 1973. Aging and cohort succession: Interpretations and misinterpretations. *Public Opinion Quarterly*, 37, 35–49.

Rose, C. L. 1965. Representativeness of volunteer subjects in a longitudinal aging study. *Hum. Develop.*, 8, 152–156.

Schaie, K. W. 1959. Cross-sectional methods in the study of psychological aspects of aging. *J. Gerontol.*, 14, 208–215.

Schaie, K. W. 1965. A general model for the study of developmental problems. *Psychol. Bull.*, 64, 92–107.

Schaie, K. W. 1970. A reinterpretation of age-related changes in cognitive structure and functioning. *In*, L. R. Goulet and P. B. Baltes (eds.), *Life-Span Developmental Psychology: Research and Theory*, pp. 486–508. New York: Academic Press.

Schaie, K. W. 1972a. Can the longitudinal method be applied to psychological studies of human development? *In*, F. Z. Moenks, W. W. Hartup, and J. DeWit (eds.), *Determinants of Behavioral Development*, pp. 3–22. New York: Academic Press.

Schaie, K. W. 1972b. Limitations on the generalizability of growth curves on intelligence, *Hum. Develop.*, 15, 141–152.

Schaie, K. W. 1973. Methodological problems in descriptive developmental research on adulthood and aging. *In*, J. R. Nesselroade and H. W. Reese (eds.), *Life-Span Developmental Psychology: Methodological Issues*, pp. 253–280. New York: Academic Press.

Schaie, K. W. 1975. Research strategy in developmental human behavior genetics. *In*, K. W. Schaie, V. E. Anderson, G. E. McClearn, and J. Money (eds.), *Developmental Human Behavior Genetics: Nature-nurture Redefined.*, pp. 205–220. Lexington, Massachusetts: D. C. Heath.

Schaie, K. W., and Gribbin, K. 1975. Adult development and aging. *Annual Review of Psychology*, 26, 65–96.

Schaie, K. W., and Labouvie-Vief, G. 1974. Generational versus ontogenetic components of change in adult cognitive behavior: A fourteen-year cross-sequential study. *Developmental Psychology*, 10, 305–320.

Schaie, K. W., Labouvie, G. V., and Barrett, T. J. 1973. Selective attrition effects in a fourteen-year study of adult intelligence. *J. Gerontol.*, 25, 171–176.

Schaie, K. W., Labouvie, G. V., and Buech, B. U. 1973. Generational and cohort-specific differences in adult cognitive functioning: A fourteen-year study of independent samples. *Developmental Psychology*, **9**, 151–166.

Schaie, K. W., and Parham, I. A. 1974. Social responsibility in adulthood: Ontogenetic and sociocultural change. *J. Pers. Soc. Psychol.*, **30**, 483–492.

Schaie, K. W., and Strother, C. R. 1968. Cognitive and personality variables in college graduates of advanced age. *In*, G. A. Talland (ed.), *Human Behavior and Aging: Recent Advances in Research and Theory*, pp. 281–308. New York: Academic Press.

Streib, G. F. 1966. Participants and drop-outs in a longitudinal study. *J. Gerontol.*, **21**, 200–201.

Wohlwill, J. F. 1970. The age variable in psychological research. *Psychol. Rev.*, 77, 49–64.

Wohlwill, J. F. 1973. *The Study of Behavioral Development.* New York: Academic Press.

3
ISSUES IN STUDYING DEVELOPMENTAL CHANGE IN ADULTS FROM A MULTIVARIATE PERSPECTIVE

John R. Nesselroade*

The Pennsylvania State University

Essays on research and statistical methodology often deal explicitly with the issue of assumptions. The most important one underlying the material to be presented here is substantive, rather than statistical, in nature. It is that behavioral change throughout the life span is a complex, multifaceted phenomenon whose proper study requires the researcher to utilize methodological tools which are sufficiently complex to match and, if necessary, even "overpower" the data. Just as gunpowder has had to give way to more effective propellants in the conduct of modern warfare, so must the social and behavioral scientists' analytic weapons be improved if more fruitful assaults are to be waged on the secrets of aging and behavioral change guarded so jealously for so long by Mother Nature.

The purpose of this chapter is to review, in a necessarily abbreviated manner, selected aspects of multivariate models and procedures as they relate, or may be made to relate, to the study

of behavioral change. Because of spatial limitations, some topics can only be highlighted; others have had to be abandoned altogether. An attempt has been made, however, to provide adequate references to steer the interested reader to a variety of pertinent source materials.

WHY A MULTIVARIATE ORIENTATION TO THE STUDY OF BEHAVIORAL CHANGE IN ADULTHOOD?

The appeal of a multivariate orientation to the study of behavior can be recognized at several levels. Two important ones are: (1) the creation or construction of a representation simply to organize a domain of variables into a dimensional framework; and (2) the definition of pertinent concepts, especially change-related ones, as profiles or patterns of a *set* of measures rather than in terms of single measures.

Behavior constitutes a vast universe of phenomena which, if considered in highly specific units, taxes our capacity for mere enumeration, not to mention for observing, recording, and searching for antecedent-consequent relationships. Moreover, behaviors are displayed neither in a vacuum nor in an environment varying *only*

*Preparation of this manuscript was supported in part by contract no. NIE-C-74-0127 from the National Institute of Education. The author gratefully acknowledges many valuable suggestions for revision made by Steven W. Cornelius.

in relative humidity, or in degrees Fahrenheit, or in amount of parental rejection, peer acceptance, or in any of a host of additional variables psychologists can readily list. It may be possible to isolate the many elements, both those in the behavior repertoire and those in the environment, into simple S-R pairs only at considerable expense to the richness of behavior concepts. An alternative is first to organize domains of pertinent variables so that, for example, one may select deliberately a level of specificity that seems most fruitful for a given purpose (Baltes and Nesselroade, 1973; Cattell, 1966b). The use of multivariate techniques to delineate an underlying structure in behavior is well represented in the psychological literature, especially in the areas of personality and ability functioning. Although lagging behind somewhat, there is also sentiment for (Frederiksen, 1972), and some attempts (Sells, 1962) to develop a dimensional taxonomy of environmental characteristics.

As one moves to the study of development and change he must face the option of whether the organism and the environment are to be represented in terms of highly specific variables or in terms of global, derived ones. One has the choice of seeking relationships either among separate variables or in terms of unique patterns manifested across a set of variables which can include more than one response dimension and, possibly, multiple stimulus dimensions. This opens the way to a consideration of different levels of complexity in concepts of change, to which we now turn.

Levels of Complexity of Change Concepts

Clearly one may elect to examine change in a single dependent variable either descriptively, as a function of age, or in a traditional experimental paradigm as a function of one or more manipulated independent variables. The shortcomings of descriptive developmental designs are well documented elsewhere (e.g., Baltes, 1968; Cattell, 1970; Nesselroade and Baltes, 1974; Schaie, 1965) and by Birren and Schaie (Chapters 1 and 2, this volume) in relation to criteria of *internal* and *external* validity of design (Campbell and Stanley, 1963). Manipu-

lative designs, given that the researcher has isolated a theoretically valuable dependent variable, may have high internal validity but often sacrifice external validity especially along the dimension of generalization from a single dependent variable to some larger subset of variables which, as a group, serve to define a psychological construct.

The examination of change in a single measurable variable, be it a global dimension such as intelligence or one as specific as reaction time, may be exceedingly worthwhile in certain contexts. It is also quite possible, however, that a single measure of, say, intelligence may be so broad as to obscure functionally distinct entities, each requiring careful attention if theory is to be advanced. Conversely, a variable such as reaction time may define a construct so narrowly that sufficiently general lawful relationships cannot be established.

An alternative is to admit from the beginning that it is risky to generalize from changes on only one measure to the nature of psychological change in a universe of measures. One may elect to design investigations which employ a carefully selected set of variables, but defining and properly sampling a variable domain is not always a straightforward task (e.g., Cattell, 1952; Humphreys, 1962; Nunnally, 1967). Utilization of multiple measures (Baltes and Nesselroade, 1973) still offers the researcher the opportunity to examine effects on separate variables but, in addition, it provides the means to explore the whole set in concert. Thus, justification for using multiple measures may range from the fear that a single measure is either too broad or too narrow to index adequately a construct to an explicit conceptualization of behavior change as inherently a multidimensional phenomenon which, perforce, requires that it be represented in a battery of measures. Cattell (1966c), for example, has argued that for learning to be integrated with clinical adjustment theory, the former must be conceptualized and measured as a multidimensional change in response to a multidimensional situation.

Through the use of multiple measures and appropriate analytic procedures, one may combine inductive and deductive methods, correlational and manipulative experiments, and the study of both inter- and intraindividual differences, and may move to a more abstract type of change concept—changes in patterns of interrelationships among variables. Wohlwill (1973), for example, has reminded us that behavioral development does not occur in isolated bits and pieces but, rather, simultaneously across many dimensions which interact closely with one another. Included are patterns of changes among stimulus variables, among response variables, and between both kinds.

Evolution of Conceptual Frameworks Adequate for the Task of Studying Behavioral Changes in Adulthood

Just how behavioral change is to be conceptualized, measured, and studied are topics that have received considerable attention in recent years (Cattell, 1966a; Cronbach and Furby, 1970; Harris, 1963b; Nesselroade and Reese, 1973; Wohlwill, 1973). *Change*, like Campbell and Stanley's (1963) characterization of experiment, connotes some type of comparison, but of what? Possibilities include a comparison of scores at Time 1 with scores at Time 2 as a reflection of intraindividual variability, a post-manipulation comparison of the mean of an experimental group with that of randomly equivalent controls, an examination of simple or rescaled observed scores as reflecting gains from an ontogenetic zero point, or "subjectivist" operations as sketched by Bereiter (1963), to mention a few general cases.

It appears too optimistic to believe that just around the corner lies some grand integration which will resolve at once the paradoxes and dilemmas that have been identified with the study of behavioral change and will chart clearly the course for subsequent research. At the same time, however, developmentalists can be encouraged by advances in measurement and scaling theory (see Cliff, 1973, for a review), reliability and validity conceptualizations (Cronbach, Gleser, Nanda, and Rajaratnam, 1972), research design (Nesselroade and Reese, 1973), and mathematico-statistical models and data-analytic techniques (e.g., Bentler, 1973; Wohlwill, 1973). Such innovations, however, vary in the explicitness with which they are

targeted toward the investigation of behavioral change and, for that reason, the developmental researcher must, at least partially, assume the burden of mastering and applying newer, more powerful tools to his own subject matter.

For the present we can suggest no more solid foundation for the study of behavioral change than a firm reliance upon structured measurement. In relation to the study of change, however, the measurement issue is far broader than simply utilizing devices, no matter how elaborate and painstaking their construction may be, to assess organisms at disparate temporal points in order to quantify changes.

An anomaly in the study of behavioral change over time is that in many instances the orientation, development, and use of measuring instruments have emphasized stability rather than lability as a target concern. One of the culprits seems to have been a failure to distinguish between the reliability of the measurement process and stability of the phenomenon being measured. In the construction of self-report measurement instruments, for instance, it is not uncommon for items which show low test-retest correlations (stability coefficients) to be discarded because they are "too unreliable" when, in fact, these items may be reliably reflecting a highly labile attribute. Bereiter (1963) gives a poignant account of his own experience with this problem in a valuable discussion of some basic issues related to the measurement of change.

One potential feature of a test-construction strategy based on utilizing only items with high stability coefficients is that there is a selection effect working toward the production of a measure which tends to be insensitive to change; yet, the measure may then be used in developmental research precisely for the purpose of studying change! There is need for considerable interplay between theoretical notions of change and the development and refinement of measurement devices; a point inherent in the theory of generalizability (Cronbach *et al.*, 1972).

Conceptually, a useful distinction related to the previous discussion of a multivariate orientation can be made between *measuring* and *structuring* change. The heart of this distinction is whether change should be cast in terms of a single measurement variable or in terms of one or more composite variables reflecting patterns of interrelationships among several measurement variables. How psychological change is to be measured is by no means an agreed upon set of procedures (Cronbach and Furby, 1970). Nevertheless, social and behavioral scientists try to make do with simple *t*-tests, analyses of variance and covariance, residual scores, etc., and are beginning to explore the potential usefulness of more elaborate statistical tools such as time-series and Markov process models. It is too early to tell where the latter models will lead but interest in measuring and describing psychological change will certainly remain a central focus of the developmentalist. Advances in understanding development may depend, however, as much on the type of change concepts that are constructed and rendered in operational terms as on the mechanics of assessing and evaluating changes. Structuring change—the elaboration and identification of change concepts embedded in networks of interrelationships of sets of variables—calls for the application of multivariate procedures.

Clearly, the identification or labeling of multivariate change concepts depends heavily upon the putative nature of observable measures. One has available for inspection, however, both convergent and divergent empirical relationships which, in addition to contributing to the identification of dimensions of change may, in turn, further help to clarify the nature of the specific observable measures. The trait-state distinction in research on anxiety (Cattell, 1973; Nesselroade and Cable, 1974; Spielberger, 1972) includes one type of change concept which has evolved, in large part, from a multivariate orientation to personality research and which, generally, has direct implications for the study of personality development across the life span (Baltes and Nesselroade, 1973).

APPLICATIONS OF CONVENTIONAL MULTIVARIATE PROCEDURES

Before introducing some uses of multivariate analysis techniques for studying change and development let us first consider briefly two general lines of application recognized explicitly in the literature—data reduction and domain structuring. These labels are used primarily for discussion purposes and need not be viewed necessarily as denoting discrete, mutually exclusive activities since in practice the distinction may frequently be blurred.

Principal Components Analysis as a Procedure for Data Reduction

Techniques for analyzing multivariate data arrays date back to the beginning of the twentieth century. Most of these can be construed in terms of constructing linear combinations of sets of variables to meet specified criterion conditions. The criteria and procedures for choosing the weights to define particular linear combinations serve to distinguish among such models as those associated with regression, canonical correlation, discriminant function, and principal components analysis. The interested reader can find more detailed discussion in Morrison (1967), Nunnally (1967), and Tatsuoka (1971).

Principal components analysis, for example, is a useful tool for the systematic reduction in number of a multiplicity of measures. The resulting components (composite variables) may then be used as variables in subsequent data analytic schemes such as regression analyses.

Various writers (Harris, 1963a; Lawley and Maxwell, 1971; Overall and Klett, 1972) have emphasized that the primary focus of principal components analysis is on analyzing variance not covariance structures, and that the useful output from a principal components analysis is a set of composite scores which provides a uniquely efficient representation of observed variability. Although it is not uncommon for researchers to transform (rotate) a set of principal components (either the full set or a partial set), individual components thus transformed no longer provide the efficient representation of variance nor are they factors in the sense of the common factor model which will be discussed next.

Factor Analysis as a Model for Domain Structuring

Thurstone (1947) identified the central purpose of factor analysis to be to ". . .discover a set of significant and meaningful parameters for describing a domain." Subsequent writers have tended to maintain this general orientation although with abundant variability in the amount of enthusiasm with which they view factor analysis to provide dimensions that are, in some sense, fundamental or real. Obviously, if the issue is resolvable at all, it cannot be done on purely empirical grounds. What is important is that the general factor analytic model represents an extremely powerful, and useful tool for representing the covariance among observed variables in terms of a smaller number of unobserved or hypothetical variables. Although it is a widely used technique, factor analysis has also accumulated a lengthy roster of vocal opponents. But, as Lawley and Maxwell (1971) pointed out, recent developments have helped to bring this "black sheep of statistical theory" into the fold of methodological respectability.

Factor analysis has wide applicability for the developmentalist, as we shall see subsequently, for imposing structure on the interrelationships of measures selected for study. Its relevance is not restricted to static, cross-sectional data by any means but, rather, appropriate factor analytic methods provide a systematic way to organize many kinds of time-related data. Bentler (1973), for example, has presented a variety of factor analytic models and applications pertinent to the study of developmental change and, at the same time, has called attention to instances in which the model may do injustice to developmental data. Before considering particular factor analytic models and procedures in relation to the study of behavioral change, however, we shall briefly present a general discussion of the model in order to identify certain concepts to be relied upon later.

EXTENSION OF CONVENTIONAL MULTIVARIATE PROCEDURES TO THE STUDY OF CHANGE

The basic linear expression of the common factor model is well enough known that it need not be reiterated here. A number of recent, excellent texts (e.g., Gorsuch, 1974; Mulaik, 1972; Rummel, 1970) as well as established ones (Harman, 1960) fully present both the model and a variety of applications. Further

discussion of the factor model set specifically in the context of developmental research issues is to be found in Bentler (1973), and Nesselroade (1970).

Invariance, Stability, and Change

Salient for the present discussion is the fact that in representing, by factor analysis, the interrelationships among a sample of observed variables from some content domain of interest, the following output is generated directly: (1) a set of factor loadings (the factor loading pattern) which defines the observed variables as linear combinations of unobserved factors; (2) a factor variance-covariance matrix which indicates the factor interrelationships and which specifies the factor variances; and (3) estimates of the portion of variance of each observed variable shared with other variables in that set. Parenthetically, it is noted that factor scores can be *estimated* for each individual on each factor but the estimation involves a set of complex issues commanding a sizeable body of literature (see e.g., Harman, 1960; McDonald, 1974; Tucker, 1971). In the remaining portion of this discussion we shall be paying attention especially to the concepts of factor loading patterns, factor covariance matrices, and factor scores as they may be interpreted to illuminate the nature of developmental change from a multivariate perspective.

Two central notions which will be briefly elaborated on are critical ones to be considered when factor analysis is used to describe developmental changes. These are factor loading pattern *invariance* and factor score *stability*. A good understanding of these two concepts will both enable the reader to grasp the logic behind using conventional factor analysis to compare time- or age-ordered structures and will serve to clarify the rationale underlying variants of the factor model developed specifically for the study of change.

Invariance of Factor Loading Patterns. Thurstone (1947) defined factorial invariance in terms of the factor loadings of a given variable remaining the same when that variable was factored in different test batteries involving the same common factors. Thurstone believed that his concept of simple structure rotation was especially conducive to the determination of factors which would display this kind of replicability. The history of factor analysis includes a considerable amount of attention being paid to the development of methods for maximizing and assessing the level of invariance achieved in substantive, factor analytic research (Harman, 1960).

What is at stake is a fundamental notion of replicability; that is, providing a basis for inferring that a dimension in one data set is the same, in some definable sense, as a dimension from a different data set. This issue becomes especially pertinent in the investigation of change where it is usually deemed crucial to establish the identity or equivalence of dimensions across time before attempting to define changes on that dimension.

Cattell (1944), for instance proposed that it should be possible to determine factors that would be invariant across populations. He suggested that if the factors are functional unities, even though they may exhibit different amounts of variance from one subpopulation to another, each factor's contributions to the variance of the observed variables should rise and fall in a consistent manner across subpopulations. Thomson (1951), Thurstone (1947), and more recently Meredith (1964a and b) have examined the issue of factor invariance in different subgroups from the standpoint of selection effects—often an unknown quantity in factor analytic studies, including cross-age comparison ones. Two rather striking points that have surfaced are: (1) The determination of invariant loading patterns may be jeopardized if variables are standardized within subsamples (e.g., if correlation matrices rather than covariance matrices are factored); and (2) the invariance of factors across different groups may be impossible to demonstrate unless the factors are allowed to covary differently from one subgroup to another. These conclusions strike at the heart of the common practice of factoring two or more correlation matrices, rotating the factors orthogonally, and then interpreting differences among factor loading patterns as indicative of, for example, ontogenetic changes rather than selection effects or even just sampling variability.

Stability of Factor Scores. Tucker (1958), in discussing the issue of factorial invariance, suggested an additional criterion to be examined in empirical research aimed at defining invariant factors—"the scores for individuals on a factor should remain invariant as the individuals are tested with different batteries which involve the factor" (p. 112). Although from a practical standpoint this criterion can be examined only in certain research schemes, it emphasizes an aspect which is often neglected in factor analytic studies—the information that may be derived from factor scores. Even though, as noted earlier, factor scores for individuals can only be estimated and not calculated directly, as in the case of principal components analysis, various relationships can be ascertained without explicitly obtaining factor scores. One such set of relationships that can be examined is the factor covariance matrix which is directly obtained in a factor analysis and is often the basis for additional, higher-order analyses. Moreover, one can estimate correlations between factors and variables measured but not included in the analysis and, by various techniques (Tucker, 1958, 1971, can estimate factor score reliability and stability coefficients, and mean differences among groups.

In focusing on individual development, information of the kind represented in factor scores has been of central concern in the development of techniques and their application to the understanding of change processes. The aforementioned trait-state distinction, for instance, has as part of its conceptual base, differences in the level of stability of factor scores (Baltes and Nesselroade, 1973; Nesselroade and Bartsch, 1976; Nesselroade and Cable, 1974).

Within a comparative factor analytic framework, Baltes and Nesselroade (1973) discussed four idealized types of factors for the study of ontogenetic changes across the life span. The four types consisted of factors which, across time, exhibited: (1) *invariant* loading patterns and stable factor scores; (2) *invariant* loading patterns and *fluctuant* factor scores; (3) *non-invariant* loading patterns and *stable* factor scores, and (4) *non-invariant* loading patterns and *fluctuant* factor scores. A variety of models and techniques can be organized around this general scheme in relation to the assumptions made (or restrictions imposed) concerning the nature of invariance of the loading pattern and degree of stability of the factor scores. Baltes and Nesselroade (1973) discussed the use of those concepts to distinguish between qualitative and quantitative changes—notions examined and further extended by Buss (1974).

Analyzing for Developmental Change. The study of change from a multivariate perspective has led to an important distinction—that between *level* and *pattern* differences or changes. Harris (1963a) drew explicit attention to this distinction and Bentler (1973), Baltes and Nesselroade (1970, 1973), Cattell (1970), Corballis and Traub (1970) and others have further discussed its implications for developmental research. Factor analytic investigation of the abilities differentiation hypothesis (Reinert, 1970), for example, represents a focus on change patterns. As Bentler (1973) has persuasively argued, however, changes or differences in level are equally germane in developmental research and conventional factor analytic solutions, unless modified, are apt to be completely insensitive to them.

Investigations of change on single measures are restricted primarily to a focus on differences in level, either for individuals or groups, and also are attended by the problems of scaling, analysis, and interpretation reviewed by such writers as Bereiter (1963) and Cronbach and Furby (1970). Moreover, such investigations raise but do not provide any clear answer for the nagging question: What has changed— the people or what the test is measuring? The issue of level must be recognized to include not only differences in distributions as reflected, for example, in group means, but also changes in the standing of individuals, relative to their fellows, as indicated by the stability coefficient.

A general approach that has been suggested for the analysis of developmental changes (Baltes and Nesselroade, 1970, 1973; Cattell, 1970), initially for descriptive purposes, is to utilize rather conventional procedures such as comparative factor analysis on multiple measures (longitudinal or cross-sectional) to look for invariant factor patterns. Invariance (or the lack of it) would be the basis for inferring whether change could be characterized as quan-

titative or qualitative. Given invariant factor patterns, one can then estimate the magnitude of differences in level on factor scores as was done, for example, by Nesselroade, Schaie, and Baltes (1972) on longitudinal data from an adult population. A variety of hypothesis-testing and model-fitting procedures to aid researchers in a systematic examination of factorial invariance are available (Cliff, 1966; Browne and Kristof, 1969; Jöreskog, 1969; Lawley and Maxwell, 1971). These procedures, as their use is extended, should help resolve many of the substantive issues centered around the distinction between qualitative and quantitative changes.

MULTIVARIATE PROCEDURES AND MODELS DESIGNED FOR DEVELOPMENTAL ANALYSIS

In addition to the relatively straightforward application of conventional multivariate techniques to various developmental problems (for reviews see McCall, 1970; Nesselroade, 1970; Wohlwill, 1973), a number of innovations in factor analytic theory and procedure established explicitly for descriptive developmental work have been witnessed in recent years. Many of these are largely untested in a variety of data contexts, but they bid fair to open up new avenues for understanding the nature of psychological change when appropriate data sets become available. Here, we will consider examples of techniques which depend for their rationale on the two kinds of distinctions made above—invariance and stability of factors, and pattern versus level differences.

Models Which Restrict Either Level or Pattern Changes to Dramatize Changes of the Other Type: Examples and Implications

Harris (1963a) presented an interesting and elegant adaptation of canonical factor analysis to the problem of identifying changes in pattern for multivariate observations obtained by repeated assessment of individuals at two points in time. In principle, the model can be applied to more than two occasions of measurement. The order of the matrix being factored, though, is equal to the sum of the orders of the separate occasion matrices and thus, becomes quite large if a number of variables are included at each occasion of measurement.

One very pertinent aspect of Harris's model is that it specifies the individual's factor score on each factor to be perfectly stable from one occasion to the next. This defines the factors to be the same for all occasions of measurement but, at the same time, the loading of a given observed measure on a particular factor may well vary from one occasion to another. Thus, the question of whether or not the same factors are involved at different points in time is obviated; they are the same by definition. However, relationships between the observed variables and the factors, as reflected in the factor loadings, can exhibit change from occasion to occasion. The point needs to be appreciated that these changes are not changes in individual differences on the factor. Differences among individuals on the factors, by definition, remain stable. Changes in individual differences on the observed variables may occur, however. Since they cannot be attributed to changes in the factor scores it is necessary, given the nature of the model, to attribute them to changes in the factor-variable relationships (loading pattern elements). This offers a rather powerful approach to studying the interesting issue of what a test is measuring at different points in time (at different age levels, for example). As noted by Bentler (1973) and by Corballis and Traub (1970), however, the procedure does not lend itself to the study of interindividual differences in intraindividual change.

Standing in marked contrast to Harris's model are those proposed by Pennell (1971) and Rozeboom (1976). Here the primary constraint imposed by the model is on the factor loading patterns rather than the factor scores. Invariance of factor loadings across data sets is literally specified by the model. In the case of longitudinal data this amounts to perfect invariance of loading patterns across occasions. Thus, a different type of constancy is defined in order to study change, viz., the factorial description of the observed variables (as represented by the factor loadings) is fixed over time with changes in the nature of factor scores and factor covariance matrices becoming objects of empirical inquiry. Rozeboom (1976), especially, has discussed the wealth of developmental information in factor covariance matrices obtained under the constraint of fixed factor loading patterns. He also addressed the reasonableness of this constraint as a model characteristic. Both of the classes of models just presented deserve the attention of developmentalists. What is clear is that, in addition to having specific data requirements, each makes rather strong assumptions about one type of change (level or pattern) in order to investigate empirically the nature of the other. In a recent paper, Hakstian (1973) discussed these and related issues and presented a series of alternative models among which researchers can choose to analyze multivariate longitudinal data.

Models Which Directly Restrict Neither Level Nor Pattern Changes: Examples and Implications

Some writers have elected to generalize techniques for studying change somewhat more than those described in the previous section by letting both factor loading patterns and factor scores vary over time. Procedures which directly restrict neither the loading patterns nor the factor scores to constancy place a special burden on the data for describing change, if one wishes to speak in some sense, about the same factors at different occasions of measurement. Alternatives, some of which were alluded to above, include trying to match up factors from different data sets either on the basis of their loading patterns (with or without some attempt to rotate them to congruence) or in terms of correlations (stability coefficients) of factor scores.

Corballis and Traub (1970) devised an analytic procedure—longitudinal factor analysis—which permits both factor loadings and factor scores to change with time but which provides a unique resolution of factors for two occasions. Corballis and Traub accomplished this by specifying factors that were uncorrelated within occasions and, save for unique pairings, uncorrelated between occasions. Thus, one factor on occasion 1 correlated to some degree with one and only one factor on occasion 2, allowing an inference that they were the same factors. Inspection of differences in loading patterns for these "matched" factors gives information concerning how the factor-construct has changed in relation to the manifest variables. The cross-occasion correlation of the factors may be interpreted as factor score stability coefficients. Nesselroade (1972) pointed out that the longitudinal factor analytic procedure achieved its unique resolution of two-occasion factors by maximizing factor score stability coefficients in a canonical correlation sense. Thus, the longitudinal factor model, while not directly imposing either pattern or factor score constancy, does place an emphasis on approximating the latter as nearly as the data permit. Corballis (1973) has recently generalized the technique to include more than two occasions of measurement. Bentler (1973) presented and tested an alternative to longitudinal factor analysis which is also applicable to data from more than two measurement occasions.

Brief Sampling of Resources for the Analysis of Multivariate Aging and Behavioral Change Data

The content oriented researcher may, at this point, feel somewhat bewildered by the array of methodological devices that has been paraded before him so fleetingly. It may be useful, therefore, to mention explicitly selected literature to consult when deciding: (a) what to do with a given set of data, or better still; (b) how to approach a given problem even before the data are collected.

Volumes by Morrison (1967) and Tatsuoka (1971) provide good coverage of the general domain of multivariate statistical analysis, and various chapters in the handbook edited by Cattell (1966a) and the symposium edited by Harris (1963b) deal generally with the measurement of change and the conduct of multivariate experimentation.

Useful discussions of the application of more abstract and technical models and procedures to the analysis of multivariate change data may be found in articles by Baltes and Nesselroade (1970), Bentler (1973), Buss (1974), Corballis (1973), Corballis and Traub (1970), Hakstian

(1973), Nesselroade (1972), and Rozeboom (1976). Selected important theoretical papers upon which these multivariate techniques depend for their rationale are those by Browne and Kristof (1969), Cattell (1944), Cliff (1966), McDonald (1974), Meredith (1964a, b), Pennell (1971), and Tucker (1958, 1971). Literally dozens of additional references could be cited here if space provided but these should serve as a useful beginning.

In light of the opening remarks of the chapter, it may be asserted that methodologists have begun to look seriously at the needs of substantive researchers in the area of development and some seemingly powerful analytic tools and concepts are awaiting trial by data. The author has tried to emphasize how multivariate models, especially factor analysis, may be employed to systematically explore concepts of aging and behavioral change. The reader is reminded that a great variety of topics, procedures, and applications simply could not be mentioned in so short a discussion. The issues presented and literature cited, hopefully, will enable developmental researchers to gain some sense of what a multivariate orientation can offer to this intriguing but complex field and will facilitate the entry of developmentalists into a sizeable and ever growing body of methodological literature.

REFERENCES

Baltes, P. B. 1968. Longitudinal and cross-sectional sequences in the study of age and generation effects. *Hum. Develop.*, 11, 145–171.

Baltes, P. B., and Nesselroade, J. R. 1970. Multivariate longitudinal and cross-sectional sequences for analyzing ontogenetic and generational change: A methodological note. *Developmental Psychology*, 2, 163–168.

Baltes, P. B., and Nesselroade, J. R. 1973. The developmental analysis of individual differences on multiple measures. *In*, J. R. Nesselroade and H. W. Reese (eds.), *Life-Span Developmental Psychology: Methodological Issues*, pp. 219–251. New York: Academic Press.

Bentler, P. M. 1973. Assessment of developmental factor change at the individual and group level. *In*, J. R. Nesselroade and H. W. Reese (eds.), *Life-Span Developmental Psychology: Methodological Issues*, pp. 145–174. New York: Academic Press.

Bereiter, C. 1963. Some persisting dilemmas in the

measurement of change. *In*, C. W. Harris (ed.), *Problems in Measuring Change*, pp. 3-20. Madison, Wisconsin: University of Wisconsin Press.

Browne, M. W., and Kristof, W. 1969. On the oblique rotation of a factor matrix to a specified pattern. *Psychometrika*, 34, 237-248.

Buss, A. R. 1974. Multivariate model of quantitative, structural, and quantistructural ontogenetic change. *Developmental Psychology*, 10, 190-203.

Campbell, D. T., and Stanley, J. C. 1963. Experimental and quasi-experimental designs for research in teaching. *In*, N. L. Gage (ed.), *Handbook of Research on Teaching*, pp. 171-246. Chicago: Rand McNally.

Cattell, R. B. 1944. "Parallel proportional profiles" and other principles for determining the choice of factors by rotation. *Psychometrika*, 9, 267-283.

Cattell, R. B. 1952. *Factor Analysis*. New York: Harper.

Cattell, R. B. (ed.) 1966a. *Handbook of Multivariate Experimental Psychology*. Chicago: Rand McNally.

Cattell, R. B. 1966b. Multivariate behavioral research and the integrative challenge. *Mult. Behav. Res.*, 1, 4-23.

Cattell, R. B. 1966c. Preface to Tucker, L. R. Learning theory and multivariate experiment: Illustration by determination of generalized learning curves. *In*, R. B. Cattell (ed.), *Handbook of Multivariate Experimental Psychology*, pp. 476-501. Chicago: Rand McNally.

Cattell, R. B. 1970. Separating endogenous, exogenous, ecogenic, and epogenic component curves in developmental data. *Developmental Psychology*, 3, 151-162.

Cattell, R. B. 1973. *Personality and Mood by Questionnaire*. San Francisco: Jossey-Bass.

Cliff, N. 1966. Orthogonal rotation to congruence. *Psychometrika*, 31, 33-42.

Cliff, N. 1973. Scaling. *In*, P. H. Mussen and M. R. Rosenzweig (eds.), *Annual Review of Psychology*, pp. 473-506. Palo Alto, California: Annual Reviews Press.

Corballis, M. C. 1973. A factor model for analyzing change. *Brit. J. Math. Stat. Psychol.*, 26, 90-97.

Corballis, M. C., and Traub, R. E. 1970. Longitudinal factor analysis. *Psychometrika*, 35, 79-98.

Cronbach, L. J., and Furby, L. 1970. How should we measure "change"—or should we? *Psych. Bull.*, 74, 68-80.

Cronbach, L. J., Gleser, G. C., Nanda, H., and Rajaratnam, N. 1972. *The Dependability of Behavioral Measurements: Theory of Generalizability for Scores and Profiles*. New York: John Wiley.

Frederiksen, N. 1972. Toward a taxonomy of situations. *American Psychologist*, 27, 114-123.

Gorsuch, R. L. 1974. *Factor Analysis*. Philadelphia: W. B. Saunders.

Hakstian, A. R. 1973. Procedures for the factor analytic treatment of measures obtained on different occasions. *Brit. J. Math. Stat. Psychol.*, 26, 219-239.

Harman, H. H. 1960. *Modern Factor Analysis*. Chicago: University of Chicago Press.

Harris, C. W. 1963a. Canonical factor models for the description of change. *In*, C. W. Harris (ed.), *Problems in Measuring Change*, pp. 138-155. Madison, Wisconsin: University of Wisconsin Press.

Harris, C. W. (ed.) 1963b. *Problems in Measuring Change*. Madison, Wisconsin: University of Wisconsin Press.

Humphreys, L. G. 1962. The organization of human abilities. *American Psychologist*, 17, 475-483.

Jöreskog, K. G. 1969. A general approach to confirmatory maximum likelihood factor analysis. *Psychometrika*, 34, 183-202.

Lawley, D. N., and Maxwell, A. E. 1971. *Factor Analysis as a Statistical Method*. New York: American Elsevier Publishing.

McCall, R. B. 1970. Addendum. The use of multivariate procedures in developmental psychology. *In*, P. H. Mussen (ed.), *Carmichael's Manual of Child Psychology*, pp. 1366-1377. 3rd Edition. New York: John Wiley.

McDonald, R. P. 1974. The measurement of factor indeterminacy. *Psychometrika*, 39, 203-222.

Meredith, W. 1964a. Notes on factorial invariance. *Psychometrika*, 29, 177-185.

Meredith, W. 1964b. Rotation to achieve factorial invariance. *Psychometrika*, 29, 187-206.

Morrison, D. F. 1967. *Multivariate Statistical Methods*. New York: McGraw-Hill.

Mulaik, S. A. 1972. *The Foundations of Factor Analysis*. New York: McGraw-Hill.

Nesselroade, J. R. 1970. Application of multivariate strategies to problems of measuring and structuring long-term change. *In*, L. R. Goulet, and P. B. Baltes (eds.), *Lifespan Developmental Psychology: Research and Theory*, pp. 193-207. New York: Academic Press.

Nesselroade, J. R. 1972. Note on the "longitudinal factor analysis" model. *Psychometrika*, 37, 187-191.

Nesselroade, J. R., and Baltes, P. B. 1974. Adolescent personality development and historical change: 1970-1972. *Monographs of the Society for Research in Child Development*, 39 (1. Serial No. 154).

Nesselroade, J. R., and Bartsch, T. W. 1976. Multivariate experimental perspectives on the construct validity of the trait-state distinction. *In*, R. B. Cattell and R. M. Dreger (eds.), *Handbook of Modern Personality Theory*. New York: Hemisphere. In press.

Nesselroade, J. R., and Cable, D. G. 1974. "Sometimes, its okay to factor difference scores"—the separation of state and trait anxiety. *Mult. Behav. Res.*, 9, 273-281.

Nesselroade, J. R., and Reese, H. W. 1973. (eds.) *Life-Span Developmental Psychology: Methodological Issues*. New York: Academic Press.

Nesselroade, J. R., Schaie, K. W., and Baltes, P. B. 1972. Ontogenetic and generational components of structural and quantitative change in adult behavior. *J. Gerontol.*, 27, 222-228.

Nunnally, J. C. 1967. *Psychometric Theory*. New York: McGraw-Hill.

Overall, J. E., and Klett, C. J. 1972. *Applied Multivariate Analysis*. New York: McGraw-Hill.

Pennell, R. 1971. Factor covariance analysis in subgroups. *Research Bulletin* (*RB-71-23*), Educational Testing Service, Princeton, New Jersey.

Reinert, G. 1970. Comparative factor analytic studies of intelligence throughout the human life-span. *In*, L. R. Goulet and P. B. Baltes (eds.), *Lifespan developmental psychology: Research and theory*, pp. 467–484. New York: Academic Press.

Rozeboom, W. W. 1976. Dynamic analysis of multivariate process data. *Psychometric Monogr*. In press.

Rummel, R. J. 1970. *Applied Factor Analysis*. Evanston, Illinois: Northwestern University Press.

Schaie, K. W. 1965. A general model for the study of developmental problems. *Psych. Bull.*, **64**, 92–107.

Sells, S. B. (ed.) 1962. *Stimulus Determinants of Behavior*. New York: Ronald.

Spielberger, C. D. 1972. Anxiety as an emotional state. *In*, C. D. Spielberger (ed.), *Anxiety: Current Trends in Theory and Research*, Vol. 1, pp. 23–49. New York: Academic Press.

Tatsuoka, M. M. 1971. *Multivariate Analysis*. New York: John Wiley.

Thomson, G. H. 1951. *The Factorial Analysis of Human Ability*. Boston: Houghton Mifflin.

Thurstone, L. L. 1947. *Multiple Factor Analysis*. Chicago: University of Chicago Press.

Tucker, L. R. 1958. An inter-battery method of factor analysis. *Psychometrika*, **23**, 111–135.

Tucker, L. R. 1971. Relations of factor score estimates to their use. *Psychometrika*, **36**, 427–436.

Wohlwill, J. F. 1973. *The Study of Behavioral Development*. New York: Academic Press.

4
HISTORY OF PSYCHOLOGICAL GERONTOLOGY

Klaus F. Riegel

University of Michigan

Treatises on the history of sciences have been traditionally restricted to intellectual changes in Europe and North America. The developments in other civilizations, based on distinctively different philosophical, political and economic conditions have been disregarded. Moreover, within the European and North American tradition, history of sciences has been described as a universal progression which through increased empirical research and abstractions would move us closer and closer to "true" scientific knowledge and enable us to detect the "laws of nature." Rarely has it been recognized that several divergent and often contradictory conceptions of these "laws" and "nature" exist even within a single cultural orientation and rarely has it been emphasized that scientific progress itself becomes possible only through confrontations between these contradictory conceptions.

As in past presentations, the following survey will be restricted to North American and European history. Within this geographical and intellectual arena, three distinct mentalities or paradigmatic orientations will be compared which are based upon different social, political

*The preparation of this chapter has been aided by the assistance of Suzanne Brumer and the constructive comments of Mary Arnold, Carol Ryff and Ruth Riegel. The author acknowledges most gratefully their valuable and kind support.

and economic conditions. For simplicity, they will be called the Anglo-American, Continental European, and Dialectical orientations (Riegel, 1972a). The argument will then be made that psychological gerontology has striven forcefully into the third orientation after realizing the first but bypassing the second. Thereby, psychological gerontology has effectively attained a far more advanced stage of design and knowledge than most of the other subdisciplines in the behavioral sciences.

PARADIGMATIC ORIENTATIONS

Anglo-American Orientation

An early indication of this mode of scientific and social philosophy is provided by Hobbes' (1558-1679) discussion of the origin of social order. At the beginning, according to Hobbes, everyone was engaged in fighting everyone else (*bellum omnium contra omnes*); the human being was compared to a selfish and untamed beast; social order had to be imposed upon the original chaotic conditions. Several centuries later, similar ideas dominated Darwin's (1809-1882) naturalistic interpretations of the "struggle for survival" and the "survival of the fittest." Not surprisingly, in social and political praxis these viewpoints originated and succeeded in societies where competition and achievement were valued so highly, i.e., as in Great Britain and in the United States.

Just as social structures were ignored as organizing principles of society, mental organizations were neglected in epistemology. The mind was compared by Locke (1682-1704) to a *tabula rasa* or an empty box upon which external contingencies impinged. Neither the environment nor the individuals themselves participated actively in the selection and organization of knowledge. Subsequently the main criterion for intellectual and personal excellence was the amount of information accumulated, just as the criterion for social respectability was the amount of wealth and property acquired.

It is also not surprising that the adult white male engaged in manufacturing or trade appeared as the most successful competitor and became the standard for comparisons. None of the other individuals and groups—the young and the old, the delinquent and the deprived, the female and the colonial subject—were evaluated in their own terms but rather compared against this single yardstick. They were described in negative terms only, as deficient, deteriorated, retarded, or simply as deviant.

This philosophy of man and society entered most distinctively into psychology through the spectacular efforts of Sir Francis Galton (1822-1911). He should also be regarded as the founder of the psychology of individual and developmental differences, including those of adulthood and aging. When merged with the pragmatic goals of stock breeding this orientation led to Eugenics which Galton justified as follows: "It may seem monstrous that the weak should be crowded out by the strong, but it is still more monstrous that the races best fitted to play their part on the stage of life, should be crowded out by the incompetent, the ailing, and the desponding" (1869, p. 343). It would be surprising, indeed, if Galton had expressed a different opinion about the aged.

Continental European Orientation

Although implied in Leibniz's (1646-1716) emphasis upon active organizing forces of the mind, the scientific and social philosophy of the alternative orientation was most clearly expressed by Rousseau (1712-1778). In contrast to the ceaseless striving for achievement, he proposed a social philosophy in which the young were considered and evaluated by independent standards rather than by those of the successful young adult. In this way, Rousseau provided an option for multiage, multigenerational and also multicultural standards.

In his romantic zeal, Rousseau refused to consider development as the taming of ineffective or asocial tendencies. The child as well as primitive man (*bon savage*) were regarded as reflecting more perfectly the inherent harmony of the human being than the acculturated adult. Civilization was seen as a restrictive cloak covering the natural beauty and knowledge of children and as the force generating social differences and injustice. Education, therefore, should treat children as children. It should keep them in their innocent state as long as possible and should not aim at making them assimilate the adult world quickly, completely and uncritically.

Through the efforts of Pestalozzi (1746-1827), Fröbel (1782-1852), Montessori (1870-1952), and many others, Rousseau's social philosophy began to influence profoundly the educational institutions on the European continent. At the same time, reformist and revolutionary movements from within various age groups led to refined age stratification and the assignment of specific roles to different groups of the society, including those of the aged.

Toward the end of the nineteenth century the widespread "youth movement" (see Hardesty, 1976) tried to liberate the adolescent, an attempt which received scholarly sanction in Spranger's influential book on adolescence. Most recently, the continental European movement has found expression in Piaget's work. His psychology is characterized by the notion of a stepwise progression in development. Each stage has to be evaluated in the framework of its own standards and, strictly speaking, is incompatible with other levels of behavior.

The Continental European paradigm emerged in societies with distinct social stratification governed by landed aristocracies. Competition within but not between classes was permitted.

The political and economic decisions were directed from the top down and as the privileges decreased the duties increased. Nevertheless, such a social organization led to an educational philosophy which was appreciative of differences between ages and social groups, and assigned selective roles to them. Undoubtedly, this orientation still needs to influence our conception of aging and the aged.

But in spite of these innovations the Continental European paradigm, like its Anglo-American counterpart, continued to focus upon the experiences of the separate individual. Development was seen as emerging from within. Although the interactions of the individual with the social world were recognized, the latter merely functioned as a testing ground and, in the philosophy of Rousseau, as a coercive power against which the individual would have to rise. But the individuals, their knowledge, motivations and feelings, do not only emerge from within, but also from without, through the collective efforts of many. Since the mutual determination of the individual and society was not sufficiently recognized both in the Anglo-American and in the Continental European paradigm, psychology has begun to depart from these orientations, most notably from the cognitive developmental psychology of Piaget.

Dialectical Orientation

The third paradigm, in trying to overcome the separation of subject and object, focuses upon the developmental interdependence of organism and environment, individual and society. The split between subject and object has characterized the psychologist's desire to imitate the conception and, thereby, the success of the natural sciences. The elimination of the observing subject from the scientific discourse contributed to the advances of the classical natural sciences up into the second half of the nineteenth century, but the creation of "objective" conditions in psychology has never been of unqualified benefit (Riegel, 1973a). Rather than generating knowledge on the basis of such a separation, the epistemological foundation for these sciences should lie in the dialectical interactions between the changing individual and the changing world (Riegel, 1975b; Rubinsteijn, 1963; Wozniak, 1975).

The topic of a dialectical psychology can be most clearly elaborated by contrasting it with three levels of psychological research. (1) The oldest and still rather common path is used by general-experimental psychologists. This approach is the most abstract form of a scientific inquiry. Both individual-developmental and cultural-historical changes are eliminated and thus, the human being represents a fictitious point in a developmental-historical vacuum. (2) Although developmental psychologists have studied age differences (and sometimes changes), commonly cultural-historical changes have been eliminated from consideration. For example, young and old persons tested at one particular historical time differ widely with regard to the cultural-sociological conditions under which they grew up. Although the impact of historical changes during an extended period of time, e.g., in education, health care, nutrition, communication, etc., is often much more dramatic than any behavioral differences between young and old persons, this factor has been disregarded in all but a few developmental studies. (3) By realizing that the study of the human being has to take account of both individual-developmental and cultural-historical changes, a dialectical approach synthesizes the two earlier orientations. It absorbs the Anglo-American paradigm of a passive organism in an unstructured world, solely directed by a relentless drive toward achievement; it absorbs the Continental European paradigm of an organism actively constructing a world which, nevertheless, remains passive and does not impose its goals and directions upon the organism but merely provides multigenerational and multicultural options. As the dialectical paradigm traces the interactions between individual and historical development to their inner-biological and outer-physical foundations, man retains much higher and humane roles than those of an untamed beast, an empty wax plate, a playful child, or a good barbarian. Through his ceaseless efforts he changes nature; the changing nature changes man.

ANGLO-AMERICAN ORIENTATION

The Study of Developmental Differences

During the second half of the nineteenth century, scientific psychology was founded in Germany by Weber, Fechner, Helmholtz, Wundt and others. Its goal was a universal analysis of the mind to be achieved either by abstracting from or by disregarding situational, individual, developmental and historical differences. As soon as this methodology and its underlying conception was grasped by American investigators (most notably by Wundt's first assistant, J. McK. Cattell), it was applied to practical ends (the selection of college students), a conversion which Wundt called "ganz amerikanisch".

As the exploration of individual differences within the conceptual framework that became known as functional psychology was set on its course, it acquired additional backing from the study of developmental differences initiated by Galton (1869) in Britain. Prior to Cattell, but similarly interested in motor performance and discrimination tasks, Galton launched the first large-scale collection of empirical data across the whole age span.

Galton, a half-cousin of Darwin, introduced evolution into psychology, especially the determining concepts of variation and selection. In America, these ideas were supported and integrated into psychology by Baldwin and Hall. Both were concerned with child development, the latter also with aging (Hall, 1922), but neither engaged in large-scale investigations of sensorimotor performance as did Galton and Cattell. Except for a few applications during and shortly after World War I, investigations of sensorimotor performances were disregarded until after World War II. At that time emphasis shifted to experimental manipulations and comparisons rather than to the collection of large population norms.

In the meantime, the study of individual and developmental differences had received a distinctly different direction through the work of Binet and Henri in France. Rather than focusing upon the "detection" and "discrimination" of smallest mental elements (sensations, images, and simple feelings in the terminology of Wundt), Binet analyzed complex performances of judgement and knowledge. He incorporated tasks measuring corresponding "capacities" in his well known intelligence test retaining only a few sensorimotor items (such as the discrimination of lines, figures and weights). Thus, the historical origin of a second major line of investigations of development and aging, i.e., of ability testing, again arose in Continental Europe. Binet's work, however, aimed at solving the rather concrete problem of selecting retarded children for special educational programs. Just as the work of the German laboratory had to be translated into the American praxis by Cattell, large-scale investigations of intelligence were conducted only after the adaptation and standardization of the test by Terman in America.

General Intelligence

The instrument prepared by Terman in 1916 was not exceptionally well suited for the study of developmental differences and changes, in particular those during adulthood and aging. The underlying concept of intelligence was that of a universal, unchanging capacity expressed by the IQ (Hunt, 1961; Riegel, 1973c). Situational variations and developmental changes were noted with misgivings since they reduced the predictive utility of the test. The observed developmental differences forced the investigators to create an artificial constancy of the IQ by fixating the maximum chronological age to be entered into the IQ formula at the early age of 12 to 18 years. Each subsequent revision of the Stanford-Binet Test introduced more complex corrections to keep the IQ constant. Nevertheless, cross-sectional data consistently showed that intelligence, as measured by this and similar instruments, declines rather rapidly during early adulthood and even more so during later years of life. Much of the subsequent research attempted to explain, modify, or reject these observations.

A common practice in contemporary psychology is to disregard farsighted earlier studies. A typical case is the investigation of adults and the aged by Foster and Taylor (1920). Here, almost all of the major issues investigated in later studies had been suggested and explored, including the speed-power relationship, the differential changes in intelligence, the dependence of change on the original level of functioning, on educational level and socioeconomic factors, etc. Few investigators paid attention to this work; instead they followed the trend set by Terman's Stanford–Binet Test and his studies of "genius" (Terman, 1925; Terman and Oden, 1959).

The studies by C. C. Miles and Miles (1932; see also W. R. Miles, 1931) enjoyed the opposite fate. They received high credit for their breadth in approach including the use of experimental methods but added less to the investigation of intellectual development. The instrument used, the Otis Test, resembles the Stanford-Binet and consists of a widely varying collection of items without any apparent conceptual organization.

In contrast to this method, Jones and Conrad (1933), beginning their work in 1926, applied an instrument much more appropriate for the measurement of adult functioning, the Army Alpha Test. This instrument—like the Wechsler Test which was going to follow it (Wechsler, 1939, 1956; see also Berkowitz, 1965; Corsini and Fasset, 1953; Doppelt and Wallace, 1955; Riegel, R. M. and Riegel, 1959)—is differentially structured and, therefore, allows for more specific inferences about intellectual variations and changes than the Binet or the Otis test. Applying this test to a large adult population in New England, Jones and Conrad were able to explore developmental differences of intellectual functions. Most notably, tasks requiring language skills and the utilization of long established habits, occasionally called "crystallized" abilities (Cattell, 1943), reveal a slow increase in performance, a late peak, and high stability or slow decline. Tasks requiring sensorimotor coordination, new learning and speedy performance, occasionally called "fluid" intelligence (Cattell, 1943), reveal a fast increase in performance, an early peak, and a rapid decline during adulthood and aging.

According to these results, the intelligence of children is dominated by "fluid" rather than by "crystallized" functions. The former are already well developed early in life; the latter are not. In contrast, the intelligence of older adults is dominated by "crystallized" rather than "fluid" performances. The findings by Jones and Conrad (1933) led to the recognition of structural changes in intelligence with age, a topic to be explored with the new technique of factor analysis which despite a multitude of inconclusive results (Balinsky, 1941; Goldfarb, 1941; Cohen, 1957; Riegel, R. M., 1960; Riegel, R. M. and Riegel, 1962; Green and Berkowitz, 1964) has not yet been laid to its deserving rest. Alternative, though more powerful theorizing has been generally disregarded (Riegel and Riegel, 1962).

C. C. Miles and Miles (1932) were among the first to analyze the dependency of growth and decline on the original intelligence level, education, and socioeconomic status (see also Cattell, 1934; Raven, 1948; Foulds, 1949; Birren and Morrison, 1961; Riegel, Riegel, and Meyer, 1963; 1967b; Berkowitz and Green, 1965; Granick and Friedman, 1967; Schaie and Strother, 1968a, b; Blum and Jarvik, 1974; Schaie and Labouvie-Vief, 1974). This issue was later elaborated in longitudinal studies of superior persons (Bayley and Oden, 1955; Terman and Oden, 1959) and led Owens (1953, 1966) and Thompson (1954) to question whether "age is kinder to the initially more able." Frequently, bright persons do not only develop faster and reach a higher than average performance level, but their skills also decline more slowly. The opposite seems to be true for persons below average intelligence (Kaplan, 1943; Muench, 1944; Bell and Zubeck, 1960). According to Riegel and Riegel (1972), these observations hold only for "fluid" intelligence. For "crystallized" functions the opposite trend was confirmed and captured by the statement that "the last will be first." Less able persons continue to gain in verbal performance over the whole span of the adult years; more able persons show relatively less improvements though little decline. Provided that the convergent and divergent trends for persons above and below average are controlled for general regression toward the means (Baltes, Nesselroade, Schaie, and Labouvie, 1972), the variance in scores between high and low individuals decreases with increasing age.

Differences in variation of scores between age groups are also responsible for the more successful prediction of survival at earlier (55 to 64 years) than at later age levels (over 65 years) (Eisdorfer, 1963; Jarvik and Falek, 1963; Riegel, Riegel, and Meyer, 1963, 1967a; Berkowitz, 1965; Palmore, 1969). The reverse conclusion was reached for test and retest participation (Jones and Conrad, 1933; Riegel, Riegel, and Meyer, 1968; Rose, 1965; Streib,

1966; Atchley, 1969; Baltes, Schaie, and Nardi, 1971). Attempts to predict survival or longevity are related to investigations of sudden decline in performance from up to a few days (Kleemeier, 1962; Lieberman, 1965) to several years prior to death (Jarvik and Falek, 1963; Riegel and Riegel, 1972).

Variations in scores between age groups have also been employed to explain differences in the results obtained either with power or speed tests (Thorndike, Bregman, Tilton, and Woodyard, 1928; C. C. Miles, 1934; Sorenson, 1938). In particular, Lorge (1936) showed that whenever speed factors were removed from the test evaluation, the average scores either became highly stable or showed improvement during the later years of life. Similar conclusions were derived by Furry and Baltes (1973) for other ability-extraneous but performance-related variables such as fatigue and subtest position. Like the following results on the impact of historical changes on intelligence, these findings seriously question the use of intelligence tests for the evaluation of adult performances. Similar arguments related to subcultural differences have been made only recently. As for many other significant insights, Lorge's contribution has been largely neglected in gerontology and psychology (for a recent appraisal see Riegel, 1973c).

During World War II, the occasion arose for testing large groups of young adults with the same instrument used on similar groups in World War I. As reported by Tuddenham (1948), the median test score of the World War II recruits coincided with the 84th percentile in the distribution of scores obtained in World War I. Thus a considerable improvement in performance with historical time had taken place, attributable perhaps, to changes in education, communication and welfare. Although not fully recognized at that time, these results revealed the fictitiousness of studies exploring developmental differences in individuals without taking into account concurrent social and historical changes. As later investigations were to show (Riegel, Riegel and Meyer, 1967b; Nesselroade, Schaie and Baltes, 1972; Riegel and Riegel, 1972; Schaie and Labouvie-Vief, 1974; Schaie, Labouvie and

Buech, 1973), cohort differences and historical changes often contribute more significantly to the observed results than individual-psychological development.

The interdependence between individual-psychological and cultural-sociological developments remained obscured because the traditional approaches for studying development, i.e., the cross-sectional and longitudinal designs, confound individual and cultural differences or changes. Only when attention was called to a third basic methodology, the time-lag design, did it become apparent that most of the interpretations of individual developmental differences or changes were based upon questionable foundations (Schaie, 1965; Baltes, 1968). If finally, as shown by Zajonc and Markus (1975) for a group of young adults, the changing family constellation has a systematic effect upon the intelligence of successive children, the concepts of intelligence in particular, and abilities in general, lose their remaining significance. What needs to be studied are the changing interactions of events within and between individuals. The investigation of this topic is the goal of a dialectical psychology.

Special Abilities

Until recently, most research efforts in psychological gerontology have been devoted to the study of intellectual development. As a byproduct, growing attention was given to vocabulary skills and occasionally to noncognitive components, such as interests, value preferences and attitudes, most notably, "rigidity," "dogmatism," "conservatism" or "attitude toward life." Although the influence of the Continental European orientation with its emphasis upon the whole person and his/her activity is apparent in these studies, by and large, they were guided by the empiricism of the Anglo-American orientation. Various traits and skills were first separated in order to analyze developmental differences; only later was their covariation to be investigated.

1. As indicated already by the comparison of "crystallized" and "fluid" intellectual functions, skills that rely on long established habits and continuous use, most notably verbal skills,

develop slowly during the early years, reach a late peak, and are very resistant to decline. Because of their unique stability the study of vocabulary attracted considerable attention among psychological gerontologists.

In 1930, Babcock developed the "level-efficiency theory of intelligence" which was applied by Gilbert (1935) to normal and senile aged. The basic idea of the theory became known as the "Babcock-Gilbert hypothesis" on the relative stability of vocabulary skill and the method proposed relies on vocabulary scores for estimating the original level of functioning of aged or pathological persons. Differences or ratios of these scores and other performance measures are used to estimate a person's intellectual deterioration on a quasi-intraindividual basis. (I am calling this procedure "quasi-intraindividual" because no repeated test scores are obtained from the same persons. Instead estimates are derived on the basis of the vocabulary which is known to remain interindividually—and presumably also intraindividually—stable over the adult life span.)

The investigations of the vocabulary created considerable interest among applied psychologists but controversy among academic investigators. Several researchers confirmed Babcock's and Gilbert's findings and supported the method (Fox, 1947; Lewinsky, 1948). Later Gilbert (1941) extended her explorations to relative age differences in memory capacities. Yakorcynsky (1941) demonstrated that the Babcock-Gilbert hypothesis holds only for the simplest form of the test, the recognition vocabulary. When more complex forms of responding are required, such as in qualitative or definition vocabularies, a differential decline in performance was observed among the aged (Feifel, 1949; Fox and Birren, 1950). In a modified form, i.e., in the comparison between "hold" and "non-hold" subtests, the Babcock-Gilbert method was retained in the early versions of the Wechsler Test of Adult Intelligence (1939).

The observed stability of vocabulary scores led this author to make specific explorations of structural changes in verbal performances and to develop a battery of verbal tests (Riegel, 1967) to measure differential changes among the aged (Riegel, 1959a, 1968c). These explorations were supported by developmental comparisons of semantic structure (Riegel, 1970), experimental investigations of set and verbal performance (Riegel and Riegel, 1964; Riegel, 1965, 1968a) and theoretical interpretations of language changes (Riegel, 1966). With few exceptions these investigations have not led to any further explorations by other investigators. Perhaps, their reluctance was caused by the attempted fusion of verbal and cognitive skills, by the emphasis upon structure (especially semantic, not syntactic) rather than function and, in general, by the use of concepts which are more characteristic for the Continental European than for the Anglo-American tradition. Similar difficulties have arisen in the study of age differences in interests and attitudes.

2. The concepts of attitudes, value preferences, and interests similar to that of cognitive, semantic structure, originated within Continental European psychology, especially in Lewin's dynamic psychology (1935) and Spranger's theory of values (1914). Lewin defines attitudes structurally as boundary conditions between different cognitive-affective "regions" representing different needs of a person in a particular situation at a particular time.

Kounin (1941) successfully translated the structural conception of one particular attitude, rigidity, into the operational terms of the laboratory and investigated developmental differences between children and mentally retarded adults. The investigation of structurally defined attitudes has remained the exception, however (e.g., Heglin's use of Luchins' Water Jar Test and the Alphabetic Maze Test, 1956; see also Schaie, 1958; Brinley, 1965; Schaie and Strother, 1968a,b). Most commonly, psychological gerontologists investigated what McAndrew (1948) has called "behavioral" properties of attitudes by questioning subjects' preference for old established habits, resistance to change, intolerance, anxiety about new situations, etc.

Most of these investigations—competently reviewed by Chown (1959), Bennet and Eckman (1973) and Botwinick (1973)—show an increase in rigidity, dogmatism, and conservatism with advancing age as well as a decline in need for achievement among men and affiliation among women, but an increase in achievement among women and in affiliation and power among men (Veroff, Atkinson, Feld, and Gurin, 1960). There are few consistent indications of how these and many other variables are structurally interrelated. Consequently, Chown (1961) has questioned the significance of these concepts. According to her findings, most of the variance attributed to "rigidity" can be accounted for by subjects' intelligence.

More recently, Brim (1974b) emphasized the significance of the mode of approach documented in studies of internal-external control of motivation. As shown by this writer for the aged population (Riegel and Riegel, 1960; for follow-up data see Riegel, Riegel, and Meyer, 1967b), it makes a marked difference whether one asks questions in the first person singular (e.g., "I much prefer to eat a familiar dish than something which I do not know at all") or in the form of impersonal phrases (e.g., "In whatever one does, the tried and true ways are always the best"). Scales built upon the second type of question show a significant increase with age, the former show a decline. The choice of approaching the individual either as an impersonal entity whose underlying traits are to be assessed or as a concrete human being in a concrete social situation, i.e., in the "testing dialogue," represents one major turning point which directs us toward a dialectical orientation.

Few of these issues entered decisively into the discussion of attitudes, value preferences, interests and other personality traits among the aged. They have also been omitted in explorations of intellectual development. Instead, and following the Anglo-American tradition, extensive investigations were launched during the late 1920's to survey in detail differences in interests and activities between age groups by administering long check lists to subjects (Strong, 1943) or by applying masculinity-femininity questionnaires (Terman and Miles, 1936). More limited investigations were conducted by Thorndike (1935).

Independent measures either of the interests expressed or of the activities performed were also applied to explore the ambiguous though important topic of personal adjustment (for reviews see Cavan, Burgess, Havighurst, and Goldhammer, 1949; Kuhlen, 1959). Adjustment can be defined by the discrepancies between one's expressed wishes and the activities actually performed. The smaller the difference, the better the adjustment. Investigations applying such a method have been conducted by Cavan *et al.* (1949), Shanas (1950) and Kleemeier (1951). Mason (1954) obtained judgmental comparisons between what has been described by Rogers as the "real" and the "ideal" self.

While these approaches aim at a structural definition of adjustment (similar to the structural definition of rigidity proposed by Lewin; see McAndrew, 1948), the majority of studies have applied functional criteria. Adjustment is either identified with general happiness or (still retaining some structured components) through judgmental comparisons of present personal and social conditions with those of the past. Many of the American investigators related these measures to the degree of a person's activity; indeed, many tried to reduce and explain adjustment by the degree of activity, especially social activity (Ju-Shu, 1952; Kutner, Fanshel, Togo and Langner, 1956). Riegel, Riegel and Skiba (1962) made a comparative analysis of different kinds of adjustment measures.

Structural evaluations of adjustment represent the Continental European conceptualization. This is also true for investigations of cognition and perception of age and aging (Giese, 1928; Havighurst, 1952; Tuckman and Lorge, 1952). In recent years, this topic has received renewed attention in the work of Ahammer and Baltes (1972) and Troll (1970). It questions the use of chronological age scales and relates to studies of roles and role perception which will be discussed further below.

Skills and Performance

The foundation for the study of intelligence and attitudes was laid in Continental Europe but large-scale investigations of developmental differences were carried out in the United

States. This application resulted from the convergence of the evolutionism of Galton, the functionalism of J. McK. Cattell, and the empiricism of both. Similar interactions occurred in the history of experimental investigations of age differences in skills and performances. Age-constant conceptions and methodologies were developed in Germany during the later parts of the nineteenth century by Weber, Fechner, Helmholtz and Wundt and in Holland by Donders. Again through the efforts of Galton and to a lesser extent of Cattell, they were applied in the study of life span differences.

Prior to Galton, Quételet (1835) had proposed the concept of "average man" and presented data from various age groups on sensory functioning, height, weight, hand strength and productivity, the latter topic was greatly extended more than a century later by Lehman (1953). Quételet was a statistician, astronomer and sociologist and is often regarded as the founder of the study of aging (Birren, 1961). In a manner advocated by his contemporary, Comte (1798–1857), and later expanded by Durkheim (1858–1917), he focused upon both biological and social determinants of man. Quételet's view that knowledge was achieved by massive empirical observations and use of statistical procedures greatly influenced Galton.

Galton's main contribution to the psychology of aging relies on data collected at the International Health Exhibition in London, 1884. Seventeen different anthropometric, sensory and psychomotor measures were obtained from 9,337 persons ranging in age from 5 to 80 years. In contrast to present research practices, Galton's subjects paid for their participation in the research. Galton's data (Ruger and Stoessiger, 1927; Elderton, Moul and Page, 1928) are still considered to be the most reliable material, for example, on age differences in simple visual and auditory reaction time across the life span. Because Galton seems to have been more interested in freely exploring ideas—many rather eccentric—than in educating students, establishing departments or professional organizations, his work was not immediately pursued by others.

During and shortly after World War I, age differences in psychomotor skills were occasionally tested for selection purposes but this work remained rather unsystematic until W. R. Miles began to direct his attention to this topic. In 1927, a committee was established at Stanford University to study the problem of older workers in industry. The committee included Stone, Strong, Terman and Miles (as chairman). In 1928, the Carnegie Corporation granted support for the Stanford Later Maturity Study.

At that time a good amount of research had already been completed on age differences in sensory capacities. Miles (1931) directed most of his attention to psychomotor functions and was led to distinguish motility, i.e., the speed of motor movements, from the speed of simple reaction. This distinction was retained in most of the following smaller studies. Major new investigations were not initiated and new interpretations were not provided until about 1950.

Two research centers became instrumental in fostering further explorations—one located in England and the other in the United States. In 1946, the Nuffield Unit for Research into Problems of Aging was organized at Cambridge University under the direction of Alan Welford. During its six-year history, the focus of research was on the measurement of skilled behavior and application to industry (Welford, 1951, 1958). In addition to its high research productivity, the unit trained many research workers who went on to other universities to teach and, thereby, to promote further investigations of the aged and aging.

In the United States, the gerontological unit of the National Institutes of Health was organized by Nathan Shock in 1946. James Birren joined the Unit in 1947 to head the psychological research division. In 1953 the Section on Aging was established in the National Institute of Mental Health under his direction. Members of this Section collaborated with the Division on Maturity and Old Age of the American Psychological Association (APA) (founded in 1945) to plan the Conference on the Psychological Aspects of Aging held in Bethesda, Maryland in 1955. The proceedings of the conference have been edited by John Anderson (1956) and influenced greatly the course of further developments in psychological gerontology.

Much of the research conducted in Birren's

laboratory aimed at identifying a general speed factor that would explain the decrease in various psychomotor performances with age (1965). For this purpose, age differences in speed of nerve conductivity were investigated (Norris, Shock and Wagman, 1953; Birren and Wall, 1956), in reflex time (Hügin, Norris, and Shock, 1960), in reaction time varying the length of the path for nerve transmission (Birren and Botwinick, 1955a) or the difficulty of the task (Birren and Botwinick, 1951a), in choice reaction time (Birren, Riegel, and Morrison, 1962) and in writing speed (Birren and Botwinick, 1951b). From this and other evidence Birren (1965) sought to explain the age decrement in speed of performance by cerebral rather than sensorimotor factors.

The work of one of his close associates in those years, Jack Botwinick, was concerned with reaction time and preparatory set (Botwinick, 1965; Botwinick and Brinley, 1962; Botwinick and Thompson, 1966), as well as with perceptual discrimination (Birren and Botwinick, 1955b; Szafran, 1951). Otherwise, the study of age differences in complex perception and perceptual integration has not been pursued much further. A few studies have been made on perceptual illusions (Comalli, 1970), ambiguous figures (Botwinick, Robbin and Brinley, 1959; Korchin and Basowitz, 1956) and form perception (Basowitz and Korchin, 1957; Axelrod and Cohen, 1961). Virtually unexplored are the topics of perception and language (Riegel, Riegel, and Wendt, 1962) and perception and cognitive set (Riegel, 1965).

Birren's work and, in particular, that of Welford and his associates was influenced by the development of information theory. Information theory led to refined analysis of choice reaction (Singleton, 1954), the effects of task difficulty (Clay, 1954; Birren, Allen, and Landau, 1954), and the sequential order of movements upon psychomotor performances (Kay, 1951). In his summarizing (1951, 1958) and generalizing (1960) interpretations, Welford made long lasting contributions not only to psychological gerontology but to general psychology as well. Furthermore, practical applications in work and training situations were explored at the Cambridge laboratory (Brown, 1957; Shooter, Schonfield, King, and Welford,

1965). Previously a few similar studies had been made in Russia (Platanoff, 1911), Germany (Weiss, 1927), France (Ehinger, 1927), Japan (Kubo, 1938), and the United States (Miles and Shriver, 1953). None of them led, however, to a comprehensive interpretation of changes in skills and performance as those proposed by Welford.

In the 1950's new explorations were also initiated on topics of memory, learning and complex performances. Some of these issues were first explored by Thorndike, Bregman, Tilton, and Woodyard (1928), Willoughby (1929, 1930) and Ruch (1933), the latter two being members of the Stanford Later Maturity Study. Also Jones and Conrad engaged in explorations of age differences in learning and memory (Jones, Conrad and Horn, 1928; Conrad and Jones, 1931) as did Gilbert (1941) whose contribution was similar to her earlier one on the relative stability of vocabulary scores and the measurement of mental decline. In general, the explorations of memory, learning and complex performance border upon those of intellectual functions and often were directly connected with them (Conrad and Jones, 1929).

Further work on these topics emphasizing verbal factors was conducted both in England and the United States. Self pacing and verbal performance (Canestrari, 1963; Eisdorfer, Axelrod and Wilkie, 1963), association strength (Canestrari, 1966), and retroactive interference (Gladis and Braun, 1958; Hulicka, 1967; Arenberg, 1967) were investigated. Short- and long-term memory was analyzed by Talland (1965) and Craik (1968) who, together with Rabbitt (1968), paid particular attention to the differential effects of the structure of the material upon the memory of old and young subjects. Also dichotic listening has been used as a method for investigating short-term memory of the aged (Inglis and Caird, 1963; Inglis, Sykes, and Ankus, 1968).

Some studies on the effects of associative and language habits upon performance showed notable improvements during continuing performance among older subjects until they exceeded the younger ones in their speed of response (Riegel and Birren, 1966; Riegel, 1965, 1968a,c). Problem solving and thinking, including concept attainment, negative information processing and switch of solution strategies, were also investigated (Wetherick, 1964; Wiersma and Klausmeier, 1965; Young, 1966; Arenberg, 1968). Occasionally, some of these investigations have been described as explorations of cognitive processes (Botwinick, 1967). In contrast to such a designation, I reserve this term for studies closely concerned with the organization and structure of thought processes best represented by the work of Piaget.

CONTINENTAL EUROPEAN ORIENTATION

The Continental European orientation interprets human development as a progression in qualitative leaps and emphasizes the active participation of the individual in structuring his own development. Although changes or shifts are not attributed to environmental inducements, these outer conditions provide the material necessary for the individual's actions; without them, the individual would operate within a physical and social vacuum. All development is brought about, however, by the activities of the organism alone and not by the activities in the environment.

The Continental European orientation is represented by theories of personality but found its most significant expression in Piaget's theory of cognitive development. In the present section, I discuss both approaches and try to show that neither of them has as yet been comprehensively implemented in the study of aging.

Cognitive Development

Although a few similar interpretations have been advanced—most notably by Heinz Werner—cognitive developmental psychology was almost single-handedly created by Jean Piaget. In his earliest period, and still under the influence of Binet, Claparède and the French sociologists led by Durkheim and Mauss, Piaget emphasized functional and social aspects. But this orientation was soon abandoned in exchange for structural, developmental interpretations. This period in Piaget's own career (see Riegel, 1975a) began toward the end of the 1930's and has

been introduced to American psychologists by Hunt (1961) and Flavell (1963). In his work during this period, Piaget described in theory and supported with his studies the well known stages of cognitive development: sensorimotor, preoperational, concrete operational and formal operational intelligence.

Until very recently (see Hooper, 1976; Papalia and Bielby, 1975), Piaget's methods and interpretations have not been applied in the study of adult development and aging. But unless new developmental periods of maturity and aging are proposed and added to his theory, all that Piaget-related research would be able to provide is some more data on intellectual stability at best or regression at worst (Flavell, 1970, Piaget, 1972). Such research would yield little over and above that contained in the conglomerate of information generated through the use of intelligence tests and similar procedures within the empiricism of the Anglo-American orientation. On the other hand, the derivation of more advanced forms of cognitive operations and developmental periods would require the dismissal of conceptions deeply rooted in Western scientific theory, i.e., those of formal or abstract logic. Historically, such a substitution has taken place with the development of dialectical logic (Kosok, 1972; Buck-Morss, 1975; Lawler, 1975). Most notably, such a logic does not reject but rather accepts contradictions as the basis of thinking, especially of mature and creative thinking. Some philosophers (Wundt, 1949) and many modern natural scientists (Bohr, Heisenberg, Jordan) have come to regard dialectical logic as the only form of thought on *par* with advances in modern natural sciences.

Recently this author (Riegel, 1973b) has proposed a fifth or final period of cognitive development. Since then, many other suggestions have appeared in the literature extending the application of dialectical analysis to most other areas of psychology, developmental psychology and, in particular, the study of adulthood and aging (for surveys see Riegel, 1975b,d). For example, extensions have been made into the areas of moral development (Meacham, 1975), language (Harris, 1975; Riegel, 1975b), learning and thinking (Clayton, 1975; Kvale, 1975) and social relations (Rappoport, 1975; Hefner, Rebecca, and Oleshansky, 1975; Van den Daele, 1975). All of these studies ask for a reorientation which rejects the one-sided emphasis upon abilities and traits and the preference for equilibrium and balance. This approach does not seek the roots of development in the single individual but in the developmental interactions between at least two individuals, for example, the mother and her child or the husband and his wife (Riegel, 1975c). In a more general sense, this approach emphasizes the interaction between individual-developmental and cultural-historical changes.

Personality Development

In his review of personality and related theories for the 1959 handbook edited by James Birren, this author compared seven major classes of theories under the following headings: constitution, unconscious, self, inner structure, learning, field, and social roles. Most of these theories are founded upon the Continental European paradigm, a few have a basic affinity to the dialectic orientation but, at the time of the writing (Riegel, 1959b), none had been extended to cover changes during adulthood and aging.

Theories of bodily constitution and temperament have continued to attract little attention among psychologists in general, and psychological gerontologists, in particular. In an early version of this theory, Kretschmer described three different constitutional types: leptosomic, pyknic, and athletic. While Kretschmer's formulations are a-developmental, the quantifying attempts by Sheldon (1954), leaning closely upon Anglo-American empiricism, have provided some information on adult development.

Theories of the unconscious, especially Freud's psychoanalytical description of developmental stages, are limited to the very early periods of life. Although some attempts have been made to apply psychoanalytical treatment to aged persons (for a review, see Rechtschaffen, 1959), Freud himself has advised against such an extension. Like Piaget's theory of cognitive development, psychoanalytic interpretations emphasize the inner activity and dynamics of the individual. Only when this theory began to

take outer social conditions into serious consideration did its extension to the study of adulthood and aging become feasible. This extension began with the Ego psychology of Hartmann. It gained additional momentum with the Individual Psychology of Alfred Adler and the sociological extension by Horney, Fromm and Sullivan. Most notably, Erikson (1963) has proposed a theory of adult developmental stages to which we will return in the following section.

Previously, I have grouped these psychoanalytical interpretations with the organismic theories of Werner and Goldstein and the intraindividual interpretations of Stern and Allport. Undoubtedly, all of these theories are Continental European in orientation and, with the exception of Allport, also in origin. Undoubtedly too, extensions by American scholars, e.g., Murray and Rogers, continue to show some influence of this tradition. Further elaborations of some of the key concepts, e.g., the concept of need in the theory of need-achievement, made Murray's interpretation susceptible to research applications in the Anglo-American tradition, e.g., in the work of Veroff, Atkinson, Feld, and Gurin (1960) in life-span psychology. The outcome was different for the theory of the self as proposed by Rogers. When this interpretation was conceptually related to role theory, a form of investigation emerged that gave due recognition to social conditions and changes. Much of the subsequent research based on this theory was carried out at the University of Chicago and led to extensive work in psychological gerontology. This extension will be considered in the next section.

Contemporary to both Stern and Allport, Charlotte Bühler (1933) explored developmental changes during the whole life span emphasizing an intraindividual approach. Corresponding to the three types of material relied upon (biological and psychological studies; production and performance records; biographical and autobiographical material), she describes three types of developmental progressions: (1) those dominated by biophysical performance, e.g., by manual workers and athletes; (2) those leading to production and achievements, e.g., by businessmen, scientists and artists; and (3) those revealing contemplative integrations, e.g., by philosophers and writers. Her approach, though with a lessened emphasis upon developmental styles, has been applied by Kuhlen (1959) and is retained in the extensive work on age and achievement by Lehman (1953).

Theories listed under the heading "inner personal structure" and "learning" elaborate the traditional psychological subsystems, introduced by Tetens (1736–1807), of cognition (intelligence), conation (motivation), and affection (emotion) as well as their structural interdependence. As investigators began to recast these concepts in terms of abilities, traits and behaviors, research investigations within the Anglo-American paradigm became possible. In the first section, some typical studies were discussed such as those on intelligence, motivation and the structural interdependence of these and other variables by means of factor analysis. While most of these explorations deviate from the Continental European perspective, the work of Thomae (1970) and his associates on the development of motivational dynamics throughout the life span (Thomae, Angleitner, Grombach, and Schmitz-Scherzer, 1973) is congruent with it.

Theories of learning, if they provide any suggestions about personality development during the adult years at all, represent clearly the Anglo-American orientation. Most pointedly, they relate to the topic of adult socialization and social learning (Brim, 1968, 1974a; Ahammer, 1973; Bengtson and Black, 1973; Emmerich, 1973; Hartup and Lempers, 1973; Looft, 1973) and, thus, provide a bridge to the last two theories to be mentioned, "field theory" and "role theory."

Field theory, developed by Kurt Lewin (1935) and applied to gerontology by Schaie (1962), places the interaction between the individual and his psychological environment at the focus of attention. But in spite of this emphasis, Lewin's theory remains individual centered. This is shown by the studies of attitudes, needs and value preferences incited by it and mentioned in the preceeding section. More promising extensions might have been expected from studies in group dynamics but few such applications have appeared in the literature on adulthood and aging. The studies reported (Burgess, 1926; Donahue, Hunter and Coons, 1953; Taietz and Larson, 1956) are more closely related to the topic of social roles than to field theory. The same holds for investigations of family structures (Albrecht, 1953; Lansing and Kish, 1957; Townsend, 1957; Lehr and Thomae, 1968; for a review see, Troll, 1971).

Role theory and its counterpart, the theory of the self, have exerted a most substantive effect upon the psychology and sociology of adulthood and aging. However, role theory has been rarely formulated in a concise and integrative manner; it consists of clusters of loosely related interpretations and represents a general theoretical orientation within the behavioral sciences rather than a well delineated model of personality or social development. With its emphasis upon the interdependence between outer-sociological and inner-psychological conditions, role theory provides the transition to research within the third, the dialectical orientation. Such an affinity is especially close, if these interdependencies are viewed in the context of individual-developmental and cultural-historical changes.

DIALECTICAL ORIENTATION

At several previous occasions, I presented research and theories that constitute transitions from the two earlier paradigmatic orientations to the one to be presently discussed. For example, in the investigations of abilities within the Anglo-American paradigm, increasing sophistication in the analysis of intellectual development led to the explication of the confounded changes in the individual and in society. This recognition directs our attention toward a dialectical interpretation. Similarly, when discussing psychoanalytical, cognitive developmental or social psychological theories, we recognized dialectical principles.

Most research and theories previously mentioned are individual centered. This holds, for example, for the single standards of excellence set within the Anglo-American paradigm but it also holds for psychological and social psychological theories within the Continental European tradition. It applies, for example, to Lewin's field theory where the environment is structured in terms of the individual's needs and where it is pointedly called the "psychological" environment. It also holds for Piaget's theory with its concept of accommodation (of the subject to the object) and assimilation (of the object by the subject). Both processes, e.g., the activities of the eater and the changes in the food eaten, are initiated, carried out and completed by the individual subject. The sharp contrast between the subject and the object that emerges here, is indicative of the individualistic or personalistic orientation. Attention is rarely given to the other subjects and hardly ever to their interactive changes. The same holds for psychoanalytical theory where "libido" provides the force to the individual for his/her confrontations with an alien and hostile world. Only when reformed psychoanalytical thinkers begin to emphasize the significance of social condition (Fromm, Horney, and Sullivan), did a reorientation take place.

Stages of Adult Development and Aging

Erikson (1963) belongs to those psychoanalytical theoreticians who moved forcefully into the new direction and thereby became seriously interested in adult development and aging. This concern is expressed by his well known "eight stages of man" of which the last three cover periods beyond adolescence, i.e., Intimacy vs. Isolation, Generativity vs. Stagnation, Ego Integrity vs. Despair. Peck (1956) and Clayton (1975) have provided modified interpretations.

Erikson regards development as constituted by the interaction of inner and outer forces. This dualistic determination implies "(1) that the human personality in principle develops in steps predetermined in the growing person's readiness to be driven toward, to be aware of, and to interact with, a widening social radius; and (2) that society, in principle, tends to be constituted as to meet and invite this succession of potentialities for interaction and attempts to safeguard and to encourage the proper rate and the proper sequence of their enfolding" (1963, p. 270). But it remains insufficient to explain the development from within by postulating a "predetermined" order of enfolding and from

without by postulating "constituting principles." We need to know the conditions which generate these shifts, their order and their structural complexity (see Van den Daele, 1969; Riegel, 1972b; Reese, 1973).

In elaborating these conditions but falling short of providing systematic explanations, Erikson introduces the concept of "crisis" or "conflict" which he describes in the following manner: "We claim only that psychological development proceeds by critical steps— 'critical' being a characteristic of turning points, of movements of decision between progress and regression, integration and retardation. . . . This indicates (1) that each critical item of psychological strength discussed here is systematically related to all others, and that they all depend on the proper development in the proper sequence of each item; and (2) that each item exists in some form before its critical time normally arrives" (1963, pp. 270–271).

Erikson's interpretation of adult development is idealistic and, generally, seen from a middle class perspective. Similar arguments can be made about Kohlberg's research and theory of stages in moral development which, likewise, have been extended into adulthood and aging (Kohlberg, 1973, Kohlberg and Kramer, 1969). While both authors strike a reasonable balance in their statements, they fail to explain why the organism grows and moves from stage to stage; they merely describe a reasonable sequence of development. In order to provide such explanations, detailed investigations of shifts and changes in both the inner-biological and the outer-sociological conditions are required. If, subsequently, these developments can be analyzed in their interactions with psychological processes, a dialectical interpretation will emerge. In psychological gerontology such explorations have been supported and advanced by two trends: the affiliation with sociological and anthropological interpretations on the one hand and with biological and medical research efforts on the other.

Sociology of Adult Development and Aging

The dependence of individual development on social conditions has been emphasized by sociologists and psychologists at the University of Chicago. Influenced by the pragmatism of James and the functionalism of Dewey, an interactionistic perspective was developed either by emphasizing social organizations such as the family, the group, and the social class (Burgess, 1926) or by searching for general principles in the determinations of the individual and society (Mead, 1934). The former perspective exerted a direct influence upon gerontology; the latter provided a general foundation for sociological and psychological interpretations.

Although a developmental conception is akin to his theory, George Herbert Mead did not provide detailed explications of the sequences of developmental events both in the individual and in society. His interpretations remained restricted to the analysis of situational interactive changes as they remained restricted to the analysis of outer interactive processes. Although he recognized the significance of inner interactions, i.e., between the individual and his biological substrata, most of his attention was directed toward outer, social interactions. This, in general, remained the trademark of the Chicago scientists who soon were to explore important issues in adult development and aging.

In the years following World War II, Mead's ideas found expression in Rogers' theory of the self and his development of the client centered, non-directive therapy. According to Rogers, psychological disturbances are brought about by discrepancies in the individual's perceptions of his "ideal" and his "real" self. Although few related investigations were initiated in psychological gerontology (Mason, 1954), this orientation influenced many scholars who began to deviate from the personalistic theories of the 1920's and 1930's, including those who began to question psychoanalytical interpretations.

At about the same time, role theory took a more explicit and precise form. More recently, explicit theories of role and status changes have been proposed by Kuypers and Bengtson (1973) and by Rosenmayr (1974). Under the influence of Burgess, Havighurst, Neugarten, Henry and others, investigations were conducted into the social situations (Lowenthal, 1964), living conditions (Carp, 1965), family life (Sussman, 1960; Rosenmayr and Koekeis,

1963; Shanas and Streib, 1965; Lehr and Thomae, 1968), career patterns and activities (Becker and Strauss, 1956) leading to explorations of the individual's engagement (or disengagement) in activities (Cumming and Henry, 1961; Neugarten and associates, 1964; Lowenthal and Boler, 1965; Maddox, 1963; Henry, 1965; Lehr and Rudinger, 1969), role changes (Neugarten and Moore, 1965; Neugarten, Moore and Lowe, 1965), retirement (Carp, 1966; Maddox, 1966; Havighurst, Munnichs, Neugarten, and Thomae, 1969; Streib and Schneider, 1971; Guillemard, 1972), bereavement and death (Kübler-Ross, 1969) and socialization in general (Brim and Wheeler, 1966; Brim, 1968; Looft, 1973). In contrast to Mead (1934), these investigations emphasized long-term changes in the individual and with their rediscovery of Mannheim's theory of generations (see Ryder, 1965; Riley, Johnson, and Foner, 1972), they emphasized cultural-historical differences and changes (Clark and Anderson, 1967; Gutmann, 1967; Meacham, 1972; Bengtson and Black, 1973; Neugarten and Datan, 1973). With this shift they prepared the way for a dialectical conception of development which is to be fully realized in conjunction with the study of the interaction between inner biological and psychological changes.

Biology of Adult Development and Aging

Since the beginning of this century, medical researchers and biologists explored the inner determinants of long-term developmental changes. Although not identifiable by a particular location and intellectual tradition, they provided the necessary counterpart to the sociological interaction model. Mutual recognition between the biologists and the behavioral and social scientists has been fostered through the interdisciplinary organization of the Gerontological Society (see Adler, 1958).

Theoretical interpretations of the biology of aging—to which we will limit our discussion—started with Minot's (1908) detailed cytological investigations and Metchnikoff's (1908) rather speculative medical treatise. In 1915, Child published experimental data on regeneration and senescence and Pearl wrote his monograph on the *Biology of Death* (1922). According to Lansing (1959) few further advances were made until the late 1930's.

Most of the early explorations were either concerned with the determinants of longevity or of death and regarded development and aging as a slow process of changes (e.g., accumulation of harmful substances in the body or in cells, decline in speed of regeneration or differentiation, and increase in vulnerability due to repeated damage) which, nevertheless, often results in a sudden breakdown in structure or a loss in functioning, i.e., in an inner-biological crisis. Repeatedly, it was argued that aging is related to a decline in endocrine functioning and that proper therapeutic treatment could delay or reverse the effects. In 1908, Metchnikoff proposed his well known theory of "intestinal putrefaction" and suggested, equally surprisingly, dietary and even surgical prescriptions. Nevertheless, his basic idea eventually was to appear in the more sophisticated form of the "accumulative waste theory." Child (1915) subscribed to the theory "that excretory mechanisms are not perfect, and that, with time, metabolic waste products injurious to cells gradually accumulate and lead to death (cf. Lansing, 1959, p. 130)." Benedict (1915) attributed the accumulation to a decrease in cellular permeability which, in turn, Lansing (1942) attributed to an increase in calcification of the cell membrane.

With Minot (1908) a different kind of interpretation was advanced, relating aging to a change in the relation between the volume of the cell nucleus and the cytoplasm. Subsequently, Cowdry (1952) supported the more general theory that aging is the result of advanced differentiation and overdifferentiation. Although not all cells are equally differentiated, they possess an equal potential for division, and age at the same rate, most scientists agree with Heilbrunn (1943) that any theory of development and aging has to be, ultimately, concerned with changes in individual cells. This holds also for one of the most recent interpretations, the irradiation theory (Failla, 1958; Szilard, 1959), concerned with the instability of chromosomes in somatic and gonadic cells. Mutations—which are generally deleterious—occur at random. The older an organism, the greater the number of mutations that have occurred and, thus, the more likely that functional and/or structural defects will have resulted. Since the mutation rate depends on the degree of irradiation to which an organism has been subjected, the amount of radioactive fallout can be regarded as a determinant of changes during development and aging.

The last formulation, although not accepted by all without reservations, suggests ways of manipulating developmental processes in the laboratory. Biologists, for example, have changed the amount of irradiation to which fruit flies were subjected and, thereby, either retarded or accelerated the aging of these organisms. When translated into the study of behavioral development (Riegel, 1966), the amount of "verbal fallout" under enriched or deprived conditions was shown to affect the rate of language acquisition in a systematic manner. In bilingual situations (Riegel, 1968b; Riegel and Freedle, 1976), the distribution of efforts, the type of bilingual environment, the time of onset of the second language and the time of switch in dominance, etc., also have to be considered. The programmed control of these parameters suggests the possibility for a refined technology of changes. Important further suggestions for the simulation of aging processes have been made by Baltes and Goulet (1971) including the use of operant techniques (Hoyer, Labouvie, and Baltes, 1973; Labouvie-Vief, Hoyer, Baltes, and Baltes, 1974; Meichenbaum, 1974).

The applications and extensions of these ideas suggest the simulation of developmental processes in the laboratory and the possibility for retarding or accelerating manipulations. The mutation theory does not consider the reversal of these processes. Most surprisingly, such a possibility has become feasible for processes considered in the other major biological theory of development and aging, the accumulative waste theory (Strehler, 1962). Basic metabolic processes of the cells lead to the production of waste materials, such as lipofuscin or "age pigment," which cannot be completely removed from the cells. These products accumulate over time until they reach a critical level and produce a slow or sudden decrease in functioning. The waste theory leads to the recognition that life itself implies growth and aging, i.e., via the accumulation of metabolic waste. The waste theory has been called an intrinsic theory of development: Biological age is determined by the amount of waste accumulation by and within the organism. But this accumulation is not irreversible. Recently, a substance has been synthesized which when injected into senile laboratory animals produced the dissolution of lipofuscin deposits in the ganglia cells and led to restoration of nearly normal performance. This drug is currently being tested on a variety of human subjects (Kugler, 1974). If proven successful, developmental and aging processes cannot only be accelerated or retarded but their reversibility has also become feasible.

The Dialectics of Development

In the preceeding sections, I presented three types of interpretations. Erikson emphasized both the outer and inner determinations of behavior but presented these as ideal states rather than in their concrete developmental and historical interactions. The psychologists and sociologists at Chicago paid attention to the outer dialectics but often neglected their inner-biological foundation. In contrast, various biologists analyzed this foundation but did not explore the codetermined and codetermining behavioral and social changes. For comprehensive synthesis, social scientists would have to investigate the structural order of events and social conditions which are experienced by the individuals as temporal markings or crises in their lives. Biologists would have to delineate inner-biological sequences leading to a gradual or sudden decline in functioning. An integrative interpretation would have to analyze the synchronization of these various sequences or their lack of synchronization in states of crises or conflicts. Such an integration would both promote formal analysis and human understanding; it would focus upon adult development and aging rather than being one-sidedly committed to the study of children.

The possibility for such synthesis has been advanced by the formulation of developmental research designs (Schaie, 1965; Baltes, 1968) and has been fostered by a series of conferences on life-span developmental psychology at the West Virginia University (Goulet and Baltes, 1970; Nesselroade and Reese, 1973; Baltes and Schaie, 1973; Datan and Ginsberg, 1975). With the publication of the new methods, accompanied by reviews of generational and historical changes (Ryder, 1965; Riley, Johnson and Foner, 1972; Meacham, 1972; Neugarten and Datan, 1973), and followed by their application in research (Riegel, Riegel and Meyer, 1967b; Schaie and Strother, 1968a,b; Riegel and Riegel, 1972; Schaie, Labouvie, and Buech, 1973; Nesselroade and Baltes, 1974; Schaie and Labouvie-Vief, 1974), the implementation of dialectical interpretations became not only possible but necessary.

Not surprisingly, such interpretations occurred first in studies of adulthood and aging. Here, more than for the short periods investigated by child psychologists, generational differences or concurrent historical changes, e.g., in education, communication, transportation, nutrition, etc., are extensive and cannot be excluded from the analysis of individual development. It has been increasingly recognized, however, that these conditions also affect childhood and adolescence (Baltes, Baltes, and Reinert, 1970; Nesselroade and Baltes, 1974). Thus, advances in psychological gerontology have begun to influence and to change major sections in the general area of developmental psychology.

The derivation of developmental research designs represents the formal aspects of a dialectical interpretation. At the same time, dialectical theory reassigns a central place to the concrete human individual, a place which had been increasingly undermined in scientific psychology. During the course of recent intellectual history, the human being was successively reduced to an abstract entity within an equally abstract system of traits and abilities. The individual's concrete activities were disregarded as were his wishes and goals, his questions and doubts. They were abandoned for the sake of describing the individual in terms of uniform, stable and equilibrated states rather than in terms of uncertainties, crises or conflicts (Lehr and Thomae, 1965; Brim, 1974a; Datan and Ginsberg, 1975; Riegel, 1975a).

A dialectical interpretation returns the individual to the center of attention. As the individual acts, e.g., as he/she speaks, both the inner-biological and outer-sociological conditions change as well. Speech has its biological basis but, as it occurs, produces an event in the outer-physical world which—if there are listeners—is, at the same time, social in nature. The changes in the social conditions induced by the speech act, in turn, change the individual. In dialogic interaction, the listener, for example, is also a speaker and the speaker is also a listener.

The role of the individual in traditional psychology is one of alienation (Riegel, 1975c). In particular, the experimenter's participatory role in his/her experiment has been denied. Diagnosticians likewise erected a screen between themselves and the testees. Whereas, in real life situations all performances (on the assembly line or in the executive session) are cooperatively determined by several and often large groups of participating members, under such "objective" conditions the experimenters like the diagnosticians are prevented from interacting with the testee in any reasonable manner.

The difficulties of such an arrangement have become all too apparent in situations in which the two-person relation is readily reversible, e.g., in the testing of aged individuals (Hamilton, 1942). As discussed at length in the earlier literature on psychoanalytic treatments of the elderly (for reviews see Rechtschaffen, 1959; Riegel, 1959b), the test administrator is commonly much younger than the testee. In terms of his age and genealogical status he might well represent the child of his client. Thus, the relationship induced is readily brought into imbalance. The tester feels insecure and, in psychoanalytical terminology, develops countertransference reviving his old child-parent relationship instead of effectively playing the superior "father" role of the psychologist. The testee feels equally unhappy and is afraid to reveal his "deficiencies"—deficiencies which more than anything else are the outcome of this particular testing arrangement and the form of its analysis.

It is conceivable to remedy the situation by placing the tester and the testee in two-person cooperative situations. The tester would receive credit for any points that the testee makes. At the same time the testee would receive credit for whatever the tester elicits from him. The mutuality between the tester and the testee transforms the testing situation into a performance dialogue in which, not only the tester asks questions and the testee gives answers but in which, eventually, both participants ask questions and receive answers. As a further implication, the rigid barrier between the diagnostic and the therapeutic part of clinical interventions is broken down. Traditionally, the first (as in "objective" testing conditions) has been dominated by a sharp subject-object separation; the second, if ever successful, aims toward an interactive dialogue. The proposed conversion does not only eliminate this artificial barrier, but also provides a more advanced basis for scientific inquiries, i.e., a basis founded upon social dialogues rather than isolated performances.

A dialectical interpretation of development gives equal emphasis to adult development and aging rather than being one-sidedly concerned with infancy, childhood or adolescence as both the Anglo-American and Continental European orientations were bound to be. In viewing individual-psychological development in its interactions with inner-biological and cultural-sociological changes, such a reorientation gives due recognition to the mature and dominant sections of society rather than being carried away by romantic glorification of youth or by blind admiration of achievements in schools and tests.

In recognizing the codetermination of experience and action by inner-biological and cultural-sociological changes, dialectical theory deemphasizes individual-psychological development in the traditional, abstract sense. Instead it focuses upon concrete human beings and the gradual modifications (neurological, physiological) or sudden shifts (accidents, diseases) in their biological make-up that force them to change constructively their individual-psychological operations and, thereby, also the social conditions under which they live. At the same time, a dialectical interpretation focuses upon gradual modifications (increase in available time) or sudden shifts (birth of children, promotion, loss of friends) in the cultural-sociological conditions that force the human beings to change constructively their individual-psychological operations and, thereby, their inner-biological state. Thus, individual-psychological development is seen in its intimate and mutual determination by inner-biological and cultural-sociological shifts and changes.

As also recognized by Baltes and Willis (Chapter 7) and Lowenthal (Chapter 6), the program of a dialectical theory of development has not yet been fully implemented. Moreover, the range of problems and topics is exceedingly wide. Nevertheless, firmly rooted trends in psychological gerontology—which I have tried to describe in this chapter—point clearly toward their convergence in dialectical theory. With the realization of this goal in research and theorizing, gerontology has become the intellectual vanguard for the behavioral and social sciences.

APPENDIX

Some Documentation for the History of Psychological Gerontology

Suzanne Brumer *University of Michigan*

Uninterrupted growth of a scientific field occurs only if a scientific community exists devoting itself to the field. A new idea is not enough to start a new field; a new role must be created. The ideas necessary for creating a new field are usually available for a long period of time and in several places, but only a few of these potential beginnings lead to further growth; growth occurs only when persons become interested in the idea as a means of establishing a new intellectual identity or role. Psychological gerontology is an example of this thesis. A new identity and role for psychological gerontology had been developing in the late 1930's; however, its development was virtually halted during World War II. Shortly after World War II, this identity became firmly established through the foundation of: the Gerontological Society (1945), the Division of Maturity and Aging of the APA (1945), the International Association of Gerontology (1948), two White House Conferences on Aging (1961, 1971) and numerous research and training centers by the government and universities.

Tables 1 and 2 summarize in a systematic manner the history of psychological gerontology. Table 1 contains a chronological listing of individuals whose names appeared eight or more times as senior authors in a reference file covering the years from 1873 to 1968 and including 3,449 publications in psychological

TABLE 1. SENIOR AUTHORS OF EIGHT OR MORE PUBLICATIONS IN PSYCHOLOGICAL GERONTOLOGY THAT APPEARED PRIOR TO 1968, ORDERED BY THEIR FIRST PUBLICATION.

1919	S. L. Pressey	1951	J. H. Britton
1926	E. W. Burgess		M. Cesa-Bianchi
	E. L. Thorndike		H. Kay
1927	K. Tachibana		R. W. Kleemeier
1928	H. E. Jones		D. O. Moberg
1929	H. S. Conrad		H. Thomae
1930	E. K. Strong	1952	J. Tuckman
1931	D. Kotsovsky	1953	A. I. Goldfarb
	W. R. Miles		V. A. Kral
1933	C. Bühler		M. E. Linden
1934	I. Lorge		K. W. Schaie
1935	J. E. Anderson	1954	E. W. Busse
	W. Dennis	1955	P. Baumgartner
	J. G. Gilbert	1956	D. B. Bromley
	H. C. Lehman		J. Inglis
	D. Wechsler		W. Schulte
1938	G. Lawton		G. F. Streib
1940	O. J. Kaplan		K. Wolff
	R. G. Kuhlen	1957	F. Clément
1943	R. A. McFarland		L. F. Jarvik
1945	N. W. Shock		K. F. H. Murrell
	A. L. Vischer	1958	E. Belbin
1947	C. Fox		S. Griew
	R. J. Havighurst		U. Lehr
1948	J. E. Birren		B. L. Neugarten
	P. Ju-Shu		K. F. Riegel
	S. Pacaud	1959	W. K. Caird
	K. Stern		S. M. Chown
1949	W. Donahue		C. Eisdorfer
	H. Feifel		G. A. Talland
	J. Szafran	1961	I. M. Hulicka
	A. T. Welford	1963	R. N. Butler
1950	N. Bayley	1964	F. I. M. Craik
1951	R. Albrecht		R. Kastenbaum
	J. Botwinick		P. M. A. Rabbitt
		1965	C. L. Goodrick

gerontology. The ordering is by the first publications of these authors. Table 2 lists the major investigations in the psychology of aging by the time of their initiation. Only those investigations have been listed that began prior to 1965 and included persons above an age of 55 years. Thus, the studies included represent large cross-sectional or longitudinal investigations.

Riegel (1973d) has provided information on the increase in the number of publications in psychological

TABLE 2. MAJOR HUMAN STUDIES IN THE PSYCHOLOGY OF AGING.[a]

Beginning year	Principal investigator Reference Title or place of study	Subjects (number, type, age range) procedures	Focus of research
1884	Galton Ruger and Stoessiger (1927), Elderton, Moul and Page (1928) Anthropometric Laboratory, London	9,337 visitors, International Health Exhibition; 5 to 80	anthropometric, sensory perceptual, motor measures
1920	Foster and Taylor (1920) Boston Study	106 hospital patients, 50 to 84; 315 men, 20 to 30; 316 children, 10 to 19	Yerkes-Bridge Point Scale
1922	Terman (1925) Terman and Oden (1959) Genetic Studies of Genius	1,500 school children with IQ's above 140; several follow-up studies into adulthood	Stanford-Binet, Concept Mastery Test, interview
1925	Jones Jones and Conrad (1933) New England Study	1191 Ss from rural communities, 10 to 60	Army Alpha, memory tasks
1927	Willoughby (1927) First Stanford Study	141 children, 13; 280 siblings and 190 parents, 5 to 60	Army Alpha
1928	Bayley and Macfarlane Maas and Kuypers (1974) From Thirty to Seventy	142 parents of children from Berkeley Growth Study and Guidance Study; 40 years follow-up	life style, personality, environmental context, health
1928	Miles (1931) Miles and Miles (1932) Stanford Later Maturity Study	863 Ss from two California cities, 6 to 95; 2 year follow-up on subsample	Otis Self Administration Test of Intelligence, perceptual and motor skills
1929	Nicholson (1929) Voluntary Motor Activity	2,000 Ss, 17 to 86	speed and control of motor ability
1930	Babcock (1930), Gilbert (1935) Measurement of Mental Deterioration	185 Ss, 20 to 29, 175 Ss, 60 to 69	Babcock Test of Mental Efficiency
1930	Sorenson (1938) Adult Abilities	5,500 students of evening classes, 15 to 60+	aptitude test, reading test, vocabulary
1931	Strong (1943) Vocational Interest	1,300 Ss, 15 to 60+; several retest studies	Strong Vocational Interest Blank
1933	Bühler (1933) Lebenslaufanalyse	256 Ss mainly from Austria and Germany; adults	biographies, life histories, interviews, personal and performance records
1934	Cattell (1934)	1,039 clerks and typists, 15 to 70	Cattell Intelligence Test
1934	Kirihara (1934) Japanese Factory Worker	25,000 workers and children, 6 to 75	intelligence test
1936	Terman and Miles (1936) Sex and Personality	3,000 Ss, 20 to 90	Attitude Interest Analysis Test
1937	Willoughby (1937)	500 women, 20 to 60+	Personality Adjustment Sexual Attitude Rigidity Tests

TABLE 2 (continued)

Beginning year	Principal investigator Reference Title or place of study	Subjects (number, type, age range) procedures	Focus of research
1939	Wechsler (1939) Doppell and Wallace (1955) Standardization WAIS	1,750 Ss from New York area, representative of white U.S. population, 7 to 64; 475 Ss from Kansas City, 68 to 75+	Wechsler-Bellevue Adult Intelligence Scale
1941	Gilbert (1941) Memory Loss	174 Ss, 20 to 29 matched on vocabulary with 174 Ss, 60 to 69	eleven memory tasks
1941	Heston and Cannell (1941) Adult Performances	643 Ss, 15 to 76	Stanford–Binet, Knox Cubes, Porteus Mazes, Ferguson Form Board
1944	Thorndike and Gallup (1944) Verbal Intelligence	2,906 Ss, national sample, 20 to 60+	Columbia Arithmetic, Vocabulary, Directions
1947	Gray (1947) Psychological Types	1,000 Ss, 10 to 60	introversion-extroversion questionnaire
1947	Kallman and Sander (1948), Jarvik and Blum (1971) Twin Studies	150 same sex twins from New York area 60 to 89; several follow-up studies	four subtests from WAIS, Stanford–Binet Vocabulary, tapping test
1948	Raven (1948), Foulds (1949) Comparative Assessment of Intelligence	4,000 skilled and unskilled men, administrators, students, 15 to 60	Progressive Matrices, Mill Hill Vocabulary
1950	Owens (1953, 1966) Iowa Study	127 college freshmen of 1919; retested after 31 and 46 years	Army Alpha
1951	Birren and Botwinick (1951a,b) Performance Speed	413 Ss, 16 to 90	addition test, writing speed
1953	Berkowitz and Green (1965) Longitudinal Study of WAIS	205 Ss below 50, 1,026 Ss above 50; retested after 10 years	Wechsler-Bellevue Adult Intelligence Scale
1953	Havighurst and Albrecht (1953) Older People	500 Ss, 20 to 60+	social roles, interests, activities
1953	Lutze and Binas (1953) Work Intensity	850 Ss, 12 to 60	addition tests
1953	Lehman (1953) Age and Achievement	several thousand exceptional individuals	biographies, performance and production records
1954	Barker and Barker (1961) Psychological Ecology	162 Ss, 65+ from three small cities	recording of action patterns
1956	Blau (1956) Age Identification	450 Ss, over 60	social status, age identification, social roles

TABLE 2 (continued)

Beginning year	Principal investigator Reference Title or place of study	Subjects (number, type, age range) procedures	Focus of research
1956	Hardesty Wechsler (1956), Riegel and Riegel (1959, 1972) Standardization HAWIE	1,831 Ss, representative of German population, 10 to 60; 360 Ss, representative of Northern German population, 55 to 75+; retested after 5 years	Hamburg-Wechsler Intelligence Test für Erwachsene
1956	Havighurst (1957) Study of Adult Life in Kansas City	124 Ss, 50 to 70, 167 Ss, 70 to 90; seven rounds of retesting	life satisfaction, level of activity, role changes
1956	Heglin (1956) Problem Solving	300 Ss, 15 to 70+	rigidity tests
1956	Kent (1956) Counseling Study	500 Ss, over 60	attitude toward life and retirement
1956	Kutner, Fanshel, Togo, and Langner (1956)	500 Ss, over 60	attitude toward life and retirement
1956	Riegel and Riegel (1972)[b] Hamburg Study	120 Ss, 16 to 19, 380 Ss, 55 to 75+ representative of population in Northern Germany; retested after 5 years; rechecked after 10 years	Intelligence (HAWIE), verbal abilities (SASKA), word associations, attitudes and interests, social and living conditions
1956	Schaie (1958) Seattle Life-Span Study	500 Ss, 21 to 70; retested after 7 years and 14 years	SRA Primary Abilities Test, behavioral rigidity, social and living conditions
1957	Busse (1970), Maddox (1963), Palmore (1970) Duke University Study of Aging and Human Development	271 community residents, 60+; ten rounds of retesting	physical, psychiatric, psychological (WAIS) and sociological measures
1957	Phillips (1957) Role Changes	500 Ss, over 60	age identification, social roles, adjustment
1958	Neugarten and Gutman (1958), Neugarten (1964) Age-Sex Roles and Personality	131 Ss, 40 to 70	Thematic Apperception Test
1958	Reichard, Livson and Peterson (1962) Aging and Personality	87 men, 55 to 72	projective tests, interviews
1959	Lowenthal (1964) Social Isolation and Mental Illness	534 patients admitted to psychiatric clinic, 60+; 600 community residents, 60+	interviews, social activities, adaptation, interaction and intimacy
1960	Birren, Butler, Greenhouse, Sokoloff, and Yarrow (1963) Granick and Paterson (1971) Healthy Aging Man	47 men, 65 to 91 11 years follow-up	medical records, EEG, psychometric, personality, psychosocial tests

TABLE 2 (continued)

Beginning year	Principal investigator Reference Title or place of study	Subjects (number, type, age range) procedures	Focus of research
1960	Gurin, Veroff and Feld (1960) Psychological Stress	2,447 Ss, 21 to 65+	interview of symptoms of distress
1960	Nyssen and Crahay (1960) Language Functions	400 Ss, 21 to 88	word definition tests
1961	Kogen and Wallach (1961) Values and Attitudes	357 college students, 154 Ss, 47 to 85	test of self-confidence and caution, evaluation of life stages
1961	Lehr (1961) Changes in Themes of Life	350 Ss, 20 to 60	ratings, attitudes toward life, marriage, family, menopause
1961	Wallach and Green (1961) Subjective Time	118 freshmen and sophomores; 160 Ss, 65 to 75	Knapp Time Metaphor Test, intelligence (WAIS)
1963	Bell, Rose and Damon (1966) Normative Aging Study	2,000 men, 24 to 84	various biological, psychological and sociological tests
1963	Lehr and Puschner (1963) Lehr (1964) Attitudes Toward Age	500 Ss, 20 to 80	interviews, questionnaires, awareness of aging
1963	Neugarten, Wood, Kraines, and Loomis (1963) Attitude Toward Menopause	267 women, 21 to 65	interview, Attitude-Toward-Menopause Check List
1964	Canestrari and Coppinger (1964) Word Association	700 Ss, 20 to 69	Kent Rosanoff Word Association Test
1964	Neugarten and Weinstein (1964) Changing Grandparents	140 grandparents, 50 to 69	comfort, significance and style of grandparental roles
1965	Thomae et al. (1973)[b] Bonn Studies	222 Ss, 59 to 78, 293 Ss, 62 to 88; retested after 1, 2, 4 and 7 years	intelligence (HAWIE), attitude and interests, social and living conditions, life histories,

[a] Initiated prior to 1965 and including persons above 55 years of age.
[b] The studies by Riegel and Riegel (1972) and Thomae et al. (1973) have been pooled, see Riegel and Angleitner (1975).

gerontology. These data were plotted as averages for two-year intervals for the period 1920 to 1968 and have been extended in Figure 1 up to the year 1972. Beginning at the present century, there has been a slight but steady increase in the number of publications. No further growth occurred during the period of World War II but, afterwards, an accelerated expansion set in lasting until 1950. Between 1954 and 1964, the rate of growth was considerable and became exceptionally large during the following few years. A maximum number of 247 articles and books were published in 1969. This figure has not been surpassed yet; on the contrary, a slight decline in productivity seems to have started.

Figure 2 lists, in an accumulative manner, all the 4,096 publications of our card file for the period from 1873 to 1972. A detailed analysis of the original numbers reveals increasing growth rates for rather distinct

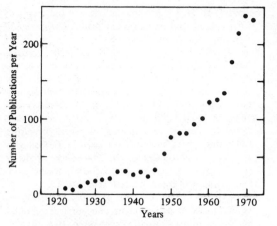

Figure 1. Fifty years of psychological geron-tology: Number of publications per year plotted as averages of 2-year intervals.

The following years saw a very marked increase in pro-historical periods. Up to the end of World War I, the growth rate was very low. It became slightly larger for the period up to the Depression, followed by a further increase that lasted until shortly after World War II.

duction. The rate of growth was not constant but accelerated continuously during this period, as can be seen by the larger and larger distances between the adjacent points on Figure 2. On the average, the num-ber of articles and books doubled after an interval of 8.3 years for the whole period from 1873 to 1972. Thus, after the first publication in 1873 we find two publications at about 1881, four at about 1890 and 4,096 up until 1972. But as indicated before, during the most recent years, growth seems to have leveled off.

REFERENCES

Adler, M. 1958. History of the gerontological society. *J. Gerontol.*, **13**, 94–100.

Ahammer, I. M. 1973. Social learning theory as a framework for the study of adult personality de-velopment. *In*, P. B. Baltes and K. W. Schaie (eds.), *Life Span Developmental Psychology: Personality and Socialization*, pp. 253–284. New York: Aca-demic Press.

Ahammer, I. M., and Baltes, P. B. 1972. Objective versus perceived differences in personality: How do adolescents, adults, and older people view them-selves and each other. *J. Gerontol.*, **27**, 46–51.

Albrecht R. 1953. Relationship of older people with their own parents. *Marr. Fam. Living*, **15**, 296–298.

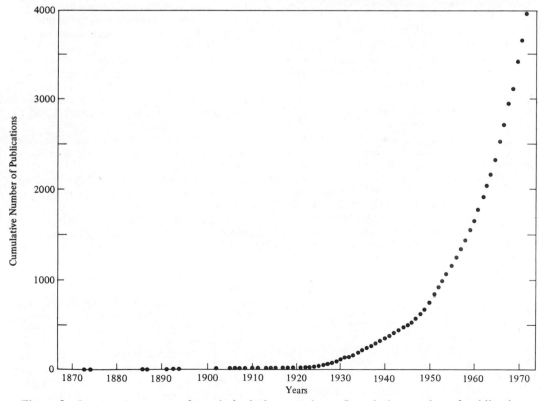

Figure 2. One hundred years of psychological gerontology: Cumulative number of publications.

Anderson, J. E. 1956. *Psychological Aspects of Aging.* Washington, D.C.: American Psychological Association.

Arenberg, D. 1967. Verbal learning and retention. *Gerontologist*, **7**, 10–13.

Arenberg, D. 1968. Concept problem solving in young and old adults. *J. Gerontol.*, **23**, 279–282.

Atchley, R. C. 1969. Respondents vs. refusers in an interview study of retired women: An analysis of selected characteristics. *J. Gerontol.*, **24**, 42–47.

Axelrod, S., and Cohen, L. D. 1961. Senescence and embedded-figure performances in vision and touch. *Perceptual Motor Skills*, **12**, 283–288.

Babcock, H. 1930. An experiment in the measurement of deterioration. *Arch. Psych.*, No. 117, 1–105.

Balinsky, B. 1941. An analysis of mental factors of various age groups from nine to sixty. *Genet. Psychol. Monographs*, **23**, 192–234.

Baltes, P. B. 1968. Longitudinal and cross-sectional sequences in the study of age and generation effects. *Hum. Dev.*, **11**, 145–171.

Baltes, P. B., Baltes, M. M., and Reinert, G. 1970. The relationship between time of measurement and age in cognitive development of children: An application of cross-sectional sequences. *Hum. Dev.*, **11**, 145–171.

Baltes, P. B., and Goulet, L. R. 1971. Exploration of developmental variables by manipulation and simulation of age differences in behavior. *Hum. Dev.*, **14**, 149–170.

Baltes, P. B., Nesselroade, J. R., Schaie, K. W., and Labouvie G. V. 1972. On the dilemma of regression effects on examining ability-level related differentials in ontogenetic patterns of intelligence. *Developmental Psychology*, **6**, 78–84.

Baltes, P. B., and Schaie, K. W. (eds.) 1973. *Life Span Developmental Psychology: Personality and Socialization.* New York: Academic Press.

Baltes, P. B., Schaie, K. W., and Nardi, A. H. 1971. Age and experimental mortality in seven-year longitudinal study of cognitive behavior. *Developmental Psychology*, **5**, 18–26.

Barker, R. G., and Barker, L. S. 1961. The psychological ecology of old people in Midwest, Kansas, and Yoredale, Yorkshire. *J. Gerontol.*, **16**, 144–149.

Basowitz, H., and Korchin, S. J. 1957. Age differences in the perception of closure. *J. Abn. Soc. Psych.*, **54**, 93–97.

Bayley, N., and Oden, M. H. 1955. The maintenance of intellectual ability in gifted adults. *J. Gerontol.*, **10**, 91–107.

Becker, H. S., and Strauss, A. L. 1956. Careers, personality, and adult socialization. *Amer. J. Sociol.*, **62**.

Bell, A., and Zubek, J. P. 1960. The effect of age on the intellectual performance of mental defectives. *J. Gerontol.*, **15**, 285–295.

Bell, B., Rose, C. L., and Damon, A. 1966. The Veterans Administration longitudinal study of healthy aging. *J. Gerontol.*, **6**, 179–184.

Benedict, H. M. 1915. Senile changes in the leaves of *Vitis vulpina* and certain other plants. *Cornell Univ. Agr. Exp. Sta. Mem.*, **7**, 273–370.

Bengtson, V. L., and Black, K. D. 1973. Intergenerational relations and continuities in socialization. *In*, P. B. Baltes and K. W. Schaie (eds.), *Life Span Developmental Psychology: Personality and Socialization*, pp. 207–234. New York: Academic Press.

Bennet, R., and Eckman, J. 1973. Attitudes toward aging: A critical examination of recent literature and implications for future research. *In*, C. Eisdorfer and M. P. Lawton (eds.), *The Psychology of Adult Development and Aging*, pp. 575–597. Washington, D.C.: American Psychological Association.

Berkowitz, B. 1965. Changes in intellect with age: IV. Changes in achievement and survival in older people. *Journal of Genetic Psychology*, **107**, 3–14.

Berkowitz, B., and Green, R. F. 1965. Changes in intellect with age: V. Differential change as functions of time interval and original score. *Journal of Genetic Psychology*, **107**, 179–192.

Birren, J. E. 1961. A brief history of the psychology of aging. *Gerontologist*, **1**, 69–77, 127–134.

Birren, J. E. 1965. Age changes in speed of behavior: Its central nature and physiological correlates. *In*, A. T. Welford and J. E. Birren (eds.), *Behavior, Aging and the Nervous System*, pp. 191–216. Springfield, Illinois: Charles C. Thomas.

Birren, J. E., Allen, W. R., and Landau, H. G. 1954. The relation of problem length in simple addition to time required, probability of success and age. *J. Gerontol.*, **9**, 150–161.

Birren, J. E., and Botwinick, J. 1951a. Rate of addition as a function of difficulty and age. *Psychometrika*, **2**, 219–232.

Birren, J. E., and Botwinick, J. 1951b. The relation of writing speed to age and to the senile psychoses. *J. Consult. Psychol.*, **15**, 243–249.

Birren, J. E., and Botwinick, J. 1955a. Age differences in finger, jaw, and foot reaction time to auditory stimuli. *J. Gerontol.*, **10**, 429–432.

Birren, J. E., and Botwinick, J. 1955b. Speed of response as a function of perceptual difficulty and age. *J. Gerontol.*, **10**, 433–436.

Birren, J. E., Butler, R. N., Greenhouse, S. W., Sokoloff, L., and Yarrow, M. R. 1963. *Human Aging.* Washington, D.C.: Public Health Service Publication, No. 986.

Birren, J. E., and Morrison, D. F. 1961. Analysis of the WAIS subtests in relation to age and education. *J. Gerontol.*, **16**, 363–369.

Birren, J. E., Riegel, K. F., and Morrison, D. F. 1962. Age differences in response speed as a function of controlled variations of stimulus condition; evidence of a general speed factor. *Gerontologia*, **6**, 1–18.

Birren, J. E., and Wall, P. D. 1956. Age changes in conduction velocity, refractory period, number of fibers, connective tissue space and blood vessels in sciatic nerve of rats. *J. Comp. Neurol.*, **104**, 1–16.

Blau, Z. S. 1956. Changes in status and age identification. *Am. Soc. Rev.*, **21**, 198–203.

Blum, J. E., and Jarvik, L. F. 1974. Intellectual performance of octogenarians as a function of education and initial ability. *Hum. Dev.*, **17**, 364–375.

Botwinick, J. 1965. Theories of antecedent conditions of speed of response. *In*, A. T. Welford and J. E. Birren (eds.), *Behavior, Aging, and the Nervous System*, pp. 67–87. Springfield, Illinois: Charles C. Thomas.

Botwinick, J. 1967. *Cognitive Processes in Maturity and Old Age*. New York: Springer.

Botwinick, J. 1973. *Aging and Behavior*. New York: Springer.

Botwinick, J., and Brinley, J. F. 1962. Analysis of set in relation to reaction time. *J. Exp. Psych.*, **63**, 568–574.

Botwinick, J., Robbin, J. S., and Brinley, J. F. 1959. Reorganization of perception with age. *J. Gerontol.*, **14**, 85–88.

Botwinick, J., and Thompson, L. W. 1966. Components of reaction time in relation to age and sex. *Journal of Genetic Psychology*, **108**, 175–183.

Brim, O. G., Jr. 1968. Adult socialization. *In*, J. A. Clausen (ed.), *Socialization and Society*, pp. 182–226. Boston: Little Brown.

Brim, O. G., Jr. 1974a. Selected theories of the midlife crisis: A comparative analysis. Unpublished manuscript. New York: Foundation for Child Development.

Brim, O. G., Jr. 1974b. The sense of personal control over one's life. Unpublished manuscript. New York: Foundation for Child Development.

Brim, O. G., Jr. and Wheeler, S. 1966. *Socialization After Childhood*. New York: John Wiley.

Brinley, J. F. 1965. Rigidity and the control of cognitive sets in relation to speed and accuracy of performance in the elderly. Unpublished doctoral dissertation. Catholic University of America.

Brown, R. A. 1957. Age and paced work. *Occupational Psychology*, **31**, 11–20.

Buck-Morss, S. 1975. Socio-economic bias in Piaget's theory and its implications for the cross-cultural controversy. *Hum. Dev.*, **18**, 35–49.

Bühler, C. 1933. *Der menschliche Lebenslauf als psychologisches Problem*. Leipzig: Hirzel.

Burgess, E. W. 1926. The family as a unit of interacting personalities. *Family*, **7**, 3–9.

Busse, E. W. 1970. A physiological, psychological, and sociological study of aging. *In*, E. B. Palmore (ed.), *Normal Aging*, pp. 3–6. Durham, North Carolina: Duke University Press.

Canestrari, R. E., Jr. 1963. Paced and self-paced learning in young and elderly adults. *J. Gerontol.*, **18**, 165–168.

Canestrari, R. E., Jr. 1966. The effects of commonality on paired associate learning in two age groups. *Journal of Genetic Psychology*, **108**, 3–7.

Canestrari, R. E., and Coppinger, N. W. 1964. The Kecoughtan age norms for responses to 100 words from Kent-Rosanoff word association test. Hamp-

ton, Virginia: Res. Unit Aging, Veterans Adm. Center, Kecoughtan Station.

Carp, F. M. 1965. Effects of improved housing on the lives of older people. *In*, *Patterns of Living and Housing of Middle Aged and Older People: Proceedings of Research Conference*, pp. 147–159. Washington, D.C.: U.S. Department of Health, Education and Welfare.

Carp, F. M. 1966. *The Retirement Process*. U.S. Department Health, Education and Welfare, PHS Publ. Washington, D.C.: U.S. Government Printing Office, No. 1778.

Cattell, R. B. 1934. Occupational norms of intelligence and the standardization of an adult intelligence scale. *Brit. J. Psych.*, **25**, 1–28.

Cattell, R. B. 1943. The measurement of adult intelligence. *Psych. Bull.*, **40**, 153–193.

Cavan, R. S., Burgess, W., Havighurst, R. J., and Goldhammer, H. 1949. *Personal Adjustment in Old Age*. Chicago: Science Research Association.

Child, C. M. 1915. *Senescence and Rejuvenescence*. Chicago: University of Chicago Press.

Chown, S. M. 1959. Rigidity–a flexible concept. *Psych. Bull.*, **56**, 195–223.

Chown, S. M. 1961. Age and rigidities. *J. Gerontol.*, **16**, 353–362.

Clark, M., and Anderson, B. G. 1967. *Culture and Aging*. Springfield, Illinois: Charles C. Thomas.

Clay, H. M. 1954. Changes of performance with age on similar tasks of varying complexity. *Brit. J. Psych.*, **45**, 7–13.

Clayton, V. 1975. Erikson's theory of human development as it applies to the aged: Wisdom as contradictive cognition. *Hum. Dev.*, **18**, 119–128.

Cohen, J. 1957. The factor structure of the WAIS between early adulthood and old age. *J. Consult. Psychol.*, **21**, 283–290.

Comalli, P. 1970. Age changes in perception. *In*, L. R. Goulet and P. B. Baltes (eds.), *Life-Span Developmental Psychology: Research and Theory*, pp. 211–226. New York: Academic Press.

Conrad, H. S., and Jones, H. E. 1929. Psychological studies of motion pictures III, Fidelity of report as a measure of adult intelligence. *University of California Publications in Psychology*, **3**, 245–276.

Conrad, H. S., and Jones, H. E. 1931. Psychological studies of motion pictures V, Adolescence and adult sex differences in delayed recall. *Journal of Social Psychology*, **2**, 433–459.

Corsini, R. J., and Fasset, K. K. 1953. Intelligence and aging. *Journal of Genetic Psychology*, **83**, 249–264.

Cowdry, E. V. 1952. Aging of individual cells. *In*, A. L. Lansing (ed.), *Cowdry's Problems of Aging*, 3rd Edition, pp. 50–88. Baltimore: Williams & Wilkins.

Craik, F. I. M. 1968. Short-term memory and the aging process. *In*, G. A. Talland (ed.), *Human Aging and Behavior*, pp. 131–168. New York: Academic Press.

Cumming, E., and Henry, W. 1961. *Growing Old.* New York: Basic Books.

Datan, N., and Ginsberg, L. H. (eds.) 1975. *Life-Span Developmental Psychology: Normative Life Crises.* New York: Academic Press.

Donahue, W., Hunter, W. W., and Coons, D. 1953. A study of the socialization of old people. *Geriatrics*, 8, 656–666.

Doppelt, J. E., and Wallace, W. L. 1955. The performance of older people on the Wechsler Adult Intelligence Scale. *American Psychologist*, 10, 338–339.

Ehinger, H. 1927. Age et decline des aptitudes. *France: Arch. Psych.*, 20, 318–323.

Eisdorfer, C. 1963. The WAIS performance of the aged: A retest evaluation. *J. Gerontol.*, 18, 169–172.

Eisdorfer, C., Axelrod, S., and Wilkie, F. 1963. Stimulus exposure time as a factor in serial learning in an aged sample. *J. Abn. Soc. Psych.*, 67, 594–600.

Elderton, E. M., Moul, M., and Page, E. M. 1928. On the growth curves of certain characters in women and the interrelationship of these characters. *Annals of Eugenics*, 3, 277–335.

Emmerich, W. 1973. Socialization and sex-role development. *In*, P. B. Baltes and K. W. Schaie (eds.), *Life-Span Developmental Psychology: Personality and Socialization*, pp. 123–145. New York: Academic Press.

Erikson, E. H. 1963. *Childhood and Society.* New York: W. W. Norton.

Failla, G. 1958. Mutation theory of aging. *Annals of the New York Academy of Sciences*, 71, 1124–1138.

Feifel, H. 1949. Qualitative differences in the vocabulary response of normals and abnormals. *Genet. Psychol. Monographs*, 39, 151–204.

Flavell, J. H. 1963. *The Developmental Psychology of Jean Piaget.* New York: Van Nostrand Reinhold.

Flavell, J. H. 1970. Cognitive changes in adulthood. *In*, L. R. Goulet and P. B. Baltes (eds.), *Life-Span Developmental Psychology: Research and Theory*, pp. 247–253. New York: Academic Press.

Foster, J. C., and Taylor, G. A. 1920. The application of mental tests to persons over 50. *J. Appl. Psych.*, 4, 29–58.

Foulds, G. A. 1949. Variations in the intellectual activities of adults. *Amer. J. Psych.*, 62, 238–246.

Fox, C. 1947. Vocabulary abilities in later maturity. *J. Educ. Psych.*, 38, 484–492.

Fox, C., and Birren, J. E. 1950. Intellectual deterioration in the aged: Agreement between the Wechsler-Bellevue and the Babcock-Levy. *J. Consult. Psychol.*, 14, 305–310.

Furry, C. A., and Baltes, P. B. 1973. The effect of age differences in ability—extraneous performance variables on the assessment of intelligence in children, adults and the elderly. *J. Gerontol.*, 28, 73–80.

Galton, F. 1869. *Hereditary Genius: An Inquiry into its Laws and Consequences.* London: Macmillan.

Giese, F. 1928. Erlebnisformen des Alterns. *Dtsch. Psychol.*, 5, 2–32.

Gilbert, J. G. 1935. Mental efficiency in senescence. *Arch. Psych.*, 188, 1–80.

Gilbert, J. G. 1941. Memory loss in senescence. *J. Abn. Soc. Psych.*, 36, 73–86.

Gladis, M., and Braun, H. W. 1958. Age differences in transfer and retroaction as a function of intertask response similarity. *J. Exp. Psych.*, 55, 25–30.

Goldfarb, W. 1941. An investigation of reaction time in older adults and its relationship to certain observed mental test patterns. *Contributions to Education*, 831. New York: Columbia University Teachers College.

Goulet, L. R., and Baltes, P. B. (eds.) 1970. *Life-Span Developmental Psychology: Research and Theory.* New York: Academic Press.

Granick, S., and Friedman, A. D. 1967. The effect of education on the decline of psychometric test performance with age. *J. Gerontol.*, 22, 191–195.

Granick, S. and Paterson, R. D. 1971. *Human Aging II.* Washington, D.C.: U.S. Government Printing Office, Publication No. 71-9037.

Gray, J. 1947. Psychological types and changes with age. *J. Clin. Psych.*, 3, 273–277.

Green, R. F., and Berkowitz, B. 1964. Changes in intellect with age: II. Factorial analysis of Wechsler-Bellevue scores. *Journal of Genetic Psychology*, 104, 3–18.

Guillemard, A. M. 1972. *La retraite: Une morte sociale.* Paris: Mouton.

Gurin, G., Veroff, J., and Feld, S. 1960. *Americans View Their Mental Health.* New York: Basic Books.

Gutmann, D. L. 1967. Aging among the highland Maya: A comparative study. *J. Pers. Soc. Psych.*, 7, 28–35.

Hall, G. S. 1922. *Senescence: The Last Half of Life.* New York: Appleton.

Hamilton, G. V. 1942. Changes in personality and psychosexual phenomena with age. *In*, E. V. Cowdry (ed.), *Problems of Aging*, 2nd Edition, pp. 810–831. Baltimore: Williams & Wilkins.

Hardesty, F. P. 1976. Early European contributions to developmental psychology. *In*, K. F. Riegel and J. A. Meacham (eds.), *The Developing Individual in a Changing World: Volume I, Historical and Cultural Issues.* The Hague: Mouton. In press.

Harris, A. E. 1975. Social dialectics and language: Mother and child construct the discourse. *Hum. Dev.*, 18, 80–96.

Hartup, W. W., and Lempers, J. 1973. A problem in life-span development: The interactional analysis of family attachment. *In*, P. B. Baltes and K. W. Schaie (eds.), *Life Span Developmental Psychology: Personality and Socialization*, pp. 235–252. New York: Academic Press.

Havighurst, R. J. 1952. Roles and status of older people. *In*, A. I. Lansing (ed.), *Cowdry's Problems of Aging*, 3rd Edition, pp. 1019–1031. Baltimore: Williams & Wilkins.

Havighurst, R. J. 1957. The social competence of middle-aged people. *Genet. Psychol. Monogr.*, 56, 297–395.

Havighurst, R. J., and Albrecht, R. 1953. *Older People*. New York: Longmans, Green.

Havighurst, R. J., Munnichs, J. M. A., Neugarten, B. L., and Thomae, H. 1969. *Adjustment to Retirement: A Cross-National Study*. Copenhagen: Assen.

Hefner, R., Rebecca, M., and Oleshansky, B. 1975. Development of sex role transcendence. *Hum. Dev.*, **18**, 143–158.

Heglin, H. J. 1956. Problem solving set in different age groups. *J. Gerontol.*, **11**, 310–317.

Heilbrunn, L. V. 1943. *An Outline of General Physiology*. Philadelphia: W. B. Saunders.

Henry, W. E. 1965. Engagement and disengagement; toward a theory of adult development. *In*, R. Kastenbaum (ed.), *Contributions to the Psychobiology of Aging*, pp. 19–35. New York: Springer.

Heston, J. C., and Cannell, C. F. 1941. A note on the relation between age and performance of adult subjects on four familiar psychometric tests. *J. Appl. Psych.*, **25**, 415–419.

Hooper, F. H. 1976. Life-span analysis of Piagetian concept tasks: The search for nontrivial qualitative changes. *In*, K. F. Riegel and J. A. Meacham (eds.), *The Developing Individual in a Changing World: Volume I, Historical and Cultural Issues*. The Hague: Mouton. In press.

Hoyer, W. J., Labouvie, G. V., and Baltes, P. B., 1973. Modification of response speed and intellectual performance in the elderly. *Hum. Dev.*, **16**, 233–242.

Hügin, F., Norris, A. H., and Shock, N. W. 1960. Skin reflex and voluntary reaction times in young and old males. *J. Gerontol.*, **15**, 388–391.

Hulicka, I. M. 1967. Age changes and age differences in memory functioning. *Gerontologist*, **7**, 46–54.

Hunt, J. McV. 1961. *Intelligence and Experience*. New York: Ronald.

Inglis, J., and Caird, W. K. 1963. Age differences in successive responses to simultaneous stimulation. *Can. J. Psych.*, **24**, 46–50.

Inglis, J., Sykes, D. H., and Ankus, M. N. 1968. Age differences in short-term memory. *In*, S. S. Chown and K. F. Riegel (eds.), *Psychological Functioning in the Normal Aging and Senile Aged*, pp. 18–33. Basel: Karger.

Jarvik, L. F., and Blum, J. E. 1971. Cognitive declines as predictors of mortality in twin pairs: A twenty-year longitudinal study of aging. *In*, E. Palmore and F. Jeffers (eds.), *Prediction of Lifespan*, pp. 199–211. Lexington, Massachusetts: D. C. Heath.

Jarvik, L. F., and Falek, A. 1963. Intellectual stability and survival in the aged. *J. Gerontol.*, **18**, 173–176.

Jones, H. E., and Conrad, H. S. 1933. The growth and decline of intelligence: A study of a homogeneous group between the ages ten and sixty. *Genet. Psychol. Monographs*, **13**, 223–298.

Jones, J. E., Conrad, H. S., and Horn, A. 1928. Psychological studies of motion pictures II, Observation and recall as a function of age. *University of California Publications in Psychology*, **3**, 225–243.

Ju-Shu, P. 1952. A comparison of factors in the personal adjustment of old people in Protestant church homes for the aged and old people living outside of institutions. *Journal of Social Psychology*, **35**, 195–203.

Kallman, F. J., and Sander, G. 1948. Twin studies on aging and longevity. *J. Heredity*, **39**, 349–357.

Kaplan, O. J. 1943. Mental decline in older morons. *Amer. J. Mental Deficiency*, **47**, 277–285.

Kay, H. 1951. Learning of a serial task by different age groups. *Quart. J. Exp. Psych.*, **3**, 166–183.

Kent, A. P. 1956. An experiment in the counselling of older people. *Geriatrics*, **11**, 44–48.

Kirihara, H. 1934. General intelligence test and its norm. *Rep. Inst. Sci. Labour*, **25**, 1–22 (Japan).

Kleemeier, R. W. 1951. The effects of a work program on adjustment attitudes in an aged population. *J. Gerontol.*, **6**, 372–379.

Kleemeier, R. W. 1962. Intellectual changes in the senium. *Proc. Soc. Stat. Sec. Amer. Stat. Assoc.*, 290–295.

Kogan, N., and Wallach, M. A. 1961. Age changes in values and attitudes. *J. Gerontol.*, **16**, 272–280.

Kohlberg, L. 1973. Continuities in childhood and adult moral development revisited. *In*, P. B. Baltes and K. W. Schaie (eds.), *Life-Span Developmental Psychology: Personality and Socialization*, pp. 180–204. New York: Academic Press.

Kohlberg, L., and Kramer, R. 1969. Continuities and discontinuities in childhood and adult moral development. *Hum. Dev.*, **12**, 93–120.

Korchin, S. J., and Basowitz, H. 1956. The judgement of ambiguous stimuli as an index of cognitive functioning in aging. *J. Pers.*, **25**, 81–95.

Kosok, M. 1972. The formalization of Hegel's dialectical logic. *In*, A. MacIntyre (ed.), *Hegel: A Collection of Critical Essays*, pp. 237–287. Garden City, New York: Anchor.

Kounin, J. S. 1941. Experimental studies of rigidity. *Character and Personality*, **9**, 251–285.

Kübler-Ross, E. 1969. *On Death and Dying*. New York: Macmillan.

Kubo, Y. 1938. Mental and physical changes in old age. *Journal of Genetic Psychology*, **53**, 101–108.

Kugler, J. (ed.) 1974. *Centrophenoxin Symposium*. Hamburg: Promonta.

Kuhlen, R. 1959. Aging and life-adjustment. *In*, J. E. Birren (ed.), *Handbook of Aging and the Individual*, pp. 852–897. Chicago: University of Chicago Press.

Kutner, B., Fanshel, D., Togo, A. M., and Langner, T. S. 1956. *Five Hundred Over Sixty*. New York: Russell Sage Foundation.

Kuypers, J. A., and Bengtson, V. L. 1973. Competence and social breakdown: A social-psychological view of aging. *Hum. Dev.*, **16**, 37–49.

Kvale, S. 1975. Memory and dialectics: Some reflections on Ebbinghaus and Mao Tse-Tung. *Hum. Dev.*, **18**, 205–222.

Labouvie-Vief, G., Hoyer, W. J., Baltes, M. M., and Baltes, P. B. 1974. Operant analysis of intellectual behavior in old age. *Hum. Dev.*, **17**, 259–272.

Lansing, A. I. 1942. Increase in cortical calcium with age in cells of *Eclodea canadensis*. *Biol. Bull.*, **82**, 385-391.

Lansing, A. I. 1959. General biology of senesence. *In*, J. E. Birren (ed.), *Handbook of Aging and the Individual*, pp. 119-135. Chicago: University of Chicago Press.

Lansing, J. B., and Kish, L. 1957. Family life-cycle as an independent variable. *Am. Soc. Rev.*, **22**, 512-519.

Lawler, J. 1975. Dialectic philosophy and developmental psychology: Hegel and Piaget on contradiction. *Hum. Dev.*, **18**, 1-17.

Lehman, H. C. 1953. *Age and Achievement*. Princeton, New Jersey: Princeton University Press.

Lehr, U. 1961. Veränderungen in der Daseinsthematik der Frau im Erwachsenenalter. *Vita Humana*, **4**, 193-228.

Lehr, U. 1964. Positive und negative Einstellungen zu einzelnen Lebensaltern. *Vita Humana*, **7**, 201-227.

Lehr, U., and Puschner, I. 1963. Untersuchungen über subjektive Alternssymptome. *Vita Humana*, **6**, 57-86.

Lehr, U., and Rudinger, G. 1969. Consistency and change of social participation in old age. *Hum. Dev.*, **12**, 225-267.

Lehr, U. and Thomae, H. 1965. *Konflikt, seelische Belastung und Lebensalter*. Köln-Opladen: Westdeutscher Verlag.

Lehr, U., and Thomae, H. 1968. Die Stellung des älteren Menschen in der Familie. *In*, G. Wurzbacher (ed.), *Familie und Sozialisation*. Stuttgart: Enke.

Lewin, K. 1935. *A Dynamic Theory of Personality*. New York: McGraw-Hill.

Lewinsky, R. J. 1948. Vocabulary and mental measurement: A quantitative investigation and review of research. *Journal of Genetic Psychology*, **72**, 247-281.

Lieberman, M. A. 1965. Psychological correlates of impending death: Some preliminary observations. *J. Gerontol.*, **20**, 181-190.

Looft, W. R. 1973. Socialization and personality throughout the life-span: An examination of contemporary psychological approaches. *In*, P. B. Baltes and K. W. Schaie (eds.), *Life-Span Developmental Psychology: Personality and Socialization*, pp. 25-52. New York: Academic Press.

Lorge, I. 1936. The influence of the test upon the nature of mental decline as a function of age. *J. Educ. Psych.*, **27**, 100-110.

Lowenthal, M. F. 1964. Social isolation and mental illness in old age. *Am. Soc. Rev.*, **29**, 54-70.

Lowenthal, M. F., and Boler, D. 1965. Voluntary vs. involuntary social withdrawal. *J. Gerontol.*, **20**, 363-371.

Lutze, E., and Binas, D. 1953. Die Entwicklung der Arbeitsintensität im Laufe des Lebens. *Psych. Rdsch.*, **4**, 99-103.

Maas, H. S., and Kuypers, J. A. 1974. *From Thirty to Seventy*. San Francisco: Jossey-Bass.

Maddox, G. L. 1963. Activity and morale; A longitudinal study of selected elderly subjects. *Soc. Forces*, **42**, 195-204.

Maddox, G. L. 1966. Retirement as a social event in the United States. *In*, J. C. McKinney and F. T. de Vyver (eds.), *Aging and Social Policy*, pp. 117-135. New York: Appleton.

Mason, E. P. 1954. Some factors in self-judgements. *J. Clin. Psych.*, **10**, 336-340.

McAndrew, H. 1948. Rigidity and isolation: A study of the deaf and the blind. *J. Abn. Soc. Psych.*, **43**, 476-494.

Meacham, J. A. 1972. The development of memory abilities in the individual and society. *Hum. Dev.*, **15**, 205-228.

Meacham, J. A. 1975. A dialectic approach to moral judgement and self-esteem. *Hum. Dev.*, **18**, 159-170.

Mead, G. H. 1934. *Mind, Self, and Society*. Chicago: University of Chicago Press.

Meichenbaum, D. 1974. Self-instructional strategy training: A cognitive prothesis for the aged. *Hum. Dev.*, **17**, 273-280.

Metchnikoff, E. 1908. *The Prolongation of Life*. New York: J. P. Putnam's Sons.

Miles, C. C. 1934. Influence of speed and age on intelligence scores of adults. *Journal of Genetic Psychology*, **10**, 208-210.

Miles, C. C., and Miles, W. R. 1932. The correlation of intelligence scores and chronological age from early to late maturity. *Amer. J. Psych.*, **44**, 44-78.

Miles, W. R. 1931. Measurement of certain human abilities throughout life span. *National Academy of Science*, **17**, 627-633.

Miles, W. R., and Shriver, B. M. 1953. Aging in Air Force pilots. *J. Gerontol.*, **8**, 185-190.

Minot, C. S. 1908. *The Problems of Age, Growth, and Death*. New York: J. P. Putnam's Sons.

Muench, G. A. 1944. A follow-up of mental defectives after eighteen years. *J. Abn. Soc. Psych.*, **39**, 407-418.

Nesselroade, J. R., and Baltes, P. B. 1974. Adolescent personality development and historical change: 1970-1972. *Monographs of the Society for Research in Child Development*, **39**, No. 154.

Nesselroade, J. R., and Reese, H. W. (eds.) 1973. *Life-Span Developmental Psychology: Methodological Issues*. New York: Academic Press.

Nesselroade, J. R., Schaie, K. W., and Baltes, P. B. 1972. Ontogenetic and generational components of structural and quantitative change in adult behavior. *J. Gerontol.*, **27**, 222-228.

Neugarten, B. L. and associates. 1964. *Personality in Middle and Late Life*. New York: Atherton Press.

Neugarten, B. L. and Datan, N. 1973. Sociological perspectives on the life cycle. *In*, P. B. Baltes and K. W. Schaie (eds.), *Life-Span Developmental Psychology: Personality and Socialization*, pp. 53-69. New York: Academic Press.

Neugarten, B. L. and Gutmann, D. L. 1958. Age-sex

roles in middle age: A thematic apperception study. *Psychol. Monographs*, **72**, 1–33.

Neugarten, B. L., and Moore, J. W. 1965. The changing age-status system. *In*, B. L. Neugarten (ed.), *Middle Age and Aging*, pp. 5–21. Chicago: University of Chicago Press.

Neugarten, B. L. Moore, J. W., and Lowe, J. C. 1965. Age norms, age constraints, and adult socialization. *Am. J. Sociol.*, **70**, 710–717.

Neugarten, B. L., and Weinstein, K. K. 1964. The changing American grandparent. *J. Marr. Fam.*, **22**, 199–204.

Neugarten, B. L., Wood, V., Kraines, R. J., and Loomis, B. 1963. Women's attitudes toward the menopause. *Vita Humana*, **6**, 140–151.

Nicholson, T. E. 1929. The increase and decline in speed and control of voluntary motor ability with advancement in age. Unpublished dissertation. Indiana University.

Norris, A. H. Shock, N. W., and Wagman, I. H. 1953. Age changes in the maximum conduction velocity of motor fibers of human ulnar nerves. *J. Appl. Psych.*, **5**, 589–593.

Nyssen, R., and Crahay, S. 1960. Etude des capacites de definition et d'evocation des mots en fonction de l'age. *Acta Psych.*, **17**, 1–23.

Owens, W. A., Jr. 1953. Age and mental abilities: A longitudinal study. *Genet. Psychol. Monographs*, **48**, 3–54.

Owens, W. A., Jr. 1966. Age and mental abilities: A second adult follow-up. *J. Educ. Psych.*, **57**, 311–325.

Palmore, E. B. 1969. Physical, mental, and social factors in predicting longevity. *Gerontologist*, **9**, 103–108.

Palmore, E. B. (ed.) 1970. *Normal Aging I*. Durham North Carolina: Duke University Press.

Papalia, D. A., and Bielby, D. D. V. 1975. Cognitive functioning in middle and old age adults: A review of research based on Piaget's theory. *Hum. Dev.*, **18**, 424–443.

Pearl, R. 1922. *The Biology of Death*. Philadelphia: J. B. Lippincott.

Peck, R. 1956. Psychological developments in the second half of life. *In*, J. E. Anderson (ed.), *Psychological Aspects of Aging*, pp. 42–53. Washington, D.C.: American Psychological Association.

Phillips, B. S. 1957. A role theory approach to adjustment in old age. *Amer. Soc. Rev.*, **22**, 212–217.

Piaget, J. 1972. Intellectual evolution from adolescence to adulthood. *Hum. Dev.*, **15**, 1–12.

Platanoff, K. I. 1911. (Experimental psychological investigation of the capacity for concentration in old age.) *Obosr. Psikkiat. Neorol.*, **16**, 204–216.

Quételet, A. 1835. *Sur l'homme et le developpement de ses facultés*. Paris: Bachelier.

Rabbitt, P. 1968. Age and the use of structure in transmitted information. *In*, G. A. Talland (ed.), *Human Aging and Behavior*, pp. 75–92. New York: Academic Press.

Rappoport, L. 1975. On praxis and quasirationality. *Hum. Dev.*, **18**, 194–204.

Raven, J. C. 1948. The comparative assessment of intellectual ability. *Brit. J. Psychol.*, **39**, 12–19.

Rechtschaffen, A. 1959. Psychotherapy with geriatric patients: A review of the literature. *J. Gerontol.*, **14**, 73–84.

Reese, H. W. 1973. Models of memory and models of development. *Hum. Dev.*, **16**, 397–416.

Reichard, S., Livson, F., and Peterson, P. 1962. *Aging and Personality*. New York: John Wiley.

Riegel, K. F. 1959a. A study on verbal achievements of older persons. *J. Gerontol.*, **14**, 453–456.

Riegel, K. F. 1959b. Personality theory and aging. *In*, J. E. Birren (ed.), *Aging and the Individual*, pp. 797–851. Chicago: University of Chicago Press.

Riegel, K. F. 1965. Speed of verbal performance as a function of age and set: A review of issues and data. *In*, A. T. Welford and J. E. Birren (eds.), *Behavior, Aging, and the Nervous System*, pp. 150–190. Springfield, Illinois: Charles C. Thomas.

Riegel, K. F. 1966. Development of language: Suggestions for a verbal fallout model. *Hum. Dev.*, **9**, 97–120.

Riegel, K. F. 1967. *Der sprachliche Leistungstest SASKA*. Göttingen: Verlag für Psychologie.

Riegel, K. F. 1968a. Changes in psycholinguistic performances with age. *In*, G. A. Talland (ed.), *Human Behavior and Aging*, pp. 239–279. New York: Academic Press.

Riegel, K. F. 1968b. Some theoretical considerations of bilingual development. *Psych. Bull.*, **70**, 647–670.

Riegel, K. F. 1968c. Untersuchungen sprachlicher Leistungen und ihrer Veränderungen. *Z. Allg. Angew. Psych.*, **15**, 649–692.

Riegel, K. F. 1970. The language acquisition process: A reinterpretation of selected research findings. *In*, L. R. Goulet and P. B. Baltes (eds.), *Life-Span Developmental Psychology: Research and Theory*, pp. 357–399. New York: Academic Press.

Riegel, K. F. 1972a. The influence of economic and political ideologies upon the development of developmental psychology. *Psych. Bull.*, **78**, 129–141.

Riegel, K. F. 1972b. Time and change in the development of the individual and society. *In*, H. W. Reese (ed.), *Advances in Child Development and Behavior*, Vol. 7, pp. 81–113. New York: Academic Press.

Riegel, K. F. 1973a. Developmental psychology and society: Some historical and ethical considerations. *In*, J. R. Nesselroade and H. W. Reese (eds), *Life-Span Developmental Psychology: Methodological Issues*, pp. 1–23. New York: Academic Press.

Riegel, K. F. 1973b. Dialectical operations: The final period of cognitive development. *Hum. Dev.*, **16**, 346–370.

Riegel, K. F. (ed.). 1973c. *Intelligence: Alternative Views of a Paradigm*. Basel: Karger.

Riegel, K. F. 1973d. On the history of psychological gerontology. *In*, C. Eisdorfer and M. P. Lawton (eds.), *Psychology of Adult Development and Aging*, pp. 37–68. Washington, D.C.: American Psychological Association.

Riegel, K. F. 1975a. Adult life crises: Toward a dialectic theory of development. *In*, N. Datan and L. H. Ginsburg (eds.), *Life-Span Developmental Psychology: Normative Life Crises*, pp. 97–124. New York: Academic Press.

Riegel, K. F. 1975b. From traits and equilibrium toward developmental dialectics. *In*, W. J. Arnold and J. K. Cole (eds.), *1974-75 Nebraska Symposium on Motivation*, pp. 349–407. Lincoln, Nebraska: University of Nebraska Press.

Riegel, K. F. 1975c. Subject-object alienation in psychological experimentation and testing. *Hum. Dev.*, 18, 181–193.

Riegel, K. F. (ed.) 1975d. *The Development of Dialectical Operations*. Basel: Karger.

Riegel, K. F., and Angleitner, A. 1975. The pooling of longitudinal studies in the psychology of aging. *Aging and Human Development*, 6, 57–66.

Riegel, K. F., and Birren, J. E. 1966. Age differences in verbal association. *Journal of Genetic Psychology*, 108, 153–170.

Riegel, K. F., and Freedle, R. O. 1976. What does it take to be bilingual or bidialectal? *In*, D. S. Harrison and T. Trabasso (eds.), *A-Seminar in Black English*, pp. 25–44, Washington, D.C.: Erlbaum.

Riegel, K. F., and Riegel, R. M. 1960. A study on changes of attitudes and interests during later years of life. *Vita Humana*, 3, 177–206.

Riegel, K. F., and Riegel, R. M. 1962. Analysis of differences in test performance and item difficulty between young and old adults. *J. Gerontol.*, 17, 97–105.

Riegel, K. F., and Riegel, R. M. 1964. Changes in associative behavior during later years of life: A cross-sectional analysis. *Vita Humana*, 7, 1–32.

Riegel, K. F., and Riegel, R. M. 1972. Development, drop and death. *Developmental Psychology*, 6, 306–319.

Riegel, K. F., Riegel, R. M., and Meyer, G. 1963. The prediction of intellectual development and death: A longitudinal analysis. *Proceedings of the 6th International Congress of Gerontology*, p. 164. Copenhagen.

Riegel, K. F., Riegel, R. M., and Meyer, G. 1967a. A study of the drop-out rates in longitudinal research on aging and the prediction of death. *J. Pers. Soc. Psych.*, 4, 342–348.

Riegel, K. F. Riegel, R. M., and Meyer, G. 1967b. Socio-psychological factors of aging: A cohort-sequential analysis. *Hum. Dev.*, 10, 27–56.

Riegel, K. F., Riegel, R. M., and Meyer, G. 1968. The prediction of retest-resisters in longitudinal research on aging. *J. Gerontol.*, 23, 370–374.

Riegel, K. F., Riegel, R. M., and Skiba, G. 1962. Untersuchung der Lebensbedingungen, Gewohnheiten und Anpassung älterer Menschen in Norddeutschland. *Vita Humana*, 5, 204–247.

Riegel, K. F., Riegel, R. M., and Wendt, D. 1962. Perception and set: A review of the literature and a study on the effects of instructions and verbal habits on word recognition thresholds of young and old subjects. *Acta Psych.*, 12, 224–251.

Riegel, R. M. 1960. Faktorenanalysen des Hamburg-Wechsler Intelligenztest für Erwachsene (HAWIE) für die Altersstufen 20–34, 35–49, 50–64 und 65 Jahre und älter. *Diagnostica*, 6, 41–66.

Riegel, R. M., and Riegel, K. F. 1959. Standardisierung des Hamburg-Wechsler Intelligenztest für Erwachsene (HAWIE) für die Altersstufen über 50 Jahre. *Diagnostica*, 5, 97–128.

Riegel, R. M., and Riegel, K. F. 1962. A comparison and reinterpretation of factorial structures of the W-B, the WAIS, and the HAWIE on aged persons. *J. Consult. Psychol.*, 26, 31–37.

Riley, M. W., Johnson, W., and Foner, A. (eds.). 1972. *Aging and Society, Vol. 3: A Sociology of Age Stratification*. New York: Russell Sage Foundation.

Rose, C. H. 1965. Representativeness of volunteer subjects in a longitudinal aging study. *Hum. Dev.*, 8, 152–156.

Rosenmayr, L. 1974. Elements of an assimilation-yield theory. Paper presented at 9th World Congress of Sociology, Toronto, Canada.

Rosenmayr, L., and Koekeis E. 1963. Propositions for a sociological theory of aging and the family. *International Social Science Journal*, 15, 410–426.

Rubinsteijn, S. L. 1963. *Prinzipien und Wege der Entwicklung der Psychologie*. Berlin: Akademie Verlag.

Ruch, F. L. 1933. Adult learning. *Psych. Bull.*, 30, 387–414.

Ruger, H. A., and Stoessiger, B. 1927. On the growth curves of certain characteristics in man (males). *Annals of Eugenics*, 2, 76–111.

Ryder, N. B. 1965. The cohort as a concept in the study of social changes. *Am. Soc. Rev.*, 30, 843–861.

Schaie, K. W. 1958. Rigidity-flexibility and intelligence: A cross-sectional study of the adult life span from 20 to 70 years. *Psychol. Monographs*, 72, No. 462.

Schaie, K. W. 1962. A field-theory approach to age changes in cognitive behavior. *Vita Humana*, 5, 129–141.

Schaie, K. W. 1965. A general model for the study of developmental problems. *Psych. Bull.*, 64, 92–107.

Schaie, K. W., Labouvie, G. V., and Buech, B. U. 1973. Generational and cohort-specific differences in adult cognitive functioning: A fourteen-year study of independent samples. *Developmental Psychology*, 9, 151–166.

Schaie, K. W., and Labouvie-Vief, G. 1974. Generational versus ontogenetic components of change in adult cognitive behavior: A fourteen-year cross-sectional sequence. *Developmental Psychology*, 10, 305–320.

Schaie, K. W., and Strother, C. R. 1968a. A cross-sequential study of age changes in cognitive behavior. *Psych. Bull.*, 70, 671–680.

Schaie, K. W., and Strother, C. R. 1968b. The effects of time and cohort differences on the interpretation of age changes in cognitive behavior. *Mult. Beh. Res.*, **3**, 259-293.

Shanas, E. 1950. The personal adjustment of recipients of old age assistance. *J. Gerontol.*, **5**, 249-253.

Shanas, E., and Streib, G. F. (eds.) 1965. *Social Structure and the Family: Generational Relations.* Englewood Cliffs, New Jersey: Prentice-Hall.

Sheldon, W. H. 1954. *Atlas of Men: A Guide for Somatotyping the Adult Male at All Ages.* New York: Harper.

Shooter, A. M. N., Schonfield, A. E. D., King, H. F., and Welford, A. T. 1965. Some field data on the training of older people. *Occupational Psychology*, **30**, 204-215.

Singleton, W. T. 1954. The change of movement timing with age *Brit. J. Psychol.*, **45**, 166-172.

Sorenson, H. 1938. *Adult Abilities.* Minneapolis: University of Minnesota Press.

Spranger, E. 1914. *Lebensformen: Geisteswissenschaftliche Psychologie und Ethik der Persönlichkeit.* Halle: Niemeyer.

Strehler, B. 1962. *Time, Cells, and Aging.* New York: Academic Press.

Streib, G. F. 1966. Participants and drop-outs in a longitudinal study. *J. Gerontol.*, **21**, 200-209.

Streib, G. F., and Schneider, C. J. 1971. *Retirement in American Society: Impact and Process.* Ithaca, New York: Cornell University Press.

Strong, E. K., Jr. 1943. *Vocational Interest of Men and Women.* Palo Alto, California: Stanford, University Press.

Sussman, M. B. 1960. Intergenerational family relationships and social role changes in middle age. *J. Gerontol.*, **15**, 71-75.

Szafran, J. 1951. Changes with age and with exclusion of vision in performance at an aiming task. *Quart. J. Exp. Psych.*, **3**, 111-118.

Szilard, L. 1959. On the nature of the aging process. *Proc. Nat. Acad. Sci. (US)*, **45**, 30-42.

Taietz, P., and Larson, O. F. 1956. Social participation and old age. *Rural Sociology*, **21**, 229-238.

Talland, G. A. 1965. Three estimates of the word span and their stability over the adult years. *Quart. J. Exp. Psych.*, **17**, 301-307.

Terman, L. M. 1925. *Genetic Studies of Genius, I: Mental and Physical Traits of a Thousand Gifted Children.* Palo Alto, California: Stanford University Press.

Terman, L. M., and Miles, C. C. 1936. *Sex and Personality.* New York: McGraw-Hill.

Terman, L. M., and Oden, M. H. 1959. *Genetic Studies of Genius, V. The Gifted Group at Mid-Life.* Palo Alto, California: Stanford University Press.

Thomae, H. 1970. Theory of aging and cognitive theory of personality. *Hum. Dev.*, **13**, 1-16.

Thomae, H., Angleitner, A., Grombach, H., and Schmitz-Scherzer, R. 1973. Determinanten und Varianten des Alternsprozesses: Ein Bericht über die Bonner Längsschnittstudie. *Aktuelle Gerontol.*, **3**, 359-377.

Thompson, D. E. 1954. Is age kinder to the initially more able? *Proc. Iowa Acad. Sci.*, **61**, 439-441.

Thorndike, E. L. 1935. *Adult Interests.* New York: Macmillan.

Thorndike, E. L., Bregman, E. O., Tilton, J. W., and Woodyard, E. 1928. *Adult Learning.* New York: Macmillan.

Thorndike, R. L., and Gallup, C. H. 1944. Verbal intelligence of the American adult. *Journal of Genetic Psychology*, **30**, 75-85.

Townsend, P. 1957. *The Family Life of Old People.* London: Routledge & Kegan.

Troll, L. E. 1970. Issues in the study of generations. *Aging and Human Development*, **1**, 199-218.

Troll, L. E. 1971. The family of later life: A decade review. *J. Marr. Fam.*, **33**, 263-290.

Tuckman, J. and Lorge, I. 1952. The best years of life: A study in ranking. *J. Psychol.*, **34**, 137-149.

Tuddenham, R. D. 1948. Soldier intelligence in World Wars I and II. *American Psychologist*, **3**, 149-159.

Van den Daele, L. 1969. Qualitative models in developmental analysis. *Developmental Psychology*, **1**, 303-310.

Van den Daele, L. 1975. Ego development in dialectic perspective. *Hum. Dev.*, **18**, 129-142.

Veroff, J., Atkinson, J. W. Feld, S., and Gurin, G. 1960. The use of thematic apperception to assess motivation in a nationwide interview study. *Psychol. Monographs*, **74**, No. 499.

Wallach, M. A., and Green, L. R. 1961. On age and the subjective speed of time. *J. Gerontol.*, **16**, 71-74.

Wechsler, D. 1939. *The Measurement of Adult Intelligence.* Baltimore: Williams & Wilkins.

Wechsler, D. 1956. *Die Messung der Intelligenz Erwachsener.* Bern: Huber.

Weiss, E. 1927. Leistung und Lebensalter. *Industrielle Psychotechnik*, **4**, 227-245.

Welford, A. T. 1951. *Skill and Age.* London: Oxford University Press.

Welford, A. T. 1958. *Aging and Human Skill.* London: Oxford University Press.

Welford, A. T. 1960. The measurement of sensory-motor performance: Survey and reappraisal of twelve year's progress. *Ergonomics*, **3**, 189-230.

Wetherrick, N. E. 1964. A comparison of the problem-solving ability of young, middle-aged and old subjects. *Gerontologia*, **9**, 164-178.

Wiersma, W., and Klausmeier, H. J. 1965. The effect of age upon speed of concept attainment. *J. Gerontol.*, **20**, 398-400.

Willoughby, R. R. 1927. Family similarities in mental test abilities (with a note on the growth and decline of these abilities). *Genet. Psych. Monographs*, **2**, 235-277.

Willoughby, R. R. 1929, 1930. Incidental learning. *J. Educ. Psych.*, **20**, 671-682; **21**, 12-23.

Willoughby, R. R. 1937. The emotionality of spinsters. *Character and Personality*, **5**, 215-223.

Wozniak, R. H. 1975. A dialectic paradigm for psychological research: Implications drawn from the history of psychology in the Soviet Union. *Hum. Dev.*, **18**, 18–34.

Wundt, M. 1949. *Hegel's Logik und die moderne Physik*. Köln: Westdeutscher Verl.

Yakorcynsky, G. K. 1941. An evaluation of the postulates underlying the Babcock deterioration test. *Psych. Rev.*, **48**, 261–267.

Young, M. L. 1966. Problem-solving performance in two age groups. *J. Gerontol.*, **21**, 505–509.

Zajonc, R. B., and Markus, G. B. 1975. Birth order and intellectual development. *Psych. Rev.*, **82**, 74–88.

5
BIOLOGICAL THEORIES OF AGING

Nathan W. Shock
Gerontology Research Center, National Institute on Aging,
National Institutes of Health and the Baltimore City Hospitals

THE ROLE OF THEORIES

Although theories may be developed without reference to observational data, more commonly theories begin to arise in a field only after a substantial body of descriptive information about a phenomenon is available. Theories play two major roles in science. The first is to systematize a range of discrete observations into a single conceptual pattern that will make possible a smaller number of generalizations. The second role of theories is to develop rational explanations for the mechanisms which will explain how or why a general phenomenon occurs. Theories are important to a science since they will have a marked influence on the nature of experiments that will be performed.

Since aging involves many diverse phenomena ranging from molecular and cellular events through physiological and psychological changes in individuals and the social problems involving interaction between different age groups, it is clear that no single theory can explain all these phenomena. A whole spectrum of biological, physiological, psychological, and social theories will be needed. This chapter will outline in general terms current theories which attempt to explain the biological and physiological changes which occur with aging.

HISTORICAL PERSPECTIVE

Comfort (1964) has listed some 20 theories of aging and has noted that unlike other sciences

which usually show a steady progression from a large number of speculative to one or two highly probable ones, theories of aging have remained multiple and numerous. In many instances the basic ideas of "wearing out" have not changed since the time of Aristotle. Only the terms have changed. A major reason for this lack of progress in eliminating some theories as untenable is that the theory has not been stated in terms that can be experimentally tested. Many of them were simply a restatement of observations made on a single phenomenon and lacked generality. In other instances analytical methods have not been available to test the theory. Consequently, only a few of these theories or hypotheses have had any real impact on aging research.

However, as the concepts and technology in molecular biology, genetics, and immunology have advanced during the past ten years it is now possible to identify and characterize a number of theories about the causes of aging which can be experimentally tested.

BIOLOGICAL AND PHYSIOLOGICAL THEORIES

Ultimately all biological theories of aging have a genetic basis. The fundamental assumption is that the life span of any animal species is ultimately determined by a program which resides in the genes of the species and ultimately in the information contained in the DNA molecules of the gene. However, for purposes of discussion one can divide these theories into two categories. In the first category the primary focus of the theories is on the way that information is transferred from DNA molecules through a variety of steps to the ultimate formation of proteins (enzymes) which are critical for the continued function of specific cells in the animal.

The second category of theories, which may be termed nongenetic, places emphasis on the changes that may occur with the passage of time in the cellular proteins after they have been formed. These theories place primary emphasis on changes that occur at the cellular and tissue level.

Physiological theories, on the other hand, place major emphasis on the interaction between cells, tissues and organ systems in attempting to explain age changes in overall response of the intact animal (Shock, 1974; Verzár, 1969). Physiologists are well aware of the fact that the ultimate explanation of the phenomena with which they are concerned may well lie at a cellular level. However, their emphasis lies in investigating the interrelationships between the performance of different organ systems in maintaining the overall performance of the animal.

GENETIC THEORIES

General Genetic Theory

There are marked differences in average age of death or life span between different species of animals. For example, the mayfly has a life span of only 1 day, the rat 2 or 3 years, the dog 12 years, the horse 25 years, and the human about 70 years (Comfort, 1964). It is therefore clear that there is some genetic program which sets the upper limit of life spans. Although it is possible by selective inbreeding to produce strains of a species with different life spans, the inbred strains usually have shorter life spans than the original wild strain (Maynard Smith, 1962). It has therefore been concluded that long life is related to many different genes and a large gene pool is advantageous for long life.

In humans, females live about 8 years longer on the average than the males. The same sex difference in favor of females also appears in a number of other species such as rats, mice, flies, and dogs. Since the primary factor that determines sex in the animal is the presence of XY chromosomes in males and XX chromosomes in females, it has been postulated that the sex difference in longevity is due to the greater amount of X chromatin in females.

Support for theories of preprogrammed aging has also been provided by studies which indicate that at least certain cells of the body when maintained in tissue cultures are capable of only a limited number of cell divisions, approximately 40 to 50, after which they age and die (Hayflick, 1965). Furthermore, cells taken from old animals can undergo only about 20 to 25 cell divisions in contrast to the 40 or 50 cell divisions possible in cells taken from young animals. These studies involving cell division provide a potential model for studying aging of cells under defined conditions, but they may not reflect the aging characteristics of cells within the intact animal.

Humans with long-lived parents and grandparents live, on the average, about 6 years longer than those with parents who die before the age of 50 (Dublin, Lotka, and Spiegelman, 1949). From the evidence available it seems clear that (1) there is a genetic program which sets the upper limits of life span in a species, (2) that there is some familial characteristic that influences differences in life span among individuals of a single species, and (3) the expression of the basic genetic program can be altered by environmental factors.

Cellular Genetic Theories—DNA Damage

It is only recently that identification of the DNA molecules as the ultimate source of all information required by the cell for the production of the essential proteins required to maintain life has led to the theory that death occurs in the cell because of damage to the cellular DNA. The information for formation of specific enzymes and other proteins depends on the precise molecular structure of different parts of the very large DNA molecules (Watson,

1969). Breaks in the chain of the DNA molecule or exchange of positions of parts of the chain would alter the message and result in the inability of the cell to manufacture essential enzymes. This could result ultimately in death of the cell.

Somatic Mutation--Radiation

Exposure to nonlethal doses of radiation substantially shortens life span. These experimental observations led to the development of the somatic mutation theory of aging (Curtis, 1966). According to this theory, exposure to radiation accelerates aging. It was postulated that even in the absence of radiation exposure some cells undergo mutations, most of which are deleterious. Although it is not possible to identify structural changes in the DNA molecule itself, Curtis and Gebhard (1959) conducted experiments with rats and mice which showed that the incidence of abnormal chromosomes increased (1) remarkably after exposure to radiation and (2) progressively with age in non-radiated animals. Furthermore, they showed that abnormal chromosomes accumulated more rapidly in short-lived species such as the rat than in longer lived species such as the dog.

The "hit" theory of aging, proposed by Szilard (1959), is a variation of the somatic mutation theory. Szilard postulated that over the lifetime of the animal "hits" occur at random which render a gene or its DNA molecules ineffective in providing the information necessary for the formation of critical proteins in the cell. According to his conception, a cell becomes ineffective when the two similar chromosomes of a pair have each suffered a "hit" in the same place or when one of the pair has been "hit" and the other carries an inherited "fault" in this locus. A "fault" is regarded as a recessive gene which renders the cell inviable or incapable of performing necessary cell functions in the adult organism only if it occurs in both genes of a pair. Death of the animal occurs when some critical fraction of the cells initially present is rendered ineffective. Szilard suggests that this fraction is of the order of $2/3$ to $11/12$. Szilard hypothesized that the main reason why some adults of a given species live shorter lives than others lies in the difference in the number of faults they have inherited. The strength of the theory lies in its mathematical basis and its ability to predict sex differences in mortality which have been observed in human populations. However, the theory requires a number of assumptions which have not been experimentally tested and may not be true for different animal species. The theory does offer a blueprint for further experiments that should be conducted.

The somatic mutation theory has largely passed from the scene for three reasons. In the first place, the effects of radiation and mutations occur primarily in dividing cells, such as red cells, leukocytes and epithelial cells of the gut and skin. Effects are seen after cell division when mutations occur. In contrast, age effects are primarily centered in cell lines that no longer divide in the adult animal, as for example, nephrons in the kidney, or neurons and muscle cells. The second reason for abandonment of the theory is that calculations on the rate at which mutations occur in the absence of exposure to radiation indicate that the number of cells which are apt to go through mutations in mammals is too small to account for overall age changes (Maynard Smith, 1966). In the third place, recent studies have shown that most cells contain mechanisms for the repair of damaged DNA molecules (Setlow, 1968; Wheeler and Lett, 1974). Consequently, it is extremely doubtful whether damage to the DNA molecule itself plays much of a role in cellular senescence.

Error Theory of Aging—Cellular

In any cell the information stored in the genetic code, as determined by the structure of the DNA molecule, must be transcribed and translated in various steps until the final protein or enzyme molecules required by the cell finally appear. The actual assembly of appropriate amino acids to form specific proteins occurs at another location in the cell, namely, on the ribosome. In order for this to occur, information from the DNA must be transferred to an appropriate location on the ribosome. This transfer occurs by the assembly of RNA molecules at specific points on the DNA molecule which then migrate to the ribosomes. Protein formed depends upon what part of the very large DNA molecule is decoded with the formation of an appropriate m-RNA.

This general theory of biology has been transferred to gerontology as the error theory of aging (Medvedev, 1964). According to this theory, aging and death of the cell are the result of errors which may occur at any step in this sequence of information transfer resulting in the formation of a protein or enzyme which is not an exact copy and therefore is unable to carry out its function properly. The error may be simply the incorporation of the wrong amino acid in the protein or a slight error in the normal sequence.

Unlike DNA molecules, which are highly stable and are maintained throughout the life span of a cell, RNA molecules have a half-life of only eight or nine days. Consequently, new RNA molecules are being formed continuously to provide replacement of enzyme molecules.

Orgel (1963) has argued that the ability of a cell to produce functional proteins, such as enzymes, depends not only on the correct genetic information contained in the DNA molecules, but also on the competence of the protein synthetic apparatus, i.e., the enzymes necessary for the translation and transcription of the information from the DNA to the final protein product. According to his theory, aging is the result of errors in enzymes involved in translation and transcription. Orgel claims that although the initial frequency of errors in a cell may be low, in the absence of cell division as in an adult animal there would be an exponential increase in the frequency of errors in the proteins synthesized with the passage of time which would lead to an "error catastrophe" and the death of the cell.

Harrison and Holliday (1967) have experimentally introduced "errors" in proteins in fruit flies by feeding analogues of certain amino acids. The analogue amino acid is introduced into the protein with a resulting "error." In general, flies with experimentally induced "errors" had shorter life spans than normals.

Although the error hypothesis is an attractive one, it suffers from a number of limitations. In the first place, there are many steps between the information source (DNA) and the final protein product and errors can conceivably occur at many points. Thus the theory is relatively non-specific (Heidrick and Makinodan, 1972; Price and Makinodan, 1973). Furthermore, the details of these transfer processes are still unknown so that the nature of the error cannot be specified. It is only recently that some investigators have claimed to have observed differences in the RNA's that have been isolated from old and young tissues (Menzies, Mishra, and Gold, 1972; Cutler, 1972). The error hypothesis is a viable one which makes predictions about aging which can be tested experimentally.

NONGENETIC CELLULAR THEORIES

At the cellular level nongenetic theories of aging presume that with the passage of time changes take place in molecules and structural elements of cells which impair their effectiveness.

Wear and Tear Theory

This theory is based on the assumption that living organisms behave like machines (Sacher, 1966). That is, from repeated use parts wear out, defects occur, and the machinery finally comes to a grinding halt. However, the man-machine analogy is not a very good one. Unlike machines which cannot repair themselves, living organisms have developed many mechanisms which permit self repair. In some tissues, such as the skin, the lining of the gastrointestinal tract, and red blood cells, new cells are continuously formed to replace old ones so that the effects of aging are minimal. In other cell systems, such as nerve cells and muscle cells, which no longer divide in the adult, repair mechanisms are present and there is a constant turnover among many of the molecules within a cell.

As far back as 1908, Rubner (1908) reported a direct relationship between the oxygen uptake in various animals and their life span and hypothesized that the rate of living as measured by oxygen consumption was an important determinant of life span. Small animals like the rat and the mouse have much higher oxygen uptakes per unit of body weight than do larger animals such as the horse and man. In fact, there is a rough correlation between the oxygen uptake per unit of body weight and life span— the higher the oxygen uptake, the shorter the life span. From this correlation Rubner concluded that the "rate of living" determined life span.

Increasing the environmental temperature significantly shortens the life span of cold blooded animals, as for example, fruit flies (Loeb and Northrop, 1917; Strehler, 1962), rotifers (Fanestil and Barrows, 1965), and *Campanularia* (Brock and Strehler, 1963). At lower environmental temperatures life span was lengthened. Since a rise in temperature increases metabolic rate in cold blooded animals, these experiments have been interpreted as evidence to support the "wear and tear" or "rate of living" hypothesis about the mechanism of aging.

In contrast to cold blooded animals who show a reduction in metabolism as environmental temperature is lowered, warm blooded animals increase their metabolism when exposed to cold temperature. Carlson, Scheyer, and Jackson (1957) and Johnson, Kintner and Kibler (1963) found that rats kept at low temperatures increased their metabolism by about 30 percent in order to maintain their body temperature and showed a comparable reduction in life span. These experiments were also interpreted as support for the "wear and tear" theory. However, all of the experiments on the effects of temperature on life span can be interpreted as evidence to support any theory of aging which involves chemical reactions, as for example, the cross-linking theory, or even error theories, since the rate of all chemical reactions is influenced by changes in temperature.

Deprivation Theories—Diffusion

Other nongenetic theories assume that aging is due to inadequate delivery of essential nutrients and oxygen to cells of the body. These theories point to the increasing prevalence of atherosclerosis with advancing age and the well known effects of vascular degeneration on cellular and tissue functions for their primary support. However, when the blood supply is shut off from a tissue by vascular disease, all of the cells in the area supplied die. This is in sharp contrast to the more or less chance distribution of cells which drop out or disappear from a tissue or organ with advancing age. Furthermore, there is no evidence for a systematic reduction in oxygen content of the blood with advancing age. Fasting blood glucose levels (Silverstone, Brandfonbrener, Shock, and Yiengst, 1957) and amounts of other nutrients present in the blood do not fall with advancing age. It seems safe to assume that even in advanced old age adequate supplies of oxygen and nutrients are available to cells and tissues of the body except under circumstances associated with diseases of the blood vessels.

Carpenter (1965; Carpenter and Loynd, 1968), however, has speculated that with advancing age, changes occur in cell membranes which limit the diffusion of oxygen and other nutrients from the blood to the inside of the living cell. There is little experimental data which would indicate that this is the case. In fact, some experiments tend to show just the reverse. At least small molecules such as glucose and oxygen tend to pass through membranes more easily in tissues taken from senescent animals than those taken from young (Kirk and Laursen, 1955). It is, therefore, extremely doubtful that senescence can be ascribed to cellular deprivation of essential materials.

Accumulation Theories

Cellular aging and senescence have also been ascribed to the accumulation of deleterious substances in the aging animals. Carrel and Ebeling (1923) first observed that serum taken from old chickens inhibited the growth of cells in tissue culture. This observation has been interpreted as evidence for the presence of some substance which accumulated in the blood with aging and is deleterious to cellular growth. However, no such substance has as yet been isolated and chemically identified.

A number of investigators have, however, reported that highly insoluble lipofuscin particles accumulate in cells of various tissues, such as neurons and muscle fibers of the heart, with advancing age (Strehler, 1964). In muscle fibers of the heart as much as $1/3$ of the total cell volume may be taken up by these insoluble pigments in senescent humans and animals. It has been argued that the presence of these insoluble particles interferes with the normal cellular metabolism and ultimately results in cell death. Up to the present no evidence of impaired physiological function associated with the presence of these age pigments has been provided. The accumulation of these large molecules has been ascribed by Carpenter (1965) to impair diffusing capacity of cell membranes with advancing age. Since the age pigments consist of varying proportions of lipids and protein molecules, it has been assumed that they represent an accumulation of non-metabolized molecules. The accumulation theory is a reasonable one to pursue, but if it is to receive serious consideration, toxic substances, present in old cells but absent in young ones, must be isolated and identified. Furthermore, physiological experiments are required to show that the presence of age pigment impairs the function of the cell.

Free Radical Theory

Harman (1968) has proposed that aging and cell death stem from the damaging effects of the formation of free radicals. Free radicals are chemical compounds which contain oxygen in a highly activated state. Hence they are very unstable and tend to react quickly with other molecules in their vicinity. As a result of these reactions enzymes and other proteins may be altered in structure and function. The rate of formation of free radicals is accelerated by radiation and inhibited by the presence of antioxidants. Harman offers as evidence for his theory the increase in average life span observed in mice which have been fed antioxidants, such as 2-mercaptoethylamine and butylated hydroxytoluene. Unfortunately, the experiments reported suffer from a number of limitations so that the theory is still unproved.

Cross-linking Theories

Many macromolecules of biological importance develop, with the passage of time, cross-linkages

or bonds either between component parts of the same molecule or between molecules themselves. The formation of these cross-links alters the physical and chemical properties of the molecules involved so that they no longer function in the same way as before. Since these cross-links are very stable they are apt to accumulate with the passage of time. The cross-linking theory first proposed by Bjorksten (1968) holds that the accumulation of these cross-link molecules is a primary cause of aging.

Most of the experimental evidence supporting this theory has been derived from studies on extracellular proteins, namely, elastin and collagen (Verzár, 1963; Bjorksten, 1968). It is well established that with aging, cross-links develop between the two intertwined strands of the collagen molecule and between adjacent strands. Formation of these cross-links results in the well known loss of elasticity with advancing age in many tissues of the body, as for example, the skin and blood vessels. It is also known that the body contains many substances, primarily aldehydes, which are effective in accelerating the rate of formation of cross-links.

From these observed facts with respect to extracellular protein, it has been assumed that similar changes occur in intracellular proteins such as enzymes and also in the DNA molecule (Bjorksten, 1968). Although cross-linking between different parts of the DNA molecule has been observed *in vitro*, no evidence has yet appeared which indicates these changes also occur *in vivo*. The cross-linking theory is, however, a viable one which may well explain molecular changes which form the basis for known changes in the characteristics of structural proteins at least. The theory leads to the search for methods whereby cross-links once formed may be broken down but, perhaps more importantly, to methods which would reduce their rate of formation in the animal and thus influence the rate of aging.

Recently Bjorksten, Weyer, and Ashman (1971) have reported the isolation of specific enzymes from soil bacteria which are capable of breaking cross-links in collagen after they have been formed. Similarly, certain chemicals, such as nitriles and penicillamine, have been found which greatly slow down the rate of formation of cross-links. Although neither of these procedures has as yet been developed to the point where they can be applied to humans, they represent important potentials for future research.

Starting with the observations that (1) collagen becomes stiffer with age and (2) collagen constitutes 25 to 30 percent of the total body protein and surrounds blood vessels and cells, Kohn (1971) has hypothesized that age changes in collagen may have far reaching effects on other physiological functions. Although this hypothesis relates molecular changes in collagen to more general physiological processes, it is highly speculative and has not been experimentally tested.

PHYSIOLOGICAL THEORIES OF AGING

Physiological theories of aging attempt to explain aging and the life span of various species of animals either on the basis of a breakdown in the performance of a single organ system or more reasonably in terms of impairments in physiological control mechanisms.

Single Organ System Hypotheses— Cardiovascular System

In the past, physiological theories of aging have focused attention on a single organ system to explain the total effects of aging. Since failure of the heart and blood vessels represents a primary cause of death, especially among the aged, failure of the cardiovascular system has long been regarded as the primary cause of aging. According to this hypothesis, aging results primarily from the progressive deterioration of blood vessels as a result of the development of atherosclerosis. However, atherosclerosis is a disease process which occurs in the young and increases progressively with advancing age. Death from this disease may occur at any age. Furthermore, aging occurs in many lower forms of animal species where no blood vessels are present, as for example, fruit flies, rotifers, and nematodes. Hence the hypothesis that aging is basically related to reduction in blood supply does not have general biological significance, even though it is an important cause of death among humans.

McFarland (1963) has advanced the hypothesis that aging is primarily the result of lowered delivery of oxygen to critical tissues such as the brain. Support for this theory of aging is drawn largely from the changes in psychomotor performance such as handwriting in older people which can be experimentally induced in young subjects when the oxygen content of the inspired air is greatly reduced. Other experimental evidence fails to support this hypothesis. The oxygen content of arterial blood does not fall with advancing age and blood flow to the brain is only slightly diminished after maturity (Kety, 1956).

Thyroid Gland

Another hypothesis assumed that aging was due primarily to slowing of metabolic processes at the cellular level. Since the rate of cellular metabolism is regulated by the thyroid gland, it was assumed that aging was due to the inability of the thyroid gland to supply adequate amounts of its hormone. This hypothesis was also supported by some of the superficial similarities between the symptoms of patients with hypothyroidism and senescent subjects, as for example, loss of hair, slower movements, lengthened reaction times, drying and wrinkling of the skin, and the presumed reduction in basal oxygen consumption with advancing age. However, more detailed studies have shown that the age related fall in basal oxygen uptake is a reflection of tissue loss with advancing age (Shock, 1955). The oxygen consumption of individual cells does not change significantly. Other experiments have shown that with the exogenous administration of thyroid stimulating hormones the thyroid of the older individual responds as well as that of the young with respect to increasing the output of thyroxin as evidenced by increased basal metabolism, heart rate, and uptake of iodine by the gland (Baker, Gaffney, Shock, and Landowne, 1959). Hence, the theory that aging is due to failure of the thyroid gland can no longer be considered as very probable.

Sex Glands

Similarly, failure of the sex glands has been looked upon as a primary cause of aging. In fact, this hypothesis has led to the adminstration of sex hormones and the transplantation of gonads in an attempt to induce rejuvenation (McGrady, 1968). In the early 1900's many attempts were made to restore sexual vigor to aging males by injection of crude extracts made from testicles. This work was first reported with great enthusiasm by Brown-Sequard (1889) based on experiments which he conducted on himself. However, even with a more highly purified male sex hormone, the side effects, as for example, the possibility of developing prostatic cancer, and the ephemeral results reported have indicated the futility of this approach to influence overall aging.

Chronic administration of female sex hormones to postmenopausal women has been urged by some endocrinologists to minimize the overall effects of aging (Greenblatt, 1965). This recommendation is based on the presumption that aging in women is related to the level of sex hormones present in the body. Although there is evidence that some of the complications of the menopause can be alleviated by the administration of female sex hormones, the possibility of inducing or activating cancer in the female genital tract by prolonged administration of the hormone has led most clinicians to utilize the treatment on the basis of relatively short-term therapy and to avoid chronic administration (Ryan and Gibson, 1973). There is little evidence that aging as a biological phenomenon can be ascribed to diminished endocrine secretion by the ovary.

Pituitary Gland—Neurohypophysis

Since the pituitary gland plays a central role in the modulation of activity of the adrenal gland, the thyroid, and the gonads, aging has been ascribed to a failure of this gland to carry out its appropriate functions (Dilman, 1971). However, methods for determining blood levels of the regulatory hormones produced by the pituitary and the hypothalamus are not yet available. Since the possibility that the pituitary plays a key role in aging cannot be ruled out at this time, recent advances in utilizing radioactive immunological techniques, which are much more sensitive than the usual biochemical methods, will resolve this problem, hopefully in the near future.

While it is true that failure of any organ system in the mammal may result in death, these failures cannot be regarded as a primary cause of aging, since aging also occurs in lower forms of organisms which may not possess the specific organ system which is assumed to be the key one in aging in the mammal. Physiological theories of aging will need to look beyond a single organ system if they are to be useful.

Stress Theory

The stress theory of aging, developed largely by Selye (1966) and his collaborators, holds that aging is the result of the accumulation over time of the effects of the stresses of living. According to Selye, any stress which requires adaptation by the organism leaves a residuum of impairment from which the animal does not completely recover. These residuals, although they may be quite small with respect to specific events, accumulate over the life span so that ultimately the reserve capacities of the animal are exhausted. The basic assumption of this theory, namely, that there is always residual damage which persists and accumulates, is not supported by some experimental data. For example, Curtis and Gebhard (1959) showed that rats who were subjected to severe but nonfatal infections repeatedly over their life span lived as long as the non-infected control animals. Furthermore, physiologists have shown that stresses oftentimes induce hypertrophy in an organ system and may therefore be beneficial. For example, the increase in blood supply to muscles and improvement in exercise performance by physical training in athletes become most marked under conditions of severe exercise.

Immunological Theories

The immune system protects the body not only against invading micro-organisms but also against atypical mutant cells which may form in the body. The immune system carries out this protective function both by generating antibodies which react to foreign organisms, proteins, etc., but also by the formation of special cells which engulf and digest foreign cells and substances. Aging has a marked impact on the capabilities of the immune system. The production of antibodies reaches a peak during adolescence and then declines (Makinodan, 1974). In some animals this decline is so dramatic that senescent animals retain only one-tenth of the immune capability of younger ones.

One assumption is that the basic impairment in the immune system is a loss in the ability to recognize slight deviations in molecular structure and cellular characteristics so that cells which have undergone mutation and would ordinarily be destroyed by the immune system are no longer recognized and are permitted to grow and develop to the detriment of the animal. By the same token, impairment of cell recognition capacity might also result in the development of antibodies which inactivate normal cells in various tissues.

It may also be hypothesized that even though recognition occurs, the immune system of the senescent animal is unable to produce an adequate supply of antibodies or phagocytic cells. Some experiments have shown that in senescent animals the supply of stem cells from which the phagocytic cells are derived, as well as the antibody producing cells, is reduced as a result of a fall in the rate of cell division in the stem cells (Heidrick and Makinodan, 1972). If this turns out to be the case, it is possible that a deficient immune system in a senescent animal could be supported by the injection of stem cells from young animals.

The *autoimmune theory of aging* (Blumenthal and Berns, 1964; Walford, 1969) proposes that aging results from the development of antibodies which react even with normal cells in the body and destroy them. This might occur either because of failure to recognize normal cells as normal or the development of errors in the formation of antibodies so that they now react with normal cells as well as the deviate ones which stimulated the immune cells to form antibodies in the first place. This hypothesis gains its greatest support from the age-related increase of autoimmune antibodies found in the blood (Walford, 1969) and the similarity between many of the so-called immune diseases (some types of anemia, rheumatoid arthritis, arteritis, maturity onset diabetes, thyroiditis, and amyloidosis) and the phenomena of aging.

Although evidence for the key role of the immune system in aging is still sketchy, the general hypothesis is an attractive one which can be experimentally tested. It has added merit that, if true, it can lead to the development of methods which could potentially influence aging in the human.

AGING AND PHYSIOLOGICAL CONTROLS

It is now becoming apparent that the overall performance of an animal is closely related to the effectiveness of a variety of control mechanisms which regulate the interplay of different organs and tissues. Frolkis (1966) has advanced the hypothesis that aging and death of an animal is the result of failure of adaptive mechanisms. Since adaptation to environmental stresses involves the appropriate functioning of control mechanisms, the adaptation hypothesis can be considered as a special case of the broader theory of control mechanism failure.

With advancing age many control mechanisms lose their effectiveness. Any control mechanism must first of all have a system which will detect changes for which adjustments must be made. In addition to the sensing device, there must also be a mechanism which can carry out the proper adjustment. In the body, there are many sensing devices which activate effective processes to carry out readjustments of body temperature, blood glucose, blood pressure, heart rate, etc. In developing theories of aging based on control mechanisms it is necessary to distinguish between alterations in the sensitivity of detecting devices and the effectiveness of the organ system or cells which initiate the changes necessary to maintain stable conditions.

In the mammal the primary control mechanisms operate either through the endocrine system or the nervous system.

Endocrine Control System

Many metabolic processes are regulated by hormones which are produced in a gland and are then transported to the target organs through the bloodstream. Although the detailed mechanisms whereby the hormone produces its effect within target organ cells is still unknown, recent studies have shown that tissues of senescent animals show a reduced binding capacity for many of the steroid hormones (Roth, 1974) so that the ultimate site of action of a breakdown of the regulatory mechanisms through endocrine control may well be at the cellular level.

There are, however, a number of examples of the breakdown of endocrine control in terms of overall physiological effects. For example, the response of the kidney to a standard amount of antidiuretic hormone is significantly less in the aged subject than in the young (Miller and Shock, 1953).

With advancing age, the rate at which excess sugar is removed from the blood is significantly reduced (Silverstone et al., 1957). The removal of the excess glucose is regulated primarily by the release of insulin from the pancreas. Extensive experiments have shown that the age deficit is due to the reduced sensitivity of the beta cells of the pancreas to a slight rise in blood sugar level (Pozefsky, Colker, Langs, and Andres, 1965; Andres, Swerdloff, and Tobin, 1969).

Nervous Control Mechanisms

The nervous system also plays an important role in regulating many physiological activities. Performances which require coordinated movements mediated through the nervous system show greater decrements with age than do component parts of the total performance. For example, the maximum breathing capacity shows a significantly greater age decrement than does vital capacity itself (Norris, Shock, Landowne, and Falzone, 1956). The maximum breathing capacity, which is measurement of the total amount of air that can be moved in and out of the lungs voluntarily within a short period of time (usually 15 seconds) requires the coordinated movement of the chest cage and the diaphragm for its performance. In contrast, vital capacity involves only a single maximum inspiration followed by an expiration, which does not involve a coordinated rate-adjusted performance. Similarly, the age decrement in a coordinated exercise such as cranking shows a greater age decrement than the static strength of the same muscle groups

which are involved in the cranking operation (Shock and Norris, 1970).

Under normal circumstances, a rise in blood pressure results in a fall in heart rate. Pressure sensitive cells located in blood vessels of the carotid sinus initiate nerve impulses which ultimately activate the vagus nerve which slows the heart rate. Animal experiments have shown that when blood pressure was increased by 50 mm Hg in both old and young unanesthetized rats by the continuous infusion of phenylephrine the lowering of the heart rate was significantly less in the senescent than in the young animals (Rothbaum, Shaw, Angell, and Shock, 1974). These experiments clearly indicate a reduction in the effectiveness of a physiological control mechanism with increasing age.

In mammals, body temperature is normally regulated within fairly narrow limits. Experimental studies in which subjects of different ages were exposed to different environmental temperatures have shown that young subjects can maintain body temperature even when environmental temperatures are either increased or decreased whereas old subjects show a significant change in body temperature (Krag and Kountz, 1950, 1952).

The ability to perform muscular work is a function of the integrated activity of the cardiovascular, respiratory, and neuromuscular systems. Many studies have shown that perhaps the greatest decrements shown with age lie in the area of exercise and maximum work performance. Although decrements can be identified within each of the organ systems involved, they are less than the decrements in total performance. In both physiological and psychological performances, the primary finding is that with increasing age the rate of adjustment or performance diminishes. The slower response observed in many organ systems in the elderly may well be a reflection of impaired integrative functions both at the neural and endocrine levels.

SUMMARY

A review of most of the theories of aging shows that, although some specific experimental evidence may be found which will support each of them, it is now clear that some are more probable than others. In some cases, critical tests of a hypothesis cannot be made at the present time because of technological limitations. This is especially true of the error hypothesis which, although it is still diffuse, is currently having considerable impact on the direction of research on aging. Methods which will permit the identification of molecules which have an error in their assembly will undoubtedly be available in the visible future. When the nature of the error and the point at which it occurs have been identified further research can be conducted to develop methods either for reducing the occurrence of error or for correcting the existing errors.

The cross-linking theory is also one which offers promise for the future. The first step is to determine whether cross-linking occurs in intracellular proteins as it does in extracellular proteins such as collagen and connective tissue. Undoubtedly further research will identify methods to both reduce the rate of formation of cross-links and even to eliminate them once they are formed.

The autoimmune theory of aging also holds great promise for the future. Although a great deal of experimental work remains to be done, the rapid developments in the field provide new methods and techniques which will make it possible to test many of the specific aspects, especially at the cellular level.

Although the ultimate cause of aging may lie at the cellular or even molecular level, current theories in this area fail to take into account the important consideration of interrelationships between cells, tissues, and organs. It is in this area that theories which focus on the role of regulatory and control mechanisms offer promise for the future. Although such theories are currently less elegant than the cellular and molecular theories, they do address themselves to the important problem of explaining aging in the total animal. When bacteria and other micro-organisms were first identified as causal agents for certain infectious diseases there was a general tendency in medical science to look for a single agent as a cause of each specific disease. However, subsequent research has shown clearly that there are many diseases

which have multiple causes and the concept of one agent as a specific cause of one disease has been abandoned in medical science. Similarly, it is extremely doubtful whether a single theory will explain all aspects of aging. Aging is a highly complex phenomenon which may require different explanatory principles for different aspects of the process.

REFERENCES

Andres, R., Swerdloff, R., and Tobin, J. D. 1969. The effects of age on plasma insulin response to hyperglycemia: studies in man with a servo-control technique. In, Proceedings of the 8th International Congress of Gerontology. Vol. I, pp. 36-39. Bethesda, Maryland: Fed. Amer. Soc. Exp. Biol.

Baker, S. P., Gaffney, G. W., Shock, N. W., and Landowne, M. 1959. Physiological responses of five middle-aged and elderly men to repeated administration of thyroid stimulating hormone (thyrotropin; TSH). J. Gerontol., 14, 37-47.

Bjorksten, J. 1968. The crosslinkage theory of aging. J. Am. Geriat. Soc., 16, 408-427.

Bjorksten, J., Weyer, E. R., and Ashman, S. M. 1971. Study of low molecular weight proteolytic enzymes. Finska Kemists. Medd., 80, 70-87.

Blumenthal, H. T., and Berns, A. W. 1964. Autoimmunity and aging. In, B. L. Strehler (ed.), Advances in Gerontological Research, Vol. 1, pp. 289-342. New York: Academic Press.

Brock, M. A., and Strehler, B. L. 1963. Studies on the comparative physiology of aging. IV. Age and mortality of some marine Cnidaria in the laboratory. J. Gerontol., 18, 23-28.

Brown-Sequard, M. 1889. Des effets produits chez l'homme par des injections sous-cutanées d'un liquide retiré des testicules de cobaye et de chien. C. R. Soc. Biol., Paris, 41, 420.

Carlson, L. D., Scheyer, W. J., and Jackson, B. H. 1957. Combined effects of ionizing radiation and low temperature on metabolism, longevity and soft tissues of white rat. I. Metabolism and longevity. Radiation Res., 7, 190-197.

Carpenter, D. G. 1965. Diffusion theory of aging. J. Gerontol., 20, 191-195.

Carpenter, D. G., and Loynd, J. A. 1968. An integrated theory of aging. J. Am. Geriat. Soc., 16, 1307-1322.

Carrel, A., and Ebeling, A. H. 1923. Antagonistic growth principles of serum and their relation to old age. J. Exp. Med., 38, 419-425.

Comfort, A. 1964. Ageing: The Biology of Senescence. New York: Holt, Rinehart and Winston.

Curtis, H. J. 1966. Biological mechanisms of aging. Springfield, Illinois: Charles C. Thomas.

Curtis, H. J., and Gebhard, K. L. 1959. Radiation induced aging in mice. In, Proceedings of the 2nd

U.N. International Conference on Peaceful Uses of Atomic Energy, Vol. 22, pp. 52–57. New York: United Nations.

Cutler, R. G. 1972. Transcription of reiterated DNA sequence classes throughout the life-span of the mouse. In, B. L. Strehler (ed.), Advances in Gerontological Research, Vol. 4, pp. 219–321. New York: Academic Press.

Dilman, V. M. 1971. Age-associated elevation of hypothalamic threshold to feedback control, and its role in development, ageing, and disease. Lancet, 7711, 1211–1219.

Dublin, L. I., Lotka, A. J., and Spiegelman, M. 1949. Length of Life: A Study of the Life Table. New York: Ronald.

Fanestil, D. D., and Barrows, C. H., Jr. 1965. Aging in the rotifer. J. Gerontol., 20, 462–469.

Frolkis, V. V. 1966. Neuro-humoral regulations in the aging organism. J. Gerontol., 21, 161–167.

Greenblatt, R. B. 1965. Estrogen therapy for postmenopausal females. New Engl. J. Med., 272, 305–308.

Harman, D. 1968. Free radical theory of aging: effect of free radical reaction inhibitors on the mortality rate of male LAF_1 mice. J. Gerontol., 23, 476–482.

Harrison, B. J., and Holliday, R. 1967. Senescence and the fidelity of protein synthesis in Drosophila. Nature, Lond., 213, 990–992.

Hayflick, L. 1965. The limited in vitro lifetime of human diploid cell strains. Exp. Cell Res., 37, 614–636.

Heidrick, M. L., and Makinodan, T. 1972. Nature of cellular deficiencies in age-related decline of the immune system. Gerontologia, 18, 305–320.

Johnson, H. D., Kintner, L. D., and Kibler, H. H. 1963. Effects of 48 F. (8.9 C.) and 83 F. (28.4 C.) on longevity and pathology of male rats. J. Gerontol., 18, 29–36.

Kety, S. S. 1956. Human cerebral blood flow and oxygen consumption as related to aging. J. Chronic Diseases, 3, 478–486.

Kirk, J. E., and Laursen, T. J. S. 1955. Diffusion coefficients of various solutes for human aortic tissue. With special reference to variation in tissue permeability with age. J. Gerontol., 10, 288–302.

Kohn, R. R. 1971. Principles of Mammalian Aging. Engelwood Cliffs, New Jersey: Prentice-Hall.

Krag, C. L., and Kountz, W. B. 1950. Stability of body function in the aged. I. Effect of exposure of the body to cold. J. Gerontol., 5, 227–235.

Krag, C. L., and Kountz, W. B. 1952. Stability of body function in the aged. II. Effect of exposure of the body to heat. J. Gerontol., 7, 61–70.

Loeb, J., and Northrop, J. H. 1917. On the influence of food and temperature upon the duration of life. J. Biol. Chem., 32, 103–121.

Makinodan, T. 1974. Cellular basis of immunosenescence. In, (Molecular and Cellular Mechanisms of Aging), pp. 153–166. Paris: INSERM, Coll. Inst. Nat. Santé Rec. Med., Vol. 27.

Maynard Smith, J. 1962. Review lectures on senescence. I. The causes of ageing. Proc. Roy. Soc. (Biol. Sci.), 157, 115–127.

Maynard Smith, J. 1966. Theories of aging. In, P. L. Krohn (ed.), Topics in the Biology of Aging, pp. 1–27. New York: Interscience Publishers.

McFarland, R. A. 1963. Experimental evidence of the relationship between ageing and oxygen want: in search of a theory of ageing. Ergonomics, 6, 339–366.

McGrady, P. M., Jr. 1968. The Youth Doctors. New York: Coward-McCann.

Medvedev, Zh. A. 1964. The nucleic acids in development and aging. In, B. L. Strehler (ed.), Advances in Gerontological Research, Vol. 1, pp. 181–206. New York: Academic Press.

Menzies, R. A., Mishra, R. K., and Gold, P. H. 1972. The turnover of ribosomes and soluble RNA in a variety of tissues of young adult and aged rats. Mech. Age. Dev., 1, 117–132.

Miller, J. H., and Shock, N. W. 1953. Age differences in the renal tubular response to antidiuretic hormone. J. Gerontol., 8, 446–450.

Norris, A. H., Shock, N. W., Landowne, M., and Falzone, J. A., Jr. 1956. Pulmonary function studies: age difference in lung volumes and bellows function. J. Gerontol., 11, 379–387.

Orgel, L. E. 1963. The maintenance of the accuracy of protein synthesis and its relevance to ageing. Biochemistry, 49, 517–521.

Pozefsky, T., Colker, J. L., Langs, H. M., and Andres, R. 1965. The cortisone-glucose tolerance test: the influence of age on performance. Ann. Internal Med., 63, 988–997.

Price, G. B., and Makinodan, T. 1973. Aging: alteration of DNA-protein information. Gerontologia, 19, 58–70.

Roth, G. S. 1974. Age-related changes in specific glucocorticoid binding by steroid-responsive tissues of rats. Endocrinology, 94, 82–90.

Rothbaum, D. A., Shaw, D. J., Angell, C. S., and Shock, N. W. 1974. Age differences in the baroreceptro response of rats. J. Gerontol., 29, 488–492.

Rubner, M. 1908. Das Problem der Lebensdauer und seine beziehungen zu Wachstum und Ernährung. Munchen: R. Oldenbourg.

Ryan, K. J., and Gibson, D. C. (eds.) 1973. Menopause and Aging. Washington: U.S. Govt. Print. Office, DHEW Publ. No. [NIH] 73–319.

Sacher, G. A. 1966. Abnutzungstheorie. In, N. W. Shock (ed.), Perspectives in Experimental Gerontology, pp. 326–335. Springfield, Illinois: Charles C. Thomas.

Selye, H. 1966. The future for aging research. In, N. W. Shock (ed.), Perspectives in Experimental Gerontology, pp. 375–387. Springfield, Illinois: Charles C. Thomas.

Setlow, R. B. 1968. The photochemistry, photobiology, and repair of polynucleotides. In, J. N. Davidson and W. E. Cohn (eds.), Progress in Nucleic Acid

Research and Molecular Biology, Vol. *8*, pp. 257–295. New York: Academic Press.

Shock, N. W. 1955. Metabolism and age. *J. Chronic Diseases*, **2**, 687–703.

Shock, N. W. 1974. Physiological theories of aging. *In*, M. Rockstein (ed.), *Theoretical Aspects of Aging*, pp. 119–136. New York: Academic Press.

Shock, N. W., and Norris, A. H. 1970. Neuromuscular coordination as a factor in age changes in muscular exercise. *In*, D. Brunner and E. Jokl (eds.), *Medicine and Sport*, Vol. *4. Physical Activity and Aging*, pp. 92–99. Basel: Karger.

Silverstone, F. A., Brandfonbrener, M., Shock, N. W., and Yiengst, M. J. 1957. Age differences in the intravenous glucose tolerance tests and the response to insulin. *J. Clin. Invest.*, **36**, 504–514.

Strehler, B. L. 1962. Further studies on the thermally induced aging of *Drosophila melanogaster*. *J. Gerontol.*, **17**, 347–352.

Strehler, B. L. 1964. On the histochemistry and ultrastructure of age pigment. *In*, B. L. Strehler (ed.), *Advances in Gerontological Research*, Vol. *1*, pp. 343–384. New York: Academic Press.

Szilard, L. 1959. On the nature of the aging process. *Proc. Nat. Acad. Sci.*, *Wash.*, **45**, 30–45.

Verzár, F. 1963. The aging of collagen. *Sci. Am.*, **208**, 104–114.

Verzár, F. 1969. Physiological control mechanisms and ageing. *In*, *Proceedings of the 8th International Congress of Gerontology*. Vol. *I*, pp. 151–161. Bethesda, Maryland: Fed. Amer. Soc. Exp. Biol.

Walford, R. L. 1969. *The Immunologic Theory of Aging*. Baltimore: Williams & Wilkins.

Watson, J. D. 1969. *The Double Helix*. New York: New American Library.

Wheeler, K. T., and Lett, J. T. 1974. On the possibility that DNA repair is related to age in non-dividing cells. *Proc. Nat. Acad. Sci.*, *Wash.*, **71**, 1862–1865.

6
TOWARD A SOCIOPSYCHOLOGICAL THEORY OF CHANGE IN ADULTHOOD AND OLD AGE

Marjorie Fiske Lowenthal
University of California, San Francisco

BACKGROUND

Traditionally, the field of aging has produced or applied concepts primarily sociological or primarily psychological. Since the early work of Arnhoff and Lorge (1960) several studies, primarily based on attitudinal research in various segments of the population, have produced generalizations about the normative climate or mores such attitudes impose on the aging individual (Axelrod and Eisdorfer, 1961; Bennett and Eckman, 1973; Cyrus-Lutz and Gaitz, 1972; Neugarten, Moore, and Lowe, 1968; Spence, Feigenbaum, Fitzgerald, and Roth, 1968). Others have applied sociological concepts to studies of the aged (Havighurst and Albrecht, 1953; Maddox, 1970; Rosow, 1967; Tibbitts, 1960; Williams, 1960). The psychological studies have most frequently used cognitive, learning or personality theory as a point of departure (Birren, 1964; Botwinick, 1973; Eisdorfer and Lawton, 1973; Kuhlen, 1968; Reichard, Livson, and Peterson, 1962).

In addition, there have been multidisciplinary studies in which sociologists, psychologists and psychiatrists have collaborated. Such research, while not proposing an integrative theory, has contributed concepts of a sociopsychological nature (Birren, Butler, Greenhouse, Sokoloff, and Yarrow, 1963; Blau, 1961, 1966; Busse and Pfeiffer, 1969; Lowenthal, Berkman, and associates, 1967). Other authors, using clinical or projective data from which developmental stages in adulthood and old age are proposed (Erikson, 1968; Gutmann, 1969), acknowledge social factors as relevant to such stages, but have not dealt with them in depth.

The most ambitious step toward a sociopsychological theory was the empirically-based and theoretically-interpreted work of Cumming and Henry (1961). It provoked interesting controversy (Maddox, 1964, 1965, 1970), and later further refinements from the authors themselves (Cumming, 1968; Henry, 1965). The study prompted other researchers to report different conclusions from their own work (Havighurst, Munnichs, Neugarten, and Thomae, 1969; Havighurst, Neugarten, and Tobin, 1968; Lowenthal and Boler, 1965; Maddox, 1963; Taber, 1965; Tallmer and Kutner, 1969). Useful new research (Carp, 1968; Kleemeier, 1964; Lehr and Rudinger, 1969; Lipman and Smith, 1968; Loeb, 1973) was also stimulated. One of the main areas of contention about the original work stemmed from its stipulation of a mutually accommodating disengagement process taking place between the aging individual and his society. Disengagement on the part of some aging individuals was empirically supported, but statements about society were primarily speculative; the term accommodating, as applied to social networks and institutions, could readily be interpreted as a euphemism for "rejecting."

The shortcomings of social and psychological theories in the field of aging reflect a serious deficiency in social psychology itself, namely lack of systematic conceptualization about the points of articulation between the individual and his society (Katz, 1967). At present, the most systematic work on this "synapse" is being undertaken by scholars concerned with stress and adaptation, such as Coelho, Hamburg, and Adams (1974), Horowitz and Becker (1972), and Lazarus (1970). Only recently have such scholars begun to develop a life course perspective.

A truly sociopsychological approach requires two simultaneous, juxtaposed perspectives: (1) close examination—through rigorous analytic conceptualization as well as empirical studies both longitudinal and cross-sectional—of how individuals at various stages of the life course perceive and affectively respond to individuals, networks and institutions within their cognitive range; and (2) study of the networks themselves as they encompass, respond to, or reject individuals at various stages of the life course. These are both formidable tasks, and as Baltes (1973), Looft (1973), McCandless (1973), Neugarten and Datan (1973), and Riegel (in press) have made clear, they do not lend themselves to simplistic models. We are somewhat further along on the individual side of this nexus than we are on the social. Psychologists, social and otherwise, in the laboratory and outside of it, have studied individual variations in perceptions of and responses to their social milieux. While much of this work has been with young people, increasing attention is being paid to a life course perspective (Thomae, 1970). Few social scientists have studied this nexus using both the individual and the societal frames of reference. Exceptions are some anthropologists working mainly in non-Euro-American cultures (Clark and Anderson, 1967; Delaney, 1974; Epstein, 1961; Hannerz, 1969; Kiefer, 1974; Morioka, 1966; Sparks, 1975). From a more strictly theoretical framework we are now beginning to have access to a growing body of dialectic concepts involving the interplay between individual and societal histories as a basis for a theory of adult development and aging (Riegel, 1972a,b, 1973a,b).

The principal focus of this chapter is on psychosocial concepts stemming from developmental theorists working in frameworks of instinct theory, stage theory, and motivational theory. These can be subsumed in a general framework provisionally labeled commitment theory expanded to include the interplay between commitment and social context as the individual moves through the successive periods of adulthood and old age. While theories of personality development and sociostructural theories are relevant to a psychosocial theory, they are being covered in other chapters in this series of volumes (Neugarten, Chapter 26, Personality and Aging; Lowenthal and Robinson, 1976), and can only be acknowledged in passing in these few pages.

CONSTRUCTS FROM DEVELOPMENTAL STUDIES

Until recently, most longitudinal studies of adulthood originated in child development research, and tended to be rather firmly rooted in personality trait theory and classical, or neoclassical, psychoanalytic theory which postulates irrevocable consequences for the adult of what happened to him or her in early life. As these subjects grew older, and as other investigators began separately to study older children and adults, it became clear that the notion of unalterable personality characteristics irrevocably predetermined in the early stages was insufficient. Out of this recognition developed, for example, Erikson's formulations in respect to what are essentially developmental stages in *interpersonal commitment*, which move progressively from dyadic to more broadly inter personal to an almost pan-human level. This anchoring of the self in a historical and broad cultural framework, called integrity, Erikson views as one end of a continuum, the other being despair (Erikson, 1959). Like many stage theories, Erikson's has been difficult to test empirically (Gruen, 1964), though his studies of individuals (*Young Man Luther*, 1958; *Gandhi's Truth*, 1969) provide brilliant exegeses of the articulation between one person and his time and culture. Berezin (1963) has developed the concept of a consultative stage in later life, which he sees as a continuation of Erikson's generative stage but with less responsibility.

Kohlberg's essentially psychosocial theory of stages in the development of *moral commitment*, also an extension of research on children, has stood up fairly well to empirical study. The stages of moral development which he proposes, however, are not proving to be progressive in the classical sense of stage theory (Kohlberg and Kramer, 1969). It may well be that regression takes place at critical periods throughout the life course, and that for some people in some life stages it augurs further growth, while for others the regression may become permanent. Indeed cross-sectional studies of values report regressive tendencies at middle age and at the preretirement stage (Lowenthal, Thurnher, Chiriboga, and associates, 1975, Chapter 10). Such regression in later life may be adaptive in the sense that it is associated with higher levels of morale than is true for people adhering to their former, more altruistic, values.

A third set of psychosocial concepts growing out of theoretical and empirical work in child development is White's (1963) postulate of what he defines as an instinct, but at the very least is a need for effectance, which may be expressed as a *commitment to competence or mastery*. Some attention has already been given to this concept in the field of adult development and aging (Kuypers and Bengtson, 1973). Again, however, we need a two-pronged approach, involving on the one hand the perceptions of individuals in various stages of the life course in regard to their own competence, and their frames of reference for such self-assessment; and on the other hand, objective information about verbal and nonverbal feedback to the individual himself. Dissonance between the individual's assessment and that of his milieu may account, as Rosow (1974) has implied, for much voluntary segregation. This area of commitment holds much promise for future gerontological research, but only if it is broadened to include satisfactions of the mastery need on much less exalted levels than

those generally implied by self-realization theorists (Allport, [1937] 1961; Bühler, 1968; Maslow, 1962).

A fourth commitment must also be added if we are to adopt a life course perspective, and that is to physical, economic, and psychological survival, a *sine qua non* for all other commitments. Of course, some people at all life stages have as a primary need the maintenance of a sense of self and self-worth so acute that it interferes or prevents genuine commitments in the other three areas, but there is evidence that self-preservation with dignity may be a major and life-preserving commitment in very advanced old age.

FLUID CONSTRUCTS

Before elaborating on areas of commitment as one promising theoretical framework, a few "fluid" constructs should be taken into account in any model for the study of psychosocial change across the life course. One such is hope, and the closely related issue of sense of time, including direction of time-focus, and projection of the life span. A second is self-concept, of which the sense of personal control and the degree of preoccupation with stress are important components, especially for a life course perspective. These constructs are termed fluid because they are both antecedents to, and outcomes of, the individual's commitments at various life stages. To the extent that they are outcomes, that they change after a change in degree of fulfillment or frustration in any one of the commitment areas, they might also be construed as measures of adaptive level.

While hope has been largely relegated to philosophers, as love and intimacy have been to the poets, the recent work of Stotland (1969) is worth noting. While the author's formal theoretical statement and, less so, his subsequent elaborations, have a rather static quality, his propositions may well be operationalizable for studies across the life course. In such perspective, his concept of hope should be supplemented by analysis of its relation to time orientation and projection of time. We would thus be elaborating and refining the concept of hope, for as in Cassirer's words, "We cannot describe the momentary state of the organism without . . . referring it to a future state for which this state is merely a point of passage" (Cassirer, 1944, p. 50). Doob (1971), discussing time perspective within the context of drive, emphasizes that undue preoccupation with time is a form of anxiety. Drawing mainly from laboratory studies, and without assuming a life course perspective, he quotes MacIver to the effect that temporal anxiety numbs the freedom to live, presumably at all life stages (MacIver, 1962). In field rather than laboratory based studies, especially of older people, it might well be more appropriate to reverse Doob's order and study drives (and goals) within the context of time orientation, rather than vice versa. There are some hints in cross-sectional data that both time focus and projections of age of probable death vary markedly (and rather unexpectedly) across the adult life course (Lowenthal, Thurnher, Chiriboga, and associates, 1975, Chapter 7). In yet unpublished follow-up data, both time focus and life span projection are found to vary over relatively short periods. We suspect, but cannot yet demonstrate, that these fluctuations are associated with change in satisfaction in one or more of the areas of commitment we are dealing with here.

The second "fluid" construct, that of self-concept, is also closely related to the spheres of commitment. As indicated in the works cited by Wylie (1961), and more recently in Gergen's work (1971), self-concept is not very precisely conceived, and the term is often used interchangeably with identity, self-esteem, and whatever is meant by ego strength. With some exceptions, as in the works of Haan (1970) and Loevinger and Wessler (1970), the area of cognitions and affects about the self is rather seriously deficient in analytic rigor. The question of consistency or inconsistency in self-concept across the life course and its effect on adaptation has been insufficiently studied. At one extreme is the not completely developed self-consistency theory of Lecky (1969); at the other is Lifton's idea that the best adapted people in our time and place are "Protean" types, constantly changing their public and self-images in an effort to adapt to accelerating social change (Lifton, [1967] 1969). In be-

tween these two extremes are some intriguing possibilities. For example, a former self may be the main referent for the quite elderly, and to reduce dissonance, this may be the self they endeavor to project through reminiscence. Landis' (1970) concept of ego boundaries may be relevant here, with inner boundaries (between past and present self) loose or diffuse, and in some way compensating for an increase in the impermeability of the boundary between the present self and others. This observer, at least, has often noted a tendency among the very old to project through reminiscence a former self (or referent self) corresponding to the life stage of whomever is present. Bengtson (1973), on the other hand, suggests that middle-aged others are the major reference group for the very old.

Despite theoretical and conceptual disagreements, however, whatever method is adopted for measuring self-concept or self-image generally yields meaningful results in studies across the adult life course (Clausen, 1972; Lowenthal, Thurnher, Chiriboga, and associates, 1975, Chapter 4). An especially important component of self-image from a life span perspective is the sense of the degree to which one feels in control of one's life (Brissett, 1972). Sense of control has been studied primarily in the laboratory, and these experiments are well reviewed, along with some pertinent survey research material and a few clinically based studies, in a recent paper by Brim (1974). A useful bibliography on the sense of personal control is the work of Throop and MacDonald (1971). A more recent study (Staats, 1974), indicates that the sense of internal control is more common for men than women, and that from childhood to age 60 it increases.

INDIVIDUAL COMMITMENT IN SOCIAL CONTEXT

Within each of the areas of commitment, to other individuals, to effectance in relation to the social and nonsocial environment, and to moral values (which are also in large part interpersonal), there are of course wide variations in degree of involvement as the young person emerges into adulthood. For now we have to leave it to the child developmentalist to explain how and why young adults vary in these three areas. The major task of a social psychology of aging is threefold: (a) to identify factors associated with change in the degree and nature of these commitments across the adult life course; (b) to measure the consequences for adaptive level of, respectively, frustration and fulfillment of these commitments at successive stages; and (c) to assess the extent to which fulfillment in one area may compensate for frustration in others. The issues are much too complex to propose a paradigm for such an inquiry at this stage of our knowledge, but this writer agrees with Riegel (1972b, 1973b) that any effective model will have to be a dialectic one.

The theoretical framework for the study of *interpersonal* commitment has a long history and is deeply rooted in classical and subsequent analytic theory, the interpersonal implications of which have been expanded into a more explicit interpersonal theory by Harry Stack Sullivan (1953). Since involvements in roles, groups, and networks are being thoroughly covered in a companion volume (Binstock and Shanas, 1976), here the focus will be primarily on dyadic relationships. An important question in this little-explored area is the extent to which different partners in a dyadic relationship may prove satisfying at successive stages of the life course. In earlier life stages, for example, the shift of interpersonal commitment from husband to child on the part of young mothers has been frequently observed. Cross-sectional study suggests that at the empty nest stage, mothers are often in conflict, and there may not only be an object shift in the offing, such as from child back to husband, but at least an inclination to move from interpersonal to mastery commitments, whereas the opposite is true for men (Neugarten and Gutmann, 1964). In any event, that the nature and intensity of the marital relationship changes across the adult life course has been well documented (Blood and Wolfe, 1960; Lowenthal, Thurnher, Chiriboga, and associates, 1975, Chapter 2). We have also been struck by the extent to which men and women, in reporting how they think their spouses would describe them, agree with each other at some life stages and disagree at

others. Blau (1961) suggests that among widowed women, same-sex friendships may satisfy the need for intimacy formerly fulfilled in marriage. For a variety of sociocultural reasons, this does not appear to be true of men in our society. This thesis runs counter to the rather prevalent concept, especially in the psychoanalytic literature, that men in our culture cannot derive a sense of being loved and worthy from a heterosexual relationship, because both men and women agree that men are the only valuable people (Miller, 1972).

Moral and altruistic commitments also constitute a promising focal point for exploring the nexus between the individual and researchable segments of his culture. Recently Kohlberg (1973) has delineated a new stage in his schema of moral development, one rather analagous to Erikson's stage of integrity, which may prove promising for studies including people in late life. Kohlberg's stages should be tested by methods in addition to the semi-projective ones which he uses, however, and certainly with older as well as young subjects. Samples should also cover a broader socioeconomic and cultural base to determine the extent to which his stages are more or less universal (Simpson, 1974).

The last stage of adulthood as Erikson sees it—integrity versus despair—seems to be the most *intra*personal of his life stages, one in which personal relationships tend to become symbolic. It involves coming to terms with one's self and one's prior interpersonal commitments and achievements, in the broader social and historical context. Such concepts seem appropriate for a Gandhi, a Luther, and Erikson himself, and not only find support in Erikson's studies of individuals (1963, 1969) but in autobiographies of gifted people (e.g., Roosevelt, 1961; Russell, 1969). These complex, almost philosophical concepts run contrary, as we have noted, to empirical data suggesting that the simple and self-protective types of individuals, and those whose values shift to the more hedonistic are those whose morale tends to be highest in later life. On the other hand, there is certainly at least anecdotal evidence in all walks of life that some kind of broad concept of integrity is a more appropriate measure of the sense of fulfillment in old age than are yardsticks of morale or happiness. Meanwhile, a number of rather concrete questions, answers to which would further contribute to theory building, should be pursued. For example, is the apparent age-linked increase in a hedonistic or "ease and contentment" value system associated with an increase in the amount of time spent with the media? Or, approaching Erikson's and Kohlberg's theses, how, in the language of the average individual, would a more cosmic or philosophical value be defined? Or will we find, as did Berenson at age 87, a certain relativity: "My values are not valuable enough to satisfy me if they are no longer valued by my fellow bipeds" (Berenson, 1963, p. 228). Berenson's observation offers beautiful support in both the moral and cognitive sphere for Riegel's insistence that the concept of dialectic stages is essential for an adult life course perspective (Riegel, 1973b).

As to *commitment to mastery* or competence, much of the relevant work has been done by scholars for whom an adult life course perspective is not necessarily the primary orientation. In the work context, the research of Chinoy (1955) is a classic, and to some extent does have a life course orientation. Subsequent studies by Soddy and Kidson (1967), Rapoport (1970), and Wilensky (1964) indicate, as does the Chinoy study, that the loss of the sense of control over the work milieu (or the recognition that one never has had it and doubtless never will) is a critical issue. While there are apparently no comparable studies of working women, there is evidence that the lack of a sense of control becomes critical for family-oriented women as their children begin to leave home, even among those who work outside the home. Indeed, in a study of people of both sexes in pre-transitional stages of the adult life course, the subjective sense of being in control of at least some aspects of the stage they were about to enter proved to be the most salient of four dimensions of the stance toward the expected transition (Lowenthal, Thurnher, Chiriboga, and associates, 1975, Chapter 11). The next and much-needed step is to learn much more about the individual's perception of internal and situational cues which induce the sense of loss of mastery or control, and whether the ratio of internal to external cues varies across the adult life course.

Turning to the largely ignored question of the interchangeability of satisfactory channels for expression within a given area of commitment, in this case mastery, competence, or creativity, a report from a longitudinal study originally centered primarily on the prediction of later adaptation from early personality traits is highly provocative. It turned out that rather than personality characteristics, it was the way free time was used in childhood that proved to be highly predictive of adaptation in later life (Brooks and Elliott, 1971). These were, or became, largely middle and upper middle class subjects who no doubt had a rather wide margin of flexibility in their work and leisure careers as adults, and might well have been satisfying their commitment to competence in both areas. By the same token we would expect that after retirement their leisure outlets would meet this need, formerly met through work as well. It may be, as Wilensky's (1961) review of organizational participation suggests, and a more recent cross-national study documents (Havighurst and de Vries, 1969), that the extent to which mastery needs are met through the uses of free time are at least as closely linked to class as they are to life stage. Indeed, were we to limit our concepts of commitment to competence to work achievement (McClelland, 1961), which we expressly wish to *avoid* in a life course perspective, we would no doubt be forced to conclude that it is indeed to a considerable extent class-linked (Lowenthal and Robinson, 1976).

While Gutmann (1969), on the basis of largely cross-cultural research among older men, conceives a continuum of mastery ranging from active to passive to magical, recent work on several life stages reveals dramatic sex differences (Lowenthal, Thurnher, Chiriboga, and associates, 1975). Among women the developmental trend appears to be from passive to active, but we do find some support for Gutmann's thesis among men—a trend from active to passive, although there are significant exceptions. These subjects are not yet old enough to have reached Gutmann's stage of "magical mastery" (a concept developed primarily from his studies of other cultures), but in earlier research, which included the very old, the people who fit the "magical mastery" category were the relatively few suffering from paranoid disorders, in turn often linked to chronic brain damage (Simon, Lowenthal, and Epstein, 1970).

Creativity may be viewed as the optimal form of commitment to mastery. This field is too vast and complex adequately to be reviewed here. Suffice it to say that, as studied among adults, creativity also appears to be class linked. In fact Maslow ([1954] 1970) had difficulty recruiting a cross-sectional group of "self-actualizing" subjects, and his eventual sample turned out to be primarily middle and upper class. In some cultures, in fact, degree of creativity appears in part to be socially defined by caste or status (Maduro, 1974, in press). There have also been some studies of productivity and creativity by age (Butler, 1967; Kogan, 1973; Dennis, 1966; Lehman, 1946). If we wish to avoid developing elitest theories, future research should be based on much more flexible definitions of creativity, as, for instance, are Barron's (1963). We also need to learn much more about the *subjective* sense of being creative and how it varies across the life course among people from all social strata.

Studies of work and leisure involvements, as well as those of creativity, implicitly acknowledge that the individual's need for mastery, or, in White's terms, effectance, has social components and probably social determinants as well. The need for feedback has been richly confirmed in the biographies and autobiographies of artists of all types. But except for this articulate and often elite source, we know almost nothing about the extent and nature of the interpersonal, or more broadly social, reinforcement needed to sustain the sense of competence among ordinary people, the ways in which the amount or nature of such social reassurance may change across the life course, and how it differs between men and women.

Turning more specifically to an adult life course perspective on commitment, the studies of McClelland (1961) have demonstrated that by early adulthood, males in our culture have some degree of potentially measurable commitment to or drive toward mastery which expresses itself through ambitions largely manifest in planning for a work career. Women have been largely ignored in these studies. Although relatively little analytic rigor has been applied to leisure commitments (as contrasted to leisure activity) the works of both de Grazia (1964) and Dumazedier (1967) are at least a start. They remain, however, a long way from answering the question posed by Havighurst (1961) and Lipset and Bendix (1959) about the extent to which mastery outlets in leisure are as gratifying as those of work. Neither de Grazia nor Dumazedier assumes a life course perspective, but there is an implicit assumption that predilections are well established by early adulthood. A more recent study (Lowenthal, Thurnher, Chiriboga, and associates, 1975, Chapter 1) suggests that high school seniors and newlyweds are nearly as active in exploring leisure styles and commitments as they are in exploring potential work commitments, though this is far more true of young men than of young women, at least in the middle and lower middle class being reported on. Most young adults have also attained a strong interpersonal commitment or commitments. In Erikson's terms, ideally they have established a mutual and intimate relationship with a person of the opposite sex, though how to assess commitments in the interpersonal sphere is a considerably thornier issue than, say, would be a measure of commitment to work.

As Kohlberg's previously mentioned studies demonstrate, young adults may also be classified on one or another level of moral development, levels which have proven to be at least partially measurable, though this reviewer is not convinced that Kohlberg's semi-projective situations actually reflect moral stages as he defines them. And the even more complex issue of the relationship between acknowledged moral values—which generally involve one's relations with others or to the broader society—and behavior has barely been touched.

By middle age, it has been suggested that, for both social and psychological reasons, there is a tendency to begin to constrict oneself in regard to mastery commitments (Pearce and Newton, 1963). This confirms our own findings in regard to middle-aged men who seemed to be moving away from mastery and toward interpersonal commitments. Few women in this study reflected this trend; on the contrary, they were reaching out for more self-assertion, but at the same time were frustrated about the opportunities for doing so in our time and society (Lowenthal, 1975). In short, both sexes reported a felt need for a strengthening of commitment in an area other than the one to which their normative sex roles had bound them, thus lending empirical support to Jung's thesis that the second half of life makes up for, or balances, the first (1933, 1957, 1960). Perhaps to reach Erikson's postulated stage of integrity both sexes have to have a sense of fulfillment in both interpersonal and mastery commitments, if not simultaneously then successively. In so saying, of course, I have contradicted myself and proposed a rather global developmental hypothesis, with a different sequence for women than for men, but it is premature because of deficiencies in the concept of mastery, and in the methods by which it is measured.

The constructs of moral development and mastery imply commitment, and in the interpersonal sphere, it has already been demonstrated that commitment to others as reflected in having a confidant and in a capacity for mutuality become increasingly important resources across the life course and far into old age (Lowenthal and Haven, 1968; Lowenthal, 1975). While one might propose that commitments in these three areas are essential for a well-rounded person, in keeping with a kind of balance theory of adaptation (Lowenthal, Thurnher, Chiriboga, and associates, 1975, Chapter 6), it is also probable that strengths in any one may offset deficiencies in the others.

The fourth area of commitment, to survival or self-protectiveness, might perhaps be viewed as merely lack of commitment in any of the other three areas, but though little studied it appears to have a strong motivational component and one of obvious importance in advanced old age. As Williams and Wirths (1965) have suggested, however, it is for some a way of life and one adopted very early. They call it "Easing Through Life with Minimum Involvement," and they found, as we did in a study of elderly San Franciscans (Lowenthal, 1964), that

men are more likely to adopt this style than women. This is contrary to the clinical observations of Moulton (1972) who reports that it is more common among women, partly because of sociocultural norms sanctioning dependency for them. Our own recent study of the values and goals of people at four stages of the adult life course (Lowenthal, Thurnher, Chiriboga, and associates, 1975) suggests a marked age-linked trend toward this kind of commitment in the middle and lower middle class and especially for men, but whether it is indeed a developmental trend is a question that must await analysis of the longitudinal data. No theoretical formulations or empirical studies that we know of have developed either clear concepts, descriptive categories or methodological approaches to the issue of self-protectiveness as a major commitment. It is occasionally touched upon tangentially in the psychoanalytic literature, sometimes in the context of dependency needs, and, at the other extreme, implied by clinicians who often mention the importance of "the will to live" but have never defined it. This writer is convinced that the commitment to self-protectiveness is a major factor in survival in very old age, and perhaps for certain severely disturbed neurotics or borderline psychotics throughout life, and that it warrants serious analytic and phenomenological attention.

While the four areas of commitment suggest a promising approach to the development of a possible framework for studying psychosocial change in the adult life course, we have analytic and methodological tasks to complete before all four of them can be simultaneously explored. The simultaneity is essential, because the challenging question for a life course perspective is whether there are developmental changes in area of commitment.

One of our tasks is to master the complex problem of relationship between commitment and attitudes on the one hand and behavior on the other. In old age, in particular, commitment without action may be a resource—especially if past behavior in the area has been rewarding. On the other hand, if a strong commitment persists and past experience in the area has not been satisfying, whether for psychological or environmental reasons, the mere persistence of the sense of commitment may become a handicap, because of the restriction in possibilities offered by the environment for continuation or restitution of commitment-connected behavior. If there are still involvements in other commitment areas, these may allow for some satisfactory substitution.

In summary, there is as yet no integrated sociopsychological theory of aging. Impressive contributions have been made by theorists, who are essentially extending the trait, personality, and stage theories of child development beyond adolescence. Some of them, notably Erikson and more recently Riegel, are making important strides toward integrating individual, developmental change with the normative social changes which take place as the individual moves across the life course, and with the broader societal changes of his particular era. Starting from the other dimension of this complex process, we have sociologists as Blau, Brim, Cumming, Maddox, Riley, Rosow, Shanas, and Streib taking increasing cognizance of personal factors as important mediators between sociostructural factors and adaptation (Lowenthal and Robinson, 1976). In between is the integrative work in the sociopsychological (Harvard and University of Chicago) tradition exemplified in the studies of Kohlberg and Neugarten, of the group at the University of California, San Francisco, and to an increasing extent, of the Institute of Human Development at the University of California, Berkeley. In the field of adult development and aging these are tentative foundations on which eventually to erect a theory or theories of psychosocial change across the life course. One of the theses of this chapter is that we are now ready to begin to incorporate further building blocks drawn from theorists and empiricists who have not necessarily addressed themselves to processes of change across the adult life course.

REFERENCES

Allport, G. W. (1937) 1961. *Pattern and Growth in Personality*. New York: Holt, Rinehart and Winston.

Arnhoff, F. N., and Lorge, I. 1960. Stereotypes about aging and the aged. *School and Society*, 88 (2167), 70–71.

Axelrod, S., and Eisdorfer, C. 1961. Attitudes towards old people: An empirical analysis of the stimulus-group validity of the Tuckman-Lorge questionnaire. *J. Gerontol.*, 16 (1), 75–80.

Baltes, P. B. (ed.) 1973. Life-span models of psychological aging: A white elephant? *Gerontologist*, 13 (4), 457–512.

Barron, F. 1963. *Creativity and Psychological Health*. Princeton, New Jersey: D. Van Nostrand.

Bengtson, V. L. 1973. *The Social Psychology of Aging*. Indianapolis: Bobbs-Merrill.

Bennett, R., and Eckman, J. 1973. Attitudes toward aging: A critical examination of recent literature and implications for future research. *In*, C. Eisdorfer and M. P. Lawton (eds.), *The Psychology of Adult Development and Aging*, pp. 575–597. Washington, D.C.: American Psychiatric Association.

Berenson, B. 1963. *Sunset and Twilight: From the Diaries of 1947–1958* (edited by N. Mariano). New York: Harcourt, Brace and World.

Berezin, M. A. 1963. Some intrapsychic aspects of aging. *In*, N. E. Zinberg and I. Kaufman (eds.), *Normal Psychology of the Aging Process*, pp. 93–117. New York: International Universities Press.

Binstock, R. H., and Shanas, E. (eds.) 1976. *Handbook of Aging and the Social Sciences*. New York: Van Nostrand Reinhold.

Birren, J. E. 1964. *The Psychology of Aging*. Englewood Cliffs, New Jersey: Prentice-Hall.

Birren, J. E., Butler, R. M., Greenhouse, S. W., Sokoloff, L., and Yarrow, M. R. (eds.) 1963. *Human Aging: A Biological and Behavioral Study*. Washington, D.C.: Government Printing Office (Public Health Service Bulletin No. 986).

Blau, D. 1961. The role of community physicians in the psychiatric hospitalization of aged patients. Unpublished manuscript read at the 14th Annual Meeting of the Gerontological Society, Pittsburgh, Pennsylvania.

Blau, D. 1966. Psychiatric hospitalization of the aged. *Geriatrics*, 21, 204–210.

Blood, R. O., Jr., and Wolfe, D. M. 1960. *Husbands and Wives: The Dynamics of Married Living*. New York: The Free Press.

Botwinick, J. 1973. *Aging and Behavior*. New York: Springer.

Brim, O. G., Jr. 1974. The sense of personal control over one's life. Invited address, 82nd Annual Convention of the American Psychological Association, New Orleans.

Brissett, D. 1972. Toward a clarification of self-esteem. *Psychiatry*, 35 (3), 255–263.

Brooks, J. B., and Elliott, D. M. 1971. Prediction of psychological adjustment at age thirty from leisure time activities and satisfactions in childhood. *Hum. Develop.*, 14 (1), 51–61.

Bühler, C. 1968. The general structure of the human life cycle. *In*, C. Bühler and F. Massarik (eds.), *The Course of Human Life: A Study of Goals in the Humanistic Perspective*, pp. 12–26. New York: Springer.

Busse, E. W., and Pfeiffer, E. (eds.) 1969. *Behavior and Adaptation in Late Life*. Boston: Little, Brown.

Butler, R. N. 1967. The destiny of creativity in later life: Studies of creative people and the creative process. *In*, S. Levin and R. J. Kahana (eds.), *Psychodynamic Studies on Aging: Creativity, Reminiscing, and Dying*, pp. 20-63. New York: International Universities Press.

Carp, F. M. 1968. Some components of disengagement. *J. Gerontol.*, 23 (3), 382-386.

Cassirer, E. 1944. *An Essay on Man*. New Haven: Yale University Press.

Chinoy, E. 1955. *Automobile Workers and the American Dream*. New York: Random House.

Clark, M., and Anderson, B. G. 1967. *Culture and Aging*. Springfield, Illinois: Charles C. Thomas.

Clausen, J. A. 1972. The life course of individuals. *In*, M. White Riley, M. Johnson, and A. Foner (eds.), *Aging and Society, Vol. Three: A Sociology of Age Stratification*, pp. 457-514. New York: Russell Sage Foundation.

Coelho, G. V., Hamburg, D. A., and Adams, J. E. 1974. *Coping and Adaptation*. New York: Basic Books.

Cumming, E. 1968. New thoughts on the theory of disengagement. *Int. J. of Psychiatry*, 6 (1), 53-67.

Cumming, E., and Henry, W. E. 1961. *Growing Old: The Process of Disengagement*. New York: Basic Books.

Cyrus-Lutz, C., and Gaitz, C. M. 1972. Psychiatrists' attitudes toward the aged and aging. *Gerontologist*, 12 (2), 163-167.

de Grazia, S. 1964. *Of Time, Work, and Leisure*. Garden City, New York: Doubleday (Anchor).

Delaney, W. P. 1974. The cultural structure of disengagement in Thai society. Unpublished manuscript read at the 27th Annual Meeting of the Gerontological Society, Portland, Oregon.

Dennis, W. 1966. Creative productivity between the ages of 20 and 80 years. *J. Gerontol.*, 21 (1), 1-8.

Doob, L. W. 1971. *Patterning of Time*. New Haven: Yale University Press.

Dumazedier, J. 1967. *Toward a Society of Leisure*. New York: The Free Press.

Eisdorfer, C., and Lawton, M. P. (eds.) 1973. *The Psychology of Adult Development and Aging*. Washington, D.C.: American Psychological Association.

Epstein, A. L. 1961. The network and urban social organization. *Rhodes-Livingston Journal*, 29, 29-62.

Erikson, E. H. 1958. *Young Man Luther, A Study in Psychoanalysis and History*. New York: W. W. Norton.

Erikson, E. H. 1959. *Identity and the Life-Cycle*. *Psychological Issues*, 1 (1), Monograph 1. New York: International Universities Press.

Erikson, E. H. 1963. *Childhood and Society*. 2nd Edition. New York: W. W. Norton.

Erikson, E. H. 1968. *Identity: Youth and Crisis*. New York: W. W. Norton.

Erikson, E. H. 1969. *Gandhi's Truth*. New York: W. W. Norton.

Gergen, K. J. 1971. *The Concept of Self*. New York: Holt, Rinehart and Winston.

Gruen, W. 1964. Adult personality: An empirical study of Erikson's theory of ego development. *In*, B. L. Neugarten and associates, *Personality in Middle and Late Life*, pp. 1-14. New York: Atherton Press.

Gutmann, D. L. 1969. *The Country of Old Men: Cultural Studies in the Psychology of Later Life*. Occasional Papers in Gerontology, No. 5. Institute of Gerontology, Ann Arbor: University of Michigan-Wayne State University.

Haan, N. 1970. Personality and intellectual changes in adulthood. *In*, J. Aronfreed and others, *Developmental Psychology Today*, pp. 465-482. Del Mar, California: CRM Books.

Hannerz, U. 1969. *Soulside: Inquiries into Ghetto Culture and Community*. New York: Columbia University Press.

Havighurst, R. J. 1961. The nature and values of meaningful free-time activity. *In*, R. W. Kleemeier (ed.), *Aging and Leisure*, pp. 309-344. New York: Oxford University Press.

Havighurst, R. J., and Albrecht, R. 1953. *Older people*. New York: Longmans, Green.

Havighurst, R. J. and deVries, A. 1969. Life styles and free time activities of retired men. *Hum. Develop.*, 12 (1), 34-54.

Havighurst, R. J., Munnichs, J. M. A., Neugarten, B., and Thomae, H. 1969. *Adjustment to Retirement: A Cross-National Study*. 2nd Edition. Assen, The Netherlands: Van Gorkum.

Havighurst, R. J., Neugarten, B. L., and Tobin, S. S. 1968. Disengagement and patterns of aging. *In*, B. L. Neugarten (ed.), *Middle Age and Aging*, pp. 161-177. Chicago: University of Chicago Press.

Henry, W. E. 1965. Engagement and disengagement: Toward a theory of adult development. *In*, R. Kastenbaum (ed.), *Contributions to the Psycho-Biology of Aging*, pp. 19-35. New York: Springer.

Horowitz, M. J., and Becker, S. S. 1972. Cognitive response to stress: Experimental studies of a "compulsion to repeat trauma." *Psychoanalysis and Contemporary Science*, 1, 258-305.

Jung, C. G. 1933. *Modern Man in Search of a Soul*. New York: Harcourt, Brace and World (Harvest Paperback).

Jung, C. G. 1957. *The Undiscovered Self*. New York: Mentor Paperback.

Jung, C. G. 1960. *On the Nature of the Psyche*. New Jersey: Princeton University Press, Bollingen Series.

Katz, D. 1967. Group process and social integration: A system analysis of two movements of social protest. *J. Soc. Issues*, 23 (1), 3-22.

Kiefer, C. W. 1974. *Changing Cultures, Changing Lives: An Ethnographic Study of Three Generations of Japanese Americans*. San Francisco: Jossey-Bass.

Kleemeier, R. W. 1964. Leisure and disengagement in retirement. *Gerontologist*, 4 (4), 180-184.

Kogan, N. 1973. Creativity and cognitive style: A life-span perspective. *In*, P. B. Baltes and K. W. Schaie (eds.), *Life-Span Developmental Psychology*, pp. 145–178. New York: Academic Press.

Kohlberg, L. 1973. Continuities in childhood and adult moral development revisited. *In*, P. B. Baltes and K. W. Schaie (eds), *Life-Span Developmental Psychology*, pp. 179–204. New York: Academic Press.

Kohlberg, L., and Kramer, R. 1969. Continuities and discontinuities in childhood and adult moral development. *Hum. Develop.*, **12**, 93–120.

Kuhlen, R. G. 1968. Developmental changes in motivation during the adult years. *In*, B. L. Neugarten (ed.), *Middle Age and Aging*, pp. 115–136. Chicago: University of Chicago Press.

Kuypers, J. A., and Bengtson, V. L. 1973. Social breakdown and competence: A model of normal aging. *Hum. Develop.*, **16** (3), 181–201.

Landis, B. 1970. *Ego Boundaries. Psychological Issues*, **6** (4), Monograph 24. New York: International Universities Press.

Lazarus, R. S. 1970. Cognitive and personality factors underlying threat and coping. *In*, S. Levine and N. A. Scotch (eds.), *Social Stress*, pp. 143–164. Chicago: Aldine.

Lecky, P. 1969. *Self-Consistency: A Theory of Personality*. Garden City, New York: Doubleday (Anchor).

Lehman, H. C. 1946. The age of eminent leaders: Then and now. *Am. J. Sociol.*, **52** (1), 342–356.

Lehr, U., and Rudinger, G. 1969. Consistency and change of social participation in old age. *Hum. Develop.*, **12** (4), 255–267.

Lifton, R. J. (1967) 1969. *Boundaries: Psychological Man in Revolution*. New York: Random House (Vintage Books).

Lipman, A., and Smith, K. J. 1968. Functionality of disengagement in old age. *J. Gerontol.*, **23** (4), 517–521.

Lipset, S. M., and Bendix, R. 1959. *Social Mobility in Industrial Society*. Berkeley: University of California Press.

Loeb, R. 1973. Disengagement, activity, or maturity? *Sociol. and Soc. Res.*, **57** (3), 367–382.

Loevinger, J., and Wessler, R. 1970. *Measuring Ego Development*, Vol. 1. San Francisco: Jossey-Bass.

Looft, W. R. 1973. Socialization and personality throughout the life span: An examination of contemporary psychological approaches. *In*, P. B. Baltes and K. W. Schaie (eds.), *Life-Span Developmental Psychology*, pp. 25–52. New York: Academic Press.

Lowenthal, M. F. 1964. Social isolation and mental illness in old age. *Am. Soc. Rev.*, **29** (1), 54–70.

Lowenthal, M. F. 1975. Psychosocial variations across the adult life course: Frontiers for research and policy. *Gerontologist*, **15** (1), Part 1 6–12.

Lowenthal, M. F., Berkman, P. L., and associates 1967. *Aging and Mental Disorder in San Francisco: A Social Psychiatric Study*. San Francisco: Jossey-Bass.

Lowenthal, M. F., and Boler, D. 1965. Voluntary vs. involuntary social withdrawal. *J. Gerontol.*, **20**, 363–371.

Lowenthal, M. F., and Haven, C. 1968. Interaction and adaptation: Intimacy as a critical variable. *Am. Soc. Rev.*, **33** (1), 20–30.

Lowenthal, M. F., and Robinson, B. 1976. Social networks and isolation. *In*, R. H. Binstock and E. Shanas (eds.), *Handbook of Aging and the Social Sciences*, pp. 432–456. New York: Van Nostrand Reinhold.

Lowenthal, M. F., Thurnher, M., Chiriboga, D., and associates 1975. *Four Stages of Life: A Comparative Study of Women and Men Facing Transitions*. San Francisco: Jossey-Bass.

MacIver, R. M. 1962. *The Challenge of the Passing Years: My Encounter with Time*. New York: Simon and Schuster.

Maddox, G. L. 1963. Activity and morale: A longitudinal study of selected elderly subjects. *Soc. Forces*, **42** (2), 195–204.

Maddox, G. L. 1964. Disengagement theory: A critical evaluation. *Gerontologist*, **4** (2), Part 1, 80–82, 103.

Maddox, G. L. 1965. Fact and artifact: Evidence bearing on disengagement theory from the Duke Geriatrics Project. *Hum. Develop.*, 8 (2-3), 117–130.

Maddox, G. L. 1970. Themes and issues in sociological theories of aging. *Hum. Develop.*, **13** (1), 17–27.

Maduro, R. 1974. Artistic creativity and aging in India. *Int. J. Aging and Hum. Devel.*, **5** (4), 303–329.

Maduro, R. Artistic creativity and Brahmin ethnicity in India. South and Southeast Asia Research Monograph Number 14. Berkeley: University of California Press. In press.

Maslow, A. H. 1962. *Toward a Psychology of Being*. New York: Van Nostrand Reinhold. (Revised Edition, 1968).

Maslow, A. H. (1954) 1970. *Motivation and Personality*. New York: Harper.

McCandless, B. R. 1973. Symposium discussion: Life-span models of psychological aging. *Gerontologist*, **13** (4), 511–512.

McClelland, D. C. 1961. *The Achieving Society*. Princeton, New Jersey: D. Van Nostrand.

Miller, J. B. 1972. Sexual inequality: Men's dilemma. *Am. J. Psychoanal.*, **32** (2), 147–155.

Morioka, K. 1966. Life cycle patterns in Japan, China, and the United States. Paper presented at the 6th World Congress of Sociology, Tokyo.

Moulton, R. 1972. Psychoanalytic reflections on women's liberation. *Contemporary Psychoanalysis*, **8** (2), 197–223.

Neugarten, B. L., and Datan, N. 1973. Sociological perspectives on the life cycle. *In*, P. B. Baltes and K. W. Schaie (eds.), *Life-Span Developmental Psychology*, pp. 53–69. New York: Academic Press.

Neugarten, B. L., and Gutmann, D. L. 1964. Age-sex roles and personality in middle age: A thematic apperception study. *In*, B. L. Neugarten and associates, *Personality in Middle and Late Life*, pp. 44–89. New York: Atherton Press.

Neugarten, B. L., Moore, J. W., and Lowe, J. C. 1968. Age norms, age constraints, and adult socialization. *In*, B. L. Neugarten (ed.), *Middle Age and Aging*, pp. 22–28. Chicago: University of Chicago Press.

Pearce, J., and Newton, S. 1963. *The Conditions of Human Growth*. New York: Citadel Press.

Rapoport, R. N. 1970. *Mid-Career Development*. London: Tavistock.

Reichard, S., Livson, F., and Peterson, P. G. 1962. *Aging and Personality: A Study of 87 Older Men*. New York: John Wiley.

Riegel, K. F. 1972a. The changing individual in the changing society. *Determinants of Behavioral Development*, pp. 239–257. New York: Academic Press.

Riegel, K. F. 1972b. Influence of economic and political ideologies on the development of developmental psychology. *Psych. Bull.*, 78 (2), 129–141.

Riegel, K. F. 1973a. An epitaph for a paradigm. *Hum. Develop.*, 16 (1-2), 1–7.

Riegel, K. F. 1973b. Dialectic operations: The final period of cognitive development. *Hum. Develop.*, 16, 346–370.

Riegel, K. F. From traits and equilibrium toward developmental dialectics. *In*, W. J. Arnold and J. K. Cole (eds.), *1974-75 Nebraska Symposium on Motivation*. Lincoln: University of Nebraska. In press.

Roosevelt, E. 1961. *This is My Story*. Garden City, New York: Doubleday (Dolphin Books).

Rosow, I. 1967. *Social Integration of the Aged*. New York: The Free Press.

Rosow, I. 1974. *Socialization to Old Age*. Berkeley: University of California Press.

Russell, B. 1969. *The Autobiography of Bertrand Russell 1944-1969*, Vol. 3. New York: Simon and Schuster.

Simon, A., Lowenthal, M. F., and Epstein, L. 1970. *Crisis and Intervention: The Fate of the Elderly Mental Patient*. San Francisco: Jossey-Bass.

Simpson, E. L. 1974. Moral development research. A case study of scientific cultural bias. *Hum. Develop.*, 17, (2), 81–106.

Soddy, K., and Kidson, M. C. 1967. *Men in Middle Life*. Philadelphia. J. B. Lippincott

Sparks, D. E. 1975. The still rebirth: Retirement and role discontinuity. *In*, D. W. Plath (ed.), *Adult Epi-*

sodes in Japan, *J. of Asian and African Studies*, 10 (1-2), 64–74.

Spence, D. L., Feigenbaum, E. M., Fitzgerald, F., and Roth, J. 1968. Medical student attitudes toward the geriatric patient. *J. Am. Geriat. Soc.*, 16, 976–983.

Staats, S., and the 1972 Experimental Psychology Class 1974. Internal versus external locus of control for three age groups. *Int. J. Aging Hum. Devel.*, 5 (1), 7–10.

Stotland, E. 1969. *The Psychology of Hope*. San Francisco: Jossey-Bass.

Stouffer, S. A., and others (eds.) 1949. *The American Soldier, Studies in Social Psychology in World War II*. Princeton, N.J.: Princeton University Press.

Sullivan, H. S. 1953. *The Interpersonal Theory of Psychiatry* (edited by H. S. Perry and M. L. Gawel). New York: W. W. Norton.

Taber, M. 1965. Application of research findings to the issues of social policy. *In*, A. M. Rose and W. A. Peterson, *Older People and Their Social World*, pp. 367–379. Philadelphia: F. A. Davis.

Tallmer, M., and Kutner B. 1969. Disengagement and the stresses of aging. *J. Gerontol.*, 24 (1), 70–75.

Thomae, H. 1970. Theory of aging and cognitive theory of personality. *Hum. Develop.*, 13, 1–16.

Throop, W. F., and MacDonald, A. P., Jr. 1971. Internal-external locus of control: A bibliography. *Psych. Reports*, 28, 175–190.

Tibbitts, C. (ed.) 1960. *Handbook of Social Gerontology*. Chicago: University of Chicago Press.

White, R. W. 1963. Ego and Reality in Psychoanalytic Theory. *Psychological Issues*, 3 (3), Monograph 11. New York: International Universities Press.

Wilensky, H. L. 1961. Life cycle, work situation, and participation in formal associations. *In*, R. W. Kleemeier (ed.), *Aging and Leisure*, pp. 213–242. New York: Oxford University Press.

Wilensky, H. L. 1964. Varieties of work experience. *In*, H. Borow (ed.), *Man in a World at Work*, pp. 125–154. Boston: Houghton Mifflin.

Williams, R. H. 1960. Changing status, roles, and relationships. *In*, C. Tibbitts (ed.), *Handbook of Social Gerontology*, pp. 261–297. Chicago: University of Chicago Press.

Williams, R. H., and Wirths, C. G. 1965. *Lives Through the Years*. New York: Atherton Press.

Wylie, R. C. 1961. *The Self Concept: A Critical Survey of Pertinent Research Literature*. Lincoln: University of Nebraska Press.

7
TOWARD PSYCHOLOGICAL THEORIES OF AGING AND DEVELOPMENT

Paul B. Baltes
and
Sherry L. Willis
Pennsylvania State University

INTRODUCTION

Efforts at theory construction occur in a context of scientific and cultural history (Coan, 1968, 1970; Kuhn, 1970; Merton, 1975; Riegel, 1972, 1973a, b) and are embedded in metatheoretical postures and arguments (Marx and Hillix, 1973; Reese and Overton, 1970; Wolman, 1973). From a pessimistic stance, therefore, an exposition on psychological theories of aging may be regarded as a Sisyphean task. First, theories are never complete or ultimate, nor has the field of psychological aging yet reached a stage of scientific development where theoretical positions are sufficiently accentuated to warrant more than the label of prototheories. Second, the *Zeitgeist* in psychology is not one of comprehensive, unitary, monistic theory building but one of pluralism dealing with the formulation of diverse and domain-specific miniature theories. To paraphrase Berger and Lambert (1968, p. 82), psychological theories do not stand serene, complete, and unchallenged at some high level of abstraction. They are part of a dynamic and pluralistic exchange between scientists and their efforts to represent a complex and continuously changing phenomenon.

It is our belief that the present state of theoretical pluralism and of metatheoretical and metamethodological concern reflected by psychology as a whole is not the mirror of a sad state of affairs or a dilemma, either for psychological theories in general or for psychological theories of aging and development. On the contrary, our position is that the present scientific forum is one which allows for novel formulations and allocations of scientific resources. The field of gerontological psychology can benefit from this context if we make explicit efforts to participate in the making of psychology. In this way, research on psychological aging can maximize its contribution both as a basic field of inquiry in its own right and as a forum for research within the conceptual framework of established theories in other areas of psychology (Birren, 1960).

The focus of this chapter, therefore, is on metatheory and a comparative analysis of major theoretical positions. This vantage point is similar to the ones taken earlier by Bromley (1970), Reese and Overton (1970), and Baltes (1973b). Specific theories or models of psychological aging and development will be mentioned only if these are relevant to the purpose of metatheoretical and comparative discourse. Readers interested in summaries of specific theoretical positions may want to consult various review chapters in the *Annual Review of Psychology* (Birren, 1960; Botwinick, 1970; Chown and Heron, 1965; Schaie and Gribbin, 1975), introductory texts (Birren, 1964a; Botwinick, 1973; Bromley, 1974; Kimmel, 1974; Lehr, 1972), edited review volumes (Baltes and Schaie, 1973a; Eisdorfer and Lawton, 1973; Goulet and Baltes, 1970; Talland, 1968), collections of readings (Chown, 1972; Neugarten, 1968a; Thomae and Lehr, 1968), and the remaining chapters in the present volume.

NATURE OF SCIENTIFIC THEORY

Objectives of Theory

Marx (1970) maintained that theory may be viewed as having two major complementary functions: It serves as a *tool* in the process of knowledge generation, and it is a *goal* of science with the implication that there is an ultimate, ideal level of knowledge represented in a theory. This distinction is useful from a didactic viewpoint. It breaks down, however, if one asserts that there is no final stage of knowledge and that knowledge is part of a dynamic, interactive system involving persons and events. With Marx and Hillix (1973, p. 3), the idea that science is not a personal but "many-sided social enterprise" is emphasized.

In the effort to organize a system of statements about objects and events, three interrelated key objectives of science are the center of attention: (a) *knowledge generation*, (b) *knowledge dissemination*, and (c) *knowledge utilization.* *

*Traditionally, the position taken on science development has been to assign primary weight to the generation and dissemination of knowledge as they flow from perspectives which are largely internal to a given theory. The intent of the present argument, asserting that knowledge utilization (in a general sense to include non-scientists) is a valid third component of theory building and evaluation, is not to downgrade the role of basic research or the traditional significance placed on a permissive context for the activity of basic researchers (see also Rozeboom, 1970, p. 74). On the contrary, we believe that an atmosphere for "basic" research is an important condition for stimulating advances in knowledge generation. The argument, however, is that aspects of knowledge utilization transcend the realm of

Conceptualizing science as an intrinsically social rather than purely academic enterprise is not generally accepted. The major implications of viewing science as a social enterprise are that the structure and function of science are not invariant but subject to complex changes with time. Furthermore, it is asserted that there is never a final set of prescriptions which defines what is scientific and what is not. As a corollary, our interpretation is that science is judged by criteria of usefulness, not only internal to the logic of the scientific method, but also external to the scientific method and related to the social context in which science occurs. In other words, our view is that science involves aspects of both knowledge generation *and* knowledge application.

The formulation and evaluation of theories are seen as being helpful or even critical to each of the three interrelated tasks involved in the making of science: knowledge generation, knowledge dissemination, and knowledge utilization. The criteria for what constitutes a theory and what represents an acceptable format of theory construction are part of the domain of the philosophy of science. Excellent reviews aimed at applying generic perspectives on theories and theory construction to the field of developmental psychology and aging are those by Bromley (1970), Langer (1969), and Reese and Overton (Overton and Reese, 1973; Reese and Overton, 1970). It is a widely held belief that there are several legitimate and useful types of theories and strategies of theory construction (see also Royce, 1970; Rozeboom, 1970).

Construction and Evaluation of Theory

Scientific theories form a deductive system. A "theory" is a set of statements including (a) general laws and principles that serve as axioms or assumptions, (b) other laws which are deduc-

activities known by a single researcher, and are valid ones in constructing and evaluating theories, and that it is desirable to consider the interactive relationships between the internal and contextual usefulness of theory formulation. A full-fledged discussion of the interactive relationship between science and societal development is contained in some recent European publications (e.g., Holzkamp, 1967, 1970), though unfortunately they are often clouded in political debate.

ible from the general axioms, and (c) coordinating definitions relating theoretical terms to observational sentences. Whenever the judgment is made that a theory is not sufficiently complete or fully consistent, one speaks of *"prototheories"* (Baldwin, 1960). Most of the theories in psychology are typically judged to be of the prototheoretical kind. A theory does not only *form* a set of statements; it is also *part* of a larger system of statements, often, but not necessarily ordered in levels. This larger system is occasionally defined as a paradigm, world view, metatheory, or metamodel. In other words, there are not only levels within a theory but also levels of models and/or theories.

In the context of describing the evaluation of theories, Kaplan (1964, p. 313) stated: "Truth itself is plainly useless as a criterion for the acceptability of a theory . . . we must proceed conversely . . . and characterize truth as the outcome of inquiry, suitably carried out." Scientific theories differ in many ways and for good reasons (Marx and Hillix, 1973): A major one is the state of development and explicitness.

The evaluation of theories proceeds along three lines. First, the evaluative examination is concerned with the *internal logic* of a theory in terms of consistency and testability. In this regard, the evaluation seems to follow the truthfulness criteria suggested by logic. Second, the evaluation centers on the *relationship between theoretical statements and empirical evidence*. It is in this regard that theories cannot be proven to be true but only supported by empirical evidence. A third aspect of evaluation of theories involves the *relationship between the three functions of a theory: knowledge generation, knowledge dissemination, and knowledge utilization*. A joint focus on knowledge generation, dissemination, and utilization in evaluating theories derives its rationale from considering science a social enterprise as described above.

There is another set of attributes which is often used (e.g., Frank, 1961; Lachman, 1963) to describe the evaluative status of theories. The three major attributes are (1) *precision*, (2) *scope*, and (3) *deployability* of theories. The level of precision of a theory refers to the accuracy and unequivocacy of prediction and control. Precision includes both aspects of theory-datum agreement and such attributes as

simplicity or parsimony. The scope or generality of a theory refers to the spectrum of subject matter which a given theory is purported to cover. Kaplan (1964) speaks of the range of heterogeneity of facts. Deployability of theories is sometimes also called fertility (Frank, 1954 in Frank, 1961) and is particularly tied to the process of knowledge dissemination and knowledge utilization.

The evaluation of a theory, then, is guided both by truth criteria of internal validity associated with the assessment of precision and by aspects of external scientific and social validity (usefulness) involving scope and deployability. Evaluation of theories, therefore, is a complex task which is never complete. The multiple functions and criteria attached to theories and their evaluation are the main reasons why theories seldom die.

Models and Theories

Some philosophers of science and researchers in the field of development and aging find it important to separate models from theories (Kaplan, 1964; Lachman, 1963; Reese and Overton, 1970)—although this distinction is far from unequivocal, and the terms "model" and "theory" are often used interchangeably.

The suggestion is made that much of the confusion and arguments surrounding specific theories and proper strategies of theory construction and theory evaluation is due to the fact that theories and models are not seen as independent structures which, however, are functionally related. According to Lachman (1963), a model is structurally separate from a theory but is part of its axioms. Axioms, as discussed earlier, represent one of the three components of a given theory. "Any theory presupposes a more general model according to which the theoretical concepts are formulated" (Reese and Overton, 1970, p. 117). Furthermore, there are levels of models and theories. If one accepts a hierarchical system, for example, any theory is formulated within a metacontext of theory building and, at the same time, any model is conceptualized within a metacontext of model building.

In our view, the distinction between models and theories is indeed a useful one. Distinguishing between models and theories helps clarify the difference between the *external context* in which theory construction and evaluation proceed and the *internal validation* of theories. In other words, separating the assumptive contextual network of a theory (its metatheory or model characteristics) from its intrinsic set of laws and concepts which are not assumptive but testable is desirable. In this vein, Reese and Overton (1970) use the term model to describe the paradigmatic context for theory building. General models such as "world views," "paradigms," or "world hypotheses" are metamodels which delineate the kind of theories which may be developed for a given subject matter by a given researcher with a given model orientation. Models, thus, circumscribe the axiomatic set of features which are a part of any complete theory at whatever level of development. Furthermore, since models are seen as representing the axiomatic metaproperties of a theory, they should not be evaluated on criteria of truth but on criteria of pragmatic usefulness.

Reese and Overton (1970; Overton and Reese, 1973; see also Looft, 1973a,b) apply the distinction between models and theories to the study of development and aging and illustrate its conceptual usefulness. For example, a recognition of the organismic model characteristics of Piagetian theory clarifies Piaget's (1970) position that his theory of cognitive development cannot be tested via behavioristic learning paradigms because these are part of a mechanistic world view. An application of the model-theory distinction also suggests that perennial dilemmas or issues in the study of development (e.g., holism *vs.* elementarism, structure-function *vs.* antecedent-consequent, discontinuity *vs.* continuity, phenotypic *vs.* genotypic, etc.) are largely a reflection of metamodel and not theory differences.

NATURE OF PSYCHOLOGY

Current Status of Psychological Theory

Psychology is a science and a profession (Clark and Miller, 1970; Graumann, 1972), and as a discipline it is, therefore, concerned with the formulation of knowledge of interest to the entire spectrum of psychological professionals.

How the behavior of organisms is studied and organized varies along many dimensions. On the one hand, there are multiple rival strategies and levels of theory formulations and theory evaluation. Such rival approaches can lead to independent structures of psychological theories. On the other hand, psychologists differ in their emphases or preferences for distinct empirical methodologies and subject matters. In the absence of a unified theory and a monolithic definition of behavior, pluralism is in vogue in current psychology (Kendler, 1970; Marx and Hillix, 1973), which leads Gilgen (1970) to conclude that psychology is still in a pre-paradigmatic (Kuhn, 1970) period. These conclusions seem valid despite occasional and important efforts at unification and integration in method and theory (e.g., Royce, 1970). A general systems view (Bertalanffy, 1968; Buckley, 1968; Sadovsky, 1972) appears to play a central role in the search for integrative formulations.

Accordingly, emphases in psychological method and theory are not seen as existing in fragmented or hierarchical units nor is reductionism (e.g., all psychological events will ultimately be accounted for on the level of biological analysis) the only acceptable strategy towards knowledge building. This change in perspective from a monolithic orientation towards a constructive-pluralistic posture is important for a discussion of psychological theories of aging. For example, the traditional focus on viewing biological mechanisms as "more basic" to the aging process than psychological or sociological mechanisms does not seem to hold up against current trends in metascience. Brunswik's (1955, p. 237) conclusion that "insistence on reductionism as a universal goal of science can only result in blighted spots on the landmap of scientific enterprise" appears to survive (see also Jessor, 1963; Kantor, 1973; Royce, 1970; Wolman, 1973). Conceptual and factual agreements, contradictions, and complementarities are all a legitimate part of the system of psychology.

Major Dimensions and Systems of Psychological Theories

Having a perspective on the scope of psychological theories is helpful in identifying and examining the status of any specific psychological emphasis such as the psychology of aging. When it comes to a comprehensive account of the substance and scope of psychological theories, there are at least three strategies to be discerned.

First, there is an effort at developing a taxonomy of psychology on the basis of metatheoretical and metamethodological grounds (Reese and Overton, 1970; Royce, 1970; Wolman, 1973). Second, the empirical method is brought to bear on examining psychologists themselves (what do psychologists do?) as demonstrated by Coan (1968, 1970). Third, efforts are made to organize psychology around schools or systems of thought or theoretical positions. This approach is typically implemented in books on the history of psychology (e.g., Boring, 1950). Each of these complementary approaches is useful in illustrating the richness and diversity of psychology as a science and profession in relation to theories of aging.

As to a metatheoretical approach, Royce (1970) has been particularly active in promoting a taxonomic analysis of representative general theories in contemporary psychology. His primary focus is on assessing the present situation in theoretical psychology in terms of underlying epistemologies (empiricism, rationalism, metaphorism) and on an evaluation of formal and empirical properties (see also Kendler, 1970). Notwithstanding the numerous pitfalls in proposing such a taxonomic and evaluative framework, it is our belief that Royce's (1970) basic

approach and intent is a useful one and deserves attention before embarking on a long journey into the construction of psychological theories in the field of aging.

The second traditional way of organizing psychological theories is to delineate empirical emphases as they are reflected in the work and conceptions of psychologists. Such an empirically based approach to identifying basic patterns of theoretical orientations in psychology was taken by Coan (1968, 1970). Using ratings from psychologists, Coan analyzed 17 factors at a first-order factor level from which, on a second-order level, five second-order bipolar factors were deduced. These were further reduced on the third-order level to one single bi-polar dimension.

The entire outcome of Coan's (1968, 1970) research on the dimensions of psychological theory is depicted in Figure 1 which shows the multidimensional space of theoretical psychology on the second and third order of factor analysis. The general third-order dimension of *Fluid versus Restrictive Orientation* is described as follows: The psychologist, for example, whose theoretical orientation is fluid tends to be concerned with conscious experience, favors dealing with wholes in both theory and research, and is willing to employ relatively loose and informal methods. The psychologist with a restrictive orientation is more inclined to confine his attention to overt behavior, favors strict be-

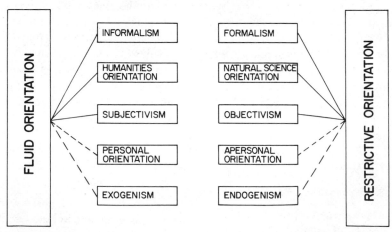

Figure 1. A bipolar hierarchy of theoretical-orientation factors in psychology at second and third-order level. On either side are terms representing two poles of five second-order and one third-order factor each. Seventeen first-order factors are not shown; dashed lines indicate relatively weaker factor connections. (After Coan, 1970.)

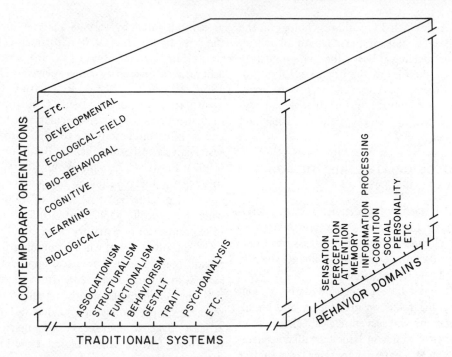

Figure 2. An illustration of pluralism in current psychological theory. (Most researchers may question whether traditional systems will lead to theories which are satisfactory in scope, precision and deployability.)

havioral terminology, prefers dealing with processes and structure abstracted from people, and favors contents and methods of the natural sciences.

A third strategy, aimed at developing a comparative framework for examining psychological theories of aging and development, is to organize a matrix containing a classification of psychological theories or orientations as reviewers see them in their assessment of contemporary research (e.g., Boring, 1950; Lowry, 1971; Marx and Hillix, 1973). Summarizing our impression both from Marx and Hillix's (1973) review of systems in psychology and the organization of various handbooks in developmental psychology (e.g., Goslin, 1969; Mussen, 1970), Figure 2 is offered as a heuristic device. It is presented in full recognition of shortcomings dealing with the number of categories given and uncertainty about internal relationships of the structural elements included.

Figure 2 is organized in terms of three categories: (1) *traditional systems* in psychology as largely described by Marx and Hillix (1973), (2) *domains of behavior processes*, and (3) major *contemporary theoretical orientations* as often found in the current psychological literature. Theoretical orientations are conceived of as having the potential to lead to major new systems of psychology in the near future if proven to sustain usefulness. The intent of Figure 2, then, is to illustrate within which sets of theoretical systems, behavior processes, and theoretical orientations a large share of current psychological research is being conducted and theories are being built. It is not asserted that all cells of the three-dimensional cube can be found in the literature; however, it is maintained that most of the combinations are available, at least in approximation, when examining both present and past psychological research. The three-dimensional scheme could be easily extended or modified, for example, by adding or using a *model of man* dimension (e.g., active *vs.* reactive) as described by Reese and Overton (1970; Overton and Reese, 1973), or a dimension containing *methodological modes of datum definition* (e.g., behavior *vs.* neurophysiological events *vs.* phenomenal experience) as suggested by Kendler (1970).

In our view, Figures 1 and 2 illustrate on a concrete level the state of current psychological theory. As indicated before, psychology in the 1970's is in a state of paradigmatic pluralism, and we are dealing at best either with miniature theories or theories of the orientational or pro- tototheoretical kind. The next step is to apply the preceding sections on metatheory and psychological theory to the field of aging and development.

PSYCHOLOGICAL THEORIES OF AGING AND DEVELOPMENT

Within the matrix of *traditional systems, developing theoretical orientations* and *behavioral domains* (Figure 2) described, the central task now is to determine the core elements for psychological theories of aging.

A first immediate conclusion deriving from the foregoing focus on metatheory and pluralism is that the way psychological aging is actually studied depends in large part on considerations which are external to aging as a subject matter. In fact, it is a major contention of this chapter that, especially in a young field such as aging, recognizing the import of the metatheoretical biases which regulate the scientific behavior of the pioneers and leaders making the field is of paramount importance. The importance of contextual variables is stressed because we see science as a many-sided social enterprise and believe that research and theory are selectively dependent not only upon a metatheoretical framework but also upon the "social, economic and political conditions of the society in which we happen to live" (Riegel, 1973b, p. 56; see also Keniston, 1971).

Historical Perspectives

In analogy to Zigler's (1963) and Bronfenbrenner's (1963) excellent analyses of the field of child development a decade ago, most recent reviews of the field of psychological aging (e.g., Bühler, Keith-Spiegel, and Thomas, 1973; Looft, 1972, 1973a; Riegel, 1973b; Schaie and Gribbin, 1975) suggest that theory in the field of aging is in a period of conceptual transition. Although the reader is referred for a detailed account to Chapter 4 of this volume on history by Riegel, a few selected observations on theoretical emphases and trends are given.

On the one hand, there is an obvious quantitative explosion in geropsychological research as demonstrated by various analyses including the ones by Charles (1970), Groffmann (1970), Looft (1972), and Riegel (1973b) which was accurately projected by earlier reviewers (Birren, 1960; Munnichs, 1966a). In addition to this quantitative explosion, there is a continued movement toward better articulation of theory and a shift from descriptive to explanatory process analysis aptly described by Bronfenbrenner (1963), Looft (1972), and Wohlwill (1973). In this regard, the psychology of aging benefited greatly from the fact that some of its pioneers were theoretically sophisticated and committed to experimental-explanatory research.

On the other hand, when examining the pluralistic matrix of psychological approaches described in Figures 1 and 2 in historical perspective, one might wonder whether Anglo-American research on psychological aging has suffered (or at least advanced unevenly) due to its close ties to strong leaders who favored experimental-behavioristic, psychometric, and bio-behavioral metamodel conceptions. Comparatively speaking, there has been a research thrust on biological-decremental views, on basic processes of the sensation-perception-information processing kind, and on the use of structuralistic and mechanistic rather than organismic and functionalistic modes of studying behavior. The study of cognitive, affective, emotional, and social behavior phenomena has, comparatively, lagged behind—as has the consideration of theoretical orientations associated with developmental learning, socialization, ecological-field, and ethological perspectives, notable exceptions notwithstanding (e.g., Bengtson and Black, 1973; Bortner, 1967; Brim and Wheeler, 1966; Goulet, 1970; Kastenbaum, 1967; Lawton and Nahemow, 1973; Lowenthal and Chiriboga, 1973; Neugarten and Datan, 1973; Schaie, 1962; Thomae, 1970).

Whatever the specific interpretation of historical trends, it seems important to project past, current, and future psychological research on aging into a pluralistic framework of psychological theory. Continuous monitoring and reflection is helpful in identifying relative strengths and weaknesses and in making the psychology of aging not only an open recipient of, but also an active and interactive contributor to, the general field of psychology as suggested in one of the early reviews of the field (Birren, 1960).

A good collection of examples for recent advances into existing theoretical niches are the increased use of cumulative and hierarchical developmental learning models (e.g., Goulet, 1970, 1973; Hoyer, 1973; Hultsch, 1974; Labouvie-Vief, Hoyer, Baltes, and Baltes, 1974); the systematic introduction of ecological and ethological perspectives (Lawton and Nahemow, 1973; Willems, 1973); the programmatic resurrection of a life-span developmental approach to the study of aging (Baltes, 1973a, Baltes and Schaie, 1973a; Goulet and Baltes, 1970; Nesselroade and Reese, 1973); the focus on a developmental approach to the study of behavior genetics (Jarvik, 1975); and the beginnings of a dynamic, dialectic view of the study of behavior-environment systems (e.g., Riegel, 1973c, 1976 in press) with its goal to capture both ontogenetic and evolutionary change components. It has been argued that research on psychological aging in some of these areas has led to novel conceptualizations which are having some impact in other domains of psychology as well.

Toward Description of Psychological Aging and Development

If one translates the definition and objective of psychology into concrete goals, psychological theory on aging should lead to a body of knowledge which facilitates the interrelated objectives of (1) description, (2) explanation, and (3) modification or optimization of aging behavior (Baltes, 1973b) at a specified level of precision, scope, and deployability.

In any discussion of aging behavior, one is initially faced with the perplexing tasks of (1) defining the target class of behaviors and (2) delineating appropriate descriptive methodologies. The boundaries limiting the area of psychological aging are indeed vague and often subject to dispute (e.g., Birren, 1964b). Birren's (1959b, p. 5) conclusion that "aging as a concept will not be defined at once and for always but will over time be redefined" is an apt characterization of a pluralistic and evolutionary view.

When evaluating the current status of the descriptive analysis of aging behavior, there are three sets of issues. The first deals with the delineation of the concept of aging itself. The second issue involves the question of adequate methodology for the study of aging behavior both with regard to the need for change analysis and for representative and fair measurement. The third issue deals with the question of which variables need observation in order to provide for a body of data suitable for explanatory analysis.

Aging as a Multidirectional Change Process. The term "aging" carries multiple meanings and, in some ways, it may be ill chosen. The major theoretical advantage which we see in the term aging (in contrast for example to gerontological psychology) is related to its implicit focus on *process* and *change* (e.g., Thomae, 1959). This is contrasted with a posture where age would only enter as a quantitative parameter into a theory of behavior of the general psychology type.

There are two major theoretical disadvantages, however, stemming from an unreflective, prescientific use of the term aging. One involves the potential to equate aging with deterioration and decrement. The second disadvantage which the term aging often produces is to suggest that the major explanatory task of aging research is to use "age" as the primary explanatory determinant for aging behavior.

Our bias is to capitalize on the primary advantage of the term aging and to conclude that the focus is on a behavioral process. In order to prevent identifying psychological aging primarily with decrement phenomena (e.g., Botwinick, 1973; Busse, 1969), it is our definite preference to combine the terms aging and development (see also Birren, 1964b) on a conceptual level or to speak simply of behavioral change in aging.

It remains to be discussed which form a behavioral process should take to be classified as aging. It is our judgment (Baltes, 1973b; Baltes and Schaie, 1973b, Baltes and Willis, in press; see also Birren, 1959b; Hoyer, 1974; Thomae, 1959) that the nature of behavioral change at all stages of the life span can take many forms in terms of directionality, range, or intensity, depending upon the class of behavior and theoretical orientation chosen. Therefore, it is desirable to refrain from the application of strict generic criteria such as unidirectionality, irreversibility, and universality when delineating aging change although these attributes may apply to *some* behavioral changes at *some* historical periods for *some* organisms. (The point here is not, for example, that sequential-directional-irreversible behavioral changes of the organismic kind [Reese and Overton, 1970] are not useful, but that these represent only a segment of the metamodels of behavioral development which can be construed.)

Descriptive Components of Behavior-Change Processes and Aging. The recognition that the form of behavioral change in aging can be multidirectional, however, does not solve the general question of which behavioral changes are to be identified with aging; it only helps prevent a stereotypic and inadequate approach to the phenomenon of psychological aging. The search for a definite set of criteria is similar to the one faced with the concept of developmental change (Baltes, Reese, and Nesselroade, 1976 in press; Birren, 1964b; Harris, 1957; Thomae, 1959; Tobach, Aronson, and Shaw, 1971).

On a descriptive level, there are a number of criteria which delineate the class of behaviors to be labeled as aging or developmental. First, the focus is on *time-trajectories of change* or on "a determinate chain of events occupying a significant portion of the life span after maturity" (Birren, 1959b, p. 5). These chains of events are assumed to express regularity. Second, we need to recognize that, for a behavioral process to be useful for aging-related theory building, it needs to exhibit some formal property of *parsimony*, *normatization*, or *generality* either on the level of nomothetic or idiographic analysis. Third, aging behavior is restricted primarily to those behavior change processes which characterize the *second part of the life span*; however, it may be useful to link late-life changes to antecedent changes in the first part of the life span in order to obtain a complete account of behavior-change functions.

Figure 3 summarizes this definitional position on aging behavior in schematic form. Behavior-change processes are seen as the crucial target phenomenon (see also Baer, 1970; Harris, 1971); traditional age-change functions (Wohlwill, 1973) are a special case of a general class of behavior-change functions. In addition, it is argued that psychologists typically conceptualize behavior-change processes on the level of indi-

vidual analysis. Accordingly, change on the individual level involves *intraindividual change*, and differences in change functions between individuals, i.e., *interindividual differences in change* (Baltes, 1973b; Baltes, Reese, and Nesselroade, 1976 in press; Buss, 1974a; Rudinger, 1976 in press). It is suggested further in in Figure 3 that one of the important features of aging is that interindividual differences typically increase with time and age resulting in progressively less age-related homogeneity (e.g., Bortner, 1967; Britton and Britton, 1972; Busse, 1969; Fozard and Thomas, 1975).

Furthermore, it is shown in Figure 3 that behavior-change can be multidirectional (incremental, decremental, curvilinear, etc.). The form and directionality of change patterns can also be conceptualized in many ways including the distinction of quantitative (more or less of a given attribute) versus structural (different sets of attributes or differing interrelations among attributes) change (e.g., Baltes and Nesselroade, 1973; Buss, 1974a; Catania, 1973; Van den Daele, 1974). Whether change is conceptualized in terms of quantitative and/or structural-qualitative components is to a large degree a function of the metamodel of development employed.

Figure 3 suggests also (see next section on explanation) that order and regularity in behavior change is produced or programmed by two interacting influence patterns: ontogenetic and biocultural systems. An underlying assumption is that a process orientation towards a psychology of aging is not desirable on *a priori* grounds but is only useful if the empirical behavior-change functions exhibit sufficient order and regularity to warrant systematic theoretic and empirical analysis (see also Baltes, Reese, and Nesselroade, 1976 in press; Fahrenberg, 1968; Wohlwill, 1970a,b; 1973).

At this time we cannot emphasize enough the statement that the construction of chronological age functions is only one way to implement time-trajectories and behavior-change approaches. Chronological age is a useful organizing parameter only if intraindividual change patterns (in form and level) are sufficiently homogeneous to yield a high correlation between chronological age and behavior change. There is nothing sacred about chronological age being a

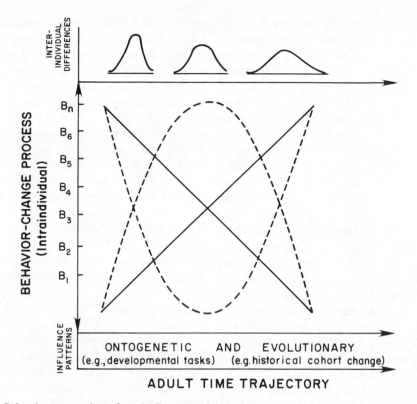

Figure 3. Selective examples of multidirectional but systematic behavior-change processes: Onto-genetic and bio-cultural influences interact in the production of normative change patterns (age functions are a special case of behavior-change processes).

sine qua non key variable as long as regularities in behavior-change functions can be detected. For example, if interindividual differences regarding age-behavior change functions (onset, schedule, etc.) are large, it is not useful to focus on chronological age-change models as representations of intraindividual change patterns. On the contrary, such behavior-change functions can be better examined outside a chronological age framework. A given class of behavior-change processes might occur at different age levels and periods for different organisms depending upon the unique schedule of life histories and the timing of critical life events.

Such an age-irrelevant but sequence-relevant approach to the study of development and aging has been argued most persuasively by operant developmentalists such as Baer (1970) but also by organicists such as Werner (1948). A persuasive example is that of the terminal drop phenomenon (Blum, Jarvik, and Clark, 1970; Jarvik, 1975; Riegel and Riegel, 1972) which suggests a determinate chain of behavior changes which, however, is less related to chronological age *per se* than to the time of death and, therefore, its onset varies widely among persons. Another example is the use of social learning theory (Ahammer, 1973) for the study of adult and gerontological personality. Furthermore, the strong focus placed by the Chicago group (e.g., Neugarten, 1968a) on contextual factors (social class, cultural settings) and interindividual differences makes a concern with intraindividual process rather than with simple and universal age change during adulthood and aging of paramount significance.

Description of Aging: Evaluation of Present Knowledge

A general assessment of the present descriptive knowledge about aging behavior leads us to conclude that the full spectrum of models of behavior change has not been explored. Considering both the pluralistic situation described in Figures 1 and 2 and the multidirectional and process-oriented perspective depicted in Figure 3, the following general observations are made.

First, from a methodological perspective (Baltes, 1968; Baltes, Reese, and Nesselroade, 1976 in press; Rudinger, 1976 in press; Schaie, 1965, Chapter 2, in this volume) it is important for gerontologists to fully recognize that research has to concentrate on strategies which indeed allow for the direct assessment of change and change processes rather than time-specific interindividual differences.

Second, with a view of theoretical orientations, the majority of descriptive data about aging have been collected within a meta-framework of biological behaviorism and/or a strong orientation towards a personological, bio-behavioral perspective rather than a contextual developmental-field view. Furthermore, the expectation has been that aging behavior is pervasively regressive or decremental. Kastenbaum (1965, 1967, 1973; see also Baltes and Labouvie, 1973) has been particularly persuasive on this point and has suggested that the prevalent meta-approaches to the study of psychological aging may have led to a body of descriptive knowledge which is unrepresentative of the universe of adult and gerontological behavioral changes.

The conclusion, then, that aging change is change toward slowness, less behavior, less acquisition, less performance, and greater dependency (e.g., Birren, 1959a, 1964a; Botwinick, 1973) may be a function of the theoretical orientations applied rather than a representative assessment of the universe of aging change itself. Data focusing on the questionable negative impact of retirement on life satisfaction (Carp, 1966), the dramatic increases in interindividual differences in behavior with age (Bloom, 1964; Britton and Britton, 1972; Busse, 1969; Fozard and Thomas, 1975), the strong impact of biocultural, historical change on the nature of adult behavior (Nesselroade and Baltes, 1974; Schaie, 1970), and the feasibility of a bi-directional model of intellectual development involving the fluid versus crystallized dimension (Horn, 1970) are all examples of an increasing body of descriptive knowledge challenging a generic decremental view of behavioral aging.

As to the need for well articulated behavior-change models, there is a dearth of them particularly if one steps outside the realm of simple quantitative age functions. Nevertheless, there is growing recognition of the need for behavior-change models however prototheoretical they may be. The formulation of psychological age concepts (Birren, 1959b; see also Kastenbaum, Derbin, Sabatini, and Artt, 1972; Nuttall, 1972), developmental-tasks models (Havighurst, 1948), and age-grade systems (Neugarten, 1968b; Neugarten, Moore, and Lowe, 1965) are commendable. Similarly, potentially useful and parsimonious behavior-change stage models have been proposed by Erikson (1959) and Bühler (1933; Bühler and Massarik, 1968) in the area of personality (see Havighurst, 1973; Looft, 1973a, for overviews) though primarily with a personological and structuralistic orientation. Furthermore, in the area of learning and cognition, Gagne (1968), Goulet (1970), and Buss (1973b) have formulated hierarchical and cumulative models which permit the systematic examination of behavior change patterns involving both structural and quantitative change attributes. Clearly, the stage is set for a concerted effort toward formulating process-oriented change functions.

There is one final comment on the adequacy of the descriptive data base in psychological research on aging. In line with Sigel's (1974) commentary on the adult-centric approach of child developmentalists and Neugarten's (1968b, 1969) concern with discontinuities between child- and adult-developmental issues, it seems fair to conclude that descriptive psychogerontological research can be characterized as being equally youth- and adult-centric, since relatively little effort has been made to construct measurement instruments with a primary view on aging. Therefore, there appears to be a host of gaps in current descriptive taxonomies of adult and gerontological behaviors. The emerging search for what is unique and representative of aging behavior is reflected, for example, in recent emphases on studying such behavioral phenomena as wisdom (Clayton, 1975), time perspectives (Bortner and Hultsch, 1974; Munnichs, 1966b; Marshall, 1974), life-review processes (Butler, 1963; Falk, 1970), personal control, mid-life crises (Brim, 1974a,b), and adult coping with professional, inter-, and intrapersonal stress (Coelho, Hamburg, and Adams,

1974; Dohrenwend and Dohrenwend, 1974; Lowenthal and Chiriboga, 1973). This selected set of examples illustrates the growing interest in a richer universe of adult-developmental behaviors.

The primary conclusions from this brief sketch of various approaches to the descriptive analysis of adult and aging behavior are two-fold. On the one hand, a greater variety of metamodels of behavior for conceptualizing adulthood and aging is desirable as is concern with change methodology. On the other hand, it is the focus on behavior-change models rather than on simple age functions which is judged to be most facilitative of vigorous theory building. Furthermore, it is asserted that a descriptive taxonomy of behavior-change patterns (including multidirectional age functions as well as in-cremental, decremental, curvilinear, cyclical and hierarchical ones which are less related to chronological age than to "age-irrelevant" de-velopmental sequences) will be the first step to-wards achieving a differentiated view of aging processes. A pluralistic but precise specification of behavior-change models is indeed seen as most crucial in moving the concept of aging from a prescientific to a prototheoretical level.

Toward Explanation of Psychological Aging and Development

The major task of explanation (Baltes, 1973b; Birren, 1959b; Reese and Overton, 1970) is the search for predictive determinants of psycho-logical aging and development ideally involving determinants of the causal type. While in de-scription the primary focus is on behavioral ob-servation, the emphasis in explanatory and ana-lytic analysis is "on the evaluation of the explanatory value of variable relationships in accounting for intraindividual change and inter-individual differences in such change sequences" (Baltes, 1973b, p. 461).

Metatheory and Explanation. The preceding sections suggest at least three preliminary ob-servations on this topic.

First, philosophers of science suggest that there is no monolithic strategy for the search of determinacy and causality nor any single causative agent for a given outcome; causality has constructive and representational features and the evaluation of predictive or explanatory

statements is guided by criteria of precision, scope, and deployability. Second, when predict-ing or explaining psychological aging and devel-opment, the focus is on change processes and not on time-specific behavioral events; explain-ing long-term behavior-change processes may require modes of inquiry which are distinct from explanatory schemes developed for ahis-torical and short-term analyses. Third, the search for causation is conducted within a con-text of metatheory; explanatory statements are different and evaluated differently within a mechanistic, organismic, personological, or etho-logical mode of conceptualizing behavior.

The decision on what is sufficient explanatory evidence is not an absolute one but monitored by metatheoretical perspectives. Consider, for example, Aristotle's specification of four causal determinants: material, efficient, formal, and final cause, with formal and final causes being explicitly teleological. Within a mechanistic concept of development, an adequate level of explanation is that of an efficient cause. An or-ganismic concept of development, on the other hand, considers an efficient causal explanation incomplete (Bunge, 1963; Overton and Reese, 1973). For organicists, formal and final cause explanations are necessary to translate their as-sumption of an active organism into systematic efforts at theory building.

Similar perspectives apply to the unique re-quirements associated with other theoretical orientations (Kendler, 1970; Royce, 1970). Consider for instance the evaluative implications for the precision and scope of statements if ethological and personological approaches to explanatory evidence are contrasted. While a personologist may be satisfied with predictive statements of the behavior-behavior type (e.g., Erikson's stage of integrity follows the stage of generativity), an ethologist (e.g., Blurton Jones, 1972) would focus on evolutionary survival characteristics and organism-environment inter-actions as acceptable forms of explanation. Similarly, a researcher committed to an oper-ant psychological orientation toward studying behavioral development (e.g., Baer, 1970, 1973; Bijou, 1970; Gewirtz, 1969; Hoyer, 1974) would only be satisfied if explanatory state-ments are available which specify the functional relationship between stimulus and response conditions in a time-ordered and programmed fashion. Therefore, for a behavior process-oriented researcher, it is "open to question whether the study of developmental problems necessarily proceeds in the two-stage process of identifying age-performance functions and then explicating age in terms of its psychological meaning" (Baltes and Goulet, 1971, p. 152; see also Wohlwill, 1973).

Change-oriented Explanations. Although we need to recognize that the explanatory component of psychological theories of aging varies according to its theoretical and methodological context, there are some generic attributes. The major attribute is that a behavior-change focus requires a corresponding change perspective with respect to explanatory determinants and mechanisms.

When presenting a general taxonomy of prototheoretical questions and paradigms in research on development and aging, Baltes (1973b) used a behavioristic framework to illustrate the key element of a change-oriented explanatory posture. Figure 4 summarizes this illustrative approach and shows how behavior and behavior change can be explained by its relationship to different classes of antecedent variables.

American behaviorism has suggested the use of three classes of variables (e.g., Spence, 1963)

for psychological analysis: (1) response or behavior variables (R), (2) stimulus or environmental variables (S), and organismic or biological variables (O). The basic postulate is that a given behavioral phenomenon can be accounted for by reference to either other behavioral variables (R), stimulus-environmental variables (S), or organismic-biological variables (O) as antecedent determinants; however, in all cases the target phenomenon to be explained is a behavior (R).

The two elements of Figure 4 which are most crucial to the present discussion are its consideration of the *time continuum*, on the one hand, and of *changes in the variable system* on the other. First, it is shown that variable relationships can be either *concurrent* or *historical* in time. Concurrent explanations focus on determinants which are close or proximal in time to the phenomenon to be explained. Historical explanations focus on determinants or chains of determinants which are distal in time. For example, loss in intellectual functioning in advanced age could be explained by concurrent aging-specific conditions such as a reduction in cerebral blood flow (which would represent a proximal form of explanation). Conversely, the same loss in intellectual functioning could be explained by recourse to an early historical life event such as absence of aging-relevant educa-

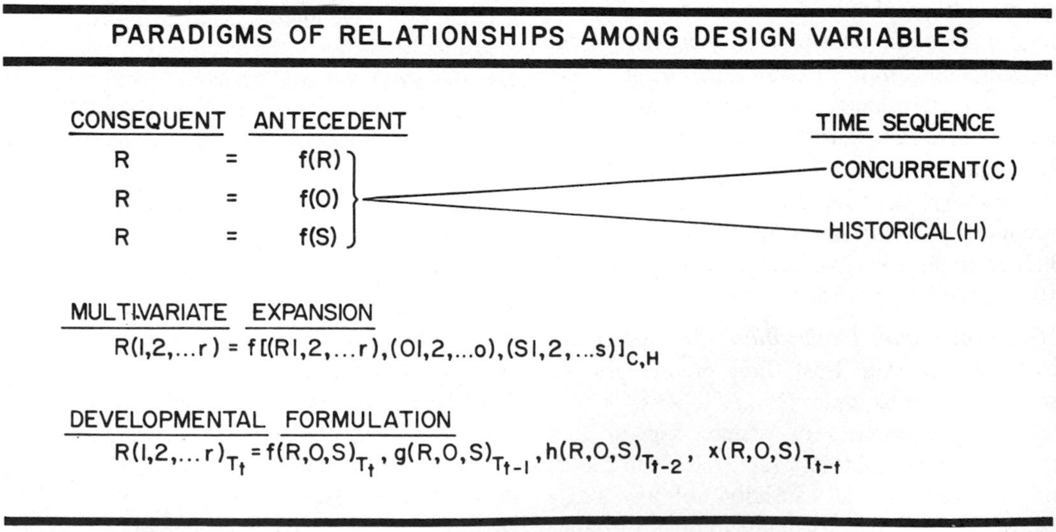

PARADIGMS OF RELATIONSHIPS AMONG DESIGN VARIABLES

CONSEQUENT   ANTECEDENT   TIME SEQUENCE

$R \quad = \quad f(R)$ CONCURRENT(C)

$R \quad = \quad f(O)$

$R \quad = \quad f(S)$ HISTORICAL(H)

MULTIVARIATE   EXPANSION

$$R(1,2,...r) = f[(R1,2,...r),(O1,2,...o),(S1,2,...s)]_{C,H}$$

DEVELOPMENTAL   FORMULATION

$$R(1,2,...r)_{T_t} = f(R,O,S)_{T_t}, g(R,O,S)_{T_{t-1}}, h(R,O,S)_{T_{t-2}}, x(R,O,S)_{T_{t-t}}$$

Figure 4. Prototypical paradigms and relationships among design variables in psychological and developmental research. (After Baltes, 1973b.)

tional experiences in childhood (which would represent a distal form of explanation).

Second, the emphasis placed in Figure 4 (see also Figure 3) on behavior-change analysis calls for explicating not only changes in the target behavior but also for explication of sequential effects of antecedent determinants. Change applies both to the consequent and antecedent side of the paradigm. It is the patterned accumulation or aggregation of effects which produces systematic behavioral change of the aging and developmental kind. The developmental change-oriented paradigm contained in Figure 4 illustrates one additional feature of a change-oriented explanatory analysis of psychological aging and development. This is the notion of *explanatory continuity vs. discontinuity* which asserts that either the same or a different set of antecedent determinants or the same or a different form of causal functions may exist at different stages or levels in the chain of antecedent-consequent events. First, different determinants (e.g., organismic versus environmental) may operate at different points in the behavior-change process. Second, the nature of the functional relationship between antecedents and consequents (f vs. g vs. h, etc.) or interaction among the determining antecedent variables may change.

For example, in the beginning of an aging chain, intellectual functioning may be largely related to early life educational experiences, whereas later elements in the chain may suggest that intellectual functioning is predominantly related to organismic-biological variables (reflecting a biological terminal drop phenomenon, etc.). An additional example of explanatory discontinuity is the postulate of structurally different processes (e.g., cognitive stages) for different levels of development. Kohlberg (1973), for instance, when presenting a life-span view of moral development uses explanatory discontinuity. He focuses on a biological-maturational explanatory orientation concerning moral development in childhood, but on an experiential explanatory orientation regarding adulthood changes in moral reasoning. As a final example, if one studies gerontological changes in personality as a consequence of environmental influences, the search for antecedents involves changing influence patterns. Neugarten's (1968b) concept of age-grading is accordingly based on a time-ordered conception of antecedents for adult personality change.

The focus of a change-oriented explanatory posture, then, is on the notion of accounting for behavior change phenomena, such as aging, in terms of time-ordered (sequential) but potentially changing systems of explanatory determinants. In our view, the explicit recognition of change in both the target behavior phenomenon and its antecedent or correlated determining processes is at the core of such concepts as developmental continuity versus discontinuity, developmental stage, developmental chain, developmental task, or developmental interaction including the dialectic kind (Riegel, 1976 in press). A similar concern with explanatory sequentiality and discontinuity is also suggested not only by the increment in interindividual differences in intraindividual change with age, but also by the pervasive effect of cohort differences in aging (Baltes, 1968; Buss, 1973a; Riley, Johnson and Foner, 1972; Schaie, 1965, 1970). Cohort effects and large interindividual differences in aging probably do occur because the developmental, time-ordered matrix of determinants producing behavioral change in aging exhibits explanatory discontinuity among persons both in terms of the key variables involved as well as their interactive relationships.

Explanation of Psychological Aging: Evaluation of Present Knowledge

Figures 3 and 4 suggest jointly that (1) a multitude of antecedent variables and processes (e.g., behavioral, biological, environmental) can be used to construct a theory of developmental and aging change; (2) a process-oriented explanatory analysis has to incorporate a perspective of change not only with regard to the behavior change to be explained but also with regard to the class of antecedent variables and their interlocking functional relationships; and (3) current pluralism does not suggest the feasibility of single-agent explanations but the usefulness of considering contingency, multiple-factor, and system-factor explanations.

The assertion is that the level of precision, scope, and deployability of theories of behavioral aging and development are in the long run not matters of untestable *a priori* assumptions but of empirical demonstration. If behavioral change in adulthood and aging could not be demonstrated to exhibit attributes of regularity and if the explanatory principles used to account for such changes could not be shown to involve systematic time-ordered, aggregated influence patterns, then a focus on change would lose its credibility as a viable and unique approach to the study of behavior in the aged.

Classes of Antecedents. Because of the intrinsic linkages between description and explanation, the main conclusions on the predominant postures in the literature regarding explanatory variables are similar to those offered regarding descriptive knowledge: (1) There is comparatively little explicit focus on developing explanatory models which could account for the pervasiveness of interindividual differences in aging change, (2) there has been an extraordinary concern with organismic (personological), biological, and endogenous rather than environmental variables, and (3) most prototheoretical explanatory attempts center on monistic, single-agent principles rather than on behavior-environment systems of multiple and discontinuous causality. Urban and Lago's (1973) summary of aging and developmental research on psychopathology, for instance, presents a persuasive case for these conclusions. The area of adult and gerontological intelligence (Baltes and Labouvie, 1973; Barton, Plemons, Willis, and Baltes, 1975; Jarvik and Cohen, 1973; Schaie, 1974) is another.

It is indeed encouraging to observe that the *chronological age variable* as the primary explanatory variable is on its way out. On the one hand, there is now overwhelming evidence questioning the descriptive and explanatory usefulness of age for methodological reasons. For example, interindividual differences in development and aging are remarkably large and can take multiple forms (see Wohlwill 1973). Moreover, with increasing age, less and less variance is age-associated but rather is related to age-irrelevant determinants such as life stress events (e.g., Dohrenwend and Dohrenwend, 1974; Lowenthal and Chiriboga, 1973) or cohort effects (e.g., Baltes, 1968; Schaie, 1965, 1970; Schaie and Gribbin, 1975). On the other hand,

there is also now widespread acceptance of the view that the use of age as an explanatory variable may inhibit vigorous theory building (even if made part of the dependent variable), in that age is a subject variable which is difficult to use for experimental-manipulative research (Baer, 1970; Baltes and Goulet, 1971; Birren, 1959b, 1970; Wohlwill, 1973).

At best, the study of age change can be seen as the first step in programmatic research as suggested by Wohlwill (1973, p. 40) or by the statement that age relations "are inevitably in transition to being explained by other variables without recourse to the use of the term age" (Birren, 1959b, p. 8). At worst, the use of chronological age as a primary antecedent variable is misleading to begin with, as it represents only an approximation to the identification of behavior-change functions and, due to its status as person variable (Kerlinger, 1964; Underwood, 1975), carries the risk of theoretical impotency. As Underwood (1975, p. 134) put it: "We cannot deal constructively with individual differences when we identify the important variables as age, sex, grade, I.Q., social status, and so on. The critical variables are process variables."

Figures 3 and 4 with their focus on pluralism also assist us in evaluating the *scope of antecedent variables* applied in current research. Taxonomies of variable systems are always arbitrary but usually involve some recognition of individual-biological, individual-psychological, cultural-sociological, and physical-environmental (Riegel, 1976) dimensions similar to the response variable, organismic variable, and stimulus variable distinction (Spence, 1963) presented earlier. For example, when jointly considering the potential import of biological and environmental determinants, several researchers (e.g., Baltes and Labouvie, 1973; Kastenbaum, 1967; Maddox, 1970; Schaie and Gribbin, 1975) have suggested that the bulk of explanatory aging research has addressed primarily the domain of biological variables even in areas where psychology has traditionally focused on the effects of experience. Environmentalism and experiential explanations are only recently surging to the forefront of explanatory research (Baltes and Lascomb, 1975; Bortner, 1967; Hoyer, 1973; Labouvie, 1973; Neugarten, 1968a). The distinction between primary and secondary aging (Busse, 1959), suggesting a "primary" biological change function and "secondary" psychological or sociological change functions, is perhaps the best symbolic illustration of the traditional conceptual bias favoring a biological and/or medical model of explanation and reductionism as a prime mode of theory building.

A final evaluative comment regarding the nature of antecedent variables involves the need for multiple-factor and systems models and a consideration of both ontogenetic and evolutionary perspectives. While it is worthwhile to continue the search for key basic antecedents for the process of "normal" aging (e.g., on the level of neurophysiology; Botwinick, 1973; Busse, 1969; Hicks and Birren, 1970), it is also equally clear that the current explanatory literature on the psychology of adult development and aging does not support the notion of a monolithic, single-agent explanatory position. As Kastenbaum (1967) maintains, we need "to lift ourselves past the mental block that we are confronting a single and inevitable process which partakes of some formidable metaphysical reality" (p. 103).

In its search for a systems-oriented rather than single-agent explanation, gerontological research can profit from lessons learned in explanatory child-development research (e.g., Bronfenbrenner, 1973; Schultz and Aurbach, 1971). In the field of child development, it is now widely accepted that long-term behavioral change is controlled by a multitude of organismic and environmental variable systems and that time-ordered influence patterns operate and interact often in a disjointed and discontinuous fashion. As Benedict (1938) already argued quite some time ago, there is both continuity and discontinuity (descriptive and explanatory) in cultural-environmental influence programs as persons move through time. Recent evidence on gene-environment interactions (McClearn, 1970; Jarvik, 1975) suggests a similar perspective in research on behavioral and developmental genetics. Accordingly, we might not expect single-agent explanations to be likely but focus in our search during the next decade on multivariate and contextual (behavior-environment systems) patterns of determinants. It is at this point, where frameworks such as those suggested by

general systems theory (Bertalanffy, 1968; Buckley, 1968) can provide a useful perspective regarding the programmatic search for and identification of key classes of antecedents and their interactive relationships.

In any case, psychological theory on development and aging is in need of explanatory work which has more scope and balance regarding the universe of classes of antecedents used than has been true over the last two decades. At the same time, the vigor and persuasion for the recognition of environmental, multivariate, and ecological approaches expressed in Eisdorfer and Lawton (1973) signals a major reorientation in explanatory posture.

Systems and Taxonomies of Explanatory Processes. While we acknowledge the fact that the building of explanatory theories of development and aging is conducted within a metatheoretical and domain-specific context, Figure 5 is presented for the purpose of providing a framework for evaluation.

Figure 5 summarizes the view that both biological and environmental influences operate and interact in the production of behavior-change processes. The argument is made that a pluralistic approach—reflecting the preparadigmatic and prototheoretical situation in gerontological psychology—toward the formulation of explanatory models should be encouraged. Furthermore, the conclusion is that greater efforts are desirable in the direction of strengthening environmental, developmental-environmental, developmental-psychobiological, and ecological conceptions of behavior-change processes. Of particular significance in Figure 5, finally, is the resurrection of considering jointly the import of ontogenetic and evolutionary influence and change systems.

Figure 5 can also be interpreted as suggesting that the two foremost niches in explanatory theory building are in (1) the area of *interindividual differences* in behavior-change and (2) the lack of well-articulated conceptions of *long-term processes* aimed at organizing chains of gene-environment events and interactions.

With regard to the question of interindividual differences in change, the conclusion corresponds to that advanced in child development (Wohlwill, 1973) and educational learning re-

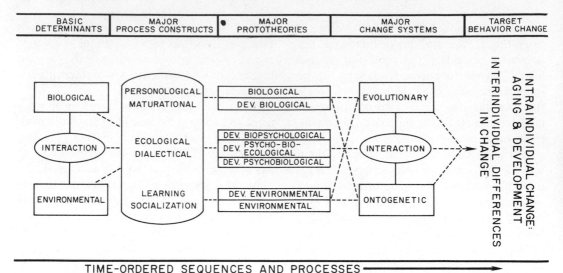

TIME-ORDERED SEQUENCES AND PROCESSES ⟶

Figure 5. Illustration of major variables, processes, and theoretical orientations in the explication of psychological aging and development (interactive, reciprocal, and feedback influence patterns can be conceived at all levels of analysis).

search (Cronbach, 1975; Underwood, 1975). It is unlikely to expect theories which are satisfactory in precision, scope, and deployability until interindividual differences are not seen as sources for error but as primary targets for explanatory process-oriented analysis (see also Baltes and Nesselroade, 1973). This argument is further supported by the recognition of both ontogenetic and evolutionary-historical change components (Bengtson and Black, 1973; Buss, 1974b; Nesselroade and Baltes, 1974; Neugarten and Datan, 1973; Riegel, 1972, 1973a, 1976) which operate jointly in a rapidly changing bio-ecological context (see also Toffler, 1970). It is the fact of pervasive interindividual differences and of developmental level or age by treatment interactions which seriously restrict the immediate usefulness of such single-factor theories as Botwinick's (1973) stimulus persistence model, or Cumming and Henry's (1961; Bromley, 1970; Cumming, 1964; Havighurst, Neugarten, and Tobin, 1968; Maddox, 1964) disengagement theory.

As to the need for the articulation of long-term change processes, the search for basic mechanisms of the information processing and learning type seems in itself insufficient. To paraphrase Birren (1959b, p. 11), the issue remains that if much of gerontological research

does not intend to explicate a process of development, then aging subjects continue to be experimental constants leading to a parametric variation of principles formulated within a framework of general experimental psychology rather than to a psychology of aging. On the contrary, the focus of explanatory aging research is on change in both the antecedent *and* consequent variables and attention must be given to the formulation of explanatory processes which are intrinsically change-oriented.

For example, one of the simplest conceptions of long-term change explanations is to invoke quantitative and cumulative learning principles such as "cumulative practice," "cumulative extinction," "cumulative reinforcement" or "increments in stimulus persistence" in order to account for acquisition or reduction in performance throughout adulthood and aging. Such linear and cumulative conceptions of the behavior-change process, however, may not be sufficient for the purpose of explaining change phenomena of the structural and qualitative kind. In fact, this is the general view taken by strong developmental researchers, such as organicists (e.g., Langer, 1969; Overton, 1973). Alternatively, it may be preferable to explicitly focus on discontinuous and qualitatively distinct mechanisms.

In the area of cognition and learning, for example, change-oriented conceptions have been proposed which entail cumulative *and* hierarchical formulations of behavior-change (e.g., Bijou, 1970; Buss, 1973b; Gagne, 1968; Goulet, 1970, 1973; Hooper, Fitzgerald, and Papalia, 1971; Jensen, 1971; Riegel, 1973c). Similarly, Reese (1973) has argued that structurally different models of memory and information processing may be most useful for distinct periods of the life span; Baltes and Schaie (1973b) have suggested that an organismic (Reese and Overton, 1970) model of development may be most applicable to early life and terminal processes in late life, whereas ecological and environmental-dialectic models seem to fit most of the adult life period in human development. Woodruff (1973), when reviewing selected aging research on psychophysiology, concluded that discontinuous antecedent-consequent relationships are evident. Finally, LeVine (1969) examining the relevance of ontogenetic and evolutionary principles of explanation drew attention to the possibility of applying a Darwinian "variation-selection" model. He argued that this principle is apt to account for some of the adaptive behavior processes shown by adults in a changing biocultural context. These examples are presented to support the assertion that an explicit concern not only with time-ordered cumulative, but also with contextual, hierarchical, and discontinuous explanatory process-mechanisms is desirable in order to maximize success in developing adequate theories of psychological aging, involving both ontogenetic and evolutionary change perspectives (see also Bengtson and Black, 1973; Lambert, 1972).

Toward Modification of Psychological Aging and Development

It was argued earlier that psychological theories involve a balanced focus on knowledge generation and knowledge utilization. Accordingly, it is a legitimate goal to search for theories of aging and development which do not only explain an existing, naturalistically occurring set of behavior-change processes but also include statements about variables and strategies apt to produce alterations in existing aging outcomes. A number of contributions have appeared over the last years (e.g., Baltes, 1973c; Birren, 1974; Birren and Woodruff, 1973; Bortner, 1975; Hultsch, 1975; Schaie, 1974; Schonfield, 1974; Urban, 1975) which have addressed or commented on issues of theory and method of intervention within a developmental and aging framework.

Metatheory and Intervention. Metatheories of development and aging set not only guidelines but also constraints for the design of intervention. Such metatheoretical constraints and guidelines involve statements about the potential *range* of modifiability, *goals* or optimization targets of intervention efforts, the scope of intervention *transfer* effects, *strategies* for the design of intervention programs, and the relative *desirability* of the intent to intervene. Second, a given theory of aging and development can be evaluated as to its intervention usefulness by considering its scope, precision, and deployability. Third, the conclusion holds that programmatic modification of behavioral aging and development is largely dependent on the extent to which explanatory research has resulted not only in internally-valid statements but also in statements with useful external validity.

Consider, for instance, metatheoretical constraints and guidelines imposed by accepting either an organismic model or mechanistic model of development as described by Overton and Reese (1973). On the one hand, when accepting a model of the organismic kind (Erikson, Piaget, etc.), there are useful prescriptions regarding the goal of intervention involving the domain and sequence (e.g., nature of psychosocial tasks and cognitive stages) of optimization. Such prescriptions (Kohlberg, 1968) are important in designing intervention programs with a view on programmatic consistency and on an active organismic-environment interchange. On the other hand, when accepting an organismic vantage point of the Erikson or Piaget kind, the anticipated range of modifiability is generally restricted due to the inherent focus on a predefined set of target (endstate-oriented) and sequential behavior-change processes and the theory-inherent preference for the optimizing power of inner-biological rather than experiential determinants (Riegel, 1976). Moreover,

Wohlwill's (1970a) organismic view goes so far as to conclude that only those behavior-change processes should be included under the heading development (or aging, the present authors infer) for which "the general course of development (considered in terms of direction, form, sequence, etc.) remains invariant over a broad range of particular environmental conditions . . . as well as genetic characteristics" (p. 52). Such a restrictive metatheoretical posture has far-reaching implications for the potential and design of explanatory research and correlated intervention efforts.

On the other extreme of a metatheoretical continuum are full-fledged mechanists and behavior designers (e.g., Baer, 1970, 1973) who are inclined to plan and implement developmental intervention with less information about the course and antecedents of development and relying largely on an arsenal of non-developmental intervention technology. It is a part of the mechanistic worldview in the behavioral sciences to focus primarily on concurrent and environmental paradigms and on target behaviors which are not related to a theoretically interrelated domain of development. Accordingly, interventionists of the mechanistic kind show less concern for the metatheoretical sacredness and/or power of a system of fixed and sequential regulatory principles of developmental behavior-change or for the contextual system of transfer effects (Bortner, 1975; Looft, 1973c; Willems, 1973). Similarly, the position has been taken by intervention-oriented social designers (e.g., Campbell, 1974; Studer and Stea, 1966) that there is little conceptual persuasion in the argument for and acceptance of "natural" systems. Therefore, becoming a planning culture and taking a vigorous approach to the design of development and aging is seen as being mandatory particularly in light of a rapidly changing ecological context.

It appears most likely that the application of both mechanistic and organismic approaches to behavioral intervention in aging will prove useful. This conclusion is in agreement with the position taken throughout this chapter that the current conceptual need in the field is one of a concerted but consistent *pluralism* in theory and method.

Theories of Aging and Intervention. The common position is to argue that a complete theory of psychological aging and development—including both descriptive and explanatory knowledge—is the key for successful intervention design. A complete theory would provide us with the necessary information about the course of behavior-change, the range of modifiability, goals of intervention, potential intervention transfer effects, and appropriate strategies of implementation and evaluation.

Descriptive and explanatory knowledge about aging processes indeed is the key prerequisite for sound intervention planning. The strength of a developmental approach to intervention (e.g., Baltes, 1973b; Brandtstadter and Schneewind, 1976 in press; Harshbarger, 1973; Urban, 1975) lies in comprehensive knowledge about the course and mechanisms of the developmental behavior-change process. Developmental knowledge permits a preventative design for optimization at all periods of the life span. In line with the arguments presented in earlier sections, the conceptual theme of a developmental approach to gerontological intervention is to recognize the contextual and process characteristics of aging as a behavioral phenomenon and to focus correspondingly on a contextual and process orientation in the design of interventive modification programs. A match between theory of development and intervention is a desirable goal.

Aside from the pervasive lack of adequate knowledge, however, the initial conclusion of aiming for a complete match between developmental-aging theory and intervention design needs modulation in light of additional issues.

First, there is the issue of *external validity* and evolutionary openness of any behavioral theory. Beyond the requirement that deployable knowledge needs an appropriate level of external validity, our position is that external validity of a behavior phenomenon is in principle unlimited and never completely marked or bounded by knowledge about existing phenomena. Recognizing that the potential range of psychological aging is not circumscribed both with regard to ontogenetic and evolutionary variation is particularly important, since the current biocultural context for aging may present us with a highly selected view of aging phenomena. Therefore, a simple translation of knowledge about "naturally" occurring aging phenomena may make intervention impotent because of the culture- and period-centric nature of the knowledge base, i.e., its restricted external validity. It is for this reason that an outright commitment to intervention theory and methodology may result in *novel* knowledge about the range (external validity) of aging which researchers committed to explaining unobstructed phenomena are not apt to generate.

There is a second reason why modification efforts are not a simple translation of aging theory into intervention practice: Designing optimal development and aging is not always a simple optimization of the conditions which are responsible for a given developmental outcome. This issue involves the degree of *isomorphy* between the production of a behavior outcome and its modification.

Isomorphy in ontogeny and intervention design refers to the degree of similarity between the variables and mechanisms which produce an outcome and the variables and mechanisms which are apt to result in outcome alterations. Human behavior has been shown not only to be rather flexible but also often a function of multiple and diverse antecedents. Baltes and Nesselroade (1973, p. 220) stated such a multivariate and developmental paradigm assumption in the following manner: "Any dependent variable (or consequent) is potentially a function of multiple determinants . . . and any determinant or antecedent has potentially multiple consequents." A developmental approach to aging as outlined in this chapter explicitly maximizes the possibility of multivariate and discontinuous relationships as reflected for example in notions involving explanatory discontinuity and age by treatment interactions (see Baltes, 1973b; Sutton-Smith, 1970; Willems, 1973).

Intervention and Knowledge Generation. Efforts aimed at modifying psychological aging, then, do not represent only application and evaluation of knowledge (Urban, 1975) generated by the study of naturalistically occurring aging phenomena. Naturalistically occurring aging is but a subset of the potential universe of aging phenomena.

On the contrary, an intervention orientation can be a vital strategy for producing novel knowledge about the range of aging (and novel aging outcomes) if conducted within the framework of a programmatic approach (Baltes and Labouvie, 1973) toward theory building. Accordingly, intervention efforts represent an important vehicle for increasing knowledge (not only in the traditional interpretation of the significance of experimental methodology *per se*) about the external validity of aging phenomena. The nature of psychological aging changes not only with a changing biocultural context but also with the range of intervention programs which researchers and social planners are able to create.

We are impressed with the constraint and/or implicit pessimism shown by most psychogerontological researchers in regard to the potential plasticity and scope of aging behavior. At the same time, we reach the conclusion that the implicit reluctance of many psychogerontologists to engage in interventive research is one of the major reasons why our knowledge base on the psychology of aging is largely descriptive and restricted in scope and external validity. A clear acknowledgment of our historical and biocultural boundaries as well as an active belief in the open dialectics of ontogenetic-evolutionary change processes seems desirable. They may represent the most fertile conditions for future theoretical advances in the field and for the creation of psychological knowledge beneficial to future aging cohorts.

SUMMARY

The central themes of this chapter were treated in the context of metatheoretical and historical issues shaping concrete efforts at theory construction in the psychology of aging and development. Some of the key arguments and conclusions advanced are the following.

On Theory Construction and Theories of Behavior

1. The making of science involves the construction of theories which incorporate aspects of knowledge generation, knowledge dissemination, and knowledge utilization.

2. Theory construction in general proceeds within a contextual framework of meta-theories and metamodels of theory building and theories of behavior.
3. Theories can be evaluated in terms of precision, scope, and deployability.
4. Psychological theories of behavior are aimed at three interrelated objectives: the description, explanation, and modification of behavior.

On Theories of Psychological Aging and Development

1. Complete theories of psychological aging and development contain statements about the description, explanation and modification of intraindividual change and interindividual differences in aging behavior.
2. All existing theories are of the prototheoretical kind and are incomplete or insufficient in precision, scope, and deployability.
3. Current research and theory construction need to become balanced and to reflect the pluralistic spectrum of current psychological theory and the diversity and multidirectionality of behavior-change phenomena observable in adulthood and aging; recognizing the impact of metatheoretical and cultural influences on the conduct of gerontological research is imperative.
4. The focus of psychological aging and development is on delineating behavior-change processes transcending a simple age-function approach; age functions are but a special case of behavior-change models.
5. Process-oriented approaches to psychological theories need to be concerned with the explication of historical, time-ordered sequences which go beyond concurrent paradigms both with regard to the description of change phenomena and their explanation and modification; this posture is known as the developmental orientation.
6. Large interindividual differences in gerontological behavior-change make monolithic, single-agent, and chronological age-related explanations not likely to be useful; the same is true for the likelihood of simple

quantitative and continuous explanatory principles.

7. Modification of psychological aging is seen not only as a simple application and evaluation of existing basic knowledge; intervention work contributes to the generation of novel knowledge by delineating and expanding on dimensions of external validity of aging phenomena.

Niches in Theories and Prospects

1. Programmatic theory building is imperative in order to advance the field; currently, the psychology of aging does not offer much evidence of well-articulated theoretical frameworks.
2. Descriptive and explanatory research on behavioral aging and development need to focus on aging-fair approaches in order to produce a representative body of knowledge; emphasis on ecological and ethological methodology is desirable.
3. Knowledge about the plasticity and modifiability of aging behavior is scarce largely due to prescientific biases about aging and a correlated lack of programmatic interventive research of the experiential kind.
4. Development and utilization of paradigms which explicitly center on biology-behavior-environment interactions appears promising; convergence of ontogenetic and evolutionary approaches to the study of aging change is also recommended.
5. Knowledge bases necessary for the design of optimal aging processes require concerted efforts aimed at constructing theory and research with a joint view on internal and external validity.

Acknowledgment. We are very grateful to Steve Cornelius and Marque Bagshaw for their valuable editorial comments. Writing of this chapter was also supported by a grant (C-74-0127) to John R. Nesselroade and Paul B. Baltes from the National Institute of Education, and participation of the first author in a committee of the Social Science Research Council on the Middle Years chaired by Orville G. Brim.

REFERENCES

Ahammer, I. M. 1973. Social-learning theory as a framework for the study of adult personality development. *In*, P. B. Baltes and K. W. Schaie (eds.), *Life-Span Developmental Psychology: Personality and Socialization.* New York: Academic Press.

Baer, D. M. 1970. An age-irrelevant concept of development. *Merrill-Palmer Quarterly of Behavior and Development*, 16, 238–246.

Baer, D. M. 1973. The control of developmental process: Why wait? *In*, J. R. Nesselroade and H. W. Reese (eds.), *Life-Span Developmental Psychology: Methodological Issues.* New York: Academic Press.

Baldwin, A. L. 1960. The study of child behavior and development. *In*, P. H. Mussen (ed.), *Handbook of Research Methods in Child Development.* New York: John Wiley.

Baltes, M. M., and Lascomb, S. L. 1975. Creating a healthy institutional environment for the elderly via behavior management: The nurse as a change agent. *International Journal of Nursing Research*, 12, 5–12.

Baltes, P. B. 1968. Longitudinal and cross-sectional sequences in the study of age and generation effects. *Hum. Develop.*, 11, 145–171.

Baltes, P. B. (ed.) 1973a. Life-span models of psychological aging: A white elephant? *Gerontologist*, 13, 457–512.

Baltes, P. B. 1973b. Prototypical paradigms and questions in life-span research on development and aging. *Gerontologist*, 13, 458–467.

Baltes, P. B. (ed.) 1973c. Strategies for psychological intervention in old age: A symposium. *Gerontologist*, 13, 4–38.

Baltes, P. B., and Goulet, L. R. 1971. Exploration of developmental variables by manipulation and simulation of age differences in behavior. *Hum. Develop.*, 14, 149–170.

Baltes, P. B. and Labouvie, G. V. 1973. Adult development of intellectual performance: Description, explanation, and modification. *In*, C. Eisdorfer and M. P. Lawton (eds.), *The Psychology of Adult Development and Aging.* Washington, D.C.: American Psychological Association.

Baltes, P. B., and Nesselroade, J. R. 1973. The developmental analysis of individual differences on multiple measures. *In*, J. R. Nesselroade and H. W. Reese (eds.), *Life-Span Developmental Psychology: Methodological Issues.* New York: Academic Press.

Baltes, P. B., Reese, H. W., and Nesselroade, J. R. 1976. *Life-Span Developmental Psychology: Introduction to Research Methods.* Monterey, California: Brooks-Cole. In press.

Baltes, P. B., and Schaie, K. W. (eds) 1973a. *Life-Span Developmental Psychology: Personality and Socialization.* New York: Academic Press.

Baltes, P. B., and Schaie, K. W. 1973b. On life-span developmental research paradigms: Retrospects and prospects. *In*, P. B. Baltes and K. W. Schaie (eds.), *Life-Span Developmental Psychology: Personality and Socialization.* New York: Academic Press.

Baltes, P. B., and Willis, S. L. Adult-gerontological intelligence and learning. *In*, B. B. Wolman (ed.), *International Encyclopedia of Neurology, Psychiatry, Psychoanalysis, and Psychology.* In press.

Barton, E. M., Plemons, J. K., Willis, S. L., and Baltes, P. B. 1975. Recent findings on adult and gerontological intelligence: Changing a stereotype of decline. *American Behavioral Scientist*, 19, 224–236.

Benedict, R. 1938. Continuities and discontinuities on cultural conditioning. *Psychiatry*, 1, 161–167.

Bengtson, V. L., and Black, K. D. 1973. Intergenerational relations and continuities in socialization. *In*, P. B. Baltes and K. W. Schaie (eds.), *Life-Span Developmental Psychology: Personality and Socialization.* New York: Academic Press.

Berger, S. M., and Lambert, W. W. 1968. Stimulus-response theory in contemporary social psychology. *In*, G. Lindzey and E. Aronson (eds.), *The Handbook of Social Psychology.* Vol. 1. Reading, Massachusetts: Addison-Wesley.

Bertalanffy, L. von 1968. *General System Theory.* New York: George Braziller.

Bijou, S. W. 1970. Reinforcement history and socialization. *In*, R. Hoppe, G. A. Milton, and E. C. Simmel (eds.), *Early Experiences and the Process of Socialization.* New York: Academic Press.

Birren, J. E. (ed.) 1959a. *Handbook of Aging and the Individual: Psychological and Biological Aspects.* Chicago: University of Chicago Press.

Birren, J. E. 1959b. Principles of research on aging. *In*, J. E. Birren (ed.), *Handbook of Aging and the Individual: Psychological and Biological Aspects.* Chicago: University of Chicago Press.

Birren, J. E. 1960. Psychological Aspects of Aging. *Annual Review of Psychology*, 11, 131–160.

Birren, J. E. 1964a. *The Psychology of Aging.* Englewood Cliffs, New Jersey: Prentice-Hall.

Birren, J. E. (ed.) 1964b. *Relations of Development and Aging.* Springfield, Illinois: Charles C. Thomas.

Birren, J. E. 1970. Toward an experimental psychology of aging. *American Psychologist*, 25, 124–135.

Birren, J. E. 1974. Translations in gerontology—from lab to life: Psychophysiology and response speed. *American Psychologist*, 29, 808–815.

Birren, J. E., and Woodruff, D. S. 1973. Human development over the life span through education. *In*, P. B. Baltes and K. W. Schaie (eds.), *Life-Span Developmental Psychology: Personality and Socialization.* New York: Academic Press.

Bloom, B. S. 1964. *Stability and Change in Human Characteristics.* New York: John Wiley.

Blum, J. E. Jarvik, L. F. and Clark, E. T. 1970. Rate of change on selective tests of intelligence: A twenty-year longitudinal study of aging. *J. Gerontol.*, 25, 171–176.

Blurton Jones, N. 1972. Characteristics of ethological behaviour. *In*, N. Blurton Jones (ed.), *Ethological*

Studies of Child Behaviour. Cambridge, Great Britain: Cambridge University Press.

Boring, E. G. 1950. *A History of Experimental Psychology.* New York: Appleton-Century-Crofts.

Bortner, R. W. 1967. Personality and social psychology in the study of aging. 1967. *Gerontologist,* 7, 23–36.

Bortner, R. W. 1975. Systems implications of improvements in adult learning. Unpublished manuscript, College of Human Development, The Pennsylvania State University.

Bortner, R. W., and Hultsch, D. F. 1974. Patterns of subjective deprivation in adulthood. *Developmental Psychology,* 10, 534–545.

Botwinick, J. 1970. Geropsychology. *Annual Review of Psychology,* 21, 239–272.

Botwinick, J. 1973. *Aging and Behavior.* New York: Springer.

Brandtstadter, J., and Schneewind, K. 1976. Optimal human development: Psychological aspects. *Hum. Develop.* In press.

Brim, O. G., Jr. 1974a. The sense of personal control over one's life. Unpublished manuscript, Foundation of Child Development, New York.

Brim, O. G., Jr. 1974b. Selected theories of the male mid-life crisis: A comparative analysis. Unpublished manuscript, Foundation of Child Development, New York.

Brim, O. G., Jr., and Wheeler, S. 1966. *Socialization After Childhood: Two Essays.* New York: John Wiley.

Britton, J. H., and Britton, J. O. 1972. *Personality Changes in Aging.* New York: Springer.

Bromley, D. B. 1970. An approach to theory construction in the psychology of development and aging. *In,* L. R. Goulet and P. B. Baltes (eds.), *Life-Span Developmental Psychology: Research and Theory.* New York: Academic Press.

Bromley, D. B. 1974. *The Psychology of Human Aging.* Baltimore: Penguin Books.

Bronfenbrenner, U. 1963. Developmental theory in transition. *In,* H. W. Stevenson (ed.), *Child Psychology.* Chicago: University of Chicago Press.

Bronfenbrenner, U. 1973. Is early intervention effective?: Report and reaction. Paper presented at the Biennial Meeting of the Society for Research in Child Development, Philadelphia, April 1973.

Brunswik, E. 1955. In defense of probabilistic functionalism: A reply. *Psych. Rev.,* 62, 236–242.

Buckley, W. (ed.) 1968. *Modern Systems Research for the Behavioral Scientist.* Chicago: Aldine.

Bühler, C. 1933. *Der menschliche Lebenslauf als psychologisches Problem.* Leipzig: Hirzel.

Bühler, C., Keith-Spiegel, P., and Thomas, K. 1973. Developmental psychology. *In,* B. B. Wolman (ed.), *Handbook of General Psychology.* Englewood Cliffs, New Jersey: Prentice-Hall.

Bühler, C., and Massarik, F. (eds.) 1968. *The Course of Human Life.* New York: Springer.

Bunge, M. 1963. *Causality: The Place of the Causal*

Principle in Modern Science. New York: World Publishing.

Buss, A. R. 1973a. An extension of developmental models that separate ontogenetic changes and cohort differences. *Psych. Bull.,* 80, 466–479.

Buss, A. R. 1973b. A conceptual framework for learning effecting the development of ability factors. *Hum. Develop.,* 16, 273–292.

Buss, A. R. 1974a. A general developmental model for interindividual differences, intraindividual differences, and intraindividual changes. *Developmental Psychology,* 10, 70–78.

Buss, A. R. 1974b. Generational analysis: Description, explanation, and theory. *J. of Soc. Issues,* 30, 55–71.

Busse, E. W. 1959. Psychopathology. *In,* J. E. Birren (ed.), *Handbook of Aging and the Individual.* Chicago: University of Chicago Press.

Busse, E. W. 1969. Theories of aging. *In,* E. W. Busse and E. Pfeiffer (eds.), *Behavior and Adaptation in Late Life.* Boston: Little, Brown.

Butler, R. 1963. The life review: An interpretation of reminiscence in the aged. *Psychiatry,* 26, 65–76.

Campbell, D. T. 1974. The social scientist as methodological servant of the experimenting society. *Policy Studies Journal.* In press.

Carp, F. M. (ed.) 1966. *The retirement process.* U.S. Department of Health, Education and Welfare, PHS Publication No. 1778. Washington, D.C.: U.S. Government Printing Office.

Catania, A. C. 1973. The psychologies of structure, function, and development. *American Psychologist,* 28, 434–443.

Charles, D. C. 1970. Historical antecedents of life-span developmental psychology. *In,* L. R. Goulet and P. B. Baltes (eds.), *Life-Span Developmental Psychology: Research and Theory.* New York: Academic Press.

Chown, S. M. (ed.) 1972. *Human Aging: Selected Readings.* Harmondsworth, England: Penguin.

Chown, S. M., and Heron, A. 1965. Psychological aspects of aging in man. *Annual Review of Psychology,* 16, 417–450.

Clark, K. E., and Miller, G. A. (eds.) 1970. *Psychology.* Englewood Cliffs, New Jersey: Prentice-Hall.

Clayton, V. 1975. Wise old men—where have they all gone? Unpublished manuscript, Gerontology Center, University of Southern California.

Coan, R. W. 1968. Dimensions of psychological theory. *American Psychologist,* 23, 715–722.

Coan, R. W. 1970. Toward a psychological interpretation of psychology. *Journal of the History of the Behavioral Sciences,* 9, 313–327.

Coelho, G. V., Hamburg, D. A., and Adams, J. E. (eds.) 1974. *Coping and Adaptation.* New York: Basic Books.

Cronbach, L. J. 1975. Beyond the two disciplines of scientific psychology. *American Psychologist,* 30, 116–127.

Cumming, E. 1964. New thoughts on the theory of

disengagement. *In*, R. Kastenbaum (ed.), *New Thoughts on Old Age.* New York: Springer.

Cumming, E., and Henry, W. E. 1961. *Growing Old: The Process of Disengagement.* New York: Basic Books.

Dohrenwend, B. S., and Dohrenwend, B. P. (eds.) 1974. *Stressful Life Events.* New York: John Wiley.

Eisdorfer, C., and Lawton, M. P. (eds.) 1973. *The Psychology of Adult Development and Aging.* Washington D.C.: American Psychological Association.

Erikson, E. H. 1959. Identity and the life cycle. *Psychological Issues*, 1, Whole No. 1.

Fahrenberg, J. 1968. Aufgaben und Methoden der psychologischen Verlaufsanalyse (Zeitreihenanalyse). *In*, K. J. Groffmann and K. H. Wewetzer (eds.), *Person als Prozess.* Bern: Huber.

Falk, J. M. 1970. The organization of remembered life experience of older people. Unpublished doctoral dissertation, University of Chicago.

Fozard, J. L., and Thomas, J. C. 1975. Psychology of aging: Basic findings and some psychiatric applications. *In*, J. G. Howells (ed.), *Modern Perspectives in the Psychiatry of Old Age.* New York: Brunner/Mazel.

Frank, P. G. 1954. The variety of reasons for the acceptance of scientific theories. *Sci. Monthly*, 79, 139–145.

Frank, P. G. 1961. *The Validation of Scientific Theories.* New York: Collier.

Gagne, R. M. 1968. Contributions of learning to human development. *Psych. Rev.*, 75, 177–191.

Gewirtz, J. L. 1969. Mechanisms of social learning: Some roles of stimulation and behavior in early human development. *In*, D. A. Goslin (ed.), *Handbook of Socialization Theory and Research.* Chicago: Rand McNally.

Gilgen, A. R. 1970. Introduction: Progress, a paradigm, and problems in scientific psychology. *In*, A. R. Gilgen (ed.), *Contemporary Scientific Psychology.* New York: Academic Press.

Goslin, D. A. (ed.) 1969. *Handbook of Socialization Theory and Research.* Chicago: Rand McNally.

Goulet, L. R. 1970. Training, transfer, and the development of complex behavior. *Hum. Develop.*, 13, 213–240.

Goulet, L. R. 1973. The interfaces of acquisition: models and methods for studying the active, developing organism. *In*, J. R. Nesselroade and H. W. Reese (eds.), *Life Span Developmental Psychology; Methodological Issues.* New York: Academic Press.

Goulet, L. R., and Baltes, P. B. (eds.) 1970. *Life-Span Developmental Psychology: Research and Theory.* New York: Academic Press.

Graumann, K. F. 1972. The state of psychology. *International Journal of Psychology*, 7, 123–134.

Groffmann, K. J. 1970. Life-span developmental psychology in Europe: Past and present. *In*, L. R. Goulet and P. B. Baltes (eds.), *Life-Span Developmental Psychology: Research and Theory.* New York: Academic Press.

Harris, D. B. (ed.) 1957. *The Concept of Development.* Minneapolis: University of Minnesota Press.

Harris, D. B. 1971. The concept of development in developmental psychology. *In*, E. Tobach, L. R. Aronson, and E. Shaw (eds.), *The Biopsychology of Development.* New York: Academic Press.

Harshbarger, D. D. 1973. Some ecological implications for the organization of human intervention throughout the life span. *In*, P. B. Baltes and K. W. Schaie (eds.), *Life-Span Developmental Psychology: Personality and Socialization.* New York: Academic Press.

Havighurst, R. J. 1948. *Developmental Tasks and Education.* New York: David McKay.

Havighurst, R. J. 1973. History of developmental psychology: Socialization and personality development through the life span. *In*, P. B. Baltes and K. W. Schaie (eds.), *Life-Span Developmental Psychology: Personality and Socialization.* New York: Academic Press.

Havighurst, R. J., Neugarten, B. L., and Tobin, S. S. 1968. Disengagement and patterns of aging. *In*, B. L. Neugarten (ed.), *Middle Age and Aging.* Chicago: University of Chicago Press.

Hicks, L. H., and Birren, J. E. 1970. Aging, brain damage, and psychomotor slowing. *Psych. Bull.*, 74, 377–396.

Holzkamp, K. 1967. *Wissenschaft als Handlung.* Berlin: de Gruyter.

Holzkamp, K. 1970. Wissenschaftstheoretische Voraussetzungen kritisch-emanzipatorischer Psychologie. *Zeitschrift für Sozialpsychologie*, 1, 5–12.

Hooper, F. H., Fitzgerald, J., and Papalia, D. 1971. Piagetian theory and the aging process: Extensions and speculations. *Aging and Human Development*, 2, 3–20.

Horn, J. L. 1970. Organization of data on life-span development of human abilities. *In*, L. R. Goulet and P. B. Baltes (eds.), *Life-Span Developmental Psychology: Research and Theory.* New York: Academic Press.

Hoyer, W. J. 1973. Application of operant techniques to the modification of elderly behavior. *In*, P. B. Baltes (ed.), Strategies for psychological intervention in old age: A Symposium. *Gerontologist*, 13, 18–23.

Hoyer, W. J. 1974. Aging as intraindividual change. *Developmental Psychology*, 10, 821–826.

Hultsch, D. F. 1974. Learning to learn in adulthood. *J. Gerontol.*, 29, 302–308.

Hultsch, D. F. 1975. What are we trying to teach adults? Unpublished manuscript, College of Human Development, The Pennsylvania State University.

Jarvik, L. F. 1975. Thoughts on the psychobiology of aging. *American Psychologist*, 30, 576–583.

Jarvik, L. F., and Cohen, D. 1973. A biobehavioral approach to intellectual changes with aging. *In*, C. Eisdorfer and M. P. Lawton (eds.), *The Psychology of Adult Development and Aging.* Washington, D.C.: American Psychological Association.

Jensen, A. R. 1971. The role of verbal mediation in

mental development. *Journal of Genetic Psychology*, **118**, 39-70.

Jessor, R. 1963. The problem of reductionism in psychology. *In*, M. H. Marx (ed.), *Theories in Contemporary Psychology*. New York: Macmillan.

Kantor, J. R. 1973. System structure and scientific psychology. *Psychological Record*, **23**, 451-458.

Kaplan, A. 1964. *The Conduct of Inquiry*. San Francisco: Chandler.

Kastenbaum, R. 1965. Theories of human aging: The search for a conceptual framework. *J. Soc. Issues*, **21**, 13-36.

Kastenbaum, R. 1967. Developmental psychology of later life. *In*, Duke University Council on Aging and Human Development (ed.), *Proceedings of Seminars*. Durham: Duke University Press.

Kastenbaum, R. J. 1973. Loving, dying, and other gerontologic addenda. *In*, C. Eisdorfer and M. P. Lawton (eds.), *The Psychology of Adult Development and Aging*. Washington, D.C.: American Psychological Association.

Kastenbaum, R., Derbin, V., Sabatini, P., and Artt, S. 1972. The ages of me: Toward personal and interpersonal definitions of functional aging. *Aging and Human Development*, **3**, 197-212.

Kendler, H. H. 1970. The unity of psychology. *Canadian Psychologist*, **11**, 30-4.

Keniston, K. 1971. Psychological development and historical change. *Journal of Interdisciplinary History*, **2**, 330-345.

Kerlinger, F. N. 1964. *Foundations of Behavioral Research*. New York: Holt, Rinehart and Winston.

Kimmel, D. C. 1974. *Adulthood and aging*. New York: John Wiley.

Koch, S. 1969. Value properties: Their significance for psychology, axiology, and science. *In*, M. Greene (ed.), Toward a unity of knowledge. *Psychological Issues*, 6 (2), 251-279.

Kohlberg, L. 1968. Early education: A cognitive-developmental view. *Child Development*, **39**, 1014-1062.

Kohlberg, L. 1973. Continuities in childhood and adult moral development revisited. *In*, P. B. Baltes and K. W. Schaie (eds.), *Life-Span Developmental Psychology: Personality and Socialization*. New York: Academic Press.

Kuhn, T. S. 1970. *The Structure of Scientific Revolutions*. 2nd Edition. Chicago: University of Chicago Press.

Labouvie, G. V. 1973. Implications of geropsychological theories for intervention: The challenge for the seventies. *In*, P. B. Baltes (ed.), Strategies for psychological intervention in old age: A symposium. *Gerontologist*, **13**, 10-15.

Labouvie-Vief, G. V., Hoyer, W. J., Baltes, M. M., and Baltes, P. B. 1974. Operant analysis of intellectual behavior in old age. *Hum. Develop.*, **17**, 259-272.

Lachman, R. 1963. The model in theory construction. *In*, M. H. Marx (ed.), *Theories in Contemporary Psychology*. New York: Macmillan.

Lambert, T. A. 1972. Generations and change: Toward a theory of generations as a force in historical process. *Youth and Society*, **4**, 21-45.

Langer, J. 1969. *Theories of Development*. New York: Holt, Rinehart and Winston.

Lawton, M. P., and Nahemow, L. 1973. Ecology and the aging process. *In*, C. Eisdorfer and M. P. Lawton (eds.), *The Psychology of Adult Development and Aging*. Washington, D.C.: American Psychological Association.

Lehr, U. 1972. *Psychologie des Alterns*. Heidelberg: Quelle.

LeVine, R. A. 1969. Culture, personality, and socialization: An evolutionary view. *In*, D. A. Goslin (ed.), *Handbook of Socialization Theory and Research*. Chicago: Rand McNally.

Looft, W. R. 1972. The evolution of developmental psychology: A comparison of handbooks. *Hum. Develop.*, **15**, 187-201.

Looft, W. R. 1973a. Socialization and personality throughout the life span: An examination of contemporary psychological approaches. *In*, P. B. Baltes and K. W. Schaie (eds.), *Life-Span Developmental Psychology: Personality and Socialization*. New York: Academic Press.

Looft, W. R. 1973b. Conceptions of human nature, educational practice, and individual development. *Hum. Develop.*, **16**, 21-32.

Looft, W. R. 1973c. Reflections on intervention in old age: Motives, goals, and assumptions. *Gerontolotist*, **13**, 6-10.

Lowenthal, M. F., and Chiriboga, D. 1973. Social stress and adaptation: Toward a life-course perspective. *In*, C. Eisdorfer and M. P. Lawton (eds.), *The Psychology of Adult Development and Aging*. Washington D.C.: American Psychological Association.

Lowry, R. 1971. *The Evolution of Psychological Theory*. Chicago: Aldine.

Maddox, G. 1964. Disengagement theory. A critical evaluation. *Gerontologist*, **4**, 80-82.

Maddox, G. 1970. Themes and issues in sociological theories of human aging. *Hum. Develop.*, **13**, 17-27.

Marshall, V. M. 1974. Age and awareness of finitude in developmental gerontology. Unpublished manuscript, McMaster University.

Marx, M. H. 1970. Observation, discovery, confirmation, and theory building. *In*, A. R. Gilgen (ed.), *Contemporary Scientific Psychology*. New York: Academic Press.

Marx, M. H., and Hillix, W. A. 1973. *Systems and Theories in Psychology*. New York: McGraw-Hill.

McClearn, G. E. 1970. Genetic influences on behavior and development. *In*, P. H. Mussen (ed.), *Carmichael's Manual of Child Psychology*. 3rd Edition. New York: John Wiley.

Merton, R. K. 1975. Thematic analysis in science: Notes on Holton's concept. *Science*, **188**, 335-338.

Munnichs, J. M. A. 1966a. A short history of psychogerontology. *Hum. Develop.*, **9**, 230-245.

Munnichs, J. M. A. 1966b. *Old Age and Finitude.* Basel: Karger.

Mussen, P. H. (ed.) 1970. *Carmichael's Manual of Child Psychology.* 3rd Edition. New York: John Wiley.

Nesselroade, J. R., and Baltes, P. B. 1974. Adolescent personality development and historical change: 1970–1972. *Monographs of the Society for Research in Child Development*, **39** (1, Serial No. 154).

Nesselroade, J. R., and Reese, H. W. (eds.) 1973. *Life-Span Developmental Psychology: Methodological Issues.* New York: Academic Press.

Neugarten, B. L. (ed.) 1968a. *Middle Age and Aging: A Reader in Social Psychology.* Chicago: University of Chicago Press.

Neugarten, B. L. 1968b. Adult personality: Toward a psychology of the life cycle. *In*, B. L. Neugarten (ed.), *Middle Age and Aging.* Chicago: University of Chicago Press.

Neugarten, B. L. 1969. Continuities and discontinuities of psychological issues into adult life. *Hum. Develop.*, **12**, 121–130.

Neugarten, B. L., and Datan, N. 1973. Sociological perspectives on the life cycle. *In*, P. B. Baltes and K. W. Schaie (eds.), *Life-Span Developmental Psychology: Personality and Socialization.* New York: Academic Press.

Neugarten, B. L., Moore, J. W., and Lowe, J. C. 1965. Age norms, age constraints, and adult socialization. *Am. J. Sociol.*, **70**, 710–717.

Nuttall, R. L. 1972. The strategy of functional age research. *Aging and Human Development*, **3**, 149–152.

Overton, W. F. 1973. On the assumptive base of the nature-nurture controversy: Additive versus interactive conceptions. *Hum. Develop.*, **16**, 74–89.

Overton, W. F., and Reese, H. W. 1973. Models of development: Methodological implications. *In*, J. R. Nesselroade and H. W. Reese (eds.), *Life-Span Developmental Psychology: Methodological Issues.* New York: Academic Press.

Piaget, J. 1970. Piaget's theory. *In*, P. H. Mussen (ed.), *Carmichael's Manual of Child Psychology.* 3rd Edition. New York: John Wiley.

Reese, H. W. 1973. Life-span models of memory. *In*, P. B. Baltes (ed.), Life-span models of psychological aging: A white elephant? *Gerontologist*, **13**, 472–478.

Reese, H. W., and Overton, W. F. 1970. Models of development and theories of development. *In*, L. R. Goulet and P. B. Baltes (eds.), *Life-Span Developmental Psychology: Research and Theory.* New York: Academic Press.

Riegel, K. F. 1972. Time and change in the development of the individual and society. *In*, H. W. Reese (ed.), *Advances in Child Development and Behavior.* Vol. 7. New York: Academic Press.

Riegel, K. F. 1973a. Developmental psychology and society: Some historical and ethical considerations. *In*, J. R. Nesselroade and H. W. Reese (eds.), *Life-Span Developmental Psychology: Methodological Issues.* New York: Academic Press.

Riegel, K. F. 1973b. On the history of psychological gerontology. *In*, C. Eisdorfer and M. P. Lawton (eds.), *The Psychology of Adult Development and Aging.* Washington, D.C.: American Psychological Association.

Riegel, K. F. 1973c. Dialectic operations: The final period of cognitive development. *Hum. Develop.*, **16**, 346–370.

Riegel, K. F. 1976. From traits and equilibrium toward developmental dialectics. *In*, W. Arnold (ed.), *Nebraska Symposium on Motivation.* Lincoln: University of Nebraska Press.

Riegel, K. F., and Riegel, R. M. 1972. Development, drop, and death. *Developmental Psychology*, **6**, 306–319.

Riley, M. W., Johnson, W. and Foner, A. (eds.) 1972. *Aging and Society: A Sociology of Age Stratification.* Vol. 3. New York: Russell Sage Foundation.

Royce, J. R. (ed.) 1970. *Toward Unification in Psychology.* Toronto: University of Toronto Press.

Rozeboom, W. W. 1970. The art of metascience, or, what should a psychological theory be? *In*, J. R. Royce (ed.), *Toward Unification in Psychology.* Toronto: University of Toronto Press.

Rudinger, G. 1976. Die Bedeutung von Längsschnitt- und Querschnitts-untersuchungen für die Messung intra- und interindividueller Differenzen. *In*, U. Lehr and F. Weinert (eds.), *Entwicklung und Persönlichkeit–Festschrift für Hans Thomae.* Stuttgart: Kohlhammer. In press.

Sadovsky, V. N. 1972. General systems theory: Its tasks and methods of construction. *General Systems*, **17**, 171–179.

Schaie, K. W. 1962. A field-theory approach to age changes in cognitive behavior. *Vita Humana*, **5**, 129–141.

Schaie, K. W. 1965. A general model for the study of developmental problems. *Psych. Bull.*, **64**, 92–107.

Schaie, K. W. 1970. A reinterpretation of age-related changes in cognitive structure and functioning. *In*, L. R. Goulet and P. B. Baltes (eds.), *Life-Span Developmental Psychology: Research and Theory.* New York: Academic Press.

Schaie, K. W. 1974. Translations in gerontology– from lab to life: Intellectual functioning. *American Psychologist*, **29**, 802–807.

Schaie, K. W., and Gribbin, K. 1975. Adult development and aging. *Annual Review of Psychology*, **26**, 65–96.

Schonfield, D. 1974. Translation in gerontology–from lab to life: Utilizing information. *American Psychologist*, **29**, 796–801.

Schultz, C. B., and Aurbach, H. A. 1971. The usefulness of cumulative deprivation as an explanation of educational deficiencies. *Merrill-Palmer Quarterly of Behavior and Development*, **17**, 27–39.

Sigel, I. W. 1974. When do we know what a child knows? *Hum. Develop.*, **17**, 201–217.

Spence, J. T. 1963. Learning theory and personality.

In, J. M. Wepman and R. W. Heine (eds.), *Concepts of Personality*. Chicago: Aldine.

Studer, R. G., and Stea, D. 1966. Environmental programming and human behavior. *J. Soc. Issues*, **22**, 127–136.

Sutton-Smith, B. 1970. Developmental laws and the experimentalist's ontology. *Merrill-Palmer Quarterly of Behavior and Development*, **16**, 253–259.

Talland, G. A. (ed.) 1968. *Human Aging and Behavior*. New York: Academic Press.

Thomae, H. 1959. Entwicklungsbegriff und Entwicklungstheorien. *In*, H. Thomae (ed.), *Entwicklungspsychologie*. Göttingen: Hogrefe.

Thomae, H. 1970. Theory of aging and cognitive theory of personality. *Hum. Develop.*, **13**, 1–16.

Thomae, H., and Lehr, U. (eds.) 1968. *Altern: Probleme und Tatsachen*. Frankfurt: Akademische Verlagsgesellschaft.

Tobach, E., Aronson, L. R., and Shaw, E. (eds.) 1971. *The Biopsychology of Development*. New York: Academic Press.

Toffler, A. 1970. *Future Shock*. New York: Random House.

Urban, H. B. 1975. Issues in human development intervention. Unpublished manuscript, College of Human Development, Pennsylvania State University.

Urban, H. B., and Lago, D. 1973. Life-history antecedents in psychiatric disorders of the aging. *In*, P. B. Baltes (ed.), Life-span models of psychological aging: A white elephant? *Gerontologist*, **13**, 502–508.

Underwood, B. J. 1975. Individual differences as a crucible in theory construction. *American Psychologist*, **30**, 128–134.

Van den Daele, L. 1974. Infrastructure and transition in developmental analysis. *Hum. Develop.*, **17**, 1–23.

Werner, H. 1948. *Comparative Psychology of Mental Development*. New York: International Universities Press.

Willems, E. P. 1973. Behavioral ecology and experimental analysis: Courtship is not enough. *In*, J. R. Nesselroade and H. W. Reese (eds.), *Life-Span Developmental Psychology: Methodological Issues*. New York: Academic Press.

Wohlwill, J. F. 1970a. The age variable in psychological research. *Psych. Rev.*, **77**, 49–64.

Wohlwill, J. F. 1970b. Methodology and research strategy in the study of developmental change. *In*, L. R. Goulet and P. B. Baltes (eds.), *Life-Span Developmental Psychology: Research and Theory*. New York: Academic Press.

Wohlwill, J. F. 1973. *The Study of Behavioral Development*. New York: Academic Press.

Wolman, B. B. 1973. Concerning psychology and philosophy of science. *In*, B. B. Wolman (ed.), *Handbook of General Psychology*. Englewood Cliffs, New Jersey: Prentice-Hall.

Woodruff, D. S. 1973. The usefulness of the life-span approach for the psychophysiology of aging. *In*, P. B. Baltes (ed.), Life-span models of psychological aging: A white elephant? *Gerontologist*, **13**, 467–472.

Zigler, E. 1963. Metatheoretical issues in developmental psychology. *In*, M. Marx (ed.), *Theories in Contemporary Psychology*. New York: Macmillan.

PART 2 BIOLOGICAL BASIS OF AGING AND BEHAVIOR

8
THE NEURAL BASIS OF AGING

William Bondareff
Northwestern University Medical School

The proper subjects for the study of behavioral events which characterize the process of an animal's aging are the neurons and neuroglial cells of the central nervous system. The numbers of these cells in a vertebrate brain are immense and their interconnections, which in large part are not known, are legion. It has been estimated that the human brain after birth contains about 10^{11} neurons, each of which makes roughly 10^4 connections with other neurons (Weiss, 1973). These cells are extraordinarily active metabolically, each containing a complement of some 10^7-10^8 protein molecules which is renewed, perhaps 10^4 times during the cell's life (Weiss, 1973). They exist in a rigidly controlled microenvironment, the properties of which they largely determine. As the neurons, especially, synthesize and degrade large amounts of protein in a lifetime, and do not themselves divide, there is ample opportunity for the production of abnormal protein, either by synthetic error or post-translational modification.

It is therefore reasonable to assume that pathology, which typically involves certain neurons at various times during the course of senescence, reflects aging of neurons, *per se.* Such neuronal pathology includes: the intracytoplasmic accumulation of lipofuscin pigment, decrements in the amounts of cytoplasmic RNA and in the activities of certain cytoplasmic enzymes, changes in the morphology, distribution or reactivity of certain cytoplasmic organelles, and in some cases death and lysis of the neuron (see Table 8). But these cellular abnormalities, in whole or in part, can also result from extraneuronal, age-associated changes of blood vessels or their associated structures, cerebrospinal fluid ventricles or their associated structures, intracellular channels, or neuroglia. Such changes, by compromising the normal supply of ions, metabolites and nutrients to and from neurons, would result in neuronal pathology similar to that following a primary change in neuronal structure or chemistry. In this review, which focuses on intracellular aspects of neuronal aging, extraneuronal elements will not be considered with the exception of the neuroglia and the immediate microenvironment of the neurons.

AGE CHANGES IN NEUROGLIA

Almost nothing is known about the aging of the neuroglia. These cells are known to accumulate lipofuscin pigment as do nerve cells although the pattern of accumulation, judging from the little that is known of it, appears to be distinct from that characteristic of neurons (Brizzee, Ordy, and Kaack, 1974). As there are essentially no data, it has been tacitly assumed for many years that the neuroglia increase in number with aging. The popularity of this assumption probably rests with the generally accepted fact that when neurons die they are replaced by neuroglia; and it has become generally accepted dogma that neuronal death accompanies aging. More recent evidence suggests that neither generalized neuronal loss nor a generalized increase in the number of glial cells are common accompaniments of aging. However, in a study of neuroglial populations in rat cerebral cortex, although no age-related increase in the numbers of astrocytes or oligodendrocytes was found, there did appear to be an increased number of microglial cells in the brains of senescent animals (Vaughan and Peters, 1974). The meaning of these findings is obscured by the finding that butyrylcholinesterase activity, present predominantly in neuroglia (Giacobini, 1964), increased in the cerebellum and cerebrum of chickens from 12 to 36 months old (Vernadakis, 1973a) and S-100 protein, also found predominantly in neuroglia (Cicero, Cowan, Moore, and Suntzeff, 1970), increased progressively in the frontal lobe, cerebellum, corpus striatum, hypothalamus and hippocampus in mice from 6 to 30 months old (Cicero, Ferrendelli, Suntzeff, and Moore, 1972). As the specificity of butyrylcholinesterase activity for neuroglia is hardly absolute and the S-100 protein has been demonstrated in neuronal cytoplasm (Hydén, 1974), it is not possible to know if there is an age-associated increase in the numbers of neuroglial cells. Whether an age-associated increase in neuroglial cells is generalized or selectively regional, as appears to be the case for the neuronal loss associated with aging, is of course a moot question.

INTRANEURONAL ACCUMULATION OF LIPOFUSCIN

By means of commonly-used histological staining reactions a globular or granular material is found in the cytoplasm of most vertebrate neurons at some stage of the life span. Depending upon specific conditions of fixation, dehydration, embedding and staining, this material will appear variously colored, structured and distributed in the neuronal cytoplasm. In the larger neurons it often will have a polar distribution. If

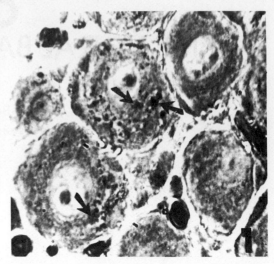

Figure 1. Photomicrograph of neurons from the second cervical spinal ganglion of a 24-month-old Sprague-Dawley rat fixed by immersion in osmium tetroxide. Representative clumps of granular lipofuscin are indicated by arrows. 1,380X. (From Bondareff, 1964. *In*, B. L. Strehler (ed.), *Advances in Gerontological Research*, Vol. I. New York: Academic Press.)

tissues are subjected to lipid solvents during histological preparation, it will appear globular; otherwise, a granular configuration is found (Figure 1) suggesting the presence of lipid which is partially dissolved during preparation. This cytoplasmic material, known generally as lipofuscin because of its lipid content and brownish coloration in unstained tissue sections, emits a characteristic yellow to orange fluorescence and is readily identified by fluorescence microscopy.

Neuronal lipofuscin has been the subject of numerous histochemical studies, which in spite of questionable chemical specificity, have shown it to contain protein, several amino acids (including tryptophan, tyrosine, arginine, lysine, histidine, cysteine and cystine), lipids, phospholipids and plasmalogens (Strehler, 1964). A few enzymes, in particular acid phosphatase and non-specific esterase have also been demonstrated histochemically as have a variety of reactive groups including sulfhydryl groups, aldehydes, acidic and basic groups, and vicinal-polyhydroxyl groups (Strehler, 1964). These constituents are responsible for staining reactions by means of which lipofuscin can be defined and reliably identified in tissue sections. Among these staining reactions are a few, which have proved especially useful for the study of lipofuscin in neurons, namely the periodic acid-Schiff reaction, staining with osmium tetroxide, Sudan Black-B or Nile-blue sulfate, the Schmorl ferric ferricyanide reaction, and the Gomori reaction for acid phosphatase (Bondareff, 1959; Strehler, 1964; Brizzee, Ordy, and Kaack, 1974). These staining reactions were useful in earlier attempts to differentiate neuronal lipofuscin from other autofluorescent pigments such as pterins and ceroids which may, under certain pathological conditions, be found in neurons. However, these stains lack chemical specificity and further analysis must depend largely upon the isolation of a purified fraction and its systematic study of specific methods of chemical analysis.

The isolation of lipofuscin from cardiac muscle, was accomplished some years ago and its analysis has been reviewed by Björkerud (1964). More recently, purified fractions of lipofuscin have been prepared from brain by Siakotos and his colleagues (Siakotos and Koppang, 1973). Initially, brain tissue is homogenized in Tris-buffered sucrose and subjected to additional high pressure disruption. By centrifugation, a supernatant and an associated brown pigment are collected from which the pigment is separ-

ated by differential centrifugation. It is layered on a linear distilled water-15 percent NaCl gradient from which an enriched fraction is collected by centrifugation. By light microscopic criteria the resulting preparation appears to be a reasonably homogeneous fraction of lipofuscin, the density of which is 1.00 to 1.03, somewhat different from that characteristic of cardiac lipofuscin. The fluorescence spectrum of this lipofuscin, also somewhat different from that characteristic of cardiac lipofuscin, has an excitation maximum of 3,600Å and an emission maximum of 4,500Å.

Neuronal lipofuscin, isolated from fractions of brain, has been shown to have a uniquely characteristic complement of cations, in particular a high concentration of zinc, and a characteristic complement of hydrolytic enzymes (Siakotos and Koppang, 1973). In addition to the acid phosphatase and esterase, known from light microscopic histochemical analyses, lipofuscin isolated from human brain has been shown to contain a number of enzymes typically found in lysosomes (see Table 1). There has been active controversy in the past as to the origin of lipofuscin pigment within nerve cells (see Bondareff, 1957), but the presence of these lysosomal enzymes now indicates that it derives from lysosomes (see Toth, 1968). Its development, however, is still not understood. It ap-

TABLE 1. COMPONENT HYDROLYTIC ENZYMES AND CATIONS OF LIPOFUSCIN PIGMENT ISOLATED FROM HUMAN BRAIN.

Enzyme	Sp. Act. (nmoles substrate hydrolyzed/ mg/protein/h)	Cation	ppm
Acid Phosphatase	5,000	Cu	20
Cathepsin D	234	Mn	1.3
β-Galactosidase	230	Ca	240
β-Hexosaminidase	310	Fe	300
β-Glucosidase	420	Zn	400
α-Glucosidase	13		
α-Mannosidase	9		
α-Fucosidase	5		
2,3,AMP-phosphohydrolase	6,200		

Reprinted with permission from, Procedures for the isolation of lipopigments from brain, heart and liver, and their properties: A review, by A. N. Siakotos and N. Koppang, *Mechanisms of Ageing and Development*, 2 (1973) 196, 198.

pears that primary lysosomes, which are abundant in the cytoplasm of nerve cells of all ages, are readily found before lipofuscin can be identified by light microscopic histochemical means or by electron microscopy. It has been suggested that these primary lysosomes, which contain the hydrolytic enzymes found later in lipofuscin particles, are the primordia of lipofuscin (Sekhon and Maxwell, 1974). The formative process may involve the formation of a secondary lysosome, either through fusion of primary lysosomal membranes with those of autophagosomes or phagosomes, or they may simply be transformed without a secondary lysosomal intermediary. In any event, the lipofuscin found in old nerve cells appears to be a residuum of some sort, probably of autophagic derivation. Whether these products of cellular metabolism, sequestered in lysosomes, are transformed in a primary or secondary lysosome is uncertain and the macromolecular events involved are not known. It has been speculated that modification of sequestered materials might be accomplished by peroxidation, polymerization and cross linking of lipoproteins or by pseudoperoxidation of catechol derivatives catalyzed by metals (Barden, 1970). Whatever the mechanism, the resultant residuum is not digested by the lysosome, perhaps because lysosomes lack the requisite lipases or phospholipases.

The progressive relative increase in lipofuscin and secondary lysosomes and the associated relative decline in primary lysosomes in nerve cells as functions of age have been well documented. In anterior horn cells of mice more than 6 months old, dense bodies, the ultrastructure of which closely resembles that of autophagosomes, are found. Sequential study of these anterior horn cells in mice from 6 months to 21 months of age has shown a progressive increase in typical lipofuscin granules and strongly suggests the gradual, progressive transformation of autophagosome-like secondary lysosomes (Sekhon and Maxwell, 1974).

Lipofuscin granules have a characteristic ultrastructure (Figure 2). In ultrathin sections of nerve cells of vertebrates fixed by vascular perfusion with aldehyde solutions and then post-

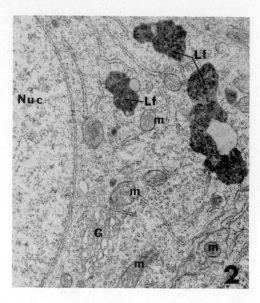

Figure 2. Electron micrograph of a Purkinje cell in the cerebellar cortex of a Fischer 344 rat, 15 months of age. Lipofuscin complexes (Lf), a Golgi complex (G) and mitochondria (m) are identified in the cytoplasm of this neuron, the nucleus of which is indicated (Nuc). 14,000X.

fixed with osmium tetroxide, lipofuscin particles appear in electron micrographs typically as complex, dense, granular structures, about 0.1 μ to as much as 5 μ in diameter. Each particle is bounded by a single membrane and contains a variable number of dense bands closely associated with a vacuolar element, which may appear empty or may contain a variable number of small dense granules. It has been presumed that lipofuscin granules increase in complexity and size by the coalescence of less complex lipofuscin particles and by the transformation of existing particles (Sekhon and Maxwell, 1974).

Although the sequential process through which lipofuscin granules (found typically in old nerve cells) form is not known, there seems to be little doubt that the number of lipofuscin particles and the size and complexity of individual particles seen in the electron microscope increase as direct functions of chronological age. A detailed electron microscopic study of lipofuscin in serial sections has not been attempted but it appears from light microscopic studies that lipofuscin does not occur in all the neurons in any nucleus or ganglion in which it is found. Why some neurons do not accumulate lipofuscin is not known. In addition, the age at which lipofuscin first appears, the site of its first appearance and the rate of its increase in involved nuclei all vary widely among vertebrates. It is not found in all neurons at the same age and its rate and manner of accumulation seem to be characteristically different in different neuronal types. In a study of rhesus monkeys at various ages, lipofuscin was found by reliable histochemical methods at 3 months in the neurons of the inferior olivary nucleus. Its sequential occurrence in medulla, hippocampus, midbrain, pons, cerebral cortex and cerebellum and its sequential increase in these nuclei as found by Brizzee, Ordy, and Kaack (1974) is summarized in Table 2.

The involvement of the Golgi complex (Figure 2) in the genesis of neuronal lipofuscin has been assumed for a number of years and the similarity between Golgi vacuoles and vesicles to those associated with lipofuscin complexes has been noted (Bondareff, 1957). The Golgi apparatus, typically well developed in neurons, tends to fragment in certain neurons in old animals, and age-related changes in staining properties of the Golgi fragments have also been noted (Sosa and de Zorrilla, 1966; Bondareff, 1959). Of greater interest perhaps, is the observation that lipofuscin often appears to occur in close association to the Golgi apparatus, further suggesting a relationship between the two. To investigate this proposed relationship Barden (1970) used a histochemical method for the Golgi-associated enzyme, thiamine pyrophosphatase (TPPase) to demonstrate the Golgi apparatus in old nerve cells and noted an inverse relationship between TPPase activity and the accumulation of lipofuscin. In the inferior olivary nucleus of aged Rhesus monkeys, the neurons of which accumulate lipofuscin early and in large amounts, there was little TPPase activity demonstrated, and the Golgi apparatus appeared to decrease as the amount of lipofuscin progressively increased.

There has as yet been no attempt to compare the chemical properties of Golgi membranes, which can be isolated by differential centrifugation from homogenates of liver (Ehrenreich, Bergeron, Siekevitz, and Palade, 1973), in homogenates of brain in young and old animals but it is reasonable to anticipate age-related changes in the Golgi complex of aged nerve cells. Novikoff and his colleagues have demonstrated the relationship between the Golgi complex lamellae, the rough endoplasmic reticulum, an intermediary group of endoplasmic reticular lamellae specifically related to the Golgi complex (GERL) and primary lysosomes (Novikoff, Novikoff, Quintana, and Hauw, 1971). If the Golgi lamellae are involved in the elaboration of primary lysosomes, which appear to be closely associated with the elaboration of lipofuscin, it is reasonable to assume a close relationship between Golgi lamellae and lipofuscin and perhaps between Golgi lamellae and the total complex of organelles associated with the synthesis of proteins and other membrane components as well (Bennett, Leblond, and Haddad, 1974).

If the accumulation of lipofuscin signals a generalized decline in neuronal metabolism such a decline has not as yet been demonstrated. Lipofuscin has been considered an inert slag product of no particular importance (see Bondareff, 1959). It has been noted that in the neurons of the inferior olivary nucleus, in which lipofuscin accumulates at an early age and is found in great abundance in old animals, there is no decline in the number of cells and no indication that lipofuscin accumulation is related to a loss of nerve cells (Brody, 1973). To date, there has been no specific attempt to relate lipofuscin content with neuronal function and perhaps it has no deleterious effect on neurons. However, in this regard the earlier observations of Murray and Stout (1947) should not be overlooked. They maintained human sympathetic neurons in culture and noted that cells containing large amounts of lipofuscin-like pigment granules migrated relatively little and their nuclei stained less intensely than normal. An age-related decline in the normal motility of certain neurons could interfere with interneuronal relationships and significantly affect function.

TABLE 2. LIPOFUSCIN ACCUMULATION EXPRESSED IN PERCENT OF CELLS IN 6 REGIONS, COMPRISING 2 NEOCORTICAL LAMINA AND 15 NUCLEI IN THE BRAIN AT 4 AGE LEVELS IN THE FEMALE RHESUS MONKEY.

Rank order of 6 regions across 4 ages	AGE IN YEARS (N = 16, n − 4) GROUP MEANS ± S.E.			
	0.64 ± 0.16	4.0 ± 0.49	9.5 ± 0.28	19.5 ± 0.95
A. Cerebellum				
1. Dentate nucleus	0	0.25	5.27	10.27
2. Cortex-Purkinje layer	0	0.17	19.40	33.17
(Mean)	(0)	(0.21)	(12.33)	(21.72)
±S.E.	−	0.07	2.82	4.70
B. Neocortex (Area 4)				
3. Lamina I	0	1.30	5.87	19.17
4. Lamina V	0	6.70	23.47	25.20
(Mean)	(0)	(4.00)	(14.67)	(22.18)
±S.E.	−	1.09)	3.39	2.13
C. Pons				
5. Superior olive	0	0.87	0.10	0.45
6. Abducens nucleus	0	1.22	4.92	30.42
7. Ven. cochlear nucleus	0	10.87	9.30	22.80
8. Lat. vestibular nucleus	0	2.92	41.30	43.97
9. Motor nucleus V	0	0.10	39.30	50.42
10. Main sensory nucleus V	0	23.97	38.02	77.30
(Mean)	(0)	(6.66)	(22.15)	(37.56)
±S.E.	−	1.88	7.87	5.38
D. Midbrain				
11. Oculomotor nucleus	0	1.52	16.70	42.42
12. Red nucleus	0	12.67	32.10	69.17
13. Mesencephalic nucleus V	0	4.70	51.95	73.55
(Mean)	(0)	(6.30)	(33.58)	(61.71)
±S.E.	−	2.51	5.19	4.91
E. Hippocampus				
14. Pyramidal layer	0	13.35	51.37	65.25
F. Medulla				
15. DMV	0	4.82	18.87	60.67
16. Hypoglossal nucleus	0	2.82	57.82	79.97
17. Inferior olive	3.3	51.12	57.22	90.52
(Mean)	(1.1)	(19.59)	(44.64)	(77.05)
±S.E.	−	7.18	6.72	5.17
(Mean)	(0.19)	(8.19)	(27.19)	(46.74)
±S.E.	−	3.10	4.72	6.49
Arc sine % of mean	2.50	12.68	28.64	42.52

From Brizzee, Ordy, and Kaack, 1974. Reproduced with permission from *Journal of Gerontology*.

ATROPHIC CHANGES AND NEURONAL DEATH

The brains of old men that come to autopsy typically demonstrate a decrement in brain weight and a decrease in brain volume resulting in a shrunken gross appearance. Although in most cases it has not been possible to know with certainty whether the apparent atrophic change has resulted from faulty preparative technique, a degenerative disease of the aged, agony, or so-called normal aging (see Bondareff, 1959), atrophic changes of some sort typically are taken as *sine qua non* of the aging process. Yet when such changes are sought among the vertebrates in a systematic manner they usually are not found (Dayan, 1971). It is true that atrophic changes are found in the brains of old men with alarming frequency. For example, the occurrence of senile plaques and neurofibrillary tangles in the brains of persons in their seventh decade (Matsuyama, Namiki, and Watanabe, 1966; cited by Terry and Wisniewski, 1972) is indeed extraordinary but may relate no more to normalcy than the comparably high incidence of atheromatous plaques in the aortae of men in their third decade (Robbins, 1967).

If neuronal atrophy, the end result of which is neuronal loss, is as obligatory an incumbency of the aging process as is the accumulation of lipofuscin, it is not as general a phenomenon as total cell counts might indicate. In cell suspensions of fixed whole mouse brain the total neuronal population was estimated at about 5.5×10^6 in young animals, as compared with about 2×10^6 neurons in 29-month-old mice (Johnson and Erner, 1972). It is more likely, however, that neuronal loss is a more exclusive process involving only selective parts of the brain. In four parts of the human brain, for example, a decrease in neuronal population is described, which is greatest in the superior temporal gyrus and least in the postcentral gyrus, with the neuronal loss in the precentral gyrus, area striata and inferior temporal gyrus being intermediate (Brody, 1955). Similarly, the neuronal loss in human frontal cortex has been found to be greater than that occurring in the diencephalon, cerebellum and brain stem (Critchley, 1942). Brody (1973), who finds a progressive decline in neuronal numbers in all cortical layers after the fifth decade has reported significant neuronal loss in the superior frontal gyrus (Figure 3), a region in which other atrophic changes are commonly found in the senium. There are, however, procedural difficulties in all these attempts to estimate total neuronal populations by morphological methods, which are difficult to evaluate and perhaps impossible to overcome. The results of other studies, which concern a variety of brain stem nuclei, the neurons of which can be counted in their entirety, are seemingly antithetic as no neuronal loss is found. In man, no age-related loss of neurons is found in the motor nucleus of the facial nerve (Van Buskirk, 1945), the ventral cochlear nucleus (Konigsmark, 1969; Konigsmark and Murphy, 1972), the dentate nucleus (Höpker, 1951) nor in the inferior oli-

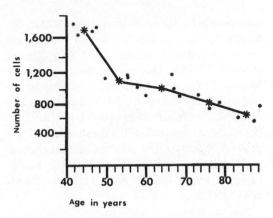

Figure 3. The relationship of age to the total number of neurons in the superior frontal gyrus of the human brain. (From Brody, 1973. *In*, M. Rockstein (ed.), *Development and Aging in the Nervous System* New York: Academic Press.)

vary nucleus (Monagle and Brody, 1974). In each of these nuclei, lipofuscin typically accumulates as a function of chronological age and seems to be a reliable index of age-related alterability.

Neuronal loss seems less reliable as an index of aging. Cowan (1973) has noted the remarkable constancy of neuronal populations in vertebrates exemplified in the lateral mammillary nuclei of adult cats where the average difference in total neuronal numbers between the right and left nuclei is only about 5 percent (Fry and Cowan, 1972). If cell numbers are so closely controlled in mammalian brains a decline in the senium may be catastrophic and more reflective of serious pathology than of normal aging. But to date most attempts to estimate neuronal populations have relied on morphological methods, which because of technical difficulties related to specimen preparation and sampling, are difficult to evaluate. Non-morphological methods, which have as yet been inadequately exploited, have only recently been applied to this problem. DNA content, for example, which has been found to decrease in the cerebellum and cerebrum of chickens after the twentieth month, may be indicative of significant neuronal loss (Vernadakis, 1973a). The loss appears selective as no change in DNA content was found in the optic lobes or in a rostral brain stem sample consisting of diencephalic and mesencephalic tissues (Vernadakis, 1973a). Selective changes in the amount of the protein 14-3-2, believed to be associated with neurons (Cicero, Cowan, Moore, and Suntzeff, 1970; Moore, 1973), indicate a slight decrease in the neuronal populations of the corpus striata and cerebral cortex of 30-month-old rats as compared with 6-month-old animals. Again, the process appears to be selective in that comparable changes were not found in the hippocampus, hypothalamus or cerebellum (Cicero *et al.*, 1972).

AGE-ASSOCIATED CHANGES IN NEURONAL ORGANELLES AND CYTOCHEMISTRY

The accumulation of lipofuscin may relate to some functional decline with actual cell death only occurring regionally as a result of special circumstances, perhaps vascular. On the other hand, the accumulation of lipofuscin should not be associated with an age-related decline in neuronal function *a priori*. While the search for other morphological indicators of neuronal physiology failure with age has not been too rewarding, it continues and recently attention has tended to focus on cellular transport phenomena and the fibrillar proteins which promote them. The frequent occurrence of neurofibrillary tangles in the brains of elderly men suggests that a change in the normal cytoskeletal elements, neurotubules and neurofilaments, may reflect neuronal functional decline in the senium.

Neurotubules, the microtubules of neurons (see Wuerker and Kirkpatrick, 1972), are tubular structures about 230Å in outside diameter which occur singly or in groups of varying dimensions in the nerve cell body and its processes. In cross-sectional profile they appear to be made up of 13 globular subunits (Tilney, Bryan, Bush, Fusiwara, Mooseker, Murphy and Snyder, 1973) and after isolation and negative staining they appear to be made up of 13 longitudinal protofilaments, helically arranged. When they occur in groups they are invariably separated by a rather uniform distance, across which they are interconnected by an ill-defined dense substance. They are rich in tubulins, specific proteins which have been isolated and characterized (Olmsted and Borisy, 1973). Under ap-

propriate conditions their outside walls react with ruthenium red (Tani and Ametani, 1970) indicating the presence of polyanionic substances presumed to be glycoproteins or glycosaminoglycans.

Neurotubules contribute to the cytoskeleton of nerve cells and are presumably determinants of cell shape. They also function in cellular motility and intracellular transport mechanisms (Goldman, 1971; Ochs, 1972; Reaven and Axline, 1973). It has been claimed that their numbers are inversely related to 100Å-filaments, which were thought to contribute directly to microtubular structure (Wisniewski, Shelanski, and Terry, 1968). But it seems more probable at present, that neurotubules and 100Å-filaments (neurofilaments in nerve cells) are distinct cellular entities with different compositions, structures and functions.

Different types of filaments are found in nerve cells (see Wuerker and Kirkpatrick, 1972; Wessels, Spooner, Ash, Bradley, Luduena, Taylor, Wrenn and Yamada, 1971). Microfilaments, about 50Å in diameter, are found immediately subjacent to the plasma membranes of many neurons and neuroglia. These appear to have a contractile property and are believed to function primarily in cellular mobility (Wessels *et al.*, 1971). Other filaments, about 100Å in diameter, are usually in groups arranged in parallel with each other, and probably are involved in intracellular transport of ions and small molecules as well as having a cytoskeletal function (Reaven and Axline, 1973; Edström, 1974). Finally, there are filaments 100–150Å in diameter, which appear to be similar to tonofilaments, that occur with great frequency especially in astroglial cells, and which presumably have a cytoskeletal function (Bondareff and McLone, 1973).

Very little is known about the neurofilaments and neurotubules in the neurons of aged animals. Neurofibrillary tangles, as has been noted, occur with almost unbelievable frequency in the neurons of people over 70 years. It is presumed that the occurrence of these neurofibrillary tangles, which are found only in human brains, represent an abnormality of the normal neurotubule-neurofibrillary element of nerve cells (Terry and Wisniewski, 1972). In these old brains, the tubules are about 220Å in outside diameter and appear to be twisted at intervals of about 800Å. Fractions enriched in twisted tubules have been prepared from hippocampal neurons isolated from human brains by sieving and differential centrifugation. These fractions contain a protein, the electrophoretic mobility of which is distinctly different from that of tubulins, but which appears similar to that of the major protein of neurofilaments normally found in human brain (Igbal, Wisniewski, Shelanski, Brostoff, Liwnicz, and Terry, 1974). Age differences in the distributions of neurofilaments and microtubules have been reported by Samorajski, Friede, and Ordy (1971) who counted them in relation to axon caliber in the pyramidal tracts of mice and found, with regression analyses, that the number of microtubules increased during 8 to 26 months of age while the number of neurofilaments decreased. Although these data may reflect a sampling error, at best difficult to control in electron microscopic studies, they are of considerable interest.

In general, microtubules appear to be related to rapid axoplasmic transport. The macromolecular mechanism which subserves rapid axoplasmic transport is not known but it appears to depend upon the structural integrity of the microtubules (Ochs, 1972). Whether transport occurs between tubules or within tubules is not known but it can be interrupted readily by drugs such as colchicine, which bind with microtubular protein and interfere with normal transport mechanisms (Sjöstrand, Frizell, and Hasselgren, 1970). There has been no detailed study of age changes in axoplasmic transport but Ochs (1973) has compared the rapid axoplasmic transport of ^{3}H-leucine-labeled protein in sensory nerve fibers of old and young dogs and cats. Ochs finds essentially no age-related changes and notes the remarkable constancy of rapid axoplasmic transport mechanisms in animals under various conditions including aging. The slight tendency toward an increased rate of rapid axoplasmic transport, which as noted by Ochs may well represent a sampling error, is especially interesting in the light of the finding of Samorajski, Rolsten, and Ordy (1971) of a relative increase in axonal neurotubules in senescent animals.

A decrease in the number of mitochondria in axons of senescent mice has been reported and there are data suggesting that mitochondria may change with age. Weinbach and Garbus (1959) found mitochondria from old animals to be less stable but the significance of these data with regard to mitochondrial function is not clear. More recently, it is claimed that mitochondria isolated from brains of old mice turn over lipids at a rate lower than that of young animals (Huemer, Bickert, Lee, and Reeves, 1971; Menzies and Gold, 1972). With these sparse data little can be said about mitochondrial function in aging animals but it would appear to remain relatively unchanged throughout life. The turnover rate of phospholipids in mitochondrial membrane fractions may also decrease in old mice (Horrocks, unpublished, reported by Samorajski and Ordy, 1972).

The common conception that neuronal aging may be equated to a decline in neuronal metabolism seems to be well documented by reports that stainable Nissl substance declines in Purkinje cells of senescent mice (Andrew, 1937) and men (Ellis, 1920) and in cerebral cortical neurons of senescent rats (Kuhlenbeck, 1954). The conclusion that neuronal aging is accompanied by a gradual loss of neuronal chromidial substance and perhaps also by a change in the distribution of Nissl substance is unfortunately controverted by other reports of no age-associated change in Nissl substance (Vogt and Vogt, 1946; Wilcox, 1959; Bondareff, 1957). The issue, which is complicated by numerous technical difficulties and sampling problems concerning variations in neuronal basophilia unrelated to cellular aging (Dolley, 1917; Kuntz,

TABLE 3. TOTAL RNA CONTENT IN HUMAN MOTOR HORN CELLS ISOLATED FROM THE NUCLEUS VENTRALIS LATERALIS OF SPINAL CORD SEGMENT C5.

Age in years	RNA in pg/cell
0–20	402 ± 28
21–40	553 ± 38
41–60	640 ± 55
61–80	504 ± 31
over 80	420 ± 30

From Hydén, 1973. *In*, G. B. Ansell and P. B. Bradley (eds.), *Macromolecules and Behavior*. By permission of Macmillan, London and Basingstoke.

1945), remains unsettled. Indeed, Hydén (1960) has published intriguing data on age-related changes in neuronal RNA content. By means of microdissection, Hydén isolated neurons from the ventral horns of the spinal cord of human traffic accident victims and found the RNA content of these cells to fall after age 60 (Table 3). With similar methods, RNA has also been measured in pyramidal cells of rats isolated from the CA3 zone of the hippocampus (Ringborg, 1966). In pooled specimens of 5-10 neurons each, total RNA was determined microspectrophotometrically (Table 4) and the base ratio composition was analyzed by microelectrophoresis on a cellulose fiber by the method of Edström (1964). Reported results suggest a significant decrement in the rate of RNA synthesis in hippocampal pyramidal neurons of senescent rats (Table 4) comparable to that found in ventral horn neurons of elderly men. According to Hydén (1973) this age-related decline in the rate of RNA synthesis suggests there may be fewer ribosomes available for protein synthesis in neurons of old animals. The change in the base composition of total RNA (Table 4) does not differentiate different species of RNA and is therefore difficult to interpret, but the increase in the guanine + cytosine/adenine + uracil ratio from 1.66 in rats 6-8 weeks old to 1.95 in rats 36-38 months old oould reflect changes In the RNA synthesized by senescent animals.

An age-related decline in neuronal RNA metabolism is indicated by the decreased capacity of Purkinje cells and anterior horn cells of mice about 20 months old to incorporate ^{3}H-cytidine. Grain counts after intraperitoneal injection of the labeled precursor were decreased over both the nucleus and the cytoplasm of neurons from old animals as compared with younger animals, about 1.5 months old. Additional data, suggesting that aging is accompanied by depressed neuronal RNA metabolism comes from a morphological study of Nissl substance in young and old rats forced to swim to exhaustion (Bondareff, 1962). Exhaustive swimming was used not only to provide a metabolic stress but to render a population of spinal ganglion cells temporarily functionally uniform so as to maximize subtle changes in functional state and minimize variables of preparation and sample (Bondareff, 1962). It was shown that although the response to initial swimming trials was similar there was a difference in the ability of young and old rats to recover. The Nissl pattern reverted to that characteristic of the normal, unexercised animal within 2 hours in young rats but remained chromatolytic in the older animals.

The decreased capacity of spinal ganglion neurons from old rats to re-establish normal patterns of Nissl substance distribution and basophilia after exhaustive swimming suggested some modification of protein or nucleic acid metabolism in neurons of senescent animals. Although no such modification has been identified precisely, Menzies and Gold (1972) have found the average half-life of ribosomal protein

TABLE 4. TOTAL RNA CONTENT AND BASE COMPOSITION OF SINGLE PYRAMIDAL CELLS ISOLATED FROM THE HIPPOCAMPAL CA3 ZONE OF RATS AT DIFFERENT AGES.

Results are Expressed as Mean Values ± Standard Error of Measurement.

Age	pg RNA / cell	BASE COMPOSITION				$\dfrac{(G + C)}{(A + U)}$	No. of Rats
		Adenine	Guanine	Cytosine	Uracil		
2-3 days prenatal	19 ± 3	20.9 ± 0.8	26.2 ± 0.5	30.8 ± 1.2	22.1 ± 0.5	1.33 ± 0.06	4
1 day	24 ± 1	21.0 ± 0.7	27.6 ± 0.8	31.0 ± 1.2	20.8 ± 0.3	1.41 ± 0.04	4
6-8 weeks	110 ± 10	17.7 ± 0.8	24.5 ± 2.0	37.8 ± 2.0	20.0 ± 0.5	1.66 ± 0.04	4
36-38 months	53 ± 1	14.9 ± 1.7	29.0 ± 1.6	36.9 ± 0.2	19.3 ± 0.3	1.95 ± 0.13	2

From Ringborg, 1966.

and RNA to be 18.2 days in 24-month-old rats as compared with 7.4 days in 12-month-old animals. These data may, of course, be variously interpreted but they are consistent with the supposition that a decline in both synthesis and degradation of protein and perhaps nucleic acid is associated with neuronal aging. A generalized decline in RNA synthesis was shown in the brain by Mackinnon, Simpson, and Maclennan (1969), who estimated ^{14}C-uridine incorporation in sections of brain with autoradiographic methods. A notable decrease in the protein/DNA ratio of 30-month-old whole mouse brain (as compared with adult animals 4-14 months old) was also reported by Kurtz and Sinex (quoted by Von Hahn, 1970).

A comparison of DNA in Feulgen-stained suspensions of cerebellar cells, measured microphotometrically showed only a very slight difference between cells of 3-month and 34-month-old rats, which was thought probably to be insignificant (Morselt, Braakman and James, 1972). A considerably greater difference, of apparently greater significance, was reported in the microspectrophoretic absorption of fast green-stained nuclei of granule cells isolated from the cerebella of young and old rats. The mean number for a population of large granule cells in young animals was about 75 percent greater than that for similar cells in old (34-month) animals. In the case of a population of large granule cells, the mean for young animals was about 67 percent greater. As fast green probably stains primarily histones in cell nuclei, these data suggest an age-related decline in the nuclei of at least some cerebellar neurons. These data are of interest as nuclear histones seem to have a regulatory role in gene activity.

If the biosynthetic capabilities of neurons are diminished as a function of aging, complementary morphological changes might reasonably be anticipated in the nucleus, nucleolus, rough endoplasmic reticulum and the Golgi apparatus, all cellular organelles which together comprise the principle machinery of protein synthesis. Some changes which have been described include: changes in the intracellular position of the nucleus, the occurrence of atypically-shaped and shrunken nuclei, changes in the distribution of chromatin and changes in staining properties of the nucleus and nucleolus (Andrew,

1956; Matzdorff, 1948; Kuhlenbeck, 1954; Klatzo, 1954). Similarly, the Golgi complex reportedly fragments and shifts from a primarily juxtanuclear to a perinuclear distribution (Sosa and de Zorrilla 1966).

SYNAPTOLOGY OF SENESCENT BRAIN

Age-related changes in biosynthetic capabilities, in particular protein metabolism, would suggest similar changes in transmitter synthesis which might effect alterations of synaptic morphology. Such changes, which have been reported, include age-associated depression of acetyl cholinesterase activity of whole brain of rat (Frolkis, Bezrukov, Duplenko, Shchegoleva, Shevtehuk, and Verkhratsky, 1973) and mouse (Samorajski, Rolsten, and Ordy, 1971); decreased concentrations of serotonin and norepinephrine in whole mouse brain (Samorajski, Rolsten, and Ordy, 1971); decreased concentrations of dopamine in mouse corpus striatum (Finch, 1973); and decreased concentrations of norepinephrine in human hindbrain (Robinson et al., 1972). In senescent mice, a reduced turnover of hypothalamic norepinephrine and dopamine has been found (Finch, 1973) and a decreased capacity of cerebral and cerebellar tissue slices to accumulate exogenous ^{3}H-norepinephrine is reported to occur in senescent chickens (Vernadakis, 1973b). What effect these changes in transmitter concentration might have on neuronal interactions or synaptic structure and function can only be conjectured as there are but few studies of neuronal interconnections and their possible alteration during the course of aging. On the one hand, Rasmussen (1959) reporting on the microscopic distribution of butons terminaux on spinal cord neurons of a a 17-year-old dog found nothing remarkable and no indication of a loss of synaptic contacts. On the other hand, in a study of human retinae of persons 70 to 85 years old, a change in the distribution of ganglion cell dendrites and axons as visualized in silver impregnated whole mounts was reported (Vrabec, 1965). Whereas these findings are not readily interpretable they suggest some age-dependent variation in neuronal processes. In this regard, it has been shown in Golgi preparations of rat visual cortex, that the numbers of spines on pyramidal cell apical dendrites was 43 spines/50μ in 29-month-old rats as compared to 67 spines/50μ in 2-month-old animals (Feldman and Dowd, 1974). In addition, there was a decrease in dendritic diameter of about 12 percent in the old rats. Whether these data indicate a decreased population of pyramidal cells in the cerebral cortex or, more specifically, an age-related decrease in the numbers of synaptic contacts is at this time moot.

Recent studies are few and as yet inconclusive. An electron microscopic study of synapses in human frontal and temporal cortices, which because of the sample are difficult to evaluate, revealed no significant age-related difference in the number of synapses/cm^3 (Cragg, 1975). Contrarily, in a study of the dentate gyrus of carefully selected Fischer 344 rats 25 months of age, a highly significant decrease in the number of synapses, as compared with normal adult animals, was found (Bondareff and Geinisman, 1976). It would appear that although significant changes in the structure and function of selective neurons are associated with the process of aging, neuronal systems may be little affected and it has now been shown with rats that the brain retains a surprising capacity for structural change well into old age. This is convincingly demonstrated by Cummins, Walsh, Budtz-Olsen, Konstantinos, and Horsfall, (1973) who compared (at 17 months) brains and behaviors of rats raised in environments enriched with an assortment of "toys" with those of rats raised in isolation. Both cerebral weight and cerebral cortical length of animals raised in the enriched environment were found to be greater and if the animals raised in the enriched environment were additionally subjected to maze testing, they were found to perform more accurately than their litter mates raised in isolation. Such testing did not additionally affect cerebral weight or cortical length of animals from the enriched environment but both were increased in animals raised in isolation. The severity of age-related changes in neuronal structure and their functional significance must, then, depend upon other factors which enhance or minimize the effects of aging on neuronal structure and function. The neuronal microenvironment may provide means through which such factors are effective.

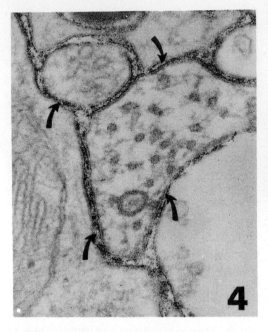

Figure 4. Electron micrograph of cerebral cortex of a normal adult Sprague-Dawley rat. The specimen was treated with ruthenium red which appears as dense particulates selectively distributed in the extracellular compartment indicated by arrows. 85,000X. (From Bondareff, 1967. *Anatomical Record*, **157**, 527–536.)

AGE CHANGES OF THE NEURONAL MICROENVIRONMENT

In the mammalian central nervous system the microenvironment of nerve cells is composed of extracellular channels which separate the plasma membranes of all cellular elements (cell bodies and their processes) from one another (Schmitt and Samson, 1969). These extracellular channels are of submicroscopic dimensions and can be visualized directly only with the aid of an electron microscope (Figure 4). They contain an ill-defined material, which appears fibrillar in electron micrographs (Bondareff, 1965), and are believed capable of transporting small molecules and ions by diffusion (Kuffler, Nicholls, and Orkand, 1966; Nicholls and Kuffler, 1964).

In an attempt to define this extracellular substance, a study was made of frozen-dried mouse cerebral cortex in which the intercellular spaces appeared empty in sections of tissues treated *in vacuo* with osmium vapors and examined in the electron microscope without prior staining (Bondareff, 1967a). When such sections were stained with uranyl acetate an intercellular substance was demonstrated. The density of this intercellular substance was noticeably reduced when uranyl acetate staining was done at low pH and it was enhanced when the pH of the staining solution was elevated. These reactions suggested the presence of a non-lipid, anionic intercellular substance in the cerebral cortex of the rat, perhaps an acidic glycosaminoglycan or a glycoprotein, both of which are known to occur in the brain. Acidic glycosaminoglycans have been demonstrated in rat cerebral cortex (Singh and Bachhawat, 1968). In the bovine brain, they have been shown to contain hyaluronic acid, chondroitin sulfate A, chondroitin sulfate C (Margolis, 1967; Margolis and Margolis, 1970), heparin (Singh and Bachhawat, 1968), heparin sulfate (Meyer, Hoffman, Linker, Grumbach, and Sampson, 1959) and a compound containing galacturonic acid (Stary, Wardi, and Turner, 1964). Similarly, glycoproteins have been demonstrated in brain and although there is some ambiguity as to their subcellular localization, available data suggest that the glycoproteins are associated with synaptosomal membranes (Brunngraber, Brown, and Aguilar, 1969; Brunngraber, Dekirjenjian, and Brown, 1967).

Age-related changes in the acidic glycosaminoglycan composition of the brain have been sought and although data are few, the relative amounts of the acidic glycosaminoglycans appear to vary with age. A significant decrease in the amount of hexosamine has been found in the acidic glycans isolated from the brains of young adults, as compared with senescent rats. No decrease in the amounts of uronic acid and galactosamine, however, were found. Since the concentration of galactosamine (presumably representing chondroitin sulfates) does not change with age, the decrease in hexosamine in the senescent rat brain may reflect the loss of a recently described keratan sulfate-like glycan (Vitello, Breen, Weinstein, and Bondareff, 1976), which might well result in a decreased water-binding capacity of the proteoglycans (Bettelheim and Plessy, 1975) in aged brains. An age-related increase was found in the sulfate/hexosamine ratio of the acidic glycosaminoglycans in the brains of old rats (Bondareff, 1973). It is not known whether this reflects age-related changes in sulfotransferase activity or in the availability of sulfate acceptors, both of which appear to decrease with age (George, Singh, and Bachhawat, 1970; Balasubramarian and Bachhawat, 1964), or whether such changes engender age-related changes in the neuronal microenvironment.

The properties of these intercellular channels in the brain are difficult to define but volume is perhaps most readily evaluated and in the cerebral cortices of Sprague-Dawley rats 10, 14 and 21 days of age, it has been estimated in electron micrographs of tissue fixed by freeze-substitution (Bondareff and Pysh, 1968). The cerebral cortices were rapidly frozen and the frozen tissue-water substituted at $-78°C$ with a 1 percent solution of osmium tetroxide in acetone. Then, in random electron micrographs of the cerebral cortex of each animal, the volume of extracellular space was estimated stereometrically and a 40.5 percent extracellular space typical of 10-day-old animals was found to diminish progressively to 31.8 percent at 14 and to 26.3 percent at 21 days (Table 5). After the third or fourth week of life an extracellular space of about 21.7 percent was found. It remained essentially unchanged until 26 months (Table 6) when the mean volume of cerebral cortex occupied by extra-

TABLE 5. VOLUME OF EXTRACELLULAR SPACE ESTIMATED IN ELECTRON MICROGRAPHS OF FROZEN-SUBSTITUTED CEREBRAL CORTEX OF RATS DURING EARLY POST-NATAL DEVELOPMENT.

Age	No. of animals	EXTRACELLULAR SPACE IN %	
		Range	Mean
10 days	3	35.0–48.0	40.5
14 days	1	27.9–35.6	31.8
21 days	3	22.6–31.0	26.3
Adult	3	17.8–26.8	21.7

From Bondareff and Pysh, 1968. *Anatomical Record*, **160**, 773–780.

TABLE 6. ESTIMATED VOLUME OF EXTRACELLULAR SPACE IN ELECTRON MICROGRAPHS OF FROZEN-SUBSTITUTED CEREBRAL CORTEX OF RATS, 26 AND 3 MONTHS OF AGE.[a]

26 months old	Volume (%)
1	13.1 ± 2.2
2	4.3 ± 0.0
3	15.0 ± 2.0
4	11.1 ± 2.2
5	6.5 ± 0.1
6	6.9 ± 0.4
7	11.0 ± 0.9
8	9.3 ± 0.9
(Average volume (%), 26 months: 9.6 ± 3.4)	

3 months old	Volume (%)
9	18.7 ± 1.5
10	22.3 ± 1.7
11	20.6 ± 1.1
(Average volume (%), 3 months: 20.8 ± 1.5)	

[a]Each estimate is based on the percentage of tissue volume occupied by extracellular space as estimated in five different electron microscopic fields. The average volumes are expressed as means ± standard deviation.
From W. Bondareff and R. Narotzky, *Science*, **176**, 1135–1136, June 9, 1972. Copyright 1972 by the American Association for the Advancement of Science.

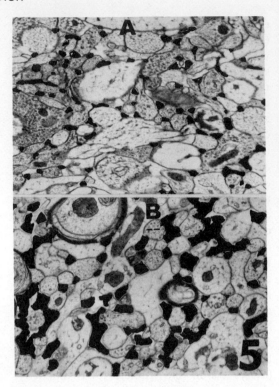

Figure 5. Electron micrographs of rat cerebral cortex fixed by freeze-substitution. The mean volume of the extracellular compartment (inked in) is about 10 percent in a 26-month-old rat (A) and about 22 percent in a 3-month-old rat (B). 14,000X. (From Bondareff and Narotzky, 1972.) *Science* **176**, 1135–1136. Copyright by the American Association for the Advancement of Science.)

cellular space was found to be 9.6 percent about one-half that typical of young adults (Figure 5) (Bondareff and Narotzky, 1972). These changes in the volume distribution of the extracellular compartment of the rat cerebral cortex as a function of chronological age have been corroborated indirectly by the report of Konigsmark and Murphy (1972) showing that the age-associated decrement in total brain volume is not necessarily a consequence of neuronal loss as was previously believed. Volume changes may, in turn, depend upon an age-related alteration in the macromolecular composition of material within the intercellular channels.

Glycoproteins and acidic glycosaminoglycans, complexed with proteins in life, are long-chain, charged molecules, which are capable of considerable conformational change (Rees, 1972; Mathews, 1964). As components of the neuronal microenvironment it can be anticipated that they play a dominant role in maintaining homeostasis. Relatively minor conformational changes associated with changes in charge, changes in hydration or perhaps even changes in mechanical sieving capability would affect electro-osmotic phenomena (Ranck, 1964), affect electrical conductance of perineuronal fluid (Wang, Tarby, Kado, and Adey, 1966) and alter the capacity of the extracellular compartment to transport metabolites and ions. To test the transport capacity of the extracellular compartment in old and young animals, exogenous catecholamines were introduced directly into brain tissue and subsequently visualized by the fluorescence histochemical method of Falck and Hillarp (Falck, Hillarp, Thieme, and Torp, 1962; Falck and Owman, 1965). No significant difference in intracerebral spread of norepinephrine in nonsenescent animals 1 to 9 months of age was found (Table 7) (Bondareff, Routtenberg, Narotzky, and McLone, 1970). The total spread found in 26-

TABLE 7. RELATIONSHIP BETWEEN CHRONOLOGICAL AGE AND INTRASTRIATAL SPREAD OF NOREPINEPHRINE AND DOPAMINE.[a]

Rat No.	Age (months)	0.5μl, NOREPINEPHRINE, 1.0μg/μl SPREAD (MM)		
		Rostral	Caudal	Total
5	1	0.54	0.36	0.90
6	1	0.45	0.54	0.99
7	1	0.54	0.54	1.08
1	1	0.45	0.54	0.99
9	3	0.45	0.36	0.81
4	3	0.45	0.36	0.81
12	9	0.54	0.45	0.99
10	9	0.18	0.27	0.45
11	26	0.27	0.27	0.54
		1.0μl DOPAMINE, 5.0μg/μl SPREAD (MM)		
20	6	1.08	1.22	2.30
35	6	0.72	2.07	2.79
55	6	0.45	0.72	1.17
74	24	0.54	0.81	1.35
75	24	0.54	0.72	1.26

[a]The catecholamine was injected into caudate nucleus of awake, feeling, moving rats. Its spread through the corpus striatum was determined by observing fluorescence in serial sections of Falck-Hillarp preparations. Data are presented as distance rostral and caudal to the site of injection.
From Bondareff, Narotzky, and Routtenberg, 1971. Reprinted with permission from *Journal of Gerontology*.

month-old senescent animals was almost half that observed in nonsenescent animals (Table 7) and the difference in spread between senescent and nonsenescent animals was significant (Bondareff, Narotzky and Routtenberg, 1971). Similarly, the total mean intrastriatal spread of dopamine (Table 7) in three senescent 24-month-old animals was also about half that found in 6-month-old animals (Bondareff, Narotzky, and Routtenberg, 1971).

Generalizing from the various neurocytological events which in one way or another are associated with neuronal aging it would appear that the aging of different populations of neurons proceeds in a manner and at a rate which varies with the population. Obviously, each population of nerve cells has a finite capacity to meet metabolic demands of functions which its genome dictates. Whether the capacity is met or exceeded must depend upon the microenvironment of the neuron and its relationship to other neurons, glial cells and non-neural elements.

As the enzymes required to transfer active sulfate to acceptor molecules appear to be located specifically in the Golgi complex, which plays a major role in sulfate metabolism (Young, 1973), it seems reasonable to predict that a relatively minor alteration in neuronal or glial metabolism might effect a change in the composition of extracellular macromolecules and profoundly affect the capacity of the extracellular space to transport ions or metabolites. It can be anticipated that such a change would result in a decreased capacity for these macromolecules to bind water and a consequent decrease in volume of the extracellular compartment, as has been demonstrated. These cascading events and the resultant neuronal pathology, illustrated in Table 8, might, of course, also result from a primary abnormality of the cerebral circulation, as does occur commonly in senescent animals (Klassen, Sung and Stadlan, 1968). In either case, the effect on hematoencephalic exchange and on the neuronal microenvironment, whether primary or secondary, would probably have the same histophysiological correlates.

Many of these changes in neuronal structure and function were recognized more than a decade ago (see review by Bondareff, 1959). At that time, the validity of some and the significance of perhaps all the neuronal changes presumed to be age-related, were equivocal. In the past decade, however, many of these changes have been more substantially documented and appear more meaningful against a background of a vastly expanded fund of basic neurobiological knowledge. It remains now to relate these abnormalities of neuronal structure and function to the changes in motor, intellectual and affective behavior which characterize senescence.

TABLE 8. HISTOPHYSIOLOGICAL CORRELATES OF AGE CHANGES IN THE EXTRACELLULAR COMPARTMENT.

Extracellular Change in Macromolecules

Change in Charge Density

Change in H$_2$O-Binding

Change in Transport of Ions, Metabolites

Change in Neuronal Metabolism

Neuronal Pathology

  Lipofuscin

  Cytoplasmic RNA

  Cytoplasmic Enzyme Activity

  Synaptic Loss
        Cell Death?

REFERENCES

Andrew, W. 1937. The effects of fatigue due to muscular exercise on the Purkinje cells of the mouse, with special reference to the factor of age. *Z. Zellforsch. Mikros. Anat.*, **27**, 534–554.

Andrew, W. 1956. Structural alterations with aging in the nervous system. *In*, The neurologic and psychiatric aspects of the disorders of aging, Chap. XI of *Proceedings of the Association for Research in Nervous and Mental Disease*, Vol. 35, pp. 129–170. Baltimore: Williams & Wilkins.

Balasubramarian, A. D., and Bachhawat, B. K. 1964. Enzymatic transfer of sulfate from 3′-phosphoadenosine 5′-phosphosulphate to mucopolysaccharides in rat brain. *J. Neurochem.*, **11**, 877–885.

Barden, H. 1970. Relationship of Golgi thiamine pyrophosphatase and lysosomal acid phosphatase to neuromelanin and lipofuscin in cerebral neurons of the aging rhesus monkey. *J. Neuropathol. Exp. Neurol.*, **29**, 225–240.

Bennet, G., Leblond, C. P., and Haddad, A. 1974. Migration of glycoprotein from the Golgi apparatus to the surface of various cell types as shown by radioautography after labeled fucose injection into rats. *J. Cell Biol.*, **60**, 258–284.

Bettelheim, F. A., and Plessy, B. 1975. The hydration of proteoglycans of bovine cornea. *Biochim. Biophys. Acta*, **381**, 203–214.

Björkerud, S. 1964. Isolated lipofuscin granules—A survey of a new field. *In*, B. C. Strehler (ed.), *Advances in Gerontological Research*, **1**, pp. 257–288. New York: Academic Press.

Bondareff, W. 1957. Genesis of intracellular pigment in the spinal ganglia of senile rats. An electron microscope study. *J. Gerontol.*, **12**, 364–369.

Bondareff, W. 1959. Morphology of the aging nervous system. *In*, J. E. Birren (ed.), *Handbook of Aging and the Individual*, pp. 136–172. Chicago: University of Chicago Press.

Bondareff, W. 1962. Distribution of Nissl substance in neurons of rat spinal ganglia as a function of age and fatigue. *In*, N. W. Shock (ed.), *Aging Around the World*. Proceedings of the Fifth Congress of the International Association of Gerontology, pp. 147–154. New York: Columbia University Press.

Bondareff, W. 1964. Histophysiology of the aging nervous system. *In*, B. L. Strehler (ed.), *Advances in Gerontological Research*, **1**, pp. 1–22. New York: Academic Press.

Bondareff, W. 1965. The extracellular compartment of the cerebral cortex. *Anat. Record*, **152**, 119–128.

Bondareff, W. 1967a. An intercellular substance in mouse cerebral cortex. *Z. Zellforsch. Mikros. Anat.*, **81**, 366–373.

Bondareff, W. 1967b. An intercellular substance in rat cerebral cortex: Submicroscopic distribution of ruthenium red. *Anat. Record*, **157**, 527–536.

Bondareff, W. 1973. Age changes in the neuronal microenvironment. *In*, M. Rockstein (ed.), *De-*

velopment and Aging in the Nervous System, pp. 1–18. New York: Academic Press.

Bondareff, W., Breen, M., and Weinstein, H. G. 1975. Changes in the neuronal microenvironment associated with aging. In, J. M Ordy and K. R. Brizzee, (eds), Neurobiology of Aging, pp. 485–504. New York: Plenum Press.

Bondareff, W., and Geinisman, Y., 1976. Loss of synapses in the dentate gyrus of the senescent rat. Am. J. Anat., 145, 129–136.

Bondareff, W., and McLone, D. G. 1973. The external glial limiting membrane in Macaca: Ultrastructure of a laminated glioepithelium. Am. J. Anat., 136, 277–296.

Bondareff, W., and Narotzky, R. 1972. Age changes in the neuronal microenvironment. Science, 176, 1135–1136.

Bondareff, W., Narotzky, R., and Routtenberg, A. 1971. Intrastriatal spread of catecholamines in senescent rats. J. Gerontol., 26, 163–167.

Bondareff, W., and Pysh, J. J. 1968. Distribution of the extracellular space during postnatal maturation of rat cerebral cortex. Anat. Record, 160, 773–780.

Bondareff, W., Routtenberg, A., Narotzky, R., and McLone, D. G. 1970. Intrastriatal spread of biogenic amines. Exp. Neurol., 28, 213–229.

Brizzee, K. R., Ordy, J. M., and Kaack, B. 1974. Early appearance and regional differences in intraneuronal and extraneuronal lipofuscin accumulation with age in the brain of a nonhuman primate (Macaca mulatta). J. Gerontol., 29, 366–381.

Brody, H. 1955. Organization of the cerebral cortex. III. A study of aging in the human cerebral cortex. J. Comp. Neurol., 102, 511–556.

Brody, H. 1973. Aging of the vertebrate brain. In, M. Rockstein (ed.), Development and Aging in the Nervous System., pp. 121–134. New York: Academic Press.

Brunngraber, E. G., Brown, B. D., and Aguilar, V. 1969. Isolation and determination of non-diffusible sialofucohexosaminoglycans derived from brain glycoproteins and their anatomical distribution in bovine brain. J. Neurochem., 16, 1059–1070.

Brunngraber, E. G., Dekirjenjian, H., and Brown, B. D. 1967. The distribution of protein-bound N-acetyl-neuraminic acid in subcellular fractions of rat brain. Biochem. J., 103, 73–78.

Cicero, T. J., Cowan, W. M., Moore, B. W., and Suntzeff, V. 1970. The cellular localization of the two brain-specific proteins, S-100 and 14-3-2. Brain Res., 18, 25–34.

Cicero, T. J., Ferrendelli, J. A., Suntzeff, V., and Moore, B. W. 1972. Regional changes in the CNS levels of the S-100 and 14-3-2 proteins during development and aging of the mouse. J. Neurochem., 19, 2119–2125.

Cowan, W. M. 1973. Neuronal death as a regulative mechanism in the control of cell number in the nervous system. In, M. Rockstein (ed.), Development and Aging in the Nervous System, pp. 19–42. New York: Academic Press.

Cragg, B. G. 1975. The density of synapses and neurons in normal, mentally defective and ageing human brains. Brain, 98, 81–90.

Critchley, M. 1942. Ageing of the nervous system. In, E. V. Cowdry (ed.), Problems of Ageing, pp. 518–534. Baltimore: Williams & Wilkins.

Cummins, R. A., Walsh, R. N., Budtz-Olsen, O. E., Konstantinos, T., and Horsfall, C. R. 1973. Environmentally-induced changes in the brains of elderly rats. Nature, 243, 516–518.

Dayan, A. D. 1971. Comparative neuropathology of ageing studies on the brains of 47 species of vertebrates. Brain, 94, 31–44.

Dolley, D. H. 1917. The recovery from depression in the Purkinje cell and the decline to senility of depression: With the incidental histogenesis of abnormal pigmentation. J. Comp. Neurol., 28, 465–494.

Edström, A. 1974. Effects of Ca^{2+} and Mg^{2+} on rapid axonal transport of proteins in vitro in frog sciatic nerves. J. Cell Biol., 61, 812–818.

Edström, J.-E. 1964. Microextraction and microelectrophoresis for determination and analysis of nucleic acids in isolated cellular units. In, D. Prescott (ed.), Methods in Cell Physiology, p. 417. New York: Academic Press.

Ehrenreich, J. H., Bergeron, J. J. M., Siekevitz, P., and Palade, G. E. 1973. Golgi fractions prepared from rat liver homogenates. I. Isolation procedure and morphological characterization. J. Cell Biol., 59, 45–72.

Ellis, R. S. 1920. Norms for some structural changes in the human cerebellum from birth to old age. J. Comp. Neurol., 32, 1–34.

Falck, B., Hillarp, N.-A., Thieme, G., and Torp, A. 1962. Fluorescence of catecholamines and related compounds condensed with formaldehyde. J. Histochem. Cytochem., 10, 348–354.

Falck, B., and Owman, G. 1965. A detailed methodological description of the fluorescence method for the cellular demonstration of biogenic amines. Acta Univ. Lund II., 7, 1–24.

Feldman, M. L., and Dowd, C. 1974. Aging in rat visual cortex: Light microscopic observations on layer V pyramidal apical dendrites. Anat. Record, 178, 355 (abstract).

Finch, C. E. 1973. Monoamine metabolism in the aging male mouse. In, M. Rockstein (ed.), Development and Aging in the Nervous System, pp. 199–218. New York: Academic Press.

Frolkis, V. V., Bezrukov, V. V., Duplenko, Y. K., Shchegoleva, I. V., Shevtchuk, V. G., and Verkhratsky, N. S. 1973. Acetylcholine metabolism and cholinergic regulation of functions of aging. Gerontologia, 19, 45–57.

Fry, F. J., and Cowan, W. M. 1972. A study of retrograde cell degeneration in the lateral mammillary nucleus of the cat, with special reference to the role of axonal branching in the preservation of the cell. J. Comp. Neurol., 144, 1–24.

George, E., Singh, M., and Bachhawat, B. K. 1970.

The nature of sulphation of uronic acid-containing glycosaminoglycans catalysed by brain sulphotransferase. *J. Neurochem.*, **17**, 189–200.

Giacobini, E. 1964. Metabolic relations between glia and neurons studied in single cells. *In*, M. M. Cohen and R. S. Snider (eds.), *Morphological and Biochemical Correlates of Neural Activity*, pp. 15–38. New York: Harper.

Goldman, R. D. 1971. The role of three cytoplasmic fibers in BHK-21 cell motility. I. Microtubules and the effects of colchicine. *J. Cell Biol.*, **51**, 752–762.

Höpker, W. 1951. Das Altern des Nucleus Dentatus. *Z. Alternsforsch.*, **5**, 256–277.

Huemer, R. P., Bickert, C., Lee, K. D., and Reeves, A. E. 1971. Mitochondrial studies in senescent mice. I. Turnover of brain mitochondrial lipids. *Exp. Gerontol.*, **6**, 259–265.

Hydén, H. 1960. The Neuron. *In*, J. Brachet and A. Mirsky (eds), *The Cell*, Vol. IV, p. 215. New York: Academic Press.

Hydén, H. 1973. RNA changes in brain cells during changes in behaviour function. *In*, G. B. Ansell and P. B. Bradley (eds.), *Macromolecules and Behavior*, p. 62. Baltimore: University Park Press.

Hydén, H. 1974. A calcium-dependent mechanism for synapse and nerve cell membrane modulation. *Proc. Nat. Acad. Sci.*, **71**, 2965–2968.

Igbal, K., Wisniewski, H. M., Shelanski, M. L., Brostoff, S., Liwnicz, B. H., and Terry, R. D. 1974. Protein changes in senile dementia. *Brain Res.*, **77**:337–343.

Johnson, H. A., and Erner, S. 1972. Neuron survival in the aging mouse. *Exp. Gerontol.*, **7**, 111–117.

Klassen, A. C., Sung, J. H., and Stadlan, E. M. 1968. Histological changes in cerebral arteries with increasing age. *J. Neuropathol. Exp. Neurol.*, **27**, 607–623.

Klatzo, I. 1954. Über das Verhalten des Nukleolarapparates und der Menschilchen Pallidumzellen. *J. Hirnforsch.*, **1**, 47–60.

Konigsmark, B. W. 1969. Neuronal population of the ventral cochlear nucleus in man. *Anat. Record*, **163**, 212–213.

Konigsmark, B. W., and Murphy, E. A. 1972. Volume of the ventral cochlear nucleus in man: Its relationship to neuronal population and age. *J. Neuropathol. Exp. Neurol.*, **31**, 304–316.

Kuffler, S. W., Nicholls, J. G., and Orkand, R. K. 1966. Physiological properties of glial cells in the central nervous system of amphibia. *J. Neurophysiol.*, **29**, 768–787.

Kuhlenbeck, H. 1954. Some histologic age changes in the rat's brain and their relationship to comparable changes in the human brain. *Confinia Neurol.*, **14**, 329–342.

Kuntz, A. 1945. Effects of lesions of the autonomic ganglia, associated with age and disease, on the vascular system. *Biol. Symp.*, **11**, 101–117.

Mackinnon, P. C. B., Simpson, R. A., and Maclennan, C. 1969. *In vivo* and *in vitro* techniques used in the study of RNA synthesis in the brains of rats and mice at various ages from birth to senility. *J. Anat.*, **104**, 351–360.

Margolis, R. U. 1967. Acid mucopolysaccharides and proteins of bovine whole brain, white matter and myelin. *Biochim. Biophys. Acta.*, **141**, 91–201.

Margolis, R. V., and Margolis, R. U. 1970. Sulfated glycopeptides from rat brain glycoprotein. *Biochemistry*, **9**, 4389–4396.

Mathews, M. B. 1964. Structural factors in cation binding to anionic polysaccharides of connective tissue. *Arch. Biochem.*, **104**, 394–404.

Matsuyama, H., Namiki, H. and Watanabe, I. 1966. Cited by Terry, R. D., and Wisniewski, H. M. *In*, C. M. Gaitz (ed.), *Aging and the Brain*, pp. 89–116. New York: Plenum Press.

Matzdorff, P. 1948. *Grundlagen zur Erforschung des Alterns*. Frankfurt am Main: Steinkopff.

Menzies, R. A., and Gold, P. H. 1972. The apparent turnover of mitochondria, ribosomes and sRNA of the brain in young and aged rats. *J. Neurochem.*, **19**, 1671–1683.

Meyer, K., Hoffman, P., Linker, A., Grumbach, M. M., and Sampson, P. 1959. Sulfated mucopolysaccharides of urine and organs in gargoylism (Hurler's syndrome). II. Additional studies. *Proc. Soc. Exp. Biol. Med.*, **102**, 587–590.

Monagle, R. D., and Brody, H. 1974. The effects of age upon the main nucleus of the inferior olive in the human. *J. Comp. Neurol.*, **155**, 61–66.

Moore, B. W. 1973. Brain-specific proteins. *In*, D. J. Schneider, R. H. Angeletti, R. A. Bradshaw, A. Grasso and B. W. Moore (eds.), *Proteins of the Nervous System*, pp. 1–12. New York: Raven Press.

Morselt, A. F. W., Braakman, D. J., and James, J. 1972. Feulgen-DNA and fast green-histone estimations in individual cell nuclei of the cerebellum of young and old rats. *Acta Histochem.*, **43**, 281–286.

Murray, M. R., and Stout, A. P. 1947. Adult human sympathetic ganglion cells cultivated *in vitro*. *Am. J. Anat.*, **80**, 225–273.

Nicholls, J. G., and Kuffler, S. W. 1964. Extracellular space as a pathway for exchange between blood and neurons in the central nervous system of the leech: Ionic composition of the glial cells and neurons. *J. Neurophysiol.*, **27**, 645–671.

Novikoff, P. M., Novikoff, A. B., Quintana, N., and Hauw, J. J. 1971. Golgi apparatus, gerl, and lysosomes of neurons in rat dorsal root ganglia, studied by thick section and thin section cytochemistry. *J. Cell Biol.*, **50**, 859–885.

Ochs, S. 1972. Fast transport of materials in mammalian nerve fibers. *Science*, **176**, 252–260.

Ochs, S. 1973. Effect of maturation and aging on the rate of fast axoplasmic transport in mammalian nerve. *In*, D. H. Ford (ed.), *Neurobiological Aspects of Maturation and Aging*, p. 349. Amsterdam: Elsevier Scientific Publications.

Olmsted, J. B., and Borisy, G. G. 1973. Microtubules. *Ann. Rev. Biochem.*, **42**, 507–540.

Ranck, J. B. 1964. Synaptic "learning" due to electro-osmosis; a theory. *Science*, 144, 187–189.

Rasmussen, G. L. 1959. Discussion. *In*, J. E. Birren, A. Imus and W. B. Windel (eds.), *The Process of Aging in the Nervous System*, p. 136. Springfield, Illinois: Charles C. Thomas.

Reaven, E. P., and Axline, S. G. 1973. Subplasmalemmal microfilaments and microtubules in resting and phagocytozing cultivated macrophages. *J. Cell Biol.*, 59, 12–27.

Rees, D. A. 1972. Shapely polysaccharides. *J. Biochem.*, 126, 257–273.

Ringborg, U. 1966. Composition and content of RNA in neurons of rat hippocampus at different ages. *Brain Res.*, 2, 296–298.

Robbins, S. L. 1967. *Pathology*, 3rd Edition, p. 574. Philadelphia: W. B. Saunders.

Robinson, A. J., Nies, A., Davis, J. N., Bunney, W. E., Davis, J. M., Colburn, R. W., Bourne, H. R., Shaw, D. M., and Coppern, A. J. 1972. Ageing, monamines, and monamine oxidase levels. *Lancet*, 1, 290–291.

Samorajski, T., Friede, R. L., and Ordy, J. M. 1971. Age differences in the ultrastructure of axons in the pyramidal tract of the mouse. *J. Gerontol.*, 26, 542–551.

Samorajski, T. and Ordy, J. M. 1972. Neurochemistry of Aging. *In*, C. M. Gaitz (ed.), *Aging and the Brain*, pp. 41–62. New York: Plenum Press.

Samorajski, T., Rolsten, C., and Ordy, J. M. 1971. Changes in behavior, brain and neuroendocrine chemistry with age and stress in C57BL/10 male mice. *J. Gerontol.*, 26, 168–175.

Schmitt, F. O., and Samson, F. E., Jr. 1969. Brain cell microenvironment. *Neurosci. Res. Prog. Bull.*, 7, 323–329.

Sekhon, S. S., and Maxwell, D. S. 1974. Ultrastructural changes in neurons of the spinal anterior horn of aging mice with particular reference to the accumulation of lipofuscin pigment. *J. Neurocytol.*, 3, 59–72.

Siakotos, A. N., and Koppang, N. 1973. Procedures for the isolation of lipo-pigments from brain, heart and liver, and their properties: A review. *Mech. Age. Dev.*, 2, 177–200.

Singh, M., and Bachhawat, B. K. 1968. Isolation and characterization of glycosaminoglycans in human brain of different age groups. *J. Neurochem.*, 15, 249–258.

Sjöstrand, J., Frizell, M., and Hasselgren, P.-O. 1970. Effects of colchicine on axonal transport in peripheral nerves. *J. Neurochem.*, 17, 1563–1570.

Sosa, J. M., and de Zorrilla, N. B. 1966. Morphological variations of the Golgi apparatus in spinal ganglion nerve cells related to ageing. *Acta Anat.*, 64, 474–497.

Stary, Z., Wardi, A., and Turner, D. 1964. Galacturonic acid in hydrolyzates of defatted human brain. *Biochim. Biophys. Acta*, 83, 242–244.

Strehler, B. L. 1964. On the histochemistry and ultrastructure of age pigment. *In*, B. L. Strehler (ed.), *Advances in Gerontological Research*, 1, p. 343–384. New York: Academic Press.

Tani, E., and Ametani, T. 1970. Substructure of microtubules in brain nerve cells as revealed by ruthenium red. *J. Cell Biol.*, 46, 159–165.

Terry, R. D., and Wisniewski, H. M. 1972. Ultrastructure of senile dementia and of experimental analogues. *In*, C. M. Gaitz (ed.), *Aging and the Brain*, pp. 89–116. New York: Plenum Press.

Tilney, L. G., Bryan, J., Bush, D. J., Fusiwara, K., Mooseker, M. S., Murphy, D. B., and Snyder, D. H. 1973. Microtubules: Evidence for 13 protofilaments. *J. Cell Biol.*, 59, 267–275.

Toth, S. E. 1968. The origin of lipofuscin age pigments. *Exp. Gerontol.*, 3, 19–30.

Van Buskirk, C. 1945. The seventh nerve complex. *J. Comp. Neurol.*, 82, 303–334.

Vaughan, D. W., and Peters, A. 1974. Neuroglial cells in the cerebral cortex of rats from young adulthood to old age: An electron microscope study. *J. Neurocytol.*, 3, 405–429.

Vernadakis, A. 1973a. Changes in nucleic acid content and butyrylcholinesterase activity in CNS structures during the life-span of the chicken. *J. Gerontol.*, 28, 281–286.

Vernadakis, A. 1973b. Uptake of ^{3}H-norepinephrine in the cerebral hemispheres and cerebellum of the chicken throughout the lifespan. *Mech. Age. Dev.*, 2, 371–379.

Vitello, L., Breen, M., Weinstein, H. G., and Bondareff, W. 1976. Proteoglycans in the aging brain: Evidence for a keratan sulfate-like glycan. *Federation Proc.*, in press.

Vogt, C., and Vogt, O. 1946. Ageing of nerve cells. *Nature*, 158, 304.

Von Hahn, H. P. 1970. Structural and functional changes in nucleoprotein during the ageing of the cell. *Gerontologia*, 16, 116–128.

Vrabec, F. 1965. Senile changes in the ganglion cells of the human retina. *Brit. J. Ophthalmol.*, 49, 561–572.

Wang, H. H., Tarby, T. J., Kado, R. T., and Adey, W. R. 1966. Periventricular cerebral impedance after intraventricular injection of calcium. *Science*, 154, 1183–1184.

Weinbach, E. C., and Garbus, J. 1959. Oxidative phosphorylation in mitochondria from aged rats. *J. Biol. Chem.*, 234, 412–417.

Weiss, P. A. 1973. *The Science of Life: The living system—a system for living*. Mount Kisco, New York: Futura Publishing.

Wessels, N. K., Spooner, B. S., Ash, J. F., Bradley, M. O., Luduena, M. A., Taylor, E. L., Wrenn, J. T., and Yamada, K. M. 1971. Microfilaments in cellular and developmental processes. *Science*, 171, 135–143.

Wilcox, H. H. 1959. Structural changes in the nervous system related to the process of aging. Present status of knowledge. *In*, J. E. Birren, H. Imus and

W. Windel (eds.), *The Process of Aging in the Nervous System.* Springfield, Illinois: Charles C. Thomas.

Wisniewski, H., Shelanski, M. L., and Terry, R. D. 1968. Effects of mitotic spindle inhibitors on neurotubules and neurofilaments in anterior horn cells. *J. Cell Biol.*, 38, 224–229.

Wuerker, R. B., and Kirkpatrick, J. B. 1972. Neuronal microtubules, neurofilaments and microfilaments. *In*, G. H. Bourne and J. F. Danielli (eds.), *International Review of Cytology*, 33, 45–76. New York: Academic Press.

Young, R. W. 1973. The role of the Golgi complex in sulfate metabolism. *J. Cell Biol.*, 57, 175–189.

9
AGING OF THE AUTONOMIC NERVOUS SYSTEM

Vladimir V. Frolkis

Institute of Gerontology AMS U.S.S.R., Kiev, U.S.S.R.

MAIN PRINCIPLES OF ORGANIZATION IN THE AUTONOMIC NERVOUS SYSTEM AND TRENDS IN ITS AGE CHANGES

The most intricate adaptive reactions, such as movement, behavior, emotions, and complex psychic acts, are followed by shifts in the cardiovascular, respiratory and other systems of the organism. This is achieved by regulatory influences in the central nervous system, realized through the pathways of the autonomic nervous system (ANS). In addition, the afferent impulses (feedback control) coming through this system substantially change the functional state of the nervous centers.

By the beginning of the nineteenth century, investigators had already come to accept the division of the nervous system into somatic (animal) and autonomic (vegetative) components. The organism's functions were thus divided into somatic activities (stimuli perception, motor reactions, etc.) and autonomic activities (digestion, blood circulation, respiration, excretion, growth, reproduction, etc.).

Such a division should not be interpreted as an opposition of one system to another. Viscerosomatic and somato-visceral reflexes, central regulation of the autonomic component of somatic reactions, complex hypothalamo-hypophyseal interrelations, and other inter-actions between the two systems form the integral neurohumoral regulation of the organism's metabolism and function.

The processes of the central nervous system are executed through the two pathways of the ANS—the sympathetic and the parasympathetic.

The most important mechanisms of the self-regulation of metabolism and function, which are the mechanisms of maintenance for the organism's homeostasis, are accomplished through the efferent and afferent pathways of the ANS in association with the higher vegetative nervous centers. In the structures of the limbic system, such as the hypothalamus, there occurs a complex synthesis of the information coming in from various areas of the central nervous system (CNS) as well as the choice of the method of regulating the internal environment. This action is accomplished through ANS and endocrine processes.

Essential changes are occurring with age in the metabolism and function of an organism, and in the regulatory mechanisms of its homeostasis. Aging is characterized by a progressive decrease in the intensity of adaptive processes. This limitation of the adaptive capacities of an aging organism promotes the development of pathology in old age as well as the possibility of an easier disruption of regulatory mechanisms.

According to the adaptive-regulatory theory, there appears to be extinctions of the organism's metabolism and function with age, in addition to the development of important adaptive mechanisms (Frolkis, 1970, 1975). The formation and tendencies of these adaptive mechanisms are determined to a great extent by neurohumoral regulation and age-related shifts in different links of the ANS. Various structures of the ANS grow old heterochronously, thus leading to the development of a qualitatively new level of nervous regulation of vegetative functions in old age.

It is through the ANS that primarily age-related changes occurring in nervous centers may induce essential shifts in metabolism and structure and function of organs in an aging organism. Furthermore, changes in the ANS and vegetative functions *per se* may lead to disruption of the activities of the nervous centers and to changes in the behavior of an aged person. Birren and Spieth (1962), Wilkie and Eisdorfer (1970), Birren (1972) and other investigators have found a clear correlation between hemodynamic shifts, a number of metabolic changes and the pattern of some of the psychic reactions in old age. It is also important to note that by acting upon the ANS it is possible to influence the mental abilities of old persons (Eisdorfer, Nowlin, and Wilkie, 1970). Thus, the investigation of the ANS might enable us to elucidate essential mechanisms of changes in milieu interieur as well as in the CNS.

One basis for age-related changes in the function of the ANS in old age rests upon the structural changes of its components. Kuntz (1938), Zhabotinsky (1953), Kazantseva (1970), Andrew (1956, 1971) and others observed degenerative changes in sympathetic and parasympathetic ganglia and in postganglionic nerve endings in various organs of human beings and animals. Of great importance is the conclusion by Andrew (1956) that structural changes with aging are more pronounced in the hypothalamus than in any other area of the CNS.

For an explanation of the age changes in the ANS, it is necessary to give the general characteristics of the reactions to and the dynamics of such changes in its various parts, such as the higher vegetative nervous centers, the efferent pathways, the vegetative ganglia, and in the afferent pathways coming from inner organs. These data are especially important for substantiation of rational pharmacotherapy.

VEGETATIVE REFLEXES WITH AGING

The ANS is responsible for reflectory regulation of inner organ functioning, or control of the most important mechanisms for maintenance of homeostasis in the internal environment. A number of vital homeostatic parameters are preserved in old age: only slight changes can be observed in blood sugar level, blood pressure, intraocular, oncotic and osmotic pressures, and in the level of cell membrane potential. Such preservation of homeostasis in old age is achieved by means of dynamic changes rather than environment stability, in addition to the development of adaptive mechanisms and irregular changes in various ANS links.

The state of the ANS can be evaluated by the character of its vegetative reflexes. Usually the reflectory changes in blood circulation, respiration, shifts in contents of catecholamines, blood sugar and fatty acids have been studied for this purpose. Despite the qualitative specificity and variability of certain vegetative reactions, there exists a general pattern in their changes with aging. In most cases the latent period of reactions is increased in old age, whereas the possible range of changes of vegetative functions as well as the rate of reactions are decreased (Chebotarev and Frolkis, 1967; Morris and Thompson, 1969; Garnier, 1972; Muravov, 1972). The reflectory changes of the vegetative functions become rigid, accompanied by wavelike shifts in the recovery period. That is why, when evaluating the age peculiarities of vegetative reactions, a continuous registration of forthcoming shifts is necessary. It has been shown in old persons that a new wave of functional changes may appear after a substantial delay, compared with young people. Subsequent recurrence of vegetative reflexes results in old persons in a pronounced decrease of their value.

It should be noted that the variability of ANS reactions increases with age in persons of the

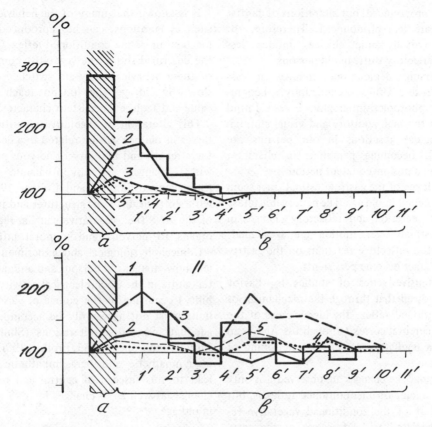

Figure 1. Changes in hemodynamics and respiration during effort (a) and in the recuperative period (b) in a 20-year-old patient (I) and in a 71-year-old patient (II) for equal work load. 1 = oxygen consumption; 2 = cardiac output; 3 = pulmonary ventilation; 4 = heart rate; 5 = respiratory rate.

same cohort. In addition to aged persons having weakened reactions, there also exists a large group of old people characterized by pronounced reflectory vegetative shifts. The characteristics of age-related changes of vegetative reactions should be based on the "strength relations law", i.e., on comparison of shifts at different levels of stimulation.

The contradictory data obtained by investigators studying the intensity of age changes in hemodynamic reactions of muscular activity, for example, are due to their not taking into account the intensity of applied load. It was found that with low intensity loads the shifts in hemodynamics and respiration were more pronounced in old persons, whereas large loads were required to produce such results in the young (Figure 1). With the substantial load increase, the old persons demonstrated marked, slowly recovered shifts in hemodynamics and respiration.

In old age, changes are observed in vegetative reflexes. A number of reflexes resulting from action of the vagal nerve on the heart (oculo-cardiac, trigeminal-vagal, etc.) are weakened. Mankovsky and Mints (1972) registered the normal oculo-cardiac reflex in only 19.8 percent of persons aged 60 and over. In old persons, the reflectory influences from superior respiratory areas on the heart are weakened. Essential hemodynamic shifts appear in an orthostatic test. These shifts are connected with hydrostatic changes on the one hand, and reflexes from vascular mechanoreceptors on the other. One of the components of this reflectory reaction is the change in heart rate. In old persons, as compared with the young, during the orthostatic test changes in blood pressure are more pronounced, but alterations of cardiac rhythm are less pronounced. Therefore, the greater hydrodynamic changes induce less marked reflectory shifts in old persons.

Old persons demonstrate changes in vascular reflexes. Using oscillography, rheography and photopletismography, it was found that with thermal, auditory and visual stimulation, vascular reactions in old persons are weakened, becoming persistent in character and having a prolonged latent period.

The reflexes of the gastrointestinal tract seem to be weakened in old age. The neurogenic phase of gastric secretion and reflectory changes in gastrointestinal tract motion are weakened. Many of the reflectory reactions on the gastrointestinal tract become persistent.

An extensive series of studies by Pavlov (1928) showed that through the mechanism of the conditioned reflex, the higher areas of the CNS and cerebral cortex (through the ANS) can produce a regulatory effect on functioning of inner organs.

With aging, the changes are observed not only in the character of unconditioned reflexes, but also in that of the conditioned vegetative reflexes associated with processes of the cerebral cortex (Parchon, 1959; Botwinick and Kornetsky, 1960; Losev, 1963; Shmavonian, Jarmat, and Cohen, 1965). The conditioned reflexes of the cardiovascular system, respiration, the galvanic skin response and gastric secretion are produced more slowly in older persons and reach lower values. To produce the conditioned vascular reflexes using cold as the unconditioned stimulus, the young person will need 3–4 couplings, while the old person will produce them only after 9–12 couplings. In old persons the conditioned-reflectory changes often acquire a more persistent character.

The conditioned-reflectory influences maintain the most mobile and flexible level of adaptation of the vegetative functions, preparing them for the forthcoming activity. Weakening of the conditioned-reflectory regulation of vegetative functions in old age results in a decrease in the organism's adaptive capacities; vegetative functions reach their optimal level more slowly, and the organism's "preparedness" for the forthcoming activity is decreased.

It is known that many of the behavioral acts, such as emotions, can be reproduced by the mechanism of the conditioned reflex. Owing to the described shifts, the vegetative components of these behavioral acts are switched on more slowly in old age; they do not reach a proper value and acquire a persistent character.

This alteration of vegetative conditioned reflexes in old age can be related to a decrease in the strength and mobility of nervous processes, with changes in hypothalamic centers (Shmavonian, Jarmat, and Cohen, 1965) and with shifts in different structures and functions of the ANS (i.e., vegetative ganglia, reaction of organs to nervous and humoral influences).

Clinical-physiological and experimental studies show that in old persons and animals, essential shifts in the CNS (electrical activity, excitability) occurring in the course of various reactions must not necessarily be accompanied by adequate vegetative alterations (Shmavonian, Jarmat, and Cohen, 1965; Frolkis, 1970). Shifts in sympathetic and parasympathetic systems lead to this discord of central and peripheral changes as well as to changes in ANS reactions in old age.

THE HYPOTHALAMIC FUNCTION IN AGING

In the visceral brain system, the hypothalamus performs the role of a motor and effector region. Experiments with stimulation or destruction of the whole hypothalamus or of its separate nuclei have revealed hypothalamic influences upon the cardiovascular system, digestive organs, thermoregulation, metabolic processes, and behavioral reactions. Hess (1954) believed that the area of anterior hypothalamic nuclei corresponded to parasympathetic centers, whereas the posterior hypothalamus corresponded to sympathetic centers. This now appears to be a relative division, since stimulation of either of the hypothalamic areas by stimuli of various strengths and frequencies can produce opposite reactions.

Within recent years, age-related changes of the hypothalamus have been found to be of great importance in the mechanism of the organism's aging (Groen, 1959; Dilman, 1971;

Everitt, 1973; Aschheim, 1972; Frolkis, Bezrukov, Duplenko, and Genis, 1972; Bezrukov, 1974). Owing to the influences realized through the ANS and endocrine system, primary hypothalamic changes seem to effect significant alterations in the functional state of milieu interieur. Changes in the hypothalamus reduce the reliability of the homeostatic control in an aging organism. Groen (1959) and Mankovsky and Mints (1972) reported an impairment of the hypothalamic function with age, and Everitt (1973) observed an exertion of hypothalamic mechanisms of regulation. Dilman (1971) supposed the development of a genetically programmed enhancement of the hypothalamic activity. Frolkis et al. (1972) and Bezrukov (1974) found irregular and even diversely directed changes in excitability of different hypothalamic areas. Thus, excitability of the anterior and posterior hypothalamus rises, while that of the lateral hypothalamus falls. Such disregulation of the hypothalamus plays an important role in the mechanism of age-related changes in the central nervous system control of vegetative functions.

It is important to note that hypothalamic regulation of body vegetative functions is also qualitatively altered in aging. Thus, the increase of cardiac output and decrease of total peripheral resistance observed after the stimulation of the anterior and posterior hypothalamus is more frequently developed in old animals than in adults.

In old age, the sensitivity of the hypothalamic structures to humoral factors rises. The role of adrenergic and cholinergic mechanisms in the function of the hypothalamus is known. After a microinjection of catecholamines and acetylcholine into the hypothalamus through chemitrodes, old animals develop more pronounced changes in hypothalamic functions. These changes include shifts in bioelectric activity and hemodynamic changes. Aschheim (1972) observed an increase in sensitivity of the hypothalamus to estrogens with aging. An increase in sensitivity of the hypothalamus to physiologically active agents may result in "hypothalamic misinformation"—a state in which shifts in the chemistry of the milieu interieur induce inadequate hypothalamic

reactions. With strong, repeated stimulation, old animals develop disturbances in the higher autonomic centers more quickly than young animals, with the hypothalamus influencing the metabolism and function of organs and tissues.

Through the hormonal systems as well as the neural pathways, the hypothalamus exerts its influence upon the activity of the genetic apparatus and protein biosynthesis in a cell. It has been found that the hypothalamic control of protein biosynthesis in old animals alters. With stimulation of the hypothalamus of these old animals, the genetic induction of many of the enzymes in the liver and kidneys appeared to be less pronounced when compared with that of adult animals; and yet, in the spleen it remained unchanged (Frolkis, Bezrukov, and Muradyan, 1974). Such irregular alteration of the genetic induction of different organs points to the fact that shifts occurring in aging are related not only with changes in the hypothalamic control centers, but also with tissue responses.

The pathways through which the hypothalamus transmits its influences on tissues are complex. With aging, the ratio of purely nervous and hormonal pathways of influence changes. Frolkis et al. (1972) compared the thresholds of the reproduction of autonomic reactions (shifts in blood pressure, respiration) employing an electrical stimulation of different CNS structures in rabbits of various ages. Judging by shifts in blood pressure, the excitability of the ANS in old rabbits shows differential change; thus, with stimulation of one structure it was found increased, while in stimulation of others decreased. The experiments concerned with cross-section have indicated that these influences upon the cardiovascular system are through ANS sympathetic and parasympathetic pathways. Irregular changes in the excitability of ANS reactions with age account for nonuniform alterations occurring in vegetative shifts during performance of various behavioral acts.

EFFERENT AND AFFERENT INFLUENCES OF THE ANS IN AGING

Most organs which are innervated by the ANS are under the control of both its parts—the

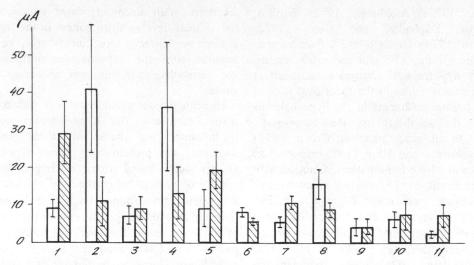

Figure 2. Threshold current values inducing pressor reactions of BP in electric stimulation of various brain structures in adult (10–12 months, open bars) and old (54–60 months, hatched bars) rabbits. 1 = sensorimotor cortex; 2 = piriform cortex; 3 = hippocampus; 4 = central amygdaloid nucleus; 5 = medial amygdaloid nucleus; 6 = anterior hypothalamic area; 7 = lateral hypothalamic area; 8 = posterior hypothalamic area; 9 = nucl. reticularis tegmenti; 10 = nucl. reticularis pontis; 11 = medulla oblongata (medial vestibular nucleus).

sympathetic and parasympathetic systems. These systems may exert inverse, antagonistic influences on many organs. Synergism of the ANS effect means that stimulation of one of its parts elevates the sensitivity of the organ to the influence of the opposite part. The peculiarities of ANS functional influences can be revealed in stimulating or switching off its efferent pathways.

The experimental and clinical-physiological data show that with aging there is a decrease in nervous, sympathetic and parasympathetic influences upon organs and tissues. Thus, the threshold of a negative chronotropic effect of the vagal nerve upon the heart rises in old age. In 2 to 3-year-old cats, slowing down of the heart rate occurs after stimulation with a current of 1.25 ± 0.42 V, whereas 10 to 12-year-old animals require 2.42 ± 0.38 V. In stimulating the g. stellatum with a current of 1.5 V, the cardiac output of adult rats rises by 28 percent, though in old animals it remains almost unchanged (5–6 percent). The impairment of tonic nervous influences, both sympathetic and parasympathetic, has been revealed in old people as well. The more intensive the tonic influence of sympathetic and parasympathetic nerves on the heart, the more significant

are the shifts which occur in the blocking of their action by atropine (blocking of cholino-receptors), and by inderal (blocking of beta-adrenoreceptors). Atropine and inderal have appeared to evoke less pronounced shifts in the heart rate of old subjects than has atropine administration (1.0 ml of 0.1 percent solution). The rhythm of heart contractions in men aged 20–24 became more frequent by 34.0 ± 2.8 contractions/minute, while in men aged 60–76 years only by 13.5 ± 1.8 contractions/minute (Dukhovichny, 1974).

With age, the sympathetic nervous system's influence on different organs changes irregularly. It was found that thresholds of sympathetic influence upon the vessels of the extremities rise, those of influence upon small intestinal vessels fall, and those upon renal vessels remain unchanged (Frolkis, Verkhratsy, and Zamostyan, 1967).

The vagal nerve, as is well known, is secretory for the gastric glands. In old dogs, gastric secretion begins at stimulation of the vagal nerve by a higher electric current than is necessary in young animals. In old people, the first phase of gastric secretion is impaired (Yakimenko, Chebotarev, and Kotko, 1972).

The ANS may exert a direct trophic influence

on tissues, which is related with regulation of their metabolism. More frequent manifestations of trophic changes, such as pigmentation, baldness and ulcers, followed by cross-section of sympathetic nerves in old rats are further evidence of changes with aging of sympathetic trophic influences.

Against the background of a decline in the influence of the central nervous system with age, one can observe an increase in the sensitivity of organs and tissues to certain hormonal factors and transmitters through which ANS influences are carried out. This can be seen in the fact that smaller doses of certain substances still induce shifts in metabolism and function in older animals. It was found that smaller doses of catecholamines, acetylcholine, serotonin and a number of hormones (thyroxine, insulin) causes changes in the hemodynamics of old animals as compared with the young (Figure 3). Besides, smaller doses of catecholamines and thyroxine administered to old animals change the rate of tissue respiration, oxidative phosphorylation, glycolysis and activity of respiratory enzymes in the liver, heart, skeletal mus-

cles, and brain (Bogatskaya, 1972). At the same time, the reaction capacity, which is a possible range of changes in the metabolism and function caused by administration of increased doses of certain substances, is higher in adult animals as compared with old animals. With age, there is a decrease in potential capacities of reactions of organs and tissues to the action of transmitter-like agents.

An increase in sensitivity to the action of many physiologically active substances of the transmitter type has also been observed in man. The data obtained by Chebotarev (1973) strongly indicate that administration of small doses of epinephrine, acetylcholine and histamine induced more pronounced shifts in blood pressure, heart rate and hemodynamics in older people than in the young. Thus, following the administration of 0.5 ml of 0.1 percent epinephrine solution, no significant changes in hemodynamics were observed in subjects aged 20–29; however in persons aged 80–89 years there was an elevation of blood pressure (from 117.9 ± 3.5 to 138.8 ± 6.3 mm Hg), a rise of cardiac output (from 2.21 ± 0.15 to

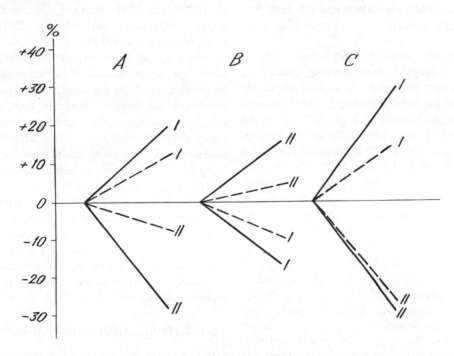

Figure 3. Changes in cardiac output (I) and total peripheral resistance (II) in adult (broken line) and old (solid line) rabbits after administration of small doses of epinephrine (A = 0.05 μg/kg), acetylcholine (B = 0.05 μg/kg) and serotonin (C = 0.5 μg/kg).

3.62 ± 0.41/minute), a fall of total peripheral resistance (from 2108.0 ± 284.0 to 1677.0 ± 180.5 dyn/sec/cm^{-5}), and an increase of heart rate (from 66.5 ± 3.22 to 82.2 ± 5 beats/minute). In young subjects, spasms of the skin vessels occurred after ionophoretic application of epinephrine in concentrations of 1.10^{-5} - 1.10^{-6} g/ml, and in old subjects after applications of 2.10^{-9} - 1.10^{-9} g/ml (Verkhratsky, 1962).

The weakening of sympathetic and parasympathetic nervous system influences, and the rise of tissue sensitivity to a number of humoral factors determine essential changes in vegetative reactions with aging. These changes include the prolongation of the latent period, the diminution of the reaction amplitude, and the persistent character of the development of these reactions. Irregular changes of sympathetic and parasympathetic influences may result in the appearance of unusual paradoxical reactions; thus, weakening of neurohumoral control is one of the leading mechanisms of an aging organism.

TRANSMITTER METABOLISM OF THE ANS WITH AGING

The influence of the ANS on tissues is accomplished through a corresponding transmitter system—the cholinergic and adrenergic. At this time, extensive literature has been accumulated on the essential changes with age in the transmitter metabolism of the ANS (Barrows, Shock, and Chow, 1958; Burkard, Gey, and Pletscher, 1966; Frolkis, 1970; Verkhratsky, 1972; Finch, 1973; Samorajski, and Rolsten, 1973). With aging, acetylcholine synthesis in postganglionic cholinergic terminals is decreased. This decrease in acetylcholine synthesis is connected primarily with the reduction of cholinesterase activity and coenzyme A content. The intensity of acetylcholine hydrolysis is decreased in old age. With aging, cholinesterase activity falls in human plasma and erythrocytes as well as in various other organs of animals. The activity of specific and nonspecific cholinesterase changes irregularly in different organs. In old age, the sensitivity of the cholinoreceptors of postsynaptic membranes rises, being connected with shifts in the content of sulfhydryl groups in them. The destruction of cholinergic nerve endings and the decrease of acetylcholine synthesis in them result in the weakening of parasympathetic influences on tissues; however, the reduction of cholinesterase activity and shifts in cholinoreceptors promote the increase of cell sensitivity to acetylcholine and to cholinomimetic substances.

The content of catecholamines in various organs changes irregularly in old age, being significantly reduced in heart and spleen (Gey, Burkard, and Pletscher, 1965; Verkhratsky, 1972). Gey, Burkard, and Pletscher (1965) showed that, due to reduction of decarboxylase of aromatic L-amine acids and dopamine-β-oxidase activities, the synthesis of norepinephrine is decreased in old age. This affects the transformation of DOPA into dopamine and of dopamine into norepinephrine. Different pathways of catecholamine metabolism change irregularly in old age; thus, the monoamine oxidase activity is increased, catechol-o-methyltransferase remains unchanged, and catecholamine uptake by sympathetic nerve endings is weakened (Novick, 1961; Burkard, Gey, and Pletscher, 1966; Gey, Burkard, and Pletscher, 1965; Verkhratsky, 1972).

Reduction of norepinephrine synthesis in adrenergic terminals and their accompanying destruction result in the weakening of nervous influences on tissues. Irregular changes of catecholamine metabolism pathways, weakening of catecholamine uptake and alteration of adrenoreceptors promote an increase of sensitivity to catecholamines as well as the development of persistent reactions.

The increase in sensitivity of innervated cells to transmitters is an important adaptive mechanism which contributes to maintenance of a certain level of nervous control of inner organs under the conditions of decreased transmitter synthesis in postganglionic sympathetic and parasympathetic endings.

VEGETATIVE GANGLIA IN OLD AGE

Vegetative ganglia are peculiar ANS mechanisms which transfer the information from preganglionic to postganglionic neurons.

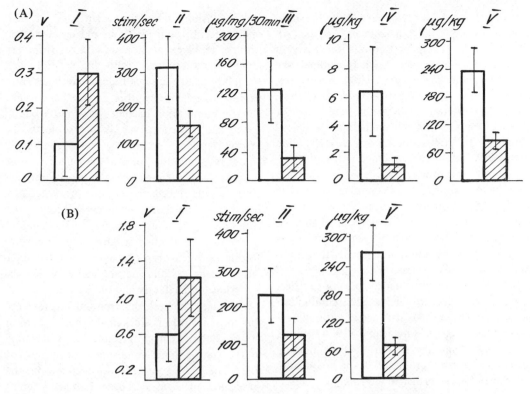

Figure 4. Age differences in functional state of superior cervical ganglion (A) and parasympathetic ganglia of heart (B) in adult (2 years) and old (10–12 years) cats. I = excitability thresholds in stimulation of preganglionic trunks; II = frequencies producing preganglionic tetanization, lability of ganglion; III = cholinesterase activity in ganglion tissue; IV = threshold doses of acetylcholine stimulating the ganglia in cats; V = threshold doses of benzohexone inhibiting the ganglionic transmission.

The excitability of vegetative ganglia is changed in old age (Frolkis, 1965; Duplenko, 1968). Figure 4 demonstrates the increased thresholds of electrical stimulation of the superior cervical ganglion and the vagal nerve in old cats. The functional state of vegetative ganglia is determined by their lability, or capacity to conduct and transform incoming excitation through preganglionic fibers. Frequencies exceeding the lability of a ganglion are transformed in it and partially or completely blocked (Skok, 1970). In old age, there is a fall of natural impulsation frequency registered in the pre- and postganglionic fibers of the sympathetic system; in addition, the lability of the autonomic ganglia and their ability to conduct and transform frequent excitation rhythms decrease in old age. Figure 4 shows that in old animals blocking of conduction (pessimum) in the superior cervical sympathetic ganglion can be observed after stimulating the preganglionic nerve at smaller frequencies than in adult animals. A decrease in the capacity of vegetative ganglia to conduct and transform the incoming excitations enables the formation of inert vegetative reactions in old age, i.e., reactions with prolonged latent and delayed recovery periods. Blockage of frequent excitation currents in the ganglionic apparatus occurring in old age protects the effectors against possible deviations of impulsation coming from nervous centers.

Age-related changes in autonomic ganglia are related to shifts in the transmitter metabolism and structural changes of the neurons. The synaptic transmission in the autonomic ganglia is related to acetylcholine metabolism. In old age, sensitivity in neurons of the autonomic ganglia to acetylcholine rises.

Smaller doses of acetylcholine induce excitation of ganglia in old animals (Figure 4). Weakening of ganglionic transmission is largely connected with the fact that in old animals the activity of the key enzyme, choline acetylase, is decreased. According to Duplenko (1968), the cholinesterase activity in the superior cervical ganglion of old animals is decreased (Figure 4). The reduction of acetylcholine hydrolysis intensity combined with the decrease of transmitter synthesis in the preganglionic terminals helps maintain the specific level of the ganglionic transmission. Any decrease in cholinesterase activity or change in cholinoreceptors results in an increase in sensitivity of the autonomic ganglia to a number of chemical substances with aging.

It is important that smaller doses of ganglion blockers can disturb the ganglion conduction in old age (Figure 4). This agrees with clinical observations by Dukhovichny (1974) which showed that administration of benzohexone leads to more pronounced hemodynamic shifts in old subjects than in the young subjects.

VISCERORECEPTION: FEEDBACK IN THE ANS

The perfect regulation of the body metabolism and function is achieved because the higher autonomic centers are informed of the most important shifts occurring in milieu interieur. It has been found that afferent signals from visceroreceptors can be transmitted through the vagal nerve and sympathetic pathways.

The reflexes from the vascular mechano- and chemoreceptors and, above all, from the aorta arch and carotid sinus, are very important in the regulation of hemodynamics and respiration. With age, the reflexes from vascular receptors change inconsistently, the sensitivity of vascular chemoreceptors increasing, and the reflexes from the mechanoreceptors decreasing (Shchegoleva, 1966; Frolkis, 1970). It has been assumed that there are two groups of vascular chemoreceptors; one which is sensitive to hypoxic substances, and the other which is sensitive to cholinomimetic substances. In old animals, smaller doses of hypoxic and cholinomimetic substances can cause the excitation of chemoreceptors of various vascular areas (Fig-

ure 5). Along with the occurrence of high chemoreceptor sensitivity in old age, one can observe rapid exhaustion of reflexes from vascular chemoreceptors following a prolonged stimulation. At the same time, the reflexes from vascular mechanoreceptors are weakened. The electric impulsation becomes even more rare in aortal and carotid nerves. In old subjects, the Hering-Hermann reflex is less pronounced (heart rate and blood pressure fall after pressing the carotid sinus area). Weakening of reflexes from vascular mechanoreceptors promotes prolonged and persistent changes in blood pressure during various hemodynamic reactions in old age. A decline in this very important feedback mechanism in hemodynamic regulation leads to the development of arterial hypertension in elderly and old persons.

With age, the reflexes from mechanoreceptors in many organs weaken. In the mechanism of age-related changes in respiration, weakening of the Hering-Breier reflex plays an important role. There is a significant decrease in the amplitude of electrical potentials in afferent pulmonary fibers of the vagal nerve. During extension of the lung the receptors get irritated, which results in the switching on of the mechanisms of expiration. Weakening of the Hering-Breier reflex maintains the amplitude of respiratory movements under the conditions of essential structural changes and decreased lung elasticity in old age. With advanced age, the reflexes from the mechanoreceptors of the stomach and intestine also become weaker.

PHARMACOTHERAPY OF THE ANS IN OLD AGE

There is a large group of pharmacological drugs which influence different links of the ANS. They are widely used in clinical settings, for it is known that disturbances of the ANS may cause the development of a number of pathological processes.

Changes in the synthesis and degradation processes of ANS transmitters, and shifts in the state of receptors lead to age-related changes in reactions to the administration of transmitter-like substances such as cholino- and adrenomimetics, as well as lytics.

Because the cholinesterase activity is decreased

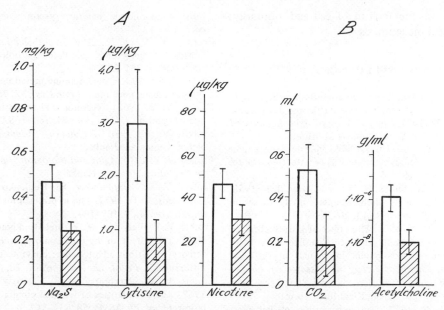

Figure 5. Threshold doses of various substances eliciting reflexes from chemoreceptors of the carotid sinus in rabbits (A) and from chemoreceptors of the intestinal vessels in cats (B). Open bars = adult animals; hatched bars = old animals.

in older persons, functional changes are provoked by administration of smaller doses of cholinesterase inhibitors, as compared with young persons. Thus, it has been shown that smaller doses of proserine and phosphamide induce changes in conductivity of cholinergic junctions. Shifts in cholinoreceptors cause hemodynamic, vascular and EEG changes in older persons and animals following administration of smaller doses of cholinolytics and cholinomimetics (acetylcholine, carbocholine, atropine, benzohexone) (Korkushko, 1969; Dukhovichny, 1974). According to Chebotarev (1973), smaller doses of catecholamines induce hemodynamic changes. Shevchuk (1974) showed that sensitivity of the cardiovascular system to β-adrenoblocker (inderal) is increased, whereas to α-adrenoblocker (regitin) it remains unchanged.

The age-related changes in the ANS necessitate the revision of dosages of a large group of pharmacological substances to be applied specifically in geriatric practice.

Conclusions

It is thus seen that, with aging, essential changes are taking place in all links of the autonomic nervous system. These changes lead to shifts in the reflectory regulation of inner organs, to a decrease in the organism's adaptive capacities, to a decrease in reliability of homeostatic regulatory mechanisms, to an easier disruption of regulatory mechanisms and to the development of pathology in old age. Owing to all of these shifts, there are irregular changes in vegetative components of various behavioral reactions, emotions, and psychic acts. Sometimes there appear paradoxical, inadequate reactions to an ordinary stimulation. Primary changes in the autonomic nervous system or in neurohumoral regulation may result in secondary shifts in other tissues. For further analyses of ANS aging, the following would be of particular concern to the researcher: elucidation of age peculiarities of vegetative reactions in various behavioral acts; psychic tensions; vegetative shifts induced by stimulation of both hypothalamus and other structures of the limbic system; establishment of an ANS/endocrine control relationship; the study of an adrenergic/cholinergic ratio in regulation of various organs; detailed analyses of limiting links of the ANS transmitter metabolism; and, elucidation of age peculiarities of ANS influences on metabolism of cell and, primarily, on protein biosynthesis.

REFERENCES

Andrew, W. 1956. Structural alterations with aging in the nervous system. *J. Chronic Diseases,* **3,** 575–582.

Andrew, W. 1971. *The Anatomy of Aging in Man and Animals.* New York: Grune & Stratton.

Aschheim, P. 1972. Un test biologique de vieilissement du controle du cycle oestral de la ratte. *Gen. Comp. Endocrinol.,* **18,** 3–5.

Barrows, C. H., Shock, N. W., and Chow, B. F. 1958. Age difference in cholinesterase activity of serum and liver. *J. Gerontol.,* **13,** 20–23.

Bezrukov, V. V. 1974. The effect of intracerebral injection of adrenalin and acetylcholine on activity of cardiovascular system in animals of different age. *In, Pharmacotherapy of Diseases of Cardiovascular System in Elderly and Old Age.* Year-Book 1973, pp. 32–36. Kiev: Inst. Geront.

Birren, J. E. 1972. The organization of behavior, adaptation and control of aging. *In, 9th Int. Congr. Geront.,* **1,** 57–61. Kiev: Inst. Geront.

Birren, J. E., and Spieth, N. 1962. Age, response speed and cardiovascular functions. *J. Gerontol,* **17,** 390–391.

Bogatskaya, L. N. 1972. Age characteristics of energy metabolism in myocardium and its regulation. *In, 9th Int. Congr. Geront.,* **2,** 77–79. Kiev: Inst. Geront.

Botwinick, J., and Kornetsky, C. 1960. Age differences in the acquisition and extinction of the GSR. *J. Gerontol.,* **15** (1), 83–84.

Burkard, W. P., Gey, K. F., and Pletscher, A. 1966. Alteration of the catecholamine metabolism of the rat heart in old age. *In, Proc. 7th Int. Congr. Geront.,* **62,** 237–239. Vienna.

Chebotarev, D. F. 1973. Prinzipien der medikamentözen Therapie im Alter. *In,* B. Steinmann (ed.), *Gerontology,* pp. 129–139. Bern: Haus Huber.

Chebotarev, D. F., and Frolkis, V. V. 1967. *Cardiovascular System with Aging.* Leningrad: Meditsina.

Dilman, V. M. 1971. Age-associated elevation of hypothalamic threshold to feed-back control and its role in development, ageing and disease. *Lancet,* **1,** 1211.

Dukhovichny, S. M. 1974. The effect of a number of neurotropic agents on arterial pressure in subjects of different age. *In, Pharmacotherapy of Diseases of Cardiovascular System in Elderly and Old Age.* Year-Book 1973, pp. 78–82. Kiev: Inst. Geront.

Duplenko, Yu. K. 1968. On some age-related peculiarities of cardiovascular response in nicotine-like and electric stimulation of nervous centers. *In, Problems of Experimental and Clinical Gerontology.* pp. 7–9. Kiev: Inst. Geront.

Eisdorfer, C., Nowlin, J., and Wilkie, F. 1970. Improvement of learning in the aged by modifica-tion of autonomic nervous system activity. *Science,* **170,** 1327–1329.

Everitt, A. V. 1973. The hypothalamic-pituitary control of aging and age-related pathology. *Exp. Gerontol.,* **8,** 265–277.

Finch, C. E. 1973. Catecholamine metabolism in the brains of aging male mice. *Brain Res.,* **52,** 261–276.

Frolkis, V. V. 1965. Neurohumoral regulation in the aging organism. *J. Gerontol.,* **21,** 161–168.

Frolkis, V. V. 1970. *Regulation, Adaptation and Aging.* Leningrad: Nauka.

Frolkis, V. V. 1975. *Aging and Biological Capacities of an Organism.* Moscow: Nauka.

Frolkis, V. V., Bezrukov, V. V., Duplenko, Yu. K., and Genis, E. D. 1972. The hypothalamus in aging. *Exp. Gerontol.,* **7,** 169–184.

Frolkis, V. V., Bezrukov, V. V., and Muradyan, Kh. K. 1974. The effect of hypothalamic stimulation on activity of various adaptive liver enzymes in rats of different age. *Fiziol. Zh. AN UkrSSR,* **20,** 646–653.

Frolkis, V. V., Verkhratsy, N. S., Zamostyan, V. P. 1967. Age peculiarities of regional circulation regulation. *Fiziol. Zh. SSSR,* **58,** 336–347.

Garnier, B. 1972. Blutdruckregulation, Nervensystem und Alter. *Actuelle Geront.,* **2,** 387–396.

Gey, K. F., Burkard, W. P., and Pletscher, A. 1965. Variation of norepinephrine metabolism of the rat heart with age. *Gerontologia,* **11,** 1–11.

Groen, J. J. 1959. General physiology of aging. *Geriatrics,* **14,** 318–331.

Hess, W. R. 1954. *Das Zwischenhirn. Syndrome, Lokalisationen, Funktionen.* Basel: Schwabe.

Kazantseva, A. G. 1970. Comparative age characteristics of internal structure of cervical sympathetic trunks in rabbits and guinea pigs. *Russk. Arkh. Anat.,* **58,** 99–107.

Korkushko, O. V. 1969. Age-conditioned changes predisposing to the development of myocardial infarction in elderly and old persons. *In, Arterial Hypertension and Coronary Insufficiency in Elderly and Old Age.* 181–198. Kiev: Inst. Geront.

Kuntz, A. 1938. Histological variations in autonomic ganglia and ganglion cells associated with age and disease. *Am. J. Pathol.,* **14,** 783.

Losev, V. A. 1963. Vascular reactions in elderly and aged persons. *In, Mechanisms of Aging,* pp. 411–412. Kiev: Zdorovye.

Mankovsky, N. B., and Mints, A. Ya. 1972. *Aging and Nervous System.* Kiev: Zdorovye.

Morris, J. D., and Thompson, L. W. 1969. Heart rate changes in a reaction time experiment with young and aged subjects. *J. Gerontol.,* **24,** 269–272.

Muravov, I. V. 1972. Regulation trophic effects of muscular activity and aging. *In, 9th Int. Congr. Geront.,* **2,** 407–410. Kiev: Inst. Geront.

Novick, W. I. 1961. The effect of age and thyroid hormones on the monoamine oxidase of rat heart. *Endocrinology,* **69,** 55–59.

Parchon, C. 1959. *Age Biology.* Bucharest: Publishing House of Literature in Foreign Languages.

Pavlov, I. P. 1928. *Lectures of Conditioned Reflexes.* New York: Liveright.

Samorajski, T., and Rolsten, C. 1973. Age and regional difference in the chemical composition of brains of mice, monkeys and humans. *In*, D. H. Ford (ed.), *Progress in Brain Research*, 40, pp. 253-265. Amsterdam-London-New York: Elsevier Scientific Publishing.

Shchegoleva, I. V. 1966. Sensitivity of carotid sinus chemoreceptors in old age. *Farmakol. Toksikol.*, 29, 404-407.

Shevchuk, V. G. 1974. The effect of stimulation and blocking of adrenoreceptors upon hemodynamic indices in animals of different age. *Farmakol. Toksikol.*, 37, 322-325.

Shmavonian, B. M., Jarmat, A. I., and Cohen, S. I. 1965. Relationship between the autonomic nervous system and central nervous system in age differences in behavior. *In*, A. Welford and J. Birren (eds.), *Behavior, Aging, and the Nervous System*, pp. 235-258. Springfield, Illinois: Charles C. Thomas.

Skok, V. I. 1970. *The Physiology of Autonomic Ganglia.* Leningrad: Nauka.

Verkhratsky, N. S. 1962. Age peculiarities of vascular sensitivity to humoral factors. *In, Problems of Gerontology and Geriatrics.* pp. 46-50. Kiev: Zdorovye.

Verkhratsky, N. S. 1970. Acetylcholine metabolism peculiarities in aging. *Exp. Gerontol.*, 5, 49-56.

Verkhratsky, N. S. 1972. Characteristics of catecholamine metabolism during aging. *In, 9th Int. Congr. Geront.*, 1, 106-109. Kiev: Inst. Geront.

Wilkie, F., and Eisdorfer, C. 1970. Blood pressure and intelligence in the aged. *Gerontologist*, 10, 11-37.

Yakimenko, D. M., Chebotarev, D. F., and Kotko, D. N. 1972. Peculiarities of cholinergic regulation of gastric motor-secretory function in the aged. *In, 9th Int. Congr. Geront.*, 3, 414.

Zhabotinsky, Yu. M. 1953. *Normal and Pathological Anatomy of Vegetative Ganglia.* Moscow: Medizdat.

10
BEHAVIOR GENETICS

Gilbert S. Omenn
University of Washington, Seattle, Washington

INTRODUCTION AND AIMS OF BEHAVIOR GENETICS

Geneticists share with poets and perhaps with psychoanalysts a consuming interest in the uniqueness of the individual. Of course, most of the differences among people are differences intuitively perceived in various aspects of their behavior. At the molecular and biochemical level one can demonstrate quite readily that no two persons, except for identical twins, are identical genetically. With only some 23 blood enzyme and antigen markers such as those used in population genetic studies or paternity testing (Omenn and Motulsky, 1972, Table 6), the probability of identical profiles for two randomly selected persons is one in 3 billion, which is the approximate world population. These 23 gene markers are only a minor sampling of the estimated 20,000 genes having variant forms potentially suitable for such testing (Omenn and Motulsky, 1972). Genetically-determined variations at the biochemical level occur not only in the blood cells but in all tissues and can be presumed to underlie anatomical, physiological, and behavioral differences in man and in animals.

Behavior Genetics has become identified as a significant field of study only over the past decade or so. The seminal text was Fuller and Thompson's (1960), with subsequent texts by Hirsch (1967), Parsons (1967), McClearn and DeFries (1973), and Ehrman and Parsons (1976),

as well as two major workshop publications (Ehrman, Omenn, and Caspari, 1972; Schaie, Anderson, McClearn, and Money, 1975). In 1970 the journal *Behavior Genetics* was established, and in 1971 the Behavior Genetics Association was founded. In fact, however, the founder of Behavior Genetics is acknowledged universally to be Sir Francis Galton. Galton was a first cousin of Charles Darwin and had made contributions as a geographer, explorer, and inventor. Greatly influenced by his cousin's book on the *Origin of Species*, Galton turned his efforts to biological phenomena and the inheritance of mental characteristics. He pioneered the study of families, leading to articles on "Hereditary Talent and Character" in 1865 and to his classic book *Hereditary Genius: An Inquiry Into Its Laws and Consequences* in 1869. He also applied the notion of a normal curve of distribution of quantitative measures and developed the twin-study method for analysis of genetic and environmental influences on behavior. Unfortunately, a long hiatus followed Galton, with unproductive controversy about the primacy of nature or nurture in the development of behavior phenotypes.

There are *two major aims* of modern behavior genetics: first, to define the degree to which genetic factors determine or predispose to specific behavioral phenotypes; and, second, to describe the mechanisms through which environmental variables interact with genetically programmed variation in cellular and metabolic functions to produce such behavioral phenotypes. Anatomical, neurophysiological, metabolic, molecular, and behavioral data must be integrated to provide detailed understanding of these mechanisms.

The interaction of genetic and environmental factors cannot be emphasized too strongly. For far too long, polemics about nature versus nurture have dominated studies of behavior, particularly of human behavior. The interaction and co-variance of genetic and environmental factors greatly complicate statistical or biometrical analyses which try to retain these important elements of variation, but the interaction becomes far more understandable as metabolic processes are elucidated. There are interactions between different animal strains and certain timed environmental treatments that produce audiogenic seizures, between the genotype for phenylketonuria or for galactosemia and the prevention of mental retardation by manipulation of the diet, and between certain enzyme deficiencies and the risk of serious complications from administration of specific pharmacological agents. These and other examples demonstrate that genetically-determined individual differences occur in animals and man that determine how certain behaviors will be influenced by specific elements in the environment.

In this *Handbook on the Psychology of Aging*, it is necessary to define the domain of "aging" and the phenomena or phenotypes suitable for analysis by the methods of behavior genetics. One definition might encompass the many diseases or disorders that befall people as they grow older. Essentially all of these disorders have a significant genetic predisposition, including heart diseases, high blood pressure, cancers, diabetes, stroke, osteoporosis with fractures, depression and senile dementia. These diseases likewise have marked effects on intellectual and emotional behaviors. Given the realization that some very old persons have remarkably intact cognitive function, one might postulate that any decline is due to recognizable or more subtle effects of cerebrovascular disease or other diseases like those just mentioned.

The editors' definition of *aging* in this *Handbook* appears to allow reference to the full spectrum of underlying mechanisms: "aging is any time-dependent change which occurs after maturity of size, form, or function is reached and which is distinct from daily, seasonal, and other biological rhythms." The gerund form of the term *aging* emphasizes the time-dimension of the phenomenon and the need to assess phenotypes of processes involved in aging over time. Clearly, different individuals bring different genetic make-up and different phenotypes to the stage of life referred to as "maturity." Many researchers interested in aging consequently consider developmental changes early in life to be highly relevant.

The great variation of ability and interests among the elderly is well known to every layman, of course. Some octagenarians are intensely active and productive, apparently still healthy of body, as well as mind. The author recently participated in a program at Stanford University heralded as "The Majesty of Man" that celebrated, against a background of neurophysiological and biochemical studies of mammalian and human brain, the remarkable prowess of pianist Arthur Rubinstein (age 88) and chemist Linus Pauling (age 74). Many less famous old persons delight their families and friends with their alertness, wisdom, and memory. On the other hand, as average life expectancy continues to increase and the proportion of the general population over age 65 and/or retired grows rapidly, our social institutions seem swamped with the numbers of older people requiring stimulation, support, or basic care.

This chapter will be devoted to highly selected data and methodology that illustrate the special perspective of behavior genetics for the psychology of aging.

METHODOLOGY OF BEHAVIOR GENETICS

Phenotypes

It is essential to describe or define the observable or measurable trait or phenotype to be analyzed. Complex phenotypes such as an intelligence score or neuroticism score or learning capability are composed of many facets of behavior and may be significantly influenced by the nature of the tasks or instruments employed. Such over-all behavioral phenotypes represent the result of a large number of biological and environmental variables, rather than reflecting specific brain functions or significant behaviors that might have been acted upon by selection during evolutionary survival of species. Psychophysiological parameters provide an intermediate level of description between the clinical/behavioral level and the biochemical/metabolic level. Thus, patterns of the electroencephalogram or of evoked potentials may be analyzed for genetic influences, even though these represent complex phenomena from large regions of the brain.

These Handbooks provide comprehensive reviews of anatomical, biochemical, physiological, hormonal, behavioral, and clinical phenomena that reflect or cause the aging process. Many of these phenomena may be susceptible to analysis of both genetic and environmental influences, from the statistical and the pathophysiological points of view.

Animal Subjects

Strain Differences. Well-defined strains of mice, rats, or other species offer the special advantage that individuals can be studied in replicates. Many kinds of strains of mice, for example, have been produced and are available. It is important to know the background of such strains, especially the inbred strains, and the different kinds of experiments for which they are well-suited.

Storer (1966) has described the average longevity and the pathological causes of death for 22 inbred mouse strains maintained by The Jackson Laboratory at Bar Harbor, Maine. These results are tabulated in Table 1. Psychologists who study mice ordinarily employ very young healthy mice and are often unaware that these strains were originally selected for their propensity to develop breast carcinoma or other diseases. Advance knowledge of the expected control survival time and characteristic pathology of each strain can allow the investigator to select appropriate strains for aging research. Strains which die early in life from a specific

disease before senescent changes have time to develop obviously should be excluded from aging studies.

Mean life span for females ranged from 276 days for strain AKR/J to 799 days for strain LP/J, a difference of nearly a factor of three. Frequency distribution plots of survival times in each strain showed the times to be reasonably normally distributed except for SWR/J and RIII/AnJ, which had bimodal distributions. Early deaths in SWR/J were due to severe polydipsia and polyuria, while early deaths in RII/AnJ were due to breast cancer. As can be seen in Figure 1, the inbred mouse strains have some common origins (Staats, 1966): the DBA/CBA/C3H group; the BALB/c; the A strains; C57 and C58; AKR and RF; SWR; and SJL. The data appear internally consistent, in that the two sexes and the related strains show very similar survival times. Among the females, for example, DBA/2J and DBA/1J ranked 20th and 21st in survival times. C57BL/6J and C57BR/cdJ ranked 18 and 19. The shorter times for C58/J are due to the very high leukemia rate (88 percent) early in life. The coefficient of correlation between the female and male survival times for each strain was .66 ($p < .001$); amended mean values excluding the four strains with bimodal patterns of death increased the correlation to .86. The high incidence of specific types of tumors in many of these strains merely reflects the fact that the strains were originally selected and bred for high tumor incidence.

Storer noted that earlier data (1948–1952) on ten of these mouse strains gave very similar results, especially in the rank order of survival times. The actual values for longevity were increased in almost all strains, presumably reflecting an improved environment. Since the extent of life lengthening was not equal across strains, genetic-environmental interaction must play a large role in the differences.

Inbred strains, ordinarily produced by 20 or more consecutive generations of brother-sister matings, also provide reliable sources for strain crosses. Strain crosses may serve any of six purposes (Green, 1966):

1. To produce uniform F_1 hybrids for use in terminal experiments. Hybrids are usually much more hardy, grow faster, live longer,

TABLE 1. LONGEVITY AND CAUSE OF DEATH IN INBRED STRAINS OF MICE.

Strain	N	Mean ± S.E.	Gross tumor incidence %	Gross pathology
a. male animals				
1. AKR/J	72	276 ± 8.9	91	90% leukemia
2. C58/J	75	351 ± 13.2	88	88% leukemia
3. SJL/J	76	395 ± 11.3	78	76% leukemia
4. PL/J	70	448 ± 13.5	71	50% leukemia
5. RF/J	81	452 ± 13.1	43	43% leukemia
6. BDP/J	75	468 ± 16.7	24	Non-specific, some kidney disease
7. SWR/J	66	496 ± 20.8	10	73% polydipsia and polyuria
8. P/J	81	510 ± 15.1	23	Non-specific, some kidney disease
9. ST/bJ	80	511 ± 15.1	6	45% polydipsia and polyuria
10. CBA/J	75	527 ± 15.4	87	75% breast tumors
11. BALB/cJ	76	575 ± 14.9	29	Non-specific, tumors varied
12. MA/J	74	585 ± 13.7	5	79% polydipsia and polyuria
13. A/J	78	590 ± 18.8	30	Non-specific, tumors varied
14. SM/J	77	591 ± 14.5	7	Non-specific
15. 129/J	78	648 ± 24.4	20	Non-specific, some massive uterine hyperplasia
16. RIII/AnJ	77	655 ± 23.1	52	45% breast tumors
17. C3HeB/FeJ	78	657 ± 14.5	55	49% late-occurring liver or breast tumors
18. C57BL/6J	75	692 ± 15.7	14	Non-specific
19. C57BR/dJ	73	694 ± 19.9	34	Non-specific, tumors varied
20. DBA/2J	80	714 ± 21.4	37	34% leukemia or breast tumors
21. DBA/1J	70	750 ± 19.9	22	Non-specific, tumors varied
22. LP/J	76	799 ± 20.3	55	Late-occurring tumors, varied type
b. female animals				
1. AKR/J	39	326 ± 15.9	81	81% leukemia
2. C58/J	75	373 ± 18.6	73	73% leukemia
3. P/J	78	384 ± 13.6	6	37% polycystic or granular kidneys
4. BDP/J	80	421 ± 12.4	5	19% polycystic or granular kidneys, others non-specific
5. ST/bJ	72	433 ± 22.9	2	27% hemorrhagic diathesis, others non-specific
6. DBA/1J	73	433 ± 30.9	2	Bimodal survival, early: hemorrhage and infection, late: non-specific
7. MA/J	76	459 ± 19.4	0	25% gross kidney disease, 12% polydipsia, polyuria
8. SJL/J	30	472 ± 25.1	28	28% leukemia
9. A/J	70	490 ± 18.4	13	Non-specific
10. PL/J	77	517 ± 17.1	19	19% leukemia, others non-specific
11. CBA/J	73	527 ± 17.0	72	64% hepatomas
12. BALB/cJ	28	539 ± 33.0	0	Non-specific
13. SM/J	75	572 ± 17.0	0	Non-specific
14. SWR/J	34	616 ± 29.2	17	Non-specific
15. RF/J	33	651 ± 24.5	49	49% leukemia
16. C3HeB/FeJ	82	652 ± 16.6	31	31% hepatomas
17. C57BL/6J	74	676 ± 20.3	7	Non-specific
18. 129/J	79	679 ± 18.9	12	Non-specific
19. RII/AnJ	76	685 ± 20.5	10	Non-specific
20. C57BR/cdJ	76	703 ± 17.4	25	25% hepatomas, otherwise non-specific
21. DBA/2J	75	707 ± 22.4	18	Non-specific, tumors varied
22. LP/J	74	748 ± 18.6	19	Non-specific, tumors varied

After Storer, 1966.

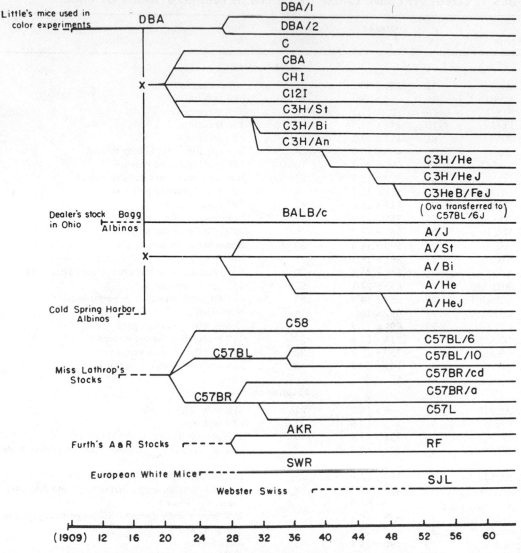

Figure 1. Origins of the older inbred strains of mice. (From Staats, 1966. *Biology of the Laboratory Mouse*, 2nd edition.)

and reproduce earlier and more abundantly than the inbred strains. Reciprocal crosses of male/female and female/male are needed to identify sex-related effects of the individual strains in the F_1 hybrid.

2. To produce F_1, F_2, back-crosses to parent$_1$ and to parent$_2$, and other generations to analyze the genetic basis of a variable trait. These crosses are most informative for traits determined by a single gene locus, as in the classical experiments of Mendel with peas.

3. To produce 2-way, 3-way, 4-way, etc., cross-bred populations as the healthy starting point for selection experiments. Here animals scoring high or low on the desired criterion are mated with similarly scored animals of the opposite sex to generate sublines of high and low scoring animals, assuming that genetic factors are involved in the trait. The stronger the genetic influence, the more rapidly selection acts to separate the characteristics of the two sublines.

4. To produce all possible F_1 generations

(diallel crosses) between several inbred strains to reveal a multiple factor genetic system determining variation especially in a continuous trait. The quantitative variation can be analyzed for several types of genetic and environmental variance (Fulker, Wilcock, and Broadhurst, 1972; Mather and Jinks, 1971).

5. To transfer a mutant gene from one genetic background to another. This approach is potentially very important to understanding the metabolic effects of a specific mutant gene. Sometimes a mutation proves nearly lethal in one strain, but is compatible with long life in another strain, albeit with characteristic abnormalities due to the mutation.

6. To decompose a complex genotype into single-locus constituents, allowing the identification of "new" genes involved in that phenotype. This approach has been most fruitful in analysis of histocompatibility loci (Snell, 1958). Actually the breeding techniques here do not isolate single loci, but do isolate successively smaller and smaller bits of heterozygous chromosomes which carry at least one pair of alleles affecting the trait of interest.

Species Comparisons. In the usual attempt to extrapolate animal data to man, it is valuable to show that behavioral phenomena and associated biochemical or physiological measures are correlated across species. Recently great efforts have been invested in developing nonhuman primate colonies for all sorts of behavioral research, since these species are closer to man in their behaviors and probably in their underlying processes. It is well-known that many drugs are metabolized differently in different species (as well as among individuals of any species); analogous differences in effects of other kinds of environmental agents may be anticipated (Omenn and Motulsky, 1976). Some researchers are less interested in extrapolation to man than in basic understanding of the evolution of behavior; for these workers detailed comparisons of closely and distantly related species have intrinsic value.

Studies of reproductive and social behavior are central to analysis of the origin of species and of reproductive isolation of newly emerging species. These phenomena have been investigated most intensively in *Drosophila* (fruit flies) (Ayala, 1970). However, such studies are highly relevant to aging research, in that social behavior within species must somehow be enhanced by the presence of older, non-reproducing individuals or the forces of natural selection would be expected to eliminate these older individuals.

Mutants. Just as inherited disorders of metabolism in man have uncovered much of what we know about normal metabolic pathways, spontaneous and induced *experiments of nature* have been analyzed in other species ranging from *E. coli* bacteria and paramecia, to earthworms, fruit flies, and mice (Ehrman and Parsons, 1976). In the case of the mouse, special efforts have produced dozens of neurological mutants, affecting cerebellar, inner ear, neuromuscular, and cortical functions (Sidman, Green, and Appel, 1965). Very often these mutant mice are poorly viable, but judicious crossing to a different genetic background can provide hardy strains carrying the mutation of interest.

Human Subjects

Epidemiological Studies. Demographic data can provide important clues to genetic influences in behavioral traits. Populations are commonly examined for differences in frequency of various traits according to sex, age, ethnic or racial group, geographic location, occupational exposure, number of siblings, and birth order. Correlational and analysis of variance methods are applied to such data. Descriptive information is far greater for man than for other species, but direct manipulation to reveal underlying mechanisms is more difficult, of course.

Family Studies. Correlations between phenotypes and degree of genetic relatedness are the basis of family investigations. For simple traits, like color blindness or ability to taste the chemical PTC, the segregation of the trait in the pedigree (i.e., who gets it and who does not get it from parents of either sex) may reveal the pattern of inheritance. Thus, color blindness is determined by an X-linked recessive gene, affecting males and carried from affected maternal grandfathers through the mother to the grandson. An autosomal dominant trait is transmitted from parent to child, without regard for sex, with a 50:50 chance that each child will manifest the trait, since one of each chromosome pair carries the particular dominant gene, while the other chromosome of the pair carries a different form of the gene. In the autosomal recessive traits, the parents are usually normal, but carry one copy of the abnormal gene; in one out of four of their children the child gets the abnormal gene from each parent (probability $\frac{1}{2} \times \frac{1}{2} = \frac{1}{4}$). These children then transmit the abnormal gene to all of their children, but these children will be affected only if the unaffected spouse-parent happens to carry the same autosomal recessive gene.

Many important behavioral traits appear to have polygenic determination (Falconer, 1960; Rosenthal, 1970). The distribution of the trait is continuous and quantitative. Here it is valuable to analyze the distribution of the trait in the relatives of individuals who are at the extremes of the quantitative distribution curve; relatives of those with very high values have a distribution curve shifted to higher values, while relatives of those with very low values have a curve shifted to a lower value.

Twin-study Method. This approach was introduced by Galton in 1883. Monozygotic (identical) twins share all the same genes, while dizygotic (fraternal) twins share half the same genes, just like ordinary siblings. To the extent that MZ twins differ there must be environmental factors which are important. To the extent that genetic factors are important, the similarity of MZ twins will be much greater than that of DZ twins. For all-or-none traits, this similarity is termed *concordance*: if one twin is affected or "has the trait," the co-twin must have it also. If the co-twin is unaffected, the twin pair is discordant. For a quantitative trait, the similarity is calculated as a correlation coefficient.

The twin method has certain difficulties. First, the results do not provide any clues to the pattern of inheritance, since transmission from generation to generation is not examined. For polygenic traits, as opposed to single-gene traits, this is not too serious a problem, since family studies will not reveal any simple segregation pattern. Second, the assumption may not be justifiable that the environmental variance is the same for MZ and like-sex DZ pairs. In this method, fraternal (DZ) pairs only of the same sex are studied, to eliminate simple differences associated with sex. The intra-pair environmental effects may be especially important in behavioral phenotypes, and over time these effects may vary.

Third, reliable assessment of zygosity often has not been documented. Nowadays there are reliable methods to prove DZ twinning and to make MZ twinning a firm diagnosis. Fourth, the between-family variance may be lost, as only the within-family variance is measured in twin studies. Cattell (1953, 1960) has introduced a Multiple Abstract Variance Analysis design (MAVA) for this problem, applicable to pairs of persons, including twins, from different families.

The estimation of the extent of genetic effect from twin studies is based upon calculation of the "heritability," ranging from 0 for no genetic effect to 1.0 for total genetic determination. Heritability is always specific to the environmental conditions observed. Several different methods have been used (Vandenberg, 1966). These utilize either intraclass correlations or within-pair variances. "Heritability" is a technical term with many complexities. Basically, however, it is the fraction of the total variance (genetic plus environmental) which is attributable to genetic variance. Thus, heritability represents $V_G/V_G + V_E$. Both V_G and V_E, the genetic and environmental variances, have subcomponents which are important for animal breeding and for detailed analysis of human behavioral traits. In addition, there are terms not to be ignored altogether which assess the genetic-environmental interaction and other effects. Finally, there is variance due to random effects of measurement or variation in the reproducibility of testing.

Heritability calculations in twins are relatively straightforward, resting, of course, upon the assumptions discussed above. Several different formulas have been utilized, which do not necessarily give identical estimates for the heritability. The first formula for heritability (h^2), as proposed by Holzinger in 1929, takes into account only the within-pair variance and not the between-pair variance:

$$h^2 = \frac{r_{MZ} - r_{DZ}}{1 - r_{DZ}} \qquad (1)$$

where r is the intraclass correlation coefficient. The more inclusive calculation, based on within-pair variances, is:

$$h^2 = \frac{\sigma^2_{w_{DZ}} - \sigma^2_{w_{MZ}}}{\sigma^2_{w_{DZ}}} \qquad (2)$$

where σ^2_w is the within-pair variance of the twins.

Adoption and Half-Sibling Studies. An exceedingly productive new research strategy has been exploited over the past ten years by Rosenthal and his colleagues at the National Institute of Mental Health and in Copenhagen (Rosenthal, 1970; Kety, Rosenthal, Wender, and Schulsinger, 1971). This strategy aims to separate the inherited factors from intrafamilial environmental factors by independently assessing the biological family and the rearing family of individuals who are adopted very early in life. There are five complementary methods, illustrated best from the work on schizophrenia.

The *adoptees' families method* begins with adoptions that took place many years earlier, usually 30 to 50 years ago. These adoptees are now adults who have lived through enough of the risk period that most who are liable to develop schizophrenia will have shown signs permitting diagnosis. The schizophrenic adoptees are identified from psychiatric histories and hospital records; such records proved to be available, on a confidential basis, in Denmark, where excellent registries are kept. These adoptees become the index cases. From among the remaining adoptees, a control group is formed, matched to the index cases with respect to age at transfer to the adoptive parents, age at time of study, sex, and social class. They are free of psychiatric disorders. Then for both the index group and the control group the incidence

of schizophrenic disorder is determined among the biological and adoptive relatives, to fill the following design cell (Figure 2):

RELATIVES

Figure 2. Design cell for adoptees' families method. Data are tabulated for incidence of disease or trait in the biological relatives and in the adoptive relatives of index cases and of controls.

Analysis is straightforward: higher incidence among the biological relatives of index cases than of controls indicates that heredity is contributing significantly; higher incidence among the adoptive relatives supports the view that rearing by, of, or with schizophrenics contributes more to the development of the disorder.

The *adoptees study method* begins with the biological parents of adoptees. Their psychiatric histories are searched to find those parents who have schizophrenic disorders. The children they gave up for adoption then become the index cases. A matched control group, as in the complementary method, is formed, differing only in that the biological parents of these adoptees have no psychiatric disorders. The two groups of adoptees are investigated. A higher incidence of schizophrenic disorder in the index group indicates that heredity is primary, assuming that the people who adopted the index and control groups of children are similar with respect to any environmental factors that might give rise to the disorder.

It should be emphasized that these two groups of adoptees can be studied intensively for a wide variety of behaviors in controlled (test or laboratory) and natural situations. Some of these additional behavioral or neurophysiological measures may be involved in the development of schizophrenia or in resistance to development of schizophrenic behavior; other measures may be unrelated but equally interesting for other investigators. In fact, this approach has been applied to studies of minimal brain dysfunction in children (Morrison and Stewart, 1973) and to other types of psychopathology of adults in Denmark (Goodwin, Schulsinger, Hermansen, Guze, and Winokur, 1973).

As the primary adoptee groups continue to age in the Denmark study, investigators interested in the genetic and environmental influences on behaviors associated with aging should seek to become involved in follow-up studies. Over the next 10 years these index cases and the control groups will be reaching the 50–70 year age bracket.

A related important research strategy is the investigation of *MZ twins reared apart*. In fact, the very first such study was reported 50 years ago by a distinguished experimental geneticist, H. J. Muller, who received the Nobel Prize for his work on mutations. Muller (1925) noted that a colleague in the Department of Psychology at the University of Texas had tested a number of twin pairs with a battery of psychological tests then available. When Muller learned of a pair of female twins, aged 30 years, who had been separated at age two weeks, did not see each other until age 18 years, and then lived quite different lives in different environments to the time of the study, he recognized that this *experiment of nature* provided an extraordinary opportunity to isolate genetic and environmental factors. He examined them carefully and calculated with high degree of certainty that they were monozygotic twins.

The twin pair yielded nearly identical and very high scores on intelligence tests (Army Alpha and Otis), despite great differences in the amount and kinds of formal education. On other tests of motor reaction time, association time, "will-temperament," emotional responses, and social attitudes, the twins gave markedly different scores. Many of the differences appeared to be related to salient differences in their past experiences and habits of life. But Muller made a far-reaching criticism of these tests: despite the diverse reactions, there were many intuitively recognized mental characteristics in which the twins would closely agree if appropriate means of measuring these characteristics were found. They seemed possessed of similar energy and tension in their daily activity, with similar mental alertness and interest in the practical problems about them, as opposed to abstractions and puzzles; they were personally agreeable and popular; they displayed similar idiosyncracies in taking the tests, their tastes in books and people were strikingly similar. Thus, we return to the point made earlier in this chapter that choice of phenotypes and development of measures for "biologically meaningful" phenotypes is crucial for research in behavior genetics.

Shields (1962) provides detailed case summaries of monozygotic twin pairs reared apart and reared together, plus results from tests of intelligence and personality (Dominoes; Mill Hill vocabulary; Extraversion; Neuroticism). Those twin pairs represented a broad age range, but many were in their thirties, forties, and even fifties at the time of study more than 15 years ago. Investigators with specific hypotheses about behavioral traits in aged persons might seek a follow-up study of these remarkable twin pairs.

Yet another aspect of this research strategy, applicable in the United States, where disease and adoption registries do not exist, is the *half-sibling approach*. Families with multiple matings and children related through only one common parent allow analogous analysis of the effects of biological transmission of genes from a parent versus cultural-rearing effects of a non-biological parent. Schuckit (1972) applied this method to studies of alcoholism, with the somewhat surprising and striking finding that the excess familial incidence of alcoholism was among the biological relatives, not the rearing, non-biological family members.

A combination of twin study and half-sibling analysis has been proposed and illustrated by Nance (1974, 1975) in the investigation of the *offspring of identical twins*. In conjunction with full-sib and parental observations, half-sib analysis permits an estimation of genetic and environmental variance and a partitioning of the genetic variance into additive and dominance components, as well as detection of interactions and maternal effects. The offspring of identical twins are related to each other in the same way as half-sibs, and the multiple relationships that exist within these kinships provide an unusual opportunity to resolve and measure potentially important sources of human variation.

The covariance between husband and wife has been used by some investigators to estimate the effects of living in a common environment, while others have used this covariance as a measure of assortative mating. Resolution of these two effects may not be important for many physical traits, but for psychological variables, the distinction is critical. Assortative (nonrandom) mating tends to inflate the additive component of the genetic variance in the offspring while environmental covariance does not (Crow and Kimura, 1970).

In Nance's model, the genetically identical twin of an assortatively mated individual should show a similar tendency to mate assortatively, when husband-wife covariance is partitioned into between- and within-twin set components. In all, some 16 relationships have been identified for analysis. The strategy has been applied thus far to analysis of birth weight and total ridge count in the fingerprint patterns, and many other applications are underway. It should be emphasized that this method draws upon long experience in the animal husbandry field, where the equivalent of offspring of identical twins have been studied extensively.

Linkage. An indirect method to investigate the genetic basis of behavioral traits is by demonstration of linkage of the putative gene(s) for the trait to some defined genetic marker, like blood groups or plasma proteins or enzyme variants. The simplest approach is demonstration of linkage to the X chromosome (sex-linkage). Growing evidence points to an X-linked dominant gene in at least some families with manic-depressive psychosis, based upon linked segregation with color blindness and blood group Xg^a markers (Mendlewicz and Fleiss, 1974). As more and more biochemical markers are identified, and as computerized analysis of complex and partial pedigrees is advanced, we may anticipate further effort to relate genetic predisposition to particular disorders or traits to specific gene markers.

Linkage, it should be emphasized, is entirely different from association (see Omenn, 1972; Omenn and Schrott, 1975). Linkage means that two genes are physically located close together on the same chromosome, so that crossing-over and recombination is unlikely and so that the chromosomes carried by the sperm or egg will likely carry the same two genes transmitted on that chromosome by the previous generation. It does *not* matter which allele (like A or B or O at the ABO blood group locus) is present; whichever allele is present will be transmitted together with the linked gene. By contrast, association of two genetic traits implies nothing about the location of the genes on the chromosome map. Association, however, may provide clues to some important pathophysiological relationships.

Linkage has been utilized in one human disorder that often affects behavior in adulthood, myotonic dystrophy, to predict the inheritance of the autosomal dominant gene for this disorder from the linked transmission of the marker gene *secretor* that determines the secretion of ABO blood group substances into body fluids, such as saliva, amniotic fluid, etc. (Schrott, Karp, and Omenn, 1973).

Search for Mechanisms

Developmental. The most important dimension to studies of underlying mechanisms for the psychology of aging is the dimension of time. It can be argued effectively that the psychology of aging embraces not just behaviors of old people but the panoply of emerging and changing behaviors from early life. Schaie (1975) has explored the implications of the developmental view for research strategies. Cross-sectional and longitudinal methods too often give conflicting results, particularly in the area of decrement with age (Schaie, 1974). In their place, Schaie recommends mixed strategies to segregate the variance due to chronological age from that attributable to cohort differences in cross-sectional studies and from non-age-related environmental or sociocultural effects in longitudinal studies. (Also see Chapter 2 in this volume.) The developmental perspective requires that anatomical, biochemical, neurophysiological and behavioral data be integrated over time. Other chapters in these Handbooks deal extensively with these levels of aging phenomena. In this section, some relevant data from our own laboratory will be cited.

Molecular. Any genetic program for development and aging must be coded in the DNA of the cells. Genetic influences set the "reaction range" within which environmental interactions have effect. For direct genetic effects there may even be some stochastic phenomena, as in formation of cell-cell connections and, certainly, in the random inactivation of the second X chromosome in females (XX).

All nucleated cells contain the same DNA. In humans there are 23 pairs of chromosomes in each somatic cell and 23 chromosomes (one of each pair) in the germ cells, the egg and the sperm. DNA in different types of cells from the same individual is identical, as has been proven chemically by DNA/DNA hybridization (McCarthy and Hoyer, 1964) and biologically by transplantation of nuclei from fully differentiated intestinal lining cells of the frog into enucleated eggs to direct development of a normal tadpole (Gurdon, 1968).

The DNA is transmitted by cell division and DNA replication to all progeny of the fertilized egg. The result of differentiation of tissues is a selection of certain genes to be active in certain tissues, other genes to be active in other tissues, and some genes to be active in all tissues. DNA/RNA hybridization shows that only part of the genome is active in any tissue at any time (McCarthy and Hoyer, 1964). Some genes are redundant, coding for large amounts of ribosomal RNA needed for protein synthesis. However, appropriate methods can determine the proportion of "unique sequence DNA" genes present in single copies and transcribed into RNA messengers which go out from the cell nucleus into the cytoplasm to direct protein synthesis on the polyribosomes.

One of the most dramatic findings of overall gene action in the nervous system has come from studies of DNA/RNA hybridization. In such tissues as liver, kidney, and spleen, only 3–6 percent of the unique-sequence DNA is transcribed into extractable RNA (Hahn and Laird, 1971; Grouse, Chilton, and McCarthy, 1972). In brain tissue, a remarkably higher proportion is transcribed: 10–13 percent in the mouse brain and approximately 20 percent in human brain (Grouse, Omenn, and McCarthy, 1973). The preliminary results suggest that the values for diversity of RNA messengers are substantially higher in the cortex than in the brain stem. Furthermore, dominant cortex appears to have higher values than non-dominant, and grossly atrophied cortex has lower values than normal-appearing cortex from a "matched" 70-year-old man (Grouse, Omenn and McCarthy, 1973). A value of 20 percent hybridization means that 40 percent of the genome (transcribing from one DNA stand *or* the other) is expressed. The amount of DNA per cell (about 6 picograms) is the same in the mouse and in man, so these data strongly indicate that evolution has been associated with an increasing assignment of the genome to functions of the central nervous system, particularly the cortex. Such a biochemical finding is certainly consistent with anatomical and psychological characterizations of the development of higher cortical functions.

Our limited data also suggest a much higher value for DNA/RNA hybridization in adults than in fetal brain. We suspect, however, that a detectable fraction of the genome may be active in fetal brain and not active later. Furthermore, there may be additional shifts in transcription as development and aging proceed. Many interesting studies of the extent of transcription in different regions of brain and in brains from individuals of various ages and certain pathological states will be carried out with these techniques. Analogous experiments can be performed with monkey and mouse brain from animals subjected to early rearing experiences of enrichment to see whether these behavior modification programs are associated with significant change in this biochemical parameter of gene expression and differentiation in brain.

Brain proteins also can be compared as a function of age and abilities. Studies of the proteins of different tissues are of essentially two kinds. First, there are comparisons of the physical properties of proteins of unknown function, simply identified as separable "bands" on polyacrylamide electrophoretic gel systems, for example. Second, there are studies of particular enzymes or other proteins whose functions are known, preferably involving key metabolic steps.

Electrophoretic profiles of proteins of brain appear significantly different from similar preparations from other tissues (Caplan, Cheung, and Omenn, 1974). Two proteins highly specific for brain have been found: the S-100 protein (named for its solubility in 100 percent saturated ammonium sulfate) in glial cells (Moore, Perez, and Gehring, 1968) and the 14-3-2 protein (named for its position on three successive chromatographic elutions) in neuronal cells (Cicero, Cowan, Moore, and Suntzeff, 1970). Unfortunately, the functional role of these two proteins remains unknown, despite much research.

The electrophoretic method has revealed developmental changes. Grossfield and Shooter (1971) and Cain, Ball, and Dekaban (1972) have reported changes during development in the profiles of aqueous-soluble and aqueous-insoluble proteins in whole brain extracts of the mouse and the rabbit, respectively. Similar techniques have shown differences among the regions of the auditory pathway in the guinea pig (Davies, 1970) and between neuronal membrane fractions of DBA and C57 mice (Gurd, Mahler, and Moore, 1972). In our laboratory, Caplan, Cheung, and Omenn (1974) have reported some differences in the electrophoretic profile of aqueous-soluble cortical human proteins between adults and fetuses or infants. In addition, affinity chromatography for glycoproteins revealed another fetal/adult difference. The profiles were identical for 100 adults ranging in age from 20 to 88 years.

Metabolic and Physiological. There are many ways in which the metabolism of brain and of other tissues may change with age. Alterations in cerebral blood flow or distribution of regional brain perfusion may trigger physiological changes and activate or inhibit certain enzymes. Accumulated mutations, affecting the structural genes for the proteins themselves or, as in the error catastrophe hypothesis, affecting the transfer RNAs or other components of the protein synthesizing system, may

have detectable effects on the protein products in tissues from aged individuals. Alternatively, repair of abnormalities in the DNA (mutations) or clearance of abnormal proteins may be impaired with age. Some of these theoretical possibilities are under intensive investigation, as will be illustrated later in the case of Werner's syndrome (see below).

Normal aging might be accompanied by changes in the expression of genes for key enzymes in metabolism. The models in man for such developmental transition include the change from fetal hemoglobin to adult hemoglobin at the time of birth (Motulsky, 1969) and the change in fetal skeletal muscle from "brain-type" isozymes of creatine phosphokinase (Eppenberger, Eppenberger, Richterick, and Aebi, 1964) and phosphoglycerate mutase (Omenn and Cheung, 1974) to adult muscle-type isozymes of these key enzymes of energy metabolism.

Changes in gene expression for iso-enzymes and for polypeptide hormones occur often in the transformation of normal cells to neoplastic cells; these changes may be important clinical features of some malignant tumors in man (Omenn, 1973). In our survey using electrophoretic methods of all eleven steps of glycolysis and of more than a dozen other enzymes intimately involved in energy metabolism in brain, we found no examples of changes in the properties of these enzymes between ages 20 and 88 years (Cohen, Omenn, Motulsky, Chen, and Giblett, 1973; Cohen and Omenn, 1972). The genetic aspects of such surveys include both the search for programmed developmental changes and the search for differences across individuals in the nature or timing of any such changes. Analogous questions may be asked about neurophysiological properties of brain, including EEGs and evoked cortical responses, and of isolated neural cells. For example, the pattern of neurotransmitter synthesis by mouse neuroblastoma clones (Amano, Richelson and Nirenberg, 1972) reflects not only the origin of the clone but also the culture conditions.

Autoimmune. An important potential mechanism for deterioration of tissue function involves immunological damage to the cells. When the antibodies or cytotoxic lymphocytes are produced by the same individual, the mechanism is termed autoimmunity. The phenomenon involves some of the basic questions of recognition of "self" and "non-self," of "tolerance" by the pregnant woman for the organ graft that is her fetus but not for the organ graft that is a kidney transplant, and of the capacity of the body to distinguish transformed or malignant cells from normal cells and thereby resist the growth of a cancer.

As reviewed by Fialkow (1969), there are many lines of evidence to suggest that tissue-specific autoimmunity has complex etiological relationships and a genetic basis. Studies of families of patients with auto-antibodies against thyroid tissue, for example, reveals that many relatives (compared with controls) have similar auto-antibodies. In addition, these individuals have auto-antibodies against stomach, adrenal, and sometimes other tissue antigens, as well as the thyroid. Organ-specific antibodies are associated with a higher incidence of chromosomal abnormalities in offspring. This effect is particularly well-documented in the case of mothers with thyroid autoimmunity and birth of children with Down's syndrome. Perhaps antibodies which affect the spindle fibers of the meiotic and mitotic apparatus during cell division lead to unequal distribution of the chromosomes of each pair; non-disjunction of the #21 pair of chromosomes would produce trisomy 21 or Down's syndrome. Analogous effects of auto-antibodies against the components of cell division in somatic cells, as opposed to the germ cells, might produce somatic chromosomal aberrations and associated abnormalities or decline in function.

Biological Rhythms. Most physical and biological phenomena are tied to certain rhythmical cycles. We are familiar, of course, with the rotation of the earth and numerous circadian (daily) rhythms in our behavior and physiology. The adrenal gland secretion of cortisol, for example, has an early morning peak and a late-afternoon and evening nadir. Deviation from this rhythmical cycle is an early sign of disease of the adrenal cortex. The levels of other circulating hormones and many other constituents of the blood vary according to the time and in conjunction with eating and sleeping patterns. On a longer scale, there may be important built-in rhythms in the hypertrophy and involution of tissues and in the migration and death of cells. These rhythms surely have a genetic basis, and they are likely to have genetically-determined individual variation.

Effects of Identifiable Exogenous Agents. Genetically-determined differences in the metabolism of the host may explain the marked individual variation in susceptibility to adverse effects from such agents as ionizing radiation, behavior-modifying and other drugs, food additives and pollutants (Omenn and Motulsky, 1976). In some cases, these differences are due to differences in the metabolism of the exogenous agent. One example is the activation of aryl hydrocarbons in cigarette smoke or air pollution to their reactive carcinogenic derivatives; those who are high inducers of the necessary hydroxylase enzyme are apparently much more likely to develop cancer of the lung. Conversely, patients who (in different steps) metabolize the antidepressant drugs nortriptyline or phenelzine faster than others are less likely to experience unwanted side effects of these agents.

Other cases of genetically-determined differences are due to different susceptibility of the tissue to damage or compromise by the drug. The classical example is deficiency of the enzyme glucose-6-phosphate dehydrogenase in red blood cells. This enzyme deficiency is quite common among Blacks and among Mediterranean populations, with the Mediterranean type of deficiency the more severe. The affected persons normally have no problem or just mild anemia, but they are susceptible to acute hemolysis (breakdown of red blood cells) if administered certain oxidizing drugs, such as those widely used in prophylaxis of malaria.

There can be little doubt that we have only begun to uncover the mechanisms for many crucial genetic-environmental interactions. Understanding of such interactions will eventually have the greatest pay-off in the area of behavioral phenotypes.

BEHAVIOR GENETICS OF AGING: STUDIES OF ANIMALS

Drosophila

The organism most studied genetically is the fruit fly. Various *Drosophila* species have provided data on a variety of behaviors, on the nature of speciation, and on the relationship of behaviors to specific chromosome or gene markers. In a few studies, age has been a critical variable.

Relatively simple or simply measured normal behaviors, such as phototaxis and geotaxis, appear to be determined polygenically. In general, it seems, normal behaviors tend to be polygenically determined, representing the concerted action of many genes and interacting physiological processes, while seriously abnormal behaviors may be caused by single abnormal genes interfering with any one of the essential normal steps.

Phototaxis (orientation toward or away from light) was analyzed in *Drosophila melanogaster* by Hirsch and Tryon (1956) and in *Drosophila pseudoobscura* by Spassky and Dobzhansky (1967). A multiple-choice apparatus was used to allow the selection of positive or negative phototaxis in inbred and outbred strains.

Parallel results, again indicating polygenic determination, were obtained for geotaxis (orientation to gravity). Using marked chromosomes, Erlenmeyer-Kimling and Hirsch (1961) demonstrated that genes of the X chromosome control positive geotaxis and genes of the third chromosome control negative geotaxis; in another strain, the second chromosome carried genes affecting positive geotaxis. Thus, three of the four chromosomes of the species were involved in this behavior. Beyond the gene effects, environment can play an important role. The beetle *Blastophagus pinniperda L.* is positively phototactic in spring (temperature 10–25°C), but negatively phototactic below and above this temperature (Perttunen, 1959). It is thought likely that such changes are mediated by hormonal changes (Petit, 1972).

The most detailed analyses of genetic and environmental interaction are provided for courtship and sexual behavior (Bastock, 1956; Dobzhansky and Streisinger, 1944). The importance of sexual selection, already emphasized by Darwin in 1871, is its contribution to speciation and to the maintenance of genetic variability among populations. Courtship in *Drosophila* involves three complex phases: (1) orientation, based upon olfactory and/or visual stimulation; (2) vibration of the male, comprising auditory and tactile stimulation; and (3) licking, just prior to copulation, involving tactile and chemical stimulation. Ablation of effectors or receptors has made it possible to define the importance of the different kinds of stimuli and of the detailed anatomy of many participating parts, such as the antennae.

One of the most curious features of mating behavior in the *Drosophila* species in the frequency-dependent "rare-male advantage" (Petit and Ehrman, 1970). A mutant type of male, present in low proportion among the males available to the female, achieves a disproportionately high frequency of mating. The phenomenon has been likened to the saying, among dark-haired populations, that "gentlemen prefer blondes." Almost all the relevant experiments, including clever demonstrations that volatile pheromones mediate the olfactory stimulation, have been carried out with young virgin females. Pruzan and Ehrman (1974), however, compared flies aged 4 days with flies aged 11 days, with "widows" of three different strains, and with males of the same and different strains. Their work has shown that both age and prior mating experience of the female can eliminate the rare-male advantage.

A major new thrust of work with *Drosophila* has been developed by Benzer and his colleagues, using attached X chromosomes, the loss of which produces a gynandromorphic mosaic fly carrying in half or some other proportion of cells various X chromosome-linked markers. These markers include mutant bristle and color phenotypes, plus an interesting array of behavioral mutations, affecting phototaxis, geotaxis, several different levels of visual function, shaking of the limbs, courting behavior, mating behavior, and circadian rhythms (Hotta and Benzer, 1970; Konopka and Benzer, 1971). Embryological questions of the relationship between neural and muscular and ocular structures and overlying or adjacent genetically marked tissues, plus neurophysiological dissection of the types of functional abnormalities in the retina or ganglia have already been productively examined. The next steps will involve elucidation of the mutant actions at the biochemical level. In the cases of mutants with abnormal circadian rhythms, results with gynandromorphs indicate that a rhythm-determining mechanism resides in the head of the fly. Some of these neurological mutants are now being studied for other general behaviors, such as activity and mating behavior (Burnet, Connolly, and Mallinson, 1974).

Mouse

A bibliography of behavioral studies using genetically defined mice has been published (Sprott and Staats, 1975). Included among the 1,222 entries are 11 primarily identified under "age: early development" and 16 under "age: maturity and senescence."

Almost all studies of the mouse, except those using age as a treatment effect, use mice of about 8 to 12 weeks of age. As we noted earlier (Table 1), mice under laboratory conditions typically live far longer, unless sacrificed or killed by aggressor mice. Sprott (unpublished) has kept mice at Bar Harbor up to 48 months until death occurred. Some interesting shifts in behavior were noted as a function of age. For example, among young mice C57BL/6 tend to be passive, compared with active DBA mice; after 6 months of age, however, C57BL/6 are more active than the DBA. Repeated behavioral testing appears to make C57BL/6 mice more aggressive and the chronic stimulation seems to greatly enhance life span. Collins (1965) also found that continued periodic stress prolonged life span; using C57BL/10J mice, electric shock plus cold stress had a greater effect than either stress alone, which in turn were associated with longer survival than for the control mice. There were changes in open-field and locomotor activity, escape avoidance conditioning, maze exploration, and adrenal weight.

It is controversial whether there is an effect of aging after maturity on the ability of rodents to learn certain tasks. Freund and Walker (1971) found decreased retention with increasing time intervals between acquisition and retention testing, using a shuttle-box learning task and C57BL/6J mice of 3 vs. 15 months of age. Similar results were obtained with DBA mice at 60 vs. 360 days (Oliverio and Bovet, 1966). Others have found no differences in avoidance learning in mice and rats, but these studies (Meier, 1964; Kirby, 1963) used animals only 150 days old.

Goodrick (1967) compared 4-month-old vs. 26-month-old C57BL/6J females; the young mice were more active, better at discriminating concentrated sucrose solutions, drank more alcohol, learned a water maze faster, and had higher response rates for dark-contingent bar pressing. There were no differences in emotional elimination during activity or in light-contingent bar pressing. Comparable data are not available for other mouse strains, but data exist for albino Wistar rats, in which the effects of aging were in the same direction on all the tests plus the emotional elimination.

Among studies of ionizing radiation, Curtis and Gebhard (1958) found that old CF-1 mice (Carworth strain) succumbed to lower doses than did young animals and that animals irradiated in youth will succumb to smaller doses when older than will an untreated animal of the same age. Radiation shortened life span both by inducing neoplasms and by seemingly "normal" degenerative processes. No such shortening was obtained with tetanus toxoid, turpentine, typhoid vaccine, or nitrogen mustard. Spalding and Brooks (1971) investigated two sublines of RFM mice selected for differing resistance to gamma radiation; resistance segregated with the H-2 locus (histocompatibility system) serotype, with $H-2^k$ more resistant than $H-2^f$. Their mean life spans were 604 ± 10.0 and 655 ± 8.2 days ($p < .01$), respectively. They differed also in spontaneous activity measures.

Prolongation of life by oral L-dopa (Cotzias, Miller, Nicholson, Maston, and Tang, 1974) has not yet been compared across strains.

Strain differences in learning tasks have been studied extensively in both the mouse and the rat. For example, McClearn found C3H mice to be poorer performers than C57BL or BALB/c mice in an elevated maze, a visual discrimination apparatus, and a tactual discrimination apparatus. Bovet, Bovet-Nitti and Oliverio (1969) extended the comparison to shuttle box avoidance learning and Lashley III maze learning. In general C3H did worse than several other strains, but C3H was superior in water-escape situations. As McClearn (1972) has emphasized, learning performance is a very complex phenotypic category demanding delineation of components of performance.

One of the most interesting behavioral studies in the mouse is the production and analysis of audiogenic seizures. There are marked strain differences in susceptibility and marked within-strain differences as a function of age. Usually these age differences have been examined only for the first 40–80 days of life, and it would be of interest to compare DBA (seizure-prone) and C57BL/6J (resistant) mice for reversal of effects later in life. Several groups have attempted to relate the phenomenon to developmental changes in brain content of the neurotransmitters gamma-aminobutyric acid, serotonin and norepinephrine and of the related enzymes (Schlesinger and Griek, 1970; Sze, 1970). The number and nature of genes involved remains to be elucidated, but Fuller (1975) has recently distinguished the inherited susceptibilities to spontaneous and to primed audiogenic seizures, using a heterogeneous stock prepared from an eight-way cross of well-established inbred strains. Spontaneous susceptibility appears to be due to a single homozygous gene (asp). Sensitivity to priming is probably polygenic.

Genetically-determined differences in the activity of three enzymes involved in catecholamine biosynthesis in adrenals and in brain were demonstrated among BALB/cJ, CBA/J, and C57BL/Ka strains (Kessler, Ciaranello, Shire, and Barchas, 1972). No relationships to age or to behaviors were investigated.

Rat

The Norway rat has been the favored animal of laboratory research in psychology, but less is known about its genetics and fewer established strains exist. Nevertheless, Broadhurst and his colleagues have developed several rat lines and

carried out biometrical analyses for such measures as open-field activity, emotional defecation, and learning and avoidance tasks (Broadhurst, 1969). Two important pairs of rat lines derived by selective breeding are widely available. The first was initiated by Tolman (1924) and Tryon (1940) to produce "maze-bright" and "maze-dull"rats. These strains have been compared by numerous investigators on other types of learning tasks, attempting to define the importance of spatial cues, of extinction in a bar-press situation, of different types of errors, and of practice. In some situations, particularly the latter, age was noted to be a significant variable (see McClearn, 1972). The descendants of the Tryon strains have been examined for neurochemical differences, as well (Rosenzweig, Krech, and Bennett, 1960). Some differences in acetylcholine content and cholinesterase activity were found, but interpretation was confounded by changes in brain weight. The second pair of rat strains is the Maudsley Reactive and Non-reactive set, developed by Hall in the 1930's on the criterion of defecation in the open field. These strains, which numerous investigators have confirmed to be high and low, respectively, for emotional elimination, have been studied for many other measures, in attempts to relate various behaviors and to interpret the adaptive role of such behavior (see Broadhurst, 1969).

The rat also serves as a convenient animal in which to test certain metabolic or pharmacologic effects deduced from studies of abnormal behavior in man. For examples, fetal and infant rats have been exposed to excess phenylalanine and excess galactose to mimic the interference by these substances with normal brain development in man in the diseases phenylketonuria and galactosemia, respectively (Chase and O'Brien, 1970; Haworth, Ford, and Younoszai, 1969). As other etiological mechanisms for differences in behavior or in rates or nature of aging are proposed, it will be important to devise direct experimental tests.

Studies comparing young and old rats, and other animals, though with little attention to genetic influences, are summarized by Jakubczak (1973). In general, after sexual maturity, various forms of spontaneous activity decrease, and activities are easier to inhibit; decrements in acquisition of instrumental responses become more prominent with age, though they may be ameliorated by distributed practice, increased sensory stimulation, and certain drugs.

Dog

A species with considerable promise for aging research is the domesticated dog. Dogs are the oldest domestic animal (about 12,000 years) adapted to as wide a range of environments as is man, and highly variable by many criteria. Unlike all the other animals described in this section, dogs are commonly kept to "old age" and monitored and treated for diseases. The book *Genetics and the Social Behavior of the Dog* (Scott and Fuller, 1965) is a gold mine of information from their 13-year breeding project at The Jackson Laboratory. The work has been continued at Bowling Green University (Stewart and Scott, in press). Five pure breeds were selected for study and mating: Central African basenjis, beagles, American cocker spaniels, Shetland sheep dogs (shelties), and wire-haired fox terriers. Because of their long history of geographic isolation and obvious differences in their behavior, the basenji and cocker spaniel were chosen for cross-breeding to produce reciprocal F_1 and F_2 generations and the back-crosses to the parental stocks. These investigators explored emotional reactivity, trainability for a variety of obedience tests, motor skills, problem-solving behavior, and social behavior underlying mother-offspring, littermate, and dog-human relationships.

Monkeys and Chimps

With the establishment of Regional Primate Centers in eight locations around the United States, most of which emphasize behavioral research, and with the obvious closer relationship of nonhuman primates to man, behavioral studies of these animals are progressing rapidly. Here at the University of Washington, for example, large projects on early infancy experiences and post-maturity changes (aging) have been initiated. The projects include breeding schemes and intensive neurophysiological and biochemical analyses, the beginnings of behavior genetics in these species.

BEHAVIOR GENETICS OF AGING: STUDIES IN MAN

Statistical Approach

Even without regard to underlying mechanisms, there is much literature showing individual differences in longevity and in psychological performance with aging. Family and twin studies suggest that such differences are genetically influenced, though the increasing variance for most measurements with age indicates increasing contribution of environmental or measurement factors.

Longevity. Genetic and familial influences on life-expectancy are well-recognized by the layman and were studied by Pearl (1922) and others who showed that the mean life-expectancy was greater if one's parents had lived to older age. Pearl estimated the "total immediate ancestral longevity" (TIAL), which is the sum of the ages attained by an individual's two parents and four grandparents; in one pedigree, a proband of age 100 had a TIAL of 599 years! Twin studies support the conclusion that genetic factors are important in longevity, as MZ twin pairs had smaller within-pair differences in life span than did DZ twins, 48.7 *vs.* 66.5 months (Kallmann and Jarvik, 1959). Actuarial tables reveal significant differences among various populations and ethnic groups, as well. Somehow there is a well-set maximum longevity for each species, even without supervening illnesses; perhaps this phenomenon was described best by Oliver Wendell Holmes in his "One Hoss Shay," which unaccountably just disintegrated one day of old age!

Phylogenetic comparisons have led to such generalizations as a rough correlation between body size and longevity, with monkeys longer-lived than cats, rats, and mice (in that order); however, cows, horses, and elephants have shorter life spans than does man. Other correlations exist between length of gestation and longevity and between rate of metabolism and heart rate and longevity. In the case of the mouse and the elephant, heart rates of 520–789/minute $\times$ 3.25 years and 25–28/minute $\times$ 70 years gave lifetime total heart beat estimates of 1×10^9 for each species (Heilbrunn, 1943). But other factors were early identified as important variables, particularly nutrition. McCay (1952) kept rats in a state of immaturity on diets containing essential nutrients but lacking sufficient calories to promote growth and maturation; these rats survived 200 days longer than controls and achieved normal growth when adequate caloric intake was provided.

Intelligence and Eminence. One of the most remarkable family studies of intellectual achievement is the classic book of Galton (1869). Galton classified men and women according to their reputation, using historical accounts and published biographical data on eminent persons. It is relevant to this discussion that very many of the cases were over 50 years of age, reflecting both time for achievement and time for recognition of achievement. In fact, there are some marked differences with type of career, with judges, statesmen, and peers generally older than commanders and men of science. Insufficient data on ages of index cases and relatives is provided to calculate these effects in detail. Galton was also obliquely interested in reproductive behavior and the extinction of family lines. The most striking case was the proclivity of English peers to marry heiresses, i.e., women who had no brothers; presumably the women and possibly both had lower over-all fertility. In all of his analyses, Galton emphasized the importance of the normal distribution, the regression toward the mean, and the usefulness of detailed study of persons at the extremes of normal variation.

Measures of Cognitive Abilities. Extensive reviews of this subject matter (Botwinick, 1967; Arenberg, 1973) deal with processes of registering, storing, retrieving information, and solving problems, usually with response-time as a critical dependent variable. In general, aged groups are less capable than younger groups on these parameters, but the pace of stimulus presentation and the state of autonomic arousal, which can be manipulated by certain drugs, have been identified as crucial technical and clinical variables (see Eisdorfer and Wilkie, Chapter 12 in this volume). Most studies compare means of groups, with little attention to the individual differences within age groups which usually are quite substantial.

Cunningham, Clayton, and Overton (1975) have tested the theory of fluid and crystallized intelligence (Horn and Cattell, 1966) for its developmental implications in an aged population. Fluid intelligence, purported to reflect functioning of neurological structures, increases until the cessation of neural maturation during adolescence and declines thereafter. Crystallized intelligence, said to reflect cultural assimilation, is highly influenced by formal and informal education factors throughout the life span. Crystallized intelligence tends to increase, but it is limited by the capacity of the fluid intelligence system so that increments become smaller with age. A reasonable test of this hypothesis was applied: the correlation between measures of these constructs should be lower in an elderly sample than in a sample of young adults. The Raven Progressive Matrices were used as an index of fluid intelligence, and the vocabulary subtest of the WAIS as an index of crystallized intelligence. The Pearson product moment correlation between these indices fell from .67 in the young to .39 in the elderly group; among the only 40 subjects in the elderly group, the correlation was lower for those in their seventies than for those in their sixties. It may be noted that both of these indices have been analyzed to have substantial heritability, .68 for the vocabulary subtest (Block, 1968) and .44 to .85 for the Raven Matrices (see Guttman, 1974).

Spatial Abilities. The tests of space and form perception and spatial manipulation on various test batteries seem to draw upon distinguishable components of spatial abilities. For the Raven Progressive Matrices, Guttman (1974) has found different familial correlations and heritabilities for the different matrices and has suggested that the genetic basis of matrix E-8 may coincide with the spatial visualizing ability assigned to the X chromosome by Bock and Kolakowski (1973). Extensive comparisons of young and elderly persons for a variety of spatial tasks have been carried out by Cohen and Schaie (unpublished).

Temperament and Related Behavior. Kallmann and his associates have reported observations on many aspects of behavior in twin pairs reaching senescence, with a registry of 2,500 senescent twin index cases and a sample of 240 index cases over age 60 years, followed for more than 6 years (Kallmann, Feingold, and Bondy, 1951). Severe maladjustment to aging, resulting in symptoms of an involutional or senile psychosis, coexisted more frequently in MZ than in DZ twin pairs, presumably due to genetic influences on a mixture of contributing factors, such as age-related personality factors, declining adaptational plasticity, and increasing emotional and socioeconomic insecurity. Discordance was the rule in the extreme maladaptation of suicide (Kallmann, Deporte, Deporte, and Feingold, 1949). A battery of tests designed to demonstrate declining intellectual function, gave smaller intra-pair differences in MZ pairs than in DZ pairs for tests measuring abstract intellectual functions (Vocabulary, Digits Backward, Digit Symbol, Block Designs, Similarities), suggesting that genetic factors are involved in the decrements. Measures of memory function showed no differences between MZ and DZ senescent pairs. Jarvik and Blum (1971) have followed these twin pairs another 20 years (see below).

Biobehavioral Approaches

Psychophysiological Studies. Thompson and Marsh (1973) have summarized much information about changes in the EEG, sleep patterns, evoked responses and autonomic nervous system responses from young adulthood to senescence and their relationships to behavioral impairment in the elderly. Associated behavioral changes are slowing in performance, deficiency in registration of raw stimuli, and decreased ability to handle inputs (Jarvik and Cohen, 1973). Wide differences among individuals characterize most studies.

One of the most consistent findings is a slowing with age in the normal alpha rhythm of the EEG, usually about 1 cycle per second. There is also a decrease in percent time alpha, with an increase of fast or beta waves. Several investigations (Obrist and Sokoloff and their colleagues) point to early atherosclerotic changes as the determinant factor, since "superhealthy" elderly subjects have cerebral blood flow equal to that of young controls and alpha frequencies nearly equal to those of the controls.

Any changes in the EEG associated with aging are superimposed upon an EEG pattern highly determined by heredity. Vogel (1970) has summarized a monumental, but largely unconfirmed, study of EEG patterns in presumably normal individuals. MZ twins share not only identical EEG patterns, but closely-timed maturational transitions in the EEGs in adolescence and in later life. Analysis of pedigrees points to a polygenic mode of inheritance, not surprising for the complex electrical activity recorded from the scalp. However, there are several specific variant EEG patterns inherited as Mendelian autosomal dominant traits (Table 2).

Four percent of the population (German and Japanese recruits, primarily) have the monotonous tall alpha pattern, determined by a single

TABLE 2. VARIANTS OF THE NORMAL HUMAN EEG.

Rhythm	Genetic basis	Population frequency	Comment
Normal alpha (8–13 cps)	Polygenic		
Low voltage alpha	Auto Dom	7%	
Quick alpha (16–19 cps)	Auto Dom	.5%	
Occipital slow (4–5 cps)	??	.1%	?Psychopathy
Monotonous tall alpha	Auto Dom	4%	?Assortative Mating
Beta waves	Multifactorial	5–10%	Sex, age ?Assortative Mating
Frontal beta groups (25–30 cps)	Auto Dom	.4%	
Fronto-precentral beta (20–25 cps)	Auto Dom	1.4%	

Adapted from Vogel, 1970.

gene, while another 5-10 percent have a beta wave pattern, with multifactorial determination. The beta wave pattern increases in prevalence in middle age, especially among females. For both of these traits, limited data suggest that individuals of that EEG type (Table 2) tend to marry individuals of the same EEG type (assortative mating). These different baseline EEG patterns have yet to be analyzed for possible correlations with psychometric measures, with response to photic, auditory, sleep, or other physiological stimuli, or with pharmacological agents that might reveal different susceptibilities to sedative or behavior-modifying actions.

Although the genetic bases of individual variation in sleep patterns and evoked cortical responses remain to be elucidated, significant changes in these parameters have been noted with age. According to Feinberg (1969) the amount of high-voltage stage 4 sleep declines and the number of arousals during the night increases linearly with age. Somewhat similar changes are noted in younger patients with organic brain disease. Averaged evoked responses with visual, somatosensory, and auditory stimuli appear to show consistent changes with aging (e.g., Dustman and Beck, 1969), perhaps indicating decreased neural inhibition with age. Finally, a number of related observations suggest depressed autonomic reactivity in the elderly, as reflected in galvanic skin response, vasomotor, and heart rate responses. The deterioration may lie in the cardiovascular and other effectors, with altered feedback to the autonomic nervous system, causing over-arousal, stress responses, free fatty acid release, and interference with learning (see Eisdorfer and Wilkie, Chapter 12 in this volume). It is likely that variation in the effector responses is under genetic influence, as well. The wide individual variability in these responses and even intraindividual variability might be better interpreted if MZ twin pairs were used for some of these studies to try to minimize genetic variation.

Cytogenetic Studies. Court Brown, Jacobs, Buckton, Tough, Kuenssberge, and Know, (1966) have reported that abnormal chromosome content of cells increases with age, indicating abnormalities in the process of mitosis (cell division). The proportion of hypomodal cells (i.e., 45 or fewer chromosomes) increases progressively in the female from 5.9 percent at age 15-24 to 11.6 percent at age 75-84 and in the male from 3.5 to 6.6 percent. Artifacts of the methods may contribute to these seemingly high values. Such artifacts are avoided in the search for hypermodal cells (i.e., 47 or more chromosomes); these were found in only 0.10 percent of the cells in the youngest age group versus 1.26 percent of the cells in the 75-84 group. The significance of these findings, which others have confirmed, must be judged in light of the fact that the chromosome most often lost in still-viable cells, capable of dividing in the laboratory, is the X or Y sex chromosome.

The possibility of sex-chromosome aneuploidy itself being a cause of aging seems unlikely, since there appears to be no premature aging in patients with Klinefelter's syndrome (XXY males) or Turner's syndrome (XO females). Jarvik (1963) drew another important distinction: neurons do not undergo mitosis and are individually old cells; blood cells, only a few weeks old, come from a stem cell line which has produced hundreds of generations of cells. Thus, there is little basis to assume that changes detected in blood cells reflect any parallel process in neurons. Nevertheless, Jarvik and her colleagues have correlated increased frequency of chromosome loss with memory impairment and cognitive impairment on various tests of both institutionalized and non-institutionalized older persons (Jarvik and Cohen, 1973). Furthermore, precipitous decline in cognitive performance has proved to be a predictor of approaching death (Jarvik and Blum, 1971).

Mutant Approach

Effects of Single Abnormal Genes on Aging

Werner's Syndrome. These individuals have an autosomal recessive disorder which provides an interesting caricature of aging. A tabular comparison of the features of Werner's syndrome and of aging is given in Table 3. More than 125 cases have been reported. Usually slim with a slow rate of growth during childhood, these

TABLE 3. COMPARISON OF FEATURES OF WERNER'S SYNDROME WITH THOSE OF AGING.

	Werner's	Aging
A. Similar Findings		
1. Atherosclerosis, arteriosclerosis and medial calcinosis		
2. Graying of the hair		
3. Hypermelanosis		
4. Cerebral cortical atrophy		
5. Lymphoid depletion and thymic atrophy		
B. Similar findings, but differences in degree:	Werner's	Aging
1. Calcification of valve rings and leaflets	Very severe	Moderate
2. Hyalinization of seminiferous tubules	Very severe	Severe only in very aged
3. Atrophy of skin appendages	Severe	Moderate
4. Osteoporosis	Generalized, but found particularly in distal extremities	Generalized, spine particularly vulnerable
5. Loss of hair	Generalized	Principally scalp
C. Features characteristic of Werner's syndrome		
1. Cataracts	"Dystrophic" type: capsular and cortical	"Senile" type: cortical or nuclear (probably different from those of Werner's syndrome)
2. Ulcerations and atrophy of extremities	Non-trophic, very frequent	Trophic, infrequent
3. Short stature	Primary	Acquired
4. Laryngeal atrophy	Common	Unusual
5. Proportion of sarcomas and connective tissue tumors among neoplasms	High	Low
6. Soft tissue calcification	Common	Unusual
7. Prostate	Atrophic epithelium	Benign prostatic hypertrophy
8. Adrenal glomerulosa	Conspicuous	Poorly demarcated
9. Parathyroid	Chief cell predominant	Oxyphils predominant
D. Features not present in Werner's		
1. Senile keratoses, senile elastosis and skin cancers, pancreatic hyalinization		Deposition of lipofuscin pigment and formation of corpora amylacea in brain.
E. Features not described in Werner's syndrome		
1. EEG analysis		Slowing of alpha rhythm
2. Psychological profile		

Adapted from Epstein *et al.*, 1966, p. 211.

persons have no adolescent growth spurt and reach their final height (mean 61 inches for men, 57 inches for women) at around 13 years of age. Gray hair is developed by age 20, cataracts by age 25, appearance of old age by 30 to 40 years of age, with mean survival 47 years. Calcification occurs in atheromatous blood vessels and in thick subcutaneous tissues, muscles become wasted with fibrous replacement, teeth are lost, and 44 percent have developed mild diabetes (Epstein, Martin, Schultz, and Motulsky, 1966).

Neurologic examinations have been recorded for only 25 percent of the 125 patients, with mild defects in about one-third, primarily loss of distal deep tendon reflexes. Three patients had meningiomas (and seven had sarcomas, while four had carcinomas). Intelligence was commented upon (not tested) in only 19 cases, with 9 regarded as retarded and some others as "infantile" emotionally, possibly related to the small stature and overall physical impression. Two patients were psychotic. Epstein *et al.* (1966) found a decreased rate of cell division and a limited total number of divisions per cell in fibroblasts cultured from a patient with Werner's syndrome, suggesting a basic defect in the life capacity of individual cells.

In fact, the limited replicative capacity of cultured human fibroblasts has provided a useful model for aging in the laboratory (Goldstein, 1971). Some studies indicate that toward the end of their replicative life span, normal fibroblasts accumulate a significant proportion of defective enzymes and incorporate increased amounts of amino acid analogues, which may make inactive proteins. Thus, fibroblasts from Werner's syndrome were studied for earlier appearance of abnormal gene products, in line with their shorter *in vitro* life-expectancy (Goldstein and Singal, 1974). Peripheral blood lymphocytes were deficient in detectable HL-A antigens upon quantitative adsorption and skin fibroblasts had 14–24 percent heat-labile G6PD (glucose-6-phosphate dehydrogenase), compared with 1 percent heat-labile G6PD in normal controls. This approach has also been applied in fibroblasts from patients with progeria (below) with similar results and to fibroblasts from patients with diabetes, with suggestive results in the same direction. Again, there is no proof that defective proteins cause rather than result from cellular aging.

Progeria. This exceedingly rare disorder, probably due to an autosomal recessive gene (McKusick, 1974), consists of alopecia (loss of scalp hair), near-absence of subcutaneous fat, skeletal hypoplasia and dysplasia, onset of generalized atherosclerosis as early as age five years, and death from what appears to be "old age." Elevated serum cholesterol, hearing loss and cataracts occur in most cases. There have been some 40–50 cases reported, with the earliest those of Hutchinson (1886) and Gilford (1904). Perhaps the earliest description of its occurrence in siblings appeared in the St. James Gazette in 1754 (Smith, 1970): "March 19, 1754, died in Glamorganshire of mere old age and a gradual decay of nature at seventeen years and two months, Hopkins Hopkins, the little Welshman, lately shown in London. He never weighed more than 17 pounds, but for three years past no more than twelve. The parents have still 6 children left, all of whom

in no way differ from other children except one girl of twelve years of age, who weighs 18 pounds and bears upon her all the marks of old age, and in all respects resembles her brother at that age." Gilford proposed the name progeria, meaning premature aging. It is extremely impressive that brain development and intelligence do not appear to be impaired. Careful review of the syndrome suggests that some extraordinary degenerative process is at work, since tissues that were fairly well-developed initially become hypoplastic or atrophic. Despite superficial similarities, the process might be quite different from senile aging.

Cockayne Syndrome. Yet another rare autosomal recessive inherited disorder is this condition, characterized by dwarfism, precociously senile appearance, pigmentary degeneration of the retina, optic atrophy, deafness, bone changes, sensitivity to sunlight, and mental retardation (Cockayne, 1946; McKusick, 1974). Growth and development proceed fairly normally in early infancy, and the pattern of defects becomes evident only at age two to four years. Abnormal regulation of glucose and cholesterol metabolism has been found in these children and adults, as in the other single-gene disorders (above) associated with early "aging," with early death due to atherosclerosis (McKusick, 1974; Fujimoto, Greene, and Seegmiller, 1969).

Xeroderma Pigmentosum. This rare autosomal recessive disease merits inclusion because of the peculiar type of metabolic errors involved. Clinically, benign and then malignant skin lesions appear on exposed parts of the body, due to sensitivity to ultraviolet radiation. Carcinomas are recognized usually in the first few years of life. Some cases have central nervous system involvement, as well; these represent a subtype, inherited within particular families. Several different mutations are responsible, all acting to interfere with the normal repair of DNA damaged by ultraviolet radiation (Cleaver, 1968; Robbins, Kraemer, Lutzner, Festoff, and Coon, 1974). The importance of this disease is its demonstration that the body's cells have the means normally to overcome environmentally-induced mutagenesis and that loss of that capacity leads to cancers and death. DNA repair mechanisms should be high on the list of metabolic pathways to be examined closely as a function of aging, since DNA repair capacity has been correlated with life span across seven species (Hart and Setlow, 1974).

In none of these four single-gene determined disorders has there been any useful psychological characterization of the patients. In addition, EEG data are lacking. As criteria are agreed upon and test protocols developed for psychological features of "normal" aging, the same criteria and tests should be applied to these rare, but potentially very interesting subjects. One may be confident that no single gene determines all the varied features of the usual aging process; yet the genes which produce the dramatic effects of these four syndromes may have less severely altered genetic forms (alleles) which contribute to the normal variation in the process of aging. Furthermore, even though the patients are rare, their cells may be studied in tissue culture *in vitro*, so that the biochemical basis of the particular defective gene action might yet be elucidated.

Single-gene Mendelian Disorders with Effects Apparently Limited to the Brain.

Alzheimer's Disease and Pick's Disease. Although these two conditions are distinct, their clinical appearances during life are so similar that they may be discussed together here. Slowly progressive dementia begins with insidious onset usually in the fifth or sixth decade, at least 10 years before the onset of senile dementia. Thus, these diseases are termed "presenile dementias." Disturbances of speech also are prominent. Focal neurological abnormalities appear, with parietal lobe signs and disturbance of gait in Alzheimer's disease and with frontal lobe signs and no gait disturbance in Pick's disease. Pathologically, they are entirely different. In Alzheimer's disease there is atrophy of all areas of the brain, loss of cells, and formation of plaques and characteristic neurofibrillary loops and tangles. Such histological changes do occur in other degenerative disorders of the brain. Pick's disease is characterized by severe atrophy and cell loss in the outer layers of the frontal and temporal regions of the cerebral cortex, glial proliferation, but no senile plaques or neurofibrillary tangles (Slater and Cowie, 1971). Alzheimer's is 20 times more common than Pick's disease, with autosomal dominant inheritance at least in some families.

Huntington's disease. This relatively common neurological disease of middle life produces involuntary movements and progressive mental deterioration, usually over about 15 years. The primary abnormality is a loss of neurons in the putamen and caudate of the basal ganglia, as well as in certain layers of the cerebral cortex. Lipofuscin pigment accumulates in the brain. Change in personality, irresponsibility, frank psychosis, and dementia occur. If involuntary movements have not yet become apparent, the patient commonly is mis-diagnosed as having schizophrenia or manic-depressive illness. Although the disease thus far appears to be limited to the central nervous system, it is striking that families and friends often exaggerate the age of affected individuals, as though they had appeared much older than their chronological ages. The disease is determined by an autosomal dominant gene, but its biochemical basis is not known.

Senile Dementia. The main clinical features are a progressive disorganization of all aspects of the mind, personality being as early and as much affected as memory, intelligence, judgment, and conceptual powers. Progression is unremitting and usually fairly even, though accompanying somatic illnesses can precipitate worsening. Pathologically, there is universal loss of neurons, accumulation of a pigmentary substance called lipochrome or lipofuscin, neurofibrillary changes identical with the plaques and tangles of Alzheimer's disease, and increase of astrocytic cells. These changes are readily distinguished from those due to cerebral vascular disease. The major genetic study of this phenotype (Larsson, Sjögren, and Jacobson, 1963) examined 377 probands and their families in Sweden. First-degree relatives have a 4.3 times risk of this disorder, but no increased risk for presenile dementias, schizophrenia, or other specific conditions. Socioeconomic factors played no part, and the genetic predisposition was postulated to be due to a major autosomal dominant gene, modified by some other genes.

The lipofuscin pigment accumulated in brains of patients with senile dementias, including Huntington's disease, is of great interest. It is a yellow autofluorescent lipid "wear and tear pigment" somehow related to the aging process. It can be produced experimentally by dietary deficiency of vitamin E; a rather similar, though distinguishable, pigment is accumulated in children with an autosomal recessive, degenerative neurological disorder called neuronal ceroid storage disease (Zeman, 1974).

Disorders Affecting the Sensory Apparatus. Without going into any detail here, it should be noted that numerous inherited conditions affect vision, hearing, inner ear function, taste, and other sensory input systems (McKusick, 1974). Visual problems and hearing loss are among the most common complaints of older people, and often reversible. As we develop sophisticated measures of neurophysiology in the central nervous system, peripheral sensory apparatus should not be neglected as behavioral changes of aging are examined for mechanisms.

Chromosomal Syndromes

Autosomal Trisomy 21, Down's Syndrome. If children with Down's syndrome (formerly called mongolism) survive the first few years (as more than 70 percent do now), the prospect for survival to middle age is quite good. Sexual development may be delayed or incomplete or both. However, there is an adolescent growth spurt, and menstruation usually begins at the average age and follows a normal course. The aging process in these individuals tends to occur early, including dryness and coarsening of the skin and recession of the gums with loss of teeth. As in other individuals of the same IQ level, the relative mortality is high after age 40, but the causes of death tend to be the same as those which effect the normal aging population. An interesting histopathological sign of early aging has been noted in the brains of adults with Down's syndrome. The typical changes associated with Alzheimer's disease or presenile

dementia—senile plaques, neurofibrillary tangles, and granulovacuolar changes in cortical and other brain cells—have been present in all brains so examined from Down's syndrome patients over age 35 (Olson and Shaw, 1969). Patients with other types of mental retardation lack such early changes in the brain.

Sex Chromosome Disorders. The aneuploidies of the sex chromosomes, including XXY, XYY, and XO men and women, are distinct syndromes with marked behavioral associations (Money, 1970). In XO women, for example, there is a remarkable deficit in space-form perception. There appear to be no clues to the aging process in the clinical or chromosomal information about these syndromes.

Genetic-Hormonal Relationships

Male/female differences are a timely subject in the general society (Ounsted and Taylor, 1972) and, of course, are notable in the elderly population, with females favored both for longevity and for good health. The sex hormones are known to act on the brain, where there are hormone-specific receptors in various regions. Furthermore, specific syndromes interfering with normal gender development or with tissue responsiveness to hormones are known. These examples demonstrate that hormone synthesis, release, and effects are under genetic influence and that individual differences in response to administered hormones may be genetically mediated as well. It is likely that much more will be learned about these relationships.

Interventionist Strategies

A number of potentially potent strategies can be proposed for slowing the aging process or reversing specific biobehavioral changes. Eisdorfer, Nowlin, and Wilkie (1970) have investigated the effects of the drug propranolol, which blocks autonomic hyperarousal thought to interfere with learning. Other agents which have been tried include anti-oxidants (vitamin E, vitamin C), antibiotics, anti-cross-linking agents, immunosuppressives, hormones, hyperbaric oxygen treatment, procaine, RNA extracts, and megavitamin therapy. None appear to be effective. Neurophysiological measures that might be tried include the new biofeedback and alpha-enhancing regimens; it would be interesting to determine whether the slowing of alpha rhythm could be reversed and, if so, whether such reversal would enhance behavioral performance. Of course, social and economic assistance may provide the most valuable and least dangerous intervention for most older people in our society.

One must stress that any measures proposed to enhance intellectual and physiological function in older people may draw millions of persons willing to try. Tight protocols for assessment of new therapies must be insisted upon. One particularly useful group of subjects consists of identical twins. One twin would receive a proposed therapy while the other would receive a placebo or an alternative therapy. The twin-control method minimizes individual variation due to genetic differences, due to chronological age differences, and due to prenatal and probably early life experiences. The effects of the intervention can be better isolated with such subjects than with any other group presently perceived.

Finally, the principle of genetic heterogeneity should be stressed (Omenn and Motulsky, 1975). Just as there are many, many causes of anemia or of mental retardation, there are probably many specific differences among individuals contributing to the processes of aging. No unitary answer to the question "what is aging" should be expected, and no single intervention, either behavioral or psychopharmacological, should be expected to be effective in all types of subjects.

REFERENCES

Amano, T., Richelson, E., and Nirenberg, M. 1972. Neurotransmitter synthesis by neuroblastoma clones. *Proc. Nat. Acad. Sci.*, **69**, 258–263.

Anderson, V. E., Siegel, F. S., Fisch, R. O., and Wirt, R. D. 1969. Responses of phenylketonuric children on a continuous performance test. *J. Abn. Psychol.*, **74**, 358–362.

Anderson, V. E., Siegel, F. S., Tellegan, A., and Fisch, R. O. 1972. Manual dexterity in phenylketonuric children. *Perceptual Motor Skills*, **26**, 827–834.

Arenberg, D. 1973. Cognition and aging: verbal learning, memory, problem solving, and aging. *In*, C. Eisdorfer and M. P. Lawton (eds.), *The Psychology of Adult Development and Aging*, pp. 74–97. Washington, D.C.: American Psychological Association.

Ayala, F. 1970. Competition, coexistence, and evolution. *In*, M. K. Hecht and W. E. Steere (eds.), *Essays in Evolution and Genetics in Honor of Th. Dobzhansky*, pp. 121–158. New York: Appleton-Century-Crofts.

Bastock, M. 1956. A gene mutation which changes a behavior pattern. *Evolution*, **10**, 421–439.

Block, J. B. 1968. Hereditary components in the performance of twins on the WAIS. *In*, S. G. Vandenberg (ed.), *Progress in Human Behavior Genetics*, pp. 221–228. Baltimore: Johns Hopkins University Press.

Bock, R. D., and Kolakowski, D. 1973. Further evidence of sex-linked major-gene influence on human spatial visualizing ability. *Amer. J. Hum. Genet.*, **25**, 1–14.

Botwinick, J. 1967. *Cognitive Processes in Maturity and Old Age*. New York: Springer-Verlag.

Bovet, D., Bovet-Nitti, F., and Oliverio, A. 1969. Genetic aspects of learning and memory in mice. *Science*, **163**, 139–149.

Broadhurst, P. L. 1969. Psychogenetics of emotionality in the rat. *Ann. NY Acad. Sci.*, **159**, 806–824.

Burnet, B., Connolly, K., and Mallinson, M. 1974. Activity and sexual behavior of neurological mutants in *Drosophila melanogaster*. *Behavior Genetics*, **4**, 227–235.

Cain, D. F., Ball, E. D., and Dekaban, A. S. 1972. Brain proteins: qualitative and quantitative changes, synthesis and degradation during fetal development of the rabbit. *J. Neurochem.*, **19**, 2031–2042.

Caplan, R., Cheung, S. C-Y, and Omenn, G. S. 1974. Electrophoretic profiles of aqueous-soluble proteins of human cerebral cortex: Population and developmental characteristics. *J. Neurochem.*, **22**, 517–520.

Cattell, R. B. 1953. Research designs in psychological genetics with special reference to the multiple variance method. *Amer. J. Hum. Genet.*, **5**, 76–93.

Cattell, R. B. 1960. The multiple abstract variance analysis equations and solutions for nature-nurture research on continuous variables. *Psych. Rev.*, **67**, 353–372.

Chase, H. P., and O'Brien, D. 1970. Effect of excess phenylalanine and of other amino acids on brain development in the infant rat. *Pediat. Research*, **4**, 96–102.

Cicero, T. J., Cowan, W. M., Moore, B. W., and Suntzeff, V. 1970. The cellular localization of the two brain specific proteins, S-100 and 14-3-2. *Brain Res.*, **18**, 25–34.

Cleaver, J. E. 1968. Defective repair replication of DNA in xeroderma pigmentosum. *Nature*, **218**, 652–656.

Cockayne, E. A. 1946. Dwarfism with retinal atrophy and deafness. *Arch. Disease Childhood*, **21**, 21–52.

Cohen, P. T. W., and Omenn, G. S. 1972. Variation in cytoplasmic malic enzyme and polymorphism of mitochondrial malic enzyme in *Macaca nemestrina* and in man. *Biochem. Genet.*, **7**, 289–301, 303–311.

Cohen, P. T. W., Omenn, G. S., Motulsky, A. G., Chen, C-Y., and Giblett, E. R. 1973. Restricted variation in the glycolytic enzymes of human brain and erythrocytes. *Nature New Biol.*, **241**, 229–233.

Collins, R. L. 1965. Longevity, aging, and environmental stress: a multivariate study. *Anat. Record*, **151**, 337–338.

Cotzias, G. C., Miller, S. T., Nicholson, A. R. Jr., Maston, W. H., and Tang, L. C. 1974. Prolongation of the lifespan in mice adapted to large amounts of L-dopa. *Proc. Nat. Acad. Sci. US*, **71**, 2466–2469.

Court Brown, W. M., Jacobs, P. A., Buckton, K. E., Tough, I. M., Kuenssberge, E. V., and Know, J. D. E. 1966. Chromosome studies on adults. *Eugenics Laboratory Memoirs XLII*, London.

Crow, J. F., and Kimura, M. 1970. *An Introduction to Population Genetics Theory*. New York: Harper & Row.

Cunningham, W. R., Clayton, V., and Overton, W. 1975. Fluid and crystallized intelligence in young adulthood and old age. *J. Gerontol.*, **30**, 53–55.

Curtis, J. J., and Gebhard, K. L. 1958. Radiation-induced aging in mice. *Proc. 2nd Intern. Conf. Peaceful Uses At. Energy*, **22**, 53–56.

Davies, W. D. 1970. The incorporation of (14C)-lysine into the protein of the guinea pig central auditory system. *J. Neurochem.*, **17**, 297–303.

Dobzhansky, T. and Streisinger, G. 1944. Experiments on sexual isolation in Drosophila. III. Geographic strains of *D. sturtevanti*. *Proc. Nat. Acad. Sci. US*, **30**, 335–339.

Dustman, R. E., and Beck, E. C. 1969. The effects of maturation and aging on the wave form of visually evoked potentials. *Electroencephalo. and Clin. Neurophysiol.*, **26**, 2–11.

Ehrman, L., Omenn, G. S., and Caspari, E. (eds.) 1972. *Genetics, Environment, and Behavior: Implications for Educational Policy*. New York: Academic Press.

Ehrman, L., and Parsons, P. A. 1976. *The Genetics of Behavior*. Sunderland, Massachusetts: Sinauer Associates.

Eisdorfer, C., Nowlin, J., and Wilkie, F. 1970. Improvement of learning in the aged by modification of autonomic nervous system activity. *Science*, **170**, 1327–1329.

Eppenberger, H. M., Eppenberger, M., Richterick, R., and Aebi, H. 1964. The ontogeny of creatine kinase isoenzymes. *Develop. Biol.*, **10**, 1–16.

Epstein, C. J., Martin, G. M., Schultz, A. L., and Motulsky, A. G. 1966. Werner's syndrome: A review of its symptomatology, natural history, pathologic features, genetics and relationship to the natural aging process. *Medicine*, **45**, 177–222.

Erlenmeyer-Kimling, L., and Hirsch, J. 1961. Measurements of the relation between chromosomes and behavior. *Science*, **124**, 835–836.

Falconer, D. S. 1960. *Introduction to Quantitative Genetics*. New York: Ronald.

Feinberg, I. 1969. Effects of age on human sleep patterns. *In*, A. Kales (ed.), *Sleep Physiology and Pathology*, Philadelphia: Lippincott.

Fialkow, P. J. 1969. Genetic aspects of autoimmunity. *Prog. Med. Genetics*, **6**, 117–167.

Freund, G., and Walker, D. W. 1971. The effect of aging on acquisition and retention of shuttle box avoidance in mice. *Life Sci.*, **10**, 1343–1349.

Fujimoto, W. Y., Greene, M. L., and Seegmiller, J. E. 1969. Cockayne's syndrome. Report of a case with hyperlipoproteinemia, hyperinsulinemia, renal disease, and normal growth hormone. *J. Pediatrics*, **75**, 881–884.

Fulker, D. W., Wilcock, J., and Broadhurst, P. L. 1972. Studies in genotype-environment interaction. I. Methodology and preliminary multivariate analysis of a diallel cross of eight strains of rat. *Behavior Genetics*, **2**, 261–287.

Fuller, J. L. 1975. Independence of inherited susceptibility to spontaneous and primed audiogenic seizures in mice. *Behavior Genetics*, **5**, 1–8.

Fuller, J. L., and Thompson, W. R. 1960. *Behavior Genetics*, New York: John Wiley.

Galton, F. 1869. *Hereditary Genius*. Reprinted 1962. New York: Meridian Books, World Publishing.

Gilford, H. 1904. Progeria: a form of senilism. *Practitioner*, **73**, 118.

Goldstein, S. 1971. The biology of aging. *New Engl. J. Med.*, **285**, 1120–1129.

Goldstein, S., and Singal, D. P. 1974. Alteration of fibroblast gene products *in vitro* from a subject with Werner's syndrome. *Nature*, **251**, 719–721.

Goodrick, C. L. 1967. Behavioral characteristics of young and senescent inbred female mice of the C57BL/6J strain. *J. Gerontol.*, **22**, 459–464.

Goodwin, D. W., Schulsinger, F., Hermansen, L., Guze, S. B., and Winokur, G. 1973. Alcohol problems in adoptees raised apart from alcoholic biological parents. *Arch. Gen. Psych.*, **28**, 238–243.

Green, E. L. 1966. *The Biology of the Laboratory Mouse*. 2nd Edition. New York: McGraw-Hill.

Grossfield, R. M., and Shooter, E. M. 1971. A study of the changes in protein composition of mouse brain during ontogenetic development. *J. Neurochem.*, **18**, 2265–2277.

Grouse, L., Chilton, M. D., and McCarthy, B. J. 1972. Hybridization of ribonucleic acid with unique sequences of mouse deoxyribonucleic acid. *Biochemistry*, **11**, 798–805.

Grouse, L., Omenn, G. S., and McCarthy, B. J. 1973. Study by DNA/RNA hybridization of the transcriptional diversity of human brain. *J. Neurochem.*, **20**, 1063–1073.

Gurd, R. D., Mahler, H. R., and Moore, W. J. 1972. Differences in protein patterns on polyacrylamide gel electrophoresis of neuronal membranes from mice of different strains. *J. Neurochem.*, **19**, 553–556.

Gurdon, J. B. 1968. Transplanted nuclei and cell differentiation. *Sci. Amer.* **219** (6), 24–35.

Guttman, R. 1974. Genetic analysis of analytical spatial ability: Raven's progressive matrices. *Behavior Genetics*, **4**, 273–284.

Hahn, W. R., and Laird, C. D. 1971. Transcription of nonrepeated DNA in mouse brain. *Science*, **173**, 158–161.

Hart, R. W., and Setlow, R. B. 1974. Correlation between deoxyribonucleic acid excision-repair and life-span in a number of mammalian species. *Proc. Nat. Acad. Sci. US*, **71**, 2169–2173.

Haworth, J. C., Ford, J. D., and Younoszai, 1969. Effect of galactose toxicity on growth of the rat fetus and brain. *Pediat. Research*, **3**, 441–447.

Heilbrunn, L. V. 1943. *An Outline of General Physiology*. 2nd Edition. Philadelphia: W. B. Saunders.

Hirsch, J., and Tryon, R. C. 1956. Mass screening and reliable individual measurement in the experimental behavior genetics of lower organisms. *Psych. Bull.*, **53**, 402–410.

Hirsch, J. 1967. Behavior-genetic or 'experimental' analysis: The challenge of science versus the lure of technology. *American Psychologist*, **22**, 118–130.

Horn, J. L., and Cattell, R. B. 1966. Refinement and test of the theory of fluid and crystallized intelligence. *J. Educ. Psych.*, **57**, 252–270.

Hotta, Y., and Benzer, S. 1970. Genetic dissection of the *Drosophila* nervous system by means of mosaics. *Proc. Nat. Acad. Sci. US*, **67**, 1156–1163.

Hutchinson, J. 1886. Congenital absence of hair and mammary glands with atrophic condition of the skin and its appendages in a boy whose mother had been almost wholly bald from alopecia areata from the age of six. *Trans. Med. Chir. Soc.*, Edinburgh, **69**, 473.

Jakubczak, L. F. 1973. Age and animal behavior. *In*, C. Eisdorfer and M. P. Lawton (eds.), *The Psychology of Adult Development and Aging*. pp. 98–111. Washington, D. C.: American Psychological Association.

Jarvik, L. F. 1963. Senescence and chromosomal changes. *Lancet*, **1**, 114–115.

Jarvik, L. F., and Blum, J. E. 1971. Cognitive declines as predictors of mortality in twin pairs: a twenty year longitudinal study of aging. *In*, E. Palmore and F. Jeffers (eds.), *Prediction of Lifespan*. Massachusetts: Heath-Lexington.

Jarvik, L. F., and Cohen, D. 1973. A biobehavioral approach to intellectual changes with aging. *In*, C. Eisdorfer and M. P. Lawton (eds.), *The Psychology of Adult Development and Aging*, pp. 220–280. Washington, D.C.: American Psychological Association.

Kallmann, F. J., Deporte, J., Deporte, E., and Feingold, L. 1949. Suicide in twins and only children. *Amer. J. Hum. Genet.*, **1**, 113–126.

Kallmann, F. J., Feingold, L., and Bondy, E. 1951. Comparative adaptational, social, and psychometric data on the life histories of senescent twin pairs. *Amer. J. Hum. Genet.*, **3**, 65–73.

Kallmann, F. J., and Jarvik, L. F. 1959. Individual differences in constitution and genetic background. *In*, J. E. Birren (ed.), *Handbook of Aging and the Individual*. pp. 216–263. Chicago: University of Chicago Press.

Kessler, S., Ciaranello, R. D., Shire, J. G. M., and Barchas, J. D. 1972. Genetic variation in catecholamine-synthesizing enzyme activity. *Proc. Nat. Acad. Sci. US*, **69**, 2448–2450.

Kety, S. S., Rosenthal, D., Wender, P. H., and Schulsinger, F. 1971. Mental illness in the biological and adoptive families of adopted schizophrenics. *Amer. J. Psych.*, **128**, 82–91.

Kirby, R. H. 1963. Acquisition, extinction, and retention of an avoidance response. *J. Comp. Physiol. Psychol.*, **56**, 158–162.

Konopka, R. J., and Benzer, S. 1971. Clock mutants of *Drosophila melanogaster*. *Proc. Nat. Acad. Sci. US*, **68**, 2112–2116.

Larsson, T., Sjögren, T., and Jacobson, G. 1963. Senile dementia: a clinical, sociomedical, and genetic study. *Acta Psychiat. Scand.*, Suppl. 167.

Mather, K., and Jinks, J. L. 1971. *Biometrical Genetics: The Study of Continuous Variation*. London: Chapman & Hall.

McCarthy, B. J., and Hoyer, B. H. 1964. Identity of DNA and diversity of messenger RNA molecules in normal mouse tissues. *Proc. Nat. Acad. Sci. US*, **52**, 915–922.

McCay, C. M. 1952. Chemical aspects of aging and the effect of diet upon aging. *In*, A. I. Lansing (ed.), *Cowdry's Problems of Aging*, pp. 139–220. 3rd Edition. Baltimore: Williams & Wilkins.

McClearn, G. E. 1972. Genetic determination of behavior (animal). *In*, L. Ehrman, G. S. Omenn and E. Caspari (eds.), *Genetics, Environment and Behavior: Implications for Educational Policy*, pp. 55–67. New York: Academic Press.

McClearn, G. E., and DeFries, J. C. 1973. *Introduction to Behavioral Genetics*. San Francisco: W. H. Freeman.

McKusick, V. A. 1974. *Mendelian Inheritance in Man: Catalogs of Autosomal Dominant, Autosomal Recessive, and X-linked Phenotypes*. 4th Edition. Baltimore: Johns Hopkins University Press.

Meier, G. W. 1964. Differences in maze performances as a function of age and strain of housemice. *J. Comp. Physiol. Psychol.*, **58**, 418–422.

Mendlewicz, J., and Fleiss, J. L. 1974. Linkage studies with X chromosome markers in bipolar (Manic-depressive) and unipolar (Depressive) illnesses. *Biol. Psych*, **9**, 261–294.

Money, J. 1970. Behavior genetics: principles, methods, and examples from XO, XXY, and XYY syndromes. *Seminars in Psych*, **2**, 11–29.

Moore, B. W., Perez, V. J., and Gehring, M. 1968.

Wallerian degeneration in rabbit tibial nerve: changes in amounts of the S-100 protein. *J. Neurochem*, **15**, 971–977.

Morrison, J. R., and Stewart, M. A. 1973. The psychiatric status of the legal families of adopted hyperactive children. *Arch. Gen. Psychiat.*, **28**, 888–891.

Motulsky, A. G. 1969. Biochemical genetics of hemoglobins and enzymes as a model for birth defects research. *Proc. 3rd Inter. Congr. Congenital Malformations*, Hague, Excerpta Medica, 199–208.

Muller, H. J. 1925. Mental traits and heredity. The extent to which mental traits are independent of heredity, as tested in a case of identical twins reared apart. *J. Heredity*, **16**, 433–446.

Nance, W. E. 1974. Genetic studies of the offspring of identical twins. A model for the analysis of quantitative inheritance in man. *Acta. Genet. Med., Gemellol.* **23**, 22.

Nance, W. E. 1975. The use of twins in clinical research. Birth Defects Original Article Series. In press.

Oliverio, A., and Bovet D. 1966. Effects of age on maze learning and avoidance conditioning of mice. *Life Sci*, **5**, 1317–1324.

Olson, M. I., and Shaw, C. M. 1969. Presenile dementia and Alzheimer's disease in Mongolism. *Brain*, **92**, 147–156.

Omenn, G. S. 1972. Linkage and association. *Ann. NY Acad. Sci.*, **197**, 125–126.

Omenn, G. S. 1973. Pathobiology of ectopic polypeptide hormone production by neoplasms in man. *Pathobiology Annual* **3**, 177–216.

Omenn, G. S., and Cheung, S. C-Y, 1974. Phosphoglycerate mutase isozyme marker for tissue differentiation in man. *Amer. J. Hum. Genet.*, **26**, 393–399.

Omenn, G. S., and Motulsky, A. G. 1972. Biochemical genetics and the evolution of human behavior. *In*, L. Ehrman, G. S. Omenn, and E. Caspari (eds.), *Genetics, Environment, and Behavior: Implications for Educational Policy*, pp. 129–172. New York: Academic Press.

Omenn, G. S., and Motulsky, A. G. 1975. Psychopharmacogenetics: experimental and clinical studies in man. *In*, B. E. Eleftheriou (ed.), *Psychopharmacogenetics*, pp. 183–228. New York: Plenum Press.

Omenn, G. S., and Motulsky, A. G. 1976. Ecogenetics: genetic variation in the susceptibility to environmental agents. *In*, B. Cohen (ed.), *Genetic Issues in Public Health*. Baltimore: Johns Hopkins University Press.

Omenn, G. S., and Schrott, H. G. 1975. Prenatal prediction of autosomal dominant diseases by linkage studies: myotonic dystrophy. *Proc. 4th Intern. Congr. Neurogenetics & Neuroophthalmology, Acta Genet. Med. Gemellol.*, **23**:225–232.

Ounsted, C., and Taylor, D. (eds.) 1972. *Gender Differences: Their Ontogeny and Significance*. Baltimore: Williams & Wilkins.

Parsons, P. A. 1967. *The Genetic Analysis of Behavior*, London: Methuen.

Pearl, R. 1922. *The Biology of Death*. Philadelphia: J. B. Lippincott.

Perttunen, V. 1959. Effect of temperature on the light reactions of *Blastophagus pinniperda* L. *Ann. Ent. Fenn.*, **25**, 65–71.

Petit, C. 1972. Qualitative aspects of genetics and environment in the determination of behavior. *In*, L. Ehrman, G. S. Omenn, and E. Caspari (eds.), *Genetics, Environment, and Behavior: Implications for Educational Policy*, pp. 27–47. New York: Academic Press.

Petit, C., and Ehrman, L. 1970. Sexual selection in Drosophila. *In*, T. Dobzhansky, M. K. Hecht, and W. E. Steere (eds.), *Evolutionary Biology, Vol. 3*, pp. 117–223. New York: Appleton.

Pruzan, A., and Ehrman, L. 1974. Age, experience, and rare-male mating advantages in *Drosophila pseudoobscura*. *Behavior Genetics*, **4**, 159–164.

Robbins, J. H., Kraemer, K. H., Lutzner, M. A., Festoff, B. W., and Coon, H. G. 1974. Xeroderma pigmentosum: an inherited disease with sun sensitivity, multiple cutaneous neoplasms, and abnormal DNA repair. *Ann. Internal Med.*, **80**, 221–248.

Rosenthal, D. 1970. *Genetic Theory and Abnormal Behavior*. New York: McGraw-Hill.

Rosenzweig, M. R., Krech, D., and Bennett, E. L. 1960. A search for relations between brain chemistry and behavior. *Psych. Bull.*, **57** (6), 476–492.

Schaie, K. W. 1974. Translations in gerontology—from lab to life: intellectual functioning. *American Psychologist*, **29**, 802–807.

Schaie, K. W. 1975. Notes on research strategy in developmental human behavior genetics. *In*, K. W. Schaie, V. E. Anderson, G. E. McClearn, and J. Money (eds.), *Developmental Human Behavior Genetics: Nature-Nurture Revisited*. Lexington, Mass. D. C. Heath.

Schaie, K. W., Anderson, V. E., McClearn, G. E., and Money, J. (eds.) 1975. *Developmental Human Behavior Genetics: Nature-Nurture Revisited*. Lexington, Mass. D. C. Heath.

Schlesinger, K., and Griek, B. J. 1970. The genetics and biochemistry of audiogenic seizures. *In*, G. Lindzey and D. D. Thiessen (eds.), *Contributions to Behavior-Genetic Analysis: The Mouse as a Prototype*. New York: Appleton.

Schrott, H. G., Karp, L., and Omenn, G. S. 1973. Prenatal prediction in myotonic dystrophy: guidelines for genetic counseling. *Clin. Genet.*, **4**, 38–45.

Schuckit, M. A. 1972. Family history and half-sibling research in alcoholism. *In*, F. A. Seixas, G. S. Omenn, E. D. Burk, and S. A. Eggleston (eds.), *Nature and Nurture in Alcoholism, Ann. NY Acad. Sci.*, **197**, 121–124.

Scott, J. P., and Fuller, J. L. 1965. *Genetics and the Social Behavior of the Dog*. Chicago: University Chicago Press.

Shields, J. 1962. *Monozygotic Twins Brought Up*

Apart and Brought Up Together. London: Oxford University Press.

Sidman, R. L., Green, M. C., and Appel, S. H. 1965. *Catalogue of the Neurological Mutants of the Mouse*. Cambridge, Massachusetts: Harvard University Press.

Slater, E., and Cowie, V. 1971. *Genetics of Neurological Disorders*. London: Oxford University Press.

Smith, D. W. 1970. *Recognizable Patterns of Human Malformation*. Philadelphia: W. B. Saunders.

Snell, G. S. 1958. Histocompatibility genes of the mouse. *In, Production and analysis of isogenic resistant lines, J. Nat. Cancer Inst.*, **21**, 843–847.

Spalding, J. L., and Brooks, M. R. 1971. The possible influence of a single gene locus on life span and its relationship to radiation resistance and activity, *Proc. Soc. Expt. Biol. Med.*, **136**, 1091–1093.

Spassky, B., and Dobzhansky, T. 1967. Responses of various strains of *Drosophila pseudoobscura* and *Drosophila persimilis* to light and to gravity. *Amer. Naturalist*, **101**, 59–63.

Sprott, R. L., and Staats, J. 1975. Behavioral studies using genetically defined mice—a bibliography. *Behavior Genetics*, **5**, 27–82.

Staats, J. 1966. The laboratory mouse. *In*, E. L. Green (ed.), *Biology of the Laboratory Mouse*, pp. 1–9. 2nd Edition. New York: McGraw-Hill.

Stewart, J. M., and Scott, J. P. *Genetics of the Dog*. In press.

Storer, J. B. 1966. Longevity and gross pathology at death in 22 inbred mouse strains. *J. Gerontol.*, **21**, 404–409.

Sze, P. 1970. Neurochemical factors in auditory stimulation and development of susceptibility to audiogenic seizures. *In*, R. L. Welch and A. S. Welch (eds.), *Physiological Effects of Noise*. New York: Plenum Press.

Thompson, L. W., and Marsh, G. R. 1973. Psychophysiological studies of aging. *In*, C. Eisdorfer and M. P. Lawton (eds.), *The Psychology of Adult Development and Aging*, pp. 112–148. Washington, D.C.: American Psychological Association.

Tolman, E. C. 1924. The inheritance of maze-learning ability in rats. *J. Comp. Psychol.*, **4**, 1–18.

Tryon, R. C. 1940. Genetic differences in maze-learning ability in rats. *Yearbook Nat. Soc. Study Educ.*, **39**, 111–119.

Vandenberg, S. G. 1966. Contributions of twin research to psychology. *Psych. Bull.*, **66**, 327–337.

Vogel, F. 1970. The genetic basis of the normal human electroencephalogram (EEG). *Humangenetik*, **10**, 91–114.

Zeman, W. 1974. Neuronal ceroid storage disease. *J. Neuropath. Exp. Neurol.*, **33**, 1–12.

11
PSYCHOPHYSIOLOGY OF AGING

Gail R. Marsh
Duke University Medical Center
and
Larry W. Thompson
University of Southern California

The field of psychophysiology embodies research and theory from a variety of disciplines. Scientists in many different fields, including anatomy, biochemistry, pharmacology, physiology and psychology to mention a few, contribute data that focus on the interrelationship of physiological and behavioral processes. Such a vast array of methodologies and theoretical positions understandably requires that some limitation be posed on the kinds of data reviewed in a chapter of this nature. Accordingly, the focus of this article will be restricted to psychophysiological studies involving traditional bioelectric measures. Other research and theory relevant to the psychophysiology of aging is discussed in chapters by Bondareff and by Frolkis in this volume.

The underlying hope implicit in studies of changes due to age in physiology and behavior is that some explanatory physiological mechanisms will be found for the observed behavioral changes. To what extent these hopes have thus far been fulfilled will be considered at the conclusion of this chapter. Many early studies provided descriptions of physiologic indicators and associated behaviors in older subjects and contrasted these results with younger controls in an attempt to provide correlational descriptions of aging changes. However, such studies provide weak theoretical links between physiology and behavior. The strongest links between these two fields will be provided by those studies which test proposed physiological mechanisms and their effects on behavior. Hopefully, in the coming years there will be a greater orientation toward the testing of physiological models and a move away from descriptive studies of the differences between old and young individuals.

ELECTROCORTICAL MEASURES

The electroencephalogram (EEG) was used as early as 1932 by Berger (1968) to describe differences between old and young subjects. Its use has continued to the present day to study the conjunction of brain physiology with behavior. While the EEG serves a useful purpose in clinical diagnosis, and while age norms have been established for this purpose, further study is still required to establish to what extent the changes in the EEG with age are an indication of pathology or merely benign changes associated with increasing age.

Changes in the EEG correlated with age have been reviewed previously in some detail (Obrist and Busse, 1965; Obrist, 1972), and more extensive information may be obtained from these reviews. Encephalographers have most often described their data by analyzing it in terms of changes in each of the usual frequency bands: alpha, beta, theta, delta, or a combination of delta and theta as "slow activity." The data will thus be presented here in like manner.

Slow Wave Activity

The general category of slow waves as used here will include all those waves from 1-7 Hz. The usual practice of the encephalographer categorizing frequencies below alpha activity as theta (4-7 Hz) and delta (1-3 Hz) is not easy to follow in studies such as those reviewed here due to the progressively decreasing amplitudes and frequencies encountered with aging. The usual lower cutoff for alpha activity, for example, is 8 Hz. However, some studies of aging have shown that healthy older subjects may slowly drift below 8 Hz in what appears to be slowed alpha activity. Thus the designation of alpha frequency in some studies has been allowed to shift to lower figures for older populations without classifying them as abnormal. However, as very low frequencies creep into the EEG, a more abnormal picture is generally described and will be noted below.

Slow waves are seen in an increasing proportion of the population as age increases (Busse, Barnes, Friedman, and Kelty, 1956; Obrist and Busse, 1965; Silverman, Busse, and Barnes, 1955). Slow activity, when it appears in several recording sites on the head, is usually referred to as diffuse slow activity. Such activity is not often found in healthy elderly subjects (e.g., community volunteers during early senescence). In fact, Obrist and Busse (1965) have reported that the amount of diffuse slowing in their subjects under 75 years of age was comparable to that seen in healthy young adults. However, in their subjects over the age of 75 at least 20 percent showed sufficient slowing to be rated abnormal. Those studies conducted on hospital patients or institutionalized populations have found a greater degree of slowing and in greater percentages of the population.

A high degree of correlation between indices of amount of slow wave activity (or simply its presence or absence) and intellectual deterioration has been found using traditional IQ scores or more all-encompassing psychiatric-rating scales (Mundy-Castle, Hurst, Beerstecher, and Prinsloo, 1954; McAdam and Robinson, 1956,

1962; Obrist, Busse, Eisdorfer, and Kleemeier, 1962; Weiner and Shuster, 1956). That such signs are evidence of brain deterioration is even more heavily reinforced by the reports that most patients with moderate or severe slowing tend to remain hospitalized or die while those with other patterns do not (McAdam and Robinson, 1956, 1962; Obrist and Henry, 1958a; Pampiglione and Post, 1958).

Such slowing has generally been associated with intellectual deterioration (Barnes, Busse, and Friedman, 1956; Silverman, Busse, Barnes, Frost, and Thaler, 1953; Thaler, 1956) but is restricted in patient populations to patients afflicted by organic brain disorders, rather than functional ones (Hoch and Kubis, 1941; Liberson and Seguin, 1945). In those patients showing signs of functional disorders (e.g., schizophrenia, depression, involutional psychosis) the majority showed faster brain rhythms and little diffuse slowing (Frey and Sjögren, 1959; Luce and Rothschild, 1953; Obrist and Henry, 1958b).

Two reports (Turton, 1958; Turton and Warren, 1960) expressing doubts about the ability to make differentiations between psychotics and organics via EEG diagnoses have been criticized by Obrist and Busse (1965) as inadequately analyzing their EEG data and using a patient sample heavily loaded with cases which could neither be differentiated on psychiatric grounds nor with EEG criteria.

Since a large number of experiments have shown that cerebral ischemia, hypoxia or anoxia produce slowing of EEG activity (Gastaut and Meyer, 1961), it was the first mechanism tested as the etiology underlying diffuse slow activity. Decreased cerebral oxygen consumption was reported in patients with senile dementia and diffuse slow activity (Lassen, Munck, and Tottey, 1957). Also cerebral oxygen uptake has been positively correlated to the peak frequency of the occipital EEG ($r = 0.74$, $p < 0.001$) in patients with diffuse slowing. Further, as percent-time spent in slow wave activity increases it has also been shown that cerebral blood flow decreases and vascular resistance increases (Obrist, Sokoloff, Lassen, Lane, Butler, and Feinberg, 1963).

Sokoloff (1966), on the basis of studies carried out by Dastur, Lane, Hansen, Kety, Butler,

Perlin, and Sokoloff (1963), has proposed arteriosclerosis or other cardiovascular diseases as responsible for the onset of this EEG slowing. He suggested that cerebral vascular insufficiency, with ensuing hypoxia, could produce loss of neurons which would then lead to a decline in oxygen utilization due to the decreased metabolic load. Obrist, Busse, and Henry (1961) provided support for this argument in showing that elderly psychiatric patients with low blood pressure (and assumed low blood flow) had significantly more diffuse slowing than patients with *mildly* elevated blood pressure. In fact, when patients develop both vascular disease and low blood pressure, 70 percent show diffuse slowing in the EEG (Obrist, 1964). Similar results have been reported by Busse and Wang (1971) on community volunteers with vascular problems.

If other patient categories such as senile deterioration are allowed to enter the picture, then cerebral vascular impairment has clearly been shown to be related to severity of intellectual deterioration (Feinberg, Lane, and Lassen, 1960; Klee, 1964; Lassen, Munck, and Tottey, 1957; Obrist, Chivian, Cronquist, and Ingvar, 1970). Similar results have been found for senile patients with EEG diffuse slow activity (McAdam and Robinson, 1962; Mundy-Castle *et al.*, 1954; Obrist *et al.*, 1970). While other endogenous factors could lead to cortical atrophy and consequent lessened metabolic consumption (Lassen, 1966), a recent review of the cerebral blood flow literature in its relation to aging indicates that vascular ischemia and hypoxia should not be discounted as contributing factors (Obrist, 1972). In order to clearly spell out the mechanism it will be necessary to determine the increase in the percentage of oxygen that must necessarily be absorbed from the cerebral circulation during periods of lessened flow in subjects passing through the early stages of deterioration. One clear possibility would be that elderly subjects may have an increased ability to respond sufficiently to such challenges. Clearly, a longitudinal design for such a study would be the most efficient. Unfortunately such data are not yet available.

Another approach to differentiate between deterioration initiated by vascular factors as opposed to atrophy from other causes would be to determine vasoreactivity to CO_2 inhalation (Novack, Shenkin, Bortin, Goluboff, and Soffe, 1953; Schieve and Wilson, 1953). One might expect a decreased vasomotor response in patients with "arteriosclerotic dementia," but recent explorations with functional tests, such as CO_2 inhalation and pharmacologic manipulations of blood pressure, have been discouraging (Simard, Olesen, Paulson, Lassen, and Skinkjl, 1971).

It should be noted that no relationship between diffuse slowing and cerebral blood flow has been obtained in healthy community volunteer subjects (Obrist, 1963; Obrist *et al.*, 1963; Wang, Obrist, and Busse, 1970). This would suggest that variation in scores on cognitive abilities and measures of physiological and metabolic function are relatively independent when kept within normal range. However, with intervening pathology as seen in hospital patient populations, the ensuing correlation between physiologic and cognitive function may be a measure of the extent of the pathology. The "discontinuity hypothesis" proposes that cognitive functioning remains independent of physiologic function until critical limits are surpassed (Birren, Butler, Greenhouse, Sokoloff, and Yarrow, 1963). The need for discriminating between healthy normal subjects and those with pathology in conducting studies of aging processes is thus highlighted by this hypothesis. As more data are reviewed below the need for such discrimination will be even more apparent. Spieth (1964, 1965) gave clear examples of such dependencies in research on reaction time. The hypothesis has been advanced that aging is due, in large measure, to the accumulation of such pathology (Obrist, 1964, 1972).

Focal Slow Activity

High voltage slow waves (1–7 Hz) appearing as episodic bursts from a small region and perhaps accompanied by sharp waves and amplitude asymmetries constitute this phenomenon. It is seen predominantly in healthy volunteers although it has been observed in hospital patients (Barnes, Busse, and Friedman, 1956; Frey and Sjögren, 1959; Harvald, 1958; Obrist and Henry, 1958a) where its distribution was more widespread. It is usually reported as having little influence on cognitive function.

It has been reported that from 30–50 percent of normal elderly may show focal slowing (Busse, Barnes, Silverman, Shy, Thaler, and Frost, 1954; Busse *et al.*, 1956; Mundy-Castle, 1962). When seen it appears approximately 75 percent of the time in the left hemisphere and predominantly in the anterior temporal region (Busse and Obrist, 1963; Kooi, Guvener, Tupper, and Bagchi, 1964; Silverman, Busse, and Barnes, 1955). The percentage of subjects showing this abnormality begins to increase at about the age of 50 (Obrist and Busse, 1965). However, in neither middle-aged nor older groups is there any correlation of this EEG abnormality with constitutional makeup or alteration in function. Other aspects or measures which have failed to show a relationship to size, presence, or extent of focal slow activity are: handedness (Kooi *et al.*, 1964; Silverman, Busse, and Barnes, 1955), seizures or aphasia (Busse and Obrist, 1963; Frey and Sjögren, 1959), intellectual or psychiatric ratings (Busse *et al.*, 1956; Mundy-Castle *et al.*, 1954; Obrist *et al.*, 1962; Thaler, 1956), or learning and recall measures (Drachman and Hughes, 1971). Obrist (1971) using two groups of elderly subjects matched for age, socioeconomic status, and education, with one group having very extensive focal slowing, could show no differences between the groups on verbal learning, memory performance, Wechsler Adult Intelligence Scale scores (WAIS), verbal-performance scale discrepancy, or longevity index.

Only two studies run counter to this general trend: Obrist (1965) showed a slowed choice reaction time in healthy volunteers with focal slowing, and Drachman and Hughes (1971) reported increased verbal-performance scale differences in a group with focal slow activity. Wang, Obrist, and Busse (1970), using well-matched controls, could not find a verbal-performance difference when age, race, and socioeconomic status were taken into account. But Wang *et al.* did find that the group with slow foci showed a significant decline in the verbal score on the WAIS over a 3.5-year period, while a matched control group actually gained slightly. Since Milner (1967) has clearly shown memory and learning mechanisms dependent on temporal lobe function, one is puzzled by the lack of studies showing significant effects. Perhaps the longitudinal method is more powerful in showing such differences. In this regard it may be significant that this anterior temporal region is the area showing the greatest reductions in blood flow in patients with organic dementia (Ingvar and Gustafson, 1970; Obrist *et al.*, 1970; Simard *et al.*, 1971). However, it has been shown that aberrant foci in other portions of the brain seem to propagate their electrical signals so as to appear as if they were located in the temporal lobe (Frantzen and Lennox-Buchthal, 1961; Strauss, Ostow, Greenstein, and Lewyn, 1955). Thus, without careful analysis and extra data gathered on those subjects showing foci, one may not state conclusively that the focus was indeed in the anterior temporal area.

It is usually assumed that these foci arise from vascular disturbances since it is known that greater numbers of cerebral vascular disturbances are found in the left hemisphere and in the temporal region (Hughes, 1960). It has also been reported that cardiovascular disease occurs more often in subjects with slow foci (Kooi *et al.*, 1964; Silverman, Busse, and Barnes, 1955). Obrist and Busse (1965) after a consideration of studies attempting to induce focal slow activity from vascular manipulations have drawn the conclusion that vascular insufficiency should be considered a prime contributor to focal slow wave production.

Alpha Frequency Activity

Alpha frequency activity is usually defined as high voltage (50–100 μV) activity falling in the frequency range of 8–13 Hz. It is found largely in the occipital, parietal, and temporal regions of the head, especially when the subject is relaxed with his eyes closed. Of the various "rhythms," the alpha rhythm has received the greatest amount of study, probably because it is the most dominant rhythm in the EEG of most subjects.

The alpha rhythm is usually seen to decrease in amplitude and slow with increasing age. The mean alpha frequency for young adults falls in the range from 10.2–10.5 Hz (Brazier and Finesinger, 1944). The older adult is more variable, but when over 70 years of age, is likely to fall in the range of 8.0–9.7 Hz (Busse and Obrist, 1963; Mundy-Castle *et al.*, 1954; Otomo, 1966) with hospital patients falling toward the low end of this range (Friedlander, 1958; Harvald, 1958). Most of the early studies of EEG changes with age were done on hospitalized patients and were of cross-sectional design (i.e., they studied different groups of people falling in different age ranges). As such, they usually were using subject populations with deteriorated mental abilities and were making the usual cross-sectional confoundings of selective subject dropout and possible influence of generational differences. Later longitudinal studies may find the mean frequencies of age-matched samples to follow the frequency decline found in the cross-sectional studies. However, thus far enough comparable data has not been accumulated to permit the needed comparison. (See Figure 1.)

The older patient not only shows slower EEG frequencies but presents alpha for a lesser percentage of the record and with a different topographical distribution (Mundy-Castle *et al.*, 1954; Obrist and Henry, 1958a,b). As the alpha

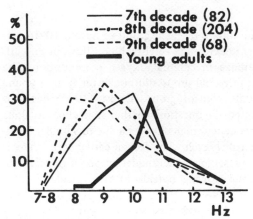

Figure 1. The distribution curves of frequencies of the dominant alpha waves (*restricted to 8 Hz and above*) in each decade of 354 normal subjects 60 years and over and those of young adults. The curve of young adults was derived from Brazier and Finesinger (1944). The numbers in parentheses indicate the number of subjects in that group. (Reproduced by permission of the publisher from Otomo, E. 1966. *Electroencephalo. Clin. Neurophysiol.*, **21**, 489–491.

activity is decreased in percent-time, slower activity replaces it—especially as the patient is rated lower in mental function. Gaches (1960) has reported alpha activity extending further into frontal and temporal areas with increasing age—especially when vascular disease was shown to be present. It would appear that the entire spectrum of frequencies produced by a subject decreases as he ages for as the dominant frequency shifts lower the higher frequencies from 10–12 have been shown to be less common (Obrist, 1954). Interestingly, no alpha slowing has been shown in hospital patients in general unless they demonstrated intellectual impairment (Mundy-Castle, 1962; Obrist, 1963). However, patients with organic deterioration (chronic brain syndrome) have been shown to have dominant alpha frequencies as low as 7 Hz (Frey and Sjögren, 1959). Slowing of alpha frequencies in conjunction with impaired memory function has also been shown by Hoagland (1954) in a study of hospital patients.

As the need for studying normal healthy subjects became apparent, longitudinal studies were instituted. Fortunately, such studies allow the gathering of data which more directly address the question of alpha frequency changes with aging. Such studies have shown that even in healthy volunteers the alpha frequency may drop with a rather linear decline over the years (Obrist and Busse, 1965; Wang and Busse, 1969; Wang, Obrist, and Busse, 1970). One such study (Wang and Busse, 1969), recording alpha frequency activity from the occiput, has described a linear decline of about .08 Hz per year in subjects passing from 60–80 years of age. However, it should also be noted that 11 of 48 subjects showed an increase in alpha frequency. Perhaps longitudinal studies may show some patterns of response not seen in cross-sectional studies.

Interestingly, while the alpha rhythm has often been described, few studies have described the entire spectrum change with aging. Clearly this is an issue of some importance since even young mature subjects produce EEG activity ranging from 8–12 Hz. Obrist (1963) has described two populations of elderly, one with no discernible health problems and another with only the mildest of symptoms. Both groups

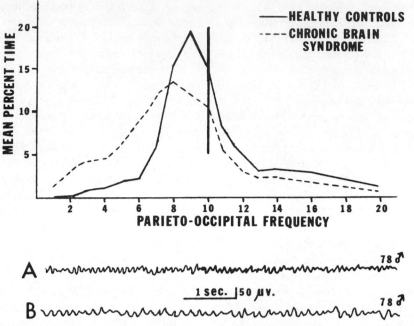

Figure 2. The distribution of EEG activity as a function of frequency for a group of healthy controls ($N = 47$) and a group with chronic brain syndrome ($N = 45$). The line marks the dominant alpha frequency reported by Brazier and Finesinger (1944). The lower portion of the figure shows a portion of an EEG record from a member of the healthy group (A) and the chronic brain syndrome group (B). In both cases the lowering of the frequencies is evident. (From Obrist, W. D. 1965. Electroencephalographic approach to age changes in response speed. *In*, A. T. Welford and J. E. Birren (eds.), *Behavior, Aging, and the Nervous System*, pp. 259–271. Courtesy of Charles C. Thomas, Publisher, Springfield, Illinois.)

show reduced production of higher and increased production of slower frequencies. However, Obrist has pointed out that peak occipital frequency is the measure which best differentiates the two groups. (See Figure 2.)

The decline in alpha frequency and amplitude with age has called for some general explanatory principles to be evolved. The decrease in the alpha rhythm is not known to be determined by any specific cause. However, the most powerful model yet developed explains the slowing due to decreased cerebral blood flow leading to ischemic and hypoxic conditions— especially during stress conditions. One early study compared age-matched males with and without arteriosclerotic diseases and showed the lower alpha frequency in the vascular disease group (Obrist and Bissell, 1955). Another study also comparing healthy subjects to those with mild vascular disease has shown a similar result (see Figure 2) (Obrist, 1963). A study of cerebral blood flow (Dastur *et al.*, 1963) showed

the mildly diseased group to have a 10–16 percent decrease in cerebral blood flow, but no difference in cerebral oxygen consumption. The healthy old group did not differ from a young adult control group. Obrist (1963) has thus raised the question whether all declines in alpha frequency might likely be due to vascular insufficiency, even when seen at earlier ages. There is at present no other model proposed to deal with alpha slowing outside of the vascular insufficiency model. However, since even the healthiest older subjects showed some slowing, it would seem that another model needs to be developed. A totally disease-dependent model seems insufficient to explain the frequency slowing seen in this and the longitudinal studies where essentially disease-free subjects are studied. Development of such a model may depend on further advances in understanding the underlying basis of the EEG itself (see, for example, Andersen and Andersson, 1968; Elul, 1972).

A mechanism of impaired cerebral circulation

would, however, fit with other deficits in behavior that are due to aphasias, strokes, etc., with a known etiology leading to central nervous system (CNS) impairment (Gerard, 1959; Reitan, 1955; Welford, 1959). WAIS performance score deficits have been related to slowed alpha frequency through a mechanism of vascular disease (Obrist et al., 1962; Obrist, 1975). Vascular disease free patients and community volunteers have shown no relationship of WAIS performance scores to the alpha frequency. Longitudinal study of a group of community volunteers has shown a significant relationship ($r = -.61$) between alpha frequency and a verbal-performance WAIS difference score (Wang and Busse, 1969). (This verbal-performance difference score is thought to be more age-sensitive than either the verbal or the performance score changes taken alone [Eisdorfer, Busse, and Cohen, 1959; Fox and Birren, 1950].) Subjecting a portion of this group to cerebral blood flow measurements has shown a significant correlation of WAIS score with blood flow ($r = .78$) in only one group—a low education, low socioeconomic group (Wang, Obrist, and Busse, 1970). However, correlation of WAIS verbal and performance score *change* over a 12-year period altered the picture to show a significant correlation ($r = .73$) between performance score change and cerebral blood flow change only in the high education, high socioeconomic group.

An extensive review of the interrelationship between cerebral blood flow and the EEG and cognitive function has been written by Obrist (1972). As outlined there, the evidence for reduced blood flow leading to neuronal loss with the consequent reduced need for oxygen and a slowed EEG is a convincing model. The initial reduced cerebral blood flow could stem from arteriosclerotic deposits or from other vascular factors. When such chronic hypoxia or ischemic episodes lead to neuronal loss this loss can be detected by a decreased need for metabolic constituents, oxygen and reduced blood flow. It is this later state that has been hypothesized to be correlated with decreased function and EEG slowing. It should be noted that a mechanism for neuronal loss remains to be detailed.

An aging factor leading to greater risk from hypoxic and ischemic conditions has been indi-cated. Sulkin and Sulkin (1967) have reported that cells from cardiac and autonomic nerve ganglia in senescent rats have swelling and fragmenting of intracellular components due to low oxygen tension for prolonged periods. Cells from young mature rats did not show such changes. Since such intracellular components are necessary for continued functioning of the neuron, a model for neuronal loss might be constructed from such data. However, one caveat might be that their losses were found only after long periods of altered oxygen tension. Also, their oxygen levels may not have been low enough to reproduce tissue hypoxic levels.

Beta Frequency Activity

Beta activity is generally described as that activity between 14–40 Hz in the human EEG. This beta activity and "low-voltage fast-frequency" activity, which is rather mixed high frequencies, are found most frequently over the anterior portion of the head. Such activity is found most frequently during periods of aroused mental activity.

While the preceding section has described a general linear decrease in alpha frequency with age, no such reports have been made for beta frequencies. Perhaps the fact that high frequency activity generally constitutes a small fraction of EEG phenomena when analyzed by spectrographic means has discouraged investigators from further study of this phenomenon.

In 1950, Gibbs and Gibbs described beta activity increasing to 25 percent of the total record by the age of 60–70 years. However, in a subject pool that extended well beyond the 80th year, it has been reported that beta activity seemed to decline in percent of the total record when subjects were beyond 80 years in age (Busse et al., 1956; Silverman, Busse, and Barnes, 1955). Mundy-Castle (1951) and Greenblatt (1944) have described an increase in beta activity during the 60–70-year period in both normal and hospitalized subjects. However, severely deteriorated hospital patients are significantly lower in amount of beta activity (Barnes et al., 1956; Frey and Sjögren, 1959; Mundy-Castle et al., 1954; Obrist and Henry, 1958a).

Wang and Busse (1969) have also reported an increase in the amount of high amplitude beta activity in a group of healthy subjects followed longitudinally. When broken down by sex and socioeconomic class, the increase in beta was especially noticeable in women of lower socioeconomic status.

This increase in beta activity has not been related to psychological variables such as arousal or anxiety. The lack of such studies is striking considering the fact that hypotheses about changes in both arousal and anxiety with age are readily at hand in the psychological literature.

EEG Reactivity

Aside from having certain frequency and amplitude properties of its own, the EEG is also reactive to stimuli presented to the subject. Of course EEG reactivity is also dependent on the state of the subject at the time of stimulation. Thus, the general theories of activation (Duffy, 1962) or arousal (Lindsley, 1960) predict certain EEG changes when a subject is called upon to respond under varying circumstances. Many early papers investigated the quenching of the alpha rhythm (alpha blocking response) and its replacement by low-voltage fast-frequency activity when various stimuli or conditions were imposed on a subject. A major step forward in understanding the underlying mechanism was made with the discovery of the role of the reticular formation in jointly driving the cortex into desynchronized low-voltage fast-frequency activity and giving rise to behavioral arousal (Moruzzi and Magoun, 1949; Lindsley, Schreiner, Knowles, and Magoun, 1950). The theory which has grown from these discoveries (Lindsley, 1960) has obvious application to gerontology. If older subjects are slower at making responses or less responsive in general, then they should show slower rhythms in their EEG reflecting their hypothesized lower levels of arousal and cortical excitability.

Alpha Blocking Response. Liberson (1944) introduced the idea that cerebral dysfunction might be tested by quantitating the alpha blocking response. Certainly decreased reactivity to sensory stimulation can be demonstrated in brain-damaged subjects (Stoller, 1949; Wells, 1962, 1963). Elderly subjects also show less reactivity to sensory stimuli (Andermann and Stoller, 1961; Verdeaux, Verdeaux and Turmel, 1961).

Another study of cortical reactivity tested the extent of the alpha blocking response in both old and young subjects in good health and of superior intelligence (Wilson, 1962). He found the older subjects less completely suppressed their alpha activity when stimulated by a light and were also faster to habituate their response to the light. However, since the older subjects initially had a lower amplitude alpha rhythm, the return to normal was less of a change for them. The lesser responsivity would fit with the precepts of activation theory since the older subjects started with a slower and lower amplitude rhythm. As for the more rapid habituation, if habituation was considered as a simple model of learning, as some theorists have proposed (e.g., Sokolov, 1959, 1963), then the faster habituation of the old group would conflict with the activation hypothesis. Again, however, a possible answer is that the older subjects had a smaller adjustment to make to return to normal.

Faster learning in the elderly would also conflict with a study carried out on EEG reactivity and verbal learning ability (Thompson and Wilson, 1966). Two groups of elderly men, matched for age, socioeconomic status and IQ, were formed on the basis of good or poor paired-associate verbal learning ability. The group showing excellent learning ability had greater reactivity to photic stimulation and higher frequency alpha activity (10 vs. 9 Hz) than did the poorer learning group. Interestingly, there were no statistical differences between the two groups in their resting EEGs.

EEG and Reaction Time

Activation theory would predict that reaction time (RT) would be faster during faster brain rhythms—or at least during periods of desynchronization (alpha blocking). Birren (1965) tested such a notion by splitting the total of reaction time trials according to: (1) presence of alpha or absence of alpha, (2) alpha frequency higher or lower than the mean for that individual, and (3) alpha amplitude greater or lesser than that individual's mean voltage. No relationship of reaction time to EEG was found in any of the cases. Thompson and Botwinick (1968) came to essentially the same conclusion after studying the relationship between EEG and reaction time in both young and old subjects.

Surwillo (1968) summarized some of his previous work (1963a,b, 1964a,b, 1966a,b) in which the hypothesis tested was of the alpha rhythm acting as (or being the indicator of) a timing mechanism. Alpha slowing (expressed as "alpha period"—the period of time for completion of one wave) was linked linearly to increase of reaction time across age (Surwillo, 1963b). Surwillo (1963a) also showed that variability in reaction time across age was correlated with alpha period. He reasoned that reaction time should increase as alpha period increases if one assumes that some portion of the information processing occurs only during a specific part of the alpha cycle since the stimulus onset could occur at any point in the alpha cycle. A further demonstration of the dependence on the alpha period in tasks requiring more complex decisions used a disjunctive reaction time and found

the correlation coefficient between age and difference between simple and disjunctive reaction time scores to be 0.26 (Surwillo, 1964a). Moreover, this relationship vanished if the period of alpha rhythm was held constant by statistical means. Finally, in a rather dubious effort to change the basic timing mechanism behind the alpha rhythm, Surwillo (1964b) provided a photic stimulus flashing at various rates (6-15 flashes per sec) in an attempt to photically drive the brain rhythms at specific frequencies. He was able to do this in only a small number of subjects and then only over a very limited range of frequencies. However, there was some evidence of having concomitantly altered reaction time. More convincingly, in several of the above studies Surwillo removed the variance dependent on the alpha rhythm and demonstrated that the correlation with age was simultaneously removed. Nevertheless, since the correlation between reaction time and alpha rhythm ranged only from .19 to .30, a great deal of variance is left unexplained due to other causes. (See Figure 3.)

Surwillo (1968) pointed out that his data had

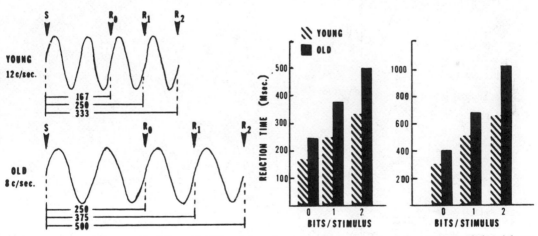

Figure 3. Comparison of EEGs and RTs of two hypothetical subjects, one a young adult with an alpha rhythm of 12 Hz and the other an elderly person with an alpha rhythm of 8 Hz. S indicates the time of the representation of the stimulus. For comparison purposes both subjects are shown receiving S at identical phases of the cycle. R_0 is the response in a simple RT experiment; R_1 and R_2 are the responses under conditions of 1 and 2 bits of information, respectively. Numbers below the waves are the hypothetical RT in milliseconds, and these values are shown in the first histogram on the right. (From Surwillo, W. W. 1968. Timing of behavior in senescence and the role of the central nervous system. *In*, G. A. Talland (ed.), *Human Aging and Behavior*, pp. 1–35. New York: Academic Press.) The histogram on the far right shows 12 young males (median age 18.5 years) and 12 old males (median age 63.0 years) in an experiment run under conditions analogous to the hypothetical example. (From Suci, G. J., Davidoff, M. D., and Surwillo, W. W. 1960. *J. Exp. Psychol.*, **60**, 242–244 with permission.)

to be collected during periods of alpha and are thus restricted by that boundary condition. Nevertheless, it is the most well developed model of behavior-EEG relationships in the aging literature.

Woodruff (1972) attempted an ingenious test and extension of Surwillo's model by the means of biofeedback training. She attempted to have one group of elderly subjects speed or slow their alpha frequency (by the aid of signaling devices to indicate when they had achieved a predetermined deviation) and to then test their reaction times during these periods. She obtained significant alterations in reaction time in the predicted directions during periods of attempted speeding and slowing of alpha rhythm despite not obtaining significant shifts in alpha rhythm frequency. Such data are difficult to interpret in terms of activation theory since reaction time and EEG activity apparently did not change concomitantly. Woodruff believes that Surwillo's changes in reaction time are too great to be accounted for by the small changes

in alpha period. The amount of EEG change in all these experiments is difficult to evaluate, however, since only the dominant frequency is reported. Frequency spectrograms or power density spectrograms would be much more informative, especially in the biofeedback study. With such spectrograms, one could evaluate the amount of frequency change through the entire EEG spectrum, especially in assessing the possible increase in frequencies closely adjacent to the dominant frequency.

Another problem that could arise in the interpretation of the joint fluctuation of RT and alpha frequency with increasing age is the possible intervention of a third determinant variable. Age related changes in sensory input systems (e.g., pupillary reflex changes [Weale, 1965; Schäfer and Weale, 1970]) might contribute to the changes in RT in a manner that would enhance the EEG-RT association in the elderly. Clearly, to make a case for the alpha rhythm being involved in some mechanism underlying RT, some experimental manipula-

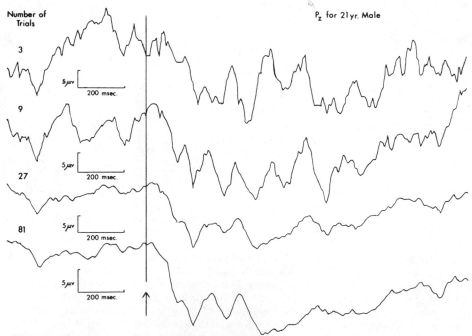

Figure 4. Illustration of the emergence of an averaged evoked potential (AEP) from background EEG. Averaging is time-locked to stimulus presentation delivered at the arrow. The increasing smoothness of the curve indicates the loss of noise contamination in the signal. In theory, the EEG baseline preceding the stimulus should eventually smooth to a horizontal line. The recording is from P_z to a linked mastoid reference.

tion showing such joint changes must be made without reliance upon statistical procedures to make an inferential argument.

EVOKED POTENTIAL MEASURES

Evoked potentials are retrieved from the EEG by an "averaging" process that is founded on two assumptions. (1) Spontaneous EEG activity is random in its voltage pattern. Thus if randomly selected epochs of the EEG, equal in length were subdivided into units and the units were summed across epochs, the sum for each *unit* would approximate zero. (2) If a stimulus were to be given at the exact moment of onset of each of the above epochs, and if the subdivisions were then summed as before, any time-locked, unchanging electrical signal elicited by the stimulus would then cumulate and emerge from the "noise" of the random waves of the EEG. Such average evoked potentials (AEP) are now commonly extracted from the EEG with stimuli being given in any of the sense modalities. Figure 4 gives examples of these complex wave forms with some examples of the amount of noise to be expected with a different number of epochs included in the average.

Passive Stimulation

The early portion of these wave forms has often been considered to be associated with processing of the physical parameters of the stimulus with later components (starting sometime about 80 msec after the stimulus) being considered more involved in complex information processing (see Lüders, 1970). While there have been different results reported for age effects on the AEP for different sense modalities, the general result has been an increase in both amplitude and latency in some components in the early portion of the AEP, and considerable diminution of the later components.

It is unclear which measurement best describes these complex wave forms: measurements of peak to peak amplitudes, baseline to peak amplitudes, area bounded by baseline and latency from stimulus onset to occurrence of a particular peak seem to be the most popular. Other approaches will be mentioned shortly. (See Figure 5.)

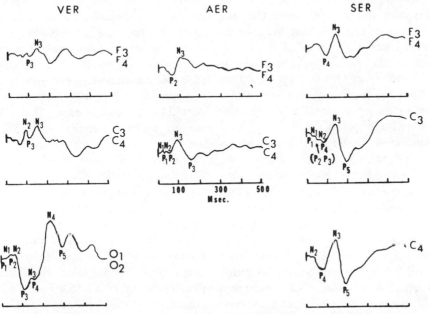

Figure 5. Examples of average evoked potentials to light (VER), sound (AER) and somatosensory (SER) stimuli recorded at frontal (F_3, F_4), central (C_3, C_4) and occipital (O_1, O_2) sites. It should be noted that different portions of the head respond differentially to different stimuli. The marking system for these AEPs should not be generalized to all studies, but are indicated here for ease of communication with the text. (Schenkenberg, 1970. Used with permission of the author.)

Somatosensory. The AEP to somatosensory stimulation recorded from centrally placed recording electrodes (approximately over somatosensory cortex) showed both amplitude and latency increases with age in several of the early components (20–80 msec) (Shagass and Schwartz, 1965; Lüders, 1970). However, this finding could not be replicated by Schenkenberg (1970) who found no increase in central (C_3 and C_4) recording sites, although he did find some increases in frontal areas (F_3 and F_4) during the same 20–80 msec interval. Shagass and Schwartz also reported females having shorter latencies in the early components than males.

Later components of the somatosensory AEP reflect a somewhat different picture. Most of the components from 100–500 msec tend to drop sharply in amplitude by 30–40 years of age and remain at these low levels. Concomitantly, their peak latencies are initially seen to increase slightly and then remain stable (Lüders, 1970; Schenkenberg, 1970). However, Schenkenberg (1970) reported that when the AEPs are measured by cumulating the total area between the AEP curve and the baseline around which it is changing, the data (μV-msec) increases in value with increasing age. The portion of the epoch examined was 300–600 msec after the stimulus. It must be noted that the cumulative measure takes into account all departures from baseline, not just specific peaks, and also includes a longer epoch than the peak amplitude analysis. Thus the discrepancy in results probably indicates increased amplitudes of later components with increasing age.

Some portion of the above changes, especially the early ones, could be due to changes in the peripheral nerves. Norris, Shock, and Wagman (1953) showed a very slight increase in conduction velocity with age (30–39 years of age) in the motor nerves. However, LaFratta (1972) has shown a rather striking decrease in afferent nerve response with age. Such changes could lead to both amplitude and latency alteration in the cortical evoked potential. Perhaps a greater dispersion of afferent input could have a significant effect, but there is no solid evidence of what should happen to the cortical AEP with such dispersed afferent input. It is difficult at present to ascribe age-related changes seen in

the cortical AEP to any specific mechanism or nervous system alteration. It is likely that the age changes observed are not associated with alterations which occur principally as a function of decreased intensity of the stimulus (see, for example, Shagass, 1972, pp. 73–74).

Auditory. The auditory AEP seems the most stable of the three major modalities for it showed no change in amplitude or in latency of any of its components across the life span from maturity to old age (Schenkenberg, 1970). Again, however, as in the somatosensory modality, the cumulative voltage of the AEP measure tended to increase with age from maturity to senescence. This was found in both frontal and central portions of the head, but not in the occipital region (Schenkenberg, 1970).

Visual. The early portion of the wave form (20–100 msec) may decrease in amplitude from age 15–45 (Schenkenberg, 1970) and then increase in size and latency in some components at least through age 80 (Straumanis, Shagass, and Schwartz, 1965; Dustman and Beck, 1966, 1969; Schenkenberg, 1970). These changes seem especially apparent in central and occipital sites. But the most characteristic change seems to be the drastic reduction in size of the AEP components from 200–300 msec. These changes are large and are seen best in the occipital area, but may also be observed in central and frontal sites. The latencies to various peaks, especially beyond 100 msec, are often seen to increase by about 20 msec (Straumanis, Shagass, and Schwartz, 1965; Dustman and Beck, 1969; Schenkenberg, 1970). Again, the cumulative voltage measurements showed increased activity for the late components in the 300–500 msec epoch for the frontal area. The central sites were highly variable while the occiput showed decreasing cumulative voltage over this same period (Schenkenberg, 1970). (See Figure 6.)

Shagass (1968, 1972) and Shagass and Schwartz (1965) have reported increasing amplitudes and latencies with age, leading them to conclude that central mechanisms must be involved in addition to any possible involvement

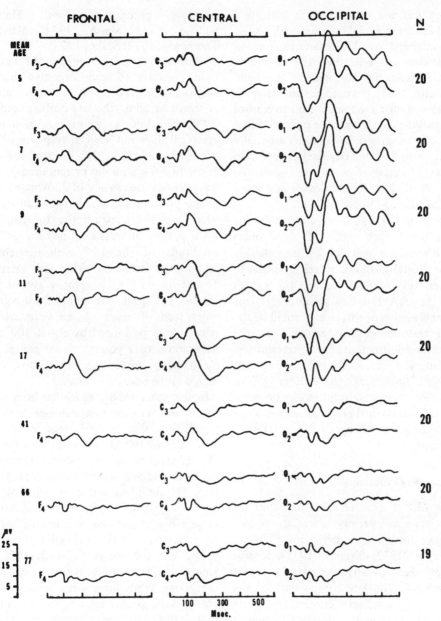

Figure 6. Composite average evoked potentials to light flash stimuli recorded at frontal, central and occipital sites from the number of subjects indicated under N in the age groups indicated at the left. Note the diminution in late waves in the older age groups. (Reproduced with permission from Schenkenberg, 1970.)

of peripheral mechanisms. If only peripheral mechanisms were involved, both latency and amplitude could not simultaneously increase (Diamond, 1964).

If a stimulus is given twice in rapid succession, the AEP to the second stimulus will be smaller in amplitude than to the first stimulus. The extent to which this AEP reacquires its full amplitude with increasing delay between the two stimuli is known as its recovery function. Shagass (1968) has reported that with increasing age most portions of the early AEP show enhanced amplitude and slowed latency recovery. Shagass (1972, pp. 87-106) has interpreted this and other data to indicate a loss of inhibition in neural function with age.

Since peripheral visual mechanisms, such as pupil diameter, can influence AEP amplitude and latency (Bergamini, Bergamosco, Mombelli, and Gandiglio, 1965), it is unfortunate that none of the above studies used any means to control for such peripheral influences (e.g., an artificial pupil or dilative drugs). This seems especially important to do since the pupillary constriction reflex may strengthen with age while the tendency to dilate becomes weaker and more sluggish (Schäfer and Weale, 1970).

Schenkenberg (1970) did not control for the peripheral mechanism, but did show male-female differences which develop over the life span. The general relationship was for males to have larger AEP in childhood and for females to show large AEP following puberty. One possible explanation of this change could be the effect of testosterone and estrogen on the production and destruction of neurotransmitters (Broverman, Klaiber, Kobayashi, and Vogel, 1968; Vogel, Broverman, and Klaiber, 1971). The effect of these steriod hormones on brain transmitters needs further investigation since they are known to change with age (Finch, 1969; Dilman, 1971).

Active Cognitive Processing

While the AEP is sensitive to various stimulus attributes such as intensity, duration, or patterning (see, for example, Perry and Childers, 1969; Regan, 1972; Shagass, 1972), it also is very responsive to what the stimulus means to the subject. The late components of the AEP are thought to reflect such stimulus aspects described as information loading, stimulus novelty, or amount of necessary cognitive processing. In general, amplitudes in these late components have been relatively large when: (1) the stimulus delivered information necessary for a decision (Chapman and Bragdon, 1964; Tueting, Sutton, and Zubin, 1970), (2) it was a signal searched for (Hillyard, Squires, Bauer, and Lindsay, 1971), (3) the stimulus (or its absence) was unexpected (Klinke, Fruhstorfer, and Finkenzeller, 1968), or (4) the stimulus was involved in extensive

cognitive processing (Poon, Thompson, Williams, and Marsh, 1974; Marsh and Thompson, 1972; Seales, 1973).

While several aspects of the AEP have been found reactive to such cognitive processing, only one aspect seems to have received attention in regard to aging—the late positive component (LPC). The LPC, or P_3 or P_{300} as it has also been called, is not seen in response to passive stimulation (perhaps due to rapid habituation in the first few stimulus presentations) and thus was not measured in any of the work mentioned in the previous section. In the auditory mode, which was the least reactive to aging effects with passive stimulation, no change in the amplitude of the LPC with age could be found in a decision-making task (Marsh and Thompson, 1972). However, a greater latency for the LPC peak was reported for a group of older men of mean age 68 years where the latency was prolonged by about 100 msec in comparison to a young mature group. No age by difficulty-of-decision interaction was observed in the latency measure.

In the visual mode, which has been reported to be most sensitive to age changes with passive stimulation, there is an increase in LPC amplitude with age (Marsh, 1974). Further extensions of this work in our laboratory have replicated the basic findings: With tachistoscopic presentations (10 msec) of verbal or spatial stimuli to either the right or left visual field which the subject had to preview and report, large LPCs were observed in the parietal region in both young and old subjects. Greater LPCs were seen at the temporal sites for the old than for the young. While there was a tendency for the old to have greater latency to the LPC peak, it was not statistically significant. It may be that when not operating under a speed set, as above, cognitive decisions proceed at a slower and more variable rate and the LPC peak latency indicates this by being less well defined and not different between the two age groups. Such an interpretation would be contrary to the finding of Donchin, Tueting, Ritter, Kutas, and Heffley (1976) who reported the LPC was reduced when a motor task response was imposed upon a decision task. No clear interpretation is apparent at the present time.

The discrepancy in decline of verbal and visuomotor performance with age on IQ tests leads to the speculation of a possible difference in decline of left and right hemisphere function. This stems from the observation that the left hemisphere is usually associated with verbal functions and the right with visuospatial functions. This speculation was not substantiated when recordings from left and right hemispheres in the temporal and parietal areas failed to show any differential asymmetry with age (Marsh, 1974).

Another set of experiments has tested the speed with which old and young can scan their memory for a target. After being given a set of digits, a probe (or target) digit is presented to which the subject must respond by indicating if it was included in the set. Sternberg (1969) has shown memory scanning speeds of about 40 msec per digit for such a task in young subjects and Anders, Fozard, and Lillyquist (1972) have shown a scanning rate of about 70 msec per digit for an older group approaching 70 years of age. Since the time required to reach a decision is dependent on the size of the set being probed, this procedure permits a test determining whether the LPC is heavily influenced by set size and whether prediction of LPC occurrence can be made from a subject's decision times. Such experiments (Marsh, 1974) have shown that the LPC does have a prolonged latency as set size increases and that the longer decision times for older subjects are reflected in their longer latency to LPC peak. This can be seen in frontal (F_z), central (C_z, C_5, and C_6), and parietal (P_z) leads, but is strongest at the frontal recording site. The increase in LPC latency does not parallel the increase in RT however, it is only a proportional increase in both age groups. The relationship is similar for both age groups but more prominently shown by the old since their RT increases more as the number of scanned digits is increased (see Figure 7 for an example in one subject).

Since the LPC has been related to the amount of cognitive processing of the information present in the stimuli and older subjects seem to be most likely to have a small LPC when the stimulation procedure calls for no cognitive processing, it might be hypothesized that the

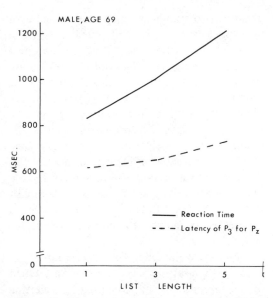

Figure 7. The reaction time and P_3 latencies for three different list lengths in a task requiring a memory scan for a decision of target match or mismatch. Both are seen to increase with increasing list length.

older subject selectively filters out or habituates more readily to the non-meaningful stimulus than does the younger subject. Wilson (1962) has already shown faster habituation of the alpha rhythm and thus it seems reasonable that other bioelectric phenomena may also show this effect. Whether such effects are related to neurotransmitter levels as mentioned earlier for age and sex differences in the AEP (Vogel, Broverman, and Klaiber, 1971; Broverman et al., 1968) remains to be shown.

Contingent Negative Variation. It has been shown by Walter, Cooper, Aldridge, McCallum and Winter (1964) that, when two stimuli are presented as a pair, in the interval between the stimuli a sustained negative shift will occur if the subject must perform some action to the second stimulus. Since the negative shift was shown to be dependent on the contingency that the second stimulus always followed the first, it was called the contingent negative variation (CNV).

This particular bioelectric phenomenon was thought to be an index of attention or arousal (Tecce, 1972). CNV is recorded in the interval between two stimuli and may thus be measured as a bioelectric correlate of preparatory set in reaction time experiments using a warning signal. Loveless and Sanford (1974a) have shown that as the foreperiod is lengthened the terminal portion of the CNV is lower for the older subject than for the young, mature subject. The suggestion has been made that the younger subject is able to time intervals as long as 15 sec and show an increase in the CNV in the last several seconds of the interval while many older subjects are unable to accomplish this (see Figure 8). The RT also reflected a difference in ability to prepare for motor action.

These same investigators also reported an early portion of the CNV wave form seemed to correspond to an orienting or alerting reaction. The older group did not differ from the younger in this aspect of their CNV measurements.

The CNV has also been measured in situations where cognitive processing was carried out. Marsh and Thompson (1973) found older subjects tended to show smaller amplitude CNV when more difficult judgments were anticipated. The same pattern was found for young, mature women, but not for men. It is unclear whether this lowered CNV amplitude in older subjects and women was illicited by the distracting task of holding stimuli in memory (Tecce and Scheff, 1969), or whether it can be traced to a greater degree of influence by instructions toward a sensory preparatory set and away from a motor preparatory set (Loveless and Sanford, 1974b). There is also the possibility of the influence of brain chemistry, as mentioned earlier.

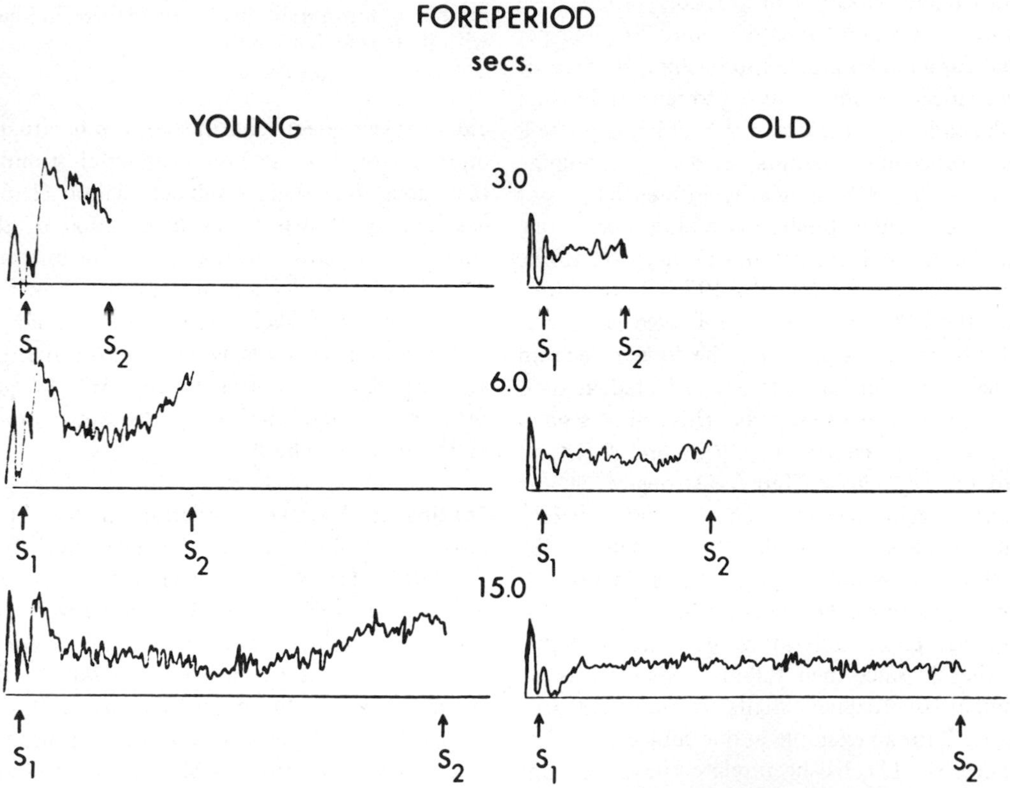

Figure 8. CNVs from a young mature and old subject at three different intervals (run in separate blocks) between a warning tone (S_1) and an imperative signal (a response-terminated burst of white noise) (S_2). The baseline is the average level of the EEG for a 1-second period preceding S_1. Each trace begins with a $-20\mu V$ calibration pulse. Note the rise in CNV preceding the imperative signal for the young subject at the longer intervals. (From Loveless and Sanford, 1974a. Reproduced with the permission of the *Journal of Gerontology*.)

Thompson and Nowlin (1973) found that age did not decrease the amplitude of the CNV as compared to a young mature control group. However, while the younger group showed the expected concordance between higher amplitude CNV and faster RT (Tecce, 1972), the older group did not. The younger group had especially quick RT when both CNV amplitude and heart rate changes were in concordance. This relationship was not apparent in the older group leading to the speculation of a possible loss of coordination between central and autonomic nervous systems. In contrast to the above study, Froehling (1974) has found a strong relationship between CNV amplitude and RT in measurements repeated over a period of three days. Since all subjects in this study were in excellent health, it may be that the reported loss of concordance in the Thompson and Nowlin study was due to health factors.

EEG Measures of Sleep

As one ages, the proportion of sleep time spent in the rapid eye movement (REM) and slow wave (SW) stages of sleep is diminished (Roffwarg,

Munzio, and Dement, 1966). This is illustrated in Figure 9 which also shows a decrease in total sleep time from childhood through young adulthood. Past the period of adolescence, the decrease in total sleep and REM is far less marked except for the very elderly (80 to 100 years of age) (Kahn, 1970). Not shown in the diagram is the decrease in proportion of stage 4, or SW sleep, that is known to occur in both normal and pathological aging (Feinberg, 1974; Feinberg, Koresko, and Heller, 1967; Feinberg and Carlson, 1968; Kales, Wilson, Kales, Jacobson, Paulson, Kollar, and Walter, 1967). It should also be noted that with increasing age the characteristic large slow waves of stage 4 are much reduced in amplitude and duration (Williams, Agnew, and Webb, 1964; Agnew, Webb, and Williams, 1967). (See Figure 10.)

Feinberg and his associates (1967) have also reported slowing of EEG spindle activity (12-15 Hz) with increasing age. The slowing seems comparable to the slowing already discussed for the alpha rhythm. Whether similar mechanisms are involved in the age-related slowing for both alpha and spindle activity is not yet known. There seem to be

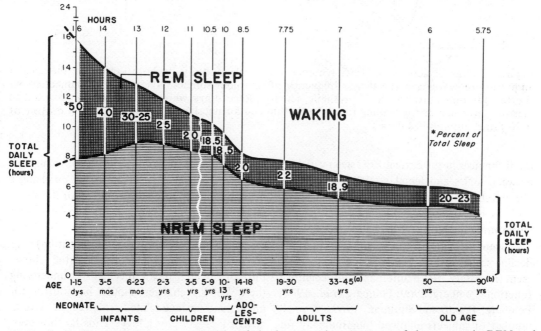

Figure 9. A diagrammatic representation of the hours and percentage of sleep spent in REM and non-REM (NREM) stages at different ages in the life cycle. (From Roffwarg, H. P., Munzio, J. N., and Dement, W. C. 1966. *Science*, **152**, 604–619. Revised. Copyright 1966 by the Association for the Advancement of Science.)

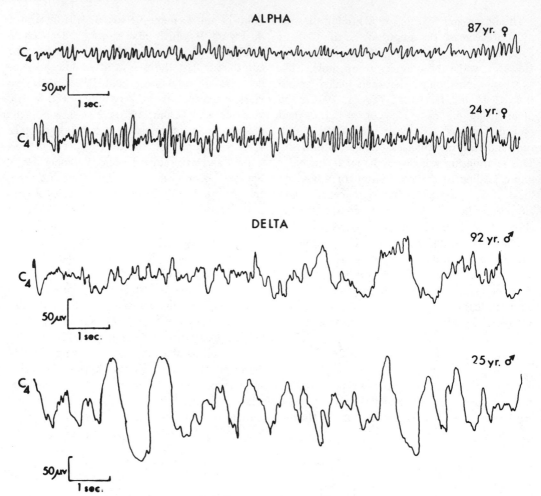

Figure 10. Age differences in EEG recorded during sleep study. In both cases note the smaller amplitude of waves and the slower frequency of the older subject. Also the older subject shows shorter duration bursts of such rhythmic activity. Recordings were made from C_4 to a linked mastoid reference during waking for alpha rhythm and during sleep for delta rhythm. (Courtesy of P. N. Prinz, unpublished data.)

no differences in the critical EEG sleep variables between males and females (Kahn and Fisher, 1969; Kahn, Fisher, and Lieberman, 1970).

It has not yet been determined what mechanism underlies this drastic decline in REM and SW sleep in later life. It is thought that the decline is deleterious in that these sleep stages seem necessary for maintenance of cognitive function (Feinberg, 1969; Feinberg et al., 1967; Feinberg, Braun, and Shulman, 1969). A small number of subjects followed longitudinally for 18 years showed a strong correlation (.8–.9) between decreases in WAIS performance scores and decreases in percentages of REM and SW sleep

(Prinz, Marsh, and Thompson, 1974). Changes in EEG sleep patterns are likely based on changes in the nuclei involved with control of the sleep-wakefulness cycle. Perhaps the large neuronal loss with aging in humans seen in the locus ceruleus (Brody, personal communication) may be related to EEG changes reported above. Further research in the mechanisms underlying these known changes should be fruitful for understanding age-related changes in several areas of psychophysiology. Thus far, however, the hypotheses linking age-related changes in sleep EEG variables to cognitive function are based only on similar results seen with organic brain disease (Feinberg and Carlson, 1968; Feinberg et al., 1967, 1969).

One precautionary note has been sounded by Mendels and Hawkins (1968) who noted that depression in the elderly subject may have a marked diminishing effect on SW sleep. Older subjects free from depressive illness in this study were found to be comparable to young, mature subjects in percentage of SW sleep.

AUTONOMIC NERVOUS SYSTEM CORRELATES

For the most part, studies involving bioelectric measures of autonomic nervous system (ANS) function in the elderly have been interpreted in the framework of arousal theory. Until recently it has been customary to conceptualize physiological correlates of arousal in a unidimensional framework from low to high levels. Under this view any of the many possible physiological measures were considered to be indicative of the momentary function of a unitary process reflecting the general level of mobilization of the organism to respond adaptively to incoming information. Cautioning against such notions, Lacey (1959, 1967) pointed out that interrelationships among various ANS measures are sufficiently low to make a unifying principle difficult to accept. Additionally, he presented evidence that differential increased activity may be seen in both the sympathetic and parasympathetic systems depending on the nature of the stress confronting the organism. Lacey, Kagan, Lacey, and Moss (1963) demonstrated this in a study in which subjects were required to perform mental activity, experience a painful stimulus (both of which involve internal awareness), or increase their attention to environmental stimuli. Increased internal awareness led to heart rate acceleration and decreased skin resistance, while increased attention to external stimuli led to heart rate deceleration and decreased skin resistance. While one autonomic component measure reacted sympathetically or parasympathetically and was dependent on the nature of the task, the other component reflected sympathetic activity in both types of task. These data led Lacey (1967) and Lacey and Lacey (1970) to introduce the concept of

"situational stereotypy" and to propose multidimensional arousal theories. Such theories may help to explain the arousal literature involving ANS measures and aging.

A number of studies in the geropsychology literature have implicated age changes in arousal as a cause for behavioral decline in the elderly, but there have been large differences of opinion regarding the mechanisms involved. The majority of papers in this area have been covered in a previous review (Thompson and Marsh, 1973). Consideration of the arousal concept involves both the CNS and ANS and must be used with an awareness that arousal may not be a unitary phenomenon. Arousal theory is in a state of transition, and Lacey (1967) has suggested that electrocortical arousal, autonomic arousal, and behavioral arousal may each be considered as complex forms of arousal independently. Furthermore, as mentioned above, Lacey has demonstrated that different forms of arousal can be separated functionally and anatomically by experimental manipulations and that many variables, including age, may affect the configurations of arousal responses both between and within these forms.

Lacey's position highlights the importance of attending to both CNS and ANS measures in attempting to account for age-related changes in behavior. In recent years some consideration has been given to complex patterning of CNS and ANS arousal responses in the elderly. These efforts have resulted in considerable controversy regarding the implications of physiological arousal for age changes in behavior.

Research Supporting the Underarousal Hypothesis

Conditioning paradigms which involve shock as the unconditioned stimulus (US) and galvanic skin response (GSR) as the major physiological dependent variable have supported the underarousal notion. Botwinick and Kornetsky (1959, 1960) reported that older subjects showed less GSR responsivity in the habituation as well as in the conditioning period, and that they extinguished the conditioned response more rapidly than younger subjects. The investigators concluded that autonomic reactivity was significantly decreased in the elderly. Similar results have been reported by Shmavonian and his co-workers. A series of studies used a paradigm in which age and sex effects were investigated. Looking at the electrodermal response, young male and female subjects showed the best discriminated conditioning followed by aged females and then aged males (Shmavonian, Miller, and Cohen, 1968). When considering the cardiovascular system these workers (Shmavonian, Miller, and Cohen, 1970) observed that young males exhibited discriminant cardio-deceleration. Young females, on the other hand, did not show conditioning, but were highly reactive. Aged males and females were poor reactors and failed to demonstrate conditioning. Shmavonian, Yarmat, and Cohen (1965) had observed decreased GSR and vasomotor reactivity in the elderly during conditioning, but noted greater activation in the EEG. There was also less responsivity in urinary catecholamines for the elderly. A slight decrease in noradrenaline and a significant increase in adrenaline levels was observed for the young while the elderly showed a decline in both. Initial levels of both were higher in the elderly in the pre-measures and remained so in the post-conditioning measures. This suggests that the elderly were more aroused than the young initially and specific reactivity to the conditioning may thus have been less.

Studies of autonomic reactivity in the elderly during vigilance tasks have also supported the underarousal hypothesis. For example, Surwillo (1966b) reported age differences in GSR, heart rate, and skin temperature during a study in which the subjects monitored a Mackworth clock over an extended period. Specifically, skin temperature changed significantly over time with the elderly showing a rise in skin temperature and the young a decline. Using a similar paradigm, other studies have shown that latency of GSR to critical stimuli is longer in the aged (Surwillo and Quilter, 1965a) and the frequency of GSR responses is less (Surwillo and Quilter, 1965b).

There are few studies showing a relationship between the level of ANS function and performance. Autonomic arousal as reflected in the GSR is positively correlated with vigilance behavior (Surwillo and Quilter, 1965b) and

with immediate memory (Shmavonian and Busse, 1963). The latter authors presented emotionally charged words to both young and old subjects. Older subjects remembered more of the words associated with marked GSRs. Although the overall GSR was less for the old than for the young, many specific responses to words were larger in an absolute sense. This suggests that highly meaningful material minimized age differences in autonomic function.

Research Supporting the Overarousal Hypothesis

For the most part, the overarousal position is based on a biochemical measure related to sympathetic function. Bogdonoff, Estes, Friedberg, and Klein (1961) have shown that free fatty acid (FFA) mobilization can be used as an indicator of autonomic nervous system activity. Studies with this measure have shown that during serial learning and stressful monitoring tasks emphasizing information overload the elderly had initially higher FFA levels, showed an increase comparable to the young during the tasks, and remained at a significantly higher level for at least one hour following the task (Powell, Eisdorfer, and Bogdonoff, 1964; Troyer, Eisdorfer, Wilkie, and Bogdonoff, 1966). From these data Eisdorfer (1967) suggested that much of the performance decrement seen in learning studies may be attributed to autonomic overarousal.

Discrepancies between the under- and overarousal positions appear on the surface to pose difficulties for integration and interpretation, but the large methodological differences between the studies make comparisons between the results almost impossible. First of all, ANS measures used to support the underarousal notions rely heavily on traditional bioelectric measures (GSR, heart rate, vasoconstriction), whereas the overarousal portion is based on a biochemical measure which is related to sympathetic function. One argument might be that ANS end organs are changed with age such that they no longer reflect adequately the arousal state within the CNS and ANS. Another point is that FFA mobilization may have different significance as an ANS measure due to changes in lipid utilization or production with age. Behavioral measures have also been decidedly different. The underarousal camp has used electric shock in conditioning paradigms or has required subjects to perform the boring task of monitoring a Mackworth clock to detect an occasional double movement of the hand. Neither task presents cognitive stress to the subjects, while the overarousal group has chosen tasks which provide a high level of cognitive stress—perhaps especially significant in the case of the elderly. Considering Lacey's position that the experimental task and behavioral situation are critical as determinants of specific patterns of ANS response, it is clear that greater commonality of methodology and measuring techniques is required before any reasonable resolution of the aging-arousal-performance controversy can be realized. It would seem reasonable, therefore, to monitor both bioelectric and biochemical measures of physiological arousal while subjects are undergoing varied cognitive and noncognitive stresses.

A second approach that may prove fruitful in dealing with this whole question of arousal would be to experimentally manipulate the degree of arousal while observing the effects on behavioral and physiological functioning. This technique has been used with mixed results. Jeffrey (1969) attempted to test the hypothesis of decreased activation in contrast to the neural noise hypothesis by having elderly subjects perform a complex RT task under varying intensities of auditory white noise and increased muscular tension, but neither hypothesis could be supported.

Eisdorfer, Nowlin, and Wilkie (1970) tested the hypothesis that excessive feedback from the ANS during stress negatively affects verbal learning in older persons, by giving an adrenergic blocking agent to one group of older subjects and a placebo to another. They reported fewer errors on a serial learning task, lower free fatty acid levels and slower heart rates in the drugged group. They concluded that learning deficits in the elderly are more likely a result of high "autonomic end organ arousal."

Froehling (1974) attempted to confirm these results using a within-subjects design. Twelve elderly subjects learned three lists of paired-associate words of equal difficulty under three conditions: administration of propranolol (6 mg), saline (6 mg) and no injection. Word lists and conditions were counterbalanced in a greco-latin square design. She reported significant changes in heart rate and FFA levels during the treatment condition when compared with the saline and control condition, but there were no differences between conditions in learning performance or in the GSR. The results of this study do not support the hypothesis that excessive end organ activity is associated with learning decrement in the elderly. However, a direct comparison between her work and that of Eisdorfer et al. cannot be made because of a difference in drug dosage.

Central-Autonomic Nervous System Interactions

Arousal in the aging nervous system can also be viewed from the perspective of the CNS as well as in terms of CNS-ANS interactions. Most CNS arousal measures in the aged have supported the hypothesis that the elderly are underaroused (Obrist, 1965; Thompson and Wilson, 1966). Surwillo (1966a) also reported that alpha blocking latency increases with age, indicating an age change in the direction of decreased CNS reactivity. The well-documented slowing of the EEG alpha rhythm has also been interpreted in terms of underarousal. It should be kept in mind, however, that most of these data come from experiments where the subject is not actively engaged in performing a task, but merely is a passive recipient of controlled stimulation.

With regard to CNS activity, a measure which has received attention as a method of assessing electrocortical responsivity is the averaged evoked potential (AEP), discussed earlier. As indicated, amplitude, latency and morphology have been found to show marked individual differences (Creutzfeldt and Kuhnt, 1967). Within subjects the AEPs are sensitive to factors such as attention and/or activation (Haider, Spong, and Lindsley, 1964; Spong, Haider, and Lindsley, 1965; Satterfield, 1965; Karlin, 1970). Typically, selective attention or a prior highly aroused state yields enhanced amplitude and shortened latency of AEP (Karlin, 1970). Only a few studies have investigated relationships between simple RT and AEP, but there is general agreement that fast RT is associated with larger amplitude AEP excursions and shorter latencies (Dustman and Beck, 1965; Morrell and Morrell, 1966).

The sensitivity of the AEP to behavioral variables such as attention, arousal and speed of behavior makes it a promising tool for investigating age relationships. The consistent trends reported in the few age studies of the AEP are of particular interest in that the amplitude of late components following the stimulus tends to decrease with age (Dustman and Beck, 1969; Lüders, 1970; Schenkenberg, 1970). These changes become evident with the onset of senescence (Lüders, 1970; Schenkenberg, 1970). Schenkenberg (1970) suggests that the decrease in late components amplitude is due to a diminished effectiveness of the reticular activating system. Marsh and Thompson (1973) found supporting evidence for this interpretation in that age differences in the amplitude of late components (200–400 msec) decreased when the subjects were in a highly alerted state.

In a recent review, Thompson and Marsh (1973) concluded that age differences in CNS reactivity may be minimal when subjects are actively processing information, but marked age differences in ANS reactivity may be apparent. This led them to speculate that a lack of congruence between CNS and ANS functioning may be associated with behavioral impairment in the elderly. Support for this position, from the same laboratory, comes from the finding that no significant relationship between an ANS measure (heart rate change) and a CNS measure (amplitude of CNV) was found in an elderly group performing an RT task, but a significant relationship was observed in a young sample (Thompson and Nowlin, 1973). Also apparent in the young group but not in the old were significant correlations between speed of response and physiological measures. Comparison of the two groups suggested no age differences in the cortical measure, but the elderly were significantly less reactive at the autonomic level. A significant finding was reported by

Shmavonian, Yarmat, and Cohen (1965) in a conditioning experiment: EEG activation was greater in old subjects, but ANS measures (GSR, vasoconstriction) were considerably less reactive for the old than the young. These comparable discrepancies between young and old subjects in two different sets of measures employed in different experimental paradigms offer support to the notion that a lack of congruence between CNS and ANS functioning may occur in the elderly, and suggest that continued investigations of CNS-ANS interactions as a possible correlate of impairment in the elderly is important.

A likely framework within which one could pursue this problem embodies the preparatory set conceptualization as reflected in the CNV paradigm used by Loveless and Sanford (1974a). These authors argued that older people have difficulty in initiating a preparatory set at an appropriate time. This was based on the absence of a CNV in long preparatory intervals. The question could be raised whether differences in autonomic responsivity may also be related to the age changes in behavior observed. It is well-known that heart rate decreases during the foreperiod of a reaction time task and that these changes are related to the CNV. Moreover, heart rate deceleration is related to response speed in young subjects (Connor and Lang, 1969; Lacey and Lacey, 1970), but not in old ones (Thompson and Nowlin, 1973). Discrepancies between young and old in terms of the interrelationships among these measures raises the question whether sensitive alignment of CNS-ANS activity may be a significant factor in preparatory set. Inclusion of autonomic measures in the paradigms similar to that of Loveless and Sanford would provide data addressed to this question. Manipulation of preparatory set by training should also provide data appropriate to this question. If elderly subjects can be trained to maximize preparatory set, then one would expect to see increased relationships between CNS and ANS measures. Simultaneous monitoring of bioelectric and biochemical measures of autonomic activity under varied conditions of cognitive and emotional stress may also enable us to reconcile the differences in physiological arousal reported in the literature. The addition of electrocortical measures would address the question of CNS-ANS interrelationships and their potential significance for cognitive deficits observed in the elderly.

Few studies have been completed where CNS-ANS comparisons have been made. The recent work of Froehling (1974) provides data indirectly related to the general line of thinking reflected above. She recorded CNV and heart rate during a traditional reaction time task with a 4-sec forewarning period. In contrast to Thompson and Nowlin (1973) and Morris and Thompson (1969), she found a significant relationship between speed of response and magnitude of heart rate change among old subjects. There was also a significant relationship between the amplitude of the CNV and RT. Discrepant results of these studies may be due to differences in health status and age. In the Morris and Thompson study, age ranged from 66 to 89, with a mean age of 73.7. In the Thompson and Nowlin investigation, the age ranged from 65 to 85. The age range in the Froehling study was 64 to 77, and they were carefully screened for health related problems. Froehling's sample may represent a biologically younger group than previous experiments which again emphasizes health status as a contributor to optimal functioning in the elderly.

The contribution of CNS-ANS interactions to reaction time remains equivocal. In the Thompson and Nowlin (1973) study, between subjects correlations of CNV and heart rate deceleration during the preparatory interval were associated with reaction time. However, in the Froehling study (1974) both between and within subjects multiple regressions indicated that substantially more of the variance of reaction time could be accounted for by CNV alone. Heart rate deceleration (HRD) and CNV X HRD showed significantly less association with reaction time than the CNV.

Following Thompson and Marsh's (1973) suggestion that correspondence between these two systems may become more crucial as one becomes older, Froehling divided her subjects according to age for internal analysis. No differences in the two age groups was found in the congruity between the two systems or their relationship to reaction time. Since all the subjects in her study were above-average in physical health, and demonstrated high levels of performance, she offered the tentative explanation that in the case of biologically younger individuals the congruity between ANS and CNS systems is less critical, whereas with older or less well-integrated persons a sensitive alignment between the two systems may be a prerequisite for optimal functioning (Froehling, 1974, pp. 122-123). It would appear that a more direct investigative effort of this notion is still in order.

CONCLUSIONS AND COMMENTS

A large number of studies looking for changes in the EEG with age indicates the zeal with which that area has been examined. If more studies are conducted in that area they would do well to cease confining themselves to the usual frequency bands. If the frequencies in the EEG are seen to slow with age, it only confuses the issue to show that alpha activity decreases while theta activity increases. Such changes would be far better described by showing the change in the entire EEG spectrum. Such descriptions would be free of the clinical connotations usually associated with the frequency band analysis.

Even such studies may be of dubious value considering the number of EEG–age studies already in the literature. Confining future such studies to longitudinal studies might be fruitful for such studies may show different patterns of change across age than the cross-sectional studies reported here. Even from the paucity of data thus far accumulated, some subjects (as mentioned earlier) have shown an increase in alpha frequency instead of the expected decrease. If cross-sectional EEG studies are to be conducted, data such as sleep EEG, brain blood flow or brain histology must be gathered so that explanatory mechanisms can begin to emerge while pure descriptive studies diminish.

As a part of the assembly of explanatory mechanisms, further studies gathering electrocortical data while the subject is engaged in specific tasks must become a more commonly used research approach. The judicious choice of tasks can begin to dissect those portions of the aged person's faculties that are undergoing change so as to allow search for the appropriate brain areas. Also, of course, the use of tasks allows at least partial control of the subject's mental state, thus avoiding the gathering of data from different subjects in widely different states. In line with Bondareff's suggestions (Chapter 8 in this volume), perhaps careful coordination between neuropsychological and psychophysiological approaches can explore brain mechanisms that neither approach could achieve on its own, especially in the area of cognitive abilities of the aging brain.

In the search for mechanisms underlying changes in function, hypotheses concerned with changing blood flow to the brain seem especially powerful. Coordinating such studies with later histological analyses for changed brain structure are sorely needed. For the present, these studies would seem to focus on human material since a proper animal model has not been presented. However, the blood flow and histological questions could likely be explored separately in an animal model.

The recent rise in popularity of the biofeedback technique may hold potential in the exploration of central and peripheral mechanisms undergoing change with age. In fact, the possibility exists that biofeedback may be useful not only for research but also for compensating for some of the deficits in performance that are known to occur with increasing age. This technique may also be of value in helping to unravel some of the relationships between the autonomic and central nervous systems. Altering some of the responses of the heart or arterial system to task stresses, for instance, may allow concomitant observation of brain responses to see if they are tied to the cardiovascular responses or to the task stresses directly.

Certainly, with the growth of knowledge of hormonal influences directly on the brain, the interaction of one of the ANS's principal output modes—glandular secretion, will have to be explored for its effects on the CNS. Since the output of hormones are known to alter greatly with age these changes and their effect on CNS function should be explored vigorously

with both pharmacological and psychophysiological techniques. Frolkis (Chapter 9 in this volume) has reported changes with age throughout the ANS which lead to "shifts in reflectory regulation." These shifts, he feels, are intricately implicated in age-related behavioral changes by virtue of disruptions in regulatory mechanisms. Such findings further emphasize the need for continued exploration of age changes in endocrine function and their impact on the contribution of CNS-ANS interrelationships to behavioral changes in the elderly.

REFERENCES

Agnew, H. W., Webb, W. B., and Williams, R. L. 1967. Sleep patterns in late middle age males: An EEG Study. *Electroencephalo. Clin. Neurophysiol.*, **23**, 168–171.

Andermann, K., and Stoller, A. 1961. EEG patterns in hospitalized and non-hospitalized aged. *Electroencephalo. Clin. Neurophysiol.*, **13**, 319.

Anders, T. R., Fozard, J. L., and Lillyquist, T. D. 1972. Effects of age upon retrieval from short-term memory. *Developmental Psychology*, **6**, 214–217.

Andersen, P., and Andersson, A. 1968. *Physiological Basis of the Alpha Rhythm*. New York: Appleton-Century-Crofts.

Barnes, R. H., Busse, E. W., and Friedman, E. L. 1956. The psychological function of aged individuals with normal and abnormal electroencephalograms. II. A study of hospitalized individuals. *J. Nervous Mental Disease*, **124**, 585–593.

Bauer, H. G., Apfeldorf, M., and Hoch, H. 1966. Relationship between alpha frequency, age, disease and intelligence. *In*, *Proceedings of the Seventh International Congress of Gerontology*, Vol 2, pp. 341–349. Vienna: Wien Medizinische Akademie.

Bergamini, L., Bergamasco, B., Mombelli, A. M., and Gandiglio, G. 1965. Visual evoked potentials in subjects with congenital aniridia. *Electroencephalo. Clin. Neurophysiol.*, **19**, 394–397.

Berger, H. 1968. On the electroencephalogram of man: Twelfth report. *Electroencephalo. Clin. Neurophysiol.*, Suppl. **28**, 267–287.

Birren, J. E. 1965. Age changes in speed of behavior: Its central nature and physiological correlates. *In*, A. T. Welford and J. E. Birren (eds.), *Behavior, Aging, and the Nervous System*, pp. 191–216. Springfield, Illinois: Charles C. Thomas.

Birren, J. E., Butler, R. N., Greenhouse, S. W., Sokoloff, L., and Yarrow, M. R. 1963. Interdisciplinary relationships: Interrelations of physiological, psychological and psychiatric findings in healthy elderly men. *In*, *Human Aging: A Biological and Behavioral Study* (USPHS Publ. No. 986), pp. 283–305. Washington, D.C.: U.S. Government Printing Office.

Bogdonoff, M. D., Estes, E. H., Jr., Friedberg, S. J., and Klein, R. F. 1961. Fat mobilization in man. *Annals of Internal Medicine*, 55, 328-338.

Boswell, R. S. 1958. An investigation of the phase of the alpha rhythm in relation to visual recognition. Unpublished doctoral dissertation. University of Utah.

Botwinick, J., and Kornetsky, C. 1959. Age differences in the frequency of the GSR during a conditioning experiment. *J. Gerontol.*, 14, 503.

Botwinick, J., and Kornetsky, C. 1960. Age differences in the acquisition and extinction of GSR. *J. Gerontol.*, 15, 83-84.

Brazier, M. A. B., and Finesinger, J. E. 1944. Characteristics of the normal electroencephalogram. I. A study of the occipital cortical potentials in 500 normal adults. *J. Clin. Invest.*, 23, 303-311.

Broverman, D. M., Klaiber, E. L., Kobayashi, Y., and Vogel, W. 1968. Roles of activation and inhibition in sex differences in cognitive abilities. *Psych. Rev.*, 75, 23-50.

Busse, E. W., Barnes, R. H., Friedman, E. L., and Kelty, E. J. 1956. Psychological functioning of aged individuals with normal and abnormal electroencephalograms. I. A study of non-hospitalized community volunteers. *J. Nervous Mental Disease*, 124, 135-141.

Busse, E. W., Barnes, R. H., Silverman, A. J., Shy, G. M., Thaler, M., and Frost, L. L. 1954. Studies of the process of aging: Factors that influence the psyche of elderly persons. *Am. J. Psychiat.*, 110, 897-903.

Busse, E. W., and Obrist, W. D. 1963. Significance of focal electroencephalographic changes in the elderly. *Postgrad. Med.*, 34, 179-182.

Busse, E. W., and Wang, H. S. 1971. The multiple factors contributing to dementia in old age. *In, Proceedings of the Fifth World Congress of Psychiatry*, 274, 818-825. *Amsterdam: Excerpta Medica.*

Chapman, R. N., and Bragdon, H. R. 1964. Evoked responses to numerical and non-numerical visual stimuli while problem solving. *Nature*, 203, 1155-1157.

Connor, W., and Lang, P. J. 1969. Cortical slow move and cardiac responses in stimulus orientation and reaction time condition. *J. Exp. Psychology.*, 82, 310-320.

Creutzfeldt, O. D., and Kuhnt, U. 1967. The visual evoked potential: Physiological, developmental and clinical aspects. *Electroencephalo. Clin. Neurophysiol.*, *Suppl.* 26, 29-41.

Dastur, D. K., Lane, M. H., Hansen, D. B., Kety, S. S., Butler, R. N., Perlin, S., and Sokoloff, L. 1963. Effects of aging on cerebral circulation and metabolism in man. *In, Human Aging: A Biological and Behavioral Study*, (USPHS Publ. No. 986), pp. 57-76. Washington D.C.: U.S. Government Printing Office.

Diamond, S. P. 1964. Input-output relations. *Ann. N.Y. Acad. Sci.*, 112, 160-171.

Dilman, V. M. 1971. Age-associated elevation of hypothalamic threshold to feedback control, and its role in development, aging, and disease. *Lancet*, 1, 1211-1219.

Donchin, E., Tueting, P., Ritter, W., Kutas, M., and Heffley, E. 1976. On the independence of the CNV and the P300 components of the human averaged evoked response. *In,* J. E. Desmedt (ed.), *International Symposium on Cerebral Evoked Potentials in Man.* In press.

Drachman, D. A., and Hughes, J. R. 1971. Memory and the hippocampal complexes: III. Aging and temporal EEG abnormalities. *Neurology*, 21, 1-14.

Duffy, E. 1962. *Activation and Behavior.* New York: John Wiley.

Dustman, R. E., and Beck, E. C. 1965. Phase of alpha brain waves, reaction time and visually evoked potentials. *Electroencephalo. Clin. Neurophysiol.*, 18, 433-440.

Dustman, R. E., and Beck, E. C. 1966. Visually evoked potentials: Amplitude changes with age. *Science*, 151, 1013-1015.

Dustman, R. E., and Beck, E. C. 1969. The effects of maturation and aging on the wave form of visually evoked potentials. *Electroencephalo. Clin. Neurophysiol.*, 26, 2-11.

Eisdorfer, C. 1967. New dimensions and a tentative theory, *Gerontologist.* 7, 14-18.

Eisdorfer, C., Busse, E. W., and Cohen, L. D. 1959. The WAIS performance of an aged sample: The relationship between verbal and performance IQs. *J. Gerontol.*, 14, 197-201.

Eisdorfer, C., Nowlin, J. B., and Wilkie, F. 1970. Improvement of learning in the aged by modification of autonomic nervous system activity. *Science*, 170, 1327-1329.

Elul, R. 1972. The genesis of the EEG. *Intern. Rev. Neurobiol.*, 15, 227-272.

Feinberg, I. 1969. Effects of age on human sleep patterns. *In,* A. Kales (ed.), *Sleep Physiology and Pathology*, pp. 39-52. Philadelphia: Lippincott.

Feinberg, I. 1974. Changes in sleep cycle patterns with age. *J. Psychiat. Res.*, 10, 283-306.

Feinberg, I., Braun, M., and Shulman, E. 1969. EEG sleep patterns in mental retardation. *Electroencephalo. Clin. Neurophysiol.*, 27, 128-141.

Feinberg, I., and Carlson, V. R. 1968. Sleep variables as a function of age in man. *Arch. Gen. Psychiat.*, 18, 239-250.

Feinberg, I., Koresko, R. L., and Heller, N. 1967. EEG sleep patterns as a function of normal and pathological aging in man. *J. Psychiat. Res.*, 5, 107-144.

Feinberg, I., Lane, M. H., and Lassen, N. A. 1960. Senile dementia and cerebral oxygen uptake measured on the right and left sides. *Nature*, 188, 962-964.

Finch, C. E. 1969. *Cellular Activities During Aging* *Mammals.* New York: MSS Information Corporation

Fox, C., and Birren, J. E. 1950. The differentia decline of subtest scores of the Wechsler-Bellevue

Intelligence Scale in 60-69 year old individuals. *Journal of Genetic Psychology*, 77, 313-317.

Frantzen, E., and Lennox-Buchthal, M. 1961. Correlation of clinical electroencephalographic and arteriographic findings in patients with cerebral vascular accident. *Acta Psychiat. Scand.*, 36 (Suppl. 150), 133-134.

Frey, T. S., and Sjögren, H. 1959. The electroencephalogram in elderly persons suffering from neuropsychiatric disorders. *Acta Psychiat. Scand.*, 34, 438-450.

Friedlander, W. J. 1958. Electroencephalographic alpha rate in adults as a function of age. *Geriatrics*, 13, 29-31.

Froehling, S. D. 1974. Effects of propranolol on behavior and physiological measures in elderly males. Unpublished doctoral dissertation. University of Miami, Florida.

Gaches, J. 1960. Etude statistique sur les traces "alpha largement developpe" en fonction de l'âge. *Presse Médicale*, 68, 1620-1622.

Gastaut, H., and Meyer, J. S. (eds.). 1961. *Cerebral Anoxia and the Electroencephalogram*. Springfield, Illinois: Charles C. Thomas.

Gerard, R. W. 1959. Aging and organization. *In*, J. E. Birren (ed.), *Handbook of Aging and the Individual*, pp. 264-278. Chicago: University of Chicago Press.

Gibbs, F. A., and Gibbs, E. L. 1950. *Atlas of Electroencephalography*. *Vol. 1. Methodology and Controls*. Cambridge, Massachusetts: Addison-Wesley.

Greenblatt, M. 1944. Age and electroencephalographic abnormality in neuro-psychiatric patients: A study of 1593 cases. *Am. J. Psychiat.*, 101, 82-90.

Haider, M., Spong, P., and Lindsley, D. B. 1964. Attention, vigilance, and cortical evoked potentials in humans. *Science*, 145, 180-182.

Harvald, B. 1958. EEG in old age. *Acta Psychiat. Scand.*, 33, 193-196.

Hillyard, S. A., Squires, K. C., Bauer, J. W., and Lindsay, P. H. 1971. Evoked potential correlates of auditory signal detection. *Science*, 172, 1357-1360.

Hoagland, H. 1954. Studies of brain metabolism and electrical activity in relation to adrenocortical physiology. *Recent Progress in Hormone Research*, 10, 29-63.

Hoch, P. H., and Kubis, J. 1941. Electroencephalographic studies in organic psychoses. *Am. J. Psychiat.*, 98, 404-408.

Hughes, J. R. 1960. A statistical analysis on the location of EEG abnormalities. *Electroencephalo. Clin. Neurophysiol.*, 12, 905-909.

Ingvar, D. H., and Gustafson, L. 1970. Regional cerebral blood flow in organic dementia with early onset. *Acta Neurol. Scand.*, 46 (Suppl. 43), 42-73.

Jeffrey, D. W. 1969. Age differences in serial reaction time as a function of stimulus complexity under conditions of noise and muscular tension. Unpublished doctoral dissertation. University of Southern California.

Kahn, E. 1970. Age related changes in sleep characteristics. *In*, E. Hartmann (ed.), *Sleep and Dreaming*, pp. 25-29. Boston: Little, Brown.

Kahn, E., and Fisher, C. 1969. The sleep characteristics of the normal aged male. *J. Nervous Mental Disease*, 148, 477-494.

Kahn, E., Fisher, C., and Lieberman, L. 1970. The sleep characteristics of the human aged female. *Comprehensive Psychiatry*, 11, 274-278.

Kales, A., Wilson, T., Kales, J. D., Jacobson, A., Paulson, M. J., Kollar, E., and Walter, R. D. 1967. Measurements of all-night sleep in normal elderly persons: Effects of aging. *J. Am. Geriat. Soc.*, 15, 405-414.

Karlin, L. 1970. Cognition, preparation, and sensory-evoked potentials. *Psych. Bull.*, 73, 122-136.

Klee, A. 1964. The relationship between clinical evaluation of mental deterioration, psychological test results and the cerebral metabolic rate of oxygen. *Acta Neurol. Scand.*, 40, 337-345.

Klinke, R., Fruhstorfer, H., and Finkenzeller, P. 1968. Evoked responses as a function of external and stored information. *Electroencephalo. Clin. Neurophysiol.*, 25, 119-122.

Kooi, K. A., Guvener, A. M., Tupper, C. J., and Bagchi, B. K. 1964. Electroencephalographic patterns of the temporal region in normal adults. *Neurology*, 14, 1029-1035.

Lacey, J. I. 1959. Psychophysiological approaches to the evaluation of psychotherapeutic process and outcome. *In*, E. A. Rubenstein and M. B. Parloff (eds.), *Research in Psychotherapy*, pp. 160-208. Washington, D.C.: American Psychological Association.

Lacey, J. I. 1967. Somatic response patterning and stress: Some revisions of activation theory. *In*, M. H. Appley and R. Trumbull (eds.), *Psychological Stress: Issues and Research*, pp. 14-42. New York: Appleton-Century-Crofts.

Lacey, J. I., Kagan, J., Lacey, B., and Moss, H. A. 1963. The visceral level: Situational determinants and behavioral correlates of autonomic response patterns. *In*, P. H. Knapp (ed.), *Expression of the Emotions in Man*, pp. 161-196. New York: International Universities Press.

Lacey, J. I., and Lacey, B. 1970. Some autonomic-central nervous system inter-relationships. *In*, P. Black (ed), *Physiological Correlates of Emotion*, pp. 205-227. New York: Academic Press.

LaFratta, C. W. 1972. Relation of age to amplitude of evoked antidromic sensory nerve potentials. *Arch. Phys. Med. Rehabil.*, 53, 388-389.

Lassen, N. A. 1966. Cerebral blood flow and metabolism in health and disease. *In*, C. H. Millikan (ed.), *Cerebrovascular Disease* (Research Publications Association for Research in Nervous and Mental Disease, 41, 205-215. Baltimore: Williams & Wilkins.

Lassen, N. A., Munck, O., and Tottey, E. R. 1957. Mental function and cerebral oxygen consumption in organic dementia. *Arch. Neurol. Psychiat.*, 77, 126-133.

Liberson, W. T. 1944. Functional electroencephalography in mental disorders. *Diseases of the Nervous System*, 5, 357–364.

Liberson, W. T., and Seguin, C. A. 1945. Brain waves and clinical features in arteriosclerotic and senile mental patients. *Psychosomat. Med.*, 7, 30–35.

Lindsley, D. B. 1960. Attention, consciousness, sleep and wakefulness. *In*, J. Field, H. W. Magoun and V. E. Hall (eds.), *Handbook of Physiology, Sec. 1: Neurophysiology, Vol. 3*, pp. 1553–1593. Washington, D.C.: American Physiology Society.

Lindsley, D. B., Schreiner, L. H., Knowles, W. B., and Magoun, H. W. 1950. Behavioral and EEG changes following chronic brainstem lesions in the cat. *Electroencephalo. Clin. Neurophysiol.*, 2, 483–498.

Loveless, N. E., and Sanford, A. J. 1974a. Effects of age on the contingent negative variation and preparatory set in a reaction-time task. *J. Gerontol.*, 29, 52–63.

Loveless, N. E., and Sanford, A. J. 1974b. Slow potential correlates of preparatory set. *Biol. Psych.*, 1, 303–314.

Luce, R. A., Jr., and Rothschild, D. 1953. The correlation of electroencephographic and clinical observations in psychiatric patients over 65. *J. Gerontol.*, 8, 167–172.

Lüders, H. 1970. The effects of aging on the wave form of the somatosensory cortical evoked potential. *Electroencephalo. Clin. Neurophysiol.*, 29, 450–460.

Marsh, G. R. 1974. Evoked potential correlates of information processing across the life span. Unpublished manuscript read at the 82nd Annual Meeting of the American Psychological Association, New Orleans.

Marsh, G. R., and Thompson, L. W. 1972. Age differences in evoked potentials during an auditory discrimination task. *Gerontologist*, 12, 44.

Marsh, G. R., and Thompson, L. W. 1973. Effects of age on the contingent negative variation in a pitch discrimination task. *J. Gerontol.*, 28, 56–62.

McAdam, W., and Robinson, R. A. 1956. Senile intellectual deterioration and the electroencephalogram: A quantitative correlation. *J. Mental Sci.*, 102, 819–825.

McAdam, W., and Robinson, R. A. 1962. Diagnostic and prognostic value of the electroencephalogram in geriatric psychiatry. *In*, H. T. Blumenthal (ed.), *Medical and Clinical Aspects of Aging, Vol. 4*. New York: Columbia University Press.

Mendels, J., and Hawkins, D. R. 1968. Sleep and depression: Further considerations. *Arch. Gen. Psychiat.* 19, 445–542.

Milner, B. 1967. Brain mechanisms suggested by studies of temporal lobes. *In*, F. L. Darley (ed.), *Brain Mechanisms Underlying Speech and Language*, pp. 122–145. New York: Grune & Stratton.

Morrell, L. K., and Morrell, F. 1966. Evoked potentials and reaction times: A study of intra-individual variability. *Electroencephalo. Clin. Neurophysiol*, 20, 567–575.

Morris, J. D., and Thompson, L. W. 1969. Heart rate changes in a reaction time experiment with young and aged subjects. *J. Gerontol.*, 24, 269–275.

Moruzzi, G. and Magoun, H. W. 1949. Brainstem reticular formation and activation of the EEG. *Electroencephalo. Clin. Neurophysiol.*, 1, 455–473.

Mundy-Castle, A. C. 1951. Theta and beta rhythm in the electroencephalograms of normal adults. *Electroencephalo. Clin. Neurophysiol.*, 3, 477–486.

Mundy-Castle, A. C. 1962. Central excitability in the aged. *In*, H. T. Blumenthal (ed.), *Medical and Clinical Aspects of Aging*, pp. 575–595. New York: Columbia University Press.

Mundy-Castle, A. C., Hurst, L. A., Beerstecher, D. M., and Prinsloo, T. 1954. The electroencephalogram in the senile psychoses. *Elecgroencephalo. Clin. Neurophysiol.*, 6, 245–252.

Norris, A. H., Shock, N. W., and Wagman, I. H. 1953. Age changes in the maximum conduction velocity of motor fibers of human ulnar nerves. *J. Appl. Physiol.*, 5, 589–593.

Novack, P., Shenkin, H. A., Bortin, L., Goluboff, B., and Soffe, A. M. 1953. The effects of carbon dioxide inhalation upon the cerebral blood flow and cerebral oxygen consumption in vascular disease. *J. Clin. Invest.*, 32, 696–702.

Obrist, W. D. 1954. The electroencephalogram of normal aged adults. *Electroencephalo. Clin. Neurophysiol.*, 6, 235–244.

Obrist, W. D. 1963. The electroencephalogram of healthy aged males. *In*, J. E. Birren, R. N. Butler, S. W. Greenhouse, L. Sokoloff and M. R. Yarrow (eds.), *Human Aging I: A Biological and Behavioral Study* (USPHS Publ. No. 986), pp. 79–93. Washington, D.C.: U.S. Government Printing Office.

Obrist, W. D. 1964. Cerebral ischemia and the senescent electroencephalogram. *In*, E. Simonson and T. H. McGavack (eds.), *Cerebral Ischemia*, pp. 71–98. Springfield, Illinois: Charles C. Thomas.

Obrist, W. D. 1965. Electroencephalographic approach to age changes in response speed. *In*, A. T. Welford and J. E. Birren (eds.), *Behavior, Aging and the Nervous System*, pp. 259–271. Springfield, Illinois: Charles C. Thomas.

Obrist, W. D. 1971. EEG and intellectual function in the aged. Unpublished manuscript read at the 25th Annual Meeting of the American EEG Society, Minneapolis.

Obrist, W. D. 1972. Cerebral physiology of the aged: Influence of circulatory disorder. *In*, C. M. Gaitz (ed.), *Aging and the Brain*, pp. 117–133. New York: Plenum Press.

Obrist, W. D. 1975. Cerebral physiology of the aged. Relation to psychological function. *In*, N. R. Burch and H. L. Altshuler (eds.), *Behavior and Brain Electrical Activity*, pp. 421–430. New York: Plenum Press.

Obrist, W. D., and Bissell, L. F. 1955. The electroencephalogram of aged patients with cardiac and cerebral vascular disease. *J. Gerontol.*, 10, 315–330.

Obrist, W. D., and Busse, E. W. 1965. The electroencephalogram in old age. *In*, W. P. Wilson (ed.), *Application of Electroencephalography in Psychiatry*, pp. 185–205. Durham, North Carolina: Duke University Press.

Obrist, W. D., Busse, E. W., Eisdorfer, C., and Kleemeier, R. W. 1962. Relation of the electroencephalogram to intellectual function in senescence. *J. Gerontol.*, 17, 197–206.

Obrist, W. D., Busse, E. W., and Henry C. E. 1961. Relation of electroencephalogram to blood pressure in elderly persons. *Neurology*, 11, 151–158.

Obrist, W. D., Chivian, E., Cronquist, S., and Ingvar, D. H. 1970. Regional cerebral blood flow in senile and presenile dementia. *Neurology*, 20, 315–322.

Obrist, W. D., and Henry, D. E. 1958a. Electroencephalographic findings in aged psychiatric patients. *J. Nervous Mental Disease*, 126, 254–267.

Obrist, W. D., and Henry, C. E. 1958b. Electroencephalographic frequency analysis of aged psychiatric patients. *Electroencephalo. Clin. Neurophysiol.*, 10, 621–632.

Obrist, W. D., Sokoloff, L., Lassen, N. A., Lane, M. H., Butler, R. N., and Feinberg, I. 1963. Relation of EEG to cerebral blood flow and metabolism in old age. *Electroencephalo. Clin. Neurophysiol.*, 15, 610–619.

Otomo, E. 1966. Electroencephalography in old age: Dominant alpha pattern. *Electroencephalo. Clin. Neurophysiol.*, 21, 489–491.

Pampiglione, G., and Post, F. 1958. The value of electroencephalographic examinations in psychiatric disorders of old age. *Geriatrics*, 13, 725–732.

Perry, W. P., Jr., and Childers, D. G. 1969. *The Human Visual Evoked Response*. Springfield, Illinois: Charles C. Thomas.

Prinz, P. N., Marsh, G. R., and Thompson, L. W. 1974. Normal human aging: Relationship of sleep variables to longitudinal changes in intellectual function. *Gerontologist*, 14, 41.

Poon, L. W., Thompson, L. W., Williams, R. B., Jr., and Marsh, G. R. 1974. Changes of antero-posterior distribution of CNV and late positive component as a function of information processing demands. *Psychophysiology*, 11, 660–673.

Powell, A. H., Eisdorfer, C., and Bogdonoff, M. D. 1964. Physiologic response patterns observed in a learning task. *Arch. Gen. Psychiat.*, 10, 192–195.

Regan, D. 1972. *Evoked Potentials in Psychology, Sensory Physiology, and Clinical Medicine*. London: Chapman & Hall.

Reitan, R. M. 1955. The distribution according to age of a psychologic measure dependent upon organic brain functions. *J. Gerontol.*, 10, 338–340.

Roffwarg, H. P., Munzio, J. N., and Dement, W. C. 1966. Ontogenic development of the human sleep-dream cycle. *Science*, 152, 604–619.

Satterfield, J. H. 1965. Evoked cortical response enhancement and attention in man. A study of responses to auditory and shock stimuli. *Electroencephalo. Clin. Neurophysiol.*, 19, 470–475.

Schäfer, W. D., and Weale, R. A. 1970. The influence of age and retinal illumination on the pupillary near reflex. *Vision Research*, 10, 179–191.

Schenkenberg, T. 1970. Visual, auditory, and somatosensory evoked responses of normal subjects from childhood to senescence. Unpublished doctoral dissertation. University of Utah.

Schieve, J. F., and Wilson, W. P. 1953. The influence of age, anesthesia and cerebral arteriosclerosis on cerebral artery activity to CO_2. *Am. J. Med.*, 15, 171–174.

Seales, D. M. 1973. A study of information processing and cerebral lateralization of function in man by means of averaged visually evoked potentials. Unpublished doctoral dissertation. University of California, Los Angeles.

Shagass, C. 1968. Averaged somatosensory evoked responses in various psychiatric disorders. *In*, J. Wortis (ed.), *Recent Advances in Biological Psychiatry*, Vol. 10, pp. 205–219. New York: Plenum Press.

Shagass, C. 1972. *Evoked Brain Potentials in Psychiatry*. New York: Plenum Press.

Shagass, C., and Schwartz, M. 1965. Age, personality, and somatosensory cerebral evoked responses. *Science*, 148, 1359–1361.

Shmavonian, B. M., and Busse, E. W. 1963. Psychophysiological techniques in the study of the aged. *In*, R. H. Williams, C. Tibbitts and W. Donahue (eds), *Processes of Aging*. New York: Atherton Press.

Shmavonian, B. M., Miller, L. H., and Cohen, S. I. 1968. Differences among age and sex groups in electro-dermal conditioning. *Psychophysiology*, 5, 119–131.

Shmavonian, B. M., Miller, L. H., and Cohen, S. I. 1970. Differences among age and sex groups with respect to cardiovascular conditioning and reactivity. *J. Gerontol.*, 25, 87–94.

Shmavonian, B. M., Yarmat, A. J., and Cohen, S. I. 1965. Relationships between the ANS and CNS in age differences in behavior. *In*, A. T. Welford and J. E. Birren (eds.), *Behavior, Aging and the Nervous System*, pp. 235–258. Springfield, Illinois: Charles C. Thomas.

Silverman, A. J., Busse, E. W., and Barnes, R. H. 1955. Studies in the process of aging: Electroencephalographic findings in 400 elderly subjects. *Electroencephalo. Clin. Neurophysiol.*, 7, 67–74.

Silverman, A. J., Busse, E. W., Barnes, R. H., Frost, L. L., and Thaler, M. B. 1953. Studies on the process of aging. 4. Physiologic influences on psychic functioning in elderly people. *Geriatrics*, 8, 370–376.

Simard, D., Olesen, J., Paulson, O. B., Lassen, N. A., Skinkjl, E. 1971. Regional cerebral blood flow and its regulation in dementia. *Brain*, 94, 273–288.

Sokoloff, L. 1966. Cerebral circulatory and metabolic changes associated with aging. *In*, C. H. Millikan (ed.), *Cerebrovascular Disease* (Research Publications Association for Research in Nervous and

Mental Disease), **41**, 237–254. Baltimore: Williams & Wilkins.

Sokolov, E. N. 1959. Neuronal models and the orienting reflex. *In*, M. A. B. Brazier (ed.), *The Central Nervous System and Behavior*. New York: Macy, Jr. Foundation.

Sokolov, E. N. 1963. Nervous function: The orienting reflex. *Ann. Rev. Physiol.*, **25**, 545–580.

Spieth, W. 1964. Cardiovascular health status, age and psychological performance. *J. Gerontol.*, **19**, 277–284.

Spieth, W. 1965. Slowness of task performance and cardiovascular diseases. *In*, A. T. Welford and J. W. Birren (eds.), *Behavior, Aging, and the Nervous System*, pp. 366–400. Springfield, Illinois: Charles C. Thomas.

Spong, P., Haider, M., and Lindsley, D. B. 1965. Selective attentiveness and cortical evoked responses to visual and auditory stimuli. *Science*, **148**, 395–397.

Sternberg, S. 1969. Memory-scanning: Mental processes revealed by reaction-time experiments. *Amer. Scient.*, **57**, 421–457.

Stoller, A. 1949. Slowing of the alpha-rhythm of the electroencephalogram and its association with mental deterioration and epilepsy. *J. Ment. Sci.*, **95**, 972–984.

Straumanis, J. J., Shagass, C., and Schwartz, M. 1965. Visually evoked cerebral response changes associated with chronic brain syndromes and aging. *J. Gerontol.*, **20**, 498–506.

Strauss, H., Ostow, M., Greenstein, L., and Lewyn, S. 1955. Temporal slowing as a source of error in electroencephalographic localization. *Journal of the Mount Sinai Hospital*, **22**, 306–315.

Suci, G. J., Davidoff, M. D., and Surwillo, W. W. 1960. Reaction time as a function of stimulus information and age. *J. Exp. Psychol.*, **60**, 242–244.

Sulkin, N. M., and Sulkin, D. 1967. Age differences in response to chronic hypoxia on the fine structure of cardiac muscle and autonomic ganglion cells. *J. Gerontol.*, **22**, 485–501.

Surwillo, W. W. 1963a. The relation of simple response time to brain-wave frequency and the effects of age. *Electroencephalo. Clin. Neurophysiol.*, **15**, 105–114.

Surwillo, W. W. 1963b. The relation of response-time variability to age and the influence of brain wave frequency. *Electroencephalo. Clin. Neurophysiol.*, **15**, 1029–1032.

Surwillo, W. W. 1964a. The relation of decision time to brain wave frequency and to age. *Electroencephalo. Clin. Neurophysiol.*, **16**, 510–514.

Surwillo, W. W. 1964b. Some observations on the relation of response speed to frequency of photic stimulation under conditions of EEG synchronization. *Electroencephalo. Clin. Neurophysiol.*, **17**, 194–198.

Surwillo, W. W. 1966a. On the relation of latency of alpha rhythm frequency and the influence of age. *Electroencephalo. Clin. Neurophysiol.*, **20**, 129–132.

Surwillo, W. W. 1966b. The relation of autonomic activity to age differences in vigilance. *J. Gerontol.*, **21**, 257–260.

Surwillo, W. W. 1968. Timing of behavior in senescence and the role of the central nervous system. *In*, G. A. Talland (ed.), *Human Aging and Behavior*, pp. 1–35. New York: Academic Press.

Surwillo, W. W., and Quilter, R. E. 1965a. The influence of age on latency time of involuntary (galvanic skin reflex) and voluntary responses. *J. Gerontol.*, **20**, 173–176.

Surwillo, W. W., and Quilter, R. E. 1965b. The relation of frequency of spontaneous skin potential responses to vigilance and to age. *Psychophysiology*, **1**, 272–276.

Tecce, J. J. 1972. Contingent negative variation (CNV) and psychological processes in man. *Psych. Bull.*, **77**, 73–108.

Tecce, J. J., and Scheff, N. M. 1969. Attention reduction and suppressed direct-current potentials in the human brain. *Science*, **164**, 331–333.

Thaler, M. 1956. Relationships among Wechsler, Weigl, Rorschach, EEG findings, and abstract-concrete behavior in a group of normal aged subjects. *J. Gerontol.*, **11**, 404–409.

Thompson, L. W., and Botwinick, J. 1968. Age and reaction time. *Journal of Genetic Psychology.*, **68**, 167–172.

Thompson, L. W., and Marsh, G. R. 1973. Psychophysiological studies of aging. *In*, C. Eisdorfer and M. P. Lawton (eds.), *The Psychology of Adult Development and Aging*, pp. 122–148. Washington, D.C.: American Psychological Association.

Thompson, L. W., and Nowlin, J. B. 1973. Relation of increased attention to central and autonomic nervous system states. *In*, L. Jarvik, C. Eisdorfer and J. Blum (eds.), *Intellectual Functioning in Adults: Psychological and Biological Influences*, pp. 107–124. New York: Springer.

Thompson, L. W., and Wilson, S. 1966. Electrocortical reactivity and learning in the elderly. *J. Gerontol.*, **21**, 45–51.

Troyer, L. W., Jr., Eisdorfer, C., Wilkie, F., and Bogdonoff, M. D. 1966. Free fatty acid responses in the aged individual during performance of learning tasks. *J. Gerontol.*, **21**, 45–51.

Tueting, P., Sutton, S., and Zubin, J. 1970. Quantitative evoked potential correlates of the probability of events. *Psychophysiology*, **7**, 385–394.

Turton, E. C. 1958. The EEG as a diagnostic and prognostic aid in the differentiation of organic disorders in patients over 60. *J. Mental Sci.*, **104**, 461–465.

Turton, E. C., and Warren, P. K. G. 1960. Dementia: a clinical and EEG study of 274 patients over the age of 60. *J. Mental. Sci.*, **106**, 1493–1500.

Verdeaux, G., Verdeaux, M., and Turmel, J. 1961. Etude statistique de la fréquence et de la réactivité des electroencephalogrammes chez les sujets agés. *Canadian Psychiatric Association Journal*, **6**, 28–36.

Vogel, W., Broverman, D. M., and Klaiber, E. L. 1971. EEG responses in regularly menstruating women and in amenorrheic women treated with ovarian hormones. *Science*, **72**, 388-391.

Walter, W. G., Cooper, R., Aldridge, V. J., McCallum, W. C., and Winter, A. L. 1964. Contingent negative variation: An electrical sign of sensorimotor association and expectancy in the human brain. *Nature*, **203**, 380-384.

Wang, H. S., and Busse, E. W. 1969. EEG of healthy old persons—A longitudinal study: I. Dominant background activity and occipital rhythm. *J. Gerontol.*, **24**, 419-426.

Wang, H. S., Obrist, W. D., and Busse, E. W. 1970. Neurophysiological correlates of the intellectual function of elderly persons living in the community. *Am. J. Psychiat.*, **126**, 1205-1212.

Weale, R. A. 1965. Un the eye. *In*, A. T. Welford and J. E. Birren (eds.), *Behavior, Aging, and the Nervous System*, pp. 307-325. Springfield, Illinois: Charles C. Thomas.

Weiner, H., and Shuster, D. B. 1956. The electro-encephalogram in dementia: Some preliminary observations and correlations. *Electroencephalo. Clin. Neurophysiol.*, **8**, 479-488.

Welford, A. T. 1959. Psychomotor performance. *In*, J. E. Birren (ed.), *Handbook of Aging and the Individual*, pp. 562-613. Chicago: University of Chicago Press.

Wells, C. E. 1962. Response of alpha waves to light in neurologic disease. *Arch. Neurol.*, **6**, 478-491.

Wells, C. E. 1963. Alpha wave responsiveness to light in man. *In*, G. H. Glaser (ed.), *EEG and Behavior*, pp. 27-59. New York: Basic Books.

Williams, R. L., Agnew, H. W., Jr., and Webb, W. B. 1964. Sleep patterns in young adults: An EEG study. *Electroencephalo. Clin. Neurophysiol.*, **17**, 376-381.

Wilson, S. 1962. Electrocortical reactivity in young and aged adults. Unpublished doctoral dissertation. George Peabody College for Teachers.

Woodruff, D. S. 1972. Biofeedback control of the EEG alpha rhythm and its effect on reaction time in the young and old. Unpublished doctoral dissertation. University of Southern California.

PART 3 ENVIRONMENTAL AND HEALTH INFLUENCES ON AGING AND BEHAVIOR

12
STRESS, DISEASE, AGING AND BEHAVIOR

Carl Eisdorfer
and
Frances Wilkie
University of Washington, Seattle, Washington

INTRODUCTION

The psychological effects of human aging are a function of many variables ranging from genetic through environmental. Operationally, studies of aging are further complicated by the fact that behavioral changes and decrements in adaptive capacity are also affected by a host of physiologic influences secondary to illness. Since older persons are more likely to be sick, the interactive effects of aging and illness continue to plague the investigator who attempts to define age-related changes in any pure sense. Busse (1969) has suggested that the term *biological aging* be used for those genetic processes which are "time-related but independent of stress, trauma, or disease," while " . . . *secondary aging* refers to those disabilities resulting from trauma and chronic illness" (p. 12). Distinctions between the effects of time or disease related degenerative changes can be only tentatively made at this time.

Recent studies in gerontology have moved from descriptions of the disabilities of older adults to analyses of the mechanisms which underlie these changes. In biology, this has taken the form of studies at the cellular and subcellular level. Cellular theories of aging propose that the cumulative effects of trauma to individual cells eventually result in organismic dysfunction and death. Thus, genetic changes, ionizing radiation, chemicals and toxins, mechanical and thermal events, a progressive accumulation of waste materials and stress have been regarded as injurious to the organism (Timaris, 1972).

While investigators have suggested that cross-sectional studies have demonstrated only a significant cohort effect (and may reflect a vastly exaggerated picture of decline among the elderly), it is generally accepted that aging postmaturity is associated with gradual decline in many psychological functions (Botwinick, 1973). The precise nature of these declines is still a question to be answered and the bases of such losses are not entirely understood.

In most physiological and psychological theories of aging, the concepts of stress and disease play elemental roles. Stress may accelerate the aging process over a given time, or it may lead to physical disease which manifests as, or interacts with aging to increase degeneration. Stress may impair the reserve capacity of the organism and compromise ability to respond, or it may be a challenge yielding improved adaptation.

The literature is vast and a review of stress and disease must be selective rather than comprehensive; illustrative rather than exhaustive. We shall focus on three approaches to this material: (1) Stress Research—Background, definitions, and methodological issues; (2) Stress and Disease—Since cardiovascular disease is the major health problem of the middle-aged and aged, psychological and psychophysiological factors associated with this disease will be emphasized; (3) Stress, Disease, and Behavior—Performance decrements have been associated with both stress and disease. An attempt will be made to evaluate the interaction of these factors.

STRESS RESEARCH

Although observations that could be categorized under the heading of stress have been made for centuries, its introduction into the life sciences as a systematic concept is credited to Hans Selye. Selye is an endocrinologist whose work (1950, 1970) describing a physiologic state which prepared the individual for "flight or fight" behavior and the possible influence this would have on more subtle behavioral and secondary physiologic events has been germinal to researchers in the social and biological sciences. For the engineer, the term stress refers to an external force directed at some physical object and strain is the result of this force, causing temporary alterations in the structure of the object (Lazarus, 1966). Behavioral scientists have defined stress less consistently or precisely (Scott and Howard, 1970). At this time, many seemingly diverse lines of inquiry (i.e., anxiety, disasters, frustration, conflict, psychosomatic disorders, disease, etc.) have been investigated under the rubric of stress research (Appley and Trumbull, 1967).

It seems notable that for the most part there has been little interdisciplinary cooperation. As a consequence, most such research can be grouped into three categories: biological, psychological, and sociological. This has produced a multitude of definitions with the result that *stress* has remained an ambiguous and somewhat vague construct (Levine and Scotch, 1970).

The multiplicity of approaches predictably leads to investigative confusion. The confusion seems reduced when investigators have focused upon one or two variables within a given discipline where the terms are operationally defined, typically within limited disciplinary parameters. As a consequence, a penalty arises in that many relevant variables may be ignored. There is emerging an increasing awareness that the stress reaction involves the physiological, psychological, and in many instances the social systems simultaneously and that there is a need to direct research accordingly (Appley and Trumbull, 1967; Lowenthal and Chiriboga, 1973).

An abbreviated description of the sequence of events in the psychological stress reaction is in order at this point. We must postulate a condition (external and/or internal) and a stimulus which indicates its presence. Typically, the investigator makes the judgment as to what is or is not stressful. The stimulus may be physical, psychological, or social and may originate from within or external to the individual (Scott and Howard, 1970). Stressful stimuli are those characterized as being novel, intense, rapidly changing, unexpected, as well as productive of fatigue, boredom, frustration, or similar states (Appley and Trumbull, 1967). For a stimulus to be stressful, it must be *perceived* in some way as potentially harmful, threatening, damaging, unpleasant, or overwhelming to the organism's adaptive capacity. Whether a given stimulus is perceived as stressful also relates to other variables such as the environmental context as well as the individual's resources (i.e., experiences, perception, intellectual ability, personality, health, education, etc.) (Lazarus, 1966; Lazarus, Averill, and Opton, 1974).

Responses to stress can be grouped into three categories: (1) physiological responses; (2) behavioral responses including expressions of affect; and (3) subjective states, self-reported (Moss, 1973). According to Selye (1956), the physiologic response to stress involves three stages: (1) the alarm reaction; (2) the stage of resistance involving an increased capacity for the organism to respond; and (3) exhaustion characterized by a loss of functional capacity to continue. Elements of this response will be discussed in greater detail in the section on physiologic reactions to stress, but it should be noted that there is an increase in central and autonomic nervous system activity as well as endocrine activity. Physiological responses indicative of stress include modification of heart rate, blood pressure, respiration, vasomotor, and galvanic skin responses, as well as changes in endocrine activity. The magnitude of this physiologic reaction has prompted observers to link it with disease. Thus, Engel (1962) and Lowenthal and Chiriboga (1973) have suggested that disease may be a response to stress or in some instances it may be the stressor.

Behavioral responses used as operational definitions of stress have included erratic performance rates, malcoordination, increases in errors, fatigue, perseverative behaviors and so on. Included among such behaviors as reflective of emotional states (and therefore of stress) are tremors, stuttering, exaggerated speech characteristics, etc. The presence of emotional activity has been used *post facto* to indicate subjective state and usually refers to any bodily changes deviating from usual or normal states such as anxiety, fear, tension, reported somatic symptoms, depression and the like. In addition, interview and test responses have been utilized for such descriptive work (Pichot, 1971).

Individual factors play a role in determining whether a specific stimulus constitutes a psychological stressor. Stress may be inferred from a sequence of events and cannot be measured *per se*, according to McGrath (1970). Certain kinds of events are likely to, but do not necessarily, constitute psychological stress.

A broad array of situations have been studied as potential stress inducers. These include: rapid cultural change, failure, frustration, competition associated with work, preparing for examinations, learning and performance tasks, battle conditions, concentration camp confinement, impending surgery, acute and chronic illnesses, isolation, life crises such as loss of a loved one, or job demotion (Mechanic, 1968), and life style transitions such as retirement, children leaving home (Lowenthal, 1975; Carp, 1972) or relocation (Lawton and Nahemow, 1973). Although relatively little attention has been paid to the cumulative effects of stressors, recent findings from investigations of psychosocial factors and disease, suggest that an accumulation of life event changes occurring within a given time frame may be related to the development of illness (Holmes and Rahe, 1967).

Many presumably routine situations may be stress inducing. Commercial airline pilots showed marked changes in endocrine and heart activity at certain points between the preliminaries for take-off and touchdown at the end of the trip; experienced car drivers with a history of coronary disease sometimes develop cardiovascular changes and even angina when driving in city traffic. Healthy racing car drivers during competition develop high-grade sinus tachycardia and show elevations in catecholamines and free fatty acids (FFA) immediately before and after racing. Public speaking induces similar changes in heart rate and rhythms and elevations in catecholamines and FFA (Sommerville, 1973). Accountants who were studied before, during and after the tax completion date had marked elevations in serum cholesterol levels and blood clotting times during the tax filing period (Friedman, Rosenman, and Carroll, 1958). Thus, the routine events encountered in daily life produce physiological stress reactions which may eventually have a "wear and tear" effect upon the organism.

There are a number of methodologic issues in stress-related research:

1. Individual differences in the perception of the stimulus. Few, if any, situations manipulated in the laboratory will be perceived by all individuals as stressful. Furthermore, a situation that is stressful to an individual one time may not be stressful at another (Appley and Trumbull, 1967). Intervening variables such as personality (i.e., defense mechanisms, etc.), intellectual ability, health, and so on may affect the subject's perception of the situation as well as the coping process (Janis, 1974; Lazarus, Averill, and Opton, 1974). We need to consider the subject's reactions to given "stressful" events, and such factors as whether they were controlled or not controlled by the subject (e.g., voluntary *vs.* involuntary retirement), state of preparedness, expectancy, etc. (Croog, 1970; Nelson, 1974)

2. Sequence of events. In distinguishing specific types of stress, little attention has been paid to temporal factors. As a consequence, it is often difficult to determine whether the event causes the stress or the stress the event. An individual may respond differently to an event before, during, and after its occurrence (Levine and Scotch, 1970). This has been one of the major methodological problems in studies of

retirement (Carp, 1972) and the "empty nest" transitions (Harkins, 1974).

3. Reactions to "stressful" events. A common, albeit erroneous assumption is that stressful events must lead to disruptive and pathological states and must invariably impair performance (Levine and Scotch, 1970). Social-psychological theories rarely consider the possibility of the positive consequences of stress (Croog, 1970). Even in performance, moderate stress or arousal may be helpful (Broadbent, 1971; Broverman, Klaiber, Vogel, and Kobayashi, 1974; Eisdorfer, 1968; Ellis, 1975).

4. Generalizable patterns of stress response. The belief that subjective affect, emotional behavior, physiologic responses and coping activities are so related that measurement of one is an adequate indicator of the others is not supported by the evidence. Low intercorrelations are found between autonomic nervous system responses (Lacey, 1967; Bridges, Jones, and Leak, 1968); and many investigators err by measuring one variable, such as galvanic skin response (GSR), heart rate (HR), or blood pressure (BP), and assuming that other measures will have changed in the same direction.

Age is generally assumed to play an important role in determining how a person reacts to stress, but the parameters and mechanisms involved are not clear. It has been pointed out that particular events may have different meaning and significance to individuals at different ages and thus whether an event is perceived as stressful or not will vary (Neugarten, 1973). Losing one's mother may have a different meaning to a child than to an adolescent, or an adult, and at each age the individual will have different resources for coping with the loss. Lazarus (1966) has suggested that to the extent that an individual's psychological structure (i.e., motive patterns) and resources for coping may change with age, there will be differences in response to stress. Caudill (1958) has suggested that the child and the elderly may have a more drastic reaction to stress than other age groups, because they are more dependent, have fewer social roles, and less differentiated behavior.

The extent to which age-related physiological and psychological changes may affect the older organism's reaction to stress is not clear. To make matters more complex, many of the response variables typically used in stress research —such as impaired behavioral performance, and physical and emotional problems—frequently occur with increasing age independent of apparent situational stress and could complicate such studies. Although we could postulate that older persons under evaluation are generally in a state of heightened arousal, it is not a very parsimonious approach to the data. In physiological studies involving young animals, prolonged stress frequently produces signs of premature aging including loss of hair, wrinkling of skin, etc. (Selye, 1970). In the older organism, measures of post-stress physical condition are extremely important, but as indicated, the pathology secondary to stress may be difficult to differentiate from changes relating to age and/or preexisting disease. While emotional states that deviate from the norm are a frequent measure of stress in the young, depression, for example, may increase with age (Busse, 1969) and this may interact with the state of the physical health (Lowenthal, Berkman, and associates, 1967; Raskind, Alvarez, Cole, and Barrett, 1974).

An example of age acting as a confounding variable in stress research is illustrated in a study of Norwegian concentration camp survivors who were not studied until about 20 years after their release. The men were being considered for government assistance if their emotional or physical health problems could be linked with their wartime experience in the concentration camps. Among the older men, it was difficult to determine whether observed decrements in intellectual performance and poor health was due to their wartime stress experiences or due to age-related changes (Strøm, 1968). It should be noted, however, that other investigators have noted signs of premature aging among concentration camp survivors (Schenk, 1963). It has been suggested that one year in war ages a man as much as two years, but a year in a concentration camp increases his age by four years. Survivors were reported to appear about 10 years older than their age, with impairment noted in their physical and mental efficiency. Undernourishment, heavy labor, the appalling conditions in the camps as well as the stress of perpetual anxiety and fear are regarded as the most important etiological factors. The symptomatology of the concentration camp syndrome observed in most survivors included: (1) failing memory and difficulty in concentration; (2) nervousness, irritability, restlessness; (3) fatigue; (4) sleep disturbances; (5) headaches; (6) emotional instability; (7) dysphoric moodiness; (8) vertigo; (9) loss of initiative; (10) vegetative lability; and (11) feelings of insufficiency (Eitinger, 1971). Apparently many of the physiological and psychological characteristics associated with a response to prolonged or severe stress are also associated with the aging process.

Much of the gerontological research under the heading of stress has tended to focus upon life crises (i.e., loss of a loved one, etc.) and transitions (i.e., children leaving home, retirement, relocation, etc.). In many of these studies, the focus has been more upon post-event adaptation with some attention paid to the intervening variables but relatively little concern with identifying the personal dimensions of the stressor in relationship to the outcome responses.

In an ongoing cross-sequential study, Lowenthal and her colleagues (Lowenthal, 1975) are attempting to identify sources of stress, coping mechanisms, and outcome parameters among men and women across the adult life span. Predictably, specific areas of concern that could be stressful differ at different ages and according to sex. Thus, for young newlyweds, a major area of concern is family oriented, such as anticipation of parenthood; for the post-parental age group, the men were concerned with work related problems while the women tended to be more concerned with children and their own personal growth. Although many women at this age were employed, they were more concerned about their husband's work related problems than their own. Studies on stress and disease have focused primarily upon this age group. Although there have been relatively few studies examining psychosocial factors related to disease among women, it has been suggested that women will be prone to the same diseases as men, now that more women are employed (Friedman and Rosenman, 1974). Lowenthal (1975) also noted that the post-parental women, independent of the apparent stress to which they were currently exposed, were the most preoccupied with it and had far more psychiatric symptoms than others across the life stages studied.

The oldest group of men and women studied were in the preretirement stage and for them, survival in good health and "no more hassles" was the dominant theme. The women at this age were also concerned about their impending retirement and the future. The number of changes in life events decreased from the newlywed stage to the post-parental stage and remained fairly stable through the imminent retirement stage which supports the findings of Holmes and Holmes (1970). Gaitz and Scott (1975) evaluated letters written to a newspaper advice columnist who had requested that senior citizens write to her about their most serious problem. They found that older people were most concerned about loneliness, rejection, interpersonal relationships, finding a new mate, and sexual problems.

Life-style transitions have been extensively studied as major sources of stress for the middle-aged and aged. The assumption that these transitions are stressful is based upon the observation that each involves relatively major changes in the interaction of the individual with the environment (Holmes and Rahe, 1967; Lowenthal, 1975).

It is not clear, however, that transitions such as retirement and children leaving home (i.e., empty nest) are always stressful to most people. Neugarten (1970) and Lowenthal and Chiriboga (1972) found no association between empty nest and emotional well being, which was supported by Harkins (1974); however, in the latter study, indices of physical health were also obtained and it was observed that women going through the empty nest period had more physical health problems than women in the pre- or post-empty nest periods. As noted by Harkins (1974), much of the earlier research failed to include individuals at all stages of the empty nest transition. In addition, many studies have frequently failed to control for relevant variables such as experience, preparedness and resources available. A distinction should be made between the response produced in anticipation of a stressful event's occurrence and the response produced upon confrontation with it, as well as after the event is past. Frequently the actual nature of the confrontation turns out to be different than what was expected (Lazarus, 1966). Among the young, marked changes in responses have been observed between the anticipatory and confrontation periods during examination time (Mechanic, 1962) including differences in catecholamine excretion levels (Frankenhaeuser and Rissler, 1970). Temporal factors are also illustrated in a study by Stokes and Maddox (1967) on adaptation to retirement. During the first year after retirement they observed that blue collar workers were more satisfied with retirement than white collar workers, but after three to five years the blue collar workers became dissatisfied while the white collar workers remained about the same. This may support Tyhurst's (1957) contention that the post-confrontation period involves the most turmoil, or Eisdorfer's (1972) suggestion that the economic state following retirement may be a basic factor in mediating adaptation. Clearly, there is a need for more research spanning the various stages of the transition process before any conclusions can be reached as to which stage is the most stressful and what factors may contribute to this.

Evidence regarding the relationship between retirement and health and other indices of adaptation is also conflicting. Eisdorfer (1972) has suggested that adaptation will fall along a continuum ranging from personality disorganization to increased adaptive capacity depending upon the individual retiree's traits and the characteristics of the situation. While some investigators suggest that retirement has a deleterious effect upon health (Ellison, 1968; Ryser and Sheldon, 1969), others find it has no consistent effect (Martin and Doran, 1967; McMahan and Ford, 1955; Thompson and Streib, 1958). Spence (1968) noted that retirement as a precipitant of mental illness in old age occurs only under rather special circumstances. He suggests that low morale and depression may well be an appropriate reaction to one's situation. Since preparation appears to be an important factor in adaptation (Coelho and Adams, 1974), pre-retirement counseling (Kalt and Kohn, 1975) may have a significant effect upon the illness behavior of the aged.

Neugarten (1970, pp. 86-87) has emphasized the importance of events being anticipated, expected, or "on time" during the life cycle. She suggests: "There are two distinctions worth making: first, that it is the unanticipated life event, not the anticipated . . . which is likely to represent the traumatic event. Moreover, major stresses are caused by events that upset the sequence and rhythm of the life cycle . . . when the empty nest, grandparenthood, retirement, major illness, or widowhood occur *off time*. In this sense then, a psychology of the life cycle is not a psychology of crisis behavior so much as it is a psychology of timing." According to this notion, a serious illness may be developmentally "on time" for an older person, possibly resulting in less psychological disturbance than for someone younger (Zarit and Kahn, 1975). On the other hand, it has been suggested that older persons are more physically and psychologically vulnerable to the effects of illness (Kleemeier, 1958). Zarit and Kahn (1975) have studied the relation of age, adaptation to illness and the severity of cerebral dysfunction among individuals aged 38 to 84 (mean age, 62 years) who had suffered cerebrovascular accidents. They found that among the minimally impaired, the older persons tended to be more depressed and to use less denial than younger individuals. Although denial increased with the severity of brain impairment, the change was greatest among the old. The investigators concluded, however, that the severity of cerebral dysfunction may be a more critical factor in determining adaptation to illness than chronological age.

Despite the high incidence of disease among the aged, it appears that the majority are able to successfully cope with most of the stresses they encounter (Meyer, 1974) and about 95 percent of them are able to continue living in the community (see Eisdorfer and Stotsky, Chapter 30).

Among the institutionalized aged, poor health does appear to be an important factor in determining whether the individual can successfully cope with major stresses. The outcome of the stress in many relocation studies is measured in terms of increased morbidity and mortality. There is a controversy as to whether relocation is a stressful experience that can lead to increased morbidity or not. According to Lawton and Nahemow's review (1973), some investigators have found that relocation does have a negative outcome while others have found no evidence or a mixed effect. It is clear that the poorest candidates for relocation included those with psychosis, brain impairment, poor mental status, and poor physical functioning.

Although there are a number of methodological issues to be considered in these studies, it does appear that the studies which found no association between relocation and morbidity or mortality tended to select patients for relocation who were in relatively good health and better prepared for the move. Aldrich and Mendkoff (1963) did observe that patients became more apprehensive when the news of a move was announced. They also noted that patients who took the move in stride or were overtly angry had the highest survival rate, while those who became anxious but did not withdraw survived only moderately well. The highest mortality rate occurred among those who regressed, became depressed or denied that the institution was closing. Miller and Lieberman (1965) also noted that depression was associated with negative outcomes after the move. Kral, Grad, and Berenson (1968) found that the mere anticipation of change could involve a negative psychological reaction which subsided markedly when the order to close the "veterans" home was rescinded.

In contrast to those in the community (Kuypers, 1972; Palmore and Luikart, 1972), institutionalized aged may feel that they have less control over their lives (Felton and Kahana, 1974). In this context, it is believed that feelings of helplessness and hopelessness may be associated with increased mortality. Thus, it is suggested that acute emotional upheavals, such as sudden fright, emotionally charged arguments and anticipation of an impending crisis may be associated with intensive vagal stimulation and cardiac standstill, or adrenosympathetically-induced ventricular fibrillation which can cause sudden cardiac arrest (Raab, 1971; Wolf, 1971).

Although the data on stress and life crises are still largely descriptive, more accurate documentation of the variables involved is yielding better data insofar as identifying social and health status, cognitive intactness, affective state and subject perception. These trends are to be encouraged and it is hoped will be followed by more precise assessment of physiologic and behavioral reactions to known precipitating events.

The results consistently suggest that relatively healthy aged individuals can successfully cope with most stressful situations that occur in life. Although some may experience low morale and depression following a major change in their life, most eventually find a solution to the problem. However, we don't know how repeated encounters with stress may affect the individual over time.

It is believed by many clinicians that psychosocial factors are associated with the development of disease and may be related to the prognosis. This presumed relationship between psychosocial factors and disease has been studied in the middle-aged male, but less attention has been paid to the aged. Our purpose in the section that follows is to examine some of the psychosocial factors related to disease among middle-aged and older individuals, pointing out the physiological mechanisms suspected in this relationship.

STRESS AND DISEASE

As a consequence of the reduction in deaths from birth defects, infectious and contagious disease (Dodge and Martin, 1970), life expectancy at birth has increased greatly in the United States during the first half of the twentieth century. Thus, a person born in 1900 had an average life expectancy of 45 years while someone born in 1971 had an average life expectancy of 71 years. Longevity for the middle-aged and the elderly has not increased substantially over this period, however, and indeed chronic and debilitating disorders have increased concomitantly with the "aging" of the population (U.S. Public Health Service publication, *Health in the Later Years of Life*, 1971).

With advancing age, there is an apparent increase in the relative incidence of deaths attributed to diseases suspected of being related to stress. Diseases of the heart, cancer, and cerebrovascular diseases (mainly stroke) are the major causes of death, accounting for about 70 percent of the deaths for those aged 45 and over, with heart disease by far the leader, causing over 40 percent of the deaths (U.S.P.H.S. publication, *Monthly Vital Statistics Report*: *Summary*, 1973, 1974).

Of some concern is the finding that the aged frequently underestimate the extent of their health problems. Ostfeld (1968) reports on an intensive study of 1,900 Old Age Assistance recipients. It was striking that less than 20 percent of the persons interviewed reported themselves as being in distress insofar as health was concerned. Physicians, however, reported that all of the aged had some readily discernible pathology and the majority needed some treatment. That study accentuates the need for more accurate definitions of physical pathology among the aged, and when intervention is required. How much illness, how much disability, how much discomfort is unmodifiable and what are we willing to accept as part of aging? How much do we wish to expend to ameliorate this situation? (Eisdorfer, 1974)

The issue raised by such questions relates to the interaction between disease and aging. It is difficult to study the physiological or psychological factors associated with various diseases in the aged because of the presence of multiple diseases and the difficulty of isolating the effects of aging from those consequent to ongoing disease or to gradual degenerative changes that develop following a history of disease or trauma.

As Levi (1971) suggests, it is well established that environmental *physical* stimuli can cause a large number of diseases. Exposure, avoidance, or manipulation of these factors increases, decreases, or removes the likelihood of becoming ill or reverses ill health when it occurs. The role that extrinsic *psychosocial* stimuli have in disease causation is not as clear despite the existing body of research. Selye's (1971) theory provides a mechanism for the process by which psychosocial factors may result in physical disease. "Stress is the non-specific response of the body to any demands made upon it . . . The intensity and duration of this stereotyped, phylogenetically old adaptation pattern, primarily preparing the organism for physical activity (e.g., flight or fight) is assumed to be closely related to the rate of wear and tear in the organism and consequently to an increased morbidity

and mortality, not in any specific disease but in a variety of diseases" (Levi and Kagan, 1971, p. 369). Regardless of how purposeful these preparatory activities may have been in the history of mankind, they have ceased to be very adequate in mediating the adaptational requirements of modern people to the socioeconomic changes, social and psychological conflicts, and other threats involved in living in a highly industrialized, modern and typically urban society. In addition, for social reasons, people often must control many emotional outlets and motor activities. This could lead to a situation in which there might be discordance between the expression of emotion, the neuroendocrine concomitants of emotion, and the psychomotor activities likely to accompany such emotion. If this "stress" pattern of response to psychosocial stimuli and/or this behavioral and physiological discrepancy lasts long enough, it may be of pathogenic significance (Levi, 1974).

The physiologic response to stress involves the nervous and endocrine systems which mediate the homeostatic regulatory mechanisms of the organism. With increasing age, there is presumed to be a loss of physiologic adaptability and the older person is reported to be less able to cope with a stress or environmental change (Marx, 1974; Timaris, 1972). Since neuroendocrine activity is a frequently used measure of stress response and is a mechanism through which psychosocial stimuli can produce physiopathology, a description of the neuroendocrine processes involved in the stress response is in order.

Figure 1 is a schematic representation used by Timaris (1972) to illustrate the postulated mechanisms of action of stressors on target tissue.

Stated simply, a stimulus would first affect the higher centers of the central nervous system (CNS), especially those involved in the perception and integration of environmental stimuli (Netter, 1970). From these CNS centers, signals would be transmitted to the posterior hypothalamus which discharges a number of releasing factors that are relayed (through vascular linkage) to the anterior pituitary (hypophysis). Each of these factors stimulates the pituitary to

STRESSOR

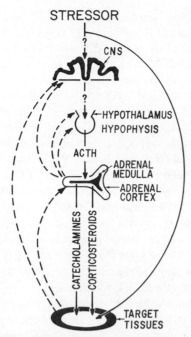

Figure 1. Schematic representation of the postulated mechanisms of action of stressors on target tissues. (Reprinted by permission from Macmillan & Company. Copyright 1972, P. S. Timiras, *Developmental Physiology and Aging*, Chapter 28, Decline in homeostatic regulation (p. 555).)

release specific hormones. Included among these hormones is growth hormone (GH), a thyrotropic hormone (TSH), three sex hormones, and the adrenocorticotropic (ACTH) hormone. ACTH stimulates the adrenal cortex to release hormones called corticosteroids or adrenocortical hormones which may be categorized into three types. The first type is the glucocorticoids of which the principal type is cortisol, the primary function of which is to influence organic metabolism. Excess of glucocorticoids leads to a rise in serum lipids and cholesterol (Netter, 1970). In this category the hormone 17-OHCS (17 hydroxycorticoid) has been extensively studied in stress research. The second group is the mineralocorticoids, with the principal type being aldosterone which has been associated with hypertension (Eisdorfer and Raskind, 1975; Selye, 1971). The third hormone group involves the sex hormones.

Regulation of corticosteroid hormones involves a feedback mechanism in that ACTH level appears to be regulated by the level of corticosteroids circulating in the blood; the higher the steroid level, the lower the ACTH secretion and vice versa. The greater the stress, the more ACTH is secreted (Netter, 1970).

The corticosteroids have diversified physiological actions. They influence carbohydrate, protein and lipid metabolism, electrolyte and water balance, and the functional capacities of the cardiovascular system, kidney, skeletal muscles and CNS. In association with other hormones, they seem to endow the organism with the capacity to resist noxious environmental changes (Brady, 1970; Kety, 1970; Netter, 1970).

According to Mason's review (1972), pituitary adrenal cortical system hormones are increased under conditions in which there appears to be a rather undifferentiated state of arousal or such involvement as anticipation of activity. This is noted in situations characterized by novelty, unpredictability, suspense, or involvement. Marked 17-OHCS responses have also been observed in psychiatric patients in association with intense, disorganizing emotional reactions. Müller and Grad (1974) found that senile patients in the 50–99 age range had higher resting plasma cortisol levels than their healthy counterparts.

Although it is best to view the entire neuroendocrine system as a functional unit rather than as an association of independent structures, neuroendocrine axes have frequently been studied as separate systems. Another system, the sympathetic-adrenal medullary system, has also been extensively studied in the young with regard to its stimulation by psychosocial factors (Mason, 1972). The adrenal medulla, under the control of the sympathetic portion of the autonomic nervous system, secretes the catecholamines, epinephrine and norepinephrine. Norepinephrine is also the transmitter substance released from sympathetic postganglionic nerve endings (Eisdorfer and Raskind, 1975, Netter, 1970).

The effects of epinephrine and norepinephrine are ubiquitous and tend to resemble those produced by stimulation of the adrenergic nerves. They differ considerably in their pharmacophysiology, however. Norepinephrine raises blood pressure through vasoconstriction and tends to decrease cardiac output. In contrast, epinephrine has less effect upon blood pressure, but increases cardiac output and initiates bronchial dilatation while inhibiting intestinal motility and insulin secretion. Both epinephrine and norepinephrine act to increase circulating free fatty acids (FFA) (Netter, 1970).

There is relatively little information on age-related changes in catecholamine levels among humans. Kärki (1956) observed an increase in resting urinary excretion of catecholamines from ages 1–50 years with a slight but consistent decrease between ages 60–90 years. Cohen and Shmavonian (1967) studied urinary catecholamine levels during performance of a psychological task among old and young. While the young showed an increase in epinephrine and a decrease in norepinephrine levels, the old had a marked decrease in both. Although the investigators did not report this finding, the old did not return to their pre-rest levels as soon as did the young during the time course of the study, which suggests that more attention should be focused upon post-stress reaction patterns among the old. A study of human autopsy material showed a reduction in norepinephrine levels in the brainstem with increasing age (Robinson, Nies, Davis, Colburn, Bourne, Shaw, and Coppen, 1972) and in synthetic enzyme levels (Coté and Kremzner, 1974).

Free fatty acids (FFA) are released into circulation from adipose tissue in response to catecholamines, the growth hormone of the pituitary, and glucocorticoids of the adrenal cortex, and are a measure of sympathetic nervous system activity (Netter, 1970). Eisdorfer and colleagues (Powell, Eisdorfer, and Bogdonoff, 1964) found pronounced and persistent FFA mobilization among the aged compared to the young during performance of a learning task. It was also demonstrated that in humans this age-related difference in FFA levels was not due to a differential ability of the old to metabolize plasma fatty acids or to respond to infused norepinephrine (Eisdorfer, Powell, Silverman, and Bogdonoff, 1965). Eisdorfer (1968) has proposed that the deficit observed in learning performance among aged men was associated with heightened autonomic nervous system (ANS)

activation secondary to increased neuroendocrine sensitivity in specific target organs as reflected in elevated FFA levels. Performance was improved in older men who were administered a beta adrenergic blocking agent (propranolol) which reduced ANS end organ activity as reflected in indices such as heart rate and FFA levels. (Eisdorfer, Nowlin, and Wilkie, 1970). Although supporting data on animals has been reported (Herr and Birren, 1973), some doubts have been raised as to the generality of these studies by work currently in progress (Froehling, 1974; Eisdorfer, Nowlin, and Wilkie, 1976). It should be noted that these recent studies using propranolol employed a lower dosage level than previously used by Eisdorfer and colleagues (1970) as well as having other methodological differences.

Although the data are meager, it appears that there is a reduction in neuroendocrine activity with increasing age. However, it is not known whether the reduction is due to reduced functional activity of the endocrine glands or metabolic rate, or to changes in the responsiveness of target tissue or organs to hormonal action, or to all of these factors (Finch, 1973; Timaris, 1972).

Most of the research on stress in the aged has focused upon different sets of nervous and endocrine system variables under a variety of experimental conditions so that conclusions are difficult to draw. The literature based upon young people and animals indicates that considerable variability exists between and within individuals in their physiological response patterns to stress (Appley and Trumbull, 1967). If advances are to be made in the understanding of the relationship of the CNS, ANS, and endocrine systems, there must be a movement toward more studies of an increasingly broad range of concurrent CNS, ANS and endocrine measurements so that relationships and patterns of the many nervous and endocrine subsystems can be defined in the aged individual.

Figure 2 shows Levi's (1974) model depicting the relationship between stress and disease. According to Levi, the combined effect of psychosocial stimuli (in block 1) and the psychobiological program (2) determines the physiological and psychological mechanisms (e.g., stress) (in

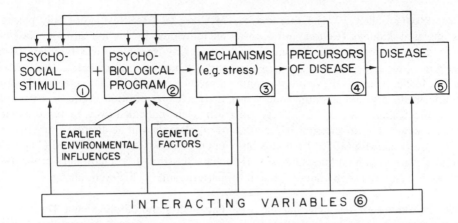

Figure 2. A conceptual model for psychosocially mediated disease. (From Levi, Lennart, Psychosocial stress and disease: A conceptual model. *In*, E. K. E. Gunderson and R. H. Rahe (eds.), *Life Stress and Illness*, 1974, p. 10. Courtesy of Charles C. Thomas, Publisher, Springfield, Illinois.)

block 3) of each person. Under certain circumstances, these may lead to precursors of disease (4) and to disease itself (5). Intervening variables can promote or counteract these sequences of events.

Even at low levels of stress, if the person pays much attention to, or misinterprets, the signals originating from such reactions, clinical symptoms may appear such as in the case of hypochondriasis. At higher stress levels, almost all subjects experience these signals as unpleasant. If such reactions are prolonged or frequent, it is claimed that they may eventually lead to structural damage. Psychosocial stimuli may also influence health by impeding recovery and aggravating disability whatever the cause of the primary disease. Such psychosocially-induced responses may involve anxiety as a reaction to the disease or situation and may become complicated by the reinforcement of secondary gains such as utilization of the disease as a means of avoiding responsibility, justifying one's incapacity and providing a release from social pressure.

Anxiety, as a reaction, is a major problem encountered in retrospective studies of stress and disease and is often a contaminant in studies investigating psychosocial factors in the etiology of coronary heart disease. Because of the number of subjects and expense in carrying out prospective research, most studies have focused upon patients with manifest coronary heart di-

sease. Since a myocardial infarction is often a life threatening event and many persons with angina pectoris experience severe chest pain, it is not surprising that most individuals who have been through such an experience appear anxious, concerned about their health, and depressed. If the physical and psychological problems are not resolved within a reasonable period of time, the individual will reportedly become a "cardiac cripple" and the psychological state a better predictor of functioning than the physiological condition (Croog, Levine, and Lurie, 1968). Although it has been suggested that such factors as anxiety, neurotic behavior and the like are precursors to the disease, one must be cautious in making this conclusion. As Halliday (1943) pointed out, the cause of an illness may be different from the basis for lack of recovery from that illness.

Although psychosocial factors are suspected in the etiology of numerous diseases, a considerable body of research in recent years has focused upon the cardiovascular diseases (e.g., arteriosclerosis, coronary heart disease and hypertension) probably because of their extensive prevalence and high mortality rate.

Blood pressure increases with age (Simborg, 1970). The hemodynamic variables affecting arterial pressure are significantly influenced by the autonomic nervous system, chiefly through its sympathetic division affecting heart rate, myocardial contractility, arterial resistance, and venous capacity (Frohlich, 1974). Other factors such as diseased kidneys (Genest and Koiw, 1972), or disturbances in neural control of blood pressure (due either to alterations in the control by higher centers of vasomotor and sympathetic medullary and hypothalamic centers or to direct alterations at these sites) can lead to increased blood pressure (Forsyth, 1974). Ito and Schanberg (1972) have also observed that elevations in blood pressure were associated with serotonin depletion in the rat brain.

Despite the volume of research that has focused upon coronary heart disease and essential hypertension, there is still much ambiguity about their etiology. Because some people develop these conditions during middle-age and others in old age, it has been suggested that the etiology of coronary heart disease in the elderly may be different from that in youth and middle-age (Acheson, 1961). It is not clear whether the primary risk factors, such as cholesterol, relative weight, hemoglobin, cigarettes smoked and EKG abnormalities usually associated with coronary heart disease have similar predictive value at all ages. Elevations in blood pressure appear to increase in predictive value with increasing age (Hyams and Loop, 1969; Truett, Cornfield, and Kannel, 1967).

Psychosocial Factors and Cardiovascular Disease

There have been an increasing number of epidemiological and clinical studies that suggest that certain social and behavioral conditions put persons at a higher risk of developing clinically manifest coronary heart disease (CHD) and hypertension, particularly during the middle-age years. It should be noted that distinct literatures are accumulating around the study of psychosocial factors associated with (1) the risk of developing CHD (Jenkins, 1971); (2) recovery or nonrecovery from CHD (Croog, Levine, and Lurie, 1968); and (3) hypertension (Benson and Gutmann, 1974; Henry and Cassel, 1969). The majority of research has involved men under the age of 65 years.

It has been suggested that psychologic factors may play a role in the development of hypertension and CHD (Dunbar, 1943; Osler and McCrae, 1920). Stress is not only placed upon an individual by his life situation but also by personality variables. The two sets of factors are themselves interrelated in that personality structure frequently has a great deal to do with the particular position in life or environment in which an individual lives. In the following section, research will be discussed that has focused upon cardiovascular disease and (1) personality characteristics; (2) a coronary-prone behavior pattern; and (3) life event changes.

Personality and Cardiovascular Disease. A number of investigators have postulated that there is a "hypertensive personality" and that characteristics such as anxiety and aggressiveness are associated with the development of heart disease. Findings have been contradictory depending in part upon the population studied, techniques used to assess behavior, whether the study was prospective or retrospective and the operational definitions of disease categories used.

Subjective descriptions of hypertensives have suggested that the hypertensive person is obsessive or compulsive, shows a lack of self-assertion, is aggressive, tense, and anxious (Brod, 1971; Palmer, 1930; Sainsbury, 1960). Torgersen and Kringlen (1971) interviewed monozygotic twins aged 33-65 years and found that the twin who had been the more submissive, quiet, withdrawn, obedient and insecure as a child had the higher systolic blood pressure. Harris and Singer (1967) in an 11-year longitudinal study observed that prehypertensive college women were more likely to have experienced tense, abrasive and hostile interactions with other people than were their normotensive counterparts.

Ostfeld and Lebovitz (1960) measured the blood pressure of 17 normotensives and 16 hypertensives every 1-2 weeks for a period of 4-12 months and used the standard deviation of each subject's readings as a measure of blood pressure lability. They found a significant positive correlation in *both* groups between lability and the scores on the hysteria, hypochondriases, and psychopathic deviation scales of the Minnesota Multiphasic Personality Inventory (MMPI). These authors suggested that those patients classified as hypertensive contained a subgroup whose blood pressure was labile and whose prognosis may be better.

It has been observed that hypertensives have exaggerated blood pressure responses to emotional or experimental stressors (Brod, 1971; Wolf, 1971). In the early stages of essential hypertension, blood pressure may be only transiently elevated but there may be exaggerated fluctuations in response to stressors (i.e., cold pressor and mental arithmetic) (Forsyth, 1974). Cardiac output during the *resting* state in early labile hypertensives is reportedly the same as in normotensives in an *acute emotional* state (Brod, 1971). Such data have led to the speculation that emotional or environmental factors play significant roles in early hypertension.

Henry and Cassel (1969) suggested that high blood pressure may occur in situations where aspirations are blocked, meaningful human interactions are restricted, and the outcome of events is uncertain. The cumulative effects of such events may lead to a sustained elevation of blood pressure. It has been suggested that the tendency toward higher blood pressure among the aged may in part be due to their ambiguous status and failure to adapt when faced with new patterns conflicting with the culture to which they were adjusted in youth.

According to Benson and Gutmann's review (1974), however, there is relatively little agreement on the significance of personality characteristics in the development of hypertension. Long-term epidemiological and family studies are needed of subjects at different points on the blood pressure continuum, in an attempt to quantify the relative contribution of emotional restraint, physique, arteriolar reactivity, and other factors. Individuals during the labile or early stages of hypertension may be more variable in their blood pressure response than normotensives or those with fully developed hypertension, and even location may be an important variable. Repeated blood pressures taken at home are being used, since some individuals have a strong emotional reaction to the physical examination (Davies, 1971; Nowlin, 1974). Tibblin (1967) found that individuals who had refused to participate

in his study had such fast pulse rates when he visited them in their home that he discontinued his evaluation of them.

Early clinical studies on coronary heart disease showed a degree of unanimity in the description of a predisposing neurotic state which upon confrontation with external stress would lead to an anxiety reaction, and cardiovascular changes which could lead to coronary heart disease. As studies increased in sample size and methodologic refinement, clinical judgments about anxiety and neuroticism were replaced by psychologic measures. The two most commonly used tests have been the MMPI and the Cattell 16 Personality Factor Inventory (16 PF) (Jenkins, 1971).

In a prospective study, Ostfeld, Lebovitz, Shekelle, and Paul (1964) administered the MMPI and the Cattell 16 PF to 1,900 working men and found that anxiety and neuroticism appeared to precede coronary disease, particularly angina pectoris. In a follow-up of these men, Lebovitz, Shekelle, Ostfeld, and Oglesby (1967) found that the manifestation of myocardial infarction or angina pectoris heightened the degree of anxiety in patients. Retrospective studies have reported similar findings (Bakker, 1968; Bakker and Levenson, 1967; Brozek, Keys, and Blackburn, 1966; Bruhn, Chandler, and Wolf, 1969).

Of particular interest is the finding in several studies involving both middle-aged and older individuals that the Cattell 16 PF, Factor O which measures anxiety, apprehension, and sensitivity to people's approval and disapproval was related to coronary disease. Among middle-aged men, Bakker (1968) found that those with angina pectoris were more apprehensive and anxious, while Caffrey (1969) found that those who died after infarction had been more apprehensive and anxious according to their pre-illness scores on the Cattell 16 PF, Factor O than those who survived. In an older population, Nowlin, Williams, and Wilkie (1973) reported on 261 men who were followed from 1968-1972 in the Duke Adaptation Study. During that period, 19 men (mean age, 65.5 years) suffered acute myocardial infarction (AMI). A comparison of their Cattell 16 PF scores as well as the physiological measures taken before the onset of illness with a group of 48 healthy old men in a multiple regression analysis indicated that those who subsequently developed AMI were more apprehensive and anxious as measured by the Cattell 16 PF, Factor O and had higher systolic blood pressure and cholesterol levels than the healthy old men.

Brown and Ritzman (1967) examined 133 aged male patients and found that a significantly larger proportion of the patients with coronary disease reported excessive stress, worry, and tension over their lifetime than those with no CHD. In addition, 83 percent of those with CHD compared to 17 percent with no CHD indicated they had been very competitive, aggressive and concerned with social status during their lifetime. Other factors associated with CHD among these elderly men included excessive eating, a family history of heart disease, lack of regular exercise and physical manifestations of generalized arteriosclerosis.

In summarizing the results of these studies, it would appear that middle-aged as well as older men who develop coronary disease are more anxious as reflected in their psychologic test profiles. Differences have been found between individuals who were about to develop angina pectoris and those with coronary disease without angina. In contrast, a few investigators have found no evidence that anxiety may be related to the development of coronary disease. Caffrey (1969) reported that monks with CHD were well adjusted and had low anxiety levels as measured by the Cattell 16 PF; however, this finding may in part be due to their less competitive environment. Rosenman (1974) maintains that the Type A coronary-prone behavior pattern does not include manifest anxiety as a characteristic, although it has been associated with heightened neuroendocrine activity.

Thus, it would appear that whether the individual who develops coronary disease is anxious or not depends in part upon how anxiety is defined and measured. We may confuse "trait" anxiety to represent neuroticism, as measured by psychological tests, with "state" anxiety as measured specific to the situation or with arousal as measured by neuro-endocrine activity. Further clarification is clearly advisable as is the use of objective measures of personality and behavior in order to avoid some of the problems currently found in the literature.

Hypertension is unrecognized by many who have it and the study sample should be representative of the population in general rather than of those who seek treatment. Identification of one's health is obviously a significant variable and the data should be interpreted in terms of the subject's overall health status. For example, Garrity and Klein (1971) observed that patients post myocardial infarction (MI) with negative attitudes toward their illness had a poorer prognosis, but they had also been in the poorest health prior to the heart attack. Among the aged, in particular, it appears that changes in personal perception, expectation, or denial may in part account for the differences in health perceptions in self-ratings as compared to the physicians' ratings (Suchman, Phillips, and Streib, 1958).

Coronary-Prone Behavior Pattern. Rosenman and Friedman have described behavior which has been associated with coronary disease among men in a prospective study. By this writing, these investigator-clinicians have published about 50 articles and books on "Type A" or coronary-prone behavior, albeit not without some criticism (Scott, 1974). Their work is noteworthy because it is perhaps the only large scale prospective study which has involved men initially aged 39–59 years that has included a behavioral measure along with numerous physiological measures.

The Type A pattern has been defined as a style of living characterized by excesses of competitiveness, striving for achievement, aggressiveness, time urgency, restlessness, acceleration of common activities (e.g., walking, eating), hostility, hyperalertness, explosiveness of speech amplitude, tenseness of facial musculature and feelings of struggling against the limitations of time and the insensitivity of the environment. The Type A person is punctual and greatly annoyed if kept waiting. In his impatience, he anticipates what others will say and frequently interrupts to answer questions before they are fully asked. The Type A behavior pattern is not a personality trait (Jenkins, Rosenman, and Zyzanski, 1974) but is associated with traits which emerge in susceptible individuals when certain challenges or conditions of the milieu arise (Rosenman, 1974).

The converse of Type A behavior pattern is Type B, characterized by the relative absence of this interplay of psychological traits and situational pressures as well as low coronary risk. About 10 percent of their subjects had a fully developed form of Type A or B behavior, while the remainder had less fully developed forms of these behavior patterns (Rosenman and Friedman, 1971a). Classification is made by a structured interview where the emphasis in scoring is more upon the style of response than the content of the answers (Rosenman, Friedman, Straus, Wurm, Kositchek, Han, and Werthessen, 1964). Although attempts have been made to develop objective tests for assessing this behavior pattern (Bortner and Rosenman, 1967; Jenkins, Zyzanski, and Rosenman, 1971), so far the interview method distinguishes better between the fully and less well developed forms of this behavior pattern and is a better predictor of coronary disease (Rosenman, 1974).

In 1960-1961, Rosenman and Friedman started a prospective study which included about 3,400 men aged 39-59 years who were free of coronary disease at intake. Subjects were classified into the behavior patterns and numerous physiological measures were obtained. Rosenman (1974) in summarizing much of this research indicated that follow-up evaluations were made at the end of 2½, 4½, and 8½ years. To date, the results indicate that Type A men have been twice as prone to develop clinical CHD as the group initially assessed as Type B. Further, the initially healthy Type A's were five times more prone to a second MI and fatal attacks occurred twice as frequently in Type A subjects as in Type B subjects.

It has been postulated that because Type A individuals without manifest CHD show biochemical changes similar to those observed in individuals with manifest CHD, this may be the mechanism whereby they subsequently develop CHD. As summarized by Rosenman and Friedman (1971b), the Type A behavior pattern has been associated with elevations in serum cholesterol, fasting triglycerides, and serum pre-beta lipoproteins, accelerated blood coagulation and higher daytime excretion of catecholamines in the working milieu.

Although in these studies CHD was associated with the standard biologic risk factors, a multiple regression analysis controlling for 12 risk factors did not seriously reduce the relation of the behavior pattern to CHD in the men aged 39-49 but it did reduce its impact sufficiently in the men aged 50-59 so that the behavior pattern alone was no longer a statistically significant predictor of CHD at the older ages (Rosenman, Friedman, Straus, Jenkins, Zyzanski, Wurm, and Kositchek, 1970).

Type A behavior alone has consistently been a poor predictor of CHD among the older subjects (Rosenman et al., 1964; Rosenman, Friedman, Straus, Wurm, Jenkins, Messenger, Kositchek, Hahn, and Werthessen, 1966). As a consequence, subjects past age 59 were apparently eliminated from the data analysis of the 8½ year follow-up study (Rosenman et al., 1970). It appears that these investigators have not completely determined the nature of the relationship between behavior and CHD among the aged. Friedman and Rosenman (1974) state that ". . . In the absence of Type A Behavior Pattern, coronary heart disease almost never occurs before 70 years of age, regardless of the fatty foods eaten, the cigarettes smoked, or the lack of exercise. But when this behavior pattern is present, coronary heart disease can easily erupt in one's thirties, or forties" (preface).

Since the relationship between behavior pattern and CHD apparently has been based upon classification of behavior at the initial evaluation (Rosenman and Friedman, 1971a), it would be interesting to know whether this behavior pattern changed with increasing age. Rosenman (1974) postulated that if the challenges or conflicts of the milieu were removed, it is possible that a Type A behavior pattern might lessen or even disappear. Lowenthal (1975) observed among her subjects, that the middle-aged men were more concerned about work related problems than older men in the pre-retirement stage. It is unclear from the Rosenman and Friedman studies whether the decrease in the predictive value of the Type A behavior pattern to CHD in the aged is due only to age-related physiological changes or whether changes in behavior may also affect this relationship. They have paid little attention to other dimensions of personality such as the role of defense mechanisms (i.e., denial, etc.) but this could be an interesting area to pursue since many Type A subjects have not developed CHD during the period studied (Rosenman and Friedman, 1971a). There is some evidence suggesting that the behavior pattern may be specific to CHD and not to diseases in general (Kenigsberg, Zyzanski, Jenkins, Wardwell, and Licciardellow, 1974). Although most of the research on this behavior pattern has been limited to middle-aged men, there is some indication that Type A women may have similar biochemical changes (Friedman and Rosenman, 1957) and CHD (Kenigsberg et al., 1974).

Life Event Changes. Further inquiry is taking place into mechanisms by which "life stress" may affect susceptibility to illness (Gunderson, 1974). Rahe (1974, p. 58) states ". . . constitutional endowment helps to explain an individual's susceptibleness to particular types of illness but does little to explain why an individual develops an illness at a particular point in time." Consequently, some investigators focus upon life event changes preceding disease onset in an attempt to explain why an illness occurs at a particular time.

Based upon the assumption that any major change in daily living may affect susceptibility to disease, Holmes and Rahe (1967) developed *The Social Readjustment Rating* Scale (SSRQ) (see Table 1) for evaluating the impact of life changes empirically determined to precede the onset of illness. This approach has now been widely used. The Holmes and Rahe scale consists of 43 items of varying consequence ranging from minor traffic violations to marriage, to death of spouse. The total score is called the "life crisis unit" and the higher the score the greater the likelihood of developing

TABLE 1. THE SOCIAL READJUSTMENT RATING SCALE.[a]

Life event	Mean value
1. Death of spouse	100
2. Divorce	73
3. Marital separation	65
4. Jail term	63
5. Death of close family member	63
6. Personal injury or illness	53
7. Marriage	50
8. Fired at work	47
9. Marital reconciliation	45
10. Retirement	45
11. Change in health of family member	44
12. Pregnancy	40
13. Sex difficulties	39
14. Gain of new family member	39
15. Business readjustment	39
16. Change in financial state	38
17. Death of close friend	37
18. Change to different line of work	36
19. Change in number of arguments with spouse	35
20. Mortgage over $10,000	31
21. Foreclosure of mortgage or loan	30
22. Change in responsibilities at work	29
23. Son or daughter leaving home	29
24. Trouble with in-laws	29
25. Outstanding personal achievement	28
26. Wife begin or stop work	26
27. Begin or end school	26
28. Change in living conditions	25
29. Revision of personal habits	24
30. Trouble with boss	23
31. Change in work hours or conditions	20
32. Change in residence	20
33. Change in schools	20
34. Change in recreation	19
35. Change in church activities	19
36. Change in social activities	18
37. Mortgage or loan less than $10,000	17
38. Change in sleeping habits	16
39. Change in number of family get-togethers	15
40. Change in eating habits	15
41. Vacation	13
42. Christmas	12
43. Minor violations of the law	11

[a]See Holmes, T. H., and Rahe, R. H. The Social readjustment rating scale, *J. Psychosomatic Res.* **11:** 213–218, 1967, for complete wording of the items. Reprinted by permission from Microforms International Marketing Corp., Inc. (p. 216).

an illness (Holmes and Masuda, 1973). The items on the test describe unpleasant and pleasant events. Levi (1971) has some evidence to support the assumption that changes of a pleasant nature as well as those of an unpleasant nature confront the organism with the necessity to adapt and that the organism reacts to both with the same physiological preparation for flight or fight. Based upon these assumptions, any significant life change may affect susceptibility to disease (Holmes and Holmes, 1970; Rahe, 1969, 1974; Rahe and Arthur, 1968). Conversely, when individuals' lives are in a relatively steady state of psychosocial adjustment with few recent life changes, little or no illness tends to be reported (Rahe, 1969; Rahe and Arthur, 1968).

In a number of retrospective studies, it has been observed that myocardial infarctions are associated with significant increases in life changes during the six-month period prior to disease onset (Theorell and Rahe, 1971) which have frequently been associated with work-related problems (Theorell and Rahe, 1974). Because retrospective studies have been criticized, Theorell and Rahe (1974) have in progress a prospective study involving 7,000 men on whom they are obtaining measures of life changes, along with psychological, social and biological measures.

Changes in life events are related to changes in neuroendocrine activity. Theorell and Rahe (1974) performed a 3-month follow-up of 21 men, aged 45 to 66 years, who had survived a MI and returned to their preinfarction life-style. For some of these subjects, changes in life events each week were related to elevated catecholamine levels. Among young, healthy men, changes in life events were associated with heightened endocrine activity during Navy training (Rubin, 1974; Rubin and Rahe, 1974).

The relationship between changes in life events and health has not been extensively studied among the aged. Neugarten (1970) has suggested that expected life events may not in themselves constitute stress. Thus, although the death of a spouse has been implicated as raising the risk of coronary disease, it may be that the aged are more psychologically prepared for such losses and would not have an adverse reaction. Heyman and Gianturco (1973) found little or no health deterioration following bereavment in those over 65 years of age. On the other hand, Parkes, Benjamin, and Fritz-

gerald (1969) found that a group of widowers had a higher death rate in the six months immediately following their spouses' deaths than did their married peers. Gerber, Rusalem, Hannon, Battin, and Arkin (1975) also found that widowers had more medical problems than widows in the six-month period after their spouses' deaths. They also noted that those aged bereaved whose spouses died after a lengthy chronic illness did less well than those whose partners died after a shorter chronic illness. Atchley (1975) observed that economic circumstances were an important factor influencing the social situation of some widows. Thus, it may be important to know the context in which life changes may occur. Life changes should be evaluated to determine to what extent the individual has control over the event, previous experience in dealing with such changes, resources for coping, health status, and degree of anticipation and preparation (Lowenthal and Chiriboga, 1973; Nelson, 1974). Since the number of life changes apparently decreases with increasing age (Holmes and Holmes, 1970; Lowenthal, 1975) one could speculate that in old age fewer changes would be required to produce health changes, particularly if the system is already weakened by disease. Thus, existing illness or a relatively more passive, less interactive pattern may result in an accentuated reaction to a given life change event in old age.

STRESS, DISEASE, AND BEHAVIOR

The relationship between physiological and cognitive functioning is a complex one. To date, the findings pertaining to this relationship have been correlational in nature, and the focus has been upon cardiovascular disease rather than other potentially relevant physiological or pathological changes.

Wang and Busse (1974) found that intellectual impairment, as measured by the Wechsler Adult Intelligence Scale (WAIS), was associated with both compensated and decompensated heart disease more so than would have been expected on the basis of the EEG and neurological findings alone. In general, however, a significant relationship between EEG and psychological test results have not been found in community aged (Birren, Butler, Greenhouse, Sokoloff, and Yarrow, 1963; Obrist, Busse, Eisdorfer, and Kleemeier, 1962).

These findings tend to support Birren and colleagues' (1963) "discontinuity hypothesis" which suggests that variations in cognitive functioning may remain largely autonomous of somatic functions until limiting levels are reached probably as a result of disease or trauma which would then result in a new set of relationships.

Szafran, in a review of his work (1968) reported that the cardiopulmonary status of healthy pilots was related to choice reaction times, sequential decision making, and the rate at which information can be processed under conditions of information overload. He suggested that decreased cardiovascular function may, because of its effect on cerebral circulation, increase "neural noise," which could in turn decrease efficient information processing. A slowing in response speed has also been associated with elevations in blood pressure (Birren, 1965; Wilkie and Eisdorfer, 1972). Botwinick and Storandt (1974) found that self-reported symptoms of cardiovascular disease were related to a slowing in response speeds.

Among men aged 35 to 59, Spieth (1965) found that subjects with cardiovascular disease did not perform as well as did healthy subjects on a variety of tasks including a serial reaction time task, the WAIS Digit Symbol and Block Design subtests. He also noted that unmedicated hypertensives performed almost as slowly as those with cerebrovascular disease, but that hypertensives whose blood pressure was kept within normotensive limits by medication performed about the same as normotensive subjects. Spieth suggested that most of the slowing occurred with the more complex problems and came not in the "doing" but rather in the "deciding what to do" phase. Despite his finding that subjects taking antihypertensive medications performed about the same as healthy subjects, Spieth's line of research has not been followed.

In a 10-year longitudinal study, Wilkie and Eisdorfer (1971) examined the relationship between blood pressure (BP) and intellectual functioning among individuals initially aged

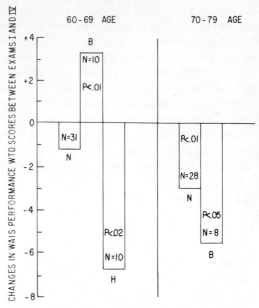

Figure 3. Intellectual change (delta scores) over a 10-year period, as measured by the Wechsler Adult Intelligence Scale (WAIS) among individuals initially examined at ages 60 to 69 and 70 to 79 with either normal (N), borderline elevated (B), or heightened (H) diastolic blood pressure on the initial examination. (From Wilkie and Eisdorfer, 1971. *Science*, **172**, 959–962. Copyright 1971 by the American Association for the Advancement of Science.)

60–79 years. In this study, diastolic BP was used and subjects were divided into a normal group with pressures between 66 and 95 mm Hg, a borderline elevated group with pressures between 96 and 105 mm Hg and a high group with pressures of over 105 mm Hg. As seen in Figure 3, the results indicate that BP was related to significant intellectual loss in performance weighted scores which was reflected in the full scale scores over the 10-year period among the subjects initially examined in their sixties. Their counterparts with normal and borderline elevations had relatively little intellectual change. For the subjects initially examined at 70–79 years of age, none with hypertension survived the 10-year follow-up program. These results suggest that severe hypertension is related to intellectual changes among the aged. Of interest was the finding that those with mild elevations of BP in the

60-69 age group showed some increase in WAIS scores over the follow-up period, which the investigators suggested supported Obrist's (1964) contention that mild elevations of BP may be valuable among the aged to maintain adequate cerebral circulation. The failure to duplicate this pattern in the group initially aged 70-79 suggests that other factors may be operating in more advanced age to compromise cerebral functioning.

Goldman, Kleinman, Snow, Bidus, and Korol (1974) observed among middle-aged men (mean age, 47.6 years) that diastolic BP was related to performance on the Categories subtest of the Halstead-Reitan Neuropsychological Test Battery. They suggested that essential hypertension is related to a type of psychological deficit that characterizes brain dysfunction.

Reitan and Shipley (1963) examined the effect of reducing cholesterol levels upon performance on the Halstead-Reitan Battery in men with serum cholesterol levels of 240 mg/100 ml or more. They found that improvement in performance was proportionately greater for the men past the fourth and fifth decades of life when their cholesterol levels were reduced by 10 percent or more.

Abrahams and Birren (1973) found that men aged 25 to 59 years who appeared to be free of cardiovascular disease but possessed the Rosenman and Friedman (1971a) Type A coronary-prone behavior pattern had significantly longer response latencies in both simple and choice reaction times and were disproportionately slower in choice reaction times than Type B subjects. Birren (1974, p. 84) suggests that ". . . while age appears to be accompanied by normal psychophysiological slowing it is exacerbated by the presence of disease, particularly those diseases of a stress character and involving the sympathetic nervous system."

Cerebral circulatory insufficiency is probably the prime factor accounting for the association between cardiovascular disease and poorer performance in humans. Since hypertension is often associated with atherosclerosis and heart disease, cerebral vascular insufficiency may in part account for poor performance. However, for the early stages of essential hypertension and in the absence of atherosclerotic lesions, the suggestion that circulatory insufficiency is the basis for psychological dysfunction is somewhat less tenable.

According to Forsyth (1974) in the early stages of essential hypertension, blood pressure may be only transiently elevated, but there may be exaggerated fluctuations in response to emotional or environmental stressors. Some investigators believe that excessive sympathetic nervous system (SNS) activity may be one of the primary mechanisms in essential hypertension (Dustan, Tarazi, and Bravo, 1972) and most treatment of clinical hypertension is now in part accomplished by interfering with SNS transmission either at the pre- or post-ganglionic level (Forsyth, 1974). This could be support for Spieth's (1965) contention that the stress of a testing situation may have more effect on the circulatory hemodynamics (and in turn on performance levels) of hypertensives than on normotensives.

There is extensive literature indicating that performance can be affected by stress or heightened arousal levels (Broadbent, 1971; Eisdorfer, 1968; Ellis, 1975; Haythorn and Altman, 1967; McKeachie, 1974) accompanied by heightened autonomic nervous system activity (Broverman et al., 1974; O'Hanlon, 1973; Troyer, Eisdorfer, Bogdonoff, and Wilkie, 1967; Troyer, Eisdorfer, Wilkie, and Bogdonoff, 1966; Eisdorfer, Nowlin, and Wilkie, 1970). Although the relationship is a complex one, it is believed that low arousal as well as high arousal produce inefficiency and that performance is best at an intermediate level of arousal. Thus, the relationship between performance and arousal is frequently illustrated by the inverted U shaped curve. This relationship may be influenced by numerous factors such as the nature of the stress, the nature of the task, and the personality of the individual (Broadbent, 1971).

Relatively little attention has been paid to the relationship between stress and performance among those with cardiovascular disease. Krantz, Glass, and Synder (1974) have observed that individuals apparently free of coronary disease but possessing the Type A coronary-prone behavior pattern performed better than

Type B's under uncontrollable, moderate stress but performed worse under high stress conditions. Since persons with cardiovascular disease often seem more anxious (at least as measured by psychological tests) than healthy individuals, the poor performance observed among individuals with cardiovascular disease may in part be due to situational stress which may be exacerbated in the face of pathological changes as the disease progresses.

CONCLUSION

There is much data to support the hypothesis that patterns of behavior including performance on tests of intellectual and cognitive functioning relate to ongoing stress, disease, and pre-disease states independent of aging. A growing body of evidence is also elucidating the relationship between disease state and a variety of situational factors leading to stress. The process by which stress (however initiated) as a transitory psychophysiological event leads to a more permanent disruption in physiologic state characteristic of disease is hypothesized, but as yet unproven. Stress as a basis for accelerated aging is also a reasonable hypothesis but one which needs more empirical study.

The implications of a relationship between stress, disease, aging, and behavior goes beyond theoretical interest. An understanding of the nature of these variables and the interactions involved, carries with it the potential for intervention not only at the behavioral level but at the somatic level as well. It is clear that stress, a physiological event, may have social and psychological antecedents as well as physical etiologies. The potential consequences of mediating stresses throughout the life span is fascinating to contemplate.

REFERENCES

Abrahams, J. P., and Birren, J. E. 1973. Reaction time as a function of age and behavioral predisposition to coronary heart disease. *J. Gerontol.*, 28, 471-478.

Acheson, R. M. 1961. Aetiology of coronary heart disease in old men. *Brit. J. Prevent & Social Med.*, 15, 49-55.

Aldrich, C. K., and Mendkoff, E. 1963. Relocation of the aged and disabled: A mortality study. *J. Am. Geriat. Soc.*, 11, 185-194.

Appley, M. H., and Trumbull, R. (eds.) 1967. *Psychological Stress*. New York: Appleton-Century-Crofts.

Atchley, R. C. 1975. Dimensions of widowhood in later life. *Gerontologist*, 15 (2), 176-178.

Bakker, C. B. 1968. Psychological factors in angina pectoris. *Psychosomatics*, 8, 43-49.

Bakker, C. B., and Levenson, R. M. 1967. Determinants of angina pectoris. *Psychosomat. Med.*, 29, 621-633.

Benson, H., and Gutmann, M. C. 1974. The relation of environmental factors to systemic arterial hypertension. *In*, R. S. Eliot (ed.), *Stress and the Heart*, Vol. 1, pp. 13-31. New York: Futura.

Birren, J. E. 1965. Age changes in speed of behavior: Its central nature and physiological correlates. *In*, A. T. Welford and J. E. Birren (eds.), *Behavior, Aging, and the Nervous System*, pp. 191-216. Springfield, Illinois: Charles C. Thomas.

Birren, J. E. 1974. Translations in gerontology—from lab to life: Psychophysiology and speed of response. *American Psychologist*, 29, 808-815.

Birren, J. E., Butler, R. N., Greenhouse, S. W., Sokoloff, L., and Yarrow, M. R. (eds.) 1963. Interdisciplinary relationships: Interrelations of physiological, psychological and psychiatric findings in healthy men. *In*, *Human Aging: A Biological and Behavioral Study* (USPHS Publ. No. 986). Washington, D.C.: Government Printing Office.

Bortner, R. W., and Rosenman, R. H. 1967. The measurement of pattern A behavior. *J. Chronic Diseases*, 20, 525-533.

Botwinick, J. 1973. *Aging and Behavior*. New York: Springer.

Botwinick, J., and Storandt, M. 1974. Cardiovascular status, depressive affect and other factors in reaction time. *J. Gerontol.*, 29, 543-548.

Brady, J. V. 1970. Endocrine and autonomic correlates of emotional behavior. *In*, P. Black (ed.), *Physiological Correlates of Emotion*, pp. 95-125. New York: Academic Press.

Bridges, P. K., Jones, M. T., and Leak, D. 1968. A comparative study of four physiological concomitants of anxiety. *Arch. Gen. Psychiat.*, 19, 141-145.

Broadbent, D. E. 1971. *Decision and Stress*. New York: Academic Press.

Brod, J. 1971. The influence of higher nervous processes induced by psychosocial environment on the development of essential hypertension. *In*, L. Levi (ed.), *Society, Stress and Disease*, pp. 312-323. London: Oxford University Press.

Broverman, D. M., Klaiber, E. L., Vogel, W., and Kobayashi, Y. 1974. Short-term versus long-term effects of adrenal hormones on behavior. *Psych. Bull.*, 81, 672-694.

Brown, R. C., and Ritzman, L. 1967. Some factors associated with absence of coronary heart disease in persons aged 65 or older. *J. Am. Geriat. Soc.*, 15, 239-249.

Brozek, J., Keys, A., and Blackburn, H. 1966. Personality differences between potential coronary and noncoronary subjects. *Ann. NY Acad. Sci.*, **134**, 1057–1064.

Bruhn, J. G., Chandler, B., and Wolf, S. 1969. A psychological study of survivors and nonsurvivors of myocardial infarction. *Psychosomat. Med.*, **31**, 8–19.

Busse, E. W. 1969. Theories of aging. *In*, E. W. Busse and E. Pfeiffer (eds.), *Behavior and Adaptation in Late Life*, pp. 11–32. Boston: Little, Brown.

Caffrey, B. 1969. Behavior patterns and personality characteristics related to prevalence rates of coronary heart disease in American monks. *J. Chronic Diseases*, **22**, 93–103.

Carp, F. M. (ed.) 1972. *Retirement*. New York: Behavioral Publications.

Caudill, W. 1958. *Effects of Social and Cultural System in Reaction to Stress*. Pamphlet No. 14. New York: Social Sciences Council.

Coelho, G. V., and Adams, J. E. 1974. Introduction. *In*, G. V. Coelho, D. A. Hamburg, and J. E. Adams (eds.), *Coping and Adaptation*, pp. xv–xxv. New York: Basic Books.

Cohen, S. I., and Shmavonian, B. M. 1967. Catecholamines, vasomotor conditioning and aging. *In*, L. Gittman (ed.), *Endocrines and Aging*, pp. 102–120. Springfield, Illinois: Charles C. Thomas.

Coté, L. J., and Kremzner, L. T. 1974. Changes in neurotransmitter systems with increasing age in human brain. *In*, *Transactions of the American Society for Neurochemistry*. 5th Annual Meeting, New Orleans, Louisiana.

Croog, S. H. 1970. The family as a source of stress. *In*, S. Levine, and N. A. Scotch (eds.), *Social Stress*, pp. 19–53. Chicago: Aldine.

Croog, S. H., Levine, S., and Lurie, J. 1968. The heart patient and the recovery process: A review of the directions of research on social and psychological factors. *Soc. Sci. Med.*, **2**, 111–164.

Davies, M. H. 1971. Is high blood pressure a psychosomatic disorder? A critical review of the evidence. *J. Chronic Diseases*, **24**, 239–258.

Dodge, D. L., and Martin, W. T. (eds.) 1970. *Social Stress and Chronic Illness*. Notre Dame; University of Notre Dame Press.

Dunbar, F. 1943. *Psychosomatic Diagnosis*. New York: Paul B. Hoeber.

Dustan, H. P., Tarazi, R. C., and Bravo, E. L. 1972. Physiologic characteristics of hypertension. *Am. J. Med.*, **52**, 610–622.

Eisdorfer, C. 1968. Arousal and performance: Experiments in verbal learning and a tentative theory. *In*, G. Talland (ed.), *Human Behavior and Aging: Recent Advances in Research and Theory*, pp. 189–216. New York: Academic Press.

Eisdorfer, C. 1972. Adaptation to loss of work. *In*, F. M. Carp (ed.), *Retirement*, pp. 245–265. New York: Behavioral Publications.

Eisdorfer, C. 1974. Strategy on health and the aged. Unpublished manuscript.

Eisdorfer, C., Nowlin, J., and Wilkie, F. 1970. Improvement of learning in the aged by modification of autonomic nervous system activity. *Science*, **170**, 1327–1320.

Eisdorfer, C., Nowlin, J., and Wilkie, F. 1976. Effects of oral propranolol on serial learning. Unpublished manuscript.

Eisdorfer, C., Powell, A. H., Silverman, G., and Bogdonoff, M. D. 1965. The characteristics of lipid mobilization and peripheral disposition in aged individuals. *J. Gerontol.*, **20**, 511–514.

Eisdorfer, C., and Raskind, M. 1975. Aging, hormones and human behavior. *In*, B. Eleftheriou and R. Sprott (eds.), *Hormonal Correlates of Behavior, Vol. I: A Lifespan View*, pp. 369–394. New York: Plenum Press.

Eitinger, L. 1971. Acute and chronic psychiatric and psychosomatic reactions in concentration camp survivors. *In*, L. Levi (ed.), *Society, Stress and Disease*, pp. 219–230. London: Oxford University Press.

Ellis, H. C., 1975. *Human Learning and Cognition*. Dubuque, Iowa: Wm. C. Brown.

Ellison, D. L. 1968. Work, retirement and the sick role. *Gerontologist*, 8 (3), Part 1, 189–192.

Engel, G. L. 1962. *Psychological Development in Health and Disease*. Philadelphia: W. B. Saunders.

Felton, B., and Kahana, E. 1974. Adjustment and situationally-bound locus of control among institutionalized aged. *J. Gerontol.*, **29**, 295–301.

Finch, C. E. 1973. Monoamine metabolism in the aging male mouse. *In*, M. Rockstein and M. L. Sussman (eds.), *Development and Aging in the Nervous System*, pp. 199–210. New York: Academic Press.

Forsyth, R. P. 1974. Mechanisms of the cardiovascular responses to environmental stressors. *In*, P. Obrist, A. H. Black, J. Brener, and L. V. DiCara (eds.), *Cardiovascular Psychophysiology*, pp. 5–32. Chicago: Aldine.

Frankenhaeuser, M., and Rissler, A. 1970. Catecholamine output during relaxation and anticipation. *Perceptual Motor Skills*, **30**, 745–746.

Friedman, M., and Rosenman, R. H. 1957. Comparison of fat intake of American men and women. *Circulation*, **16**, 339–347.

Friedman, M., and Rosenman, R. H. 1974. *Type A Behavior and Your Heart*. New York: Alfred A. Knopf.

Friedman, M., Rosenman, R. H., and Carroll, V. 1958. Changes in the serum cholesterol and blood-clotting time in men subjected to cyclic variation of occupational stress. *Circulation*, **17**, 852–861.

Froehling, S. 1974. Effects of propranolol on behavioral and physiological measures in elderly males. Unpublished doctoral dissertation. University of Miami, Miami, Florida.

Frohlich, E. D. 1974. Hemodynamic concepts in hypertension. *Hospital Practice*, **9**, 59–72.

Gaitz, C. M., and Scott, J. 1975. Analysis of letters to

"Dear Abby" concerning old age. *Gerontologist*, **15** (1), 47–51.

Garrity, T., and Klein, R. F. 1971. A behavioral predictor of survival among heart attack patients. *In*, E. Palmore and F. C. Jeffers (eds.), *Prediction of Life Span*, pp. 215–222. Lexington, Massachusetts: Heath.

Genest, J., and Koiw, E. (eds.) 1972. *Hypertension–1972*. New York: Springer-Verlag.

Gerber, I., Rusalem, R., Hannon, N., Battin, D., and Arkin, A. 1975. Anticipatory grief and aged widows and widowers. *J. Gerontol.*, **30**, 225–229.

Goldman, H., Kleinman, K. M., Snow, M. Y., Bidus, D. R., and Korol, B. 1974. Correlation of diastolic blood pressure and signs of cognitive dysfunction in essential hypertension. *Diseases of the Nervous System*, **35**, 571–572.

Gunderson, E. K. E. 1974. Introduction. *In*, E. K. E. Gunderson and R. H. Rahe (eds.), *Life Stress and Illness*, pp. 3–7. Springfield, Illinois: Charles C. Thomas.

Halliday, J. L. 1943. Principles of aetiology. *Brit. J. Med. Psychol.*, **19**, 367–380.

Harkins, E. B. 1974. Stress and the empty nest transition: A study of the influence of social and psychological factors on emotional and physical health. Unpublished doctoral dissertation. Duke University, Durham, North Carolina.

Harris, R. E., and Singer, M. T. 1967. Interaction of personality and stress in the pathogenesis of essential hypertension. *Hypertension, Proc. Counc. High Blood Pressure Res.*, **16**, 104–115.

Haythorn, W. W., and Altman, I. 1967. Personality factors in isolated environments. *In*, M. H. Appley and R. Trumbull (eds.), *Psychological Stress*, pp. 363–399. New York: Appleton-Century-Crofts.

Henry, J. P., and Cassel, J. C. 1969. Psychosocial factors in essential hypertension: Recent epidemiological and animal experimental evidence. *Am. J. Epidemiol.*, **90**, 171–200.

Herr, J. J., and Birren, J. E. 1973. Differential effects of epinephrine and propranolol on shuttle box avoidance learning in rats of different ages. Unpublished manuscript read at the 26th Annual Meeting of the Gerontological Society, Miami, Florida.

Heyman, D. K., and Gianturco, D. T. 1973. Long-term adaptation by the elderly to bereavement. *J. Gerontol.*, **28**, 359–362.

Holmes, T. H., and Masuda, M. 1973. Life change and illness susceptibility. *In*, J. P. Scott and E. C. Senay (eds.), *Symposium on Separation and Depression*, pp. 161–186. (Publication No. 94.) Washington, D.C.: American Association for the Advancement of Science.

Holmes, T. H., and Rahe, R. H. 1967. The social readjustment rating scale. *J. Psychosomatic Res.*, **11**, 213–218.

Holmes, T. S., and Holmes, T. H. 1970. Short-term intrusions into the life style routine. *J. Psychosomatic Res.*, **14**, 121–123.

Hyams, L., and Loop, A. 1969. The epidemiology of myocardial infarction at two age levels. *Am. J. Epidemiol.*, **90**, 93–102.

Ito, A., and Schanberg, S. M. 1972. Central nervous system mechanisms responsible for blood pressure elevations induced by *p*-chlorophenylalanine. *J. Pharmacol. Exp. Ther.*, **181** (1), 65–74.

Janis, I. L. 1974. Vigilance and decision making in personal crisis. *In*, G. V. Coelho, D. A. Hamburg, and J. E. Adams (eds.), *Coping and Adaptation*, pp. 139–175. New York: Basic Books.

Jenkins, C. D. 1971. Psychologic and social precursors of coronary disease. *New Engl. J. Med.*, **284**, 244–255; 307–317.

Jenkins, C. D., Rosenman, R. H., and Zyzanski, S. J. 1974. Prediction of clinical coronary heart disease by a test for the coronary-prone behavior pattern. *New Engl. J. Med.*, **290**, 1271–1275.

Jenkins, C. D., Zyzanski, S. J., and Rosenman, R. H. 1971. Progress toward validation of a computer-scored test for the Type A coronary-prone behavior pattern. *Psychosomat. Med.*, **33**, 193–202.

Kalt, N. C., and Kohn, M. H. 1975. Pre-retirement counseling: Characteristics of programs and preferences of retirees. *Gerontologist*, **15**, 179–181.

Kärki, N. T. 1956. The urinary excretion of noradrenaline and adrenaline in different age groups, its diurnal variation and the effect of muscular work on it. *Acta Physiol. Scand.*, **39**, (Suppl. 132) 7–96.

Kenigsberg, D., Zyzanski, S. J., Jenkins, C. D. Wardwell, W. I., and Licciardello, A. T. 1974. The coronary-prone behavior pattern in hospitalized patients with and without coronary heart disease. *Psychosomat. Med.*, **36**, 344–351.

Kety, S. S. 1970. Neurochemical aspects of emotional behavior. *In*, P. Black (ed.), *Physiological Correlates of Emotion*, pp. 61–71, New York: Academic Press.

Kleemeier, R. W. 1958. Somatopsychologic effects of illness in the aged person. *Geriatrics*, **13**, 441–448.

Kral, V. A., Grad, B., and Berenson, J. 1968. Stress reactions resulting from the relocation of an aged population. *Canadian Psychiatric Association Journal*, **13**, 201–209.

Krantz, D. S., Glass, D. C., and Snyder, M. L. 1974. Helplessness, stress level, and the coronary-prone behavior pattern. *J. Exp. Soc. Psychol.*, **10**, 284–300.

Kuypers, J. A. 1972. Internal-external locus of control and ego functioning, and personality characteristics in old age. *Gerontologist*, **12** (2), Part 1, 168–173.

Lacey, J. I. 1967. Somatic response patterning and stress: some revisions of activation theory. *In*, M. H. Appley and R. Trumbull (eds.), *Psychological Stress*, pp. 14–37. New York: Appleton-Century-Crofts.

Lawton, M. P., and Nahemow, L. 1973. Ecology and the aging process. *In*, C. Eisdorfer and M. P. Lawton (eds.), *The Psychology of Adult Development and Aging*, pp. 619–674. Washington, D.C.: American Psychological Association.

Lazarus, R. S. 1966. *Psychological Stress and the Coping Process*. New York: McGraw-Hill.

Lazarus, R. S., Averill, J. R., and Opton, E. M., Jr. 1974. The psychology of coping: Issues of research and assessment. *In*, G. V. Coelho, D. A. Hamburg, and J. E. Adams (eds.), *Coping and Adaptation*, pp. 249–315. New York: Basic Books.

Lebovitz, B. Z., Shekelle, R. B., Ostfeld, A. M., and Oglesby, P. 1967. Prospective and retrospective psychological studies of coronary heart disease. *Psychosomat. Med.*, **29**, 265–272.

Levi, L. (ed.) 1971. *Society, Stress and Disease*. London: Oxford University Press.

Levi, L. 1974. Psychosocial stress and disease: A conceptual model. *In*, E. K. E. Gunderson and R. H. Rahe (eds.), *Life Stress and Illness*, pp. 8–33. Springfield, Illinois: Charles C. Thomas.

Levi, L., and Kagan, A. 1971. A synopsis of ecology and psychiatry: Some theoretical psychosomatic considerations, review of some studies and discussion of preventive aspects. *Psychiatry (Part I) Proceedings of the Fifth World Congress of Psychiatry*, pp. 369–379. Amsterdam: Excerpta Medica.

Levine, S., and Scotch, N. A. (eds.) 1970. *Social Stress*. Chicago: Aldine.

Lowenthal, M. F. 1975. Psychosocial variations across the adult life course: Frontiers for research and policy. *Gerontologist*, **15** (1), Part 1, 6–12.

Lowenthal, M. F., Berkman, P. L., and associates. 1967. *Aging and Mental Disorder in San Francisco*. San Francisco: Jossey-Bass.

Lowenthal, M. F., and Chiriboga, D. 1972. Transitions to the empty nest: Crisis, challenge, or relief? *Arch. Gen. Psychiat.*, **26**, 8–14.

Lowenthal, M. F., and Chiriboga, D. 1973. Social stress and adaptation: Toward a life-course perspective. *In*, C. Eisdorfer and M. P. Lawton (eds.), *The Psychology of Adult Development and Aging*, pp. 281–310. Washington, D.C.: American Psychological Association.

Martin, J., and Doran, A. 1967. Perception of retirement: Time and season. Unpublished manuscript. Pilkington Research Project on Retirement, University of Liverpool.

Marx, J. 1974. Aging research (II): Pacemakers for aging? *Science*, **186**, 1196–1197.

Mason, J. W. 1972. Organization of psychoendocrine mechanisms: A review and reconsideration of research. *In*, N. S. Greenfield and R. A. Sternbach (eds.), *Handbook of Psychophysiology*, pp. 3–91. New York: Holt, Rinehart and Winston.

McGrath, J. E. (ed.) 1970. *Social and Psychological Factors in Stress*. New York: Holt, Rinehart and Winston.

McKeachie, W. J. 1974. Instructional Psychology. *Annual Review of Psychology*, **25**, 161–193.

McMahan, C. A., and Ford, T. R. 1955. Surviving the first five years of retirement. *J. Gerontol.*, **10**, 212–215.

Mechanic, D. 1962. *Students Under Stress*. New York: The Free Press.

Mechanic, D. 1968. *Medical Sociology*. New York: The Free Press.

Meyer, G. G. 1974. The closing of the cycle: Old age. *In*, C. L. Bowden and A. G. Burstein (eds.), *Psychological Basis of Medical Practice: An Introduction to Human Behavior*, pp. 203–214. Baltimore: Williams & Wilkins.

Miller, D., and Lieberman, M. A. 1965. The relationships of affect state and adaptive capacity to reactions to stress. *J. Gerontol.*, **20**, 492–497.

Moss, G. E. 1973. *Illness, Immunity & Social Interaction*. New York: Wiley-Interscience.

Müller, H. F., and Grad, B. 1974. Clinical-psychological, electroencephalographic, and adrenocortical relationships in elderly psychiatric patients. *J. Gerontol.*, **29**, 28–38.

Nelson, P. D. 1974. Comment. *In*, E. K. E. Gunderson and R. H. Rahe (eds.), *Life Stress and Illness*, pp. 79–89. Springfield, Illinois: Charles C. Thomas.

Netter, F. H. 1970. *The Ciba Collection of Medical Illustrations: Endocrine System and Selected Metabolic Diseases*, **4**, New York: CIBA.

Neugarten, B. 1970. Adaptation and the life cycle. *Journal of Geriatric Psychiatry*, **4**, 71–100.

Neugarten, B. L. 1973. Personality change in late life: A developmental perspective. *In*, C. Eisdorfer and M. P. Lawton (eds.), *The Psychology of Adult Development and Aging*, pp. 311–335. Washington, D.C.: American Psychological Association.

Nowlin, J. B. 1974. Anxiety during a medical examination. *In*, E. Palmore (ed.), *Normal Aging II*, pp. 77–86. Durham, North Carolina: Duke University Press.

Nowlin, J. B., Williams, R., and Wilkie, F. 1973. Prospective study of physical and psychological factors in elderly men who subsequently suffer acute myocardial infarction (AMI). *Clin. Res.*, **21**, 465.

Obrist, W. D. 1964. Cerebral ischemia and the senescent electroencephalogram. *In*, E. Simonson and T. H. McGavack (eds.), *Cerebral Ischemia*, pp. 71–98. Springfield, Illinois: Charles C. Thomas.

Obrist, W. D., Busse, E. W., Eisdorfer, C., and Kleemeier, R. W. 1962. Relation of the electroencephalogram to intellectual function in senescence. *J. Gerontol.*, **17**, 197–206.

O'Hanlon, J. F. 1973. Interrelationships among performance circulating concentrations of adrenaline, noradrenaline, glucose, and the free fatty acids in men performing a monitoring task. *Psychophysiology*, **10**, 251–259.

Osler, W., and McCrae, T. 1920. *The Principles and Practice of Medicine*. New York: Appleton.

Ostfeld, A. M. 1968. Frequency and nature of health problems of retired persons. *In*, F. M. Carp (ed.), *The Retirement Process* (USPHS Publ. No. 1778), pp. 83–96. Washington, D.C.: U.S. Department of Health, Education, and Welfare.

Ostfeld, A. M., and Lebovitz, B. Z. 1960. Blood pressure lability: A correlative study. *J. Chronic Diseases*, **12**, 428–439.

Ostfeld, A. M., Lebovitz, B. Z., Shekelle, R. B., and Paul, O. 1964. A prospective study of the relationship between personality and coronary heart disease. *J. Chronic Diseases*, **17**, 265–276.

Palmer, R. S. 1930. The significance of essential hypertension among young adult males. *J. Am. Med. Assoc.*, **134**, 9–13.

Palmore, E., and Luikart, C. 1972. Health and social factors related to life satisfaction. *J. of Health and Soc. Behavior*, **13**, 68–80.

Parkes, C. M., Benjamin, B., and Fritzgerald, R. G. 1969. Broken heart: a statistical study of increased mortality among widowers. *Brit. Med. J.*, **1**, 740–743.

Pichot, P. 1971. Quantification of psychological stress responses. *In*, L. Levi (ed.), *Society, Stress and Disease*, pp. 49–52. London: Oxford University Press.

Powell, A. H., Eisdorfer, C., and Bogdonoff, M. D. 1964. Physiologic response patterns observed in a learning task. *Arch. Gen. Psychiat.*, **10**, 192–195.

Raab, W. 1971. Preventive myocardiology—proposals for social action. *In*, L. Levi (ed.), *Society, Stress and Disease*, pp. 389–394. London: Oxford University Press.

Rahe, R. H. 1969. Multi-cultural correlations of life change scaling: America, Japan, Denmark, and Sweden. *J. Psychosomatic Res.*, **13**, 191–195.

Rahe, R. H. 1974. Life change and subsequent illness reports. *In*, E. K. E. Gunderson and R. H. Rahe (eds.), *Life Stress and Illness*, pp. 58–78. Springfield, Illinois: Charles C. Thomas.

Rahe, R. H., and Arthur, R. J. 1968. Life changes surrounding illness experience. *J. Psychosomatic Res.*, **11**, 341–345.

Raskind, M. A., Alvarez, C., Cole, L. A., and Barrett, R. R. 1974. Geriatric crisis intervention: The experience of an outreach team. Unpublished manuscript read at the Gerontological Society 27th Annual Scientific Meeting, Portland, Oregon.

Reimanis, G. 1967. Increase in psychological anomie as a result of radical and undesirable change expectancy. *J. Pers. Soc. Psychol.*, **6**, 454–457.

Reitan, R. M., and Shipley, R. E. 1963. The relationship of serum cholesterol changes to psychological abilities. *J. Gerontol.*, **18**, 350–357.

Robinson, D. S., Nies, A., Davis, J. M., Colburn, R. W., Bourne, H. R., Shaw, D. M., and Coppen, A. J. 1972. Aging, monoamines and monamine-oxidase levels. *Lancet*, **1**, 290–291.

Rosenman, R. H. 1974. The role of behavior patterns and neurogenic factors in the pathogenesis of coronary heart disease. *In*, R. S. Eliot (ed.), *Stress and the Heart*, pp. 123–141. New York: Futura.

Rosenman, R. H., and Friedman, M. 1971a. Observations on the pathogenesis of coronary heart disease. *Nutrition News*, **34**, 9–14.

Rosenman, R. H., and Friedman, M. 1971b. The

central nervous system and coronary heart disease. *Hospital Practice*, **6**, 87–97.

Rosenman, R. H., Friedman, M., Straus, R., Jenkins, C. D., Zyzanski, S., Jr., Wurm, M., and Kositchek, R. 1970. Coronary heart disease in the western collaborative group study. A follow-up experience of 4½ years. *J. Chronic Diseases*, **23**, 173–190.

Rosenman, R. H., Friedman, M., Straus, R., Wurm, M., Jenkins, C. D., Messinger, H. B., Kositchek, R., Hahn, W., and Werthessen, N. T. 1966. Coronary heart disease in the western collaborative group study. A follow-up experience of two years. *J. Am. Med. Assoc.*, **195**, 86–92.

Rosenman, R. H., Friedman, M., Straus, R., Wurm, M., Kositchek, R., Han, W., and Werthessen, N. T. 1964. A predictive study of coronary heart disease. The western collaborative group study. *J. Am. Med. Assoc.*, **189**, 15–22.

Rubin, R. T. 1974. Biochemical and neuroendocrine responses to severe psychological stress. *In*, E. K. E. Gunderson and R. H. Rahe (eds.), *Life Stress and Illness*, pp. 227–241. Springfield, Illinois: Charles C. Thomas.

Rubin, R. T., and Rahe, R. H. 1974. U.S. Navy underwater demolition team training: Biochemical studies. *In*, E. K. E. Gunderson and R. H. Rahe (eds.), *Life Stress and Illness*, pp. 208–226. Springfield, Illinois: Charles C. Thomas.

Ryser, C., and Sheldon, A. 1969. Retirement and health. *J. Am. Geriat. Soc.*, **17** (2), 180–190.

Sainsbury, P. 1960. Psychosomatic disorders and neurosis in outpatients attending a general hospital. *J. Psychosomatic Res.*, **4**, 261–273.

Schenk, E. G. 1963. The problems of premature senescence after a life under extremely difficult conditions. *In*, *Pathology of the Captivity of the Prisoners of War II*. Int. Confeder. Ex-Prisoners of War, Paris.

Scott, R. C. 1974. Doctor's bookshelf: Useful, "if somewhat biased," Type A behavior and your heart. *Med. World News*, May 17, p. 56.

Scott, R., and Howard, A. 1970. Models of stress. *In*, S. Levine and N. A. Scotch (eds.), *Social Stress*, pp. 259–278. Chicago: Aldine.

Selye, H. 1950. *The Physiology and Pathology of Exposure to Stress*. Montreal: Acta.

Selye, H. 1956. *The Stress of Life*. New York: McGraw-Hill.

Selye, H. 1970. Stress and aging. *J. Am. Geriat. Soc.*, **18**, 660–681.

Selye, H. 1971. The evolution of the stress concept—stress and cardiovascular disease. *In*, L. Levi (ed.), *Society, Stress and Disease*, pp. 299–310. London: Oxford University Press.

Simborg, D. W. 1970. The status of risk factors and coronary heart disease. *J. Chronic Diseases*, **22**, 515–552.

Sommerville, W. 1973. Emotions, catecholamines and coronary heart disease. *Early Diagnosis of Coronary Heart Disease, Adv. Cardiol.*, **8**, 162–173.

Spence, D. L. 1968. Patterns of retirement in San Francisco. *In*, F. M. Carp (ed.), *The Retirement Process* (USPHS Publ. No. 1778), pp. 63–75. Washington, D.C.: U.S. Government Printing Office.

Spieth, W. 1965. Slowness of task performance and cardiovascular diseases. *In*, A. T. Welford and J. E. Birren (eds.), *Behavior, Aging and the Nervous System*, pp. 366–400. Springfield, Illinois: Charles C. Thomas.

Stokes, R. G., and Maddox, G. L. 1967. Some social factors on retirement adaptation. *J. Gerontol.*, **22**, 329–333.

Strøm, A. (ed.) 1968. *Norwegian Concentration Camp Survivors*. New York: Humanities Press.

Suchman, E., Phillips, B., and Streib, G. 1958. An analysis of the validity of health questionnaires. *Soc. Forces*, **36**, 223–232.

Szafran, J. 1968. Psychophysiological studies of aging in pilots. *In*, G. A. Talland (ed.), *Human Aging and Behavior*, pp. 37–71. New York: Academic Press.

Theorell, T., and Rahe, R. H. 1971. Psychosocial factors and myocardial infarction. I. An inpatient study in Sweden. *J. Psychosomatic Res.*, **15**, 25–31.

Theorell, T., and Rahe, R. H. 1974. Psychosocial characteristics of subjects with myocardial infarction in Stockholm. *In*, E. K. E. Gunderson and R. H. Rahe (eds.), *Life Stress and Illness*, pp. 90–104. Springfield, Illinois: Charles C. Thomas.

Thompson, W. E., and Streib, G. 1958. Situational determinants, health and economic deprivation in retirement. *J. Soc. Issues*, **14** (2), 18–34.

Tibblin, G. 1967. High blood pressure in men aged 50. *Acta Med. Scand.*, (Suppl. 470), 5–84.

Timaris, P. S. 1972. *Developmental Physiology and Aging*. New York: Macmillan.

Torgersen, S., and Kringlen, E. 1971. Blood pressure and personality. A study of the relationship between intrapair differences in systolic blood pressure and personality in monozygotic twins. *J. Psychosomatic Res.*, **15**, 183–191.

Troyer, W. G., Eisdorfer, C., Bogdonoff, M. D., and Wilkie, F. 1967. Experimental stress and learning in the aged. *J. Abnorm. Psychol.*, **72**, 65–70.

Troyer, W., Eisdorfer, C., Wilkie, F., and Bogdonoff, M. D. 1966. FFA responses in the aged individual during performance of a learning task. *J. Gerontol.*, **21**, 415–419.

Truett, J., Cornfield, J., and Kannel, W. 1967. A multivariate analysis of the risk of coronary heart disease in Framingham. *J. Chronic Diseases*, **20**, 511–524.

Tyhurst, J. S. 1957. The role of transition states—including disasters—in mental illness. *In*, *Symposium on Preventive and Social Psychiatry*, pp. 149–169. Washington, D.C.: Walter Reed Army Institute of Research.

U.S. Public Health Service. 1974. *Health in the Later Years of Life*. Washington, D.C.: Government Printing Office. Stock No. 1722–0178.

U.S. Public Health Service. *Monthly Vital Statistics Report: Summary, 1973.* **22** (13).

Wang, H. S., and Busse, E. W. 1974. Heart disease and brain impairment among aged persons. *In*, E. Palmore (ed.), *Normal Aging II*, pp. 160–167. Durham, North Carolina: Duke University Press.

Wilkie, F., and Eisdorfer, C. 1971. Intelligence and blood pressure in the aged. *Science*, **172**, 959–962.

Wilkie, F., and Eisdorfer, C. 1972. Blood pressure and behavioral correlates in the aged. Unpublished manuscript read at the 9th International Congress of Gerontology, Kiev, USSR.

Wolf, S. 1971. Psychosocial forces in myocardial infarction and sudden death. *In*, L. Levi (ed.), *Society, Stress and Disease*, pp. 324–330. London: Oxford University Press.

Zarit, S. H., and Kahn, R. L. 1975. Aging and adaptation to illness. *J. Gerontol.*, **30**, 67–72.

13
THE IMPACT OF
THE ENVIRONMENT ON
AGING AND BEHAVIOR

M. Powell Lawton
Philadelphia Geriatric Center

There has been a strong surge of interest in environment and aging during the past decade. It seems fair to date the beginning of this interest from the chapter by Kleemeier (1959) in the original *Handbook of Aging and the Individual* (Birren, 1959). Kleemeier emphasized the sensory-perceptual mediation of man-environment transactions, the definition of milieu in social terms, the self as it interacts with different environmental contexts, and more specific social and physical aspects of housing and institutions. Thus, a real debt is owed to him for his early recognition of the possibilities for both theory development and application inherent in such a transactional view of the behavior of older people.

DEFINING THE ENVIRONMENT

"Environment" has been a convenient term to use in general discussions of behavior, but by virtue of its overgeneralized quality, its use masks many ambiguities. New housing, institutionalization, and relocation have been the most frequently studied environmental phenomena. To be sure, each of these involves a change of physical scene, but also a change in the available social network of the individual who moves. We speak of the new environment as "unfamiliar" to the relocated individual. Is the unfamiliarity an environmental phenomenon or an intrapersonal phenomenon? The change of physical scene may involve new movable objects, a new dwelling unit, new patterns of light and sound, new facilities for eating, shopping, toileting, new pathways to these resources, and so on. By considering "environment" as a unitary independent variable in our research, we are clearly doing an injustice to the complexity of the concept. Further precision of definition is necessary both to be able to distinguish among quite different aspects of the environment and to allocate some processes to the proper domain, that is, to the environment, to the individual, or to their interface.

In addition, there are persistent problems in operationalizing environment due to lack of specificity about the scale and complexity of the environmental phenomenon being studied. Relocation, institutionalization and housing are complex and relatively large-scale. The opposite end of the scale and complexity dimensions is represented by the laboratory experiment where context is standardized as much as possible so that the effect of specific stimulus variations may be studied.

Between the microlevel (e.g., of length of exposure of a paired associate) and the macrolevel (e.g., of enforced institutionalization) is a variety of phenomena whose study has both basic and applied relevance: the comprehensibility of graphic material, the orientational cues given by room decor, the relationship between the presence of artifacts from the past and the maintenance of a sense of continuity of self, and so on.

THE INTERFACE OF INDIVIDUAL AND ENVIRONMENT

The number of aspects of individuals subsumed in the P term of the ecological equation $B = f$ (P, E) is as many as have been studied in all the literature of human behavior. Some aspects are closer to the man-environment interface than others, however, such as sensory-perceptual processes and personal style.

Sensory-Perceptual Processes

The decline of some sensory and perceptual functions with age results in less total incoming environmental information and a consequent risk of maladaptive behavior. While we surmise that compensatory adaptations are made to minimize the negative effects of loss of acuity, little is known about the process or the extent to which such personal coping efforts succeed in counteracting maladaptation. On the environmental side, compensatory stimulus modifications such as larger type or loud telephone bells are commonplace.

Personal Style

A personal style is a readiness to process either internal or external stimuli in a particular manner; where a trait describes the content of an individual's potential behavior, style refers to typical mechanisms used by the individual to organize stimuli. The general literature in this area was reviewed by Klein, Barr, and Wolitzky (1967) and a summary chart of characteristics of these styles which have been identified was presented and discussed in Lawton (1975a).

While the significance of personality style for the environmental transactions of the elderly cannot be said to have been validated, one may hypothesize that personality styles

1. regulate the intensity of environmental stimulation.
2. regulate the complexity of stimulation that the individual attempts to process.
3. regulate the relative proportions of total processed stimulation that originate from within the individual and from the environment.
4. regulate the content of environmental information that is perceived, cognized, or acted upon.

THE RESOURCE ENVIRONMENT

Perhaps the most salient single aspect of the older person's living environment aside from his personal habitat is the resources available to him within accessible distance, whether they be life-sustaining facilities such as shops, medical care and police protection, or life-enriching facilities, such as family, friends, cultural opportunities, or a senior center. Before considering the extensive research in this area, however, it is necessary to sharpen definitions of the resource environment, or "social space."

The *physical resource environment* consists of all such facilities located within a physically-defined area, such as that bounded by city limits, specific streets, or a standard radius. The *functional resource environment* is the aggregate of facilities that are actually used. Its physical boundaries are typically irregular and even discontinuous, but this environment decreases in density as distance from the individual's residence increases. The *perceived resource environment* is the individual's definition of his "neighborhood," which is a physical area presumed to be constructed of a varying mix of physical, functional, and symbolic attributes. The *salient resource environment* consists of the resources that are valued highly by the individual, whether because of need or affective attachment. The position of a resource in the hierarchy of salience may be conditioned by realistic limitations on access, such as distance, income, or health. While the physical resource environment exists independently of the individual, the functional, perceived, and salient environments clearly are interactive terms in a modification of the ecological equation $B = f (P, E, P \times E)$. They also may be either idiosyncratic to a particular individual or consensual, that is, areas defined in terms of the agreement of a majority of persons living within a given area.

Regnier, Eribes, and Hansen (1973) and Regnier (1974) found some consensual agreement in the perceived neighborhoods of older people, as well as significant tendencies for males, automobile drivers, higher-income subjects, the healthier, and longer-term residents of the area to indicate larger perceived neighborhoods. Although use was not related directly to perceived neighborhood by Regnier, Eribes, and Hansen (1973), these findings imply that privileged statuses do enlarge one's internal representations of social space. From the fairly large body of material on resource-use by the elderly, the conclusion is that the shorter the distance between a subject and a resource, the greater the likelihood that he will use it.

A full understanding of the dynamics of social space use requires the collation of data from a number of investigations in order to provide baseline estimates of such factors as (a) the proportion who utilize various resources, (b) the frequency of use of resources, (c) the distance to the resources and/or (d) the time required to get to the resource. Information has been drawn from Nahemow and Kogan (1971), Newcomer (1973), Lawton and Nahemow (1975), Regnier (1974), Carp (1973, 1975), Cantor (1975), and Bourg (1975) to provide the consensual material in Table 1. The values shown are approximate medians of the modal values reported by the researchers mentioned above; estimates could not be made of all values.

Some of the processes underlying these data are illustrated schematically in Figure 1, which shows the subject's location in the center (S) of a set of concentric circles. The radial distances from S roughly indicate (a) the percentages of subjects who make trips to a particular resource (open circles), (b) the travel-time (distance) from subject to resource (dark circles), and (c) the frequency with which resources are used (crossed circles). These radial distances actually superimpose on one another three incommensurate scales; some comparability of scales was attained simply by subdividing the distributions of the three attributes and plotting them on a single scale. Arrows are drawn outward from the center to indicate resources that tend to be located relatively

TABLE 1. MODAL USE, TIME AND DISTANCE TO RESOURCES FROM SEVERAL STUDIES.

	Median % using	Modal freq. of use (users)	Modal freq. of use (all)	Modal travel time (users)	Modal use distance-NYC[a]	Modal nearest distance-PH[b]
Grocery	87	2/week	1 or 2/week	7 min.	1 to 3 blocks	1 to 3 blocks
Physician	86	"several"/year	several/year	15 min.	>20 blocks	4 to 10 blocks
Visit one or more children	98	1/week	1/week to never	20 min.	<10? blocks	
Other shopping	70	1 or 2/month	never			
Church	67	1/week	1/week	12 min.	4 to 6 blocks	
Bank	64	1/month			4 to 6 blocks	4 to 10 blocks
Visit friends	61	2 or 3/week	never	7 min.	4 to 6? blocks	
Visit other relatives	57	several/year	never	35 min.		
Beauty/barber shop	40					1 to 3 blocks
Restaurant	31	several/year			>20 blocks	1 to 3 blocks
Park	30				1 to 3 blocks	
Clubs, meetings	29	1/month	never	15 min.	>20 blocks	
Entertainment	19	1/month	never	20 min.	>20 blocks	>11 blocks
Library	18					>11 blocks

[a]Cantor (1975), New York City poverty-area residents.
[b]Newcomer (1973), public housing tenants.

Functional distance
exceeds
physical distance

Functional distance
equals
physical distance

Physical distance
exceeds
functional distance

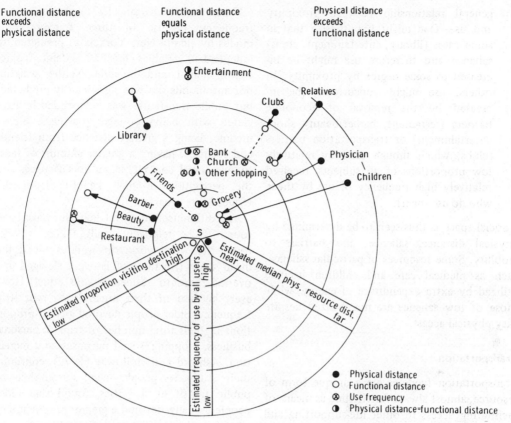

Figure 1. Schematic representation of deviations between physical resource distance, functional resource distance (indexed by proportion of all older people who visit a destination once a year or more), and frequency of use by all who use the resource.

close to most subjects but are used by relatively few older people (negative use-deviation). Arrows drawn from the periphery toward the center indicate resources that, while used by relatively low proportions of all subjects, received relatively high frequency of use by those who do use them.

A certain regularity appears among the use-location relationships portrayed:

1. All of the resources with positive use-deviation are of high salience to the individual, whether by need (medical care), affective ties (children, relatives) or to a small degree, attractiveness (clubs).

2. Among the resources with negative use-deviations, the barber/beauty shop and restaurant are associated with strong economic barriers to use, and library use is probably filtered by sociocultural back-

ground. The negative deviation for friends is produced by the sizeable numbers of isolates (people who name no friends); when one considers those who have any friends, frequency of contact is very high (crossed circle very close to center).

3. Among the resources with no use-deviation, both percentage who use and frequency of use are roughly proportional to (a) distance from subject and (b) presumed salience to the subject—grocery shopping is the most obligatory resource and entertainment the least.

4. Three discretionary activities (Hammer and Chapin, 1972), show relatively high use frequency among users—friends, church, clubs. Even though the proximity effect is strong with each of these three, their high salience for users potentiates use. Thus, barriers and attractions modify the

general relationship between proximity and use. One might hypothesize that in some cases (library, entertainment, clubs) salience and therefore use might be increased to some degree by proximity. In others, use might concurrently be increased by the removal of economic barriers (restaurant, barber/beauty shop, entertainment) or transportation barriers (clubs, which though used by relatively low proportions of all subjects, received relatively high frequency of use by those who do use them).

Social space is thus seen to be determined by physical distance, salience, and barriers to mobility. Some resources of particular salience, such as medical care and children become utilized by extra expenditure of energy, while those of low salience are not utilized despite easy physical access.

Transportation

Transportation facilities are a unique form of resource, almost always functioning as means of facilitating access to other life-supporting and life-enriching facilities, rather than being ends in themselves. Adequate transportation may act as a functional equivalent to proximity to the resource, as seen in the virtually unlimited accessibility of far-flung resources to the affluent automobile driver.

The specifics of transportation behavior have been dealt with more extensively by Cantilli and Shmelzer (1971), Nahemow and Kogan (1971), Carp (1973), Bourg (1975), and Golant (1976). This section will consider only studies that have examined the environmental and personal correlates of transportation behavior.

Carp (1973) found frequency of trips and satisfaction to be most associated with good health, distance from city center, and car ownership. Use of public transportation was most highly associated with living in the city center, good health, relative youth, and nearness to a bus stop. Walking was done most by males, those who lived in the city center, and were in good health. Among city-center residents 50 percent walked every day, while in the suburbs fully 50 percent never walked.

Nahemow and Kogan (1971) also examined frequency of use of three transportation modes by elderly New Yorkers as predicted by independent variables classified as demographic, environmental, and life-style. Neither walking nor automobile use was significantly predicted, but public transit use was independently associated with being younger, having a higher income, being a greater distance from friends and relatives, having a greater amount of face-to-face social contact, larger social space, and the perception of high benefits from the reduced-fare program.

Age differences in travel behavior have been found to be relatively small. Golant (1972) found that when work trips were excluded, the mean daily trip rates of late middle-aged and over-65 Toronto residents were equal. However, because of their much lower work-trip frequency, older people devoted greater proportions of their total number of trips to personal business, shopping, social purposes, and recreation. Ashford and Holloway (1972), confining their study to people using automobile or public transit in six cities, found that older people actually devoted a greater proportion of all trips to central-city destinations and to destinations outside the zone of their own residences; their trips were no different in length from those of other adults. This study did not deal with the restricted social space of the immobile older person or the walker, but the findings showed a most important exception to the generalization that old age is associated with a restriction of functional space: once the set of personal, financial, and environmental barriers to initiating an automobile or transit trip have been overcome, social space if anything expands with the freedom from time constraints consequent to retirement. Distant resources retain their attractions for the most mobile elderly.

Activity Patterns

Knowing the locations where different behaviors occur and their relative frequency can give important clues regarding the attraction of the locations and the degree of congruence of these environments with the needs of specific user groups. Satisfactory exploration of place-specific behavioral patterns requires an adequate taxonomy of both locations and behaviors, neither of which is presently available. A major problem in such efforts is the level of generality of the rubrics under which specific behaviors may be categorized. For some purposes, gross or highly abstracted categories may be most suitable, as Lawton (1970a) attempted in the hierarchical representation of the behaviors of older people shown in Figure 2. The columns represent very general types of behavior, arranged from left to right in an order roughly representing an increase in the level of complexity of each behavior type. Within a given behavior type, specific behaviors may also be ranked on a vertical axis in terms of their degree of complexity; examples of such behaviors are shown within the columns. It is clear that the types overlap greatly in their complexity, although the hierarchy among types is indicated by the increasing heights of the columns. No attempt was made in this scheme to classify specific behaviors exhaustively or to relate them to spatial locations.

Chapin and Brail (1969) and Hammer and Chapin (1972), on the other hand, began with highly specific behaviors (referred to as "activity patterns") to evolve an activity classification system at several levels of abstraction. One early system had 217 entries grouped under headings labeled homemaking, vacation, religious and cultural activities, visiting, leisure and recreation, movement, public affairs, health, and miscellaneous activities. A later one was reduced to 38 categories. Among these, "obligatory" activities are self-maintaining and instrumental behaviors that are relatively highly programmed and whose time demands are, for the adult population, considered relatively invariant as compared to the social and personal leisure-time activities included in the "discretionary" group. Chapin and Brail (1969) found in a large sample from 43 different metropolitan areas that older people engaged more in relaxation, reading and television watching, and less in work-related and out-of-home obligatory activities than did younger people. Adults spent 80 percent of their discretionary time at home—ranging from 64 percent for childless couples and unattached single people to 85 percent for the unemployed, for full-time workers, for people engaged in child-rearing, and for people 65 and over. Thus once again, the image of the

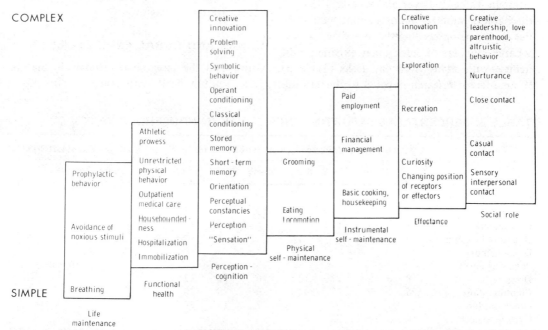

Figure 2. Schematic diagram of sublevels of individual organization. (From Lawton, 1970a. Reproduced with permission from *The Gerontologist*.)

TABLE 2. WITHIN-DWELLING-UNIT BEHAVIORS, DAY PRIOR TO INTERVIEW.[a]

Behavior	% engaged in behavior	Median hours spent by all engaged
Eating, cooking	99	2.5
Personal care	97	1.0
Television	70	3.0
Housework	67	2.0
Reading	61	1.0
Napping, idleness	56	2.0
Radio, records	17	1.5
Handiwork	15	2.0
Entertaining	9	2.5
Writing	8	1.5
Crafts, collections	1	2.0

[a]From Beyer and Woods, 1963, p. 9.

older person as being grossly housebound as compared to other segments of the population is disproved. One does, however, need to have similar information about obligatory time in order to gain a full picture of time use across the age range.

A rough idea of the within-dwelling-unit behavior of a large number of elderly people is given in Table 2 (Beyer and Woods, 1963), on the basis of subjects' reports about their activities on the day preceding the interview.

Large numbers of elderly may experience difficulty with many everyday tasks (Table 3). Human-factor research devoted to the bathtub, toilet, sink, counter, storage-space, appliances, bed, chairs and other furnishings ought to result in design improvements that could enhance their usability by the competent and make the critical difference between independence and dependence among the marginally competent.

Careful study of energy expenditure in different spatial and structural arrangements in relation to the competence of the individual should lead to a better understanding of optimal person-dwelling unit matching. Salvosa, Payne, and Wheeler (1971) studied subjects wearing heart-rate integrators, which gave a continuous record of rate of energy expenditure over about 36 hours. Energy expenditure was greater among older women living alone in scattered dwelling units than among institution residents, and greater in women with separate-bedroom flats as compared to those living in efficiencies. While the first finding confounds environmental type and individual competence, the one-bedroom versus efficiency difference is clearly related to the amount of space to be traversed and the greater opportunity for varying behavior given in the larger flat.

Very few of these studies of activity patterns have included information on the basic ingredient required for an ecological study, that is, the location of behavior.

URBAN AND RURAL ENVIRONMENTS

Almost all the research referred to in the previous section dealt with issues of city life or

TABLE 3. PERCENTAGES REPORTING DIFFICULTY IN HOUSEHOLD TASKS.

	NATIONAL SAMPLE[a]				NATIONAL SAMPLE[b]			LOW-INCOME COMMUNITIES[c]	
	65–69	70–74	75–79	80+	65–69	70–74	75+	Poor	Near-Poor
Doing things around the house					13	28	37		
Bathing self	7	8	13	19	8	11	17	9	8
Household cleaning								28	23 (females)
Doing laundry								32	28
Preparing meals								16	13 (females)
Dressing	8	8	7	13	10	12	12		
Climbing stairs	26	29	33	42	9	18	20		
Going outdoors					7	13	20		
Cutting toenails	14	17	22	34					

[a]Shanas, Townsend, Wedderburn, Friis, Milhøj, and Stehouwer, 1968.
[b]Schooler, cited in *Indicators of the Status of the Elderly in the United States* (1972).
[c]National Council on the Aging (1971).

utilized urban-dwelling subjects. Studies by Kutner, Fanshel, Togo, and Langer (1956), Cumming and Henry (1961), Cantor (1975), Bourg (1975), Lopata (1975), and Carp (1975) are rich with detail about the personal, social, and economic aspects of living in the city. They all especially highlight the exceptional burdens under which non-majority, aged, subcultural groups live.

National concern with crime has risen from 4 percent viewing it as the country's major problem in 1948 to 13 percent in 1973; in urban areas it was 21 percent (*Gallup Opinion Index*, 1973). The elderly have frequently been singled out for attack because of their physical vulnerability. On the other hand, some studies showed a lower overall rate of victimization for older people (U.S. Department of Justice, 1974; Forston and Kitchens, 1974), though some have shown slightly higher rates among the elderly for minor larceny or robbery. None of these has controlled rate of exposure to crime, which clearly varies with amount and type of mobility, and therefore may be lower among the elderly.

The negative aspects of city life for the elderly must be balanced against the positive stimulation provided by the city, the relative accessibility of resources and the transportation necessary to utilize them, and the lifelong familiarity of most older city dwellers with their environments. Almost two-thirds of the nation's older people do cope with such an environment. Impact must inevitably be assessed not in terms of an overall net effect but in terms of the extent to which individual needs can be satisfied by the opportunity to select an optimal ecological niche from the many that are theoretically possible within the city.

Far less is known regarding the environmental transactions of older people living in rural, small-town, and suburban environments. Since aging in suburbia has been treated primarily in speculative fashion thus far, this section will discuss only small-town and rural areas, wherever possible dealing with their contrasts to city living.

The Small Town

About one-sixth of the older population lives in small towns. There are almost no national data on the parameters of behavior in such locales, so that one must examine data on individual or nonrepresentative samples to gain any idea of how older people differ in urban, small-town, and rural environments. Barker and Barker (1961) studied the "behavior settings" (standing patterns of behavior occurring in specific locations) of two small towns. By direct observation they concluded that the territorial range (percentage of behavioral settings occupied) and extent of active participation of older people in "Midwest" were restricted with respect to the adult population (about the same as that for people 12–17 years old), and that the mean occupancy time in all behavior settings of the elderly was equivalent to that of the pre-school child. They refer to these changes as "behavioral regression." However, the kinds of behavior settings to which they were exposed were roughly equivalent to those of the total population, though proportionally less in those characterized by social interaction, professional leadership, government and recreation.

The most extensive study of small towns is reported by Pihlblad and Rosencranz (1967, 1969), who interviewed 1,716 older people living in a probability sample of Missouri towns with populations of 250 to 5,000. These studies provide a picture of the small-town elderly resident as being lower in income, more likely than the urban dweller to own his own home, to be somewhat poorer in health, and yet to receive less frequent medical care. On the environmental side, fewer institutionalized service facilities are available and basic household amenities are more frequently missing. Their life satisfaction (Pihlblad and Rosencranz, 1969) did not differ from that found in the Kansas City urban group reported by Neugarten, Havighurst, and Tobin (1961).

Rural Areas

Rural elderly are even more deprived than the small-town elderly in income, health, health care, access to both institutionalized services and basic resources, housing quality, and household facilities, and they express a greater need for access to resources (Youmans, 1963; Langford, 1962).

Youmans (1963) and Bultena (1969) found contact with children to be somewhat more frequent in their urban samples than in their small-community samples. Both, however, also found a tendency for children to live closer to urban residents. Langford (1962), Youmans (1963), Bultena (1969), and Schooler (1970) all found contact with friends to be greater in smaller size communities (including cross-generational relationships in Langford's study). In addition, the level of such contact found by Pihlblad and Rosencranz (1969) in small towns was greater than that found in the Kansas City sample (Havighurst, 1963). This higher lever of social integration may be partly due to the longer residence of people in smaller communities in their dwelling-units (which is, in turn, correlated with number of local friends). Langford (1962) found that most of the friends of 60 percent of her residents of communities under 30,000 population lived in the same neighborhood, as compared to 32 to 52 percent of those living in larger communities.

Langford obtained information on activities performed outside the home on the day prior to the interview. The number of people mentioning each activity decreased as community size decreased. Schooler's (1970) basic distinction was between rural and non-rural residents. Rural residents saw resources as more distant, and were less knowledgeable about available social services but, paradoxically, the urban dwellers showed a slight tendency to perceive services as *less* convenient.

It is difficult to say what effect the complex set of pluses and minuses associated with living in communities of different sizes has on the psychological state of the individual. Being poor and living in an environment that brings stress to threshold levels of tolerance has been found to be associated with lower morale in the city resident (Lawton, Kleban, and Singer, 1971) and with anomie and a negative attitude toward being old (Youmans, 1963). Schooler (1970) found anomie, but not three other aspects of low morale, to be greater among rural residents.

POPULATION MIXES—THE SUPRAPERSONAL ENVIRONMENT

An essential aspect of the environment is the dominant characteristics of the other people in proximity to the individual. For relatively young people, there may be many different suprapersonal environments (environments defined by the dominant characteristics of the individuals populating them, [Lawton, 1970a]) as a consequence of their mobility—their living environment, work environment, or recreational environment. For some older people, economic, physical, and social limitations may restrict movement to a point where their neighborhoods are the only salient suprapersonal environments. Can one expect the older individual's behavior to vary significantly as a function of whether he lives among people of similar or dissimilar economic, racial, ethnic, age, or health status?

Age Context

One of the most influential findings from social gerontological research has been Rosow's (1967) study of the social integration of 1,200 aged apartment-dwellers in Cleveland. His basic hypothesis was that social integration would increase as the number of age-peers living in close proximity to the older person increased—a late-life persistence of the age-grading phenomenon that characterizes our society. This relationship was expected to be moderated by the socioeconomic background of the individual, such that working-class people would choose friends within a more limited social space than would middle-class people. The age-concentration of each multi-unit apartment building was characterized as normal (1-15 percent elderly household heads) concentrated (3-49 percent elderly; this level was studied only for middle-class elderly) and dense (50 percent elderly or greater). The dependent variables were the number of neighbor-friends named and the ages of friends. He found that the number of friends and the number of elderly friends were both direct functions of the age-density of the apartment. Thus the critical factor in the ability of the older apartment-dweller to maintain an active social life seems to be proximity of age peers. Working-class subjects were also more likely to have neighbor friends than middle-class subjects.

Rosenberg (1970) examined a similar phenomenon on the next larger environmental scale, that is, the city block. His sample consisted of about 1,100 white working-class people ages 45 to 79 from a sample of 230 Philadelphia blocks, whose demographic characteristics were also surveyed. While all subjects were from a blue-collar background and were of limited income, they were classified as "poor" or "solvent" according to current income and family size. He counted the number of friends or neighbors within or outside the city block with whom each subject reported a personal or telephone contact within the past week. The poor were affected by age context in the same way as Rosow's apartment-dwellers were, while the solvent were less affected by age context than the poorer group.

Since proximity is such a major determinant of social behavior, one would expect the age-context effect to become less marked as the scale on which density is calculated increases. Rosow's scale consisted of a single building; his age-density effects appear to be somewhat stronger than Rosenberg's, whose scale was the city block. Whether the effect would continue to be evident if one progressed to the level of neighborhood (aggregates of blocks) or community is not certain. There are no data to enlighten us here.

In planned housing environments, a direct comparison between older tenants in an age-integrated and in an age-segregated public housing project (Messer, 1967) found a considerably higher level of social interaction in the age-segregated environment. The picture is less clear in the case of morale and life satisfaction, where a lack of relationship to age mix was found by both Rosow (1967) and Messer (1967). Messer, however, found such a positive relationship in a subset of his subjects, and looked further for their relationships with moderating variables. When examining morale as a function of activity level, he found no relationship between the two within the age-segregated setting, but in the integrated setting, high activity was associated with high morale. Messer saw the segregated setting as one whose age-appropriate normative system allowed tenants the option of participating or not, as they chose. In the integrated setting, low activity levels were negatively judged according to the standards set by the younger society, producing low self-esteem in the inactive person. Teaff, Lawton, and Carlson (1973) looked at the effect of degree of age integration on

housing satisfaction, neighborhood mobility, functional health, activity participation, and interaction with family among 2,000 public housing tenants in 101 sites. With a large number of personal and environmental variables controlled, high age-density was associated with housing satisfaction, mobility, high morale, and high level of participation in activities.

Economic Context

Rosenberg also found that aged men of both income levels showed the least isolation in consonant socioeconomic and racial contexts. However, the solvent were proportionately more isolated in the dissonant context than were the poor, for reasons that are not immediately apparent. It is of particular interest to note that there was almost no socioeconomic contextual effect on friendships for women. In contrast to men, women do not experience a suddenly stronger orientation to the neighborhood for friendships following retirement.

Racial Context

All who have studied public housing have been impressed with the ease with which people of different races live together when occupancy is limited to the elderly. Nash, Lawton, and Simon (1968) in a sociometric study of four public housing sites whose percentages of black tenants ranged from 26 to 56 percent found that of all tenants naming one or more friends, 31 percent named at least one friend of a different race. There was of course, a strong tendency for both blacks and whites to choose friends of their own race; blacks showed a stronger tendency to choose one another than did whites in three of the four sites. This evidence supports the viability of racial mixing, at least in age-segregated settings. The one reservation applies to situations of extreme splits, where either blacks or whites constitute a very small minority of all tenants. In these situations where a given individual may have a very small pool of like-status peers with whom to interact, there may be a tendency for social isolation to occur.

Status homophilies of all types are important determinants of social behavior in planned housing. Where deviations occur, by far the great majority of tenants appear to deal constructively with the situation. Two major questions remain regarding status heterogeneity. First, while some risks of heterogeneity have been identified, no substantial effort has been made to determine the extent to which mixing results in enriching or stimulating effects. Second, more research is needed to determine whether the choice of age-segregated situations may be for some people an attempt to reduce the level of stress to which they are exposed.

PLANNED HOUSING

Planned housing for older people has been studied by a number of investigators, beginning with Carp's (1966) study of Victoria Plaza in San Antonio, one of the first public housing environments built explicitly for older people. Behavioral research findings have been incorporated into the thinking of recent books on housing directed toward the planner, designer, and administrator (Gelwicks and Newcomer, 1974; Lawton, 1975b; Lawton, Newcomer, and Byerts, 1976).

Impact of Planned Housing

Carp (1966) studied 352 applicants for a new public housing project, of whom 204 were selected as occupants of Victoria Plaza (VP) and 148 were turned down. The results of a variety of assessment techniques were analyzed to assess change after one year, using the appropriate covariance design; the results leave no doubt that, as reported by the Ss themselves, positive change was perceived by the VP tenants and, usually, no change by the group that stayed in the community. Housing had disappeared as a major problem for VP tenants, but remained the same for controls. Most other indices acted similarly: housing and neighborhood satisfaction, satisfaction with life-sustaining resources, morale, level of activity participation, social interaction, and health. Money appeared to become more of a problem to tenants, though they paradoxically claimed a greater feeling of financial security. VP tenants expressed a decreased need for all types of services after occupancy, as compared to controls, except in the case of meal services, where their need increased slightly. The one obvious limitation of these findings is the absence of any criterion of change independent of the Ss' own report. The indices of activity and social interaction were designed to be as objective as possible, and are very convincing in their support of the favorable effect of the new environment. However it is still plain that tenants may have felt both a need to speak well of VP to please the interviewer and the administrator, as well as attempting to achieve cognitive harmony between their attitudes and their new circumstances—neither effect would be particularly reasonable among the unsuccessful group. The tenants' realization that their home was the center of much national attention, as well as a research project, may also have encouraged a positive response set. The positive effect is unquestionably maximized by this approach and requires comparison with criterion measures from sources other than the respondent.

One of the most comprehensive studies was done on a unique public housing site planned to give maximum support to both the elderly and to younger physically-handicapped individuals (Sherwood, Greer, Morris, and Sherwood, 1972). The original occupants were matched through an effective multivariate procedure to a group of applicants who either refused occupancy when offered one or who accepted but remained on the waiting list during the nine-month period between preoccupancy assessment and follow-up. A comprehensive assessment battery revealed an overall relative gain among the rehoused group in housing satisfaction, self-rated health, rate of transfer to long-term care facilities, formal activity participation, and satisfaction with level of social activity. Scattered positive effects were found in functional health and morale. No difference was observed in mortality, acute hospitalization, informal social activity, cognitive performance, or most aspects of morale. As compared to other studies, this study is unique in assessing the impact of an environment designed to serve the needs of a particularly vulnerable group of tenants.

Lawton and Cohen (1974) studied tenants in five housing sites before and 12 months after occupancy, comparing them to three groups of community residents who had not applied for planned housing. The groups were not matched, but background characteristics, including initial health status and preoccupancy scores on the dependent variables, were controlled for in a multiple-regression design. The dependent variables were nine factor scores derived largely, but not completely, from tenant responses to an interview schedule. Tenants' well-being after 12 months exceeded that of the community comparison subjects on self-assessed change for the better, housing satisfaction, external involvement, and satisfaction with the *status quo*. No group differences after one year were found on morale, loner status, orientation to children, or activity breadth, while the rehoused declined significantly more in functional health. These results extend Carp's findings over a wider variety of housing types, but the magnitude of the favorable effect attributable to rehousing was considerably less than Carp found.

One may conclude that enough different sites, different methods, and different comparison groups have been utilized to allow the fairly firm conclusion that planned housing has a favorable impact on older people, particularly in their level of expressed satisfaction with life and their social behavior. It would still be desirable to test the impact further by the use of longitudinal measures not obtained from subjects, such as directly observed behavior, standardized tests, or blind ratings.

Location of Planned Housing

Unfortunately there are few hard research findings to guide the planner in making the critical decision about location of new housing. For some years the major guideline has been the study of Noll (reported in Niebanck, 1965), who asked 117 housing administrators to estimate the distance from a number of resources beyond which elderly tenants expressed dissatisfaction. Only recently has there been any attempt to validate these estimates in terms of the actual behavior of tenants. Newcomer (1973) obtained data on the distance of the nearest of 24 different facilities from each of 154 elderly housing projects. He also obtained frequency-of-use information from about 600 tenants living in these projects. Location-by-use tabulations enabled him to validate some of

Noll's estimates. Of particular interest were facilities where no critical distance could be established: church, physician, library, and restaurant. In the case of the first three, the individual's personal choice seems to override distance considerations, while for the latter, socioeconomic limitations override distance (see section on the resource environment above). Newcomer suggests that planned transportation, rather than a locational decision, be the method by which access is assured to church, medical care and library.

Sherman (1973) classified six sites in terms of their proximity to an urban center and examined tenants' functional space in terms of the proportion of activities engaged in on the site as compared to off the site. In general, there was more off-site social visiting, more off-site club memberships, and some tendency for more activities to be performed off-site in the more centrally-located environments.

Lawton, Nahemow, and Teaff (1975) found small but significant tendencies for public housing located in smaller communities to be associated with tenants' greater housing satisfaction and more contact with neighbor-friends than in housing located in larger communities, when tenant demographic characteristics were controlled.

We clearly need more research on aspects of the location of planned housing with respect to barriers to ambulation, transportation facilities, social and medical service resources, neighborhood resources, land-use patterns, crime exposure, demographic characteristics of the neighborhood, terrain, and the esthetic and interest appeal of the site.

Building Structure and Behavior

Newman (1972) studied crime in public housing as a function of site layout and building design. With varying degrees of support from empirical data, he concluded that a variety of physical aspects of site and building were associated with low crime risk, including low-rise structures (low-density land use), few units sharing the same entrance, single-loaded corridors, high surveillance capability of public spaces inside and outside the building, high (but controlled within site boundary) level of traffic, and clearly-marked territories "belonging" to a single unit.

Lawton, Nahemow, and Teaff (1975) studied the relationship of size and building height to tenant well-being, controlling for a number of tenant characteristics (demographic characteristics, health, and current welfare status), the size of the community, suprapersonal characteristics of the tenant population (age mix and socioeconomic mix), and a few physical site characteristics. Of the six criteria of tenant well-being, building size was not associated with any, while greater building height was associated with lower housing satisfaction and less neighborhood mobility. It may well be that higher projects discourage energy expenditure in channels that open up boundaries between the project and the larger community. The size of these effects was small, however, and they serve primarily as reminders to administrators that counteractive measures may be required in high-rise buildings, rather than as contraindications to building these types of structures. It is noteworthy that there was no effect of these variables on tenant morale.

In a study of 12 high-rise projects for the elderly, Lawton (1970b) used behavior maps (Ittelson, Rivlin, and Proshansky, 1970b) to note the location and behavior of tenants in the indoor and outdoor public spaces of the buildings by time-sampled direct observation. Among all buildings, a median of about 11 percent of the building's population was visible during the average tour of public spaces, ranging from 3 percent in a building with strong off-site competition (an oceanfront boardwalk) to 18 percent in a building located in a very high-crime area. High rates of public space occupancy occurred significantly more often in projects where tenants were in poorer health. Among buildings with both centrally- and peripherally-located lounges, occupancy was almost five times greater in the more central locations. In one site, social behavior was enhanced by a single-loaded corridor with apartments opening onto an open gallery, as compared to the totally enclosed double-loaded corridors in another part of the same building. Lawton and Simon (1968) found the well-known propinquity effect to manifest itself quite strongly in

both the friendship choices and active social behavior of tenants in five of the same sites. This tendency did not diminish with tenants' length of residence. Nahemow and Lawton (1975) documented the propinquity effect in an age- and race-integrated project, and examined its moderating effect on status similarity (age, race, sex) as a basis for sociometric choices. Cross-status friendship choices occurred frequently, but much more often between people living in proximate apartments than in distant apartments.

One manipulable aspect of the housing environment is the choice of whether to leave one's apartment door open. Lawton and Simon (1968) found that the frequency with which a tenant's door was found open was highly related to the number of sociometric choices made by the occupant. Across 10 sites, Lawton (1970b) found that the percentage of doors observed to be left open in a site was positively related to the percentage of tenants observed in social interaction and the mean number of within-building friends named by tenants. These replicated findings on the open-door phenomenon illustrate nicely the concordance between the spatial and social behaviors of tenants.

Services within the Housing Environment

A major policy issue in the development of federal housing programs has been whether housing should be limited to shelter or whether it should include a variety of supportive services, such as on-site meals, personal care, medical services, or social services. Policymakers and gerontologists both have been concerned about the effect of too-easy availability of services on the independence of tenants. Further, the needs and wishes of potential tenants for various service packages have not always been clear.

Lawton (1969), Sherman (1974), and Grimes (1973), surveying the preferences of tenants and community residents for various services, found that the desire for some kind of on-site medical service was very high, as compared to on-site meal services. Tenants living in sites where these services were provided were strongly in favor of their continuation.

Assessment of the effect of the provision of such services on the tenant population is difficult, since it is virtually impossible to make random assignment of tenants to service and no-service programs. Lawton (1969) studied three sites with Jewish tenant populations from urban areas. The original tenants in the site offering no services were younger, more healthy, more active in organizations, more mobile in one of two measures, and "happier" in self-rating than those in the two sites that offered a substantial package of supportive services. These findings suggest that older people attempt to match their competence with an appropriate level of environmental support when choosing a living situation. They further suggest that planning decisions regarding the level of support to be built into a prospective housing environment will determine to some extent the character of the tenant population that will be recruited.

This demonstration of initial differences in the populations recruited by service-rich and service-sparse housing environments led Lawton (1975c) to study the impact of service. He compared two of the three sites mentioned above in terms of the change in well-being of their original tenant populations over their first year of occupancy, using tenant background characteristics, health, and initial scores on each dependent variable as covariates. One year after residence was established, tenants in the housing without services reported higher levels of discretionary activity by two indices than those in the housing with services. Tenants in the site with services showed small relative gains in morale and housing satisfaction. Thus, there was no strong effect in a single direction, but the pattern of findings suggests that the two environments had selective effects on different individuals.

Predicting the Effects of Planned Housing from Preoccupancy Characteristics

Beyond the assessment of the generalized impact of housing on older people, one may ask whether there are differential impacts on different tenants. Theoretically there should be combinations of environmental situation and individual characteristics that would optimize congruence and therefore lead to better outcomes from the point of view of either the individual tenant or the collective housing environment, just as there might be incongruities which should be avoided. It is a natural step from this reasoning to a search for preoccupancy indicators that can be utilized to screen applicants in terms of potential optimal vs. nonoptimal matches.

Carp's impact study of Victoria Plaza (1966) and an eight-year follow-up (1974) included a search for predictors of post-occupancy adjustment as judged by self-reported happiness, sociometric popularity, and ratings by administrator, staff, and research workers. For the eight-year follow-up, the 22 preoccupancy self-ratings and interviewer ratings constituted one set of predictors and five staff consensus ratings done at the 18-month follow-up constituted a second set. There was relatively little shrinkage in prediction after eight years. Over this longer period, self-rated happiness was predicted significantly by preoccupancy self-ratings of self-attitude, positive feeling about the future, and middle-age identification. Sociometric popularity after eight years was predicted by consensual staff ratings on several qualities clearly related to the capacity for group living: tidiness, lack of snobbishness, and lack of tendency to gossip. Finally, administrator-rated adjustment after eight years was best predicted by earlier staff-consensus ratings of high nosiness (sic), lack of snobbishness, and degree of activity participation prior to occupancy. These results are particularly meaningful when one sees that some predictions were based on totally independent data sources, such as those relating to peer popularity.

A similar study by Storandt, Wittels, and Botwinick (1975) utilized 23 tests, ratings, and self-reports relating to cognition, personality, health, and activities, of which 11 were significantly related to the interviewer-rated 15-month follow-up criterion. Those judged most vital at follow-up had been more flexible, less compliant, felt more "in control of things," rated themselves as better in health, higher (sic) in alcohol consumption, and performed better on 6 of the 10 cognitive tests prior to occupancy. A discriminant analysis revealed that the WAIS Comprehension subtest and a crossing-off test of psychomotor speed contributed maximally to the prediction of vital functioning. In general, measures of cognitive status were more likely to forecast the vitality outcome than the personality or social measures.

Administrators might well be able to use carefully-chosen measures of competence to select a maximum percentage of those who would adjust well. One may wonder, however, whether such a practice would achieve any constructive purpose. First, many initially healthy people would at some point begin to decline. Even more importantly, to what kind of environment should the less initially competent be directed, if they are screened out of elderly housing? Predictive studies seem useful primarily for the advancement of knowledge rather than as guides to selection, unless much more compelling evidence than is now available comes to suggest that such screening can both maximize person-environment congruence and produce differential increments in well-being.

Change of Residence

Despite the strong public image of older people moving to retirement areas, as a class, older people move far less frequently than do younger adults (Brotman, 1976). Movers among older people tend to be separated or divorced, of low income, have less education, are renters, are in better health, and have earlier histories of mobility (Goldscheider, 1966; Golant, 1972). Estimates of the desire to move vary widely among subgroups and with different ways the question is asked, ranging from 29 percent in a geographically dispersed sample (Langford, 1962) to 81 percent in a distressed urban center (Lawton, Kleban, and Singer, 1971).

Some of these data allow inferences about reasons for moving or staying. Home ownership seems to be one of the most important factors in keeping an older person in his residence. Langford (1962) found that while poor condition of the dwelling unit was strongly correlated with the desire to move among renters, it was unrelated to this wish among homeowners. She found that social ties to the neighborhood were also important. Since poor health is associated with failure to move across the whole

later span of life, we may infer that many will prefer up to a certain point to cope with problems of housekeeping, access, and neighborhood decline rather than face the stress of dealing with a new environment.

The most extensive study of the consequences of "normal" moving was done by Schooler (1975), who reinterviewed 3 years later over 500 movers and non-movers of a national sample of 4,000 older people. His outcome variables were a series of factor scores of health and morale. His results were very complex, and not always consistent, but the following conclusions were drawn:

1. There was some tendency for mobility to result in decreases in morale and health. The results were inconsistent and in a few instances increases in morale followed mobility.
2. Anticipation of moving also was associated with a mixed pattern of change in morale and health, with the weight of the findings in the direction of a decline in health.
3. Favorably perceived environmental change (especially change in dwelling-unit quality, whether by change in the same residence or by a move from one residence to another) was associated with an improvement in some measures of morale.
4. Anticipating a move and actually moving was strongly associated with a decline in morale.
5. Within the most-vulnerable group who both expected to and actually did move, those whose environment declined in quality following the move were the most likely to decline in both morale and health.
6. The association between mobility and environmental change on the one hand, and morale on the other, is mediated by social relationships. That is, having a confidant reduces the likelihood of a negative effect from a change of environment.

INVOLUNTARY RELOCATION, MORBIDITY, AND MORTALITY

Urban Renewal

Niebanck (1965) found a significant drop in income and rise in rentals among elderly relocatees. Retrospective reports also indicated post-relocation dissatisfaction with the new housing, especially in those with the lowest income. Those with the most friends in the old neighborhood were least satisfied with the new housing, but those best able to maintain their old contacts experienced less post-relocation distress.

Institutional Relocation

There have been enough studies documenting the unfavorable effects of mass relocation on vulnerable institutionalized elderly people to enable us to accept the relocation mortality hypothesis as being generally upheld, especially for those who have significant physical and mental impairments. Such studies have been reviewed by Blenkner (1967), Kasl (1972), and Lawton and Nahemow (1973), and more recent studies (Bourestom and Pastalan, undated; Marlowe, 1973) have concurred. The remainder of the discussion will be devoted to studies of changes short of death following relocation, the quality of the new environment as a factor in the relocation effect, methods of counteracting excess mortality, the positive relocation effect, and the relocation of less-vulnerable populations.

Marlowe's (1973) study is by far the most complete in its longitudinal view of changes in physical health, mental status, self-care, and social capacities of both relocated and nonrelocated mental hospital patients. When surviving patients were classified as improved, stable, or deteriorated, the relocated and nonrelocated did not differ appreciably, except for the deterioration's being spread over more areas in the relocated group. The differential fate of the two groups' subjects differed markedly, however, when viewed as a function of their status as of the time of original evaluation. At the time of follow-up, the initially most-adequate relocated patients had changed most; they had either improved or deteriorated. The originally least adequate had either died or remained stable. By contrast, the non-relocated initially-adequate group had either improved or remained stable, while the less-adequate had deteriorated. Thus, Marlowe concluded that relocation was a make-or-break affair. The break outcome for the relocated was more destructive (death or deterioration) than the corresponding outcome (deterioration) for the group that had not faced relocation.

Post-relocation Environmental Quality

Slover (1972) measured the environmental qualities of 26 settings to which a group of elderly mental patients were transferred. The settings were rated by an environmental anthropologist on 189 physical, social, and service-related qualities on the basis of a day's observational visit to each. Decline following relocation was greatest in those who had been placed in environments lacking in warmth, individuation, and autonomy.

Marlowe (1973) utilized a similarly comprehensive set of environmental ratings to assess the 142 community facilities, long-term care institutions and other state hospital units to which her patients were transferred. Like Slover, she found the environmental variables to predict follow-up well-being more powerfully than the personal predictors. The degree of autonomy of the individual over his behavior seemed to be the critical factor. She also found some instances of optimal matching of cluster-analytically defined patient and environment types. For example, a patient cluster characterized by high social contact had a lower death rate and a greater improvement rate in an environmental type that was low-average in both interpersonal adequacy and dehumanization.

Counteracting the Relocation Mortality Effect

Bourestom and Pastalan (undated) divided one relocation population into two matched relocation-preparation groups. The maximum-preparation group experienced four visits to the new location, where they had conducted tours, saw their own new facilities and interacted with the new staff and other residents. The minimum-preparation group had only one tour, but were shown slides and pictures of the new institution. Both groups met for discussion of the impending move, and programs were held for the staffs of both groups, as well as for the relatives of residents. Twelve-month mortality was 27 percent for the maximum and 52 percent for the minimum group.

Positive Relocation Effects

In Schooler's studies described in the preceding section on mobility, there were several instances where moving was associated with greater improvement in morale, either with or without a simultaneous decrement in dwelling-unit quality, than non-moving. Marlowe's study showed particularly clearly that improvement occurred in a fortunate subgroup of her originally most adequate relocatees; these changes were associated with a move to the kinds of favorable environments described above. Thus evidence seems to be slowly accumulating to suggest that there is such a thing as favorable stimulation consequent to a change of scene.

Low-risk Environmental Change

Some studies utilizing less vulnerable Ss have failed to show excess mortality (Miller and Lieberman, 1965; Lieberman, Tobin, and Slover, 1971). Planned housing especially is noteworthy for its failure to show such effects (Lawton and Yaffe, 1970; Wittels and Botwinick, 1974).

Relocation is probably with us to stay. One of the most difficult choices facing society today is that of choosing between the mortality risk of closing substandard facilities and the continued threat to physical, social, and personal well-being inherent in their continued operation. Dual channels of continued research are necessary to determine how existing institutions can be improved short of closing and how the relocation shock itself can be minimized.

INSTITUTIONS

Despite the fact that only 5 percent of the elderly population is institutionalized, institutions have been studied far more than any other environmental exemplar. This section will make no attempt to cover the entire literature on institutions, but will be limited to research attempts to define institutional milieu, to evaluate their quality, and to assess their impact, and to studies that examine the behavioral consequences of particular physical and spatial aspects of institutions.

The Components of Institutional Milieu

Kleemeier (1959) posited three dominant institutional characteristics. The *segregate* dimension represented the extent to which institution members are separated from, or integrated with, the larger society. Indicators of segregate quality would include the presence of members who differ grossly in age, health, and other statuses from the population at large; infrequent excursions by members into the surrounding community; and limited penetration of the institution by outsiders. The *congregate* dimension was the degree to which members tended to perform the same activities at the same time in the same places. High congregate quality would be seen in the maintenance of schedules for waking, eating, or activities; the serving of meals in a common dining room; the provision of standard furnishings, clothing, and accommodations. The *control* dimension referred to the extent to which individual behavior is standardized by staff and organizational rules and procedures.

In a factorial study Pincus (1968) obtained milieu dimensions labeled public versus private, structured versus unstructured, resource-sparse versus resource-rich, personalization versus impersonalization, and isolated versus integrated with the outside world. In a later study, Pincus and Wood (1970) further articulated these dimensions at two levels. On the data-source level, they obtained independent estimates from administrators, staff, residents, and a research observer. They also measured each dimension as shown in staff attitudes, the physical plant, institutional rules and regulations, the activity program, the behavior of residents, and the evaluations of residents. Across eight institutions the milieu estimates from all but the residents' level were combined into consensus estimates, which were compared to the residents' report of (a) how they behaved in relation to each dimension and (b) their satisfaction with the milieu in each dimension. Residents made more use of and were better satisfied with resources in resource-rich homes, and similarly in the case of high-privacy homes. There was no concordance in the other dimensions. Considering the small number of institutions and the diversity of the measures, a fairly strong degree of support was demonstrated for the pervasiveness of these basic dimensions in the institutional system.

Kahana (1975) operationalized 18 aspects of the milieu as measured by staff consensus, as well as the residents' views of their personal needs along each dimension. Her hypothesis was that congruence between resident needs and environmental opportunities to exercise the need would be associated with high morale. The hypothesis was upheld in two of the three long-term care institutions. Especially important areas of person-environment congruence were privacy, impulse control, stimulation, continuity with the past, and change versus sameness.

None of the research reviewed maintained the operational independence of physical and other aspects of milieu throughout all phases of the study. Unquestionably the physical, the social, and the organizational levels have areas of functional equivalence and are interdependent. However, we need to know how the different levels reinforce, counteract, or operate independently of each other in order to be able to design a maximally effective institutional system.

Assessment of Institutional Quality

With all the study of institutions, no dependable quality criterion has yet been defined. Most institutions for the aged are one-way streets, where death rate (or length of remaining life) is the only possible ultimate criterion. Given the wide variation among residents in their input characteristics, remaining life span is at present an almost useless criterion for comparing one institution to another. Perhaps the most relevant set of criteria would involve the definition of desirable behaviors or mental states of residents, and the measurement of change in these criteria over two points in time. The magnitude of such a task has effectively deterred the completion of any such project.

Thus, the search for quality criteria has inevitably resulted in the choice of process variables with only a *presumed* relationship to ultimate quality, such as number of employees, high cost, diversity of programming, number of ser-

vices given, or staff attitudes ("structural variables"–Donabedian, 1966). This has, indeed, been the approach of most reports that have appeared in the literature; it is of interest how little some lists of such characteristics overlap (Holmberg and Anderson, 1968; Levey, Ruchlin, Stotsky, Kinloch, and Oppenheim, 1973).

Linn (1974) appears to have been the only one to attempt to establish a relationship between structural quality criteria such as these and "process criteria" in the form of consensual judgments of overall quality. She reported a study of 40 nursing homes which were rated for quality of care by six social workers who were very familiar with them but not attached to the institutions. This consensual criterion was related to research workers' ratings on a 71-item Nursing Home Rating Scale. The strongest independent correlates of quality were ratings of the physical plant, staffing ratio, and ratings of meals and administrative policies.

Another type of criterion of quality has already been discussed in connection with relocation: the institutional dimensions studied by Slover (1972) and Marlowe (1973). These dimensions proved to be related to longitudinally measured change in residents' well-being, and are thus perhaps the best-validated indices of institutional quality. Both of these investigators dealt primarily with broad psychosocial aspects of the environment, while those reviewed in this section tended to be much more concrete and specific. Inclusion of both the psychosocial milieu characterizations of institutional environments as well as the more concrete physical aspects in any multi-institution impact study is highly desirable. While the resident change (longitudinally measured) is the most on-target kind of quality criterion, the structural criteria and the judged-quality criteria give additional views of institutional quality.

Effects of Institutionalization

It is nothing short of astonishing that to date no complete longitudinal control-group study allowing a critical test of the effects of institutionalization has been reported. By far the most informative writing on institutional impact is contained in two critical reviews (Lieberman, 1969; Kasl, 1972), where recurrent problems of conceptualization and execution are discussed. Both writers point out the irrelevance to the impact question of cross-sectional comparisons between institutionalized and noninstitutionalized people. They further note that even with the ideal longitudinal control-group design it would remain unclear whether the relocation phenomenon or the effect of the institution itself were being tested.

One major study traced changes within subjects from a point when they joined the waiting list for admission to the time when they had been institutionalized for 12 months. Tobin (1971) found stability, rather than gross change, to characterize many sectors of functioning, such as self-descriptions and cognitive functioning. In the affective area, however, negative feelings such as abandonment were prevalent during the waiting-list period, succeeded by body preoccupation and death fantasies shortly after admission. The following period of becoming an "old-timer" saw further shifts in the affective area, leading to a slightly lesser general feeling of well-being. No report has yet appeared comparing change in the admission group with changes in a non-applicant group. Thus, the post-admission changes in the waiting-list group cannot conclusively be attributed to institutionalization.

Turner, Tobin, and Lieberman (1972) added further detail to the congruence concept by relating a cluster of traits regarded as enhancing adaptation to institutional life to 12-month outcome by physical, psychological, and behavioral criteria (improvement, no change, or mild negative change versus extreme negative change or death). Earlier literature plus study of the characteristics of successfully adapted "old-timers" led them to define nine personality characteristics that should be relatively congruent with the demands of institutional life (high activity or high status drive, for example), including some that are traditionally thought of as being negatively related to mental health (narcissism, distrust, aggression). The good-outcome group had a higher total score on this adaptive cluster prior to admission than did the poor-outcome group. Thus, passivity and conformity appear to be maladaptive, given the milieu of these relatively high-quality institutions. It must be noted, however, that initial health status was not reported; it is conceivable that the passivity and conformity of the poor-outcome group might have been an expression of a lesser biological vitality associated with vulnerability.

There are major difficulties standing in the way of constituting an "ideal" control group, since applicants are certain to differ systematically from non-applicants. A suitable comparison group might be subjects who were also candidates for institutionalization but whose admission was deferred by some factor external to them, such as long-term unavailability of beds.

Spatial Aspects of Institutional Behavior

Relatively few formal research explorations have been done thus far on space and behavior in institutions. Sommer and Ross (1958) rearranged chairs in a geriatric ward around four-person tables, in contrast to their usual position lined up on the periphery of the dayroom. Observation of behavior before and after the change was made showed a significant rise in the amount of patient-to-patient interaction. Lawton, Liebowitz, and Charon (1970) studied the spatial and social behavior of six residents before and after extensive remodeling of the area. With no apparent change in staff behavior, residents were more mobile following the remodeling. However, there was less staff-patient interaction. The explanation for this finding seemed to lie in the longer line of sight allowed nurses in monitoring residents' behavior following the removal of a partition; they could see residents from a distance rather than having to go into their rooms.

A significant experiment was done by Kahana and Kahana (1970), who controlled the suprapersonal environments of two admission wards in a mental hospital. As compared to their status on admission, elderly patients randomly placed on an age-integrated ward were rated as significantly more responsive three weeks later than those placed on an age-segregated ward.

No research data are available on the behavioral consequences of private versus shared rooms in institutions for the elderly, although a study by Ittelson, Proshansky, and Rivlin (1970) with younger mental patients resulted in findings that may be relevant for older people. Contrary to what one might expect, they found that social behavior was more likely to be observed in rooms with fewer patients. They reasoned that when privacy was more easily attainable, a patient was more likely to exercise the option of having a visitor in his room. Multiple-occupancy rooms were most likely to be treated as private rooms in the sense of observed occupancy typically being limited to only one of its nominal residents at any given time. Lawton and Bader (1970) inquired about preferences for single rooms among a number of different institutional residents and about hypothetical preference among community residents of different ages. Older community residents, middle-class institutional residents, people given a hypothetical response set toward good health, and current single-room residents were more likely to prefer single rooms, although the overall preference for multiple-bed rooms of institutional residents who currently occupied multiple-bed rooms was surprisingly high (about 50 percent). The authors hypothesized that future cohorts of older people, with an increasingly high valuation of privacy during their earlier lives, would prefer single accommodations.

This handful of studies has only begun to break ground in research that will lead toward better understanding of design principles and institutional treatment.

THEORIES OF MAN-ENVIRONMENT RELATIONS

A particularly useful overview of the function of theory in man-environment relations and the scope of current theory-types was given by Rapoport (1973), who emphasized the lack of comprehensiveness of any one model and the necessity for utilizing many models concurrently in the search for a satisfactory meta-model. Rapoport identified some issues with which any theory must contend: the meaning of space, the phenomena of territoriality, crowding, and privacy, environmental preference, environment as communication, and the effects of environments on specific user-groups.

Some recent beginnings have been made in applying these concepts to gerontology. Three such statements will be reviewed here.

The Person-Environment Congruence Model

Kahana (1975) has proposed that behavior varies as the result of an interaction between an individual's personal needs and the capability of environmental press in fostering the gratification of such needs. Thus, the "optimal environment" is person-specific, and its characteristics are defined by the degree of congruence it offers with the needs of the individual. She sees congruence as being an intermediate process whose outcome is the individual's perception of well-being. The individual's behavior is an adaptive mechanism by which congruence is maximized, whether by changing the environment or by altering one's own hierarchy of needs. Congruence was operationalized in terms of the deviation of personal preferences from consensual staff ratings of the same environmental dimensions. Congruence is most important under threshold conditions where options are limited either by personal vulnerability, environmental restrictions, or the individual's perception of a high degree of external control.

Kahana's formulation was based on empirical research on institutions, although its relevance to other situations is clear. Perhaps the most provocative aspect of her thinking to date is her consideration of a variety of models that attempt to relate the quality of outcome to person-environment congruence in a more precise fashion. Three models are discussed, which differ in their assumptions regarding the relationship between the size of the person-environment deviation and outcome:

1. The cumulative difference model. Zero deviation between need and press is optimal, and deviations are cumulative across different need-press combinations.
2. The critical-difference model. Deviations lead to nonoptimal outcomes only when they exceed a critical level.

3. The optimal congruence model. Both zero deviation and extreme deviations are associated with negative outcome, while optimal outcome is associated with a range of deviations falling in between each extreme and the zero-point range. This was described by Wohlwill (1966) and has its origin in adaptation-level theory (Helson, 1964). In contrast, the preceding two models may be characterized as tension-reduction models.

Each of the above may take three forms, depending on the assumption made regarding the relationship between the direction of the person-environment deviation and outcome:

1. Nondirectionality. The absolute size of the deviation is assumed to be the best measure of congruence, whether the deviation is positive or negative.
2. Undirectionality. Only an "undersupply" of the environmental attribute contributes to outcome, while an "oversupply" has the same effect as a perfect match.
3. Bidirectionality. A deviation in the positive direction (oversupply) has one outcome, and a deviation in the negative direction has a different outcome. Kahana gives the example in which an environment that is too stimulating for an individual's preference can arouse anxiety, while one too unstimulating evokes apathy.

The nine models resulting from the combinations of the above types provide the framework for a large variety of empirical tests, although Kahana suggests the probability that some will be found to characterize particular situations better than others, as contrasted to the less likely possibility that a single one will be validated as a general expression of the dynamics of man-environment interaction.

Kahana's congruence theory is closely tied to concepts that have evolved from empirical research and that to some extent have been operationalized. "Need" has posed a persistent problem of definition and measurement in general psychology, however, and her use of overtly expressed preference as an index of need is less than completely satisfactory. Her environmental dimensions are largely from the personal, suprapersonal, and social domains: staff attitudes, organizational structure, resident characteristics, and administrative practices. No attempt has been made, as Pincus and Wood (1970) did, to devise parallel physical and social aspects of the same press, or to deal conceptually with the physical environment as such. Despite these limitations, Kahana's model is the most fully articulated to date.

Adaptation Theory

Closely related to many of Kahana's concepts is the model of adaptation and aging of Lawton and Nahemow (1973), elaborated in Nahemow and Lawton (1973) and Lawton (1975a). This conception views outcome in the dual terms of adaptive behavior (outer criterion) and positive versus negative affect (inner criterion), which are related, but not perfectly correlated. The model is schematized in Figure 3. Lawton and Nahemow suggest a limited aspect of the individual, *competence,* and a limited aspect of environmental press, *demand quality,* as the transactional terms that are most palpable, both conceptually and operationally. Lawton (1975a) defined *competence* as "the theoretical upper limit of capacity of the individual to function in the areas of biological health, sensation-perception, motoric behavior, and cognition." Explicitly excluded are needs and personality traits. *Demand quality* is the aspect of environmental press that refers to the potential of a given environmental quality for activating behavior. Press are operationalized in normative terms, that is, empirical demonstration that a given environmental quality does activate the behavior of some people (for example, proximity, an architectural barrier, or relocation). Mediating this person-environment transaction and the behavioral and affective outcome are two interactional phenomena, personality style and environmental cognition (Lawton, 1975a). Outcome (behavior or affect) is the point defined by an individual of a particular level of competence dealing with a press of a given strength (Figure 3). Positive outcomes fall within the shaded area, where the individual's competence is adequate to deal with the press level at a given time. As competence decreases, quality of outcome becomes increasingly deter-

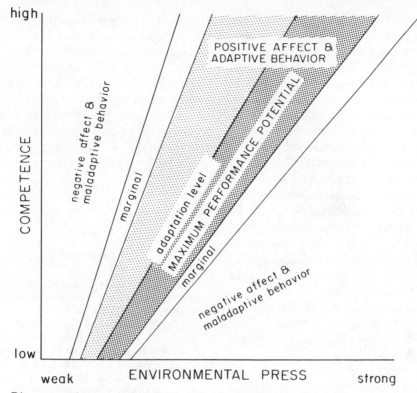

Figure 3. Diagrammatic representation of the behavioral and affective outcomes of person-environment transactions (From Lawton and Nahemow, 1973. Copyright 1973 by the American Psychological Association. Reprinted by permission.)

mined by environmental press (as shown in Figure 3 by the wide band of negative outcomes associated with even mild press levels for the least competent). As press strength increases beyond a given level, no level of personal competence allows a positive outcome. The model is bipolar, in that both excessively high press (stress) and excessively low press (stimulus deprivation) are associated with negative outcomes. The model also utilizes the concept of adaptation level to define the "indifference" point at which positive outcome occurs with little awareness of the environmental press occurring (the central diagonal line in the shaded area). At press strengths above adaptation level the environment is perceived as stimulating, with increased behavioral activation and positive affect ("zone of maximum performance potential"). At press strength below adaptation level, the environment is perceived as supporting, rather than stimulating ("zone of maximum comfort"), but positive affect also increases. Changes in competence or in press strength tend to be accompanied by a

shift in adaptation level, so that a new indifference point is established. Personality style and environmental cognition are not portrayed graphically, but are seen as processes mediating the dynamics of changing adaptation levels and dealing with changes in press level.

While many aspects of this conception are compatible with Kahana's model, neither competence nor press strength is as clearly defined as the critical variables in Kahana's need-press conception. Competences are many, and are not always distinguishable from the outcome variable, adaptive behavior. There are many aspects of both the individual and of the environment that are not accounted for by competence and press strength. Like Kahana's model, there is no explicit statement about the relationship between the physical and other aspects of the environment.

Stress Theory

Schooler (1975) has used the stress theoretical frameworks of Lazarus (1966) and Cassel

(1975) as bases for a cognitive model of man-environment relations. The ecological sequence is presumed to begin with an external stimulus which is appraised for its threat potential, either in terms of the perceived characteristics of the environment or the self. The appraisal of a stimulus as a threat to the self might for the older person be the cognition of biological, psychological and social changes consequent to the process of growing old (host vulnerability). Such a perception might also have an external referent in perceiving environmental change as a state where confirmation that one's behavior is evoking familiar environmental responses is lacking (Cassel, 1975). Thus, the person-environment interaction is a cognitive process. If no threat is perceived, behavior goes on without change toward a positive outcome as indexed by morale and health. The perception of threat defines the stimulus as a stressor, leading to coping behavior and a process of "secondary appraisal" which may (a) lead directly to a positive outcome, (b) to a negative outcome, or (c) be modified by environmental buffers, such as the quality of social relationships.

Schooler's research leading to this formulation has already been described in the section on relocation. Schooler's model has both psychological and sociological components, but unlike Kahana or Lawton and Nahemow, he places the individual's cognitive organization of environmental events in the most central position. He appears to minimize direct stimulus-response elements such as one might find when an individual's behavior is determined by physical barriers, or when environmental contingencies shape behavior without awareness.

It should be obvious that theoretical statements regarding man-environment relations among the elderly are just beginning to become useful in organizing the scattered research findings. All of the approaches discussed have relevance beyond gerontology, but each has extended general environmental theorizing by emphasizing the special outcomes that may ensue under threshold conditions of either personal capability or environmental stimulus strength. There are major gaps, such as Kahana's limitation to institutional settings and Lawton's and Nahemow's definition of person-character-istics solely in terms of competence. Each also suffers from dependence on some problematic concepts: need, competence, press, threat. Finally, despite their explicit environmental focus, none has gone very far in enabling us to identify which of the many facets of the physical environment are potentially relevant independent or dependent variables in the behavioral system. Some useful models are with us, but theory is yet to come.

REFERENCES

Ashford, N., and Holloway, F. M. 1972. Transportation patterns of older people in six urban centers. *Gerontologist,* **12,** 43–47.

Barker, R. G., and Barker, L. S. 1961. The psychological ecology of old people in Midwest, Kansas, and Yoredale, Yorkshire. *J. Gerontol.,* **61,** 231–239.

Beyer, G., and Woods, M. E. 1963. *Living and Activity Patterns of the Aged.* Ithaca, New York: Cornell University Center for Housing and Environmental Studies.

Birren, J. E. (ed.) 1959. *Handbook of Aging and the Individual.* Chicago: University of Chicago Press.

Blenkner, M. 1967. Environmental change and the aging individual. *Gerontologist,* **7,** 101–105.

Bourestom, N. C., and Pastalan, L. Undated. *Death and Survival.* Relocation Report No. 2. Ann Arbor: University of Michigan, Institute of Gerontology.

Bourg, C. 1975. Elderly in a southern metropolitan area. *Gerontologist,* **15,** 15–22.

Brotman, H. B. 1976. Every tenth American—the "problem" of aging. *In,* M. P. Lawton, R. J. Newcomer, and T. O. Byerts (eds.), *Community Planning for an Aging Society.* Stroudsburg, Pennsylvania: Dowden, Hutchinson, & Ross.

Bultena, G. L. 1969. Rural-urban differences in the familial interaction of the aged. *Rural Sociology,* **34,** 5–15.

Cantilli, E. J., and Shmelzer, J. L. (eds.) 1971. *Transportation and Aging.* Washington, D.C.: Administration on Aging.

Cantor, M. H. 1975. Life space and the social support system of the inner-city elderly of New York. *Gerontologist,* **15,** 23–26.

Carp, F. M. 1966. *A Future for the Aged.* Austin: University of Texas Press.

Carp, F. M. 1973. Life-style and location within San Antonio. Mimeo report. Berkeley, California: The Wright Institute.

Carp, F. M. 1974. Short-term and long-term prediction of adjustment to a new environment. *J. Ger-*

ontol., **29**, 444–453.

Carp, F. M. 1975. Life style and location within the city. *Gerontologist,* **15**, 27–34.

Cassel, J. 1975. The relation of the urban environment to health: Toward a conceptual frame and a research strategy. Mimeo report. Chapel Hill: University of North Carolina, School of Medicine.

Chapin, F. S., and Brail, R. K. 1969. Human activity systems in the metropolitan United States. *Environ. and Behav.*, **1**, 107–130.

Cumming, E., and Henry, W. E. 1961. *Growing Old.* New York: Basic Books.

Donabedian, A. 1966. Evaluating the quality of medical care. *Milbank Memorial Fund Quart.*, **44** (Part 2), 166–206.

Forston, R., and Kitchens, J. 1974. *Criminal Victimization of the Aged: the Houston Model Neighborhood Area.* Denton: North Texas State University, Department of Sociology.

Gallup Opinion Index. 1973. Special report on crime in the U.S. Gallup Poll, Report No. 91 (January).

Gelwicks, L. E., and Newcomer, R. J. 1974. *Planning Housing Environments for the Elderly.* Washington, D.C.: National Council on the Aging.

Golant, S. M. 1972. *The Residential Location and Spatial Behavior of the Elderly.* Research Paper No. 143. Chicago: Department of Geography, University of Chicago.

Golant, S. M. 1976. Intraurban transportation needs and problems of the elderly. *In,* M. P. Lawton, R. J. Newcomer, and T. O. Byerts (eds.), *Community Planning for an Aged Society.* Stroudsburg, Pennsylvania: Dowden, Hutchinson, & Ross.

Goldscheider, C. 1966. Differential residential mobility of the older population. *J. Gerontol.*, **21**, 103–108.

Grimes, M. 1973. *Supportive Services in Federally Assisted Housing for the Elderly.* Philadelphia: Philadelphia Geriatric Center.

Hammer, P. G., and Chapin, F. S. 1972. *Human Time Allocation: A Case Study of Washington, D.C.* Chapel Hill: University of North Carolina, Center for Urban and Regional Studies.

Havighurst, R. 1963. Successful aging. *In,* R. H. Williams, C. Tibbitts, and W. Donahue (eds.), *Processes of Aging,* Vol. 1, pp. 299–320. New York: Atherton.

Helson, H. 1964. *Adaptation Level Theory.* New York: Harper & Row.

Holmberg, R. H., and Anderson, N. N. 1968. Implications of ownership for nursing home care. *Medical Care,* **6**, 300–307.

Indicators of the Status of the Elderly in the United States. 1972. Minneapolis: Institute for Interdisciplinary Studies.

Ittelson, W. H., Proshansky, H. M., and Rivlin, L. G. 1970. Bedroom size and social interaction of the psychiatric ward. *Environ. and Behav.*, **2**, 255–270.

Ittelson, W. H., Rivlin, L. G., and Proshansky, H. M. 1970. The use of behavioral maps in environmental psychology. *In,* W. H. Ittelson, H. M. Proshansky, and L. G. Rivlin (eds.), *Environmental Psychology,* pp. 658–668. New York: Holt, Rinehart and Winston.

Kahana, B., and Kahana, E. 1970. Changes in mental status of elderly patients in age-integrated and age-segregated hospital milieus. *J. Abnorm. Psychol.*, **75**, 177–181.

Kahana, E. 1975. A congruence model of person-environment interaction. *In,* P. G. Windley, and G. Ernst (eds.), *Theory Development in Environment and Aging.* Washington, D.C.: Gerontological Society.

Kasl, S. 1972. Physical and mental health effects of involuntary relocation and institutionalization—a review. *American Journal of Public Health,* **62**, 379–384.

Kleemeier, R. W. 1959. Behavior and the organization of the bodily and the external environment. *In,* J. E. Birren (ed.), *Handbook of Aging and the Individual,* pp. 400–451. Chicago: University of Chicago Press.

Klein, G. S., Barr, H. L., and Wolitzky, D. L. 1967. Personality. *Annual Review of Psychology,* **18**, 467–560.

Kutner, B., Fanshel, D., Togo, A. M., and Langer, T. S. 1956. *Five Hundred Over Sixty.* New York: Russell Sage Foundation.

Langford, M. 1962. *Community Aspects of Housing for the Aged.* Ithaca, New York: Cornell University Center for Housing and Environmental Studies.

Lawton, M. P. 1969. Supportive services in the context of the housing environment. *Gerontologist,* **9**, 15–19.

Lawton, M. P. 1970a. Assessment, integration, and environments for the elderly. *Gerontologist,* **10**, 38–46.

Lawton, M. P. 1970b. Public behavior of older people in congregate housing. *In,* J. Archea and C. Eastman (eds.), *Environmental Design Research Association II,* pp. 372–380. Pittsburgh: Carnegie-Mellon University.

Lawton, M. P. 1975a. Competence, environmental press, and the adaptation of older people. *In,* P. G. Windley and G. Ernst (eds.), *Theory Development in Environment and Aging.* Washington, D.C.: Gerontological Society.

Lawton, M. P. 1975b. *Planning and Managing Housing for the Elderly.* New York: Wiley-Interscience.

Lawton, M. P. 1975c. *Social and medical services in housing for the elderly.* Mimeo report. Philadelphia: Philadelphia Geriatric Center.

Lawton, M. P., and Bader, J. 1970. Wish for privacy among young and old. *J. Gerontol.*, **25**, 48-54.

Lawton, M. P., and Cohen J. 1974. The generality of housing impact on the well-being of older people. *J. Gerontol.*, **29**, 194–204.

Lawton, M. P., Kleban, M. H., and Singer, M. 1971. The aged Jewish person and the slum environment. *J. Gerontol.*, **26**, 231–239.

Lawton, M. P., Liebowitz, B., and Charon, H. 1970. Physical structure and the behavior of senile patients following ward remodeling. *Aging and Human Development*, 231-239.

Lawton, M. P., and Nahemow, L. 1973. Ecology and the aging process. *In,* C. Eisdorfer and M. P. Lawton (eds.), *Psychology of Adult Development and Aging,* pp. 619-674. Washington: American Psychological Association.

Lawton, M. P., and Nahemow, L. 1975. *Cost, structure, and social aspects of housing for the aged.* Final report to the Administration on Aging. Philadelphia: Philadelphia Geriatric Center.

Lawton, M. P., Nahemow, L., and Teaff, J. 1975. Building characteristics and the wellbeing of elderly tenants in public housing. Manuscript submitted for publication. Philadelphia: Philadelphia Geriatric Center.

Lawton, M. P., Newcomer, R. J., and Byerts, T. O. (eds.), 1976. *Community Planning for an Aging Society.* Stroudsburg, Pennsylvania: Dowden, Hutchinson & Ross.

Lawton, M. P., and Simon, B. B. 1968. The ecology of social relationships in housing for the elderly. *Gerontologist*, 8, 108-115.

Lawton, M. P., and Yaffe, S. 1970. Mortality, morbidity, and voluntary change of residence by older people. *J. Am. Geriat. Soc.*, 18, 823-831.

Lazarus, R. 1966. *Psychological Stress and the Coping Process.* New York: McGraw-Hill.

Levey, S., Ruchlin, H. S., Stotsky, B. A., Kinloch, D. R., and Oppenheim, W. 1973. An appraisal of nursing home care. *J. Gerontol.*, 28, 222-228.

Lieberman, M. 1969. Institutionalization of the aged: Effects on behavior. *J. Gerontol.*, 24, 330-340.

Lieberman, M., Tobin, S. S., and Slover, D. 1971. *The effects of relocation on long-term geriatric patients.* (Final Report, Project No. 17-1328). Chicago: Illinois Department of Health and Committee on Human Development, University of Chicago.

Linn, M. W. 1974. Predicting quality of patient care in nursing homes. *Gerontologist*, 14, 225-227.

Lopata, H. Z. 1975. Support systems of elderly urbanites. *Gerontologist*, 15, 35-41.

Marlowe, R. A. 1973. Effects of environment on elderly state hospital relocatees. Paper presented at annual meeting of the Pacific Sociological Association, Scottsdale, Arizona, May, 1973.

Messer, M. 1967. The possibility of an age-concentrated environment becoming a normative system. *Gerontologist*, 7, 247-251.

Miller, D., and Lieberman, M. A. 1965. The relationship of affect state and adaptive capacity to reactions to stress. *J. Gerontol.*, 20, 492-497.

Nahemow, L., and Kogan, L. S. 1971. *Reduced Fare for the Elderly.* New York: Mayor's Office for the Aging.

Nahemow, L., and Lawton, M. P. 1973. Toward an ecological theory of adaptation and aging. *In,* W. F. E. Preiser (ed.), *Environmental Design Research,* Vol. 1, pp. 24-32. Stroudsburg, Pennsylvania: Dowden, Hutchinson & Ross.

Nahemow, L., and Lawton, M. P. 1975. Similarity and propinquity in friendship formation. *J. Pers. Soc. Psychol.*, 32, 205-213.

Nash, G., Lawton, M. P. and Simon, B. 1968. Blacks and whites in public housing for the elderly. Paper presented at annual meeting of the Gerontological Society, Denver.

National Council on the Aging. 1971. *The Golden Years—a Tarnished Myth.* Washington, D.C.: National Council on the Aging.

Neugarten, B. L., Havighurst, R. J., and Tobin, S.S. 1961. The measurement of life satisfaction. *J. Gerontol.*, 16, 134-143.

Newcomer, R. J. 1973. Housing, services, and neighborhood activities. Paper presented at the annual meeting of the Gerontological Society, Miami Beach.

Newman, O. 1972. *Defensible Space.* New York: Macmillan.

Niebanck, P. L. 1965. *The Elderly in Older Urban Areas.* Philadelphia: University of Pennsylvania, Institute for Environmental Studies.

Pihlblad, C. T., and Rosencranz, H. A. 1967. *The Health of Older People in the Small Town.* Columbia: University of Missouri, Department of Sociology.

Pihlblad, C. T., and Rosencranz, H. A. 1969. *Social Adjustment of Older People in the Small Town.* Columbia: University of Missouri, Department of Sociology.

Pincus, A. 1968. The definition and measurement of the institutional environment in homes for the aged. *Gerontologist*, 8, 207-210.

Pincus, A., and Wood, V. 1970. Methodological issues in measuring the environment in institutions for the aged and its impact on residents. *Aging and Human Development*, 1, 117-126.

Rapoport, A. 1973. An approach to the construction of man-environment theory. *In,* W. F. E. Preiser (ed.), *Environmental Design Research,* Vol. 2, pp. 124-135. Stroudsburg, Pennsylvania: Dowden, Hutchinson & Ross.

Regnier, V. A. 1974. Neighborhood settings and neighborhood use: Cognitive mapping as a method for identifying the macro-environment of older people. Paper presented at annual meeting of the Gerontological Society, Portland, Oregon.

Regnier, V. A., Eribes, R. A., and Hansen, W. 1973. Cognitive mapping as a concept for establishing neighborhood service delivery locations for older people. Paper presented at eighth annual Association for Computing Machinery symposium, New York City.

Rosenberg, G. S. 1970. *The Worker Grows Old.* San Francisco: Jossey-Bass.

Rosow, I. 1967. *Social Integration of the Aged.* New York: The Free Press.

Salvosa, C. B., Payne, P. R., and Wheeler, E. F. 1971. Energy expenditure of elderly people living alone or in local authority homes. *Am. J. Clin. Nutrition*, 24, 1467-1470.

Schooler, K. K. 1970. *Residential Physical Environment and Health of the Aged.* Final report, USPHS Grant EC 00191. Waltham, Massachusetts: Brandeis University, Florence Heller School for Advanced Studies in Social Welfare.

Schooler, K. K. 1975. Response of the elderly to environment: a stress-theoretic perspective. *In,* P. G. Windley, and G. Ernst (eds.), *Theory Development in Environment and Aging.* Washington, D. C.: Gerontological Society.

Shanas, E., Townsend, P., Wedderburn, D., Friis, H., Milhøj, P., and Stehouwer, J. 1968. *Old People in Three Industrial Societies.* New York: Atherton.

Sherman, S. R. 1973. Housing environment for the well-elderly: Scope and impact. Paper presented at annual meeting of the American Psychological Association, Montreal.

Sherman, S. R. 1974. Provision of on-site services in retirement housing. Mimeo report. Albany: New York State Department of Mental Hygiene, Mental Health Research Unit.

Sherwood, S., Greer, D. S., Morris, J. N., and Sherwood, C. C. 1972. *The Highland Heights Experiment.* Washington D.C.: U.S. Department of Housing and Urban Development.

Slover, D. 1972. Relocation for therapeutic purposes of aged mental hospital patients. Paper presented at annual meeting of Gerontological Society, San Juan, Puerto Rico.

Sommer, R., and Ross, H. 1958. Social interaction in a geriatrics ward. *Int. J. Soc. Psychiat.,* **4,** 128–133.

Storandt, M., Wittels, I., and Botwinick, J. 1975. Predictors of a dimension of well-being in the relocated healthy aged. *J. Gerontol.,* **30,** 97–102.

Teaff, J. D., Lawton, M. P., and Carlson, D. 1973. Impact of age integration of public housing projects upon elderly tenant well-being. Paper presented at annual meeting of the Gerontological Society, Miami.

Tobin, S. S. 1971. Community to institution. Paper presented at annual meeting of the Gerontological Society, Houston, Texas.

Turner, B. F., Tobin, S. S., and Lieberman, M. A. 1972. Personality traits as predictors of institutional adaptation among the aged. *J. Gerontol.,* **27,** 67–68.

U.S. Department of Justice. 1974. *Crime in the Nation's Five Largest Cities.* Washington, D.C.: U. S. Department of Justice, Law Enforcement Administration.

Wittels, I., and Botwinick, J. 1974. Survival in relocation. *J. Gerontol.,* **29,** 440–443.

Wohlwill, J. F. 1966. The physical environment: a problem for a psychology of stimulation. *J. Soc. Issues,* **22,** 29–38.

Youmans, E. G. 1963. *Aging Patterns in a Rural and Urban Area of Kentucky.* Bulletin 681. Lexington: University of Kentucky, Agricultural Experiment Station.

14
THE CROSS-CULTURAL PERSPECTIVE:
Notes Toward a Comparative Psychology of Aging

David Gutmann
University of Michigan

INTRODUCTION: METHODS, SHORTCOMINGS, AND POSSIBILITIES OF CROSS-CULTURAL STUDIES

The comparative psychology of aging is a field that lacks concepts, methods, and investigators. Indeed, the useful literature is mainly produced by ethnographers and sociologists, by those with, at best, incidental interest in the psychology of aging. Where these investigators have considered the psychological condition of aging populations, they have—in line with their theoretical interests—treated these states as the dependent outcomes of externally imposed sociocultural conditions. Paradoxically, the few psychologists who have attempted cross-cultural studies usually join the anthropologists and sociologists in derogating the independent status of psychological variables. Thus we find almost no comparative studies—those conducted by the same investigator(s) using the same tools and theoretical conceptions across cultures—of the sort required to either test or generate a developmental, "species" conception of aging psychology.

Certainly, geriatric psychologists have abundant reasons for avoiding the discomforts, methodological pitfalls and dubious rewards of cross-cultural research. Neugarten and Bengtson (1968) discuss these in detail. Along with the formidable problem of creating constructs and instruments that have cross-cultural validity, there is also the hard task of obtaining truly equivalent data from a variety of cultural settings, particularly when the investigators represent different social backgrounds and scientific traditions. Also noted is the problem of defining comparable samples, plus the difficulty of making interpretations which will be meaningful in the context of each society. Overtly similar behaviors noted in different cultures can have markedly different functions relative to their setting, just as seemingly different behaviors can have similar functions, across cultures. Furthermore, the difficulties of cross-cultural research are compounded by the drawbacks inherent in the study of later life *per se:* the lack of well-developed research methods and sophisticated conceptions in this field.

While acknowledging these limitations, Neu-

302

garten and Bengtson argue that cross-cultural studies are a necessary corrective to the cultural blindspots of theory builders; that they pay off in greater generality of findings, and in greater richness of conceptions. Though deficient on the side of theory testing, such research still provides a unique means for developing hypotheses and for identifying powerful variables whose effects can be rigorously tested in single cultures, or in those controlled settings where these same variables *could not have been initially identified*. Cross-cultural, comparative studies help to generate explanatory frameworks which illuminate hitherto unobserved regularities and relationships at the local level.

The cross-cultural approach is particularly important in establishing a developmental psychology of aging: such studies vary, and thus control for social or extrinsic contributions to the aging process and any residual transcultural regularities can be logically referred to intrinsic, or developmental forces. Thus, the developmental armatures of aging personality—if these exist—can be identified through (preferably longitudinal) studies of aging populations across disparate cultural settings.

Clark (1967) believes that the study of aging personality—within or across cultures—has been neglected because of the common bias among personality theorists towards the "formative years." This "child-centered" bias has blinded social scientists to the orderly changes in personality that occur across the entire life span, progressions that are provoked and regulated by the cultural age-grading systems which prescribe the proper phrasing of personality and behavior for each major life stage.

In sum, authors who agree on the need for cross-cultural studies of aging also differ in the uses that they would make of them. Neugarten and Bengtson might use the comparative approach to trace the "natural" trajectories of psychological change in the latter half of life; while others (like Clark) would use this same cross-cultural approach to study the effects of social nurture on the psychological outcomes of that same period. The "human nature" approach, which treats specific behaviors as phenotypic expressions of the genotypes that guide human development, has mainly in-

formed the study of infancy and early childhood—those periods when the conditions of nurture have not had time enough to account for patterned behavior. But most trans-social studies of later life have been guided by the "reactive" conception of personality, which treats psychological dispositions as dependent outcomes of extrapersonal social pressures. The features of personality in later life are viewed as outcomes of the parochial economic, age-grading kinship and ideological arrangements maintained by particular societies. This view of adult psychology as the consequence rather than the shaper of its social ecology is upheld by the majority of psychological researchers in cross-cultural gerontology.

Thus, Eckensberger (1973) asserts that cross-cultural psychological studies must treat cultural conditions as the independent variables. He thus assigns all essential dynamism to the social conditions of nurture. The social order is primary: it alone is organized and coherent; and it sponsors, through its various functions, as these bear on individuals, the necessary psychological preconditions for its own continuity. Individual psychology thus becomes a very junior partner of the imperious social process. This ultimately totalitarian idea dominates the meager cross-cultural research undertaken thus far.

But this socio-centric view of aging personality was formed in those largely urbanized, Western European settings where the great majority of cross-national studies have been carried out. In these complex, impersonal milieux, the aged are in a relatively victimized position: they must react to a fate that they cannot shape. It is not surprising that the "reactive" view of the aged would be persuasive for psychologists who meet them largely on urban and Western ground. However, if there are psychological genotypes, aspects of human nature specific to the aged, these will not be identified in cross-national studies, but in more genuinely cross-cultural studies, particularly those undertaken in traditional, preliterate societies, where the aged tend to have the greatest social power, and the greatest leverage over the conditions of their own nurture. Thus, the subsequent review of the literature concerning the life of the aged in traditional and "folk" societies may provide some corrective to the reactive conceptions that dominate the field of psychological gerontology. Accordingly, this chapter will largely focus on data sources from those simple societies which provide evidence of psychological genotypes in aging personality. We will also consider the general transformations, the phenotypic outcomes of such genotypes under the impact of modernization and urbanization.

In addition, we will use cross-cultural, cross-national, cross-ethnic and rural-urban comparisons in order to shed light on important questions in gerontological psychology: persistence and change in adult personality; the universality and adaptive value of disengagement; psychological coordinates of longevity; the religiosity of later life. This review will not end controversy on these issues, but hopefully it will underline the value of the cross-cultural approach by bringing some new perspectives to these debates.

We start by reviewing age-grade prescriptions from agrarian, preliterate societies. Such systems are age-qualified recipes for proper social behavior, but in such usually gerontocratic societies these prescriptions may be crafted by the aged to their own specifications. If there are common themes in aging psychology, we should expect to find their metaphors in those age-grade systems that meet and reflect the needs of older people. Thus, by reviewing the conditions of social nurture, we may pinpoint some underlying conditions of human nature, some psychological universals that characterize the latter half of the human life cycle.

THE AGE-GRADING OF MALE PASSIVITY

Asian Systems

This review begins with societies most distant in the geographic and cultural sense from our own—those of East Asia. We will compare age-grade systems from that sector, note any consistencies, and ask if persistent themes are replicated in culture areas remote from the Orient, and closer to our own. We then consider some generalizations concerning the "species" psychology of aging that can be derived from this review of thematic regularities in cultural systems.

Mead (1967) reports that younger Chinese men are expected to be achievement-oriented and aggressive, whereas older men are expected to be relaxed, meditative, and "noble." Similarly, Yap (1962) reports that elderly Chinese are expected to abstain from meat and sex, and to practice self-cultivation, worship and meditation. In exchange for this "moral work," they will receive food and shelter. Rustom (1961) reports that four major stages of life are recognized by Burmese villagers: until puberty the task of the individual is to respect parents and elders and to acquire their wisdom. The next, or "virgin" age is centered around the search for a spouse. During the third stage, the young husband's duty is to acquire property, to "give, show, teach," and to provide. Parents are expected to remain economically active until all their children have been married. In the fourth stage, the older Burman leaves mundane tasks to younger family members and devotes himself to religious activities, to merit-acquiring deeds and to meditation. Inner life changes in step with public behavior: the older Burman presumably loses interest in worldly affairs and curbs his former appetites. The last period is regarded as the peak: a long life is proof of "good karma" and augurs well for the next existence. The elders have provided for their children, and it is now the duty (and the pleasure) of the children to care for them (Rustom finds few old age homes among the Burmese, and these have small populations). Along similar lines, Cowgill (1968) notes that, despite a continuing deference to the Thai aged, the real leadership is in the hands of the middle-aged. Following their abdication, many older Thai men will enter the priesthood.

The Hindu *Asrama*, or life cycle, has four major stages: the student, the married householder, the "forest" state, and finally *Sanyasa*, involving the complete renunciation of worldly attachments. Steed (1957) elicited somewhat similar views of the Indian life cycle in a Gujurat village. Younger men are expected to be impetuous and driven by a need to succeed; maturity brings a more peaceful nature, followed by a return of peevish anger and egocentricity in old age.

Thus, the Oriental versions of the life cycle cluster towards a consensus. Young men are expected to push and sweat for success in the pragmatic world; but in later life they are expected to shift their concern to the next world, and to their relationship with God.

Middle Eastern and African Societies

The belief that younger men should fulfill the productive style of their culture while old men should contemplate the productive powers of God is not limited to Asian societies. Thus, Gutmann (1974) notes a similar pattern among elderly Druze, a Levantine sect defined by religious beliefs which are held secret even from younger Druze. After his initiation into the religious society, the outward behavior and the inner life of the older Druze are devoted to the service of Allah: he shaves his head, adopts special garb, gives up tobacco, devotes much time to prayers, and dwells on God's mercy, while forgetting his own past grossness and stupidities.

Sub-Saharan tribes institutionalize, within rigid age-set and age-grade systems, some equivalent conceptions. Thus, Spencer (1965) found that Samburu males are divided into age-sets, composed of peers who move together through the sequential age grades which define their rights, their duties and even their attitudes. The most important distinction is cut between the *Moran*, the age-set of young unmarried warriors, flamboyant predators of other men's herds and wives, and the moderate, responsible "bourgeois" householder. The *Moran* are kept in line by the elders of the most advanced age grades, who cannot match them in physical strength, but who can deploy potent curses against them.

Spencer discovers that these patterns are repeated wherever polygamy gives older men a monopoly over younger wives. Thus, among the Groote Eylandt of Australia, the young men are secluded from the mainstream of social life, their energy and aggression is directed outwards towards prey and enemy, and if they challenge the political and sexual prerogatives of their seniors, the older men will retaliate against them with sorcery.

Prins (1953) finds the age-sets of the Kikuyu (Kenya) moving through the same cycle of age-graded transitions: the younger men are organized into warrior societies and their form of "production" is to steal from the enemy. In their turn, the elder's age grade deals with the possibly disastrous consequences of any breach of *tabu*. The younger men deal with the threats from enemy power, while the older men deal with threats from supernatural power.

Amerindian Age Grading

Kardiner and Linton (1945) found an equivalent age-grading pattern among the Comanche, horse soldiers of the American Southwest. While young men initiate war parties, two roads are open to the older ex-warrior: he can either become the "Peace Chief," or the "bad old man," who substitutes sorcery for the lost prowess of the warrior. In either case, the older Comanche has the task of controlling external power: he either restrains the warriors, or he matches their innate strength with power "borrowed" from totemic sponsors.

In sum, there appears to be a certain unanimity among the prescriptions for the various age grades maintained by quite disparate cultures: young men are expected, through their *own* energies, to wrest resource and power from physical nature, from enemy or from both; older men are expected, through rituals or through postures of accommodation, to coax power—whether for good or malign purposes—from the supernaturals. In each society, the age-graded expectations for appropriate behavior operate as rules and norms to which all proper men must conform; but the thematic solidarity across separate sets of rules suggests that age-grading systems are responsive to trans-cultural universals, some *intrinsic* sequences which are independent of the cultural institutions that they shape.

THE INFORMAL AGE-GRADING OF MALE PASSIVITY

Asian Studies

The relatively sparse ethnographic evidence concerning the informal and personally expressive behavior of aging men tends to replicate the tentative findings developed by our review of the more formal age-grading structures, and suggests that men tend to age psychologically along an activity-passivity continuum. Thus, Quain (1948) observed that Fijian men bestow increasing time and affection on the women of their household and on their gardens as they age. They become more "domesticated," less interested in the company and affairs of men, and their productive efforts shrink to the household garden.

Murdock (1935) demonstrates that, in simple societies, any domestic task is usually defined as "women's work." Accordingly, this "tend your own garden" attitude of the elder Fijian suggests that, as part of their burgeoning passivity, they take on interests hitherto reserved for women. This "feminization" of older men can go forward even without social approval— Simmons (1945) notes that an aged Arawak warrior who cooked was insultingly referred to as "an old woman."

Amerindian and Meso-American Studies

The androgyny of old men shows up in a different culture area, encompassing Mexico, and the American Southwest. Powers (1877) writes: "When a Pomo Indian becomes too infirm to serve any longer as a warrior or hunter, he is henceforth condemned to the life of a menial and scullion. He is compelled to assist the squaws in all their labors. . . . These superannuated warriors are under the woman's control as much as children and are obliged to obey their commands implicitly." Simmons (1945) found that older Hopi men, unable to go to the fields, would knit, card wool, or make sandals at home. Cornshelling was woman's work, but old Hopi men would routinely do it.

Southwards, in Yucatan, Press (1967) observed that older Mayan men turn to Catholicism, typically the woman's religion, giving it priority over the native Mayan religion which is more pragmatic and instrumental, oriented to the cultivation of the productive earth, rather than a pure soul. In the same village, this author (Gutmann, 1966) found corresponding feminine identifications in the Thematic Apperception Test responses given by the older men.

Independently administered psychological tests produce further evidence of an intersexual shift in another sector of Mexico. Thus, Lewis (1951), describing the results of Rorschach tests administered in Tepoztlan, a Mexican village, reports that men are "likely to be more exuberant than women, but also more anxious and insecure. As they grow older they lose their dominant position and the older adults appear disturbed, impulsive and anxious. They seem to be losing the grip on society that the older women are taking over."

Similarly, Butler (1963) was impressed by the use of denial as an ego defense among the older Maya of the Guatemalan Highlands. Again, denial is a primitive defense which protects an essentially passive position: security is preserved by illusory rather than practical means.

Using the Kluckhohn and Strodtbeck values scale in the urban sector of South America, Webber, Coombs, and Hollingsworth (1974) found that older community leaders in three Colombian cities were more apt than younger leaders to favor harmony with nature over mastery of nature; past time over present time; "being" over "doing"; and collateral (familistic) over individualistic relationships. While these results could reflect secular trends, the experimental design supports a developmental interpretation: the leaders of the most traditional city showed as strong an association between older age and "passive mastery" values as that found among the leaders of the more modern cities. If cohort effects alone accounted for the age variance, then we would expect the age differences to be most marked among the leaders of the rapidly modernizing cities, and weakest in traditionalist Popoyán, where young and old alike have been socialized towards similar values.

Israeli and Western Studies

In sum, older men, whether traditional-urban or rural-preliterate, move towards values, interests and activities which are no longer stereotypically masculine. Confirmatory evidence comes from students of the inner and social life of Israelis, a sophisticated, Westernized people. Thus, Abarbanel (1972) found that younger Israeli farmers were more achievement-oriented than their fathers, a difference which led to friction over the management of the family farm. Again, this conflict could reflect an age rather than a cohort effect: the cautious fathers were once the pioneering generation of Israel.

Furthermore, in Israel—as in Fiji—Talmon-Garber (1962) has noted the upwelling of domestic interests, though among the pioneer *kibbutzniks* this development makes for psychic trouble rather than tranquility. However, Wershow, (1969) who restudied Talmon-Garber's original sample, found that in the eight years between Talmon-Garber's work and his restudy, the aging *kibbutzniks* had presumably completed the transfer of power to the young and were more tolerant of their own placid, domesticated life. Another Israeli, Shanan, (1968) carried out an important inter-ethnic, inter-generational study of aging psychology. His Jerusalem sample, consisting of Sephardic and Ashkenazi Jews subdivided as to sex and level of education, was tested with questionnaire and projective instruments. His data analyses indicate that older men, regardless of ethnic background or education, show reduced future orientation, as well as a decline in "active coping."

Studies of aging European populations generate further evidence of the older male's need to give priority to community over agency: Havighurst (1960) finds that German men—like aging *Yucatecos*—spend more time in church than do women of equivalent age, a reversal of the usual sex differences in that country. Studying the themes of German adult life, Thomae (1962) finds that younger white collar workers look to their jobs for change, contact and satisfying activity, whereas men fifty and over chiefly desire job security. Thomae's German findings are confirmed by Bergler (1961). This placid work orientation is also noted by Heron and Chown (1962): English supervisors and foremen prefer older workers, who cooperate with management, over younger employees, who "work for themselves."

Studies in U.S. Subcultures

Turning to inter-ethnic and interracial studies within the United States, Youmans, Grigsby, and King (1969) found that both older blacks and whites in rural Florida share a heightened interest in "familistic" values. The same later life tug towards familism may reactivate earlier ties to the family of orientation: an inter-ethnic study conducted by Clark and Anderson (1967) in San Francisco showed that strong sibling ties reappear in later life, following the thinning out of membership in the family of procreation.

The older males' drift towards the passive stance has been noted in older middle class, American men by Lipman (1962) who found that elderly retirees take pleasure in domestic activities; by Giambra (1973) who found that daydreams regarding heroic action or personal advancement decline steadily with age; by DeGrazia (1961), who found that gardening becomes the favored activity of the older American male; and by Lovald (1962) who found that older skid row residents are less likely than their younger companions to get in trouble with the police.

Psychotherapy with American patients also leads to formulations consistent with those independently derived from the trans-cultural study of normal aging. Thus, Wolff (1959) refers to a return of infantile demands in old age, such that the older male patient will seek support from parental surrogates. The upwelling of infantile demands, and the falling off of competitive drives both contribute to later life feelings of inferiority. Senescent neurosis and psychosis are organized around metaphors of denial: the manic escape into confabulated happiness and/or the regression to infantilism, where the end is denied in the fantasy of a new beginning. Other psychiatrists—Meerloo (1955), Zinberg and Kaufman (1963), Berezin (1963)—all stress the aging American's withdrawal from active engagement with the world in favor of more cerebral, introversive and arbitrarily defended positions.

TOWARDS A SPECIES PSYCHOLOGY OF MASCULINE AGING

These first soundings on a species psychology of aging are based on a *potpourri* of studies, undertaken by different investigators, using different sites. This motley collection underlines the need for more orderly and truly comparative research. One such attempt has been made by this author, who has kept investigator, methods, hypotheses and analytic frameworks fairly constant across disparate cultures. The overall aim has been to establish, through application of the comparative method, some basis for a developmental psychology of aging (see Gutmann, 1966, 1967, 1969, 1971 a and b, 1974). The program has involved intensive interviewing and projective testing of younger (aged 35-54) and older (aged 55 and over) men—and some women—of traditional and usually preliterate societies: the lowland and highland Maya of Mexico, the Navajo, and the Druze of Israel, including the Golan Heights. These societies differ from each other in ethnic composition, the content of culture, and their physical environment. They are alike in that they are composed of isolated marginal agriculturalists who hold to their traditional ways. Thus, those cultural values and practices that might influence individual personality tend to remain constant across the generations. Accordingly, if standard psychological differences appear between the younger and older individuals of such static societies, the age variation may be imputed to intrinsic (developmental) rather than extrinsic social variations.

This series of studies is incomplete, and the methodological flaws that attend cross-cultural work are compounded with each foray into a new society. However, this author feels that the developmental conceptions have been supported by his cross-cultural, cross-sectional and longitudinal surveys. Though the subject societies vary in the degree to which they emphasize active, passive or magical mastery as cultural *motifs*, there is in all cases some age shift away from active mastery and towards the passive and/or magical forms.

In sum, we see traces of an autonomous current in human development that urges men in their younger and middle years towards competitiveness, agency and independence, and in later life towards some reversal of these priorities: familism takes priority over agency; a receptive stance, particularly in regard to women, tends to replace independence; passive affiliation with supernatural power tends to replace the control and deployment of individual strength.

TOWARDS A COMPARATIVE PSYCHOLOGY OF LONGEVITY

We can only infer the psychic constitution of long-lived men from superficial reports. These do, however, suggest a coherent picture of aged survivors: consistently, they eschew the various aspects of passivity. They remain active; they insist—at least in token ways—on their continued independence; and they are pugnacious. Russia has many reputed centenarians and Sachuk (1965) notes that these survivors are found in the severest regions of Siberia, where they had known lifelong difficulties. There were no gluttons, and work was still a *vital* necessity. Pitskelauri (1966) states that longevous Russians are usually mountaineers, descended from long-lived parents, moderate in their diet, and still active in work and sports. Leaf's (1973) observations of reputed centenarians among the Abkhasians (Caucasus region), the Hunzukuts (Himalayan foothills) and the Villacambans (Ecuadorian highlands) add to the portrait of the survivor. He finds them moderate in their appetites, hard-working, still interested in sex, esteemed for their wisdom, and enjoying high status in their communities. It should be noted, however, that there has been criticism of these observations of reputed centenarians on the grounds that none of these cases of super-longevity can be said to be scientifically valid (Medvedev, 1974).

This author (see Gutmann, 1971a) noted similar characteristics among longevous Druze and Navajo: almost invariably, they force themselves to continue a regimen of hard physical work, particularly in the service of a younger relative. Then too, Talmon-Garber (1962) has noted that *kibbutzniks* in their seventies often volunteer as instructors in new settlements manned by young pioneers. In these cases, the old survivor demonstrates his independence by maintaining a "parental" stance towards the young.

Survival and the Need for an Enemy

Integral to active mastery, and perhaps to longevity, is the capacity to externalize aggression, to turn potentially debilitating inner conflicts into external struggles. This author has observed that surviving traditionalists frequently complain about a faceless "someone" who is trying to rob or kill them. In some cases this "enemy" is clearly a metaphor of death. Thus, an 80-year-old Druze rants against "thieves"—possibly including this investigator—who plague him. When asked, "Old man, why do you always speak of thieves? Who is the real thief?", he points mutely to heaven. Ultimately, for him, God is the thief.

Lieberman, (1973) working with residents of a Jewish old people's home in Chicago, has come independently to similar conclusions concerning this "adaptive paranoia" of later life: "grouchiness," he concludes, "is a survival asset." In effect, the curmudgeons may survive because they do not accept death as an inevitable presence within their bodies. Rather, they turn it into an outer enemy, who can be fought, or evaded. This magic may have clear practical advantages: the old man with an enemy has good reason to turn anger away from his own aging self. By adopting the paranoid position, he avoids the much more lethal depressive position. Furthermore, being vigilant and active, he tunes up his cardiovascular system, and he avoids the vegetative position that is perhaps prodromal to death.

Indeed, the capacity to externalize anger might be a survival asset at any age. Thus, evidence from the Nazi death camps indicates that communists and Zionists had much better survival chances than bourgeois internees. The activists saw their plight as part of a continuing historical struggle against a familiar enemy, whereas the bourgeois inmates could not mobilize rage against the authorities that they had been taught to respect as leaders and protectors. Nardini (1952) made similar observations in Japanese prison camps: again, most forms of passivity were contra-survival, even in the absence of lethal clinical conditions. The symptoms of fatal withdrawal occurred a few days before death, when the victim lay inert, refusing food. Systematic needling to arouse anger was successfully used as a lifesaving measure; and the "natural" survivors tended to be the more combative individuals. On the other hand,

"those who developed depression for psychologic reasons were very likely to rapidly develop physical illness."

THE AGE GRADING OF FEMALE DOMINANCE

The available trans-cultural evidence suggests that women may reverse the order of male aging: where adult men start from active mastery and move towards passive mastery, women start from passive mastery—characterized by dependence on and deference to the husband—but move in later life to active mastery. Across cultures and with age they seem to become more domineering, more agentic, and less willing to trade submission for security.

We cannot (as we could with men) study the "masculinization" of the older woman by reviewing the content of formal age-grading systems. Though these exist for women, their content is rarely studied or reported. However, looking across cultures at actual behavior, we do find mid and late life "women's liberation," even where this development is not given formal recognition. Again, we will start with the data from Asian societies, and end by considering our own Western culture.

Asian Studies

Yap (1962) reports that when a woman heads the Chinese equivalent of a retirement home, she is addressed as a male patriarch; and when the aging husband retires from the management of the family, he concedes control to his wife and oldest son. Apparently, older Chinese women are less likely than Chinese men to move to a contemplative old age. Similarly, Okada (1962) finds that the old widow has great power in the traditional Japanese family: as in China, she runs the family jointly with the oldest son.

This oriental matriarchy may have psychological coordinates. Tachibana (1962) finds that Japanese men are more extroversive than women until age 60 when a marked decline in these terms puts their scores below the female mean, which rises steadily across age groups. The extroversion of the older Japanese woman may be the result of, or the precondition for matriarchy: in either case it implies a greater interest in the nature and management of external affairs. This Japanese arrangement is replicated in Burma: Rustom (1961) finds that the Burmese widow becomes the head of the household and is responsible for family affairs as long as she remains interested.

DeBeauvoir (1972) cites further evidence of this Oriental pattern: sex differences disappear with age. The older Balinese woman can occupy hitherto exclusively patriarchal slots, and govern entire households. Among the neighboring Samoans, "a group of older women may say things that no one else would dare to say."

From the Hindu sector, Rowe (1961) reports that older village women may attain the status of *malikin* and control family affairs. Despite *de jure* patriarchy, Harlan (1964) discovers that the older man's status in the Indian family is finally upheld by his wife, who ensures that his edicts are obeyed.

Similar developments occur in Highland, Muslim India. Pehrson reports (personal communication) that the Baluchi, a nomadic group of the Northwest frontier, are strongly patriarchal. Yet in later life the chief—while retaining nominal control—gives over the management of the tribe's daily affairs to his wife and older son, and spends his time in discourse with the priests.

The Older African Woman

The older woman's domestic rule, particularly in league with her oldest son, is not restricted to Asia. Spencer (1965) reports that older Samburu women acquire status through alliance with their *Moran* sons against the fathers. Indeed, throughout Africa older women are bonded to younger men, either as allies or as antagonists. Nadel (1952) tells us that the Nupe recognize two kinds of supernatural power. Bad power is exercised by domineering older women—who also engage in trade. Men use good power to combat witchcraft; but the older women use deadly power to attack younger men. This variation suggests that older women may enact their "rebirth" as a man either through alliances with virile young males and/or

direct competition with them. This rebirth may be explicitly recognized: Goody (1962) finds that only post-menopausal women, who have "become men" are allowed to wash corpses. Social authority, he adds, is generally vested in men, or in those elderly Lodagaa women who are most like men.

The Older Meso-American and Amerindian Woman

In the Americas, the trend holds: Kardiner and Linton (1945) report that among the warrior tribes of the Southwest, matrons were called "manly hearted women." Levy (1967) notes an Amerindian pattern of giving post-menopausal women greater sexual freedom and the right to participate in ritual and healing practices. Mexican Americans also concede social power to older women, despite the official *machismo* of Chicano culture. Thus, Leonard (1967) finds that the *Chicana* is very important in the home; and this importance increases as she ages.

The Older Woman in Western European Society

Evidence for the "matriarchy of later life" comes from societies closer in values and organization to our own. Cesa-Bianchi (1962) reports that female residents of Italian old age homes do more institutional work than older male residents, that they have more intellectual efficiency and autonomy, and that they are more extrapunitive, with a greater tendency to externalize blame for subjective trouble.

Studies of U.S. suicide rates (DeGrazia, 1961) confirm that men are more likely than women to commit suicide at any age, and that the male lead increases steadily over successive age groups. Psychoanalytic doctrine holds that suicide represents a deployment of murderous aggression against the self, and away from its original target in the outer world. If so, then older U.S. men—like the Japanese men studied by Tachibana and the Italians studied by Cesa-Bianchi—are more apt to manage their rage introversively, even to the point of self-murder, while older U.S. women take the extroversive position, and turn their aggression against others.

The superior vigor of older women is captured in Townsend's (1957) description of English old people on an outing: "The women clearly had more bounce." Objective findings suggest that English "bounce" and longevity go hand in hand. Kleemeier (1960) states that elderly English women are less likely to die in mental hospitals than their male age peers.

The Aging Woman in American Ethnic Subcultures

Turning to comparative U.S. studies, Clark and Anderson (1967) find that, across San Francisco ethnic groups, old women are more likely than old men to describe themselves in positive terms and show a higher degree of social participation. Contrasting black and white elderly, Rubenstein (1971) finds that single women score higher on a measure of morale than do solitary men. Such findings suggest a greater autonomy, a greater ability to live off one's own psychic resources among older women, regardless of race.

Studies of American middle class women suggest that the sex-role reversals noted in other societies appear in this country as well: thus, Kuhlen (1964) finds less evidence of need affiliation among older American women than in their male age-peers; Kerchoff (1966) notes a later life "reversal," in that older husbands show a greater sensitivity to human relationships than their wives, who are interested in practical affairs; and Lowenthal, Thurnher and Chiriboga (1975) observe that middle-aged women become more dominant in the family, even as the husbands become more self-indulgent, move into the filial niche that has been vacated by their grown children, and look to interpersonal rather than inner resources for remedy. Consistent with these shifts towards the normal unisex of later life, Cameron (1967) and Kelly (1955) find increasing "masculinity" in middle-aged women. And at the more subjective level, Brenneis (1975) finds in the dreams of older women a striking increase in robust, active representations of the dreamer.

Finally, Kaufman (1940), a psychoanalyst, notes the emergence of the "reverse Oedipus" in older women, where the son is related to as though he were a father, and the daughter related to as though she were the mother. This syndrome could be the clinical echo of the overt mother-son alliance against the father-husband that has been noted in the trans-cultural materials.

THE OLDER WOMAN AS WITCH

To test the scope of senescent matriarchy, Gold (1960) questioned 27 anthropologists as to whether they had observed age variations in the sex-role patterns of the cultures they had studied. Fourteen reported matriarchal shift, and the rest reported no change. None reported greater male dominance in later life.

But Simmons (1945) denies any "feminine partriarchy." Reviewing data from 71 preliterate groups, he finds women—whether young or old—holding high office in only two of them.

However, Simmon's figures are based on indices of formal prestige, whereas we have found that the older woman's power increases most dramatically in informal, domestic settings. Mead (1967) resolves this apparent discrepancy: "old women are usually more of a power within the household than older men. Older men rule by ascribed and titular authority, but wives and sisters rule by force of personality and knowledge of human nature."

Furthermore, if older women are disbarred from prestige positions in public life, it is not because they lack dominance needs, but because—according to the rest of society—they may be too imperious. Increased aggression is not a social asset for older women, but a liability which can make them vulnerable to charges of sorcery. Thus, LeVine (1963) tells us that young men among the Gusii of Kenya routinely suspect their mothers-in-law of casting spells against them. Similarly, the Yoruba of Nigeria *only* ascribe witchcraft to older women, and older men may exile their wives to avoid being poisoned. Fortes (1962) reports that Tallensi matrons (of Kenya) become completely ego-centric, and will curse anybody who crosses them.

The Moroccans capture the African consensus on the lethal nature of old women in this parable: each boy is born surrounded by a hundred devils and each girl is born surrounded by a hundred angels. However, with each passing year, a devil is exchanged for an angel; when a man reaches a hundred years of age, he is surrounded by angels, and the woman by devils. In the same vein, Westermarck (1926) has concluded, "Old age inspires a feeling of mysterious awe which tends to make the man a saint, and the woman a witch."

Some old women may actually resort to black arts because they envy young, powerful males; or because, having the name they also want the game. But the near-universal ascription of evil motives to old women in simple societies must have other, less "rational" sources, such as the sex-role reversals of later life, which render older men mild, even "motherly," while endowing women with the "paternal"dominance that the old men are abandoning. But while male aggression (in orderly societies) is directed outside the community, toward socially valued purposes, female aggression emerges in the most intimate precincts, and is accordingly feared. The long-closeted anger of old women, generally repressed during their childbearing years, may revive, in others, archaic fears of the "bad mother," as expressed in the *persona* of the witch.

AGE-SEX ROLES AND THE PARENTAL IMPERATIVE

This author (Gutmann, 1975) has proposed a tentative schema, based on a concept of parenthood, to explain shifts in male and female sex roles that shape the trans-cultural data. The sharp sex role distinctions of early parenthood are presumably based on the vital needs of the young for physical and emotional security. These requirements are a formidable stimulus to younger parents, causing each sex to surrender to the other the qualities that would interfere with the provision of their special mode of security. Male providers of physical security give up the dependency needs that would interfere with their courage and endurance; these they live out through identification with their wives and children. By the same token, women, the providers of emotional

security, give up the aggression that could alienate their male providers or that could damage a vulnerable and needful child. Each sex lives out, through the other, those aspects of their nature that could interfere with adequate performance in their parental role, and that could therefore be lethal to their children.

But as children take over the responsibility of their own security, the chronic sense of parental emergency phases out, and both sexes can afford to live out the potentials that they once had to relinquish in the service of their parental task. Men recapture the "femininity" that was previously repressed in the service of productive instrumentality; and women generally become more domineering and independent. In effect, "masculine" and "feminine" qualities are distributed not only by sex but by life period. Men are not forever "masculine"; rather, they can be defined as the sex that shows "masculine" traits before the so-called "feminine" pattern. The reverse is true for women.

PRELITERATE GERONTOCRACY: THE OLD MAN AS HERO

However, despite the older man's inner migration away from aggressive forms of authority, in preliterate societies his official powers increase. Simmon's (1945) review of 71 distinct tribes shows that chieftainship by old men is nearly universal at this level of social development.

But, while "some degree of prestige for the aged seems to be practically universal in all known societies," Simmons has also identified ecological and social factors associated with wide variations in gerontocracy. Thus, extremes of climate appear to reduce gerontocracy, as does impermanency of residence. Conversely, male gerontocracy increases as society becomes more stable and more complex. In organized folk settings, the usefulness and prestige of the aged depends on their wisdom, their experience, their acquired property rights, and their ritual powers.

Implicitly, Simmons accuses the preliterate aged of sharp practice: they declare the best foods off limits to the young; they hold onto their property; they marry off their children to their own advantage; and in many societies they have acquired a monopoly over the youngest, most attractive women.

Simmon's belief that gerontic status is based on possession and social stability is essentially shared by Cowgill (1971), and both account for preliterate gerontocracy in the most parsimonious terms. In the small, static society old age leads to social power because of the long lead time required to build up the property, exploits, ritual power and wisdom on which prestige is based. But such common-sense explanations leave the psychologist, who believes that human phenomena can have less rational bases, with unanswered questions. For example, older women become awesome across the human scene, even though (as Simmons himself reminds us) they have *not* acquired much formal status and possession. Moreover, in Asian societies the prestige of older persons is enhanced precisely because they *put aside* the temporal power and possessions upon which, in the anthropologist's view, status is mainly based.

In effect, the anthropologist's explanation of primitive gerontocracy is very much a *young man's* explanation: old men are powerful because they control more of the symbolic and material goods that the young man is least likely to have and is most likely to want. To the anthropologist, the old man is only a young man who has had time to become successful in terms of those achievement criteria that he shares with his sons and with the culture in general. But our foregoing review shows that old men do not invariably share younger men's definitions of success, problem or remedy. And while they value prestige, they may conceive of it and move towards it in ways that would not occur to the young.

The Old Man as "Power Broker"

Possibly then, there is not only an age shift in the sheer amount of status, but also some orderly change in the bases for status ascription, such that older tribesmen acquire power via routes unavailable even to rich young men. To clarify this point, we must digress to con-

sider preliterate conceptions of *power*. In the folk mind, the *mana* which sustains the pragmatic world has its ultimate origin in supernatural, extra-communal sources—in the spirits of ancestral dead, in the mythic past, in totemic animals, in enemy, and in the gods. The particular power sources vary culturally, but wherever this world view holds, anointed figures are required to live on the interface between the mundane and supernatural worlds, so as to "attract" the benevolent aspect of supernatural power, and make it available to the community and its ecosystem. The human metaphors of *mana* are those residents of the pragmatic community who "extend" beyond it, and represent the various extraordinary domains within it. Here, quite apart from his wealth, is the crux of the aged traditionalists's social power. Unlike the young, who are bonded through action to the immediate world, the aged merge and blend with the domains of *mana*.

In some cultures the aged blend with the revered, deified figures of the ancestors; and they were born in the semi-mythic past, another storehouse of power. Thus, Durkheim noted that old people are the only witnesses to the acts of the holy ancestors—therefore, they are unique intermediaries between the present and the past. Shelton   (1965) finds that the revered tribal elders of the Nigerian Ibo are closest to the spiritualized forefathers, who are closest to the gods. Here again, the aged merge with the mythic time when the people emerged from the sacred into the banal world; thus, they carry the power that moved events in those special times.

As Levy-Bruhl (1928) put it, in the preliterate society the old man is "encircled by a kind of mystic halo," an essence so pervasive that even his body parts can take on supernatural power. Thus, the climax of the Hottentot initiation ritual comes when an old man urinates on the young candidate, who receives the liquid with joy, rubbing it vigorously into his skin. His sponsor assures the youth that he will be fruitful, and that his beard will grow. Clearly, urine "marinates" the young Hottentot with the phallic powers of the old man, thus bringing him in turn to manhood.

Senescent *mana* is not confined to the older man's body, but dominates a *tabu* zone around him. Cowgill (1968) reports that younger Thai crouch before aged men in order to avoid the *tabu* power which surrounds the elder's head. This elder power is strong enough to harm even its possessor. According to Hurlbert, (1962) the Hare Indians of northwest Canada believe that a medicine man's power will increase with age to the point where it blinds him.

If the old man's powers threaten him, they also make him invulnerable to *tabu* influences that could harm the young. Thus, Simmons cites many instances where the choicest foods were made *tabu* for the young and were reserved for the old. Faithful to rationalism, Simmons implies that the aged have in effect bamboozled the young into believing that the best foods will be bad for them. But the food *tabus* of various cultures contain a common but less "common-sense" theme: some foods contain *tabu* power and can only be ingested by the aged, who have *tabu* power of their own. For example, four of the foods tabooed for the young by the Arunta of Australia were believed to cause premature aging.

But the final paradox of the gerontocrat's power is that it stems as much from weakness as from the particular wisdom or skills that he may have acquired over time. Precisely *because* of their frailty, the aged are moving into the country of the dead; they take on some of the fearsome aura of the corpse that they will soon become. Furthermore, in old age, a strong spirit is revealed in its own terms, no longer masked by the vitality of a young body. Thus, besides intersecting the mythic past, the aged overlap the spirit world which they will soon enter; and as they blend with that world they acquire its essential physiognomy and powers. Accordingly, Mead (1967) found the Balinese life-cycle to be circular: both the child and the grandsire are at the "highest point" of life because each is closest to the other world.

By the same token, older men gain status *because* of the very passivity that becomes prominent in their psychic life. Róheim (1930) cites much data from preliterate societies which shows that the power broker typically exhibits abasive and even masochistic behavior. Across cultures, the gods mainly give power to those men who approach them submissively, even in the guise of women. Thus, in the religious community it is the older men, cleansed of sex and aggression, humble in bearing (and not the Promethean young men), who can draw good influences from the gods without offending them. In the folk mind, the power bringer must be a metaphor of the power that he would attract. Accordingly, the "maternal" old man becomes a vessel for nutritive "good power," while the angry old woman becomes a vessel for bad supernatural power, and is suspected of witchcraft. The folk mind transforms the older traditionalist's passivity—in urban cultures the badge of his psychic weakness—into the very pivot of his social strength.

Furthermore, just as they utilize his passivity, traditional societies can also articulate into executive capacities the older man's quotient of magical mastery, an ego stage founded on the (developmentally) primitive belief that the universe and its powers are coerced by symbolic, metaphoric forms of control. In a secular society, magical mastery mainly takes the form of aberrant and psychotic acts; but in the religious and traditional society, magical mastery as a personal style is readily assimilated to a conventionalized symbol and ritual system, through which important events are presumably regulated.

TRUST AND SURVIVAL IN LATER LIFE

Clearly, the old traditionalist's power does not depend on his ability to dominate men, but on his ability to influence God. But the cross-cultural data also suggest that social power, however gained, is neither a necessary or sufficient condition of the older person's security. This depends on his claim not only to the love of God but also to the love of his children. As DeBeauvoir (1972) observes, "A surer protection—than magic or religion—is that which their children's love provides their parents." However, despite the crucial importance of filial ties, social scientists who study the bases of later life security usually ignore the "soft," not easily quantified topic of the emotions. In their view, where the aged are treated harshly, it is not because they are unloved, but because they are a luxury that a hardship society cannot afford. For example, Simmons (1945) holds that senilicide among nomadic groups "was not necessarily a sign of disrespect ... harshness of life rather than hardness of heart was the basic reason." Eskimo aged, left dying on ice floes, are also cited to support this "rationalist" thesis. Thus, Mirsky (1953) tells us that among the Ammassalik of Greenland an old man who cannot hunt will survive only if he has sons who *choose* to look after him. Again, it is assumed that the Eskimos, like pastoral nomads, do not have enough resources to feed a useless person and only let him die out of necessity. But the Ammassalik are psychological as well as cultural primitives. Mirsky states that they are interested only in power and possession, and so egocentric that murder at any age goes unpunished, *even by kinsmen of the slain.* Clearly, the Ammassalik are not *objects* to each other in the matured, internalized sense—they exist to be manipulated and exploited, and when they are out of sight they are out of mind.

By contrast, Lantis (1953) tells us that the Nunivak Eskimos of the Bering Sea defer even to the post-productive aged, giving them the best food. Clearly, the Bering are not discriminated from Greenland Eskimos by degree of hardship, but by the capacity for *object relations;* where the Ammassalik are emotional retardates, the Nunivak are emotionally advanced, with warm kindred ties *at all age levels.* Apparently, close social relationships will extend to and safeguard the aged, even in a harsh climate. Thus, the Yaghan of Tierra Del Fuego live in a bleak region but cherish their children and their aged. Similarly, the Aranda of the Australian Desert practice late weaning and maintain their aged into senility.

Conversely, a benign environment does not guarantee the welfare of the weak and unproductive. Thus, the Thonga (Bantu-speakers) neglect their young and do away with useless aged. Again, the dominant personality type of the society seems to account for the hard fate of both the young and the old. Chiefly valued

among Thonga are the fattest, the strongest, and the richest individuals—and none other.

Similarly, according to Williams and Calvert (1859), cannibalism was a common Fijian practice, widows were immolated, the sick were buried before their death, and the aged would beg for release: ". . . a repugnance on the part of the sound, the healthy and the young to associate with the maimed, the sick, and the aged is the main cause of sacrifice." Again, in Fiji, objects have no *constancy:* become sick or old and you'lose your humanity. And like the Ammassalik or Thonga, the egocentric Fijian is turned towards self-aggrandisement, at the expense of others. Consequently, the aged in this paradise are much worse off than their age-peers among the Nunivak of the cold Bering Sea.

This author's work among two Mexican Indian groups made him aware of the geriatric implications of a society's affective quotient. Thus, relationships among the Highland Maya are marked by chronic envy and mistrust, and while the aged acquire much ritual and political power, they live in a state of terror only partially alleviated by heavy drinking. By contrast, the Yucatan Maya are an orderly, responsible, and quietly warm people. Age does not bring wealth or formal status—*but it does command love.* Political power is in the hands of younger *Yucatecos,* but the aged are content, they say, because "we have good sons who maintain us well in our old age."

In sum, societies that sponsor an egocentric, self-seeking spirit in the population will be lethal to young and old alike. But societies which sponsor altruism, and the formation of internalized objects, provide security to these vulnerable cohorts. The internal object, an emotionally invested representation abstracted from a long history of shared interaction, has constancy and relates the past to the present. Accordingly, the older person who acquired true object status transcends his immediate condition. His child does not see in the parent a useless, ugly old person. Rather, he still relates to the vigorous, sustaining parent that he once knew, as well as the weak person immediately before him. By keeping his object status the older person avoids becoming the *stranger,* and is thereby protected against the fear and revulsion aroused by the "other." There is a much noted tendency for the aged to reminisce, and even to relive their earlier life. Though taken as a sign of egocentricity, this may be an adaptive move to escape the lethal condition of "otherness." As they reminisce, the elders seem to be saying, "See me not as I am, but as a total *history*, and as someone who was once like you."

In effect, those social scientists who have studied the aged trans-culturally have been Ammassalik rather than Nunivak. They have looked at the aged egocentrically, from the standpoint of the power and prestige variables that social scientists can most easily quantify. But (perhaps out of fear of encountering the "strangeness" of the aged) they have not taken the "inside" view, to consider the *affectional* variables that might be most important to older people.

THE INTEGRATION OF NATURE AND SOCIAL NURTURE IN LATER LIFE

The trans-cultural overview demonstrates that no single perspective can account for the forms and variations of geriatric prestige and security in the preliterate society. Environmental features play some part, as does the advantage that accrues to the aged in static societies; but the consequences of these factors for the older person's power and well-being are clearly mediated by an independent constraint—the nature and level of affectional bonds, of object relations, in a particular society. Thus, old men can control property and rituals even in societies where envy is a dominant *motif,* but they will be in constant danger—the rich old shaman will be accused of being a sorcerer as well as a healer, and in times of plague or famine his life will be at risk. He will be feared and respected for his powers, but also hated for the malice that presumably went into their acquisition.

Finally, to account for phenotypic variations in aging psychology we must consider the *interactions* among important variables, for example, the developmental potentials of later life and the cultural *value* setting in which they emerge. Thus, Clark (1967) reminds us that

aging should be studied in those contexts where the values that the aged are *naturally* prone to adopt are already the core values of the society. Thus, where social norms and values interface with the affiliative and "magical" potentials released by the older man's withdrawal from the instrumental-productive life, then new personal configurations are possible, registered in renewed ego identity, and in forms of social prestige unavailable to the young. Conversely, where cultures devalue the "passive" male potentials, these are more likely to emerge as the basis of mid-life crisis or psychosomatic illness. By the same token, the revived, uncloseted aggression of the older woman can lead either to her stigmatization as the witch, or to her elevation as the *Malikin*, again depending on the culture's attitude towards female aggression.

The importance of this coordination between developmental "givens" and the value consensus which "receives" them is highlighted by the work of Hsu (1951), who found that the aged were *particularly* revered in traditional China, a society based on mutual cooperation and *dependence* among family members. Wolff (1959) supports him with clinical evidence: Chinese patients with chronic brain syndrome (CBS) rarely show the psychotic reactions that often accompany CBS in our society.

Another fortunate nature-nurture matching is found by Shelton (1965) among the Nsukka Ibo, an African society which emphasizes both achievement and interpersonal skills. In effect, the Ibo male has two lives: first as an instrumental leader, later as a socio-emotional leader—and Ibo culture encourages each mode in its proper, developmentally ordained season. (Arth (1968) contradicts Shelto. The Ibo, he claims, are not dual valued, but unilaterally favor achievement. Accordingly, the young high achievers are ambivalent towards the elders, whose achievement days are over.)

Another optimal personal-social matching is revealed in Leonard's (1967) observations of the Mexican-American elderly, whose subculture elevates the principles of passive mastery to an ethic, and there is no celebration of work *per se.* Accordingly, old age is honored as a time to rest and to dole out accumulated wisdom. Thus, older *Chicanos*—unlike their Anglo age peers—feel no compunction about receiving help from their children.

This "interactionist" perspective may shed new light on the long standing debate in the gerontological literature on the religious predilections of the aged. The trans-cultural reviews suggest that the aged are not innately "religious'" but that they develop potentials which are best sponsored—translated into executive capacities—in a religious atmosphere. Thus, Abarbanel (1972) analyzed the relationship between the prestige of old persons and their control over cultural resources in 62 cultures. His preliminary findings are that older people replace their decreased involvement in economic production with increased involvement in the form of "moral production" represented by religion. Again, the sources of phenotypic behavior are not finally founded either in nature or nurture, but in some dynamic, constantly shifting interplay between them.

SHORTCOMINGS OF DISENGAGEMENT THEORY

Although disengagement theory was not tested cross-culturally, Cumming and Henry (1961) claimed universal application for their conception. However, the foregoing review of continuities and discontinuities between social values and personal modalities in later life underlines the value of the comparative approach even as it casts doubt on the universal validity of disengagement theory. This theory does not extend to societies (e.g., the Druze) which maintain a strong traditional armature; and it does not apply to societies (e.g., the Chinese or Mexican) where human relationships are structured along lines consistent with the themes of passive and/or magical mastery.

Disengagement theory views overt social withdrawal and the loosening of internal controls as linked parts of the same overall process. But trans-cultural studies indicate that *detachment* on the social level does not inevitably lead to the predicted decoupling from internalized norms and values. Thus, Delaney (1974) found that elderly Thai become self-pre-

occupied and remote—though unfailingly polite—in social occasions, and are centrally concerned with a transition to the next life that must be gracefully accomplished according to traditional forms. Clearly then, Thai withdrawal from the human arena does not imply concurrent separation from normative control. As Delaney puts it, "When an aging individual began to truly confront death, and began to work with the material of dying, he did so under the guide of Buddhist ideology and within the religious action system of Buddhist ritual."

By the same token, cohorts who still maintain social contacts, but who become detached from the crucial norms and values of a traditional society, can demonstrate arbitrary thinking, one of the major signs of disengagement. Thus, Cole and Gutmann (1975), analyzing TAT data from middle-aged and older Druze women, found that stories given by those over 60 showed a sharp degradation towards arbitrary interpretations of the stimuli, while the age shift in Druze males towards magical interpretations was less drastic. Significantly, these signs of "internal" disengagement appear in women at about the time when Druze men enter the exclusive ranks of the religious elders and detach themselves from their wives. Thus, their religious preserve seems to provide the older Druze men with meaningful norms that retard disengagement, while the women, still socially active, but lacking this particular normative order, show some striking *stigmata* of this condition. In this case, it is the decay of the subjective relationship with internalized norms, rather than the loss of external social relationships, that sponsors disengagement.

MODERNIZATION AND DISENGAGEMENT

The foregoing examples suggest that the loss of traditional culture, rather than the retirement from social interaction *per se,* is the precondition for disengagement. Since the static folk society is the usual framework for traditional culture, do contemporary changes in such communities erode the communitarian and religious principles which sponsor engagement in later life? Is disengagement a side effect of urbanization and modernity, rather than a developmental imperative, as claimed by Cumming and Henry? With these questions in mind we will review some geriatric effects of modernization in folk, traditional and rural societies.

Modernization in Asia

Reviewing Asian studies, Mead (1967) suggests that modern medical advances may be a mixed blessing for the aged. Before Western medicine arrived, the aged were by definition survivors who had prevailed by virtue of their own rather than medical resources. As such, they conveyed a positive image of aging. Now the infirm aged survive in Bali and sponsor a bad image of their life stage. Smith (1961) concurs that elderly Asians are becoming more numerous just when the traditional and familial bases of their authority and emotional security are breaking down.

Rowe (1961) also finds an erosion of village gerontocracy as a result of Indian modernization. The young men find wage work in the cities and return impatient with tradition and with the slow paced village life. Furthermore, the wealth that they bring back undercuts the traditional association between affluence and advanced age.

Harlan (1964) warns against "glib generalizations" that link the troubles of the aged to industrialization and urbanization. Even in traditional Indian villages, he finds that income and education had more to do with leadership than did age *per se*. In general, the aged are only deferred to on ritual occasions, and are abused in daily life. However, two out of the three villages that Harlan studied are close enough to cities for the younger men to seek urban wage work. Harlan may actually be studying the erosive effects of modernization within the traditional village, thus supporting the point that he means to refute.

Okada (1962) finds that the Japanese rural family functioned successfully in the past, when impersonal social institutions were weak. The elder maintained and increased his property while training his successor, and he turned patriarchy over to his oldest son at a time of his own choosing. But currently, farming becomes more mechanized, and control passes earlier to the son because of his technical sophistication.

Modernization in Africa and the Levant

Modernization has similar effects in Africa: Arth (1968) finds that young Ibo, acquiring independent wealth from wage work, no longer rely on their fathers for the bride price. Consequently, the prestige of the father declines. Noting prevalent "psychosenility" among elderly Ibo, Arth links this to the corrosive effects of modernization. Nahemow and Adams (1972) believe that the loss of other prestigious roles led the aged in Uganda to emphasize grandparenthood. However, this compensatory role is undercut as generational discontinuities increase in step with the modern "liberation" of the young.

Modernization can mean limitation rather than freedom for the young; but in either case the traditional balance of generational relations is upset. Thus, according to Spencer (1965), the virtual monopoly over young women held by older Samburu men did not provoke generational tensions so long as the young *Moran* were free to be warriors, and the aggression fostered by their exclusion from women was turned towards prey and enemy. But with the modern restrictions on raiding, the *Moran* are "angry young men" within the tribe, and their anger is aimed against the traditional authorities who have not yet surrendered their sexual prerogatives.

In the Middle East, Datan *et al* (1970) measured the psychological adjustment of women in five Israeli subcultures to their climacterium. Her sample was divided by ethnic subgroups and by degree of modernity within these. Surprisingly, the most modern and the most traditional women responded best to the menopausal "crisis." The "transitional" women responded worst. Datan believes that these women had lost the advantages that come with traditional aging, but had not yet gained the liberation that comes with modernity.

Meso-American and Amerindian Modernization

Reviewing the status of the aged Meso-American Indian, Press and McKool (1972) find that modernization effects are accelerated when the traditional town installs a small factory. Shifting from agriculture to wage work, the young men can buy land before their father is ready to surrender the family holding. The father now comes to live in the son's house, rather than granting the son's family a place in the patriarchal compound. Such decline in the acquired statuses, based on control of resources, leads to a decline in the *residual* statuses that automatically accrue with age. Often, the village *Principal*—until recently a mighty figure—becomes a "has-been," and aging fathers who refuse to surrender land to their sons are sometimes murdered.

Boyer, Klopfer, and Boyer (1965) used Rorschach measures to study the interaction of modernization and aging in two Amerindian groups, the Mescalero and Chiricahua Apache. Their findings suggest a clear advantage in ego strength among the traditional men, aged 50 and over. Some portion of this difference may have to do with the older men's continuing allegiance to the shamanistic culture, which supplies routes for focusing hostility. Having lost this traditional legitimation, the younger men are more apt to rely on alcohol to sponsor the expression of rage.

Levy (1967) found that the government's stock reduction policy (instituted to counter over-grazing) motivates older Navajo to surrender their grazing permits—and the associated prestige—to the young in exchange for welfare benefits. The Navajo religion is based on healing rituals known mainly to older traditionals, but now the singer's role is declining in competition with government hospitals, and with the *Peyote* religion, which makes ceremonial roles available at low cost to young Navajo. Furthermore, the traditionalist loses his educational role—his grandchildren now go to Indian Agency boarding schools and learn "white man" knowledge that he lacks. Finally, the old Navajo becomes a source of strife among clan members who compete for his custody so as to get his welfare check. The old age assistance program was designed to safeguard the welfare and prestige of the aging Indian; instead, it gives him the image of a dependent rather than a wise man.

The effects of modernization on the aged have been further explored by application of the Equality Index (E.I.), a measure designed by Palmore and Morton (1974) to estimate gerontic status relative to the young. The E.I. indicates reduced status for the aged in the more modern countries as opposed to the less advanced ones. However the relationship between the E.I. and modernization is "J" shaped rather than linear. As Datan found in her Israeli studies, early modernization brings about a sharp decline in E.I., with some resurgence in countries that have reached the later stages. In rapidly industrializing countries the aged lose the traditional bases of honor and have not yet learned to content themselves with the material benefits that result from industrialization.

RURAL AND URBAN AGING

Rural-urban transformations, within "advanced" societies, have consequences similar to those observed when traditional societies modernize. Reviewing the effects of modernization *within* Western society, Burgess (1960) states that the "roleless role" of the aged reflects shifts from home to family production; from rural to urban residence; from the extended to the conjugal family; from small to large organizational structures; and the marked increase in leisure time.

Burgess' generalizations are borne out by Aldrich (1974) who found that rural-urban differences were more powerful than cultural differences in determining family attitudes in Portugal and Brazil. While rural subjects maintained "traditional, familistic and intergenerational deferential patterns," respect for elders decreased with education and in the urban milieux of both societies.

At the heart of Western Europe, Kooy (1962) observes the same effect. The urban-proximal regions of Holland provide less status to the aged than do the urban-remote enclaves, where the extended family predominates. Similarly, Baumert (1962) finds more multigenerational, coresidential families in farming areas of Germany, and less exclusion of rural elders. Likewise, Havighurst (1960) concludes that older rural people of Western Europe have less need for institutionalized ego supports since family and work already provide these.

The U. S. findings replicate those from Western Europe. Jackson (1970) reports that black aged in the rural south will turn first to their families, even in time of illness. This pattern is reversed in the southern city where the older black is more likely to turn to the hospital or to the church for remedy.

Perhaps, in keeping with their "familism," and out of a wish to sponsor their own "re-engagement," older men—even those reared in the city—are apt to migrate away from urban settings and back to the countryside, the ecology of the extended family. This author has observed a "return to the blanket" among older men of the Amerindian, Mexican Indian and Druze groups. By the same token, Chevry (1962) notes a tendency among Frenchmen aged 65 and over to migrate to rural areas. It is mainly the younger men who vacate the French countryside for the cities.

The urban milieu provides such skimpy emotional support that Rosow (1962) warns against scattering the aged throughout urban neighborhoods, where psyche-groups are not composed of cross-generational kin, but of age-peers. Paradoxically, in industrialized neighborhoods with a "normal" age-distribution, the aged tend—because of their infirmity and fear—to be walled off from each other and cannot form their own peer communities. Thus, contrary to much conventional wisdom, Rosow favors pooling older people in retirement communities which are more apt to provide the "raw materials" of a significant group life.

Paraphrasing Rosow, the aged do not naturally disengage; like other cohorts, they seek community. It is the industrialized city that changes the bases of association and that makes associates unavailable to the aged, thus bringing about their apparent "disengagement." Contrary to the predictions of disengagement theory, when the barriers of association are removed, the aged will bond to each other. Again, disengagement appears to be a way station in a natural process that leads to phase-specific forms of re-engagement in the static and traditional society, but that is aborted to become a terminal stage of life in the industrialized and urban community.

THE MATRIARCHY OF THE CITIES

Urbanization and industrialization may have different effects with respect to disengagement in each sex. Generally, we find that the patriarchal organization of the folk-traditional or rural society is very vulnerable to even glancing contact with modern ways. But the unofficial matriarchy that has been noted even in some folk societies may survive the transition to modern ways. Generally, cities are settled by young refugees liberated from the stifling control exercised in the small community by old men, religious leaders and omnipresent extended family. The city represents among other things the outcome of a revolution against male gerontocracy. Not surprisingly then, as the patriarch declines in the city, hitherto disadvantaged groups, including women, may find their freedom there.

This matriarchy of the cities becomes more apparent as we compare various socio-emotional arrangements along the rural-urban continua of the West. Thus, Sheldon (1960) discovers that the increase in life expectancy brought about by modernization is most impressive in the case of women. Also, Kooy (1962) discovers that, *save in rural areas*, older Dutch women outnumber older Dutch men. Likewise Chevry (1962) reports that the proportion of aged men, *particularly widowers*, increases in step with the agricultural character of the French municipality.

Rural life may be more lethal for women and less lethal for men because of the hard physical labor and continuous child-bearing that are borne by the peasant wife. But Youmans' (1967) work suggests that sex differences in mortality have more to do with the unequal distribution of love, rather than labor, along rural-urban continua. Reviewing patterns of association in the Western world, he concludes that men are likely to be the recipients of emotional supplies in rural areas, and that this pattern is reversed in the cities. Jackson's (1971) comparisons of rural and urban American blacks also suggest a correlation between later life survival and familial bonds. Again, rural black men outlive women; and the urban shift towards superior female longevity is accompanied by a corresponding shift in the patterning of affectional ties. In the city, these are strongest between mothers and daughters; and this close bond pays off in the form of greater direct assistance to the aging black mother at all social class levels.

Other theorists, commenting on aging in Western nations, make equivalent points. Burgess (1960) notes that the matrilocal extended family can function in stable working class neighborhoods as the urban equivalent of the patriarchal extended family of the countryside. The urban family is based on strong bonds between grandmothers, mothers and daughters. In the city, Burgess says, "men have friends; women have relatives."

Similarly, Young and Geertz (1961), reviewing family ties in San Francisco and London, assert: "the mother-daughter bond is the central nexus of kin ties in industrial societies." and Shanas, Townsend, Wedderburn, Friis, Milhøj and Stehouwer (1968) find that modified extended family networks are common in all urban centers of the industrialized West. For the elderly widow, disengagement is not obligatory —bereavement draws reintegrating responses from separately domiciled family members who still maintain strong mutual ties. Citing his Austrian studies, Rosenmayr (1973) terms this pattern "intimacy at a distance." Townsend (1962) notes the "repair" function of this family format: since urban women typically outlive men, the modified extended family helps to compensate the English widow for the loss of her spouse.

The decline of patriarchy has usually been linked to the older male's loss of control over urban financial, cognitive and ritual resources. The city is a young man's terrain, and old men (except tycoons and successful politicians) presumably lose prestige because they lose access to urban power. However, we now find that urban matriarchy is founded on women's superior capacity for intimacy, rather than acquisition. Again, the students of the social life—perhaps out of masculine bias—seem to have downplayed intimacy in favor of power as a determinant of the reduced status, morale and viability of urban men.

PASSIVE MASTERY IN URBAN MALES

While cutting older men off from the emotional resources of the community, urban living may also release other, contrasurvival masculine tendencies. Scattered findings suggest that the urban decline in patriarchy may be linked to the more passive-dependent bent of the city

man of any age, in contrast to his country cousin. Thus, Kreps (1968) reports that after age 65, 70 percent of male residents of agricultural countries are still employed as against only 38 percent for men of industrialized countries. Since these figures may reflect the urban retirement norm, a more meaningful comparison deals with the uses of leisure. Thus, Youmans (1967) finds that the tendency to "sit and think" increases with age, in Kentucky, more markedly for urban than for rural men.

Religious leanings are a possible expression of dependent yearnings; and Jackson (1970) found that urban blacks are more likely than their rural age peers to turn to the church for remedy in later life. The passive propensities of urban men also appear at the more "appetitive" level of personality. This author (Gutmann, 1971b) found that oral-incorporative tendencies increased in his Navajo and Druze male samples as a function of age, but also as a function of the closeness to cities. Empirical evidence from both groups confirms the orality score as a register of passive-dependency; and this trait increases dramatically in the urban-proximal sectors of two very different cultures.

AGING AND THE MIND OF THE CITY

In order to understand the concomitant variation between social life and individual psychology, researchers have neglected rural-urban or folk-urban comparisons in favor of intercultural comparisons. However, the admittedly minimal evidence supports this generalization: urbanization within cultures seems to replicate the psychological effects of aging across cultures. On the one hand, it appears to sponsor masculine passivity and early mortality; on the other hand, it increases the authority and freedom of older women and the young. Cities may be founded by bold young emigrés, masculine rebels against patriarchy; but their urban descendants, particularly in later life, appear less self-reliant than their rural counterparts.

Like the folk society, the city is more than a characteristic arrangement of social and economic institutions. It is also the habitat for mental and affective dispositions strikingly different from those found in the small, tradition-directed community. No writers have systematically considered the relationship between aging and urban forms of mentation. However, the changes in the situation of the aged across folk-urban continua are so consistent that they warrant some brief speculations of the sort that might guide future work.

Two lines of psychological development seem to be engendered in the city, each of which results in a heightened emphasis on the primacy of the individual as a center of experience, of exploit and of possession. On the one hand, urban experience sponsors the development of ego boundaries, which are vital to the sense of individual *separateness;* in addition, urban experience seems to sponsor manifest narcissism, pivotal to the individual sense of *uniqueness* and centrality. At the convergence of these developmental lines the urban individual appears: self-conscious, aware of his inner life and more apt to serve his own purposes rather than the larger purposes of his community or his kin.

The emergence of the modern, urban individual seems to have crucial consequences for the aged. The city-sponsored boundaries that define the self not only separate individuals but also sexes, races, ethnic groups, and generations. The "generation gap" that is strikingly absent in the village and folk society bisects the heart of the nuclear and modified-extended family in the city. These divisions are sharpened by narcissism. In the city, the sense of familiarity does not proceed along the lines of natural, transgenerational groupings—clan, family, or neighborhood—but is organized along egocentric principles. Urban individuals mainly confer the sense of community, of "we-ness," on those who share with them the most concrete and visible tokens of sex, age, skin color or sexual preference. The politics of the city become the politics of narcissism: Youth Liberation, Women's Liberation, Black Liberation, or Gay Liberation.

The conjunction of narcissism and individuation creates the flamboyant individualist, focused on personal power and possession, that we have already identified in those groups that practice senilicide and infanticide—the Amassalik, the Thonga, and the Fijians. We do not know how or why these folk groups pushed individualism to its most destructive extreme (though we are not surprised to find that primi-

tive culture and primitive psychology can go hand in hand). But in the urban case we are faced with a clear paradox: the most sophisticated arrangements at the social level often lead to the most primitive and narcissistic psychological configurations at the individual level.

Predictably then, our urban alienation has reached the point where—judging from the increase in child abuse—even babies are often at risk from their own parents. Thus, it is not surprising that the aged should also be major casualities of urbanization. The aged are always in danger of becoming the *other*, of being regarded—like strangers everywhere—with a mixture of awe and revulsion. In the preliterate mind, which conceives the human community englobed in sacred power, the awe of the aged predominates. But in urban societies, where power is secularized, where heroes or rarefied spirits are not required to man some sacred perimeter of the community, revulsion takes precedence over awe. The narcissistic *ethos* of the city, which asserts that "nothing strange is human," further crystallizes the tendency to put the aged in this potentially lethal position of the "other." Stripped of the magical powers that ratify their strangeness, or—particularly in the case of men—of the affectional bonds that minimize it, the urban aged tend to be dehumanized, and are increasingly ignored, (or worse, sentimentalized) and warehoused in retirement homes, nursing homes or back wards. "Disengagement" may be the most recent term that we have invented to excuse and disguise this process.

Finally, this comparative review suggests that neither the general decline in gerontic status, nor the apparent reshuffling of psychological traits by age and sex that takes place along folk-urban or traditional-secular continua can be accounted for by our usual models of personal-social interaction. Clearly, there are modes of thinking and relating that change across these continua and that mediate between social facts and private needs to determine the individual's ultimate psychosocial condition. We do not yet comprehend the origins, the nature or the functioning of those interface institutions—whether termed "superego," "boundary," "identity" or, more simply, "conscience"—that modulate individual capacities for love, rage, narcissism, or influence as independent variables the social contexts from which they originally derive. These psychic institutions render the collective life available to the individual in the forms of symbols which standardize his subjectivity and so make him available, in turn, to the collective life. Furthermore, psychologists do not adequately comprehend—or even recognize the need to comprehend—the metaphoric relationship between psychosocial ecologies, the kinds of cognition that these sponsor and the role played by forms of mentation in shaping objective features of the social life. These mediating structures are not concretely available to psychologists in the form of overt behavior, or codified social norms; yet they account for much variance in those collective or individual behaviors that *are* observable and quantifiable. We must develop better ideas of the origins, functions and variations in these interface or ego functions; otherwise our measures and our data analyses will remain inadequate in regard to the aged or any other cohort.

REFERENCES

Abarbanel, J. 1972. Aging, family phase, and intergenerational relations in an Israeli farming cooperative. Paper presented at the December, 1972 meetings of the American Gerontological Society, San Juan, Puerto Rico.

Aldrich, D. 1974. Familism and the prestige of the aged in two societies. Paper presented at the October, 1974 meetings of the American Gerontological Society, Portland, Oregon.

Arth, M. 1968. Ideals and behavior. A comment on Ibo respect patterns. *Gerontologist*, 8, 242-244.

Baumert, G. 1962. Changes in the family and the position of older person in Germany. *In*, C. Tibbetts and W. Donahue (eds.), *Social and Psychological Aspects of Aging: Aging Around the World*, pp. 415-425. New York: Columbia University Press.

Berezin, M. 1963. Some intra psychic aspects of aging. *In*, N. Zinberg (ed.), *Normal Psychology of the Aging Process*, pp. 93-117. New York: International Universities Press.

Bergler, R. 1961. Beiträge Zur Psychologie Des Erwachsenen Alters. *Bibliotheca Vita Humana*. Basel: Karger.

Boyer, B., Klopfer, B., Boyer, R., Brawer, F., and Kawai, H. 1965. Effects of acculturation on the personality traits of the old people of the Mescalero and Chiricahua Apaches. *Int. J. Soc. Psychiat.*, 11, 264-272.

Brenneis, C. B. 1975. Developmental aspects of aging in women. *Arch. Gen. Psychiat.*, 32, 429-435.

Burgess, E. 1960. Aging in western culture. *In*, E. Burgess (ed.), *Aging in Western Societies*, pp. 3-28. Chicago: University of Chicago Press.

Butler, R. 1963. Some observations on culture and personality in aging. *Social Work*, 8, 79-84.

Cameron, P. 1967. Introversion and egocentricity among the aged. *J. Gerontol.*, 22, 465-468.

Cesa-Bianchi, M. 1962. A further contribution to the study of adjustment in old age. *In*, C. Tibbetts and W. Donahue (eds.), *Social and Psychological Aspects of Aging: Aging Around the World*, pp. 623-627. New York: Columbia University Press.

Chevry, G. 1962. One aspect of the problem of older persons: housing conditions. *In*, C. Tibbetts and W. Donahue (eds.), *Social and Psychological Aspects of Aging: Aging Around the World*, pp. 98-110. New York: Columbia University Press.

Clark, M. 1967. The anthropology of aging: a new area for studies of culture and personality. *Gerontologist*, 7, 55-64.

Clark, M., and Anderson, B. 1967. *Culture and Aging: An Anthropological Study of Older Americans*. Springfield, Illinois: Charles C. Thomas.

Cole, J., and Gutmann, D. 1975. The later life of Druze women: a TAT study. Unpublished manuscript, Department of Psychology, University of Michigan, Ann Arbor.

Cowgill, D. 1968. The social life of the aging in Thailand. *Gerontologist*, 8, 159-163.

Cowgill, D. 1971. A theoretical framework for consideration of data on aging. Paper delivered at meetings for the Society for Applied Anthropology, Miami, Florida, April, 1971.

Cumming, E., and Henry, W. 1961. *Growing Old: The Process of Disengagement*. New York: Basic Books.

Datan, N., Maoz, B., Antonovsky, A., and Wijsenbeek, H. 1970. Climacterium in three culture contexts. *Tropical and Geographical Medicine*, 22, 77-86.

DeBeauvoir, S. 1972. *The Coming of Age*. New York: J. P. Putnam's Sons.

DeGrazia, S. 1961. The uses of time. *In*, R. Kleemeier (ed.), *Aging and Leisure*, pp. 113-154. New York: Oxford University Press.

Delaney, W. 1974. Aging and the cultural structure of disengagement in Thai society. Paper presented at the October, 1974 meetings of the American Gerontological Society, Portland, Oregon.

Eckensberger, L. 1973. Methodological issues of cross-cultural research in developmental psychology. *In*, Nesselroade and H. Reese (eds.), *Life-Span Developmental Psychology*, pp. 43-64. New York: Academic Press.

Fortes, M. 1962. *The Web of Kinship Among the Tallensi*. London: Oxford University Press.

Giambra, L. 1973. Daydreaming in males from seventeen to seventy-seven: a preliminary report. *Proceedings of the 81st Annual Convention of the American*

Psychological Association, Montreal, Canada, 8, 769-770.

Gold, S. 1960. Cross-cultural comparisons of role change with aging. *Student J. Hum. Dev.* (University of Chicago), 1, 11-15.

Goody, J. 1962. *Death, Property and the Ancestors.* Stanford: Stanford University Press.

Gutmann, D. 1966. Mayan aging: a comparative TAT study. *Psychiatry*, 29, 246-259.

Gutmann, D. 1967. On cross-cultural studies as a naturalistic approach in psychology. *Hum. Develop.*, 10, 187-198.

Gutmann, D. 1969. The country of old men: cross-cultural studies in the psychology of later life. *In, Occasional Papers in Gerontology, No. 5.* Ann Arbor: Institute of Gerontology, University of Michigan-Wayne State University.

Gutmann, D. 1971a. Navajo dependency and illness. *In,* E. Palmore (ed.), *Prediction of Life Span.* Lexington: Heath.

Gutmann, D. 1971b. The hunger of old men. *Trans-Action*, 9, 55-66.

Gutmann, D. 1974. Alternatives to disengagement: aging among the highland Druze. *In,* R. LeVine (ed.), *Culture and Personality: Contemporary Readings,* pp. 232-245. Chicago: Aldine.

Gutmann, D. 1975. Parenthood: key to the comparative psychology of the life cycle? *In,* N. Datan and L. Ginsberg (eds.), *Life Span Developmental Psychology,* pp. 167-184. New York: Academic Press.

Harlan, W. 1964. Social status of the aged in three Indian villages. *Vita Humana*, 7, 239-252.

Havighurst, R. 1960. Life beyond family and work. *In,* E. Burgess (ed.), *Aging in Western Societies,* pp. 299-353. Chicago: University of Chicago Press.

Heron, A., and Chown, S. 1962. Semi-skilled and over forty. *In,* C. Tibbitts and W. Donahue (eds.), *Social and Psychological Aspects of Aging: Aging Around the World,* pp. 195-207. New York: Columbia University Press.

Hsu, F. 1951. *The Challenge of the American Dream: The Chinese in the U.S.* Belmont: Wadsworth.

Hurlbert, J. 1962. *Age as a Factor in the Social Organization of the Hare Indians of Fort Good Hope, Northwest Territories.* Ottawa, Ontario, Canada: Northern Co-ordination and Research Centre, Department of Northern Affairs and National Resources.

Jackson, J. 1970. Aged Negroes: their cultural departures from statistical stereotypes and rural-urban differences. *Gerontologist*, 10, 140-145.

Jackson, J. 1971. Sex and social class variations in black aged parent-adult child relationships. *Aging and Human Development*, 2, 96-107.

Kardiner, A., and Linton, R. 1945. *The Psychological Frontiers of Society.* New York: Columbia University Press.

Kaufman, M. 1940. Old age and aging: the psychoanalytic point of view. *Am. J. Orthopsychiat.*, 10, 73-79.

Kelly, E. L. 1955. Consistency of the adult personality. *American Psychologist*, 10, 659-681.

Kerchoff, A. 1966. Family patterns and morale. *In,* I. Simpson and J. McKinney (eds.), *Social Aspects of Aging,* pp. 173-192. Durham: Duke University Press.

Kleemeier, R. 1960. The mental health of the aging. *In,* E. Burgess (ed.), *Aging in Western Societies,* pp. 203-270. Chicago: University of Chicago Press.

Kooy, G. 1962. The aged in the rural Netherlands. *In,* C. Tibbitts and W. Donahue (eds.), *Social and Psychological Aspects of Aging: Aging Around the World,* pp. 501-509. New York: Columbia University Press.

Kreps, J. 1968. Comparative studies of work and retirement. *In,* E. Shanas and J. Madge (eds.), *Methodological Problems in Cross-National Studies in Aging,* pp. 75-99. Basel: Karger.

Kuhlen, R. 1964. Developmental changes in motivation during the adult years. *In,* J. Birren (ed.), *Relations of Development to Aging,* pp. 209-246. Springfield, Illinois: Charles C. Thomas.

Lantis, M. 1953. The Nunivak Eskimos of the Bering Sea. *In,* A. Sanders and I. Sanders (eds.), *Societies Around the World,* pp. 74-99. New York: Dryden.

Leaf, A. 1973. Search for the oldest people. *National Geographic*, 143, 92-119.

Leonard, O. 1967. The older Spanish-speaking people of the Southwest. *In,* E. Youmans (ed.), *The Older Rural Americans,* pp. 239-261. Lexington: University of Kentucky Press.

LeVine, R. 1963. Witchcraft and sorcery in a Gusii community. *In,* J. Middleton and E. Winter (eds.), *Witchcraft and Sorcery in East Africa.* London: Routledge and Kegan-Paul.

Levy, J. 1967. The older American Indian. *In,* E. Youmans (ed.), *The Older Rural Americans,* pp. 231-238. Lexington: University of Kentucky Press.

Levy-Bruhl, L. 1928. *The "Soul" of the Primitive.* New York: Macmillan.

Lewis, O. 1951. *Life in a Mexican Village: Tepoztlan Restudied.* Urbana: University of Illinois Press.

Lieberman, M. 1973. Grouchiness: a survival asset. *University of Chicago Alumni Magazine*, April, 1973, 11-14.

Lipman, J. 1962. Role concepts of couples in retirement. *In,* C. Tibbitts and W. Donahue (eds.), *Social and Psychological Aspects of Aging: Aging Around the World,* pp. 475-485. New York: Columbia University Press.

Lovald, K. 1962. The social life of the aged on skid row. *In,* C. Tibbitts and W. Donahue (eds.), *Social and Psychological Aspects of Aging: Aging Around the World,* pp. 510-517. New York: Columbia University Press.

Lowenthal, M. Thurnher, M. and Chiriboga, D. 1975. *Four Stages of Life.* San Francisco: Jossey-Bass.

Mead, M. 1967. Ethnological aspects of aging. *Psychosomatics*, 8 (supp.), 33-37.

Medvedev, Z. A. 1974. Caucasus and Altay Longevity:

A biological or social problem? *Gerontologist*, **14**, 381-387.

Meerloo, J. 1955. Psychotherapy with older people. *Geriatrics*, **10**, 583-590.

Mirsky, J. 1953. The Ammassalik Eskimo of Greenland. *In*, A. Sanders and I. Sanders (eds.), *Societies Around the World*, pp. 62-73. New York: Dryden.

Murdock, G. 1935. Comparative data on the division of labor by sex. *Soc. Forces*, **15**, 551-553.

Nadel, S. 1952. Witchcraft in four African societies: an essay in comparison. *Am. Anthropologist*, **54**, 18-29.

Nahemow, N., and Adams, B. 1972. Grandparenthood in transition: the Ugandan case. Paper given at the October, 1972 meetings of the American Gerontological Society, San Juan, Puerto Rico.

Nardini, J. 1952. Survival factors in American prisoners of war of the Japanese. *Am. J. Psychiat.*, **109**, 241-248.

Neugarten, B., and Bengtson, V. 1968. Cross-national studies of adulthood and aging. *In*, E. Shanas and J. Madge (eds.), *Methodological Problems in Cross-National Studies of Aging*, pp. 18-36. Basel: Karger.

Okada, Y. 1962. The aged in rural and urban Japan. *In*, C. Tibbitts and W. Donahue (eds.), *Social and Psychological Aspects of Aging: Aging Around the World*, pp. 454-458. New York: Columbia University Press.

Palmore, E., and Morton, K. 1974. Modernization and the status of the aged: international correlations. *J. Gerontol.*, **25**, 205-210.

Pitskelauri, G. 1966. Some factors of longevity in Soviet Georgia. *Proceedings of the International Congress of Gerontology*, **5**, 93-95.

Powers, S. 1877. Tribes of California. *In*, *Contributions to North American Ethnology, Vol. III*. Washington, D.C.: Department of the Interior.

Press, I. 1967. Maya aging: cross-cultural projective techniques and the dilemma of interpretation. *Psychiatry*, **30**, 197-202.

Press, I., and McKool, M. 1972. Social structure and status of the aged: toward some valid cross-cultural generalizations. *Aging and Human Development*, **3**, 297-306.

Prins, A. 1953. *East African Age-Class Systems*. Groningen: Walters.

Quain, B. 1948. *Fijian Village*. Chicago: University of Chicago Press.

Róheim, G. 1930. *Animism, Magic and the Divine King*. London: Kegan-Paul.

Rosenmayr, L. 1973. Family relations of the elderly. *Zeitschrift Für Gerontologie*, **6**, 272-283.

Rosow, I. 1962. Retirement housing and social integration. *In*, C. Tibbitts and W. Donahue (eds.), *Social and Psychological Aspects of Aging: Aging Around the World*, pp. 327-340. New York: Columbia University Press.

Rowe, W. 1961. The middle and later years in Indian society. *In*, R. Kleemeier (ed.), *Aging and Leisure*, pp. 104-112. New York: Oxford University Press.

Rubenstein, D. 1971. An examination of social participation found among a national sample of black and white elderly. *Aging and Human Development*, **2**, 172-188.

Rustom, C. 1961. The aging Burman. *In*, R. Kleemeier (ed.), *Aging and Leisure*, pp. 100-103. New York: Oxford University Press.

Sachuk, N. 1965. The geography of longevity in the U.S.S.R. *Geriatrics*, **20**, 605-606.

Shanan, J. 1968. *Psychological Changes During the Middle Years-Vol. I.* (In Hebrew). Jerusalem: Gons and Grafica.

Shanas, E, Townsend, P. Wedderburn, D., Friis, H., Milhøj, P., and Stehouwer, J. 1968. *Old People in Three Industrial Societies*. New York: Atherton Press.

Sheldon, H. 1960. The changing demographic profile. *In*, C. Tibbitts (ed.), *Handbook of Social Gerontology*, pp. 27-61. Chicago: University of Chicago Press.

Shelton, A. 1965. Ibo aging and eldership: notes for gerontologists and others. *Gerontologist*, **5**, 20-23.

Simmons, L. 1945. *The Role of the Aged in Primitive Society*. New Haven: Yale University Press.

Smith, R. 1961. Japan: the later years of life and the concept of time. *In*, R. Kleemeier (ed.), *Aging and Leisure*, pp. 84-112. New York: Oxford University Press.

Spencer, P. 1965. *The Samburu: a Study of Gerontocracy in a Nomadic Tribe*. Berkeley: University of California.

Steed, G. 1957. Notes on an approach to personality formation in a Hindu village in Gujurat. *In*, M. Marriott (ed.), *Village India*, pp. 102-144. Chicago: University of Chicago Press.

Tachibana, K. 1962. A study of introversion-extraversion in the aged. *In*, C. Tibbitts and W. Donahue (eds.), *Social and Psychological Aspects of Aging: Aging Around the World*, pp. 655-656. New York: Columbia University Press.

Talmon-Garber, Y. 1962. Aging in collective settlements in Israel. *In*, C. Tibbitts and W. Donahue (eds.), *Social and Psychological Aspects of Aging: Aging Around the World*, pp. 426-441. New York: Columbia University Press.

Thomae, H. 1962. Thematic analysis of aging. *In*, C. Tibbitts and W. Donahue (eds.), *Social and Psychological Aspects of Aging: Aging Around the World*, pp. 657-663. New York: Columbia University Press.

Townsend, P. 1957. *The Family Life of Old People*. Glencoe: The Free Press.

Townsend, P. 1962. The purpose of the institution. *In*, C. Tibbitts and W. Donahue (eds.), *Social and Psychological Aspects of Aging: Aging Around the World*, pp. 378-399. New York: Columbia University Press.

Webber, I, Coombs, D, and Hollingsworth, J. 1974. Variations in value orientations by age in a developing society. *J. Gerontol.*, **29**, 676-683.

Wershow, H. 1969. Aging in the Israeli Kibbutz. *Gerontologist.*, **9**, 300–304.

Westermarck, E. 1926. *Ritual and Belief in Morocco* (2 Vols.). London: Kegan-Paul.

Williams, T., and Calvert, J. 1859. *Fiji and the Fijians.* New York: Appleton.

Wolff, K. 1959. *The Biological, Sociological and Psychological Aspects of Aging.* Springfield, Illinois: Charles C. Thomas.

Yap, P. 1962. Aging in under-developed Asian countries. *In*, C. Tibbitts and W. Donahue (eds.), *Social and Psychological Aspects of Aging: Aging Around the World*, pp. 442–453. New York: Columbia University Press.

Youmans, E. 1967. Disengagement among older rural and urban men. *In*, E. Youmans (ed.), *The Older Rural Americans*, pp. 97–116. Lexington: University of Kentucky Press.

Youmans, E., Grigsby, S., and King, M. 1969. Social change, generation, and race. *Rural Sociology*, **34**, 305–312.

Young, M., and Geertz, H. 1961. Old age in London and San Francisco: some families compared. *British Journal of Sociology*, **12**(2), 124–141.

Zinberg, N., and Kaufman, I. 1963. Cultural and personality factors associated with aging: an introduction. *In*, *Normal Psychology of the Aging Process*, pp. 17–71. New York: International Universities Press.

15
THE IMPACT OF SOCIAL STRUCTURE ON AGING INDIVIDUALS*

Vern L. Bengtson,
Patricia L. Kasschau,
and
Pauline K. Ragan
University of Southern California

Three decades of research in social gerontology have provided many examples of how variations in social context may be related to differences in patterns of behavior with age. It has often proven difficult, however, to summarize the precise ways in which factors of social location are linked to specific variations in psychological processes associated with aging. Even more problematic is the statement of overarching perspectives from which to examine the complex interplay among social forces and aging individuals.

In this chapter, we suggest three major themes or perspectives arising from current research in the sociology of aging which have particular relevance for psychologists examining the impact of social structure on behavior in maturity and old age.

*We wish to acknowledge the assistance of Richard Verdugo and Eileen Walsh in preparing this manuscript, and of James Dowd, Stephen McConnell, and Judith Treas for helpful criticisms to an earlier draft. Original data reported in this chapter are from studies supported by the National Science Foundation's RANN program (#APR-21178) and the 1907 Foundation of the United Parcel Service.

The first concerns *social definitions of age and aging*. Reality is socially constructed; humans think, feel, and act in the context of shared expectations. Aging as it is experienced depends to a great extent on socially defined patterns just as it reflects alterations in bio-psychological structure and function with the passage of time. Aging thus must be examined in the context of *events* which are socially defined, events which gain meaning by reference to the individual's location within the broader social structure.

A second and related theme concerns the importance of social differentiation as it relates to aging. *Patterns of aging vary according to location in the social structure*. Such location is indexed by socioeconomic status, ethnic group membership, and sex. In this chapter we will review some of the available evidence linking variations in these social status categories to data on differences in perceptions of aging, life satisfaction and social adjustment, social networks and community participation, and demographic characteristics.

A third theme centers on *social and histor-*

ical changes and their relation to aging. To adequately understand the aging individual, it is necessary to consider ways in which the social structure itself changes through time. First, the context of aging is influenced by unplanned and often unanticipated macrosocial alterations which affect an entire society: shifts in population distribution, technological innovations, and historical or political events. These alter the configurations of social structure—for example, social institutions, roles, positions, even values—in which individuals grow up and grow old. Second, one must consider the impact of "planned" social change in the form of purposive intervention: alterations over time of the social system through political or social policies which have implications for the aged.

SOCIAL DEFINITIONS OF TIME AND AGING

To begin with it is well to highlight a perspective central to much current social theory: *the sociology of knowledge* (or, as this tradition has more popularly become known, the "social construction of reality") (Berger and Luckmann, 1966). A pioneer sociologist, W. I. Thomas (1931), noted that situations are real insofar as they are *defined* as real, by individuals or by groups. The way humans categorize events or individuals they encounter—the designation of a person as mad or sane, old or not-yet-old, masculine or feminine—are seen to derive not merely from "objective" cues but also from the perceiver's subjective definitions of the situation. Such evaluations are conditioned by what Thomas (1931) called the "intersubjective construction" of events; that is, the learned and shared definitions of situations which influence action or behavior with the passage of time. The classic experiments of Sherif (1936) and Asch (1951) provide empirical support for the assertion that "objective" events are interpreted according to shared norms which develop through interaction.

The "social construction of reality" perspective has several implications for those studying aging. First, the social categorization of individuals by age (as young, middle-aged, or elderly) varies according to location in the social system. As has been demonstrated in the social psychology of person perception, at least three parameters structure such definition (Bengtson, 1971): characteristics of the individual who is the target stimulus (for example, male or female, blue-collar or white-collar); characteristics of the individual or social group categorizing the object (e.g., working class, ethnic minority, young or old); and the social context of the attribution (family, politics, or work). The 48-year-old Canadian Prime Minister was perceived as somewhat "young" to accede to his office, but "old" to be marrying a 23-year-old woman (Schoenfeld, 1974). Empirical studies indicate that definitions concerning the ascription of "old age," as well as characteristics attributed to the aged, vary among social categories (see Ahammer and Baltes, 1972; Blau, 1973; Nardi, 1973; Neugarten and Moore, 1968). Such evidence suggests that social age should be examined as a dependent variable, just as it is more often employed as an independent variable to examine behavioral correlates of differences in chronological age (Wohlwill, 1970).

Second, the sociology of knowledge perspective also reminds us that time, while usually defined in terms of chronological events such as sunrise to sunrise, or birthday to birthday, can be behaviorally defined in terms of developmental or historical events which have influenced an individual's life (Bengtson and Black, 1973). The *occurrence* of such events, as well as their *meaning* for the person, varies among groups and between individuals. Thus the basic constructs of interest to gerontologists (time and aging) may have quite different meanings for one group of humans in contrast to another.

A third implication concerns the definition of "social problems." What is or is not seen as a difficulty associated with aging reflects what is collectively defined as normal or deviant—and this may vary across societies, across locations in the social structure, and across historical periods. So also do the solutions proposed to deal with problematic aspects of aging—how much, for example, it is the responsibility of the collectivity (such as governmental agencies) to provide needed assistance to older individuals, and how much it is the responsibility of the older person himself or his family (Kasschau and Bengtson, 1976; Ragan and Grigsby, 1976).

Thus the public recognition of problems, and of their appropriate amelioration, is a complex social and political process based on the emergence of collective definitions of the situation.

In short, aging represents one of many aspects of reality which are socially defined; and old age is a social category whose properties and problems are constructed within the context of shared expectations particular to specific groups.

Social Organization and Aging: Conceptual Tools

Social organization refers to the patterns of relationships that can be observed among groups and between individuals. Several concepts are particularly useful in examining social organization as it is related to aging and change over time (for a more detailed exposition see Atchley, 1972; Bengtson, 1973; Berger and Berger, 1972; Maddox, 1970; Riley, 1971; Riley, Johnson, and Foner, 1972; Streib, 1976). Throughout this chapter we will frequently refer to seven concepts used in analysis of social organization: status, value, stratification, roles, institutions, values, and norms.

In examining human aging, it would seem natural to begin with the individual as a unit of analysis. But in order to understand what happens in that individual's life history, it is necessary to view biographical events as related to his or her position in the social structure. What has been termed *status* refers to the manner in which individuals are located in the network of social relations on the basis of characteristics such as sex, age, ethnicity, occupation, and level of education (Blau and Duncan, 1967). Such statuses are often hierarchically arranged, reflecting the *values* or conceptions of the desirable shared by the social group; thus status designates in shorthand fashion how the individual fares within the system of stratification (Lenski, 1966).

By *stratification* is meant the system of differential distribution of resources, prestige, and power among individuals, according to their status characteristics. But individuals also are located in the social structure by virtue of occupying certain *positions*, such as mother,

student, worker, spouse; to each position is attached a *role*, a commonly recognized repertoire of rights and responsibilities.

Stratification is manifest within a number of spheres of social activity, such as the family, religion, education, and the political-legal system. These social networks are examples of *institutions*, broad systems of patterned social relationships which endure over time and are based on shared values. These in turn are regulated by *norms* or expectations regarding behavior (Homans, 1964). And all such factors—institutions, roles, norms, values—can be seen to exhibit both continuity and change over time.

Social Dimensions of Aging: Change and Continuity

Sociological approaches to individual change and continuity through time address a central theme: how to understand the aging process and the succession of cohorts as individuals mature, die, and are replaced by new members of the group (Cain, 1964; Elder, 1975; Riley, Johnson, and Foner, 1972). In addressing this problem, investigators apply the conceptual tools discussed above. With the construct of "role," for example, one may view an individual biography as a sequence of roles which the individual enters, learns to perform, and from which he eventually exits (Blau, 1973). In fact, the individual occupies sets of roles at given times, and the patterned sequencing of roles appears to reflect "stages" in the sequence of life events.

The attribution of behavior as appropriate or inappropriate (through "norms," statements of what individuals should or should not do) is often tied to the age of those individuals. The age-specificity of norms is seen in casual expectations concerning dress and entertainment as well as in the timing of major life events such as entry to and eventual relinquishment of the work role (Neugarten and Moore, 1968).

The application of concepts such as role, norms, and stratification can be a useful procedure in revealing the process of aging as socially organized. Before reviewing studies illustrating specific ways in which patterns of aging vary by dimensions of social stratification, however, we need to look at the concepts of time, change, and continuity as they apply to both the personal system and the social system of individuals (Bengtson, 1973).

Chronological and Social Age. The biography of an individual reflects periods of both change and stability. Some sequences of life stages and accompanying roles are commonly expected and experienced by most individuals. Others vary according to location in the social structure, as indexed by such characteristics as occupational status, ethnicity, and sex. Continuity reflects not only the patterned succession of roles occupied by an individual through time, but also the fact that each period of life is partly determined by all that has gone on before in the developing history of an individual's adaptation to life events (Maddox, 1970).

The dimensions of time against which the sequencing of life events and changes are played out are reflected in different ways of viewing age (Baltes and Schaie, 1973; Neugarten and Datan, 1973; Riegel, 1969).

Chronological age refers to calendar age, the number of years an individual has lived. Chronological age is an arbitrary, if objective, indicator of life events (Bengtson and Black, 1973). It is not without relevance as a rough predictor of life events, for it corresponds, within a range of individual variation, to certain biological events such as puberty, the climacterium, and mortality. Those events provide the limits within which sociocultural variations on a common theme, for example the institution of family relations, may be played.

Chronological age may become a determining factor in the sequencing of life events because in some cases an arbitrary age has become institutionalized and even legalized. This is evident with the age at which one reaches legal majority, or faces compulsory retirement, or becomes eligible to receive Social Security (Cain, 1964; Neugarten and Moore, 1968).

Social age, by contrast, involves definitions overlaid on biological markers and chronological age, and is based on social positions and roles (Neugarten and Datan, 1973). The progression through family roles from being single to marriage to widowhood, from parenthood through the "empty nest" to grandparenthood, provides markers for the definition of the individual as young, middle-aged, or old. Similarly the statuses of student, worker, seniority in a work occupation, and retirement, are interpreted as indicators of advancing age, as are declining health status and perceived longevity. Those indicators influence whether others will perceive the individual as young, middle-aged, or old, and act toward him accordingly. They affect as well the individual's own concept of his age, and the behavior that follows from that self concept (Cain, 1964; Gergen and Back, 1964; Riley, Johnson and Foner, 1972).

Social and environmental constraints, determining to some extent the ordering of events through the life cycle, can predominate over intrinsic biological factors of maturation in producing characteristic patterns of aging. In this sense, social age becomes a status or social position in itself, determining social relationships and conceptions of identity.

Group Variations in Patterns of Aging. That aging is socially defined suggests a second fundamental consideration in examining the social context of aging individuals: the process of aging varies according to specified social parameters. Three such factors will be discussed here. First are locations in the social structure reflective of social differentiation (Streib, 1976), for example, ethnicity, socioeconomic status, sex. Second are characteristics of the broader sociocultural setting, as evidenced in cross-cultural investigations in patterns of aging (see Cowgill and Holmes, 1972; Havighurst Munnichs, Neugarten, and Thomas, 1969; Shanas, Townsend, Wedderburn, Friis, Milhøj and Stehouwer 1968; Streib, 1976; Gutmann, Chapter 14 in this volume). A third source of variation concerns contrast attributable to historical period (Baltes and Nesselroade, 1972; Cutler and Bengtson, 1974; Elder, 1974, 1975; Laslett, 1976; Schaie, 1965) as social systems themselves change through time.

Certain processes of aging appear to be relatively consistent among individuals within a common sociocultural context. It is this similarity to which we refer when we speak of *patterns of aging.* Individuals within a social system share expectations, definitions, and norms regarding the appropriate sequencing of events through the life cycle (Rosow, 1967). Individuals are fitted into the pattern through a process referred to as "socialization," the learning of new behaviors and orientations as one moves into successive positions in the social structure (Bengtson, 1973; Rosow, 1974).

The consensus of shared definitions regarding age has been investigated in terms of perceptions of aging (Bengtson, 1971; Bennet and Eckman, 1973; McTavish, 1971; Nardi, 1973; Peters, 1971) and of stereotypes regarding aging (Atchley, 1972; Bengtson, 1973; Maddox, 1973). Definitions of aging can be viewed as an example of shared expectations which influence behavior toward older people as well as behaviors of older people themselves. Stereotypes are, of course, expectations about individuals in a social category which are overly generalized and often negative; they are used in organizing thinking about aging, but they may be too rigid and may be false. Examples of common stereotypes that persist in American society are the following: older people are isolated from their children; a great proportion of older people are in institutions; most are in poor health; retirement is a crisis. These shared definitions of aging, however they may be unsupported in fact, do organize attitudes and behavior toward aged individuals. In addition they influence the definition of policy and programs directed toward the elderly (Kasschau and Bengtson, 1976).

SOCIAL DIFFERENTIATION AND AGING: GROUP VARIATIONS IN PATTERNS OF AGING

The Location of the Individual in the Social Structure

Much social science research documents that an individual's beliefs, values, attitudes, and behaviors vary according to his or her position in the social structure. Three primary social status locations, or what can be called stratum variables, persistently explain the greatest amount of variation in the attitudes and behaviors of individuals: sex, social class (or socioeconomic status), and ethnicity (racial or national origin group). These stratum variables represent in a shorthand fashion a summary of the life-experiences that an individual is likely to encounter by virtue of his membership in one social category and not another.

Specifically, stratum location influences what might be called *life chances*: the probability that an individual will be born healthy, or live to age 75, or get married, or have children, or have a comfortable income—all tend to be correlated with social class, ethnicity, sex, and age (or cohort membership). Stratum location also influences certain *life-style* experiences reflected in an individual's interpersonal and broader social relationships. For example, the nature of family interaction or the pattern of voluntary association membership is known to be different for young as opposed to old people, or men vis-à-vis women, or low-income relative to high-income persons. Thus an individual's membership in a particular social stratum will influence his life chances and his life styles, as he progresses through stages of the life course.

One initial focus of research in social gerontology has been to demonstrate how age functions in much the same way as sex, socioeconomic status (SES) and ethnicity do, as a location in the social structure that influences the individual's share of prestige, power, responsibilities, and resources. and thus his life chances and life-style experiences. Early research studies tended to treat the aged population as a single, homogeneous group and made comparisons to several younger age strata to understand how life course stage or maturation influence one's attitudes, values, and behavior.

Yet the aged do not constitute a homogeneous population; In many ways, the old as a group appear to be even more varied than younger age strata (Kalish, 1975; Neugarten and Moore, 1968). Aging does not eradicate sex, race and class distinctions; rather, it adds another dimension of social differentiation to these distinctions of middle age. A retired schoolteacher may still identify himself more as a schoolteacher (SES remains the dominant stratum variable) than retired (age, the new stratum variable) (Bengtson, Chiriboga, and Keller, 1969). Many political analysts have underscored this point with their repeated observations that the aged are too diverse a population in terms of SES, ethnicity, political and religious affiliation, to coalesce solely on the basis of an age identification (Binstock, 1974; Campbell. 1971; Ragan and Dowd, 1974). The aged retain much of the heterogeneity inherited from their middle years to which is added the substantial individual variability of biological, psychological, and social processes attendant to aging.

Thus it is of considerable importance to investigate variations in patterns of aging associated with social differentiation. In the remainder of this section, we will review literature on the influence of three stratum variables (sex, SES, and ethnicity) along five dimensions: (a) population and demographic characteristics; (b) perceptions of aging—the subjective definition of age; (c) life satisfaction and social adjustment; (d) social networks and interaction; and (e) community participation.

Sex-Related Contrasts in Patterns of Aging

Although contrasts between males and females in social aspects of aging have seldom been systematically examined, we begin with this aspect of social differentiation because sex is perhaps the most fundamental status identification a person carries with him throughout his lifetime. The importance of sex as a stratification variable can be seen in probability statements concerning the differential *life chances* (e.g., life expectancy, health status) and the differential personal resources or prestige (e.g., income or marital status) likely to accrue to males or females as they age. Similarly, knowing a person's sex enables us to suggest certain modal *life styles* and life experiences he or she is more likely to follow throughout the course of life.

Population and Demographic Characteristics. Women have a longer life expectancy at all ages than men. In 1974, the average life expectancy at birth was 68.9 for men and 76.6 for women in the United States (U.S. Bureau of the Census, 1976). At the age of 50, men had an additional life expectancy of 23.1 years in 1970, compared to 28.9 years for women (*Social Indicators*, 1973). At age 65, the average remaining lifetime is 13.4 years for men, 17.6 for women.

The gap between male and female mortality rates (and hence male-female life expectancy) has been increasing since 1920 (Enterline, 1961; Retherford, 1975). This is partly due to decreases in the causes of death that affect mostly women (e.g., maternal mortality, cancer of the uterus) and increases in death rates from certain causes that affect mostly men (car accidents, lung cancer, and coronary heart disease). It has been suggested that employment-related stress is a major factor in deaths from cardiovascular diseases. There are indications that as women approach the male profile of labor force participation (entering the labor force at upper occupational levels and staying in for prolonged periods of time) they may exhibit death rates from stress-related diseases and occupational hazards more similar to those of men. Still another factor is smoking. Retherford (1975) estimates that one-half of the sex differential in mortality after age 37 is derived from males' higher consumption of tobacco. An increase in the number of women smoking throughout their lifetime may lead to future convergence in mortality rates between the sexes.

Whatever the reasons, biological or environmental, for today's marked difference in life expectancy between men and women, there are several important ramifications of this differential. The first concerns marital status: older women are far more likely to be widowed than older men. Whereas nearly three-quarters (73 percent) of all men over 65 are married less than half (37 percent) of all women over 65 are married; at the same time, more than half (53 percent) of women over 65 are widowed (U.S. Bureau of Census, 1976). There are three widows to every widower over the age of 65. The average age at which widowhood occurs in America is 56 years, and of those women widowed at age 65 over half can expect to live 15 years longer, while a third have 20 or more years of life ahead of them (statistics reported in Kalish, 1975;

Lopata, 1973). Moreover, a widowed male is likely to remarry within 3 years of the death of his spouse, whereas a widowed woman is still likely to be unmarried 7 years following the death of her spouse (McKain, 1969; Cleveland and Gianturco, 1975). This is due, of course, to the significant contrasts between males and females in numbers of available partners. The rate of remarrying for widowers over the age of 65 is eight times as high as for widows (Treas and Van Hilst, 1976).

A second consequence of the differential mortality rates between men and women concerns living arrangements. Many more women than men come to live alone (36 to 15 percent); 15 percent of older women, compared to only 7 percent of men, live in the household of a relative other than spouse (Cutler and Harootyan, 1975). The percentages of older women living alone has risen from 28 percent in 1960 to 36 percent in 1971, a reflection of both the increased mortality gap and growing decline in living arrangements with other relatives (Cutler and Harootyan, 1975).

A third consequence, poverty, is often related to surviving one's spouse and living alone or in families where other relatives or nonrelatives are heads of the household. Over 45 percent of single, divorced, and widowed women live below poverty level compared to 33 percent of the men. Unrelated individuals comprised 60 percent of the aged low-income group, and 83 percent of them were women (Cutler and Harootyan, 1975). Single or widowed women clearly suffer the major burden of poverty within the older population. The financial disadvantage of elderly women may be traced in large part to lack of employment history and lower earnings on which to base Social Security benefits. Although labor force participation drops off for both men and women after 50, slightly more men (12.8 percent) than women (9.0 percent) continue to work full time after age 65. It has been predicted that males born in 1960 will spend an average of 46 years in the labor force and 25 years outside of it compared to 20 and 53 years respectively for women (*Social Indicators*, 1973).

Fourth, despite their longer life expectancy, women are less likely than men to rate their health as good between the ages of 60 and 94 (Maddox, 1962). Kalish (1975), however, reports from HEW data that older men are far more likely than older women to report being unable to carry on major work and maintenance activities due to chronic health conditions. This seeming paradox reflects the fact that men are prone to such life-threatening illnesses as cardiovascular disease while women are more likely to suffer conditions such as arthritis which seldom lead to death (Vebrugge, 1975).

In sum, demographic contrasts between the sexes suggest women are advantaged over men in longevity and perhaps in health status. If one examines the quality of life of those women surviving into advanced old age, however, we might ask whether this added longevity is indeed a blessing. Less likely to maintain independent living arrangements, more likely to be living without the companionship and support of a spouse, and typically suffering from greatly lowered incomes, the woman's life in old age may be qualitatively less desirable than that of the older man. Such a proposition may be tested by examining life-style considerations, to which we now turn.

Perceptions of Aging. How do women vis-à-vis men feel about aging and being old? Shanas (1962) reports that the U. S. public more frequently considers women old before age 65 than it does men, in spite of the greater longevity for women. Older women do not, however, appear to label themselves "old" any more often than older men do: one survey found that 40 percent of both sexes over 65 considered themselves younger than their actual age (unpublished study by Batten, Barton, Durstein and Osborn, reported in Riley, Foner, and associates, 1968, p. 303). Several studies have concluded that older women have more negative self-images than do men (Pollack, Karp, Kahn, and Goldfarb, 1962; Gurin, Veroff, and Feld, 1960). McTavish (1971) concludes that the weight of the evidence suggests women in general hold more negative stereotypes about aging and old people than do men. This is consistent with the demographic portrait of sex status related to aging reviewed above.

Life Satisfaction and Social Adjustment. Because men and women in the middle and late years are making adjustments to different life events, and thus typically exhibit contrasting life styles, it is difficult to compare men and women on variables such as life satisfaction, morale or adjustment in old age, or to have confidence in the validity of findings about their relative happiness. It would be more appropriate, therefore, to evaluate adjustment to specific age-related events in life such as retirement, marital satisfaction in the later years, widowhood, or one's own impending death. But there are few studies that compare both male *and* female adjustment to the same social role transition.

In considering adjustment to a particular role loss, it appears crucial to examine how central the role is and the individual's commitment to the role. For example, in adjusting to loss of the primary role as mother, psychiatric disturbance (while rare) is most common during the onset of the empty nest stage of life for those women who have been preoccupied with the rearing and socialization of their children to the exclusion of other activities and involvement (Bart, 1968). For men, similarly, the desire to retire and initial adjustment to retirement from their primary work role seem to be inversely related to their involvement or commitment to work (Simpson, Back, and McKinney, 1966).

Retirement from the labor force may be less traumatic for women than men, because a woman has effectively retired once before from her primary family role as mother and thus by age 65 has already negotiated one more or less successful transition. Indirect support for this assertion comes from several sources including data from the Social Security Administration's 1963 Survey of the Aged which documents that more older women than older men retire from the labor force and do so for voluntary reasons. Moreover, married women retire more frequently at earlier ages than do single women, suggesting that married women may be retiring on the occasion of their husband's retirement (Palmore, 1965). Women tend to hold lower work and achievement commitment than do men at all ages, and this is true for working women as well as for those not working (Cyrus-Lutz and Gaitz, 1972).

Retirement frequently has consequences for the marital relationship and manifest satisfaction in the later years. Retirement of the husband often means that the wife must readjust her routines to accommodate her husband's presence in and involvement around the house. Kerckhoff (1966) found that preretirement husbands looked forward to retirement more than did their wives. And after retirement, older women who assumed an instrumental role in the home (e.g., emphasis on responsibility for home maintenance) evidenced considerably lowered morale following their husbands' retirement than did women who stressed the expressive aspects of their role (e.g., love, understanding and companionship) (Lipman, 1961). The first group apparently resented their husbands' intervention and participation in their household duties. Heyman and Jeffers (1968) suggest the majority of wives were sorry that their husbands had retired. Lipman (1961) concluded that morale in old age was related to the couples' attainment of consensus regarding the husbands' new role in domestic activities at home.

Widowhood is generally considered a problem of older women rather than men, and in terms of demographic probability of being widowed, we have seen this is true. But in terms of the qualitative life experience of this event and subsequent adjustment to widowed status, there are data to suggest that widowers and widows face somewhat different adjustment problems. For example, the bereavement of the surviving husband may require greater life-style changes since he must begin to manage all household affairs for which neither his previous life experiences nor his self-image prepare him (Berardo, 1970). Recent widowers also appeared to exhibit greater difficulty than widows in adjustment to loss of spouse after long-term illness (Gerber, Rusalem, Hannon, Battin, and Arkin, 1975).

Older widows may find some compensation in having a rather large potential group of other widows who might provide companionship, while widowers are likely to find no such group available to meet their emotional needs. But this lack of companionship and support is less problematic for men who seek the companionship of any of a large number of widows (Kalish, 1975). We observed earlier that older widowers remarry significantly earlier than do older widows. This is due to the differential likelihood of remarrying by older females (Treas and Van Hilst, 1976). A nationwide 1965 Harris Poll found that among pre-retired persons, women were significantly more likely than men to report that they had thought about the possibility of losing their spouse (reported in Riley, Foner, and associates, 1968, p. 540). Thus the role transition may be more expected—and thus easier—for women than men (for a specific discussion of adjustment to widowhood see Lopata, 1973, Chapter 7).

Social Networks. Aged males and females appear to have different patterns of social participation. As indicated earlier, the proportion of women becoming widowed after age 64 is increasing with each passing year. The wife was the surviving partner in 70 percent of the marriages terminated by death of the spouse in 1960, compared to 56 percent in 1930 (Riley, Foner, and associates, 1968, p. 166). Dependence on family contact seems most important for this segment of the elderly population. Most widows live alone, but are more likely than widowers to live with their children, most frequently with a daughter (Britton and Britton, 1972; Shanas, 1962; Shanas et al., 1968). Women are likely to take responsibility for maintaining contact within the family over the life cycle, a pattern which continues well into old age (Adams, 1968; Hill, Foote, Aldous, Carlson, and MacDonald, 1970; Komarovsky, 1964). Older women do, in fact, tend to see their children and other kin more than older men do (Langford, 1962; Rosenberg, 1970).

Outside the family, older women have more friends than do men (Itzin, 1970). In sum, older women seem to have greater emotional involvement and experience than older men, not only in family relationships, but also in neighbor and friend relationships.

Community Participation. Sex-related differences in community participation vary according to the sphere of participation one examines. For example, in the realm of politics using voting as criterion for continued activity, older males remain more active than older females (U. S. Bureau of the Census, 1965).

The decline in voting behavior comes later and is less severe for men than for women. Men aged 65-74 are still voting at their peak rate of 80 percent; it is only after age 75 when the voting rate declines substantially to a level of about two-thirds of the eligible male voters. For women, on the other hand, voting participation drops from 75 percent of the eligibles in the middle years to a plateau of two-thirds by age 65 and then declines further after age 75 to only 50 percent of the eligible female voters. Because these data are not longitudinal they may, of course, reflect a cohort (rather than aging) effect (Bengtson and Cutler, 1976).

If one looks at religious participation, however, older women are more active than older men. Women of all ages attend church more often and more regularly than do men (Britton and Britton, 1972; Orbach, 1961). Moreover, women are more likely to report that religion is important to them.

In other kinds of voluntary associations (formal and informal) it appears that, on the average, older women belong to more organizations and that their membership shows considerably less decline than male memberships after age 55 or 65 (Atchley, 1972; Beyer and Woods, 1963; Rubenstein, 1972).

In sum, older women generally seem to evidence greater engagement than older men in community-level organizations and activities, while men maintain greater political activity.

The general conclusion from this review of the literature is that many aspects of aging are different for men than women. Sex appears to be an extremely important aspect of social differentiation in examining behaviors associated with age; indeed, patterns of aging may be quite different for males than females in our society.

Socioeconomic Differences in Social Aging Process

Socioeconomic status (measured in terms of income, education, or occupation) accounts for considerable variation in the attitudes and behavior of aging individuals. Numerous studies have focused on the very poor, marginally poor or institutionalized elderly (the most disadvantaged segments of the aged population).

It is unfortunate that fewer studies have included samples of lower-middle (or blue collar) and middle-income (or white collar) classes of elderly, who constitute the majority of the aged population. Even less information is available concerning what aging is like when money is no problem. This group is larger than is usually considered: in 1972, 18.5 percent of elderly households reported incomes in excess of $10,000, and 3.5 percent reported incomes of more than $25,000 (*Social Indicators*, 1973).

Despite this somewhat truncated perspective of socioeconomic status (SES) afforded in current gerontological literature, and the many differing operationalizations of SES, a consistent theme clearly emerges from the literature: the decrements associated with aging come later in chronological life for those with higher SES than for those of lower SES. This proposition is consistently supported in the five areas reflecting patterns of aging reviewed below.

Population and Demographic Characteristics. Not all of America's elderly are poor, but many are; moreover, the differential between the lowest one-fifth (living below the poverty line) and the highest one-fifth (living comfortably on their retirement income) is dramatic indeed. While it is obvious that income limits the kind of life style an elderly person may maintain in his later years, it is no less true that income influences the most basic life chances, including longevity, health status, housing, and marital status.

For example, health status varies inversely with SES. Epstein and Murray (1967) confirmed the findings of previous studies in their National Survey of the Aged in 1963 to the effect that the number of days in which more than half of the daylight hours were spent in bed or in the hospital is inversely related to income for all sex and age categories between the ages of 25 and 74. However, this inverse relationship between SES and disability does not hold for aged persons over the age of 75. Another measure of health status—limitation on major physical activity of non-institutionalized older persons due to chronic conditions—shows a similar relationship with

individuals' SES: 45.7 percent of older persons with incomes less than $3,000 experience limited mobility as contrasted with only 30.5 percent of those with incomes exceeding $15,000 (*Social Indicators*, 1973).

Longevity is similarly related to socioeconomic status. Palmore and Stone (1973) found that three SES variables (education, occupation, and continued employment) accounted for more than two-thirds of the variance in the longevity of older persons. Mortality rates for males generally show an inverse relationship to occupation although the evidence is not conclusive (Riley, Foner, and associates, 1968, p. 3).

Living arrangements and housing also vary by socioeconomic status. There are indications that low income resources are a factor in old people's decision to share a household (Epstein and Murray, 1967). Older persons with higher income are, of course, more likely to own houses than persons with lower incomes, and the lower the household income the greater proportion of older persons' houses that are substandard. Older people who had once owned homes but in later years shifted to other quarters cite financial problems as the chief reason. There is an inverse relationship between SES on the one hand and residential mobility on the other: lower status people over 50 move twice as often as the higher status elderly (Goldscheider, Van Arsdol, and Sabagh, 1965).

Higher income or upper status persons seem to possess a configuration of advantages associated with their greater financial resources: better health, extended longevity, independent living arrangements and better housing. All of these personal advantages facilitate independent living into advanced old age for persons of advantaged status compared to lower income status elderly who suffer the decrements associated with aging not only earlier but more severely. Given such contrasts, how do upper and lower status individuals perceive the aging process and their own aging?

Perceptions of Aging. In an extensive review of the available literature, McTavish (1971) concluded that there tends to be a negative relationship between SES and stereotyping old people: higher status persons tend to hold less negative attitudes toward old age and aging than do lower status persons. This is consonant with the probable life experiences each will face in old age.

Several studies have confirmed that lower SES elderly are more likely to identify themselves as old than the better off elderly. Neugarten and Peterson (1957) concluded that there was some consensus among respondents that old age began at 70 for the middle class and at 60 for the working class. Rosow (1967) found similar class differences in his Cleveland study. He concluded:

> This involves no social psychological aberration, but reflects genuine class differences in life styles and life chances, in life expectancy and illness, and the greater physical toll of manual labor than white collar employment. . . It is not surprising that members of both classes perceive the onset of old age differently, for they do age at effectively different rates (Rosow, 1967, p. 267).

From a slightly different perspective, Neugarten and Moore (1968) also confirm this quickened timing of the life cycle among those of lower class standing. The lower the individual's SES the earlier each of the following events in life had been reached: leaving parental home, marriage, birth of first child and birth of last child, and retirement.

Life Satisfaction and Social Adjustment. Lower SES elderly tend to exhibit less satisfaction or happiness, even when health and other relevant factors are controlled (Alston and Dudley, 1973; Gurin, Veroff, and Feld, 1960; Kutner, Fanshel, Togo, and Langer, 1956; Streib, 1956). Of all the socioeconomic characteristics that might be considered relevant contributors to reported life satisfaction or morale, Edwards and Klemmack (1973) note that family income was the single most important determinant of life satisfaction. Further they found that when SES was held constant many independent variables frequently found to be statistically correlated with life satisfaction became statistically nonsignificant or were eliminated altogether.

Though preretirement attitudes are related to the subjects' socioeconomic status, the relationship is not a simple one. Simpson, Back, and McKinney (1966) suggest that persons in upper status occupations (e.g., professional/managerial) are least likely to want to retire because the nonmonetary satisfactions of work that constitute their primary rewards for working are not easily found in substitute retirement activities. Despite such reluctance to retire, retirees from upper level occupations still have the best retirement experience because they have ample income resources and good health status. In contrast, mid-level occupation retirees are the most responsive to the idea of retirement before the fact, though their actual retirement experience is less satisfactory than that of the upper level retirees and is closely pegged to the perceived adequacy of their income and health resources. Persons from the lowest level occupations seem essentially passive to the idea of retirement (e.g., resigned to its inevitability), and they tend to make few or no plans for it. As could be expected, their actual experiences with retirement are the least satisfying and they are far more likely to hold negative feelings about retirement after the fact than either of the higher occupational levels.

Social Networks. Contact with family, friends, and neighbors appears to be both more widespread and frequent among upper SES elderly when compared to lower status persons. Those of higher status will show less decline in their interpersonal contacts in old age than will lower status persons, but there are some exceptions to this general rule. First, considering contact with kin, higher income elderly are less likely than lower-class elderly to live with their children (Beyer and Woods, 1963). Among those elderly not living with their kin, we also find social class differences in patterns of family contact. Adams (1968), for example, reports that middle class individuals are more likely to give monetary support to their kin while lower income persons provide in-kind/ service assistance. Shanas et al. (1968) report help patterns are more likely to flow both ways between the older and middle generations in upper status than lower status families. Rosenberg (1970), Aldous and Hill (1965), Kerckhoff (1965) and others report that actual kin contact, however, is more frequent among blue collar people than white collar or upper status persons. Adams (1970) suggests, however, that much of this visiting occurs with siblings rather than with parents, and thus the elderly in blue collar families may in fact receive less direct attention than do the elderly in higher status families.

Rosow (1967) offers a different perspective, contrasting norms with actual assistance between generations among families of differing social status. When asked who should help out and take care of older people if they have problems, middle class respondents consistently indicated the family, while the working class people mentioned outside organizations (public and private including government agencies, churches, unions, and lodges). Personal sources of help other than the family (e.g., neighbors or friends) were relatively infrequently mentioned. However, when one contrasts norms that prescribe ideal or expected behavior with actual behavior, 30 percent of the working class and 41 percent of the middle class reported having received *no* help from their children. Thus, Rosow found that in fact working class older people receive more help from their children than do middle-class older individuals.

Turning to nonfamily social networks, it appears that middle class aged have significantly more friends and more close friends than those in the working class. In Rosow's (1967) Cleveland-based study, one-sixth of the older working class persons reported that they had *no* good friend, and only 25 percent of the lower class versus 44 percent of the middle class reported having more than ten good friends. Moreover, he found that the working class aged were more dependent on their neighbors in the immediate area for friendship, whereas the middle class aged were more likely to have good friends outside of the immediate locale (see also Blau, 1961; Rosenberg, 1970). Rosow concluded that the entire social life of working class elderly persons was much more locally focused than was the social life of those elderly who were of middle class background.

Community Participation.   Just as with social networks, upper SES elderly appear to retain higher involvement and participation in community activities into old age than do lower SES elderly.

Political participation is related to socioeconomic status at all stages of the life cycle. Riley, Foner, and associates (1968, p. 467) report census data to indicate that among the elderly, the best educated are likely to continue voting whereas among the lesser educated, voting drops off with age.

Membership in voluntary associations is also positively correlated with higher SES, especially among men (Beyer and Woods, 1963; Rubenstein, 1972). Taietz and Larson (1965) phrase it somewhat differently: the decline in voluntary association membership with advancing old age is less precipitous for upper status than lower status elderly.

Videbeck and Knox (1965) suggest that SES reflects an implicit opportunity system available to the older adult. Each of the following were positively correlated with the SES of the older respondent: number of voluntary associations, time spent in voluntary associations, number of public meetings attended, time spent reading magazines, number of books read in the preceding year, and political participation. Only church activity showed no significant differences among persons in the three SES groupings.

Ethnic Differences Among The Aged

Moore (1971) observes that "whether we talk about individuals, group behavior, or the aged as a collectivity, most of our generalizations are based on the study of a limited sample—primarily middle-class, majority Anglos. We do not really know how much such sample limitations constrain these generalizations." Specifically, we know relatively little about the minority aged and about ethnic group differences in patterns of aging (Jackson, 1970, 1974; Streib, 1976).

The National Urban League (1964) introduced the concept of "double jeopardy" to describe the situation of minority aged as one of additive disadvantage: minority aged face not only the problems associated with being old, and often poor, but also the accumulated problems of a lifetime of membership in a minority group. The validity of this observation can be explored by examining available data concerning ethnic or racial group contrasts in patterns of aging. This review will focus on black and Mexican-American groups because of their greater visibility in the literature: but our major point—that there are substantial differences in aging among ethnic groups—applies to other racial minorities, as well as to the increasingly discussed "white ethnics."

Population and Demographic Characteristics.
Adequate statistics are frequently not available for each of the minority aged populations, among whom one would include blacks, Mexican-Americans, other Spanish-speaking, Asians, and Native American aged at least. Census data often subsume all of these groups together under a "non-white" category, or at best separate out merely a few racial or ethnic groups. With the exception of the black aged population which is sufficiently dispersed throughout the U.S. to have visibility in all areas, other minority groups tend to be restricted to certain geographical regions of the country (e.g., Mexican-Americans in the Southwest, Puerto Ricans in the East, Asian Americans on the West Coast). Thus, except where specific surveys have made distinctions among the minority groups under discussion, we will have to be content with examining white/nonwhite or black/white differences.

At birth the average life expectancy of a white person is 71.9 years, whereas for nonwhites it is 65.2. However, the difference in additional life expectancy is reduced when one looks at persons already 50 years of age: whites show an additional life expectancy of 26.4 years, while nonwhites have an average of 23.8 years (*Social Indicators*, 1973). At the age of 70 the life expectancy of nonwhites catches up to whites, and for over age 70 it actually exceeds it (Vital Statistics, 1972). The apparent gains in longevity made by nonwhites in the later years perhaps reflect survival of the most fit among disadvantaged minorities.

Black aged comprise well over 90 percent of the nonwhite population; hence one may have considerably more confidence in attributing nonwhite data to the black aged than to any other minority aged group. However, the

New York Times Encyclopedia Almanac (Kurtz, 1970) reports the average life expectancy for Mexican-Americans in 1960 was 56.7 years, as compared to 67.5 years for all other Americans, and 65.2 for all nonwhites.

The reduced longevity of minority aged explains in part why 11 percent of white Americans are over the age of 65, but only 7.4 percent of the Negro population (U.S. Bureau of the Census, 1975) and merely 4 percent of the Spanish surnamed population (Moore, 1971). In 1970 there were 1.5 million blacks and Mexican-Americans over the age of 65 in the U.S., out of the total population of 65 and above numbering 21,000,000. Moore (1971) compares the ethnic groups' aged-dependency ratios (the number of 65+ per 1,000 divided by the number of individuals between ages 20 and 64): whereas it is 17 for whites, it is only 11 for nonwhites and less than 9 for the Spanish surnamed. She attributes the differences in these ratios, especially as regards the Mexican-Americans, to higher mortality, higher fertility and repatriation (some elderly returning to Mexico to live out their remaining days in old age).

Income data provide additional indication of multiple jeopardy. Nonwhite aged are far more likely than white aged to be poor. The U.S. Senate Special Committee on Aging (1971) published data to indicate that blacks over the age of 65 are more than twice as likely to be poor as the white elderly. In 1974, 36 percent of black persons 65 years of age and over fell below the poverty level, compared to 14 percent of older whites (U.S. Bureau of the Census, 1974).

Similarly, there are substantial differences in white-nonwhite levels of educational attainment among the aged. While 33 percent of white males and 37 percent of white females over 65 have completed high school, only 10 percent of black older men and 13 percent of black older women have attained a high school level of education (U.S. Bureau of the Census, 1974). Moore (1971) predicts that this gap between Anglo (white) and minority elderly in terms of resources such as education, linguistic fluency, etc., will *increase*, not abate, in future decades. That is, multiple jeopardy will persist to the disadvantage of the minority elderly.

Poor housing frequently accompanies low

income. Kent (1971) observed that in 1966, 8 percent of whites of all ages lived in dilapidated housing versus 29 percent of the blacks; he concluded that the percentages of black and white aged living in substandard housing would be much the same. Rubenstein (1971) reports that nearly one-half (48 percent) of the black elderly live in the inner city and few of these urban blacks own homes. Based on figures from the 1960 census, Riley, Foner, and associates (1968, p. 131) report that whereas nearly 70 percent of the white aged heads of households own their home, only 50 percent of the black aged do.

Finally, the issue of health status provides another striking picture of ethnic contrasts in aging. In a Southern California study contrasting 1,269 black, Mexican-American, and Anglo respondents in three age groups, questions were asked concerning both self-perceived and functional health status (for a description of this sample see Bengtson, Cuellar, and Ragan, 1977). Anglos in the 45–54 age range were much more likely to report good health (85 percent) than either the Mexican-Americans (61 percent) or the blacks (58 percent). At higher ages the contrasts were greater (see Table 1). In the 65–74 age group 27 percent of the blacks considered their health poor or very poor; 23 percent of the Mexican-Americans, but only 4 percent of the Anglos reported being in poor health, by their own definition.

Using a functional measure of health, including for example the ability to walk up three flights of stairs, the Southern California study suggests older blacks are substantially more likely to experience serious difficulties than are older Anglos. In addition there are striking differences in the percentages who reported they retired because of *poor health*: 55 and 49 percent of the blacks and Mexican-Americans respectively, compared to only 27 percent of the Anglos.

Multiple jeopardy or multiple disadvantage certainly appears to characterize accurately the life chances of minority elderly compared to white aged (Dowd and Bengtson, 1975). Not only do they face a shorter lifetime, but also they enjoy fewer advantages and comforts while they are alive. Against the backdrop of these objective conditions, how do minority elderly personally (or subjectively) perceive aging in general and their own aging in particular?

Perceptions of Aging. Subjective assessments of aging appear to vary considerably by ethnicity. In the Southern California study, respondents were asked whether they considered themselves as young, middle-aged, elderly, or old. Over 30 percent of the Mexican-Americans answered "old" at age 60, blacks at age 65, and Anglos not until nearly age 70 (see Figure 1). Jackson (1970) suggests that blacks perceive themselves as "old" at a considerably earlier chronological age than whites because of the repeated hardships they have faced through a lifetime of economic and social disadvantage.

The number of years an individual expects to live may be considered another indicator of self-assessment of age. In the Southern California study, Mexican-Americans are again subjectively the oldest, and in this case blacks subjectively the youngest (see Figure 2). Mexican-Americans began indicating reduced expectations of longevity at age 60 (less than 60 percent expecting to live 10 years or more) while the Anglos did not reach this proportion

TABLE 1. PERCEIVED HEALTH STATUS BY ETHNICITY.

	ETHNICITY		
Percent who consider their health to be poor or very poor:	Black (*n*: 413)	Mexican-American (*n*: 449)	Anglo (*n*: 407)
Ages: 45–54	13.8%	16.9%	1.7%
55–64	15.2	20.8	9.1
65–75	27.0	23.2	4.0

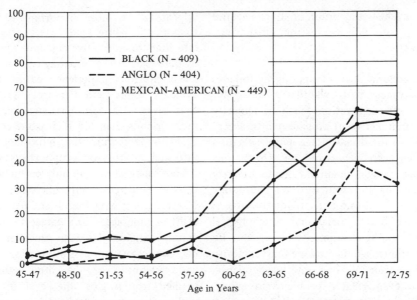

Figure 1. Percent considering themselves "old" or "elderly."

until about age 69. Even at age 75, 70 percent of the blacks voiced an expectation of living 10 years or more. Similar findings are reported by Reynolds and Kalish (1974) in a sample that included Asian-Americans as well. Such subjective assessments coincide with data on life expectancy after age 50 and with the "survival of the most fit" hypothesis, both discussed earlier.

Turning to stereotyping concerning old age, McTavish (1971) found some indication that blacks are more likely to hold negative evaluations of older people and aging than are whites. In the Southern California study, both blacks and Mexican-Americans tended to evaluate aging less favorably than did Anglos. This suggests another dimension to the "multiple jeopardy" argument: elderly minority

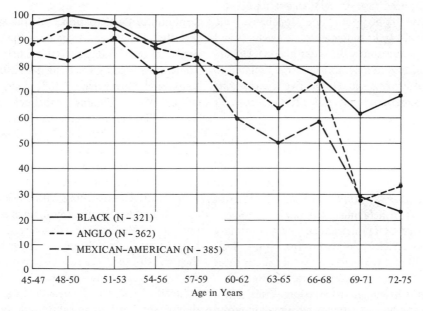

Figure 2. Percent expecting to live over 10 more years.

persons may bear the brunt of more negative perceptions of old age within their own communities.

Life Satisfaction. Two competing hypotheses may be advanced as to whether a life of disadvantage and deprivation (such as minority peoples commonly face) prepare one to accept and adjust to the disadvantage and deprivation which often accompanies old age. On the one hand some would maintain that minority elderly, drawing on resources developed during a lifetime of adjustment to disadvantages, would make better social and psychological adjustment to the decrements of old age. By contrast others would argue that minority elderly, by virtue of their multiple jeopardy, experience even greater problems in adjustment than do the white majority: thus they would evidence lower life satisfaction in old age.

The Southern California study provides some support for the second position (Ragan, Bengtson, and Solomon, 1975). Older Mexican-Americans in the sample demonstrated the most negative evaluations of the quality of their lives, in terms of feelings of sadness and worry, that life is not worth living, and that things get worse with advancing age. However, such feelings are expressed at lower age levels as well: the middle-aged (age 45–54) Anglos report difficulties with boredom and loneliness, the middle-aged blacks indicate greater sadness and worry (as compared with older blacks). Unhappiness and low morale appear closely related to feelings of being old (subjective age) among Mexican-Americans but not among blacks or Anglos.

Social Networks. Are minority aged more likely than white aged to belong in an extended family structure or to have more family contact and assistance? Jackson (1970) suggests that for aged blacks with families, the family is the primary source of (1) assistance and (2) primary group contact. By way of interpretation, Sussman (1970, p. 315) suggests, "the Negro faces severe economic depression, racial stigmatization, deprivation and frustration. Thus active participation and acceptance within a kin group

appear to be more important to the Negro than to the White aged." He goes on to speculate that the normative demands for reciprocity in the Negro kin group may be more easily met given previous experience earlier in the life cycle. O'Reilly and Pembroke (1970) report that black Old Age Assistance recipients had more friends than did their white counterparts, again underscoring the importance of these informal, interpersonal support systems.

These suggestions are only partially supported by the Southern California study. Frequency of interaction with friends and neighbors across eight of nine age X SES categories was greatest among Anglos. Mexican-Americans generally had the lowest rates of interaction with friends and neighbors of the three ethnic groups studied; for Anglos, the level of interaction with children, grandchildren, and relatives was less than for blacks or Mexican-Americans (Dowd and Bengtson, 1975). The authors interpret these findings as indicating that individuals seem to seek, and usually find, an *optimum level* of social interaction. Viewing interaction with friends and neighbors as compensation for the lower levels of contact with kin, it becomes clearer why the frequency of interaction of Anglos with friends, neighbors, and acquaintances is considerably greater than either Mexican-Americans or blacks.

Community Participation. Several analyses suggest that black aged may have higher rates of organizational and political participation than do whites, when SES is held constant (Hirsh, Kent and Silverman, 1968; Jackson, 1970; Olsen, 1970; Williams, Babchuck, and Johnson, 1973). Mexican-Americans, however, have shown a lesser likelihood of either political participation or voluntary association membership than blacks or Anglos (Antunes and Gaitz, 1975). Data from the Southern California study support these conclusions with one major exception. When the analysis compares Anglos with only those Mexican-Americans who were either born in the United States or who speak English, the previously noted differential between Anglos and Mexican-Americans was significantly reduced. However, Rubenstein (1972) found that fewer black than white elderly belong to institutional formal social activities (such as clubs and fraternities). Low-income black elderly, as expected, evidenced the lowest level of overall participation. On the other hand, more blacks attended church and participated in church-related social activities each week than did white elderly. Hirsch, Kent, and Silverman (1968) concur that the black aged, relative to the white elderly in their sample, did participate more and receive more from their church. They observed that their active participation in this institutional sphere was probably related to the fact that the chuch, unlike many formal organizations such as lodges and business-affiliated groups, is characterized by multiple, local affiliations that do not necessarily coalesce in a central national organization: hence, the blacks have been able to establish their own, independent and intimate church institutions.

Antunes and Gaitz (1975) examined 11 kinds of social participation and concluded that ethnicity independently accounted for more variance, on the average, than did either social class or age. They found that after controlling for social class, black levels of participation equalled or exceeded those for whites in 9 of the 11 areas, while Mexican-Americans exceeded the whites' level of participation on only 4 of the 11. Relative to whites, the black aged were most active in voting, church attendance, enjoyment of clubs and political discussion. The areas of participation in which whites showed higher participation rates than blacks were in attempts to influence decision-makers and attendance at cultural events. Relative to whites, the Mexican-American aged were most active in church attendance, recreational interaction with friends, cultural participation and helping relatives.

There is a noticeable gap of information on the black and other minority aged. Jackson (1970) and Moore (1971) have underscored the need to develop more appropriate methodological instruments and techniques with which to study these minority groups. Not only demographic, but attitudinal and behavioral studies are required to present a more complete view of minority aging. Furthermore, the trend that has already come to research on white aged—

namely to emphasize the heterogeneity rather than the homogeneity of the population under study—must be extended to the consideration of minority aged groups as well, for they are no more homogeneous in character than is the white aged population. Finally, the only way to disentangle the unique effects of race on aging from the effects of income or other social class factors is by looking at comparable SES ethnic segments within the aged population. (Bengtson, Cuellar, and Ragan, 1977).

SOCIAL CHANGE AND AGING

A third major theme of this chapter is that the passage of time produces changes in groups as well as in individuals. At the same time men and women progress through patterned sequences of roles, institutionalized within a particular social system, the very social system itself is undergoing change. Such change is seen in virtually every society today, and the pace of that change itself accelerates (Cottrell, 1960; Cowgill and Holmes, 1972; Palmore, 1975). Consequently, on the one hand we observe consistency in terms of patterns of aging, consensus among individuals on expectations and norms of aging, and the process of socialization by which individuals are inducted into their places in a socially defined sequence of positions. On the other hand we must consider the added complexity that accrues when social change produces shifts in the social structure within which patterns of aging are defined.

It is essential to separate at the conceptual level, historical events and developmental or life-cycle events (Bengtson and Black, 1973). Riley, Johnson, and Foner (1972) make this distinction by contrasting age-related processes and structural change. Neugarten and Datan (1973) discuss historical time, those long-term processes and social events that shape the age norms and age-grade system in which the individual life cycle is played out. Change over time, then, involves not only those biological, psychological, and sociological events that mark the biography of the *individual* from birth to death, but also involves the *historical* events that mark off periods of the social system (Bengtson, 1973).

Change in the social system may involve the substitution of new patterns and expectations for old, or it may involve the disintegration of stable patterns without the emergence of equivalent forms. Norms, values, and social institutions that at one time made the meaning of growing older quite clear may give way over time to a situation of "anomie," or normlessness (Burgess, 1950; Havighurst and Albrecht, 1953; Rosow, 1967).

Historical and Cultural Changes

Technological Innovations. Every change considered relevant to the situation of the aged is related to the complex of technological development, industrialization, and urbanization set in motion some 200 years ago. This is true of population shifts, changes in the functions of institutions such as the family and religion, modifications in the pattern of role sequencing which accompanies aging, and the changing system of values that surround aging (Cottrell, 1960).

Social change by its very nature is a factor in age stratification (Riley, Johnson, and Foner, 1972). In the situation of rapid technological advance, there is often a loss of prestige and power attached to the status of old age; accumulated knowledge, a valued resource of the aged in stable societies, becomes obsolete (Bengtson, Dowd, Smith, and Inkeles, 1975; Cowgill and Holmes, 1972; Palmore and Manton, 1974; Simmons, 1945).

The effects of technology on population, longevity, and the structure of work roles must be viewed as a complex whole. The combined impact of several changes that are taking place and may be expected to continue for the next several decades include: (1) mandatory retirement at an arbitrary age (65 or 62 in most countries); (2) mandatory or voluntary retirement at increasingly earlier ages; (3) unemployment rates increasing for the entire age range of workers; (4) increased longevity; and (5) changing population structure reflecting greater proportions of older people. The result is a growing economically dependent older age stratum, increasing in both absolute numbers and relative proportion of the population, which results in increased demands on the resources available to the entire population.

One indication of the growing allocation of resources to the aged sector is the increased expenditure of the federal government for programs for the aged, which rose from 16 percent to 20 percent of the total budget in the five years between 1967 and 1972 (Brotman, 1971). A secondary effect to be monitored is the possible development of a backlash effect against the dependence of the older population (Shanas and Hauser, 1975; Ragan, 1976).

Population Shifts. In the United States, changes in the age composition represent the single most dramatic social change related to aging in this century. Changes in the proportion of the aged to the total population are displayed in age profiles at different periods (see figure 3).

The proportion of the 65 and over segment of the population has increased from 4.1 percent in 1900 to 9.9 percent in 1970. Current projections of the proportion of the aged in the year 2020 range from 8.9 to 10.6 depending on the level of fertility on which the projection is based (Cutler and Harootyan, 1975). The primary cause of the change in the population structure is the decreased birth rate; increased longevity and changing immigration rates also contribute to the change.

The absolute number of older persons in the population, as well as the proportion, has also increased dramatically, from 3.1 million in 1900 to 20.2 million in 1970; the projected estimate of the population 65 and older is 40.2 million in the year 2020 (Cutler and Harootyan, 1975).

Some probable effects of these population changes are: (1) increased attention to the aged, particularly as far as problems in health and income are concerned; (2) increased dependency ratio—the proportion of the nonworking to the working population; (3) increased demand on resources: social security, welfare, medical facilities, recreational facilities; (4) enhanced possibility of the emergence of older people as a social movement and political force (Bengtson and Cutler, 1976; Ragan and Dowd, 1974; Kasschau and Bengtson, 1976).

In addition to the shift to an older population, a steady change in the sex ratio in the 65 and older age group can also be observed. In 1900 there were 102 males for every 100 females in the 65 and over population, and in

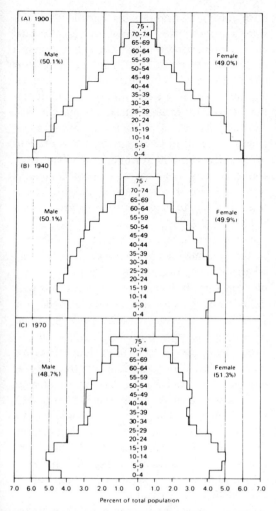

Figure 3. Age-sex population pyramids for the United States: 1900, 1940, 1970. (United States Bureau of the Census. *Census of Population: Characteristics of the Population.* 1940, 1970). Reprinted from Cutler and Harootyan, 1975.

1970 there were 139 women per 100 males 65 and over. It is clear that the role structure in which older persons experience aging is quite different as a result of this population change. The sequencing of the roles of marriage, widowhood, and remarriage, for example, depends on and reflects the differential mortality of the sexes and the resulting availability of marriage partners (Treas and Van Hilst, 1976).

Changes in Social Institutions. Social changes such as industrialization and urbanization com-

bine to alter major institutions of the social system, such as the family. Since some of the major roles that we identify in role-sequencing with aging occur within the institution of the family, the aging process is directly affected by these changes (Cain, 1964; Troll, 1971). People marry younger; have their first child at a younger age; have fewer children; and spend more time in the post-parental period (Neugarten and Moore, 1968). In 1890 the median age of a woman when her last child married was 55 years (Glick, Heer, and Beresford, 1963). Her life expectancy was such that she would probably live on for only another year or two after launching the last of her children (Neugarten and Moore, 1968). Women today see their last child married at about the age of 48 and may expect another 31 years of life.

The fact that the mother is younger in age and has a greater number of years to live after her youngest leaves home has produced a relatively new phenomenon, the "empty nest," which may represent the equivalent of the retirement crisis for women. This is especially true of those women whose major occupation has been childbearing and who are not prepared to make a transition to working outside the home. On the other hand, with more and more women working through the child-rearing years, the "retirement" crisis of the empty nest may prove to have been a temporary phenomenon of our time.

Culture Change. Ideological revolutions can produce an apparent generation gap because a particular generational unit seems to adopt values and norms that conflict seriously with those of the older generation. For example, Reich (1970) speaks of a "revolution of consciousness" during the 1960's that was comparable to the Protestant Reformation and Industrial Revolution. Toffler (1970) has suggested that one of the effects of the acceleration of change in producing "Future Shock" is the segmenting of the community along age lines. He argues that as the pace of change in the external environment steps up, differences between young and old become necessarily more marked.

However, empirical analyses cast doubt on sharp value cleavages between age groups. Bengtson (1975) notes substantial overlap between generations in global value orientations. He suggests that, in a rapidly-changing society, the young and the old may change together, rather than in opposition, in responding to common socio-historical events.

Cultural change may directly affect the role sequencing that occurs with age. Consider the effects of the women's movement on both men and women, as women enter the labor force and adopt the work-retirement pattern of men, and as men in turn experience roles beyond the work role in their increased participation in homemaking and child rearing. One result may be quite different patterns of adjustment to retirement than we have described as occuring at present.

Effects of the Aging Process on Further Social Change. Just as social change affects the system of age stratification and the aging process, so do these developments in turn bring about further social change. "Strain" in the system may occur, as in "age-specific imbalances between role expectations and trained capacities, or between supplies of people and of roles" (Riley, Johnson, and Foner, 1972). Allocation of roles on the basis of age may result in dissatisfaction of sizeable segments of the population. Exclusion from work roles in the middle and later years is one example. Several studies have documented an emerging re-definition of mandatory retirement as an unconstitutional violation of the older person's right to work (Kasschau, 1976).

A combination of changes in the age structure may result in proportionately more older persons being allocated fewer rewards, in terms of resources, power, and prestige, than they consider just. In the Southern California study, a majority of elderly respondents from all ethnic backgrounds agreed with the statement that "age discrimination is common in American society" and a sizeable minority claimed to have personally experienced such discrimination since arriving at middle age (Kasschau, in press). Such instances suggest again the possibility of the emergence of older people as a political force for social change.

Directed Social Change

Accompanying social changes that seem to have a momentum of their own—the drop in the birth rate, urbanization, the knowledge explosion—societies also attempt to direct social change along certain lines. Man is not merely a passive observer and participant in the effects of social change. He is also, to varying degrees, an agent of change as he anticipates and directs the effects of technological, population, and cultural changes. The ability to direct social change depends in large part on the limitations of knowledge, on the formation of collectivities and coalitions, their access to power, and the responsiveness of governmental and private sectors of power to demands for change (Etzioni, 1968).

Attempts to direct social change in the favor of the aged may come from older people themselves, as they organize together or vote as a bloc on specific issues, join organizations with lobbyists at the state and federal level, or form social movements such as the "Gray Panthers" to attempt to raise the level of consciousness about aging. Beyond the flourishing of various special interest organizations of the aged at federal, state, and local levels (as effective as these attempts may be in specific instances), there is little evidence for the emergence of a powerful political force based on old age itself (Binstock, 1972; Campbell, 1971; Ragan and Dowd, 1974). The organizing and lobbying efforts of older people could significantly affect the enactment of social policy.

Usually, however, policies which benefit the aged (such as with Social Security and Medicare) are enacted because of a combination of change agents, such as legislators who are motivated to enact legislation and economic forces which require the proposed change. Cottrell (1960) suggests that the Social Security Act of 1935 was a product not so much of the pressure of older people themselves but of the need to remove the aged from jobs that younger men needed and to remove the cost of their support from family heads. Similarly, in spite of ongoing pressure by the older population for national health insurance, Medicare was not enacted until 1965, when there occurred a convergence between the needs of the medical care system itself, and the efforts of coalitions which went far beyond the aging population in their bases of support (Marmor, 1973).

Change may be promoted in the social structure itself, for example in attempts to develop "new roles" for the roleless aged; to arrange services for disabled older people in order to make possible their living independently; to modify the stratification systems (e.g., by encouraging the employment of older workers and fostering second careers); and to effect change in the very system of values attached to aging (attempting to replace negative attitudes toward old age with more positive attitudes).

Efforts to bring about change inevitably create some conflict. Several pressures operate to resist change: political orientations unfavorable to welfare programs in general; the finite capacity for dependency in any population; and the scarcity of resources, such as money, jobs, and positions of influence. Certainly consensus does not exist on programs for the elderly. In fact, one may begin to discern some "backlash" effects, although minor, against the increased demands on societal resources occasioned by the growing population of dependent elderly (Ragan, 1976).

Importance of Social Change in the Study of Aging

Social change is an essential consideration in the understanding of the process of aging from methodological, theoretical, and practical points of view. It is necessary to separate the effects of age cohort membership from the effects of aging itself. Changes in the last 50 years account for many of the differences we observe in age cohorts. For example, the mean level of education attained by succeeding cohorts has risen rapidly; while in 1972, 30 percent of those over 65 had a high school education, over 86 percent of the elderly in the year 2020 will have 12 years of education (Bengtson and Cutler, 1976). Level of education accounts for many of the differences we observe in political attitudes, leisure activity patterns, and participation in community and formal organization networks among age strata. Medical and dental care have improved substantially in recent decades; the relatively poorer health of older persons reflects not only the effects of aging but the accumulation of years of inadequate medical care. Many of today's older populations are immigrants who came to the United States (often in poverty) in the early decades of this century. The younger generation are likely to be native born or first generation Americans, and are consequently different from the older immigrants in their life experiences.

It is theoretically as well as methodologically important to distinguish between the changes the individual experiences in a lifetime as he moves through a succession of roles and participates in social institutions, and the changes in the role structure and basic institutions themselves that are occurring at the same time.

Looking ahead to future generations of old people, we can expect even greater differences between the old and young as the pace of social change increases. It would be a grave error to take the older age stratum as it appears today as a model of tomorrow's aged. Better educated, in better health, with different work experiences, having experienced a distinctive historical milieu in growing up, the aged of tomorrow may little resemble today's older people. Social planning for the aged will need to anticipate those differences.

IMPLICATIONS FOR RESEARCH AND THEORY

In this chapter we have reviewed some ways in which location in the social structure influences patterns of behavior among aging individuals. We have stressed, first, the value of recognizing that aging is socially defined, and that many of the behavioral patterns associated with aging can be better understood within the context of socially defined events which vary according to location in the social structure. The "sociology of knowledge" perspective underscores the importance of explicitly considering perceptions of aging, both in what are considered as normative events in the aging process and in what are defined as problems requiring intervention of social institutions. Second, we have reviewed evidence concerning social differentiation and patterns of aging, noting that statuses such as sex, social class, and ethnicity are linked to variations in many aspects of behavior: longevity, quality of life, perceptions of aging, life satisfaction, social networks, and community participation. Third, we have emphasized the role which social and historical change plays in shaping the patterns of human aging. These themes suggest several implications for further research and theory.

A first implication that emerges from examining patterns of aging in different social groupings is the *heterogeneity of the aged population*. Of course there is danger in any life-cycle developmental research if one considers a given age cohort as a homogeneous group; but in research designs focusing on the aged there is special difficulty in not recognizing the patterns of diversity that occur among social strata. Such social variations are not merely "noise" in the system (as was once argued of age effects in psychophysiological research) but rather variations which assume discernible patterns once sufficiently isolated for examination. Unfortunately much social-psychological research has ignored such diversity, or attempted only to match subjects and thus "control" for variations, without focusing directly on the implications of stratum variables on the behavioral measures in question. An important feature of any stratification system is the particular history of social class and racial categories within the broader system. From such shared experience through time come collective orientations which, if properly understood, help explain distinctive patterns in particular aspects of behavior in old age (Elder, 1975; Riley, Johnson, and Foner, 1972; Streib, 1976).

Second, there is need for greater awareness of *continuity manifest as one moves from middle into old age*. Discontinuity is apparent as one notes the distinctive role transitions evident in aging: retirement, widowhood, the empty nest, and declines in the social network participation. However, as Neugarten (1965) has noted, the aging individual can be viewed as a "socio-emotional institution" unto himself as he or she moves through the course of life. This "institutional" quality involves "an individuated pattern of strategies for dealing with the changing world within and without, strategies which transcend many of the intra-psychic changes and (social) losses that appear" (Neugarten, 1965, p. 16).

The perspective on social differentiation draws attention to the fact that aging individuals exhibit some degree of continuity precisely because of their ongoing location with repect to dimensions of stratum characteristics. Age does not eradicate sex, race, and class distinctions; rather, aging adds another dimension of social differentiation of these differentiations so apparent in middle age. Thus, the unfolding biography of aging individuals is better understood by examining factors of continuity resulting from ongoing membership in long-term social categories.

Third, future research should more systematically reflect the important advantages of considering *the aged as a stratum category* in itself. Indeed, comparative research concerning aging which explicitly treats age as a stratum variable on a par with other stratification variables, such as socioeconomic status, constitutes perhaps the most important conceptual development in the last decade within social gerontology (as articulated in Riley, 1971; Riley, Johnson, and Foner, 1972). The age structure within a society is an essential dimension for understanding human behavior. Four decades ago, Linton (1936) noted the universal significance of age structures for the study of social organization. Since that time many studies have supported the idea that all societies provide unique rights and responsibilities for members of different age groups, and that the relations between age groups are governed by sets of rules and expectations.

Fourth, a corollary of treating age as a stratum variable involves consideration of distinctive cohort or *generational patterns in behavior*. This perspective calls attention to the interface between specific historical events, occurring during a particular period, and development stages or the life cycle location of individuals experiencing those events (Bengtson and Cutler, 1976; Elder, 1975; Ryder, 1965). As argued by Mannheim (1952), occasionally some events are of such magnitude as to create out of the age group experiencing them a "generational unit," a cohort collectively activated in a conscious effort to produce specific social changes. This interpretation was frequently employed in analyses of the youth movements of the 1960's. Such "generation units" also might be manifest at the older end of the life cycle, as the demographic changes and historical events (especially as related to economic considerations) may cause the elderly of tomorrow to identify themselves as a group and thus take collective action (Ragan and Dowd, 1974). In short, a "gerontocratic generation unit" may emerge (Laufer and Bengtson, 1974).

Many researchers in the psychology of maturity have taken seriously the notions of historical effects and generational or cohort effects in aging (see Baltes and Nesselroade, 1972; Baltes and Schaie, 1973; Riegel, 1969; Schaie, 1965, 1973, Chapter 2 in this volume). Psychologists have been less successful in examining a fifth implication for research and theory reflected in this chapter, that of *aging as an intersubjective perception*. Biological events and social-psychological processes are not always clearly related to each other. Neugarten, Wood, Kraines, and Loomis (1963) for example, found that menopause is not the major determinant of behavior in the lives of older women, as had once been assumed. Similarly, it has become well established that organic changes and the decreased capacities associated with age do not necessarily produce depression (Pearlin and Butler, 1963). Biological models of the life course are inadequate by themselves to account for individual behavior and attitudes because of the considerable influence exercised by social definitions and situational variables as reviewed in this chapter.

Aging should be examined as a dependent variable, a social category varying by characteristics of perceiver and target, since this is the way aging is in fact defined by individuals. Too little research, however, has focused on perceptions of aging in the sense that person perception and attribution theory have occupied a significant place in the literature of personality psychology in the last two decades. Systematic focus on the broader social context within which such perceptions are evolved and reinforced is useful in understanding individual patterns of aging.

REFERENCES

Adams, B. N. 1968. *Kinship in an Urban Setting*. Chicago: Markham.

Adams, B. N. 1970. Isolation, function, and beyond: American kinship in the 1960's. *J. Marriage & Fam.*, 32, 575-597.

Ahammer, I. M., and Baltes, P. B. 1972. Objective vs. perceived differences in personality. *J Gerontol.*, 27, 46-51.

Aldous, J., and Hill, R. 1965. Social cohesion, lineage type, and intergenerational transmission. *Soc. Forces*, 43, 471-482.

Alston, J. P., and Dudley, C. J. 1973. Age, occupation and life satisfaction. *Gerontologist*, 13, 58-61.

Antunes, G., and Gaitz, C. M. 1975. Ethnicity and participation: a study of Mexican-Americans, Blacks, and Whites. *Am. J. Sociol.*, 80, 1192-1211.

Asch, S. E. 1951. Effects of group pressure upon the modification and distortion of judgment. *In*, H. Guetzkow (ed.), *Groups, Leadership, and Men*. Pittsburgh: The Carnegie Press.

Atchley, R. 1972. *Social Forces in Later Life*. Belmont, California: Wadsworth.

Baltes, P. B., and Nesselroade, J. R. 1972. Cultural change and adolescent personality development: an application of longitudinal sequences. *Life-Span Developmental Psychology*, 32, 366-395.

Baltes, P. B., and Schaie, K. W. 1973. On life-span developmental research paradigms: retrospects and prospects. *In*, P. B. Baltes and K. W. Schaie (eds.), *Developmental Psychology: Personality and Socialization*. New York: Academic Press.

Bart, P. 1968. Social structure and vocabularies of discomfort: what happened to female hysteria? *J. of Health and Soc. Behavior*, 9, 188-193.

Bengtson, V. L. 1971. Inter-age differences in perception and the generation gap. *Gerontologist*, 11, 85-90.

Bengtson, V. L. 1973. *The Social Psychology of Aging*. Indianapolis: Bobbs-Merrill.

Bengtson, V. L. 1975. Generation and family effects in value socialization. *Am. Soc. Rev.*, 40, 358-371.

Bengtson, V. L., and Black, K. D. 1973. Intergenerational relations and continuities in socialization. *In*, P. B. Baltes and K. W. Schaie (eds.), *Life-Span Devel. Psy., Personality and Socialization*. New York: Academic Press.

Bengtson, V. L., Chiriboga, D. C., and Keller, A. C. 1969. Occupational differences in retirement: patterns of role activity and life-outlook among Chicago retired teachers and steelworkers. *In*, R. J. Havighurst, M. Thomae, B. L. Neugarten, and J. K. A. Munnichs (eds.), *Adjustment to Retirement: A Cross-National Study*. Assen, The Netherlands: Van Gorkum.

Bengtson, V. L., Cuellar, J. B., and Ragan, P. K. 1977. Contrasts and similarities in attitudes toward death by race, age, social class, and sex. *J. Gerontol.*, 32, 204-216.

Bengtson, V. L., and Cutler, N. E. 1976. Generations and intergenerational relations: perspectives on age groups, and social change. *In*, R. Binstock and E. Shanas (eds.), *Handbook of Aging and the Social Sciences*. New York: Van Nostrand Reinhold.

Bengtson, V. L., Dowd, J. J., Smith, D. H., and Inkeles, A. 1975. Modernization, modernity, and perceptions of aging: a cross-cultural study. *J. Gerontol.*, 30, 688-695.

Bennet, R., and Eckman, J. 1973. Attitudes toward aging: a critical examination of recent literature and implications for future research. *In*, C. Eisdorfer and M. P. Lawton (eds.), *The Psychology of Adult Development and Aging*. Washington, D.C.: American Psychological Association.

Berardo, F. M. 1970. Survivorship and social isolation: the case of the aged widower. *Family Coordinator*, 19, 11-25.

Berger, B. and Berger, P. L. 1972. *Sociology: A Biographical Approach*. New York: Basic Books.

Berger, P. L., and Luckmann, T. 1966. *The Social Construction of Reality*. New York: Doubleday.

Beyer, G. H., and Woods, M. E. 1963. Living and activity patterns of the aged. *Research Report No. 6.* Ithaca, New York: Center for Housing and Environmental Studies, Cornell University.

Binstock, R. H. 1972. Interest-group liberalism and the politics of aging. *Gerontologist*, 12, 265–280.

Binstock, R. H. 1974. Aging and the future of American politics. *Annals of the Am. Acad. of Pol. and Soc. Sci.*, 415, 199–212.

Blau, P. M., and Duncan, O. D. 1967. *The American Occupational Structure*. New York: John Wiley.

Blau, Z. S. 1961. Structural constraints on friendship in old age. *Am. Soc. Rev.*, 26, 429–439.

Blau, Z. S. 1973. *Old Age in a Changing Society*. New York: New Viewpoints.

Britton, J. H., and Britton, J. O. 1972. *Personality Changes in Aging*. New York: Springer.

Brotman, H. B. 1971. *Facts and Figures on Older Americans: Federal Outlays in Aging, Fiscal Years 1967-72*. Washington, D.C.: U.S. Department of Health, Education and Welfare.

Burgess, E. W. 1950. Personal and social adjustment in old age. *In*, M. Derber (ed.), *The Aged and Society*. Champaign, Illinois: Industrial Relations Research Association.

Cain, Jr., L. D. 1964. Life course and social structure. *In*, E. Faris (ed.), *Handbook of Modern Sociology*. Chicago: Rand McNally.

Campbell, A. 1971. Politics through the life cycle. *Gerontologist*, 11, 112–117.

Cleveland, W. P., and Gianturco, D. T. 1976. Remarriage probability after widowhood: a retrospective method. *J. Gerontol.*, 31, 99–103.

Cottrell. 1960. The technological and societal basis of aging. *In*, C. L. Tibbits (ed.), *Handbook of Social Gerontology*, pp. 92–119. Chicago: University of Chicago Press.

Cowgill, D. O., and Holmes, L. D. (eds.) 1972. *Aging and Modernization*. New York: Appleton-Century-Crofts.

Cutler, N. E., and Bengtson, V. L. 1974. Age and political alienation: maturation, generation and historical effects. *Annals of the Am. Acad. of Pol. and Soc. Sci.*, 415, 160–175.

Cutler, N. E., and Harootyan, R. 1975. Demography of the aged. *In*, D. Woodruff and J. E. Birren (eds.), *Aging: Scientific Perspectives and Social Issues*. New York: D. Van Nostrand.

Cyrus-Lutz, C., and Gaitz, C. M. 1972. *Lifetime Goals: Age and Ethnic Considerations*. Houston: Texas Research Institute of Mental Sciences.

Dowd, J. J., and Bengtson, V. L. 1975. Social participation, age and ethnicity: an examination of the "double jeopardy" hypothesis. Paper presented at the Annual Meeting of the Gerontological Society.

Edwards, J. N., and Klemmack, D. L. 1973. Correlates of life satisfaction: a re-examination. *J. of Gerontol.*, 28, 497–502.

Elder, G. H. 1974. *Children of the Great Depression*. Chicago: University of Chicago Press.

Elder, G. H. 1975. Age differentiation and the life course. *In*, A. Inkeles, J. Coleman, and N. Smelser, (eds.), *Annual Review of Sociology*, Vol. 1. Palo Alto: Annual Reviews.

Enterline, P. E. 1961. Causes of death responsible for recent increases in sex mortality differentials in the United States. *Milbank Memorial Fund Quarterly*, 39, 312–328.

Epstein, L. A., and Murray, J. H. 1967. *The Aged Population of the U.S.: the 1963 Social Security Survey of the Aged*. Washington, D.C.: U.S. Department of Health, Education and Welfare, U.S. Government Printing Office.

Etzioni, A. 1968. *The Active Society: A Theory of Societal and Political Processes*. London: Collier-Macmillan.

Gerber, I., Rusalem, R., Hannon, N., Battin, D., and Arkin, A. 1975. Anticipatory grief and aged widows and widowers. *J. Gerontol.*, 30, 225–229.

Gergen, K. J., and Back, K. W. 1966. Communications in the interview and the disengaged respondent. *Public Opinion Quarterly*, 30, 385–398.

Glick, P. C., Heer, D. M., and Beresford, J. C. 1963. Family formation and family composition: trends and prospects. *In*, M. B. Sussman (ed.), *Sourcebook in Marriage and the Family*. 2nd Edition. New York: Houghton Mifflin.

Goldscheider, C., Van Arsdol, M. D., and Sabagh, G. 1965. Residential mobility of older people. *In*, *Patterns of Living and Housing of Middle-Aged and Older People*. Bethesda, Maryland: U.S. Department of Health, Education and Welfare, National Institute of Child Health and Human Development.

Gurin, G., Veroff, J., and Feld, S. 1960. *Americans View Their Mental Health*. Joint Commission on Mental Illness and Health, Monograph Series No. 4. New York: Basic Books.

Havighurst, R. J., and Albrecht, R. 1953. *Older People*. New York: Longmans, Green.

Havighurst, R. J., Munnichs, J. K. A., Neugarten, B. L., and Thomas, M. 1969. *Adjustment to Retirement: A Cross-National Study*. Assen, The Netherlands: Van Gorkum.

Heyman, D., and Jeffers, F. 1968. Wives and retirement: a pilot study. *J. Gerontol.*, 23, 488–496.

Hill, R., Foote, N., Aldous, J., Carlson, R., and MacDonald, R. 1970. *Family Development in Three Generations*. Cambridge, Massachusetts: Schenkman.

Hirsch, C., Kent, D. P., and Silverman, S. L. 1968. Homogeneity and heterogeneity among low income Negro and White aged. Paper presented at the Annual Gerontological Society Meetings, Denver, Colorado.

Homans, G. C. 1964. Contemporary theory in sociology. *In*, R. Faris (ed.), *Handbook of Modern Sociology*, pp. 951–977. Chicago: Rand McNally.

Itzin, F. 1970. Social relations. *In*, A. M. Hoffman (ed.), *The Daily Needs and Interests of Older People*. Springfield, Illinois: Charles C. Thomas.

Jackson, J. J. 1970. Aged Negroes: their cultural departures from statistical stereotypes and rural-urban differences. *Gerontologist*, **10**, 140-145.

Jackson, J. J. 1974. NCBA, black aged and politics. *Annals of the Am. Acad. of Pol. and Soc. Sci.*, **415**, 138-159.

Kalish, R. 1975. *Late Adulthood: Perspectives on Human Development*. Monterey, California: Brooks-Cole.

Kasschau, P. L. 1976. Perceived age discrimination in a sample of aerospace employees. *Gerontologist*, **16**, 166-173.

Kasschau, P. L. Race and age discrimination reported by middle-aged and older persons. *Soc. Forces*. In press.

Kasschau, P. L., and Bengtson, V. L. 1976. *The New American Dilemma: Decision-makers View Aging and Social Policy*. Final Report to the National Science Foundation. October, 1976.

Kent, D. 1971. The Negro aged. *Gerontologist*, **11**, 48-51.

Kerckhoff, A. C. 1965. Nuclear and extended family relationships: normative and behavioral analysis. *In*, E. Shanas and G. Streib (eds.), *Social Structure and the Family: Generational Relations*. Englewood Cliffs, New Jersey: Prentice-Hall.

Kerckhoff, A. C. 1966. Husband-wife expectations and reactions to retirement. *In*, I. H. Simpson and J. C. McKinney (eds.), *Social Aspects of Aging*, pp. 160-172. Durham, North Carolina: Duke University Press.

Komarovsky, M. 1964. *Blue Collar Marriage*. New York: Random House.

Kurtz, S. (ed.). 1970. In Other Americas: Mexican Americans. *In*, *The New York Times Enclyclopedic Almanac*, p. 301. New York: New York Times, Book and Educational Division.

Kutner, B., Fanshel, D., Togo, A., and Langer, T. 1956. *Five Hundred Over Sixty: A Community Survey on Aging*. New York: Russell Sage Foundation.

Langford, M. 1962. Community aspects of housing for the aged. *Research Report No. 5*. Ithaca, New York: Center for Housing and Environmental Studies, Cornell University.

Laslett, P. 1976. Societal development and aging. *In*, R. Binstock and E. Shanas (eds.), *The Handbook of Aging and the Social Sciences*. New York: Van Nostrand Reinhold

Laufer, R., and Bengtson, V. L. 1974. Generations, aging and social stratification: on the development of generational units. *J. Soc. Issues*, **30**, 181-206.

Lenski, G. 1966. *Power and Privilege: A Theory of Social Stratification*. New York: McGraw-Hill.

Linton, R. 1936. *The Study of Man*. New York: Appleton-Century-Crofts.

Lipman, A. 1961. Role conceptions and morale of couples in retirement *J. Gerontol.*, **16**, 267-271.

Lopata, H. Z. 1973. *Widowhood in an American City*. Cambridge, Massachusetts: Schenkman.

Maddox, G. L. 1962. Some correlates of differences in self-assessment of health status among the elderly. *J. Gerontol.*, **17**, 180-185.

Maddox, G. L. 1970. Themes and issues in sociological theories of human aging. *Hum. Develop.*, **13**, 17-27.

Maddox, G. L. 1973. Growing old: getting beyond the stereotypes. *In*, R. R. Boyd and C. G. Oakes (eds.), *Foundations of Practical Gerontology*, pp. 5-16. 2nd Edition. Columbia: University of South Carolina Press.

Mannheim, K. 1952 [1928]. The problem of generations. *In*, P. Kecskemeti (ed. and trans.), *Essays in the Sociology of Knowledge*. London: Routledge & Kegan-Paul.

Marmor, T. R. 1973. *The Politics of Medicare*. Chicago: Aldine.

McKain, W. C. 1969. Retirement marriages. *Agriculture Experiment Station Monograph No. 3*. Storrs, Connecticut: University of Connecticut.

McTavish, D. G. 1971. Perceptions of old people: a review of research methodologies and findings. *The Gerontologist Third Report, 1971-72*, pp. 90-101.

Moore, J. 1971. Mexican Americans. *Gerontologist*, **11**, 30-35.

Nardi, A. H. 1973. Person-perception research and the perception of life-span development. *In*, P. Baltes and K. W. Schaie (eds.), *Life Span Developmental Psychology: Personality and Socialization*. New York: Academic Press.

National Urban League, The. 1964. *Double Jeopardy: The Older Negro in America Today*. New York: National Urban League.

Neugarten, B. L. 1965. Personality changes in the aged. *Catholic Psychological Record*, **3**, 9-17.

Neugarten, B. L. 1974. Age groups in American society and the rise of the young-old. *Annals of the Am. Acad. of Pol. and Soc. Sci.*, **415**, 187-198.

Neugarten, B. L., and Datan, N. 1973. Sociological perspectives on the life cycle. *In*, P. Baltes and K. W. Schaie (eds.), *Life-Span Developmental Psychology*, pp. 53-71. New York: Academic Press.

Neugarten, B. L., and Moore, J. 1968. The changing age status system. *In*, B. L. Neugarten (ed.), *Middle Age and Aging*. Chicago: University of Chicago Press.

Neugarten, B. L., and Peterson, W. 1957. A study of the American age-grade system. *Fourth Congress of the International Association of Gerontology. Vol. III. Firenzi, Italy. Tito Mattioli.*

Neugarten, B. L., Wood, V., Kraines, R. J., and Loomis, B. 1963. Women's attitudes toward the menopause. *Vita Humana*, **6**, 140-151.

Olsen, M. E. 1970. Social and political participation of Blacks. *Am. Soc. Rev.*, **35**, 682-697.

Orbach, H. L. 1961. Aging and religion: a study of church attendance in the Detroit metropolitan area. *Geriatrics*, **16**, 530-540.

O'Reilly, C. T., and Pembroke, M. M. 1970. O.A.A. profile: the old age assistance client in Chicago. *In*, A. M. Hoffman (ed.), *The Daily Needs and Interests of Older People*, pp. 51–67. Springfield, Illinois: Charles C. Thomas.

Palmore, E. B. 1965. Differences in the retirement patterns of men and women. *Gerontologist*, 5, 4–8.

Palmore, E. B. 1975. *The Honorable Elders*. Durham, North Carolina: Duke University Press.

Palmore, E. B., and Manton. 1974. Modernization and status of the aged. *J. Gerontol.*, 29, 205–210.

Palmore, E. B., and Stone, V. 1973. Predictors of longevity: a follow-up of the aged in Chapel Hill. *Gerontologist*, 13, 88–90.

Pearlin, S., and Butler, R. N. 1963. Psychiatric aspects of adaptation to the aging experience. *In*, J. E. Birren *et al* (eds.), *Human Aging: A Biological and Behavioral Study* (NIMH Publ. No. HSM 71-9051). Washington. D.C.: Government Printing Office.

Peters, G. A. 1971. Perceptions of old people: a review of research methodologies and findings. *The Gerontologist Third Report, 1971-72*, pp. 69–73.

Pollack, M., Karp, E., Kahn, R., and Goldfarb, A. 1962. Perception of self in institutionalized aged subjects: response patterns to mirror reflection. *J. Gerontol.*, 17, 405–408.

Ragan, P. K. 1976. On the politicizing of old age: can we expect a backlash effect? Paper presented at the Annual Meeting of the Society for the Study of Social Problems.

Ragan, P., Bengtson, V. L., and Solomon, B. 1975. Life satisfaction, age identification, and attitudes toward aging. Paper presented at the Gerontological Society Annual Meeting.

Ragan, P. K., and Dowd, J. J. 1974. The emerging political consciousness of the aged: a generational interpretation. *J. Soc. Issues*, 30, 137–158.

Ragan, P. K., and Grigsby, E. 1976. Responsibility for meeting the needs of the elderly for health care, housing, and transportation: a survey of Blacks, Mexican Americans, and whites. Paper presented at the Annual Meeting of the Western Gerontological Society.

Reich, C. 1970. *The Greening of America*. New York: Random House.

Retherford, R. D. 1975. *The Changing Sex Differential in Mortality*. Westport, Connecticut: Greenwood Press.

Reynolds, D. K., and Kalish, R. A. 1974. Anticipation of futurity as a function of ethnicity and age. *J. Gerontol.*, 29, 224–231.

Riegel, K. F. 1969. History as a nomothetic science: some generalizations from theories and research in developmental psychology. *J. Soc. Issues*, 25, 99–127.

Riley, M. W. 1971. Social gerontology and the age stratification of society. *Gerontologist*, 11, 79–87.

Riley, M. W., Foner, A., and associates. 1968. *Aging and Society, Vol. I: An Inventory of Research Findings*. New York: Russell Sage Foundation.

Riley, M. W., Johnson, M., and Foner, A. 1972. *Aging and Society, Vol. III: A Sociology of Age Stratification*. New York: Russell Sage Foundation.

Rosenberg, G. S. 1970. *The Worker Grows Old*. San Francisco: Jossey-Bass.

Rosow, I. 1967. *Social Integration of the Aged*. New York: The Free Press.

Rosow, I. 1974. *Socialization to Old Age*. Berkeley: University of California Press.

Rubenstein, D. I. 1971. An examination of social participation among a national sample of black and white elderly. *Aging and Human Development*, 12, 172–188.

Rubenstein, D. I. 1972. The social participation of the black and white elderly in social groups and organizations. Paper presented at the Annual Gerontological Society Meetings, San Juan, Puerto Rico.

Ryder, N. 1965. The cohort as a concept in the study of social change. *Am. Soc. Rev.*, 30, 843–861.

Schaie, K. W. 1965. Age changes and age differences. *Psych. Bull.*, 65, 92–107.

Schaie, K. W. 1973. Methodological problems in descriptive developmental research on adulthood and aging. *In*, J. R. Nesselroade and H. W. Reese (eds.), *Life-Span Developmental Psychology: Methodological Issues*, pp. 253–280. New York: Academic Press.

Schoenfeld, A. E. D. 1974. Translations in gerontology—from lab to life: utilizing information. *Amer. Psychol.* 29, 796–801.

Shanas, E. 1962. *The Health of Older People: A Social Survey*. Cambridge: Harvard University Press.

Shanas, E., and Hauser, P. M. 1975. Zero population growth and the family life of old people. *J. Soc. Issues*, 30, 79–92.

Shanas, E., Townsend, P., Wedderburn, D., Friis, H., Milhøj, P. and Stehouwer, J. 1968. *Old People in Three Industrial Societies*. New York: Atherton Press.

Sherif, M. 1936. *The Psychology of Social Norms*. New York: Harper & Row.

Simmons, L. W. 1945. *The Role of the Aged in Primitive Society*. New Haven: Yale University Press.

Simpson, I. H., Back, K. W., and McKinney, J. C. 1966. Attributes of work involvement in society and self-evaluation in retirement. *In*, I. H. Simpson and J. C. McKinney (eds.), *Social Aspects of Aging*, pp. 55–74. Durham, North Carolina: Duke University Press.

Social Indicators. 1973. Executive Office of the President: Office of Management and the Budget. Washington, D.C.: U.S. Government Printing Office.

Streib, G. F. 1956. Intergenerational relations: perspectives of the two generations. *J. Marriage & Fam.*, 27, 469–476.

Streib, G. F. 1976. Social stratification and aging. *In*, R. H. Binstock and E. Shanas (eds.), *Handbook of Aging and the Social Sciences*. New York: Van Nostrand Reinhold.

Sussman, M. 1970. Family relations and the aged. *In*, A. M. Hoffman (ed.), *The Daily Needs and Interests of Older People*. Springfield, Illinois: Charles C. Thomas.

Taietz, P., and Larson, O. 1965. Social participation and old age. *Rural Sociology*, **21**, 229–238.

Thomas, W. I. 1931. *The Unadjusted Girl*. Boston: Little, Brown.

Toffler, A. 1970. *Future Shock*. New York: Random House.

Treas, J., and VanHilst, A. 1976. Marriage and remarriage rates among older Americans. *Gerontologist*, **16**, 132–136.

Troll. 1971. The family in later life: a decade review. *J. Marriage & Fam.*, **33**, 263–290.

U.S. Bureau of the Census. 1965. *Current Population Reports*. Series P-20, No. 143. Washington, D.C.: U.S. Government Printing Office.

U.S. Bureau of the Census. 1974. *Current Population Reports*. Series P-23, No. 57. Social and economic characteristics of the older population, 1974. Washington, D.C.: U.S. Government Printing Office.

U.S. Bureau of the Census. 1975. *Current Population Reports*. Series P-25, No. 493. Projections of the population of the United States by age and sex: 1972-2020. Washington, D.C.: U.S. Government Printing Office.

U.S. Bureau of the Census. 1976. *Current Population Reports*. Series P-23, No. 59. Demographic aspects of aging and the older population in the United States. Washington, D.C.: U.S. Government Printing Office.

U.S. Senate Special Committee on Aging. 1971. *The Multiple Hazards of Age and Race: The Situation of Aged Blacks in the United States*. Washington, D.C.: U.S. Government Printing Office.

Verbugge, L. 1975. Sex differentials in morbidity and mortality in the United States. Paper presented at the Annual Meeting of the Population Association of America.

Videbeck, R., and Knox, A. B. 1965. Alternative participatory responses to aging. *In*, A. Rose and W. A. Peterson (eds.), *Older People and Their Social World*, pp. 37–48. Philadelphia: F. A. Davis.

Vital Statistics of the United States, Vol. II, Sec. 5, Life Tables: 1972. Rockville, Maryland: U.S. Department of Health, Education and Welfare.

Williams, J. A., Babchuck, N., and Johnson, D. R. 1973. Voluntary associations and minority status: a comparative analysis of Anglo, Black, and Mexican-Americans. *Am. Soc. Rev.*, **38**, 637–646.

Wohlwill, J. F. 1970. The age variable in psychological research. *Psych. Rev.*, **77**, 49–64.

4 BEHAVIORAL PROCESSES

16
MOTIVATION AND ACTIVITY

Merrill F. Elias
and
Penelope Kelly Elias*
Syracuse University, New York

INTRODUCTION

The aging literature on motivation and activity has increased appreciably since Botwinick (1959) presented his comprehensive review in the *Handbook of Aging and the Individual*. A beneficial outcome of this increase in literature is a growing realization among aging researchers that the elderly are not necessarily less motivated than the young, and that increased motivation, as well as decreased motivational states, in the aged may contribute to apparent differences in cognitive functioning and performance.

The major advance provided by aging research since 1959 is an awareness of the implications of age-related differences in motivational states for studies of learning, cognition, and social interaction in humans and animals. Less progress has been made in understanding the underlying physiological mechanisms of need and drive states. Theory construction in motivation and aging is in its infancy. Thus, few manipulative studies have been conducted in an effort to test theories. Unfortunately, research efforts in the areas of human and animal motivation are largely unrelated.

The difficulty in integrating the literature, to the point that empirically generated theoretical formulations are forthcoming, is related to a problem inherent in all areas of motivational research. Different investigators have different definitions of motivation based on theoretical or intuitive biases. They often use the same terms and constructs in different ways. The terms *drive* and *need* may have very different meanings for investigators who approach research from a Hull-Spence versus Lewinian point of view. For this reason it seems important to provide a definition of the way in which various motivational terms are used and defined in the present chapter.

DEFINITIONS

Motivation

Several basic terms will be used: *motivation, drive, incentive, need,* and *general activity*. Motivation will be used as a general term which includes the specific terms, drive, incentive, and need.

There are, as Bolles (1967) points out, three basic areas of correspondence in the motivational theories of Freud, Lewin, and Murray. Behavior is pushed through the action of moti-

*Much appreciation is extended to Mrs. Nicole Maier and Mrs. Ann Kunkle for their careful typing and editing of this manuscript. The authors wish to thank Mr. Wayne Watson and Dr. Charles Goodrick for helpful suggestions with regard to the preparation of this chapter. Penelope Kelly Elias is an NICHD Postdoctoral Fellow (HD-06024).

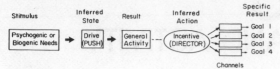

Figure 1. The authors' "push" and "direction" notion of motivation. The push concept of drive is strongly influenced by Spence's concept of drive, although incentive is used in a quite different sense. Incentive, as defined here, directs responses to specific goals and incentive-stimuli gain incentive value *via* past reinforcement history or by virtue of the fact that they evoke reflexive responses in some instances, e.g., withdrawal of the hand from heat. This simplistic concept is not presented either as a theoretical framework or as a summary of an existing theory of motivation. Rather it is a composite of several theories and it is offered solely to clarify the use of terms in this chapter.

vating drives and pulled through the perception of valuable objects, valences or goals in the environment. As may be seen by inspection of Figure 1 which presents the authors' notion of motivation, the push concept will be emphasized in the present paper. Drive is viewed as a hypothetical energy state or "push" resulting from psychological or biological needs, or from external stimulation leading to a heightened state of arousal. Drive stimulates activity. Behavior is directed toward a specific goal or goals by incentives. Performance may be tied intrinsically to an incentive (e.g., food—eating), it may become tied to an incentive by means of reinforcement history (e.g., money—work), or it may constitute a reflex response (e.g., escape from shock). Thus incentives motivate specific responses and may interact with general drive level. For example, drive could be increased by food deprivation, but shock could be used as an incentive to produce a *specific* food choice. Drives result in increased activity. Incentives are tied to specific activities.

Activity and Exploration

Quite often the rhythmic variations in activity level which are observed for all species and vary with age are referred to as "spontaneous activities." This term implies that there are no stimuli pushing or pulling on the organism to

cause these fluctuations in activity. The term *general activity* will be used in this chapter because it is equally descriptive and does not make these assumptions (Bolles, 1967).

The work of Harlow (1950) and others has raised serious questions as to whether "exploratory behavior" is reflective of a general drive state or constitutes an autonomous drive which need not be tied to either induced arousal resulting from external stimulation or deprivation. In this chapter it will be assumed that exploratory behavior can result from autonomous exploratory drive, but it is not a necessary condition. Increase in drive for a variety of reasons may increase activity level and thus influence goal-directed exploratory behavior.

EMPHASIS AND ORGANIZATION

This chapter is organized into two general sections; one deals with animal research and the other with human research. This organization reflects the dichotomization of these two areas of research as reflected in the literature. Animal research has concentrated heavily on basic or primary needs such as hunger and thirst. Human research has been concerned with complex social relationships involving higher order (psychogenic) needs and drives produced by aversive stimulation and task stress. Perhaps the one area of greatest potential for integration of animal and human studies will be provided by the laboratory studies of stress-induced drive states.

ANIMAL RESEARCH: MOTIVATION AND ACTIVITY

HUNGER-INDUCED DRIVE

Hunger drive is produced by food deprivation for a period of time prior to testing or until the animal dies of starvation (terminal food deprivation). Hunger-induced drive is associated with a specific goal such as food, but it also has a diffuse and generalized effect on activity level.

In comparison to the extensive literature on food deprivation for young animals, studies of hunger-induced motivation and behavior for different age groups are relatively few in number. One of the first studies by Margolin and Bunch (1940) was done with three age groups of male albino rats of an unspecified strain or stock: 1 to 1.3 months (prepubescent), 5 to 5.8 months (postpubescent), and 10 to 11.7 months (adult). Animals were deprived of food for varying numbers of days. Then the number of crossings over an electrified (or nonelectrified) wire runway to obtain food was recorded. Results of the study were reviewed and discussed extensively by Botwinick (1959). Generally, age trends after 1 day of food deprivation were essentially the same regardless of shock conditions. The two older groups showed a similar number of crossings but significantly fewer crossings than the prepubescent group. Unfortunately, absence of a nondeprived control group made it impossible to separate effects of 1-day deprivation from those which may have resulted from no deprivation.

Noting that the nonshock condition was the most important condition from the standpoint of hunger motivation and activity, Botwinick (1959) reanalyzed the performance of the older age groups for the nonshock control group. The rationale for the analysis was as follows. The two older groups did not differ for 1 day of deprivation. Thus, the number of crossings for the 3- and 5-day deprivation conditions could be referred to a common index of crossing despite the fact that a nondeprived control group was not employed. Botwinick's reanalysis of these data indicated that the adult rats made fewer crossings than the postpubescent rats for both deprivation conditions. Consequently, it appears that food deprivation in excess of a single day produces unequal motivation strength for young and old animals. Later studies provide an indication as to why this may be true. More important, they indicate that number of days of food deprivation constitutes an inadequate operational definition of hunger drive when animals of different ages are compared.

Weight Loss

More recent experiments provide strong support for the notion that hunger motivation is largely a function of relative weight loss rather than the period of food deprivation *per se* (e.g., Capaldi and Robinson, 1960; Raymond, Carlton and McAllister, 1955). Consequently, it is advisable to maintain records of weight loss as an index of effective motivational level. This practice is particularly appropriate for aging studies involving strain and species comparisons. Body weight may increase or decrease at various points in the life span, and inbred strains within a species often differ significantly in initial body weight. Most important, an equal number of days of deprivation may not result in equal weight loss at all ages.

The importance of weight loss as opposed to days or amount of deprivation has been demonstrated by Jakubczak (1967b). Relative body weight refers to a percentage drop in body weight relative to initial body weight prior to deprivation. Jakubczak (1967b) tested five age groups of male Sprague-Dawley rats: 2, 3, 6, 11, and 26 months. Age differences were observed for the effects of food deprivation and the (a) maximum levels of running activity, (b) number of days to reach maximum levels of activity, and (c) the increase in activity per day to maximum activity. Consistent with Margolin and Bunch's (1940) findings, and a later experiment by Campbell, Teghtsoonian, and Williams (1961), the 2- and 3-month-old groups manifested significantly greater values for each of these performance measures than did the 6-, 11-, and 26-month-old groups. The latter three groups did not differ significantly among themselves.

The two youngest age groups (2 and 3 months) lost relative body weight at a significantly greater rate and survived for a significantly shorter time than did the older groups (6, 11, and 26 months). However, there were no age differences in the percentage body weight loss at death (approximately 43 percent). Moreover, maximum activity for all age groups occurred with approximately equal values of percent weight loss. It seems, then, that *percent (relative) weight loss is indeed a more comparable way of expressing degree of hunger motivation in rats of different ages than is duration of deprivation.* Energy stores appear to deplete much more rapidly in the younger animal following a given number of days of deprivation; and, consequently, hunger motivation is greater than that observed for older animals given the same number of days of deprivation.

Amount Consumed and Latency to Eat

In view of the problems associated with the operational definition of hunger drive in terms of days of deprivation, other indices of deprivation have been used, e.g., amount eaten after deprivation and latency to start eating. Studies examining these indices have revealed important age-hunger relationships. For example, Jakubczak (1973a) tested three age groups of female Sprague-Dawley rats (4, 11, and 24 months). They were placed on 24-, 48-, and 96-hour food deprivation schedules and then fed again for 7 days. Regardless of duration of deprivation, latency to eat decreased with age. The 4-month-old rats took a significantly longer time to start eating than did the 24-month-old rats. The 11-month-old group did not differ significantly from either the 4- or 24-month-old groups. Regardless of the deprivation schedule and the number of days of refeeding, the 4-month-old group weighed and ate less than the 11- and 24-month-old groups.

Jakubczak's (1967b) results are inconsistent with Jerome's (1959) hypothesis that degree of hunger accompanying a given duration of food deprivation is greater for younger than for older animals. However, as Jakubczak points out, Jerome's hypothesis may only be valid when animals differing significantly in rate of growth are compared. This growth rate hypothesis is supported by studies which indicate that weight loss is inversely related to age and that survival time is positively related to age between 2 and 6 months, but remains invariant with age after 6 months (Campbell, Teghtsoonian and Williams, 1961; Jakubczak, 1967b; Jakubczak, 1969). This age-growth rate relationship makes considerable sense in view of the finding that metabolic rate per unit body weight does, in fact, decrease with age between 2 and 6 months of age (Kleiber, Smith, and Chernikoff, 1956). Age differences in survival time and weight loss between 1 and 6 months may well reflect age differences in the rate at which bodily energy

stores are utilized during starvation. However, it should be noted that growth rate may not terminate for all species and all strains of a species beyond 6 months. Under some circumstances mice of strain C57BL/6J continue to show growth beyond 6 months.

While relatively few data exist with regard to the relationship of hunger drive to food deprivation for extremely old animals, there is reason to believe that the relationship is possibly even more complicated than for very young animal subjects (Jakubczak, 1973b). Old rats of the Fischer strain exhibit less preference for calorically dense diets than do young Fischer rats. In contrast, ACI/Mai (Microbiological Associates) rats exhibit no significant age differences for degree of preference. Lower preference of the Fischer rats may reflect terminal changes in preference for fat as a thermoregulatory response, food conversion, basal metabolism, or any combination of these factors (Jakubczak, 1973b) or more general health factors.

Feedback Effects of Activity on Drive

While age differences in metabolic rate appear to play an important role in the degree of motivation induced by hunger states, age differences in activity level may also affect the rate at which bodily energy stores are utilized and thus affect hunger motivation. This posibility has important implications for aging studies which use wheel running as a behavioral index of deprivation-induced drive level.

Jakubczak (1969) found that age differences in wheel running in response to food deprivation do contribute to age-related differences in weight loss. Male Sprague-Dawley rats, ages 2, 3.5, and 5.1 months, were either confined in the living compartment of a wheel running apparatus or permitted free access to the activity drum. After an adaptation period, all mice were totally deprived of food. Among those groups given free access to the activity wheel, the 2-month-old rats differed significantly from the older groups in the direction of increased activity. This active 2-month-old group also exhibited greater weight loss per day as compared to the confined 2-month-old group. They also took significantly fewer days to lose 35 percent of their predeprivation weight. However, weight differences between confined and nonconfined animals were not significant for the older two groups.

Jakubczak's data: (a) confirm Reid and Finger's (1957) hypothesis that wheel running activity may itself increase drive by depleting energy stores at a higher rate than would normally be the case in the home cage, and (b) indicate that utilization of change in activity resulting from a given amount of food deprivation, as an index of age differences in drive level, is a practice which may actually lead to an overestimation of age differences in drive when younger animals are compared with mature and old animals. Clearly, a measure of the effectiveness of drive manipulation (deprivation) which is independent of the behavioral consequences of drive manipulation is necessary. At present, percent loss of predeprivation body weight appears to be the best candidate.

One problem encountered in the use of percent deprivation body weight as an index of effective drive level is that prolonged data collection involves normal weight variations for aging animals. Thus predeprivation levels are not reflective of normal weight gain during the testing period. This problem can be solved by the adjusting of percent body weight in experimental subjects based on daily changes in body weight for nondeprived control subjects of the same age. On a particular day of deprivation, the mean percentage of increase or decrease of body weight of the nondeprived control animals is added (or subtracted) from the percentage of initial weight loss exhibited by experimental subjects.

Water Deprivation

Not much work has been done in the area of water deprivation. Total water deprivation in young rats results in dehydration, anorexia, lowered temperature, and approximately 40 to 60 percent weight loss at death.

Jakubczak (1970a) investigated the effects of water deprivation on wheel running activity, weight loss, and survival time for male Sprague-Dawley rats, ages 3, 10.7, and 25.8 months, at the start of the experiment. The youngest animals lost relative body weight at a faster rate and tended to survive a shorter time than the older groups. The percentage of weight loss at death was approximately constant for all age groups. Percent survival time and percent body weight were highly correlated regardless of age. Basal levels of running activity (ad libitum) were inversely related to age. Water deprivation increased running activity relative to the basal level but only for the two older age groups. Thus for water deprivation, as for food deprivation, weight loss is a more precise index of drive state in water-deprived rats than is length of deprivation.

Further Work

For the most part, research on hunger- and thirst-induced motivation, activity level, and aging has been methodological and descriptive in nature. It has concentrated on (1) characterization of the relationship between motivation and behavioral changes, (2) appropriate operational definitions of hunger motivation, (3) appropriate time sampling techniques. These studies must necessarily precede studies concerned with the underlying mechanisms of hunger motivation as it interacts with age. Future studies may deal with the latter question once basic methodological controls have been established.

GENERAL ACTIVITY LEVEL

Wheel Running

Wheel running activity has been a popular means of assessing the general drive state of the organism in the absence of food and water deprivation. It is clear, however, that the term spontaneous activity is inappropriate because it suggests that the behavior is not influenced by internal drive states which may be dictated by prior reinforcement history.

Jones, Kimeldorf, Rubadeau, and Castanera (1953), and Botwinick (1959) have reviewed the very early work dealing with the relationship between wheel running activity and age in the rat (Slonaker, 1970; Richter, 1922; Shirley,

1928). It is clear from these studies that wheel running activity is low at about 1 month, increases to a maximum somewhere between 2.3 and 10 months, and decreases for old animals. However, it is difficult to assess the contribution of age to activity in these studies because some studies were done with single animals, random bred stocks were used and often not identified, and the experimental designs did not permit separation of activity differences related to age from other experimental variables which covaried with age. One early study departed significantly from the usual finding of increased activity beyond 1 month. Anderson and Smith (1932) using an unspecified stock of male rats found a decrease in activity from 1 to 5 months of age. However, they only recorded activity for 1 hour a day and thus it is difficult to compare their findings with previous studies in which relatively long recordings were obtained. It would seem appropriate to obtain at least a 24-hour record, and perhaps longer, in view of the influences of time of day (Jakubczak, 1970b), temperature, and barometric pressure (Sprott, 1967) on wheel running behavior.

Brief samples of wheel running activity are biased by virtue of the fact that daytime activity scores for different age groups may yield very different results than nighttime activity scores. Adult albino rat strains appear to exhibit a single major activity peak during the dark hours of a 24-hour period (Calhoun, 1946). This nocturnal pattern changes with age. At the time of weaning, activity periods were distributed throughout the 24-hour period and concentrated in the dark hours. By the eighth month almost all activity was confined to the night hours. After 8 months, there was a leveling of the curve and a spreading of activity into the daylight hours. This loss of rhythmicity was accentuated from 24 months until death.

In a more recent investigation of the interaction of food deprivation and distribution of activity, Jakubczak (1970b) tested three age groups of Sprague-Dawley rats, 2, 10, and 24 months, who were either deprived by total food withdrawal or provided food *ad libitum*. Regardless of presence or absence of food deprivation, the youngest rats ran a greater total amount, a greater number of hours, and at a higher hourly rate than did the older rats. The food-deprived rats ran a greater total amount, a greater number of hours, and at a greater hourly rate than the nondeprived rats, but each of these measures was invariant with age. The young rats exhibited significantly greater dark-running versus light-running difference scores than did the mature and older rats. This was true for total amount of activity and for the number of hours of activity. Food deprivation increased the dark-light difference in number of hours of activity, but the increase was proportionate across age groups. These data emphasize the importance of obtaining large time samples of wheel running activity when age and deprivation variables are examined as the baseline levels of activity do change with age both with respect to the total amount and distribution of daily running activity.

Longitudinal findings have been reported by Browman (1942). Male albino rats (unspecified stock) on an *ad libitum* food and water schedule were observed from 1 to 9 months. The highest level of activity wheel performance was observed between 2.3 and 3.3 months with lower activity for older and younger animals. The major problem with the study was that experience in the activity wheel affects performance and interacts with age. Jones *et al.* (1953) explored the effects of extensive activity wheel experience on wheel running activity for male Sprague-Dawley rats that were 1.7, 2, 3.3, 4.7, and 7 months of age when they were placed in the activity wheel. The nondeprived animals were observed for 7 weeks. The highest peak of activity was obtained with the 1.7-month group, but age interacted with experience. The greater the initial age of each age group tested, the shorter was the time required to obtain a maximum activity level.

Questions have been raised concerning the experimental and environmental factors which contribute to the decrease in activity for very old animals. Botwinick (1959) has listed age-related changes in factors such as variations in musculature, proprioception, endocrine function, and central nervous system mechanisms. Few studies have examined these and other variables, e.g., isolation in wheel running apparatus, which represent underlying potential causes of decreased or increased wheel running activity. Hunt and Schlosberg (1939) reported that stocks of Wistar male rats, which were experimentally blinded, were less active than normal males. Browman (1942) reported the opposite for both male and female rats. The two studies are essentially impossible to compare because testing and blinding ages were different. Browman's animals were blinded during their first day of life and tested at 3 months. Hunt and Schlosberg's rats were blinded at various ages after 200 days and tested immediately. Moreover, different stocks of animals were used in each study.

Locomotor Activity

More recent studies have been concerned with locomotor activity in the open field. Generally, under *ad libitum* food and water schedules, activity decreases with increasing age over a broad range of the life span. At least one study indicated that females are generally more active than males, but that activity decreases with age for both sexes (Barrett and Ray, 1970).

Clearly, strain differences interact with age and affect activity level and thus the influence should be taken into consideration when generalizations are drawn from single strain studies. It does appear that the percent decline with age beyond one year is relatively uniform for strains C57BL/6J and DBA/2J, although initial activity levels are different. Sprott and Eleftheriou (1974) found that both strains exhibited a decrease in activity level after 6 months of age and that DBA/2J showed a moderate decrease from 2 to 6 months. Elias, Elias, and Eleftheriou (1975) replicated Sprott and Eleftheriou's findings for strain C57BL/6J but obtained somewhat different results for strain DBA/2J. The latter strain exhibited an increase in activity from 6 to 12 months and a highly significant decrease from 12 to 24 months. Failure to replicate Sprott and Eleftheriou's findings for DBA/2J mice may be related to the use of different open field testing procedures, e.g., Sprott and Eleftheriou tested only locomotor activity. The latter investigators examined the relationship between exploratory activity, locomotor activity, and emotionality. This necessitated a change in the open field configuration which involved the use of a darkened area in which the animal could retreat. Presence of the dark retreat area resulted in an overall decrease in the activity level of strain DBA/2J relative to Sprott and Eleftheriou's study.

Elias, Elias and Eleftheriou (1975) found that activity level for a limited sample of 37-month-old C57BL/6J mice was similar to that of the 24-month-old DBA/2J mice. The DBA/2J mice have a shorter life span than C57BL/6J mice (Storer, 1966; Less, 1969) and thus the possibility is raised that activity level reflects a more rapid functional aging for the DBA/2J mice.

Not only does genotype influence the relationship between age and open field behaviors, but environment interacts with genotype and age. This interaction is illustrated in a study performed by Sprott and Eleftheriou (1974). Two mouse strains, C57BL/6J and DBA/2J, were obtained from a common breeding source, but housed and tested in two laboratories ten miles apart. Housing, day-night cycle, and temperature conditions in the colony rooms were identical, and open field testing procedures were the same. However, a number of laboratory routines varied as well as environmental parameters such as the playing of a radio 18 hours a day in the colony room of one laboratory.

Two age groups were compared: 2 and 18 months. The activity level of DBA/2J mice was similar for both laboratories and at both ages. The activity level of young C57BL/6J mice was similar for both laboratories. However, activity levels for the 18-month-old mice of strain C57BL/6J were quite different for the two experiments. Moreover, the variability in performance was much greater for the older animals. The younger animals were housed in separate laboratory environments for a considerably shorter time prior to testing than were the older animals (1.5 months versus 8 to 10 months). Thus, one might expect the effects of environmental differences to be observed for the oldest group. It is interesting to note, however, that greater variability "occurred in the most 'protected' of the two laboratories."

The Sprott-Eleftheriou investigation has very important implications for the practice of shipping animals from a production source at similar ages and then testing them at a different age. As Sprott and Eleftheriou (1974, p. 160) point out, "The effects of these environmental differences (e.g., noise levels, diet, temperature, humidity, etc.) may well be cumulative over time and produce much larger effects in aging studies than in more typical short-term studies."

Play Activities

Few systematic studies have been reported in the aging literature *per se*, that deal with play activities of infrahuman mammals in a systematic manner. An interesting example of this research area is provided by Lockwood's quasi-naturalistic study of wolves. Lockwood (1975) gathered data on 11 captive packs of wolves in order to characterize their social organization across the life span. Play behavior, most frequently observed in pups less than 1 year of age, decreased steadily across age groups. Gross motor activity increased in wolves up to 2 years of age and declined thereafter. Although aging wolves (5+ years) displayed less synchronous behavior than younger wolves, i.e., their daily activity rhythms were out of phase with the rest of the group, they remained active participants in the pack. The oldest wolves were most often the recipients rather than emitters of submissive behaviors in their encounters with their younger packmates. Moreover, they were as successful as the younger wolves in their competition for food.

Other studies dealing with play activities in animals may be available in specialty journals, but they have not been cited in various bibliographies on aging studies and they do not appear in the specialty journals in aging. Thus, it is difficult to assess the extent to which a formalized literature exists for this potentially important research area.

Needed Research with Primates

It is apparent from the preceding section that little research of an organized experimental nature has been done for species other than the rat and mouse when questions concerning drive, exploratory behavior, activity level, and emotionality in old and senile animals have been raised. The situation exists for the obvious reasons that small animals are less expensive and more convenient subjects for studies which involve the entire life span. To some extent it also reflects a concentration on the rat and

mouse in psychological research to the exclusion of other *infrahuman* species (Bitterman, 1960). This is an unfortunate state of affairs as the question of generality of findings across species is important, particularly for those species which are close to man phylogenetically.

The primate has received relatively little attention in the context of motivation and aging despite the fact that it provides an excellent model for curiosity, emotional, and sexual behavior in humans because of the diversity of behavioral response and the advanced level of social interaction relative to species lower on the phylogenetic scale (Bernstein and Mason, 1962).

Studies by Bernstein and Mason (1962) illustrate the usefulness of the primate model and provide hypotheses for research with old and senile primates. They point out that, in the course of ontological evolution of primates, emotional responses develop a degree of functional specificity and that the same environmental conditions may be expected to elicit different emotional patterns in different age groups because one set of environmental conditions which permit adaptation for the mature animal may not permit adaptation for the immature animal. In an examination of responses to fear stimuli and frustration (food out of reach) with male and female rhesus monkeys aged 3, 7, 16, and 25 months, they found that directed responses become tied to these stimuli with increasing age and that the contrast between fear and frustration increases with age. Frustration in the 25-month animals was associated with response patterns indicative of a less mature level of emotional adaptation. These studies were not extended to elderly and senile primates. Such studies may be particularly important in view of the suggestion that the emotional and motivational behavior of the senile organism represents a retrogression to infantile, or less mature, developmental stages. Furthermore, it is possible that any "apparent" decrease in emotionality with increasing age in rats and mice does not reflect increased behavioral rigidity, but the fact that general stress responses (defecation) are reduced relative to a diversity of learned responses specifically directed to particular objects.

It is clear that the emotional responsiveness

of the primate and its relationship to complex social interactions and stimuli is a good model for the relation of emotionality and drive in the human. It is thus unfortunate that more in the way of a formal aging-motivation literature does not exist for primates.

Exploration, Activity, and Food Deprivation

Goodrick (1966) emphasized two important points regarding the measurement of exploratory behavior: (1) in many studies valid measures of exploratory behavior have not been obtained because exploratory behavior is often inferred from locomotion scores; (2) locomotion may be inversely related to exploratory behavior under certain conditions such as those which elicit fear. In several experiments designed to separate exploratory or investigatory behavior from locomotion *per se,* Goodrick (1966) tested three age groups of male albino rats (Experiment 1–1.5, 10, and 22 months; Experiment 2–3, 11, and 24 months). The oldest animals were of the Wistar rat strain and the youngest two groups were Sprague-Dawleys.

In Experiment 1, young food-deprived rats (1.5 months) tended to exhibit less open field locomotor activity than controls of the same age, while the oldest group of deprived rats (22 months) engaged in *more* locomotor activity than aged controls. Goodrick related this age difference in locomotion to the increased amount of exploratory behavior observed for all deprived animals, i.e., the normally more active, younger animal may slow down in order to explore; the less active, older animal may be stimulated to explore by food deprivation, and hence, activity is increased.

Experiment 2 was primarily concerned with exploration and thus locomotion scores were not observed. All animals were tested using the "free exploratory method" which involves the possibility for free entry into a darkened portion of the field. For control groups, exploration was a decreasing function of increasing age. This was largely due to the higher mean exploratory (sniffing in the bright portion of the field) and lower mean nonexploratory (lying and grooming) scores for the youngest animals in comparison with the two older groups (11 and

24 months). No age-related differences were found between deprived animals of the three age groups for exploratory behavior or nonexploratory behavior. The effect of deprivation was to increase exploratory behavior across all age groups and to reduce the magnitude of differences among age groups.

The increase in exploratory responses was greater for the oldest animals (12 and 24 months) than for the 3-month-old animals. This phenomenon is most likely related to the fact that the young animals, under deprivation conditions, reached a ceiling level which they could not surpass regardless of amount of deprivation. While age differences in exploration for the control group of Experiment 1 were minimal where age groups 1.5, 10, and 22 months were compared, they were quite significant for the control group of Experiment 2 where 3-, 11-, and 24-month-old groups were compared. This was largely related to the young 3-month control group which showed increased exploration relative to the young 1.5-month-old group. Goodrick argues that comparisons between old and young groups should use animals within the age range of 3 to 24 months. If younger animals are used, the failure to obtain differences between young and old animals may result from rapid behavior changes which occur between 1 month and 3 months rather than absence of age differences from young adulthood to old age.

In a later experiment, Goodrick (1967) used Sprague-Dawley male rats for all age comparisons and examined a wider range of young animals for comparison with old animals. Age groups were 1, 1.7, 2.4, 3.0, 12, and 24.3 months of age. Exploration was high at 1 month, decreased to a minimum at 1.7 months, and reached a level comparable with the 1 month level of activity at 3 months. The bright area of the field was explored progressively less with increasing age between 3 and 24.3 months. Nonexploratory responses were inversely related to exploratory responses under all conditions. These data suggest that rats, prior to sexual maturity, engage in exploration less than young mature rats, and that a narrow range of young animals should serve as "young controls."

While Goodrick's point with regard to the missing of age differences as a result of selection of particular young groups for comparisons with old groups is well taken, the rate of growth and the age at which pre- and post-pubescence and old age is reached are influenced by genotype, and the generality of data drawn from a single inbred strain is limited because, genetically, all subjects in the sample represent a single "individual." Strain (genotype) and age differences do interact for exploratory behavior.

This point is illustrated by a recent study comparing the open field performance of two strains of mice, C57BL/6J and DBA/2J, of four age groups: 2.5, 6, 12, and 24 months of age (Elias, Elias, and Eleftheriou, 1975). In this study the measure of exploratory behavior was the number of crossings to and from an illuminated area and a dark area. Locomotor behavior was defined as number of open field squares traversed. The exploratory measure was adjusted statistically for its correlation with locomotor behavior *per se*. For the C57BL/6J mice (adjusted scores) there was a drop in exploratory behavior between 2.5 and 6.5 months of age and no age-related differences thereafter. In contrast, strain DBA/2J exhibited no differences in adjusted exploratory scores as a function of age. Consequently, the generalization that exploratory behavior decreases with advancing age may apply only to specific strains and for specific periods of the life span.

Factors Influencing Age Differences in Exploratory Responses

Goodrick (1971) has investigated environmental test factors which influence exploratory behavior with increasing age. Wistar rats showed increased exploration at 1 and 3 months relative to 1.7 and 2.4 months. Exploration of the low scoring adolescent rats (1.7 and 2.4 months) was increased dramatically when testing was done in the dark cycle. However, low scoring older rats (12 and 24 months) remained at the same level. Thus, it appears that the dark cycle influences exploratory behavior to a greater extent for initially low scoring adolescent Wistar rats.

Compared with individually tested controls, adolescent male rats (1.7 months) that were tested in pairs exhibited higher exploration scores (and lower nonexploration scores), but no differences were observed for adolescent (2.4-month) males. Goodrick (1971) interprets these differences in terms of changing dominance-subordination behavior for the adolescent animals.

Gentling did not result in changes of exploration scores relative to controls for low scoring older rats (12 and 24 months), but both groups of low scoring adolescent rats (1.7 and 2.4 months) were comparable with high scoring immature (1 month) and mature (3 months) rats as a result of handling. Emotionality scores (boluses) indicated that the groups for which exploration was facilitated were significantly less emotional. Gentling had no effect on elimination scores for the older male and female rats (12 and 24 months). Goodrick (1971) concluded that these data are compatible with the hypothesis that general behavior rigidity was greater for old than young animals because of a failure of environmental manipulation to initiate changes in exploration and emotionality in these older groups. We suggest that the term *behavioral stability* may be more accurate as it does not suggest cognitive inflexibility. The term "rigidity" may be more accurately applied to the perseveration of inappropriate behavior.

In an earlier study, Goodrick (1965) found that group versus isolated housing did not affect the decrease in exploratory behavior with age that was observed for individually tested mice that were not subject to isolation. Isolation and paired testing *increased* the exploration scores for the 24-month-old rats and *decreased* the exploration scores for the 3-month-old rats. Examination of dominance-submissive relationships with a sniffing-lying score (SL) indicated that the youngest group of isolated animals paired during testing evidenced a decrease in mean exploratory activity because of an increase in dominance-subordination behavior, i.e., one member of the pair lay quietly while the other engaged in sniffing and other activities. Presumably, the paired-tested, isolated, aged rats explored more than did the singly tested and paired-tested, nonisolated groups, because of their decreased dominance-submissive hierarchies. It is clear from these studies that exploratory behavior is influenced by a variety of factors including time of measurement, genotype, dominance-submissive hierarchies established by caging, paired versus nonpaired testing, sex, the measure of exploration used, emotionality, and general activity.

Emotionality

Age and strain differences in emotionality appear to influence activity and exploratory behavior. Several studies have explored differences in emotionality for different age groups of rats and mice in the open field. For Sprague-Dawley rats, Werboff and Havlena (1962) found a *decrease* in emotionality level (defecation, urination, rearing, crouching) with increasing age beyond 6 months, but an *increase* from 3 to 6 months. However, their data were based on repeated testing of the same animals and thus the results may be explained in terms of adaptation to the testing situation rather than decrease in emotionality level. The increase in emotionality at 9 months may have been related to a stressful testing procedure which was introduced after animals reached 3 months of age. It is difficult to draw conclusions regarding age changes in activity level from Werboff and Havlena's longitudinal data because subjects were exposed to a variety of experiences such as water maze learning between 3 and 6 months of age and attempts at mating at 12 months.

One of the difficulties in studying the relationship between emotionality, exploratory behavior, and locomotion, is that locomotion *per se* has been used to infer all three phenomena. Generally, decreased exploratory behavior is inferred from decreased locomotion and decreased locomotion is attributed to increased fear responses. However, in some strains of rats, separate measures of emotionality (defecation, crouching, urinating, rearing) and locomotor activity (quadrants entered in open field) are positively related rather than inversely related (see Werboff, 1962; Broadhurst, 1961), and in some instances they are unrelated. Thus, as Werboff (1962) and Goodrick (1966) suggest, it is important to have separate measures of each. Changes in circulating levels of plasma corticosterone levels may be a more sensitive index of fear than defecation alone (Elias and Elias, 1975). Many strains defecate very little at any

age (Werboff, 1962; Elias, Elias and Eleftheriou, 1975). Clearly, measures of locomotion as indices of fear are compromised by age and strain differences in activity level and exploratory behavior. Moreover, there is some question as to the extent to which defecation scores represent a valid or sensitive measure of emotionality (Collins, 1966; Hunt and Otis, 1953).

Feedback Relationships

In the previous section dealing with hunger motivation, studies were cited which indicate that although wheel running activity is often used as an indicator of heightened appetitive drive, wheel running activity itself may further heighten hunger drive and thus exaggerate differences in drive between animals of different growth (metabolic) rates, e.g., young and old animals. A similar feedback relationship exists for open field indices of locomotion, exploratory behavior, and emotionality. This relationship exists because open field behaviors, often used to evaluate drive level or stressors applied *prior* to open field, are affected by the stress of the open field itself.

A study by Eleftheriou (1974) illustrates this point. C57BL/6J mice and DBA/2J mice, ages 2, 6, 9, 12, 18, 24, and 30 months were placed in the center of an open field. They were allowed to move freely for 5 minutes, and then returned to their respective home cages. At the end of 30 minutes in the home cage, the mice were removed and plasma was collected for fluorometric analyses of corticosterone levels. At 12 and 18 months of age, both strains subjected to open field stress exhibited essentially the same levels of circulating plasma corticosterone. At 6 and 9 months, significant differences between the two strains were found with a significant rise from 2 months for the C57BL/6J mice as compared to a moderate rise for strain DBA/2J. Plasma corticosterone levels were higher for the DBA/2J mice at 2 months of age. At 30 months of age both strains exhibited levels that were essentially identical to those found at 2 months. The point is that the task used to measure drive level may differentially increase drive level for older and younger animals of different strains by virtue of the fact that the stress response may be quite different for different strains of different ages.

AVERSIVE STIMULATION

In many learning experiments, escape from and/or avoidance of aversive stimulation provides an incentive to perform. Thus, an important question with regard to motivation and age has to do with the effectiveness of a given drive stimulus or incentive for various age groups.

Shock and Auditory Stimulation

Several studies provide data with regard to age differences in response to different shock levels and auditory stimuli. Birren (1955) obtained reaction time data to electric shock and auditory stimuli for different age groups of male and female Sprague-Dawley rats. Data were analyzed for three age groups: approximately 1-2, 5-8, 21-30 months. A significant slowing in reaction to shock was found in the oldest as opposed to the two younger groups. For auditory reaction time there was a slight decrease in reaction time (RT) from the youngest age to approximately 15 months and then an increase in RT from 15 to 30 months. No relationship was found between body weight, sex and reaction time. These data have clear implications for the equating of motor response to aversive stimulation for various age groups when aversive stimulation is used as an incentive for learning.

Paré (1969) designed an experiment to evaluate the relative effect of two shock intensities (.5 ma and 1.0 ma) on the acquisition of a discrimination bar press response for Sprague-Dawley rats: 1.3, 3.0, and 11.8 months of age. All animals were placed on a deprivation schedule resulting in 20 percent body weight reduction relative to *ad libitum* controls (not tested). CS+ and CS- were beeping tones of 2,000 and 850 Hz respectively. For both shock intensities, speed of acquisition of the discrimination bar press response was inversely related to age. Discrimination between CS+ and CS- was poorer under the high shock than under the low shock condition for the oldest, but not for the younger groups of rats. Thus, Paré questioned whether the incentive-inducing attributes of shock were

the same for young and old animals. Campbell (1967) failed to find age-related differences in the aversive threshold to grid shock in the rat, but the age range 1.0 to 3.3 months was quite limited. Doty and O'Hare (1966) report data suggesting that the aversive threshold is higher in 12-month-old rats than 2-month-old rats.

Decreased threshold for older animals may explain poorer discrimination performance for these animals, but it does not account for the poorer performance under high- as opposed to low-shock conditions for the oldest group in Paré's experiment. If decreased sensitivity to shock accounts for inferior discrimination performance, increased shock should result in improved discrimination. It is possible that older subjects in Paré's study were operating at a generally higher drive state or arousal state. This interpretation is consistent with findings for elderly human subjects (Eisdorfer, Nowlin and Wilkie, 1970), that increased motivation, beyond an optimum level for efficiency, may account for performance decrements on stressful laboratory tasks.

Paré found that age differences were abolished when discrimination complexity was decreased. He did not manipulate both food deprivation and shock incentive. Thus, information regarding the interaction of general drive level and incentive was not obtained.

Stimulation with Light

While stimulation with light is generally considered far less aversive than shock stimulation, escape and/or avoidance of light intensity can act as an incentive for performance in albino rats and mice (Lockard, 1963). It has been repeatedly demonstrated that these animals will learn a bar press response (Goodrick, 1970) and simple escape-avoidance responses (see Botwinick, 1959) in order to escape from light into darkness.

Botwinick, Jerome, Birren and Brinley (1957) found no differences between 12- and 24-month-old male and female Sprague-Dawley rats in a simple light avoidance task. Similarly no age differences or age by sex interactions were significant.

Goodrick (1970) has reported that comparisons of mature (6 months) and senescent (26 months) albino rats of the Wistar strain did not result in a significant difference in dark contingent bar press behavior.

Recently, Goodrick (1970) found that light onset had a reward value which was similar to that for light offset. His results suggest that stimulus change, rather than light aversion, may be an incentive for bar press behavior. This hypothesis is entirely consistent with the notion that drive level increases when mean level of environmental stimulation falls below a threshold level. Goodrick's study indicated that the amount of light contingent and dark contingent bar press behavior was invariant over age when 6-month-old versus 26-month-old Wistar albino rats were compared. Generally, these data suggest that change in stimulus intensity, as well as light aversion, may constitute drive stimuli.

Water Escape

Studies of swimming speed in animals as a function of increasing age provide an opportunity to examine psychomotor activity of a somewhat different nature than that which is involved in measures of open field locomotion and wheel running activity. Similar to the latter activities, swimming involves a prolonged sequence of psychomotor movements under stress, rather than quick and limited responses to aversive stimulation, e.g, response to electric shock. However, for water escape behavior, the motor performance is more closely tied to the survival of the animal than it is for volitional locomotion, e.g., wheel running and open field behavior. If the animal fails to swim, it eventually sinks and dies. If it fatigues more readily than another animal, it dies sooner. Further, it must learn the specific directional movements which lead to escape.

Birren and Kay's (1958) and Kay and Birren's (1958) data on water escape behavior provide information with regard to age differences in serial motor performance, which is intimately tied to survival, affected by elementary learning, and limited by fatigue. These studies provide a baseline for the evaluation of later studies in which incentive motivation to escape is manipulated by varying the strength of aversive stimulation (water temperature).

In the first experiment (Birren and Kay, 1958), male Sprague-Dawley rats of six groups varying from 5 to 30 months were given five swimming trials (one minute between trials) for two days. They were placed in one end of a long metal trough and the time to escape was measured. Maximum (fastest swimming time) and median swimming times were reported. Females were generally faster swimmers and the greatest differences between males and females occurred for the oldest group. Old rats of both sexes were slower than young rats. This was true for both maximum and median swimming times, although differences were more exaggerated for the latter scores. The greatest age difference was observed between 15 and 27 months for both sexes.

In a second study, using the same apparatus and rat strains, Kay and Birren (1958) examined the effects of fatigue and practice. Two important questions were raised: (1) is slower swimming a compensatory response which conserves the strength of older animals so that they fatigue less quickly than younger animals; (2) does practice eliminate or reduce age differences?

Two age groups of males and females, 7-8 months and 23-27 months were given "fatigue" and "recovery" trials after an initial habituation to the task. For the fatigue task, each rat was given 30 consecutive trials but removed from the apparatus prior to 30 trials if it was no longer able to swim or swimming exceeded 60 seconds. After fatigue trials, animals were rested for 5 minutes and then given 5 additional (recovery) trials. Results indicated that the old rats were more susceptible to fatigue and that the old males were considerably more susceptible than the old females. Performance on the recovery trials was the same but the differences were even more exaggerated. Thus, as concluded by Kay and Birren, it does not appear that the older organisms' slower swimming speed results from conservation of resources "in the nature of an adaptive strategy to meet continuous environmental demands" (1958, p. 380). Even though they swam at an initially slower rate, the old males became easily exhausted. Most important, the effects of fatigue accentuated differences between groups. Kay and Birren attributed the superiority of the old females to a difference in vigor between the two sexes and the longer average life span for the females.

The phase of Kay and Birren's study which considered practice effects utilized two age groups of males and females, 11 months and 23 to 24 months. Old and young animals of the same sex were matched for body weight and given 15 trials a day for 15 days. Practice effected a reduction in escape times for old males, although the rank order of age and sex groups remained the same. Thus, it would seem that age differences in performance, which are induced by water escape incentive, may be exaggerated by many massed trials and reduced by many widely distributed trials.

Somewhat different results were obtained when continuous swimming to submersion was examined for C57BL/6J mice (Wright, Werboff, and Haggett, 1971). The relationship between age and time to submersion was nonlinear from 11.6 to 20 months and then decreased in a linear fashion from a maximum at 20.5 months to a minimum at 28 months. Wright, Werboff, and Haggett (1971, p. 368) offer an interesting hypothesis in explanation of their findings:

> "These observations may be explained by the hypothesis that the age threshold after which one may expect to see evidence of debilitation occurring is after the mean life-span age (676 days) for this strain. Prior to this age, there is a selective factor operating so that animals that survive after 50% of their life-span are more resistant to severe experiences. This selective factor operates also at the older end of the life-span scale but the debilitating effects of age are now so severe as to mask the selective factor."

The mean life span of any inbred strain or hybrid stock is dictated by laboratory conditions (Less, 1969) and must be determined for the experimenter's colony. Under ideal conditions, mean life span for C57BL/6J mice is greater than the 676 days cited by Wright, Werboff, and Haggett. Nevertheless, Wright, Werboff, and Haggett's comments have considerable validity for all aging studies with animals as they point to changes in sample characteristics with age as important factors to be taken into consideration when age changes or differences are explained.

In a second phase of the Wright, Werboff, and Haggett experiment, three water temperatures were used in order to explore the relationship between incentive to swim and time to submersion. Time to submerge decreased with increased incentive to swim. The old animals showed the least notable effects for the three temperature incentive conditions. Wright, Werboff, and Haggett concluded, because of the decreased capacity of the old group, i.e., their strength, resistance to fatigue, and energy reserves, that the differential demands of the water temperature conditions were minimal. It is clear that higher motivation results in faster swimming and that faster swimming results in more rapid fatigue.

The relationships noted for a single inbred rodent strain by Birren and Kay and by Wright and his associates cannot necessarily be generalized to the rat and mouse species as a whole. Studies in our laboratory (Elias and Eleftheriou, 1975a, 1975b, 1975c) and by others (Festing, 1974; Winston and Lindzey, 1964) indicate a wide range of strain differences for rats and mice in water escape performance.

Age Differences in Thermoregulation

One of the problems in the area of incentive manipulation *via* temperature extremes or shock is that the "effective" stimulation produced by equal values of temperature or electric current may not be the same at all ages. Thus, baseline differences in thermoregulation and shock threshold for various age groups represents a basic methodological prerequisite to refined studies of incentive motivation and aging. This problem is analogous to the definition of hunger motivation in terms of weight loss rather than days of food deprivation *per se*.

There is some degree of inconsistency in the literature on thermoregulation. Several reports indicate that older rats have a lower rectal temperature at room temperature than young rats and are less efficient in the maintenance of body temperature in a cold environment (Bourlière, 1947; Hügin and Verzár, 1957). However male Sprague-Dawley (NIH) rats in age groups of 7, 12, and 28 months showed equal heat loss as inferred by rectal temperature in a cold stress (2°C refrigeration) study by Jakubczak (1966). Moreover, lever pressing to turn on a heat source was invariant with age.

Differences in the results of the above studies

may be attributed to sex differences, age differences, or the use of different ambient temperatures. Hügin and Verzár (1957) used lower ambient temperatures than Jakubczak (1966). Jakubczak (1963) did report age differences in an earlier study in which 32-month-old female Sprague-Dawley rats were used. Further studies involving both sexes, similar cold stress temperatures, and more than one inbred strain of mice may resolve conflicting findings. The important point is that the same level of cold or heat source may be a less effective motivator of performance for older animals.

SEXUAL DRIVE AND ACTIVITY

Despite the increasing recognition of the role of social factors in the change in sexual activities with advancing age, one must consider the effects of sex hormones on sexual drive and sexual behavior in the aged. Animals have provided a convenient model for the study of hormonal changes as they relate to sexual activity. Recently, Elias and Elias (1975) reviewed the literature on hormones and behavior in aging mammals. Thus, only a brief summary of this literature will be presented here.

Pattern of Activities

Behavioral manifestations of sexual activity involved in mating consist of a number of partially independent components (e.g., frequency of mounts, intromissions, frequency and latency of ejaculations, intercopulatory and postejaculatory intervals). These components are organized into temporal and spatial patterns which are characteristic of a given sex and species. The rate of decline with age varies for these different components. In the male albino rat, the number of ejaculates per unit time exhibits an increase from puberty to 1 year, a gradual decrease during the second year, and rapid decline in the third year (Larsson, 1956). The pattern is different for the guinea pig. After puberty, the frequency of intromissions increases the first year and decreases notably in the next 2 years (Antliff and Young, 1957). Findings for other investigations with the rat and guinea pig (Jakubczak, 1964) are consistent with Antliff and Young's (1957) findings which indicate

that in the rat and guinea pig, mating behavior increases in intensity with maturity and then declines, and the various components of mating behavior change at different rates with advancing age.

Basis of Decline

Much of the animal research directed toward an understanding of the factors affecting a reduction in sexual activities with advancing age for infrahuman mammals has been concentrated on the identification of the physiological basis for this decline. This work has been summarized by Jakubczak (1967a), Timiras and Meisami (1972), Korenchevsky (1961) and others. It is clear that, for males, sexual activity and mating are under control of the testes and that onset of mating behavior at puberty is correlated with maximal androgen secretion of the testes. It is also well known that androgens of adrenal origin influence sexual behavior of females as well as males (Tepperman, 1973). Indirect evidence for the role of androgens in declining sexual activity with increasing age has been provided by the observation that a decrease in the production of androgen also occurs with increasing age (Young, 1961).

Androgen deficiencies produce changes in the accessory sex glands which may, in turn, be related to decreased sexual activities. However, androgen deficiencies with increasing age affect a wide range of biological systems (Timiras and Meisami, 1972) other than those involved in reproductive behavior. Moreover, despite the important role of androgens in reproductive activity, there are age-associated changes in accessory sexual glands which are not necessarily related to decreases in androgen levels. The accessory sex glands are affected by the intrinsic cellular processes that are characteristic of other aging tissues (Timiras and Meisami, 1972; Finch and Girgis, 1974; Huggins and Clark, 1940).

Neither androgen deficiency nor aging of the accessory sex glands is a necessary condition for a decrease of all types of sexual activity. Jakubczak (1964), for example, found that older (30 months) guinea pigs performed as well as younger (6 months) guinea pigs in terms of nuzzling, abortive mounting, and successful mounting. However, older males exhibited lower intromission and ejaculation scores, and large doses of exogenous testosterone for four weeks failed to increase these activities. Jakubczak concluded that old and young animals were equally sexually aroused and that decreased mating behaviors were related to factors other than lowered levels of androgen. Jakubczak (1964) has reviewed a number of studies of the role of androgen versus nonandrogen factors. These studies indicate that age changes in mating behavior occur prior to demonstrable deficit in androgen. When animals reach an age where androgen deficit is observed, the level of mating behavior decreases further.

The important question in a life span developmental context is the nature of the hormonal events prior to androgen deficiency which are related to decreased copulatory behavior. Evidence from a variety of sources (e.g., Jakubczak, 1964; Timiras and Meisami, 1972) indicates that there are age decrements in the mechanisms that mediate the temporal summation of excitatory neuronal impulses from the central nervous system which lead to ejaculation. Further, it appears that age changes in mediating mechanisms in the central nervous system occur earlier in the life of the animal than do changes in androgen levels.

In a summary of animal and human research on changes in sexual behavior with advancing age, Timiras and Meisami (1972) pointed out that sexual behavior in humans is more complex and hence more difficult to assess because it is governed by numerous psychosocial factors which act in contradiction to physiological competence. Nevertheless, it should not be concluded that complex social factors do not affect the mating behaviors of lower animals. Few studies with animals have explored the effects of early experience, isolation, conditions of housing or enriched environment on the sexual behavior of aging animals, although animals, particularly primates (Bernstein and Mason, 1962) have been used to study the effect of these psychosocial factors on other behaviors of adult animals. Although research with aging primates may be very expensive, it may be particularly useful with regard to manipulative studies which attempt to separate effects of sex

hormone and central nervous system changes from psychosocial factors, such as changes in housing patterns and social isolation. The latter conditions represent two major environmental events in the lives of the human elderly (Lowenthal, 1968; Rosow, 1968) and have a potentially important influence on sexual behavior.

HUMAN MOTIVATION STUDIES

Research on motivation in aging humans, from the standpoint of controlled laboratory investigation using reliable psychometric and psychophysiological measurement techniques, has been less systematic than motivational research with animals.

ANXIETY-AROUSAL

The most significant contribution to a systematic laboratory study of motivation has been made by Eisdorfer and his colleagues (Eisdorfer, 1966, 1968; Eisdorfer, Nowlin, and Wilkie, 1970; Eisdorfer, Conner, and Wilkie, 1968; Troyer, Eisdorfer, Bogdonoff and Wilkie, 1967). Their work can be loosely placed in the context of the anxiety and arousal concepts of drive (Spence, 1958, 1964; Duffy, 1957).

It appears to have been precipitated by observations of (1) the nature of performance decrements for elderly persons in verbal learning experiments, and (2) the specific circumstances under which these decrements were observed. Errors of omission exceeded errors of commission and both kinds of errors were exaggerated when the rate of task pacing (interstimulus intervals) was high (Eisdorfer, 1968; Troyer et al., 1967). Eisdorfer (1968) hypothesized that omission errors represented response inhibition related to heightened situational anxiety. Evidence in favor of this hypothesis was provided by the observation that performance of elderly persons improved appreciably when task pacing was reduced. Most important, the improvement was generally larger for omission errors than for commission errors, and when longer intervals between stimuli were used as a means for decreasing task pacing, mean response times fell well within a time period required for responding under rapidly paced stimulus presentation conditions (Eisdorfer, Axelrod, and Wilkie, 1963; Troyer et al., 1967; Arenberg, 1965).

These data are consistent with the notion that rapid task pacing results in increased anxiety and concommitant reduction in performance efficiency due to departure from optimal drive levels. However, in order to test this hypothesis, the experimenter must have a measure of arousal (drive) which is independent of performance measures. Eisdorfer and his group employed free fatty acid (FFA) levels and measures of heart rate and galvanic skin responses as indices of arousal.

Plasma levels of FFA are thought by some investigators to reflect level of autonomic arousal because FFA mobilization constitutes one of the metabolic processes associated with release of catecholamines from the adrenal medulla in response to stress. Using FFA as an indicator of arousal, Powell, Eisdorfer, and Bogdonoff (1964) conducted a serial verbal learning study with older (60+) and younger male subjects (20-48 years). The older group exhibited higher FFA levels than the younger group and performed more poorly. After the experiment the younger subjects exhibited a decrease in FFA level, but older subjects continued to exhibit an increase in FFA level. In a second study, limited only to older subjects (60+, mean age = 68 years), degree of arousal as inferred from FFA levels was related to performance in a curvilinear manner (Troyer, Eisdorfer, Wilkie, and Bogdonoff, 1966).

These data provide additional support for the hypothesis that older subjects are more stressed by task demands than younger subjects, but they do not provide evidence for a cause and effect relationship between poor performance and arousal. In order to do this, one must demonstrate that experimental lowering of arousal level results in an improvement of performance. To achieve this objective, Eisdorfer, Nowlin, and Wilkie (1970) selected a drug, propranolol (Inderol), which blocks autonomic nervous system arousal but seems to have minimal direct influence on central nervous system activation or deactivation.

Older men (60-78 years) were given propranolol during performance of a rote verbal learn-

ing task and their FFA levels, performance, heart rate and galvanic skin responses (GSR) were compared to those obtained for an elderly placebo control group. They were also given the Wechsler Adult Intelligence Scale, the Taylor Anxiety Scale (to assess their general level of state anxiety), and a test of organic brain impairment. No Propranolol versus control (placebo) group differences were observed for these preliminary measures, but there was a significant decrease in total number of errors for the older men given the drug. Moreover, the FFA levels showed a decrease for older men in the drug group after they were given the drug. In contrast, FFA levels for control subjects rose during the experiment and remained at a comparatively high level. Heart rate and GSR exhibited a response pattern similar to FFA level, but differences were not significant for GSR.

These data provide considerable support for the contention that autonomic nervous system activation associated task demands may contribute to performance decrement, although a finding that errors of omission were even more favorably affected by drug treatment than were errors of commission would have provided even stronger evidence in support of the anxiety-arousal interpretation. Moreover, it is unfortunate that a group of younger subjects was not tested under drug and placebo conditions. Use of a young control group would permit analysis of motivational versus cognitive factors as important determinants of age differences in performance.

Data provided by Eisdorfer and his coworkers do not exclude the possible influence of non-motivational factors on performance differences between old and young subjects. However, they do point out the following: (1) contrary to the notion that decrements in performance are due only to cognitive factors or to decreased motivation to perform, older subjects may be performing at such a high level of motivation that they perform less well than they are capable of performing (arousal); and (2) failure in task performance may further increase anxiety-induced arousal (drive) in a vicious cycle (Troyer et al., 1966).

A major problem in connection with the concept of general arousal is related to the fact that the assumptions of simultaneous arousal for all systems and uniform arousal in one system for all subjects have been challenged (Lacey and Van Lehn, 1952). It seems clear that unique autonomic response patterns emerge in response to stress for individual subjects and thus interpretations of group means are compromised. Further studies should incorporate other indices, "individual and task specific," of arousal patterns such as secretion of several steroids (e.g., cortisol and testosterone), response of the biogenic amines, and a variety of psychophysiological measurements which are collected at the same time and related to each other.

Task Involvement and Meaningfulness

One popular explanation for inferior learning or impaired sensory detection and discrimination performance in elderly subjects is that they are simply less involved in laboratory tasks. There is some evidence that this may be true for tasks that have little meaning for the older person. However, older persons may be even more involved than younger persons under circumstances in which the task at hand has meaning for them.

Shmavonian and Busse (1963) measured GSRs under various conditions of sensory stimulation. GSRs were considered to be indices of arousal states. Older men (60 to 70 years) exhibited less GSR activity than younger men (20 to 24 years) and thus a conclusion was reached that they were less involved with the laboratory task. This finding is not consistent with Powell, Eisdorfer, and Bogdonoff's (1964) findings of increased arousal as inferred from FFA in older as compared to younger subjects. However, Powell *et al.'s* stimulus materials may have been more meaningful to the subjects or the tasks may have been intrinsically more challenging. When Shmavonian and Busse (1963) used spoken phrases rather than simple tones, the differences between age groups diminished but did not disappear altogether. It appears then that older persons may be disproportionately more affected by decreases in task meaningfulness than young persons. However, a question may be raised as to the extent to which increased GSR activity reflects involvement in a cognitive sense.

Support for increased performance decrement

with meaningful material was provided in a later study of memory span by Craik and Masani (1967). In this experiment, subjects ranged in "decade" age groups from 20 to 79 years. Three types of stimuli were presented: (1) meaningful sentences, (2) color names, and (3) proverbs in scrambled word order. The hypothesis was that aged subjects would do relatively well with color names because they lend themselves *less* to organization based on familiarity. This hypothesis was confirmed by their findings.

In the same study, stimulus meaningfulness was varied by manipulating contextual constraints between words. Five lists of words were presented, each differing in an approximation to a standard English list. They ranged from a list of randomly chosen words to a meaningful English text. Both young and old subjects exhibited better performance with the meaningful list, but the greatest performance differences between young and old subjects were observed for the meaningful stimuli. It should be noted however that this trend did not generally hold for older subjects with superior verbal ability.

Generally then, it appears that improvement in performance for older subjects is sometimes observed when material is more meaningful, but in some instances the reverse is true, particularly when the more meaningful material lends itself to organization. The major problem with regard to interpretation of these findings in terms of increased motivation induced by meaningfulness or involvement is that task difficulty covaries with meaningfulness. Increases in concreteness of stimulus content and less rapid pacing or the opportunity to self-pace may involve decreased demands on abstract reasoning processes and attention. On the other hand, when task difficulty does not exceed a certain level, increased opportunity to organize or encode material may actually result in greater age differences even though overall performance level is enhanced for both young and old persons. At best, then, these studies indicate that motivational factors related to stimulus meaningfulness may influence performance decrements in the elderly, but they do not eliminate alternate explanations involving age-associated changes in central nervous system structure and function.

The ideal experimental paradigm would maintain constant task difficulty while manipulating task meaningfulness. An experiment by Wittels (1972) was designed to maintain task difficulty and at the same time vary stimulus meaningfulness for older and younger subjects. Word meanings change over time and the typical stimulus materials for paired associate tasks were designed for young subjects. Thus, Wittels questioned whether the difficulty observed for older persons with paired associate learning is due to the fact that they deal with less meaningful materials than do younger subjects in the typical paired associate task.

Word lists were obtained in a manner designed to ensure familiarity. Each person in the old (60 to 82) and the young (18 to 24) age groups was given 15 meaningful words and asked to provide his own response associations. The fifth response association to each word was taken as the paired associate to that word. Each person had a different list with stimuli which were common to all lists but response associates which were peculiar to the responder. The assumption was that lists were different from person to person but similar with regard to their strength of associations. When the person was given his own list it was called a personal list. When it was given to persons of the same age it was called a generational list, and when it was given to persons of a different age it was called a cross-generational list.

Wittels expected that the elderly persons would perform poorly on the cross-generational list, better on the generational list, and in a superior manner on the personal list. This hypothesis was not confirmed. Elderly subjects performed more poorly than younger subjects with each of the lists. These data provide evidence which is not consistent with the hypothesis that poor performance of the elderly on paired associate learning tasks is related to stimulus meaningfulness. This is not to say that increased meaningfulness does not result in increased motivation for older subjects. Rather, it seems to improve performance to an equal extent in younger subjects. However, too few systematic studies have been conducted to allow firm generalizations. To obtain conclusive evidence, it is necessary that studies first separate parameters of task meaningfulness and task difficulty.

CLASSICAL DRIVE STUDIES

Few studies with old subjects have been done with the experimental paradigm typically employed for manipulating drive and incentive in the context of Spence's motivation theory (1958). In this paradigm, strength of the unconditioned stimulus in an aversive stimulus avoidance paradigm is used as an incentive to respond (Elias, 1965). The stimulus (shock or a puff of air to the pupil of the eye) may be avoided or escaped by making the unconditioned response (finger withdrawal or eyeblink).

The few classical drive studies involving older adults have employed eyelid conditioning (Braun and Geiselhart 1959; Kimble and Pennypacker, 1963). For both studies, elderly subjects did not acquire a conditioned response to the same level as that observed for the younger subjects, i.e., the percentage of conditioned responses was lower for aged subjects. Kimble and Pennypacker (1963) have suggested that the UCR habituates more quickly for the older subjects, i.e., over time the eyeblink reflex becomes more susceptible to adaptation and this results in poorer conditioning. However, neither study manipulated strength of the UCS over a wide range of values. Thus, the possibility that some level of UCS intensity is optimal for elderly subjects was not determined. These studies were not designed as studies of anxiety-induced drive *per se*. Thus, a measure of anxiety level was not obtained prior to the experiment. Further studies with different age groups in which anxiety measures are obtained and UCS intensities are varied over a wide range would provide further information regarding the Eisdorfer (1968) arousal hypothesis discussed in a preceding section of this chapter. Avoidance conditioning, anxiety measures, and manipulation of UCS strength represent major tools in the investigation of drive for young subjects, but they have not been employed for aging studies to any significant extent.

A study by Botwinick, Brinley, and Robbin (1958) provides a more direct test of the relationship between incentive strength (shock) and performance for different age groups. Young (18 to 37 years) and old subjects (65 to 79 years) were required to press their fingers on a response key after hearing a warning signal. The key press set off a warning light followed by a preparatory interval and an auditory stimulus which terminated with the lifting of the finger. After a series of trials, shock was applied to the subject's wrist at a time after the warning light which was equal to the subject's median reaction time during preliminary trials. Shock reduced reaction times but did not differentially affect old and young subjects. While the older subjects were slower, the shock incentive did not reduce reaction time disproportionately for the old subjects. This result was repeated in a later study under the same conditions of irregular preparatory intervals and with a new set of irregular preparatory intervals (Botwinick, Brinley, and Robbin, 1959). However, when constant intervals were used, the older group reduced their reaction times more than the younger group. The authors do not comment on the implications of this study for motivation and aging. Presumably, older subjects are capable of responding more rapidly under proper conditions of incentive, but only under circumstances in which preparatory intervals are presented in a regular series.

It is obvious that many more studies need to be done in this area before the relationship between UCS-induced motivation and aging can be clarified. Moreover, it would be particularly useful if these studies were done in the context of a well-defined drive theory such as that developed by Spence (1958) for simple laboratory tasks. Ethical considerations may dictate the use of less noxious stimulation than shock, e.g., intensity of air puff and eyelid responses.

ACTIVITY: SEX DRIVE

Extensive discussions and reviews of the literature are available in the area of sexual behavior and aging (e.g., Pfeiffer, 1969). Thus, only a general summary will be presented in order to fit this literature into the context of drive research with the aged.

Capability

The first issue of concern when one considers sexual motivation among older persons is their biological capabilities to engage in sexual behavior. Certainly, the increased incidence of

physical and psychological illness, (e.g., myocardial infarction and depression) with advancing age necessarily places at least temporary restrictions on the total amount of sexual behavior occurring among the elderly (Pfeiffer, 1974). Nonetheless, there exists a substantial body of literature which indicates that both sexual interest and behavior decline among *healthy* aging individuals (e.g., Kinsey, Pomeroy, and Martin, 1948; Masters and Johnson, 1966). It is becoming increasingly apparent, however, that a significant proportion of this decline may be attributed to social, cultural, and psychological factors which adversely affect the expression of sexual drives. Some of these factors (e.g., lack of privacy) may be quite easily modified; others are exceedingly difficult to remedy (e.g., number of available sexual partners for the aging female).

Studies of the erection cycle during sleep in healthy men over 70 have shown them capable of both sexual arousal and erection, although the correlation between age and proportion of full erections was $-.49$ (Kahn and Fisher, 1969). Interestingly, correlations between nocturnal erections and actual sexual behavior during waking did not reach significance. Furthermore, the existence of physical changes in the male pattern of sexual responses with advancing age (e.g., increased time to arousal, erection, and ejaculation) has been well established (Masters and Johnson, 1966). Clinical evidence also exists for analogous changes in aging females (e.g., increased time to nipple erection and clitorical engorgement), although the capacity to reach orgasm does not appear to diminish, especially among women who have sources of regular sexual stimulation (Masters and Johnson, 1966). Furthermore, there is substantial agreement among researchers that both healthy males and females are usually *capable* of sexual activity, including intercourse, well into the seventh decade and not infrequently into the ninth decade (Pfeiffer, 1974).

Interest

Capabilities are only one aspect of sexual behavior in elderly persons. As with young and middle-aged adults, one must consider the interaction of capabilities and interest which may be dictated by psychological needs and complex social factors. Studies of sexual interest and behavior among the elderly reveal that there is a decline in both with advancing age, although the range of sexual activity is probably just as great as in any other age group. Based upon the current literature regarding sexuality in aging persons, a number of generalizations may be advanced. First, frequency of sexual activity declines for both sexes (Finkle, Tobenkin, and Karg, 1959; Christenson and Gagnon, 1965), although the sharpest drop occurs earlier for women, i.e., late sixties, than for men, i.e., late seventies (Verwoerdt, Pfeiffer, and Wang, 1969b). Second, men maintain higher levels of interest and activity than women at all ages up to the ninth decade (Newman and Nichols, 1960; Verwoerdt, Pfeiffer, and Wang 1969a,b; Cameron and Biber, 1973). Third, aging men exhibit a relatively large discrepancy between expressed interest in sex, which tends to be sustained well into the eighties, and actual sexual performance. Women do not exhibit as large a discrepancy. Both interest and behavior tend to decline at approximately the same rate (Verwoerdt, Pfeiffer, and Wang, 1969a,b). Fourth, marital status affects the frequency of sexual activity and interest for women, but is of less significance for men (Verwoerdt, Pfeiffer, and Wang, 1969a,b).

A few investigators have attempted to determine the factors which may account for the overall decrease in sexuality with advancing age. Generally, these factors differ for men and women. For men, the determinants of sexual behavior appear to be very complex. For example, between 45 and 69 years of age, present health status, past and present life satisfaction, and social class correlate positively with sexual functioning, while concern over physical well-being and taking of antihypertensive drugs correlate negatively with sexual functioning (Pfeiffer and Davis, 1972). For women, the overwhelming determinant of sexual expression in the middle and later years is marital status. While both single and married men report approximately the same rates of sexual interest and activity, single women report much lower rates of interest and activity than married women (Verwoerdt, Pfeiffer, and Wang, 1969a, b; Pfeiffer and Davis, 1972). Thus, the fact that many elderly women are widowed or divorced may account for their extensive decrease in sexual behavior and interest. Further, Pfeiffer and Davis (1972) note that the decline in sexual interest *per se* may be a result of defensive reaction, i.e., adaptation is to some extent dependent upon the ability to inhibit sexual strivings when no socially sanctioned partners are available. Perhaps the most significant finding in the current literature is that amounts of past sexual activity and enjoyment are excellent predictors of sexual activity and enjoyment in old age (Christenson and Gagnon, 1965; Verwoerdt, Pfeiffer, and Wang, 1969a,b; Pfeiffer and Davis, 1972). The critical implication of this finding is that those persons who failed to enjoy sex in their younger years, for whatever reason, may retreat into the myth of a sexless old age (Berezin, 1969), thus taking advantage of the taboo against sexual behavior among the elderly. However, those who previously derived pleasure from sexual behavior may find the taboo a considerable hindrance to their present activity.

Evidence for cohort differences in attitudes towards the taboo against sexual behavior in the aged has been presented by Wood (1971). She reported the results of a questionnaire study which indicated that older persons tended to be less self-accepting of "unconventional" behaviors (e.g., remarriage of a widower of 70 in the face of objections from his children) in themselves than were young persons, i.e., the young persons appeared to be more able to accept unconventional behavior in old persons. Furthermore, the elderly group perceived the young group as far less accepting than they actually were. Thus, while it may be possible to provide an environment which is more accepting of sexual behavior among elderly persons, one must be aware of the fact that for old and young persons, attitudes as well as incentives influence sexual activity. Perhaps in some instances the attitudes, themselves, may be essentially adaptive. For example, the number of single women over 65 far exceeds the number of men available as sexual partners and many of these women adopt an attitude of waning sexual interest. While some solutions such as polygamous marriages have been advanced (Berezin, 1969), it appears more realistic to concentrate efforts on prolonging the life span of men (Pfeiffer and Davis, 1972) and on modifying attitudes towards sexual expression. Attitude modifications may provide increased incentive for engaging in sexual activities dictated by sexual drive.

Finally, it should be noted that decline in sexual interest and behavior with advancing age is not an isolated psychological phenomenon that can be reduced to simple questions of motivation and attitude. Rather, it is related to the whole life social-psychological situation. For example, Butler (1967) reported that many elderly persons are involved in deteriorating marriages which may be the result of many factors including rejection, fear or anger concerning physical and mental changes in self and spouse, fear that sexual relations will bring on heart attacks or strokes, and resentment of the social admonition to "grow old gracefully." All of these psychological factors represent a severe withdrawal of the personal incentives to engage in sexual relations. Attempts to restore incentives can only be accomplished on an individual basis which includes a consideration of the aging person's entire life situation. Investigations in this area must be done in the context of social theories of motivation which emphasize complex life forces and social value systems.

ACTIVITY, WORK, AND LEISURE

In contrast to animal research which has concentrated heavily on general decrease in psychomotor activity as a result of functional changes with age, human studies of activity have been concerned with the social psychological factors involved in the substitution of some activities for others. At the infrahuman level, concern centers about physical activity. At the human level, decline in psychomotor activity level appears to be an accepted generalization. The major issues involve the qualitative and quantitative changes in social activities. This literature is far too extensive to deal with in any detail in this chapter. It has been reviewed in texts and papers falling in the general category of sociology or social-psychological studies of aging. Thus, only a summary of the most relevant conclusions is presented.

The notion that older subjects are motivated to decrease a broad range of activities has not received much support (Yarrow, Blank, Quinn, Youmans, and Stein, 1963; Lehr and Rudinger, 1969; Palmore, 1968; Youmans and Yarrow, 1971; Maddox, 1968). Given good health and opportunity, some type of activity is almost always associated with greater life satisfaction, although the repertoire of activities changes considerably as the person ages (Havighurst, Neugarten, and Tobin, 1964; Palmore, 1968; Lipman and Smith, 1968). Even after retirement, aging is characterized by substitution of activities by choice and necessity rather than a diminuation of a wide range of activities (Maddox, 1968; Dawson and Baller, 1972; Hearn, 1972). General decline in activity, when it occurs, is often dictated by poor health or economic constraints (Youmans, 1968; Tissue, 1971; Sherman, 1974).

CONCLUSIONS

There has been little in the way of integration of human and animal research in aging and motivation. In part, this state of affairs is related to the fact that motivational factors of importance are quite different for verbal and nonverbal animals. It is not possible, for ethical and moral reasons, to manipulate deprivation schedules and aversive motivational stimuli in human studies. Moreover, for many persons, complex social motivations are often more important determinants of everyday behavior than are basic physiological needs.

Despite the advantages of animals for studies of deprivation and aversive stimuli, animal research has not taken full opportunity of the special advantages offered by the animal model for the manipulation of life history variables. The generality of many animal studies is limited by failure to provide information about genotype. Many studies used only a single inbred strain of mice or rats, limiting general conclusions to be made and failing to allow capitalization on the possibilities for assessing genotype-environment interactions and behavior genetic techniques (Bailey, 1971; Elias and Eleftheriou, 1972; Elias and Schlager, 1974; Elias, Elias and Schlager, 1975; Manosevitz, Lindzey, and Thiessen, 1969; Henderson, 1969).

Expansion of research to include infrahuman species other than rats and mice may be of value in the construction of ontological models based on the study of phylogenetic similarities and differences. Increased use of primates in manipulative studies would constitute an important step toward better understanding of aging and social-motivational factors such as sex drive, fear, frustration, and play.

Despite limitations in the use of the animal model, several generalizations of importance have evolved from the animal literature. Weight loss appears to be a better way to equate hunger deprivation conditions across age groups than are amount of food and water consumed following deprivation, days of deprivation, latency to eat, and activity level. The basic problem with activity level is that activity itself influences drive in a feedback relationship.

A frequently replicated finding is that locomotor activity decreases with advancing age after sexual maturity has been reached, but a significant decrement does not occur until senility. However, increases and decreases in activity occur between weaning and postadolescence, and thus it is important to compare a range of ages rather than extremely young and old animals.

Exploratory behavior, emotionality, and locomotor activity in the open field are not always related in the same manner at different ages. Consequently, it is important to obtain separate measures of these variables, and all three should never be inferred from the locomotion score. Decreased exploratory behavior has been reported in some strains of rats and mice, but not others. Basic problems exist with regard to the measurement of emotionality and exploratory behavior.

It is not clear yet as to whether or not aversive stimuli are equally motivating for all age groups. A particularly interesting finding is that old and young animal subjects, even rodents, will perform in order to produce a change in level of stimulation.

Research with sex drives in animals has concentrated on the identification of the physiological bases of this decline; however, indirect evidence exists that early experience variables can affect various components of sexual activity with advancing age.

A number of rather firm generalizations about motivation and aging may also be gleaned from the human literature. We have learned that too much motivation can be as bad as too little, and that overinvolvement or overarousal resulting in a heightened drive state may impair performance for the elderly relative to the young. Thus, cognitive factors do not *necessarily* account for age differences in laboratory performance. Older subjects may be more cautious or more threatened and aroused by laboratory tasks. In some instances laboratory tasks may have less meaning for elderly subjects. However, data do not provide consistent support for these propositions, and quite clearly they do not hold for all older subjects or in all situations. One difficulty encountered in manipulating the meaningfulness of stimulus materials is that task difficulty often varies with changes in stimulus materials. Caution is difficult to separate from decreased competence. Reduction in task pacing often makes the task less difficult. Thus, further experiments are necessary to resolve issues of task difficulty and task meaningfulness, and many more studies need to be concentrated on individual differences in cautiousness behavior and their relationship to functional rather than chronological indices of age.

Research on sexual drive has concentrated on psychosocial factors as opposed to hormonal factors. It is quite clear that for many older persons, competence continues long after activity ceases. The best predictor of sexual activity and interest in old age is sexual activity and interest at a younger age. There are, of course, other determinants of continued sexual activities. Two of the most important predictors of continued activity for men are health and socioeconomic status, while for women marital status seems to be the best predictor of continued sexual activity. Often sexual activity falls drastically for women after their husbands die. Limited choice of mates, decreased number of men in the population, decreased mobility, and society's attitudes toward sex among unmarried individuals, particularly elderly individuals, are among the factors that preclude the resumption of sexual activities for elderly widows.

In general, animal and human research has forced a realization that age differences in a variety of human activities may be related to motivation rather than intellectual or physiological competence. Hopefully, then, researchers in areas such as learning, perception, cognitive processes, and social interactions will become increasingly sensitive to the need to control for unequal levels of motivation across age groups and to account for age-related motivational differences in the interpretation of their data.

REFERENCES

Anderson, J. E., and Smith, H. H. 1932. Relation of performance to age and nutritive condition in the white rat. *J. Comp. Psychol., 13,* 409–446.

Antliff, H. R., and Young, W. C. 1957. Internal secretory capacity of the abdominal testis in the guinea pig. *Endocrinology, 61,* 121–127.

Arenberg, D. 1965. Anticipation interval and age differences in verbal learning. *J. Abnorm. Psychol., 70,* 419–425.

Bailey, D. W. 1971. Recombinant inbred strains. *Transplantation, 11,* 404–407.

Barrett, R. J., and Ray, O. S. 1970. Behavior in the open field, Lashley III Maze, Shuttle-Box, and Sidman avoidance as a function of strain, sex and age. *Developmental Psychology, 3,* 73–77.

Berezin, M. A. 1969. Sex and old age: A review of the liturature. *Journal of Geriatric Psychiatry, 2,* 131–149.

Bernstein, S., and Mason, W. A. 1962. The effects of age and stimulus conditions on the emotional responses of rhesus monkeys: Responses to complex stimuli. *Journal of Genetic Psychology, 101,* 279–298.

Birren, J. E. 1955. Age differences in startle reaction time of the rat to noise and electric shock. *J. Gerontol., 10,* 438–440.

Birren, J. E., and Kay, H. 1958. Swimming speed of the albino rat: I. Age and sex differences. *J. Gerontol., 13,* 374–377.

Bitterman, M. E. 1960. Toward a comparative psychology of learning. *American Psychologist, 15,* 704–712.

Bolles, R. C. 1967. *Theory of Motivation.* New York: Harper & Row.

Botwinick, J. 1959. Drives, expectancies and emotions. *In,* J. E. Birren (ed.), *Handbook of Aging and the Individual,* pp. 739–768. Chicago: University of Chicago Press.

Botwinick, J., Brinley, J. F., and Robbin, J. S. 1958. The interaction effects of perceptual difficulty and stimulus exposure time on age differences in speed and accuracy of response. *Gerontologia, 2,* 1–9.

Botwinick, J., Brinley, J. F., and Robbin, J. S. 1959. Further results concerning the effect of motivation by electrical shocks on reaction-time in relation to age. *Amer. J. Psych., 72,* 140.

Botwinick, J., Jerome, E. A., Birren, J. E., and Brinley, J. F. 1957. Light aversion motivation in psychologic studies of aging in rats. *J. Gerontol., 12,* 296–299.

Bourlière, F. 1947. Quelques caractéristiques physiologiques de la sénescence chez le rat. *Rev. Canad. de Biol., 6,* 245–259.

Braun, H. W., and Geiselhart, R. 1959. Age differences in the acquisition and extinction of the conditioned eyelid response. *J. Exp. Psych., 57,* 386–388.

Broadhurst, P. L. 1961. Analysis of maternal effects in the inheritance of behavior. *Animal Behav., 9,* 129–141.

Browman, L. G. 1942. The effect of bilateral optic enucleation on the voluntary muscular activity of the albino rat. *J. Exp. Zoöl., 91,* 331–334.

Butler, R. N. 1967. Research and clinical observations on the psychologic reactions to physical changes with age. *Mayo Clin. Proc., 42,* 596–619.

Calhoun, J. B. 1946. Twenty-four hour periodicities in the animal kingdom: Part II. The vertebrates. *J. Tennessee Acad. Sci., 20,* 373–378.

Cameron, P., and Biber, H. 1973. Sexual thought throughout the life-span. *Gerontologist, 13,* 144–147.

Campbell, B. A. 1967. Developmental studies of learning and motivation in infra-primate mammals. *In,* H. W. Stevenson, E. H. Hess and H. L. Rheingold (eds.), *Early Behavior: Comparative and Developmental Approaches,* pp. 43–71. New York: John Wiley.

Campbell, B. A., Teghtsoonian, A. R., and Williams, R. A. 1961. Activity, weight loss, and survival time of food-deprived rats as a function of age. *J. Comp. Physiol. Psychol., 54,* 216–219.

Capaldi, E. J., and Robinson, D. E. 1960. Performance and consummatory behavior in the runway and maze as a function of cyclic deprivation. *J. Comp. Physiol. Psychol., 53,* 159–164.

Christenson, C. V., and Gagnon, J. H. 1965. Sexual behavior in a group of older women. *J. Gerontol., 20,* 351–356.

Collins, R. L. 1966. What else does the defecation score measure? *Proceedings of the Annual Meeting of the American Psychological Association, 2,* 147–148.

Craik, F. I. M., and Masani, P. A. 1967. Age differences in the temporal integration of language. *Brit. J. Psychol., 58,* 291–299.

Dawson, A. M., and Baller, W. R. 1972. Relationship between creative activity and the health of elderly persons. *J. Psychol., 82,* 49–58.

Doty, B. A., and O'Hare, K. M. 1966. Interactions of shock intensity, age and handling effects on avoidance conditioning. *Perceptual Motor Skills, 23,* 1311–1314.

Duffy, E. 1957. The psychological significance of the concept of "arousal" or "activation." *Psyc. Rev., 64,* 265–275.

Eisdorfer, C. 1966. New dimensions and a tentative

theory. A paper presented at the Symposium: Learning and memory. 19th Annual Meeting, Gerontological Society, New York.

Eisdorfer, C. 1968. Arousal and performance: Experiments in verbal learning and a tentative theory. *In,* G. A. Talland (ed.), *Human Aging and Behavior,* pp. 189–216. New York: Academic Press.

Eisdorfer, C., Axelrod, S., and Wilkie, F. L. 1963. Stimulus exposure time as a factor in serial learning in an aged sample. *J. Abn. Soc. Psychol.,* 67, 594–600.

Eisdorfer, C., Conner, J. F., and Wilkie, F. L. 1968. The effect of magnesium pemoline on cognition and behavior. *J. Gerontol.,* 23, 283–288.

Eisdorfer, C., Nowlin, J., and Wilkie, F. 1970. Improvement of learning in the aged by modification of autonomic nervous system activity. *Science,* 170, 1327–1329.

Eleftheriou, B. E. 1974. Changes with age in pituitary adrenal responsiveness and reactivity to mild stress in mice. *Gerontologia,* 20, 224–230.

Elias, J. W., Elias, M. F., and Schlager, G. 1975. Aggressive social interaction in mice selected for blood pressure extremes. *Behavioral Biology,* 13, 155–166.

Elias, M. F. 1965. The relation of drive of finger-withdrawal conditioning. *J. Exp. Psych.,* 70, 109–116.

Elias, M. F., and Eleftheriou, B. E. 1972. Reversal learning and RNA labeling in neurological mutant mice and normal littermates. *Physiol. Behav.,* 9, 27–34.

Elias, M. F., and Eleftheriou, B. E. 1975a. A genetic analysis of water maze discrimination learning for *Mus musculus:* Polygenes and albinism. *Physiol. Behav.,* 14, 833–838.

Elias, M. F., and Eleftheriou, B. E. 1975b. Separating measures of learning and incentive in water maze experiments with aging inbred strains of mice. *Psych. Reports,* 36, 343–351.

Elias, M. F., and Eleftheriou, B. E. 1975c. A genetic analysis of simple water escape behavior: Test of a major gene hypothesis. *Physiol. Behav.,* 15, 737–740.

Elias, M. F., and Elias, P. K. 1975. Hormones, aging and behavior in aging mammals. *In,* B. E. Eleftheriou and R. E. Sprott (eds.), *Hormones Correlates of Behavior,* pp. 395–439. New York: Plenum Press.

Elias, M. F., and Schlager, G. 1974. Discrimination learning in mice genetically selected for high and low blood pressure. Initial findings and methodological implications. *Physiol. Behav.,* 13, 261–267.

Elias, P. K., Elias, M. F., and Eleftheriou, B. E. 1975. Emotionality, exploratory behavior, and locomotion in aging inbred strains of mice. *Gerontologia,* 21, 46–55.

Festing, M. F. W. 1974. Water escape learning in mice. III. A diallel study. *Behavior Genetics,* 4, 111–124.

Finch, C. E., and Girgis, F. G. 1974. Enlarged seminal vesicles of senescent C57BL/6J mice. *J. Gerontol.,* 29, 134–138.

Finkle, A. L., Tobenkin, MI., and Karg, S. J. 1959. Sexual potency in aging males: I. Frequency of coitus among clinic patients. *J. Am. Med. Assoc.,* 170, 113–115.

Goodrick, C. L. 1965. Social interactions and exploration of young, mature, and senescent male rats. *J. Gerontol.,* 20, 215–218.

Goodrick, C. L. 1966. Activity and exploration as a function of age and deprivation. *Journal of Genetic Psychology,* 108, 239–252.

Goodrick, C. L. 1967. Exploration of nondeprived male Sprague-Dawley rats as a function of age. *Psych. Reports,* 20, 159–163.

Goodrick, C. L. 1970. Light and dark-contingent bar pressing in the rat as a function of age and motivation. *J. Comp. Physiol. Psychol.,* 73, 100–104.

Goodrick, C. L. 1971. Variables affecting free exploration responses of male and female Wistar rats as a function of age. *Developmental Psychology,* 4, 440–446.

Harlow, H. F. 1950. Learning and satiation of response in intrinsically motivated complex puzzle performance by monkeys. *J. Comp. Physiol. Psychol.,* 43, 289–294.

Havighurst, R. J., Neugarten, B. L., and Tobin, S. S. 1964. Disengagement, personality and life-satisfaction in the later years. *In,* P. F. Hansen (ed.), *Age with a Future.* Copenhagen: Munksgaard.

Hearn, H. L. 1972. Aging and the artistic career. *Gerontologist,* 12, 357–362.

Henderson, N. D. 1969. Prior treatment effects on open field behavior of mice: a genetic analysis. *In,* M. Manosevitz, G. Lindzey and D. Thiessen (eds.), *Behavioral Genetics: Methods and Research.* New York: Appleton-Century-Crofts.

Huggins, C., and Clark, P. J. 1940. Quantitative studies of prostatic secretion II. The effect of castration estrogen injection on the normal and on the hyperplastic prostate glands of dogs. *J. Exp. Med.,* 72, 746–761.

Hügin, V. F., and Verzár, F. 1957. Versagen der Warmeregulation bei alter Tieren. *Gerontologia,* 1, 96–106.

Hunt, H. F., and Otis, L. S. 1953. Conditioned and unconditioned emotional defecation in the rat. *J. Comp. Physiol. Psychol.,* 46, 378–382.

Hunt, J. McV., and Schlosberg, H. 1939. The influence of illumination upon general activity in normal, blinded and castrated male white rats. *J. Comp. Physiol. Psychol.,* 28, 285–298.

Jakubczak, L. F. 1963. The physiological determinants of age differences in behavioral control of body temperature. *American Psychologist,* 18, 324.

Jakubczak, L. F. 1964. Effects of testosterone propionate on age differences in mating behavior. *J. Gerontol.,* 19, 458–461.

Jakubczak, L. F. 1966. Behavioral thermoregulation in young and old rats. *J. Appl. Physiol.,* 21, 19–21.

Jakubczak, L. F. 1967a. Age, endocrines and behavior.

In, L. Gitman (ed.), *Endocrines and Aging,* pp. 1–15. Springfield, Illinois: Charles C. Thomas.

Jakubczak, L. F. 1967b. Age differences in the effects of terminal food deprivation (starvation) on activity, weight loss and survival of rats. *J. Gerontol., 22,* 421–426.

Jakubczak, L. F. 1969. Effects of age and activity restriction on body weight loss of rats. *Am. J. Physiol.,* **216** (5), 1081–1083.

Jakubczak, L. F. 1970a. Age differences in the effects of water deprivation on activity, water loss and survival of rats. *Life Sci.,* 9, 771–780.

Jakubczak, L. F. 1970b. Age, food deprivation and the temporal distribution of wheel running of rats. Proceedings, 78th Annual Convention, *American Psychological Association,* 689–690.

Jakubczak, L. F. 1973a. Frequency, duration, and speed of wheel running of rats as a function of age and starvation. *Animal Learn. Behav.,* **1,** 13–16.

Jakubczak, L. F. 1973b. Age differences in caloric-density preference as a function of strain of rats. *Bull. Psychon. Soc.,* **1,** 395–396.

Jerome, E. A. 1959. Age and learning-experimental studies. *In,* J. E. Birren (ed.), *Handbook of Aging and the Individual,* pp. 655–699. Chicago: University of Chicago Press.

Jones, D. C., Kimeldorf, D. J., Rubadeau, D. O., and Castanera, T. J. 1953. Relationships between volitional activity and age in the male rat. *Am. J. Physiol.,* **172,** 109–114.

Kahn, E., and Fisher, C. 1969. REM sleep and sexuality in the aged. *Journal of Geriatric Psychiatly,* **2,** 181–199.

Kay, H., and Birren, J. E. 1958. Swimming speed of the albino rat II. Fatigue, practice, and drug effects on age and sex differences. *J. Gerontol.,* 13, 378–385.

Kimble, G. A., and Pennypacker, H. S. 1963. Eyelid conditioning in young and aged subjects. *Journal of Genetic Psychology,* **103,** 283–289.

Kinsey, A. C., Pomeroy, W. B., and Martin, C. R. 1948. *Sexual Behavior in the Human Male.* Philadelphia: Saunders.

Kleiber, M., Smith, A. H., and Chernikoff, H. N. 1956. Metabolic rate of female rats as a function of age and body size. *Am. J. Physiol.,* **186,** 9–12.

Korenchevsky, F. 1961. *Physiological and Pathological Aging.* New York: Hafner; Basel: Karger.

Lacey, J. I., and Van Lehn, R. 1952. Differential emphasis and somatic responding to stress: an experimental study. *Psychosomat. Med.,* **14,** 71–81.

Larsson, K. 1956. Conditioning and sexual behavior in the male albino rat. *Acta Psychologia Gothoburgensia,* pp. 77–100 Stockholm: Almgvist & Wiksell.

Lehr, U., and Rudinger, G. 1969. Consistency and change of social participation in old age. *Hum. Develop.,* **12,** 255–267.

Less, E. S. 1969 . Effect of pasturized diet on the lifespan of inbred mice. Paper presented at the Twentieth Annual Meeting of the American Association for Laboratory Animal Science, Dallas, Texas. (Paper in preparation for *Laboratory Animal Science.*)

Lipman. A., and Smith, K. J. 1968. Functionality of disengagement in old age. *J. Gerontol., 23,* 517–521.

Lockard, R. 1963. Some effects of light on the behavior of rodents. *Psych. Bull., 60,* 509–529.

Lockwood, R. 1975. Social organization in captive wolves: A dyadic and pack analysis of cohesive and divisive behaviors. Unpublished doctoral dissertation, Washington University, St. Louis, Missouri.

Lowenthal, M. F. 1968. Social isolation and mental illness in old age. *In,* B. L. Neugarten (ed.), *Middle Age and Aging,* pp. 220–234. Chicago: University of Chicago Press.

Maddox, G. L. 1968. Persistence of life-style among the elderly: A longitudinal study of patterns of social activity in relation to life satisfaction. *In,* B. L. Neugarter (ed.), *Middle Age and Aging,* pp. 181–183. Chicago: University of Chicago Press.

Manosevitz, M., Lindzey, G., and Thiessen, D. (eds.) 1969. *Behavioral Genetics: Methods and Research.* New York: Appleton-Century-Crofts.

Margolin, S. E., and Bunch, M. E. 1940. The relationship between age and the strength of hunger motivation. *Comp. Psychol. Monogr.,* **16,** 1–34.

Masters, W. H., and Johnson, V. E. 1966. *Human Sexual Response.* Boston: Little, Brown.

Newman, G., and Nichols, C. R. 1960. Sexual activities and attitudes in older persons. *J. Am. Med. Assoc., 173,* 33–35.

Palmore, E. B. 1968. The effects of aging on activities and attitudes. *Gerontologist, 8,* 259–263.

Paré, W. P. 1969. Interaction of age and shock intensity on acquisition of a discrminated conditioned emotional response. *J. Comp. Physiol. Psychol., 68,* 364–369.

Pfeiffer, E. 1969. Sexual behavior in old age. *In,* E. W. Busse and E. Pfeiffer (eds.), *Behavior and Adaptation in Late Life.* Boston: Little, Brown.

Pfeiffer, E. 1974. Sexuality in the aging individual. Paper presented as part of the Symposium on Sexuality in the Aging Individual at the 31st Annual Meeting of the American Geriatric Society, Toronto, Canada.

Pfeiffer, E., and Davis, G. C. 1972. Determinants of sexual behavior in middle and old age. *J. Amer. Geriat. Soc., 20,* 151–158.

Powell, A. H., Eisdorfer, C., and Bogdonoff, M. D. 1964. Physiologic response patterns observed in a learning task. *Arch. Gen. Psychiat., 10,* 192–195.

Raymond, C. K., Carlton, P. L., and McAllister, W. R. 1955. Feeding method, body weight, and performance in instrumental learning. *J. Comp. Physiol. Psychol., 48,* 294–298.

Reid, L. S., and Finger, F. W. 1957. The effect of activity restriction upon adjustment to cyclic food deprivation. *J. Comp. Physiol. Psychol., 59,* 491–494.

Richter, C. P. 1922. A behavioristic study of the activity of the rat. *Comp. Psychol. Monogr., 1,* 1–55.

Rosow, I. 1968. Housing and local ties of the aged. *In,*

B. L. Neugarten (ed.), *Middle Age and Aging*, pp. 382–389. Chicago: University of Chicago Press.

Sherman, S. R. 1974. Leisure activities in retirement housing. *J. Gerontol., 29*, 325–335.

Shirley, M. 1928. Studies in activity. II. Activity rhythms, age, and activity: activity after rest. *J. Comp. Psychol., 8*, 159–186.

Shmavonian, B. M., and Busse, E. W. 1963. The utilization of psycho-physiological techniques in the study of the aged. *In*, R. H. Williams, C. Tibbetts and W. Donahue (eds.), *Process of Aging Social and Psychological Perspectives*, pp. 160–183. New York: Atherton Press.

Slonaker, J. R. 1970. The normal activity of the white rat at different ages. *J. Comp. Neurol. Psychol., 17*, 342–359.

Spence, K. W. 1958. A theory of emotionally based drive (D) and its relation to performance in simple learning situations. *American Psychologist, 13*, 131–141.

Spence, K. W. 1964. Anxiety (drive) level and performance in eyelid conditioning. *Psych. Bull., 61*, 129–139.

Sprott, R. L. 1967. Barometric pressure fluctuations: effects on the activity of laboratory mice. *Science, 157*, 1206–1207.

Sprott, R. L., and Eleftheriou, B. E. 1974. Open field behavior in aging inbred mice. *Gerontologia, 20*, 155–160.

Storer, J. B. 1966. Longevity and gross pathology at death in 22 inbred mouse strains. *J. Gerontol., 21*, 404–409.

Tepperman, J. 1973. *Metabolic and Endocrine Physiology*. 3rd Edition. Chicago: Yearbook Medical.

Timiras, P. S., and Meisami, E. 1972. Changes in gonadal function. *In*, P. S. Timiras (ed.), *Developmental Physiology and Aging*, pp. 527–541. New York: Macmillan.

Tissue, T. 1971. Disengagement potential: Replication and use as an explanatory variable. *J. Gerontol., 26*, 76–80.

Troyer, W. G., Eisdorfer, C., Bogdonoff, M. D., and Wilkie, F. L. 1967. Experimental stress and learning in the aged. *J. Abnorm. Psychol., 72*, 65–70.

Troyer, W. G., Eisdorfer, C., Wilkie, F. L., and Bogdonoff, M. D. 1966. Free fatty acid responses in the aged individual during performance of learning tasks. *J. Gerontol., 21*, 415–419.

Verwoerdt, A., Pfeiffer, E., and Wang, H. S. 1969a. Sexual behavior in senescence. I. Changes in sexual activity and interest of aging men and women. *Journal of Geriatric Psychiatry, 2*, 163–180.

Verwoerdt, A., Pfeiffer, E., and Wang, H. S. 1969b. Sexual behavior in senescence. II. Patterns of sexual activity and interest. *Geriatrics, 24*, 137–154.

Werboff, J. 1962. Reply to "comment on 'effects of aging on open field behavior'. " *Psych. Reports, 10*, 862.

Werboff, J., and Havlena, J. 1962. Effects on aging on open field behavior. *Psych. Reports, 10*, 395–398.

Winston, H. D., and Lindzey, G. 1964. Albinism and water escape performance in the mouse. *Science, 144*, 189–191.

Wittels, I. 1972. Age and stimulus meaningfulness in paired-associate learning. *J. Gerontol., 27*, 372–375.

Wood, V. 1971. Age-appropriate behavior for older people. *Gerontologist, 11*, 74–78.

Wright, W. E., Werboff, J., and Haggett, B. N. 1971. Aging and water submersion in C57BL/6J mice: Initial performance and retest as a function of recovery and water temperature. *Develop. Psychobiol., 4*, 363–373.

Yarrow, M. R., Blank, P., Quinn, Q. W., Youmans, E. G., and Stein, J. 1963. Social psychological characteristics of old age. *In*, J. E. Birren, R. N. Butler, S. W. Greenhouse, L. Sokoloff and M. R. Yarrow (eds.), *Human Aging: A Biological and Behavioral Study* (USPHS Publ. No. 986.). Washington, D.C.: Public Health Service.

Youmans, E. G. 1968. Objective and subjective economic disengagement among older rural and urban men. *J. Gerontol., 21*, 439–441.

Youmans, E. G., and Yarrow, M. 1971. Aging and social adaptation: A longitudinal study of healthy old men. *In*, S. Granick and R. D. Patterson (eds.), *Human Aging II: An Eleven-year Follow-up Biomedical and Behavioral Study*, pp. 95–103. U.S. Department of Health, Education, and Welfare, Publ. No. (HSM) 71-9037.

Young, W. C. 1961. The hormones and mating behavior. *In*, W. C. Young (ed.), *Sex and Internal Secretions*. Baltimore: Williams & Wilkins.

17
AGE DIFFERENCES IN HUMAN MEMORY

Fergus I. M. Craik
University of Toronto

INTRODUCTION

This chapter is concerned with experimental studies of adult age differences in human memory, and the implications of these studies for theories of memory and aging. While the major focus is on "normal" aging, examples are also drawn from the literature on the psychopathology of memory and from the literature on child development; experimental studies on animals are not covered in this review. Also, the focus is on behavioral studies and theories, although implications for the neurophysiology of brain function will be pointed out. Finally, the work described is drawn largely from research published in the last 15 or 20 years.

The years 1958 and 1959 were important ones for students of memory and aging. In 1959, the first handbook on the behavioral aspects of aging was published (*Handbook of Aging and the Individual*, edited by J. E. Birren), and the chapters by Kay and Jerome provide excellent summaries of the literature up to that time. Also, 1958 saw the publication of Broadbent's *Perception and Communication* and Welford's *Ageing and Human Skill*, two

*The author is most grateful for helpful comments on a previous draft from David Schonfield, George Schlotterer, Morris Moscovitch and Betty Ann Levy. He also gratefully acknowledges technical help from Sharon White and Eileen Simon.

extremely influential books describing experiments and theories in the information-processing tradition. In the mid-1970's, human experimental psychology is dominated by information-processing ideas; thus 1958 was something of a watershed, marking the beginnings of information-processing ideas as a major force, and also dividing, to some extent, earlier work in the Gestalt and S-R traditions from later work conducted in the information-processing framework. Naturally, much excellent work in human learning and memory has continued in the S-R tradition since 1958, and many studies of the aging process have been carried out within the S-R framework. It is the case, however, that information-processing notions have grown in importance over the last 20 years and these notions form the principal theoretical orientation of the present chapter.

Running parallel to the change in emphasis from S-R to information-processing theories, there has been a change in emphasis from studies of learning to studies of memory. Within the general framework of S-R theories, human learning and retention have been described and analyzed in terms of interference theory (e.g., Postman, 1961; Postman and Underwood, 1973); this theory focuses attention on the hypothesized association between stimuli and responses (or, at least, between their internal representations). Thus, empirical work in this tradition has been directed toward elucidating the factors relevant to the acquisition and breakdown of the associative bond; "learning" is the formation of new associations and "forgetting" is their loss or inhibition. In human learning, much of the experimental work has used the paired-associate paradigm in which stimuli and responses are verbal units—numbers, letters, words or nonsense syllables; short lists of such stimulus-response pairs are typically presented for several learning trials and this acquisition phase is then followed by a task to measure retention or transfer. By way of contrast, information-processing studies of memory have more often involved situations in which the material to be learned is presented for one trial only—the focus has thus been on factors which affect the subject's *memory* for once-presented events: factors concerned with registration, storage and retrieval of the events.

While plainly the processes of "learning" and "memory" must rely on the same underlying mechanism—they are different aspects of one basic phenomenon—it is conceptually useful to distinguish them. Thus "learning" may be thought of as referring to the acquisition of general rules and knowledge about the world, while "memory" refers to the retention of specific events which occurred at a given time in a given place. We have learned that Paris is the capital of France, that $8 \times 9 = 72$, that our telephone number is 864-2968—the time and place of learning is not important for our utilization of these pieces of knowledge. On the other hand, time and place is of the essence when we recall a specific incident—who was at the party last Saturday or what we were doing on July 7, 1973. In this sense, acquiring the knowledge that 5 and BEJ go together in a paired-associate list may be considered "learning" although the learning is specific to a certain situation (the experimental laboratory), just as the pairs DOG-CHIEN and DOG-HUND are specific to French and German contexts respectively. This distinction between the retention of general rules and the retention of events was made by Tulving (1972) under the respective headings of "semantic" and "episodic" memory. These two aspects of learning

and memory should not be considered separate memory systems—what we store about a specific event must depend on our perception and interpretation of what took place, and that in turn depends on semantic memory; nevertheless the distinctions between semantic and episodic memory and between "learning" and "memory" are conceptually useful ones.

To summarize, this chapter reviews experimental studies of age differences in memory—where memory is defined as the retention of specific incidents and events. The work is largely described and interpreted within the framework of information-processing views of memory. However, since that general framework has evolved rapidly and contains many confusing and sometimes contradictory details, some space will be taken up outlining current views on memory, before the work on aging is described.

MODELS OF MEMORY

Three-Stage Models

The essential aspects of the three-stage model were discussed by Murdock (1967)—his "modal model" is shown in Figure 1. Information is received and transduced by the senses and is then held briefly in one of several modality-specific sensory stores—for example, auditory information is held in an auditory sensory store ("echoic memory"), visual information is held in a visual sensory store ("iconic memory") and so on. If the information is retrieved from sensory storage by the attention process before it is lost by decay or is overwritten by subsequent stimuli, it is passed on to short-term memory—a limited-capacity store in which verbal stimuli are held in terms of their auditory or articulatory features. Further rehearsal of the stimuli has the effect of transferring information about the items to a relatively permanent long-term store.

The arguments for distinguishing among three discrete stages in memory have usually been framed in terms of differences in (a) capacity, (b) encoding characteristics and (c) the rate and mechanism of forgetting. With regard to the sensory memories, the notion of capacity has not been well defined, and it is

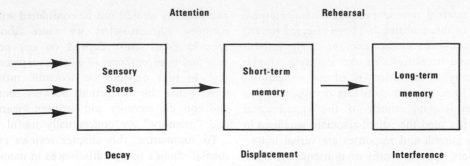

Figure 1. A generalized three-stage model of memory. (From Murdock, 1967.)

even doubtful whether "capacity" is a valid metaphor in this case. In one classic experiment, Sperling (1960) found a capacity of 9.1 letters in visual sensory memory, but that figure may depend on task-specific factors. It is clear that encoding at the sensory stage is modality-specific—the idea is that these stores hold relatively "raw" copies of the impinging patterns. The dominant characteristic of sensory traces is their very rapid forgetting rate—from 1/3 second to 1 second for iconic storage (e.g., Haber, 1970; Neisser, 1967) and about 2 seconds for echoic memory (Crowder and Morton, 1969; Neisser, 1967); the mechanism of forgetting is usually presumed to be spontaneous decay or overwriting by subsequent stimuli (Neisser, 1967).

In the late 1950's and early 1960's, short-term memory was characterized as a limited-capacity store, in which verbal items were coded acoustically; items were lost either by decay (Brown, 1958) or by a process of active displacement (Waugh and Norman, 1965) over a period of approximately 20–30 seconds (Peterson and Peterson, 1959). By contrast, long-term memory was thought of as having no capacity limitations; it was postulated that items in this store were encoded semantically (Baddeley, 1966) and forgetting was attributed either to interference (e.g., Postman, 1961) or to loss of accessibility—a failure of retrieval (Tulving and Pearlstone, 1966). The dichotomy between short-term memory (STM) and long-term memory (LTM) was further supported by reports of clinical cases in which one memory system is apparently normal while the other is grossly deficient (Milner, 1970; Warrington and Shallice, 1972).

However, Melton (1963) took issue with the "dual-process" view of memory. He opposed the dichotomy on the grounds that the same phenomena are found in short-term and long-term memory situations; if the systems share the same characteristics, what is the point in treating them as separate? Waugh and Norman provided an answer in 1965. They suggested that Melton (and most other theorists at the time) had confused the notions of short-term *retention* with a postulated short-term *mechanism*. While it had been assumed that items held for a few seconds or minutes were necessarily retrieved from the short-term store, Waugh and Norman suggested that information could be copied into the permanent memory system rather rapidly, while it was also maintained in the short-term stage. This means that information about an item can reside in both systems and that, even a short time after presentation, recall performance will reflect the characteristics of both stores. In this way, Waugh and Norman argued that while Melton's examples dealt with "short-term memory" (in terms of the task or the retention interval) the information was being drawn in part from the long-term store, and thus classic learning and interference effects were reflected in performance. Waugh and Norman thus proposed that the notion of two stages was a viable one, but that the characteristics of the short-term stage should be defined more precisely. In particular, the definition must be in terms of the *processes* carried out, not in terms of the retention interval or the experimental paradigm. Thus it is no longer satisfactory to state that retention over 30 seconds, or recall of a 20-word list reflects "short-term memory"; even immediate retention can involve a "long-term" component by Waugh and Norman's argument. To avoid confusions with previous concepts, they termed the initial stage "primary memory" and the subsequent stage "secondary memory." Items in primary memory are still in conscious awareness; they may be maintained in primary memory by a process of rehearsal and this process also serves to transfer information about the items to the more commodious and permanent secondary memory system. Defined in this way, primary memory holds only 2–4 verbal items (see Watkins, 1974 for a review), but this fragment of memory is extremely important as it serves a crucial control function for information, both during its registration into the main memory system (secondary memory) and during its retrieval from that system. Primary memory may thus be viewed more as a temporary holding and organizing *process* than as a structured memory *store*.

These notions have been described in some detail for two reasons: (a) the primary memory/secondary memory (PM/SM) distinction serves an important clarifying role in understanding the current literature on memory research, and (b) in the aging literature the results from several paradigms loosely defined as testing "short-term memory" can be better understood in the light of the PM/SM distinction. For example, many findings suggest that PM functioning is unimpaired in the elderly (provided that the material does not require reorganization) but that there are age decrements in SM. Thus to the extent that a "short-term memory" task reflects PM functioning only (e.g., digit and word span), no age decrements will be observed; to the extent that short-term retention involves a large SM component (e.g., the immediate free recall of a supra-span list of words) older subjects will perform less well.

To summarize, the literature on age differences in memory will be examined within the framework of current information-processing models of memory. By and large, these models involve three discrete stages in mnemonic processing: a modality-specific sensory memory stage followed by primary memory (or short-term store) and then by secondary memory (or long-term store). Results from the aging litera-

ture will be interpreted as demonstrating integrity or impairment of the three stages, the transfer of information from one stage to the next and the registration and retrieval processes associated with each stage. However, since most studies were conducted in the context of a specific *problem* (e.g., are older subjects more vulnerable to interference effects in memory?) or in the setting of a specific experimental paradigm (e.g., dichotic listening) the literature will be organized under headings of problems and paradigms, although findings will be interpreted in the light of the three-stage model.

SHORT-TERM RETENTION

Sensory Memory

Visual sensory memory ("iconic memory") has been investigated by means of several techniques. Sperling (1960) exposed a 3 × 4 array of digits or letters for 50 milliseconds and then, at various times after stimulus offset, cued the recall of one row only, by means of an auditory tone. The subject's ability to reproduce the row declined rapidly over 300–500 milliseconds after stimulus offset and Sperling attributed this result to the rapid decay of a visual sensory trace. Using a different procedure, Haber (1970) also concluded that the visual trace decays in about 250 milliseconds. While Haber's results are thus in agreement with those of Sperling, a further technique developed by Posner (e.g., Posner, Boies, Eichelman, and Taylor, 1969) gives a rather longer estimate of visual trace decay. Posner showed subjects two single letters, one after the other; the subject's task was to say whether the two letters shared the same name—thus AA and Aa would both be "yes" responses. Posner found that response latency was shorter (for positive responses) when "same name" letters were also in the same case, but that this advantage declined as the interval between presentation of the first and second letters was lengthened. When the letters were 1½ seconds apart, latencies were the same for AA and Aa. Posner attributes the "same case" advantage to a rapidly decaying visual trace—but obviously the characteristics of this trace are somewhat different from the trace described by Sperling and Haber. First, in Posner's study the trace decayed over a much longer time (1,500 milliseconds as opposed to 250–300 milliseconds) and, second, while in Sperling's work the trace was easily masked by further visual stimuli, this result was not found in Posner's studies. One possibility is that the two sets of results reflect retrieval from different stages or stores. Another possibility (which will be developed throughout this chapter) is that the discrete stage model has outlived its usefulness; and that these results are better described by a model which states simply that the durability of the memory trace depends on how "deeply" the stimulus has been processed; the more analysis and processing that is carried out, the longer-lasting the consequent trace (Craik and Lockhart, 1972).

Very little work has been reported which examines age differences in this area. Botwinick (1973) describes a study by Abel in which subjects of different ages were tested on a modified version of the Sperling paradigm. The stimulus array was exposed for a much longer time (500 milliseconds) than in Sperling's experiments and it thus seems more likely that performance was mediated by primary memory—this interpretation is supported by the observation that performance declined very little as probe delay was varied from 0–300 milliseconds. The rates of decline did not differ as a function of age (Botwinick, 1973, p. 264).

While Abel's study thus gives little indication of age differences in visual sensory memory, a recent experiment by Schonfield and Wenger (1975) is suggestive of such an age decrement. They found a dramatic increase in the time required to identify a visually presented letter string in an older group, when the string was increased from 4 to 5 letters. No such increase was found for young subjects, although an increase did occur at 6 or 7 letters in the young. The authors point out that a sensory storage deficit may underlie the shorter "perceptual span" in the elderly. Further work using the paradigms of Sperling, Haber or Posner would be very welcome, although it seems likely (in the light of further age-related work discussed in the Chapter) that the root cause of learning and other cognitive difficulties in the elderly does not lie at peripheral stages, but deeper in the system.

With regard to other sensory modalities, memory for tactile information has been investigated by Gilson and Baddeley (1969) and memory for smell has recently been studied by Engen and Ross (1973); the present reviewer is not aware of age-related experiments in these areas. Auditory sensory memory ("echoic" memory) has been implicated in a number of paradigms. In both free recall (e.g., Murdock and Walker, 1969) and serial recall (Crowder and Morton, 1969) the last 1–3 items in the list are recalled at higher levels after auditory presentation as opposed to visual presentation; this augmentation has been ascribed to a relatively long-lasting echoic trace. While no work with older subjects appears to have been done to assess the "capacity" or durability of echoic memory directly, there are some related studies. First, experiments using short-term memory paradigms have generally shown slighter age losses with auditory presentation (e.g., Arenberg, 1968; McGhie, Chapman, and Lawson, 1965); these studies are reviewed below. Second, several experiments have been reported which examine age differences in dichotic listening performance, and these studies will now be described.

Dichotic Listening Studies

In the dichotic listening experiment (Broadbent, 1958), two short series of digits, letters or words are presented simultaneously, one series to each ear. The subject attempts to recall both series and he typically recalls all available items from one ear before recalling the other series, provided the rate of presentation is one pair per second or faster. As a rule, more words are recalled from the first "half-set." Broadbent's original suggestion was that one "channel" (that is, digits presented to one ear) is selected by the attention mechanism and that these items are then perceived and given back as responses; meanwhile, digits from the unattended ear are held briefly in a preperceptual storage system (echoic memory) until the attention mechanism and central perceptual channel are clear. Since items in the preperceptual store are subject to rapid decay, fewer items are recalled from the second half-set.

Inglis and his colleagues have carried out an extensive series of studies to explore the effects of aging on dichotic listening performance. Inglis and Sanderson (1961) showed that a group of elderly patients with a memory disorder recalled as many digits as a control group (elderly patients without a memory disorder) from the first half-set, but that the memory disordered group were poorer than the controls on the second half-set. This finding was corroborated by Caird and Inglis (1961) and extended to the situation where one half-set was presented auditorily and one visually. Inglis and Caird (1963) published the classic demonstration that normal aging is associated with no decrement in the first half-set recalled, but that performance on the second channel drops progressively with age. Their results are shown in Figure 2. The finding was replicated by Mackay and Inglis (1963). One conclusion which Inglis (1964) drew from the results was that short-term storage deficits in the elderly cannot all be due to loss of motivation, since in the dichotic listening situation older subjects are as accurate as their young counterparts on the first half-set. Inglis (1964) also ruled out the possibility of a unilateral hearing loss in the elderly, by finding the typical pattern of results when the first half-set was specified before presentation. In the same paper he rejected the further possibility that older subjects might choose to attend to one ear only, from the finding that typical results were again obtained when the ear to be recalled first was not specified until *after* the digits were presented. Caird (1966) reported the same pattern of results when words, rather than digits were used as stimuli. The general conclusion from all these studies was that the first half-set shows no age decrement since it is not held in the preperceptual store; the second half-set is held in store and shows more rapid loss from that store with increasing age.

Later studies have generally confirmed Inglis' findings, with some minor differences. Craik (1965) found age decrements in both half-sets; from an analysis of the types of errors made, Craik concluded that the age decrements were due to deficits during storage. Clark and Knowles (1973) investigated the possibility that

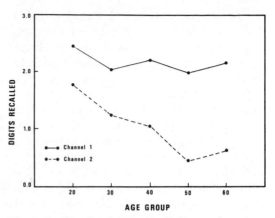

Figure 2. Recall of dichotic digits as a function of age and order of report. (From Inglis and Caird, 1963.)

spoken recall of the first half-set was especially disruptive to second half-set recall for older subjects. They found higher recall levels when recall was written, but there was no differential enhancement for older subjects. Clark and Knowles (like Craik, 1965) found age decrements in both half-sets. Using a recognition procedure for dichotically presented word lists, Schonfield, Trueman and Kline (1972) also found age decrements on both half-sets. The question naturally arises as to the difference between those studies finding an interaction between age and channels 1 and 2 (e.g., Inglis and Sanderson, 1961; Inglis and Caird, 1963; Caird, 1966) and those finding age decrements in both channels and no interaction (e.g., Craik, 1965; Clark and Knowles, 1973; Schonfield, Trueman and Kline, 1972; Inglis and Tansey, 1967). One obvious procedural difference between the sets of studies is that in earlier studies (e.g., Inglis and Caird, 1963) the recall order was unspecified—subjects could choose which ear to attend to and give back first—while in later studies (e.g., Clark and Knowles, 1973), channel 1 was specified, either before or after presentation. This difference in procedure may be important; while all subjects tend to show a right-ear superiority in dichotic listening, perhaps due to left hemisphere dominance for verbal material (Bryden, 1963), older subjects show a greater discrepancy between right and left ear performance. That is, older subjects are particularly bad at recalling digits presented to the left ear (Clark and Knowles, 1973). Thus, when ear order is unspecified, older subjects may tend to concentrate on their better (right) ear, and recall that channel first—thereby giving rise to very poor performance on the second (left) channel; whereas when the order *is* specified, the preferred ear is channel 1 on half of the trials only. In support of this suggestion, Clark and Knowles' data are presented in Figure 3. In their study, recall order was specified after presentation; thus subjects may have perceived and registered right-ear digits more clearly. When the right ear was asked for first, results resembling Inglis' original findings are observed (Figure 3A). When the right ear was second, however, there were no differences between channels; if anything there was a slight superiority for channel 2 in the older group (Figure 3B). Thus, *overall*, approximately equal age decrements were found in both channels. While this argument gives a good account of most of the data, it must be pointed out that Inglis and Ankus (1965) found no support for the notion that laterality differences might account for the discrepancy in findings.

Schonfield, Trueman and Kline (1972) investigated the possibility that age losses in dichotic listening reflect retrieval failures. However, they found age decrements in both channels when a recognition test was given and thus argued that, since recognition procedures minimize retrieval difficulty, the age decrements were attributable to input difficulties—failures of registration, not storage or retrieval. Clark and Knowles (1973) also argued for a "perceptual deficit" explanation of their results.

There is no doubt that the dichotic listening paradigm provides a sensitive index of age-related decrements, but it is not clear which processes are involved. It was originally suggested (Inglis and Caird, 1963) that the second half-set was held in a preperceptual auditory store and that material in this store was lost more rapidly with age. The notion that channel 2 messages are held in a "preperceptual" echoic memory is not appealing on a number of grounds. First, the same general pattern of results was obtained at rates of 30 pairs/minute and 90 pairs/minute (Craik, 1965). It is unreasonable to suppose that, at the slower rate, digits from the second channel were not perceived until 5–8 seconds after presentation. Also, since older subjects were not especially penalized by the slower rate of presentation (which would give more time for decay to occur), an explanation in terms of "more rapid fading of the trace in the elderly" is not convincing. Weiss (1963) also found that rate of presentation had little effect on older subjects' dichotic listening performance.

A second hypothesis is that older subjects are more vulnerable to interference, in this case from channel 1 responses. Although this idea is supported by the results of an ingenious

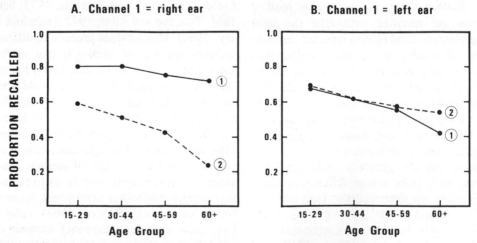

Figure 3. Proportion of dichotic digits recalled as a function of age, order of report, and laterality. (From Clark and Knowles, 1973. Reproduced by permission of the *Journal of Gerontology*.)

study by Taub and Greiff (1967), the notion gets little support from Clark and Knowles' (1973) result that older subjects did not benefit differentially from written as opposed to spoken responding. Also, it does not provide an account of the observed age losses in channel 1 performance. A third possibility, favored by the present reviewer, is that the durability of a memory trace depends on how "deeply" the stimulus is processed (Craik and Lockhart, 1972). "Depth" in this sense refers to the number and qualitative nature of perceptual analyses carried out on the input. Treisman (1964) has suggested that division of attention is associated with shallower levels of analysis of the unattended stimulus and thus to more rapid loss of the information; put another way, trace strength is determined by the amount of attention allocated to the stimulus. There is much evidence that older subjects are especially penalized in situations where they must divide their attention; perhaps their capacity is largely taken up in "programming" the division of attention leaving relatively little capacity to process the stimuli (Craik, 1973). If older subjects' processing capacity is differentially reduced in this way, they would process one or both of the dichotic channels less deeply, and this, in turn, would lead to poorer retention.

Age Differences Under Conditions of Divided Attention

One of the clearest results in the experimental psychology of aging is the finding that older subjects are more penalized when they must divide their attention, either between two input sources, input and holding, or holding and responding. One classic experiment relating division of attention to aging was carried out by Kay (1953, cited by Welford, 1958) and replicated by Kirchner (1958). In these studies, subjects watched a display of 12 light bulbs; a morse key was positioned below each bulb, and the subjects' task was to press the key when its corresponding light came on. Pressing the key extinguished the light, but caused another light to come on. Older subjects could perform this serial task without trouble, but when the task was complicated by asking sub-

jects to press the key corresponding to the *previous* light, the older group performed less well than the young group. When the memory load was increased by making subjects work "two back" or "three back" the age decrement was even more severe; apparently the division of attention between memory and response was especially disruptive to the performance of older subjects.

Further experiments have led to the same conclusion. Broadbent and Heron (1962) required subjects to perform a visual letter cancellation task while monitoring a series of auditory letters for a repeated letter. Young subjects coped moderately well with both tasks while older subjects tended to concentrate on one task while performance on the other deteriorated markedly. Talland (1962) also showed that older subjects were especially poor at performing two tasks simultaneously. The results of these and similar experiments led Welford (1958, 1962, 1964) to formulate the influential notion that one major source of performance decrements in the elderly is the disruption of short term memory by shifts of attention between perception and recall.

The dichotic listening studies reviewed above provide one set of results which bears out the important negative effects of divided attention. In a similar study, Broadbent and Gregory (1965) presented three visual and three auditory items simultaneously. The visual items were a digit, a letter and a digit while the auditory items were a letter, a digit and a letter. When subjects were asked to recall the visual items and then the auditory items, performance remained at a constant level with age up to 45, and then dropped significantly. When subjects were asked to recall the letters first and then the digits, performance fell off more steeply with age. McGhie, Chapman, and Lawson (1965) also used a bisensory paradigm. They presented five numbers visually and simultaneously presented five other numbers auditorily at a 2-second rate. One number was repeated (either within one sensory channel or between channels) and the task was to detect and write down the repeated number. No age differences were found when the repeated number occurred first on the auditory channel (AA or

AV) but there were substantial age losses when the first occurrence was visual (VV or VA).

Two further studies in this area may be described briefly. Brinley and Fichter (1970) found that older subjects were more penalized than a younger group when a memory load was added to a cognitive task. Craik (1973) reported two experiments in which the subject's attention was divided between a detection task and a memory task. In both experiments the memory task consisted of a serial string of letters or digits followed immediately by a probe letter or digit. The subject's task was to judge whether the probe had been in the preceding string. Memory performance declined with age in both experiments—more especially in Experiment II where the memory task was presented visually.

While all these experiments show that the deleterious effects of division of attention increase with age, some qualifying statements should be made. The studies by Craik (1973) and McGhie, Chapman, and Lawson (1965) showed that divided attention was less harmful when the memory task was presented auditorily. This result was also found in free recall by Anderson and Craik (1974), and it may be interpreted as showing that auditory inputs can be held briefly whether they are attended to or not. Older subjects can also make use of this "cost-free" encoding. When the input is visual, however, attention is required; older subjects have less processing capacity to spare in the divided attention situation, thus their performance on visual memory tasks is especially poor. This factor was also present in the Broadbent and Gregory (1965) experiment. Performance was even worse, however, when subjects had to reorganize the material into letters and digits—the necessity to reorganize the contents of the short-term store added a further complication and led to poorer performance in the older group.

Age Differences in Primary Memory

The general position adopted in this chapter concerning the distinction between "short-term" and "long-term" memory is that of Waugh and Norman (1965). That is, for material which has been adequately perceived and registered, the only useful distinction within memory functioning is between primary and secondary memory. Primary memory (PM) is involved when the retained material is still "in mind," still being rehearsed, still at the focus of conscious attention. By this definition, some items are no longer in PM when the immediate memory span is exceeded. For example, immediate recall of a list of 20 words will largely involve retrieval from secondary memory (SM).

Although PM, defined in this way, deals with a minute portion of remembered events, that portion is of critical importance for the encoding and retrieval of information; it constitutes the control system for all thinking and remembering (Atkinson and Shiffrin, 1971). The memory literature—especially reports of applications to clinical and educational research—has been in conceptual chaos for the last 20 years, with a proliferation of loosely defined terms such as "short-term memory," "recent memory," "immediate memory" and the like. The strong argument put forward here is that PM (defined in the way suggested above) is subserved by different processes to those underlying SM performance, and that the PM-SM distinction clarifies many findings which are otherwise confusing and contradictory. It is further suggested that SM functioning in *short-term retention* situations reflects the same characteristics as "long-term memory" in the sense of retention over hours or days. The point is that qualitative distinctions within memory functioning must be made in terms of processes (e.g., PM and SM) and not in terms of retention intervals or experimental paradigms. Recent reviews of primary memory have been provided by Craik (1971b), Murdock (1974) and Watkins (1974).

In the following sections, it is argued that the age differences in PM are negligible. Since the original experiments were not conducted within the PM-SM framework, they are described in terms of experimental paradigms, but the results will be interpreted in the light of the PM-SM distinction. Free recall is one experimental paradigm which yields a relatively pure measure of PM functioning (Watkins, 1974). After several practice lists, subjects typically recall the last few words in the list first of all, thereby giving rise to a marked "recency effect." Both Craik (1968b) and Raymond (1971) have demonstrated that older subjects show as much recency as do young subjects; they concluded that primary memory (or "the short-term store" in Raymond's case) was unimpaired by aging. Craik (1968a) reached the same conclusion on the basis of a somewhat different analysis.

Memory Span Studies

The immediate memory span for digits, letters or words is typically taken as the longest string of items that can be reproduced in serial order. Since digit and word spans are about 7 and 5 items respectively, and since estimates of primary memory capacity range from 2.6 to 3.4 words (Watkins, 1974, Table 1), it could be concluded that even immediate memory span involves the retrieval of one or more items from secondary memory. If the span technique largely reflects PM functioning but has a small SM component, it would be expected that memory span performance would fall off slightly with age, but that losses would be much less severe than under conditions which reflected SM functioning entirely. Published reports bear out this analysis; some investigators have found no significant age differences in digit span (e.g., Bromley, 1958; Craik, 1968a; Drachman and Leavitt, 1972; Kriauciunas, 1968) while others have found slight but reliable age decrements (e.g., Botwinick and Storandt, 1974; Friedman, 1974; Gilbert, 1941; Gilbert and Levee, 1971; Taub, 1973). With other materials, Botwinick and Storandt (1974) found a reliable age loss in letter span, and Talland (1965) found no age differences in word span. The data reported by Botwinick and Storandt are typical and are shown in Table 1. Taub investigated the hypothesis that older subjects would benefit more from practice in the digit span situation (Taub and Long, 1972; Taub, 1973). He found that all age groups improved their performance with practice but, if anything, young subjects showed greater improvement. Thus the conclusion from immediate memory span studies is that age decrements are slight. It should be stressed that it is the pattern of age differences which is important for theoretical interpretation, not the finding (or absence) of statistical significance.

TABLE 1. MEMORY SPAN FOR LETTERS PRESENTED AUDITORILY.

	AGE (YEARS)					
	20's	30's	40's	50's	60's	70's
Span	6.7	6.2	6.5	6.5	5.5	5.4

Botwinick and Storandt, 1974.

Some investigators have also measured "backward span"—that is, requiring subjects to repeat the string in reverse serial order. The typical finding here is that older subjects perform less well than a young group. Bromley (1958) found that backward span scores declined faster than forward span scores with increasing age. Botwinick and Storandt (1974) also found age decrements in backward span; again, the backward span decrements were slightly greater than those for forward span, although not reliably so in this case. It seems plausible that if subjects must reorganize the contents of their primary memory system, old subjects should be at a greater disadvantage; as well as maintaining the material, subjects must demonstrate mental flexibility and agility in order to rearrange the items. Evidence has already been cited (Broadbent and Gregory, 1965) to show that when this mental reorganization is required, older subjects are more penalized. Friedman (1966, 1974) has also made the point that older subjects show poorer organization in immediate memory, although his use of supraspan material could be interpreted as showing an age decrement in retrieval from secondary memory.

In "running memory span" the subject is given a relatively long string of items of unknown and variable length. When the string ends, the subject's task is to reproduce as many items as possible from the end of the string. This task is similar to reproduction of the recency items in free recall, but with the additional constraint that the items must be reproduced in their correct serial order; thus "running span" can be classified as a primary memory task which requires some reorganization. Talland (1968) reported a series of studies using this paradigm; in general terms, he found relatively slight but reliable age losses in this version of the span task.

Talland (1965) introduced a further technique for the study of age differences in word span situations. He presented word lists in which each item in the first half of the string, except one, was repeated in a different order in the second half; the subject's task was to reproduce the words, but hold to the end the word that was presented only once. This task thus involves a division of attention between holding the words, detecting the nonrepeated item and reorganizing the words to some extent before recall. Given that the task involves division of attention and reorganization, strong effects of aging would be expected, and indeed were found.

So far in this section it has been argued that the performance of older subjects is unimpaired on primary memory tasks which do not involve division of attention or reorganization of the material. While this observation remains valid where performance is indexed by amount recalled, some studies using the more sensitive index of response latency have recently been reported. In this situation, age decrements in performance have been found. Sternberg (1966) devised a paradigm in which a short set of digits or letters is presented to the subject; immediately after presentation of this memory set, a test item is presented. The subject's task is to decide as quickly as possible whether the test item was a member of the memory set. Sternberg found that decision latency increased linearly as the size of the memory set increased. He suggested that the slope of this linear function indexed the rate of a serial search or scan through the contents of primary memory, while the intercept of the function indexed factors such as encoding of the test stimulus, response execution and nerve conduction time.

Anders, Fozard and Lillyquist (1972) carried out Sternberg's experiment on subjects of different ages. Subjects were given a set of 1 to 7 digits to hold in memory, followed by a test digit; their results are shown in Figure 4. Both the intercepts and the slopes of the functions

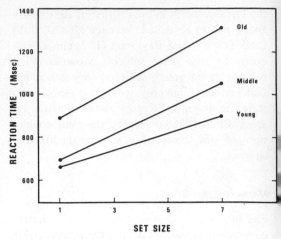

Figure 4. Mean response times as a function of age and set size. (From Anders, Fozard, and Lillyquist, 1972. *Developmental Psychology*, **6**, 214–217. Copyright 1972 by the American Psychological Association. Reprinted by permission.)

increased significantly with age. The reciprocal of the slope constant gives the rate at which subjects allegedly scan the contents of the memory set ("allegedly" since other interpretations of the result are possible, e.g., parallel rather than serial retrieval processes [Townsend, 1971]). Further studies by Eriksen, Hamlin, and Daye (1973) and Anders and Fozard (1973) confirmed that both the intercept and the slope of the scanning function increase with age.

Kirsner (1972) reported an ingenious study which casts some doubt on the conclusion that memory scanning rates are slower in the elderly. He presented four words followed by a test word; the subject's task was either to decide whether the test word had occurred in the list, or to simply *name* the test word. Kirsner argued that the subtraction of naming latency from decision latency yields a relatively pure measure of memory comparison time—the common perceptual and response factors have been eliminated. Using this technique, Kirsner found that whereas "uncorrected" decision latency increased from 25 to 60 years, the "corrected decision latency" measure showed no such increase. The implication is that aging affects perception and response factors, but not comparison times. This conclusion is, of course, at odds with the findings of steeper slopes in the Sternberg paradigm.

In summary, memory span tasks show either no decrements or very slight losses with increasing age. Since span tasks largely reflect PM functioning, these findings are in accord with the notion that PM is unaffected by the aging process. The exceptions to this rule occur when the task demands reorganization of the material or division of attention between two or more mental operations. Although the *number* of items retrieved from PM thus remains stable across age groups, the *speed* of retrieval may decline in older subjects.

Short-term Retention of Supraspan Material

Once the memory span is exceeded, the majority of presented items must be retrieved from secondary memory—even in an immediate retention test. It will be argued that older subjects show deficits both of acquisition into SM and retrieval from that system; the extent of these deficits will depend on features of the material and the experimental situation. In the present section some studies are described which examine the immediate retention of supraspan strings of verbal items.

Friedman (1966) presented letter strings, 4–12 items in length, to a group of young subjects (20–34 years) and to a group of older subjects (60–81 years); the groups were matched on letter span. Friedman's hypothesis was that the older group's performance on a serial recall task ("recall the letters in their correct order") would be more disrupted by supraspan lists due to their lower level of memory organization. This result was found with serial recall scoring, although there were no age differences when the data were scored without regard to order. Friedman attributes this result to the lesser organizational demands of free recall.

For somewhat different reasons, Craik (1968a) also hypothesized that supraspan lists would disrupt recall performance to a greater extent for old subjects. Craik's reasoning followed suggestions by Welford (1958) and Kay (1959) that older subjects may be more vulnerable to the effects of interference from further presented items, once the span is ex-

ceeded. Craik reported the results of a study in which two groups of 50 subjects (in their 20's and 70's respectively) were matched on digit span performance, and then given lists of 4–9 digits for serial recall. Young subjects performed better than the older group on the longer lists, but the interaction between age and list length did not approach significance. This latter result gives no support to the notion that older subjects are more affected by supraspan interference. However, in a later study, Craik (1968a) showed that the interaction between age and list length did appear when the list items were drawn from a larger set of words. The materials used were digits, English county names, animal names and unrelated words; list length varied from 5 to 20 (5–10 for digits) and the task was free recall. The results (Figure 5) showed some tendency toward a larger interaction between age and list length as the vocabulary from which words were drawn increased in size. The age difference was slight with digits (thereby replicating Friedman's (1966) and Taub's (1968) results for the free recall of letters) and the age decrements increase with larger word pools. However, the old subjects' performance does not drop as list length increases; it simply fails to increase at the same rate as that of the younger group. Thus it does not make any sense to talk about "an increased liability to supraspan interference" on the part of older subjects; it appears rather that younger subjects are less penalized by the inadequate retrieval information inherent in large word

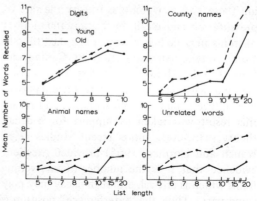

Figure 5. Mean recall scores as a function of age, list length, and type of material. (From Craik, 1968a.)

pools. This notion of an age decrement in retrieval from secondary memory unless the retrieval information is particularly effective was proposed by Schonfield (1965), Laurence (1967b) and Craik (1968a,b). Evidence for the idea is discussed further in a later section.

The ability of older subjects to benefit from repeated presentations of a digit string has been investigated by several workers using a paradigm devised by Hebb (1961). In this situation a long series of digit strings is presented for immediate serial recall; one identical string is presented on several occasions throughout the series thus affording an opportunity for cumulative learning. The clear prediction here is that younger subjects should show a faster rate of learning, but the evidence on the point is contradictory (Caird, 1964, 1966; Heron and Craik, 1964). However, using the more straightforward technique of repeated presentation of a 15-digit string for serial recall, Drachman and Leavitt (1972) have more recently provided clear evidence for faster learning in younger subjects.

Short-term Forgetting

How is material lost from primary memory? It was originally hypothesized that material in the short-term store simply decays unless it is refreshed by rehearsal (Brown, 1958; Broadbent, 1963). This position may be contrasted with an "interference" view, which states that it is not time as such, but intervening material, which gives rise to forgetting. One obvious way of testing these two viewpoints is to vary the rate of presentation and recall; in this way the number of items may be held constant and the "time in store" varied. An early study by Conrad and Hille (1958) showed that fast presentation coupled with fast recall led to higher performance levels than slow presentation and recall; this result was taken as support for a decay theory. However, more recent studies (e.g., Waugh and Norman, 1965) provided excellent evidence that it is the number of intervening items which is critical, although decay may play some part. Thus, the "interference" position is now generally accepted, to the point that in a recent review Murdock (1974, pp. 156-157)

stated: " . . . the evidence for decay has been weak at best, and one could even make the flat statement that forgetting through the passage of time *per se* just does not occur in short-term memory."

At a time when decay theory was more popular, it seemed possible that older subjects would exhibit a faster rate of decay. This conclusion was reached by Fraser (1958) on the basis of a study in which presentation and recall rates were varied. Fraser found no difference between young and old subjects' performance on an immediate recall test at fast rates, but that the old group's recall level dropped more than the young group's performance at slow rates. However, a recent study by Kinsbourne (1973) showed quite the reverse. Older subjects were generally poorer than a young group at recalling an 8-letter sequence, but while the young group was unaffected by variations in presentation rate (from 1 per 2 second to 4 per second), the older group performed disproportionately poorly at the faster rate. Since both Fraser and Kinsbourne used auditory presentation, the source of the discrepancy is not obvious. It seems reasonable, however, that older subjects would have greater difficulty in perceiving and registering items at very fast presentation rates (such as the 4 per second rate used by Kinsbourne). Schonfield and Donaldson (1966) also concluded that older subjects are more vulnerable to decay in short-term memory situations. They used an ingenious technique in which the first and second halves of a short digit string were presented at different rates. While all subjects recalled more digits under the "slow-fast" condition (in which digits are in store for a shorter time on average), the advantage of "slow-fast" over "fast-slow" was significant only in the old group. This is weak evidence for the conclusion, however, as no *interaction* between age and the presentation conditions is reported. Finally, while some authors have interpreted a greater age decrement on the second channel reported from a dichotic listening task as evidence for faster decay (e.g., Inglis, 1965), other workers have argued against this view (Taub and Greiff, 1967).

The position at present is thus that decay plays a rather little part in short-term forgetting and that the evidence for faster decay in the elderly is not strong. With regard to the effects of rate of presentation on short-term retention, it seems likely that rate has no major effect on memory span and primary memory performance, at least with auditory presentation (see Murdock, 1974 for a review). This is the result reported by Kinsbourne (1973) for young subjects although older subjects' performance was disrupted at very fast rates. With visual presentation, there is evidence that slower rates benefit short-term recall (e.g., Mackworth, 1962). This result was also reported by Taub (1966); however, both old and young subjects benefited equally from a slower presentation rate.

If interference, in the sense of disruption caused by futher inputs to the system, is the major cause of short-term forgetting, are older subjects more vulnerable to such interference effects? This question was given a strong affirmative answer by Welford (1958). He argued persuasively that many of the age-related deficits in cognitive and motor skills might arise essentially from an increased vulnerability to such interference effects. However plausible that view may be, it has not been supported by empirical studies carried out since 1958 and the view must now be rejected.

Results from two short-term interference paradigms will be discussed to illustrate this last statement. In the Brown-Peterson paradigm, the subject is presented with three letters to remember; he then counts backwards (as a rehearsal-preventing activity) for 0-20 seconds, and finally attempts to recall the letters. The rate of forgetting may be taken as an index of vulnerability to interference. Schonfield (1969b) has reported data of this kind with age as a variable; they are shown in Figure 6A. It may be seen that the rates of forgetting are identical for all age groups. The finding of no age decrement in this situation has also been reported by Keevil-Rogers and Schnore (1969), Kriauciunas (1968), and by Talland (1967). The second paradigm used as an illustration is the recognition probe technique in which seven 2-digit numbers are presented auditorily, followed by a test number. The subject's task is to decide whether the test number has occurred in the preceding series. Ability to recognize the test probe varies as a function of the target's serial position in the 7-item series; recognition is highest when the target is at the end of the list, and declines as the target is placed at earlier serial positions. This serial position effect may again be taken as an index of the rate of short-term forgetting. Craik (1971a) conducted such an experiment, and the data are shown in Figure 6B. The conclusion, once again, is that older subjects do not exhibit faster rates of short-term forgetting. Craik's findings have been confirmed by Binks and Sutcliffe (1972) and have also recently been extended in a continuous recognition experiment carried out by Wickelgren (1975). This latter author found evidence for poorer acquisition in an elderly group, but identical forgetting rates in the younger and older groups over a 2 hour period. There is no evidence here that older subjects are more vulnerable to the effects of interference.

It has also been suggested that older subjects may be more affected by response interference; that is, initial responses from memory may interfere with the remaining memory items to a greater degree in the elderly. This notion was investigated by Taub and Walker (1970) by requiring subjects to always write the prefix "O" before recalling a 6- or 8-letter string. The critical interaction between age and condition (prefix vs. no prefix) was found, but only in the second half of 8-letter strings, and only within a subset of subjects matched on control performance on the task. Thus, although the authors found support for their hypothesis, they had to work rather hard to obtain that support! Finally, it may be noted that output interference has also been implicated in dichotic listening, but Bryden (1971) has recently shown that output interference plays a minimal role in second channel performance.

Modality Effects

Murdock (1966) showed that short-term retention was higher when the items were presented auditorily as opposed to visually; this finding has since been replicated in a number of experimental settings (e.g., Craik, 1969; Crowder and Morton, 1969; Murdock and Walker, 1969).

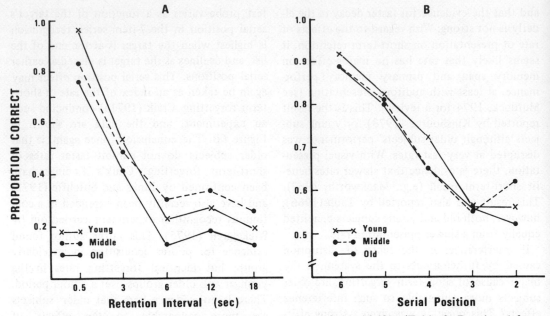

Figure 6. Forgetting rate as a function of age. A, Schonfield, 1969b. (Table 3. Reprinted from Proceedings of Seminars 1965–69, Duke University Council on Aging and Human Development with permission from the Duke University Center for the Study of Aging and Human Development.) B, Craik, 1971a. (Table 1. Reprinted from the *Quarterly Journal of Experimental Psychology*, 1971, **23**, 316–323.)

Several explanations have been proposed to account for the auditory superiority. Murdock's view (e.g., Murdock and Walker, 1969) is that there are separate prelinguistic auditory and visual stores, and that the auditory store is in some sense larger. Other suggestions have been in terms of an additional echoic component for auditory presentation (Crowder and Morton, 1969) or the notion that the short-term encoding of verbal material is phonemic and that while auditory information is highly compatible with that storage format, visual information requires some extra translation step to convert it into a phonemic representation (e.g., McGhie, Chapman, and Lawson, 1965).

On the basis of these findings, it would be expected that older subjects should also benefit from auditory presentation. Indeed, they might benefit *more*, since auditory information might require less attention or processing (due to its higher salience) or is more compatible with a phonemic code. Some of these expectations are upheld by the experimental results. Bromley (1958) found a faster decline with age for a short-term visual task than for an auditory task

and suggested that visual memory was more impaired by aging than auditory memory. However, the two tasks are not very comparable—the auditory task was digit span while the visual task was recognition of 10 geometrical shapes—thus there are PM/SM differences, recall/recognition differences and possibly familiarity differences involved in the comparison too. Bromley's findings are therefore interesting and suggestive, but not conclusive. Stronger support for an interaction between presentation modality and age comes from the study by McGhie, Chapman, and Lawson (1965) described earlier. In their divided attention task, more repetitions were detected by the older subjects if the first occurrence was auditory (it should be noted, however, that on a similar split-attention monitoring task reported by Fozard, Carr, Talland, and Erwin, 1971, old subjects performed better on the visual channel).

In memory span and serial recall tasks, it has usually been reported that while subjects of all ages show a slight auditory superiority, older subjects do not benefit disproportionately. The results reported by Talland (1968, p. 106),

Craik (1968a) and Taub (1972, 1975) fit this pattern. Contrary to the general trend, Botwinick and Storandt (1974) found superior digit- and letter-span performance when presentation was visual; it seems quite possible that this result stems from their technique of presenting all visual digits simultaneously on the presentation card. Again, however, Botwinick and Storandt found no interaction between age and presentation modality.

An excellent study in this series was reported by Arenberg (1968). He hypothesized that recall performance might be aided more for older than for younger subjects by the addition of auditory information to a visually-presented series of digits; and further, that the old group might benefit disproportionately if the auditory information was added "actively," by the subject reading the digits aloud. The 4 digits to be remembered were followed by a distractor activity (reading aloud 3 further irrelevant digits). Arenberg's results are shown in Table 2. He found a reliable age decrement, and also an interaction between age and presentation modality—older subjects benefited more from the two conditions in which auditory information was added. While both age groups improved their performance further when the auditory information was added "actively" (spoken by the subject) as opposed to passively (spoken by the experimenter) the old subjects did not gain a special benefit from active responding. Interestingly, performance on this task correlated with *backward* digit span, but not forward span, suggesting that the storage and manipulation processes involved in backward span are quite similiar to the abilities involved in holding a short string of items while reading 3 further items.

The conclusions regarding age and modality of presentation in short-term retention tasks may be stated briefly. While all subjects show slightly superior retention under auditory presentation conditions, old subjects do not appear to benefit disproportionately unless they must divide their attention between storage operations and other input or output operations (Arenberg, 1968; McGhie, Chapman, and Lawson, 1965). In this latter case, the auditory input may provide an additional rather "passive"

TABLE 2. TOTAL NUMBER OF DIGITS RECALLED OUT OF 32.

	PRESENTATION CONDITION		
	Visual Only	Passive Auditory	Active Auditory
Young	22.8	24.5	26.2
Old	18.0	22.1	23.3

Arenberg, 1968.

(in the sense of "attention-free") source of information to compensate for the older subject's reduced ability to cope with the divided attention situation.

Conclusions on Age Differences in Short-term Retention

The argument presented in this chapter follows from Waugh and Norman's (1965) analysis of the memory processes; recent items are still held and rehearsed in "primary memory" while previous items must be retrieved from "secondary memory." Thus even short-term retention situations will reflect secondary memory functioning to some extent. The literature reviewed above supports the contention that age differences in primary memory are minimal; given that the items have been fully perceived and that no reorganization is required, age decrements occur only in the recognition latency paradigm (e.g., Anders, Fozard, and Lillyquist, 1972). When the material to be remembered exceeds the capacity of primary memory, age differences are observed, thereby implicating acquisition or retrieval difficulties in secondary memory. Older subjects are especially penalized in divided attention situations, and it was suggested that such results reflect an attentional deficit which results in relatively poorer acquisition of the non-attended material. The other type of situation which leads to disproportionate difficulty in the elderly is where the stored material must be manipulated or reorganized (e.g., Broadbent and Gregory, 1965; Talland, 1965).

Thus, to the extent that the experimental (or real life) situation requires manipulation and reorganization of the input, Welford's

(1958) suggestion that "short-term memory" deficits underlie the poorer performance of older subjects on a variety of tasks has been borne out by the subsequent data. However, Welford's other suggestion, that older subjects are more vulnerable to interference effects, is not well supported in cases where the memory items have been adequately registered.

AGE DIFFERENCES IN SECONDARY MEMORY PERFORMANCE

The term secondary memory (SM) is used here in the sense described by Waugh and Norman (1965). Thus, even in "immediate" retention situations, items will be retrieved from SM provided that 5-6 further items have been processed by the subject. As outlined in previous sections, retention of the initial segments of a free-recall list depends on SM, as does the retention of supraspan material. However, SM should not be thought of as an "intermediate memory" store or process; the position adopted here is that the *qualitative* characteristics of SM performance after 30 seconds of interpolated activity are identical to those observed after months or years. Thus SM and "long-term memory" are equivalent terms; Waugh and Norman's (1965) contribution was to show that SM mediated performance, in part, even in immediate retention. From the work reviewed above, it was concluded that older subjects perform less well than young subjects when SM is involved; this conclusion is further supported in the present section. Some tentative proposals will then be made about the nature and locus of the age decrements in SM performance.

Age Differences in Recall and Recognition

Results from a number of studies agree that substantial age decrements are found under conditions of single-trial free recall. Typically, a list of 12–30 words is presented and the subject is asked to recall them in any order. No age differences are found in recall of the last few items (the recency effect) but older subjects recall fewer words from the beginning and middle of the lists—that is, from the SM portion (Craik, 1968b; Raymond, 1971). Schonfield

and Robertson (1966), Laurence (1966, 1967a, b) and Botwinick and Storandt (1974) have all presented data which show lower recall levels in the elderly. Before turning to a consideration of the locus of the deficit, some studies will be described that demonstrate an attenuation of the age decrement under certain conditions.

Laurence (1967a) presented lists of 12 words for immediate recall to groups of young and elderly adults. Under one condition the list was made up of words from a single conceptual category (e.g., animals, articles of clothing) and under another condition all 12 words were drawn from different categories. Laurence found rather slight age differences in recall for the single concept lists, but a substantial age decrement in recall of unrelated words; the interaction between age and list composition was highly reliable. One interpretation of Laurence's data is in terms of the availability of retrieval cues; that is, perhaps older subjects are less penalized when they can group the list items under one concept and then use this concept to aid their retrieval. This interpretation is supported by the results of a further study by Laurence (1967b), in which she found that the age decrement in recall was eliminated under cued recall conditions (that is, where category names of list items were provided at retrieval.)

The notion that older subjects' recall is differentially aided by the provision of good retrieval information gains further support from a study reported by Craik (1968a,b). He manipulated the size of the pool from which list items were drawn (digits, English county names, animal names and unrelated words) and found some tendency for the age decrement in recall to be attenuated for the smaller word pools. The relatively small age decrement in the recall of letters reported by Taub (1968) could also be taken to support the idea that old subjects' recall performance benefits disproportionately when the retrieval pool is small. Both Laurence's results and those of Craik and Taub can be interpreted as showing that when good retrieval information is made available—either by the provision of retrieval cues or by the use of a limited set of items—older subjects' retention is less impaired. This point will be reconsidered after some data from recognition studies are examined.

Schonfield and Robertson (1966) presented some extremely interesting data comparing recall and recognition scores at various ages. Subjects were presented with a list of 24 words to learn; the acquisition phase was followed either by free recall or recognition. The recognition test was a forced-choice task in which each list word was presented in a group with 4 distractor items. Schonfield and Robertson found a large and systematic drop in recall performance with increasing age, but no age decrement in recognition. Their data are shown in Figure 7. The authors had initially postulated that retrieval from storage constituted a special difficulty for older subjects and thus, since recognition does not require retrieval, smaller age decrements would be observed in recognition than in recall. Their findings obviously support this postulation thus Schonfield and Robertson concluded that retrieval from storage is one major cause of poor memory performance in older people. They also suggested that the elderly may compensate for this deficit by utilizing extra cues—a suggestion in line with observations of Welford (1958). Finally, it should be noted that Schonfield and Robertson's argument depends simply on *greater* age losses in recall than in recognition—their hypothesis would not be disconfirmed by the finding of age decrements in recognition under some conditions. Similarly, the notion that retrieval constitutes one source of difficulty for older subjects does not deny the possibility that other deficits may also occur.

Since Schonfield and Robertson's study was published, further experiments have generally confirmed the notion that age decrements are more severe for recall tasks than for recognition tasks; however, age decrements have usually been found in recognition as well as in recall. While Craik (1971a) reported no significant age differences in the recognition of 25 words, the number of subjects per group was small (*n* = 10) and recognition scores did drop systematically with increasing age. Significant age decrements in word recognition have been reported by Crenshaw (1969), Fozard and Waugh (1969), Gordon and Clark (1974a,b), Botwinick and Storandt (1974) and Erber (1974). Similarly, age decrements in recognition memory for line drawings or pictures have been reported by Harwood and Naylor (1969) and by Howell (1972). Finally, a rather different type of study yielding the same result has been described by Warrington and Sanders (1971). They did not present the material to be learned, but asked subjects about events or faces which had been in the news either recently or many years ago. While all age groups showed higher performance levels for more recent material, older subjects did less well than the younger groups, even when a recognition test was employed. On the basis of all these results, there seems no doubt that under most conditions, there are age decrements in recognition of both words and pictures.

Several workers have found greater age decrements in recall than in recognition. For example, Harwood and Naylor (1969) presented 20 line drawings of objects until subjects could recall at least 16 of the objects' names. Four weeks later, subjects were asked to recall the names again, and then to recognize the 20 drawings from a set of 60. The mean recall of the older subjects was 74 percent of the young group's level, while recognition was 87 percent of the level achieved by the young group. Erber (1974) reported that age accounted for more of the variance in a recall test (25 percent) than in a recognition test (10 percent). In a question-

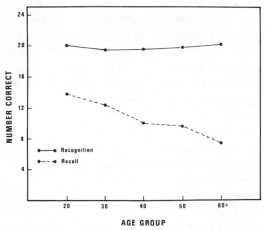

Figure 7. Recognition and recall scores as a function of age. (From Schonfield and Robertson, 1966.)

naire designed to measure retention of "items in the news" Warrington and Silberstein (1970) found that recall declined with increasing age, whereas performance on a multiple-choice version of the test did not. In a later study, however, Warrington and Sanders (1971) found age decrements in both recall and recognition although they noted that the recall decrements were more severe. Finally, Crenshaw (1969) reported a significant interaction between age and type of retention test (again, recall declined more with age than did recognition). There is thus general agreement that aging has a greater detrimental effect on recall performance than on recognition. From the data, this seems to be a reasonable conclusion, although some caution should be exercised in comparing recall and recognition scores directly. It is well known that recognition performance is not absolute, but depends on such factors as the nature of the "distractor" or "lure" items; similarly recall level varies with the adequacy of the retrieval information provided—recall may even be higher than recognition in certain circumstances (Tulving and Thomson, 1973).

Tentative conclusions about the effects of aging on recall and recognition in secondary memory may be drawn. Older subjects appear to be at the greatest disadvantage relative to younger groups when little retrieval information is provided by the experimental situation. In this case, they must rely on self-generated "reconstructive" activities (e.g., Bartlett, 1932) to retrieve the items; it may be postulated that older people are less intellectually flexible and creative in these mental operations (e.g., Chown, 1961; Lehman, 1953) and thus their memory performance is impaired. By this analysis, age decrements should be greatest in free recall, where no retrieval cues are provided, and this seems to fit the observed facts. On the other hand, age decrements should be less in cued recall and in recognition where more retrieval information is provided by the situation and less need be generated by the subject; this is also borne out by the data. The present analysis of age deficits in memory thus leans toward an explanation in terms of retrieval failure in the elderly. This may not be the whole truth, however. Further discussion is deferred until more data and arguments are considered.

Age Differences in Acquisition and Organization

If it is accepted that the age differences in primary memory are minimal, it follows that most age-related deficits in memory are not due to difficulties of perception or initial registration of the material. That is, the search for the major locus of difficulty should not take place at the level of peripheral processing or sensory storage, but deeper in the system. While the adequacy of registration or acquisition in the elderly may be sufficient to support immediate recall, it is possible that the more elaborate encoding necessary for longer-term retention is not carried out so well by older subjects. If this is the case, then age deficits in secondary memory and learning may be attributable to deficiencies in acquisition processes, not to decrements during storage or at retrieval. This notion of poorer initial learning in older subjects was suggested by Jerome (1959) and has received empirical support from studies by Wimer and Wigdor (1958), Hulicka and Weiss (1965) and Moenster (1972). All these studies showed no age differences in retention after initial learning had been equated. This issue is discussed further below.

In the context of information-processing theories, secondary memory acquisition depends on such factors as organization of the material (e.g., Tulving, 1962; Mandler, 1967) and formation of a rich, elaborate encoding (e.g., Paivio, 1971; Craik and Tulving, 1975). Thus if older subjects show acquisition deficits, these deficits would be manifested in a lessened ability to organize incoming items into mental clusters and hierarchies, and also in less spontaneous (or less efficient) use of such mnemonic techniques as verbal mediators and images. There is indeed some evidence that older persons show decrements both in organization and in their use of mediators. The experiments on organization will be described following a brief discussion of the effects of meaningfulness on memory.

While it makes excellent intuitive sense that older subjects should be less penalized when the material to be learned and remembered is meaningful and familiar to them, the evidence on this point is somewhat confused (see Botwinick, 1973, for a review). Several studies of paired-associate learning have yielded the finding that older subjects are at their greatest disadvantage with materials of low associative strength (Canestrari, 1966; Zaretsky and Halberstam, 1968). Similarly, Howell (1972) found that age decrements in recognition of pictorial material were greatest with unfamiliar material and least with familiar objects. A further approach to meaningfulness has been through the use of strings of letters or words which differ in their degree of approximation to the structure of written English (Miller and Selfridge, 1950). At one end of the scale, the words or letters are selected randomly, while at the other, the word strings are taken from coherent prose passages and the letter strings reflect the sequential dependencies of the language. Using letter material, Kinsbourne (1972) found some evidence to support the view that older subjects were disproportionately helped by increasing approximations to English, although, in his data, the age decrements in recall do not decline systematically with increasing approximation (the differences are $1 \cdot 6$, $2 \cdot 8$, $2 \cdot 0$, and $1 \cdot 5$ letters, for zero, 1st 2nd, and 6th orders of approximation, respectively). In a subsequent study (Kinsbourne, 1973), no interaction was found between age and order of approximation. On the other hand, Craik and Masani (1967) used sequences of words and reported that older subjects of lower verbal intelligence showed the greatest decrement with *higher* orders of approximation to English, although no such interaction was found in a further study (Craik and Masani, 1969). Given these contradictory results, the most reasonable conclusion at present appears to be that while older subjects generally do less well than a young group at recalling long strings of words or letters, both groups can make equally good use of the linguistic rules inherent in higher orders of approximation to English.

The pattern of results linking aging with familiarity and meaningfulness is likely to be complex and may depend on specific features of the subjects, task and materials. In the cases where old subjects benefit disproportionately from the use of meaningful material, the argument is that older subjects refuse to try to learn the meaningless material, and that more meaningful materials reflect real-life situations more

validly (Hulicka, 1967). On the other hand, both Gilbert and Levee (1971) and Taub (1974) found *greatest* age losses with more meaningful verbal material. Also Craik (1968a) found greater age losses in the retention of text sentences than in memory for lists of color names; he also found that older subjects were poorer at guessing a sentence letter by letter—it seemed that older subjects could not make such good use of the learned rules and redundancies inherent in language. Whereas both old and young groups recall more items when the material is meaningful, young subjects can benefit more in some situations (this statement is qualified by the contradictory results from the studies involving approximations to English). Craik suggested that, with some materials and tasks, older subjects exhibited a deficit of encoding or "chunking" the material in secondary memory.

Craik and Masani (1969) tested the hypothesis of an encoding deficit by breaking down the total recall scores from word lists differing in order of approximation to English, into the number of "adopted chunks" recalled, and the number of words per adopted chunk. Following Tulving and Patkau (1962) a chunk was defined as a string of words recalled in the same order as it was presented. Craik and Masani found that older subjects recalled fewer chunks, but did not differ from the young group in the "words per chunk" measure. The authors concluded that aging thus had a detrimental effect on retrieval processes (fewer chunks retrieved by older groups) but that aging did not affect encoding (no differences in the number of words encoded into each chunk). However, it is quite possible that the adopted chunk measure is not a very sensitive index of encoding efficiency (it does not allow for recombination of words into more compatible groupings, for example) and that more sophisticated measures *would* show deficits in organization and recoding of the material.

The issue of age differences in organization has been dealt with mainly by Laurence (1966, 1967a; Laurence and Trotter, 1971) and Hultsch (1969, 1971a,b, 1974). Laurence (1966) found that while young adult subjects learned faster and recalled more than older subjects, the groups did not differ in the amount of organization shown by Tulving's (1962) measure of "subjective organization." The finding of age differences in recall but not in organization is surprising in light of Tulving's (1962) conclusion that learning and organization are highly correlated. Laurence and Trotter (1971) investigated the recall of word lists which contained pairs of homophones (e.g., surplus, surplice) and acoustically similar words (e.g., morning, warning). They found that young subjects were superior to an older group under all conditions but that the age difference was least with homophone pairs—this result might again be interpreted as showing the disproportionate benefits to the elderly when retrieval information is good.

Hultsch (1969) gave subjects of different ages a 22-word list to learn, either (1) under standard free recall conditions, (2) with instructions to "try to organize the list" or (3) with instructions to associate each word with its first letter. The last two conditions gave rise to higher recall and there was some evidence that older subjects of lower verbal intelligence benefited disproportionately from the alphabetic instructions. Thus instructions which helped subjects to organize the list more efficiently were most beneficial to the older group. In a more direct test of age differences in organization and recall, Hultsch (1971b) utilized Mandler's (1967) technique of requiring subjects to sort 52 words into 2-7 categories until they had achieved two identical sorts. Hultsch found no age differences on the sorting behavior, but found that older subjects recalled fewer words in a subsequent retention test. The age decrement was greater for other subjects who did not sort the words into categories, but simply inspected the word list for the same number of trials as "sorting" subjects (see Figure 8). The interaction between age and experimental condition was significant, showing that age differences in recall are attenuated under conditions that encourage subjects to organize the material meaningfully. At first sight the result of no age differences in sorting behavior ("organization"), yet differences in recall, is puzzling since Mandler (1967) had reported a strong relationship between sorting and recall. In other words, given that subjects were induced to perform the same mental operations

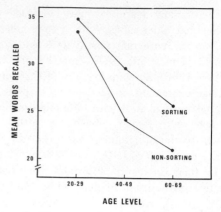

Figure 8. Mean number of words recalled as a function of age and experimental treatment. (From Hultsch, 1971b. *Developmental Psychology*, **4**, 338–342. Copyright 1971 by the American Psychological Association. Reprinted by permission.)

during categorization, retention should also have been equated. The resolution to this puzzle may depend on the fact that the experiment was run under intentional learning conditions; young subjects may have carried out further learning operations which then benefited their recall. Another possibility is that sorting performance did not index "organization" very accurately. This possibility is supported by Hultsch's (1974) finding of age decrements in organization when a more appropriate measure was used (the ITR measure of Bousfield and Bousfield, 1966). Hultsch suggests that use of an inappropriate measure of organization may also have given rise to Laurence's (1966) puzzling results. He comments:

... previous studies used Tulving's (1962) measure of subjective organization, which is sensitive to the number of words recalled on the two trials. Recalling words on trial $t + 1$ that were not recalled on trial t lowers Tulving's index. Since younger subjects generally acquire new words more rapidly than older subjects, this characteristic of the index tends to penalize them to a greater degree. The present measures do not suffer from this disadvantage and, hence, are probably more useful for developmental research. (Hultsch, 1974, p. 307)

Thus, Hultsch's recent work suggests that at least part of the older person's greater difficulty with recall tasks lies at the acquisition stage; older people fail to organize the material as effectively, and this failure leads to poorer recall levels. Other evidence supporting an acquisition deficit comes from studies in which presentation rates were varied. Most of these experiments are paired-associate learning studies and will not be reviewed in detail; they are described and discussed by Botwinick (1973, Chapter 15). Canestrari (1968) has shown that older subjects benefit disproportionately from slower rates of presentation, supporting the notion of an acquisition failure at faster rates, although it should also be noted that other workers have found no disproportionate advantage to an older group at slower rates (e.g., Monge and Hultsch, 1971).

Finally, a number of studies support the view that older subjects are less adept at using verbal and imaginal mediators to enhance their levels of retention. Hulicka and Grossman (1967) compared the performance of young and old subjects on a paired-associate learning task, either with no special instructions or with instructions to use mediators. When no instructions were given, Hulicka and Grossman found that older subjects showed a lesser tendency to use mediators spontaneously (36 percent *vs.* 68 percent of the pairs for old and young respectively). When subjects were asked about the mediators they had employed, it transpired that older subjects had a greater tendency than the young group to use verbal connections, but a lesser tendency than the young subjects to use imagery. These results were generally confirmed in a further study by Hulicka, Sterns, and Grossman (1967). Surprisingly, the second study failed to find a disproportionate improvement in the older group when unpaced association and response times were permitted; it seems likely that older subjects would require more time to form adequate mediators. The proportions of pairs recalled in the Hulicka and Grossman study are shown in Table 3. The table shows that older subjects do appear to benefit more from mediation instructions; they are able to perform the mental operation required for the formation of a mediator, but do not typically carry out these operations. This failure may be described as increasing cognitive rigidity (Chown, 1961) or perhaps decreased

TABLE 3. PERCENTAGES OF PAIRED ASSOCIATES RECALLED WITH AND WITHOUT MEDIATORS.

	No Mediator	Mediator
Young	63	83
Old	13	65

Hulicka and Grossman, 1967.

"depth of processing" (Craik and Lockhart, 1972) in the aged.

Hulicka's conclusions concerning age differences in the use of mediators were very largely confirmed by Canestrari (1968). He also found that older subjects benefited more from mediation instructions, although their level of performance remained lower than that of young subjects under both verbal and imaginal mediator conditions.

From this evidence, there seems little doubt that some part of the age decrement in secondary memory stems from less effective acquisition procedures. There is no failure to perceive the material in the elderly; it seems, rather, that the more elaborate encoding procedures involved in "organization" and in the formation of mnemonic mediators are not carried out spontaneously by older persons. In terms of the three-stage model of memory, it might be said that older subjects fail to "transfer information from primary memory to secondary memory" so effectively. That description is somewhat empty, however, since the mechanism of "transfer" has never been elucidated. It is preferable to state that older subjects fail to carry out those mental operations that result in deeper, elaborative encoding of the material to be learned. It is known that such failures result in poor retention (Craik and Lockhart, 1972; Jenkins, 1974; Eysenck, 1974). This theme will be taken up again after a review of age differences in rates of forgetting.

Age Differences in Forgetting from Secondary Memory

In the classical verbal learning literature, failure to remember was attributed largely to interference arising either from previously learned material (proactive inhibition, PI) or from subsequent material (retroactive inhibition, RI). At the time of recall, several responses have been associated to one stimulus, thereby giving rise to response competition; also there may be a failure of a "selector mechanism" to differentiate between appropriate and inappropriate responses. In this tradition, "forgetting" is thus seen as taking place during storage of the material and at the time of its retrieval. Information-processing paradigms are less amenable to an analysis in terms of stimuli and responses—for example, it is unclear what the stimulus term is in the free recall of words or in the recognition of pictures. The notion that forgetting occurred during storage persisted for some time as decay theory (e.g., Broadbent, 1963), and in the "acid-bath" model of Posner (1967). However, more recent information-processing theories have seen the major loci of memory failure as acquisition on the one hand and retrieval on the other (see Murdock, 1974 and Tulving, 1974 for recent reviews).

With regard to aging, one frequently repeated conclusion is that old subjects are more vulnerable to the disruptive effects of interference. This statement was made in the form of a plausible speculation by Welford (1958) and Jerome (1959), but has been echoed uncritically many times since then, and has increasingly been treated as established fact rather than as a proposition to be tested. The general acceptance of the notion is a tribute to the powerful ascendancy of ideas over observations!

An exception to this generally uncritical approach is a first-class review by Kausler (1970) in which the author points out the methodological weaknesses of some early studies on which the "increased interference susceptibility" hypothesis is based, and generally makes it clear that this interesting speculation is no more than that. The relevant experiments are largely in the paired-associate learning tradition and will not be reviewed in detail here. In general, however, it may be stated that one major flaw with earlier studies was the failure to equate initial learning between young and old groups. Once this is done, longer-term remembering is also equated (Wimer and Wigdor, 1958; Hulicka and Weiss, 1965; Hulicka, 1967;

Moenster, 1972) although exceptions to this conclusion have been reported (Wimer 1960; Arenberg, 1967; Harwood and Naylor, 1969). In a recent study, Smith (1974) also found no evidence for greater response interference with organized recall in an older group.

A further source of difficulty in evaluating the notion that older persons are more vulnerable to the effects of interference is the failure of theorists to agree on what exactly is meant by "interference." In S-R terms, interference is seen as response competition; this competition is more severe if the postulated selector mechanism fails to differentiate between currently appropriate and inappropriate response sets (Postman and Stark, 1969). The greater the number of potential responses associated with each stimulus term (either due to previous or subsequent relevant learning, or to a failure of differentiation) the less likely is the stimulus to evoke the desired response. A very similar idea from the information-processing literature is that a retrieval cue becomes less effective as more items are nested under it (Tulving and Pearlstone, 1966).

Despite the lack of good empirical evidence, it is still an attractive idea that older subjects may fail to remember an event because of the greater *functional* number of items associated with each retrieval cue (or stimulus term). The number of items may be functionally greater, thereby giving rise to greater "cue overload" in the elderly (1) because they fail to utilize retrieval information effectively and thus do not sharpen the cue until it adequately specifies the desired event in memory; also (2) because they fail to differentiate between appropriate and inappropriate sets of responses—there may be greater inertia and less discriminative power in the older person's selector mechanism. It should be stressed that this version of the "greater susceptibility to interference" hypothesis is put forward tentatively, but it may help to focus research activities on what this reviewer sees as relevant issues.

Some evidence from the literature is at least in general agreement with the "functional overload" notion. Tulving and Pearlstone (1966) found that when a list of nouns falling into various categories was presented for free recall, the proportion of words recalled from each category dropped systematically as the number of presented words per category increased. Hultsch (1975) has recently reported a similar study in which a 40-word list, comprising 10 categories each with 4 exemplars, was presented for recall. Under noncued conditions, the proportions of words recalled per category were .89, .79 and .70 for young, middle-aged and old subjects respectively; under cued conditions, the proportions were .80, .61 and .57 respectively. Cuing resulted in retrieval of more categories, but fewer exemplars from each category. Putting Hultsch's result together with the Tulving and Pearlstone finding, it could be said that older subjects behave as if they were retrieving from larger categories. A similar conclusion may be drawn from a study by Craik (1968b) in which list length was manipulated. Craik reported that the proportion of words retrieved from secondary memory was substantially smaller for an older group of subjects.

If the hypothesized selector mechanism works less efficiently for older subjects so that they cannot differentiate current responses from old responses, it would be expected that the number of intrusions from previous lists would rise with age. This finding is mentioned by Kay (1959) and was reported by Taub (1966). Supportive evidence also comes from a paired-associate study by Lair, Moon, and Kausler (1969). These workers found that older subjects were less able to learn a list made up of re-paired high associates (e.g., table-queen; king-chair). As a parallel observation from the work on amnesia, Warrington and Weiskrantz (1970) and Winocur and Weiskrantz (1976) have suggested that forgetting in amnesics may be largely attributable to the patients' inability to edit out items from previous lists. Also, more directly on the issue of inertia of the selector mechanism, Kinsbourne and Wood (1975) have reported that amnesic subjects do not show "release from PI" (Wickens, 1970) on the first shift trial, but they do show release on the *next* trial (for example, if 3 trials on "animals" are followed by 3 on "professions," normals show release on trial 4 while amnesics show release on trial 5). While

it would be interesting indeed if older subjects also exhibited this "delayed release" effect, the present evidence is against it. Goggin (1975) has carried out the "release from PI" experiment on subjects of various ages; she found that older (55+) subjects who scored above 50 on the Wechsler Memory Scale did show normal buildup and release from PI, but that a senile old group did not. The senile group was defined as older subjects (mean age = 74) who scored less than 50 on the Wechsler test. This group exhibited attenuated build-up and release effects, but showed no evidence of a delayed release effect.

To summarize this section on forgetting, many workers have concurred with the general idea that the elderly are more vulnerable to the effects of interference (Welford, 1958; Jerome, 1959; Schonfield, 1969a; Botwinick, 1973). The underlying assumption has usually been that prior or subsequent learning somehow weakens the strength of the memory trace, and that this process occurs more rapidly in older subjects. Despite the popularity of this view, however, there is essentially *no* good evidence to back it up. Recently, Tulving (1974) has argued persuasively that forgetting may be more a matter of decreasing retrieval cue effectiveness than loss of "trace strength"; when retrieval information is improved, the event is remembered. In this vein, it has been suggested in the present section, that older subjects may indeed be more vulnerable to interference—but where the interference arises from greater cue overload. This increased overload, in turn, may come from (1) a failure to utilize retrieval information effectively and (2) decreased effectiveness of the selector mechanism. Two points should be stressed in conclusion: first, the present account suggests that the locus of forgetting is at retrieval rather than during storage; second, the present account is again a *plausible speculation* which must be backed by experimental evidence before it is accepted or rejected.

The Locus of the Age Decrement in Secondary Memory

Before turning briefly to further topics, it may be helpful to bring together some arguments concerning the nature of the secondary memory deficit in the elderly. Schonfield and Robertson (1966) found a large age decrement in recall but none in recognition. Since it has been argued that recall depends on an active retrieval process whereas this is much less true for recognition (e.g., Kintsch, 1970), Schonfield and Robertson suggested that their results pointed to retrieval as being the major locus of difficulty in the older subject's memory performance. This conclusion was contested by McNulty and Caird (1966), however, who suggested that since recognition can be mediated by partial information, older subjects may have learned enough of the material to support recognition but not recall. The present reviewer finds this an unappealing argument as a description of Schonfield and Robertson's results. For example, if acquisition were the *only* cause of the age decrement in remembering, it is difficult to see why the elderly are also poorer at remembering information from "semantic memory" (Tulving, 1972)—that is, familiar faces, names, news items and objects. Such information has been highly overlearned, yet older subjects are often less able to recall it (Warrington and Sanders, 1971; Schonfield, 1972; Bahrick, Bahrick, and Wittlinger, 1975; Hurwitz and Allison, 1965). Also, an ingenious study by Buschke (1974) has demonstrated a retrieval failure in an older group. Buschke had his subjects attempt repeated recall trials from a 20-word list which was presented only once. Older subjects showed greater variability in the pool of words they recalled consistently from trial to trial—the words must therefore have been in storage but not retrieved on certain trials.

In a reply to McNulty and Caird, Schonfield (1967) makes it clear that he is fully in agreement that age decrements in acquisition do occur; his point is that retrieval processes are also less effective in the elderly. From the work reviewed in previous sections, it does indeed seem clear that both acquisition and retrieval processes are impaired in older subjects. Hultsch's (1974) study showed that organizational processes are poorer in the aged, while the work of Hulicka and Grossman (1967) and Canestrari (1968) showed deficits in the con-

struction of mediators. Buschke's (1974) recent study provides further convincing evidence of impaired retrieval. On the other hand, the present reviewer can find no good evidence for the notion that older subjects exhibit faster loss of material from storage, either through decay or interference processes. In fact, several theorists have recently suggested that once material is registered in secondary memory, the information is never lost from the system, although it may normally be inaccessible (Shiffrin and Atkinson, 1969; Tulving, 1974). The present conclusion, then, is that increasing age is associated with deficits in both acquisition and retrieval; a possible link between these stages of processing is outlined in a later section.

There is no point in prolonging the debate on whether age deficits are due to acquisition *or* retrieval. Undoubtedly some situations can be found in which acquisition is the major problem (e.g., Drachman and Leavitt, 1972) while in others, retrieval will be the major source of difficulty (Schonfield and Robertson, 1966; Hultsch, 1975). The next phase of research in this area must attempt to elucidate the interactions between experimental situations and the postulated memory processes.

Age Differences in Nonverbal Memory

One of the liberating effects of the switch from S-R to information-processing approaches to memory has been the much greater range of materials studied. As well as memory for linguistic material, recent experiments have examined memory for pictures, voices, tones, the modality of presentation, the time of presentation, spatial position, touch and smell. Some of this work is reviewed by Neisser (1967) and Murdock (1974). As yet, there are few studies linking nonverbal memory abilities with adult aging; some workers have studied age differences in memory for geometric designs, and there are several experiments on the retention of more meaningful pictorial material.

In general, the ability to reproduce or recognize geometric designs declines with age, but the loss is gradual until the 60's or 70's when the loss becomes greater. This pattern of results was reported for reproduction of the designs by

Kendall (1962), Heron and Chown (1967) and Davies (1967). Slightly different results were found by Botwinick and Storandt, 1974. They reported a decline with age in the reproduction of both recognizable forms (geometric designs) and meaningless shapes, but did not find a disproportionate decline after age 50. Although comparisons of reproduction and recognition are of doubtful validity, performance on recognition of designs appears to decline less with age than scores on reproduction tests (Bromley, 1958; Gilbert and Levee, 1971; Botwinick and Storandt, 1974). There is thus some slight evidence that the finding of differential age losses in recall and recognition applies to memory for designs as well as to linguistic material.

With regard to more meaningful pictorial material, several workers have presented line drawings of objects for later recall (Laurence, 1966; Harwood and Naylor, 1969). Age decrements in recall were observed in both studies. In this case, the subject may simply "recode" the picture and retain its verbal label, although the extra pictorial information may benefit recall (Paivio, 1971). Given the evidence that older subjects are poorer at constructing images as mediators (Hulicka and Grossman, 1967), it would be informative to ascertain whether older persons benefit disproportionately from the addition of pictorial information to the list of object names. Farrimond (1968) showed subjects 25 short scenes recorded on silent cine-film (e.g., a 4-second shot of a boy inflating a bicycle tire). Subjects did not expect a recall test; thus learning was incidental, although the primary task (lip-reading silent shots of a commentator after each scene was presented) necessitated attention to and comprehension of each visual scene. Farrimond's results are shown in Table 4. He found significant declines in recall both with advancing age and with lower verbal intelligence groups, although it is noteworthy that there is very little decline with this task until the 60's.

Studies on the recognition of meaningful pictorial material have generally shown slight deficits with increasing age. Botwinick and Storandt (1974) found no reliable decline in the recognition of 4 line drawings, although

TABLE 4. PERCENTAGE RECALL OF VISUAL SCENES BY SUBJECTS OF HIGH AND LOW VERBAL INTELLIGENCE.

	AGE (YEARS)				
	20's	30's	40's	50's	60+
High vocabulary	54	57	57	52	42
Low vocabulary	46	48	48	44	34

Farrimond, 1968.

there were undoubtedly ceiling effects operating in this test. In a similar task, Harwood and Naylor (1969) had subjects learn a series of 20 line drawings; after 4 weeks, young subjects recognized 19.0 of the drawings on average, while the older group's score was 16.6. The difference was significant although in absolute terms the age loss is not great. Finally, Howell (1972) found an age decrement in the recognition of pictures of common objects and of unfamiliar patterns, but no decrement in the recognition of pictures reproduced from the 1908 Sears Roebuck Catalogue. She concluded that recognition performance was related to the familiarity and meaningfulness of the materials used.

Age Differences in Long-term Retention

One rather widely accepted notion about the effects of aging is that while the elderly are deficient on tasks of recent memory, their memory for remote events is unimpaired. The evidence for this belief is entirely anecdotal—usually it is based on the recollection of a few highly salient childhood incidents. Before valid comparisons can be made between recent and remote memories some care should be taken to equate the nature of the material to be remembered, and the conditions of its acquisition. Another flaw in the anecdotal argument is that the childhood events have inevitably been recalled many times since they occurred; the older person is not remembering from 50 years ago, but partially at least, from the time of his last rehearsal. Fortunately, three sets of independent investigators have recently examined the question of remote memories more rigorously; all three have concluded that older subjects are poorer than younger controls at recalling and recognizing events from the past. The notion that memory for remote events is unimpaired in the elderly must thus now be rejected—although all investigators were surprised at the high levels of retention exhibited by the older groups. The studies in question are described briefly below.

Schonfield (1972) described an informal study in which subjects of various ages were asked to recall the names of all their school teachers. He found a systematic decline in the percentage of names recalled, from 67 percent for subjects in their 20's to 45 percent for subjects aged over 70. Although the scores dropped with age, recall levels were thus still quite high for the oldest group. A more elaborate study in the same vein was reported recently by Bahrick, Bahrick and Wittlinger (1975). These investi-

gators gave subjects a variety of tests for the names and faces of their high school graduating class. The information was verified from the relevant high school yearbook. The tests were (1) free recall of all names, (2) recognition of faces, (3) recognition of names, (4) matching faces and names, (5) name recall cued by a photograph of the person's face. An attempt was made to adjust the retention scores for such uncontrolled variables as size of class, meeting classmates since graduation, frequency and recency of looking at the yearbook. The results are shown in Figure 9. It should be noted that free recall is on a different scale from the other measures—the true proportion of names retrieved in free recall was only 0.15. Figure 9 shows that performance on the recognition and matching tasks remained quite stable for at least 15 years after graduation. In this

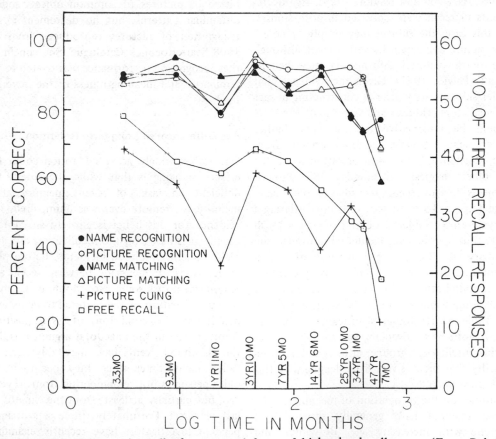

Figure 9. Recognition and recall of names and faces of high-school colleagues. (From Bahrick, Bahrick, and Wittlinger, 1975. *Journal of Experimental Psychology*, **104**, 54–75. Copyright 1975 by the American Psychological Association. Reprinted by permission.)

study, the age of the subjects and the length of the retention interval are necessarily confounded, but Bahrick, Bahrick, and Wittlinger (1975) suggest that the decline in recognition performance for the oldest group is suggestive of degenerative changes. The recall measures decline more gradually with age, although this decline is largely attributable to the forgetting of names of classmates who had been known only vaguely. A further interesting finding was an increase with age in the number of intrusions of names from the preceding and succeeding class (2 percent for subjects 6 months after graduation as opposed to 19 percent for subjects 48 years after graduation). Bahrick, Bahrick, and Wittlinger (1975) comment that this finding reflects a "declining ability to differentiate temporal context"—it is nicely in line with the suggestion made in a previous section that the "selector mechanism" is less efficient in older subjects.

Warrington and Silberstein (1970) devised a questionnaire to study the retention of news items which had been current from 1 month to 2 years previously. They found a decline in recall of the events, both with increasing retention interval and with increasing age of the subjects; however, there was much less decline in *recognition* performance with either variable (Table 5). In an extension of this technique, Warrington and Sanders (1971) tested subjects of various ages on memory for events and also on recognition of well-known faces. Again, they found that performance declined with remoteness of the event and with increasing age; in this case, there were age decrements in recognition as well as in recall. The authors concluded that "No evidence was obtained to support the widely held belief that memory is inversely related to the remoteness of events in older subjects" (Warrington and Sanders, 1971, p. 432).

Age Differences in Cognitive Operations

Although "discrete-stage" models of memory have been extremely heuristic in the past, there are signs that the splitting up of memory into separate stores may have outlived its usefulness. For example, Craik and Lockhart (1972) put forward a series of arguments against multistore models, and suggested instead that memory be thought of as a continuum. They further suggested that the durability of the memory trace is simply a function of the "depth of processing" carried out on the stimulus, where greater "depth" implies more elaborate, semantic analyses. If memory performance depends only on the depth (or "breadth") of encoding of the item, knowledge of a subsequent memory test or intention to learn should be unimportant; the only critical factor would be inducing the subject to carry out the optimal mental operations on the material. Thus, if incidental learning tasks were devised which necessitated either shallow, peripheral encoding or deep, elaborate encoding, the subject's memory performance should be poor in the first case and good in the other. Results in good agreement with this notion have recently been reported by Jenkins (1974), Schulman (1971) and by Craik and Tulving (1975). In these experiments, shallow encoding was induced by requiring the subject to make a physical or structural judgment about a word (e.g., "is it in capital letters?" or "does it contain the letter E?") while deep encoding was induced by means of a semantic or categorical judgment (e.g., "is the word an animal name?" or "rate the word for pleasantness"). The use of the incidental learning paradigm gives the experimenter control over the mental operations (Kolers, 1973) carried out by the subject.

This line of research has extremely important implications for the analysis and possible rectification of age deficits in memory. It seems highly likely that one major source of the deficit is poorer acquisition of the material in

TABLE 5. PERCENTAGE RETENTION OF PUBLIC EVENTS AFTER THREE TIME INTERVALS.

Retention Interval (months)	RECALL			RECOGNITION		
	6	12	18	6	12	18
age group { <40	48	37	32	77	72	69
40–54	45	35	31	80	71	68
55+	36	29	26	75	69	68

Warrington and Silberstein, 1970

secondary memory, and that this failure may be thought of as a "production deficiency" (Flavell, Beach, and Chinsky, 1966; Kausler, 1970). That is, older subjects are capable of performing the optimal mental operations associated with good retention, but fail to carry them out spontaneously (Hulicka and Grossman, 1967). The present analysis suggests that if older subjects were not simply instructed to "learn" the material, but were given an appropriate task to perform, their resulting memory performance would be closer to the level reached by a younger group.

Several studies of age differences in incidental learning have been carried out. The results are confused and contradictory; some studies found an age decrement (Bromley, 1958; Farrimond, 1968; Peak, 1968) while others found no age differences (Wimer, 1960; Hulicka, 1965). One weakness of these studies is the underlying assumption that incidental learning is a different "type" of learning from intentional learning, whereas the present analysis leads to the point of view that there is no difference between incidental and intentional learning, except insofar as the mental operations performed are themselves different. A second weakness, from the present viewpoint, is that most of the studies cited above did not require the subjects to perform operations on the material that was later tested. There is thus no guarantee that older subjects treated the material in the same way; in fact, a reasonable conclusion would be that they did not. For example, Bromley (1958) suggests that due to a "reduction in surplus intellectual resources" older subjects do not process irrelevant details to the same extent as a younger group would. Similarly Hulicka comments: "it is likely that attention to incidental details tends to decrease with increased age, for reasons including the older person's concentration on a narrowed range of problems, and particularly his increased knowledge of the environment which reduces his need to attend to perhaps interesting but irrelevant or incidental stimuli" (Hulicka, 1965, p. 646). From the present point of view, incidental tasks are needed which require the subject to deal with the presented material in a specific way. From Craik and Lockhart's

(1972) analysis, this would then lead to control over the encoding operations carried out by subjects of different ages. If a production deficiency is indeed a major source of age decrement, then equating acquisition in this manner should attenuate age differences; any remaining differences could then be more confidently attributed to another source.

So far, few studies have been carried out which meet these requirements. One study is by Johnson (1973) who asked subjects to classify words as nouns or verbs; this task was followed by an unexpected memory test. Johnson found no age differences in either free recall, cued recall or recognition after the incidental learning task. This result could be interpreted as showing that retention was equated since acquisition was equated. Younger subjects showed a disproportionate improvement in their free recall scores under intentional learning conditions, perhaps demonstrating that the young group performed more additional operations under instructions to learn.

A study carried out in the present author's laboratory by Sharon White will be briefly described. Following the techniques of Craik and Tulving (1975), White presented a series of single words to subjects under one of four instructional conditions. Before each word was presented, the experimenter asked the subject to make one of the following judgments: (1) Is the word in capital letters? (2) Does the word rhyme with _____? (3) Does the word belong to the _____ category? Although each word was then presented for the same time after the question had been asked, it was hypothesized that the judgments required deeper processing from (1) to (3) and that performance in a later unexpected memory test would reflect the benefits of this deeper processing. The fourth presentation condition was the instruction to "learn this word." Thus, subjects expected a memory test for one quarter of the words presented, but thought they were simply making judgments about the remaining words. After all words were presented, subjects were first asked to recall as many words as they could from *all* conditions, and were then given a recognition list. The results are shown in Figure 10.

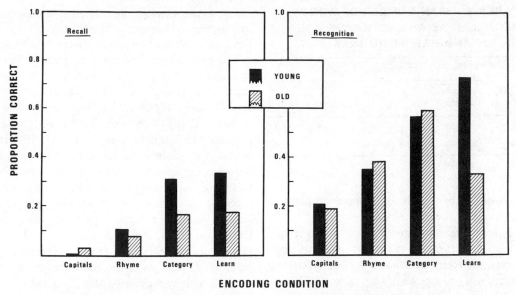

Figure 10. Age differences in recall and recognition as a function of "depth of processing." (From Sharon White, unpublished data.)

In the recall test, performance increased from "capitals" judgments to "category" judgments; the "learn" condition yielded the same level of recall as the deepest incidental task (category judgment). Further, an age decrement was found under three of the four conditions. This result could be interpreted to mean that older subjects showed a retrieval deficit; performance was poorer for them even though acquisition is assumed to be equivalent for both age groups in the first three conditions. In the recognition test, however, the age decrement disappeared in the incidental conditions although it was still present in the "learn" condition. Tentatively, it could be concluded that when acquisition is equated (conditions 1 to 3) and when retrieval information is adequate (recognition), age decrements are eliminated. The finding of an age decrement under the "learn-recognition" condition is puzzling, but may reflect the fact that in this experiment, old subjects simply repeated the words to themselves under "learn" instructions, while young subjects encoded the words in a semantic fashion. That is, "learning" for the older subjects was equivalent to processing the words at the level of their sounds, while the younger group encoded the words at a deeper, semantic level.

Finally, an excellent study by Eysenck (1974) has recently been reported. It is similar in conception to White's study but is interpreted somewhat differently. Eysenck proposes a "processing-deficit hypothesis" of age decrements in memory; namely, that older subjects are at their greatest disadvantage with deeper, semantic forms of encoding. This notion was tested by giving subjects incidental tasks which necessitated either relatively shallow processing (counting letters of words and generating rhymes) or more semantic processing (generating appropriate adjectives and images to word stimuli). In addition, a control group was simply instructed to learn the list of words. All groups subsequently recalled the words; the results are shown in Table 6. Eysenck's results are obviously very similar to White's recall data (Figure 10). However, whereas Eysenck interprets his results as showing a semantic processing deficit, White's recognition results cast some doubt on this interpretation.

Further experiments must be carried out to clarify the picture. In any event, the present reviewer feels that this type of incidental learning study can make a major contribution to our understanding of age decrements in memory processes. Finally in this section, the possible

TABLE 6. MEAN NUMBER OF WORDS RECALLED AS A FUNCTION OF AGE GROUP AND ORIENTING TASK.

Age Group	ORIENTING TASK				
	Letter Counting	Rhyming	Ad-jective	Imagery	Con-trol
Young	6.5	7.6	14.8	17.6	19.3
Old	7.0	6.9	11.0	13.4	12.0

Eysenck, 1974.

application of "depth of processing" ideas to retrieval may be pointed out.

It seems certain that the elderly suffer from a retrieval deficit in secondary memory performance. Retrieval failures occur in relatively short-term situations (e.g., Schonfield and Robertson, 1966), long-term situations (e.g., Warrington and Sanders, 1971) and in clinical settings (Hurwitz and Allison, 1965). In all these cases, older persons benefit disproportionately from the provision of good retrieval information. It seems as if older subjects fail to elaborate minimal retrieval cues in order to make them more effective; while the younger person can actively reconstruct aspects of the initial situation, the older person either does not or cannot engage in these reconstructive activities. In this sense, it could be speculatively suggested that the retrieval deficit is due to the same basic processing failure as the acquisition deficit, namely, a failure to engage in deep, semantic processing when presented with either the material to be learned or the retrieval cue.

BROADER IMPLICATIONS

In conclusion, some comments are made about points of contact between research on age differences in memory and other areas. Also, some questions for future research are pointed out.

Relation to Other Areas

There are some beguiling similarities between the pattern of results shown by old subjects in memory tasks and other groups of "non-normals" (i.e., other than young college students). During the next few years, it will be an important task to ascertain the extent to which

these similarities are associated with similar underlying differences in brain structure and function. The most obvious comparison is between children and older adults. Here the outstanding similarity is the finding of a "production deficiency" in children (Flavell, Beach, and Chinsky, 1966) and in the elderly (e.g., Kausler, 1970). A second finding with older subjects which is echoed in work with children is that a developmental trend has been found between the ages of 5 and 10 for performance to increase on the second channel of a dichotic listening task while performance on the first half-set remains relatively constant with age (Inglis and Sykes, 1967). A third point of contact is the potential usefulness of regarding memory failures in both the elderly and in younger children as being due to a failure to encode "deeply" (Hagen, Jongeward and Kail, 1975). Fourth, the extremely influential ideas of Piaget are now being extended to age changes in cognitive abilities (e.g., Hooper, Fitzgerald and Papalia, 1971; Storck, Looft and Hooper, 1972). It seems likely that this area of research will grow in importance.

Research on pathological populations has also yielded similarities to findings from older normals. Several workers have explored the relations between results from brain-damaged subjects and the elderly (e.g., Inglis, 1965; Hurwitz and Allison, 1965; Davies, 1968). This comparison may have particular validity since it is widely assumed that the effects of normal aging are due in part to the loss of brain tissue. Davies (1968) reported the results of an extensive series of tests showing the similarities and differences between the two groups of subjects. One plausible reason for the lessened efficiency of the aged brain is that the brain tissue has been chronically starved of oxygen, due to poorer vascular circulation in the elderly. This notion is particularly appealing since techniques of hyperoxygenation may lead to restoration of normal functioning (e.g., Jacobs, Winter, Alvis, and Small, 1969). In a less extreme form, a comparison could be made between healthy and non-healthy older people. It is possible that poor health might lie behind some of the alleged "age decrement." Hulicka (1967) investigated this notion specifically for memory disorders and found some support for the hypothesis; only one out of four learning tasks continued to show significant age-related decrements when differences in health status were eliminated by statistical techniques.

Finally, some classes of amnesic patients show patterns of memory impairment which bear a strong resemblance to the decrements observed in the elderly. For example, Baddeley and Warrington (1970) have argued that primary memory functioning is essentially intact in amnesic patients and that the memory decrements are associated with secondary memory deficits. In line with Waugh and Norman's (1965) analysis, secondary memory deficits can also manifest themselves in some short-term retention situations, and this result has been reported in amnesic subjects (Cermak and Butters, 1972). There is also accumulating evidence that many memory decrements in amnesic subjects are due to retrieval failures (Warrington and Weiskrantz, 1970; Kinsbourne and Wood, 1975). While normal elderly subjects are not necessarily identical to younger amnesics in their memory functioning, the similar pattern of results in amnesics may point to useful exploratory research which might be undertaken with the aged.

Future Research

The main need is for more data from well-controlled experimental studies. Large-scale parametric investigations establishing normative data for a variety of tasks would be especially welcome; the programs of research reported by Heron and Chown (1967) and by Botwinick and Storandt (1974) have been extremely useful in this regard. Otherwise the need is for theorists and empirical workers who are contributing to current work in "mainstream" memory research to turn their attention to the age variable. It is almost inevitable that applied workers fall behind the very latest ideas in the parent discipline, and this is especially likely to happen in memory research which presents a voluminous and highly confusing literature to the non-expert.

The present reviewer's biases and prejudices have been made fairly explicit throughout this chapter but, in conclusion, some main points will be reiterated in the form of focal issues for future research.

1. The nature of the age decrement in divided attention situations. Is the deficit best thought of as a reduction in effective capacity, loss of processing power or loss of mental flexibility?

2. Age differences in the ability to manipulate and reorganize the contents of primary memory. The notion of "working memory" has recently been revived (Baddeley and Hitch, 1974) linking primary memory with other cognitive abilities, and these concepts might be usefully extended to research in aging. A reduction in flexibility (possibly allied with a generalized slowing of mental functioning, e.g., Welford, 1958; Botwinick, 1973) again seems a possible description of the deficit.

3. Flexibility and inertia may also play a part in the postulated reduced effectiveness with age of Postman and Stark's (1969) selector mechanism. The failure to suppress responses which are no longer appropriate also bears a resemblance to perseveration defects found in patients with frontal-lobe damage (e.g., Luria, 1973).

4. Age differences in the qualitative nature and relative effectiveness of various types of rehearsal. Recent work has shown the usefulness of the distinction between primary or maintenance rehearsal and secondary or elaborative rehearsal (Craik and Watkins, 1973; Woodward, Bjork and Jongeward, 1973). These notions could be usefully applied to memory research with elderly subjects.

5. The nature of the retrieval deficit in older persons. The suggestion has been made in the present chapter that old subjects fail to process retrieval information "deeply," and thus to utilize it effectively. This description, and others, should be sharpened into empirically testable propositions.

6. Finally, the commonalities among studies of child development, amnesia, brain damage and aging should provide a further focus for future research.

REFERENCES

Anders, T. R., and Fozard, J. L. 1973. Effects of age upon retrieval from primary and secondary memory. *Developmental Psychology*, 9, 411–415.

Anders, T. R., Fozard, J. L., and Lillyquist, T. D. 1972. The effects of age upon retrieval from short-term memory. *Developmental Psychology*, 6, 214–217.

Anderson, C. M. B., and Craik, F. I. M. 1974. The effect of a concurrent task on recall from primary memory. *J. Verb. Learn. Verb. Behav.*, 13, 107–113.

Arenberg, D. 1967. Age differences in retroaction. *J. Gerontol.*, 22, 88–91.

Arenberg, D. 1968. Input modality and short-term retention in old and young adults. *J. Gerontol.*, 23, 462–465.

Atkinson, R. C., and Shiffrin, R. M. 1971. The control of short-term memory. *Sci. Am.*, 224, 82–90.

Baddeley, A. D. 1966. The influence of acoustic and semantic similarity on long-term memory for word sequences. *Quart. J. Exp. Psych.*, 18, 302–309.

Baddeley, A. D., and Hitch, G. 1974. Working memory. *In*, G. H. Bower (ed.), *The Psychology of Learning and Motivation*, Vol. VIII, pp. 47–89. New York: Academic Press.

Baddeley, A. D., and Warrington, E. K. 1970. Amnesia and the distinction between long- and short-term memory. *J. Verb. Learn. Verb. Behav.*, 9, 176–189.

Bahrick, H. P., Bahrick, P. O., and Wittlinger, R. P. 1975. Fifty years of memory for names and faces: A cross-sectional approach. *J. Exp. Psych.: General*, 104, 54–75.

Bartlett, F. C. 1932. *Remembering: A Study in Experimental and Social Psychology*. Cambridge: Cambridge University Press.

Binks, M. G., and Sutcliffe, J. 1972. The effects of age and verbal ability on short-term recognition memory. Paper presented at the annual conference of the British Psychological Society, Nottingham.

Birren, J. E. (ed.) 1959. *Handbook of Aging and the Individual: Psychological and Biological Aspects.* Chicago: University of Chicago Press.

Botwinick, J. 1973. *Aging and Behavior.* New York: Springer.

Botwinick, J., and Storandt, M. 1974. *Memory, Related Functions and Age.* Springfield, Illinois: Charles C. Thomas.

Bousfield, A. K., and Bousfield, W. A. 1966. Measurement of clustering and of sequential constancies in repeated free recall. *Psych. Reports*, 19, 935–942.

Brinley, J., and Fichter, J. 1970. Performance deficits in the elderly in relation to memory load and set. *J. Gerontol.*, 25, 30–35.

Broadbent, D. E. 1958. *Perception and Communication.* New York: Pergamon Press.

Broadbent, D. E. 1963. Flow of information within the organism. *J. Verb. Learn. Verb. Behav.*, 2, 34–39.

Broadbent, D. E., and Gregory, M. 1965. Some confirmatory results on age differences in memory for simultaneous stimulation. *Brit. J. Psychol.*, 56, 77–80.

Broadbent, D. E., and Heron, A. 1962. Effects of a subsidiary task on performance involving immediate memory in younger and older men. *Brit. J. Psychol.*, 53, 189–198.

Bromley, D. B. 1958. Some effects of age on short-term learning and memory. *J. Gerontol.*, 13, 398–406.

Brown, J. 1958. Some tests of the decay theory of immediate memory. *Quart. J. Exp. Psych.*, 10, 12–21.

Bryden, M. P. 1963. Ear preference in auditory perception. *J. Exp. Psych.*, 65, 103–105.

Bryden, M. P. 1971. Attentional strategies and short-term memory in dichotic listening. *Cog. Psychol.*, 2, 99–116.

Buschke, H. 1974. Two stages of learning by children and adults. *Bull. Psychon. Soc.*, 2, 392–394.

Caird, W. K. 1964. Reverberatory activity and memory disorder. *Nature*, 201, 1150.

Caird, W. K. 1966. Aging and short-term memory. *J. Gerontol.*, 21, 295–299.

Caird, W. K., and Inglis, J. 1961. The short-term storage of auditory and visual two-channel digits by elderly patients with memory disorder. *J. Mental Sci.*, 107, 1062–1069.

Canestrari, R. E. 1966. The effects of commonality on paired-associate learning in two age groups. *Journal of Genetic Psychology*, 108, 3–7.

Canestrari, R. E. 1968. Age changes in acquisition. *In*, G. A. Talland (ed.), *Human Aging and Behavior*, pp. 169–187. New York: Academic Press.

Cermak, L. S., and Butters, N. 1972. The role of interference and encoding in the short-term memory deficits of Korsakoff patients. *Neuropsychologia*, 10, 89–95.

Chown, S. M. 1961. Age and the rigidities. *J. Gerontol.*, 16, 353–362.

Clark, L., and Knowles, J. 1973. Age differences in dichotic listening performance. *J. Gerontol.*, 28, 173–178.

Conrad, R., and Hille, B. A. 1958. The decay theory of immediate memory and paced recall. *Can. J. Psych.*, 12, 1–6.

Craik, F. I. M. 1965. The nature of the age decrement in performance on dichotic listening tasks. *Quart. J. Exp. Psych.*, 17, 227–240.

Craik, F. I. M. 1968a. Short-term memory and the aging process. *In*, G. A. Talland (ed.), *Human Aging and Behavior*, pp. 131–168. New York: Academic Press.

Craik, F. I. M. 1968b. Two components in free recall. *J. Verb. Learn. Verb. Behav.*, 7, 996–1004.

Craik, F. I. M. 1969. Modality effects in short-term storage. *J. Verb. Learn. Verb. Behav.*, 8, 658–664.

Craik, F. I. M. 1971a. Age differences in recognition memory. *Quart. J. Exp. Psych.*, 23, 316–323.

Craik, F. I. M. 1971b. Primary memory. *Brit. Med. Bull.*, 27, 232–236.

Craik, F. I. M. 1973. Signal detection analysis of age

differences in divided attention. Paper presented at the meeting of the American Psychological Association, Montreal.

Craik, F. I. M. and Lockhart, R. S. 1972. Levels of processing: A framework for memory research. *J. Verb. Learn. Verb. Behav.*, **11**, 671–684.

Craik, F. I. M., and Masani, P. A. 1967. Age differences in the temporal integration of language. *Brit. J. Psychol.*, **58**, 291–299.

Craik, F. I. M., and Masani, P. A. 1969. Age and intelligence differences in coding and retrieval of word lists. *Brit. J. Psychol.*, **60**, 315–319.

Craik, F. I. M., and Tulving, E. 1975. Depth of processing and the retention of words in episodic memory. *J. Exp. Psych.: General*, **104**, 268–294.

Craik, F. I. M., and Watkins, M. J. 1973. The role of rehearsal in short-term memory. *J. Verb. Learn. Verb. Behav.*, **12**, 599–607.

Crenshaw, D. A. 1969. Retrieval processes in memory and aging. Doctoral thesis, Washington University.

Crowder, R. G., and Morton, J. 1969. Precategorical acoustic storage (PAS). *Percept. and Psychophys.*, **5**, 365–373.

Davies, A. D. M. 1967. Age and memory-for-designs test. *Brit. J. Soc. Clin. Psychol.*, **6**, 228–233.

Davies, A. D. M. 1968. Measures of mental deterioration in aging and brain damage. *In*, S. M. Chown and K. F. Riegel (eds.), *Psychological Functioning in the Normal Aging and Senile Aged*, pp. 78–90. Basel: Karger.

Drachman, D., and Leavitt, J. 1972. Memory impairment in the aged: Storage versus retrieval deficit. *J. Exp. Psych.*, **93**, 302–308.

Engen, T., and Ross, B. M. 1973. Long-term memory of odors with and without verbal descriptions. *J. Exp. Psych.*, **100**, 221–227.

Erber, J. T. 1974. Age differences in recognition memory. *J. Gerontol.*, **29**, 177–181.

Eriksen, C. W., Hamlin, R. M. and Daye, C. 1973. Aging adults and rate of memory scan. *Bull. Psychon. Soc.*, **1**, 259–260.

Eysenck, M. W. 1974. Age differences in incidental learning. *Developmental Psychology*, **10**, 936–941.

Farrimond, T. 1968. Retention and recall: Incidental learning of visual and auditory material. *Journal of Genetic Psychology*, **113**, 155–165.

Flavell, J. H., Beach, D. R., and Chinsky, J. M. 1966. Spontaneous verbal rehearsal in a memory task as a function of age. *Child Development*, **37**, 283–299.

Fozard, J. L., Carr, G. D., Talland, G. A., and Erwin, D. E. 1971. Effects of information load, sensory modality, and age on paced inspection performance. *Quart. J. Exp. Psych.*, **23**, 304–310.

Fozard, J. L., and Waugh, N. C. 1969. Proactive inhibition of prompted items. *Psychon. Sci.*, **17**, 67–68.

Fraser, D. C. 1958. Decay of immediate memory with age. *Nature*, **182**, 1163.

Friedman, H. 1966. Memory organization in the aged. *Journal of Genetic Psychology*, **109**, 3–8.

Friedman, H. 1974. Interrelation of two types of immediate memory in the aged. *J. Psychol.*, **87**, 177–181.

Gilbert, J. G. 1941. Memory loss in senescence. *J. Abn. Soc. Psych.*, **36**, 73–86.

Gilbert, J. G., and Levee, R. F. 1971. Patterns of declining memory. *J. Gerontol.*, **26**, 70–75.

Gilson, E. Q., and Baddeley, A. D. 1969. Tactile short-term memory. *Quart. J. Exp. Psych.*, **21**, 180–184.

Goggin, J. P. 1975. The effects of aging on short-term memory. Paper presented at the Midwestern Psychological Association Annual Convention, Chicago.

Gordon, S. K., and Clark, W. C. 1974a. Application of signal detection theory to prose recall and recognition in elderly and young adults. *J. Gerontol.*, **29**, 64–72.

Gordon, S. K., and Clark, W. C. 1974b. Adult age differences in word and nonsense syllable recognition memory and response criterion. *J. Gerontol.*, **29**, 659–665.

Haber, R. N. 1970. How we remember what we see. *Sci. Am.*, **222**, 104–112.

Hagen, J. W., Jongeward, R. H., Jr., and Kail, R. V., Jr. 1975. Cognitive perspectives on the development of memory. *In*, H. Reese (ed.), *Advances in Child Development and Behavior*, Vol 10. New York: Academic Press.

Harwood, E., and Naylor, G. F. K. 1969. Recall and recognition in elderly and young subjects. *Australian J. Psychol.*, **21**, 251–257.

Hebb, D. O. 1961. Distinctive features of learning in the higher animal. *In*, J. F. Delafresnaye (ed.), *Brain Mechanisms and Learning*, pp. 37–46. New York: Oxford University Press.

Heron, A., and Chown, S. M. 1967. *Age and Function*. London: Churchill.

Heron, A., and Craik, F. I. M. 1964. Age differences in cumulative learning of meaningful and meaningless material. *Scand. J. Psychol.*, **5**, 209–217.

Hooper, F. H., Fitzgerald, J., and Papalia, D. 1971. Piagetian theory and the aging process: Extensions and speculations. *Aging and Human Development*, **2**, 3–20.

Howell, S. C. 1972. Familiarity and complexity in perceptual recognition. *J. Gerontol.*, **27**, 364–371.

Hulicka, I. M. 1965. Age differences for intentional and incidental learning and recall scores. *J. Am. Geriat. Soc.*, **13**, 639–648.

Hulicka, I. M. 1967. Age differences in retention as a function of interference. *J. Gerontol.*, **22**, 180–184.

Hulicka, I. M., and Grossman, J. L. 1967. Age group comparisons for the use of mediators in paired-associate learning. *J. Gerontol.*, **22**, 46–51.

Hulicka, I. M., Sterns, H., and Grossman, J. 1967. Age group comparisons of paired-associate learning as a function of paced and self-paced association and response times. *J. Gerontol.*, **22**, 274–280.

Hulicka, I. M., and Weiss, R. 1965. Age differences in retention as a function of learning. *J. Consult. Psychol.*, **29**, 125–129.

Hultsch, D. F. 1969. Adult age differences in the

organization of free recall. *Developmental Psychology*, **1**, 673–678.

Hultsch, D. F. 1971a. Organization and memory in adulthood. *Hum. Develop.*, **14**, 16–29.

Hultsch, D. F. 1971b. Adult age differences in free classification and free recall. *Developmental Psychology*, **4**, 338–342.

Hultsch, D. F. 1974. Learning to learn in adulthood. *J. Gerontol.*, **29**, 302–308.

Hultsch, D. F. 1975. Adult age differences in retrieval: Trace-dependent and cue-dependent forgetting. *Developmental Psychology*, **11**, 197–201.

Hurwitz, L. J., and Allison, R. S. 1965. Factors influencing performance in psychological testing of the aged. *In*, A. T. Welford and J. E. Birren (eds.), *Behavior, Aging and the Nervous System*, pp. 461–475. Springfield, Illinois: Charles C. Thomas.

Inglis, J. 1964. Influence of motivation, perception and attention on age-related changes in short-term memory. *Nature*, **204**, 103–104.

Inglis, J. 1965. Immediate memory, age, and brain function. *In*, A. T. Welford, and J. E. Birren (eds.), *Behavior, Aging and the Nervous System*, pp. 88–113. Springfield, Illinois: Charles C. Thomas.

Inglis, J., and Ankus, M. N. 1965. Effects of age on short-term storage and serial rote learning. *Brit. J. Psychol.*, **56**, 183–195.

Inglis, J., and Caird, W. K. 1963. Age differences in successive responses to simultaneous stimulation. *Can. J. Psych.*, **17**, 98–105.

Inglis, J., and Sanderson, R. E. 1961. Successive responses to simultaneous stimulation in elderly patients with memory disorder. *J. Abn. Soc. Psych.*, **62**, 709–712.

Inglis, J., and Sykes, D. H. 1967. Some sources of variation in dichotic listening performance in children. *J. Exp. Child Psychol.*, **5**, 480–488.

Inglis, J., and Tansey, C. L. 1967. Age differences and scoring differences in dichotic listening performance. *J. Psych.*, **66**, 325–332.

Jacobs, E. A., Winter, P. M. Alvis, H. J., and Small, S. M. 1969. Hyperoxgenation effects on cognitive functioning in the aged. *New Engl. J. Med.*, **281**, 753–757.

Jenkins, J. J. 1974. Can we have a theory of meaningful memory? *In*, R. L. Solso (ed.), *Theories in Cognitive Psychology: The Loyola Symposium*, pp. 1–20. Potomac, Maryland: Lawrence Erlbaum Associates.

Jerome, E. A. 1959. Age and learning—experimental studies. *In*, J. E. Birren (ed.), *Handbook of Aging and the Individual: Psychological and Biological Aspects*, pp. 655–699. Chicago: University of Chicago Press.

Johnson, L. K. 1973. Changes in memory as a function of age. Doctoral thesis, University of Southern California.

Kausler, D. H. 1970. Retention—forgetting as a nomological network for developmental research. *In*, L. R. Goulet and P. B. Baltes (eds.), *Life-Span Developmental Psychology*, pp. 305–353. New York: Academic Press.

Kay, H. 1959. Theories of learning and aging. *In*, J. E. Birren (ed.), *Handbook of Aging and the Individual*, pp. 614–654. Chicago: University of Chicago Press.

Keevil-Rogers, P., and Schnore, M. 1969. Short-term memory as a function of age in persons of above average intelligence. *J. Gerontol.*, **24**, 184–188.

Kendall, B. S. 1962. Memory-for-designs performance in the seventh and eighth decades of life. *Perceptual Motor Skills*, **14**, 399–405.

Kinsbourne, M. 1972. Contrasting patterns of memory span decrement in ageing and aphasia. *J. Neurol., Neurosurg. Psychiat.*, **35**, 192–195.

Kinsbourne, M. 1973. Age effects on letter span related to rate and sequential dependency. *J. Gerontol.*, **28**, 317–319.

Kinsbourne, M., and Wood, F. 1975. Short term memory processes and the amnesic syndrome. *In*, J. A. Deutsch (ed.), *Short-term Memory*. New York: Academic Press.

Kintsch, W. 1970. Models for free recall and recognition. *In*, D. A. Norman (ed.), *Models of Human Memory*, pp. 333–374. New York: Academic Press.

Kirchner, W. K. 1958. Age differences in short-term retention of rapidly changing information. *J. Exp. Psych.*, **55**, 352–358.

Kirsner, K. 1972. Developmental changes in short-term recognition memory. *Brit. J. Psychol.*, **63**, 109–117.

Kolers, P. A. 1973. Remembering operations. *Memory and Cognition*, **1**, 347–355.

Kriauciunas, R. 1968. The relationship of age and retention interval activity in short term memory. *J. Gerontol.*, **23**, 169–173.

Lair, C., Moon, W., and Kausler, D. H. 1969. Associative interference in the paired associate learning of middle-aged and old subjects. *Developmental Psychology*, **1**, 548–552.

Laurence, M. W. 1966. Age differences in performance and subjective organization in the free recall of pictorial material. *Can. J. Psych.*, **20**, 388–399.

Laurence, M. W. 1967a. A developmental look at the usefulness of list categorization as an aid to free recall. *Can. J. Psych.*, **21**, 153–165.

Laurence, M. W. 1967b. Memory loss with age: A test of two strategies for its retardation. *Psychon. Sci.*, **9**, 209–210.

Laurence, M. W., and Trotter, M. 1971. Effect of acoustic factors and list organization in multitrial free recall learning of college age and elderly adults. *Developmental Psychology*, **5**, 202–210.

Lehman, H. C. 1953. *Age and Achievement*. Princeton, New Jersey: Princeton University Press.

Luria, A. R. 1973. *The Working Brain*. London: Allen Lane The Penguin Press.

Mackay, H. A., and Inglis, J. 1963. The effect of age on a short-term auditory storage process. *Gerontologia*, **8**, 193–200.

Mackworth, J. F. 1962. Presentation rate and immediate memory. *Can. J. Psych.*, **16**, 42–47.

Mandler, G. 1967. Organization and memory. *In*, K. W. Spence and J. T. Spence (eds.), *The Psychology of Learning and Motivation: Advances in Research and Theory*, Vol 1, pp. 327–372. New York: Academic Press.

McGhie, A., Chapman, J., and Lawson, J. S. 1965. Changes in immediate memory with age. *Brit. J. Psychol.*, **56**, 69–75.

McNulty, J. A., and Caird, W. 1966. Memory loss with age: Retrieval or storage? *Psych. Reports*, **19**, 229–230.

Melton, A. W. 1963. Implications of short-term memory for a general theory of memory. *J. Verb. Learn. Verb. Behav.*, **2**, 1–21.

Miller, G. A., and Selfridge, J. A. 1950. Verbal context and the recall of meaningful material. *Amer. J. Psych.*, **63**, 176–185.

Milner, B. 1970. Memory and the medial temporal regions of the brain. *In*, K. Pribram and D. Broadbent (eds.), *Biology of Memory*, pp. 29–50. New York: Academic Press.

Moenster, P. A. 1972. Learning and memory in relation to age. *J. Gerontol.*, **27**, 361–363.

Monge, R., and Hultsch, D. 1971. Paired associate learning as a function of adult age and length of anticipation and inspection intervals. *J. Gerontol.*, **26**, 157–162.

Murdock, B. B., Jr. 1966. Visual and auditory stores in short-term memory. *Quart. J. Exp. Psych.*, **18**, 206–211.

Murdock, B. B., Jr. 1967. Recent developments in short-term memory. *Brit. J. Psychol.*, **58**, 421–433.

Murdock, B. B., Jr. 1974. *Human Memory: Theory and Data*. Potomac, Maryland: Lawrence Erlbaum Associates.

Murdock, B. B., Jr., and Walker, K. D. 1969. Modality effects in free recall. *J. Verb. Learn. Verb. Behav.*, **8**, 665–676.

Neisser, U. 1967. *Cognitive Psychology*. New York: Appleton-Century-Crofts.

Paivio, A. 1971. *Imagery and Verbal Processes*. New York: Holt, Rinehart and Winston.

Peak, D. T. 1968. Changes in short-term memory in a group of aging community residents. *J. Gerontol.*, **23**, 9–16.

Peterson, L. R., and Peterson, M. J. 1959. Short-term retention of individual verbal items. *J. Exp. Psych.*, **58**, 193–198.

Posner, M. I. 1967. Short-term memory systems in human information processing. *Acta Psychol.*, **27**, 267–284.

Posner, M. I., Boies, S. J., Eichelman, W. H., and Taylor, R. L. 1969. Retention of visual and name codes of single letters. *J. Exper. Psychol. Monogr. Suppl.*, **79**, Part 2, 1–16.

Postman, L. 1961. The present status of interference theory. *In*, C. N. Cofer (ed.), *Verbal Learning and Verbal Behavior*, pp. 152–179. New York: McGraw-Hill.

Postman, L., and Stark, K. 1969. Role of response availability in transfer and interference. *J. Exp. Psych.*, **79**, 168–177.

Postman, L., and Underwood, B. J. 1973. Critical issues in interference theory. *Memory and Cognition.*, **1**, 19–40.

Raymond, B. 1971. Free recall among the aged. *Psych. Reports*, **29**, 1179–1182.

Schonfield, D. 1965. Memory changes with age. *Nature*, **208**, 918.

Schonfield, D. 1967. Memory loss with age: Acquisition and retrieval. *Psych. Reports*, **20**, 223–226.

Schonfield, D. 1969a. Learning and retention. *In*, J. E. Birren (ed.), *Contemporary Gerontology: Issues and Concepts*. Los Angeles: University of Southern California Press.

Schonfield, D. 1969b. Age and remembering. Duke University Council on Aging and Human Development. Proceedings of Seminars.

Schonfield, D. 1972. Theoretical nuances and practical old questions: The psychology of aging. *Canadian Psychologist*, **13**, 252–266.

Schonfield, D., and Donaldson, W. 1966. Immediate memory as a function of intraseries variation. *Can. J. Psych.*, **20**, 218–227.

Schonfield, D., and Robertson, B. A. 1966. Memory storage and aging. *Can. J. Psych.*, **20**, 228–236.

Schonfield, D., Trueman, V., and Kline, D. 1972. Recognition tests of dichotic listening and the age variable. *J. Gerontol.*, **27**, 487–493.

Schonfield, D., and Wenger, L. 1975. Age limitation of perceptual span. *Nature*, **253**, 377–378.

Schulman, A. I. 1971. Recognition memory for targets from a scanned word list. *Brit. J. Psychol.*, **62**, 335–346.

Shiffrin, R. M., and Atkinson, R. C. 1969. Storage and retrieval processes in long-term memory. *Psych. Rev.*, **76**, 179–193.

Smith, A. D. 1974. Response interference with organized recall in the aged. *Developmental Psychology*, **10**, 867–870.

Sperling, G. 1960. The information available in brief visual presentations. *Psychol. Monogr.*, **74**, (11, Whole No. 498).

Sternberg, S. 1966. High-speed scanning in human memory. *Science*, **153**, 652–654.

Storck, P. A., Looft, W. R., and Hooper, F. H. 1972. Interrelationship among Piagetian tasks and traditional measures of cognitive abilities in mature and aged adults. *J. Gerontol.*, **27**, 461–465.

Talland, G. A. 1962. The effect of age on speed of simple manual skill. *Journal of Genetic Psychology.*, **100**, 69–76.

Talland, G. A. 1965. Three estimates of the word span and their stability over the adult years. *Quart. J. Exp. Psych.*, **17**, 301–307.

Talland, G. A. 1967. Age and the immediate memory span. *The Gerontologist*, **7**, 4–9.

Talland, G. A. 1968. Age and the span of immediate recall. *In*, G. A. Talland (ed.), *Human Aging and Behavior*, pp. 92–129. New York: Academic Press.

Taub, H. A. 1966. Visual short-term memory as a

function of age, rate and schedule of presentation. *J. Gerontol.*, **21**, 388–391.

Taub, H. A. 1968. Aging and free recall. *J. Gerontol.*, **23**, 466–468.

Taub, H. A. 1972. A comparison of young and old groups on various digit span tasks. *Developmental Psychology*, **6**, 60–65.

Taub, H. A. 1973. Memory span, practice and aging. *J. Gerontol.*, **28**, 335–338.

Taub, H. A. 1974. Coding for short-term memory as a function of age. *Journal of Genetic Psychology*, **125**, 309–314.

Taub, H. A. 1975. Mode of presentation, age, and short-term memory. *J. Gerontol.*, **30**, 56–59.

Taub, H. A., and Greiff, S. 1967. Effects of age on organization and recall of two sets of stimuli. *Psychon. Sci.*, **7**, 53–54.

Taub, H. A., and Long, M. 1972. The effects of practice on short-term memory of young and old adults. *J. Gerontol.*, **27**, 494–499.

Taub, H. A., and Walker, J. B. 1970. Short-term memory as a function of age and response interference. *J. Gerontol.*, **25**, 177–183.

Townsend, J. T. 1971. A note on the identifiability of parallel and serial processes. *Percept. and Psychophys.*, **10**, 161–163.

Treisman, A. 1964. Selective attention in man. *Brit. Med. Bull.*, **20**, 12–16.

Tulving, E. 1962. Subjective organization in free recall of "unrelated" words. *Psych. Rev.*, **69**, 344–354.

Tulving, E. 1972. Episodic and semantic memory. *In*, E. Tulving and W. Donaldson (eds.), *Organization of Memory*, pp. 381–403. New York: Academic Press.

Tulving, E. 1974. Cue-dependent forgetting. *Amer. Scient.*, **62**, 74–82.

Tulving, E., and Patkau, J. E. 1962. Concurrent effects of contextual constraint and word frequency on immediate recall and learning of verbal material. *Can. J. Psych.*, **16**, 83–95.

Tulving, E., and Pearlstone, Z. 1966. Availability versus accessibility of information in memory for words. *J. Verb. Learn. Verb. Behav.*, **5**, 381–391.

Tulving, E., and Thomson, D. M. 1973. Encoding specificity and retrieval processes in episodic memory. *Psych. Rev.*, **80**, 352–373.

Warrington, E. K., and Sanders, H. I. 1971. The fate of old memories. *Quart. J. Exp. Psych.*, **23**, 432–442.

Warrington, E. K., and Shallice, T. 1972. Neuropsychological evidence of visual storage in short-term memory tasks. *Quart. J. Exp. Psych.*, **24**, 30–40.

Warrington, E. K., and Silberstein, M. 1970. A questionnaire technique for investigating very long term memory. *Quart. J. Exp. Psych.*, **22**, 508–512.

Warrington, E. K., and Weiskrantz, L. 1970. *In*, J. A. Deutsch (ed.), *The Physiological Basis of Memory*, pp. 365–395. New York: Academic Press.

Watkins, M. J. 1974. Concept and measurement of primary memory. *Psych. Bull.*, **81**, 695–711.

Waugh, N. C., and Norman, D. A. 1965. Primary memory. *Psych. Rev.*, **72**, 89–104.

Weiss, A. D. 1963. Auditory perception in relation to age. *In*, J. E. Birren, R. N. Butler, S. W. Greenhouse, L. Sokoloff, and M. R. Yarrow (eds.), *Human Aging: A Biological and Behavioral Study*, pp. 111–140. Bethesda, Maryland: U.S. Department of Health, Education and Welfare.

Welford, A. T. 1958. *Ageing and Human Skill.* London: Oxford University Press.

Welford, A. T. 1962. On changes of performance with age. *Lancet*, **1**, 335–339.

Welford, A. T. 1964. Experimental psychology in the study of aging. *Brit. Med. Bull.*, **20**, 65–69.

Wickelgren, W. A. 1975. Age and storage dynamics in continuous recognition memory. *Developmental Psychology*, **11**, 165–169.

Wickens, D. D. 1970. Encoding categories of words: An empirical approach to meaning. *Psych. Rev.*, **77**, 1–15.

Wimer, R. E. 1960. A supplementary report on age differences in retention over a 24 hour period. *J. Gerontol.*, **15**, 417–418.

Wimer, R. E., and Wigdor, B. T. 1958. Age differences in retention of learning. *J. Gerontol.*, **13**, 291–295.

Winocur, G., and Weiskrantz, L. 1976. An investigation of paired-associate learning in amnesic patients. *Neuropsychologia*, **14**, 97–110.

Woodward, A. E., Jr., Bjork, R. A., and Jongeward, R. H., Jr. 1973. Recall and recognition as a function of primary rehearsal. *J. Verb. Learn. Verb. Behav.*, **12**, 608–617.

Zaretsky, H. H., and Halberstam, J. L. 1968. Age differences in paired-associate learning. *J. Gerontol.*, **23**, 165–168.

18
LEARNING AND AGING

David Arenberg

and

Elizabeth A. Robertson-Tchabo

National Institute on Aging, NIH

If the adage, "You can't teach an old dog new tricks," was not buried in the previous handbook (Birren, 1959), the research reported since then should complete the interment. This is not to suggest that the performance of old and young learners is indistinguishable. In most studies of human learning and in many studies of animal learning, performance comparisons of different age groups favor the young adult. Recent studies, however, have identified variables which improve or impair the learning performance of the older individual, and these studies are emphasized in the present chapter.

There are three general types of questions which are asked in studies of learning and aging: (1) Is the learning of older individuals affected by specific conditions (experimental or organismic variables)? (2) Is the magnitude of the age differences affected by specific conditions? (3) Does learning change with age, and are age changes affected by specific conditions? Most of the studies in the literature on aging and learning have been cross-sectional, that is, addressed to variations of the second question. Very few studies have used the longitudinal approach which is appropriate to answer the third question.

LONGITUDINAL STUDIES

The term "longitudinal" is used here in the broad sense, i.e., independent samples from the same cohort as well as repeated measures of the same sample are considered longitudinal. Virtually all learning research in aging has been cross-sectional; samples of different ages born at different times have been compared. This is not to say that important gerontological questions cannot be answered by the cross-sectional approach. Such questions are discussed later in this chapter. Nevertheless, many investigators in learning seem to believe that despite the uncontrolled variables, and the difficulties in matching groups in cross-sectional studies, if the age differences are substantial, it is likely that at least some part of those differences represent age changes.

Discomfort about these beliefs is reduced by research showing brain differences with age, by observation of old individuals whose cognitive behavior has changed markedly, and, for some investigators, by awareness of their own changes in performance. But longitudinal findings of maintenance of performance on psychometric measures of intelligence over much of the life span, and recent findings of substantial cohort effects in such measures (Schaie and Strother, 1968a,b; Schaie, Labouvie, and Buech, 1973; Schaie and Labouvie-Vief, 1974) have questioned the assumptions held by many investigators that at least some part of the age differences in learning studies are attributable to age changes. The term "the

421

myth of intellectual decline" with age is readily over-generalized to "the myth of cognitive decline," and there is a danger that the many cross-sectional learning studies in which age differences have been demonstrated will be ignored or attributed to cohort differences on the basis of the psychometric longitudinal findings. Furthermore, there is the argument that unless a function changes in individuals as they become older, age differences do not represent "aging." Therefore, despite the current paucity and incomplete status of longitudinal learning data, their inclusion here is deemed warranted. These data are reported early in the chapter so that the evidence for age decrements in learning late in life are kept in mind as the reader encounters and attempts to assess the cross-sectional findings.

Gilbert's Follow-Up Study

Gilbert (1973) reported a study which included longitudinal results on learning and retention tasks. Fourteen of the young participants in a large-sample study of age and mental performance (Gilbert, 1936) were available for retesting 35 to 40 years later. The 29 subtests of the Babcock-Levy Test of Mental Efficiency were administered when the subjects were in their twenties or early thirties and again when they were 60 to 74 years of age. Unfortunately the longitudinal data were reported only for six composite scores; among them were "initial learning" and "retention." Each of these two composite measures showed statistically significant declines. On the other hand, vocabulary scores remained high. Although the retested sample was probably not representative of the initial young sample, it is more likely that such a sample would be positively biased than negatively biased. Typically, previous performance of survivors has been superior to that of nonsurvivors; and similarly, individuals who return for retest have exceeded dropouts in previous performance (see, e.g., Riegel, Riegel, and Meyer, 1967).

The Baltimore Longitudinal Study

The most extensive body of adult longitudinal learning data known to the authors is incom-

plete and unpublished. These data are from the Baltimore Longitudinal Study of men who are for the most part, well educated and of high socioeconomic status.

The learning data consist of paired-associate and serial performance at two different anticipation intervals for each task. Cross-sectional analyses showed small age differences prior to age 60 and large age differences thereafter, particularly at the short anticipation interval for both tasks (Arenberg, 1967).

Data pertinent to questions about age changes were of two types: (a) conventional longitudinal data based on repeated measures at least 6 years apart, and (b) independent subsamples of the same cohorts measured during two separate periods. The second subsample of each cohort was comprised of men who entered the study after the first sample. Two advantages of comparing independent subsamples born in the same time periods are: (a) elimination of retest effects, and (b) elimination of effects of noncomparability of learning material. A disadvantage of comparing independent subsamples from the same cohort is that age becomes a between-subjects variable and any precision attributable to the within-subjects design is lost. Schaie and his colleagues (Schaie, Labouvie, and Buech, 1973; Schaie and Strother, 1968b) advocated the merits of the independent-subsamples approach to estimate age changes. It is argued here that if the repeated-measures data indicate performance changes over time, and the intra-cohort differences are similar to the repeated-measures change, then the evidence for age changes is compelling.

Dates of birth between 1885 and 1932 were categorized into six equally spaced cohorts for the early sample (measured between 1960 and 1964). Data for only five of the six cohorts were available for the later sample (measured between 1968 and 1974). The comparisons of independent samples from the same cohort are shown as solid lines in Figures 1, 2, 3, and 4. The six subsamples with repeated measures consist of the men from the early sample for whom two valid measures were available; means of the first measure are connected to means of the second measure by dashed lines in Figures 1, 2, 3, and 4.

Analyses of the conventional longitudinal

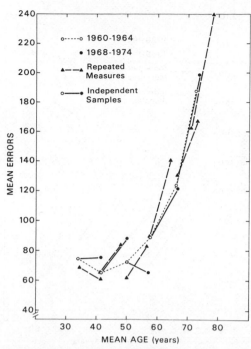

Figure 1. Paired-associate learning errors—short anticipation interval. (From Baltimore Longitudinal Study, unpublished data.)

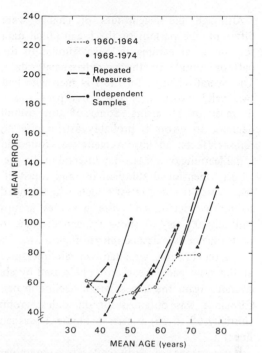

Figure 2. Paired-associate learning errors—long anticipation interval. (From Baltimore Longitudinal Study, unpublished data.)

data for the paired-associate task showed overall increases in errors (declines in performance) at both anticipation intervals. For the 102 men assigned to the fast pace who had two valid measures, the mean increase in errors was 27 over their mean interval of 6.8 years. The youngest group (initially 30 to 38) showed a small mean improvement, and the other two groups of men initially below 54 years of age showed moderate mean declines. The three oldest groups showed larger mean declines with the largest decline found for the oldest group (initially 69 to 76).

For the 111 men assigned to the slower pace in the early sample who had two valid measures, the mean increase in errors was 27 over the mean interval of 6.7 years. The three youngest groups (initially 30 to 55) showed the smallest mean declines and the two oldest groups (initially 61 to 74) showed the largest mean declines (see the dashed lines in Figure 2).

Although the two paired-associate lists were selected for their formal similarity (in structure and frequency of the words), List II (the list used for the second measure) may have been somewhat more difficult (based upon prelim-

inary data in a study of list and retest effects). However, the comparison of subsamples born in the same period but measured approximately 7 years apart is not subject to list differences. Inasmuch as such data are all first measures, the same list could be used. The results (indicated by solid lines in Figures 1 and 2) were similar to the longitudinal analyses of changes. For the men who learned at the fast pace, the smallest differences within cohorts were found for the three latest born cohorts (1909-1932) and the largest differences favoring the younger group within each cohort were found for the two earliest born cohorts (1893-1908). The mean WAIS Vocabulary raw scores were similar—66.7 ($n = 134$) for the early (1960-1964) sample and 65.0 ($n = 65$) for the later sample.

For the men who learned at the slower pace, the smallest difference within cohorts was found for the latest born cohort (1925-1932) and large differences favoring the younger subsample within cohorts were found for the two earliest born cohorts (1893-1908). Again the mean WAIS Vocabulary raw scores were quite similar—67.4 ($n = 141$) for the early sample and 66.0 ($n = 50$) for the later sample.

Although the magnitudes of change were different, the pattern of the longitudinal data for the serial-learning task was similar to the pattern found for the paired-associate data. The overall changes for the 104 men who had two valid measures at the faster pace was a decrease of 15 errors. Some of this overall decrease in errors is probably attributable to retest effects; an improvement was found in serial learning over a one-day interval in the previously mentioned study of list and retest effects. Despite these retest effects which tended to improve performance, the two oldest groups (initially 63 to 76) showed mean declines in performance (see dashed lines in Figure 3).

For the 102 men who had two valid measures at the slow pace, mean errors increased by six overall. Again the largest mean decline in performance was obtained for the oldest group (initially 68 to 76) as seen in Figure 4 (dashed lines).

Comparisons of early and late subsamples from the same cohort yielded similar results (unconfounded by list differences) for the men who learned the list at the faster pace. The largest increases in mean errors were found for the two earliest born cohorts (see solid lines in Figure 3). For the men who learned the list at the slow pace, all cohorts showed age differences. Mean errors were consistently greater for the older subsample within each cohort. Although no clear pattern emerged between the magnitude of the mean age differences and the birth periods of the cohorts, the earliest born cohort showed the largest age difference (see solid lines in Figure 4).

These studies were not originally designed to provide comparisons of independent samples within cohorts. As a result the samples may not have been equivalent (although their mean WAIS Vocabulary raw scores are quite comparable). Nevertheless, the overall picture for paired-associate and serial learning seems clear. Age declines were found in conventional longitudinal comparisons for the oldest age groups; and the within-cohort comparisons showed that for early born cohorts, older subsamples performed less effectively than younger subsamples from the same cohort. The evidence indicates a deficit in verbal learning in the later years of life.

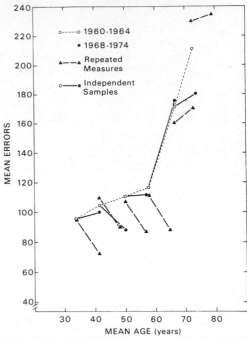

Figure 3. Serial learning errors—short anticipation interval. (From Baltimore Longitudinal Study, unpublished data.)

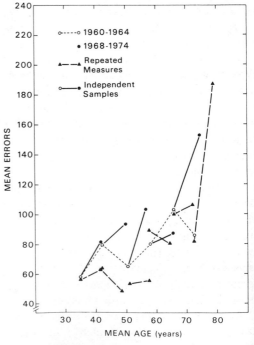

Figure 4. Serial learning errors—long anticipation interval. (From Baltimore Longitudinal Study, unpublished data.)

THEORETICAL DEVELOPMENTS AND TRENDS

Gerontological learning research during the past 15 years, not surprisingly, has followed the trends in the psychology of learning and memory. Emphasis has been on verbal processes, especially short-term memory. Welford (1958) concluded that an age decrement in short-term memory could account for the observed decline in learning ability, in problem solving, and in skilled performance. Since then, there has been a shift in the focus of research from rote learning to short-term memory studies emphasizing factors which affect age differences in learning (see Craik, Chapter 17).

Changes in performance in rote learning seem to represent a balance between the processes of registration or acquisition of information and the apparent forgetting of this information. The task now is to identify the specific contributions of registration, storage, and retrieval processes and their interactions which produce the trial-to-trial changes observed in many learning experiments. Recently, performance changes during a learning experiment have been described as increased resistance to forgetting (Kintsch, 1970; Murdock, 1974), but this interpretation has been applied only to verbal learning.

There is still no widely accepted definition of "learning," but we shall consider learning in the very broad, theoretically neutral, terms defined by Botwinick (1967, p. 48), as "the acquisition of information or skills" measured by an improvement in some overt response. Short-term memory, unless qualified, will be used in an atheoretical sense to describe the system that is used to register, encode, store, and retrieve information over brief periods of time. Obviously, the production of an overt response in an experiment is the dependent variable from which conclusions regarding memory and learning are drawn; that is, learning can only be inferred from an overt change in behavior or performance. The learning-performance distinction is particularly important with respect to the interpretation of age differences in learning ability, and this distinction has been a pervasive issue especially since the publication of the previous handbook (Birren, 1959).

Currently, no formal systematic or elaborated theory has been proposed to account for age-related differences in learning, probably because model or theory building is premature in relation to the empirical base of knowledge. Many specific independent variables which have been demonstrated to affect acquisition and/or retention of verbal material in young adults have not been investigated with the old. Nevertheless, gerontological investigators tend, either explicitly or implicitly, to adopt from the general area of learning one of two approaches to the study of verbal processes: a stimulus-response (S-R) orientation or an information-processing framework. The S-R and information-processing views have been discussed by Craik (see Chapter 17) and also by Tulving and Madigan (1970).

In the early 1960's many studies of age differences in rote paired-associate and serial learning were carried out within the S-R framework, and particular attention was paid to the pacing conditions. Due to a substantial motor element involved in paced anticipation paradigms, it is possible for a subject to "know" an item and still fail to produce the overt response under rapidly paced conditions. The older individual was particularly disadvantaged by the paced task. Thus, what appeared to be an age-related deficit in learning capacity was then attributed to the particular performance deficit obtained under paced conditions (e.g., Canestrari, 1963; Eisdorfer, Axelrod, and Wilkie, 1963). The implication was that, given enough time to respond, an older individual would be capable of performing as well as a younger individual.

The S-R verbal-learning approach as well as information-processing views assume that a subject transforms or encodes presented information to optimize his performance. Atkinson and Shiffrin (1968) identified two dimensions of central processing: structural features and control processes. The former refer to permanent features of the system (including both the physical system and the built-in processes that are fixed from one situation to another). Control processes, on the other hand, refer to features that can be modified readily or reprogrammed by an individual and may vary substantially from one situation to another depending upon such factors as the nature of instructions, the meaningfulness of the information, and the individual's experience. This distinction between permanent and modifiable aspects of learning has important ramifications for research in aging. It is important to distinguish those aspects of learning which the individual can vary or control from the structural features which he cannot. There is a long-standing, tacit assumption that age-related changes in the central nervous system (for example, the loss of neurons, Andrew, 1956) account for age-related declines in cognitive functioning; and no doubt part of the decrements observed is attributable to age differences in structural features. However, the contribution of the use of control processes to age differences in learning is important. Currently, we should concentrate on age differences in control processes inasmuch as these are the only variables that can be manipulated in the experimental laboratory situation and in life, generally. An older individual may be able to improve his learning by modifying his use of control processes.

AGE DIFFERENCES IN VERBAL PROCESSES

We will now review the effects of selected independent (treatment) variables on age differences in learning performance with a particular emphasis on studies of verbal, rote learning. For the most part, these studies have been carried out within the framework of verbal learning, i.e., the early approach based on associationism; but we will attempt to emphasize the implications of age differences in a treatment effect for encoding, storage, and retrieval of information. Encoding refers to the symbolic representation of one thing by another; that is, it is the unknown internal code of the nervous system for physical objects or events. Storage refers to the persistence of information over time, and retrieval refers to the recovery and utilization of stored information. Studies employing an information-processing view usually measure memory and have been considered elsewhere in this handbook (see Craik, Chapter 17).

Rate and Pacing

Rate variables have been the focus of many studies of age differences in learning. In studies of aging it is particularly important to distinguish the effects of input rate (presentation pacing) from those of output rate (response pacing).

In some rote learning tasks, it is possible to isolate the effects of input rate from those of output rate. For example, in a paired-associate learning paradigm each item in the list is presented in two parts: the stimulus alone, and the stimulus together with its response. The task is to produce the response that has been paired with a particular stimulus when the stimulus is presented alone. The time between the onset of the stimulus display and the onset of the stimulus-response display is designated the anticipation interval, that is, the time interval within which an individual must produce the appropriate response. The time between the onset and offset of the stimulus-response display is referred to as the inspection interval, that is, the time available for an individual to learn the response and association. It is assumed that the duration of the anticipation interval determines the time available to search for and retrieve a correct response. The duration of the inspection interval, on the other hand, limits the time to register a response as well as the time to establish an association between the stimulus and response, seek a mnemonic, and rehearse.

Canestrari (1963) reported that when both the inspection and anticipation intervals were relatively long (3.0 seconds each), fewer errors occurred for both young and old learners than when both intervals were short (1.5 seconds each); and the old group benefited more than the young from the slower pace. In a third (unpaced) condition, an old and a young group were permitted to interrupt the stream of experimental events to extend the duration of any inspection or anticipation interval. This resulted in even fewer errors for both groups; and the old benefited more than the young even more than at the slow pace. The young learners interrupted the sequence less frequently than the old, as expected; but surprisingly, the latter group increased the anticipation interval much more frequently than the inspection interval. In other words, the older learners often increased the time available to make a response, but seldom took more time to study the stimulus-response together.

Canestrari (1963) manipulated the duration of the inspection and anticipation intervals jointly. But in a more recent study, Monge and Hultsch (1971) varied both the anticipation and inspection intervals independently. Each interval could be 2.2, 4.4, or 6.6 seconds in all combinations. They found that either a longer inspection interval or a longer anticipation interval reduced the number of trials required by the older individuals to reach the criterion of an errorless trial. It is interesting to note that a longer inspection interval benefited both young and old groups about the same, whereas increasing the anticipation interval was particularly beneficial to the older individuals.

Kinsbourne and Berryhill (1972) investigated the performance of old groups in a paired-associate study in which each learner was tested under three treatment conditions. The duration of the inspection interval was varied, (2.0, 4.0, or 6.0 seconds) but the duration of the anticipation interval was held constant (2.0 seconds). Their results indicate that increasing the duration of the inspection interval improves the performance of the old.

In addition, two studies in which only one performance trial was administered also showed that the old groups benefited from increased study time (Canestrari, 1968; Hulicka, Sterns, and Grossman, 1967).

The results of these studies indicate that both old and young groups benefit when more time is available during the inspection interval (Kinsbourne and Berryhill, 1972; Monge and Hultsch, 1971). Certainly, more time to study an item provides more opportunity to rehearse a response and an association and increases the probability that information will be encoded in a manner that facilitates subsequent search. The old seem to benefit even more than the young when more time is available during the anticipation interval (Canestrari, 1963; Monge and Hultsch, 1971), suggesting that retrieval and/or response production require more time in older individuals.

Arenberg (Study I, 1965) found that when the inspection interval was fixed (1.9 seconds) and only the anticipation interval was varied (1.9 or 3.7 seconds), the old learners benefited substantially at the slower pace. The results of this study and Canestrari's study (1963) are consistent with the interpretation that the age-related performance decrement can be attributed to a retrieval rather than a storage difficulty and reflects the older individual's need for additional time to search for, recover, and produce a stored response. Such an interpretation gains indirect support from the fact that the additional errors at the fast pace in Canestrari's study were predominantly omission errors (failures to respond).

In a direct test of his hypothesis, Arenberg (Study II, 1965) investigated whether the higher frequency of errors at a short anticipation interval could be attributed to insufficient time to produce learned responses. After each paced trial (in which the anticipation interval was either 1.9 or 3.7 seconds), a self-paced test trial was administered. In these test trials, the learners were given as much time as they needed to respond to each stimulus (although no confirmation of a correct response was provided as the response was not displayed together with its stimulus). If responses were equally available with short and long anticipation intervals and the paced performance age differences were due solely to insufficient time to make a response, then the performance of both anticipation-interval groups should have been equivalent during the self-paced test trials when an individual had as much time as he needed to respond. The results did not support this hypothesis. Groups that learned at the shorter anticipation interval did not substantially reduce their errors in the self-paced test trials. Even under the self-paced condition, the mean number of errors for the old group that was assigned the short anticipation interval treatment far exceeded the mean number of errors for the old group that was assigned the long anticipation interval treatment. These findings suggest that individuals must also learn how to search for and produce a required response; the production of the correct response seems to increase the probability that that item will be correctly recalled on succeeding trials. It may be that when an individual makes the correct association and produces the correct response, it is functionally equivalent to an additional experimental presentation of the particular stimulus-response pair.

Other evidence suggests that an increase in the frequency of correct responses during training improves performance only when the additional responses are the result of a successful search of secondary memory. Arenberg (1967) described studies in which two procedures increased correct responding for old groups during training trials but neither improved performance on subsequent test trials (which were subject-paced). Both procedures depended on a recent display of the item to increase correct responding in the training trials. The search for a correct response was minimal because it had been seen quite recently. Together these studies suggest that additional time to respond results in more effective learning for the old only if it leads to a successful search from secondary memory.

There is a non-cognitive interpretation of the finding that older individuals make fewer correct responses than young adults especially under paced conditions, namely that the older person is more reluctant to venture a response. Frequency of omission errors has been used as an index of such reluctance. Taub (1967) attempted to reduce omission errors by instructing learners to respond to every item, but that procedure was not successful in increasing the responsiveness of the older group. Leech and Witte (1971), however, were successful in reducing omission errors by paying older participants for incorrect as well as for correct responses. Moreover, those who were paid for incorrect as well as correct responses also learned the task in fewer trials than those who were paid only for correct responses. These results need corroboration, but they suggest that older individuals sometimes do not emit learned responses, particularly at a fast pace, but can be induced to respond under appropriate incentive conditions.

Paced serial-learning procedures have been used by Eisdorfer and his colleagues to develop an intriguing model of over-arousal and response suppression in the older learner (see Eisdorfer, 1968). The argument in over-simplified terms is: (a) the older learner responds less frequently and performs less effectively at a fast pace; but, (b) he is capable of responding fast enough at the fast pace; (c) higher and more persistent levels of an index of autonomic arousal are found for old than for young groups during and after learning; therefore, (d) the level of arousal of the old is too high for optimal learning, particularly at a fast pace, resulting in response suppression. A recent study in which a drug was administered to reduce autonomic arousal provided evidence in support of this model (Eisdorfer, Nowlin, and Wilkie, 1970). Immediately prior to a serial-learning task, a drug (which blocks autonomic arousal) was administered to one group of old learners and a placebo to another group. The group which received the arousal blocking drug made fewer errors than the control group. It was concluded that much of the reported age deficits in learning is attributable to the over-arousal of the older individual in a laboratory learning task.

It would not be surprising to find that arousal has different effects on different types of learning. Classical conditioning, which seems to be little affected by selective attention or cognitive effort, is likely to be more directly affected by autonomic arousal than verbal learning, which is substantially affected by control processes such as attention, rehearsal, and other cognitive effort. It seems likely that the effects of autonomic arousal on verbal learning would be indirect and operate on performance via control processes; that is, arousal influences control behaviors which, in turn, affect performance.

It is reasonable to assume that conditions which produce over-arousal should be avoided to approach optimal performance by the elderly. Shooter, Schonfield, King, and Welford (1956, p. 215) concluded that ". . . difficulties and failures owing to unsuitable methods in training may introduce anxiety and lead to failure which will so shake older people's confidence that they are then unable to do jobs which they would otherwise have been able to tackle well." In this regard, there is some evidence that supportive instructions facilitate the performance of older individuals (Ross, 1968; Lair and Moon, 1972).

Use and Effectiveness of Control Processes

Recently, psychologists have become interested again in the effect of organizational variables upon learning and memory performance. In the context of information-processing models, the amount of information which can be stored and retrieved from memory is determined by organizational processes. Organizing incoming information into temporal groups, semantic clusters, or hierarchies, and using mnemonic devices are strategies which generally may be used at the discretion of the individual; that is, they are control processes. Obviously rate variables (discussed above) have considerable impact on the opportunity for and complexity of organization. Organization of information into higher-order mnemonic groupings serves to increase memory performance, and fast pacing decreases opportunity for organization.

An obvious but very important point is that the organization imposed by an individual on a set of to-be-remembered items depends on his perception of the structure of the material. Perceptual, semantic, or conceptual categories must be discovered before such groupings can be used. This point is particularly relevant to the performance of older individuals. Learning to attend to relevant cues in order to optimize encoding is, in fact, the essence of the so-called "discovery method," proved successful in retraining middle-aged and older workers (Belbin, Belbin, and Hill, 1957; Belbin, 1958; Belbin and Shimmin, 1964; Belbin and Downs, 1964). Crovitz (1966) found that performance in a discrimination task was facilitated by training older subjects to verbalize the critical dimensions of the stimuli to be discriminated.

Age-related differences in the tendency to encode information in addition to an item itself have important implications for subsequent recall performance. There is evidence for encoding specificity which means that the specific encoding operations performed on the perceived material determine what information is stored, and what has been stored determines which retrieval cues can be effective in providing access to what has been stored (Tulving and Thomson, 1973). Therefore, any age-related decrease in the amount of information encoded about an item, whether due to insuffi-

cient time to carry out the operations or to an inability to devise an efficient encoding strategy, necessarily limits the variety of retrieval cues available to direct the search process at the time of recall.

Evidence that older persons tend not to use mnemonics was found in a study by Hulicka and Grossman (1967). Old subjects did not spontaneously verbalize attempts to mediate associational relationships between paired-associate items as frequently as did young subjects; and when mediations were formed, they were often inappropriate and confusing to the old. In a study specifically designed to investigate age differences in the use of mediators in paired-associate learning, they found that without specific instructions to use mediators, older individuals reported use of associations only half as often as younger individuals. The old improved more than the young when given specific instructions to increase the use of verbal mediators, but performance differences favoring the young were still found.

Canestrari (1968) reported the results of a study by Knill (1966) which explored the use of verbal and visual (imaginal) mediators supplied by the experimenter. Knill found that providing subjects with mediators resulted in a differentially greater improvement in the performance of the older as compared to the younger group, but age differences were found even with the mediators supplied. Contrary to the hypothesis, the results did not support the relative superiority of visual to verbal mediators for either age group.

In another approach to the study of age differences in the use of visual mediators, Rowe and Schnore (1971) investigated the spontaneous (uninstructed) use of mediators in learning pairs of nouns, comparing concrete with abstract pairs. Increased concreteness or image-arousing capacity of stimulus material previously had been shown to improve learning and memory in young individuals (Paivio, 1969). Rowe and Schnore found that their young group performed significantly better than their middle-aged group who performed significantly better than their old group. Pairs of concrete nouns were easier to learn than pairs of abstract nouns for all age groups. Age differences also were found in the reported use of three types of strategies: repetition, visual mediation or imagery, and verbal mediation. The young and middle-aged groups reported a greater use of all types of strategies than the old group.

Why are older individuals reluctant to adopt spontaneously the more efficient elaborative encoding strategies even though these plans subsequently yield superior performance? (Elaboration coding refers to mnemonics which make information more memorable by adding additional information to a to-be-remembered item; for example, adding a visual image or a verbal association to the item information.) The answer seems to be that, initially, the additional information increases the storage load and may even over-load the older central processing system. Until an older individual has extensively practiced using an unfamiliar mnemonic device he has more information to remember, and he is unable to make optimal use of the additional cues to direct the search.

All the evidence cited indicates that organization aids recall, and the old tend to organize less frequently or less effectively than the young. A second point for which there is considerable support is that increasing the organization of a list improves recall performance for all age groups. Much of the evidence for this view has been provided by studies of multitrial free recall, and these experiments have been described elsewhere in this volume (see Craik, Chapter 17).

In summary, what can we conclude about the age differences in learning and memory from what has been reviewed thus far? Pacing the response phase of a task clearly contributes to the age differences in learning—strong evidence of an age-related difficulty in search and retrieval processes. However, this is not the whole story, for even under self-paced conditions there are still age differences in learning performance. Second, the degree of organization imposed on incoming information affects the probability of successful retrieval at the time of recall, and the aged do not use effective encoding strategies. Finally, a comment on the learning-performance distinction seems in order. Learning, memory, and their component processes must be inferred from measures of some overt behavior, that is, performance. However, the important issues in aging (and potential contributions to understanding learning) depend upon the identification of age-related difficulties. Having identified retrieval as a source of special difficulties for an older individual, for example, appropriate steps may be taken to minimize the difficulty. Retrieval, however, is an integral component of central processing and should not be considered simply a "performance" variable which is external to "true" learning.

TRANSFER AND INTERFERENCE

As an Explanation of Age Differences in Learning

It can be argued that all adult learning is transfer of training—the effect of learning one task upon the acquisition of a second task. Transfer may be positive, that is, facilitate subsequent learning, or negative, that is, impede subsequent learning. Two other classifications of transfer should be distinguished: (1) specific transfer which refers to the effect of a particular aspect of one task upon another task, for example, a high degree of response similarity; and (2) nonspecific transfer which refers to more general aspects of inter-task relationships, such as warm-up effects or learning-to-learn. Goulet (1972) has discussed the importance of specific and non-specific transfer factors in gerontological studies.

A topic closely related to transfer of training is interference, which refers to the effect of learning one task upon the retention of another task. Retroactive interference refers to the effects generated by learning information subsequent to the to-be-remembered material. Proactive interference refers to the effect of information presented prior to the to-be-remembered material on the retention of that material. The terms proactive and retroactive interference should not be considered theoretical concepts but rather descriptive terms which simply refer to detrimental effects generated by prior or subsequent material.

Despite some evidence that there are age differences in the rate of decay of information (Fraser, 1958), the most frequent explanation of age differences in learning and memory is an increased susceptibility to the effects of interference (Welford, 1958; Inglis, 1965; Kay, 1954, 1968; Kirchner, 1958; Arenberg, 1973; Kausler, 1970). The difficulty with "interference proneness" as an explanation of age differences in forgetting is that it does not specify the locus or loci of the effect.

Interference—Substantive Findings

Before reviewing the experimental studies of age differences in the effects of interference, one critical methodological consideration must be mentioned. In order to compare age groups in retention or in susceptibility to interference, they must be equated for the degree of original learning. It has been assumed that groups are equated for the degree of original learning when the material is learned to a common criterion of mastery. However, as Underwood (1964) pointed out, there is a problem comparing the retention of different individuals who learned the original material to a common criterion at different rates. Obviously this concern is pertinent to aging studies for frequently the rates of acquisition of different age groups vary considerably. Furthermore, the common practice in gerontological studies of adjusting age differences in the rate of original list learning by analysis of covariance is inappropriate when the treatment is correlated with the covariate (Evans and Anastasio, 1968). It is important to remember these points in considering the evidence for age differences in the susceptibility to interference. Unfortunately there have been relatively few studies of age differences in the parameters assumed to generate interference within the interference theory framework, but we will consider these now.

Proactive Interference. One method of studying the effect of established habits on performance and aging is to vary the associative strength of the pairs of items. When one word frequently elicits another word in free association, the pair is said to have high associative strength. For example, "chair-table" is high

whereas "chair-moon" is low. Several studies have shown that older groups benefit more than young adults when performance on lists composed of high associative strength is compared to that with lists of low strength (Canestrari, 1966; Kausler and Lair, 1966; Zaretsky and Halberstam, 1968). In a closely related study, Lair, Moon, and Kausler (1969) constructed lists in which the correct response was a high strength response to some other stimulus in the list. For example, from pairs such as "blossom-flower" and "hot-cold," new pairs such as "blossom-cold" were created. The old learners experienced great difficulty in learning the list constructed to maximize associative interference. These studies indicate that when well-established habits are beneficial for learning for the young, they are even more beneficial for the old; and when the well-established behavior interferes with learning for the young, it is even more interfering for the old.

Perhaps the most important age-related source of interference is from well-established, non-specific habits which manifest themselves in the older person's general approach to an experimental situation. Such behavior is frequently seen when instructions are given to older individuals in a laboratory task. If the instructions are complicated, the older person may develop misconceptions about the task. When that occurs, it is often difficult for the experimenter to correct those misconceptions. Frequently older subjects have difficulty in maintaining the instructional set and revert to their own strategies which are inappropriate because they are not consistent with the information provided.

Retroactive Interference. Two retroaction studies of aging published in the same year attempted to explore the interfering effects of learning a second task on the recall or relearning of the primary task (Gladis and Braun, 1958; Wimer and Wigdor, 1958). Gladis and Braun found no age differences in retroaction when recall scores were adjusted for vocabulary level and rate of original and interpolated learning, whereas Wimer and Wigdor found that an old group encountered greater difficulty relearning the first list than did a group of young adults. Both used paired-associate lists but that was the extent of procedural similarity. One of the differences in the studies was the length of the anticipation interval. Gladis and Braun used a 4-second anticipation interval whereas Wimer and Wigdor used a 1-second interval. Arenberg (1967) used lists from the study of Gladis and Braun and presented them at anticipation intervals of 1.9 or 3.7 seconds. Only at the short interval did the old group require more trials than the young to relearn the first list. These results essentially agree with the results of Gladis and Braun and of Wimer and Wigdor.

Hulicka (1967) reported age differences in retroaction effects only when young and old groups learned paired-associate lists for a fixed number of trials. When learning was carried out to a criterion, the procedure used in all three of the retroaction studies cited above, no age difference in interference from learning an interpolated list was found, although there was a significant age difference in trials to criterion on original learning. Hulicka's results are consistent with the other studies in that she used a long anticipation interval, a condition which had not been found to produce age differences in retroaction.

Traxler and Britton (1970) using a self-paced, written, modified method of free recall (MMFR test) studied age differences in three transfer paradigms (A-B, A-C; A-B, C-B; and A-B, C-D) at a fast (2-second) and a slow (4-second) anticipation interval. They found statistically significant age differences in trials to criterion for both original and interpolated learning. For all transfer conditions, the mean number of items recalled by the older individuals on the MMFR test was significantly fewer than the mean items recalled by younger individuals. However, any observed age difference in retention is unfortunately confounded with the rate of learning original and interpolated lists. The results were consistent with previous work showing that for the old individuals in the A-B, A-C paradigm there was a significant difference in mean recall favoring the slower anticipation interval condition compared to the fast anticipation interval condition but there was no difference in mean recall between anticipation interval conditions for young subjects.

Boyarsky and Eisdorfer (1972) attempted to extend McGovern's (1964) analysis of the components of transfer to an old group. They investigated the relative interfering effects in four paradigms (A-B, A-C; A-B, A-Br; A-B, C-B; and A-B, C-D) on the modified free recall (MFR) performance of old, well-educated individuals. They concluded that for older individuals the interfering effect of response learning (which McGovern attributed to interfering contextual associations) seemed to contribute more to forgetting than was the case for McGovern's young sample. However, the statistical test of the hypothesis was inappropriate so the conclusion is tentative. In any case, McGovern's controversial assumption that interference with contextual associations accounts for the difficulty in response learning has yet to be established.

On the basis of these studies, it is not possible to evaluate the view that older individuals are more susceptible to interference than are younger individuals due to the methodological difficulty of equating individuals of different ages for the rate of learning of to-be-retained information. The data are consistent with those from rote learning studies that there are age differences in the effect of pacing the response output.

ANIMAL LEARNING

Animal studies of learning and aging have been conducted to provide: (a) environmental control prior to and between measurements, (b) genetic control, and (c) control and experimental manipulation of motivation. Furthermore, as Jerome (1959) pointed out in the previous handbook, the universality of the age-learning decrement hypothesis requires evidence from many infra-human organisms.

Animal studies also avoid many of the methodological problems inherent in human studies. For example, education is frequently an important variable in human learning experiments; but it is difficult to deal with this variable definitively in a single study of age comparisons in learning. It is possible to control previous experience of laboratory animals to avoid such problems. Unfortunately, a price must be paid for this advantage; age studies of animals are not free of their own inherent methodological problems.

Motivation and activity level are frequently important variables in animal learning experiments. Age differences in activity level between young-mature and senescent animals are typical, and such differences can create difficulties in interpretation of age differences in learning. Equating motivation level in animals which vary in age is another pervasive problem (see Elias and Elias, Chapter 16).

In 1959, Jerome tabulated 13 animal-learning studies in which age groups had been compared on maze learning, discrimination, or problem solving; a few of those studies included relearning comparisons. Jakubczak (1973), in his review of the animal behavior literature after 1959, tabulated 51 studies in which old and young animals were compared on instrumental behavior, and cited two other studies of Pavlovian conditioning and aging. The animal literature in learning and aging, like its human counterpart, has proliferated since the previous handbook; but the rate appears to have declined somewhat in the last few years.

Emphasis in the present chapter is on studies since 1959 of maze learning, discrimination learning, and shock-avoidance learning requiring discrimination. Although many studies of bar pressing and aging have been reported since 1959, less weight is given to them here, partly because the effects of motivation and activity levels on such behavior make the interpretation of age differences particularly difficult.

No attempt is made here to define an old animal. The typical age range for rats and mice, the animals most frequently used, has been 2 to 8 months for young groups and 1 to over 2 years for older groups. For those studies described in some detail, the ages of the animals are indicated. In some of those studies, very young groups were included, but they have been omitted for the purposes of this chapter.

Task Complexity

There is a pervasive idea in the psychology of aging that age differences in performance are related to task difficulty; that is, the more difficult the task, the more likely an age difference will be found. This is only partially true in animal learning. The evidence from studies of maze learning and of discrimination learning with positive reinforcement suggests that age differences depend upon complexity defined as the number of choice points in a maze or the number of concurrent discriminations in a trial.

Complexity: Number of Choice Points. One of the few consistent findings in the animal-learning and aging literature since Jerome's (1959) review can be seen when complexity is indexed by the number of choice points. Age differences rarely have been found in learning tasks involving 1 or 2 choice points, small age differences have been found for 4-choice tasks, and substantial age differences have been reported for 8- and 14-choice tasks.

Several of the studies described below included reversal learning following initial learning. The initial learning results are discussed in this section, and discussion of the results of reversal learning is deferred until the next section.

Botwinick, Brinley, and Robbin (1962) reported no age difference in initial learning of a single-choice Y-maze in two studies with three age groups of female rats. In the first study, the rats were 3 to 4 months, 8 to 12 months, and 22 to 27 months old. The animals were food deprived and a food reward was provided for each correct choice. Five successive trials per day were given until the criterion of at least four correct (of five) was attained for three consecutive days. The mean number of days to reach criterion was virtually the same for all three age groups in initial learning. Similar results were found for the second study in which the food reward was larger.

Birren (1962) reported two studies of two-choice, water-maze learning in which three age groups were compared. In the first study, age differences were found. The oldest rats (24+ months) showed a higher mean error curve and required more days to reach the criterion (four errorless trials out of five per day for two successive days) than either a group aged 15 months or a group aged $2\frac{1}{2}$ to 4 months. Because the age difference could have been attributed to initial response tendencies, a second study was carried out with a modified maze.

The three age groups were 2 to 3 months, 12 months, and 24 to 26 months. Age differences were not found for mean error curves over trials or for median days to reach the criterion.

In a study of four-choice maze learning of three age groups of female rats (3 months, 12 to 14 months, and 23 to 25 months), Botwinick, Brinley, and Robbin (1963) found substantial age differences in original learning. The animals were food deprived and a food pellet was provided at the fourth choice point in the maze. Five trials were presented per day, and the criterion of mastery was four out of five errorless trials on three successive days. Median days to attain this criterion were greatest for the oldest group and least for the youngest group.

Maze learning was one of the tasks included in Goodrick's (1967) comparison of two age groups of mice. The mice were females 4 months or 26 months old. A water maze with eight choice points was used. Two trials were given for three consecutive days; and on the fourth day, four trials were given at 1-hour intervals. Both age groups showed a decline in mean errors during the experiment, but the young group consistently committed fewer errors than the old.

Jordan and Sokoloff (1959) compared large samples of rats 3 months of age with rats aged 20 to 27 months using a 14-choice water maze. They presented one trial per day for 15 days and found many more mean errors for the old rats than the young when the animals were under normal atmospheric conditions. The acquisition curve for the old group reached a plateau of mean errors mid-way through the experiment with no further improvement. When rats were placed in negative ionized air for 3 hours prior to each trial, the performance of the young animals was similar to that of the young control group, but the old ionized animals committed fewer errors than the old controls. The acquisition curve for the old ionized group was similar to those for both young groups.

Goodrick (1968) reported substantial age differences in rats learning a 14-choice maze; he then showed that the extent of age deficits was related to number of choices (Goodrick, 1972). Rats aged 6 to 8 months were maintained at

80 percent of their weight and senescent rats (26 to 27 months) were maintained at 75 percent of their weight. Milk with sucrose was the reward throughout. The two groups were compared on three tasks involving choice behavior. For a 1-choice T-maze, no age difference was found. For 4-choice mazes, age differences were small on the first two mazes, and only for the first trials on the third and fourth mazes were the mean errors for the senescent group substantially larger than for the young. For the 14-choice maze, at one trial per day, 15 of 16 young rats mastered the maze, whereas only 6 of 16 old rats reached the criterion (zero or one error on the last trial of 20 trials). The old rats made many more perseverative errors than the young.

Goodrick (1968, 1972, 1973a,b, 1975), in a systematic series of learning studies using his modification of Stone's (1929a) 14-choice maze, showed: (1) consistent age differences in learning curves between young-mature and senescent rats, with the young animals reducing their mean errors in fewer trials than the old; (2) that the performance of those old rats learning the maze with difficulty was characterized by perseverative errors; (3) that the maze learning of old rats, particularly slow-learning ones, was enhanced by massed practice, that is, multiple trials per day; and (4) that by preventing the animals from entering culs-de-sac during training trials, old rats committed few errors on test trials (when access to the culs-de-sac was permitted). In these studies (except Goodrick, 1975), the age groups were differentially deprived in an effort to equate for motivation.

In the earliest paper of the Goodrick series, several studies were reported (Goodrick, 1968). In the first, rats (6 months and $\geq$ 26 months) were given 4 trials per day. The interval between trials on the same day was between 60 and 80 minutes. Within 8 days all of the 24 young animals reached the criterion (four or fewer errors for the 4 daily test trials). In contrast, by the end of the tenth day, 18 of the 36 senescent animals had failed to reach that criterion. The performance of those old animals which failed to master the maze was characterized by perseverative errors, i.e., repetition of errors at specific choice points over many consecutive trials. Old animals which attained the

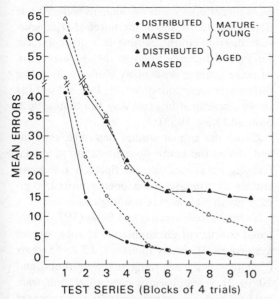

Figure 5. Mean errors (in blocks of four trials) in 14-choice maze. (From Goodrick, 1973. Copyright 1973 by the American Psychological Association. Reprinted by permission.)

criterion made fewer perseverative errors, and young animals rarely made such errors. Twelve of the old "slow learners" then were switched to a more distributed schedule of trials (one per day, for 12 days) to explore the effects of distibuted practice. No evidence of further learning was found. When these same animals subsequently were placed on a 12-trial per day schedule with 4 consecutive trials per block and 90 minutes between blocks, 11 of the 12 rats met the original criterion by the third day.

Later, Goodrick (1973b) reported an experiment explicitly designed to assess the unexpected result that old rats benefited from massed trials (Goodrick, 1968). The previous results were confirmed. Two age groups of rats (6 months and 26 months), differentially deprived of food, were given either 1 trial or 4 trials per day for 40 trials. Under both conditions, the younger group learned the maze more quickly, but the result of particular interest was the different effect of the distribution of trials on the two age groups. Moderately massed practice (4 trials per day) resulted in impaired performance for the young but in enhanced performance for the old. With 1 trial per day, the acquisition curve for the old animals reached a plateau; errors did not decrease in

the late trials. At 4 trials per day, the old group continued to improve throughout the experiment. Again perseverative errors were more frequent for old than for young animals. In a second study, 24 old rats (26 to 28 months) which had not mastered the maze in 20 trials with 1 trial per day were divided into three equal groups matched for performance on the last 4 trials. All 24 animals were given 36 additional trials; one group continued at 1 trial per day, one group was switched to 4 trials per day, and one group was switched to 12 trials per day. The group which continued at 1 trial per day showed little evidence of further learning. The learning curves of the two groups with multiple trials per day were quite similar. After initial increases in errors during the first block of 4 trials, both groups reduced mean errors thereafter.

Goodrick interpreted the consistent finding of a high frequency of perseverative errors among senescent rats as behavioral rigidity. He hypothesized that if errors were prevented during training by blocking all culs-de-sac, then in subsequent test trials, when incorrect choices were accessible, senescent rats would make few errors (Goodrick, 1975). The hypothesis was confirmed. Both young (5-month) and aged (25-month) rats were maintained at 75 percent of initial body weight. After 20 training trials in which all incorrect choices were blocked (only errors due to retracing the correct path could occur), 16 test trials were given in which incorrect choices could be made. In the first 2 test trials, the old animals committed few errors; but the young animals made many errors which were probably due to exploratory behavior in the culs-de-sac, areas which were accessible to them for the first time. Thereafter, old and young animals committed very few errors.

Distribution of test trials was also varied in this study, but differences between one and four trials per day were small and not in agreement with Goodrick's (1968, 1973b) earlier studies. When choice errors were prevented during training, old and young groups had already learned the maze to near mastery at the time that the variable of distribution of trials was introduced. Massing trials in complex maze learning seems to have beneficial effects for old rats when error rates are high and much learning remains.

Complexity: Number of Concurrent Discriminations. Age differences typically have not been found in tasks requiring discrimination of only a single pair of stimuli, although learning such tasks is difficult. Even young rats commit many errors before mastering such tasks. In two studies of discrimination learning, Kay and Sime (1962) found no age difference in initial learning. In the first study, two age groups of male rats were compared (5 to 6 months and 18 to 20 months). The animals learned to discriminate a circle from an inverted triangle. They were food deprived and rewarded with food for each correct choice which was the circle in the initial learning phase. Both age groups learned the discrimination with about the same number of errors. In the second study, the rats were males 8 to 9 months and 20 to 23 months. This time in the initial learning, the inverted triangle was the reinforced choice. Although many more mean errors were committed before this discrimination was learned, again no age difference was found.

In another study, Sime and Kay (1962) found the direction of age differences related to specific discrimination tasks. Groups of male rats 5 to 6 months and 15 to 16 months were compared. When shape was the relevant dimension, the young group committed fewer mean errors than the older group; but when height was the relevant dimension, the older group learned the discrimination in fewer mean errors than the young. This reversal of age differences has not been explained.

Fields (1953) compared two age groups of male rats on concurrent discrimination problems. First he demonstrated that both age groups (30 days and 450 days) could learn to discriminate vertical stripes from horizontal stripes and from no stripes. When these groups were 60 and 480 days old, five different problems (pairs of patterns) were exposed in constant order for 33 trials (165 discriminations). In each pair, one pattern was correct. The young group made many more correct choices than the older group (on all trials combined and on the last 10 trials). Similar results were obtained for a second series of five new

pairs of patterns when the animals were 90 and 510 days old. It should be noted that concurrent discrimination learning is a difficult task for rats and shares some of the characteristics of maze learning with many choice points. Age differences were found for this task but not for single discriminations (see Kay and Sime, 1962; Sime and Kay, 1962).

All of the animal studies described thus far and almost the entire aging literature in animal learning have used rats or mice. A few aging studies of primates have been reported, typically involving complex learning tasks.

Medin, O'Neil, Smeltz, and Davis (1973) compared concurrent discrimination learning of two age groups of rhesus monkeys, 13 to 15 years ("middle-aged" according to the authors) and 20 to 21 years. Twenty pairs of stimuli were used in each series; but some stimuli appeared in more than one pair. Unlike the series in Fields' (1953) rat study, the order was changed from trial to trial. Furthermore, after the first series (presented on four consecutive days with four trials, that is, 80 discriminations per day), three other series with different stimuli were learned in the same manner with one day of rest between series. Both age groups demonstrated equivalent learning during the four trials on the first day of a series. On subsequent days, the older group made fewer correct choices on the first trial than on the last trial of the previous day; the younger group did not. Although both age groups reduced their errors equivalently during subsequent trials on the second day, the age difference on the first trial was maintained for all four trials. The overall age effect was not statistically significant by analysis of variance, but each of the three "middle-aged" monkeys made more total correct choices than any of the four "old" animals. This age difference was attributable to the increase in errors between days by the old monkeys. Similar between-day increases in errors were reported by Goodrick (1968) for old rats successfully learning a 14-choice maze with multiple trials per day. Apparently, forgetting occurred between days for old rats and monkeys on complex tasks.

Medin (1969) had previously reported four studies of pattern discrimination with rhesus monkeys. Each pattern consisted of 1, 2, or

4 lighted panels in a 4 × 4 matrix. The mean age of the younger group was 10 years, and the older group consisted of five monkeys approximately 17 to 18 years old. In all four studies, the delay between offset of the pattern and opportunity to respond (push the previously lighted panels for food rewards) was varied. When only 1 of the 16 panels was lighted, the older group performed at least as well as the younger group at 0, 1, and 2 seconds, but performed more poorly at 5, 10, and 20 seconds delay. When the pattern consisted of 2 or 4 of the 16 panels, the older group was consistently more impaired than the younger group from delays as short as 2 seconds. Both complexity of the stimulus and delay of responding affected the performance of the older monkeys in this study.

Riopelle and Rogers (1963, 1965) studied the performance of chimpanzees in a variety of choice-behavior tasks, some of which were learning tasks. The animals were between 7 and 41 years old, a range described by the authors as . . . "from prepuberty to old age" . . . as determined by growth, x-ray and microscopic structure of bones, and observation of behavior. The first task was rather simple (for the chimpanzee). Two stimuli were presented simultaneously and one was food rewarded. Each pair was presented four times, and 200 such problems were presented (16 per day). The data reported for the second trial of the last 50 problems (the first opportunity in each problem for learning to be demonstrated) showed no age decline.

The second task required learning concurrent discriminations. Ten pairs of stimuli were presented in serial order; that is, all ten discriminations were presented before the same ten were repeated. The same order was presented ten times on the same day. Again correct responding was unrelated to age.

The next learning task did show a decline with age. Five identical stimuli were used, but the food was placed under one of them in direct view of the animal. When a 5-second delay was imposed between placing the food and presenting the stimuli, several of the younger animals but none of the group over 20 had high percentages of correct responses. A positive relation between age and errors also was found when a 10-second delay was used. The delay required memory, but even when the stimuli were presented immediately after the food was placed, the age relation was found. Riopelle and Rogers (1965) interpreted this as a deficit in attention rather than in memory.

The clearest age relation in this series of learning studies of chimpanzees was found in an oddity task. Four stimuli, three identical and one different, were presented simultaneously; and the food was always located behind the one that was different. All of the animals over 20 performed poorly on this task, some little better than chance. Only one of the ten younger animals performed as poorly as any of the older group.

The following conclusions can be drawn from the animal studies reviewed thus far. Several studies of maze learning indicate that when number of choices is used as an index of complexity, substantial age deficits are found only with 8- and 14-choice tasks. Age deficits are rarely found even for difficult discrimination tasks involving only one pair of stimuli. A few studies indicate that concurrent discrimination tasks, which require several pairs of stimuli to be discriminated within trials, result in age deficits for rats and also for monkeys (when the order is changed), but not for chimpanzees (when the order is not changed). Imposed delays in responding impair older monkeys and chimpanzees more than their younger counterparts; but for the chimpanzee, the effect may be attributable to attention rather than memory. Oddity problems require learning a principle; the old chimpanzee is particularly impaired in that task.

Reversal Learning

Reversal learning requires that previously learned responses be changed. For example, in a maze, choice points at which left turns were previously correct are changed to require right turns. In a discrimination task, a previously rewarded choice typically becomes an unrewarded choice.

If aging results in greater susceptibility to interference or in increased behavioral rigidity, then reversal learning should be more difficult for old animals than for young. There was suggestive evidence for age differences in reversal learning at the time of Jerome's review (1959). Stone (1929b) reversed the correct cue in his serial discrimination task from the illuminated alternatives to the dark alternatives. The error curves for his three age groups diverged in the later stages of reversal learning, probably due to the failure of a few old rats to learn the reversal task. The evidence for age differences in reversal learning since that study, however, is far from compelling. Several studies described in the previous section included one or more reversal-learning procedures, and those results are presented here.

In the second of Birren's (1962) studies of two-choice water-maze learning, the correct path was reversed. Only those rats which had reached the criterion for initial learning on the same day were included; that is, all animals were matched on performance in initial learning. Mean errors did not differ among the three age groups (2 to 3, 12, and 24 to 26 months) in the reversed maze.

Botwinick, Brinley, and Robbin (1962) included four reversals following initial learning of a single-choice Y-maze. After age differences had not been found in initial learning among three age groups of female rats (3 to 4, 8 to 12, and 22 to 27 months), the oldest group required more days than the younger two to learn the reversed choice on the first and second reversal. On the third and fourth reversal, however, the oldest group learned as readily as the two younger groups. In a second experiment, in which the food reward was larger (and the animals were in the goal box less time), no age difference was found on any of the four reversals.

Botwinick, Brinley, and Robbin (1963) also included four reversals following initial learning in their study of a four-choice Y-maze. In this study, age differences were found in initial learning; the oldest group (23 to 25 months) required the most days to reach criterion and the youngest group (3 months) the least. Similar results were found for the first reversal in which all four choices were reversed; but on the subsequent three reversals, the oldest group learned as readily as the two younger groups. All groups substantially reduced their errors on the second reversal (iden-

tical with the initial maze) and maintained about the same level for the last two reversals.

Kay and Sime (1962) reversed the rewarded choice five times after their rats (5 to 6 and 18 to 20 months) learned to discriminate between a circle and a triangle. No age difference was found in initial learning or on the first two reversals. On the third and fifth reversals, however, all of the older rats learned more readily than any of the younger rats. In a second experiment, involving 29 reversals, both age groups (8 to 9 and 20 to 23 months) learned to reverse from triangle rewarded and circle unrewarded to square rewarded and triangle unrewarded. Both groups decreased their mean errors dramatically, particularly with the earlier reversals. The older group learned the reversals with as few errors as the younger group.

Sime and Kay (1962) reported a reversal study which was complicated in both procedure and results. The paired stimuli varied not only in shape (triangle and cross) but in relative vertical position, one being higher than the other. Reversals were from dimension to dimension; for example, if initially the higher stimulus was rewarded (and the shape irrelevant), then on the first reversal the cross was rewarded (and the height was irrelevant). Such reversals result in 50 percent correct responding if the animal consistently responds to the stimulus cue previously rewarded prior to reversal. For the groups which learned the shape problem first, the older animals (15 to 16 months) made more errors initially, and even more errors on the reversal problem, than the younger group (5 to 6 months). For the groups which learned the height problem first, however, the younger animals made more errors initially and even more errors on the reversal problem than the older group.

It is difficult to summarize these reversal findings, but it seems safe to say that, typically, younger rats learn reversal tasks no more readily than older rats.

Avoidance Learning

Age differences in learning to avoid shock depends to some extent on the nature of the response to be learned and the interval between trials. Specific ages of the groups compared is also a factor. For example, Bättig and Grand-jean (1959) reported age differences in learning a simple avoidance task with the oldest rats (25 months, about 760 days) performing more poorly than rats of any of their seven younger age groups; and Kirby (1963) found no difference in acquisition of a simple avoidance between rats 100 and 500 days old.

In a study of irradiation, Furchtgott and Wechkin (1962) found age differences in simple avoidance conditioning among three age groups of rats (3 to 4, 14, and 20 months). In the control group, the youngest animals required fewest trials to reach the criterion (five consecutive avoidances of the shock), and the oldest group required the most trials. Although the interaction between treatment and age was not statistically significant, the age differences were small for the animals which had been irradiated *in utero*. Sex interacted with age; the difference between the young and old groups was larger in females than in males.

Doty and her colleagues reported an extensive series of age studies of shock avoidance. In two studies (Doty, 1966a,b), age differences were found in a delayed discrimination avoidance task, but simple and discrimination avoidance without delay did not show age differences consistently. Five age groups of rats were included in one study (Doty, 1966a) but only the three oldest (250, 450, and 650 days) are discussed here. In the discrimination task, a light appeared in one of two compartments, and the animal could avoid the shock by moving to the lighted compartment within 5 seconds. If the appropriate response was not made, the animal was shocked for 10 seconds; but the shock terminated if the lighted compartment was entered. Thirty trials per day (interval between trials unspecified) were given until the criterion of nine avoidances in ten consecutive trials was attained. No age difference was found in mean number of trials to reach criterion. In the delayed discrimination task, the light was presented in one of the compartments for 5 seconds, but the animal was not permitted to move toward the goal for 3 seconds after the light terminated. If the previously lighted compartment was entered within 5 seconds after the barrier was withdrawn, the shock was avoided. The other features of the task were

similar to the discrimination task. On the delayed task, the mean number of trials to reach the criterion was highest for the oldest group (650 days) and lowest for the youngest group (250 days).

In a similar study, the interval between trials was varied, and a simple avoidance task was added (Doty, 1966b). The simple avoidance task was the same as the discrimination problem except that both goal compartments were lighted, and the task was to enter either compartment. The interval between trials was 10 seconds, 1 hour, or 4 hours. Three age groups of rats were included, but only the two older groups (150 and 750 days) are discussed here. All animals received 40 trials at one combination of the three tasks and the three inter-trial intervals. In the simple avoidance task, the mean number of avoidance responses was quite similar for the young and old group when the interval was 1 hour or 4 hours; an age deficit was found only at the 10-second interval. The results for the discrimination task were somewhat similar. This task was more difficult than simple avoidance; but again when the interval between trials was 4 hours, the mean number of avoidance responses was about the same for both age groups. In the discrimination task, however, the young group made more avoidance responses than the old not only at the 10-second interval, but also at the 1-hour interval. Age differences were found in the delayed discrimination task (with a 2-second delay); but mean avoidance responses were low for the young group, and near zero for the old at all three inter-trial intervals.

In another experiment (Doty and Doty, 1964), three age groups of rats were compared on the simple avoidance task at five inter-trial intervals (10 seconds, 30 minutes, 1 hour, 3 hours, and 24 hours). Only the results of the two oldest groups (120 days and 600 days) are included here. The younger group was impaired only at the 10-second interval. The older animals made about as many avoidance responses as the young at the 3-hour and 24-hour intervals, but were impaired at the shorter intervals.

Age differences in shock-avoidance tasks could result from an age deficit in learning, but there are other plausible explanations for such differences (see Elias and Elias, Chapter 16). For example, Paré (1969a) has shown that the aversive threshold of shock is age-related. Although Furchtgott and Wechkin (1962) found a near-zero correlation between shock threshold and avoidance conditioning in 14-month-old rats, sensitivity to shock could account for age differences in an avoidance task, particularly at low or moderate shock intensities. In addition, the more an animal moves around prior to shock, the more likely it is to enter the area that avoids the shock; therefore, the activity level or exploratory behavior of the young animal is more likely to improve its performance on that basis. Furthermore, the reaction to high intensities of shock could also be age related. If strong shock is likely to induce young animals to move and old animals to freeze, age differences in opportunity to learn could result because the old animal is less likely to experience the contingency of correct responding and cessation of shock.

These possible explanations for age differences in avoidance performance would be more tenable if such age differences were unrelated to task and procedural differences. When, however, the same level of shock intensity results in age differences only at specific combinations of tasks and inter-trial intervals (e.g., Doty, 1966b), it seems likely that at least some part of the age differences in performance is attributable to learning differences.

In those studies discussed previously in which distribution of trials was included as an independent variable, massed practice has been found deleterious to the old rat in simple avoidance learning (Doty, 1966b; Doty and Doty, 1964) but beneficial to the old rat in complex maze learning (Goodrick, 1968, 1972). There was a procedural detail in the avoidance studies which may have contributed to this difference. In those studies, the goal compartment of one trial could serve as the start compartment of the next trial. Doty's procedure with a 10-second interval did not require the animal to be removed from the goal compartment of the previous trial. This procedure may have contributed to the confusion of the old animals and impaired their performance. A similar procedure was used in the study by Furchtgott

and Wechkin (1962) and may have contributed to the age difference they found with a 1-minute interval.

Doty and her colleagues used avoidance conditioning in a series of age comparisons of the effects of drugs, animal handling, and cage environment. In a study of the effects of chlorpromazine hydrochloride administered at four different intervals after daily simple avoidance trials, all age groups of rats were impaired when the drug was administered 10 seconds after each trial (Doty and Doty, 1964). The oldest group (600 days), however, was impaired even when the drug was administered $1/2$, 1, or 2 hours after each trial; these longer intervals did not affect the performance of the younger age groups (120, 280, and 365 days). This result was interpreted to mean that memory consolidation requires more time for old animals.

Dye (1969) reported the effects of ether on retention of discrimination avoidance learning. Three age groups were included, but only the results for two (11 to 12 months and 20 to 22 months) are described here. The younger group committed fewer total errors in 25 trials than the old in initial learning. Ether was administered 3, 15, or 30 minutes after initial learning. On the following day, 25 more avoidance trials were given. Both control groups committed few errors, but the effects of ether on retention were substantial for both age groups. The shorter the interval between the end of initial learning and the administration of ether, the greater the impairment in relearning—but the drug effects were equivalent for both age groups. Although Doty and Doty (1964) reported an interaction between age and interval with chlorpromazine for rats of similar ages as those in this study, Dye found no such interaction with ether. Thus, the hypothesis that memory consolidation requires more time for old animals was not supported by Dye's results.

Other studies by Doty and her colleagues have shown that some drugs have facilitative effects on avoidance conditioning, particularly for old animals. Amphetamine sulfate was administered daily after ten trials of simple or discrimination avoidance for 4 days (Doty and Doty, 1966). Three age groups of rats (120, 500, and 730 days) were included. Performance improved compared with controls on both tasks for all three age groups when the drug was administered 10 seconds after each block of ten trials. The oldest group made more correct avoidances than the two younger groups: (1) when the drug was administered 1 hour after the trials on the simple task; and (2) when the drug was administered 4 hours after the trials on the discrimination task.

Doty and Johnston (1966) also reported facilitative effects of physostigmine salycilate (eserine) on simple and discrimination avoidance, particularly for old rats. The drug was administered daily for 4 days at one of three intervals (10 seconds, 1 hour, and 4 hours) after a block of ten avoidance trials. Compared with controls, both age groups (120 and 730 days) improved on simple avoidance performance when the drug was administered 10 seconds after each block of trials. Both age groups also improved on discrimination avoidance at the 10-second drug interval, but the old group improved even at the 1-hour and 4-hour drug intervals.

Two of the four drug studies of rats reported by Gordon, Tobin, Doty, and Nash (1968) included age comparisons of avoidance learning. In one study, procainamide injected 45 minutes prior to acquisition trials had no effect on mean avoidance responses for rats (60 to 90 days or 420 to 450 days). Diphenylhydantoin (Dilantin), however, improved the performance of old rats (700 to 730 days). They performed at least as well as the younger groups (60 to 90 and 300 to 330 days) which did not improve under the drug, whereas the control old group made fewer avoidance responses than the two younger groups. In the other learning study (see also Doty and Dalman, 1969), drugs, dosages, age, and task were varied and retention as well as acquisition performance was reported; but the use of "avoidances . . . to a criterion of seven out of ten consecutive avoidances" as the dependent measure makes the results difficult to interpret.

Doty (1968, 1972) also showed that discrimination avoidance learning can be facilitated for old rats by handling, and that reversal learning in an avoidance task can be facilitated for old rats by caging them in large groups in an enriched environment. In the study of the effects of handling (Doty, 1968), control rats 620 days old required more trials to learn a discrimination avoidance task than rats 270 or 420 days old. Daily handling (for 20 days prior to the first learning trial), however, decreased the number of trials to criterion required by the oldest animals. In the handling condition, the oldest group performed as well as the younger groups.

Doty (1972) compared the performance of rats housed in different environments for 360 days beginning at 300 days of age. Some groups consisted of nine rats of the same sex housed in large containers furnished with toys. The other groups consisted of pairs of the same sex housed in standard wire cages. All animals learned three consecutive avoidance tasks in the same order: (1) a discrimination avoidance (to light or dark); (2) a reversal task in which the previously correct and incorrect light conditions were switched; and (3) a passive avoidance task in which the correct response was to remain in the start compartment when a light was presented. Each task was learned to a criterion of eight correct out of ten consecutive trials. The two housing conditions had no effect on the initial discrimination performance. On both the reversal task and the passive avoidance task, however, the animals housed in large groups (the enriched condition) required fewer trials to learn than the animals housed in pairs. The results supported the hypothesis that environmental enrichment increases behavioral flexibility of aged animals as evidenced by superior performance on tasks which require a change in the correct response from the previous task.

Retention and Relearning

Some of the maze studies reviewed by Jerome (1959) in the previous handbook included relearning data (Stone, 1929a; Verzár-McDougall, 1957). Their findings, although not compelling, tended to show that old rats committed more errors in relearning than young rats or that a minority of old rats had deficits in relearning.

In view of the importance of the question of

whether retention declines with age, surprisingly few animal studies have included retention data. One deterrent to such studies is the high mortality loss when senescent animals are used. The methodological problems in assessing retention for groups that differ in initial learning may be another deterrent.

Goodrick (1968) reported recall and relearning data for young and old survivors which had reached the criterion of learning his 14-choice maze 45 days earlier. On the first day of relearning, mean errors increased from the level at the end of initial learning, and the increase was larger for the old than the young rats. By the third day of relearning, however, both age groups returned to their mean levels at the end of initial learning.

Doty (1966a, 1968) also reported relearning data. In the earlier study, the oldest animals had learned the initial discrimination avoidance in about the same number of trials as the younger groups; the oldest group improved equivalently in relearning 30 days after initial learning and again 60 days after the first relearning. In delayed avoidance, a more difficult task, age differences were found for initial learning and for relearning. The decrease in trials during the first relearning was small for the oldest group, whereas the younger groups substantially reduced their trials to learn. During the second relearning, all age groups further reduced their mean trials to learn, but the largest reduction was found for the oldest groups.

Doty (1968) also included two relearning series in the study of the effects of daily handling 20 days prior to initial learning. At the beginning of learning, the ages of the three groups discussed here were 270, 420, and 620 days. Initially, the oldest control group required more trials to learn the discrimination avoidance task than the younger groups; and, although all age groups improved in the first relearning and again in the second relearning series, the oldest reduced their trials to learn about the same as the next younger group and only slightly less than the youngest of the three groups discussed here. For the handled animals, the oldest group learned initially in as few trials as the other two groups and improved at least as much in the two relearning series.

Two groups of rats in Doty's (1972) study of

enriched environments learned the three avoidance tasks at age 300 days (before they were introduced to their respective environments) and relearned these tasks a year later. The performance means did not change. (It should be noted, however, that the three avoidance tasks were learned in the same sequence at both times. As a result, two reversal tasks were learned between the initial learning and relearning of each task.)

From these studies of relearning, there is little evidence to support the hypothesis of decrements in retention for old rats.

Bar Pressing

In Jakubczak's (1973) review, he cited several papers on bar-pressing performance and aging. Surprisingly, there were at least as many studies which failed to find age differences in bar pressing as studies which found that young animals bar press more than old. Both general activity level and motivational differences would be expected to result in age differences in performance on a bar-pressing task.

Goodrick (1965, 1969, 1970) anticipated that young animals would bar press more than senescent animals, and included a non-rewarded bar as well as a bar rewarded with light in an attempt to separate general response levels from responses specific to the reward. In the first study, Goodrick (1965) found age differences in mean operant level (spontaneous bar pressing) and in mean number of responses on both the rewarded and the non-rewarded bar. The young group (6 months) responded more than the old ($\geqslant$ 24 months), and the difference was found in both deprived and non-deprived conditions. (No attempt was made in this paper to adjust the age differences in number of responses to the rewarded bar by using the age differences in bar pressing without rewards.)

In later two-bar studies (Goodrick, 1969), the rats were neither food nor water deprived, and sweetened milk was used as a reward. In one study (Experiment 2), old rats (28 months) either responded more than younger rats (10 months) or equivalently depending upon their previous training histories. The unrewarded bar proved to be unnecessary because so few responses were made to that bar by either age group. In another study (Experiment 3), no age difference was found on either bar; but there was some evidence of an age difference in learning the time contingency of the task. At each of the three fixed-interval schedules the old group responded more per reward than the young. Inasmuch as only one response per reward was necessary, the lower response frequency per reward for the younger group suggested that they, to a greater degree than the old group, had learned the relationship between the interval and the response requirements.

Goodrick (1970) also used the two-bar procedure in a study in which the reward for bar pressing was a change in lighting conditions. Again the precaution of using two bars to adjust for lower responding by the old rats proved unnecessary. Total responses were as high for the old (25 to 27 months) as the young (6 months) under all conditions of the experiment.

Corke (1964) reported a study of bar pressing in which three bars were used and the reward was presented only if they were pressed in the proper order. Two age groups (90 to 130 days and 600 to 640 days) were compared on mean total responses and on mean number of correct responses "during the last eight stabilization trials." The older rats made more total responses, but the young group made more correct responses. At least part of the age difference in total responses was attributed to the greater time spent by the young animals in eating because they received more rewards. It is interesting to note that "The older animals . . . seemed to repeat erroneous sequences more than did the younger ones" (p. 375). Such behavior is similar to the perseverative errors that Goodrick (1968, 1972) described for the old rats in his 14-choice maze.

It is not at all apparent why some studies of bar pressing have shown more responding by young than by old animals, whereas others have shown no age difference or even somewhat more responding by the old animals.

Classical Conditioning

In the two reports of Pavlovian conditioning and aging in animals since the 1959 handbook, both used a conditioned emotional response (CER) procedure. This procedure measures the suppression of bar pressing during a conditioned stimulus (e.g., a tone) which is followed by an inescapable unconditioned stimulus (usually a shock). The response suppression measure is a ratio based upon the response rate immediately before, and the rate during, the conditioned stimulus. Such a measure is presumably independent of general activity and response levels which may differ with age.

Solyom and Miller (1965) reported that young rats (4 to 5 months) not only bar pressed more than older rats ("approximately 20 months"), but suppressed a higher proportion of responses than the older group. A weak shock was used in the CER procedure. If an older animal is less sensitive to shock than a young one, as suggested by Paré (1969a), then some of the decreased response suppression of the older rats might be attributable to their functionally lower shock intensity.

In a carefully designed study, Paré (1969b) attempted to control the motivational levels affecting bar-pressing rates and used two shock intensities in the CER procedure. Furthermore, two stimuli were used (2,000 cps and 850 cps) and only the higher tone was followed by shock. This provided a comparison between response suppression to a shocked and a nonshocked stimulus. The older rats (only 354 days) suppressed more to both stimuli than the young rats (about 3 months) and were less discriminating in their suppression to the shocked and unshocked tones. It was also found that when the tones were made more discriminable, and a weak shock intensity was used, response suppression to the stimulus paired with shock was about the same for the two age groups, and little response suppression was found for either group with the unshocked stimulus. Paré's studies would have contributed more to the aging literature had a senescent group been included.

On the bases of these studies, there is little evidence that classical conditioning decreases with increasing age in the rat.

Extinction

Extinction is defined as the reduction in responding after learning when the reinforcement is no longer presented. Resistance to extinction has been used as a measure of the initial learning. An argument can be made, however, that rapid extinction is an indication of learning the change in response-reinforcement contingency. In aging, resistance to extinction can also be an index of behavioral rigidity, that is, continued responding which is no longer appropriate under the changed conditions. Hypotheses about extinction and aging depend upon how extinction is interpreted.

Solyom and Miller (1965), in their study of the conditioned emotional response, added extinction trials following the training trials. In the extinction trials, the shock did not follow the conditioned stimulus. They found that the older rats extinguished faster than the young group. The young rats suppressed responding more during training and returned to the non-suppression level much more slowly than the older rats. This was interpreted as evidence for greater initial learning by the young.

Goodrick (1968) gave unrewarded trials to young and old rats which previously had learned and relearned a 14-choice maze. Prior to the extinction trials (4 trials per day for 3 days), all animals were brought to "equivalent numbers of asymptotic trials." On the day before extinction, the young group (6 months at the beginning of the study) was committing fewer errors than the old (> 26 months). On the first day of extinction, the old increased their errors very little, but the young increased their errors substantially. Both groups increased their errors on the second and third days of extinction trials, but the young increased their errors more than the old group. This was interpreted as greater behavioral rigidity in the old rats.

In a study of bar pressing, Goodrick (1969, Experiment 2) reported extinction data for young (10 months) and old (28 months) rats following rewarded trials during which the old groups had bar pressed as much as or more than the young. This was a two-bar study. In mean total responses, the old groups bar pressed more than the young groups during the early extinction trials, but less than the young groups during the later extinction trials. However, the proportion of bar presses to the previously rewarded bar was higher for the old than the young rats on all extinction trials. These results were interpreted as equivalent retention of learned responses by senescent and young rats.

In these studies of extinction, young rats extinguished a conditioned emotional response more slowly than old rats, increased errors in a complex maze more rapidly than the old when the reward was not presented, and bar pressed less than the old in early extinction trials but more than the old in later extinction trials. Evidence for more extinction with age, less extinction with age, and equivalent extinction has been reported; and the interpretations as well as the results of these studies were quite varied.

Summary and Comments—Animal Learning

In a review of this kind, an attempt is made to impose some organization on the literature, but the organization of the animal learning studies may be more apparent than real. Kay (1959, p. 621) in his comments on the status of learning and aging at the time of the previous handbook stated, " . . . learning experiments with animals in aging studies have rarely had the rigor and continuity of attack that has been devoted to them in other spheres." Although there are many examples of improved rigor in the more recent studies, continuity of attack remains a problem with but few exceptions; and, given the decrease in the number of animal studies published in the past few years, the situation does not appear headed for improvement.

Maze learning is one of the few areas of learning and aging with consistent results for a substantial number of studies. Typically age differences were not found when 1 or 2 choice points were required, small age differences were found when 4 choice points were required, and (with the exception of Stone, 1929a) those studies with 8 or more choice points showed substantial age differences favoring the young. Performance of senescent rats on a 14-choice maze was facilitated by massed practice; and preventing errors at choice points during training resulted in few errors in performance by old rats in test trials when incorrect turns could be made.

On concurrent discrimination problems,

middle-aged rats performed more poorly than young rats, old monkeys performed more poorly than middle-aged monkeys, but no age relation was found for chimpanzees ranging in age from young to old.

Age differences in avoidance learning depended upon the avoidance task and the intertrial interval. In simple avoidance and in discrimination avoidance, some studies found less effective performance with old than young animals, but other studies found no age difference. In delayed discrimination avoidance, however, the old group invariably performed less effectively than the young. Short intervals between trials impaired discrimination avoidance learning more for old than for young animals.

Drugs which had selectively beneficial effects for avoidance learning in old animals included amphetamine sulfate, eserine, and Dilantin. Chlorpromazine impaired memory consolidation over longer periods between avoidance learning and drug administration for old than young rats, but no age difference was found for ether's effect on memory consolidation. Handling prior to learning had a facilitative effect on avoidance learning for old rats.

Little evidence has been found for age differences in animal studies of relearning. Results of studies of bar pressing, extinction, and classical conditioning have been quite variable.

CONCLUSIONS

Verbal Learning

In human learning studies, the effects of stimulus presentation (input) rate and of output rate on age differences in performance have been studied extensively. Although input rate is more important than output rate in learning for all ages, older individuals are particularly disadvantaged when time to respond is short. Little of this interaction, however, is accounted for by the old failing to respond in time with learned responses. This indicates an age-related difficulty in retrieving stored information.

However, age differences in performance are found even under self-paced conditions when speed is not a consideration. Clearly, rate is not the only factor limiting the perfor-

mance of the aged. Performance is also limited by the amount of information encoded about an item, and it is this information which determines the effectiveness of retrieval. There is evidence for age decrements in the use of encoding strategies. Older individuals (at least in the experimental situation) tend not to use mediators spontaneously. Even when explicit instructions to develop mediators are given, older people are less likely to generate associations for as many of the items in a list. Furthermore, the old seem to have more difficulty in using mediators generated by the experimenter and tend to reject "bizarre" associations. The consequence of such age differences in elaborative encoding is that there is a qualitative, age-related difference in the nature of the potential retrieval cues. Infrequent or ineffective use of organizational strategies means that the retrieval cues are minimal.

In all experimental tasks, it is important to distinguish task-specific and non-specific factors which affect performance. Do older subjects need more time because central processing requires more time, that is, due to structural features of the system, or do older subjects require more time to make adjustments to the demands of the task because the situation is unfamiliar? Since it is now accepted that control processes can have a tremendous effect on the amount of information retained, it should be informative to compare older subjects who differ in performance on a learning task with respect to their use of control processes. It is important to remember that the performance of some 70-year-olds is indistinguishable from that of younger individuals. If we study individual differences within an older group, we may further delineate the nature and scope of any age-related learning deficit.

Transfer and Interference

In view of the frequent evocation of interference proneness as an explanation of age decrements in learning and memory, it will be necessary to analyze task requirements in more detail in order to specify the source of the interference. Within the interference theory framework with its focus on list retention, the methodological problem of equating age groups in the rate of learning has severely limited age comparisons of the effects of interference. Fortunately, there are several ways to circumvent this problem. One approach, rarely used, is to consider only the performance of the aged and to establish the relative contribution of the interfering effects of unlearning and of response competition to their performance decrement (Kausler, 1970; Schonfield, 1969).

A second approach to equating age groups in the rate of learning is to train older learners until they can learn any list at a rate equal to that of younger learners (Goulet, 1972). This strategy emphasizes the use of multiple testing sessions and the intensive study of a few subjects as a way to analyze processes in more detail. The criteria for the selection of subjects to participate in such studies must be given extra careful consideration.

Third, and more readily applicable, Kay (1968, p. 73) has suggested that a more sensitive index of the rate of learning is to consider the acquisition rate of each item rather than that of the list as a whole. Using this method, one can compare the recall-retention history of items correctly anticipated the same proportion of times, for example, items recalled four out of ten times by one subject with those recalled four out of ten times by other subjects. One advantage of using the item as the unit for analysis is that one may also relate the effect of a particular method of encoding an item to the recall and retention history. This is particularly important in view of the fact that there is high inter-item variability in the facility of older individuals to generate and to use mediators.

Animal Studies

Kay (1959) advocated a more extensive use of animals in investigations of age-learning relationships. However, the emphasis in human studies on verbal processes to the exclusion of other types of learning precludes comparative analyses of animal and human data. Nevertheless, animal studies of age changes in learning throughout the life span would be important in their own right. Apart from the obvious economy in the time required to carry out a longitudinal animal study, one may more readily document and control an animal's history. Particularly if one were to select tasks for which age differences have been documented consistently, the information would be invaluable.

REFERENCES

Andrew, W. 1956. Structural alterations with aging in the nervous system. *J. Chronic Diseases,* **3**, 575–596.

Arenberg, D. 1965. Anticipation interval and age differences in verbal learning. *J. Abnorm. Psychol.,* **70**, 419–425.

Arenberg, D. 1967. Age differences in retroaction. *J. Gerontol.,* **22**, 88–91.

Arenberg, D. 1973. Cognition and aging: Verbal learning, memory, and problem solving. *In,* C. Eisdorfer and M. P. Lawton (eds.), *The Psychology of Adult Development and Aging*, pp. 74–97. Washington, D.C.: American Psychological Association.

Atkinson, R. C., and Shiffrin, R. M. 1968. Human memory: A proposed system and its control processes. *In,* K. W. Spence and J. T. Spence (eds.), *Advances in the Psychology of Learning and Motivation Research and Theory*, Vol. II, pp. 90–197. New York: Academic Press.

Bättig, V. K., and Grandjean, E. 1959. Beziehung zwischen Alter und Erlernen einer bedingten Fluchtreaktion bei der weissen Ratte. (Relation between age and learning of a conditioned flight reaction in the white rat.) *Gerontologia,* **3**, 266–276.

Belbin, E. 1958. Methods of training older workers. *Ergonomics,* **1**, 207–221.

Belbin, E., Belbin, R. M., and Hill, F. 1957. A comparison between the results of three different methods of operator training. *Ergonomics,* **1**, 39–50.

Belbin, E., and Downs, S. M. 1964. Activity learning and the older worker. *Ergonomics,* **7**, 429–437.

Belbin, E., and Shimmin, S. 1964. Training the middle aged for inspection work. *Occupational Psychology,* **38**, 49–57.

Birren, J. E. (ed.) 1959. *Handbook of Aging and the Individual.* Chicago: University of Chicago Press.

Birren, J. E. 1962. Age differences in learning a two-choice water maze by rats. *J. Gerontol.,* **17**, 207–213.

Botwinick, J. 1967. *Cognitive Processes in Maturity and Old Age.* New York: Springer.

Botwinick, J., Brinley, J. F., and Robbin, J. S. 1962. Learning a position discrimination and position reversals by Sprague-Dawley rats of different ages. *J. Gerontol.,* **17**, 315–319.

Botwinick, J., Brinley, J. F., and Robbin, J. S. 1963. Learning and reversing a four-choice multiple Y-Maze by rats of three ages. *J. Gerontol.,* **18**, 279–282.

Boyarsky, R. E., and Eisdorfer, C. 1972. Forgetting in older persons. *J. Gerontol.*, 27, 254–258.

Canestrari, R. E., Jr. 1963. Paced and self-paced learning in young and elderly adults. *J. Gerontol.*, 18, 165–168.

Canestrari, R. E., Jr. 1966. The effects of commonality on paired-associate learning in two age groups. *Journal of Genetic Psychology*, 108, 3–7.

Canestrari, R. E., Jr. 1968. Age changes in acquisition. *In*, G. A. Talland (ed.), *Human Aging and Behavior*, pp. 169–188. New York: Academic Press.

Corke, P. P. 1964. Complex behavior in "old" and "young" rats. *Psych. Reports*, 15, 371–376.

Crovitz, E. 1966. Reversing a learning deficit in the aged. *J. Gerontol.*, 21, 236–238.

Doty, B. A. 1966a. Age and avoidance conditioning in rats. *J. Gerontol.*, 21, 287–290.

Doty, B. A. 1966b. Age differences in avoidance conditioning as a function of distribution of trials and task difficulty. *Journal of Genetic Psychology*, 109, 249–254.

Doty, B. A. 1968. Effects of handling on learning of young and aged rats. *J. Gerontol.*, 23, 142–144.

Doty, B. A. 1972. The effects of cage environment upon avoidance responding of aged rats. *J. Gerontol.*, 27, 358–360.

Doty, B., and Dalman, R. 1969. Diphenylhydantoin effects on avoidance conditioning as a function of age and problem difficulty. *Psychon. Sci.*, 14, 109–111.

Doty, B. A., and Doty, L. A. 1964. Effect of age and chlorpromazine on memory consolidation. *J. Comp. Physiol. Psychol.*, 57, 331–334.

Doty, B. A., and Doty, L. A. 1966. Facilitative effects of amphetamine on avoidance conditioning in relation to age and problem difficulty. *Psychopharmacologia*, 9, 234–241.

Doty, B. A., and Johnston, M. M. 1966. Effects of post-trial eserine administration, age and task difficulty on avoidance conditioning in rats. *Psychon. Sci.*, 6, 101–102.

Dye, C. J. 1969. Effects of interruption of initial learning upon retention in young, mature, and old rats. *J. Gerontol.*, 24, 12–17.

Eisdorfer, C. 1968. Arousal and performance: Experiments in verbal learning and a tentative theory. *In*, G. A. Talland (ed.), *Human Aging and Behavior*, pp. 189–216. New York: Academic Press.

Eisdorfer, C., Axelrod, S., and Wilkie, F. L. 1963. Stimulus exposure time as a factor in serial learning in an aged sample. *J. Abn. Soc. Psych.*, 67, 594–600.

Eisdorfer, C., Nowlin, J., and Wilkie, F. 1970. Improvement of learning in the aged by modification of autonomic nervous system activity. *Science*, 170, 1327–1329.

Evans, S. H., and Anastasio, E. J. 1968. Misuse of analysis of covariance when treatment effect and covariate are confounded. *Psych. Bull.*, 69, 225–234.

Fields, P. E. 1953. The age factor in multiple-discrimi-nation learning by white rats. *J. Comp. Physiol. Psychol.*, 46, 387–389.

Fraser, D. C. 1958. Decay of immediate memory with age. *Nature*, 182, 1163.

Furchtgott, E., and Wechkin, S. 1962. Avoidance conditioning as a function of prenatal X irradiation and age. *J. Comp. Physiol. Psychol.*, 55, 69–72.

Gilbert, J. G. 1936. Mental efficiency in senescence. *Arch. Psych.*, 27, (188).

Gilbert, J. G. 1973. Thirty-five-year follow-up study of intellectual functioning. *J. Gerontol.*, 28, 68–72.

Gladis, M., and Braun, H. 1958. Age differences in transfer and retroaction as a function of intertask response similarity. *J. Exp. Psych.*, 55, 25–30.

Goodrick, C. L. 1965. Operant level and light-contingent bar presses as a function of age and deprivation. *Psych. Reports*, 17, 283–288.

Goodrick, C. L. 1967. Behavioral characteristics of young and senescent inbred female mice of the C57BL/6J strain. *J. Gerontol.*, 22, 459–464.

Goodrick, C. L. 1968. Learning, retention, and extinction of a complex maze habit for mature-young and senescent Wistar albino rats. *J. Gerontol.*, 23, 298–304.

Goodrick, C. L. 1969. Operant responding of nondeprived young and senescent male albino rats. *Journal of Genetic Psychology*, 114, 29–40.

Goodrick, C. L. 1970. Light- and dark-contingent bar pressing in the rat as a function of age and motivation. *J. Comp. Physiol. Psychol.*, 73, 100–104.

Goodrick, C. L. 1972. Learning by mature-young and aged Wistar albino rats as a function of test complexity. *J. Gerontol.*, 27, 353–357.

Goodrick, C. L. 1973a. Error goal-gradients of mature-young and aged rats during training in a 14-unit spatial maze. *Psych. Reports*, 32, 359–362.

Goodrick, C. L. 1973b. Maze learning of mature-young and aged rats as a function of distribution of practice. *J. Exp. Psych.*, 98, 344–349.

Goodrick, C. L. 1975. Behavioral rigidity as a mechanism for facilitation of problem solving for aged rats. *J. Gerontol.*, 30, 181–184.

Gordon, P., Tobin, S. S., Doty, B., and Nash, M. 1968. Drug effects on behavior in aged animals and man: Diphenylhydantoin and procainamide. *J. Gerontol.*, 23, 434–444.

Goulet, L. R. 1972. New directions for research on aging and retention. *J. Gerontol.*, 27, 52–60.

Hulicka, I. M. 1967. Age differences in retention as a function of interference. *J. Gerontol.*, 22, 180–184.

Hulicka, I. M., and Grossman, J. L. 1967. Age-group comparisons for the use of mediators in paired-associate learning. *J. Gerontol.*, 22, 46–51.

Hulicka, I. M., Sterns, H., and Grossman, J. 1967. Age-group comparisons of paired-associate learning as a function of paced and self-paced association and response time. *J. Gerontol.*, 22, 274–280.

Inglis, J. 1965. Sensory deprivation and cognitive disorder. *Brit. J. Psychiat.*, 111, 309–315.

Jakubczak, L. F. 1973. Age and animal behavior. *In*, C. Eisdorfer and M. P. Lawton (eds.), *The Psychology of Adult Development and Aging*, pp. 98–111. Washington, D.C.: American Psychological Association.

Jerome, E. A. 1959. Age and learning–Experimental studies. *In*, J. E. Birren (ed.), *Handbook of Aging and the Individual*, pp. 655–699. Chicago: University of Chicago Press.

Jordon, J., and Sokoloff, B. 1959. Air ionization, age, and maze learning of rats. *J. Gerontol.*, **14**, 344–348.

Kausler, D. H. 1970. Retention-forgetting as a nomological network for developmental research. *In*, L. R. Goulet and P. B. Baltes (eds.), *Life-Span Developmental Psychology: Research and Theory*, pp. 305–353. New York: Academic Press.

Kausler, D. H., and Lair, C. V. 1966. Associative strength and paired-associate learning in elderly subjects. *J. Gerontol.*, **21**, 278–280.

Kay, H. 1954. The effects of position in a display upon problem solving. *Quart. J. Exp. Psych.*, **6**, 155–169.

Kay, H. 1959. Theories of learning and aging. *In*, J. E. Birren (ed.), *Handbook of Aging and the Individual*, pp. 614–654. Chicago: University of Chicago Press.

Kay, H. 1968. Learning and aging. *In*, K. W. Schaie (ed.), *Theory and Methods of Research on Aging*, pp. 61–82. Morgantown: West Virginia University Press.

Kay, H., and Sime, M. E. 1962. Discrimination learning with old and young rats. *J. Gerontol.*, **17**, 75–80.

Kinsbourne, M., and Berryhill, J. L. 1972. The nature of the interaction between pacing and the age decrement in learning. *J. Gerontol.*, **27**, 471–477.

Kintsch, W. 1970. *Learning, Memory, and Conceptual Processes*. New York: John Wiley.

Kirby, R. H. 1963. Acquisition, extinction, and retention of an avoidance response in rats as a function of age. *J. Comp. Physiol. Psychol.*, **56**, 158–162.

Kirchner, W. K. 1958. Age differences in short-term retention of rapidly changing information. *J. Exp. Psych.*, **55**, 352–358.

Knill, F. P. 1966. The effect of visual and verbal mnemonic devices on the paired associate learning of an aged population. Unpublished master's thesis, University of Richmond.

Lair, C. V., and Moon, W. H. 1972. The effects of praise and reproof on the performance of middle aged and older subjects. *Aging and Human Development*, **3**, 279–284.

Lair, C. V., Moon, W. H., and Kausler, D. H. 1969. Associative interference in the paired-associate learning of middle-aged and old subjects. *Developmental Psychology*, **1**, 548–552.

Leech, S., and Witte, K. L. 1971. Paired-associate learning in elderly adults as related to pacing and incentive conditions. *Developmental Psychology*, **5**, 180.

McGovern, J. B. 1964. Extinction of associations in four transfer paradigms. *Psychol. Monogr.*, **78**, (16, Whole No. 593).

Medin, D. L. 1969. Form perception and pattern reproduction by monkeys. *J. Comp. Physiol. Psychol.*, **68**, 412–419.

Medin, D. L., O'Neil, P., Smeltz, E., and Davis, R. T. 1973. Age differences in retention of concurrent discrimination problems in monkeys. *J. Gerontol.*, **28**, 63–67.

Monge, R., and Hultsch, D. 1971. Paired-associate learning as a function of adult age and the length of the anticipation and inspection intervals. *J. Gerontol.*, **26**, 157–162.

Murdock, B. B. 1974. *Human Memory: Theory and Data*. Potomac, Maryland: Lawrence Erlbaum Associates.

Paivio, A. 1969. Mental imagery in associative learning and memory. *Psych. Rev.*, **76**, 241–263.

Paré, W. P. 1969a. Age, sex and strain differences in the aversive threshold to grid shock in the rat. *J. Comp. Physiol. Psychol.*, **69**, 214–218.

Paré, W. P. 1969b. Interaction of age and shock intensity on acquisition of a discriminated conditioned emotional response. *J. Comp. Physiol. Psychol.*, **68**, 364–369.

Riegel, K. F., Riegel, R. M., and Meyer, G. 1967. Sociopsychological factors of aging: A cohort-sequential analysis. *Hum. Develop.*, **10**, 27–56.

Riopelle, A. J., and Rogers, C. M. 1963. Behavior of chimpanzees of differing ages. *Activitas Nervosa Superior*, **5**, 260–263.

Riopelle, A. J., and Rogers, C. M. 1965. Age changes in chimpanzees. *In*, A. M. Schrier, H. F. Harlow, and F. Stollnitz (eds.), *Behavior of Nonhuman Primates*, pp. 449–462. New York: Academic Press.

Ross, E. 1968. Effects of challenging and supportive instructions on verbal learning in older persons. *J. Educ. Psych.*, **59**, 261–266.

Rowe, E. J., and Schnore, M. M. 1971. Item concreteness and reported strategies in paired-associate learning as a function of age. *J. Gerontol.*, **26**, 470–475.

Schaie, K. W., Labouvie, G. V., and Buech, B. U. 1973. Generational and cohort-specific differences in adult cognitive functioning: A fourteen-year study of independent samples. *Developmental Psychology*, **9**, 151–166.

Schaie, K. W., and Labouvie-Vief, G. 1974. Generational versus ontogenetic components of change in adult cognitive behavior: A fourteen-year cross-sequential study. *Developmental Psychology*, **10**, 305–320.

Schaie, K. W., and Strother, C. R. 1968a. A cross-sequential study of age changes in cognitive behavior. *Psych. Bull.*, **70**, 671–680.

Schaie, K. W., and Strother, C. R. 1968b. The effect of time and cohort differences on the interpretation of age changes in cognitive behavior. *Multi. Behav. Res.*, **3**, 259–294.

Schonfield, D. 1969. Learning and retention. *In*, J. E. Birren (ed.), *Gerontology: Issues and Concepts*. Los Angeles: University of Southern California Press.

Shooter, A. M. N., Schonfield, A. E. D., King, H. F., and Welford, A. T. 1956. Some field data on the training of older people. *Occupational Psychology*, **30**, 204–215.

Sime, M. E., and Kay, H. 1962. Inter-problem interference and age. *J. Gerontol.*, **17**, 81–87.

Solyom, L., and Miller, S. 1965. The effect of age differences on the acquisition of operant and classical conditioned responses in rats. *J. Gerontol.*, **20**, 311–314.

Stone, C. P. 1929a. The age factor in animal learning. I. Rats in the problem box and the maze. *Genet. Psychol. Monogr.*, **5**, 1–130.

Stone, C. P. 1929b. The age factor in animal learning. II. Rats on a multiple light discrimination box and a difficult maze. *Genet. Psychol. Monogr.*, **6**, 125–202.

Taub, H. A. 1967. Paired associates learning as a function of age, rate, and instructions. *Journal of Genetic Psychology*, **111**, 41–46.

Traxler, A. J., and Britton, J. H. 1970. Age differences in retroaction as a function of anticipation interval

and transfer paradigm. *Proceedings of the 78th Annual Convention of the American Psychological Association*, **5**, 683–684.

Tulving, E., and Madigan, S. A. 1970. Memory and verbal learning. *Annual Review of Psychology*, **21**, 437–484.

Tulving, E., and Thomson, D. M. 1973. Encoding specificity and retrieval processes in episodic memory. *Psych. Rev.*, **72**, 352–373.

Underwood, B. J. 1964. Degree of learning and the measurement of forgetting. *J. Verb. Learn. Verb. Behav.*, **3**, 112–129.

Verzár-McDougall, E. J. 1957. Studies in learning and memory in ageing rats. *Gerontologia*, **1**, 65–85.

Welford, A. T. 1958. *Ageing and Human Skill*. London: Oxford University Press.

Wimer, R. E., and Wigdor, B. T. 1958. Age differences in retention of learning. *J. Gerontol.*, **13**, 291–295.

Zaretsky, H., and Halberstam, J. 1968. Effects of aging, brain-damage, and associative strength on paired-associate learning and relearning. *Journal of Genetic Psychology*, **112**, 149–163.

19
MOTOR PERFORMANCE

A. T. Welford

University of Adelaide, South Australia

INTRODUCTION

The psychological study of motor performance in relation to age stands at the meeting point of two lines of research that have been vigorously pursued during the last 30 years. One has yielded what is now a substantial body of physiological, behavioral, and social knowledge about the nature and processes of aging; the other is the approach known as "skills research" which has greatly enhanced the general understanding of human performance both in the laboratory and in certain applied fields such as industrial work and, more recently, sports and athletics. The second line is probably the more coherent and systematic at the present time, and it is in terms of this, therefore, that the treatment in this chapter will be structured.

Figure 1 summarizes the results of a great many investigations into human performance designed to identify the main functional mechanisms involved and the manner of their interaction (Welford, 1968, 1976). The sense organs shown at the extreme left of the diagram fall into two groups. One consists of those which receive data from external sources—eyes, ears, nose, mouth, and skin. The other includes, first, internal receptors in muscles, tendons and joints which, although they seldom impinge upon consciousness, play an important part in the control of movement; and second, a number of less understood sensors which measure the state of blood chemistry, hydration, and other bodily conditions.

The effectors shown at the extreme right of the diagram also fall into two groups—one including the hands, feet, vocal organs, and other instruments of "voluntary" muscle, the second consisting of the various reactors of the auto-nomic system, which are not normally under voluntary control.

Between these lies a chain of three main central mechanisms which it seems intuitively obvious should be distinguished from each other in function: it is one thing to perceive that an event has occurred, another to decide what to do about it, and still another to carry out the action decided upon. It is envisaged that, in the perceptual mechanism, data from the various sense organs are analyzed, coordinated, and supplemented by data from the memory stores. The processed data are fed through to the translation mechanism, so called because it translates them into action by triggering a decision and computing a response. The orders for this response are passed to the central effector mechanism which programs a phased sequence of muscular actions to execute them. The "gate" shown between the perceptual and translation mechanisms appears to close while the latter is computing a response, preventing interference with this process by further data coming from the perceptual mechanism, until the responding action has been initiated. The short-term store holds data while the gate is closed and also seems to play an important part in immediate memory. The long-term store appears to be fed from the translation mechanism in the sense that little is retained unless some response is made to it, and what is retained bears the marks of the response rather than of the original material.

The various feedback loops emphasize that performance hardly ever consists of only a single run through the chain of mechanisms from sense organs to effectors. Even relatively simple actions such as picking up a glass or opening a door involve an iterative process in

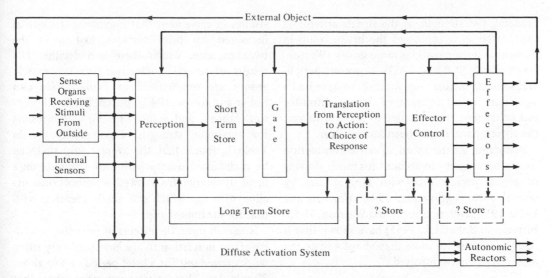

Figure 1. Hypothetical block diagram of the human sensorimotor system.

which an initial action, such as making a reaching movement, is followed by a series of smaller adjustments each of which depends for its precise form on the outcome of the one before. In other words, data from the effector action and its results on the external world are fed back as part of the sensory input for the next run through the chain. The data fed back appear to be compared with the original aim of the action, and the fresh "orders" for action passed to the translation and central effector mechanisms take account of any discrepancy. In this way errors are corrected and the whole sensorimotor system behaves as a self-correcting servomechanism.

The diffuse activation system appears to be the basis of *arousal*, not only mediating the difference between sleep and wakefulness, but providing subtle changes in the level of general activation of the organism from moment to moment. It has its center in the brain stem and generates diffuse impulses which increase the sensitivity and responsiveness of the cortex. The center receives inputs from the various sensory channels so that it responds to external situations. It also seems to have connections from the perceptual mechanism so that it reacts to any situation seen as requiring effort or threatening departure from optimum conditions. It is thus the mediator of generalized reactions to stress and motivation. Subjectively its activities

are associated with emotions and feelings. It appears to have connections to all the main central stages, enhancing their activity at times of high demand and reducing it under monotonous conditions. It also has connections with the autonomic nervous system, whose activities are commonly used as indices of arousal.

The system outlined in Figure 1 makes it clear that the motor performance with which this chapter is concerned does not depend on motor factors alone but on activities in the whole system, any part of which may limit motor performance in particular circumstances. However, the main limitations seem usually to lie in the second and third mechanisms in the chain—the translation and central effector links. Probably the most important change of motor performance that comes with age is in *speed*, and the main framework of this chapter will be an attempt to locate the sources of, and reasons for, this change.

LIMITATIONS DUE TO PERIPHERAL MECHANISMS

A number of well-known changes in the sense organs associated with age have been outlined in Chapters 20–23. These changes obviously limit the performance of older people in some cases and may well do so more widely than is commonly recognized. For example, they may, by reducing the strength of the signals arriving at the central mechanisms of the brain, result in these mechanisms working more slowly (Weston, 1948, 1949; Sheldon, 1963). However, peripheral sensory factors seem unlikely to have had a significant effect in most of the sensorimotor tasks that have been studied in relation to age: the signals have usually been far too clear.

Reduction in the speed of nerve conduction would be unlikely to account for much slowing of actual performance with age. Studies by several authors (Sommer, 1941; Wagman and Lesse 1952; Norris, Shock, and Wagman, 1953; Birren and Botwinick, 1955) have shown that it rarely accounts for more than about 4 msec per meter of the nerve involved.

Effector Organs

Speakman (1956) in a survey of research, including that upon bodily strength, found all studies in agreement that maximum strength as measured by brief tests is highest in the twenties, after which there is a decline. The results of several studies using various muscle groups are summarized in Table 1 (see also Fisher and Birren, 1947). Burke, Tuttle, Thompson, Janney, and Weber (1953), whose results for maximum strength of grip are shown in Table 1, found that the average grip that can be maintained over a period of 1 minute on a hand dynamometer showed a proportional decline with age which was nearly identical with that for maximum grip.

Research upon the effects of intensive muscular effort in relation to age have used very tiring work carried out for a brief period—up to about 30 minutes. These studies commonly show that with increasing age there is a decline in the amount of work done in a given time or until some criterion of exhaustion is reached (e.g., Szakall, 1944).

TABLE 1. MAXIMUM STRENGTH AT DIFFERENT AGES AS A PERCENTAGE OF STRENGTH AT AGES 20-29.

Author and muscle group	AGE RANGE					
	20-29	30-39	40-49	50-59	60-69	70-79
1. Uffland (1935):						
Grip, right hand	100 (41.6)[a]	96.4	90.9	78.0	64.9	–
Biceps, right flexor	100 (31.8)	93.4	83.6	66.0	54.1	–
Wrist, right flexor	100 (29.3)	96.9	93.1	85.9	75.4	–
Thumb, right flexor	100 (12.4)	96.8	96.8	85.3	79.8	–
Wrist, right extensor	100 (24.3)	99.2	94.2	88.9	79.3	–
Back strength	100 (134.6)	95.4	89.8	79.2	64.3	–
2. Galton; see Ruger and Stoessiger (1927):						
Grip, right hand	100 (37.4)	99.8	97.8	93.2	85.9	74.9
Pull (across chest)	100 (33.7)	99.4	95.1	87.9	78.0	65.5
3. Cathcart et al. (1935):						
a) Employed men:						
Grip, right hand	100 (52.7)	99.4	96.3	91.3	82.2	–
Back strength	100 (171.6)	100	97.0	93.1	85.3	–
b) Unemployed men:						
Grip, right hand	100 (46.1)	97.1	94.1	87.2	80.9	–
Back strength	100 (150.2)	99.3	93.7	87.7	84.9	–
4. Burke et al. (1953):						
Maximum grip strength	100 (56.3)	95.0	91.5	86.9	78.8	64.4
	AGE RANGE					
	23-27	28-32	33-37	38-42	43-47	48-52	53-68
5. Fisher and Birren (1947):						
Grip, right hand	100 (56.0)	96.8	95.2	93.5	89.9	86.2	83.6

[a]Numbers in parentheses are kilograms.

Maximum strength and capacity for continued exertion may well be important factors limiting energetic pursuits and work involving heavy muscular effort by older people. This is likely to be true even though the average work load is less than maximum: work load inevitably fluctuates from moment to moment and hour to hour, and the limitations will apply to the peaks rather than the average. Further, subjective feelings of overload tend to precede the attainment of maximum exertion and will thus tend to keep normal performance well short of this level. It is therefore not surprising that Åstrand (1967) found that the levels of work load spontaneously chosen by building workers varied with the maximum capacities of the individuals concerned, tending to be about 40 percent of their capacities for continuous exertion. For lighter work and most everyday activities, maximum capacities are likely to be of little importance until well into old age. In line with this, Birren and Spieth (1962) found little relationship between speed of performance and either blood pressure or pulse rate, either before or after exercise.

Other subtle effector limitations, for example, stiffness of joints leading to difficulty of action or reduced mobility of the neck resulting in the need to turn the whole body to see sideways, doubtless affect some sensorimotor performances, although the extent to which they do so has not, so far as the author is aware, been studied. There are also factors which enter into gait and posture which show well-known changes with age. Their effects on some tasks may be substantial, but again it seems likely that, compared with central factors, the limitations imposed are relatively small.

LIMITATIONS DUE TO CENTRAL MECHANISMS

From what has been said so far, it seems clear that the main sources of limitation for most normal performances lie in the central mechanisms. All the stages appear to be involved although to different extents in different cases: the balance between one and the other depends upon the relationships of the task concerned to the capacities of the particular individual performing it.

Usually, the time taken by the perceptual mechanism is short compared with that of the other stages. It can, however, be substantial in two sets of circumstances. One is where identification of incoming data involves an extensive search of memory (Birren, 1955; Wallace, 1956; Riegel and Birren, 1965, 1967; Gekoski and Schultz, 1965). The other is where fine discriminations have to be made. The reason appears to be that random activity in the nervous system—so-called "neural noise"—disturbs the incoming signals so that if, for example, two lines A and B of slightly differing lengths have to be distinguished, one will at some moments appear longer and at others shorter than the other. In these circumstances, the best the subject can do is to make a number of inspections of the lines—evidence suggests at a rate of about 10 times per second—and to accumulate the results until eventually the tally of $A > B$ or $B > A$ reaches some criterion value (Vickers, Nettelbeck, and Willson, 1972). The finer the discrimination or the greater the random noise, the longer the accumulation will have to be for any given degree of accuracy. Accumulation can occur from the actual stimuli only so long as they are present to be inspected, except insofar as the aftereffects of stimulation provide a brief "iconic" storage. If, therefore, the stimuli are exposed only briefly, the time taken to decide between the alternatives rises relatively little as the discrimination becomes finer, but there is an increase of errors, and the number of errors made in such circumstances can be used as the basis of a measure of neural noise.

It is possible in these terms to interpret results obtained by Botwinick, Brinley, and Robbin (1958b) who required subjects aged 18–35 and 65–79 years to decide which was the longer of a pair of lines differing by between 1 and 20 percent. Two exposures were used, one of 2 seconds, which was longer than most times taken to make a decision, the other of 0.15 second. They found that with the longer exposure the mean difference of the decision times taken by the two age groups rose progressively as the difference between the lines fell from 10 to 1 percent, but that the groups did not differ in accuracy. With the short exposure the difference of times between the groups remained roughly constant at all levels of discrimination, but the older became progressively less accurate as the discrimination became finer. Vickers, Nettelbeck, and Willson calculated that the randomness with the short exposure was about 0.14 degrees of visual angle for the younger subjects and about 0.21 for the older. With the longer exposure the figure was about 0.10 for both age groups. In short, it looks as if the older subjects had effectively compensated for their greater neural noise by averaging their input over a longer time. The constant mean difference of about 0.16 second between the decision times of the two age groups with the short exposure was presumably due to some slowing with age in the processes of responding.

This example has been treated in some detail because, although with clear signals specified in advance limitations on the speed of performance lie mainly in the translation and central effector mechanisms, similar effects of exposure time on speed of performance are found.

Simple Movements

Change with age in the speed of simple movements varies greatly between different studies. For a single thrusting movement 11 inches long at maximum speed Pierson and Montoye (1958) found a roughly linear increase of time taken from the late teens to the seventies and early eighties in a group of men. The change was from about 0.18 second in the twenties to about 0.34 in the sixties—an increase of 89 percent. On the other hand Galton, who obtained results from visitors to an exhibition, found that what he termed "swiftness of blow" increased from about 56 msec per foot at age 25 to about 67 msec at age 65—an increase of only about 20 percent (see Ruger and Stoessiger, 1927). For discrete movements of some 23 inches aimed at a target, Hodgkins (1962) again found a roughly linear increase of time from the late teens onwards in a group of women with a change from 193 msec in those aged 18–21 to 249 msec in those aged 55–69, an increase of 29 percent.

Singleton (1955), who studied men from the twenties to the sixties moving a lever rapidly from side to side in an 18-inch slot, found a similar rise of 29 percent in the time taken be-

tween these age groups. Detailed examination of the form of the movement revealed that the times taken over the first quarter of the movement did not change with age, implying that the older subjects accelerated as quickly as the younger. During the last quarter of the movement the older subjects tended to be quicker. The extra overall time taken by the older subjects was due to their taking longer for the middle part of the movement and for changing direction at the end stops. The picture was of older people attaining lower maximum rates of movement and using the end stops to arrest their actions instead of making graded decelerations—a strategy which was to some extent successful in reducing their overall time.

Impetus was given to the quantitative study of simple movements alternately between two targets by Fitts (1954), who suggested a theoretical formulation in terms of the sizes of the targets and the distance between them. Several slightly different variations on this formulation have been put forward, but the one which has given the most consistent fit to the results of several studies has been:

$$\text{Movement time} = k \log \frac{(A + \frac{1}{2} W)}{(W)}$$

$$= k \log \left(\frac{A}{W} + .5 \right) \quad (1)$$

where A is the distance between target centers, W is the width of the targets and k is a constant. This formula makes the time a linear function of the information, in the information theory sense, gained in distinguishing between the distances from the starting point to the near and far edges of a target; and if logarithms to base 2 are used, the results can be expressed in bits per second. The quantity W needs to be corrected for errors if any shots fall outside the target areas—as a few of them usually do. The formula is discussed and the method of correcting for errors is described by Welford (1960; see also Welford, Norris, and Shock, 1969).

The results of two studies in which subjects of different ages tapped alternately on two circular targets are shown in Table 2. It can be seen that, in both, the increases of time taken with age were substantial, being about 30 percent between the twenties and the sixties in

TABLE 2. TIMES PER MOVEMENT (IN MSEC) FOR TAPPING ALTERNATELY ON TWO CIRCULAR TARGETS.
(Rates of information gain according to Equation (1) in bits per second are shown in parentheses.)

	Data from Singleton (1955)	Data from N. T. Welford (see A. T. Welford, 1958)			
Target diameter (inches)	1	2	1	2	1
Distance between centers (inches)	18	12	12	24	24
Age groups (years)					
20–29	486 (8.7)	293 (9.2)	370 (9.8)	401 (9.1)	491 (9.4)
30–39	512 (8.2)	357 (7.6)	435 (8.4)	443 (8.2)	547 (8.4)
40–49	494 (8.5)	455 (5.9)	544 (6.7)	568 (6.4)	656 (7.0)
50–59	573 (7.3)				
60–69	631 (6.7)	558 (4.8)	661 (5.5)	716 (5.1)	798 (5.8)
Percent increase of time from 20–29 to 60–69	30	90	79	79	63

Singleton's case and from 63 to 90 percent in the other. The steeper rise in the latter case may have been due to the fact that the targets, instead of being flush with their surrounds, were recessed slightly, and also that errors were corrected instead of being left uncorrected.

Studies in which subjects have tapped alternately between targets which were not circular but consisted of strips perpendicular to the direction of movement have shown rather smaller changes with age. Morikiyo and Nishioka (1966) using all combinations of $A = 4$ and 16 inches, and $W = 0.25$ and 2 inches found rises in time taken between the twenties and fifties of around 16 and 13 percent for men and women respectively, as shown in Table 3, and falls in bits per second from about 7.5 to 6.25 among

the men and from about 6.75 to 6.25 among the women. Welford, Norris, and Shock (1969), using all combinations of $A = 50$, 142, and 402 mm and $W = 32$, 11, and 4 mm found a rise in time taken of 8 percent between the twenties and sixties for men, as shown in the last line of Table 4. Both studies found that the loss of speed with age tended to be accompanied by increased accuracy—a compensatory tendency which has been found in several other studies of sensorimotor performance with age (see Welford, 1958).

In the study by Welford, Norris, and Shock, the targets, instead of being plates let into a surround and tapped with a stylus as in previous studies, were drawn on paper and the subject tapped to and fro with a pencil. He thus

TABLE 3. TIMES PER MOVEMENT (IN MSEC) AND PERCENTAGE ERRORS (SHOWN IN PARENTHESES) IN A RECIPROCAL TAPPING TASK.[a]

	Target width (inches)	2	2	0.25	0.25
	Distance between centers (inches)	4	16	4	16
Sex	Age group				
Men	20–29	194 (3)	331 (5)	444 (33)	650 (42)
	50–57	219 (2)	381 (3)	513 (19)	781 (23)
	Percent difference	13	15	16	20
Women	20–29	231 (1)	394 (3)	469 (31)	675 (46)
	50–57	250 (1)	425 (1)	575 (24)	763 (44)
	Percent difference	8	8	23	13

[a]From Morikiyo and Nishioka, 1966. The times are calculated from graphs given in their paper.

left a detailed record of the shots made. W was therefore taken not as the presented target width but as the width of the scatter of shots on the target, neglecting any occasional wild deviant. Similarly A was taken as the distance between the centers of the scatters on the two targets. This enabled a much more precise and detailed analysis to be made. An example of the results obtained is given in Figure 2, from which it will be seen that equation (1) using the modified quantities W and A gives a reasonable fit, but that the small targets take rather too long. If we join the points for any one target for different values of A, we obtain much lower slopes than if we join the points for different targets at any one value of A. This suggests that two control processes ought perhaps to be distinguished: a faster distance-covering phase and a slower phase of "homing" onto the target. It seems reasonable to regard the former as similar in speed to that of a ballistic movement of a given amplitude and the latter as implying an additional process of visual control. If so, the appropriate equation would be of the type:

$$\text{Movement time} = a \log A + b \log \frac{1}{W} \quad (2)$$

where a and b are the slope constants for amplitudes and targets respectively. Since ballistic movements show substantial accuracy without current visual control, we should probably write in place of equation (2):

$$\text{Movement time} = a \log \frac{A}{W_0} + b \log \frac{W_0}{W}$$

$$= a \log A - b \log W$$

$$+ (b - a) \log W_0 \quad (3)$$

when W_0 is the scatter of shots for ballistic movements of amplitude A. There is evidence that the accuracy with which ballistic movements are made is independent of their extent, depending upon some absolute appreciation of end position rather than upon distance moved (Marteniuk and Roy, 1972). If so, W_0 can be taken as constant.

The data from Figure 2 plotted in terms of equation (3) are shown in Figure 3. It can be seen that the fit is good except for the leftmost

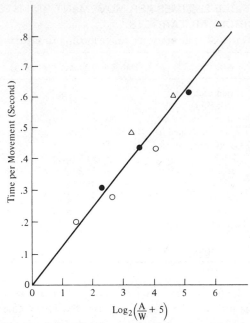

Figure 2. Times for tapping alternately on two targets plotted in terms of equation (1). Subjects aged 40–49. ○, 32 mm targets; ●, 11 mm targets; △, 4 mm targets. The distances from the center of one target to the far edge of the other were, for each target width from left to right, 50, 142 and 402 mm. (Data from Welford, Norris, and Shock, 1969.)

point. The time taken by short movements between wide targets is commonly longer than predicted in tasks of this kind, and it seems as if there is some minimum duration of aimed movements below which they do not fall, no matter how little demand is made for accuracy. An estimate of W_0 can be obtained from Figure 3 since the distance from zero to where the regression line cuts the abscissa = $(b - a) \log W_0$. In the example shown, W_0 worked out at 24 mm, which is certainly of the right order of magnitude. The rates of gain of information implied by the slope constants a and b are respectively 9.6 bits per second and 5.6 bits per second. The latter is close to that found by Hick (1952) and others for choice reaction times. One may suppose that the former represents the capacity of the effector mechanism and that the latter represents control involving the translation mechanism.

The constants a, b, and W_0 calculated for the different age groups are shown in Table 4. It

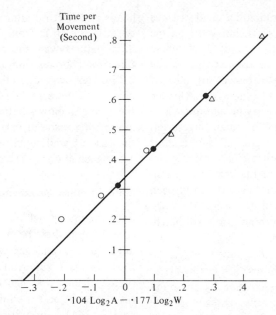

Figure 3. The data of Figure 2 plotted in terms of equation (3) with W_0 taken as constant for all target widths and distances.

can be seen that W_0 is at a minimum in the twenties, a in the thirties, and b in the forties.

The reasons for the age changes observed and for their variation in different studies are not clear. At present, however, it seems fair to note four points:

1. Muscular limitations might play an important part in rapid, unaimed movements such as those required by Pierson and Montoye but are likely to be less important than central limitations in aimed movements.

2. Consistent with this, age changes appear to be greater when the targets are circular and thus demand accurate aiming in two dimensions than when they are strips and thus require accuracy in one dimension only.

3. The age effect cannot be due to increased

TABLE 4. TIMES (IN SECONDS) AND PARAMETERS IN TERMS OF EQUATION (3) FOR A RECIPROCAL TAPPING TASK.

| | Totals for 9 combinations of target width and distance | | Parameters[a] | | | | |
| | | | W constant bits per | | A constant bits per | | W_0 |
Age group	Time	$Log_2\ W$	a	second	b	second	(mm)
20–29	440	9.41	0.113	8.86	0.201	4.98	20.4
30–39	414	9.62	0.103	9.75	0.181	5.53	23.4
40–49	419	9.31	0.104	9.65	0.177	5.65	23.7
50–59	421	9.47	0.106	9.45	0.187	5.35	24.0
60–69	475	9.44	0.116	8.65	0.195	5.14	28.2
70–79	535	9.12	0.131	7.63	0.205	4.89	26.9
Percentage difference between 20–29 and 60–69	8		3	2	–3	–3	38

[a]From Welford, Norris, and Shock, 1969.

tremor. Any tremor would add a small variance to the aim, so that the scatter of shots on the target would be a function of $\sigma_x^2 + \sigma_t^2$ where σ_t^2 is the variance due to tremor and σ_x^2 the variance from other disturbances of aim. If σ_t^2 rose with age, it would reduce the effective target size for older people by an amount which would be relatively large for small targets and relatively small for large ones. It should thus have lowered the speed of performance by older subjects with the small targets proportionately more than with the large. It can be seen from Table 2 that this did not occur: the slowing with age was, if anything, proportionately less for the smaller targets.

4. Movements aimed at a target appear to consist of a series of impulses each lasting about 100 msec. The distances covered by these impulses become progressively shorter as the movement proceeds: the first covers about half the distance from the starting point to the target area, the second covers about a quarter, the third an eighth, and so on until the movement can terminate within the target limits (Crossman and Goodeve, 1963). In young people, these impulses tend to run into each other to make a fairly smooth progression, whereas in older people they tend to be more separated, with intermittent decelerations and accelerations marking the transition from each to the next (Murrell and Entwisle, 1960).

Simple Movements Carried Out at Less Than Maximum Speed. The studies reviewed so far have all been of tasks carried out as fast as possible consistent with accuracy. It is a relevant question to ask whether the fall with age noted in maximum speeds is reflected in a fall in what are regarded as "comfortable" speeds of action. Four tasks used with subjects aged 11–88 years by Fieandt, Huhtala, Kullberg, and Saarl (1956) provide some answers to this question. These tasks and the percentage differences between the 21–24 and 59–67 age groups were (a) tapping with the forefinger on a table, the subject's arm resting on the table and movement being from the wrist, 10.3; (b) tapping with the ball of the foot on the floor while standing on the other foot and supporting himself by holding the edge of a table, 26.7; (c) clapping the

hands in a rhythm alternately on the knees and twice in the air in front, 22.6; and (d) "walking in a natural way the subject had to convey three matchboxes one at a time, a distance of 2.25 meters from one table to another, 5.7. The percentage increases are all within the range of the changes shown between the same ages for movements made at maximum speed, except in the case of walking. For this the change with age was small until the seventies.

More Complex Movements

Experiments in which complex sensorimotor coordination has been required have shown much greater changes with age than most of those we have surveyed so far. The magnitude of the change that can occur is well shown in the results of an experiment by Birren and Botwinick (1951a) on writing speed. They required their subjects to copy digits and words, each arranged at random, for periods of up to 2 minutes as fast as possible compatible with legibility. Their results are shown in Table 5 from which it is evident that there was a profound slowing after the thirties. The percentage change in time per digit between the twenties and the sixties was 97 and in time per word 118.

Change of writing speed with age has, however, been found to differ with occupation: LaRiviere and Simonson (1965), whose results are shown in Table 6, found no appreciable change in time taken to write digits by clerical

TABLE 5. SPEED OF WRITING.[a]

Age group	Seconds per digit	Seconds per word
16–20	.60	2.65
20–29	.62	2.50
30–39	.61	2.54
40–49	.78	3.16
50–59	.97	4.08
60–69	1.22	5.46
70–79	1.75	7.24
80–89	2.04	7.87
Percentage difference between 20–29 and 60–69	97	118

[a]Adapted from Birren and Botwinick, 1951a.

TABLE 6. WRITING SPEED (SECOND PER DIGIT) IN RELATION TO AGE AND OCCUPATION.[a]

Age group	40–49	50–59	60–69	Percentage difference between 40–49 and 60–69
Occupational group				
Clerical without supervisory duties	.70	.68	.70	0
Executive, supervisory, managerial and professional	.55	.62	.67	22
Skilled trades, machine operation and laboring	.71	.75	.85	20

[a]From LaRiviere and Simonson, 1965.

workers in their forties, fifties and sixties, but substantial increases among both those holding executive, supervisory, managerial or professional positions, and those classified as skilled tradesmen, machine operators and laborers. Even among the latter groups the percentage changes from the forties to the sixties were less than those found earlier by Birren and Botwinick between the same ages—about 21 as opposed to about 50. It seems possible that the older subjects in the later study had more need to write than did those in the earlier one who were residents in a home for indigent aged. If so, the difference is probably attributable to effects of familiarity and practice. Similar findings that age changes in speed of writing are less among those for whom writing is a familiar daily task have been reported by Smith and Greene (1962).

In any case, it has to be admitted that actual speeds of writing are not easy to interpret, since it is difficult to assess the quality of writing accurately; and, without doing so, we cannot say how far younger subjects have sacrificed quality to speed. Indications of speed and accuracy together were obtained in a figure tracing experiment by Brown (see Welford, 1958). The subjects traced first over a set of figures 1, 2, 3, 4, 5, 6, 7, 8, 9, 0, then over another set each of which was reversed from left to right, and then again over the normal figures. The times taken are shown in Figure 4, and the numbers of errors made are set out in Table 7. Taking these two together, it can be seen that the thirties maintained speed at the

TABLE 7. ERRORS MADE IN TRACING TEN FIGURES FIFTEEN TIMES.[a]

Age range	Mean errors per subject
20–29	20.5
30–39	54.3
40–49	29.7
50–59	8.8
60–69	17.4
70–79	7.3

[a]From an experiment by Brown (see Welford, 1958).

expense of accuracy, but from the forties onward accuracy was restored at the expense of speed.

Results from the same experiment also throw light on the effects of familiarity in two ways. First, the percentage difference of time taken between the twenties and the sixties on the first run was 124. By the fifth run over normal figures it was only about 50. On the first run with reversed figures it rose to 65, but by the fifth run with these it had dropped again to 55. Second, the task of tracing is less demanding than that of writing since, when tracing, the subject has merely to follow a display provided for him, whereas in writing he has to guide his actions by means of an internally conceived display. This is true even when copying since the subject cannot look simultaneously at the digit or word he is copying and at his own writing. Before the tracing task, subjects wrote the figures 1–0 once on paper the usual way, and both before and after tracing the reversed

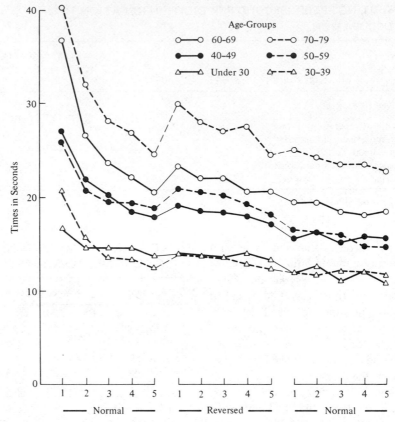

Figure 4. Times taken to trace ten figures (1-0) fifteen times. (After an experiment by Brown [see Welford, 1958].)

figures they wrote them reversed. The times taken for the three writing tasks are shown in Table 8. The times for normal writing were intermediate between those obtained by Birren and Botwinick and by LaRiviere and Simonson, while those for reversed writing were much

TABLE 8. TIME TAKEN PER SUBJECT TO WRITE TEN FIGURES (1-0) ONCE.[a]
(In Seconds)

Age range	Normal way round	Reversed first time	Reversed second time
20–29	7.3	21.3	12.4
30–39	7.7	20.3	14.5
40–49	9.3	33.8	20.9
50–59	7.7	31.9	22.8
60–69	11.7	34.9	25.1
70–79	12.5	55.5	37.2

[a]From an experiment by Brown (see Welford, 1958).

slower. Somewhat surprisingly, the proportional change with age for the first writing of the reversed figures was similar to that for the normal figures—64 and 60 percent respectively from the twenties to the sixties; the age change for the second reversed writing was much greater—102 percent over the same age range. Presumably the older subjects took longer to learn to write the reversed digits efficiently. In line with these results, Smith and Greene (1962) found little change with age until the seventies in speed of repeatedly writing the letter *a* the right way round, but appreciable rises with the less familiar tasks of writing *a* reversed or drawing triangles.

Age changes in the times taken for simple and more complex movements can be compared in results obtained by Miles (1931a,b). Percentage changes from the twenties to the sixties in the times required for simple movements made in response to a sound were: 9.5 for releasing a key, 18 for lifting the foot, and 22 for pressing a key. For more complex responses the percentage changes over the same range were: 18 to raise the finger from a key then transfer a pencil from one vertical hole to another and finally move the hand back to the key, 26 and 68 respectively to turn the crank of a hand-drill mechanism with the dominant and subdominant hands, and 79 to raise and lower the forefinger of the dominant hand.

More cogent comparisons are possible when the component actions within a complex performance are measured separately. For example, Simon (1960) compared two groups of subjects aged 18-24 and 59-85 years at a task in which they had to adjust two circular dials in turn to bring marks on the dials into coincidence with lines on the panel on which the dials were mounted. The percentage difference between the two groups in the time taken to manipulate the dials once they had been grasped was 45, whereas in the time to move the hand from one dial to another—a much simpler action—it was only 15. Smith and Greene (1962) similarly found that the times taken to write letters or draw triangles in a series rose with age substantially more than did the times to move the hand and pen from the end of one letter or triangle to the beginning of the next.

The longer times presumably imply more "work" by the translation and central effector mechanisms and are in line with the finding that, in continuous tasks, the times spent making actual movements change less with age than those spent stationary between one movement and the next—the times during which decisions about the next movement are presumably made. Three experiments will suffice as examples.

The first of these was by Szafran (1951). The subject sat in a kind of cockpit facing a panel of small lights and targets—one corresponding to each light—around him at nearly arm's length. As soon as one of the lights went out, the subject had to move a stylus from a small metal plate directly in front of him to the corresponding target. The experiment was perfomed under two different conditions—one with full vision and one with the subject wearing goggles which left the lights visible but obscured everything else. For our present purpose the difference between these two conditions is unimportant. The interesting result is that, while the time between the light going out and the subject lifting the stylus from the plate rose with age, the actual movement time between leaving the plate and reaching the target did not. The results are contained in Table 9. They have since been confirmed in an experiment by Griew (1959a) mentioned later.

The second experiment, which was by Leonard (1953), compared groups of subjects in a serial reaction task where the subject sat facing a display panel with five neon bulbs at the corners of a regular pentagon. On a table in front of him was a board with a brass disk corresponding to each light bulb and another similar disk in the center. The task was presented under two conditions. In one, the subject slid the stylus from the center disk to one of the other disks indicated by the corresponding light being on; he then returned to the center disk as quickly as possible, whereupon the light changed, indicating that the stylus should be moved to a different disk; and so on

TABLE 9. REACTION TIMES AND MOVEMENT TIMES IN AN AIMING TASK.[a]
(In Seconds)

	AGE GROUP			
	Twenties	Thirties	Forties	Fifties
Time from appearance of signal to beginning of responding movement	0.86	0.99	1.29	1.37
Duration of responding movement	1.18	1.20	1.14	1.22

[a]From Szafran, 1951.

TABLE 10. ANALYSIS OF CYCLE TIMES IN A SERIAL-REACTION EXPERIMENT.[a]
(In Seconds)

	LIGHT CHANGING WHEN CENTER DISK TOUCHED			LIGHT CHANGING WHEN INDICATED DISK TOUCHED		
	Twenties	Sixties	Percentage difference	Twenties	Sixties	Percentage difference
Total time per cycle	.85	1.24	46	.69	1.10	59
Made up of:						
Time on disks	.59	.92	56	.38	.79	108
Time moving between disks	.26	.32	23	.31	.31	0

[a]From Leonard; see Welford, 1958.

for a series of 100 signals. In the other condition the task was similar except that the light changed as soon as the indicated outer disk was touched, thus providing the subject with advance information of the direction in which he would have to move after returning to the center. Leonard's results are given in Table 10. It can be seen that the older subjects took substantially longer than the younger but that the percentage increases of time with age were much greater on the disks than in moving between them.

The third example is an experiment by Singleton (1954, 1955). The subject sat with a vertical joystick between his knees. On a panel in front of him were two lights. A run of trials started when one of the lights came on. The subject had immediately to pull the joystick towards him in a slot, and then push it in another slot to the side on which the light appeared. When he reached the end of the slot the light disappeared, whereupon he had to return by the same route to his starting point. As soon as he reached it a further signal light appeared, either the same as before or the one on the other side at random, and so on for a series of 64 lights. The times spent at the various points at which the joystick changed direction increased much more with age than did the times taken to move between these points. The percentage changes between the twenties and the sixties were 133 and 27 respectively.

It is reasonable to regard these stationary times as decision times and to regard the serial performance as made up of the two components, decision times and movement times. Such a view needs qualification, however, for two reasons. First, Jeeves (see Welford, 1958),

who used a modification of Singleton's apparatus, found that if he delayed giving the next signal by 100 or 200 msec after the subject returned the joystick to the starting point, the time taken to move away again was lengthened by less than the amount of the delay. The amount was less by about 30 msec for subjects aged 18–33 and about 50 msec for those aged 58–71. It looked, in fact, as if some process taking time after the end of the preceding movement had to be completed before the subject could deal with the ensuing signal and that the time taken by this extra process increased with age. What the process was cannot be determined from Jeeves' results alone: it might be that some neural aftereffect of the preceding response impaired the capacity to deal with a subsequent signal coming immediately after, or it might be that the subject spent time monitoring the completion of his response before turning attention to the next signal. We shall consider these possibilities later. Meanwhile it should be noted in passing that Jeeves' results sound a warning against oversimple conceptions of sensorimotor performance: while the delays reduced the times taken to react to the signal lights after they had occurred, they also shortened the movement times. In other words they affected the whole pattern of performance.

The second qualification to regarding the stationary times in Leonard's and Singleton's experiments as decision times arises from an experiment by Birren, Riegel, and Morrison (1962) who compared the times taken by subjects aged 18–33 and 60–80 to press in turn a series of 10 buttons in a row, with the times to press the same buttons in response to 10 lights presented in random order. The first task showed a rise in the time taken of about 46 percent from the younger group to the older. The second task took both groups substantially longer, but the rise was only 27 percent. The absolute increase in time with age was about the same in both tasks despite the much longer decisional component in the second. Presumably times taken to make decisions and to control movement can to some extent overlap.

Reaction Times

The reaction time, that is the period elapsing between the appearance of a signal and the beginning of a responding movement, is commonly regarded as a measure of the time taken by central processes. Obviously, it includes some time taken by peripheral processes as well, but as we have seen, this is usually short compared with that taken by perception, translation from perception to action, and the shaping and initiation of the responding movement. The central processes which take place during reaction time may be of greater or less complexity, and the length of the reaction time is commonly regarded as a measure of this.

Traditionally a distinction has been made between two main types of reaction time: *simple* (in which only one signal and one corresponding response are used) and *disjunctive*. The main case of the latter is the *choice* reaction in which several signals are each associated with a corresponding response. Other types of disjunctive reaction are where several signals all call for the same response, or where a response has to be made to only one or some of the signals presented. In all cases, the typical experimental method is to measure the time from the appearance of each signal to the initiation of the corresponding response so that the reaction time is a measure of the time taken by central processes. However, studies of choice reactions have also been made with subjects sorting packs of cards into different classes, and taking the time over the whole pack, so that the time includes also the time taken to move the cards.

Simple Reaction Times. In these, the signal and response are both known in advance, and the

reaction time is therefore essentially the time needed to recognize that the signal has occurred and to initiate a previously prepared response. The results of several studies in relation to age are summarized in Table 11. It is noticeable that the percentage increase of reaction time with age tends to be higher in the later studies, probably reflecting more rigorous techniques. Certainly some of the early results can be questioned on these grounds. For example, those by Bellis (1933) are not comparable with the rest because the times are the averages of only the shortest five by each subject; Galton (1899) obtained his subjects from visitors to an exhibition where they paid a small fee to "try their powers," and one may expect that older subjects volunteered only if they were fairly confident they would do well; De Silva's (1936) measure included a substantial movement component. Of the studies done since 1958, the median percentage increase of reaction time from the twenties to the sixties has been about 26.

Five other points may be noted about the entries in Table 11.

1. There is some discrepancy in the evidence about whether age changes of simple reaction time are greater or less than those of reflex times, but the more recent is in favor of their being greater, implying that the changes are due to central processes (Magladery, Teasdall, and Norris, 1958; Feinberg and Podolak, 1965).

2. The percentage changes with age do not appear to differ systematically with the sense organ stimulated, implying that the changes are either common to all sensory and perceptual mechanisms or are concerned with mechanisms of perception and response lying beyond the point at which the various sensory modes converge.

3. Slowness with age is not due to lack of motivation. Studies by Botwinick, Brinley, and Robbin (1958a) and by Weiss (1965) in which electric shocks were given for slow reactions caused both young and older subjects to react faster. In one of the studies, the speeding of the older was greater than that of the young, in the other study, the opposite occurred. In neither was the difference large. Parallel to this is perhaps the finding by Davies (1973) that older people speeded up to the same ex-

TABLE 11. SIMPLE REACTION TIMES. (In Seconds)

Author	Type of Reaction[a]	Teens	Twenties	Thirties	Forties	Fifties	Sixties	Seventies	Eighties	PERCENTAGE CHANGES 20s–50s	20s–60s	20s–70s	Notes
Galton (1899); see also Koga and Morant (1923)	Press key in response to light	.187	.182	.181	.190	.186	.206	.205	–	2	13	13	Subjects were visitors to an international health exhibition. The figures have been calculated approximately from those given by Koga and Morant.
	Press key in response to sound	.158	.154	.158	.159	.157	.167	.174	–	2	8	13	
Miles (1931a)	Press key in response to sound	–	.23	.24	.22	.20	.28	.30	.28	-13	22	30	100 subjects: fewer in the twenties and eighties than other ranges. The twenties ranged from 25 to 29 only.
	Release key in response to sound	–	.21	.22	.22	.22	.23	.26	.28	5	10	24	
	Lift foot in response to sound	–	.22	.22	.24	.24	.26	.27	.30	9	18	23	
Bellis (1933)	Press key in response to light												20 subjects in each age range except the highest which had 10. Equal numbers of men and women in each range. Scores are means of best five readings by each subject.
	Men	.24	.22	.26	.27	.38	–	–	–	73	–	–	
	Women	.32	.26	.34	.36	.44	–	–	–	59	–	–	
	Press key in response to sound in headphones												
	Men	.23	.19	.24	.25	.37	–	–	–	95	–	–	
	Women	.31	.20	.30	.30	.42	–	–	–	110	–	–	
De Silva (1936)	"Brake reaction time" in a test designed to simulate car driving (subject raised foot from accelerator pedal and transferred it to brake on seeing red flash of a traffic light)	.418	.418	.428	.442	.455	.465	–	–	9	11	–	2000 subjects. The age range of the teens is 16–19 and of the sixties, 61–65. The figures are approximate only, having been taken from a graph included in De Silva's paper.
Goldfarb (1941)	Raise finger from key and move to press another key in response to light	.376	.321	.334	.366	.387	–	–	–	21	–	–	Age groups were 18–24, 25–34, 35–44, 45–54, 55–64.
Obrist (1953)	Raise finger to sound of click and buzzer	–	.122	–	–	–	–	.131	.145			7	Age groups were 18–39, 65–75, 76–86.
Birren and Botwinick (1955)	Respond to 1,000 cps tone with												Age groups were 19–36, 61–91.
	Finger	–	.182	–	–	–	–	.232	–	–	–	27	
	Jaw	–	.194	–	–	–	–	.254	–	–	–	31	
	Foot	–	.202	–	–	–	–	.260	–	–	–	29	
Cesa-Bianchi (1955)	Response to light	–	.215	.186	.202	.207	.214	–	–	-4	0	–	268 subjects mostly between 30 and 59. The oldest age range was 60–66. Very full scores given for individual subjects.
	Response to sound	–	.157	.161	.179	.167	.187	–	–	6	19	–	
Fieandt et al. (1956)	Press button in response to light	.228	.201	.201	.217	.212	.217	.245	.353	5	8	22	The age ranges were 11–14, 21–24, 29–36, 39–47, 49–56, 59–67, 69–79, and 80–88. Each of the 120 subjects gave five readings. The two extremes of these were excluded and the scores were the means of the remaining three.

Reference	Response[a]												Comments
Botwinick, Brinley, and Robbin (1958b)	Lift finger to 1,000 cps tone		.177										32	Age groups were 18–37, 65–79.
	Same with shock for failure to react quickly		.157										40	
Pierson and Montoye (1958)	Lift hand to light	.28	.26	.27	.28	.32	.34	.33		23	31			400 male subjects aged 8–85. Figures read off graph. Those for subjects under 11 years not shown.
Magladery, Teasdale, and Norris (1958)	Flex foot to touch		.170				.189					11		Response measured by EMG potentials. Age groups 22–46, 61–85. Percentage changes shown are between these groups.
	Reflex to scratch on foot		.207				.279					35		
Griew (1959c)	Lift stylus in response to light: Light on until reaction made	.23	.23	.25						9				In the first experiment there were 12 subjects in each age group 19–26 and 52–59. In the second there were 8 aged 21–25 and 8 aged 50–57. The same 16 were subjects in the third experiment. All subjects were industrial workers roughly matched for occupation and background.
	Another similar experiment	.20	.20	.23						15				
	Light on for about 115 msec only	.21	.21	.22						5				
Hugin, Norris, and Shock (1960)	Flex left foot to touch on right foot	.210	.178	.177	.184	.192	.214	.222	.229	8	20	25		Responses measured from muscle action potentials.
	Reflex to scratch on Foot	.088	.090	.101	.099	.101	.099	.097	.095	12	10	8		
	Abdomen	.060		.071		.065	.059	.074	.082	−7	−16	6		
Talland and Cairnie (1961)	Press key in response to light		.253			.309			.328		22			Age ranges were 20–40, 65–75, 77–89 with means of 26.4, 69.8, 80.9.
Jalavisto et al. (1962)	Press contact in response to light		.235			.287		.320		22		36		Age groups 20–26, 44–64, 65–83.
	Catch ruler when dropped (visual cue)		.210			.242		.250		15		19		
	Catch ruler—further experiment Visual cue only		.195		.236						21			Mean ages were 22 and 69.5
	Visual and tactile		.137		.187						36			
	Tactile only		.121		.160						32			
Hodgkins (1962)	Release key to light	.224	.203	.214	.240	.253		.307			25	43		Subjects all women. Age groups 12–17, 18–21, 22–38, 39–54, 55–69, 70–84.
Weiss (1965)	Lift finger to 1,000 cps tone.		.174				.228					31		Figures are means of individual medians. Age groups 18–30, 65–80.
	Same with shock for failure to react quickly		.156				.196					26		
Onishi (1966)	Jumping in response to light: Male rural dwellers	.460	.470	.491	.554	.584				20	27			Subjects had to jump with whole body. Totals of subjects in the three groups were 205, 102 and 103 respectively. Factory workers in the fifties aged 50–56 only.
	Female rural dwellers	.515	.598	.611	.624					21				
	Male factory workers	.397	.415	.442	.472					19				
Morikiyo, Iida, and Nishioka (1967)	Press key in response to light	.211	.228	.267	.279					32				Subjects were 393 industrial workers.

[a]All reactions are made with the hand unless otherwise stated.

tent as younger in the performance of a maze under instructions for speed.

4. Weiss (1965) and Onishi (1966) used EMG techniques to analyze reaction time into a component of central time before muscular effects began, and one of the time between the beginning of innervation of the muscles and muscle action becoming effective. Weiss' results and those of Onishi's male rural dwellers are shown in Table 12. It can be seen that in Weiss' case the premotor time increased proportionally more with age than the motor, but that in Onishi's case this was not so. The difference is presumably due to the latter's task of jumping being more complex and involving a much greater amount of musculature than Weiss' task of merely lifting a finger. If so, the balance between premotor and motor components appears likely to vary with the motor requirements of the response, and this may account for some of the variation in the results listed in Table 11.

5. Some of the variation in Table 11 may also be due to the fact that some studies used warning signals before the signal to react, while others did not. The effects of warning signals

vary somewhat with age, as will be discussed later.

Disjunctive Reaction Times. We may begin by disposing of the two subsidiary types of disjunctive reaction mentioned earlier. Griew (1958c) used a task in which subjects had to lift a stylus from a metal disk whenever any one of several signals occurred. He compared conditions in which only 1 or any of 2, 4, or 8 signals might occur, and found that the times taken rose with the number of signals both for subjects aged 19-26 years and for those aged 52-59. The rise among the latter was somewhat greater—20 as opposed to 13 percent—suggesting that the older subjects found it more difficult to refrain from paying attention to the irrelevant information about *which* signal had occurred. Support for this view was obtained by Rabbitt (1965) who, in a task in which subjects sorted cards according to letters printed on them, found that the performance of older subjects was more impaired than that of younger subjects by additional, irrelevant letters on the cards. However, Rabbitt (1964b) in another card-sorting task found that

TABLE 12. ANALYSIS OF SIMPLE REACTION TIMES INTO CENTRAL TIMES BEFORE MUSCULAR EFFECTS BEGIN (PREMOTOR TIMES) AND TIMES FOR MUSCULAR ACTION (MOTOR TIMES).
(All figures In msec)

Data from Weiss (1965)

Age groups	18-30			65-80	Percentage difference
Without shock for slow reaction					
Premotor time	109			153	40
Motor time	65			75	15
With shock for slow reaction					
Premotor time	98			125	28
Motor time	59			72	22

Data from Onishi (1966)[a]

Age groups	20-29	30-39	40-49	50-59	60-72	Percentage difference between 20-29 and 60-72
Premotor time	155	162	163	171	183	18
From EMG innervation to beginning of muscular contraction	189	197	197	214	221	17
Muscular contraction	301	309	331	381	400	33

[a]Note that the sums of the components exceed the mean reaction times in Table 11 because the measured reaction time includes only part of the muscular contraction time.

although the rise in time taken with age increased with the number of stimuli calling for any one response, it was much less than that associated with an increase in the number of different *responses* to be made, implying that the perceptual factors were less important than those concerned with choice of response. A further study by Griew (1959c) suggests that the tendency of older people to attend to irrelevant information is similar to their tendency, noted by Botwinick, Brinley, and Robbin (1958b), to inspect incoming data for a longer time before making a decision, and that shortening exposure time so that extra data cannot be accumulated tends to bring the performances of older and younger closer together. Griew repeated his 1958 study but with signals lasting only 150 msec instead of lasting until the response was made. Under these conditions the increase of time from 1 to 8 signals was closely similar for subjects aged 21–25 and 50–57 years.

The second subsidiary type of disjunctive reaction is exemplified in an experiment by Surwillo (1973) who presented a series of tones, either 250 or 1,000 cps in random order, and required subjects to respond to the higher while ignoring the lower. The need to discriminate between the tones made reaction time longer than in the simple reaction situation when only one tone was used, but the rise was roughly proportional with age—about 16 percent in the simple case and 19 percent in the disjunctive, between the ages of 30 and 70 years.

Any disjunctive reaction involves two main processes: first the identification of which signal has occurred, and second the choice and initiation of a corresponding response. The types of disjunctive reaction surveyed so far have attempted to study the first of these processes by varying the number of signals while keeping the response constant. The main type of disjunctive reaction, where each of several signals is uniquely related to a corresponding response, does not usually allow this separation to be made, so that it is questionable whether any observed age change is due to the processes of identification or choice or both. Some evidence that both are affected and to a roughly

equal extent is provided by Naylor (1973) and his associates who compared the times taken to *recognize* a digit 1–9 shown tachistoscopically, with the reaction time to press one of 9 keys in *response* to a digit. The recognition times were .355 and .450 second respectively for groups aged 18–28 and 65–75 years—a difference of about 27 percent. The reaction times were 1.075 and 1.360 seconds respectively. Deducting the recognition times from these we obtain .720 and .910 second for choice and initiation of response—an age difference of 26 percent. The implications are that the identification times are shorter than the corresponding times for choice and initiation of response, but that the percentage change with age is the same in both.

Several theoretical models put forward since the early 1950s have treated choice reaction times in terms of variants on the equation:

$$\text{Reaction time} = a + bx \qquad (4)$$

where a denotes time taken by peripheral processes outside the actual process of choice, b denotes the directness with which responses are coupled to signals, and x is a measure related to the degree of choice. It has recently been suggested that most—perhaps all—choice reaction time data can be fitted if

$$x = \log \left(n \frac{C}{E} + 1 \right) \qquad (5)$$

where n is the number of equiprobable signals, C is the criterion of responding—high when the subject is cautious, lower when he is willing to risk errors—and E denotes the strength of the signal (Smith, in press; see also Welford, 1976). The signal E is assumed to accumulate with time until the level C is reached at which a response is triggered. When C is large or E is small the effect of the +1 becomes negligible.

The question for our present purpose is whether age effects are to be described in terms of changes in a, b, or x. A completely general slowing of processes in the organism should lead to proportional changes in both a and b. A change confined to the process of choice should affect b, while one which affected only other links in the chain from input to output should affect a. Any rise of criterion for responding (C) or fall of signal strength (E) in the sense organs or brain would tend to affect x to the extent of shifting it from $\log (n + 1)$ to $\log n$, although the change would be small and probably difficult to detect. More important, a rise in C or fall in E could also produce an *apparent* rise of a. The reason can be seen if, ignoring for simplicity the $+1$, we rewrite equation (5)

$$x = \log n + \log C - \log E \qquad (6)$$

Unless C or E varied with n, any change in these would be independent of the degree of choice and thus virtually indistinguishable from changes in a.

The evidence is by no means entirely clear. The earliest results are those of Goldfarb (1941). His subjects sat pressing a button in the center of a semicircle of five keys. Above each key was a light. The subject was given a warning sound, and then at a randomly varied interval, between 2 and 4 seconds later, one of the lights would come on. The subject was required to move his hand as quickly as possible from the central key to the key under the light. The experiment is not a typical reaction experiment because movement from the central key to the others involved a substantial arm movement, and the results shown in Table 13 are not well fitted with x as defined in equation (5). It is clear, however, that the rise with age is roughly constant for all age groups except the youngest. In other words it is in a rather than b.

The next results obtained were those of Crossman and Szafran (1956) for a card-sorting task. The subject sorted an ordinary pack of playing cards into either red or black, the four

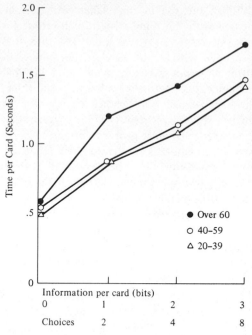

Figure 5. The average times of different age groups for sorting playing cards into different numbers of classes. (After Crossman and Szafran, 1956.)

suits, or the four suits separating picture cards from the others. These arrangements provided 2, 4, and 8 choices, respectively. As a control, the cards were dealt alternately into two piles to give a measure of time taken to make the movements of sorting without having to make discriminations or choices. The results are shown in Figure 5 with $x = \log n$. There is no sign of a rise in b with age from 2 to 8 choices, but there is a substantial rise of a from the 40–59 to the over 60 age group. This rise cannot be

TABLE 13. COMPARISON OF SIMPLE AND CHOICE REACTION TIMES.[a]
(Mean Times in msec)

	AGE GROUP				
	18–24	25–34	35–44	45–54	55–64
Simple	376	321	334	366	387
Two-choice	394	380	395	436	451
Five-choice	429	418	432	472	495
Difference between simple and two-choice	18	59	61	70	64
Difference between two-choice and five-choice	35	38	37	36	44

[a]From Goldfarb, 1941.

due to an increase of movement time with age since the rise of dealing time is small.

A rise of a but not of b with age was also found by Szafran (1966a) in a more conventional reaction time task in which the subjects pressed microswitches in response to a series of neon lights presented one at a time in random order. The regressions he found for reaction times between 3, 5, and 8 choices were $.272 + .085 \log_2 n$ second for subjects under 40 (mean age 32.3 years), and $.288 + .082 \log_2 n$ for those over 40 (mean age 47.7). When at the same time as this serial reaction task, subjects had to perform a subsidiary task involving short-term retention or making statements with delayed auditory feedback, the regressions became $.393 + .089 \log_2 n$ second and $.477 + .087 \log_2 n$, respectively.

An age effect predominantly in a was also observed by Botwinick, Robbin, and Brinley (1960) in a card-sorting task in which packs of playing cards (without the picture cards) had to be sorted into from 2 to 10 classes by number. The results, plotted with $x = \log_2 n$, are shown in Figure 6. The reaction time regressions are $.510 + .188 \log_2 n$ second per card for a group aged 19-35 years, and $.745 + .242 \log_2 n$ for one aged 65-81. There is some rise of b with age but it is clearly not as striking as that of a.

On the other hand, age effects predominantly in b were obtained by Griew (1959a, 1964). His subjects had to respond in different runs to any of 1, 2, 4, or 8 lights arranged in a semicircle on a vertical board some 3 feet away by moving a stylus from a central brass disk to the corresponding one of 8 disks arranged in an 8-inch radius semicircle. The reaction time measured was from the appearance of the light to the moving of the stylus from the disk. Examples of the reaction times he obtained are $.288 + .073 \log_2 n$ second for subjects aged 20-28 years and $.307 + .094 \log_2 n$ for those aged 48-62. Similar results were obtained by Suci, Davidoff, and Surwillo, (1960) for a task in which subjects responded by speaking nonsense syllables on the disappearance of one of a set of 4 lights. They compared conditions in which the same light went off in each trial with those in which either of 2 or any of 3 or 4 might go off. They obtained reaction times of $.323 + .179 \log_2 n$ second for a group aged 17-38 (median 18.5) years and $.387 + .302 \log_2 n$ second for one aged 60-70 (median 63). It should be noted that their results can also be described well with $x = \log (n + 1)$ and $a = 0$, so that the regressions become $.30 \log_2 (n + 1)$ and $.41 \log_2 (n + 1)$ second, respectively. Again Talland and Cairnie (1961) who compared two-choice manual reactions to red and green lights with simple manual reactions to green light found regressions for three age groups 20-40, 65-75, and 77-89 years of $.253 + .080 \log_2 n$, $.309 +$

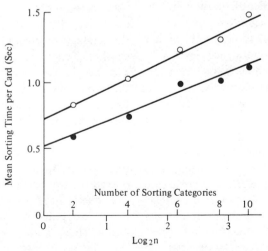

Figure 6. Times taken to sort playing cards (excluding picture cards) into 2–10 classes by number. ●, subjects aged 19–35 years; ○, subjects aged 65–81 years. (Data from Botwinick, Robbin, and Brinley, 1960.)

TABLE 14. CHOICE REACTION TIMES IN TERMS OF EQUATION (4).[a]

All figures in msec

$(x = \log_2 n)$

	a	b
Teens	209	191
Twenties	199	193
Thirties	205	207
Forties	191	233
Over 50	216	234

[a]From Morikiyo, Iida, and Nishioka, 1967.

.114 $\log_2 n$, and .328 + .215 $\log_2 n$ second respectively. Rises predominantly in b have also been found by Morikiyo, Iida, and Nishioka (1967) for factory workers with a task in which they responded by pressing keys under their fingers to numerals shown on a Nixie tube: 2, 4, and 8 choices were compared. The regressions of reaction times obtained are shown in Table 14.

Any resolution of the conflict between the results showing the main rise with age to be in a and those showing it to be in b must be speculative. It seems possible to distinguish between the two groups of results in terms of the effective length of exposure of the stimulus, and so link them with the effects of length of exposure in the discrimination task of Botwinick, Brinley, and Robbin (1958b) discussed earlier. In all cases where the main age effect was in b, the signal had to be identified fully by the subject before he could begin to respond, and he would therefore accumulate data until he had attained an adequate confidence level. The conditions thus resembled those of Botwinick, Brinley, and Robbin (1958b) using a long exposure. On the other hand, in all cases except Szafran's (1966a) where the age effect was mainly in a, the conditions enabled the subject to begin his response after only a brief look at the display: in the card-sorting tasks he had to move towards the area where the card was to be placed, while in Goldfarb's (1941) task he had to move towards the button he was to press. In all these cases, therefore, his inspection of the display was likely to be brief and the conditions would be like those of a brief signal in the study by Botwinick, Brinley, and

Robbin (1958b). The situation in Szafran's case is unclear because he does not state the conditions of his experiment in detail, but it seems likely from his description that the signals he used were brief.

Two further results are anomalous, but appear to be special cases. The first is a card-sorting experiment by Rabbitt (1964b) using cards each of which bore a single letter in one of nine positions. Comparing two- and four-choice conditions and age groups of 17-25 and 68-82 years, he found the main age effect was in b; but the task appears to have required much closer scrutiny of the cards than in other card-sorting experiments where the main age change was in a. The second anomalous case is that of a more normal reaction time experiment by Deupree and Simon (1963) in which the age effect was not reduced by brief exposure as opposed to exposure terminated by the response. The short exposure they employed— 50 msec—was, however, too short to be fully effective at the low intensity they used: Vickers, Nettelbeck, and Willson (1972) have shown that exposures less than about 100 msec pose special problems.

Explanations of the Lengthening of Reaction Time with Age

Finding reasons for the changes in reaction time with age is not easy. The main question appears to be whether the changes are due to some basic deterioration in the sensorimotor mechanisms, or whether they result from changes in the strategy of performance such as increased caution. The two are not mutually exclusive and may be compensatory as, for example, in the experiment by Botwinick, Brinley, and Robbin (1958b) already mentioned on discrimination, where longer reaction times by older people appeared to compensate for greater neural noise. The question we should ask therefore appears to be: How far does each factor operate in any particular set of circumstances? The question is important, not only from a theoretical point of view, but because fundamental changes are essentially a physical problem whereas changes of strategy may be amenable to training.

As regards changes of capacity, there is now

abundant evidence that cardiovascular impairments are associated with the slowing of several types of performance, both motor and intellectual, and that the likelihood of these impairments increases with age (e.g., Birren and Spieth, 1962; Spieth, 1964, 1965; Simonson, 1965; Simonson and Anderson, 1966; Botwinick and Storandt, 1974). With regard to the parameters of choice reaction time, Szafran (1966b), using the task already mentioned, found that in addition to the rise of a with age there was also a rise of b among subjects showing cardiac deficiency after exercise. Similarly Abrahams and Birren (1973) found that both a and b were higher among subjects judged to be predisposed to coronary heart disease by Friedman's Standard Situation Interview. As the author has already suggested, a change of a may imply either a change in some ancillary process in the chain from input to output, or a rise of criterion for responding (C) or a fall of signal strength (E) in equation (5). A rise of C would be in line with increased caution, while a fall of E seems entirely plausible from what is known about the loss of active elements with age in sense organs and brain. A change of b, however, implies a change in the actual process of choice.

Botwinick and Thompson (1968a) found that while the reaction times of a group of subjects aged 68–86 years were significantly slower than those of young athletes ages 18–27, they were not significantly slower than those of young men of the same age who were not athletes. This finding suggests at first sight that part at least of the slowness shown by older people is attributable to lack of physical fitness, which might be associated with poorer blood supply to the brain. There is certainly evidence that exercise can increase physical capacities in older people (Barry, Daly, Pruett, Steinmetz, Page, Birkhead, and Rodahl, 1966a; Stamford 1972) and that this has in some cases been accompanied by improvements in performance at other tasks such as making simple ballistic movements (Barry, Steinmetz, Page, and Rodahl, 1966b) and, among seniles, intellectual performance (Powell, 1974). Among normal older people, however, physical exercise has not been shown to improve intellectual performance (Barry

et al., 1966b), and Botwinick and Storandt (1974) found that exercise was associated with reaction times only in young subjects and had no association with amount of exercise normally taken among subjects aged 64–74. De Vries (1970) has suggested that where exercise improves intellectual performance it does so less by physical conditioning than by causing central stimulation. This, in terms of the model outlined in the Introduction, would be expected to raise the subject's arousal level and thus his sensitivity and responsiveness. As noted in the Introduction such arousal is associated with optimal performance at moderate levels— performance tends to be poor if the level is either too low or too high. Other evidence, not related to age, is in accord with this view: vigorous exercise over a period of 2–5 minutes has been found to improve intellectual performance, but to impair it if continued longer (Davey, 1973). Such periods are far too short for physical conditioning to occur, but are likely to have substantial central stimulating effects (Cooper, 1973).

An alternative explanation sometimes offered is that older people fail to realize their full capacities because they are out of practice, and it is often further assumed that sufficient practice would equate the performances of old and young. There is, however, no sound evidence for this view. For example, practice at tracing tasks studied by Brown (Figure 4) and by Szafran (see Welford, 1958), although only over short periods, reduced absolute differences between age groups but gave no indication that performance would eventually reach equality. Studies of the effects of practice upon reaction times have shown that older subjects may become substantially faster, but much of the evidence is unsatisfactory. For example, Botwinick and Thompson (1967a) found that their younger subjects tended to produce *longer* reaction times after practice, suggesting that the task was boring. Again Hoyer, Labouvie, and Baltes (1973), who demonstrated gains in speed among subjects with a mean age of 70, used no younger group as a control. Murrell (1970), who did show an age difference disappearing with long practice, used only two younger subjects, aged 17 and 18, and one aged 57—an age at which other studies have shown little slowing of reaction is to be expected. The most thorough study, by Noble, Baker, and Jones (1964), found that reaction times diminished with practice in all age groups from childhood to the seventies and eighties, but that the asymptotes of the learning curves fitted to their results tended to rise with age after the late teens—in other words, the curves did *not* converge upon a common level of speed.

On the neurological side, Hicks and Birren (1970) have surveyed the relationships between age changes in psychomotor performance and the symptoms of various kinds of brain deficiency, and several authors, especially Obrist (1965) Surwillo (1961, 1963, 1964) and Mankovsky and Belonog (1971), have studied relationships between changes of EEG and performance with age. Surwillo has shown a close correlation between reaction time, both simple and choice, and the frequency of the alpha rhythm, and has argued that the slowing of this can account for the lengthening of reaction time with age. He suggests that the alpha rhythm can be used as a kind of metric for reaction times, implying that it consists of "modules" of about 0.1 second. This suggestion tallies with the findings of Vickers, Nettelbeck, and Willson (1972), who postulated that discrimination could be regarded as a process in which data accumulated in modules of about 0.1 second and of the present author (Welford, 1971, 1975), whose data suggested modules of about the same duration for the choice of response.

On the other hand, there seems to be evidence of strategies by older people aimed consciously or unconsciously at optimizing performance and minimizing the effects of more basic changes. For instance, we have already noted a tendency to compensate for loss of speed by increased accuracy which will lead to less time being wasted in correcting errors. The tendency can be seen as parallel to that noted by Szafran (see Welford, 1958) for older people to look at objects they are picking up instead of trusting to touch alone, and to several studies which have shown older people to be reluctant to make a positive, accepting response. Thus Silverman (1963) found that older people,

when shown words briefly and instructed to identify them if they could but not to reply if doubtful, tended to make fewer replies than did younger subjects, but also fewer errors. Again Botwinick (1966), who obtained opinions from people of different ages as to what they would do in a number of risky real life situations, found older people to be more cautious.

Perhaps most cogent is the finding that in a series of trials in which, after a warning, subjects had to decide whether or not a faint tone had been sounded, older subjects gave a higher proportion of negative replies, even though the tones had been equated beforehand for audibility for each individual; in terms of "Signal Detection Theory," the detectability (d') did not differ with age but the parameter β, indicating bias against giving positive responses, became higher (Craik, 1969; Rees and Botwinick, 1971). Craik (1969) also reanalyzed data by Belbin and Shimmin (1964) who had found in an inspection task in which faulty articles had to be rejected and accurate ones accepted that older people tended to reject articles that should have been accepted. He found again that the difference between the performance of older and younger subjects was to be accounted for in terms of β rather than d'. The finding is of special interest in that Belbin and Shimmin had shown that the overstrictness of judgement among the older inspectors could be corrected by training, and Craik found that when it was, the change was indicated in a reduction of β, leaving d' unaffected.

Of other possible reasons for a rise of reaction time with age the most widely canvassed is the view that, for one reason or another, older people are less able than younger to prepare their responses before the signal to make them arrives. Evidence in favor of such a view comes from the fact that in reaction time tasks where a warning is given at a variable time before each signal, reaction is slower when the interval is short or very long than when it is of moderate length. This is true of both old and young subjects, but the slowing at very short intervals tends to be more pronounced among the older (Botwinick, Brinley, and Birren, 1957; Botwinick, Brinley, and Robbin, 1959; Brinley and Botwinick, 1959; Botwinick and Brinley,

1962). Somewhat similar effects appear when signals are given at irregular intervals in a continuous series: reactions to signals which follow others at very short or long intervals tend to be slower than to those which follow at intermediate intervals, and the slowness at short intervals has again been shown to be more pronounced among older subjects (Brebner and Szafran, 1961). The lengthening of reaction time with short intervals between warning and signal does not occur if the interval is kept the same for a whole block of trials, presumably because the subject in fact reacts to the warning rather than to the signal itself (Botwinick, Brinley, and Robbin, 1959, Botwinick and Brinley, 1962, Botwinick and Thompson, 1966). Several possible reasons, not mutually exclusive, for these results will be considered in turn:

1. It has been noted in studies not concerned with age that reaction is especially slow when a short interval between warning and signal follows a long one in the previous trial, and Botwinick, Brinley and Birren (1957) found that this was especially so among older subjects. This might imply that older subjects relied more on *expectations* than did younger, and that their expectations tended not to be well founded. It has, in fact, been shown in tasks where the subject has to guess which will be the next signal in a series that older subjects tend to guess less correctly (e.g., Sanford and Maule, 1973). Consistent with this view, variability of interval between warning and signal from trial to trial has been found to make for somewhat greater variation of reaction time in older than in younger subjects (Botwinick and Thompson, 1968b). Inaccurate expectations might result from failures of short-term retention, well known to increase with age, which would mean that less account could be taken of any trend in previous signals in the series.

2. Morris and Thompson (1969) found that the slowing of heart rate while waiting for a signal, commonly taken as an indicator of preparation, was less among older subjects than among younger ones. The implication is that older subjects do not prepare so *intensively* as young. In line with this view, Loveless and

Sanford (1974) found that older subjects failed to show an anticipatory electrocortical potential between a warning and a signal to respond. Also, Rabbitt (1964a) found that a warning which conveyed information, such as that 1 of 4 out of a possible 8 responses would be called for, shortened reaction times for younger but not older subjects.

3. What at first sight might be an interpretation of the results outlined in the previous paragraph is that the diffuse activating system shown in Figure 1 is less effective in older people, so that they are less *aroused* than are younger people by the warning signals. However, Surwillo and Quilter (1965) showed that although the latency of the galvanic skin response, commonly taken as a measure of arousal, was longer for older than for younger subjects, there was no relationship between this and reaction time. A similar lack of correspondence has been found for EEG measures of arousal and reaction time by Thompson and Botwinick (1968). while Surwillo (1969), who did find relationships in some individuals, found they were unrelated to age. More generally, the evidence about whether older or younger people show higher arousal levels is equivocal (van der Valk and Groen, 1950; Surwillo, 1965). An amphetamine-like drug, "Meretran," which would be expected to raise arousal level, was found to make action more vigorous but not to increase its speed in a group of elderly men (Kleemeier, Rich, and Justiss, 1956); again, the effects of monotonous conditions which tend to lower arousal differ little between young and old (Griew and Davies, 1962; Davies and Griew, 1963; Kemp, 1973), and any individual changes of vigilance under these conditions do not appear to be related to speed of reaction (Surwillo and Quilter, 1964).

Such evidence makes it unlikely that lack of arousal plays any significant part in the slow reactions by older people to signals coming at short intervals after warnings or previous signals. One further line of evidence confirms this view: if arousal were important, reactions should be faster and age changes less in continuous performance tasks. An experiment by the present author has shown that they are not so.

TABLE 15. TWO-CHOICE REACTION TIMES (MSEC) IN RELATION TO INTERVALS BETWEEN SIGNALS, FOR THREE GENERATIONS.

		NEXT SIGNAL ARRIVED:		
Generation	Mean age (years)	2 seconds after release of previous key	Immediately after release of previous key	On pressing previous key
Younger	19	278	393	321
Middle	46	273	398	342
Older	73	340	520	472
Percentage differences from younger:				
Middle		−2	+1	+7
Older		+22	+32	+47

Ten trios of subjects, one member of each trio from each of three generations of the same family—daughter, mother, and mother's mother, or son, father, and father's father—performed a two-choice reaction task under two conditions. The signals were two pairs of neon lights, each pair corresponding to one of two response keys. The lights within each pair came on alternately, and between pairs came on in random order. In one condition each signal arrived 2 seconds after the key pressed in response to the previous signal was released. In another, the next light appeared immediately when the previous key was released. The results are shown in Table 15. The reaction times in the second condition were significantly longer than in the first for all three generations and became disproportionately longer for the oldest (Welford, in press).

4. A plausible interpretation of the last result, and also of the greater slowing of reaction among older subjects when the interval between warning and signal is very short, is that some aftereffects, increasing with age, of the processes concerned with the decision to respond or the observation of the warning, continue for a brief period and act as noise, blurring any decision process which follows shortly after (Welford, 1965). The same effect could account for Jeeves' result mentioned earlier—the aftereffect would be dissipated during the delay between the completion of the previous response and the appearance of the next signal. We should expect such aftereffects to impair performance less when the

following response is the same as the one just made: they should rather facilitate it since the processes for its initiation would already be operating to some extent. Such an explanation has been put forward for the so-called repetition effect observed in several studies of reaction time not concerned with age: reaction times for responses repeated within about 0.5 second tend to be quicker than those for different responses (for reviews see Welford 1976, and in press). The same type of explanation could account for the perseveration effects observed in senility (Hurwitz and Allison, 1965). If this is the correct explanation of the age effects previously mentioned as obtained by the present author (Welford, in press), we should expect repetition effects to increase with age, especially when the next signal follows immediately upon the release of the previous key. However, scrutiny of the results revealed no such tendency. A lack of increase in repetition effect with age has also been reported by Waugh, Fozard, Talland, and Erwin (1973). It seems clear, therefore, that perseverative aftereffects of these kinds cannot account for the slowing with age.

5. Perhaps the most likely explanation of the slower reactions by older people when a new signal follows a very short time after the making of a previous response or the giving of a warning is, first, that the translation mechanism is busy monitoring the previous response or data from the warning so that data from the new signal are delayed at the gate shown in Figure 1; and second that the time taken by

such monitoring is longer for older subjects. This might be so partly because of a greater tendency to monitor, parallel to Szafran's findings already noted that older people tended to look more at what they were doing; and partly that when the monitoring occurred it took longer, parallel to the finding of longer reaction times. Some indication in favor of this type of view is contained in the finding by Talland and Cairnie (1961) and by Talland (1964) that although warnings shortened reaction time among younger subjects, they tended to lengthen them among older. Further indications come from additional results, shown in Table 15. All age groups were slower when the next signal was given on the *release* of the key used for the previous response than when there was a 2-second interval. Surprisingly, however, the times when the next signal arrived upon *pressing* the key for the previous response were intermediate between the other two. For the youngest subjects, reaction times in this last condition approached those with the 2-second interval after release, while for the oldest they approached the times taken when the next signal came immediately on release of the previous key. It has been shown that, for young subjects, time tends not to be spent monitoring responses when the next signal arrives *before* the response to the previous signal has begun (Leonard, 1953; Welford, 1968), and it is probably reasonable to suppose that monitoring would also tend to be suppressed if the next signal arrived at the moment the previous response began. If so, the results in Table 15 can be taken to mean that older subjects are less able—or less willing—to omit such monitoring.

What appears to be an interesting parallel to these results in a different context has been obtained by Rabbitt and Rogers (1965), who compared times for movement to one of two alternative end points, one further away than the other in the same direction, with times for return movements to a single end point. They found that, when making the former movements, subjects aged 19–29 could overlap the time required to make the choice between alternatives with the initial stages of the movement. Subjects aged 63–76 appeared less able

to do this, seemingly because they needed to monitor their movements more closely and were unable to combine this with making choices. A similar parallel is contained in the results obtained by Rabbitt and Birren (1967) whose subjects responded to regular, continuous sequences of signal lights in different positions by pressing corresponding keys thus: 1, 2, 1, 2, 1, 2 ... or 1, 2, 3, 4, 3, 2, 1, 2, 3, 4 .... They found that subjects aged 60–81 were slower and less accurate than those aged 17–28, especially with the 4-item sequence, but were less affected by occasional deviations from the regular pattern. It seemed that younger subjects programmed and monitored the regular series as wholes, whereas the older tended to react to and monitor each signal individually.

Continuous Performance. The foregoing discussions imply that in tasks such as tracing over figures, or making serial reactions, speed of performance depends upon the sum of movement times, decision times (which are essentially reaction times), and some time for monitoring movements; but that in certain cases decision times for one signal can overlap the movements in response to a previous signal, and monitoring can be at least partly suppressed. It seems, however, difficult to perform continuously without *some* monitoring of action. The situation is well summed up in the task of tracking a continuously moving target by adjusting a pointer to coincide with it. What appears to happen in this case is that the subject perceives a discrepancy between the positions of the target and the pointer, decides upon a correction and makes it. He then observes again and the cycle is repeated, for a subject in his twenties, at intervals of about 0.5 second. This time appears to be made up of about 0.3 second reaction time plus 0.2 second monitoring the movement—the actual movement is usually somewhat longer than 0.2 second although it is clearly intermittent at a frequency of about 2 movements per second (Welford, 1968).

Experiments on tracking in relation to age have shown that performance at this kind of task changes a great deal with age at high speeds of target movement although very little at low speeds (Welford, 1958). The subject was required to "drive" a ballpoint pen along a track on paper drawn downward past a window. His control was a steering wheel, and the apparatus was arranged in such a manner that more or less of the track could be seen ahead of the pen. The course of the target or the track could in all cases be conceived as that of an approximate sine wave with irregularities or harmonics.

At low speeds the subjects could track in step with the target, but, as the speed was raised, they began to lag farther and farther behind, and their "swings" became progressively shorter. The shortening of the swing was of such a nature that the amount of movement made per minute remained approximately constant, although this meant that, as the excursions of the target rose in frequency, the subject's responding movements became individually smaller. Performance at high speeds was substantially better with preview than without for all ages, but the older subjects still moved less than the younger.

At first sight these results seem to permit three possible explanations. First, that the older subjects were more cautious than the younger; second, that they were unable to swing sufficiently fast because they could not make the necessary movements in the time allowed; and, third, that the experiment was measuring a rather fundamental capacity to transmit information from the track to the control and that this capacity falls with age. The first of these explanations seems to be excluded because, although it might reasonably apply where preview was not given, it could hardly be the explanation where the track could be seen well ahead, unless some other limitation was operating also. If the subject can see the track far enough ahead, he should have plenty of time to prepare his actions as carefully as he wishes unless other factors are limiting the extent to which he can usefully look ahead. This, as we shall see, seems likely to be the case. The second possibility was shown by control experiments to be unimportant. We therefore assume the change of performance with age to be due to a change of capacity.

The capacity concerned seems to be of two different kinds: first, the rate of transmission and second, the storage of information. Both these may need a little explanation. The first means that, as we have already seen, the observation of a display and the shaping of accurate movements in response to it take time, and that only a certain amount of such "work" can be done in any given amount of time. As the track is speeded up, this limit is gradually reached and then passed. When this happens, some breakdown of accuracy will occur. The shorter swings made by the subject in response to the excursions of the target appear to represent a lessening of the differentiation between one responding movement and another. In this way the amount of information transmitted from display to control is reduced, and the time taken per swing is shortened. The subject is thus able to continue to make the correct *number* of swings, although at some sacrifice of accuracy in their *extent*. Adequate preview of the track may enable him to avoid tracking late and so keep his swings in time with the excursions of the target, but it cannot overcome the limits of his capacity to transmit information. The amount of preview which can usefully be given is thus limited in amount.

Even where the limit of capacity to transmit information is not reached, the amount of preview likely to be used is limited by the fact that any information seen ahead has to be stored in a kind of running short-term memory until it can be used. The capacity of this short-term memory seems to become lower with age. Evidence for this is contained in an experiment by Griew (1958a) using the same apparatus. He gave a preview of the track for a substantial way ahead, but obscured the portion just ahead of the pen, thus forcing the subject to store data over a brief period. Under these conditions older subjects were at a relatively severe disadvantage.

The concept of capacity and of its change with age implied by these tracking results has a number of implications of which three deserve mention.

Pacing. Tracking is a paced task in which signals for action arrive at times which are not controlled by the subject and have to be responded to within a restricted period if action is not to be too late. Substantial falls of performance with age have also been found in other paced tasks. The one closest to the tracking task already discussed is that of the *pursuit rotor* in which the subject tries to keep a stylus on a small circular area near the periphery of a rotating turntable. Gutman (1965) found that performance at this task by subjects aged 60–91 (mean 74.3) years was very poor compared with that of subjects aged 17–25 or 36–46.

A different type of paced task is that used by Talland (1966), who required subjects to detect the digit 4 among digits which might appear in any of nine positions. He found no systematic change with age from the twenties to the sixties when signals appeared at rates of 27 or 54 per minute, but an increase from each decade to the next in the number of signals missed when the rate was 109 per minute.

What is perhaps the most detailed study of paced performance in relation to age is an experiment by Brown (1957). The subject sat in front of an apparatus on which were two pieces of 6 × 4-inch graph paper. On one of these was a small steel ball. The subject's task was to plot the position of this ball on the other by means of a pointer carrying a small black spot. When the subject thought he had plotted correctly, he pressed a button on the handle of the pointer and, if the position was correct, the ball started to move until it was stopped by pressing a key at the side of the apparatus. The subject then began to plot the new position of the ball, thus beginning the cycle of operations over again.

Observing the subjects, it was clear that the method adopted by the younger and older tended to be very different. The young subjects acted rapidly, swinging the pointer into position and pressing the button almost immediately. If they had plotted accurately, this procedure was, of course, fast and economical. Often, however, the first attempt did not make the ball move and had to be followed by several other attempts leading to errors before success was achieved. The older subjects were much more careful and meticulous. They tended to plot on the two dimensions separately, swinging the pointer first one way and then at right an-

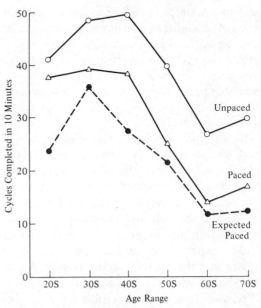

Figure 7. Comparison of paced and unpaced performance at a plotting task. The "expected" paced score was calculated by taking, for each subject, the proportion of cycles he completed unpaced in the allowed time of 8 seconds and multiplying by the maximum possible paced score. This gave the paced score that would have been attained if the distribution of cycle times in the paced performance had been the same as the distribution in the unpaced. It can be seen that the observed paced performance was a little higher than the expected, which means that the pacing speeded performance up a little, at least in the sense of reducing the number of long cycle times. (After Brown, 1957.)

gles, and when they had it in position they usually checked, often counting the squares on the "grids," before making any attempt to start the ball.

Brown compared results under the conditions just described with those when the time allowed for each plot was rigidly fixed: the ball started to move automatically after 8 seconds, whether or not the subject had plotted its position accurately. Figure 7 shows that under the unpaced conditions subjects in their fifties performed about as well as those in their twenties, whereas under the paced conditions they did very much worse. The reason was that the careful, meticulous method that older subjects tended spontaneously to adopt was too slow, and they were forced either to adopt a method somewhat similar to that of younger subjects or else to fail to complete a high proportion of plots. The slight improvement of both unpaced and paced performances from the sixties to the seventies probably reflects the fact that subjects in their seventies tend to be a selected group who are unusually fit.

Pacing may also have some arousing effect, and results obtained by Brebner and Szafran (1961) suggest that this effect may increase with age. They required subjects to react by pressing a Morse key to signals which appeared at regular intervals and by pressing a micro-switch with the other hand to other signals which appeared at irregular intervals. They found that the reactions to the irregular signals were faster when the regular signals came every 2 seconds than when they came every 4.5 seconds, and that the speeding up was greater for the older subjects. Increased arousal may also be the reason why the paced performances of Brown's subjects were better than expected, although in her case the improvement did not increase with age.

Interference. A tracking experiment by Griew (1958b) has taken up the question of whether, if when tracking a subject has also from time to time to react to other signals, the interfering effect of these increases with age. His subjects were required to respond by pressing a key as quickly as possible to the sound of a buzzer given at irregular intervals while they were tracking. He found that tracking performance was about equally impaired by the distracting task in two groups of subjects aged 24–31 and 42–50. The two groups also showed very similar reaction times to the buzzer given apart from the tracking task. It seemed as if the performance at the double task could be adequately accounted for in terms of performance at the tracking and the reaction time tasks separately and that there was no additional handicap to the older subjects from combining them.

Coordination in Time. This last result implies that when two tasks are carried out together at maximum speed but with the pace determined by the subject, the performance attained will depend on the amount of decision and monitor-

ing required by each and the extent to which such decisions and monitoring can be coordinated or interdigitated. Some evidence is given by Talland (1962), who presented subjects with three tasks: (A) working a manual counter held in the nondominant hand, (B) picking up beads, one at a time with tweezers held in the dominant hand, from a bowl of red beads and transferring them to another bowl, and (C) doing the same with blue beads mixed with an equal number of yellow beads. Each task was done singly, and also (A) was combined with (B) and with (C). It can be seen from Table 16 that the older subjects performed more slowly than the younger. The percentage differences with age for (B) and (C), both with and without (A) were, however, closely similar: the main change with age when the tasks were combined was in (A) implying, first, that subjects gave priority to (B) and (C), and second that older subjects had less capacity to spare for (A). The tendency for a relatively easy task such as (A) to suffer more than a more difficult one when they are combined has been noted in studies not concerned with age (Mowbray, 1953). It appears to result from the fact that, because of the operation of the gate shown in Figure 1, the central mechanisms alternate rapidly between the two tasks, and since the time taken by the more difficult is relatively long, there is little spare time left for the easier.

Relations Between Signal and Response

We have argued earlier that all sensorimotor performance involves translation from perception to action and that some cases appear to be simple and direct but that others involve more or less elaborate intermediate steps which may cause difficulty. These effects have been studied among young subjects by many authors and have been shown to be substantial. Several experiments will be surveyed here in which such translation processes have been studied in relation to age. They fall into two broad classes: spatial transpositions and symbolic translations.

Spatial Transpositions. Several studies of these have been concerned with mirror effects, for example, those of Snoddy (1926) on mirror

TABLE 16. MEAN RATES OF PERFORMANCE (IN SECONDS PER ITEM) FOR THREE TASKS SINGLY AND IN COMBINATION.[a]
(Percentage Differences from Early Twenties Are Shown in Parentheses.)

Age groups	Early 20s	40–63	76–89
Tasks			
(A) Operating counter	.30	.32 (7)	.42 (40)
(B) Transferring beads	1.44	1.89 (31)	2.34 (62)
(C) Transferring beads of one color selected from mixture of two	1.55	2.17 (40)	2.74 (77)
(A) + (B) (A)	.36	.53 (47)	.69 (92)
(B)	1.54	2.09 (36)	2.62 (70)
(A) + (C) (A)	.36	.55 (53)	.81 (125)
(C)	1.64	2.31 (41)	3.01 (84)
Percentage increases			
(A) with (B)	20	66	64
with (C)	20	72	93
(B) with (A)	7	11	12
(C) with (A)	6	6	10

[a]Adapted from Talland, 1962.

tracing and of Ruch (1934) using a pursuit rotor. The latter author found that the time for which subjects managed to keep their tracking stylus on the target of the pursuit rotor fell by about 16 percent from a group aged 12–17 to one aged 60–82 when the target could be seen directly, but by about 47 percent when it had to be viewed in a mirror. Similar results analyzed in somewhat greater detail were obtained by Szafran (see Welford, 1958) for throwing at a target. The task was presented under three different conditions: (a) throwing directly at the target; (b) throwing over a bar, which slightly complicated the motor task; and (c) throwing over a screen of the same height as the bar which hid the target from view so that it could be seen only via a mirror close behind it. Szafran found that performances from the late teens to the fifties were not significantly different in the first two tasks, but that there was a rise with age of the errors in the third condition in terms of throwing too far or too near. This was accompanied by a number of other changes in performance, for example, some slowing and a tendency toward "rigidity" in the sense of making insufficient correction for errors.

Snoddy attributed the lower performance of older people in mirror tasks to their being slower at learning the required new coordination, while Ruch regarded the mirror as introducing a conflict with previous habits. Both these factors doubtless play a part but would seem to miss the core of the problem. The subject is required in a mirror task to, as it were, "turn the display round mentally" or to employ some rule of procedure. The mirror does, in short, require that some additional stage or process be inserted in the translation from display to action, and the fundamental questions would seem to be why such an extra stage causes difficulty for older people and whether some types of stage cause more difficulty than others. If we admit that this formulation is correct, the studies of mirror tasks link with a number of others. We may divide these into two classes, which will be considered in turn.

Some evidence of established motor habits as a source of difficulty in mirror tasks is given by the tracing experiment, the results of which are shown in Figure 4. The older subjects were slowed down to a greater extent by the reversed figures than were the younger and tended to treat them as normal figures reversed and to trace them as such, while the younger subjects treated them as "nonsense" shapes and traced them in any way which was convenient. The age difference was, however, small compared with that in writing reversed figures shown in Table 8. It seems that the essential difference between the two tasks was that, in tracing, the subject had a definite display to follow, while, in writing, he had to construct his own imaginary display.

The relationship between display and action in mirror tasks was further explored in a series of experiments by Szafran (see Welford, 1958):

A. The subject moved a stylus along a wavy groove pressed into a metal plate. The plate was screened from direct view but visible in a mirror.

B. The groove was replaced by a wavy double line along which the subject traced with a pencil.

C. The figures from the tracing experiment of Figure 4 were used, screened from direct view, and seen in a mirror. This made the reversed figures appear normal and the normal ones appear reversed.

D. The subjects wrote figures 1, 2, 3, 4, 5, 6, 7, 8, 9, X, so that they appeared normal when seen in the mirror.

The first of these tasks did not really require the subjects to use the mirror at all, since they could "feel" their way along the groove. For the second and third, the use of the mirror was essential. For the fourth, the subject had either to use the mirror or to make a mirror-image reversal in imagination.

Taking these together with the experiment of Figure 4, we have a total of eight tasks in which the performance of two age ranges can be compared. Three of the tasks did not require the use of any mirror-image reversal. One involved a reversal but without using a mirror, and four necessitated the use of the mirror. The comparisons are set out in Table 17. The performances of the older subjects were little different from those of the younger in the first group of tasks; they were somewhat slower in tracing but also somewhat more accurate. The differences in the last group were, however, substantial, as regards both speed and accuracy. Writing reversed figures was intermediate between the two groups. Within the groups the age differences seem to have been closely similar. It appeared, therefore, that there were substantial differences in the age changes of performance asso-

TABLE 17. PERCENTAGE DIFFERENCES BETWEEN SCORES BY SUBJECTS AGED 40-59 AND 20-39 IN EIGHT TASKS INVOLVING DIFFERING RELATIONSHIPS BETWEEN PERCEPTION AND ACTION.

	Times	Errors
1. *Tasks not requiring mirror-image reversal*		
Brown's experiment:		
Writing figures normal way	13	
Tracing figures	37	-49
Szafran's experiment:		
Following groove with stylus	12	
2. *Task requiring mirror-image reversal "in imagination" but not use of mirror*		
Brown's experiment:		
Writing figures reversed	60	
3. *Tasks requiring use of mirror*		
Szafran's experiments:		
Following track on paper	100	
Drawing figures so that they are seen normally in mirror	120	
Tracing figures:		
Seen unreversed in mirror	110	309
Seen reversed in mirror	107	309

ciated with the relationship between display and action, and that these were much greater than age changes associated with differences in features of the display or of the responding action alone within the groups.

Other experiments have studied the effects of spatial transposition between display and control on reaction time. For example, Simon and Wolf (1963), who measured two-choice reactions with display lights rotated at various angles from 0 to 180 degrees relative to response keys, found that times became longer as the angular discrepancy became greater, and that older subjects were slower than younger, but that there was no disproportionate increase of reaction time with age as the angle increased. However, different results were obtained by Griew (1964) in an extension of a study discussed earlier in which subjects had to move a stylus to one of several disks indicated by signal lights. Instead of requiring that the response to each light was to touch the corresponding disk, he arranged that response to the leftmost light was with the disk corresponding to the right-most light, and so on. He found that reactions were not only slower in this latter condition but tended to become disproportionately so with age. The regressions of reaction time upon degree of choice for 2, 4, and 8 choices were $0.296 + 0.127 \log_2 n$ second for subjects aged 20-28 years and $0.301 + 0.171 \log_2 n$ for those aged 48-62. The increases in the slope b of equation (4) over the straightforward condition were 74 and 82 percent respectively. Percentage changes of a were +3 and −2 respectively.

Two other studies show greater proportional differences with age in line with Griew's. The results of one by the present author in extension of the experiment on which Table 15 is based, are shown in Table 18. The results of the other, by Kay (1955), are shown in Table 19. He used two boxes, one containing 12 light bulbs and the other having 12 keys, one for each bulb. One of the bulbs was on, and the subject's task was to press the key corresponding to it, whereupon the bulb would go out and another light up, and so on through a series in which the various bulbs lit in random order. The performances of different age groups were compared (a) with the lights immediately above the keys; (b) with the lights 3 feet away

TABLE 18. TWO-CHOICE REACTION TIMES (MSEC) WHEN SIGNALS ON RIGHT WERE RESPONDED TO WITH THE LEFT HAND AND *VICE VERSA*.
(The Subjects Were the Same as for Table 15.)

Percentage increases of time compared with the corresponding condition with relationships unreversed, shown in Table 15, are given in parentheses.

	NEXT SIGNAL ARRIVED:	
Generation	2 seconds after release of previous key	Immediately after release of previous key
Younger	425 (53)	527 (34)
Middle	448 (64)	545 (37)
Older	607 (79)	732 (41)
Percentage differences from younger		
Middle	5	3
Older	43	39

TABLE 19. TIMES AND ERRORS IN A SPATIAL TRANSPOSITION TASK.[a]
(Means per Subject per Run of 30 Responses)

	CONDITION		
	a	b	c
Age range	Times (in Seconds)		
15–24	22.8	38.4	75.9
25–34	23.9	37.7	86.5
35–44	23.4	38.6	76.6
45–54	24.3	37.6	85.9
55–64	25.5	44.8	92.9
65–72	26.9	47.5	126.7
	Errors		
15–24	0	5.5	9.1
25–34	0	4.2	10.1
35–44	0	3.9	8.3
45–54	0	4.5	10.6
55–64	0	3.5	7.8
65–72	0	2.4	8.2

[a]From Kay, 1955.

across a table; and (c) with the lights 3 feet away and the box turned through 180 degrees. The percentage changes of time taken with age from the combined 15-24 and 25-34 year age groups to the 65-72 group were 15 for (a), 25 for (b), and 56 for (c).

Why Simon and Wolf's results should have differed from the rest is not clear.

Symbolic Translations. These are in many ways akin to the translations involved in digit-symbol and other substitution tasks and thus form a link between sensorimotor performance and the material of other chapters.

A comparison of movement time and tenchoice reaction time, both with a straightforward relationship between signal and response and with a symbolic translation between the two, is provided in results by Birren *et al.* (1962). The apparatus used in these experiments was modeled on that used by Kay. It can be seen from Table 20 that the percentage increase of time taken by the older subjects was about 45 for movements, about 27 for straightforward choices, and about 50 for choices involving symbolic translation between signal and re-

TABLE 20. MEAN TIMES PER ITEM (SEC) FOR SEVERAL TEN-ITEM TASKS.[a]

Tasks	AGE RANGE 18–33	AGE RANGE 60–80	Percentage difference
1. Pressing 10 buttons in order	.32	.46	44
2. Same 3 times continuously	.70	1.03	47
3. 10-choice reaction time: lights numbered randomly. Buttons with same numbers in corresponding positions.	.64	.81	27
4. Same with different random order	.58	.73	26
10-choice reaction times with symbolic translation between signal and response:			
5. Lights numbered randomly, buttons numbered in order	1.04	1.58	52
6. Both lights and buttons numbered randomly	1.42	2.14	51
7. Same as 5 but with letters instead of numbers	1.05	1.59	51
8. Same as 6 but with letters instead of numbers	1.51	2.22	47
9. Lights numbered randomly. Buttons with symbols to be matched to numbers with code card.	2.88	4.34	51
10. Same as 6 but with syllables instead of numbers	1.29	1.87	45
11. Same as 10 but with words instead of syllables	1.33	1.92	44
12. Same as 6 but with colors or pairs of colors instead of numbers	1.74	3.38	94
13. Same as 6 but with one of 5 colors together with letter X or Y instead of numbers	1.53	2.84	86

[a] Adapted from Birren, Riegel, and Morrison, 1962.

sponse. The percentage increase for tasks involving color coding was somewhat higher. Why this was so is not clear, but it is well recognized that color coding is inefficient in that only about eight different hues can be distinguished both reliably and quickly (see Miller 1956).

The increase with age of about 50 percent was similar to that found by Kay (1954) for a symbolic translation using the same apparatus as in his experiment already described. In the present case, as well as the two boxes, one of lights and one of keys, there was a card with the numbers 1–12 in random order placed as shown on the left of Figure 8. The subject was told:

Think of the lights as being numbered 1–12.
When the light goes on, decide which number it is.
Find the number on the card.
The correct key to hit is the key in line with the number on the card.

The results are shown in the column headed "Condition 1" of Table 21.

The other condition of Kay's experiment, the results of which are shown under the column headed "Condition 2" of Table 21, indicates that adding a symbolic translation to a spatial transformation produces a far greater age effect than the sum of the two effects separately. This was achieved by moving the card to the posi-

TABLE 21. TIMES AND ERRORS IN KAY'S (1954) EXPERIMENT.
(Means per Subject per Run of 20 Responses)

Age range	CONDITION 1	CONDITION 2
	Times (in Seconds)	
15–24	56.4	84.8
25–34	54.2	111.6
35–44	62.0	137.1
45–54	54.1	174.7
55–64	73.7	229.3
65–72	84.7	445.3
	Total Errors	
15–24	1.2	4.0
25–34	1.3	8.5
35–44	2.6	13.6
45–54	2.6	23.5
55–64	3.6	33.6
65–72	3.1	47.9

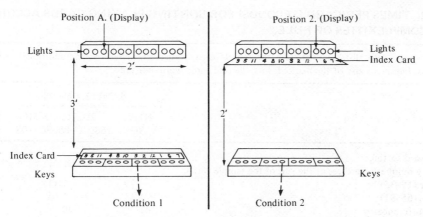

Figure 8. Layout of apparatus in an experiment by Kay (1954) combining spatial transposition with symbolic translation. Examples of keys corresponding to two light-positions are shown by arrows.

tion shown on the right of Figure 8. The instructions were the same, so that the subjects had not only to find the correct number on the card, but also to align across the 3-foot gap in a manner similar to that required in condition (b) of Kay's (1955) experiment. The percentage rise of time from the combined 15–24 and 25–34 year age groups to the 65–72 age group which had been 25 for condition (b) and 53 for condition 1 was no less than 353 for condition 2. Similar results were obtained in a replication of Kay's experiment by Ross, Vicino, and Krugman (1960).

Older subjects tended in Kay's condition 2 to avoid the double task of both using the card and aligning across the 3-foot gap between the lights and the keys. They did this by methods which led to two recognizable types of error. One type resulted when they imagined the *keys* to be numbered and pressed the key corresponding to the number on the card opposite the light which was on. The other type occurred when they pressed the key immediately opposite the light, either because they omitted to use the card at all or because they used it twice by finding the number corresponding to the light and then pressing the similarly numbered key instead of the key opposite the number on the card.

Two further examples of what can be regarded as symbolic translations in a broad sense may be mentioned briefly. The first is an experiment by Szafran (see Welford, 1958) involv-

ing the translation of data from one sensory mode to another. Subjects were blindfolded and required to move their hand a distance of some 12 inches sideways to a stop, and then to return to the starting point. In some trials, they were allowed to observe the accuracy of their movement as a guide to their next attempt. In others no knowledge of results was given. The errors made in the latter condition were not very different between the age groups. Younger subjects, however, benefited much more than older subjects from the knowledge of results. It seemed that they found the translation from vision to kinesthesis easier than did the older.

The second is a further card-sorting task by Botwinick, Robbin, and Brinley (1960). Cards had to be sorted into slots marked with sample cards such as the 7 of clubs or the 4 of diamonds. Subjects were told to " match the cards by number and color if the number is even, but if the number is odd, then match number and opposite color." The results are shown in Table 22 where they are compared with those for sorting the cards so that both number and color had to match straightforwardly. All cards which did not fall into the categories indicated by sample cards were classed as "the rest." It can be seen that the percentage increases of time taken with age were greater in the less straightforward condition.

Not only times but also errors tend to rise with age in tasks where complex translations between signal and action are required. This is

TABLE 22. TIMES PER CARD (SECONDS) FOR SORTING PLAYING CARDS ACCORDING TO TWO COMPLEXITIES OF RULE.[a]

Cards were sorted into slots marked with the sample cards indicated. There was an additional slot for cards which did not belong to any of the marked slots. Picture cards were omitted.

Task	SAMPLE CARDS		Percentage difference
	4D, 7C 9C	2D, 3C, 4D, 5H 6S, 7C, 8S, 9C, 10S	
Straightforward sorting:			
all cards by number regardless of the suit of the sample cards:			
Younger (19–35)	.79	1.11	41
Older (65–81)	1.11	1.65	49
Percentage difference	41	49	
Sorting conditional upon whether number is odd or even,			
and color:			
Younger	.82	1.49	82
Older	1.29	2.47	91
Percentage difference	57	66	

[a]Adapted from Botwinick, Robbin, and Brinley, 1960.

clearly seen for Kay's results in Table 21. A further example is shown in the results of an experiment by Pacaud (1955a,b). Subjects were required to:

1. Press with the left foot on seeing a red light.
2. Raise the right foot on seeing a green light.
3. Make both movements on seeing a yellow light.

When these responses had been learned the task was further complicated by the requirement that when a light signal was accompanied by a sound of metallic quality, a key was to be pressed and the normal reaction to the light omitted. When the sound was of a lower tone, however, the subject had to respond as to the light signals above. Accuracy fell steadily from the early twenties onwards. Some indication of the extent can be gained from the fact that about 83 percent of the subjects aged 19-24 years but only 37 percent of those over 49 made more than 80 percent of their responses correctly—an age difference of 46 percent. The corresponding percentages for a more straightforward reaction time task by the same author were 92 and 76—a difference of 16 percent. The times taken for the complex reactions have not been published, but the present author understands they increased with age, so that there is no question of errors by older subjects having been due to faster performance.

Why spatial transpositions and symbolic translations should cause difficulty is not clear, but a possible lead to explanation is contained in the fact that they all seem to require the holding of a quantity of data in mind while some manipulation of it occurs. Thus, for example, in Kay's experiments the number or the position of a light had to be retained while the subject tracked with his eyes across the gap between the signal lights and the response keys, and in the card-sorting experiment by Botwinick, Robbin, and Brinley (1960) the rule about colors and numbers had to be held while the numbers were identified. The tasks can therefore be plausibly regarded as making demands upon the capacity for short-term storage of data. This has been shown to be adversely affected by age, especially when attention has to be switched to other data or action during the period of retention (e.g., Inglis and Ankus 1965; Smith, 1975). If so, it is understandable that tasks involving transposition or translation would become easier as they became familiar and the relationships were "built into" the subjects' memories—as, for instance, occurs with the association between the visual and auditory patterns of letters or digits which because of long experience has become seemingly "automatic." Results obtained by Schonfield and Robertson (1968) are perhaps in line with this view. They found that a group of subjects aged 60-90 years responded faster to digits—a familiar class of symbol—displayed on a screen by pressing keys bearing the same digits, than they responded to unfamiliar symbols by pressing keys bearing the same symbols.

RELATIONSHIP OF SENSORIMOTOR PERFORMANCE TO OTHER VARIABLES

Studies relating age changes of sensorimotor performance to variables of sex, education, and socioeconomic status appear to have yielded somewhat equivocal results. As regards sex, Bellis (1933) in his investigation of reaction times found that, although women's times were a little longer than men's, there was no real evidence of a differential rate of change with age between the sexes. Noble *et al.* (1964) found women to be slower than men between the ages of 18 and the 60s, but to be slightly faster in a group aged 71-87, perhaps because at that age women, who tend to live longer than men, are relatively fitter. On the other hand, Engel, Thorne, and Quilter (1972) found average differences of reaction time for men and women of 3 and 20 percent between groups aged 20-30 and 55-65. Botwinick and Storandt (1974) found no difference between the reaction times of men and women in their twenties, but women were slower in a group aged 64-74; there was, however, no significant age-by-sex interaction.

Pacaud (1953, 1955a,b) in her extensive studies of French railway personnel found substantial differences in tests of intellectual, memory, and learning functions associated with different levels of educational achievement, separating those who had obtained the Certificat d'Études Primaire from those who had undergone "instruction primaire" but who had not obtained the diploma. These differences either remained about the same in different age groups from the twenties to the fifties or tended to lessen in the older groups; she found no case in which they increased. However, no differences were found between the different educational grades at sensorimotor tasks, although the differences between age groups in these were substantial.

Similar findings to Pacaud's were obtained by Clément (1969) for a group of factory workers. Those who had obtained the Certificat d'Études scored much higher on a coding test and somewhat higher on a test of memory than those who had not, while there was little difference as regards reaction time or strength of grip. For all tests the differences between groups of subjects with mean ages of 29.5 and 49.75 years were similar with either level of educational attainment. Clément found that age changes were less among schoolteachers than among factory workers for all tests except reaction time. However, the teachers had shorter reaction times than the factory workers in the corresponding age groups. Why the teachers' performances should have been superior in these ways is not clear. Clément himself attributed it to the fatiguing effects of factory work as opposed to what he regarded as the less onerous task of teaching. Alternatively, it can be argued that those who find their way into higher occupational strata such as teaching as opposed to factory work are, on the average, the more able members of society and are better endowed biologically and thus likely to age more slowly. Botwinick and Storandt (1974) also found shorter reaction times among older people with more years of education, which presumably tends to go with higher socioeconomic status.

Be this as it may, Nuttall and Fozard (1971) have shown that age and socioeconomic status are not equally associated with the 12 tests which make up the General Aptitude Test Battery of the U.S. Department of Labor. Scores on the tests concerned with dexterity were associated with age but virtually not at all with socioeconomic status. The opposite was true of vocabulary and arithmetic reasoning. The remaining tests showed some association with both variables.

Correlations Between Different Performances

Many studies besides those of Pacaud, Clément, and Nuttall and Fozard have included both sensorimotor and other measurements made on the same subjects. For example, Galton's data included body measurements such as height and weight, several measures of visual and auditory acuity, and tests of perceptual judgement. Goldfarb's subjects performed, in addition to reaction-time tasks, the CAVD Scale, the Otis Self-administering Test, a simple directions test, an arithmetic additions test, an easy same-difference test, and the Wechsler-Bellevue Scale. Harwood and Naylor (1969) and Mortimer-Tanner and Naylor (1973) tested their subjects with the Wechsler Adult Intelligence Scale as well as with their information-processing tasks. Fieandt et al. (1956) included in their battery of tests: judgements of time interval, assessment of the "pleasant" speed of the ticking of a metronome, EEG measurements, and the Rorschach test. Age changes with these other tasks and variables do not seem to provide a sufficient explanation of the age changes observed in sensorimotor performance, but some of the same characteristic changes do occur. The widespread loss of speed with age is an obvious example, but more subtle similarities are also shown. For instance, Horn and Cattell (1966) have noted a tendency for older subjects to display increased carefulness in a wide variety of tasks.

Of more interest are studies which have correlated measures of different performances and considered the ways in which the correlations change with age. Three patterns appear to be distinguishable:

(a) Two performances which both change with age do not correlate with each other when age is held constant. An example is provided by Botwinick and Thompson (1967b), who showed that auditory reaction time and scores for depression on the Minnesota Multiphasic Personality Inventory both correlated with age but not with each other. Botwinick and Storandt (1973) found a similar pattern in the relationships of scores for vocabulary and digit-symbol substitution from the Wechsler Adult Intelligence Scale with simple auditory reaction time and performance at a writing task, and also between these latter two performances themselves. The implication is that several age changes, each affecting a different performance, are taking place simultaneously but independently.

(b) Two performances correlate with each other and the correlations remain roughly the same as age increases. Botwinick and Storandt found this relationship between the vocabulary and digit-symbol substitution scores already mentioned. Such a pattern of correlation implies that both performances are affected by one or more common sources of limitation which change with age.

(c) Correlations between performances increase with age. Examples of this relationship have been provided by Birren and Botwinick (1951b) for speed of writing and rate of addition, and by Cesa-Bianchi (1955; see also Gemelli and Cesa-Bianchi, 1952) who gives unusually complete data with full individual results for a number of measures, including visual and auditory reaction times; performance at two coordination tasks; measures of tachistoscopic, stereoscopic, and other perceptual ability; tests of memory and calculation; and the solution of "technical" problems. Correlation coefficients between all these tests and between two or more scores from each are given for three age groups: 20–29, 45–49, and over 59. The absolute coefficients vary greatly but show a clear tendency to rise with age. The increasing correlations suggest that some limitation which affects the tasks concerned is trivial when young but becomes more severe as age increases. Examples might be visual acuity which could affect both sensorimotor tasks requiring fine discrimination and also performances which involve reading, and loss of mobility in joints which would affect most performances involving substantial activity. More subtly, any increase with age of random activity in the brain (neural "noise") would affect a wide range of both sensorimotor and intellectual performances.

INDUSTRIAL STUDIES RELATING TO SENSORIMOTOR PERFORMANCE

The primary interest of much of the research on sensorimotor performance in relation to age has been to assess the extent to which older people are likely to find difficulty at work, and how such difficulty might be removed. It is hazardous to make inferences about work done day in and day out from brief laboratory studies, and experimental results need to be checked by actual field observations before policy decisions can be made with any reasonable safety. It has become clear, however, that, without the pointers gained from laboratory work, field studies are very difficult to make and interpret. Studies of aging in industry can in their turn validate results obtained in the laboratory.

Studies of output by those of different ages engaged in production work in industry have shown that both speed and accuracy increase up to the age of about 35–45. Thereafter accuracy remains high, but speed either remains constant (Breen and Spaeth, 1960) or declines slowly (Wackwitz, 1946; Clay, 1956; Mark, 1956, 1957; de la Mare and Shepherd, 1958). The increase up to middle age implies that the learning of an industrial job does not cease when the period of initial training is over, but continues for many years after.

The decline of speed in later middle and old age is much less than that found in laboratory experiments. This is probably due in part to increased experience compensating for loss of capacity (Murrell, Powesland, and Forsaith, 1962), but is almost certainly due also to people leaving jobs they can no longer perform well, so that those who continue at later ages represent the "survival of the fittest." Evidence in favor of this view is that the numbers employed in production jobs fall sharply from the late forties onward, that those who remain tend to have performed better than average during earlier years (King, 1956), and that those who leave tend to be less fit than those who remain (Powell, 1973). Also, the variability of performance between individuals tends to remain steady with age (Breen and Spaeth, 1960) or to fall (Wackwitz, 1946) instead of rising as it almost invariably does in laboratory studies.

Clearer evidence would be obtained if the same individuals in industry could be followed over a period of years instead of comparing those of different ages at one point in time, but to do this is seldom possible on practical grounds. We therefore have to turn to other indications of change with age in industrial performance. Of these, the age distributions of those employed on particular jobs, although sometimes misleading if a job has expanded or contracted rapidly, are probably the best simple measures available of how suitable jobs are for older people (Welford, 1958; Murrell, Griew, and Tucker, 1957; Murrell and Griew, 1958; Griew, 1959b; Smith 1973).

One of the earliest attempts to relate age distributions to the characteristics of jobs was made by Belbin and Shooter (Belbin, 1953; see also Welford, 1958), who found very few men or women over 50 in production work where there was severe pressure for speed, especially if this was combined with continuous bodily activity. Their results, shown in Figure 9 and Table 23, are in line with the slowing of performance found in laboratory experiments and are confirmed and amplified by other studies using different approaches:

(a) Murrell and Forsaith (1960), who made detailed time studies of industrial work, found that the slowing lay not so much in the speed at which actual movements were executed as in the times required to plan and decide what actions to take.

(b) Featherstone and Cunningham (1963) confirmed that "pacing" by the machinery used was one of the factors associated with a low mean age of those employed on a job, and Heron and Cunningham (1962) noted that a far lower proportion of men over 40 than under went into piecework following a work reorganization.

(c) Whitfield (1954) found that young coal miners who had high accident rates tended to have good physique and to perform well at laboratory tasks so that their accidents seemed to be due to their taking undue risks, while older miners who sustained accidents tended to be slow at laboratory tasks, which suggests that their accidents were due to failing capacity. Again King (1955), in a study of agricultural accidents, results of which are set out in Table 24, found that those which increased in frequency with age could be explained by slowness in getting out of the way of hazards or recovering balance, whereas those which became less frequent with age were attributable to carelessness. The trend of road accidents is in the same direction; accidents typically sustained by

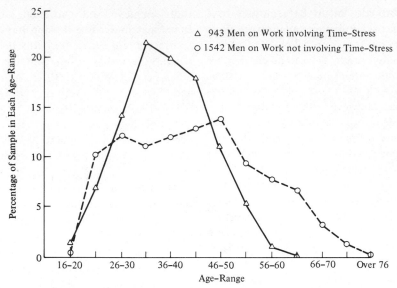

Figure 9. Age distributions on operations with and without pressure for speed or rigid pacing. (From a study by Shooter and Belbin [see Welford, 1958].)

older drivers seem to be due to slowness and tendency to confusion, whereas those characteristic of younger drivers are due to various kinds of recklessness (McFarland and O'Doherty, 1959; McFarland, Tune, and Welford, 1964). Similar causes seem to lie behind

TABLE 23. RELATIONSHIP BETWEEN OPERATIONS FROM WHICH THERE WERE MOVES WITH AGE AND THOSE ON WHICH THERE WERE PACING OR A DEMAND FOR CONTINUOUS BODILY MOVEMENT AND ACTIVITY.[a]

	Moves with age	No moves with age
Operations involving both pacing and continuous bodily movement and activity	10	1
Operations involving pacing without continuous bodily movement and activity	3	3
Operations involving continuous bodily movement and activity without pacing	6	7
Operations involving neither continuous bodily movement and activity nor pacing	0	77

[a]From Belbin, 1953.

the traffic violations characteristic of older and younger drivers (Planek and Fowler, 1971; Road Traffic Board of South Australia, 1972).

Belbin and Shooter's study revealed a further, and very surprising, result that the men engaged in relatively heavy work tended to be older than those on light work. This finding was difficult to believe at first but is confirmed by several other studies. The tendency had been noted many years before by Barkin (1933) in New York State. Social survey results in Britain had shown that, while older people tended not to be doing very strenuous work, a high proportion was found in moderately heavy jobs (Thomas and Osborne, 1950). Belbin himself in a subsequent study (1955) found older men tended to prefer relatively heavy work under conditions where they were free to choose. He analyzed work done among a group in a factory making storage batteries, where the danger of lead poisoning made it necessary for jobs to be changed around at frequent intervals. He found that practically all the heavy work was done by older men and all the light work by younger ones. An analysis of the jobs done is given in Table 25. Richardson (1953), in a study of miners and foundry-workers, observed that moves from heavy to lighter work came on an average about 10 years later than the moves from fast-paced work noted by Belbin. The rea-

TABLE 24. CAUSES OF AGRICULTURAL ACCIDENTS.[a]

Cause	No. of cases	PERCENTAGES OF EACH KIND OF ACCIDENT BY AGE GROUPS					
		15-20	21-30	31-40	41-50	51-60	61-80
Significant increases with age:							
Falls from heights or machines	252	7.6	8.4	10.5	14.5	19.2	16.4
Falls through slipping or tripping on ground	201	3.8	6.3	9.4	13.4	11.0	16.4
Hit by falling or moving object	339	14.0	15.7	13.9	17.6	21.4	21.3
Significant decreases with age:							
Caught in machine	202	13.4	11.8	11.5	9.1	7.9	6.6
Injury inflicted by own tool	184	13.4	11.8	10.7	5.8	6.6	9.3
Continued activity	127	4.5	9.2	7.9	6.2	2.8	4.4
Starting an engine	98	12.7	7.9	4.1	4.5	1.3	1.1
No significant change with age:							
Moving heavy objects	103	3.2	4.8	6.8	4.2	7.5	1.6
Knocked against, or trod on, object	90	6.4	3.6	5.3	4.9	3.4	3.8
Action of animals[b]	79	1.3	3.9	4.3	4.2	5.3	2.7
Trapped, other than in machine	48	1.3	3.1	1.9	2.7	1.6	3.8
Miscellaneous	127	9.5	6.0	7.7	4.7	6.0	6.0
Cause not specified	141	8.9	7.5	6.0	8.2	6.0	6.6
Total	1991	100	100	100	100	100	100

[a]From King, 1955.
[b]Some cases in which animals were involved were classified under "Hit by falling or moving object." This group constitutes the remainder.

son seems to be that heavy work tends to be slow, so that moderately heavy work is often less exacting for older people than light work carried out under pressure for speed (Nuffield Foundation, 1963).

Richardson's observations serve to emphasize, however, that very strenuous work can also be unfavorable to older people, presumably because of changes in physical capacity with age. The point has been demonstrated by Powell (1973) in a study of underground workers in coal mines, in which he compared numbers leaving and staying on particular jobs over a 12-month period. Table 26 shows numbers of men of different ages staying and leaving for four types of underground jobs ranked in terms of difficulty defined as a combination of energy cost, pace of work, environmental heat, and difficulty of access. It can be seen that the proportion of older men leaving was higher for the more exacting jobs. Among the colliers the tendency for older men to leave was higher for the more difficult coal-faces. These results do not contradict those of Belbin. Powell points out

TABLE 25. PERCENTAGES OF JOB CARDS FOR WORK GRADED IN TERMS OF DEMAND FOR PHYSICAL EXERTION.[a]

	I[b]	II	III	IV	V
No. of operations in each grade	4	4	11	12	3
No. of persons who worked in each grade	35	63	283	312	90
Percentage of work done by under fifties	35.8	81.7	71.1	73.5	89.5
Percentage of work done by age group 50–54	23.5	14.2	17.7	13.8	10.5
Percentage of work done by age group 55–59	23.4	3.9	9.1	7.5	0
Percentage of work done by age group 60 and over	17.3	0.2	2.1	5.2	0

[a]From Belbin, 1955.
[b]I = very heavy, . . . , V = light.

TABLE 26. PERCENTAGE OF MEN OF DIFFERENT AGES ON FOUR TYPES OF UNDERGROUND WORK RANKED FROM MOST TO LEAST DIFFICULT.[a]

Type of work	Number of men	PERCENTAGES OF TOTAL IN AGE RANGES			
		34 and under	35–44	45–54	55 and over
Tunneling (most difficult)	67	53.8	40.3	4.4	1.5
Coal-face—Colliers	946	45.9	34.3	10.8	9.0
Coal-face—other workers	1087	35.8	26.8	20.9	16.5
Transport (least difficult)	311	6.3	9.2	43.2	41.3

[a]From Powell, 1973.

that even the least severe of these jobs was probably more physically demanding than any of those studied by Belbin.

Further studies of industrial work in relation to age and methods of overcoming limitations for older people in industrial work have been summarized by Welford (1966).

SUMMARY CONCLUSIONS

Looking back over the studies surveyed in this chapter, it seems appropriate to summarize the evidence in ten statements:

1. Movements of large extent made at maximum speed show substantial slowing with age, due seemingly to muscular limitations. Most movements studied in the laboratory and most of those occurring in everyday manipulatory tasks are not limited by muscular factors but by the speed of decisions required to guide movements and the time taken to monitor them.

2. When movements of this latter type can be prepared in advance, changes with age are relatively small. Such preparation is possible when the movements required are relatively simple and are either made in response to signals well separated in time, as in many reaction time tasks, or form a simple repetitive sequence as in reciprocal tapping tasks.

3. Greater changes occur with age when the movements cannot be prepared in advance, especially when a rapid series of different movements too long to be programmed as a whole is called for, as in tracing over a complex pattern. In these cases, while part of the extra time taken may represent longer decision times, much of it appears to be due to time taken in monitoring the various stages of the movement

sequence as they occur. The tendency to monitor movement increases with age.

4. Monitoring appears to be an aspect of caution. Older people appear to show greater caution than younger persons not only in monitoring but also in their tendency to inspect signals for a longer time before responding, if the signal is available. Doing so enables them to compensate for increased randomness or "neural noise" and reduced signal strength in the sense organs and central nervous system.

5. When opportunities to monitor and to inspect signals for as long as they wish are available, older people tend to be slower but more accurate than younger. When such opportunities are lacking, older people tend to be less accurate than younger.

6. Relationships between signals and responses which are not straightforward but require complex spatial transpositions or symbolic translations between perception and action have a disproportionately adverse effect on the performance of older people, which becomes both slower and less accurate. The limitation appears to result from a fall with age in the capacity to effect complex recodings, possibly as the result of a diminished capacity for short-term retention. It may be substantially mitigated by familiarity with the recoding required.

7. Age changes, at least in relatively simple sensorimotor performances, show little consistent relation to sex, educational level, or socioeconomic status, although absolute levels of performance are related to all these variables.

8. Sensorimotor performances correlate to varying extents with intelligence test scores and other measures of cognitive or intellectual abil-

ity, but clearly also show substantial degrees of independence from them. Some of the correlations remain at the same level with increasing age, while others increase.

9. Laboratory findings are reflected in the industrial work done by older people: they tend not to be found on jobs which demand rapid decisions or continuous activity paced by the machinery used. Demands for speed seem to be more adverse than demands for moderately heavy physical effort.

10. The types of industrial and road accidents and road traffic violations which increase with age can be attributed mainly to slowness in making decisions rather than to any sensory or motor impairment.

REFERENCES

Abrahams, J. P., and Birren, J. E. 1973. Reaction time as a function of age and behavioral predisposition to coronary heart disease. *J. Gerontol.*, **28**, 471-478.

Åstrand, I. 1967. Degree of strain during building work as related to individual aerobic work capacity. *Ergonomics*, **10**, 293-303.

Barkin, S. 1933. *The Older Worker in Industry*. New York Legislative State Document No. 60. Albany: Lyon.

Barry, A. J., Daly, J. W., Pruett, E. D. R., Steinmetz, J. R., Page, H. F., Birkhead, N. C., and Rodahl, K. 1966a. The effects of physical conditioning on older individuals. I. Work capacity, circulatory-respiratory function, and work electrocardiogram. *J. Gerontol.*, **21**, 182-191.

Barry, A. J., Steinmetz, J. R., Page, H. F., and Rodahl, K. 1966b. The effects of physical conditioning on older individuals. II. Motor performance and cognitive function. *J. Gerontol.*, **21**, 192-199.

Belbin, E. and Shimmin, S. 1964. Training the middle aged for inspection work. *Occupational Psychol.*, **38**, 49-57.

Belbin, R. M. 1953. Difficulties of older people in industry. *Occupational Psychol.*, **27**, 177-190.

Belbin, R. M. 1955. Older people and heavy work. *Brit. J. Indust. Med.*, **12**, 309-319.

Bellis, C. J. 1933. Reaction time and chronological age. *Proc. Soc. Exp. Biol. Med.*, **30**, 801.

Birren, J. E. 1955. Age changes in speed of simple responses and perception and their significance for complex behaviour. *In, Old Age in the Modern World:* Rep. 3rd Cong. Internat. Ass. Gerontol., London 1954, pp. 235-247. Edinburgh: Livingstone.

Birren, J. E., and Botwinick, J. 1951a. The relation of writing speed to age and to the senile psychoses. *J. Consult. Psychol.*, **15**, 243-249.

Birren, J. E., and Botwinick, J. 1951b. Rate of addition as a function of difficulty and age. *Psychometrika*, **16**, 219-232.

Birren, J. E., and Botwinick, J. 1955. Age differences in finger, jaw, and foot reaction time to auditory stimuli. *J. Gerontol.*, **10**, 429-432.

Birren, J. E., Riegel, K. F., and Morrison, D. F. 1962. Age differences in response speed as a function of controlled variations of stimulus conditions: Evidence of a general speed factor. *Gerontologia*, **6**, 1-18.

Birren, J. E., and Spieth, W. 1962. Age, response speed, and cardiovascular functions. *J. Gerontol.*, **17**, 390-391.

Botwinick, J. 1966. Cautiousness in advanced age. *J. Gerontol.*, **21**, 347-353.

Botwinick, J., and Brinley, J. F. 1962. Aspects of RT set during brief intervals in relation to age and sex. *J. Gerontol.*, **17**, 295-301.

Botwinick, J., Brinley, J. F., and Birren, J. E. 1957. Set in relation to age. *J. Gerontol.*, **12**, 300-305.

Botwinick, J., Brinley, J. F., and Robbin, J. S. 1958a. The effect of motivation by electrical shocks on reaction-time in relation to age. *Amer. J. Psychol.*, **71**, 408-411.

Botwinick, J., Brinley, J. F., and Robbin, J. S. 1958b. The interaction effects of perceptual difficulty and stimulus exposure time on age differences in speed and accuracy of response. *Gerontologia*, **2**, 1-10.

Botwinick, J., Brinley, J. F., and Robbin, J. S. 1959. Maintaining set in relation to motivation and age. *Amer. J. Psychol.*, **72**, 585-588.

Botwinick, J., Robbin, J. S., and Brinley, J. F. 1960. Age differences in card-sorting performance in relation to task difficulty, task set, and practice. *J. Exp. Psychol.*, **59**, 10-18.

Botwinick, J., and Storandt, M. 1973. Speed functions, vocabulary ability, and age. *Percep. Mot. Skills*, **36**, 1123-1128.

Botwinick, J., and Storandt, M. 1974. Cardiovascular status, depressive affect, and other factors in reaction time. *J. Gerontol.*, **29**, 543-548.

Botwinick, J., and Thompson, L. W. 1966. Components of reaction time in relation to age and sex. *J. Genet. Psychol.*, **108**, 175-183.

Botwinick, J., and Thompson, L. W. 1967a. Practice of speeded response in relation to age, sex and set. *J. Gerontol.*, **22**, 72-76.

Botwinick, J., and Thompson, L. W. 1967b. Depressive affect, speed of response and age. *J. Consult. Psychol.*, **31**, 106.

Botwinick, J., and Thompson, L. W. 1968a. Age difference in reaction time: an artifact? *Gerontologist*, **8**, 25-28.

Botwinick, J., and Thompson, L. W. 1968b. A research note on individual differences in reaction time in relation to age. *J. Genet. Psychol.*, **112**, 73-75.

Brebner, J., and Szafran, J. 1961. A study of the "psychological refractory phase" in relation to ageing. *Gerontologia*, **5**, 241-249.

Breen, L. Z., and Spaeth, J. L. 1960. Age and productivity among workers in four Chicago companies. *J. Gerontol.*, **15**, 68–70.

Brinley, J. F., and Botwinick, J. 1959. Preparation time and choice in relation to age differences in response speed. *J. Gerontol.*, **14**, 226–228.

Brown, R. A. 1957. Age and 'paced' work. *Occupational Psychol.*, **31**, 11–20.

Burke, W. E., Tuttle, W. W., Thompson, C. W., Janney, C. D., and Weber, R. J. 1953. The relation of grip strength and grip strength endurance to age. *J. Appl. Physiol.*, **5**, 628–630.

Cathcart, E. P., Hughes, D. E. R., and Chalmers, J. G. 1935. The physique of man in industry. *Industrial Health Research Board Report No. 71*. London: H.M.S.O.

Cesa-Bianchi, M. 1955. Contributo allo studio delle modificazioni psichiche in raporto con l'eta. *Contrib. Lab. Psicol. dell'Univ. Catt. del Sacre Cuore*, **19**, 127–189.

Clay, H. M. 1956. A study of performance in relation to age at two printing works. *J. Gerontol.*, **11**, 417–424.

Clément, F. 1969. The relative development of several psycho-physiological and psychometric variables with different occupations and intellectual levels. *In*, A. T. Welford and J. E. Birren (eds.), *Decision Making and Age*, pp. 57–65. Basel: Karger.

Cooper, C. J. 1973. Anatomical and physiological mechanisms of arousal, with special reference to the effects of exercise. *Ergonomics*, **16**, 601–609.

Craik, F. I. M. 1969. Applications of signal detection theory to studies of ageing. *In*, A. T. Welford and J. E. Birren (eds.), *Decision Making and Age*, pp. 147–157. Basel: Karger.

Crossman, E. R. F. W., and Goodeve, P. J. 1963. Feedback control of hand-movement and Fitts' Law. Communication to the Experimental Psychology Society.

Crossman, E. R. F. W., and Szafran, J. 1956. Changes with age in the speed of information intake and discrimination. *Experientia Suppl.*, **4**, 128–135.

Davey, C. P. 1973. Physical exertion and mental performance. *Ergonomics*, **16**, 595–599.

Davies, A. D. M. 1973. Age and temperament effects on maze performance under speed and accuracy stress. *Percep. Mot. Skills*, **37**, 502.

Davies, D. R., and Griew, S. 1963. A further note on the effect of aging on auditory vigilance performance: the effect of low signal frequency. *J. Gerontol.*, **18**, 370–371.

de la Mare, G. C., and Shepherd, R. D. 1958. Ageing: changes in speed and quality of work among leather cutters. *Occupational Psychol.*, **32**, 204–209.

De Silva, H. R. 1936. On an investigation of driving skill. I. *Human Factor*, **10**, 1–13.

Deupree, R. H., and Simon, J. R. 1963. Reaction time and movement time as a function of age, stimulus duration and task difficulty. *Ergonomics*, **6**, 403–411.

de Vries, H. A. 1970. Physiological effects of an exercise training regimen upon men aged 52 to 88. *J. Gerontol.*, **25**, 325–336.

Engel, B. T., Thorne, P. R., and Quilter, R. E. 1972. On the relationships among sex, age, response mode, cardiac cycle phase, breathing cycle phase, and simple reaction time. *J. Gerontol.*, **27**, 456–460.

Featherstone, M. S., and Cunningham, C. M. 1963. Age of manual workers in relation to conditions and demands of work. *Occupational Psychol.*, **37**, 197–208.

Feinberg, R., and Podolak, E. 1965. Latency of pupillary reflex to light stimulation and its relationship to aging. *In*, A. T. Welford and J. E. Birren (eds.), *Behavior, Aging and the Nervous System*. Springfield, Illinois: Charles C. Thomas.

Fieandt, K. von, Huhtala, A., Kullberg, P., and Saarl, K. 1956. Personal tempo and phenomenal time at different age levels. *Reports from the Psychological Institute*, No. 2. University of Helsinki.

Fisher, M. B., and Birren, J. E. 1947. Age and strength. *J. Appl. Psychol.*, **31**, 490–497.

Fitts, P. M. 1954. The information capacity of the human motor system in controlling the amplitude of movement. *J. Exp. Psychol.*, **47**, 381–391.

Galton, F. 1899. On instruments for (1) testing perception of differences of tint and for (2) determining reaction time. *J. Anthropol. Inst.*, **19**, 27–29.

Gekoski, W. L., and Schultz, K. 1965. Differences in associative reaction time as a function of task instruction, stimulus word type, age, and sex. *University of Michigan Center for Human Growth and Development*. Report No. 3.

Gemelli, A., and Cesa-Bianchi, M. 1952. Disadattamento del vecchio alla vita individuale, familiare e sociale. *In*, *II Convegno Nazionale di Gerontologia e Geriatria*, Milano.

Goldfarb, W. 1941. An investigation of reaction time in older adults and its relationship to certain observed mental test patterns. *Teachers College Contributions to Education*, No. 831. New York: Teachers College Columbia University, Bureau of Publications.

Griew, S. 1958a. Age changes and information loss in performance of a pursuit tracking task involving interrupted preview. *J. Exp. Psychol.*, **55**, 486–489.

Griew, S. 1958b. A note on the effect of interrupting auditory signals on the performance of younger and older subjects. *Gerontologia*, **2**, 136–139.

Griew, S. 1958c. Uncertainty as a determinant of performance in relation to age. *Gerontologia*, **2**, 284–289.

Griew, S. 1959a. Complexity of response and time of initiating responses in relation to age. *Amer. J. Psychol.*, **72**, 83–88.

Griew, S. 1959b. Methodological problems in industrial ageing research. *Occupational Psychol.*, **33**, 36–45.

Griew, S. 1959c. A further note on uncertainty in relation to age. *Gerontologia*, **3**, 335–339.

Griew, S. 1964. Age, information transmission and the

positional relationship between signals and responses in the performance of a choice task. *Ergonomics*, 7, 267–277.

Griew, S., and Davies, D. R. 1962. The effect of aging on auditory vigilance performance. *J. Gerontol.*, 17, 88–90.

Gutman, G. M. 1965. The effects of age and extraversion on pursuit rotor reminiscence. *J. Gerontol.*, 20, 346–350.

Harwood, E., and Naylor, G. F. K. 1969. Rates of information-transfer in elderly subjects. *Austral. J. Psychol.*, 21, 127–136.

Heron, A., and Cunningham, C. M. 1962. The experience of younger and older men in a works reorganisation. *Occupational Psychol.*, 36, 10–14.

Hick, W. E. 1952. On the rate of gain of information. *Quart. J. Exp. Psychol.*, 4, 11–26.

Hicks, L. H., and Birren, J. E. 1970. Aging, brain damage, and psychomotor slowing. *Psychol. Bull.*, 74, 377–396.

Hodgkins, J. 1962. Influence of age on the speed of reaction and movement in females. *J. Gerontol.*, 17, 385–389.

Horn, J. L., and Cattell, R. B. 1966. Age differences in primary mental ability factors. *J. Gerontol.*, 21, 210–220.

Hoyer, W. J., Labouvie, G. V., and Baltes, P. B. 1973. Modification of response speed deficits and intellectual performance in the elderly. *Hum. Develop.*, 16, 233–242.

Hugin, F., Norris, A. H., and Shock, N. W. 1960. Skin reflex and voluntary reaction times in young and old males. *J. Gerontol.*, 15, 388–391.

Hurwitz, L. J., and Allison, R. S. 1965. Factors influencing performance in psychological testing of the aged. *In*, A. T. Welford and J. E. Birren (eds.), *Behavior, Aging and the Nervous System*, pp. 461–475. Springfield, Illinois: Charles C. Thomas.

Inglis, J., and Ankus, M. N. 1965. Effects of age on short-term storage and serial rote learning. *Brit. J. Psychol.*, 56, 183–195.

Jalavisto, E., Forsén, A., Lindqvist, C., Makkonen, T., and Tallqvist, M. 1962. Age and the simple reaction time in response to visual, tactile and proprioceptive stimuli. *Ann. Acad. Sci. Fenn. Series A, V*, Medica No. 96.

Kay, H. 1954. The effects of position in a display upon problem solving. *Quart. J. Exp. Psychol.*, 6, 155–169.

Kay, H. 1955. Some experiments on adult learning. *In, Old Age in the Modern World:* Rep. 3rd Cong. Internat. Ass. Gerontol., London 1954, pp. 259–267. Edinburgh: Livingstone.

Kemp, B. J. 1973. Reaction time of young and elderly subjects in relation to perceptual deprivation and signal-on versus signal-off conditions. *Develop. Psychol.*, 8, 268–272.

King, H. F. 1955. An age-analysis of some agricultural accidents. *Occupational Psychol.*, 29, 245–253.

King, H. F. 1956. An attempt to use production data

in the study of age and performance. *J. Gerontol.*, 11, 410–416.

Kleemeier, R. W., Rich, T. A., and Justiss, W. A. 1956. The effects of alpha-(2-piperidyl) benzhydrol hydrochloride (Meratran) on psychomotor performance in a group of aged males. *J. Gerontol.*, 11, 165–170.

Koga, Y., and Morant, G. M. 1923. On the degree of association between reaction times in the case of different senses. *Biometrika*, 15, 346–372.

La Riviere, J. E., and Simonson, E. 1965. The effect of age and occupation on speed of writing. *J. Gerontol.*, 20, 415–416.

Leonard, J. A. 1953. Advance information in sensorimotor skills. *Quart. J. Exp. Psychol.*, 5, 141–149.

Loveless, N. E., and Sanford, A. J. 1974. Effects of age on the contingent negative variation and preparatory set in a reaction-time task. *J. Gerontol.*, 29, 52–63.

Magladery, J. W., Teasdall, R. D., and Norris, A. H. 1958. Effect of aging on plantar flexor and superficial abdominal reflexes in man—a clinical and electromyographic study. *J. Gerontol.*, 13, 282–288.

Mankovsky, N. B., and Belonog, R. P. 1971. Aging of the human nervous system in the electroencephalographic aspect. *Geriatrics*, 26 (8), 100–116.

Mark, J. A. 1956. Measurement of job performance and age. *U.S. Dept. Lab., Monthly Lab. Rev., Dec. 1956.*

Mark, J. A. 1957. Comparative job performance by age. *U.S. Dept. Lab., Monthly Lab. Rev., Dec. 1957.*

Marteniuk, R. G., and Roy, E. A. 1972. The codability of kinaesthetic location and distance information. *Acta Psychol.*, 36, 471–479.

McFarland, R. A., and O'Doherty, B. M. 1959. Work and occupational skills. *In*, J. E. Birren (ed.), *Handbook of Aging and the Individual*, pp. 452–500. Chicago: University of Chicago Press.

McFarland, R. A., Tune, G. S., and Welford, A. T. 1964. On the driving of automobiles by older people. *J. Gerontol.*, 19, 190–197.

Miles, W. R. 1931a. Correlation of reaction and coordination speed with age in adults. *Amer. J. Psychol.*, 43, 377–391.

Miles, W. R. 1931b. Measures of certain human abilities throughout the life span. *Proc. Nat. Acad. Sci.*, 17, 627–633.

Miller, G. A. 1956. The magical number seven, plus or minus two: some limits on our capacity for processing information. *Psychol. Rev.*, 63, 81–97.

Morikiyo, Y., Iida, H., and Nishioka, A. 1967. Age and choice reaction time. *J. Sci. Lab.*, 43, 636–642.

Morikiyo, Y., and Nishioka, A. 1966. An analysis of the control mechanism on simple movement of the hand (2). *J. Sci. Lab.*, 42, 238–243.

Morris, J. D., and Thompson, L. W. 1969. Heart rate changes in a reaction time experiment with young and aged subjects. *J. Gerontol.*, 24, 269–275.

Mortimer-Tanner, R. S., and Naylor, G. F. K. 1973. Rates of information acceptance and executive response in youthful and elderly subjects. *Austral. J. Psychol.*, **25**, 139–145.

Mowbray, G. H. 1953. Simultaneous vision and audition: the comprehension of prose passages with varying levels of difficulty. *J. Exp. Psychol.*, **46**, 365–372.

Murrell, K. F. H. 1970. The effect of extensive practice on age differences in reaction time. *J. Gerontol.*, **25**, 268–274.

Murrell, K. F. H., and Entwisle, D. G. 1960. Age differences in movement pattern. *Nature*, **185**, 948.

Murrell, K. F. H., and Forsaith, B. 1960. Age and the timing of movement. *Occupational Psychol.*, **34**, 275–279.

Murrell, K. F. H., and Griew, S. 1958. Age structure in the engineering industry: a study of regional effects. *Occupational Psychol.*, **32**, 86–88.

Murrell, K. F. H., Griew, S., and Tucker, W. A. 1957. Age structure in the engineering industry: a preliminary study. *Occupational Psychol.*, **31**, 150–168.

Murrell, K. F. H., Powesland, P. F., and Forsaith, B. 1962. A study of pillar-drilling in relation to age. *Occupational Psychol.*, **36**, 45–52.

Naylor, G. F. K. 1973. The anatomy of reaction time and its relation to mental function in the elderly. *Proc. Austral. Ass. Gerontol.*, **2**, 17–19.

Noble, C. E., Baker, B. L., and Jones, T. A. 1964. Age and sex parameters in psychomotor learning. *Percep. Mot. Skills*, **19**, 935–945.

Norris, A. H., Shock, N. W., and Wagman, I. H. 1953. Age changes in the maximum conduction velocity of motor fibres in human ulnar nerves. *J. Appl. Physiol.*, **5**, 589–593.

Nuffield Foundation. 1963. *Workers Nearing Retirement.* London: The Nuffield Foundation.

Nuttall, R. L., and Fozard, J. L. 1971. A re-examination of the structure of the General Aptitude Test Battery aptitudes. *Indust. Gerontol.*, **8**, 1–18.

Obrist, W. D. 1953. Simple auditory reaction time in aged adults. *J. Psychol.*, **35**, 259–266.

Obrist, W. D. 1965. Electroencephalographic approach to age changes in response speed. *In*, A. T. Welford and J. E. Birren (eds.), *Behavior, Aging and the Nervous System*, pp. 259–271. Springfield, Illinois: Charles C. Thomas.

Onishi, N. 1966. Changes of the jumping reaction time in relation to age. *J. Sci. Lab.*, **42**, 5–16.

Pacaud, S. 1953. Le vieillissement des aptitudes: déclin des aptitudes en fonction de l'age et du niveau d'instruction. *Biotypologie*, **14**, 65–94.

Pacaud, S. 1955a. Experimental research on the ageing of psychological functions. *In*, *Old Age in the Modern World:* Rep. 3rd Congr. Internat. Ass. Gerontol., London 1954, pp. 279–289. Edinburgh: Livingstone.

Pacaud, S. 1955b. Le vieillissement des aptitudes. *In*, L. Binet and F. Bourlière (eds.), *Précis de Gérontologie*, pp. 40–67. Paris: Masson.

Pierson, W. R., and Montoye, H. J. 1958. Movement time, reaction time, and age. *J. Gerontol.*, **13**, 418–421.

Planek, T. W., and Fowler, R. C. 1971. Traffic accident problems and exposure characteristics of the aging driver. *J. Gerontol.*, **26**, 224–230.

Powell, M. 1973. Age and occupational change among coal-miners. *Occupational Psychol.*, **47**, 37–49.

Powell, R. R. 1974. Psychological effects of exercise therapy upon institutionalized geriatric mental patients. *J. Gerontol.*, **29**, 157–161.

Rabbitt, P. M. A. 1964a. Set and age in a choice-response task. *J. Gerontol.*, **19**, 301–306.

Rabbitt, P. M. A. 1964b. Age and time for choice between stimuli and between responses. *J. Gerontol.*, **19**, 307–312.

Rabbitt, P. M. A. 1965. An age-decrement in the ability to ignore irrelevant information. *J. Gerontol.*, **20**, 233–238.

Rabbitt, P., and Birren, J. E. 1967. Age and responses to sequences of repetitive and interruptive signals. *J. Gerontol.*, **22**, 143–150.

Rabbitt, P. M. A., and Rogers, M. 1965. Age and choice between responses in a self-paced repetitive task. *Ergonomics*, **8**, 435–444.

Rees, J. N., and Botwinick, J. 1971. Detection and decision factors in auditory behavior of the elderly. *J. Gerontol.*, **26**, 133–136.

Richardson, I. M. 1953. Age and work: a study of 489 men in heavy industry. *Brit. J. Indust. Med.*, **10**, 269–284.

Riegel, K. F., and Birren, J. E. 1965. Age differences in associative behavior. *J. Gerontol.*, **20**, 125–130.

Riegel, K. F., and Birren, J. E. 1967. Age differences in choice reaction times to verbal stimuli. *Gerontologia*, **13**, 1–13.

Road Traffic Board of South Australia. 1972. The Points Demerit Scheme as an Indication of Declining Skill with Age.

Ross, S., Vicino, F. L., and Krugman, A. D. 1960. Effects of position in a display on problem-solving ability in aged subjects. *J. Gerontol.*, **15**, 191–194.

Ruch, F. L. 1934. The differentiative effects of age upon human learning. *J. Gen. Psychol.*, **11**, 261–286.

Ruger, H. A., and Stoessiger, B. 1927. Growth curves of certain characteristics in man. *Ann. Eugen.*, **2**, 76–111.

Sanford, A. J., and Maule, A. J. 1973. The concept of general experience: Age and strategies in guessing future events. *J. Gerontol.*, **28**, 81–88.

Schonfield, D., and Robertson, E. A. 1968. The coding and sorting of digits and symbols by an elderly sample. *J. Gerontol.*, **23**, 318–323.

Sheldon, J. H. 1963. The effect of age on the control of sway. *Gerontol. Clin.*, **5**, 129–138.

Silverman, I. 1963. Age and the tendency to withhold response. *J. Gerontol.*, **18**, 372–375.

Simon, J. R. 1960. Changes with age in the speed of performance on a dial setting task. *Ergonomics*, **3**, 169–174.

Simon, J. R., and Wolf, J. D. 1963. Choice reaction time as a function of angular stimulus-response correspondence and age. *Ergonomics*, **6**, 99–105.

Simonson, E. 1965. Performance as a function of age and cardiovascular disease. *In*, A. T. Welford and J. E. Birren (eds.), *Behavior, Aging and the Nervous System*, pp. 401–434. Springfield, Illinois: Charles C. Thomas.

Simonson, E., and Anderson, D. A. 1966. Effect of age and coronary heart disease on performance and physiological responses in mental work. *Proc. 7th Internat. Cong. Gerontol., Vienna*, paper No. 279.

Singleton, W. T. 1954. The change of movement timing with age. *Brit. J. Psychol.*, 45, 166–172.

Singleton, W. T. 1955. Age and performance timing on simple skills. *In, Old Age in the Modern World*: Rep. 3rd Cong. Internat. Ass. Gerontol., London 1954, pp. 221–231. Edinburgh: Livingstone.

Smith, A. D. 1975. Aging and interference with memory. *J. Gerontol.*, 30, 319–325.

Smith, G. A. Studies in compatibility and a new model of choice reaction time. *In*, S. Dornic (ed.), *Attention and Performance VI*. Hillsdale, New Jersey: Lawrence Erlbaum Associates, in press.

Smith, J. M. 1973. Age and occupation: The determinants of male occupational age structures—hypothesis H and hypothesis A. *J. Gerontol.*, 28, 484–490.

Smith, K. U., and Greene, D. 1962. Scientific motion study and ageing processes in performance. *Ergonomics*, 5, 155–164.

Snoddy, G. S. 1926. Learning and stability. *J. Appl. Psych.*, 10, 1–36.

Sommer, J. 1941. Synchronisierung motorischer Impulse und ihre Bedeutung fur die neurophysiologische Forshung. *Ztschr. Ges. Neur. u. Psychiat.*, 172, 500–530.

Speakman, D. 1956. *Bibliography of Research on Changes in Working Capacity with Age*. London: Ministry of Labour and National Service.

Spieth, W. 1964. Cardiovascular health status, age, and psychological performance. *J. Gerontol.*, 19, 277–284.

Spieth, W. 1965. Slowness of task performance and cardiovascular diseases. *In*, A. T. Welford and J. E. Birren (eds.), *Behavior, Aging and the Nervous System*, pp. 366–400. Springfield, Illinois: Charles C. Thomas.

Stamford, B. A. 1972. Physiological effects of training upon institutionalised geriatric men. *J. Gerontol.*, 27, 451–455.

Suci, G. J., Davidoff, M. D., and Surwillo, W. W. 1960. Reaction time as a function of stimulus information and age. *J. Exp. Psychol.*, 60, 242–244.

Surwillo, W. W. 1961. Frequency of the 'Alpha' rhythm, reaction time and age. *Nature*, 191, 823–824.

Surwillo, W. W. 1963. The relation of simple response time to brain-wave frequency and the effects of age. *EEG Clin. Neurophysiol.*, 15, 105–114.

Surwillo, W. W. 1964. The relation of decision time to brain wave frequency and to age. *EEG Clin. Neurophysiol.*, 16, 510–514.

Surwillo, W. W. 1965. Level of skin potential in healthy males and the influence of age. *J. Gerontol.*, 20, 519–521.

Surwillo, W. W. 1969. Relationship between EEG activation and reaction time. *Percept. Mot. Skills*, 29, 3–7.

Surwillo, W. W. 1973. Choice reaction time and speed of information processing in old age. *Percept. Mot. Skills*, 36, 321–322.

Surwillo, W. W., and Quilter, R. E. 1964. Vigilance, age, and response-time. *Amer. J. Psychol.*, 77, 614–620.

Surwillo, W. W., and Quilter, R. E. 1965. The influence of age on latency time of involuntary (galvanic skin reflex) and voluntary responses. *J. Gerontol.*, 20, 173–176.

Szafran, J. 1951. Changes with age and with exclusion of vision in performance at an aiming task. *Quart. J. Exp. Psychol.*, 3, 111–118.

Szafran, J. 1966a. Age differences in the rate of gain of information, signal detection strategy and cardiovascular status among pilots. *Gerontologia*, 12, 6–17.

Szafran, J. 1966b. Age, cardiac output and choice reaction time. *Nature*, 209, 836.

Szakall, A. 1944. Maximale Leistung und maximale Arbeit. *Arbeitsphysiologie*, 13, 9–41.

Talland, G. A. 1962. The effect of age on speed of simple manual skill. *J. Genet. Psychol.*, 100, 69–76.

Talland, G. A. 1964. The effect of warning signals on reaction time in youth and old age. *J. Gerontol.*, 19, 31–38.

Talland, G. A. 1966. Visual signal detection, as a function of age, input rate, and signal frequency. *J. Psychol.*, 63, 105–115.

Talland, G. A., and Cairnie, J. 1961. Aging effects on simple, disjunctive and alerted finger reaction time. *J. Gerontol.*, 16, 370–374.

Thomas, G., and Osborne, B. 1950. *Older People and Their Employment*. Social Survey Report No. 150. London: Central Office of Information.

Thompson, L. W., and Botwinick, J. 1968. Age differences in the relationship between EEG arousal and reaction time. *J. Psychol.*, 68, 167–172.

Uffland, J. M. 1935. Einfluss des Lebensalters, Geschlechts, der Konstitution und des Berufs auf die Kraftverschieder Muskelgruppen. *Arbeitsphysiologie*, 6, 653–663.

van der Valk, J. M., and Groen, J. 1950. Electrical resistance of the skin during induced emotional stress. *Psychosomat. Med.*, 12, 303–314.

Vickers, D., Nettelbeck, T., and Willson, R. J. 1972. Perceptual indices of performance: the measurement of "inspection time" and "noise" in the visual system. *Perception*, 1, 263–295.

Wackwitz, J. D. 1946. *Het Verband Tusschen Arbeidsprestatie en Leeftijd*. Delft: Waltman.

Wagman, I. H., and Lesse, H. 1952. Maximum conduction velocities of motor fibers of ulnar nerve in human subjects of various ages and sizes. *J. Neurophysiol.*, 15, 235–244.

Wallace, J. G. 1956. Some studies of perception in relation to age. *Brit. J. Psychol.*, 47, 283–297.

Waugh, N. C., Fozard, J. L., Talland, G. A., and Erwin, D. E. 1973. Effects of age and stimulus repetition on two-choice reaction time. *J. Gerontol.*, **28**, 466–470.

Weiss, A. D. 1965. The locus of reaction time change with set, motivation, and age. *J. Gerontol.*, **20**, 60–64.

Welford, A. T. 1958. *Ageing and Human Skill*. Oxford University Press for the Nuffield Foundation. (Reprinted 1973 by Greenwood Press, Westport, Connecticut).

Welford, A. T. 1960. The measurement of sensory-motor performance: survey and reappraisal of twelve years' progress. *Ergonomics*, **3**, 189–230.

Welford, A. T. 1965. Performance, biological mechanisms and age: a theoretical sketch. *In*, A. T. Welford and J. E. Birren (eds.), *Behavior, Aging and the Nervous System*, pp. 3–20. Springfield, Illinois: Charles C. Thomas.

Welford, A. T. 1966. Industrial work suitable for older people: some British studies. *Gerontologist*, **6**, 4–9.

Welford, A. T. 1968. *Fundamentals of Skill*. London: Methuen.

Welford, A. T. 1971. What is the basis of choice reaction-time? *Ergonomics*, **14**, 679–693.

Welford, A. T. 1975. Display layout, strategy and reaction time: tests of a model. *In*, P. M. A. Rabbitt and S. Dornic (eds.), *Attention and Performance V*. pp. 470–484. New York: Academic Press.

Welford, A. T. 1976. *Skilled Performance*. Glenview, Illinois: Scott Foresman.

Welford, A. T. Serial reaction times, continuity of task, single-channel effects and age. *In*, S. Dornic (ed.), *Attention and Performance VI*. Hillsdale, New Jersey: Lawrence Erlbaum Associates, in press.

Welford, A. T., Norris, A. H., and Shock, N. W. 1969. Speed and accuracy of movement and their changes with age. *Acta Psychol.*, **30**, 3–15.

Weston, H. C. 1948. The effect of age and illumination upon visual performance with close sights. *Brit. J. Ophthalmol.*, **32**, 645–653.

Weston, H. C. 1949. On age and illumination in relation to visual performance. *Trans. Illum. Eng. Soc.*, **14**, 281–297.

Whitfield, J. W. 1954. Individual differences in accident susceptibility among coal miners. *Brit. J. Indust. Med.*, **11**, 126–139.

20
VISUAL PERCEPTION AND COMMUNICATION

James L. Fozard
Veterans Administration Outpatient Clinic,
Boston, Massachusetts, and
Harvard Medical School, Boston, Massachusetts

Ernst Wolf
Retina Foundation, Boston, Massachusetts,
and Harvard Medical School, Boston, Massachusetts

Benjamin Bell
Veterans Administration Outpatient Clinic,
Boston, Massachusetts, and
Boston University School of Medicine

Ross A. McFarland
Harvard School of Public Health, Boston, Massachusetts

Stephen Podolsky
Veterans Administration Outpatient Clinic,
Boston, Massachusetts, and
Boston University School of Medicine

Visual perception refers to those processes required to sense, interpret, and to respond to visual information, while visual communication refers to the physical and psychosocial processes involved in the transfer of visual information among individuals and groups.

The present review concerns three issues: (a) the differences in visual perception and communication processes with age; (b) the significance of these differences for the behavioral and biological scientists who study aging; and (c) some implications of the research for environmental engineering and intervention.

Three organizing concepts will be employed in this chapter. The first is that man may be considered as an information processing device. Adopting an information processing framework replaces in part the traditional distinctions between sensation and perception. The distinction between the two largely reflects variations in the specificity of the task requirements and in the amount of utilization of memorized information in the perceptual process.

The second concept is that the major age differences in perceptual functioning are mediated by two classes of changes in the structure of the eye (Bell, 1972; McFarland, 1963, 1968; Wolf, 1960, 1967). The first concerns changes in the transmissiveness and accommodative power of the eye that begin to assume importance between the ages of 35–45 years; such changes affect distance vision, sensitivity to glare, binocular depth perception, and color sensitivity. The second class of change concerns the retina and nervous system and begins to be important between 55–65 years of age. Changes in the circulation and therefore the metabolism of the retina are reflected in changes in size of the visual field, sensitivity to low quantities of light, and sensitivity to flicker.

The third descriptive concept concerns the relationship between perceptual processes and the experiences and expectations of an individual (Fozard and Thomas, 1975; Lawton

This chapter was prepared while Drs. Fozard and Bell were members of the staff of the Veterans Administration Normative Aging Study. Preparation of the chapter was supported in part by NIH Grant HD7296. The authors are grateful to Drs. R. A. Weale, T. Gunderson and P. E. Comalli, Jr. for their reviews of earlier drafts of this chapter.

and Nahemow, 1973). For many purposes, man and his environment should be viewed as a system. As man ages, he becomes better adapted to one kind of environment and more poorly to another. In general, greater adaptation implies greater interdependence of the system components. As adaptation to an environment increases, so does the ability to utilize external information in it when making decisions. On the other hand, changes in the environment may be relatively more disruptive to the individual who is well adapted to it.

The research to be summarized emphasizes material published since the chapters by Braun (1959) and Weiss (1959) in Birren's earlier handbook. The emphasis in the present chapter will be on the normal human eye, but some consideration will be given to changes in visual functioning associated with pathology.

Surveys of the incidence of blindness and problems of visual acuity in various age groups show that both of these problems are associated with older age. A study by the National Society for the Prevention of Blindness (1966) revealed

that the incidence of legal blindness increases from about 250 to 500 to 1,450 per 100,000, respectively, in groups 40-64, 65-69, and 69 years and over.

The incidence of poorer visual acuity as defined by conventional clinical standards also increases with older age (United States National Health Survey, 1968; Anderson and Palmore, 1974). In Figure 1 the corrected visual acuity in the better eye is plotted. Visual acuity of 20/20 is optimal and 20/50 or worse is serious enough so that some states impose restrictions on driver's licenses issued to such individuals.

Results of reexaminations of 93 of the persons whose data are summarized on the right panel of Figure 1 revealed that after 10 years, the incidence of visual acuity of 20/50 or worse in the better eye increased by 13 percent in the group 60-69 years of age while the corresponding figure was 32 percent for the group that was 70-80 years of age. While the results of such surveys highlight visual problems, they do not tell much about their causes nor of the practical significance of such problems.

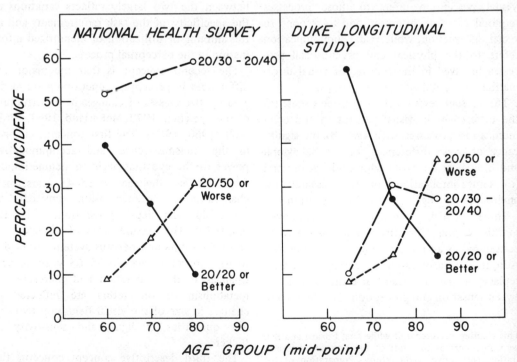

Figure 1. Percentage of individuals with different visual acuity levels (Snellen values) in three age groups. (Data from U.S. National Health Survey, 1968; Anderson and Palmore, 1974.)

STRUCTURAL CHANGES AND THEIR BEHAVIORAL SIGNIFICANCE

A strong subjective impression of an individual's age is provided by the physical appearance of the eye and its surrounding tissue. Because the various tissues of the eye are differentiated from all three germinating layers during development, many patterns of aging may be observed.

The eyebrows and eyelashes both serve protective functions. The small amount of graying in the eyelashes in comparison to the eyebrows or hair is due in part to the specialization of the cilia as tactile sense organs.

The loss of elasticity of the skin on the eyelids accounts for their wrinkled appearance and the loss of subcutaneous fat and fluids accounts for their greater transparency. There is some loss in the tonus and elasticity of the muscle of the eyelid. When the eyelid does not follow the movement of the globe, tears are more likely to spill over the margin of the lower lid resulting in reddening, irritation, and swelling of the lid which in turn leads to further reddening, etc.

The eye may appear more sunken in old age, and the enlargement of the nose with advancing age may enhance the appearance.

Chamberlain (1970) measured the upward and downward limit of gaze by observing the extent to which an individiual follows the movement of a light. The average upward gaze for monocular vision was 40°, 33°, 26°, and 16° in groups of subjects 5-14, 35-44, 55-64, and 75-94 years of age, respectively. There were no differences in the lower limits of gaze. Chamberlain's explanation of his results is that the elevator muscle of the eyeball atrophies with age due to disease. He found that persons who were stooped or bent over so that they had to elevate their gaze to see straight ahead could do much better than age peers without marked kyphosis. Smaller visual fields would also account for part of the difference. The practical significance of this age trend has not been studied, but it would seem that older persons would be handicapped in reading overhead street signs.

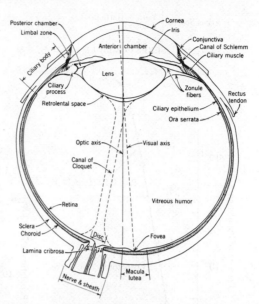

Figure 2. Diagram of the eye referred to in text. (From Brown, 1965, p. 42, adapted from a figure by Walls, 1942).

Cornea

The cornea, transparent and normally without blood vessels, has a greater curvature than the rest of the eye (Figure 2). In addition to being the principal refracting surface of the eye, the cornea serves a protective function. The sensitivity of the corneal surface to mechanical stimulation decreases with age (Jalavisto, Orma, and Tawast, 1951; Sedan, Farnarier, and Ferrand, 1958).

The appearance of the cornea frequently changes with age in two ways. The first is a loss of lustre which may reflect changes in its refractive power and a decrease in the amount of fluid bathing the corneal surface (e.g., Henderson and Prough, 1950).

The second change is the development of a gray ring (arcus senilis) on the border between the bulbar conjunctiva and the cornea. It results from the accumulation of lipids on the cornea.

The results of a survey of the prevalence of arcus senilis in British subjects by Burch, Murray, and Jackson (1971) and some data from the Johns Hopkins Hospital study by Macsareg, Lasagna, and Snyder (1968) are summarized in the panels of Figure 3. The cumulative propor-

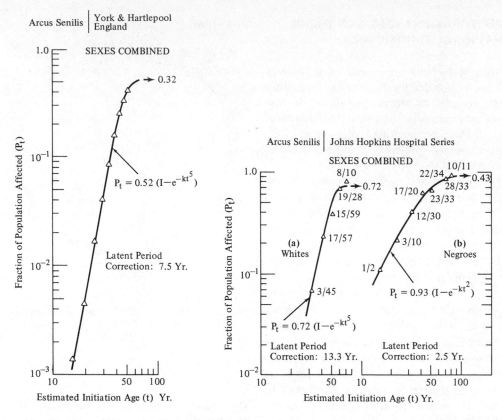

Figure 3. Incidence of arcus senilis in a British and two United States samples. The fitted functions are estimated from the stochistic equations shown. (From Burch, Murray, and Jackson, 1971. Reproduced with the permission of the *Journal of Gerontology*.)

tion of cases is plotted against age and indicates that arcus senilis is not a universal aging phenomenon.

The fitted functions in Figure 3 are theoretical values generated by the stochastic equations shown in the figures. The hypothesis is that the manifestation of arcus senilis results from somatic gene mutations that have occurred in one or more distinctive stem cells. Note that the age of initiation is not observed directly.

There is some evidence that both the curvature and the thickness of the cornea vary somewhat with age (Marin-Amat, 1956; Löpping and Weale, 1965). The curvature of the cornea is relatively flatter in infancy and in old age than in middle age. One result of such variations in curvature is increased astigmatism with an increase in blurred vision, independent of near or farsightedness. In old age, the astigmatism resulting from irregularities of the corneal surface result in greater refraction in the horizontal than in the vertical meridian. The opposite is true in children (Kapoor, 1965).

The thickness of the cornea increases between the ages of 25 and 65 years (von Bahr, 1956), probably from an increase in the amount of water in the tissue (Adler, 1965, Chapter 3).

Corneal guttata are deposits on the posterior endothelial layer of the cornea that contribute to the scattering of light in the eye. Anderson and Palmore (1974) report that marked or moderate incidence as defined clinically was found in only 3 percent, 2 percent, and 9 percent of the Duke Longitudinal study participants who were 60-69, 70-79, or 80 and over years of age. In the 10-year follow-up, the incidence increased to 10 and 21 percent respectively in the two younger groups.

Aqueous Humor, Sclera, and Intraocular Pressure

The anterior chamber is between the cornea and the lens, and the posterior chamber between iris and the lens (Figure 2). The depth of the anterior chamber declines from about 3.6 to 3.1 mm between the ages of 25-85 years (Rosengren, 1950). Both chambers are filled with a clear fluid, the aqueous humor, which provides nutrients to the lens and transportation of the waste products of metabolism from the chambers.

The aqueous humor originates in the blood vessels of the eye, particularly the ciliary body. Its elimination occurs through tissues located at the place where the iris, ciliary muscles, and the cornea converge, and its end points are the aqueous vein. Under normal conditions the filtration angle is large enough that flow is unimpeded even when the iris is fully dilated. The chemical reactions governing the outflow of the aqueous humor are of considerable importance, because glaucoma may result from inadequate passage of the aqueous humor into the canal of Schlemm (Adler, 1965, p. 137).

Intraocular Pressure and Glaucoma. The normal intraocular pressure of the eye is about ten times that of any other tissue; its functional value is the maintenance of uniform refractive properties of the cornea. Excessively high intraocular pressure is associated with glaucoma.

Glaucoma is not intrinsically related to aging. Anderson and Palmore (1974) report an incidence of glaucoma in only 3 percent and 1 percent of subjects 60-69 and 70-79 years of age, respectively, and after 10 years the incidence increased to 12 percent and 6 percent, respectively. Other estimates for groups older than 65 years ranged from 5-13 percent (e.g., Harrison and Wolf, 1964). For younger subjects Leydhecker (1959) reported incidences of glaucoma ranging from .04 to 4.5 percent for age groups between the 20's and the 60's. The wide variation reflects differences in criteria for diagnosis.

The type of glaucoma most typically associated with old age is gradual in onset and is generally unrelated to problems of refraction which might bring a person to the attention of a specialist (Harrison and Wolf, 1964). For this reason, the best protection against this disease is for the appropriate examination, including tonometry, to be included in a regular physical examination (Gordon, 1965).

Iris, Ciliary Body and Pupil

Iris. With aging there is a decrease in the permeability of the iris, a factor that some believe to be contributory to glaucoma. There is also depigmentation. Epithelial cells loosen and scatter on the surface of the iris, the lens capsule, and the posterior surface of the cornea, thereby contributing to scattering of light.

Ciliary Muscle. The ciliary muscle increases in depth and length until age 18 and increases in volume for another 15 years, after which its length diminishes and some of the muscular tissue is replaced by connective tissue (Fuchs, 1928; Stieve, 1949). The atrophy of the ciliary muscle may be functional inasmuch as the increasing immobility of the lens makes the muscle less effective (Weale, 1963, p. 63).

Pupil Size. The pupil increases in size between the second year of life and adolescence and decreases thereafter. The size of the pupil is constantly fluctuating according to variations in the amount of ambient light. The effect of the smaller size of the pupil with age on limiting the amount of light illuminating the retina therefore depends on the adaptation of the eye. The left panel of Figure 4 shows the average amount of decrease in pupillary area at different levels of adaptation. The amount of decrease in area is greater for lower levels of illumination. The right hand panel of Figure 4 shows that the ratio of pupillary area in the fully dark adapted eye to that of the light adapted eye changes very little after age 40. The significance of these data is that much of the contradictory evidence about age differences in visual acuity and sensitivity to be presented later may be attributed to differences in the adaptation of the eye under the conditions of testing. The decrease in pupillary size with age, called senile miosis, cannot be explained by sclerosis of iridal tissues. Weakening of the muscles controlling dilation proceeds more rapidly with age than those controlling contraction (Schäfer and Weale, 1970).

Pupillary Reflex. By using lenses it is possible to bring about contraction of the pupil with

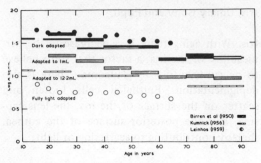 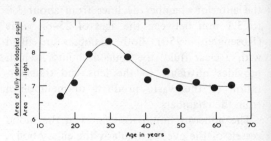

Figure 4. Left: Decrease in average diameter of pupil with age under various levels of dark adaptation. (From Birren, Casperon, and Botwinick, 1950; Kumnick, 1956; Leinhos, 1959.) Right: Ratio of pupillary area in dark adapted to that in light adapted eye. (From Weale, 1961; Weale, 1963, pp. 12, 56.)

convergence of the visual axes without accommodation. Normal convergence may also be prevented by use of prisms (Renard, 1947). In either case the pupillary contraction occurs when the object comes within about 0.5 meter of the eye.

The time between light increase and the contraction of the pupil defines the latency of the pupillary reflex. With the exception of Kumnick (1956), many investigators have found that the latency increases with age. Estimates of the latency of the reflex depends upon many factors other than age, e.g., the diameter of the pupil when the light change occurs, the rapidity of change of the size of the pupil, the intensity of the stimulating light, and the adaptation level of the eye.

Feinberg and Podolac (1965) measured pupillary reflex latencies in a group of 86 subjects ranging in age from 14–67 years, employing a procedure designed to give results independent of either the diameter of the pupil or its color.

Pupillary latencies ranging from about 214–314 msec were observed, and longer latencies correlate with older age ($r = .54$). Pupil diameter decreased with age ($r = .-55$).

Lens

The lens, differentiated from epithelial tissue, continues to grow throughout life but, unlike the hair, nails, and skin, the cells of the lens are not shed. If it were not for the compacting processes, the lens would grow too large for the eyeball. The left panel of Figure 5 shows that with increased growth the lens becomes more dense at its center (see Weale, 1971, 1973, and Fisher, 1973 for reviews).

The growth of the lens is marked by regular increases in the number and the position of the lenticular strata. Each stratum requires about 4 years to form, and older strata get pushed toward the center of the lens (Goldmann, 1937).

After birth, the lens does not respond to deleterious physical or chemical agents or inflammatory or allergic processes. Moreover, it has no blood supply, because of which the metabolic basis for its work is of interest to biochemists (see Adler, 1965, p. 236 and p. 274; and Weale, 1963, pp. 86–102). It has the highest protein content of any organ in the body. One chemical characteristic of particular behavioral interest results from the extreme sensitivity of the lens to water. Lowering of the blood sugar may induce transitory hyperopia and when it rises, myopia may develop. These sudden changes may occur in cases of diabetes.

Functional Significance. Three aspects of aging in the lens are of importance to visual functioning. The most important is that the growth of the lens contributes to a decrease in its accommodative power. This will be discussed in greater detail later in the chapter.

Second, the refractive index of the lenses of many mammals increases with age, although the evidence is less clear in humans. Differential rates of hardening of the nucleus and cortex of

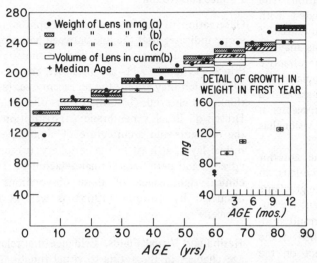
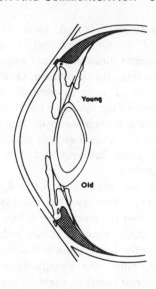

Figure 5. Left: Growth of mass and volume of the human lens. (From Salmony and Weale (a), 1961; Scammon and Hesdorffer (b), 1937; Johansen (c), 1947.) Right: Ciliary (shaded) and lens of the eye in the second and seventh decades. (From Weale, 1963, p. 69.)

the lens in humans may lead to uneven refractive properties of the lens which in some cases result in double images in one eye (Paton and Craig, 1974).

Third, the yellowing of the lens with age reduces the amount of light which reaches the retina as well as changing its composition. Said and Weale (1959) estimated the optical density of living lenses at different wavelengths by analyzing photographs of reflections from the anterior and posterior surfaces of the lens. Their results, summarized in Figure 6, indicate that the older eye loses its sensitivity to shorter wavelengths because wavelengths from the blue-green end of the spectrum are absorbed by the yellowing lens.

There is at present no completely satisfactory explanation of the yellowing of the lens. It may reflect increases in the amount of cholesterol in the lenticular tissue to changes in the relative quantity of different proteins (see Weale, 1963, pp. 86–102 for a review).

Cataracts. An opacity of the lens that impairs vision is a cataract. Although some 90 percent of cataracts are classified as senescent as distinguished from congenital, juvenile, or secondary to other diseases, their incidence in persons over 65 is not high. In the Duke University

study, the initial incidence as clinically defined was 9, 18, and 36 percent, respectively, for participants in their 60's, 70's, and 80's. Over a 10-year follow-up, the incidence increased by only 3 percent in the group initially in their 70's and not at all in the youngest group.

The consequences of a cataract for visual

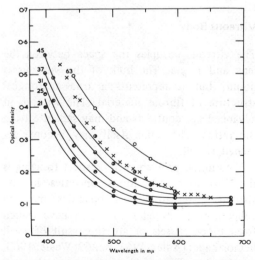

Figure 6. Transmitted light from human lenses for various wavelengths. Numbers indicate the age of subjects; the crosses represent data from an extirpated lens. (From Weale, 1963, p. 84, based on data from Said and Weale, 1959. *Gerontologia*, 3, 213–231. Basel: S. Karger.)

functioning depend upon its location. The most common cataract is associated with excessive nuclear sclerosis. Prior to any onset of cataracts, the hardening of the lens may be associated with an increase in the refractive power of the eye and a resultant myopia which, because it counteracts the hyperopia associated with the normal growth of the lens, results in individuals believing that their near vision has improved.

If the cataract is located in the anterior cortex rather than the nucleus of the lens, an acquired hyperopia may occur. If the gradients of opacity between cortex and nucleus are sufficiently large, double vision may result. Finally, when the opacification occurs on the posterior cortex, there is no effect on the refractive power of the lens, but rather a distortion of light which makes it difficult to locate a source of light.

When cataracts are surgically removed, a substitute lens is required for the aphakic eye. The use of contact lenses is desirable, particularly when one cataract is removed, because the image size associated with it is, in comparison to the normal lens, only about 8 percent larger as opposed to 25 percent larger for a spectacle lens (Paton and Craig, 1974).

Vitreous Body

The vitreous occupies the space between the lens and retina. The bulk of the vitreous is liquid, but it represents a true anatomical structure of fibrous material. The vitreous in advanced age contracts and may separate from the retina. The retina itself may become detached as well.

A common problem with respect to aging is the formation of various opacities in the vitreous. Nonpathological opacities may be collections of blood cells which have leaked from blood vessels or are the result of small hemorrhages (Adler, 1965, p. 269; Weale, 1963, pp. 21–28). The effect of opacities, whatever their cause, is to impair image quality, usually by reducing the amount of light illuminating the retina. In time surgical treatment of these difficulties may be possible.

Fundus and Retina

Observation of the fundus with an ophthalmoscope indicates that the line between pathology and "normal" age change is very uncertain. Prince (1965, pp. 11–12) lists five characteristics which may typify the senescent eye: (a) a thickened choroid; (b) retinal veins dilated; (c) Drusen on Bruch's membrane; (d) disruption of the elements and architecture of almost every retinal layer, at least in the periphery; (e) some vitreous and peripheral retinal detachment. The clinical significance of these observations is discussed by Gordon (1965) as well as by Prince.

Retina and Visual Fields. Evidence that relates age changes in the retina to visual functioning comes from determinations of the size of the visual field (Burg, 1968; Wolf, 1967). The boundaries of the field (isopters) are defined by determining the positions at which an observer, who, while fixating a central point, first detects a target light moved from the light insensitive to light sensitive area of the retina. In addition to the influence of anatomical factors (Fisher, 1968), the estimated size of the visual field depends upon: (a) the size, luminance, and color of the target; (b) the contrast between the target and its background; (c) the state of adaptation of the eye; and (d) individual differences in criteria adopted for making judgments of the presence of the test light.

Wolf (1967) employed constant conditions of illumination (3.3 ml for the target and .02 ml for the field) to determine the isopter for 24 points equally spaced around the perimeter of the right eye.

The mean isopters for a 1 mm^2 target for age decades from 16–96 years are shown in the left panel of Figure 7. The field shrinks most rapidly in the three oldest groups. To the extent that the older persons were more cautious in making judgments in the testing situation, the age effects reported may be exaggerated.

Many of the same subjects were used to determine the size of the blind spot. Harrison and Wolf (1964) report that its size increases regularly for subjects over 40.

In order to provide a description of age-

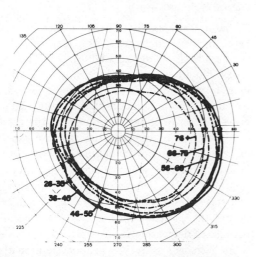
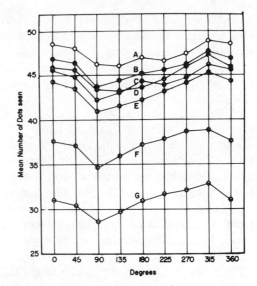

Figure 7. Left: Mean perimeter of right eyes in six age groups. Right: Mean number of dots identified in .04 sec. displays each consisting of 4 lights shown at various distances from center of field. Mean ages of youngest to oldest age groups indicated by letters A-H. (Data from Wolf, 1967.)

related differences in sensitivity between the center and extremes of the visual fields, Wolf (1967) employed a display of four illuminated dots (white light). The observer's task was to report the number of dots seen on each .4-second presentation. The displays varied in luminance, size, distance, and orientation from the center of the field.

The mean number of dots seen for groups between 16 and 91 years are displayed in the right panel of Figure 7. The horizontal axis indicates the eight positions of the visual field where measures were made. Sensitivity was greatest in the temporal field and lowest on the upper vertical meridian. With older age the mean number of dots seen decreased. Sensitivity decreased markedly in the decades from 60 to 90 years.

If the age differences in sensitivity of the peripheral fields could be accounted for entirely by changes in the amount of light reaching the retina as suggested by Weale (1963, Chapter 8), performance should fall off faster with age as target size, and therefore retinal illumination, decreased. Wolf's data are not compatible with this hypothesis; when the data are averaged across radial position and luminance levels, the functions relating the three dot sizes to age are essentially parallel.

Wolf suggests that his data are evidence for a decrease in retinal metabolism in persons older than 60 because the abrupt decline in sensitivity occurs beyond the age effects related to loss of accommodation and yellowing of the lens.

Electroretinography (ERG). Straub (1957), analyzing the ERGs of 1,205 eyes, found two distinct groups, one from 10-50 and a second from 50-80 years. To produce an a-wave, photopic luminances are required, and the older group needed more light to obtain an equal response. The b-wave shows the following age-dependent changes: (a) latency and peak time are functions of stimulus intensity and are distinctly different for the two age ranges; (b) the duration of the b-wave is longer for the older group; (c) the amplitude depends on the strength of the light stimulus. When stimulus strength is correlated with age, amplitude undergoes a considerable decrease in the older group.

Lehnert and Wuensche (1966) studied the ERG on 187 normal individuals divided into six groups of mean ages 15 to 65 years. Visual acuity was normal. Pupils were dilated to at least 6 mm. A 10-minute period of light adaptation and subsequent stay in complete darkness for 30 minutes preceded the tests in a dimly lit room. The results are shown in Figure 8. *A* represents the amplitudes of the total b-wave (from the a-trough to maximum); *B* the amplitude of the partial b-wave (from base line to maximum); and *C* the amplitude of the a-wave. Amplitudes decrease with advancing age. The b-wave shows a marked drop at mean age 45 years and a faster decline into advanced age. Curve *A* shows some change before 45 years, curve *B* does not. The amplitude of the a-wave in curve *C* decreases rather smoothly from 15 to 65; no change in rate is indicated.

The a- and b-waves usually employed in ERG analyses offer only a partial picture of electrical events following light stimulation. Information presently available is inadequate to support any valid conclusions about the significances of age changes.

Macular Disease. Gordon (1965) estimates that macular disease accounts for some 45 percent of the vision problems in elderly persons. Because the cones are located in the macula of the retina, macular diseases may have a large

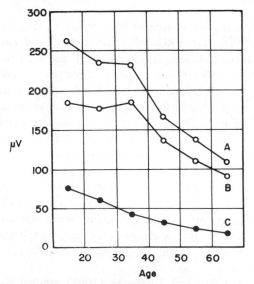

Figure 8. Mean amplitude (microvolts) of electroretinogram in six age groups: A, total b-wave; B, partial b-wave; C, a-wave. (Data from Lehnert and Wuensche, 1966.)

effect on vision for detail. Most macular degeneration is progressive.

Diabetic Retinopathy. The incidence of diabetes mellitus increases with older age; it is characterized by accelerated aging of the arteries. Blindness is perhaps the most devastating long term complication of diabetes. Some 2 percent of the population of the United States has diabetes. In about 40 percent of the cases, the condition is unrecognized due to a variety of causes, including the absence of symptoms, individual neglect, and inadequate medical care (Marble, 1971). "Asymptomatic" middle-age diabetes is not infrequently first recognized during the patient's visit to an eye specialist because of decreasing vision.

In a recent survey, diabetic retinopathy ranked fourth behind senile macular degeneration, cataracts, and glaucoma among causes of legal blindness, accounting for 11 percent of new patients (Welch, 1969). The development of retinopathy is more frequent in patients in whom the onset of the diabetes occurred in early life. The presence of retinopathy occurs in 93 percent of juvenile diabetics having the disease for 20–40 years (White, 1960) and in 85 percent of all patients with diabetes for 25 years or longer (Bryfogle and Bradley, 1957). Krall and Podolsky (1971) reported that less than one-fifth of patients with diabetic retinopathy actually became blind after a mean interval of 10 years with retinopathy.

The chief causes of visual impairment of diabetes are macular edema, vitreous hemorrhage, retinal detachment, and neovascular glaucoma (Davis, 1971). The common nonproliferative or background retinopathy of typical maturity onset diabetic patients consists of microaneurysms, hemorrhages, and exudates and can also seriously impair vision, although causing actual blindness in a lesser percentage of patients than does neovascular or proliferative retinopathy.

On the basis of their studies of experimentally produced retinopathy in dogs, Engerman, Davis, and Bloodworth (1971) conclude that diabetic microangiopathy is a complication of the metabolic abnormalities caused by insulin deficiency. If retinopathy and other vascular changes are secondary to the metabolic abnormalities of diabetes, these vascular changes can be somewhat prevented or ameliorated by correction of metabolic abnormalities.

SENSITIVITY AND ADAPTATION OF THE EYE TO LIGHT

The quality of the retinal image and hence the visual information extracted from it are largely determined by the amount of illumination falling upon the retina. The sensory elements of the retina have a capability to respond to luminances of between 10^{-5} and 10^4 footcandles. This large range of sensitivity is based on the power of adapting and on the division of the retinal elements into rods, responding to low luminances in the scotopic, and cones, responding to high luminances in the photopic range of vision.

The retinal periphery contains predominantly rods, while the central retinal contains a dense population of cones. Loosely speaking, the peripheral retina may be thought of as acting as a catch basin for excitation, inducing the turning of gaze toward the stimulus and examining the details with the fovea. As soon as more than rough perception of movement or form is required, the image of an object must fall onto the fovea.

Besides element distribution and density on the retinal surface, the quality of the retinal image depends on: (a) the refractive power of the cornea and lens; (b) the control of incident luminance by the pupil; and (c) the transmissiveness of the ocular media. Defects in the optical system such as refractive errors and spherical and chromatic aberrations reduce image clarity.

Sensitivity to Low Levels of Illumination

The determination of the minimum amount of light to which the eye can respond requires explicit control of the following: (a) the region of the retina which is stimulated; (b) the stimulus size intensity, duration, and wavelength of both the light used to preadapt the eye and the test light itself; and (c) the time spent in the dark (dark adaptation). The effects of all three factors interact with age.

Data on age differences in dark adaptation were obtained by McFarland, Domey, Warren, and Ward (1960) using the same procedures described by McFarland and Fisher (1955). The level of preadaptation of the eye and the time and the intensity of the test light were held constant, and an artificial pupil was employed. Data were obtained from 240 subjects ranging in age from 16 to 90 years.

The results, shown in the left panel of Figure 9, suggest that both the rate and the final level of adaptation varied with age. The correlations between sensitivity and age after 2, 5, and 40 minutes were .71, .80, and .84, respectively.

The prediction of the final level of adaptation on the basis of age and the time elapsed from the beginning of dark adaptation is possible on the basis of a simple mathematical model (Domey, McFarland, and Chadwick, 1960a, 1960b), and the results of the application of the model to the data of McFarland et al. (1960) are shown on the right of Figure 9.

On the basis of the high correlations with age, Domey and McFarland (1961) were able to recommend the use of a short test consisting of 3 minutes of preexposure and a measure of sensitivity after 10 minutes that, together with age, would account for about 83 percent of the variance in the level of adaptation after 40 minutes.

Three factors have been postulated to explain the age differences in dark adaptation; they are not mutually exclusive (Burg, 1967).

Age-related decrements in retinal metabolism are considered most important by McFarland et al. (1960). The basic argument is that the supply of oxygen to the retina diminishes with age, particularly in the rod dense area. The hypothesis rests at this time partly on analogies between the effect of decreased oxygen supply on dark adaptation and shrinkage of the visual fields observed in high altitudes and those observed in advanced age (McFarland, 1963). Since the efficiency of dark adaptation varies as a function of anoxia, hypoglycemia, and vitamin A deficiency (McFarland, 1963) and the functioning of the central nervous system depends upon the oxidation of blood sugar, any reduction of blood sugar would decrease the rate of oxidation.

Other factors contributing to the age differ-

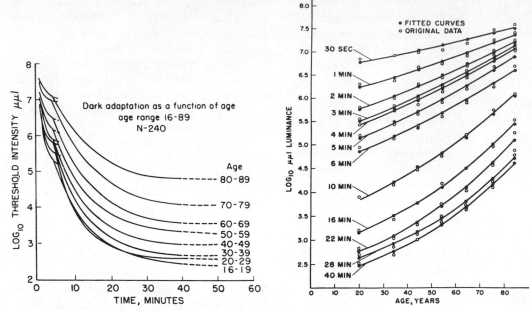

Figure 9. Left: Mean luminance required for identification of target light by seven age groups after various amounts of time in dark. (From McFarland, Domey, Warren, and Ward, 1960.) Right: Estimated and observed thresholds after 0.5 to 40 min. in dark function of age. (From Domey, McFarland, and Chadwick, 1960a.) Reproduced with the permission of the *Journal of Gerontology*.)

ence in final level of sensitivity include senile miosis and age-related increases in the degree of yellowing of the lens. Although McFarland *et al.* (1960) employed an artificial pupil, a violet test lens was used. As a result, the effective illumination of the retina under standard conditions would be less for older subjects because the opacity of the lens is relatively greater with lights of short wavelengths.

As seen in Figure 9, the degree of difference between thresholds for the aged and for the young appears to be geometrically progressive as a function of adaptation time.

The argument that both rate and final level of dark adaptation vary with age implies that the control mechanisms in dark adaptation are sugar metabolism and oxygen transportation and utilization. The evidence for age differences in rate of adaptation has been disrupted (e.g., Weale, 1965). The procedure for estimating rate from drop scores confounds rate of change of adaptation with displacement of the functions with age (Birren and Shock, 1950; McFarland and Fisher, 1955). Domey, McFarland, and

Chadwick (1960a,b) have presented a mathematical analysis of the functions relating rate of adaptation to time in the dark, from which they concluded that there is an age related difference in the rate of adaptation of both rods and cones. They provide a detailed analysis of the hypothesis of Birren and Shock that there is no age difference in rate of adaptation. It is clear that the procedures for estimating rate of adaptation have a strong bearing on the conclusion reached with respect to age differences in rate of adaptation.

The practical significance of these data is in tasks that require partial adaptation; for instance, the operation of motor vehicles at night under conditions of unpredictable changes of luminance (Bouma, 1947; Lewis, 1972). The range of luminances involved in such tasks commonly requires crossing over from rod to cone vision and vice versa. Rate of adaptation then becomes exceedingly important, because it is precisely in this region that the terminal level of adaptation of the cone cells almost defines the moment when three-dimensional vision, acuity, and color vision cease and the moment before the rod cells have generated any useful degree of sensitivity.

Glare

Loss of distinct vision results from too much illumination as well as from too little, e.g., the temporary loss of vision experienced when one leaves a darkened theater for daylight. Holladay (1926) has described the physical properties of glare, and more recently the relationships between age and the effect of glare on visual performance and the transmissiveness of the ocular media have been studied (Wolf, 1960; Wolf and Gardiner, 1965).

Selected results from 112 subjects ranging in age from 5 to 85 years are shown in Figure 10. The panel on the left shows the luminance of the target required to detect the break in a Landolt ring at different levels of glare for subjects in eight different age groups. The shift in threshold as a function of age is illustrated in the right panel of Figure 10. The rise in sensitivity to glare is slight up to age 40 years but increases much more between 40 and 70 years.

After surgical removal of the opaque lens an aphakic individual will often show a sensitivity equal to or greater than that of a normal peer (Wolf, 1960), suggesting that the increasing

opacity in the lens is the primary cause for the increasing sensitivity to glare. Related evidence comes from the results of a study demonstrating a correlation between a psychophysical response to glare and photometric measurements on scattering of light in lens and vitreous (Wolf and Gardiner, 1965).

The turbidity of the vitreous remains practically unchanged in the normal eye until advanced age. Under abnormal conditions, however, as for instance in postoperative retina patients, vitreous turbidity can contribute materially to the sensation of glare. Irritation or changes in the cornea also can produce glare (Miller and Wolf, 1969; Miller, Wolf, Gair, and Vesallo, 1967).

Flicker

Age-related differences in the sensitivity of the eye to light have also been studied by determining the threshold for detecting flicker in an intermittent light source. The threshold called the critical flicker frequency (CFF) obtained at any specific retinal point is a function of: (a) luminance of the flicker target and its surround; (b) spectral characteristics of the flickering light; (c) angular area of the flickering object; (d) the light time/dark time ratio in each flicker cycle; and (e) retinal position.

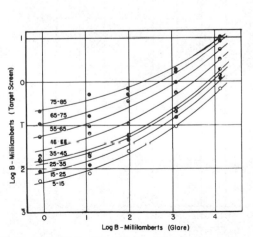 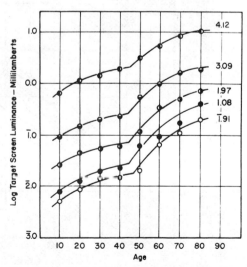

Figure 10. Left: Target illumination necessary to detect gap in Landolt ring by seven groups in five levels of glare. Right: Data of left panel plotted as a function of age. (From Wolf, 1960. Copyright 1960 by the American Medical Association. Reproduced with permission.)

Wolf and Schraffa (1964) have determined the CFF at 49 points of the visual field in 302 subjects in nine age groups ranging from 6–15 to 86–95 years.

Figure 11 displays the decrease in the mean CFFs obtained in the fovea and extrafoveal points 10°, 20°, 30°, 40°, 50°, and 60° from fixation on the horizontal and vertical meridians of the right eye for mean ages 10, 20, 30, 40, 50, 60, 70, 80, and 90 years. Levels of response are related to specific retinal positions: the individual flicker field is neither radially symmetrical nor symmetrical in relation to the vertical meridian of the field.

As shown in Figure 11, the size of the age differences increases more rapidly beyond age 60. The uniform change in the profiles associated with age is in sharp contrast with variations in the profile associated with specific pathologies. In such cases, abnormal CFF pro-

files, after corrections for age, were shown to be restricted to particular locations in the field. In contrast, in another part of the study, a comparison was made of the flicker patterns obtained on trained young subjects breathing normal air and/or gas mixtures contain 5 percent or 100 percent oxygen. With less oxygen, CFF was reduced at all retinal points, a finding reminiscent of the aging effect, but not of the ones associated with pathology. Breathing 100 percent oxygen, on the other hand, did not elevate CFF values.

McFarland, Warren, and Karis (1958) investigated age differences in CFF as a function of the percentage of light- and dark-time during the flicker cycle. The method of limits was employed. Male subjects, 108 in number, were divided into eight groups ranging from 13–89 years.

As seen in Figure 12, the effects of percent-

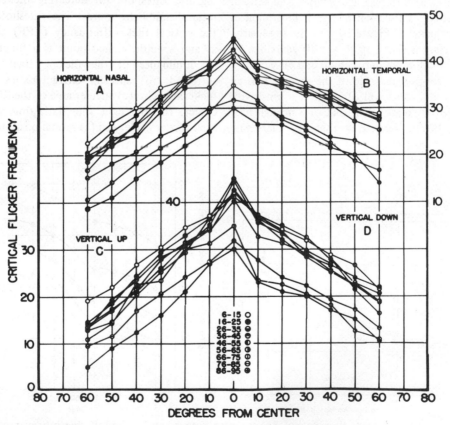

Figure 11. Critical flicker fusion thresholds at the fovea and six extrafoveal points in nine age groups for the horizontal and vertical meridians. (From Wolf and Schraffa, 1964. Copyright 1964 by the American Medical Association. Reproduced with permission.)

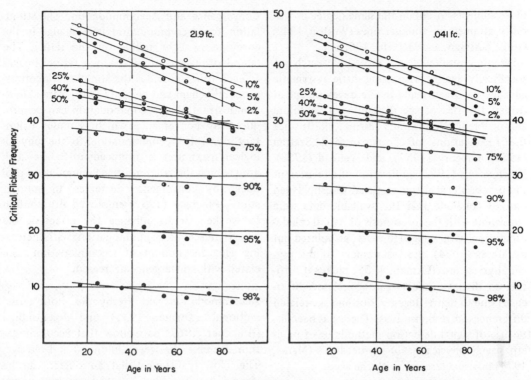

Figure 12. Critical flicker frequency values for eight age groups under high (left) and low (right) levels of background illumination as a function of percentage of time that light was on during the flicker cycle. (From McFarland, Warren, and Karis, 1958. Copyright 1958 by the American Psychological Association. Reprinted by permission.)

age of light in flicker cycle had a similar effect on the magnitude of the age difference at both levels of illumination, the difference being largest when the percentage of light was small. Increasing the percentage of illumination clearly decreased the age differences in CFF. The similarity of the age profiles for two rather different levels of illumination suggests that the effect of percentage of light could not entirely be accounted for by age-related differences in the amount of light reaching the retina. Other evidence that senile miosis does not entirely account for the effect comes from the comparisons of CFF when the observer's eyes were dilated or natural (Weekers and Roussel, 1946). With dilated pupils, the difference between the average CFFs of groups ranging in age from 25 to 65 years could only be decreased by about half.

The evidence to support neurological explanations of the age difference in CFF available is indirect (Adler, 1965, pp. 739–750; Simonson, Anderson, and Keiper, (1967). Both McFarland, Warren, and Karis (1958) and Wolf and Schraffa (1964) have pointed out that the relative variability of CFF judgments increases with age, even under conditions where the average level of the age groups is very similar. Thus, part of the age-related differences in criteria for these threshold judgments may account for part of the observed differences, a point that is also made by Weale (1963, pp. 150–151).

Differential Sensitivity

Age differences in sensitivity to intensity changes in light above threshold levels have received little recent attention. Gregory (1957) found an increase in the Weber fraction with age that was most pronounced in subjects in their 60's and 70's. A relatively greater increase in the intensity of illumination is required for older subjects to obtain the same degree of visibility attained by younger ones (Weston, 1949; Guth, Eastman, and McNelis, 1956).

Despite considerable advances in research not specifically dealing with aging, little systematic advance has been made in the development of formal theories of age differences in absolute and differential thresholds (Birren, 1970) since the formulations of Crossman and Szafran (1956), Gregory (1957), and Welford (1958). Hinchcliffe's (1962) application of a revision of the psychophysical law to visual thresholds led him to conclude that the available data were consistent with the hypothesis of neural cell degeneration with aging. However, as pointed out by Marks (1974), the restatement of the psychophysical law (Ekman, 1955) makes it difficult to distinguish between age-related differences due to neural degeneration and age-related differences in response bias. There has been little use of signal detection methods or of modern psychophysical scaling procedures (Marks, 1974) in visual research with the aged.

BASIC VISUAL FUNCTIONS

Attaining and maintaining a focused image on the retina involves three processes: (a) variations in the diameter of the pupil; (b) altering the focal length of the lens by changing the refractive power of the cornea and/or lens, and (c) changes in the convergence of the two eyes as the object of regard moves from a distance at which light rays are effectively parallel to a point close to the viewer. Although all three processes normally function in a coordinated way, their innervation and relationships to age are different.

Focusing and Maintaining an Image

Pupil. Constriction of the pupil can improve the quality of the retinal image by excluding light from the peripheral parts of cornea and lens, by reducing the amount of light falling on the retina, and by increasing the depth of focus of the eye, i.e., the distance of an object from the retina that may occur without producing a perceptible blur. Because pupil size decreases with age, the amount of its effect on changing depth of focus becomes smaller.

Convergence and Accommodation. The stimulation for accommodation is a change in the envelope of light falling on the retina. The lateral displacement of the two retinal images to each other provides the stimulus for convergence. Fincham and Walton (1957) were able to demonstrate that accommodation can be produced by convergence which is under voluntary control. Accommodation to the physiological maximum is produced up to the 20's, after which the amount of accommodation produced by convergence decreases. In another study, Fincham (1937) employed drugs either to weaken or to enhance the effect of the ciliary muscle on accommodation. With increasing age, the amount of accommodation associated with convergence decreased.

Accommodation and Presbyopia. Both cross-sectional (Duane, 1931) and longitudinal (Brückner, 1967) data show that accommodation decreases between childhood and old age. The closest distance that an object can be viewed without blur is called the near point, and from it the maximum accommodative power of the lens is measured in diopters. Its value decreases with age. Brückner's (1967) data indicate that the sharpest decline was between 40–55 years, over which values the mean changed from approximately 5 to 2 D. Brückner's measurements take into account a correction for near or farsightedness and pupil size, distance of the corrective lens from the cornea, and the level of illumination.

The trends of the longitudinal data were similar to those of the cross-sectional data except that the decline in accommodation with age was greater. The reason for the difference is not clear (Corso, 1971). Because of selective drop out of persons in older cohorts, the cross-sectional data may have underestimated the true aging trend.

There is some evidence that the speed of accommodation decreases with age. The relevant data come from measuring the interval between individuals' reports of having a near object and then a distant one in focus (Allen, 1956; Robertson, 1937). Because of some methodological difficulties indicated by Weale (1965), the practical significance of these data is not clear.

The mechanism of accommodation and therefore its relation to presbyopia is complex (Weale 1962, 1971). Fisher (1969a, b) has shown that the loss of accommodation is associated with a decrease in the elasticity of the lenticular capsule. This and other senile changes in the mechanical properties of the lens and lens capsule (Fisher, 1971, 1973) account for most of the senile changes in the balance of forces that control accomodation.

Refraction. Walton (1950) found that the average spherical lens power had to be increased in four groups of patients, 1-20, 21-40, 41-60, and 61 years and above. Most of the changes in hyperopic eyes were for increased hyperopia while only about 40 percent of the myopic changes represented increased myopia. The author concludes that the increase in hyperopia reflects declines in the strength of the ciliary muscle. In contrast to hyperopia, myopia increases until age 20, remains static until 60, and then decreases.

Static Acuity. One critical variable that determines acuity is the brightness gradient of the image on the retina. Acuity may be improved by increasing the contrast between the target and its surround. Increasing contrasts affects the visibility of larger targets relatively more than that of smaller ones. Fankhauser and Schmidt (1957) showed that increasing retinal luminance improved acuity, both for persons in their 20's and those in their 60's; however, the values for the older group never reached those for the younger one. From the research on glare sensitivity summarized earlier in this chapter, high levels of ambient illumination may reduce visibility relatively more for older than for younger subjects (see also Weale, 1971, 1975.)

Temporal Factors in Acuity. With constant illumination and size, the time required to identify a target increases with age (Eriksen, Hamlin, and Breitmeyer, 1970). As shown in the left panel of Figure 13, the oldest group required almost ten times as long a presentation as the youngest to reach the same level of performance. Earlier research by Eriksen and Steffy (1964) suggests that presentation times of 300 to 500 msec are required for subjects in their 60's to attain the same level of performance as those in their 20's. Similar age trends have been observed in other studies which have employed different stimuli (Abel, 1972; Rajalakshmi and Jeeves, 1963; Reading, 1972). The results of Figure 13 may be partially explained on the basis that less light reached the retina of the older subjects (an artificial pupil was employed, however).

Eriksen, Hamlin, and Breitmeyer (1970) hypothesized that older subjects may have more time than younger ones to obtain information from a stimulus and provided a test of this idea in a second experiment in which the size of the Landolt ring was adjusted for each

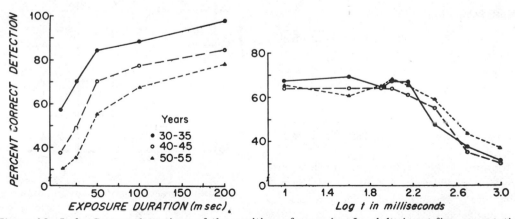

Figure 13. Left: Correct detections of the position of a gap in a Landolt ring at five presentation times for subjects in three age groups. Right: Correct detections of gap when luminance of the target decreased with larger presentation times so that total energy was constant. (From Eriksen, Hamlin, and Breitmeyer, 1970.)

subject so that his detection level was 75 percent with a 10 msec exposure at 1.3 ml. For each of the presentations shown on the right hand panel of Figure 13 the intensity values were adjusted so that the total energy of each combination of presentation time and intensity was constant. The time-intensity reciprocity relationship breaks down at about 146 msec for all three age groups, but the slope of the decay function for the oldest group was less than that of the two younger ones. The results suggest, therefore, that older subjects can trade time for intensity in making judgments for longer periods than younger ones. The authors interpret their results in terms of a central scanning process which is slower for older subjects.

Dynamic Acuity. The age difference in the time required to identify detail in a stationary target is relatively larger if the target is moving (Reading, 1972). Increasing velocity had a relatively greater deleterious effect on the acuity of a group in their 40's than on adults in their 20's. By employing static acuity data, available on the subjects, the contribution of static and dynamic components to the observed results was estimated for each velocity. The correlations decreased with higher target velocities, the amount of decrease being greater in the older group. The practical significance of the findings are that measures of static acuity have limited value in predicting the ability of older persons to detect details in moving targets.

Depth Perception

Information on the relative location of objects in the visual space is obtained by each eye singly on the basis of cues such as object size, overlap, shadows, atmospheric haze, and relative motion. Information to both eyes depends, in addition to the monocular cues, on the binocular cues of convergence and retinal disparity.

Gibson's (1950) concept of visual texture gradients provides one way of interpreting possible age differences in the effectiveness of monocular cues. The gradient of visual texture, defined as the changes with distance in the amount of discriminable small detail, is the major determinant of judgments of apparent size and distance. Losses in acuity and increased susceptibility to glare could accordingly reduce the value of the monocular cues for distance.

In a study of size constancy Leibowitz and Judisch (1967a) found that the size matches of older adults (51–88 years) were, if anything, closer to constancy than those of the group of college students. The judgments were not affected by age-related differences in acuity. The relationship between depth perception based on monocular cues and age requires further research in which the cues contributing to visual texture are varied.

Depth perception that depends on binocular cues has also received little attention with respect to age. Because the quality of stereopsis depends on brightness and contrast, any age related processes that reduce retinal illumination would diminish binocular depth perception.

Jani (1966) tested depth perception in more than 7,000 normal individuals. A device consisting of three short cylindrical rods on a transilluminated surface was pointed in the direction of the eye of an observer who had to distinguish a longer rod from two shorter ones. The mean percentage of correct choices averaged over several distances are shown in curve A of Figure 14. After age 45 a deterioration in stereopsis is seen.

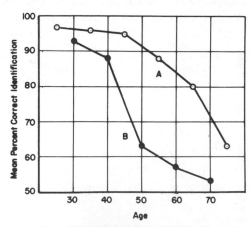

Figure 14. Correct detections of a rod closer or further away from two others in several age groups; data averaged over several viewing distances. (A: Data from Jani, 1966; B: Data from Bell, Wolf, and Bernholz, 1972.)

Bell, Wolf, and Bernholtz (1972) first studied a group of 96 students (18–25 years) and a group of 73 veterans between 45–65 years with a Titmus vision tester. Because the Titmus vision tester is a stereoptic device not requiring accommodation and convergence, two important factors influencing stereopsis, no age-related difference in depth perception was found.

In order to identify the relationship between age and accommodation and convergence, Bell, Wolf, and Bernholtz (1972) then employed a Verhoeff stereopter in which three vertical black bars were seen against a transilluminated screen. The spatial position of the bar that was either in front or behind the plane of the other two had to be recognized. Curve *B* in Figure 14 shows the mean percentage of correct judgments for distances ranging from .25 to 1 meter for 164 males from the Normative Aging Study (Bell, Rose and Damon, 1972) ranging in age from 30–70 years.

As in the case of Jani's data, a drastic change in stereopsis between 40 and 50 years is indicated, whereas before and after this critical decade the changes are much smaller. Because of the coincidence of the changes in stereopsis with changes in the power of accommodation, the authors assume that the changes described are part of the functional changes of the anterior segment of the eye including accommodation convergence, transmissiveness of lens, scatter of light, and sensitivity to glare.

Color Vision

Gilbert (1957) found that with older age there was differential loss of discrimination at the blue end of the spectrum (See also Figure 6) as well as a loss of sensitivity over the entire spectrum. Between 60 and 70 years and between 80 and 90 years mean discrimination scores were 76 percent and 56 percent, respectively, of those obtained by young adults.

Dalderup and Fredericks (1969) studied color vision in 136 elderly residents of two homes for the aged, one for individuals of low socioeconomic status, the other for those of high socioeconomic status. Stilling's pseudoisochromatic tables were used for testing under prevailing daylight. Starting at about age 70 a definite loss in color sensitivity was observed which increased with age. Near age 90 color sensitivity was greatly deficient; less than 50 percent of the colored objects could be identified correctly by individuals in that group. No definite protan, deutan, or tritan anomaly could be discerned. The elderly individuals required about twice as much time to complete the task than young adults. Monocular tests revealed that the two eyes may differ significantly, suggesting that color vision loss proceeds at different rates in the two eyes.

Many of the observations on the elderly are similar to those made in pathological cases of central retinal degenerations: loss of acuity, acquired anomalous trichromacy, protanomaly, deuteranomaly, and tritanomaly are often observed, and it is difficult at this time to decide where the border between normal aging and pathology is to be drawn. On the basis of color discrimination of young and elderly aphakic patients, Lakowski (1962) demonstrated that senile changes in spectral sensitivity of the lens cannot completely account for losses in color vision with age.

Combined Effects of Visual Deficits

Laboratory and clinical determinations of age-related deficits in light sensitivity, acuity, and color vision do not by themselves provide an appreciation of the combined impact of such difficulties on an older individual's overall visual functioning.

Pastalan and his associates (Pastalan, Mautz and Merrill, 1973) have attempted to simulate the combined effects on visual functioning of lens yellowing, opacities, and light scattering by applying special coatings to the lenses of spectacles and cameras. The lenses, created for architects and human factors specialists who plan environments for the elderly, were designed to simulate the visual appearance of scenes to the eyes of a person in their late 70's or early 80's.

The photographs in Figure 15 show comparable views of scenes made through a clear lens and a lens with the special coating. The acuity measured through the lens is about equivalent

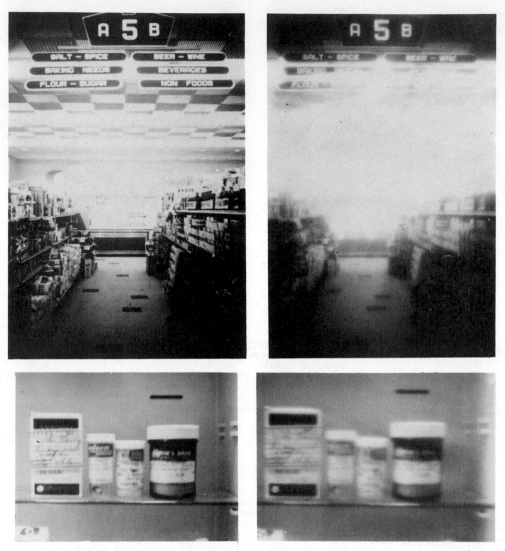

Figure 15. Photographic simulation of scenes as seen by a modal person in their late 70's or early 80's is shown in the right hand member of each pair. The increased susceptibility to glare by the elderly is illustrated in the upper panel, while problems of acuity associated with poor contrast is illustrated in the lower pair. The prints were made from color slides prepared by Dr. Leon Pastalan.

to a Snellen rating of 20/40. The black and white photographs shown in the figure do not convey the effect of the selective absorption of short wavelengths by the lens apparent in the original color photographs but they do illustrate the effects of lowered contrast associated with opacities and the blurring of retinal images.

The research by Pastalan, Mautz and Merrill (1973), Reading (1972), and Wolf (1967) all point to limitations with visual testing devices

that are typically used in connection with driver's tests. For example, many older persons or anyone with a condition which would lead to excessive scattering of light in the eye might perform satisfactorily on the standard acuity and depth perception tests. Yet they could experience appreciable difficulties in driving because of reduced tolerance for glare either in daylight or in the evening where the illumination levels change frequently and unpredictably. Properly validated tests for glare, dark adaptation, dynamic acuity and other visual functioning would add appreciably to the value of visual screening for older drivers.

Overview. Advances have been made toward specifying two groups of structural changes in the eye which affect visual functioning. The first group, beginning in the 30's to 40's, affect the amount of light reaching the retina as well as the refractive power of the eye. New data have become available concerning the effects of glare on perception, the specification of spectral absorption of the lens, and astigmatism, acuity, and depth perception. A quantitative description of the combined effects of these variables on visual functioning is required. Also, many basic questions remain unanswered relative to mechanisms of presbyopia and age changes in acuity and to binocular and monocular cues for depth perception.

The second class of age-related changes occurs in the retina itself, usually becoming evident in the 50's and 60's. Evidence on age-related differences in the size of the visual fields, in dark adaptation, and in extrafoveal sensitivity to CFF has provided the most important new information pointing to changes in the retina.

There is more than a superficial similarity between the physiological and psychological behavior observed in both oxygen want and in aging, because in both there is a diminished availability, or utilization, of oxygen in the central nervous system.

Reduction in the total number of cells, for any reason, is another cause for decreased oxygen uptake. According to this theory, hypoxia may be a result rather than a cause of aging (Himwich and Himwich, 1959). However, in some diseased conditions hypoxia precedes the cell destruction. While oxygen want is not the sole factor in aging, it may be one of the most important single factors

Correlational studies of the age-related differences in pulmonary function (Bell, 1972) indicated that smaller visual fields were correlated with decreased pulmonary function when age was held constant, but subsequent studies failed to demonstrate a significant correlation between blood gases and pulmonary function as measured directly in the arteries.

A direct assessment of the oxygen transfer between the arterial and venous processes of the retina is needed. Another possibility is to study the effects of hyperbaric oxygenation on visual functioning. The emphasis of much current research in this area is on global assessments of cognitive functioning rather than on sensory functioning.

VISUAL INFORMATION PROCESSING

The following sections describe age differences in identifying single alphanumeric targets either in isolation or in the context of static or changing displays in order to provide information on the interaction between the early perceptual process involved in target identification and subsequent decision-making, memory, and response processes.

Briefly Presented Targets

The total amount of time available for an observer to extract information from a display, sometimes called the icon (Neisser, 1967), includes the presentation time of a display itself plus the duration of the positive afterimage. The requirement of older persons for longer presentations could result from greater delays between the presentation of the target and the beginning of the period when information is extracted from the stimulus. It could also result from a shorter afterimage following presentation of the target. Neither possibility excludes the other, but the data of Eriksen, Hamlin, and Breitmeyer (1970) cited earlier suggested that older subjects can extract information from the icon (under conditions of constant energy) for longer periods of time than younger ones.

Using a direct procedure for estimating visual persistence, Walsh and Thompson (1975) found that younger adults stored information for about 40 msec. longer than older ones. Another line of research that bears on the question is called backward visual masking. In this procedure a target stimulus (TS) is presented. Shortly thereafter a second, interfering stimulus called the masking stimulus (MS) is presented which effectively terminates the icon.

The interstimulus interval (ISI) between the TS and MS defines the duration of the icon.

Welsandt, Zupnick, and Meyer (1973) presented one of four letters E, H, K, and X for 8 msec followed by an MS also presented for 8 msec. The ISIs ranged from 0 to 150 msec. In the control condition, no MS was presented. Age groups with mean ages of 5, 10, 16, 19, 22, 35, and 55 years were selected on the basis of acuities of 20/30 or better and at least 85 percent correct responses in the control condition.

For all age groups the performance remained at a chance level between 0 and 25 msec ISIs and then increased sharply with ISIs greater than 50 msec. In the two youngest groups, the slope relating ISI to the fraction of correct identifications increased more slowly than the others and that of the youngest group never reached its no mask asymptote. The oldest group also performed more poorly than the young adults although the age-related differences were confined to performance at ISIs longer than 50 msec. The authors attribute the poorer performance of the children to lack of experience in extracting information from visual displays. The results for the oldest adult group are consistent with the hypothesis that their rate of extracting information from the icon is slower.

Kline and Szafran (1975), using two digit numbers as TSs, varied the presentation times of both the ISI and the TS to determine the combinations of TS and ISI that yielded 50 percent correct identifications of the TS. Two groups, 21–30 and 61–76 years of age, had acuities of 20/25 or better and were screened on the procedure. The MS was presented for 100 msec.

In the no masking control condition, younger subjects required shorter presentations than the older ones. The results for the masking conditions are summarized in Figure 16, which displays the mean ISIs required to detect the TS presented at the values shown on the horizontal axis. The range of time over which the MS exerted its effect was greater for the older group as was the duration of the ISI. The sharp rise in the isoperformance functions at presentation times of the TS below 5 to 8 msec is similar to the results of Welsandt, Zupnick, and Meyer (1973) for very short ISIs.

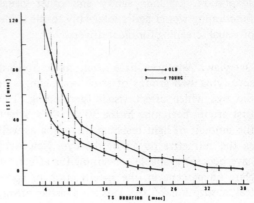

Figure 16. Mean interval (ISI) between the presentation of a two-number digit (TS) and the presentation of a visual masking pattern (MS), required for 50 percent correct identification of the digit in two age groups. Presentation times of the TS are shown on the horizontal axis. The vertical lines indicate values for 1 standard deviation. (From Kline and Szafran, 1975. Reproduced with the permission of the *Journal of Gerontology*.)

Kline and Szafran interpret their results to mean that older subjects require more time to "clear" a stimulus through the nervous system, pointing out that the backward masking occurred at stimulus onset asynchronies sufficiently long so that the sensory message elicited by the TS would have reached the visual cortex by the time the MS was presented.

Walsh (1976), employing a dichoptic backward masking procedure to identify central as opposed to peripheral mechanisms as defined by Turvey (1973), observed that the ISI required to overcome the effects of the MS was 24% longer in adults 60–68 years of age than in a group 18–23 years. On the basis of his reanalysis of Kline and Szafran (1975) data according to Turvey's criteria, Walsh concluded that Kline and Szafran demonstrated age differences in peripheral rather than central perceptual processes (Walsh, 1976, pp. 183–184).

The data of all three studies are consistent with the general hypothesis presented earlier that there is a time frame or psychological moment during which information can be extracted from the icon that is longer for older persons. They are also consistent with the stimulus persistency hypothesis of Botwinick (1973). Application of Turvey's procedure to the problem represents an increase in understanding of central and peripheral factors in age differences in information processing.

Identifying Targets in Complex Displays

Except for the psychologist's laboratory, there are few if any situations in which a person simply identifies a single target presented in the constant background provided by the tachistoscope. Rather, objects are identified in the context of a complex visual background which is itself changing over time.

If the duration of the psychological moment (Stroud, 1949; Kristofferson, 1965; Surwillo, 1968) increases with age, the number of times that portions of a complex visual display can be sampled for a particular target in a given period of time necessarily decreases. Accordingly, longer search times for a target imbedded in a complex static display would be expected for older persons. In a changing display, the fraction of correct identifications of a target would decrease with age because the probability that the target would be sampled in a given period of time is lower.

The role of possible age differences in a central scanning mechanism in identification tasks is difficult to assess because of the relative complexity of the responses typically required in such tasks.

Duration and Presentation Rate. Talland (1966) required groups of 40 men in each age decade from the 20's to the 70's to monitor a circular display of nine continuously changing numerals for the occurrence of the numeral "4" presented on about 20 percent of the trials. In one condition, numerals in the display changed about 54 times per minute; in a second, the rate of change was twice as fast.

Noticeable age declines in performance occurred only in the two oldest groups. The major determinant of identification performance for all subjects was the time that a signal was presented. Results of auxiliary experiments indicated that performance improved in all groups when the rate was lowered to 27 display changes per minute rate and decreased when the density of signals was increased. There were no age differences in strategies or in pattern of commission of errors, nor were there any trade-offs among the effects of frequency of occurrence, the duration, and rate of presentation of the signal. Clearly, the time that a signal was available is the dominant variable determining the age effect.

Number of Items in Display. Rabbitt (1965) investigated age differences in the speed with which subjects in their 20's or 70's could locate one of two letters *A* or *B* on a card, and then place it in one of two stacks. The number of other letters on each card was varied. In a second condition, eight targets (A–H) rather than two were employed. With two response categories, increasing the total number of letters on the card decreased speed of sorting for the older subjects more than that for the younger ones (left panel of Figure 17), a result consistent with the hypothesis of age differences in scanning rates. With eight categories (right panel), the relative difference between the response time of the two groups was less, probably because the successive decision making and movement processes could overlap more.

Rabbitt, noting the interaction between age and the number of irrelevant stimuli when in the two- and eight-category conditions, suggested that the older subjects had smaller perceptual spans. Whether the number of items perceived in a "glance" varies with age or just the scanning rate itself requires an appropriate experimental test. In Rabbitt's experiment, the rate of turning over cards was subject paced, while in the studies by Talland (1966) the subject had no control over the duration of the presentation of either the target stimulus or the irrelevant stimulus.

Slow Rates of Signal Presentation and Response Bias. While monitoring a continuously changing display, the number of correct identifications may change over time even though the demands of the task remain the same. The effect depends on the frequency of presentation of signals and duration of the task. When both are high, as in the study of Talland (1966), some practice effects were observed. In contrast, when the number of signals is very low, performance may decline over time.

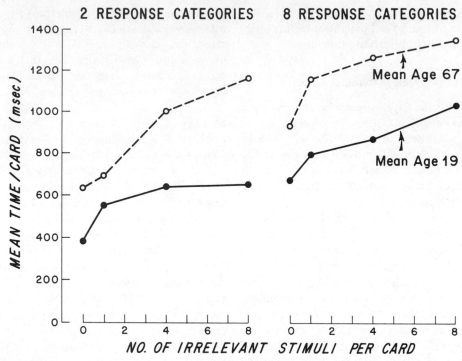

Figure 17. Mean time per card to sort decks of cards with letters into two (left panel) or eight (right panel) piles by two age groups. The number of other (irrelevant) letters on each card in addition to the target letters is indicated on the horizontal axis. (Data from Rabbitt, 1965.)

Surwillo and Quilter (1964) required 106 men 22–88 years of age to monitor the movement of a hand on a faceless clock which rotated 28 minutes of arc each second. About once every 2.6 minutes the hand moved 56 minutes of arc, and the subject was to report those events by pressing a key. Between the first and fourth quarters of an hour-long test period, performance of the older subject dropped from 78 percent to about 57 percent while that of the younger dropped from about 82 percent to 71 percent. There were no age differences in the latencies of the responses nor the number of errors. With these very low rates of signal presentation, age difference in performance is not attributable to difficulties in remembering the target, because the task provided a constant reference for judgments of the unique event. Rather the effect appears to be associated with boredom with the task or fatigue.

Target Identification with Memory Load. In the experiments cited above, the observer monitored a display for the occurrence of a single target. In other paced inspection tasks (Davies, 1968) the target is defined as a series of two or more sequentially presented letters or digits that are similar by some arbitrary rule, e.g., two consecutive letters the same, three consecutive odd digits, etc. The subject accordingly must store and evaluate perceptual information over several discrete stimulus events in order to identify the target. When such requirements are superimposed upon the monitoring task, the age effect on performance becomes more pronounced (Canestrari, 1963; Szafran, 1968; Thompson, Opton, and Cohen, 1963; Davies, 1968; Fozard, Carr, Talland, and Erwin, 1971; Fozard, Nuttall, and Waugh, 1972; Harkins, Nowlin, Ramm, and Schroeder, 1974). Results of all the experiments indicate that older subjects simply require more time to complete all of the psychological processes involved in making their responses. The major age difference in performance is in the number of missed signals rather than strategies. The alternative hypotheses suggested by Davies

(1968) to explain the age differences observed in such experiments require experimental evaluation.

Continuous Perceptual-Motor Tasks. The effects of perceptual factors on continuous tracking performance has been studied in relation to a pursuit tracking task by Welford (1958, pp. 85-96). Subjects were required to keep a pointer aligned with a track that resembled a curving road by controlling a handwheel. The perceptual variable manipulated was the amount of the moving track that could be seen by the subject. The response or output variable was the amount of gain that was possible in the steering wheel. Increasing the amount of track that the subject could see decreased the amount that the subject "lagged" behind the track by the same absolute amount for subjects of all ages. On the other hand increasing the gain helped the older subjects relatively more than younger ones only when the subject could preview the track. Neither manipulation brought the performance of the older subjects to the level of the youngest ones. The results are consistent with the hypothesis that the limiting effects of performance of stimulus variables are constant across age.

Finally, Welford, Norris, and Shock (1969) required subjects to strike alternatively two rectangular targets with a stylus. The size and separation of the two rectangles varied. The speed and variability of performance was related to age groups of male subjects covering a span from 20 to 70 years. They concluded that: "... factors of positional sense and motor control decline more with age than do the decisional processes responsible for ... the accuracy of homeing in on a target" (p. 13).

The research summarized in this section leaves many questions unanswered about the role of perceptual variables in age differences in information processing. In particular the central scanning hypothesis needs direct experimental test if it is to be more than an after-the-fact explanatory concept. It will be important to determine the sufficient conditions for obtaining a masking effect in older persons. Another relevant experimental procedure would be to use perceptual judgments of temporal discrimination to identify the resolving power of the nervous system (e.g., Efron, 1973; Yund and Efron, 1974).

Future research based on a visual information processing model would also provide a reasonable approach to the three neglected areas of perceptual research that were identified in Comalli's (1967) review: perceptual constancies, adaptation, and visual factors in social perception.

Little information is available on the relationship between perceptual processes and other sources of individual differences in perceptual processes such as social class or education. Research with the Primary Mental Abilities Test (Schaie, 1970) indicates that age differences in the spatial factors in that test are sensitive to cohort effects. The fluid intelligence component of intelligence as defined by Cattell (1963) contains many perceptual tasks that on a cross-sectional basis do not appear to be related to education. Cross-sectional research with the General Aptitude Test Battery (Fozard and Nuttall, 1971, 1972; Fozard, Nuttall, and Waugh, 1972) indicates that measures of spatial visualization and perceptual matching are factorially distinguishable from perceptual motor tasks involving guidance of repetitive finger and hand movements. Neither factor correlated strongly with differences in education, and both correlated differently with age. The significance of these data requires elucidation in further research.

Except for some work relating performance on paced inspection tasks to measures from standard intelligence or ability tests (Thompson, Opton, and Cohen, 1963; Fozard, Nuttall, and Waugh, 1972), there has been little work relating performance on laboratory-based tasks to intelligence test scores.

CONTEXT EFFECTS IN PERCEPTUAL JUDGMENTS AND INFORMATION PROCESSING

Perceptual judgments are made on the basis of stimulus information that may be incompatible with expectations or incomplete or both. Perceptual whole-part differentiation, set, and closure are defined using stimulus materials constructed according to these principles.

Perceptual Flexibility and Stimulus Satiation

Age-related differences have been reported in the ability to switch between two alternative views that may be seen in a single test object. In addition, age differences in the threshold for and duration of the perceptual aftereffects resulting from inspection of a test object have been reported. Central processes are significant in such judgments because the behavior occurs either in response to a test object that does not itself change or after the stimulus object has been removed from view.

Necker Cube. Heath and Orbach (1963) required institutionalized men and women 65 to 90 years of age to report any reversals in the perspective of the two-dimensional drawing of the cube. The 6 of the 31 subjects who were able to recognize the sketch as three-dimensional, to understand the instructions, and to report reversals reported 1 to 48 reversals, values that are lower than those reported for young adults but are comparable to those for patients with frontal lobe damage. The authors believe that their results indicate the presence of a nonspecific central neural fatigue factor, but their findings may have other explanations. The act of counting the number of reverses in perspective of a static figure is highly incongruous with the everyday experiences of most persons and may be more so for an elderly individual. In their study, no systematic attempt was made to determine minimal conditions under which the target behavior would occur.

Ambiguous Figures. Botwinick, Robbin, and Brinley (1959) showed a drawing of a face that could be seen either as a young or an old woman to one group of male subjects 19–34 years old and to another 65–81 years of age. When the subject saw one of the faces in the ambiguous figure, he was told to try to identify the other; if he failed, he was shown an unambiguous version of the other figure and then shown the ambiguous figure a second time and asked if he could now identify the second figure.

During the initial presentation of the ambiguous picture, the vast majority of subjects in both groups saw the young woman first and very few changed perspective.

Of the younger subjects who had to be shown the unambiguous figure of the other figure, almost 80 percent saw the other figure; the corresponding figure for the older subjects was 24 percent. Most older subjects failed to see the second figure in the unambiguous picture.

The ambiguous figure was clearly not very ambiguous to subjects in either age group with the result that there was a response bias against the shift. Also there are few occasions in life in which one expects to observe two figures in a single drawing, especially when the drawing involves a face. The question of defining the sufficient conditions for a threshold effect therefore remained unclear.

In later research Botwinick (1961) reduced the response bias by using a different stimulus figure. Botwinick (1973, p. 148), in discussing both studies, concluded that the difficulty in seeing the old person in the composite reflected greater difficulty in perceiving it in the first place.

Another problem concerned the interpretation of the use of the unambiguous view of the second figure. Without data from suitable control conditions in which the subject was shown the other figure in the ambiguous figure itself, it is difficult to specify what perceptual effects the exposure to the unambiguous figure may have produced. The question of possible age differences in perceptual flexibility is not answered by these studies.

Binocular Rivalry. Observers ranging in age from 40 to 93 years viewed a green patch in one side of a stereoptic viewer and a red one in the other (Jalavisto, 1964). Binocular rivalry, as indicated by frequency of oscillations reported, decreased in older subjects, while fusion, as indicated by reporting a grey color, increased. Since fusion and rivalry occur centrally, Jalavisto concluded that the reduction in rivalry represented an age difference in brain function. Jalavisto's work failed to establish the sufficient conditions defining age differences for fusion and rivalry. Older persons may be more likely to expect a single rather than an oscillating figure. Another factor that may have increased the likelihood of fusion in older subjects is that the green patch may not have been as bright to older subjects as to the younger ones. Enough is known about stereopsis and binocular vision (e.g., Aafjes, Hueting, and Visser, 1966; Adler, 1965, pp. 853–858; and Graham, 1965) so that the relative contributions of central and peripheral factors to the understanding of age-related differences in perceptual processes is possible.

In the three studies summarized above the subject was required to perceive changes in a single figure. In the experiments to be described below, age differences in perceptual aftereffects resulting from inspection of a test figure were assessed by studying perceptual judgments in a second one.

Figural Aftereffects. Eisdorfer and Axelrod (1964) required subjects to fixate a dot while viewing rectangles on either side of it. An inspection figure was placed between one of the two figures and the fixation dot for a minute. After the inspection figure was removed, the observer adjusted the rectangle on the side of the fixation dot opposite that in which the inspection figure had been placed so that both rectangles appeared equidistant from it. The aftereffect is such that the rectangle should appear farther away from the fixation point after inspection. When the adjustment was made just after the removal of the inspection figure, the average displacement of a group in their 20's was about twice that of a group in their 60's, but the difference disappeared after a 2-minute interval. The older subjects' performance stayed about the same over all intervals.

The significance of the age trends is difficult to interpret partly because of the complexity of the procedures and partly because of questions about the interpretation of figural aftereffects. The sufficient conditions for establishing the aftereffect in older persons are not clear; the occasions on which one consciously encounters apparent displacement of a figure in space because it has been viewed next to another for a 60-second period are slight. Also, without the use of data from control conditions in which the variable and constant errors associated with

the matching judgments were made without the satiation figure, it is difficult to identify the perceptual aspect of the effect. Finally, on the basis of results of research in which both the size and location of the inspection and test figures were varied, Freeman (1964) has presented evidence indicating that the figural aftereffect is best explained by size contrast effects rather than displacements. His interpretation mitigates against a satiation hypothesis which was the original basis for the research procedure and its interpretation.

Spiral Aftereffects. Griew, Fellows, and Howes (1963) reported that duration of the aftereffect in a group 18–25 years old increased linearly as the logarithm of the duration of the stimulus (15–60 seconds), a typical result (see Fozard, Fuchs, Palmer, and Smith, 1965). The older subjects, 60–81 years of age, had a mean aftereffect identical to the younger group at the shortest duration, but it increased much more slowly with increasing duration until 30 seconds and then exceeded that of the younger group at the 60-second inspection time. The results may be due to possible age differences in response bias and acuity; yet there is little doubt that both young and old subjects usually gave a positive response to the stimulus. Because it is known that the average duration of the aftereffect may be manipulated by varying either the rate of convergence of the spiral or its speed of rotation (Fozard et al., 1965), the Archimedes spiral may be a promising method for assessing age differences in perceptual aftereffects.

Botwinick (1973, pp. 138–142) interprets the data on aftereffects in terms of a stimulus persistence hypothesis according to which higher thresholds for altered perceptions and aftereffects are attributable partly to a greater time required to establish a perception in older persons. Corso (1971) concluded that because there is little age difference in the perceptual responses once the threshold for eliciting them is exceeded, the data provide little support for the idea that the aftereffect can be used as an index of age differences in central nervous system activity. The finding that the figural aftereffects are very specific to modality support Corso's view.

Stimulus-Response Incompatibility

Unconventional arrangements of display and control elements in man-machine systems result in increased operator errors and slower responses (Tolin and Simon, 1968). In a normal condition of a two-choice reaction task, the subject was to respond to the presentation of a light on his right with his right hand by pushing the key just below it, and vice versa. In the reversed condition, the stimulus-response relationship was the opposite. In a group of subjects with an average age of 20 and another with a mean age of 72 years, reversal of the conventional stimulus-response relationships increased reaction times above that observed with normal stimulus relationships by the same absolute amount. Simon and Wolf (1963) systematically varied the angular orientation of two stimulus lights between normal and reversed conditions with reference to two fixed response levers. The reaction times for a young and elderly group increased as the angular displacement changed from normal to reversed. Again, the absolute difference between the reaction times of young and old subjects across conditions remained the same. As there was no statistically significant interaction between stimulus conditions and age in either study, it would appear that the strategies of the young and old subjects were similar; the older persons were simply slower.

In one control condition of the Stroop color-word test, the subject reads the names of colors printed in black ink; in another he names the colors of patches shown. In the experimental condition, he names the color of the ink which is different from the color named, e.g., responding "blue" if the word "green" is printed in blue ink.

Comalli, Wapner, and Werner (1962) reported results from groups of subjects ranging from a mean age of 5 to 86. In all cases, the time taken to perform on the experimental task was greater than on the two control tasks, but the relative difference was greater in the two oldest groups and in the youngest group of children than in the teenagers and the young

and middle-aged adults. The finding has been confirmed by other investigators (e.g., Bettner, Jarvik, and Blum, 1971). One explanation for the results is that older adults, who have had relatively more experience with conventional relations between names of colors and the colors of the ink in which they are printed, would require relatively more time than younger ones to adapt to the novel requirements of the task. Practice effects are not usually studied in the task in relation to age, partly because only the total time for all responses is recorded.

Schonfield and Trueman (1974) created three variations on the task. Two involved making the color of either the first or second half of the letters of the word the same as the color named by the word. In the third, the colors of both halves of the word differed from the color named by it. Average reading speeds for groups in their 20's to their 60's increased least with age when the color of the first half of the word corresponded to the color named by the word and most when neither color was the same. In comparison to younger adults, older ones are better adapted to conventional color-name configurations and are, accordingly, relatively more sensitive to disruptive context effects.

Geometrical Illusions

Susceptibility to the four geometric illusions shown in Figure 18 has been evaluated in both children and adults. In Figure 18, the pairs of line segments or circles to be compared in each illusion are objectively equal, but because of the context effects produced by the figures or lines adjacent to or abutting them, they appear different. At present, there is no satisfactory theory of the illusions which permits a systematic classification of them, either in terms of their stimulus properties (Graham, 1965, pp. 564-566) or the age-related differences in responses to them that have been reported (Pollack, 1969; Eisner, 1972a).

Consistent age-related differences in susceptibility to the Müller-Lyer illusion in adulthood have been demonstrated. Wapner, Werner, and Comalli (1960) concluded that susceptibility to the illusion is greater in childhood and old age than it is in young and middle adulthood. In this and many subsequent studies, subjects were

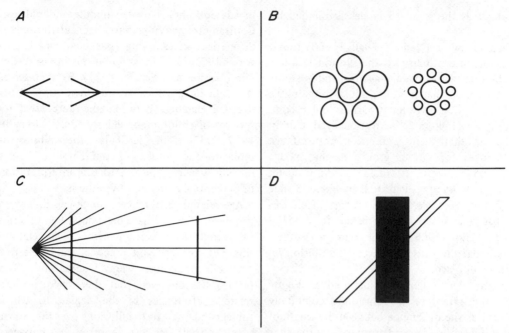

Figure 18. The geometric illusions discussed in the text. A: Müller-Lyer illusion; B: Satellite Circles or Titchner Circles illusion; C: Ponzo illusion; D: Poggendorf illusion.

instructed to adjust the segment with the angles pointing out until it appeared subjectively equal to the fixed segment with the angles pointing in. The difference was lowest in a group of adults ranging in age from 20-40 years and larger in children under 10 and adults over 50 years. The observed age trends were not entirely systematic, e.g., the mean scores of a group with an average age of 42 years was almost the same as those of children 5-10 years old. Using the same procedure, Comalli (1965) and Comalli, Krus, and Wapner (1965) found no differences among various groups of institutionalized and community dwelling elderly residents although the elderly groups appeared to be more susceptible to the illusion than the young adults. No direct statistical comparison of the mean values of all the age groups was made.

Gajo (1966), using the same stimuli and procedures, found that susceptibility to the illusion was significantly greater in groups of 30 men and women 60-77 years than in either of two younger groups (30-44 and 45-59 years, respectively). Using the same subjects Gajo obtained almost the identical results when the method of limits rather than the method of adjustment was employed.

Eisner and Schaie (1971) found that susceptibility to the illusion increased in males ranging in age from 55-75 years. The identical test was readministered to the same subjects 6 months later. There was no significant change in the degree of susceptibility to the illusion. The overall age trend based on the averages of both tests was statistically significant. Direct comparison of the results of this study with the others is difficult because the simple main effects for age for the separate test occasions were not reported. The authors hypothesized that generational rather than maturational differences account for a substantial part of the significant cross-sectional age effect observed, but 6 months is probably too short a time interval for estimating possible age changes in the responses to the illusions.

In each of the studies of the Müller-Lyer illusion described above, susceptibility of the Satellite Circles illusion was also measured (Figure 18B). The method of limits was employed to determine the diameter of a variable circle surrounded by eight circles that appeared as small as the standard circle surrounded by five circles.

Wapner, Werner, and Comalli (1960) found that the susceptibility to the illusion was less in children whose average age is 6 and in adults older than 50 than in young adults in their 20's and 30's. Comparison of various older community-dwelling and institutionalized elderly indicated that there were no significant age differences for various groups ranging in age from 65–81 years (Comalli, 1965; Comalli, Krus, and Wapner, 1965). Eisner and Schaie (1971) were unable to find any age differences in groups of males ranging in age from 55–74 years. Gajo (1966), using two procedures, found that the susceptibility to the illusion *increased* with age.

In the Ponzo illusion illustrated in Figure 18C, the extent of the illusion is commonly defined as the difference between the length of the standard line located farther from the apex and that of the variable line located closer to the apex.

Research by Leibowitz and Judisch (1967b) confirms earlier findings that susceptibility to the illusion increases from a negligible amount at ages younger than 5 years to a maximum in early adulthood. They also observed a substantial drop in the magnitude of the illusion in adult groups aged between 58 and 82 years, a finding that was not confirmed in a subsequent study by Farquhar and Leibowitz (1971). The conservative conclusion is that susceptibility to the illusion remains stable over the adult age range.

Leibowitz and Gwozdecki (1967) studied age differences in susceptibility to the Poggendorf illusion (Figure 18D) using the same subjects employed in the study of the Ponzo illusion reported by Leibowitz and Judisch (1967b). Subjects adjusted the upper right segment of the diagonal line so it appeared as a straight line with a lower left segment. The average setting of the variable segment was similar for adults in different age groups.

The results of all of the studies reviewed are consistent in showing that the susceptibility to geometrical illusions decreases between childhood and adulthood, but only one of them, the Müller-Lyer illusion, shows subsequent increase

in susceptibility between middle and old age. Contradictory results have been attributed to differences in sampling (Farquhar and Leibowitz, 1971) and in stimulus materials (Gajo, 1966; Eisner and Schaie, 1971). By themselves the data on illusions provide little support for drawing parallels between the perceptual responses of children and elderly adults (Comalli, 1967; 1970). In particular the failures to replicate the results of the Satellite Circles illusion weaken the case for the interpretation of perceptual regression hypothesis.

Age-related differences in susceptibility to geometric illusions have been described in terms of overall mean constant errors. The relationship between age and practice, variable errors and discrimination were studied by Gajo (1966). He observed that there were no age-related differences in the degree to which subjects adapted to the illusions over the course of eight trials. He also reported that between-subject variability in the oldest group was less than in the others even though those individuals were more susceptible on the average to the illusion. Intrasubject variability did not differ significantly across age.

The effect of errors of discrimination associated with age that were independent of the effect of the illusion were measured by having the subjects adjust the lengths of the lines without the arrows attached before the trials of the illusion test were administered. Gajo concluded that there are age differences in the perceptual components of the responses to the illusion beyond discrimination errors. A similar analysis of the data from the Satellite Circles illusion in which the age differences in matching the size of the two circles was the same both with and without the surrounding circles showed that the discrimination errors accounted for a much larger portion of the age differences reported. Thus a greater set for accuracy in the oldest group could account for the age-differences observed.

Gajo's analysis of age differences in the Müller-Lyer illusion are consistent with the hypothesis of Fozard and Thomas (1975) which states in effect that older persons are more susceptible to the effects of unusual variations in stimulus configurations than are younger ones. An adequate evaluation of this hypothesis would require an experiment in which the response set of the subject with respect to the criterion for his judgments is systematically varied. In addition to the above hypotheses that are based essentially on supposed age differences in response biases, the role of age differences in acuity and brightness contrast effects merit investigation (e.g., Sjostrom and Pollack, 1971).

Judgments of Verticality

Investigators have compared age groups in judgments of verticality of a stimulus object such as a rod or their own bodies either when the frame surrounding the rod or when the chair or the room in which the observer is seated is tilted. Comalli, Wapner, and Werner (1959) and Comalli (1965) studied the effect of varying the tilt of the chair in which the subject was seated on judgments of the verticality of a luminescent rod in a dark room. For teenagers and young and middle-aged adults, the rod appeared vertical when it was tilted opposite to the side of tilt of the body. In elderly adults and young children, the rod was judged vertical when its orientation was the same as that of the body. These results were not obtained in a similar study by Davies and Laytham (1964). The explanation of these trends by Comalli (1970) is that the elderly and children appear to have a relatively more egocentric organization of space. Another possible explanation for the adults is that they were more likely to compromise conflicting postural and visual cues in a highly unconventional task setting. Experiments in which instructions for practice and adaptation were varied would clarify the interpretation.

In a variation of the task, a luminous frame surrounding the test rod was tilted as well as the chair in which the subject was seated. From ages 20 through 70, the contextual effects of the tilted frame and chair on judged verticality increased, the effect being largest when both body and frame were tilted to the same side and least when the body was erect and the frame alone was tilted. The results show again that in contrast to young adults older persons were relatively more sensitive to the unusual context for perceptual judgments provided by the procedures.

Closure

Identification of objects or words on the basis of incomplete or mutilated figures are examples of perceptual closure. Comalli (1963) found that groups in their 50's or older performed relatively more poorly than younger adults on the most difficult closure tasks. As Comalli (1970, p. 224) points out, the age difference could be due to lessened integrative ability or more a function of factors such as cautiousness or giving up or becoming fixated on isolated parts of the stimulus. The age effects were largest in the case of the most familiar stimuli, i.e., the mutilated words, as would be expected on the basis of the view of Fozard and Thomas (1975).

Age differences were also reported in the recognition of familiar pictures, but not designs, when parts of the picture were presented sequentially (Wallace, 1956). This finding is consistent with the hypothesis that the functioning of older subjects is relatively more disrupted by unconventional task requirements.

The opposite side of the coin to closure is flexibility, usually defined by the ability to change perception of a familiar figure as its representations metamorphose to those of a different figure. In a sequence of drawings, an initial picture of a cat was changed so that the final picture represented a dog (Korchin and Bosowitz, 1956). Older subjects changed their perceptual judgments later in the series than did younger ones. Botwinick (1962), using different stimuli and instructions, found just the opposite. The result of the Botwinick study was to demonstrate that the effect depends heavily on the set given the subjects. Little attention has been given to constructing stimulus series which have elements that are equally discriminable to young and old. This is especially important when drawings of familar objects are used in the sequence, as older observers might be less likely either to attend to small details which constitute the changes or even able to detect them.

Most of the research reviewed on closure, whole part differentiation, flexibility, and illusions has been guided by the Werner-Wapner-Comalli theory of perceptual regression, the Witkin perceptual style framework, or the Piagetian developmental model. The similarities between the performance of children and the elderly reported are not yet explained satisfactorily. A useful approach would be to identify the conditions in which perceptual judgments can be modified in either young children or the elderly. Although the hypothesis of perceptual regression rests largely on the observation of age similarities in performance on several different perceptual tasks, there has with few exceptions (Eisner, 1972b,c) been little systematic study of the correlations among the tasks employed.

Many of the tasks required the observer to assume a highly unconventional frame of reference for his judgments; accordingly, more attention ought to be paid to possible age-related differences in interpretations of the task requirements (Blenkner, 1967). Meaningful theories await a better understanding of these effects.

PRACTICAL APPLICATIONS

The level of illumination required for various tasks varies over a wide range depending on the details of the task. Perhaps the single most difficult design problem in planning visual environments suitable for the elderly centers around determining suitable levels of illumination for various activities (e.g., see Welford, 1958). As Guth (1957) and Weston (1949) have shown, the level of illumination required for various tasks by the elderly is greater than for young persons. Because of his greater susceptibility to glare, the older person cannot benefit from increased illumination in many situations. Practical information was given by Guth, Eastman, and McNelis (1956) and by Guth and McNelis (1969). The general principle that should guide practice in this area is to allow for more individual control of lighting so that the illumination of particular tasks may be varied independently of that for the total area. The needed research in this area is straightforward, but, with few exceptions noted earlier, it has not been performed. In designing visual environments for heterogeneous populations, one principle would be to design for the average older eye rather than for the average young one (McFarland, 1968; Fozard and Thomas, 1973).

The data on age changes in accommodation, refraction, astigmatism, and color vision reviewed in the chapter make clear what the ophthalmologist and optometrist have realized from clinical practice for years, i.e., it is often more difficult to provide spectacle prescriptions for older patients because multiple visual problems may make it difficult to achieve an optimal prescription. In addition, the question of the relationship of the conditions of testing to those experienced in the everyday visual world becomes more critical. Despite the large number of relevant clinical surveys reported, little if any systematic follow-up research has been described.

Early detection and intervention is possible to a larger degree than is now practiced in glaucoma and diabetic retinopathy. While the incidence of these diseases is relatively low in the elderly, it seems clear that in both cases routine tests by the general practitioner could help identify them when they occur.

The cumulative bibliography published in the *Journal of Gerontology* includes many applied articles concerning the optimal professional advice on visual problems that can be given to the elderly and the possibilities for rehabilitation for elderly who develop visual handicaps. However, to our knowledge, no controlled clinical studies evaluating alternative approaches to counseling or rehabilitation involving comparisons across age groups has been reported. There is clinical evidence suggesting that considerable care is required in explaining to the elderly patients the limitations of spectacles and, more importantly, low vision aids (Bell, 1968).

CONCLUSIONS

The major issues which have been addressed in this review include: (a) the relationship between age-related structures of the eye and visual functioning; (b) psychophysiological theories of visual thresholds and discrimination; (c) gestalt and life-span approaches on perceptual research and intelligence testing; and (d) the application of information processing and ecological theories of behavioral development to understanding visual perception.

The size of the reference list and level of detail in the review attest to the advances that have been made in the first two of the four areas mentioned above. Research in relation to the second two has emerged in importance mostly in the last decade and shows promise as a conceptual tool for analyzing age differences in perceptual processes. In the next decade, major scientific advances could be achieved if an adequate account of age differences in oxygen utilization and transport by the retina and nervous system is achieved and if the improvement in our understanding of relationship between presbyopia and the mechanisms of accommodation made by Fisher (1971, 1973) continue.

Elucidation of the relationships among the various physiological factors which affect age differences in vision and the psychological factors relating response bias to perceptual judgments need a unifying theoretical concept and a common set of measurement procedures. Many opportunities exist for useful work in this area.

At a practical level, very little has been done to use existing information to improve visual functioning of the elderly. The needs for applied research, improved specifications of lighting requirements, and improved procedures for medical intervention are great. The development of surgical procedures to reduce opacities in vitreous would be of great benefit. The work of the last decade and earlier years summarized in this chapter will provide a good basis for the needed advances in both research and applications.

REFERENCES

Aafjes, M., Hueting J. E., and Visser, P. 1966. Individual and interindividual differences in binocular retinal rivalry in man. *Psychophysiology*, 3, 18–22.

Abel, M. 1972. The visual traces in relation to aging. Unpublished doctoral dissertation, Washington University, St. Louis, Missouri.

Adler, F. H. 1965. *Physiology of the Eye*. 5th Edition. St. Louis, Missouri: C. V. Mosby.

Allen, M. J. 1956. The influence of age on the speed of accomodation. *Am. J. Optom.*, 33, 201–208.

Anderson, B., and Palmore, E. 1974. Longitudinal evaluation of ocular function. *In*, E. Palmore (ed.), *Normal Aging*, pp. 24–32. Durham, North Carolina: Duke University Press.

Bell, B. 1968. Maintenance therapy in vision and hearing for geriatrics patients. *In*, J. Rudd and R. J. Margolins (eds.), *Maintenance Therapy for the Geriatrics Patient*, pp. 187–201. Springfield, Illinois: Charles C. Thomas.

Bell, B. 1972. Retinal field shrinkage, age, pulmonary function and biochemistry. *Aging and Human Development*, 3 (1), 103–111.

Bell, B., Rose, C. L., and Damon, A. 1972. The normative aging study: An interdisciplinary and longitudinal study of healthy aging. *Aging and Human Development*, 3, 5–17.

Bell, B., Wolf, E., and Bernholz, C. D. 1972. Depth perception as a function of age. *Aging and Human Development*, 3 (1), 77–88.

Bettner, L. G., Jarvik, L. F., and Blum, J. E. 1971. Stroop color-word-test, non-psychotic organic brain syndrome and chromosome loss in aged twins. *J. Gerontol*, 26, 458–469.

Birren, J. E. 1970. Toward an experimental psychology of aging. *American Psychologist*, 25, 124–135.

Birren, J. E., Casperson, R. C., and Botwinick, J. 1950. Age changes in pupil size. *J. Gerontol.*, 5, 267–271.

Birren, J. E., and Shock, N. W. 1950. Age changes in rate and level of dark adaptation. *J. Appl. Physiol.*, 26, 407–411.

Blenkner, M. 1967. Environmental change and the aging individual. *Gerontologist*, 7, 101–105.

Botwinick, J. 1961. Husband and father-in-law—a reversible figure. *Amer. J. Psych.*, 74, 312–313.

Botwinick, J. 1962. A research note on the problem of perceptual modification in relation to age. *J. Gerontol.*, 17, 190–192.

Botwinick, J. 1973. *Aging and Behavior*. New York: Springer.

Botwinick, J., Robbin, J. S., and Brinley, J. F. 1959. Reorganization of perception with age. *J. Gerontol.*, 14, 85–88.

Bouma, P. J. 1947. Perception on the road when visibility is low. *Philips Tech. Rev.*, 9, 149–157.

Braun, H. W. 1959. Proceptual processes. *In*, J. E. Birren (ed.), *Handbook of Aging and the Individual*, Chap. 16. Chicago: University of Chicago Press.

Brown, J. L. 1965. The structure of the visual system. *In*, C. H. Graham (ed.), *Vision and Visual Perception*, pp. 39–59. New York: John Wiley.

Brückner, R. 1967. Longitudinal research on the eye. *Gerontol. Clin.*, 9, 87–95.

Bryfogle, J. W., and Bradley, R. F. 1957. The vascular

complications of diabetes mellitus: A clinical study. *Diabetes*, 6, 159.

Burch, P. R. J., Murray, J. J., and Jackson, D. 1971. The age prevalence of arcus-senilis, greying of hair, and baldness: Etiological considerations. *J. Gerontol.*, 26, 364–372.

Burg, A. 1967. Light sensitivity as related to age and sex. *Perceptual Motor Skills*, 24, 1279–7288.

Burg, A. 1968. Lateral visual field as related to age and sex. *J. Appl. Psych.*, 52, 10–15.

Canestrari, R. E. 1963. The relationship of vigilance to paced and self-paced learning in young and elderly adults. *Dissertation Abstr.*, 24, 2130–2131.

Cattell, R. B. 1963. Theory of fluid and crystallized intelligence: A critical experiment. *J. Educ. Psych.*, 54, 1–22.

Chamberlain, W. 1970. Restriction in upward gaze with advancing age. *Trans. Am. Opthalmol. Soc.*, 68, 235–244.

Comalli, P. E., Jr. 1963. Perceptual closure in middle and old age. Presented at the Gerontological Society, Boston, Massachusetts, October, 1963.

Comalli, P. E., Jr. 1965. Cognitive functioning in a group of 80–90 year old men. *J. Gerontol.*, 20, 14–17.

Comalli, P. E. 1967. Perception and age. *Gerontologist*, 7 (2), 73–77.

Comalli, P. E., Jr. 1970. Life-span changes in visual perception. *In*, L. R. Goulet and P. B. Baltes (eds.), *Life-Span Developmental Psychology*, pp. 211–226. New York: Academic Press.

Comalli, P. E., Jr., Krus, M., and Wapner, S. 1965. Cognitive functioning in two groups of aged: One institutionalized, the other living in the community. *J. Gerontol.*, 20, 9–13.

Comalli, P. E., Jr., Wapner, S., and Werner, H. 1959. Perception of verticality in middle and old age. *J. Psych.*, 47, 259–266.

Comalli, P. E., Jr., Wapner, S., and Werner, H. 1962. Interference effects of Stroop color-word test in childhood, adulthood, and aging. *Journal of Genetic Psychology*, 100, 47–53.

Corso, J. F. 1971. Sensory processes and age effects in normal adults. *J. Gerontol.*, 26, 90–105.

Crossman, E. R. F. W., and Szafran, J. 1956. Changes with age in the speed of information-intake and discrimination. *Experientia*, Suppl. IV, 128–135.

Dalderup, L. M., and Fredericks, M. L. C., 1969. Colour sensitivity in old age. *J. Am. Geriat. Soc.*, 17, 388–390.

Davies, A. D., and Laytham, G. W. 1964. Perception of verticality in adult life. *Brit. J. Psychol.*, 55, 315–320.

Davies, D. R. 1968. Age differences in paced inspection tasks. *In*, G. A. Talland (ed.), *Human Aging and Behavior*, pp. 217–238. New York: Academic Press.

Davis, M. D. 1971. Opthalmic problems in diabetes mellitus. *In*, S. S. Fajans and K. E. Sussman (eds.), *Diabetes Mellitus: Diagnosis and Treatment*, Vol. III, pp. 323–328. New York: American Diabetes Association.

Domey, R. G., and McFarland, R. A. 1961. Dark adaptation as a function of age: Individual prediction. *Am. J. Opthalmol.*, 51, 1262–1268.

Domey, R. G., McFarland, R. A., and Chadwick, E. 1960a. Dark adaptation as function of age and time: II. A derivation. *J. Gerontol.*, 15, 267–279.

Domey, R. G., McFarland, R. A., and Chadwick, E. 1960b. Threshold and rate of dark adaptation as functions of age and time. *Human Factors*, 2, 109–119.

Duane, A. 1931. Accommodation. *Arch. Opthalmol.*, 5, 1–14.

Efron, R. 1973. Conservation of temporal information by perceptual systems. *Percept. and Psychophys.*, 14, 518–530.

Eisdorfer, C., and Axelrod, S. 1964. Senescence and figural aftereffects in two modalities: A correction. *Journal of Genetic Psychology*, 104, 193–197.

Eisner, D. A. 1972a. Developmental relationships between field independence and fixity-mobility. *Perceptual Motor Skills*, 34, 767–770.

Eisner, C. A. 1972b. Explanations of visual illusions in middle and old age. *Journal Supplement Abstract Service*, 2, 106.

Eisner, D. A. 1972c. Life-span age differences in visual perception. *Perceptual Motor Skills*, 34, 857–858.

Eisner, D. A., and Schaie, K. W. 1971. Age change in response to visual illusions from middle to old age. *J. Gerontol.*, 26, 146–150.

Ekman, G. 1955. Two generalized ratio scaling methods. *J. Psych.*, 45, 287–295.

Engerman, R. L., Davis, M. I., and Bloodworth, J. M. B., Jr. 1971. Retinopathy in experimental diabetes: Its relevance to diabetic retinopathy in man. *In*, R. R. Rodriguez and J. Valence-Owen (eds.), *Diabetes*, pp. 261–267. Amsterdam: Excerpta Medica.

Eriksen, C. W., Hamlin, R. M., and Breitmeyer, R. G. 1970. Temporal factors in visual perception as related to aging. *Percept. and Psychophys.*, 7, 354–356.

Eriksen, C. W., and Steffy, R. A. 1964. Short-term memory and retroactive interference in visual perception. *J. Exp. Psych.*, 68, 423–434.

Fankhauser, F., and Schmidt, T. 1957. Die Untersuchung der Funktionen des dunkeladaptierten Auges mit dem Adoptometer Goldmann-Weekers. *Opthalmologica*, 133, 264–272.

Farquhar, M., and Leiboiwtz, H. 1971. The magnitude of the Ponzo illusion as a function of age for large and small stimulus configurations. *Psychon. Sci.*, 25, 97–99.

Feinberg, R., and Podolac, E. 1965. Latency of pupillary reflex to light and its relationship to aging. *In*, A. T. Welford and J. E. Birren (eds.), *Behavior, Aging and the Nervous System*, pp. 326–339. Springfield, Illinois: Charles C. Thomas.

Fincham, E. F. 1937. The mechanism of accommodation. *Brit. J. Opthalmol.*, Suppl. No. 8, 5–80.

Fincham, E. F., and Walton, J. 1957. The reciprocal actions of accommodation and convergence. *J. Physiol.*, 137, 488–508.

Fisher, R. F. 1968. The variations of the peripheral visual fields with age. *Docum. ophthal.*, **24**, 41–67.

Fisher, R. F. 1969a. Elastic constants of human lens capsule. *J. Physiol.*, **201**, 1–19.

Fisher, R. F. 1969b. The significance of the shape of the lens and capsular energy in accommodation. *J. Physiol.*, **201**, 21–47.

Fisher, R. F. 1971. The elastic constants of the human lens. *J. Physiol. (Lond.)* **212**, 147–180.

Fisher, R. F. 1973. Presbyopia and the changes with age in the human crystalline lens. *J. Physiol.*, *(London)* **228**, 765–779.

Fozard, J., Carr, G. D., Talland, G. A., and Erwin, D. E. 1971. Effects of information load, sensory modality and age on paced inspection performance. *Quart. J. Exp. Psych.*, **23**, 304–310.

Fozard, J. L., Fuchs, M., Palmer, M., and Smith, A. M. 1965. Effects of six presentation conditions on the duration of the spiral aftereffect. *U.S. Gov. Res. and Develop. Rep.*, A. D. 623–647.

Fozard, J. L., and Nuttall, R. L. 1971. General Aptitude Test Battery scores by age and socioeconomic status. *J. Appl. Psych.*, **55**, 372–379.

Fozard, J. L., and Nuttall, R. L. 1972. General Aptitude Test Battery scores for men in different age and socioeconomic status groups. *In*, G. Shatto (ed.), *Employment of the Middle Aged*, pp. 117–140. Springfield, Illinois: Charles C. Thomas.

Fozard, J. L., Nuttall, R. L., and Waugh, N. C. 1972. Age-related differences in mental performance. *Aging and Human Development*, **3**, 19–44.

Fozard, J. L., and Thomas, J. C. 1973. Why aging engineering psychologists should get interested in aging. Presented at American Psychological Association, Montreal, Ontario, Canada, August, 1973.

Fozard, J. L., and Thomas, J. C. 1975. Psychology of aging: Basic findings and their psychiatric applications. *In*, J. G. Howells (ed.), *Modern Perspectives in the Psychiatry of Old Age*, pp. 107–169. New York: Brunner-Mazel.

Freeman, R. B. 1964. Figural after-effects: Displacement or contrast? *Amer. J. Psych.*, **70**, 607–613.

Fuchs, E. 1928. Über den Ciliarmuskel. *V. Graefes. Arch. Opthalmol.*, **120**, 733–741.

Gajo, F. D. 1966. Visual illusions. Unpublished doctoral dissertation, Washington University, St. Louis, Missouri.

Gibson, J. J. 1950. *The Perception of the Visual World*. Boston: Houghton Mifflin.

Gilbert, J. G. 1957. Age changes in color matching. *J. Gerontol.*, **12**, 210–215.

Goldmann, H. 1937. Studien uber die Alterskernstreifen der Lense. *Arch. Augenheilk.*, **110**, 405–414.

Gordon, D. M. 1965. Eye problems of the aged. *J. Am. Geriat. Soc.*, **13**, 398–417.

Graham, C. H. (ed.) 1965. *Vision and Visual Perception*. New York: John Wiley.

Gregory, R. L. 1957. "Neurological noise" as a factor in aging. *Proceedings of the Fourth Congress of the International Association of Gerontology*, Vol. 1, pp. 314–324. Merano, Italy: International Association of Gerontology.

Griew, S., Fellows, B. J., and Howes, R. 1963. Duration of spiral aftereffect as a function of stimulus exposure and age. *Perceptual Motor Skills*, **17**, 210.

Guth, S. K. 1957. Effects of age on visibility. *Am. J. Optom.*, **34**, 463–477.

Guth, S. K., Eastman, A. A., and McNelis, J. F. 1956. Lighting requirements for older workers. *Illum. Eng.*, **11**, 656–660.

Guth, S. K., and McNelis, J. F. 1969. Visual performance, subjective differences. *Illum. Eng.*, **24**, 576–578.

Harkins, S. W., Nowlin, J. B., Ramm, D., and Schroeder, S. 1974. Effects of age, sex, and time on watch on a brief, continuous performance task. *In*, E. Palmore (ed.), *Normal Aging*, II, pp. 140–150. Durham, North Carolina: Duke University Press.

Harrison, R., and Wolf, E. 1964. Ocular studies with special reference to glaucoma in a group of 107 elderly males. *Am. J. Opthalmol.*, **57**, 235–241.

Heath, H. A., and Orbach, J. 1963. Reversibility of the Necker Cube: IV. Responses of elderly people. *Perceptual Motor Skills,* **17**, 625–626.

Henderson, J. W., and Prough, W. A. 1950. Influence of age and sex on flow of tears. *Arch. Opthalmol.*, **43**, 224–231.

Himwich, W. A., and Himwich, H. E. 1959. Neurochemistry of aging. *In*, J. E. Birren (ed.), *Handbook of Aging and the Individual*, pp. 187–215. Chicago: University of Chicago Press.

Hinchcliffe, R. 1962. Aging and sensory thresholds. *J. Gerontol.*, **17**, 45–50.

Holladay, L. L. 1926. The fundamentals of glare and visibility. *J. Opt. Soc. Am.*, **12**, 271.

Jalavisto, E. 1964. The phenomenon of retinal rivalry in the aged. *Gerontologia*, **9**, 1–8.

Jalavisto, E., Orma, E., and Tawast, M. 1951. Aging and relationship between stimulus intensity and duration in corneal sensitivity. *Acta. Physiol. Scand.*, **23**, 224–233.

Jani, S. N. 1966. The age factor in stereopsis screening. *Am. J. Optom.*, **43**, 653–655.

Kapoor, P. M. 1965. Total astigmatism and its components: Its changes with age. *Indian J. Med. Res.*, **53**, 10.

Korchin, S. J., and Basowitz, H. 1956. The judgment of ambiguous stimuli as an index of cognitive functioning in aging. *J. Pers.*, **25**, 81–95.

Kline, D. W., and Szafran, J. 1975. Age differences in backward monoptic visual noise making. *J. Gerontol.*, **30**, 307–311.

Krall, L. P., and Podolsky, S. 1971. Long-term clinical observations of diabetic retinopathy. *In*, R. R. Rodriguez and J. Vallence-Owen (eds.), *Diabetes*, pp. 268–275. Amsterdam: Excerpta Medica.

Kristofferson, A. B. 1965. Attention in time discrimination and reaction time. Bolt Beranek and Newman, Inc., *NASA Rep.* CR-194.

Kumnick, L. S. 1956. Aging and the efficiency of the pupillary mechanism. *J. Gerontol.*, **11**, 160–164.

Lakowski, R. 1962. Is the deterioration of colour discrimination with age due to lens or retinal changes? *Farbe,* **11,** 69–86.

Lawton, M. P., and Nahemow, L. 1973. Ecology and the aging process. *In,* C. Eisdorfer and M. P. Lawton (eds.), *The Psychology of Adult Development and Aging,* pp. 619–674. Washington, D. C.: American Psychological Association.

Lehnert, W., and Wuensche, H. 1966. Das Electroretinogramm in verschiedenen Lebensaltern. *Graefe Arch. Clin. und Exp. Opthalmol.,* **170,** 147–155.

Leibowitz, H., and Judisch, J. M. 1967a. Size constancy in older persons: A function of distance. *Amer. J. Psych.,* **80,** 294–296.

Leibowitz, H., and Judisch, J. M. 1967b. The relation between age and the magnitude of the Ponzo illusion. *Amer. J. Psych.,* **80,** 105–109.

Leibowitz, H. W., and Gwozdecki, J. 1967. The magnitude of the Poggendorff illusion as a function of age. *Child Development,* **38,** 573–580.

Lewis, E. M., Jr. 1972. Interaction of age and alcohol on dark adaptation time. *Department of Health Education and Welfare. Injury Control Res. Lab. Rep.* ICRL-RR-70-9.

Leydhecker, W. 1959. Zur Verzeitzung des Glaucoma Simplex in der scheinbar gesunden augenärztlich nicht behandelten Bevöekerung. *Doc. Ophthalmol.,* **13,** 359–380.

Löpping, B., and Weale, R. A. 1965. Changes in corneal surface during occular convergence. *Vision Res.,* **5,** 207–215.

McFarland, R. A. 1963. Experimental evidence of the relationship between ageing and oxygen want: In search of a theory of aging. *Ergonomics,* **6,** 339.

McFarland, R. A. 1968. The sensory and perceptual processes in aging. *In,* K. W. Schaie (ed.), *Theory and Methods of Research on Aging,* pp. 3–52. Morgantown, West Virginia: West Virginia University Press.

McFarland, R. A., Domey, R. G., Warren, A. B., and Ward, D. C. 1960. Dark adaption as a function of age: I. A statistical analysis. *J. Gerontol.,* **15,** 149–154.

McFarland, R. A., and Fisher, M. B. 1955. Alterations in dark adaptation as a function of age. *J. Gerontol.,* **10,** 424–428.

McFarland, R. A., Warren, A. B., and Karis, C. 1958. Alterations in critical flicker frequency as function of age and light: dark ratio. *J. Exp. Psych.,* **56,** 529–538.

Macsareg, P. V. J., Jr., Lasagna, L., and Snyder, B. 1968. Arcus not so senilis. *Ann. Internal Med.,* **68,** 345–354.

Marble, A. 1971. Current concepts of diabetes. *In,* A. Marble, P. White, R. F. Bradley, and L. P. Krall (eds.), *Joslin's Diabetes Mellitus, Eleventh Edition,* pp. 1–9. Philadelphia: Lea & Febiger.

Marin-Amat, M. 1956. The physiological variations of the corneal curvature during life; their significance in ocular refraction. *Bull. Soc. Belge. Opthalmol.,* **113,** 251.

Marks, L. E. 1974. *Sensory Processes: The New Psychophysics.* New York: Academic Press.

Miller, D., and Wolf, E. 1969. A model for comparing the optical properties of different sized cornea. *Am. J. Opthalmol.,* **67,** 724–728.

Miller, D., Wolf, E., Gair, S., and Vesallo, V. 1967. Glare sensitivity related to the use of contact lenses. *Arch. Opthalmal.,* **78,** 448–450.

National Society for Prevention of Blindness. 1966. Estimated statistics on blindness and vision problems. New York: National Society for the Prevention of Blindness, Inc.

Neisser, U. 1967. *Cognitive Psychology.* New York: Appleton-Century-Crofts.

Pastalan, L. A., Mautz, R. K., and Merrill, J. 1973. The simulation of age related-losses: A new approach to the study of environmental barriers. *In,* W. F. E. Preiser (ed.), *Environmental Design Research, Vol. 1.,* pp. 383–392. Stroudsberg, Pennsylvania: Powden, Hutchinson and Ross.

Paton, D., and Craig, J. A. 1974. Cataracts: Development, diagnosis, management. *CIBA Clinical Symposia,* **26** (3), 1–32.

Pollack, R. H. 1969. Some implications of ontogenetic changes in perception. *In,* D. E. Elkind (ed.), *Studies in Cognitive Development.* New York: Oxford University Press.

Prince, J. H. 1965. *Introduction to Aging and Pathology of the Retina.* Springfield, Illinois: Charles C. Thomas.

Rabbitt, P. 1965. An age-decrement in the ability to ignore irrelevant information. *J. Gerontol.,* **20,** 233–238.

Rajalakshmi, R., and Jeeves, M. A. 1963. Changes in tachistoscopic form perception as a function of age and intellectual status. *J. Gerontol.,* **18,** 375–378.

Reading, V. M. 1972. Visual resolution as measured by dynamic and static tests. *Pflüg. Arch.,* **333,** 17–26.

Renard, G. 1947. La synérgie pupillaire à la convergence. *Rev. Otoneuroophtalmol,* **19,** 240.

Richards, O. W. 1966. Vision at levels of night road illumination. XII. Changes of acuity and contrast sensitivity with age. *Am. J. Optom.,* **43,** 313–319.

Robertson, C. J. 1937. Effect of fatigue on the adjustment of the eye. *Arch. Ophthalmol.,* **17,** 859–876.

Rosengren, B. 1950. Studies in depth of the anterior chamber of the eye in primary glaucoma. *Arch. Ophthalmol.,* **44,** 523.

Said, F. S., and Weale, R. A. 1959. The variation with age of the spectral transmissivity of the living human crystalline lens. *Gerontologia,* **3,** 213–231.

Salmony, D. and Weale, R. A. 1961. Data cited in R. A. Weale, *The Aging Eye.* London: W. K. Lewis.

Scammon, R. E., and Hesdorffer, M. B. 1937. Growth in man and volume of the human lens in postnatal life. *Arch. Ophthalmol.,* **17,** 104–112.

Schäfer, W. D., and Weale, R. A. 1970. The influence of age and retinal illumination on the pupillary near reflex. *Vision Res.,* **10,** 179–191.

Schaie, K. W. 1970. A reinterpretation of age related

changes in cognitive structure and functioning. *In*, L. R. Goulet and P. B. Baltes (eds.), *Life-Span Developmental Psychology: Research and Theory*, pp. 485–507., New York: Academic Press.

Schonfield, D., and Trueman, V. 1974. Variations on the Stroop theme. Presented at the Gerontological Society, Portland, Oregon.

Sedan, J., Farnarier, G., and Ferrand, G. 1958. Contribution à l'étude de la keratesthesie senile. *Acta XVIII Int. Cong. Ophthalmol., Bruxelles*, 1, 385–387.

Simon, J. R., and Wolf, J. D. 1963. Choice reaction time as a function of angular stimulus-responses correspondence and age. *Ergonomics*, 6, 99–105.

Simonson, E., Anderson, D., and Keiper, C. 1967. Effect of stimulus movement on critical flicker fusion in young and older men. *J. Gerontol.*, 22, 353–356.

Sjostrom, K. P., and Pollack, R. H. 1971. The effect of simulated receptor aging on two types of visual illusions. *Psychon. Sci.*, 23, 147–148.

Stieve, R. 1949. Über den Bau des menschlichen Ciliarmuskels, seine Veränderungen während des Lebens und seine Bedeutung für die Akkommodation. *Anat. Anz.*, 97, 69–79.

Straub, W. 1957. Über den gegenwärtigen stand der Klinischen Elektroretinographie. In H. Sautter (ed.), *Bibliotheca Ophthomologica Elektroretinographie*. Symposium 26-27 Mai, 1956, Hamburg, H.R.S.G. Vol. 48, pp. 137–160. Basel: Karger.

Stroud, J. 1949. The psychological moment in perception. *In*, V. Foerster (ed.), *Conference on Cybernetics, Transactions of the Sixth Conference*, pp. 27–63. New York: Josiah Macy Jr. Foundation.

Surwillo, W. W. 1968. Timing of behavior in senescence and the role of the nervous system. In G. A. Talland (ed.), *Human Aging and Behavior*, pp. 1–36. New York: Academic Press.

Surwillo, W. W., and Quilter, R. E. 1964. Vigilance, age and response time. *Amer. J. Psych.*, 77, 614–620.

Szafran, J. 1968. Psychophysiological studies of aging in pilots. *In*, G. A. Talland (ed.), *Human Behavior and Aging*, pp. 37–74. New York: Academic Press.

Talland, A. 1966. Visual signal detection, as a function of age, input rate, and signal frequency. *J. Psych.*, 63, 105–115.

Thompson, L. W., Opton, E. M., Jr., and Cohen, L. D. 1963. Effects of age, presentation speed and sensory modality on performance of a "vigilante" task. *J. Gerontol.*, 18, 366–369.

Tolin, P., and Simon, J. R. 1968. Effect of task complexity and stimulus duration on perceptual-motor performance of two disparate age groups. *Ergonomics*, 11, 283–290.

Turvey, M. T. 1973. On peripheral and central processes in vision: Inferences from an information-processing analysis of masking with patterned stimuli. *Psychological Rev.*, 80, 1–52.

United States National Health Survey. 1968. Monocular-binocular visual acuity of adults. Public Health Service Pub. No. 100-Series 11-No. 30. 1960-62.

Washington, D.C.: U.S. Department of Health, Education and Welfare.

von Bahr, G. 1956. Corneal thickness, its measurement and changes. *Am. J. Opthalmol.*, 42, 251–269.

Wallace, J. G. 1956. Some studies of perception in relation to age. *Brit. J. Psychol.*, 47, 283–297.

Walls, G. L. 1942. *The Vertebrate Eye*. Bloomfield Hills, Michigan: Cranbrook Institute of Science.

Walsh, D. A. 1976. Age differences in central perceptual processing: A dichoptic backward masking investigation. *J. Geront.*, 31, 178–185.

Walsh, D. A. & Thompson, L. W. 1975. Age differences in the persistence of visual storage. Paper presented at the Gerontological Society Meeting, Louisville, Ky., October.

Walton, W. G. 1950. Refractive changes in the eye over a period of years. *Amer. J. Optom.*, 27(6), 267–286.

Wapner, S., Werner, H., and Comalli, P. E. 1960. Perception of part-whole relationships in middle and old age. *J. Gerontol.*, 15, 412–416.

Weale, R. A. 1961. Retinal illumination and age. *Trans. Illum. Eng. Soc.*, 26, 95–100.

Weale, R. A. 1962. Presbyopia. *Brit. J. Ophthalmol.*, 46, 660–668.

Weale, R. A. 1963. *The Aging Eye*. London: H. K. Lewis.

Weale, R. A. 1965. On the eye. *In*, A. T. Welford and J. E. Birren (eds.), *Aging, Behavior and the Nervous System*, pp. 307–325. Springfield, Illinois: Charles C. Thomas.

Weale, R. A. 1971. The aging eye. In, *The Scientific Basis of Medicine: Annual Reviews*. British Postgraduate Medical Federation, pp. 244–260. Atlantic Highlands, New Jersey: Athlone Press (Humanities).

Weale, R. A. 1973. The effect of the ageing lens on vision. In, The Ciba Foundation Symposium 19, *The Human Lens—in relation to cataract.*, pp. 5–24. Amsterdam, North Holland: Elsevier.

Weale, R. A. 1975. Senile changes in visual acuity. *Trans. ophthal. Soc. U.K.*, 95, 36–38.

Weekers, R., and Roussel, F. 1946. Introduction à l'étude de la fréquence de fusion en clinique. *Ophthalmologica*, 117, 305–319.

Weiss, A. P. 1959. Sensory functions. *In*, J. E. Birren (ed.), *Handbook of Aging and the Individual*, Chap. 15. Chicago: University of Chicago Press.

Welch, R. J. 1969. Causes of blindness in additions to MRA Registers for 1967. Proceedings of the 1969 Conference of Model Reporting Area for Blindness. Washington, D.C.: U.S. Government Printing Office.

Welford, A. T. 1958. *Ageing and Human Skill*. London: Oxford University Press.

Welford, A. T., Norris, A. H., and Shock, N. W. 1969. Speed and accuracy of movement and twin changes with age. *Acta Psychol.*, 39, 3–15.

Welsandt, R. F., Zupnick, J. J., and Meyer, P. A. 1973. Age effects in backward visual masking. *J. Exp. Child Psychol.*, 15, 454–461.

Weston, H. C. 1949. On age and illumination in relation to visual performance. *Trans. Illum. Eng. Soc.* (London), **14**, 281–297.

White, P. 1960. Childhood diabetes: Its course, and influence on the second and third generations. *Diabetes*, **9**, 345.

Wolf, E. 1960. Glare and age. *Arch. Ophthalmol.*, **64**, 502–514.

Wolf, E. 1967. Studies on the shrinkage of the visual field with age. *Highway Res. Rec.*, **167**, 1–7.

Wolf, E., and Gardiner, J. S. 1965. Studies on the scatter of light in the dioptric media of the eye as a basis of visual glare. *Arch. Opthalmol.*, **74**, 338–345.

Wolf, E., and Schraffa, A. M. 1964. Relationship between critical flicker frequency and age in flicker perimetry. *Arch. Opthalmol.*, **72**, 832–843.

Yund, E. W., and Efron, R. 1974. Dichoptic and dichotic micropattern discrimination. *Perceptual Motor Skills,* **15**, 383–390.

21
AUDITORY PERCEPTION AND COMMUNICATION

John F. Corso
State University of New York, Cortland

INTRODUCTION

In adults the most common source of auditory deficiency is probably presbycusis. Presbycusis is characterized by a progressive bilateral loss of hearing for tones of high frequency due to degenerative physiological changes in the auditory system as a function of age. With increasing knowledge on the complex sensory and behavioral changes which occur with age (Corso, 1968, 1971), the problems related to presbycusis and other hearing disorders emerge in new perspective since the implications of these disorders cannot be isolated from the aging person's total repertoire of behavior.

Prevalence of Deafness

United States. Any attempt to specify the prevalence of deafness in the United States or elsewhere is at best an approximation. There are three major reasons for this: (1) the definition of deafness has not been universally accepted by authorities in the field; (2) sampling procedures in large-scale studies have often been inadequate; and (3) survey data on hearing abilities tend to lack precision due to measurement problems. Nevertheless, within these limitations, some tentative generalizations may be made.

At present there are approximately 236,000 deaf individuals in the United States, including 38,000 children in schools for the deaf. In addition, there are approximately 6 million persons who have a bilateral hearing loss of sufficient magnitude to produce a social handicap and approximately 2.5 million individuals who do not have a severe handicap, but show unilateral hearing impairments (U.S. Department of Health, Education, and Welfare, 1969).

There are now at least 17 million people in the United States who are 65 years or over and by 1980 this age group will number approximately 24 million (U.S. Department of Health, Education, and Welfare, 1963). Given that approximately 13 percent or more of this age group will show advanced signs of presbycusis, the need for expanding present audiological services becomes readily apparent.

Figure 1 shows the increase in the incidence of deafness from 1945 to the present, with a projection to the year 2000. It is estimated that by the end of the century there will be 80 percent more hard of hearing persons in the United States than exist today (Watson and Tolan, 1967).

Other Countries. Except for a few isolated studies, reliable data are lacking on the prevalence of hearing disorders in other countries. In England, Scotland, and Wales, a large-scale study indicated that 1,765,000 persons or ap-

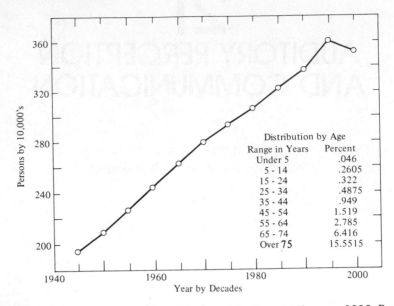

Distribution by Age	
Range in Years	Percent
Under 5	.046
5 - 14	.2605
15 - 24	.322
25 - 34	.4875
35 - 44	.949
45 - 54	1.519
55 - 64	2.785
65 - 74	6.416
Over 75	15.5515

Figure 1. Estimate of the increase in the incidence of deafness to the year 2000. Population forecasts prepared by U.S. Bureau of the Census in cooperation with the Scripps Foundation for Research in Population Problems. Distribution of deafness by age categories based upon National Health Survey (Beasley, 1938). (Adapted from Watson and Tolan, 1967.)

proximately 4.9 percent of the population were hard of hearing or deaf. Approximately 1 percent of the 20-year-olds and 9 percent of the 65-year-olds were found to have hearing impairments (Wilkins, 1950).

In Sweden, it is estimated that 1.5 percent of those 67 years or over have serious hearing problems, but in Denmark the estimate is considerably higher at 6 percent (Liden, 1968).

Voice Communication: The Interrelation of Speech and Hearing

Hearing is a major sensory modality and any serious impairment of this modality will probably produce a concomitant problem in voice communication. Hearing disorders interact with speech disorders and the communication process which is vital for effective social interaction tends to be impaired in older adults. Thus, problems of hearing impairment should no longer be viewed in purely statistical or theoretical terms, but in personal terms since they affect both the social and psychological adjustment of the older individual. The kind and magnitude of the adjustment problem will be

related directly to the severity of the hearing disorder and the time of its inception.

Figure 2 outlines in a highly simplified manner, the functional aspects of the human nervous system in voice communication. The nervous system is arbitrarily divided into three sections and Figure 2 illustrates the information flow from the receptor subsystem, through the central processing subsystems, to the effector subsystems. The significance of Figure 2 is that it shows how the successful execution of the sequence of activities in voice communication depends upon the integration of auditory and oral processes. Both processes must operate at an appropriate level for each individual in the given situation; if there is a serious impairment in either process, effective communication cannot be maintained.

Statement of Purpose

The purpose of this chapter, therefore, is threefold: (1) to consider the basic physiological and functional changes which occur with age in man's vocal and auditory systems; (2) to determine how these changes may affect

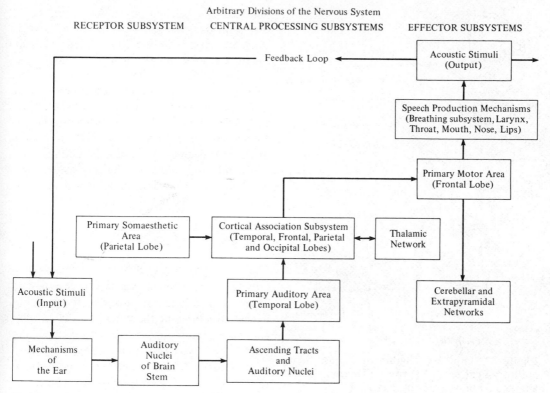

Figure 2. Schematic diagram of the functional aspects of the human nervous system in voice communication.

auditory perception and the process of speech communication; and (3) to examine the psychological implications of speech and hearing disorders in older adults, with attention directed towards vocal and aural rehabilitation programs as a means of effecting more adequate personal and social adjustment in the presence of these disorders.

CLINICAL FEATURES OF THE AGING AUDITORY SYSTEM

The human auditory system consists of the ear and its associated neural pathways. These pathways are organized into afferent and efferent subsystems, with the fiber tracts of the two subsystems running parallel to each other at all levels without intermixing (Desmedt, 1960). The primary function of the afferent subsystem is to encode the information in the acoustic stimulus into neural patterns which are transmitted to the auditory cortex in the temporal lobes of the cerebral hemispheres; the efferent subsystem appears to provide a feedback control function (excitatory and inhibitory) on the effectiveness of the acoustic input (Whitfield, 1967).

A schematic representation of the ascending auditory pathway is shown in Figure 3. With age, deterioration may occur in the neural structures at any level, as well as in the peripheral components of the ear that are directly involved in sound transmission. Some of the major changes will be described in this section.

Outer Ear

Pinna. In older adults the pinna often appears hard and inflexible, with an alteration in size and shape. The length and breadth of the pinna may increase by several millimeters (Tsai, Chou, and Cheng, 1958). However, the functional significance of these changes, if any, has not been ascertained.

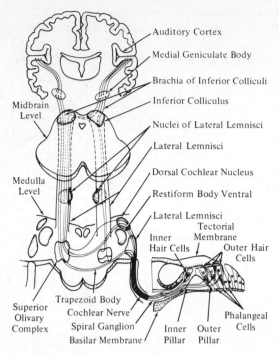

Figure 3. Simplified diagram of the ascending auditory pathways. (From Flanagan, 1965; adapted from drawings by Nettler.)

External Auditory Meatus. Atrophic changes have been reported in the supporting walls of the external auditory meatus (Magladery, 1959) and excessive accumulations of cerumen have been frequently observed in the elderly (Richards, 1971). The impacted wax may produce a conductive loss in hearing ability, thereby confounding the effects of presbycusis which is essentially a sensori-neural problem.

Middle Ear

Eustachian Tube. Another common finding in the elderly, as well as in young children, is the accumulation of fluid in the middle ear due to an obstruction in the Eustachian tube, usually in conjunction with a cold. As long as the tube remains closed, a hearing impairment will be present (Richards, 1971).

Ossicular Chain. Histological study of the middle ear joints in individuals ranging from infancy to 96 years shows that arthritic changes occur in the incudomalleal and incudostapedial joints of the ossicular chain. As age increases, the arthritic changes become more severe. These changes, however, do not seem to impair sound transmission through the middle ear (Etholm and Belal, 1974).

Otosclerosis is also found in older persons and adds a component of conductive hearing loss to the sensori-neural loss of presbycusis (Gross, 1969). Since older individuals with otosclerosis often have decreased cochlear functioning, the treatment of otosclerosis by a stapedectomy operation may be beneficial but it will not completely restore the hearing process.

Inner Ear

Cochlea. According to Schuknecht and Igarashi (1964), four general classes of disorders may be observed as a function of age in the morphological structures of the inner ear: (1) atrophy and degeneration of hair cells and supporting cells in the basal coil of the cochlea (sensory presbycusis); (2) loss of auditory neurons (neural presbycusis); (3) atrophy of the stria vascularis in the scala media with corresponding deficiencies in the bioelectric and biochemical properties of the endolymphatic fluids (metabolic presbycusis); and (4) atrophic changes in the structures associated with vibration of the cochlear partition (mechanical presbycusis). The tectorial membrane may also show a marked thickening with restrictive adhesions (Hansen and Reske-Nielsen, 1965).

For each of these classes of disorders, audiometric data show a characteristic hearing pattern. Sensory presbycusis produces a high frequency loss, but does not involve speech frequencies; neural presbycusis affects speech discrimination without a parallel loss in pure tone thresholds; metabolic presbycusis shows a nearly uniform threshold loss for all frequencies with loudness recruitment; and mechanical presbycusis produces increasing hearing loss values from low to high frequencies.

Retrocochlear Structures. Contradictory findings have been reported regarding the loss of neurons in the ventral cochlear nucleus (VCN) with advancing age. Kirikae and Shitara (1961) and Hansen and Reske-Nielsen (1965) observed the loss of cells in the VCN, as well as other degenerative changes, but Konigsmark and Murphy (1970) did not. While the mean neuronal population of the VCN remained constant at 63,000 cells, the volume was found to vary with age from a maximum of 12.1 cubic millimeters at 50 years to 8.2 cubic millimeters at 90 years. The decrease in VCN volume was attributed to a decrease in the number of myelinated axons and not to a loss of auditory cells.

With increasing age the ganglion cells of the medial geniculate body show a reduction in number and shrinkage in size, with an accumulation of pigment. Beyond 68 years the size of the ganglion cells is also reduced in the superior olivary nucleus. In the inferior colliculus, the medium-size nerve cells become irregular in shape and the small-size cells show an increase in the ratio between the size of the nucleus and that of the cell body (Kirikae, Sato, and Shitara, 1964).

The functional significance of retrocochlear disturbances involves the impairment of directional hearing and decreased speech discrimination, even when pure tone thresholds remain normal (Kirikae, 1969).

Central Auditory Pathways and Brain. There are relatively few studies with aged individuals concerning the pathological and anatomical alterations in the central auditory pathways and brain. Scheidegger (1963) maintains that as a consequence of arteriosclerosis both diffuse and localized changes occur in the brain and suggests that these alterations affect the cerebral pathways and auditory centers in the same way. More specifically, Hansen and Reske-Nielsen (1965) have reported severe degeneration in the glial part of the acoustic nerve, as well as in the white matter of the brain stem and hearing centers. The temporal lobes show normal stratification of the cortex, but ganglion cell loss is present; with the deterioration of cells there is an accumulation of degenerative products in the cytoplasm. The alterations appear to be bilaterally symmetrical.

Vascular System. Aging of the auditory system also involves vascular changes. In presbycusis

there is a marked loss of capillaries in the spiral ligament of the scala vestibuli, with a less pronounced loss in the scala tympani. The radiating arterioles of the scala vestibuli may also atrophy, becoming narrower with thickened walls, but no changes typical of arteriosclerosis have been found (Johnsson and Hawkins, 1972).

With the loss of vessels, there is a loss of nuclei and cell substance in the spiral ligament and atrophy of the stria vascularis is observed. Strial atrophy is most severe in the middle and apical turns of the cochlea, whereas the degeneration of hair cells is most marked in the basal turn (Johnsson and Hawkins, 1972). In some instances, atrophy of the spiral ligament is accompanied by sensori-neural hearing losses which are greater than those that can be attributed to the loss of hair cells or ganglion cells. This finding is interpreted in terms of a cochlear conductive hearing loss (Wright and Schuknecht, 1972).

Further observations have involved the fundus of the internal auditory meatus in the region of the basal coil of the cochlea (Krmpotic-Nemanic, 1969). With age, there is an accumulation of bony substance at the entrance of the cochlear branch of the auditory artery which appears to produce degenerative changes in the walls of the arterial vessels. However, many other age-related factors may influence the blood supply in the inner ear structures so that the functional significance of these changes remains unknown (Fitsch, Dobozi, and Greig, 1972).

Despite the general lack of evidence, the possibility remains that arteriosclerosis may occur in the cochlea. Bochenek and Jachowska (1969) suggest that arteriosclerosis may be not only an essential concomitant of presbycusis, but a causative factor. Recent data indicate, however, that age-dependent changes in vision and audition occur independently of cardiovascular abnormalities (Webster, 1974).

Temporal Bone. According to the hypothesis of Sercer and Krmpotic-Nemanic (1958) on the pathogenesis of presbycusis, aging produces a progressive bone apposition in the fundus of the internal auditory canal which gradually reduces the number of holes accommodating the nerve fibers of the spiral tract; consequently, the nonaccommodated nerve fibers degenerate. It is estimated that from 2 to 26 years there are on the average 32,500 acoustic nerve fibers; but from 44 to 60 years, only 30,300 fibers. By 80 or 90 years, the channels for the nerve bundles are almost completely closed by osteoid and contain few, if any, fibers (Krmpotic-Nemanic, 1969). The changes in the structure of the temporal bone are reported to be correlated with audiometric data on presbycusis.

AUDITORY PSYCHOPHYSICS IN OLDER ADULTS

Basic Functions of Hearing

Threshold Sensitivity. In recent years there has been considerable interest in attempting to specify normal threshold values for non-noise exposed individuals of increasing age. Data from eight studies (American Standards Association, 1954; Beasley, 1938; Corso, 1963a; Glorig and Nixon, 1962; Glorig, Wheeler, Quiggle, Grings, and Summerfield, 1957; Hinchcliffe, 1959; Jatho and Heck, 1959; Johansen, 1943) have been selected and statistically combined by Spoor (1967) to provide derived values showing the relation between hearing level and age at different frequencies. The presbycusic data based on the combined studies were modified by Lebo and Reddell (1972) to conform to the 1969 calibration data of the American National Standards Institute (1970) and are presented in Figure 4 for men. The corresponding data for women are shown in Figure 5.

The curves indicate that for frequencies up to 1,000 Hz the increase in hearing level (poorer hearing) is less than 5 dB to 50 years and, regardless of sex, is essentially independent of frequency. Above 1,000 Hz, hearing level increases with frequency for all groups, but the increases to 40 years are less than approximately 10 dB for both men and women. Up to 50 years, the highest hearing level is at 4,000 Hz and 6,000 Hz, beyond this age the highest level is at 8,000 Hz.

As previously reported (Corso, 1963b), the hearing level for men is higher than that for

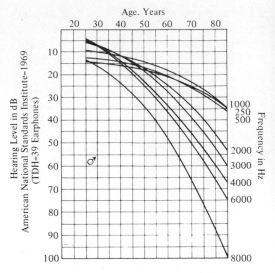

Figure 4. Spoor's (1967) composite presbycusis curves for men, modified to conform to ANSI-1969 standard. (From Lebo and Reddell, *Laryngoscope*, 1972, Figure 3, p. 1403.)

women, age held constant, for 2,000 Hz and above; at and below 1,000 Hz, the hearing level for women tends to be slightly higher than that for men. Similar results have been obtained for subjects ranging from 70 to 88 years (Schaie, Baltes, and Strother, 1964). After about 32 years for men and 37 years for women, some

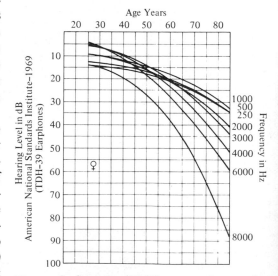

Figure 5. Spoor's (1967) composite presbycusic curves for women, modified to conform to ANSI-1969 standard. (From Lebo and Reddell, *Laryngoscope*, 1972, Figure 3, p. 1403.)

degree of hearing loss is nearly always present. As shown in Figures 4 and 5, with advancing years, the decline in hearing ability includes progressively lower frequencies.

The combined data from five selected studies (American Standards Association, 1954; Beasley, 1938; Corso, 1963a; Glorig et al., 1957; Glorig and Nixon, 1962), show that the dispersion in hearing levels is almost identical for men and women, with the spread increasing as a linear function of age at all frequencies. However, as frequency increases from 250 to 8,000 Hz, the increase in spread for 65-year-olds is approximately 3.5 times greater than that for 25-year-olds (Spoor and Passchier-Vermeer, 1969).

Some data are available on a comparison of presbycusis in American Negroes and whites (Eisdorfer and Wilkie, 1972). Initial testing occured when the subjects were in their sixties or seventies with retesting 7 years later. Pure tone audiometric data at six frequencies from 500 to 6,000 Hz showed that at each evaluation Negroes had significantly better hearing than whites at all frequencies, with less decrement in the 7-year span except for 4,000 Hz. These results, however, appear contrary to those of the National Health Survey of 1960–1962 (National Center for Health Statistics, 1967) in which it was found that past age 55, there were no racial differences for the better ear at or above 3,000 Hz. A possible explanation for these apparently contradictory findings may lie in the use of a nonrandom sample in the Eisdorfer and Wilkie (1972) study and the small sample size of Blacks (14 men and 13 women).

An interview study of 270 centenarians revealed that loss of hearing is more gradual than loss of sight, but adjustment to loss of hearing is more difficult (Beard, 1969).

Pitch Discrimination. The ability to detect small changes in the pitch of sounds is not only important for musical listeners and performers (Corso, 1954), but is a significant factor in the perception of speech. Konig (1957) has provided pitch discrimination data for subjects ranging from 20 to 89 years. The method of constant stimuli was used and the tones were presented at a sensation level (SL) of 40 dB, i.e., 40 dB above the threshold of hearing.

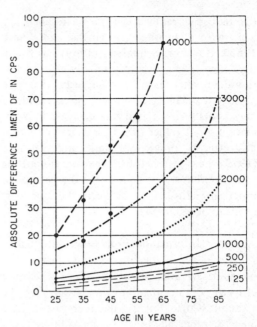

Figure 6. Absolute difference limen (DF) for pitch discrimination at 40 dB Sensation Level, with frequency in hertz as the parameter. (From Konig, 1957.)

The results for 70 subjects are shown in Figure 6. The absolute difference limen (DF) for pitch discrimination begins to deteriorate as early as the fourth decade. From 25 to 55 years, the DF for a given frequency increases approximately as a linear function of age; beyond 55 years, there is a marked increase in the size of DF particularly for the higher frequencies. The question remains, however, whether the impairment in pitch discrimination is related to the peripheral effects of aging, e.g., degeneration of sensory hair cells, or to deteriorated central processes.

Dichotic Listening. In a dichotic listening situation, the two ears of the listener are stimulated simultaneously, but different material is presented to each ear. For experimental purposes, dichotic listening tasks have been used to determine the basis for memory impairment in the elderly.

Inglis (1962) has proposed that the impairment is due to the inability of the elderly to maintain items in short-term storage; he has found that in dichotically-presented halved digit-spans of increasing length, the digits in the half-span recalled second are recalled less well with increasing age (Inglis and Caird, 1963). However, Schonfield (1969) has found that the decline occurs primarily for the left (nondominant) ear. This suggests that the presumed memory problems of the elderly may actually be related to a decrease in information input rather than to impaired retention or retrieval processes. Clark and Knowles (1973) have offered further data supporting this hypothesis. The reasons for the perceptual processing differences between the two ears needs to be explored.

Auditory Information Processing. Although a wide variety of qualitative and quantitative measures are available by means of which the efficacy of information processing may be assessed (Corso, 1973), the literature in this area for older adults is extremely limited, except perhaps for studies on reaction time.

In studying the relations among hearing, reaction time, and age, Feldman and Reger (1967) have found that in male subjects there is a significant increase in simple reaction time to a 500 Hz tone. The increase is relatively linear from 0.20 second at 20 years to 0.37 second in the seventh decade, followed by a sharp increase to 0.53 second in the eighth decade. The changes in reaction time are taken as behavioral indicants of generalized deterioration in the auditory nervous system. This position is consistent with that of Bauer (1965) and others who contend that reaction time is centrally rather than peripherally determined.

When the information to be processed is more complex, older persons may or may not show a performance decrement, depending upon the particular task requirements. In a vigilance experiment, older subjects (fourth to sixth decades) did less well than young adults when they were required to listen to a series of digits and to write the digits which occurred in each sequence of three odd numbers; however, when the occurrence was reported by pressing a key, no difference between age groups was obtained. Thus, it appears that the writing task imposes an additional load on the short-term retention which tends to deteriorate the performance of older subjects (Griew and Davies, 1962).

In studying professional pilots, Szafran (1968) has challenged the notion that age-related changes in the auditory and visual systems necessarily lead to a deteriorated level of information processing. He suggests that, as a cumulative effect of prolonged experience, changes in strategy may occur when distorted signals are to be detected. Presumably this ability to adapt to new situations remains relatively unaffected by the adverse effects of aging, at least for some individuals.

Age differences do appear to exist in strategies for the perceptual processing of speech when words or phrases are continuously repeated (Warren and Warren, 1971). Children respond to the repetitious stimuli in terms of English sounds but may transform the test material into nonsense syllables, whereas adults report only meaningful words as illusory transformations. These findings suggest that older people utilize different processing mechanisms which mediate more accurate auditory perception; the mechanisms appear to be dependent upon the individual's functional capacity and familiarity with language.

Thus, the question arises whether age-related decrements in human performance reflect impaired sensory functions or modifications in decision-making processes. An approach to the problem may be made in terms of the theory of signal detectability (TSD) (Tanner and Swets, 1954). TSD yields two independent measures that statistically describe an observer's performance in a given judgmental situation. One measure (d') indicates the individual's sensitivity to the characteristics of the stimulus; the other (β) indicates the individual's decision criterion. Craik (1966) and Rees and Botwinick (1971) found that young and old adults did not differ in their ability to detect a pure tone in the presence of noise (d'), but showed a significant difference in their decision criterion (β). It appears that older persons use more conservative (cautious) criteria in experimental situations and try to be fairly certain of a correct judgment before making a response.

Although the data are limited, the findings to date strongly suggest that any attempt to explain decrements in adult performance solely on the basis of the physiological deterioration of sensory systems is likely to be overly restrictive. The availability of sensory input is unquestionably a significant factor in effective performance, but a broader explanatory approach is required in which experimental and theoretical consideration must be given not only to the delivery of sensory input, but to the perceptual and cognitive processes that utilize the input to mediate behavioral responses.

Noise Exposure and Presbycusis. Numerous studies have now established that a significant relation exists between excessive noise exposure and permanent hearing loss (Kryter, 1970). Consequently, for medical and legal reasons (Corso, 1958), there is a growing demand for the etiological evaluation of hearing losses in occupational workers of all ages so that the effects of noise exposure may be quantitatively separated from those of aging. The problem, however, is complex since the pathological processes for the two conditions are, in part, remarkably similar; both involve the loss and degeneration of sensory hair cells and damage to related cochlear structures for which there is no known cure. The basic question, then, is whether the hearing losses due to noise exposure and to age are additive, or interactive.

The American Standards Association (1954) favors the additive hypothesis. Macrae (1971) has provided further support for this hypothesis by finding that in a longitudinal study, the threshold values for 1,000 Hz and 4,000 Hz were increased by approximately the amounts predicted by Spoor's (1967) equations for presbycusis, even though the initial hearing levels for the two frequencies were markedly different. Glorig and Davis (1961) and others consider it permissible to estimate the effects of noise by subtracting the presbycusis effect from the obtained audiometric threshold value. Two formulas for calculating the age correction factor have been provided (Lebo and Reddell, 1972).

Others hold to the hypothesis of interaction. Goldner (1953) has reported that older workers are more susceptible to noise. Schmidt (1969) found that after an initial exposure period of 15 years, the hearing loss at 4,000 Hz is not changed appreciably for a noise exposed group,

but for a non-noise exposed group there is an increasing loss even after the initial 15 years. However, when appropriate deductions were made for presbycusis, Mollica (1969) failed to find differential effects of acoustic trauma in younger and older workers having similar length of service (2 to 40 years).

A penetrating analysis of this problem has recently been presented by Corso (1976). While aging and noise exposure may both affect the hair cells of the organ of Corti, the totality of physiological evidence indicates that there are marked differences in the locus of lesions and the extent of neural damage produced by the two factors which appear to operate as separate causative agents, among others, in producing permanent hearing loss.

In terms of audiometric sensitivity, Corso (1976) has taken the position that hearing loss due to noise exposure and to aging may or may not be additive depending upon the locus and extent of hair cell destruction following noise exposure of given intensity, duration, and frequency characteristics. When destruction of sensory cells following exposure is essentially complete in a given region of the basilar membrane, subsequent noise exposure, aging, or other deleterious factors may not be expected to add further deficits in hearing functions unless new areas of injury are implicated.

Data from Corso, Wright, and Valerio (1973) on auditory temporal summation in older subjects tend to support this hypothesis. Temporal summation involves a reciprocal relationship between stimulus intensity and stimulus duration such that, up to some critical value, a threshold response may be maintained by decreasing one factor and increasing the other.

Figure 7 presents threshold-duration functions at 4,000 Hz for three groups of subjects: (1) a non-noise exposed sample, 51 to 57 years, (2) a noise exposed sample, 51 to 57 years, and (3) a noise exposed sample of young adults (mean age 29.5 years). For the three groups there are no significant differences in the threshold-duration functions, but the groups differ significantly from the theoretical curve for a normal ear (Zwislocki, 1960).

Thus, the temporal summation measure reveals similar deficits in the auditory system

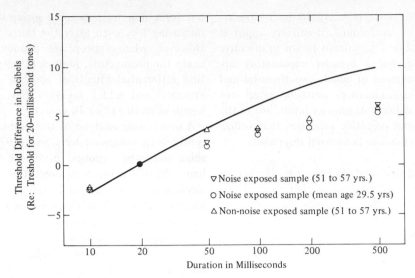

Figure 7. Threshold-duration functions at 4,000 Hz for three groups of subjects, compared with a theoretical curve (Zwislocki, 1960) for a normal ear. (From Corso, Wright, and Valerio, 1973.)

for aging and noise exposure. It appears that the effects of age and noise exposure are independent and nonadditive, at least for this age group. Corso (1975) views the effects of noise exposure as similar in certain respects to "premature presbycusis."

LANGUAGE AND SPEECH COMMUNICATION

Psychophysical Measurements of Speech

Speech Reception Threshold (SRT). One measure of the listener's hearing ability is the threshold of speech reception or intelligibility. This is typically taken as the speech intensity required to produce a 50 percent correct response for a standard list of words, e.g., Central Institute for the Deaf (C.I.D.) Auditory Tests W-1 or W-2 consisting of 36 spondee words (Hirsh, 1952). For young adults (18 to 24 years) the mean threshold for speech on Test W-2 was found to be approximately 18.5 dB *re* 0.0002 microbar (Corso, 1957a); this value is in excellent agreement with the 1969 normative threshold of the American National Standards Institute (1970) set at 19 dB Sound Pressure Level (SPL) for the Western Electric 705-A earphone.

Similar data for older age groups are very limited. For men ranging from 60 to 74 years

with a negative history of cardiovascular disease, the SRT was found to be approximately 16.5 dB SPL (Welsh, Luterman, and Bell, 1969). Other data (Punch and McConnell, 1969) show that the SRT for subjects with presbycusis from 69 to 79 years is approximately 42 dB SPL. As measured by words imbedded in sentences, the hearing ability for speech for men over 40 years is dependent upon the ability to hear pure tones below 500 Hz (Farrimond, 1961).

Speech Discrimination. In presbycusis there is not only a decrease in auditory sensitivity, but a decrease in the ability to understand speech. Clinically, this ability is measured by administering a speech discrimination test, e.g., C.I.D. Auditory Test W-22 consisting of 200 phonetically balanced (PB) monosyllabic words, to determine the maximum speech-perception score (PB max) as the intensity of the test words is increased. To provide a normative baseline for evaluating this effect, Corso, (1957b) tested untrained young adults from 18 to 24 years, and found that the mean discrimination loss for monaural listening on Test W-22 at 78 dB SPL was 2.3 percent (about 2 words wrong in 100). For the same test material, Feldman and Reger (1967) found that between the ages of 20 and 50 years the ability to understand speech was relatively stable, but by age 80 there was a discrimination loss of 25 percent.

Pestalozza and Shore (1955) compared the discrimination loss for speech for a group of older patients and a group of younger patients with perceptive hearing losses similar to those in presbycusis. For a given amount of hearing loss, speech discrimination for PB words was 9 to 20 percent better in the younger group. Also, for easier speech material (e.g., spondees), the discrimination loss for the younger group could be predicted from the pure tone audiograms; but for the older group, the loss was greater than predicted.

Among others, Farrimond (1961) has proposed a series of equations for predicting hearing loss for sentences from pure tone thresholds at various frequencies. For men over 40 years, the multiple correlation between pure tone thresholds at 250, 1,000, and 4,000 Hz and hearing loss for sentences is 0.82. The addition of a variable for vocabulary level significantly improves both the multiple regression correlation coefficient and the corresponding predictive accuracy.

For diagnostic purposes, speech discrimination is often measured at several levels of intensity. By plotting percent intelligibility as a function of increasing speech intensity, a gain function (intelligibility function) is obtained. Pecularities in the shape of the function, when compared to that for a normative group, provide diagnostic information regarding the possible sites of auditory lesions.

For Test W-22 and a normative young group, intelligibility in the steeper portion of the gain function increases at a rate of approximately 4 to 5.5 percent per decibel. The functions begin to "level off" at an intensity level of about 25 dB above the SRT (Eby and Williams, 1951). In comparison, elderly subjects (mean age 74.9 years) with minimal hearing loss show a gain of about 2.2 percent per decibel for speech presented 10 to 20 dB above threshold; whereas a second group (mean age 74.0 years) with presbycusis gained only 1.6 percent per decibel over the same intensity range. Moreover, while the first group attained a maximal discrimination score of 90 percent at 40 dB SL, the second achieved only 65.5 percent at the

same intensity level (Punch and McConnell, 1969).

When the degree of pure tone hearing loss is held constant, there is a progressive decline with age in maximal intelligibility for PB words (Jerger, 1971). It appears, therefore, that older individuals have a considerably flatter intelligibility function and a restricted functional range of speech intensity.

Speech Intelligibility Under Stressful Listening Conditions. The decrement in speech intelligibility in older individuals is even more marked under stressful listening conditions. Bergman (1971) tested 282 adults ranging in age from 20 to 79 years and found very little decline in their ability for hearing test sentences that were undistorted or did not compete with other stimuli. However, when words overlapped or were interrupted eight times per second with a speech-on time ratio of 50 percent, changes in performance were observed starting in the fourth decade; by the seventh decade, the performance of the older adults declined to less than half that of the younger. These effects are shown in Curve D of Figure 8.

Figure 8 also shows the aging effects of reverberation time on speech intelligibility (Curve B). With a reverberation time of 2.5 seconds and speech presented at 80 dB SPL, the percent intelligibility shows a marked downward trend starting in the fifth decade. Thus, while unaltered speech (Curve A) shows only a minor decrement in intelligibility through the eighth decade, substantial decrements are produced by deviations in speech involving distortion, time alteration or competing signals (Curve C).

Reduced speech perception in the aged seems to be due, in part, to the increase in time required to process information in the higher auditory centers. The magnitude of this effect has been studied by presenting individuals with accelerated speech, i.e., an increase in the word rate per minute. For young subjects, it is possible to offset the decrease in discrimination by slightly increasing speech intensity. This equalizing effect is not possible in older subjects. For those over 70 years, 100 percent intelligibility can be obtained for normal word rates (140

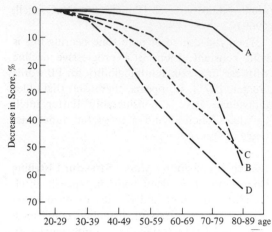

Figure 8. Decrease in percent intelligibility for speech as a function of age. Curves: A—unaltered speech; B—reverberated speech; C—overlapping speech with spondaic words; D—interrupted speech. For each curve normal subjects 20–29 years served as zero reference. (From Bergman, M. 1971. Hearing and aging. Implications of Recent Research Findings. *Audiology*, **10**, 164–171. Basel: Karger.)

words per minute) if the intensity is high enough; but, for accelerated speech (350 words per minute) intelligibility does not exceed 45 percent regardless of intensity (Calearo and Lazzaroni, 1957).

In a study of filtered speech (Welsh, Luterman, and Bell, 1969), four listening conditions were used with two age groups (mean age 21.7 and 67.7 years). When Test W-22 was presented at 70 dB SL, both groups did poorer in a monaural low pass condition (540 Hz) than a monaural high pass condition (2,160 Hz). However, the greatest difference between groups was obtained in a binaural filtered condition with low pass to one ear and high pass to the other (66 percent for younger group *vs.* 39 percent for older group). The data of this study not only show age differences in filtered speech intelligibility, but emphasize the information processing difficulties of older individuals which must be taken into account in the application of filtered speech tests in clinical audiology.

As expected from numerous studies with normal hearing subjects, phoneme discrimination under noise conditions should produce poorer performance in older adults, even if pure tone

thresholds at speech frequencies are essentially normal. Smith and Prather (1971) tested this hypothesis for 16 consonants in a consonant-vowel (CV) context at six sensation levels of noise over four signal-to-noise (S/N) ratios. The results for monotic listening showed that an older group (60 years or above) had significantly fewer correct responses than a younger group (18 to 30 years) for all listening conditions. However, the relative performance remained the same as either sensation level was increased or the S/N ratio was decreased. The lack of significant interactions between groups, therefore, failed to support the expectancy that the older group would do progressively poorer as the listening conditions became less favorable. It should be noted, however, that the subjects in this study were screened for normal hearing and therefore, the older group did not represent a random sample from the population. Groen (1969) also failed to find a significant interaction for phonemes as the S/N ratio was reduced, although subjects between 62 and 81 years scored 40 percent lower than a normal group at a S/N ration of -5.0 dB.

Central Versus Peripheral Factors. The major question regarding the results of experimental studies on speech discrimination is whether the decrements for older individuals are attributable to central or peripheral changes in the auditory nervous system. Hinchcliffe (1962) hypothesizes that central factors are predominantly involved and correlates the age deficit in speech intelligibility with decreased cell count of the temporal lobe. Fournier (1954) has suggested that in older persons there is a lengthening of the time required for the central identification and processing of a message, so that speech rates faster than normal (phonemes delivered at a rate of approximately 10 per second) will produce some difficulty. Calearo and Lazzaroni (1957) attribute the lengthening of the time requirement to synaptic delays in the auditory pathways and cortex. Jerger (1971) also supports a central interpretation since loudness recruitment, a symptom of cochlear disorder, does not appear to account for the disproportionate loss in speech intelligibility for older adults.

Other investigators point to peripheral factors to explain the findings on speech discrimination. Schuknecht and Igarashi (1964) suggest that the discrimination loss is characteristic of neural degeneration. Bocca and Calearo (1963) indicate that poor discrimination for traditional speech material, when accompanied by a normal pure tone audiogram, is of particular significance for lesions at the midbrain level.

Thus, the issue of central versus peripheral factors in hearing disorders of the elderly is unresolved. As an alternative in this controversy, the hypothesis is offered that both peripheral and central components are involved, with the components being intermingled in various degrees at different age levels. It is anticipated that the development and refinement of new techniques in speech audiometry, in conjunction with established clinical measures, will lead to marked progress in the differential diagnosis of hearing disorders, thereby providing a more exact specification of the locus of lesions in the auditory pathways of older individuals (Carhart, 1973).

Language and Voice Impairments

If the later years of life are to remain profitable and purposeful, language and communication processes must be maintained at an effective social level as long as possible. With age, the ability to communicate does not lessen in importance; instead, the older individual may become increasingly dependent on his ability to communicate as his perceptual-motor skills begin to decline.

Classification of Speech Disorders. Deviations from normal speech generally fall into one or more of the following disorder areas (DeWeese and Lillywhite, 1968): (1) articulation, in which the production of sound combinations is impaired; (2) stuttering, in which nonfluency occurs with excessive repetition of phonemes; (3) voice, in which the processes of phonation and resonation are altered with deviations in pitch, loudness, and vocal quality; and (4) symbolization, in which an individual is unable to associate meaning with language symbols in a normal manner (aphasia).

Pathology of Language Impairment. In older individuals problems of articulation may arise from a variety of causes, including vascular insufficiency, trauma, neoplasms, and progressive degenerative illness, e.g., Parkinson's disease. Cancer of the larynx may also occur in young and old adults, but most individuals who require a laryngectomy are usually between 55 and 60 years of age (Darley, 1963). Until an alternative mode of communication is acquired, these individuals feel severely handicapped. Fortunately, the majority are able to develop esophageal or pharyngeal speech without an electronic or mechanical device. For those who are unsuccessful in mastering laryngeal speech due to poor health, impaired intellectual ability, lack of motivation or other factors, satisfactory voice communication often can be achieved by means of an artificial larynx.

In older individuals and in the young, communication may be seriously disrupted by aphasia. The majority of cases of aphasia are due to extensive vascular lesions or disease in the brain. Aphasia may be divided into two main types: (1) motor or expressive aphasia, which involves a decrease in the capacity to transform language concepts into speech or writing; and (2) sensory or receptive aphasia, which involves a deficit in understanding the intended concepts of speech or writing. Anatomically, motor aphasia involves lesions that destroy the foot of the third frontal gyrus of the left cerebral hemisphere; while sensory aphasia involves damage to the posterior portion of the first temporal gyrus on the left side.

The aphasia of older persons may involve both kinds of damage so that mixed aphasia (motor and sensory) may be present. In this case, the individual has difficulty both in understanding language and in its formulation. The auditory retention span may be reduced to one or two words and reading comprehension may be severely curtailed. The problems of communication are further complicated if dysarthria, presbycusis, and presbyopia are also present.

Auditory Modifications of the Aging Voice. In older individuals, altered communication processes are not restricted to language and hearing impairments, but may also involve the acoustic characteristics of the voice. The frequency range becomes smaller, vocal intensity is decreased, and voice quality is impoverished depending upon the kind and extent of organic changes which have occurred in the larynx (Luchsinger and Arnold, 1965). Ryan (1972), however, failed to confirm the reported decrease in vocal intensity; instead, vocal intensity increased with age and subjects in the seventh decade had a greater intensity than those in the three preceding decades. There is also some evidence that the mean level of voice frequency for individuals above 80 years is significantly higher than that for individuals 65 to 79 years of age (Mysak, 1959). While Charlip (1968) did not find any change in the fundamental frequency characteristics of women, Segre (1971) has reported that after the menopause, i.e., at about 50 years, the hormonal balance shows a predominance of androgenous corticoids from the adrenal glands and the voice becomes more masculine, with a drop in fundamental frequency. The singing voice is also adversely affected by age-related changes, with vocal alterations occurring more frequently and at a much earlier age than in speaking.

The changes which occur in the human voice with age are sufficiently discriminable that college students can make reliable judgments of chronological age for individuals 20 to 89 years solely on the basis of voice cues. Direct magnitude estimates yield a correlation of 0.88 between chronological age and perceived age as judged from recorded speech samples (Shipp and Hollien, 1969).

Vocal Misuse. In patients over 60 years, vocal strain and vocal fatigue, i.e., "tired voice," are frequently encountered. Vocal misuse may interfere with the communication process and may lead to organic dysphonia such as nodes, polyps, and contact ulcer on the vocal folds (Cooper, 1970).

THE PSYCHOLOGY OF DEAFNESS AND COMMUNICATION DISORDERS IN OLDER ADULTS

Auditory Deficits and Interpersonal Behavior

Levels of Adaptation. From a systematic viewpoint, human behavior may be considered in relation to the physical and social forces in the environment. The task of psychology then is to determine the manner in which these forces elicit, modify, and sustain behavior and to understand how, in turn, the resulting behavior acts upon the environment (Corso, 1967).

Within this context, human behavior may reflect different levels of adaptive ability. The lowest level is primarily motor activity which is mediated by the efferent nervous system. e.g., walking, manipulating tools, and performing routine daily tasks. At an intermediate level, adaptation requires social contact with other individuals through oral and written communication or some form of nonverbal communication, such as facial expressions and gestures. The most complex adaptive behaviors involve cognitive, perceptual, and emotional processes which enable the individual not only to react appropriately to particular environmental circumstances, but to utilize feedback information resulting from these behaviors to enhance the adaptive effectiveness of the behavioral sequence.

Loss of Auditory Contact. The impairment of speech, language, or auditory processes, therefore, may significantly alter an individual's adjustment. In effect, the loss of hearing places the individual in a new and strange natural environment, one in which auditory localization is impaired and the familiar sounds of work and play are absent. Without the warning signals that typically occur in the physical environment, personal security is greatly reduced and self-preservation becomes dependent upon other sensory modalities.

Furthermore, hearing deficits in speech reception and discrimination substantially alter the individual's social environment and undermine his ability to maintain normal interpersonal relations. Thus, enjoyment of life dwindles and the restricted physical and social environment tends to become monotonous and depressive. These changes often occur at a time in life when other socioeconomic problems are increasing and, consequently, personal adjustment is strained.

Psychological Correlates of Communication Disorders. Elderly individuals with impaired speech or hearing ability are extremely sensitive to their decreased capacity for effective communication and social interaction. If an individual has any paranoid tendencies, they may be accentuated by a hearing problem so that suspicious and hostile attitudes are reinforced; deafness alone, however, is insufficient to produce paranoia. Knapp (1948) has found that patients with a chronic hearing loss of more than 50 dB tend to have relatively severe emotional disturbances. While these include compulsive, anxious, and hypochondriacal states, depressive reactions are predominant. The possibility of using voice intensity as a behavioral measure of personality disorder, as in depression, has been explored by Hanf and Corso (1966).

Thus, social interactions tend to diminish in scope and quality with age and the behavioral consequences of the impairments become apparent. The older individual finds himself incapable of maintaining control in social situations and, therefore, his feelings of inferiority tend to be increased. Furthermore, his inability to use language effectively produces a decline in the release of emotional tension through verbal expression. Given these circumstances, the older person may begin to show maladaptive behavior (Hyams, 1969).

Rehabilitation of Hearing

Planning Procedures. The proper management of antisocial behaviors due to speech and hearing disorders requires both vocal and aural rehabilitation. Aural rehabilitation should be predicated upon a good personal history and a careful medical examination accompanied by adequate tests (Parker, 1969). The results of these tests will indicate whether or not the patient can utilize otological and audiological services and, if so, whether he can be helped by medico-surgical procedures or by professional consultation, a hearing aid, and rehabilitative therapy (Ronis, Liebman, and Lindsay, 1971).

Rehabilitation Programs. Following an orientation period and group counseling sessions on problems of impaired hearing and their possible remediation, two training programs should be initiated: (1) speechreading (lipreading) and (2) auditory training. The dual aspects are impor-

tant, since in most conversations both vision and hearing are employed to obtain information. Speechreading is a skill which enables a person to understand language by carefully observing the speaker (face-to-face or via motion-picture). It is one of the primary compensatory behaviors that is practiced by older individuals to alleviate the effects of hearing loss. The format of an apparently successful training program in speechreading skills for older people has been presented by Phythyon and McConnel (1969), and Sanders (1971) has described a plan for auditory training. For some older patients the tasks of the rehabilitation program may be difficult so that a concomitant program of drug therapy, e.g., hormone-vitamin drugs, may be advisable (Niemeyer, 1968).

Technological Advances. Recent technological advances have contributed substantially to the alleviation of certain kinds of hearing impairments in the elderly. Wearable electric hearing aids are available in binaural as well as monaural models and several varieties of mountings may be obtained. For some listeners, the binaural hearing aid provides better sound localization and easier speech discrimination in noise. The more elaborate models of hearing aids may provide a telephone pick-up device which activates the hearing aid amplifier during telephone conversations and eliminates interference from ambient noise. Improvements in telephone reproductive characteristics have also been made, based upon the kinds of frequency losses which occur in presbycusis (Salama, 1964). For hearing-impaired telephone users without a hearing aid, special receiver-amplifiers may be obtained to improve speech reception.

Rehabilitation of Speech and Language Disorders

There are at least two major problems which tend to mitigate against the successful rehabilitation of older adults with speech and hearing problems: (1) while the majority of sufferers believe they need professional assistance, many indicate they have neither the time, the money, nor the inclination to attend a rehabilitation program; (2) those who do attend may be treated in such a passive manner that they are made to feel incapable of managing their own lives due to senile deterioration. Nevertheless, given an appropriate rehabilitative program, the patient can usually make rapid progress in developing and maintaining the speaking and listening skills which are required for effective communication.

Psychological Counseling. The counseling portion of the rehabilitation program should be considered as the essential core for the success of the program. The older individual with a speech or hearing problem usually does not voluntarily seek professional services, but does so on the urging of family and friends. Following a clinical examination, the patient should be given a simple explanation of the findings and their implications. This tends to reduce the patient's anxiety and enables him to share his problem with others. Psychological counseling should also be extended to the members of the immediate family, since they may not realize the patient's limitations and are unaware of the assistance they can render. The rehabilitation plan should encourage the patient to maintain old social contacts and to develop new ones. If the impairment poses a problem regarding employment or professional activities, vocational counseling should be provided.

Speech and Language Training. The major component of vocal rehabilitation is speech training; the details of training programs are available in numerous sources, e.g., Brodnitz, 1961. The older patient with presbycusis gradually loses his ability to use auditory monitoring to effect the more or less automatic adjustment of the vocal articulators required for normal speech sounds. The two sounds most often affected are *s* and *r*. Since the patient cannot use acoustic cues to monitor correct articulator placements, he must be taught to use other cues to regulate his speech. "Phonetic placement" is the primary method for accomplishing this objective. In this method, the patient is instructed on the proper placement of his articulators and is encouraged to utilize the associated kinesthetic sensations while speaking (Mysak, 1966). For maximal effectiveness, speech training for older persons should be initiated before presbycusis reaches an advanced

level so that tactile and kinesthetic feedback may be augmented by residual auditory cues. In this way, it may be possible to maintain good speech into later years. If instrumentation is available, learning techniques based upon operant conditioning and programmed instruction may be extremely useful in the vocal rehabilitation program.

CONCLUSIONS

Although reliable data on the incidence of deafness in the United States and other countries are limited, population studies indicate that at least until the turn of the century a marked increase is to be expected in the number of individuals with socially-debilitating hearing disorders, including presbycusis.

With age, clinical manifestations of deterioration are increasingly evident in the human auditory and vocal systems. The available data show that the major functional changes in hearing are associated with disturbances in the inner ear and related neural pathways. Mechanical processes are altered and other deficiencies occur in the metabolic and neuronal processes which are essential for normal hearing. Vascular changes are also implicated, especially in the cochlea.

The physiological changes in the auditory system produce functional decrements in several areas: absolute thresholds for pure tones and for speech, differential thresholds for pitch discrimination, speech discrimination, and information processing as in dichotic listening. The decrements for speech become more pronounced for older individuals under adverse listening conditions, including speech acceleration, interruption, filtering, distortion, and reverberation. In complex perceptual tasks, changes in response strategy may be used by older individuals to maintain an effective level of performance.

Age-related changes also occur in the vocal system which further tend to disrupt the communication process. In addition, vascular insufficiency, trauma, neoplasms, degenerative illnesses, cancer and other etiological factors may alter the larynx or other structures of the vocal system. These conditions may produce speech disorders in articulation, fluency, phonation and resonation, and language symbolization. The aging voice is characterized by a higher fundamental frequency in men and a lower frequency in women, a smaller frequency range, a change in vocal intensity, and a modification in voice quality.

With advancing years, the functional changes in speech and hearing significantly interfere with the communication process and the aging individual is, therefore, inclined to restrict the degree and scope of his social interaction. The proper management of these behaviors involves effective training in both vocal and aural rehabilitation programs, in conjuction with hearing aids or other technological devices. Psychological and vocational counseling are also usually required to support the rehabilitation programs. The success of these programs leads to an optimistic prognosis for the older individual who is motivated to continue to live a happy and useful life in his later years.

While the auditory and vocal processes are significantly altered by the physiological changes which occur over time, the problems of speech and hearing cannot be isolated from the individual's total pattern of behavior. Thus, any theoretical attempt to explain age-related changes in behavior should not be restricted to a consideration of a single process or modality; more appropriately, the approach should be sufficiently broad to encompass a wider range of variables, as in motivational, cognitive, or other psychological processes which serve as functional mediators in the processing of information that determines human behavior.

REFERENCES

American National Standards Institute. 1970. *American National Standard Specifications for Audiomotors, ANSI S3.6-1969* New York: American National Standards Institute.

American Standards Association. 1954. *The Relation of Hearing Loss to Noise Exposure.* Report Z.24-X-2. New York: American Standards Association.

Bauer, H. G. 1965. Measurements of brain wave period and auditory reaction time as related to advancing age. *Electroencephalo. Clin. Neurophysiol.*, 19, 318 (Abst.).

Beard, B. B. 1969. Sensory decline in very old age. *Gerontol. Clin.*, 11, 149–158.

Beasley, W. C. 1938. *National Health Survey (1935-36) Preliminary Reports, Hearing Studies Series*, Bulletins 1–7. Washington, D.C.: U.S. Public Health Service.

Bergman, M. 1971. Hearing and aging. *Audiology*, 10, 164–171.

Bocca, E., and Calearo, C. 1963. Central hearing processes. *In*, J. Jerger (ed.), *Modern Developments in Audiology*, pp. 337–370. New York: Academic Press.

Bochenek, Z., and Jachowska, A. 1969. Atherosclerosis, accelerated presbyacusis, and acoustic trauma. *Internat. Audiol.*, 8, 312–316.

Brodnitz, F. S. 1961. *Vocal Rehabilitation*, for the American Acad. of Ophthal. and Otolaryngol. 2nd edition. Rochester, Minnesota: Whiting Press.

Calearo, C., and Lazzaroni, A. 1957. Speech intelligibility in relationship to the speed of the message. *Laryngoscope*, 67, 410–419.

Carhart, R. 1973. Updating special hearing tests in otological diagnosis. *Arch. Otolaryngol.*, 97, 88–91.

Charlip, W. S. 1968. The aging female voice: Selected fundamental frequency characteristics and listener judgments. Unpublished Ph.D. dissertation, Purdue University.

Clark, L. E., and Knowles, J. B. 1973. Age differences in dichotic listening. *J. Gerontol.*, 28, 173–178.

Cooper, M. 1970. Voice problems of the geriatric patient. *Geriatrics*, 25, 107–110.

Corso, J. F. 1954. Scale position and performed melodic octaves. *J. Psychol.*, 37, 297–305.

Corso, J. F. 1957a. Confirmation of the normal threshold for speech on C.I.D. Auditory Test W-2. *J. Acoust. Soc. Am.*, 29, 368–370.

Corso, J. F. 1957b. Confirmation of normal discrimination loss for speech on C.I.D. Auditory Test W-22. *Laryngoscope*, 67, 365–370.

Corso, J. F. 1958. Proposed laboratory standard of normal hearing. *J. Acoust. Soc. Am.*, 30, 14–23.

Corso, J. F. 1963a. Age and sex differences in puretone thresholds. *Arch. Otolaryngol.*, 77, 385–405.

Corso, J. F. 1963b. Aging and auditory thresholds in men and women. *Arch. Environ. Health*, 6, 350–356.

Corso, J. F. 1967. *The Experimental Psychology of Sensory Behavior*, pp. 461–507. New York: Holt, Rinehart and Winston.

Corso, J. F. 1968. The sensory effects of aging in man. *Scientia: Internat. Rev. of Sci. Synthesis*, 103, 362–393.

Corso, J. F. 1971. Sensory processes and age effects in normal adults. *J. Gerontol.*, 26, 90–105.

Corso, J. F. 1973. Hearing. *In*, B. B. Wolman (ed.), *Handbook of General Psychology*, pp. 348–381. Englewood Cliffs, New Jersey: Prentice-Hall.

Corso, J. F. 1976. Presbycusis as a complicating factor in evaluating noise-induced hearing loss. *In*, D. Henderson, R. P. Hamernik, D. S. Dasanjh, and J. H. Mills (eds.), *Effects of Noise on Hearing*. New York: Raven Press.

Corso, J. F., Wright, H. N., and Valerio, M. 1973. Temporal summation function in presbycusis. Paper presented at the 85th Meeting of the Acoustical Society of America, Boston.

Craik, F. I. M. 1966. The effects of aging of the detection of faint auditory signals. *Proceedings of the 7th International Congress of Gerontology, Vol. 6,* Vienna.

Darley, F. L. 1963. Speech problems in the aging. *Postgrad. Med.,* 294–300.

Desmedt, J. E. 1960. Neurophysiological mechanisms controlling acoustic input. *In,* G. L. Rasmussen and W. F. Windle (eds.), *Neural Mechanisms of the Auditory and Vestibular Systems,* Chap. II. Springfield, Illinois: Charles C. Thomas.

DeWeese, D. D., and Lillywhite, H. 1968. Speech disorders. *In,* D. D. DeWeese and W. H. Saunders (eds.), *Textbook of Otolaryngology.* Saint Louis, Missouri: C. V. Mosby.

Eby, L. G., and Williams H. L. 1951. Recruitment of loudness in the differential diagnosis of end organ and nerve fiber deafness. *Laryngoscope,* 61, 400–414.

Eisdorfer, C., and Wilkie, F. 1972. Auditory changes in the aged: A follow-up study. *J. Am. Geriat. Soc.,* 20, 377–382.

Etholm B., and Belal, A., Jr. 1974. Senile changes in the middle ear joints. *Ann. Otol. Rhinol. Laryngol.,* 83, 49–54.

Farrimond, T. 1961. Prediction of speech hearing loss for older workers. *Gerontologia,* 5, 65–87.

Feldman, R. M., and Reger, S. N. 1967. Relations among hearing, reaction time, and age. *J. Speech Hearing Res.,* 10, 479–495.

Fitsch, V., Dobozi, M., and Greig, G. 1972. Degenerative changes of the arterial vessels of the internal auditory meatus during the process of aging. *Acta Oto-Laryngol.,* 73, 259–266.

Flanagan, J. L. 1965. *Speech analysis, Synthesis, and Perception.* New York: Academic Press.

Fournier, J. E. 1954. L'analyse et l'identification du message sonore. *J. Franc, Oto.-Rhino.-Laryngol.,* 3, 257.

Glorig, A., and Davis, H. 1961. Age, noise and hearing loss. *Ann. Otol. Rhinol. Laryngol.,* 70, 556–571.

Glorig, A., and Nixon, J. 1962. Hearing loss as a function of age. *Laryngoscope,* 72, 1596–1610.

Glorig, A., Wheeler, D., Quiggle, R., Grings, W., and Summerfield, A. 1957. *1954 Wisconsin State Fair Hearing Survey.* Subcommittee on Noise in Industry of the American Academy of Ophthalmology and Otolaryngology, Los Angeles.

Goldner, A. J. 1953. Deafness in shipyard workers, *Arch. Otolaryngol.,* 57, 287–309.

Griew, S., and Davies, D. R. 1962. The effect of aging on auditory vigilance performance. *J. Gerontol.,* 17, 88–90.

Groen, J. J. 1969. Social hearing handicap: Its measurement by speech audiometry in noise. *Internat. Audiol.,* 8, 182–183.

Gross, C. W. 1969. Sensori-neural hearing loss in clinical and histologic oterosclerosis. *Laryngoscope,* 79, 104–112.

Hanf, C., and Corso, J. F. 1966. Intensity of voice and the theory of activation. *Amer. J. Psych.,* 79, 226–233.

Hansen C. C., and Reske-Nielsen, E. 1965. Pathological studies in presbyacusis. *Arch. Otolaryngol.,* 82, 115–132.

Hinchcliffe, R. 1959. The threshold of hearing as a function of age. *Acustica,* 9, 303–308.

Hinchcliffe, R. 1962. The anatomical locus of presbycusis. *J. Speech Dis.,* 27, 301–310.

Hirsh, I. J. 1952. *The Measurement of Hearing,* pp. 119–153. New York: McGraw-Hill.

Hyams, D. E. 1969. Psychological factors in rehabilitation of the elderly. *Geront. Clin.,* 11, 129–136.

Inglis, J. 1962. Effects of age on responses to dichotic stimulation. *Nature,* 194, 1101.

Inglis, J., and Caird, W. K. 1963. Age differences in succes╕ive responses to simultaneous stimulation. *Can. J. Psych.,* 17, 98–105.

Jatho, K., and Heck, K. H. 1959. Schwellenaudiometrische untersuchungen über die progredienz und charakteristik der alterschwerhörigkeit in der verschiedenen lebensabschnitten. *Z. Laryng., Rhinol., Otolog.,* 38, 72–89.

Jerger, J. 1971. Audiological findings in aging. Paper presented at the International Oto-Physiology Symposium, Ann Arbor, Michigan.

Johansen, H. 1943. *Den Altere Bedingete Tunghored.* Copenhagen: Munksgaard.

Johnsson, L. G., and Hawkins, J. E., Jr. 1972. Symposium on basic ear research: II. Strial atrophy in clinical and experimental deafness. *Laryngoscope,* 82, 1105–1125.

Kirikae, I. 1969. Auditory function in advanced age with reference to histological changes in the central auditory system. *Internat. Audiol.,* 8, 221–230.

Kirikae, I., Sato, T., and Shitara, T. 1964. A study of hearing in advanced age. *Laryngoscope,* 74, 205–220.

Kirikae, I., and Shitara, T. 1961. Recent advances in the study on presbycusis. *Ronenbyo,* 5, 18. (As cited in Kirikae, Sato, and Shitara, 1964.)

Knapp, P. H. 1948. Emotional aspects of hearing loss. *Psychosomat. Med.,* 10, 203–222.

Konig, E. 1957. Pitch discrimination and age. *Acta Oto-Laryngol.,* 48, 475–489.

Konigsmark, B. W., and Murphy, E. A. 1970. Volume of the ventral cochlear nucleus in man: Its relationship to neuronal population and age. *J. Neuropathol. Exp. Neurol.,* 31, 304–316.

Krmpotic-Nemanic, J. 1969. Presbycusis and retrocochlear structures. *Interat. Audiol.,* 8, 210–220.

Kryter, K. 1970. *The Effects of Noise on Man.* New York: Academic Press.

Lebo C. P., and Reddell, R. C. 1972. The presbycusis component in occupational hearing loss. *Laryngoscope,* 82, 1399–1409.

Liden, G. 1968. The geriatric-audiological problems of modern society. *In*, G. Liden (ed.), *Geriatric Audiology*, pp. 9–15. Stockholm: Almquist & Wiksell.

Luchsinger, R., and Arnold, G. E. 1965. *Voice-Speech-Language*. Belmont, California: Wadsworth.

Macrae, J. H. 1971. Noise-induced hearing loss and presbyacusis. *Audiology*, 10, 323–333.

Magladery, J. 1959. Neurophysiology of aging. *In*, J. Birren (ed.), *Handbook of Aging and the Individual*, pp. 173–186. Chicago, Illinois: University of Chicago Press.

Mollica, A. 1969. Acoustic trauma and presbyacusis. *Internat. Audiol.*, 8, 305–311.

Mysak, E. D. 1959. Pitch and duration characteristics of older males. *J. Speech Hearing Res.*, 2, 46–54.

Mysak, E. D. 1966. *Speech Pathology and Auditory Feedback*, pp. 71–83. Springfield, Illinois: Charles C. Thomas.

National Center for Health Statistics. 1967. *Hearing levels of adults by race, region, and area of residence, United States; 1960–1962*. U.S.P.H.S. Publ. No. 1000, Series 11, No. 26 (September). Washington, D.C.: Government Printing Office.

Niemeyer, W. 1968. Probleme der gerontologischen Hörprothetik. *Electromedica*, 4, 116–119.

Parker, W. 1969. Hearing and age. *Geriatrics*, 24: (4) 151–157.

Pestalozza, G., and Shore, I. 1955. Clinical evaluation of presbyacusis on basis of different tests of auditory function. *Laryngoscope*, 65, 1136–1163.

Phythyon, M. J., and McConnell, F. 1969. Hearing rehabilitation for older people. *Gerontologist*, 9, 66–68.

Punch, J. L., and McConnell, F. 1969. The speech discrimination function for elderly adults. *J. Aud. Res.*, 9, 159–166.

Rees, J. N., and Botwinick, J. 1971. Detection and decision factors in auditory behavior of the elderly. *J. Gerontol.*, 26, 133–136.

Richards, S. 1971. Deafness in the elderly. *Geront. Clin.*, 13, 350–358.

Ronis, M. L., Liebman, E. P., and Lindsay, C. H. 1971. The rehabilitation of the aged deaf. *Geriatrics*, 26: (12) 57–59.

Ryan, W. J. 1972. Acoustic aspects of the aging voice. *J. Gerontol.*, 27, 265–268.

Salama, I. 1964. Telephone communication to meet the needs of the aged with defective hearing. *In*, *Yearbook XVI*, pp. 8–18. Helsinki: Societas Gerontologica Fennica. (English summary, 1966).

Sanders, D. A. 1971. *Aural Rehabilitation*. Englewood Cliffs, New Jersey: Prentice-Hall.

Schaie, K. W., Baltes, P., and Strother, C. R. 1964. A study of auditory sensitivity in advanced age. *J. Gerontol.*, 19, 453–457.

Scheidegger, S. 1963. Präsenile spongiöse gehirnatrophie schweiz. *Arch. Neurol. Psychiat.*, 91, 211. (As cited in Hansen and Reske-Nielsen, 1965.)

Schmidt, P. H. 1969. Presbycusis and noise. *Internat. Audiol.*, 8, 278–280.

Schonfield, D. 1969. Recognition tests of dichotic listening. Paper presented at the International Congress of Psychology, London.

Schuknecht, H. F., and Igarashi, M. 1964. Pathology of slowly progressive sensori-neural deafness. *Trans. Am. Acad. Ophthalmol. Otolaryngol.*, 68, 222–242.

Segre, R. 1971. Senescence of the voice. *Eye, Ear, Nose, Throat Monthly.*, 50 (6), 223–227.

Sercer, A., and Krmpotic-Nemanic, J. 1958. Über die ursache der progressiven altersschwerhörgkeit (Presbyacusis). *Acta Oto-Laryngol. Suppl.*, 143, 1–36.

Shipp, T., and Hollien, H. 1969. Perception of the aging male voice. *J. Speech Hearing Res.*, 12, 703–710.

Smith, R., and Prather, W. F. 1971. Phoneme discrimination in older persons under varying signal-to-noise conditions. *J. Speech Hearing Res.*, 14, 630–638.

Spoor, A. 1967. Presbyacusis values in relation to noise induced hearing loss. *Internat. Audiol.*, 6, 48–57.

Spoor, A., and Passchier-Vermeer, W. 1969. Spread in hearing-levels of non-noise exposed people at various ages. *Internat. Audiol.*, 8, 328–336.

Szafran, J. 1968. Psychophysiological studies of aging in pilots. *In*, G. A. Talland (ed.), *Human Aging and Behavior—Recent Advances in Research and Theory*. New York: Academic Press.

Tanner, W. P., and Swets, J. A. 1954. A decision-making theory of visual detection. *Psych. Rev.*, 61, 401–409.

Tsai, H. K., Chou, F. S., and Cheng, T. J. 1958. On changes in ear size with age, as found among Taiwanese-Formosans of Fukienese extraction. *J. Formosan Med. Assoc.*, 57, 105–111.

U.S. Department of Health, Education, and Welfare. 1963. *Information Service Series, No. 63-11*. Washington, D.C.: Vocational Rehabilitation Administration.

U.S. Department of Health, Education, and Welfare. 1969. *Human Communication and its Disorders*. Bethesda, Maryland.

Warren, R. M., and Warren R. P. 1971. Some age differences in auditory perception *Bull. N. Y. Acad. Med.*, 47, 1365–1377.

Watson, L. E., and Tolan, T. 1967. *Hearing Tests and Hearing Instruments*. New York: Hafner.

Webster, I. W. 1974. The age-prevalence of cardiovascular abnormalities in relation to the aging of special-sense function. *J. Am. Geriat. Soc.*, 22, 13–17.

Welsh, O. L., Luterman, D. M., and Bell, B. 1969. The effect of aging on responses to filtered speech. *J. Gerontol.*, 24, 189–192.

Whitfield, I. C. 1967. *The Auditory Pathway*. London: Edward Arnold.

Wilkins, L. T. 1950. The prevalence of deafness in England, Scotland, and Wales. *Acta Oto-Laryngol. Suppl.* 90, 97–114.

Wright, J. L., and Schuknecht, H. F. 1972. Atrophy of the spiral ligament. *Arch. Otolaryngol.*, 96, 16–21.

Zwislocki, J. 1960. Theory of temporal auditory summation. *J. Acoust. Soc. Am.*, 35, 691–699.

22
TASTE AND SMELL

Trygg Engen
Brown University

Tasting and smelling are necessary to judge the adequacy of food; and olfaction especially may be indispensable in warning the person of dangers associated with the air he breathes. Man's sense of smell and taste are sometimes more sensitive than physical instruments. For this reason human observers are used in laboratories and field studies concerned with the evaluation of food and air, as well as whiskey and cosmetics.

These modalities appear to be at their best in discriminating between qualitatively different substances and poorest in discriminating between concentrations of single substances. Yet most studies of taste and smell, those concerned with the effects of age included, have involved the latter ability. The reason for this is partly that one tends to study all modalities with the methods applied to vision and audition, i.e., with classic psychophysical methods for measuring ability to resolve small physical differences in one variable or substance (see Corso, 1971; Comalli, 1967).

However, the most important role of the sense of taste and smell may be in motivating the person to action after a certain quality of substance has been detected. Pleasantness and unpleasantness, approach and avoidance, is what one ought to measure in these modalities rather than acuity. Such an approach would also seem consistent with the close physiological connections between these modalities and

emotional behavior. A change in emphasis in research may be afoot, and although the present reviews will include a preponderance of studies of detection and discrimination, it will at least be possible to show that the study of hedonic changes with age has been started.

DETECTION AND DISCRIMINATION

Taste

The studies reported here involve various psychophysical procedures to determine the so-called threshold concentration necessary for an observer either to identify a certain taste quality, for example, what concentration of sucrose is required to make it taste sweet, or to distinguish this substance from water even though the concentration may be so weak that he may not be able to judge whether it is salty or sweet. The keener the sensitivity, the lower the concentration defining threshold. Usually the so-called primary taste qualities, mixtures of which may presumably match any other taste, are used in this research. Thus, sucrose may be used for sweet, quinine for bitter, hydrochloric acid for sour, and sodium chloride for salty. These substances are diluted in water and usually presented to the subject for sipping and tasting in a more or less natural manner. (Variations on method will be presented in context.)

In their early work, Richter and Campbell (1940) found that both the ability to discriminate between sucrose and water and the ability to identify sucrose by its sweet taste could be done at lower concentrations by adults 19 to 50 years old than children between 7 and 11 although both of these groups were more sensitive than older adults ranging in age from 52 to 82.

These results were verified by Bourliére, Cendron, and Rapaport (1958) for both sweet and salty. Byrd and Gertman (1959), who grouped their subjects in ages between 18 and 25, 60 and 70, and 80 and 90, found the latter group consistently less likely to make correct identification of all the four primaries with no significant differences between them. Cooper, Bilash, and Zubek (1959) observed 100 subjects ranging from 19 to 89 years of age and found a significant age-effect, which seemed largely due to the sharp increase in threshold concentration after the late fifties. The results were about the same in all four taste qualities, except for an indication that the drop in sensitivity to sour takes place later than to sweet, salty, and bitter. It is worth noting in this connection that most anecdotal reports seem to suggest that with age there is an increase in the sensitivity to bitter, but this has apparently not been documented in experimental threshold studies.

In this field, as in many others in psychology, different methods have produced different results. In addition to the ages observed, the most important is the psychophysical procedure involved (Engen, 1971). Hermel, Schönwetter, and Samueloff (1970) used a different method of presenting the sapid substances. They presented drops of the substance on the subject's tongue and then asked for an identification of the taste quality. With this procedure sensitivity to salt was found unchanged over ages which ranged from 4 to 60. Adults over 48 were found to be less sensitive to sweet and bitter than children from 7 to 11, but the statistical significance of the differences is not reported.

In order to avoid the time-consuming and fatiguing aspects of these psychophysical procedures which demand repeated observations with each concentration of each quality whether presented in drops or sips, Hughes (1969) used a weak galvanic current presented on the tongue with an electrode. This electrical stimulation produces a taste sensation which varies with the amperage of the stimulus in a manner analogous to the concentration of sapid substances. Hughes found that young control subjects, 29 medical students less than 30 years of age, would experience a taste sensation at less than 10 microamps, while elderly people, 88 subjects ranging in age from 62 to 96, required stimulation at a higher level. Finer grouping of these subjects indicates that there was a continuous decrease of sensitivity from age 60 to 90. Once again, however, even when the methodology has been the same, different experimenters have not obtained the same results. Thus, Kranz, Berndt, and Wagner (1968) did not observe an age-effect in such electrical taste thresholds.

The same uncertainty applies to studies using animals as subjects. Considering the potential importance of using an animal model, the observation by Richter and Campbell (1940) that the rat and man have similar thresholds for sucrose is important. But here, too, more data are required. Brindley and Prior (1968) observed the effects of color related to age in the Bobwhite quail. Some of the subjects responded adversely to red. Yet these investigators did not observe any age differences in taste discrimination for any of the four taste qualities.

Despite the lack of uniformity of results, there have been attempts to make generalizations. In their work on the ability of man to detect phenylthiourea (PTC), which is known to be genetically determined, Harris and Kalmus (1949) reported that the threshold concentration of this substance would have to be doubled for every 20 years of age. In a later study, Kalmus and Trotter (1962) describe the change as being of the order of 3 percent in concentration per year.

Hinchcliffe (1962), who may have done the most extensive work as far as psychophysical theory is concerned and who made extensive observations of many modalities, including taste, hearing, vision, and corneal sensitivity (but not olfaction), concluded that "all sensory threshold sensitivities seem to show an exponential decrement with age when the intensity of the threshold stimulus is expressed in terms of a quantity, $(\phi-\phi_k)$, where ϕ is the physical intensity of the threshold stimulus and ϕ_k is the physical intensity of some reference level, which is constant for a given type of stimulus" (p. 50).

Smell

Weiss' conclusion, based on his review in 1959, that "the data on age changes in the sense of smell are sparse and contradictory" still applies, but a few studies have been added, and these may on balance support the hypothesis that this sense is not seriously affected by age *per se* but perhaps primarily by other factors associated with age.

As early as 1904 Vaschide reported that odor sensitivity declined with age, and, perhaps partly because this result is what one would expect, it seems to have been a generally accepted conclusion for smell as well as for all other modalities. Megighian (1958) also reported evidence that odor sensitivity decreases with age, as did Kimbrell and Furchgott (1963), Bartalena and Bocci (1964), Springer and Dietzmann (1970), and Rous (1969). Overall, the results are not inconsistent with Hinchcliffe's (1962) suggestion that sensitivity shows an exponential decrement with age.

Nevertheless, as early as 1943 Mesollela reported that he could not verify Vaschide's (1904) findings. Even the studies reporting decrement with age did not observe this in all cases. As noted by Kimbrell and Furchgott (1963), there are large individual differences. In addition, when these authors asked subjects to select by sniffing which of four test tubes contained an odorant (with the other four containing an odorless diluent), they found that the form of the function relating age to this ability differed for the two odorants they used. In the case of *n*-butanol the threshold increased monotonically with age, but in the case of iso-amyl acetate an asymptote was reached at the age of 70 with the threshold apparently unaffected with age from that point on.

Chalke, Dewhurst, and Ward (1958), who were concerned that a decrement in odor sensitivity might be an important factor in accidental poisoning, examined people over 65 years old in apparent good health who were members of so-called old folk's clubs. They compared them with 77 in- and out-patients in a hospital with various complaints (not specified) for their ability to detect town gas. For this purpose they developed an olfactometer which enabled them to present quantities of gas measured in parts per million (ppm) in air. Their results show that people under 65 were, in general, able to detect the gas at a lower concentration than those over 65, and they conclude that "about 30% of persons over 65 may be incapable of recognizing gas by smell" (p. 27). However, based on further analysis of the differences between patients and subjects from the old folks' club they indicate that the change in sensitivity may not be the result of age *per se*, but may be compounded with the health and the sex of the subject. The recognition thresholds were 25 ppm for patients over 65 and 10 for patients under 65, and the comparable figures for the subjects in the old folks' clubs were 10 versus 5. Differences between the sexes will be considered further below.

This study, like several others, calls attention to the important problem of the state of health of the subject. This point has also been emphasized since illness may be the reason for the apparent decrement of sensitivity with age. In a paper just prepared for publication, Rovee, Cohen, and Shlapack (1975) describe the stability in olfactory sensitivity involving 120 subjects ranging in age from 6 to 94. This study involved judgments that perceived the intensity of supra-threshold concentrations of *n*-propanol diluted in diethyl phthalate rather than its detection. The subject was asked to judge the intensity of seven concentrations ranging from 1.56% to 100% by producing varying length by markers on a slide such that the greater the perceived intensity the greater the length. No evidence was found that perceived intensity decreased as a function of age; in fact, two groups of older subjects, 60 to 70 and 80 to 90, were apparently more sensitive than subjects of intermediate ages, 20 to 50. These older subjects consisted primarily of retired faculty and staff members of the university, who represented a physically superior population.

One final but also as yet unpublished experiment (Engen and Zweban) also indicates that normal old subjects may show little if any sensory deficit. In this case, the task was detection as in the other studies reported above. Six subjects ranging in age from 60 to 74 were compared with a group of subjects of college age (20 to 22) in a difficult signal-detection task. Odor sensitivity was assessed by presentation of 0.08 millimoles of guaiacol (used for its smoky odor in a study of smoke detection) diluted in ethyl phthalate, and a so-called blank containing only the diluent, ethyl phthalate. Each substance was presented 50 times to each subject in a random sequence of 100 trials. Since only a small group of subjects was available, the potential significance of differences observed are dubious, but the older subjects did slightly less well than the college students. Individual differences are large in both groups so that any attempt to sort out the subjects in terms of age either for false positives (incorrectly identifying the blank as having a smoky odor) or for hits (correctly identifying the odor) would be difficult and probably of little practical consequence.

PREFERENCE

In this section we shall present the studies reported on hedonic properties of stimuli, as distinguished from their intensities, which are involved in discrimination and detection. Preference, of course, implies intensity discrimination and may be more significant in understanding the function of the modalities of taste and smell.

Taste

It is generally assumed that preference in taste depends on characteristics inherent in the stimulus (for example, sweet seems almost universally liked and bitter disliked), and also on habit and need. Habit and need might be of primary interest in the present case. Young (1957) stated that "New habits tend to form in agreement with body needs, but established habits tend to persist as regulators of food selection even when the selections are out of line with bodily needs."

In the case of the rat, Bloomquist and Cand-land (1965) could not find the effect of age on taste preferences for water, sucrose, quinine, salt, and hydrochloric acid they had expected from a review of a number of animal studies. In man there are to date apparently no published studies on the development of preferences with age. However, Susan S. Schiffman (personal communication) has recently performed several experiments involving aging and food preferences. In one study she presented common foods, such as apples, corned beef, fish, and cheese to blindfolded subjects by a method similar to that used by Hermel, Schönwetter, and Samueloff (1970) above. All foods were processed in a blender and presented by eye dropper in order to eliminate textural as well as visual clues. Schiffman obtained data both on the subject's ability to identify the food and the liking of the food by subjects selected for age and obesity. Her reports indicate that old people were the least able to identify these foods and the obese the best. But what is of greatest interest in the present context is the evidence that old subjects may dislike bitter more than the young. She suggests that the reason for this might be that age is associated with an increase in sensitivity to bitterness relative to a decrease in sensitivity to sweet and saltiness.

Smell

Based on developmental work with children, experiments indicate that taste preferences, for example, liking sweet, and aversions, for example, disliking bitter, may be innate, while odor preferences may be largely a result of cultural influences (Engen, 1974). Moncrieff (1966a,b), who has done the most extensive work on this topic, however, appears to favor explanations based on innate mechanisms, although he does not elaborate. His method was to instruct his subjects to rank-order odors sniffed from bottles from those liked best to those liked least. Based on a study of 132 odors with 550 people he concludes that age is one of the most important factors in odor preference, more important, for example, than sex. Regarding differences between adults and children, he observed that children less than 15 years old prefer odors of flowers much more than the fruity odors preferred by adults. For example, the liking of strawberry essence reaches it peak before age 10, then decreases to its minimum preference value at age 30 and remains stable from then on through the age of 60. For adults, there was a trend toward greater liking of "sophisticated flower smells." For example, the average preference for lavender oil tends to decrease from about 5 to 14, but then suddenly a liking for it develops, which reaches its asymptotic value at about age 30 and then remains there to old age. Thus, it is important to note that these changes take place relatively early in life and cannot be considered part of aging.

As a part of a study of objectionable traffic odors, Springer and Dietzmann (1970) asked observers, grouped according to age ranging from 15 to 65, to give hedonic ratings of diesel exhaust fumes presented in a mobile laboratory ("The Sniffmobile") which was utilized in large metropolitan areas such as San Antonio and Chicago. The response was made on a pictorial rating scale consisting of cartoon drawings of a person looking and being described as feeling that the odor was "neutral," "pleasant," "unpleasant," "very unpleasant," and "unbearable." According to their ratings, people over 65 found the odor less objectionable than younger people. Their ratings were similar to those subjects who, regardless of age, described themselves as in poor health. Springer assumes that health and age may be related and that they may reduce sensitivity to odor which in turns leads to higher preference ratings. This is not inconsistent with the interpretation suggested that it is health rather than age which is the crucial variable.

POSSIBLE EXPLANATIONS FOR AGE EFFECTS IN TASTE AND SMELL

Many, perhaps most, of the authors referred to above assume that there is a decrement of sensitivity with age and that it is based on anatomical and physiological changes associated with growing old. It must be borne in mind, of course, that some studies find no such change with age. Three factors associated with age and changes in taste and smell sensitivity are mentioned in this literature, namely, atrophy, sex, and smoking.

Atrophy

Many investigators have suggested that deterioration of nerves may explain decreased sensitivity with age, and they cite studies in which degenerative changes have been observed. For example, Arey, Tremaine, and Monzingo (1936, p. 18) reported that they observed in cadavers a "striking decline of taste buds in extreme old age (74-84)." Smith (1942) made similar observations in the case of olfactory nerves and suggested that there might be an even greater degeneration in the case of these fibers than in the case of other nerve fibers because of the inhalation of pollutants and diseases associated with the respiratory system.

Byrd and Gertman (1959) observed that hypergeusia may occur mainly in the oldest people observed in the kind of study reviewed here and suggest that "It may well be that the elevated threshold for groups of older persons, as indicated by the average, may be due to extremely high thresholds of a few individuals in the group." Unfortunately, neither they nor anyone else seem to be able to suggest any anatomical and physiological reason for such individual differences.

Megighian (1958) is another investigator who suggests that disease may be the reason for decrease in olfactory sensitivity. He found higher thresholds for people 70 to 90 years old but could propose no specific pathogenic hypothesis. Complicating matters still further, Kranz, Berndt, and Wagner (1968) performed histological examinations in connection with their study of electrical taste and concluded that disease will affect sensitivity, but increases and decreases have been associated more with some diseases than with others. In particular, Henkin (1969) has presented cases in which disease has *increased* sensitivity. Some sensory anomalies are genetic in nature (Amoore, 1971). (Although the data pertain only to development in infancy, an interesting paper on methods for observing morphological changes in olfaction with age is presented by Naessen, 1971.)

Hinchcliffe (1962) argues that the peripheral changes, for example in taste buds and olfactory nerves, are not correlated with functional changes and he speculates that degeneration of brain cells could be correlated with the exponential decrease in sensitivity observed in his psychophysical studies. In this connection, consideration of recent studies of cell replacement is relevant. The general view has been that nerve cells, such as sensory receptors, do not regenerate if destroyed. However, according to Beidler (1965), the taste bud "is seldom damaged permanently." Although cells of the taste bud only have an average life of about 250 hours, they are continually replaced, making it possible for the taste bud to remain sensitive despite noxious stimuli which are likely to be placed in the mouth. In addition, he states that the taste bud also has the power of regeneration and concludes that "it is useful to remember that the cells we are dealing with are not inanimate transducers but living structures that have many of the characteristics associated with other cells of the living body" (p. 198). It has also been suggested that replacement and regeneration may be possible in case of the sense of smell, but the research has not yet produced definitive data. However, histological evidence is suggestive (Takagi, 1971; Moulton, 1974).

Sex

As noted, the results by Chalke, Dewhurst, and Ward (1958) indicated higher olfactory thresholds for town gas in patients than in other old subjects of similar ages, but they suggest that this difference may be related to a sex difference. As they put it, "...since the expectation of life for women over 65 is somewhat greater than that for men of the same age, their faculties deteriorate less rapidly, and [that] the lower threshold of recognition for the 'non-institutionalized' might have been influenced by the proportion of women to men" (p. 27–28).

Differences associated with sex hormones seem well documented and have received increased attention recently (e.g., Vierling and Rock, 1967). Women are apparently most sensitive to odors 7 to 9 days before menses

and least sensitive during menstruation. Differences between children and adults may also be related to sex hormones (Koelega and Köster, 1974). Most of these studies, of course, have been done with young people, and there is apparently no information on the potential change in such sex hormones with older adults and their potential effect on odor sensitivity in old age.

In taste, Kalmus and Trotter (1962) observed that women seem to be more sensitive to PTC than men, a result also observed by Leguébe (1960). Cooper, Bilash, and Zubek (1959) found no such differences associated with sex, but Glanville, Kaplan, and Fischer (1964) did. Their subjects ranged from 3 years of age and it was observed that taste sensitivity increased up to an age of about 20, and then started decreasing, more rapidly for men than for women. A year later these investigators performed another experiment (Kaplan, Glanville, and Fischer, 1965) and concluded that it was smoking rather than sex which was the source of the difference in taste sensitivity.

Smoking

Kalmus and Trotter (1962) also noted that one might expect that the effect of such harmful agents and disease would decrease one's sensitivity to taste and smell. In their review, Kaplan, Glanville, and Fischer (1965) indicated that since men tend to smoke more than women, as documented by Matarazzo and Saslow (1960), the difference observed may be the result of duration and amount of smoking rather than age and sex. However, Hughes (1969) did not observe any effect of smoking in his study of older subjects. Likewise, Pangborn, Trabue, and Barylko-Pikielna (1967) found no effect in younger subjects. According to Moncrieff (1968), the effect of smoking might be specific such that one may only observe a decrease in sensitivity to test substances, for example, pyridine, which is also part of tobacco smoke.

CONCLUSIONS

1. Although the literature on the present topic has increased substantially during the last decade, there is as yet not enough information

to make generalizations which may be of practical value, for example, in diagnosing sensory deficits or influencing diets. In addition, different investigators have used different methods with the result that the available information is both incomplete and unsystematic. One would expect this field to benefit from (a) modern psychometric procedures which make it possible to separate the effects of aging on sensory capacity from other effects, and (b) more emphasis on measuring preference rather than sensitivity.

2. Although a number of investigators have observed that taste sensitivity decreases with age, one must view this conclusion cautiously. Not all experiments have been able to verify it. The evidence of changes in taste preferences such as increased aversion for bitter is worthy of further study, for preference may be more characteristic of these modalities than detection.

3. As in the case of taste, no firm conclusions can be drawn about smell. However, odor sensitivity seems very stable over age. Observed decreases with age may have been the result of other factors such as disease, sex differences, and smoking. Odor preferences do seem to change with age but relatively early in life and more under the influence of maturation or learning than aging.

4. Atrophy is associated with aging and is often mentioned as a possible reason for decrement of sensitivity with age. However, the evidence is uncertain and, in addition, regeneration is possible so that transducers of taste and smell may not be depleted with age.

REFERENCES

Amoore, J. E. 1971. Olfactory genetics and anosmia. *In*, L. M. Beidler (ed.), *Handbook of Sensory Physiology*, *Vol. IV, Chemical Senses 1, Olfaction*, pp. 245–256, New York: Springer Verlag.

Arey, L. B., Tremaine, M. J., and Monzingo, F. L. 1936. The numerical and topographical relations of taste buds to human circumvallate papillae throughout the life span. *Anat. Record*, **64**, (1), Suppl. 1.

Bartalena, G., and Bocci, C. 1964. L'Acutezza e la fatica olfactoria in relazoine alla'etta anagrafica e biologica. *Clin. Otorinolaring.*, **16**, 409–415.

Beidler, L. M. 1965. Comparison of gustatory receptors, olfactory receptors, and free nerve endings. *In, Cold Spring Harbor Symposia on Quantitative Biology*, **30**, 191–200.

Bloomquist, D. W., and Candland, D. K. 1965. Taste preferences measured by tongue licks and bar presses as a function of age in the rat. *Psychon. Sci.*, **3**, 393–394.

Bourliére, F., Cendron, H., and Rapaport, A. 1958. Modification avec l'âge des senils gustatifs de perception et de reconnaissance aux saveurs salée et sucrée chez l'homme. *Gerontologia*, **2**, 104–112.

Brindley, L. D., and Prior, S. 1968. Effects of age on taste discrimination in the bobwhite quail. *Animal. Behav.* **16**, 304–307.

Byrd, E., and Gertman, S. 1959. Taste sensitivity in aging persons. *Geriatrics*, **14**, 381–384.

Chalke, H.D., Dewhurst, J. R., and Ward, C. W. 1958. Loss of sense of smell in old people. *Public Health*, London, 72(6), 223–230.

Comalli, P. E., Jr. 1967. Perception and Age. *Gerontologist*, 7(2), 73–77.

Cooper, R. M., Bilash, I., and Zubek, J. P. 1959. The effect of age on taste sensitivity. *J. Gerontol.*, **14**, 56–58.

Corso, J. F. 1971. Sensory processes and age effects in normal adults. *J. Gerontol.*, **26**, 90–105.

Engen, T. 1971. Olfactory psychophysics. *In*, L. M. Beidler (ed.), *Handbook of Sensory Physiology*, *Vol. IV, Chemical Senses 1, Olfaction*, pp. 216–244. New York: Springer-Verlag.

Engen, T. 1973. The sense of smell. *Annual Review of Psychogy*, **24**, 187–206.

Engen, T. 1974. Method and theory in the study of odor preferences. *In*, J. W. Johnston, Jr., D. G. Moulton, and A. Turk (eds.), *Human Responses to Environmental Odors*. New York: Academic Press 1974.

Frisch, K. von. 1934. Über den geschmackssinn der beine. Ein beitrag zur vergleichenden physiologie des geschmacks. *Z. Vergleich. Physiol.*, **21**, 1–156.

Glanville, E. V., Kaplan, A. R., and Fischer, R. 1964. Age, sex, and taste sensitivity. *J. Gerontol.*, **19**, 474–478.

Harris, H., and Kalmus, H. 1949. The measurement of taste sensitivity to *phenylthiourea* (P.T.C.). *Annals of Eugenics*, Cambridge, **15**, 24–31.

Henkin, R. I. 1969. The metabolic regulation of taste acuity. *In*, C. Pfaffmann (ed.), *Olfaction and Taste*, Proceedings of the Third International Symposium, pp. 575–586. New York: The Rockefeller University Press.

Hermel, J., Schönwetter, S., and Samueloff, S. 1970. Taste sensation identification and age in man. *J. Oral Med.*, **25**, 39–42.

Hinchcliffe, R. 1962. Aging and sensory threshold. *J. Gerontol.*, **17**, 45–50.

Hughes, G. 1969. Changes in taste sensitivity with advancing age. *Gerontol. Clin.*, **11**, 224–230.

Kalmus, H., and Trotter, W. R. 1962. Direct assessment of the effect of age on P.T.C. sensitivity. *Ann. Human Genet.*, **26**, 145–149.

Kaplan, A. R., Glanville, E. V., and Fischer, R. 1965. Cumulative effect of age and smoking on taste sensitivity in males and females. *J. Gerontol.*, **20**, 334–337.

Kimbrell, G. McA., and Furchgott, E. 1963. The effect of aging on olfactory threshold. *J. Gerontol.*, **18**, 364–365.

Koelega, H. S., and Köster, E. P. 1974. Some experiments on sex differences in odor perception. *Ann. N.Y. Acad. Sci.*, **237**, 234–246.

Kranz, D., Berndt, H., and Wagner, H. 1968. Studies on age-dependent changes of the taste threshold. *Archiv fur Klinische und Experimenteele Ohren-, Nasen, und Kehlkopfheilkunde*, **192**, 258–267.

Leguébe, A. 1960. Génétique et antropologie de la sensibilité á la phenylthiocarbamide. *Bull. Inst. Roy. Sci. Vat. Belingeuque*, **36**, 1–27.

Matarazzo, J. D. and G. Saslow. Psychological and related characteristics of smokers and non-smokers. *Psychol. Bull.* (1960), **57**, 493–513.

Megighian, D. 1958. Variazioni della soglia olfattiva nelleta senile. *Minerva Otorinolaringolica*, Torino, **8** (9), 331–337.

Mesolella, V. L'olfatto nelle diverse età. *Archivo Italiano di Otologia Rinologia e Laringologia*, **46**, 43–62.

Moncrieff, R. W. 1966a. *Odour Preferences.* New York: John Wiley.

Moncrieff, R. W. 1966b. Changes in olfactory preferences with age. *Revue de Laryngologie Otologie Rhinologie*, **86**, 895–904.

Moncrieff, R. W. 1968. Sensory discrimination and smoking. *Food Process. Mkt.*, **37**, 303–305.

Moulton, D. G. 1974. Cell renewal in the olfactory epithelium of the mouse. *Ann. N.Y. Acad. Sci.*, **237**, 52–61.

Naessen, R. 1971. An enquiry on the morphological characteristics and possible changes with age in the olfactory region of man. *Acta Oto-laryngol.*, **71**, 49–62.

Pangborn, R. M., Trabue, I. M., and Barylko-Pikielna, N. 1967. Taste, odor, and tactile discrimination before and after smoking. *Percept. and Psychophys.*, **2**, 529–532.

Richter, C. P., and Campbell, K. H. 1940. Sucrose taste thresholds of rats and humans. *Am. J. Physiol.*, **128**, 291–297.

Rous, J. 1969. Effect of age on the functional state of the olfactory analyser. *Ceskoslovenska Otolaryngologie*, **18**, 248–256.

Rovee, C. K., Cohen, R. Y., and Shlapack, W. 1975. Life span stability in olfactory sensitivity. *Developmental Psychology*, **11**, 311–318.

Schiffman, S. S. 1973. The dietary rehabilitation clinic: A multi-aspect, dietary and behavior approach to the treatment of obesity. Presented at the Association for Advancement of Behavior Therapy, Miami, Florida.

Smith, C. S. 1942. Age incidence of atrophy of olfactory nerves in man. *J. Comp. Neurol.*, **77**, 589–595.

Springer, K. J., and Dietzmann, H. E. 1970. Correlation studies of diesel exhaust odor measured by instrumental methods to human odor panel ratings. Presented at the Odor Conference at the Korlinska Institute, Stockholm, Sweden.

Takagi, S. F. 1971. Degeneration and regeneration of the olfactory epithelium. *In*, L. M. Beidler (ed.), *Handbook of Sensory Physiology, Vol. IV, Chemical Senses 1, Olfaction*, pp. 75–94. New York: Springer-Verlag.

Vaschide, N. 1904. L'état de la sensibilité olfactive dans la vieillesse. *Bull. Laryng.*, **7**, 323–333.

Vierling, J. S., and Rock, J. 1967. Variations in olfactory sensitivity to Exaltolide during the menstrual cycle. *J. Appl. Physiol.*, **22**(2), 311–315.

Weiss, A. D. 1959. Sensory functions. *In*, J. E. Birren (ed.), *Handbook of Aging and the Individual: Psychological and Biological Aspects.* Chicago: University of Chicago Press.

Young, P. T. 1957. Psychogenic factors regarding the feeding process. *Am. J. Clin. Nutrition*, **5**, 154–161.

23
AGE CHANGES IN TOUCH, VIBRATION, TEMPERATURE, KINESTHESIS AND PAIN SENSITIVITY

Dan R. Kenshalo*
Florida State University

INTRODUCTION

Somesthesis includes those sensations that arise from normal and intensive stimulation of the skin, the viscera, and kinesthesis—the muscle and joint sense. Changes in somesthetic sensitivity that may occur with advancing age can be better understood when described in the context of the changes in the anatomical and physiological characteristics of the aging skin, muscles, joints, viscera, and nervous system. While the primary concern of this chapter is with changes in somesthetic sensitivitiy that might be associated with advancing age, consideration will also be given to the changes in the skin, receptors, and peripheral nerves that might account for these changes in sensitivity.

The implication of the title of this chapter is that changes in somesthetic sensitivity are the direct consequence of growing old. It should be borne in mind, however, that these may not be due directly and exclusively to aging, per se, but may also result from the increased probability, with added years of life, of the occurrence of injury or pathological conditions that affect

the skin, the receptors, or the nervous system. For example, peripheral neuropathies are known to be associated with disorders such as pernicious anemia (Lockner, Reizenstein, Wennberg, and Widen, 1969), diabetes (Thomas and Lascelles, 1965, 1966), and occlusive vascular disease involving the vaso nervorum and connective tissue outgrowth (Cottrell, 1940). Mild neuropathies may go undetected by standard clinical neurological tests (Lockner et al., 1969).

In the peripheral nervous system neuropathies result in the loss of as much as 32 percent of the axons in the dorsal and ventral roots and neuron cell bodies in the dorsal root ganglia in 80-year-old humans (Corbin and Gardner, 1937; Gardner, 1940). These observations could not be replicated in aged cats* or rats (Birren and Wall, 1956). Abnormally short internode lengths for nerve fibers of a given diameter have been observed in apparently normal, aged humans (Lascelles and Thomas, 1966) and are even more pronounced in diabetics (Thomas and Lascelles, 1965). The authors suggest that the anomalous internode lengths may have re-

*Preparation of chapter was assisted by USPHS Grant NS-02992 and NSF Grant GB-30610

*See Dr. Moyer's discussion (Birren et al., 1959, p. 64).

sulted from segmental demyelination and re-myelination or as a result of complete degeneration and subsequent regeneration of the peripheral nerve fibers. The abnormally short internode lengths may account for the mildly slower conduction velocity in the ulnar nerves of apparently normal aged compared to young humans observed by Norris, Shock, and Wagman (1952). Others, however (Birren and Wall, 1956; Wayner and Emmers, 1958), have been unable to demonstrate slowed conduction velocities in the peripheral nerves of rats. But the slowing of nerve conduction observed in elderly humans is small, and the length of any rat peripheral nerve is much less than that of the human ulnar nerve, both of which make any possible differences due to the age of the rats difficult to detect.

Data that demonstrate a loss of somesthetic sensitivity with advancing age can be attributed to age only in a broad sense. Beyond that it is yet to be determined if the loss is the direct result of aging, as in the case of presbyopia, or of specific neuropathies due to disease or injury, whose probabilities of occurrence increase with age and, therefore, make the loss only the indirect result of aging.

CUTANEOUS SENSITIVITY

Qualitative studies in the clinical literature describe a general degradation of somesthetic sensitivity with advancing age. According to some clinicians, measurements of the two-point, tactile, vibratory, thermal, and pain thresholds all show increased values in the elderly. The sensitivity of the feet starts to decrease at an earlier age than that of the forearm to all stimuli (Critchley, 1931; Enomoto, 1969). The expectation that these deficiencies occur in most aged persons, however, appears to be erroneous. Skre (1972) reports impaired vibratory sensitivity in the upper extremities in only 5 percent and in the lower extremities in 40 percent of his 64 to 73-year-old subjects, while Himel and MacDonald (1957) found impaired vibratory sensitivity of the lower extremities in approximately 23 percent of their 31 subjects who were 80 years of age and older. Howell (1949) conducted standard neurological

tests on 200 elderly male subjects ranging in age from 65 to 91 years. Twenty-four percent (48 subjects) showed impaired cutaneous sensitivity of one type or another. Ten percent did not register pain, and 10 percent did not appreciate changes in temperature, while only 5 percent failed to perceive light touch. In some, pain and temperature sensations were diminished over the same area of the body. In others, one modality appeared to be normal while the other was impaired. Findings of sensory loss were most frequent in the men beyond the eighth decade in age. At that age vibratory sensitivity was practically normal at the wrist, elbow, and shoulder but showed marked deterioration at the ankle (10 percent), shin (28 percent), knee (28 percent), and especially the sacrum (90 percent).

Thus, reports of increased mean thresholds for a particular modality with advancing age may be misleading. Reports of the frequency of occurrence of significant changes in somesthetic sensitivity are more meaningful in assessing the degeneration of function as related to age.

Touch

Sensitivity. Ronge's (1943a) is the only report seen in which a systematic investigation of touch was carried out as a function of age. Unfortunately, his subject population was small; he had only 10 subjects ranging from 12 to 76 years of age. The stimulus area was 2 cm^2, divided into a 10 × 10 grid, on the ulnar aspect of the volar wrist. An aesthesiometer (von Frey hairs) was used to deliver tactile stimuli of five intensitities, from 1.4 to 6.3 gm/mm^2, to each square of the grid. There seemed to be a reduction in the number of touch spots responding at all intensities of stimulation in the subjects up to the sixth decade of age. The subjects in the sixth and seventh decade age groups showed an increase in the number of touch spots. In this small sample the trend could have resulted from a sample bias. However, since the subjects in the sixth and seventh decade showed a greater number of spots responding with intensity increases than the younger subjects, and because the older subjects also gave pain responses at lower intensities of stimulation than the younger subjects, Ronge suggested that structural changes in the skin at the older ages made the skin easier to deform.

Sensitivity to light touch, measured by an aesthesiometer, on both the palm and thumb has been found to be significantly less ($p < 0.01$) in old (63 to 78 years old) than in young (20 to 36 years old) subjects (Axelrod and Cohen, 1961). No data were presented on the frequency of occurrence of a loss in touch sensitivity in their old subjects. In both groups the palm was slightly, though not significantly, less sensitive than the thumb.

The cornea of the eye provides a unique opportunity to study changes in the sensitivity of free nerve endings as a function of age. The cornea is known to possess a uniform population of fine branching fibers without special end organs—free nerve endings (Zander and Weddell, 1951). Two investigations of this type have been found. Zobel (1938) measured the sensitivity of the cornea in terms of the pressure required by von Frey hairs to elicit a report of a sensation within 1 to 2 seconds. A total of 531 corneas of subjects who ranged from 5 to 90 years of age were used. He found that the center of the cornea was most sensitive to the applied pressure and that sensitivity decreased the more peripherally the stimulus was placed. He described sensitivity changes with age as first increasing to the fifth decade and then decreasing "sharply" thereafter. Unfortunately, he reported only means, and it is not clear that the increase in sensitivity between age 15 and 50 was statistically significant. The increase in sensitivity was only 0.2 gm/mm^2 (from 0.7 to 0.5 gm/mm^2) for stimuli placed in the center of the cornea. Sensitivity decreased by 0.45 gm/mm^2 (from 0.5 to 0.95 gm/mm^2) from age 50 to 80.

Jalavisto, Orma, and Tawast (1951) measured the corneal sensitivity by air puffs of controlled pressure and duration in 43 subjects, divided into three age groups: 11 subjects aged 11 to 20, 6 aged 39 to 50, and 26 aged 65 to 81 years. The durations of the air puffs were 500, 100, 50, 25, 16.7, and 10 msec. Virtually identical chronaxies of 0.113, 0.093, and 0.095 were found for the young, middle, and old age groups. However, at short durations of

air puffs (<50 msec) the old group was significantly less sensitive than the middle and young age groups. The authors interpret their findings as indicating a decrease in corneal sensitivity with advancing age. An alternate interpretation suggests that older subjects require longer times for temporal summation, a process that is thought to be an integrative function of the central nervous system (Zwislocki, 1960). Such integrative functions have been found to be adversely affected by age (Axelrod, Thompson, and Cohen, 1968).

Anatomy. In an attempt to account for the increased number of touch spots and reports of pain in subjects beyond the sixth decade, Ronge (1943a) suggested that structural changes in the skin at the older ages made the skin easier to deform. Changes of this type might result from a thinning of the epidermis, a decrease in the collagen, or a decrease in the elastic fibers in the superficial layers of the dermis, or all three.

There is no general agreement that thinning of the epidermis and the dermis is a general characteristic of aged skin. Some maintain that by age 60 a general thinning of the epidermis has occurred. It is especially noticeable on the dorsum of the hands, where prominent blue veins and yellow tendons may be seen through the translucent skin. Likewise, the dermis has also thinned and has become inelastic with advancing age (Jackson, 1972). Others, however, have failed to note any consistent thinning of the epidermis or dermis with advancing age (Montagna, 1965; Whitton, 1973). There may well be inconsistent effects of age upon skin thickness, and Ronge's suggestion may be correct that structural changes of the skin of his few elderly subjects account for their increased tactile sensitivity.

Decreased amounts of both collagen (Pearce and Grimmer, 1972) and elastin (Ma and Cowdry, 1950) are found in aged skin. The decreased amount of elastin is more evident in the subepithelial elastic plexus than in the deeper fiber layer. The elastic fibers tend to split into component fibrils in the subepithelial plexus, and this is consistent with the notion that the material that binds them has

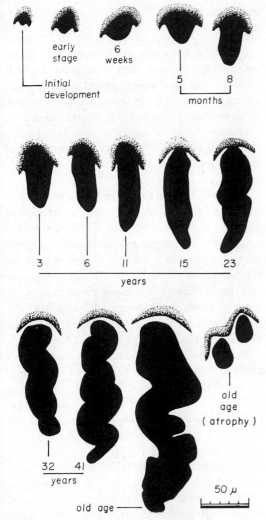

early
stage   6
weeks

└─ Initial
development

5   8

months

3   6   ll   l5   23

years

32   4l
years

old age ──

old
age
(atrophy)

50 μ

Figure 1. Changes of size, shape, and relation-ship to the epidermis of Meissner corpuscles from birth to old age. Scale drawing from mi-crograph and wax plate reconstruction. ×240. (From Cauna, 1965, Figure 20.)

loosened (Ma and Cowdry, 1950; Pearce and Grimmer, 1972). These changes agree with the observation that the skin of young rats is stronger (tensile strength) than that of old rats (Sussman, 1973).

Changes in the morphology and the decreased numbers of Meissner corpuscles that attend advancing age appear to account for the de-creased sensitivity of thumb and thenar emi-nence with age reported by Axelrod and Cohen (1961). As seen in Figure 1, Meissner corpus-cles, which are suggested as the receptor respon-sible for the exquisite sensitivity to light touch and the small two-point limen found in the palmar and plantar skin of the hands and feet (Cauna, 1954; Winkelmann, 1956), are oval capsular endings located almost exclusively in the dermal papillae of glabrous skin (Bolton, Winkelmann, and Dyck, 1966). Each corpuscle is surrounded by an elastic capsule which, in the young, is attached to the epidermis above and the general elastic framework of the dermis below. In old skin the attachment of the cor-puscle to the epidermis is loose and may even become nonexistent (Cauna, 1954).

Figure 2 shows the density and the relation to dermal ridges and to sweat pores of Meissner corpuscles identified in the skin of the distal phalanx of the index finger taken from subjects 3, 32, and 83 years old.

The results of all investigations seen agree that there is a continuous decrease in the num-ber of Meissner corpuscles from the first decade to old age (Cauna, 1965; Dickens, Winkelmann, and Mulder, 1963; Hunter, Ridley, and Malle-son, 1969; Martinez, 1931; Meissner, 1853; Quilliam and Ridley, 1971; Ridley, 1968; Ronge, 1943b). Furthermore, there are differ-ences in the concentrations of these capsules in various parts of glabrous skin. The concen-tration in the palmer skin of the digits is greater than in the thenar eminence and they are more numerous in the hand than in the plantar sur-face of the great toe of adults. There are also marked regional differences in their concen-tration in great toe specimens. The peak con-centration appears to occur at about the center of the pad (Bolton, Winkelmann, and Dyck, 1966).

Free nerve endings form a considerable net-work in the upper layers of the dermis. Intra-epidermal free nerve endings are usually not found after birth (Cauna, 1965), although they may be encountered in certain adults (Quilliam and Ridley, 1971). Throughout adult life the density and morphology of dermal free endings seem to remain relatively unchanged (Cauna, 1965; Hunter, Ridley, and Malleson, 1969). Their enduring character with advancing age may well account for the lack of an unquivocal decrease in the sensitivity of the cornea at advanced ages.

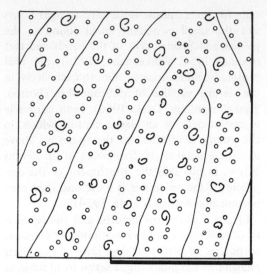

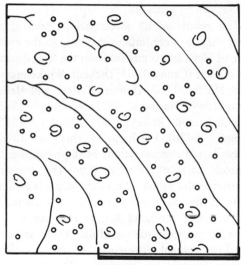

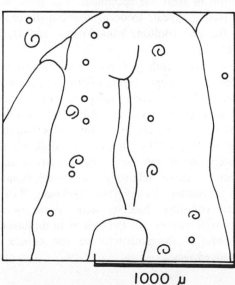

1000 μ

Vibration

Sensitivity. Changes in sensitivity to vibratory stimuli with advancing age have enjoyed somewhat greater interest than light touch in both clinical and laboratory investigations. This interest is probably because changes in vibratory sensitivity have been found to be of diagnostic value in assessing disorders of the nervous system. Furthermore, the instrument used to measure it is convenient and portable (a tuning fork).

In normal, young subjects sensitivity to vibration is a function of its frequency. As seen in Figure 3 the threshold of a vibrating stimulus applied to the finger pad or thenar eminence decreases at a moderate rate as frequency is increased up to 50 to 90 Hz. At higher frequencies the threshold decreases more rapidly to reach a minimum between 200 and 300 Hz; thereafter it increases rapidly (Mountcastle, La-Motte, and Carli, 1972; Perret and Regli, 1970; Talbot, Darian-Smith, Kornhuber and Mountcastle, 1968; Verrillo, 1968). The frequency curve of vibratory sensitivity measured on the great toe yields a similarly shaped function, except the toe is, overall, less sensitive than the finger pad or thenar eminence (Perret and Regli, 1970; Rosenberg, 1958).

Clinical and experimental measurements agree that there is a definite loss of sensitivity to vibration in a significant proportion of aged subjects apparently free of disease or detectable neuropathy (Goff, Rosner, Detre, and Kennard, 1965; Keighley, 1946; Laidlaw and Hamilton, 1937b; Newman and Corbin, 1936). The loss appears to start at about 50 years of age and is more severe in the lower than the upper extremities (Cosh, 1953; Howell, 1949; Pearson, 1928; Perret and Regli, 1970; Rosenberg, 1958; Steiness, 1957). Figure 4 shows that with advancing age the frequency function

Figure 2. The distribution pattern of Meissner corpuscles (small circles) in relation to the papillary ridges and sweat duct orifaces (spirals) in the central area of the distal phalanx of the index fingers of a 3-year-old child (top), a 32-year-old female (middle), and an 83-year-old male. The density of Meissner corpuscles are about 69, 27, and 8 per mm^2, respectively. X32. (From Cauna, 1965, Figures 33, 34, and 35.)

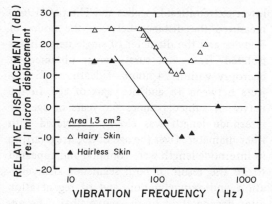

VIBRATION FREQUENCY (Hz)

Figure 3. Comparison of vibrotactile thresholds on hairy and glabrous skin for a contactor area of 1.3 cm². (The horizontal lines through 14 and 25 dB represent the curves obtained using a contactor area of 0.2 cm². Curves drawn to fit the experimental data have a slope of − 12 dB.) (From Verrillo, 1966. *Journal of Experimental Psychology,* 72, 47–50. Copyright 1966 by the American Psychological Association. Reprinted by permission.)

of vibratory sensitivity decreases more or less uniformly at all frequencies (Goff *et al.*, 1965; Keighley, 1946; Perret and Regli, 1970) although Goff *et al.* found that the loss in females was confined to frequencies above 150 Hz.

Anatomy. The frequency function of vibratory sensitivity appears to be a duplex curve and suggests that two different types of receptor, each with its own operating characteristics, co-operate to form the complete curve (Talbot, *et al.*, 1968; Verrillo, 1968). Convincing evidence has been presented that the receptors involved are superficial, quick adapting receptors (QA) that entrain impulses well at frequencies up to 90 Hz while the responses at higher frequencies are attributed to the more deeply placed Pacinian corpuscles (Mountcastle, LaMotte, and Carli, 1972; Talbot *et al.*, 1968; Verrillo, 1968). In glabrous skin the QA receptors may be free nerve endings, Meissner corpuscles, or both, and the Pacinian corpuscles found in the deep dermis and subcutis. In hairy skin the QA receptors may be free nerve endings, hair follicle receptors, or both, and the Pacinian corpuscles involved are those lying close to the periosteum, tendons, and joints. The position of these Pacinian corpuscles accounts for the greater

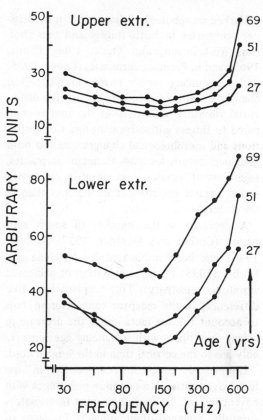

FREQUENCY (Hz)

Figure 4. Vibrotactile thresholds, plotted in arbitrary units, measured on the styloid process and the internal malleolus of the preferred side as a function of age. (From Perret and Regli, 1970. *European Neurology,* 4, 65–76. Basel: Karger.)

success observed in eliciting a vibratory sensation when the foot of the tuning fork is firmly placed against one of the bony prominences than when applied to soft tissue. It has led some to label vibratory sensitivity the "bone sense" (Minor, 1904).

Several explanations have been advanced for the difference in vibratory sensitivity of the fingers and toes and for the loss of vibratory sensitivity with advancing age. The markedly lower concentration of Meissner corpuscles in the great toe than in the finger pad may account for the differences in vibratory sensitivity in the fingers and toes. Were this true, then a difference in vibratory sensitivity should appear only at frequencies up to about 100 Hz, unless there is a similar difference in the concentration of Pacinian corpuscles, a circumstance for which there is no evidence.

Marked morphological changes occur in Meissner corpuscles in both fingers and toes (Bolton, Winkelmann, and Dyck, 1966; Cauna, 1965) and in Pacinian corpuscles (Cauna, 1965) with advancing age. These morphological changes do not seem to account for the differential vibratory sensitivity in the toes as compared to fingers with advancing age. Concentrations and morphological changes occur in both Meissner corpuscles and Pacinian corpuscles, regardless of location, yet vibratory sensitivity shows greater impairment in the toes than in the fingers.

A decrease in the number of spinal root nerves (Corbin and Gardner, 1937; Gardner, 1940) has been implicated by Newman and Corbin (1936) in the explanation of decreased vibratory sensitivity. This explanation, like differences in the receptor concentration, fails to account for the facts unless the decrease in spinal root fibers with advancing age is markedly less in the cervical than in the lumbar cord.

Diminished circulation, especially in the lower extremities, is a common occurrence with advancing age. Even though most investigators carefully screened their subjects for signs of circulatory disorders, it is possible that changes in the microcirculation of the legs (Rosenberg, 1958) or of the lower spinal cord (Pearson, 1928) went undetected and thus account for the decreased sensitivity to vibration in the toes of the aged.

Magladery (1959) also suggested that ischemia due to impaired circulation may be responsible for the loss of vibratory sensitivity in the feet. He cites data that light touch (yet to be satisfactorily demonstrated) and vibratory sensitivity are both decreased in aged subjects. In studies of sensory dissociation, usually produced by ischemia, these sensations are the first to be affected, and they disappear after about the same length of ischemia. However, in the several studies that screened the subjects for circulatory defects impaired vibratory sensitivity was nevertheless demonstrated (Goff et al., 1965; Rosenberg, 1958; Perret and Regli, 1970).

Yet another morphological change associated with aging has been suggested to account for the loss of vibratory sensitivity especially in the lower extremities. Lascelles and Thomas (1966) measured the distance between the nodes of Ranvier and the diameter of single nerve fibers isolated from the sural nerve, obtained at necropsy within 24 hours of death, of 15 subjects between 18 and 80 years of age. In the nerves of subjects under 65 years of age the internode length was closely correlated with fiber diameter. Over the age of 65, irregularities in internode length were common and appeared to be the result of both segmental demyelination and remyelination and of regeneration after degeneration of the nerve fiber. The unequal involvement of the nerve fibers, especially the larger ones, will lead to a temporal dispersion of an impulse volley at higher nervous centers due to slowed conduction velocities in the affected fibers. The changes in conduction velocity, they suggest, are likely to result in the loss of tendon reflexes and vibration sensitivity, both of which depend on the conduction of synchronous volleys of impulses. The longer the conduction path the more this synchrony may be disrupted.

Vibratory sensitivity is known to be diminished uniformly across frequency, independent of age, in individuals suffering from diabetes and pernicious anemia (Goff et al., 1965). In advanced stages both conditions are known to produce neuropathies.

Some evidence indicates that decreased vibratory sensitivity may be due to dietary deficiencies, such as that of thiamin, a deficiency more common among the aged than in the young (Horwitt, Liebert, Kreisler, and Wittman, 1946).

Temperature

Sensitivity. The ASHRAE (American Society of Heating, Refrigeration, and Air-Conditioning Engineers) Handbook (1967), which sets the standard conditions to attain comfort in heated and air conditioned spaces, states that the preferred temperature for persons over 40 years old is about 0.5°C higher than that desired by younger persons. However, in a survey conducted on 64 subjects whose mean age was 75 years, Rohles (1969) found that their rating of thermal comfort gave distributions identical to college and middle age adults.

Although thermal comfort criteria may not change with advancing age, the ability of the elderly temperature regulating system to cope with extreme environmental temperature appears to be impaired. Elderly subjects (57–91 years) are less able to maintain body core temperature when exposed to cold (5°–15°C) for periods of 60 to 90 minutes. Core temperature was lowered by as much as 1°C in the elderly while no change could be detected in the core temperature of the young subjects (Krag and Kountz, 1950).

Measurements of the detectability of radiant warm stimuli have been made by Clark and Mehl (1971) on groups of subjects that they classed as young and old. The young group ranged from 18 to 30 years, and the old group ranged from 30 to 67 years. The method of signal detection was used. This method allows an assessment of detectability of the stimulus independent of attitudinal or response biases, motivation, or criteria (Egan and Clarke, 1966). Clark and Mehl found that their "old" subjects detected the warm stimuli almost as well as the young subjects. Their "old" subjects, however, were not as advanced in age as those in other studies on the effects of aging.

Classical psychophysical methods have been used to measure the sensitivity of aged people to warm and cool stimuli applied to the dorsal forearm close to the elbow (Kenshalo, 1970). Only three subjects were tested (age 74, 73, and 70 years) but, as seen in Figure 5, no differences were encountered between these and college aged subjects that could not be attributed to the decision process. One of the older subjects was significantly more sensitive to cool stimuli than any of the college subjects tested.

Pain

Sensitivity. The sensitivity to pain as a function of age is the most actively investigated of the skin senses. Yet reports of threshold vary strikingly between subjects, between experimenters, and between experimental conditions.

In this section, similarities and differences in the measurements of pain tolerance and pain threshold will be considered. The discussion of pain will also be divided into cutaneous and

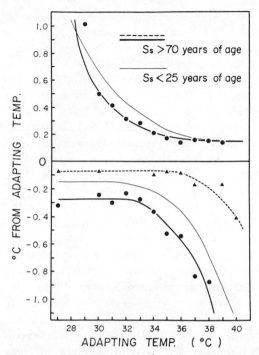

Figure 5. Comparison of the temperature sensitivity of one male, age 75, and one female, age 71 (combined), and the cool threshold of one female, age 75, with the mean thermal thresholds of seven young males. The skin was first adapted to one of the adapting temperatures shown along the x axis. The intensity of changes in the temperature of the thermode sufficient to elicit a threshold warm or cool sensation are shown on the y axis. (From Kenshalo, 1970. *In*, W. D. Neff (ed.), *Contributions to Sensory Physiology*. New York: Academic Press.)

deep pains, not that they are necessarily different in receptors, pathways, or other operating characteristics, but because they are frequently subject to different experimental treatments.

Pain Tolerance and Threshold. Pain is more than a sensory phenomenon. In addition to its sensory component it has cognitive and motivational aspects that play important roles in how a subject responds to noxious stimuli (Melzack and Casey, 1968; Melzack and Wall, 1965). Much of the outcome of experiments on the pain threshold, and especially pain tolerance, depends on how the subject views the experimental situation, the experimenter, and even upon the instructions given (Gelfand, 1964).

A question arises as to whether pain threshold and pain tolerance are measures of different aspects of a noxious experience or are measures of the same aspects. The proposition has been tested. When pain tolerance was defined as the time from the onset of a noxious stimulus (heat, mechanical, and electrical) to withdrawal, Clark and Bindra (1956) obtained significantly high correlations between times to the pain threshold and to the pain tolerance level. This result indicates that pain threshold and pain tolerance hold some variables in common. One is the time required to achieve the pain threshold. So, when time from the occurrence of the pain threshold to time of withdrawal was used as a measure of pain tolerance, the correlation became insignificantly small (Gelfand, Ullmann, and Krasner, 1963). This result was interpreted to mean that many of the variables that determine pain tolerance are different from those that determine pain threshold. Benjamin (1958) has also presented evidence that pain tolerance and pain threshold are probably not highly related.

Measurements of pain tolerance are markedly affected by "instructions to the subject" whereas the effect on pain threshold is not so great. Other situational and interpersonal variables such as the type of subject, the nature of the pain experience, the personality and prestige of the experimenter, and his relationship to the subjects play larger roles in determining pain tolerance than pain threshold (Gelfand, 1964).

These results do not necessarily indicate that attitudinal factors do not influence pain thresholds. Hall and Stride (1954) found that their anxious patients reported pain at lower stimulus intensities than nonanxious patients, that instructions to the subjects could make both age and sex differences disappear and reappear, and that subjects not informed that the experiment involved pain had higher pain thresholds than those so informed.

Cognitive and motivational factors clearly play a significant role in determining pain thresholds and play an even greater role in determining pain tolerance as measured in experimental situations. However, many clinicians maintain that investigations involving experimentally produced pain minimize these cognitive-motivational aspects, whereas in clinical investigations of pathologically produced pain the contribution of these aspects is considerably greater (Beecher, 1959). The role of these situational variables is considerable in determining experimental pain thresholds, and it is even greater in determining experimental pain tolerance levels. Their role in clinical pain may, as Beecher suggests, be still greater.

Cutaneous Pain. The sensitivity to painful stimuli with advancing age has been extensively investigated. Unfortunately, convincing evidence is lacking that it decreases, remains unchanged, or increases with age. Radiant energy has been, by far, the most frequently used method of inducing experimental pain. In these studies several investigations have found no difference in pain sensitivity between young and old subjects (Birren, Schapiro, and Miller, 1950; Hardy, Wolff, and Goodell, 1952). Clark and Mehl (1971) reported similar results except that older women were found to be less sensitive to the heat-pain stimulus than young men and women, and than older men. Other investigators report that heat-pain sensitivity showed a marked decrease in advanced age which commenced at about the fifth to sixth decade (Chapman, 1944; Chapman and Jones, 1944; Hall and Stride, 1954; Procacci, Bozza, Buzzelli and Carte, 1970; Sherman and Robillard, 1960; Schludermann and Zubeck, 1962). The only other possible outcome, that heat pain sensitivity increased with advancing age, has also been reported (Collins and Stone, 1966).

Tolerance of heat-pain has been reported to increase with age (Sherman and Robillard, 1960) and to decrease with age (Collins and Stone, 1966). Tolerance of Achilles' tendon compression has also been found to decrease with age (Woodrow, Friedman, Siegelaub, and Collen, 1972).

These conflicting and highly variable results permit no firm conclusions to be made about changes in pain threshold and tolerance as a function of advancing age. Instructions to the subjects and the definition of pain tolerance play important roles in determining the results of these measurements. Subject attitudes have also been cited as an important variable. Race (Sherman, 1943; Woodrow *et al.*, 1972), ethnic background (Sherman and Robillard, 1960), and socioeconomic status (Schludermann and Zubek, 1962) have all been cited as variables of sufficient importance in measurements of pain threshold and pain tolerance that in cross-sectional studies, where different age groups are not equated for these variables, the effects of age, if any, may be obscured (see Melzack, 1973, for a review of these variables).

One way in which the influence of these extraneous variables might be circumvented is to use animal subjects. The measurement of nociceptive thresholds is not difficult. Nicák (1971) has used the occurrence of vocalization, the "squeek point," as an indicator of nociception in five groups of rats. The groups were 9 to 11, 21, 42, 90, and 440 days old. The stimuli were electric shock to the feet and a mechanical stimulator. (A variable weighted hammer was dropped from a constant distance onto the hind foot dorsum. The ventral foot pad rested on a blunt conical elevation in a foot rest.) As seen in Figure 6 significantly higher voltage was required to achieve the squeek point for the 440-day-old rats than was required for those of the four younger groups. The weight of the mechanical stimulus was significantly heavier to reach the squeek point in the 42-day-old rats than for the two younger groups, and further increases in the weight of the hammer were required for the older groups to reach the squeek point.

A second method that accounts for cognitive and motivational factors employs signal detection procedures. It is applicable to both humans and animals. The procedure yields two numerical indices of the subjects' performance. One (d') is a relatively pure measure of the sensitivity of the sensory system and remains unaltered during manipulations of such nonsensory variables as the subjects' criterion for the occurrence of the sensory event and the subjects' motivations. The second index, the likelihood ratio (β), measures the attitudinal biases or response sets of the subjects (Egan and Clarke, 1966).

The only investigation seen that had employed a signal detection procedure to measure the

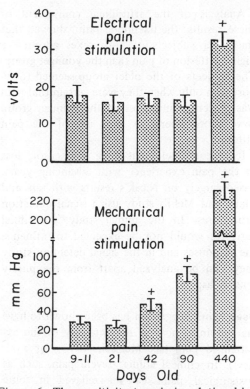

Figure 6. The sensitivity to pain in relationship to the postnatal development in rats after different pain stimulation. + represents statistically significant increases in the pain threshold. (From Nicák, 1971, Figure 2.)

effect of age on pain sensitivity is that by Clark and Mehl (1971). They divided their 32 male and 32 female subjects into two groups according to age. The mean ages of the four groups were as follows: young females, 22.2 years; young males, 23.9 years; old females, 49.4 years; and old males, 43.8 years. The subjects were asked to rate, on an 11 point scale, seven intensities of radiant heat applied to the blackened forearm. The results indicated that the d' (the purely sensory component) of the young males and females did not differ and that males' d' did not change with age while the d' for the older females was significantly lower than that for the younger females. (A smaller d' indicates a reduced ability to detect the stimulus.) This indicates that only the older females underwent a loss in their sensory input and that they actually experienced less pain for the same intensity of stimulation than the males and the younger females.

Analysis of the attitudinal component of these results, the likelihood ratio, showed that the older subjects of both sexes adopted a higher criterion of pain than the younger group. The subjects of the older group seemed to report pain only when they were certain that pain was present while those of the younger group were more liberal in their use of the pain criterion.

It appears likely that there is a sensory loss in the pain experience with advancing years, based largely on Nicák's results with rats and Clark and Mehl's study using signal detection procedures. In the animal study, attitudinal variables would not be expected to influence the responses and in the signal detection study they can be analyzed apart from the purely sensory aspects.

Deep Pain. Suggestion has been shown to have marked influence on the intensity of the experienced pain (see Melzack, 1973, for a review). In clinical studies severe pain, such as postsurgical pain, can be relieved in some patients by giving them a placebo (usually some nonanalgesic substance such as lactose or isotonic saline) in place of an active analgesic (Beecher, Keats, Mosteller, and Lasagna, 1953). About 35 percent of the patients reported marked relief after receiving a placebo. Morphine, even in large doses, will relieve pain in only about 75 percent of the patients. It appears, therefore, that nearly half of the effectiveness of the morphine is really a placebo effect.

Several investigations have found that age may play an important role in the occurrence of the response to placebos. In addition to finding a significantly higher incidence of pain relief from morphine in placebo reactors (perhaps the placebo response plus the pharmacological effect) than in the placebo nonreactors, Lasagna, Mosteller, von Felsinger, and Beecher (1954) also found that the placebo reactors were, on the average, 5 years older than the nonreactors (52 vs 47 years). Bellville, Forrest, Miller, and Brown (1971) also report that of the variables considered in their study (height, weight, body surface area, type of surgery, variation among hospitals) age was the most important variable in determining the degree of pain relief afforded by a potent analgesic. They infer that because their older patients experience a greater pain relief from active drugs one should expect perceptual changes with age. A more direct statement that accounts for the results of both studies seems more defensible. Older patients tend to respond to placebos with greater frequency than do younger patients. The placebo response added to that of the active agent would predict a greater pain relief from a standard dose of an analgesic in older patients (Lasagna, 1971.)

KINESTHESIS

One of the important and distressing problems of older adults is their susceptibility to falls and the complications, sometimes fatal, that occur as a consequence. Such falls may be occasioned by dizziness, muscular weakness, or a decreased input from the muscle and joint receptors. Disturbed gait due to cerebral vascular problems may also make the older adult more susceptible to falls. It is conceivable that a decreased or outright failure of an input from the kinesthetic receptors may be a contributing factor.

The matter of the receptors that are responsible for the kinesthetic sense is still a matter of debate. Originally it was assumed that both muscle stretch receptors and the Golgi tendon organs together with those receptors in and around the joints were responsible for relaying information to the nervous system concerning limb position. However, the contribution of the muscle afferents came under question (Browne, Lee and Ring, 1954; Gelfand and Carter, 1967; Mountcastle and Darian-Smith, 1968; Mountcastle and Powell, 1959; Merton, 1964; Provins, 1958). Recently, however, strong evidence has been presented that muscle afferents, as well as the joint receptors, participate in kinesthesis (Goodwin, McClosky, and Matthews, 1972).

Passive Movement

Clinical tests of passive movement of the great toe in 200 subjects ranging in age from 65 to 91 years failed to produce any evidence of a

TABLE 1. MODAL THRESHOLD VALUES FOR EACH JOINT.

	SUBJECTS UNDER 40		SUBJECTS OVER 50	
	UP	DOWN	UP	DOWN
	Degrees	Degrees	Degrees	Degrees
Shoulder	0.4	0.3	0.5	0.5
Elbow	0.4	0.4	0.5	0.7
Wrist	0.3	0.5	0.5	0.5
First metacarpophalangeal joint	0.5	0.6	0.5	0.5
Second metacarpophalangeal joint	0.5	0.5	0.5	0.5
Third metacarpophalangeal joint	0.4	0.4	0.6	0.5
Fourth metacarpophalangeal joint	0.4	0.5	0.6	0.6
Fifth metacarpophalangeal joint	0.5	0.7	0.5	0.5
Hip	0.2	0.2	0.4	0.5
Knee	0.3	0.3	0.5	0.6
Ankle	0.3	0.3	0.6	0.6
First metatarsophalangeal joint	0.7	0.7	not done	

progressive deterioration in perception of movement with advancing age (Howell, 1949). However, a more extensive study of the kinesthetic sense in several joints showed some deterioration with age (Laidlaw and Hamilton, 1937a). Forty subjects between 17 and 35 years old and 20 subjects between 58 and 85 years old were tested. Laidlaw and Hamilton found that older subjects made more errors in judging the direction of the movement of both the knee and hip joints in order to detect the movement than the younger group. Little or no increase in the threshold of movement detection of the upper extremities was found in the older group.

Any interpretation of impaired movement detection of the great toe should be tempered by the knowledge that wide variations in the threshold of movement detection may occur even in healthy young subjects. Browne, Lee, and Ring (1954) report that while the average threshold angle was 4.4°, about 12 percent of their young subjects yielded average threshold angles of 15° or more. Appreciation of active movement did not appear to be impaired.

Active Movement

Deficiencies in such clinical tests as finger-to-nose, heel-to-knee, and finger-to-heel have been interpreted as deficiencies in motor coordination. The possibility of a kinesthetic deficiency in active movement appreciation, however, should not be overlooked. Howell (1949) has found that up to 4 percent of his 200 subjects were unable to touch their noses accurately when their eyes were closed. The resulting movement was not an intention tremor but a definite dysmetria. Up to the age of 85, increasing years had no effect on the frequency of this deficiency. No other investigations of the effect of age on active movement judgment have been found.

While it is obvious that kinesthesia is directly involved in reporting the relative positions during active or passive movement of body parts, it is not so obvious that at least some of these same receptors are involved in feelings of strain added to the total kinesthetic picture when resistance to limb movement is encountered. When something more than the normal demand for moving bones occurs, as when a weight must be lifted, sensations originating in the muscular and tendinous tissue become evident. Another means of testing the effect of age on the kinesthetic acuity is available, that is, discrimination of lifted weights.

In the only study found on this topic Landahl and Birren (1959) found that young subjects (18 to 32 years old) were only slightly more accurate in judging the heavier of two weights than were the old subjects (58 to 85 years old). The old subjects were as accurate as the young subjects when the weight differences were small. When a fast judgment time was required, the percent of correct judgment of the old group suffered only slightly.

COMPLEX SENSITIVITIES

Here are considered those sensitivities that require some degree of central integration of the afferent input from several sensory channels.

Localization

No studies have been seen that assess the effect of age on the ability to identify the part of the body subjected to a single punctate stimulus.

A study of a more complex type of localization has been reported by Bender, Fink, and Green (1952). With his eyes closed, the subject was simultaneously touched or stroked on the cheek and on the ipsilateral or contralateral hand. Subjects were than asked to identify whether there were one or two stimulations. On the first few trials both children and adults reported only facial stimulation, termed "face dominant." On subsequent stimulations both children (3 to 6 years old) and elderly adults (61 to 96 years old) continued to give a high percentage of face dominant responses, while older children and young adults reported double stimulations. Face dominant responses in these young adults were observed only when heterogeneous body parts (face and hand) were stimulated. Two sensations were experienced when either both hands or both cheeks were stimulated (Bender and Green, 1952). The loss of ability to distinguish two stimulations is somewhat greater when homolateral stimuli (face and hand on same side) are given than when stimuli are contralateral (both cheeks or both hands). Patients with diffuse brain damage give a frequency of face-dominant responses comparable to young children and old normal adults (Bender and Green, 1952). Fot, Richard, Tissot, and DeAjuriaguerra (1970) suggest that the test is a sensitive measure of approaching senility. The loss appears to be established when the subjects are still functioning at a relatively high cognitive level.

Two-Point Limen

Two-point limen of the palm and thumb of 30 young (20 to 36 years old) and 30 elderly (63 to 78 years old) subjects has been investigated (Axelrod and Cohen, 1961). In the young the two-point limen on the palm was 6.3 mm and significantly smaller than the 7.82 mm found in the elderly. Similarly, the two-point limen of 2.26 mm on the thumb of the young was significantly smaller than the 3.95 mm of the elderly. Bolton, Winkelmann, and Dyck (1966) likewise found that the two-point limen on the pad of the little finger increased from 2 mm in children to 6 mm in the elderly and from 2 mm on the great toe pad of children to 30 mm in the elderly.

Stereognosis

The ability to recognize the form of an object is thought to tap such individual sensitivities as two-point limen, light touch, and kinesthesis. A capacity closely allied to stereognosis is the ability to recognize tactually a figure embedded in a more complex geometrical form. This capacity has been shown to be consistently poorer in the elderly (age 63 to 78 years) than in the young (age 20 to 36 years) (Axelrod and Cohen, 1961). Not only were the elderly unable to identify correctly as many of the figures as the young, but they also took more time in making correct identifications. Correlations of measurements of tactile sensitivity and two-point limen, with performance on the hidden-figure test, were low and insignificant except between the hidden-figure score and two-point limen on the thumb. However, analysis of covariance, with the two-point limen on the thumb used as the predictor variable, showed that the lower limen of the young group could not account for their superiority on the hidden-figure task. Axelrod and Cohen concluded that the deficit on the hidden figure test was independent of age related decline in basic sensitivity or acuity and suggested that the poorer performance of the elderly is due to their poorer capacity to visualize the tactually presented figures.

Deterioration in the elderly for recognition of geometric forms placed in the mouth has also been reported (Williams and LaPointe, 1971; McDonald and Aungst, 1967), but no assessment was made of the basic acuities that might be involved.

SUMMARY, CONCLUSION, AND COMMENTS

1. The current clinical descriptions of the effect of age on somesthetic acuity are ones of uniform decreasing sensitivity. These descriptions differ little from those of Critchley (1931), given more than 40 years ago. Numerous reports cited in this review have shown that losses in several measures of somesthetic sensitivity are by no means general in the aged population. In these instances the possibility should not be overlooked that neuropathies produced by disease, injury, or circulatory insufficiency may account for these losses, even though standard clinical tests fail to evidence the disorders.

Loss in touch sensitivity (appreciation of cotton wool applied to the hairy skin) has been reported to occur in a small percent (25 percent) of an aged population. The possibility of occlusive vascular disorders should not be overlooked in their account.

2. The few quantitative studies conducted on the loss of touch sensitivity with advancing age suggest that there may be a sensitivity decrement in glabrous skin of the palm and sole, but not in hairy skin. This differential loss in glabrous skin may be the result of degenerative changes in Meissner corpuscles that have been described in aged skin. Although free nerve endings are present in glabrous skin, the greater sensitivity of these areas is thought to be the result of the presence of Meissner corpuscles. On the other hand, absence of a loss in touch sensitivity in hairy skin may be the result of the enduring functional capacity of free nerve endings with advancing age. Reports of a loss of touch sensitivity in the cornea are not convincing that the loss is of receptor origin. These considerations suggest that future studies of touch sensitivity take into account the body site tested compared to other body sites, as well as the frequency of occurrence of a demonstrable loss in old subjects.

3. Loss of vibratory sensitivity, like the loss of touch sensitivity, is not a universal concomitant of growing old. There is a greater frequency of occurrence of a loss in the lower extremities than in the upper extremities (roughly 25 percent *vs.* 5 percent except on the sacrum where it may be as high as 90 percent). These facts suggest that the loss of function is due to specific pathologies rather than being a general result of age.

Sensitivity to vibrating stimuli has been shown to result from the stimulation of two types of receptors, depending on the frequency of the vibration. Quick adapting mechanoreceptors of the dermis are more sensitive than Pacinian corpuscles to frequencies of up to about 100 Hz while the Pacinian corpuscles are more sensitive to higher frequencies of vibration. They reach a peak sensitivity at about 250 Hz. Pacinian corpuscles are to be found in the deep layers of the dermis and in the subcutis as well as around the joint ligaments and periosteum in glabrous skin. In hairy skin they are absent in the dermis and subcutis. These considerations suggest that adequate tests of vibratory sensitivity must include several frequencies of vibration (at least one well below 100 Hz and one at 250 Hz) applied to soft tissue, e.g., finger or toe pad, by a stimulator of sufficient area to set up traveling waves in the adjacent tissue.

Loss of vibratory sensitivity in the aged appears to be uniform across the frequencies of vibration. Since vibratory sensitivity appears to result from a duplex receptor system, losses in sensitivity are likely the result of a dysfunction in the neural transmission system rather than in the receptors.

4. An extreme thermal environment places an additional stress on the body temperature regulatory center. As the subject grows older he is less able to overcome the additional stress. The result is that body core temperature cannot be maintained. On the other hand, the elderly do not appear to require a higher ambient temperature than the young in order to be comfortable. What scant information there is also indicates that the elderly are about as sensitive as the young to mild warm or cool stimuli applied to limited areas of the body.

In a small percentage of the elderly, temperature and pain sensitivity may be impaired. The low frequency of occurrence, however, suggests that peripheral neuropathies, spinal cord, or brain lesions may be involved.

5. Sensitivity to noxious stimulation appears to undergo a real decrement with advancing age. However, most of the studies of pain sensi-

tivity, as measured by threshold or tolerance limits, have not employed adequate controls for the powerful effects of suggestion, attitude, motivational, and cognitive factors that have been shown to strongly bias these measurements. At the very minimum double-blind control procedures should be employed in future measurements, and subjects should be matched for ethnic and socioeconomic backgrounds. Signal detection theory offers an alternate method, which, in some respects, appears to be superior to the classical psychophysical methods that have heretofore been employed. According to the theory, such measurements provide separate estimates of sensitivity for (a) the purely sensory aspects of the response and (b) the motivational, response biases, and criteria aspects of the response to noxious stimuli. The one study to employ this design, in assessing the effect of age on pain sensitivity, showed a small but significant loss of sensitivity to noxious stimulation in older females and a large increase in the criterion of what is painful in older compared to younger subjects, regardless of their sex.

Increased susceptibility to suggestion is a concomitant of advancing age. The mean age of placebo reactors (those who report relief from postsurgical pain when an inert substance was administered) is higher than that of non-placebo reactors. The amount of relief reported for postsurgical pain from a standard dose of an analgesic has also been found to increase with age. This result could be explained by the analgesic action of the drug plus an increased placebo reaction.

6. The two-point threshold on the thumb, fingertips, and toes has been found to increase with age. This task is usually considered to depend on higher nervous system processes, especially the cerebral cortex. It is yet to be determined if this deficit is related to a reduction in the cutaneous receptor population (Meissner corpuscles) or impaired nervous system function.

7. Other deficits in complex identification tasks, such as tactile identification of a geometric figure embedded in a more complex design, and oral stereognosis have been noted in the elderly. Generally, however, these have not

been found to result from impaired peripheral cutaneous function. The deficits have been suggested to arise from impairment of more central neurological processes.

8. Kinesthetic capabilities, identification of the direction and amount of passive joint rotation, were found to be impaired in the lower limbs of elderly subjects. Judgments of tension or differing degrees of muscle or tendon strain produced by discriminations of weights, however, was relatively unaffected by age. Additional studies in this area, to compare active and passive joint rotation, discriminations, and weight discriminations in the young and the elderly, are sorely needed.

REFERENCES

ASHRAE Handbook of Fundamentals. 1967. New York: American Society of Heating, Refrigeration, and Air-Conditioning Engineers.

Axelrod, S., and Cohen, L. D. 1961. Senescence and embedded-figure performance in vision and touch. *Percept. and Psychophys.*, **12**, 283–288.

Axelrod, S., Thompson, L. W., and Cohen, L. D. 1968. Effects of senescence on the temporal resolution of somesthetic stimuli presented to one hand or both. *J. Gerontol.*, **23**, 191–195.

Beecher, H. K. 1959. *Measurement of Subjective Responses.* New York: Oxford University Press.

Beecher, H. K., Keats, A. S., Mosteller, F., and Lasagna, L. 1953. The effectiveness of oral analgesics (morphine, codeine, acetylsalicylic acid) and the problems of placebo reactors and non-reactors. *J. Pharmacol. Exp. Therap.*, **109**, 393–400.

Bellville, J. W., Forrest, W. H., Miller, E., and Brown B. W. 1971. Influence of age on pain relief from analgesics. A study of postoperative patients. *J. Am. Med. Assoc.*, **217**, 1835–1841.

Bender, M. B., Fink, M., and Green, M. 1952. Patterns in perception on simultaneous tests of the face and hand. *Arch. Neurol. Psychiat.*, **66**, 355–362.

Bender, M. B., and Green, M. A. 1952. Alterations in perception in the aged. *J. Gerontol.*, **7**, 473 (abstract).

Benjamin, F. B. 1958. Effect of aspirin on suprathreshold pain in man. *Science,* **128**, 303–304.

Birren, J. E., Imus, H. A., and Wendle, W. R. (eds.) 1959. *The Process of Aging in the Nervous System.* Springfield, Illinois: Charles C. Thomas.

Birren, J. E., Schapiro, H., and Miller, J. 1950. The effect of salicylate upon pain sensitivity. *J. Pharmacol. Exp. Therap.*, **100**, 67–71.

Birren, J. E., and Wall, P. D. 1956. Age changes in conduction velocity, refractory period, number of fibers, connective tissue space and blood vessels in sciatic nerve of rats. *J. Comp. Neurol.*, **104**, 1–16.

Bolton, C. F., Winkelmann, R. K., and Dyck, P. J. 1966. A quantitative study of Meissner's corpuscles in man. *Neurology*, 16, 1–9.

Browne, K., Lee, J., and Ring, P. A. 1954. The sensation of passive movement at the metatarso-phalangeal joint of the great toe in man. *J. Physiol., Lond.*, 126, 448–458.

Cauna, N. 1954. Nature and functions of the papillary ridges of the digital skin. *Anat. Record*, 119, 449–468.

Cauna, N. 1965. The effects of aging on the receptor organs of the human dermis. *In*, W. Montagna (ed.), *Advances in Biology of Skin*, Vol. VI: *Aging*, pp. 63–96. New York: Pergamon Press.

Chapman, W. 1944. Measurement of pain sensitivity in normal control subjects and in psychoneurotic patients. *Psychosomat. Med.*, 6, 252–255.

Chapman, W. P., and Jones, C. M. 1944. Variations in cutaneous and visceral pain sensitivity in normal subjects. *J. Clin. Invest.*, 23, 81–91.

Clark, J., and Bindra, D. 1956. Individual differences in pain thresholds. *Can. J. Psych.*, 10, 69–76.

Clark, W. C., and Mehl, L. 1971. Thermal pain: A sensory decision theory analysis of the effect of age and sex on d', various response criteria, and 50 percent pain threshold. *J. Abnorm. Psychol.*, 78, 202–212.

Collins, L. G., and Stone, L. A. 1966. Pain sensitivity, age and activity level in chronic schizophrenics and in normals. *Brit. J. Psychiat.*, 112, 33–35.

Corbin, K. B., and Gardner, E. D. 1937. Decrease in number of myelinated fibers in human spinal roots with age. *Anat. Record*, 68, 63–74.

Cosh, J. A. 1953. Studies on the nature of vibration sense. *Clin. Sci.*, 12, 131–151.

Cottrell, L. 1940. Histologic variations with age in apparently normal peripheral nerve trunks. *Arch. Neurol. Psychiat.*, 43, 1138–1150.

Critchley, MD. 1931. Neurology of old age. *Lancet*, 1, 1221–1230.

Dickens, W. N., Winkelmann, R. K., and Mulder, D. W. 1963. Cholinesterase demonstration of dermal nerve endings in patients with impaired sensation: A clinical and pathological study of 41 patients and 37 control subjects. *Neurology*, 13, 91.

Egan, J. P., and Clarke, F. R. 1966. Psychophysics and signal detection. *In*, J. B. Sidowski (ed.), *Experimental Methods and Instrumentation in Psychology*, pp. 209–246. New York: McGraw-Hill.

Enomoto, A. 1969. A study by quantitative sensory examinations on patients with subacute myelo-optico-neuropathy (SMON) with abdominal symptoms—especially on two-point threshold. *Clin. Neurol.*, 4, 179–185.

Fot, K., Richard, J., Tissot, R., and DeAjuriaguerra, J. 1970. Le phénomène de l'extinction dans la double stimulation tactile de la face et de la main chez les déments dégénératifs du grand âge. *Neuropsychologia*, 8, 493–500.

Gardner, E. 1940. Decrease in human neurones with age. *Anat. Record*, 77, 529–536.

Gelfand, S. 1964. The relationship of experimental pain tolerance to pain threshold. *Can. J. Psych.*, 18, 36–42.

Gelfand, S., and Carter, S. 1967. Muscle sense in man. *Exp. Neurol.*, 18, 469–473.

Gelfand, S., Ullmann, L. P., and Krasner, L. 1963. The placebo response: An experimental approach. *J. Nervous mental Disease*, 136, 379–387.

Goff, G. B., Rosner, B. S., Detre, T., and Kennard, D. 1965. Vibration perception in normal man and medical patients. *J. Neurol. Neurosurg. Psychiat.*, 28, 503.

Goodwin, G. M., McCloskey, D. I., and Matthews, P. B. C. 1972. The persistence of appreciable kinesthesia after paralysing joint afferents but preserving muscle afferents. *Brain Res.*, 38, 326–329.

Hall, K. R. L., and Stride, E. 1954. The varying response to pain in psychiatric disorders: A study in abnormal psychology. *Brit. J. Med. Psychol.*, 27, 48–60.

Hardy, J. D., Wolff, H. G., and Goodell, H. 1952. *Pain Sensation and Reactions*. New York: Hafner.

Himel, H., and MacDonald, R. I. 1957. A fallacy in clinical medicine–vibration sense in the aging and aged. *Can. Med. Assoc. J.*, 77, 459–462.

Horwitt, M. K., Liebert, E., Kreisler, O., and Wittman, P. 1946. Studies of vitamin deficiency. *Science*, 104, 407–408.

Howell, T. H. 1949. Senile deterioration of the central nervous system; clinical study. *Brit. Med. J.*, 1, 56–58.

Hunter, R., Ridley, A., and Malleson, A. 1969. Meissner corpuscles in skin biopsies of patients with Presenile Dementia: A quantitative study. *Brit. J. Psychiat.*, 115, 347–349.

Jackson, R. 1972. Solar and senile skin: Changes caused by aging and habitual exposure to the sun. *Geriatrics*, 27, 106–112.

Jalavisto, E., Orma, E., and Tawast, M. 1951. Aging and relation between stimulus intensity and duration in corneal sensibility. *Acta Physiol. Scand.*, 23, 224–233.

Keighley, R. 1946. An instrument for measurement of vibration sensation in man. *Milbank Mem. Fund Quart. Bull.*, 24, 36–48.

Kenshalo, D. R. 1970. Psychophysical studies of temperature sensitivity. *In*, W. D. Neff (ed.), *Contributions to Sensory Physiology*, pp. 19–74. New York: Academic Press.

Krag, C. L., and Kountz, W. B. 1950. Stability of body functions in the aged. I. Effect of exposure of the body to cold. *J. Gerontol.*, 5, 227–235.

Laidlaw, R. W., and Hamilton, M. A. 1937a. A study of thresholds in appreciation of passive movement among normal control subjects. *Bull. Neurol. Inst.*, 6, 268–273.

Laidlaw, R. W., and Hamilton, M. A. 1937b. Thresholds of vibratory sensibility as determined by the pallesthesiometer. *Bull. Neurol. Inst.,* **6**, 494–503.

Landahl, H. D., and Birren, J. E. 1959. Effects of age on the discrimination of lifted weights. *J. Gerontol.,* **14**, 48–55.

Lasagna, L. 1971. Influence of age on analgesic pain relief. *J. Am. Med. Assoc.,* **218**, 1831.

Lasagna, L., Mosteller, F., von Felsinger, J. M., and Beecher, H. K. 1954. A study of the placebo response. *Am. J. Med.,* **16**, 770–779.

Lascelles, R. G., and Thomas, P. K. 1966. Changes due to age in internodal length in the sural nerve in man. *J. Neurol. Neurosurg. Psychiat.,* **29**, 40–44.

Lockner, D., Reizenstein, P., Wennberg, A., and Widen, L. 1969. Peripheral nerve function in pernicious anemia before and after treatment. *Acta Haematol.,* **41**, 257–263.

Ma, C. K., and Cowdry, E. V. 1950. Aging of elastic tissue in human skin. *J. Gerontol.,* **5**, 203–210.

McDonald, E. T., and Aungst, L. F. 1967. Studies in oral sensorimotor function. *In,* J. F. Bosma (ed.), *Symposium on Oral Sensation and Perception,* pp. 202–220. Springfield, Illinois: Charles C. Thomas.

Magladery, J. W. 1959. Neurophysiology of aging. *In,* J. E. Birren (ed.), *Handbook of Aging and the Individual,* pp. 173–186. Chicago: University Chicago Press.

Martinez, P. R. 1931. Contribution a l'étude des terminations nerveuses dans la peau de la main. *Trab. Lab. Invest. Biol. Univ. Madr.,* **27**, 187.

Meissner, G. 1853. *Beitraege zur Anatomie und Physiologie der Haut.* Leipzing: Leopold Voss.

Melzack, R. 1973. *The Puzzle of Pain.* New York: Basic Books.

Melzack, R., and Casey, K. L. 1968. Sensory, motivational, and central control determinants of pain. *In,* D. R. Kenshalo (ed.), *The Skin Senses,* pp. 423–443. Springfield, Illinois: Charles C. Thomas.

Melzack, R., and Wall, P. D. 1965. Pain mechanisms: A new theory. *Science,* **150**, 971–979.

Merton, P. A. 1964. Human position sense and sense of effort. *Symp. Soc. Exp. Biol.,* **18**, 387–400.

Minor, L. 1904. Uber die localisation und klinische bedeutung der sog. "Knockensensibilität" oder das "Vibrationsgefühls." *Neurol. Centralbl.,* **23**, 199.

Montagna, W. 1965. Morphology of the aging skin: The cutaneous appendages. *In,* W. Montagna (ed.), *Advances in Biology of Skin,* Vol. VI: *Aging,* pp. 1–16. New York: Pergamon Press.

Mountcastle, V. B., and Darian-Smith, I. 1968. Neural mechanisms in somesthesia. *In,* V. B. Mountcastle (ed.), *Medical Physiology,* Vol. 2. pp. 1372–1423. St. Louis: C. V. Mosby.

Mountcastle, V. B., LaMotte, R. H., and Carli, G. 1972. Detection thresholds for stimuli in humans and monkeys: Comparison with threshold events in mechanoreceptive afferent nerve fibers innervating the monkey hand. *J. Neurophysiol.,* **35**, 122–136.

Mountcastle, V. B., and Powell, T. P. S. 1959. Neural mechanisms subserving cutaneous sensibility with special reference to the role of afferent inhibition in sensory perception and discrimination. *Johns Hopkins Hosp. Bull.,* **185**, 201–232.

Newman, H. W., and Corbin, K. B. 1936. Quantitative determination of vibratory sensibility. *Proc Soc. Exp. Biol. Med.,* **35**, 273–276.

Nicák, A. 1971. Changes of sensitivity to pain in relation to postnatal development in rats. *Exp. Geront.,* **6**, 111–114.

Norris, A. H., Shock, N. W., and Wagman, I. H. 1952. Age changes in the maximum conduction velocity of motor fibers of human ulnar nerves. *J. Appl. Physiol.,* **5**, 589–593.

Pearce, R. H., and Grimmer, B. J. 1972. Age and the chemical constitution of normal human dermis. *J. Invest. Dermatol.,* **58**, 347–361.

Pearson, G. H. J. 1928. Effect of age on vibratory sensibility. *Arch. Neurol. Psychiat.,* Chicago, **20**, 482–496.

Perret, E., and Regli, F. 1970. Age and the perceptual threshold for vibratory stimuli. *Eur. Neurol.,* **4**, 65–76.

Procacci, B. G., Bozza, G., Buzzelli, G., and Corte, M. D. 1970. The cutaneous pricking pain threshold in old age. *Gerontol. Clin.* **12**, 213–218.

Provins, K. A. 1958. The effect of peripheral nerve block on the appreciation and execution of finger movements. *J. Physiol.,* Lond., **143**, 55–67.

Quilliam T. A., and Ridley, A. 1971. The receptor community in the finger tip. *J. Physiol.,* Lond., **216**, 15–17.

Ridley, A. 1968. Silver staining of the innervation of Meissner corpuscles in peripheral neuropathy. *Brain,* **91**, 539–552.

Rohles, R. H. 1969. Preference for the thermal evironment by the elderly. *Human Factors,* **11**, 37–41.

Ronge, H. 1943a. Altersveränderungen des berührungs sinnes. I. druchpunktschwellen und bruckpunktfrequenz. *Acta Physiol. Scand.,* **6**, 343–352.

Ronge, H. 1943b. Altersveränderungen der Meissnerchen Körperchen in der Fingerhaut. *Z. Mikrosk-anat. Forsch.,* **54**, 167–177.

Rosenberg, G. 1958. Effect of age on peripheral vibratory perception. *J. Am. Geriat. Soc.,* **6**, 471–481.

Schludermann, E., and Zubek, J. P. 1962. Effect of age on pain sensitivity. *Perceptual Motor Skills,* **14**, 295–301.

Sherman, E. D. 1943. Sensitivity to pain. *Can. Med. Assoc. J.,* **48**, 437–441.

Sherman, E. D., and Robillard, E. 1960. Sensitivity to pain in the aged. *Can. Med. Assoc. J.,* **83**, 944–947.

Skre, H. 1972. Neurological signs in a normal population. *Acta Neurol. Scand.,* **48**, 575–606.

Steiness, I. 1957. Vibratory perception in normal subjects. *Acta Med. Scand.,* **158**, 315–325.

Sussman, M. D. 1973. Aging of connective tissue: Physical properties of healing wounds in young and old rats. *Am. J. Physiol.,* **224**, 167–171.

Talbot, W. H., Darian-Smith, I., Kornhuber, W. H., and Mountcastle, V. B. 1968. The sense of flutter-vibration: Comparison of the human capacity with response patterns of mechanoreceptive afferents from the monkey hand. *J. Neurophysiol.*, **31**, 301-334.

Thomas, P. K., and Lascelles, R. G. 1965. Schwann-cell abnormalities in diabetic neuropathy. *Lancet*, **1**, 1355-1357.

Thomas, P. K., and Lascelles, R. G. 1966. The pathology of diabetic neuropathy. *Q. J. Med.*, **140**, 489-509.

Verrillo, R. T. 1966. Vibrotactile thresholds for hairy skin. *J. Exp. Psych.*, **72**, 47-50.

Verrillo, R. T. 1968. A duplex mechanism of mechanoreception. *In*, D. R. Kenshalo (ed.), *The Skin Senses*, pp. 139-159. Springfield, Illinois: Charles C. Thomas.

Wayner, J. J., and Emmers, R. 1958. Spinal synaptic delay in young and aged rats. *Am. J. Physiol.*, **194**, 403-405.

Whitton, J. T. 1973. New values for epidermal thickness and their importance. *Health Phys.*, **24**, 1-8.

Williams, W. N., and LaPointe, L. L. 1971. Intraoral recognition of geometric forms by normal subjects. *Perceptual Motor Skills*, **32**, 419-426.

Winkelmann, R. K. 1956. The neuroanatomy of the skin: A morphologic basis for sensation. Thesis, Graduate School, University of Minnesota.

Woodrow, K. M., Friedman, G. D., Siegelaub, A. B., and Collen, M. F. 1972. Pain tolerance: Differences according to age, sex and race. *Psychosomat. Med.*, **34**, 548-556;

Zander, E., and Weddell, G. 1951. Observations on the innervation of the cornea. *J. Anat.*, **85**, 68-99.

Zobel, H. 1938. Die sensibilität der kornhaut in den verschledenen lebensaltern. *Albrecht v. Graefes Arch. Ophthal.*, **139**, 668-676.

Zwislocki, J. S. 1960. Theory of temporal auditory summation. *J. Acoust. Soc. Am.*, **32**, 1046-1060.

24
INTELLECTUAL ABILITIES

Jack Botwinick
Washington University

DOES INTELLIGENCE DECLINE IN OLD AGE?

An earlier review of studies on intellectual abilities was introduced with the question: "Does intelligence decline in old age?" It was followed by the statement: "In the study of aging, no problem has received greater attention than that of intelligence; yet in spite of the abundance of research data gathered, many questions remain" (Botwinick, 1967, p. 1). This statement notwithstanding, the introductory question was largely rhetorical since evidence was mustered that many, but not all, abilities do decline with age. Wechsler (1958, p. 135) was even more emphatic: "nearly all studies ... have shown that most human abilities ... decline progressively after ... ages 18 and 25."

Since then more research data have been added to the already abundant literature, yet the initial question, "Does intelligence decline in old age?" no longer is rhetorical. There is a growing controversy as to the answer, or, at least, to what its emphasis ought to be. For example, Green (1969, p. 618) wrote: "It is surprising that ... (so much evidence) ... has not seriously eroded belief in the decline hypothesis .... It seems that if belief in the decline hypothesis is to be finally discouraged, Wechsler's work (of decline) will have to be directly attacked." In like manner, several

important articles emphasizing little or no decline with age have become prominent; each could be described by the title of one of them— "Aging and IQ: The Myth of the Twilight Years" (Baltes and Schaie, 1974). Others have lined up on the "no decline" side of the controversy; it catches the imagination and seems to please.

Nevertheless, after reviewing the available literature, both recent and old, the conclusion here is that decline in intellectual ability is clearly part of the aging picture. The more recent literature, however, is bringing attention to what has been under-emphasized in the older literature, viz., these declines may start later in life than heretofore thought and they may be smaller in magnitude; they may also include fewer functions.

Controversy as to whether intelligence declines in old age centers around several related factors, which, unfortunately, are often overlooked. Among these factors are inconsistencies regarding (1) what is meant by age or aging, (2) types of tests used, (3) definitions of intelligence, (4) sampling techniques, and (5) research methods and their pitfalls.

Age and Aging

Generalizations as to whether intelligence declines with age depend upon where in the age spectrum one chooses to look. Historically, intelligence testing was begun in the early part of this century and was largely directed to assessing the ability of children in order to predict school achievement. The concept of mental age (MA) was evolved as was the concept of IQ that was related to it. These concepts were instrumental in spuriously pointing to a decline in intelligence beginning as early in life as the teens.

It was natural for child psychologists, now called developmental psychologists, to extend their interests to adults. Using different tests and different concepts of IQ, they soon discovered that intellectual decline is not a teenage phenomenon. It is hard now to believe that it was not until the mid-1950's that this was clearly demonstrated (Bayley, 1955). Based on periodic testings of children grown to adulthood, Bayley reported that growth continued to at least age 36; she even developed a "theoretical curve of the growth of intelligence" to demonstrate this (Bayley, 1970). Her studies were most impressive to child psychologists raised in the tradition of MA and the related IQ concept. But psychologists not reared in this tradition seemed less impressed with constancy or even rise in test scores to age 36, or even to age 50 as indicated by later studies. For psychologists interested in the later years—for gerontologists—50 might be a starting point to look for age patterns, not an end point.

It is clear that in what is meant by age and aging, vastly different conclusions will be drawn. Between ages 20 and 40, and between 60 and 80, different age patterns hold. Those who argue for "no decline" in intellectual ability often focus either on the earlier adult years or on "life span" data. Those arguing for "decline" may point to the later years. If ameliorative measures are possible for the elderly, then the later years are where the focus may best be.

Types of Tests Used

Generalizations as to whether intelligence declines with age also depend upon the types of tests used. It is very clear that however intelligence may be defined, the specific test used is crucial to what inferences and generalizations will or may be drawn: some functions peak early and are maintained well into old age, others may show recession beginning in early adulthood. Clearly, inferences and generalizations regarding intellectual ability would be very different if only tests of the first kind were given, and not the other. Test scores which fall with age often involve perceptual-motor and speed functions; those holding with age tend to involve verbal functions. The reasons for emphasizing one set of functions and not the other relates to the definition of intelligence. Not everyone agrees that perceptual-motor and speed functions are part of what is called intelligence. This will be elucidated later.

Defining Intelligence

Different Views. Most everyone seems to know what is meant by intelligence, but efforts to provide a formal definition that is both meaningful and useful are elusive. On one extreme, intelligence is an unseen, inferred attribute of a person, part or all of which is genetically given. Experience and biological change modify the basic potentialities, but precisely how and how much is not easily determined. The emphasis is on *capacity*—a theoretical limit when health, educational opportunity, social background, motivation, and other factors do not detract from performance. An alternate definition of intelligence focuses on *ability* rather than capacity. Nothing is said here of potential or biological limit. The emphasis is simply on what a person can do now—at the present time of testing.

Generalizations and inferences of test performances may take forms related to definitions of intelligence. One can make inferences regarding capacity; it is here that controversy and emotionality are most severe. Another type of inference is of ability. Thus, for example, old people doing well on Vocabulary tests and poorly on Digit Symbol tests may suggest that broad, general verbal skills are performed well and perceptual-integrative ones are not. Knowing this, jobs, roles, problems needing aid and improvement are highlighted for meaningful decision. No reference need be made to capacity, or to intellectual potential, or even to biological change; certainly no reference need be made to genetic determination. This emphasis on relative ability should encourage emphasis on ameliorative change and should minimize controversy.

Modifiers. There is no question that the test performances of the elderly are modified or altered by a large number of important factors. What these modifiers mean depends on whether the issue is one of capacity or ability. For example, Furry and Baltes (1973) investigated what they called an "ability-extraneous" variable—in this case, test fatigue. They showed that older people may tire in the course of extended testing and this could impair their performances.

These results indicate that inferences regarding intelligence (capacity) are wrong if reference is not made to the modifying fatigue factor. However, if intellectual performance in the ability sense is stressed, then fatigue is not "ability-extraneous." Older people in their work roles, in retraining programs, must account for their fatigability—it is part of their overall intellectual skill. Roles and functions that do not permit proper rest are to be avoided or minimized if intellectual performance is to be of a high level. Further research questions may then be directed to the issue of fatigability, but efforts to ignore or negate this modifying factor may well be harmful.

There are many other test performance modifiers, among which are education, socioeconomic status, and cohort or cultural-generational factors. They are so important, in fact, that they can be more important than age itself in test performance. Birren and Morrison (1961), for example, reported a higher correlation between intelligence test scores and education level than between these scores and age. Others have also emphasized the role of education (e.g., Granick and Friedman, 1973). Modifiers such as education and fatigue have different meaning when intelligence is viewed in the ability sense than when viewed as capacity.

Sampling Techniques

Just as the specific tests and evaluation of modifiers are crucial in forming generalizations regarding intellectual ability, so are the criteria of subject recruitment for investigation. For example, choosing subjects of specific education levels can alter age relationships drastically.

Green (1969) compared cross-sectional age curves based on subjects who were recruited by stratified random selection to age curves based on subjects matched for education level. The random sample reflected overall age decline, while the matched education sample did not. Which is the more correct?

Again, if intelligence in the sense of capacity is meant, then the matched groups might be given emphasis. If intellectual ability as it is distributed currently in the "real world" is the concern, then the random sample is to be emphasized. Any random sampling of people of different ages would likely result in samples of decreasing education level with increasing age of group. This reality exists now; it may not exist in the future. Now, it has to be said that older people, as they have been educated, tend to be lower in ability as measured by a particular test such as the WAIS.

Sampling problems are present in longitudinal research also. A main one is selective subject dropout (mentioned briefly in the next section and discussed fully later with Figures 3 and 4). The specific samples of subjects that are examined and, to an extent, the particular age pattern that is observed, depend on when in the course of time in the longitudinal research one chooses to analyze the data.

Research Methods

The problem of subject sampling relates to the issue of method of investigation used in aging research, i.e., cross-sectional or longitudinal. And the method used has a direct bearing on the controversy regarding intelligence and age; the method relates to what the results may be. The cross-sectional method may spuriously magnify age decline, and the longitudinal method may minimize it.

The cross-sectional method may even manufacture age decline because the different age groups have their origins and upbringing in different eras. A cohort born in 1900, for example, may score less well on a test than a cohort born in 1950, not because of being older but because of social and educational experiences less adequate for good test performance. Thus, a presumed age effect may be due to cohort experience. However, this argument in extreme form fails to recognize the obvious fact that cohort and age are inseparable; at best, only approximations to the isolation of the two effects are possible. In the world outside the laboratory where abstractions differentiating between cohort and age do not exist, age and cohort are one. Age is not synonomous with biology, nor is cohort synonomous with sociocultural influences.

Negative age patterns tend to be less apparent in longitudinal research than in cross-sectional research. One reason for this is the selective subject dropout, noted earlier. Not all individuals remain equally available for retest; it is mainly the more able ones who are available, thus providing the investigator with increasingly biased samples for examination as the age of the sample subjects increases (e.g., Riegel, Riegel, and Meyer, 1967). A method of investigation combining cross-sectional and longitudinal research has been developed by Schaie (1965) and modified by Baltes (1968); it is called sequential analysis and holds much promise. A major goal of this method—sequential strategy research—is to disentangle the effects on performance that could be attributed to age and to the different cohort groups (cultural backgrounds). Sequential analysis has the potential for doing much toward the goal of disentangling these effects but the very nature of the entanglements precludes total or absolute solution. In human investigations, at least, some ambiguity in determining the effects of age isolated from cohort must always remain.

CROSS-SECTIONAL INVESTIGATIONS

General Trends

Age Differences. Testing adult intelligence was begun in full force with World War I and many cross-sectional age studies have been reported since then. These will not be reviewed here, having been summarized already by Jones (1959), Botwinick (1967) and others. Their overall impact was very clear; as suggested in the very first paragraph of this chapter, most of the

earlier investigators had little doubt that increasing adult age brought about intellectual decline.

This belief was reinforced with the advent of what had become the most widely used test of adult intelligence—the WAIS (or its predecessor, the WB; see, e.g., Wechsler, 1958). This test comprises 11 subtests, each measuring an ability which is correlated to some extent with the others. Although the test has been available since 1939, it was not until 1955 that norms became available for age groups older than 55 to 64 years (Doppelt and Wallace, 1955).

Six of the 11 WAIS subtests comprise the Verbal scale and 5 the Performance scale. Scores on these scales and the combination of the two, the Full scale, may be seen in Figure 1. The Performance tests show greater age differences than do the Verbal tests, and the meaning of this will become clear later. For the present, it is simply well to realize that higher Verbal than Performance scores by elderly sub-

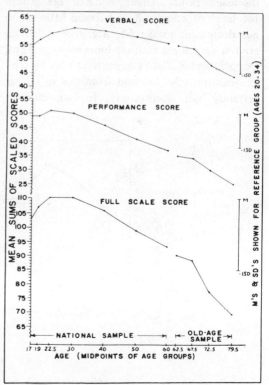

Figure 1. Verbal, Performance and Full Scale scores as a function of age. (WAIS norms from Doppelt and Wallace, 1955. Copyright 1955 by the American Psychological Association. Reprinted by permission.)

jects has been called a "classic aging pattern" because it has now been demonstrated many times. In fact, it constitutes one of the best replicated results for normal aging populations. Eisdorfer, Busse, and Cohen (1959) reported that this aging pattern holds for men and women, for white and black subjects, for different socioeconomic statuses, and for people in mental hospitals as well as those residing in the community.

From Figure 1 and the individual subtest data which formed this figure, Doppelt and Wallace concluded that, overall (Full Scale), it is not until age 70 that scores drop sharply. Furthermore, even after this age, the decline on most of the six Verbal tests is not a full standard deviation below the peak performances of younger people.

This emphasis is in contradistinction to the conclusion of major age-deficits beginning early in life. As such, it is not at variance with Green's (1969) data and the sampling issue discussed earlier. Green equated age groups for level of education and found little or no age decrement to age 64, after having demonstrated decrement with random sampling. Thus, Doppelt and Wallace's conclusion may be seen as quantitatively different from that of Green, certainly not qualitatively. In like manner,

Doppelt and Wallace's conclusion of sharp decline beginning only late in life suggests that cross-sectional and longitudinal studies do not provide vastly different information as is frequently thought. Again, the difference is quantitative, not qualitative, as will be elucidated toward the end of this chapter.

Of the many cross-sectional studies that have concluded that there is an age decline in intellectual functioning, one study is especially important because it formed the basis of longitudinal and sequential studies which followed. Schaie (1958) gave the Primary Mental Abilities (PMA) test to 500 people, 50 in each of ten 5-year intervals. The PMA, developed by Thurstone and Thurstone (1949), consists of 5 subtests believed to measure independent functions. The mean of these five may be seen in Figure 2. This figure shows a cross-sectional PMA age pattern not often recognized: no appreciable age decline was observed from 20 to 50 years. After age 46–50, decline is clear, being more or less systematic. From the early twenties to the early thirties there may be a rise in ability, but if there is, it is not great. Very important here, however, is the fact that it is not until after age 60 that scores are more than one standard deviation lower than peak performance at age 31 to 35.

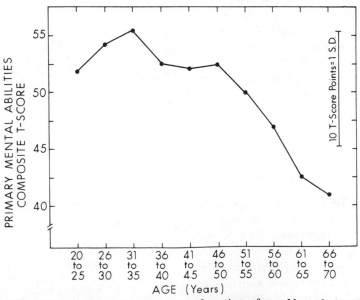

Figure 2. Composite Primary Mental Abilities as a function of age. Note that systematic decline is not seen until age 46–50 years. (From Table 5 of Schaie, 1959.)

Selective Availability. While the cohort effect in cross-sectional research may exaggerate age decline, Riegel and Riegel (1972) pointed to an effect which may work in the opposite direction: as people age they become less available for testing.

Take, as an extreme example, the study of visual perception. People completely blind cannot be tested and people with very poor eyesight, or those nearly blind, may not show up for the experiment. If such people are represented more in an old age group than in a young one, then the lower ends of the distributions of visual perception will be missing, showing up as less age decline than is actually so in the overall population.

Riegel and Riegel also indicated that selective subject availability can work in the other direction—that of spuriously showing age declines in cross-sectional studies. They called to bear the concept "terminal drop," which they defined as a decline in test performance some few years prior to death, due perhaps to "physiological deterioration or damage." Since "terminal drop" is "an increasing occurrence ... during the later years," Riegel and Riegel suggested that if only the test scores of people surviving at least 5 years following cross-sectional testing were analyzed, much or all of the age decline seen in cross-sectional studies would disappear. According to this formulation, age decline is largely a matter of those test-takers who are in the process of dying; those who are full of life, so to speak, with long lives ahead of them, show little or no age decline.

Our position is the only practical one. Living and dying is part of the description of aging. We cannot tell in advance who is to be excluded from testing on the basis of death within the next 5 years. Those whose test performances were poor and who died soon after taking the test, as well as those to whom tests were not given but who would have scored poorly had they been, constitute part of the only reality we have. Other considerations make for highly abstract, artificial samples for study.

The Individual. The studies by Green and others demonstrated how important individual factors can be—an old person can be extra-ordinarily intelligent as compared to a person of any age. Individual differences are great. For example, the correlations between age and intelligence test score tend to be between .40 to just more than .50 (Wechsler, 1958, p. 139; Miles, 1934; Weisenburg, Roe, and McBride, 1936, pp. 82–83), indicating that if only the age of the person is known and nothing else, approximately only 20 percent of intelligence test score variance can be predicted. Eighty percent cannot be predicted, leaving much unknown.

Differential Performance

A Variety of Abilities. All that has been discussed so far points to the fact that whatever the view regarding decline, different intellectual functions are related to age in different ways. By and large, verbal functions were seen to hold up well with age, while nonverbal, psychomotor ones, especially when involving speed, hold up less well. This may be differentiated further by an examination of the 11 individual subtests making up the WAIS totals of Figure 1.

The Classic Pattern. As reported by Doppelt and Wallace, among the six Verbal subtests, only the scores on Similarities and Digit Span, even for the very oldest group—those aged 75 years and older—are more than one standard deviation below the mean of the optimally performing group. On none of the other four subtests is performance decline appreciable. The situation is otherwise with the five subtests in the Performance grouping. By age 60 years, on all of these subtests, decline of at least one standard deviation is seen. By age 75 and over, the decline is greater than this.

Stability of Classic Pattern. The relatively large age difference in Performance ability and little or no age difference in Verbal ability was seen in an interesting demonstration. Harwood and Naylor (1971) matched almost exactly a group aged 60–69 years and a group aged 70–89 years, each with a young control group on the basis of Total WAIS scale scores. In other words, each old group was similar in overall WAIS intelligence to a young adult group to which it was compared. Comparisons were then made between respective old and young age groups in regard to Verbal and Performance abilities.

Information, Comprehension and Vocabulary of the Verbal subtests were significantly higher in the old groups than in their respective young control groups. On the other hand, Digit Symbol, Picture Completion and Picture Arrangement of the Performance subtests were lower. The fifth subtest of the group, Object Assembly, was significantly lower only in the older group (70-89) as compared to the young control, but numerically it was lower in the other old group too. Thus, even in age groups matched for Total WAIS ability, the robust classic pattern of age differences was seen.

Rank Order of Abilities. What does this mean in terms of a more generalized pattern of intellectual ability? Before an attempt is made to answer this important but difficult question it is well to examine the specific order of subtest performance decline in regard to age. To do this, 10 WAIS and WB studies, including the one by Doppelt and Wallace, were compared with respect to the subtest age patterning (Botwinick, 1967). The results of these studies, reported between 1945 and 1963, were remarkable in their similarity. The Verbal subtests, Information and Vocabulary, tend to reflect the least age difference (or none at all) among the 11 WAIS subtests. The Performance subtests, Picture Arrangement and Digit Symbol, reflect the greatest age difference among the 11.

The maintenance and rise of scores in Verbal subtests such as Information and Vocabulary, and the decrement scores on Performance subtests such as Picture Arrangement and Digit Symbol, led many investigators to argue for a no decline hypothesis. A major basis for this argument is the fact that, in one form or another, the Performance subtests involve speed in carrying out the task requirements.

This argument is epitomized in an early study by Lorge (1936). He used power and speed tests (not the WAIS or WB) and equated three age groups on the basis of scores made on a power test. He then found that the groups were different with respect to their scores on speed tests—the older groups performing less well.

Lorge's conclusion was not that older people perform relatively well in one aspect of intelligence and poorly in another, but "speed obscures sheer mental power in older adults" (p. 105). This notion of the role of speed in intellectual ability will be argued subsequently, but first, the PMA subtest pattern:

Each of the five PMA subtests reflects what the composite (Figure 2) does in showing decline beginning at age 46-50 years and continuing to at least age 66-70. However, the five are different in regard to patterns up to age 46-50. Two of the subtests—Word Fluency and, even more so, Number—show an increase in ability from age 20-25 to age 41-45. The Verbal Meaning subtest reflects the composite, i.e., some rise to about age 30, then the beginning of decline. Only the Reasoning subtest and perhaps the Space subtest show decline beginning early in adulthood. Overall, the individual subtests indicate that not much change is to be expected until the middle or late forties, but then, age decline begins.

Suitability of Tests. We now come to a most controversial part, and perhaps the most important, in evaluating the results of cross-sectional studies, and the conclusions that have been drawn from them. Basically, there are two opposing viewpoints—one represented here by Lorge (1936), Green (1969), and others who deemphasized speed and perceptual-motor functions in intelligence; the other viewpoint represented by Birren (1952) and by Botwinick and Storandt (1973) who examined the WAIS Performance subtests (and similar measures) and found them important in intelligence testing.

Green, it will be recalled, compared WAIS scores among different age groups (ranging from 25 to 64 years) after matching them on the basis of education level. He found a small but statistically significant rise with age in the combined six Verbal tasks, and no statistically significant age difference in the Performance tasks. However, the mean scores of each of the five Performance subtests were lower for the old than the young, with the Digit Symbol subtest reflecting statistical significance. The latter Green called a test of "purely speeded functions," indicating greater valuation of the Verbal task performances as an index of intelligence in later life than those of the Performance tasks.

Lorge similarly held speed to be of less value; so did Corsini and Fassett (1953) who tested a prison population of subjects because they believed that this would make for a better age sampling. As did Green with special sampling, they found a rise in Verbal scores with age, and they also found a Performance scale decline. But the latter they attributed to "nonintellectual factors" and concluded that the "Performance tests are clearly unsuited for the purpose of between-age research on intelligence" (pp. 262-263).

This, in essence, is at the heart of the no-decline hypothesis—this and the related issues of sampling implicit in the cross-sectional method. Are the WAIS Performance subtests and those tests similar to them unsuited for testing older people?

Speed of Response. A person with visual defects or specific motor disabilities is inappropriately tested by most standard tests and should not be included in "normal" representative samples. But slowing of response speeds with age is "normal" and, it would seem, part of intellectual *ability*. It may also be part of intellectual capacity. Three sets of WAIS or PMA data will be considered here in relation to this contention, but it is well to note that there is an extensive literature on the significance of the slowing of response speeds in later life, irrespective of intelligence test results (see, for example, Botwinick, 1973, pp. 154-180).

First, data of a PMA study will be examined. Schaie, Rosenthal, and Perlman (1953) compared four age groups of subjects on the basis of each of the five PMA subtests. The age groups were 53-58, 59-64, 65-70, and 71-78 years. The tests (except for Word Fluency) were given both in the regular manner, i.e., with the prescribed time limits, and in an irregular manner whereby the subjects were allowed to finish the tests in their own time and to gain credit for correct answers. The results were interesting in that when the time limits affected the magnitude of the age decline, they *minimized* them. Thus, for the Space and Reasoning

subtests, removing the time limits and allowing everyone to complete the test made for greater age differences. Speed of response in this instance could not explain differential test performances with age.

Data on the WAIS might be more to the point. When Doppelt and Wallace (1955) gave the test to subjects aged 60 to 75 years and older, they examined the effect of allowing additional time for response on five of the subtests involving speed: Arithmetic, Picture Completion, Block Design, Picture Arrangement and Object Assembly. Of these five, all but one (Arithmetic) are Performance subtests. Only the Digit Symbol subtest of the Performance group was missing (because its nature precluded such analysis). Doppelt and Wallace compared "regular" scores and irregular ones; both were based on accuracy alone, i.e., additional time was allowed for completing the tasks in the case of irregular scores, but no bonus for quick response was given in either case.

They found that except for the Block Design, there were hardly any differences between "regular" and irregular scoring. With Block Design, there was a slight difference, but it was similar among the four elderly age groups that were compared. Klodin (1975) replicated part of this study and extended it. Unlike Doppelt and Wallace, Klodin found a significant difference between timed and untimed scoring of both the Object Assembly and the Block Design subtests. However, no significant difference in scoring the Object Assembly task was found when the timed condition included bonus points for quick response, as is traditional.

These were the only two speed WAIS subtests used, but Klodin tested a young control group in addition to the elderly one. With both subtests the magnitude of age differences was reduced with the untimed scoring. The older subjects benefited more than the younger with the additional time, the younger being better able to score nearer peak performance with time limitations. The important point, however, is that despite the greater benefit to the older subjects of additional time, they never reached the high performance levels of the younger subjects.

It seems, therefore, that when speed is important in the scores of the WAIS Performance tests, it tends to magnify differences between age groups. Eliminating speed requirements from a task might reduce the magnitude of these age differences, but not negate them. Thus, the classic aging pattern might be reduced but not extinguished if speed requirements were eliminated.

A third study, one specific to the Digit Symbol subtest, was carried out by Botwinick and Storandt (1973). It will be recalled that this subtest involves speed, and of the 11 WAIS subtests is the most reflective of age decline. The Digit Symbol subtest was given to a young adult group and to an elderly one, as were two other speed tasks and the WAIS Vocabulary subtest (one of the tests showing maintenance and even rise with age). The two other speed tasks were designed to have less cognitive or perceptual demand placed on the subject than the Digit Symbol subtest, and thus made the speed demand relatively more important.

Performances on the four tests were intercorrelated (Vocabulary, Digit Symbol, and two speed tests), with the effects of age removed by way of partial correlation. Contrary to the notion that the Digit Symbol subtest is a test of "pure speed," the correlation between performances on this subtest and those on Vocabulary was approximately .50: 25 percent of the variance of scores on one of these tests could be accounted for by the variance of scores on the other. Digit Symbol performance and Vocabulary ability, therefore, have quite a bit in common. This fact was underscored when the correlations between Digit Symbol and the other two speed tests, and between the latter two speed tests and Vocabulary, were found to be not reliably greater than zero.

The relationship between speed and nonspeed tasks was seen in another type of analysis. A major study was carried out in which 32 measurements were made, among them the 11 WAIS subtests. The 32 measures were intercorrelated and organized by principal components analysis. It was found that the three lowest-ranked WAIS subtests (Digit Symbol, Picture Arrangement, and Block Design)—all involving speed—were represented with most of the Verbal subtests on the first component (Birren, Botwinick, Weiss, and Morrison, 1963, p. 147).

The foregoing, then, suggests that the Performance decrement part of the classic aging pattern is not to be attributed to peripheral, nonintellective factors, but to intellectual ones.

Verbal Functions. What may be said regarding the Verbal abilities which are maintained by the elderly? Birren (1952, p. 404) concluded that they are "determined by what (elderly people) already know rather than by what new information they can elicit from the situation." These Verbal abilities reflect "stored information or general intellectual achievement . . ." (Birren *et al.*, 1963, pp. 150-151). This interpretation was based on the nature of the Verbal subtests: they seem "simple and unambiguous; the subject either knows or doesn't know or recognize what is called for." Verbal tests seem to measure the manipulation of familiar materials in familiar ways. On the other hand, as suggested in one study, tests such as the Digit Symbol seem to measure the manipulation of unfamiliar materials, perhaps in unfamiliar ways (Schonfield and Robertson, 1968).

A recent study supported this conclusion regarding Verbal functions, but at the same time indicated that extension was necessary. Botwinick and Storandt (1974a) gave the WAIS Vocabulary test to young and older adults, but instead of the traditional method of "quantitative" scoring based on "a simple, unambiguous knowing what is called for," a "qualitative" scoring was carried out. Each response to a test word was scored on the basis of six levels of correct response. The highest level was that of an excellent synonym; the lowest level, but still correct, response was that of an illustration, a demonstration by hands or body, or by correct repetition of the word in sentences. One of the three middle-level responses was a relatively poor explanation.

This study was distinguished from others in that when a young adult and an elderly age group were compared for qualitative Vocabulary response, they were first matched on the basis of their regular "quantitative" scores. The results of this study cast doubt as to the validity of the generalization that vocabulary function is maintained throughout adult life. The best possible response, i.e., superior synonym, was seen to decline with age. "This decline, however, was compensated for by very satisfactory, although less good, performance" (p. 303). It was speculated that if performances on the other Verbal tasks could be analyzed for response precision, Verbal functions might resemble Performance functions as to age pattern. This important notion should be put under further test.

Organization of Abilities

There is now a sizable literature reflecting the effort in organizing abilities into groups based upon correlations among test scores, i.e., factor analysis. Many of these studies were reviewed elsewhere in great detail (e.g., Botwinick, 1967, pp. 13-20; Matarazzo, 1972, pp. 261-276) and they will not be reviewed here except to point out a few specific, important results.

Fluid and Crystallized Intelligence. One organization of intelligence involves the categories "fluid" and "crystallized"—the latter presumably based primarily on learned abilities, and the former based more directly on physiological structure. Horn and Cattell (1967) tested people aged 40 to 61 years with a wide variety of different tests (not including the WAIS or WB) and their basic findings may be thought of as compatible with the classic aging pattern seen with the WAIS. The fluid function tests are similar in some ways to the Performance subtests, and these declined with age. The crystallized functions are largely verbal, and these held and even increased with age.

Memory and General Ability. Verbal and Perceptual factors have been identified in most factor analytic WAIS studies. Thus, the results are not vastly different from the organization of Verbal and Performance that Wechsler suggested originally. However, additional factors have been identified; problems in intellectual performance in later life may derive from memory loss. To the extent that an older person has a memory problem, a wide variety of cognitive functions will be impaired (see Botwinick and Storandt, 1974b).

An additional point is compatible with the conclusion by Green (1969) in regard to education, and with the previous commentary under the heading, The Individual. It is General Ability, the conglomerate rather than any one specific ability, that most characterizes intelligence test performances. Of utmost importance, the cross-sectional factor-analytic studies *do not* necessarily point to age as being important in conglomerate intelligence. For example, Birren and Morrison (1961) factor analyzed the WAIS standardization data based on subjects ranging in age to 64 years. They extracted a large General intellectual component accounting for approximately half of all the test score variance. None of the other factors accounted for more than 11 percent. Age was *not* an important contributor to the General intellectual factor. Education level, on the other hand, was so important as to contribute as much as did any one subtest.

What does this mean, then, in view of all that was said up to now; does this contradict all the foregoing? The answer is simply that when an age-intelligence relationship is seen, it is more a matter of certain specific functions than of overall intelligence. A summary of the cross-sectional literature suggests that the age-intelligence relationship tends to be small, with decline not setting in until relatively late in life. When it does, memory, speed of response and perceptual-integrative functions are involved. How crucial even these test abilities are in the daily business of carrying out life's responsibilities is the important question not answered by the investigations carried out to date.

LONGITUDINAL STUDIES

Recent longitudinal age studies have forced a review and re-emphasis of the interpretations of cross-sectional studies. Part of this may be seen in contrasting the views presented just above with those seen in previous reviews of cross-sectional studies where interpretations of decline starting early in adult life were more prominent (as for example, Jones, 1959; Botwinick, 1967; and more obviously, Wechsler, 1958, quoted in the beginning of the present chapter). Thus, the interpretations of the longitudinal data and their analyses which follow are not very different from those of the cross-sectional studies as summarized above. Differences are quantitative: by and large, longitudinal studies show less decline than do cross-sectional ones; they may also show the decline starting later in life. Where maintenance or improvements in function are seen cross-sectionally, they are also seen longitudinally.

Sampling Bias: Selective Dropout

Whereas previous interpretations of cross-sectional data underemphasized cohort or cultural effects, current interpretations of longitudinal data tend to underemphasize a sampling bias intrinsic to this method of investigation. While this sampling bias is now very well known, having been reported in a variety of contexts (e.g., Jarvik and Falek, 1963; Riegel, Riegel, and Meyer, 1967; Baltes, Schaie, and Nardi, 1971), too few investigators seem to be sufficiently impressed with how great a problem this can be.

A Reversal of Age Difference. The sampling bias is one of selective dropout in longitudinal research. For different reasons, people who perform poorly tend to be less available for longitudinal retesting than those who perform well.

Thus, as a longitudinal study continues over time, superior-performing older people remain and this may make for spurious conclusions. Observe Figure 3 of PMA test data collected during three test periods, each 7 years apart. Note a most extreme example of selective dropout in the case of Word Fluency.

In 1956, Schaie (1958) tested 500 subjects representing several age groups; in 1963 he retested them (Schaie and Strother, 1968), but only 302 of them were available for this retest. In 1970, the subjects were again tested, but this time only 161 were available (Schaie and Labouvie-Vief, 1974). In Figure 3, two age groups of the several that were tested are compared—the open circles represent subjects aged approximately 25 years at the time of the first testing in 1956, and the closed circles represent subjects aged approximately 67.

Figure 3 may be understood this way: the mean scores made by the subjects within these two age groups during the first test session in 1956 are represented on the abscissa by the number 1. When their numbers were reduced in the second testing, 7 years later, *the means of the 1956 scores, but of the remaining subjects only* (N = 302), were higher than those of the total group tested in 1956 (N = 500). This is seen in Figure 3 as 1956, number 2. With the

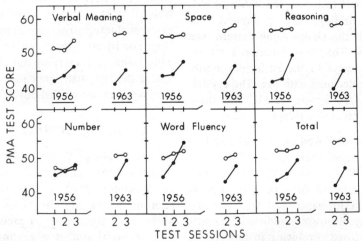

Figure 3. An example of selective dropout in longitudinal research. See text for explanation. The original 1956 data were regrouped from Table 5 of Schaie (1959). The data based on the second testing were regrouped from photocopies provided by ASIS National Publication Service, c/o CCM Information Sciences (Order NAPS Document No. 00160). The third testing data were provided by Schaie in personal communication. His study of selective dropout provides additional information (Schaie, Labouvie, and Barrett, 1973).

third testing in 1970, *the same 1956 scores of the still remaining subjects* ($N = 161$) were even higher. This may be seen on the abscissa of Figure 3 as 1956, number 3. The important thing to remember is that 1, 2, and 3 of 1956 represent the same two age groups at the same time of testing—only the numbers of subjects within the age groups are different.

In Figure 3, the 1963 data are interpreted similarly. Those subjects retested in 1963 made scores represented by the number 2 of that year. The retest 7 years later was based on fewer subjects. The 1963 scores of these remaining subjects were higher than the 1963 scores of the total sample tested then. Moreover, this was more so for the 67-year-olds (in 1956) than the 25-year-olds.

Looking at Word Fluency, the 67-year-olds performed less well in 1956 than did the 25-year-olds. When their numbers were reduced in 1963 (second testing), the 1956 scores of those remaining showed cross-sectional age decline, but to a lesser extent. When their numbers were further reduced in the 1970 testing, the remaining 1956 scores were *higher* for the old than the young! Here we see a reversal in the age difference: the very same cross-sectional data, but based on only those people who did not drop out over the 14-year longitudinal period, show an age pattern different from the original one. Following up only these superior 67-year-olds, and not all those originally tested, can yield longitudinal data from which only very limited generalizations may be made. While these Word Fluency data are extreme in pointing to this, it may be seen that the general pattern of retest availability of superior old subjects holds for each of the 5 PMA abilities and the average or total of these 5.

(Later, it will be seen that the aging patterns of high and low ability people were similar, at least over the first 7-year retest interval. If the aging patterns of the elderly who were retested and those who dropped out of the study were also similar, then the problem of subject attrition might be less severe than indicated above. While there is no sure way to determine this, Figure 4 based on WAIS data suggests that the subject attrition problem is important. Also, in Figure 5, the difference between repeated and independent PMA measurements, especially with Cohorts V and VI, suggests the importance of dropout considerations.)

Terminal Drop. Why this relative unavailability for longitudinal retesting of those performing poorly, especially those among the aged? There are several reasons. One may be that those performing poorly, or those who have declined from former levels, tend to die sooner than those maintaining function and performing well. The former are thus not available for retesting later on. Kleemeier (1962) was the first to provide data emphasizing the relationship between test performance and survival.

Using the WB, he tested elderly men on four separate occasions in the course of 12 years. Each of the men showed a decline in score over the 12-year period, but some declined more than others. Kleemeier compared the decline scores between those who later died and those who survived, and found that the decline (terminal drop) scores were greater for the deceased.

Terminal drop is but one sampling factor making the longitudinal method imperfect—there are others, e.g., health and interest in being tested. As already indicated, these sampling biases tend to increase as the study continues, and probably do so more for the old than the young. The expectation, therefore, is that longitudinal studies, while accurately reflecting changes among those people available for retesting, do not accurately reflect changes of more complete populations. This is the reason why it was said earlier that the longitudinal method may minimize age differences, just as the cross-sectional method may exaggerate them.

Early Life Age Changes

In this and in the next section most of the important longitudinal studies on intellectual ability in adulthood will be presented. It will be seen that there are not many of them.

Childhood to Age 30. Several of the longitudinal studies on early adult development came from a common data pool begun in 1931 by Terman. In that year, children aged from 2 to 5½ years were tested with the Stanford-Binet intelligence test. Ten years later, in 1941, most of these children were retested. Then, in 1956, 15 years later when the children were grown (about age 30), they were given a third testing. Different forms of the Binet test were used in the course of the three test periods, and, in addition, in 1956 the WAIS was given.

About half of the original 1931 sample was available for all three tests. For this remaining group, no change in the Stanford-Binet IQ was seen in the first 10-year interval (from approximately the ages of 4 to 14 years), and an increase was seen during the next 15-year interval. The Binet IQ scores increased from approximately 113 to 124 (Bradway, Thompson, and Cravens, 1958).

Mid-Life Patterns.

To the Mid-Forties. The above study was continued by Kangas and Bradway (1971). In 1969 there was a fourth test session, the children approximately 4 years old at the start were now near 42 years old. Their Stanford-Binet IQs were estimated at 130, a growth of another 6 IQ points. Their WAIS scores also increased— the change over the previous 13 years was from 110 to 118. Important to note is that from age 30 to 42, *both* the WAIS Verbal and the WAIS Performance scores increased.

The subjects in these studies were of relatively high IQ. In fact, most of the data of early and middle age development are of intellectually superior subjects, and this limits the generalizations which may be made. The next three studies taken together bear this out.

The first study was that of Nisbet (1957) who reported two testings of graduate students covering a 24-year period (from age 22½ to age 47). The Simplex Group Test was used which essentially is a test of verbal functions. The second study is that of Bayley and Oden (1955) who also used verbal tests in their study of intellectually superior subjects. Their subjects were so superior that they were classed as "gifted;" they had been selected when they had been children by Terman and his associates for the study of "genius" (Terman and Oden, 1947). Their ages in the Bayley-Oden study were from about 29 to 41 years.

Both Nisbet and Bayley and Oden reported that test scores increased with age. Since these two studies were of intellectually superior adults tested for verbal skills, the results might have been anticipated from the literature of cross-sectional studies. What would studies on more average people given nonverbal tests show? The third study, that of Tuddenham, Blumenkrantz, and Wilkin (1968), helps answer this question. Men retiring from the army after 20 years of service were given the Army General Classification Test (AGCT). This test has four parts; three could be classed as verbal and one nonverbal. Over a period of 13 years, from the approximate ages of 30 to 43, each of four parts of the AGCT showed age decline, but only one was statistically significant—the nonverbal one.

During this relatively early part of adult life, studies more varied with respect to subject populations might well point to what was indicated by the cross-sectional literature—relative maintenance of verbal functions and decline of nonverbal ones, especially when speed is involved. Most studies of later life show this.

To Age 50 and Beyond. Under a different heading, studies of subjects of advanced age will be reviewed. First, however, two studies which included subjects aged 50 and over will be highlighted separately, because they were the first to draw attention to the fact that even to this relatively late age, decline is not a necessary eventuality.

The gifted subjects in Bayley and Oden's study were tested, on the average, when they were approximately 29 years old and then again when they were 41. Since there was a spread in the ages of these subjects—some were in their early twenties at the first test, and some were in their late forties at the second test—Bayley and Oden were able to divide their samples into 3 or 4 age groups, depending upon the specific analysis. "The impressive thing that comes out of this division into age groups is that all groups show similar and significant tendencies to increase in scores over the twelve-year interval" (p. 104). Bayley and Oden also concluded, "Our material does not . . . cover the later ages at which real senescent decrements in intellectual functioning are to be expected. Further, our material is not concerned with speed, either in physical action or in intellectual processes." But, at least during the age period 20 to 50, superior adults improve in "knowledge of symbols and abstractions and in ability to use these in relation to each other" (p. 106).

A second study which made an important impact when first reported was by Owens (1953). In 1919, 363 students entering Iowa State College were given the Army Alpha intelligence test. Thirty years later, Owens was able to locate and retest 127 of them, thus making for a two-point longitudinal study—at the approximate ages of 19 and 49.

The Army Alpha test that Owens used comprised eight subtests, most seemingly more similar to the WAIS Verbal subtests than the Performance, but with speed a more important factor. With one exception (Arithmetical Problems) all of the subtests showed increased scores over the period of 30 years, with four or five of these (depending on criterion) being statistically significant. The overall total score of the eight subtests showed a significant increase as well.

Owens (1966) was able to retest 97 of the 127 some 11 years later, when the subjects were near 61 years of age. He reported that none of the subtest scores changed significantly over this period, thus suggesting a plateau was reached and maintained during the fifties. However, Owens grouped the data in accord with a reported factor analysis by Guilford, and found that of the three factors representing the eight subtests, one showed age decline. A Numerical factor showed a significant, although slight, decline from age 49 to 61, but the factors labeled Verbal and Reasoning did not show decline—in fact, the Verbal score showed nonsignificant improvement.

Owens then carried out an interesting second analysis on these data. He compared the original 1919 scores with those made by students of similar age (19 years) who were tested for the first time in 1961. He found improvement in most of the Army Alpha subtest scores in the newer sample when compared to the 1919 sample, and he labeled this "cultural change." Owens then subtracted these cultural change scores from the longitudinal age difference

scores that he obtained with the original group. When he did this he found that while the Verbal factor score showed gain over the period from age 19 to about 61, a small loss was seen in the Numerical factor score and a larger one with the Reasoning. The latter factor score was based more on the speeded test items than the other factor scores: in this way it was more similar to the WAIS Performance subtests than the Verbal.

Cunningham (1974) carried out an almost identical study which he modeled after Owens'. College student subjects tested during 1944 were located and tested again 28 years later in 1972. The test used was also the Army Alpha, but in a somewhat different version. The results of the two studies were similar in several important ways. From both, it is possible to conclude that a type of classical age pattern was seen to hold longitudinally as well as cross-sectionally. In this case, it held from the period of late teen-age to mid-life and beyond.

LATER LIFE CHANGES

We have seen how to age 50 and even beyond there is little or no decrement in intellectual performance in the use of information and skills already achieved. Some decrement, however, was seen in speeded tests, especially nonverbal ones. We now turn to those longitudinal studies which focus, either in part or in whole, on late life—the basic concern of gerontology.

Research Based on the Wechsler Scales.

Continued Testing: Different Results with Short- and Long-Interval Retests. Eisdorfer and Wilkie (1973) reported WAIS results of a longitudinal study covering a 10-year period. Measurements were made on four occasions in the course of the 10 years on subjects of two age groups—60 to 69 and 70 to 79. The results may be seen as the closed circles in Figure 4. An interesting commentary on longitudinal research in general may be made in comparing these data points with the open circles in the same figure. The open circles represent these same subjects already tested four times who were also available for three subsequent test sessions, covering a total period of 15 years

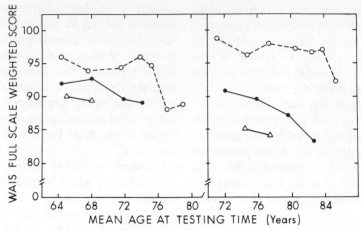

Figure 4. Subjects aged 60 to 69 years ($N = 61$) and 70 to 79 ($N = 37$) at the start of the study were tested four times (solid circles) over a 10-year period (Eisdorfer and Wilkie, 1973). The study continued for another 5 years with three additional testings (open circles): 35 subjects of the younger group and 15 of the older group were available for all seven test sessions (Wilkie and Eisdorfer, 1973). Note age decline in the course of the first four testings (10 years) and no decline during that *same* period among those tested seven times. Triangles represent two consecutive test sessions (values calculated from Eisdorfer, 1963).

(Wilkie and Eisdorfer, 1973). Those subjects unavailable for these subsequent retests dropped out for a variety of unspecified reasons.

Observe the 10-year age patterns by comparing the closed and open circles. The selective subject dropout during the last 5 years of the study functioned to obfuscate the pattern of age decline that was present In the course of the first 10 years. Figure 4 suggests that, as longitudinal research continues, and as only certain people are available for retest, age decline patterns that were seen previously may become progressively diminished (except, perhaps, in extreme late life).

In the 10-year longitudinal study by Eisdorfer and Wilkie (Figure 4, closed circles), there were statistically significant Full Scale score declines from the first to the fourth test session. For those aged 60 to 69 years at the start of the study, the weighted score loss was 2.6 points, and for those aged 70 to 79 years, the loss was 7.3 points. These declines were made up of the classic aging pattern in the younger group, not the older. Of the 2.6-point loss of the younger group, 2.0 points comprised the Performance scale and 0.6 the Verbal. Of the 7.3-point loss of the group aged 70 to 79 years at

the start, the Performance and Verbal scales were nearly equal. Other data soon to be discussed also show that in very late life the classic aging pattern may give way to overall decline.

Figure 4 also shows triangle data points covering a 3-year period of only two longitudinal test sessions (Eisdorfer, 1963). During this brief retest interval, decline patterns were not observed; the 3-year retest (triangles) did not reflect statistically significant differences in performance over time. Note the progressively higher scores made by the subjects at the first test period for those remaining progressively longer in the study. As already seen in Figure 3, selective dropout makes for subsequent longitudinal comparisons mainly of superior-performing subjects.

The different age effects in long- and short-interval testing were also seen by Jarvik, Kallmann, and Falek (1962) who tested older people on three occasions. They used several of the WB subtests, the Vocabulary test of the Stanford-Binet (List 1 of the 1916 version), and a speed of tapping test. Originally, 134 twins (268 subjects) were tested, but only 48 pairs were available for all three test periods. The first and second testings were just short of 1 year apart, and the third testing was 7.3 years after the second one. The mean ages of the subjects at the time of the three test periods were. 67.5, 68.4 and 75.7 years.

Between the first and second testing approximately 1 year later, all but two tests showed *age-increases*. The two were Digit Symbol which showed a decline, and Digit Span Forward which was unchanged. Jarvik, Kallmann, and Falek suggested that "test wiseness" may have underlain the age pattern of increase. From the first to the third testing (about 8 years) an age decline was seen in Digit Symbol performance, tapping speed and Block Design, the former two being statistically significant but the latter not. None of the other tests showed age decline. Thus, again, Performance type of tests showed decline patterns and the Verbal type did not. Jarvik (1973, p. 65) concluded, ". . . our longitudinal studies have led us to rediscover the classical pattern of aging."

A Single Long-Interval Retest. Jarvik's data are particulary interesting when viewed with the results of a later testing, almost 20 years after the first one. This later testing was not of subjects who had been tested three times previously, as just discussed; it was of subjects tested the first time who might or might not have been tested in the interim. "Over the 20-year period, mean ages 64.8–84.3 years, statistically significant declines in mean scores occurred on all subtests" (Blum, Fosshage, and Jarvik, 1972, p. 180). Thus, this study, like that of Wilkie and Eisdorfer, suggests that in very late life the general decline, rather than the differential decline, is manifest.

The very long retest interval of 20 years in Blum, Fosshage, and Jarvik's study did not obfuscate the decline seen after 7 years; in fact, it showed greater decline. This might be seen as data at variance with the data of Wilkie and Eisdorfer. Among the several differences between the two studies, one especially stands out: greatly different demands were made on the subjects. Blum, Fosshage, and Jarvik analyzed the data of a first testing and one 20 years later irrespective of whether or not the subjects were tested in the interim. Wilkie and Eisdorfer, on the other hand, included only

subjects who had already been tested four times in the first 10 years and who had been tested three times in the next 5 years—7 times in 15 years. It seems that extended longitudinal testing will obfuscate age patterns seen earlier only when the availability of subjects is stressed through requirements such as frequent testing in the course of the study.

Institutionalized Subjects. These WAIS and WB studies were based on noninstitutionalized, community-residing older people. At the time of the 20-year retest by Blum, Fosshage, and Jarvik, only 4.5 percent of the subjects were in nursing homes or homes for the aged. None of the other subjects in these studies were institutionalized. It seems that the age patterns seen with such subjects are seen also with institutionalized ones, including the different age patterns derived from short-interval and long-interval results. For example, Berkowitz and Green (1965) compared retests averaging less than 6 months and more than 8 years. As in the Jarvik, Kallmann, and Falek study, the short-interval retest showed age increments, while the long-interval retest showed decrements.

Overall then, Figure 4, and other data as well, show longitudinal age decline of subjects beginning at least in the sixties, but this decline may not be apparent if the test-retest interval is relatively brief.

Faulty Conclusions. Incomplete, if not faulty, conclusions may be drawn from longitudinal investigation if proper care is not taken. If the test-retest interval is too variable, confusion may result rather than clarification. For example, Rhudick and Gordon (1973) tested men and women aged 58 to 88 years initially, and then again, 1 to 8 years later. They found that the 1 to 8 year test interval resulted in "slight gains on Verbal, Performance, and Full-Scale WAIS scores . . ." (p. 8).

Rhudick and Gordon recognized the disparity of results that might result between longitudinal periods of 1 year and of 8 years and, accordingly, divided their sample into those who were retested within 2 years, between 2 and 6 years, and between 6 and 8 years. When this was done, Full and Verbal scale scores were found unchanged, but the Performance scores changed in a way to emphasize the importance of the length of test-retest interval. The interval of 2 or less years showed a significant *age-increase* while the interval of 6–8 years showed a significant *age-decrease*.

The less than 2 years group showed a paradoxical pattern: some decrease was seen in the Verbal score and increase in the Performance, resulting in the no age change of the Full Scale—just the opposite of the classical aging pattern. A possible explanation was the finding that "males dropped significantly on the Performance scale, while females did not" (pp. 9–10). The relative ages of men and women were not reported—perhaps the men were older than the women.

This highlights but a few of the many factors which must be considered in longitudinal investigations. The factor of age range of the subjects is of special importance. A range from 58 to 88 years, as in the Rhudick-Gordon study, is too broad. The obvious question is whether those in the fifties, eighties or in-between contributed most to the age-change results. The two sexes should be represented equally or at least proportionately in each age grouping.

The Babcock Test of Mental Efficiency (BTME). More extended longitudinal testing, it seems, does not always show decline patterns very different from the classic one. It appears to depend on the age groups in question. Blum, Fosshage, and Jarvik's 20-year interval data were of subjects aged in their eighties at the time of last testing, as were the subjects of Wilkie and Eisdorfer. When younger subjects are retested after a long interval, other results may be seen.

Gilbert (1973) gave the BTME to subjects in their twenties or early thirties and then gave it again 35 to 40 years later! Only 14 subjects were available for the retest and these "were of definitely superior intelligence." They were of relatively high socioeconomic level and ranged in age from 60 to 74 years at retest, with the average age being 65.

The BTME uses the Stanford-Binet vocabulary test and includes 29 short tests combined into six groupings: "easy and quick recall of

well-learned material, repetitions, initial learning, retention, motor reactions, and easy continuous tasks." These are averaged to produce a "mental efficiency score."

The results of this unique longitudinal study were interesting in that after 35 to 40 years, the Vocabulary ability was maintained—it even showed a slight insignificant rise. Perhaps the selective dropout with the obvious intellectual superiority of the subjects accounted for this. In any case, this result is not incompatible with cross-sectional data, especially when the subjects are highly selected, as in the study by Green (1969).

All other BTME scores and combinations of scores showed statistically significant age decline, except those of quick recall of easy, well-learned material and of repetitions. These showed insignificant age decline.

The Primary Mental Abilities Test (PMA). The best planned and excuted longitudinal investigation concerned the PMA. Beginning with an initial testing in 1956, Schaie and collaborators tested those available again in 1963, and again in 1970. In addition to a uniform pattern of test schedules (every 7 years), they tested so many subjects across the whole adult life span that they were able to categorize these subjects into uniform age groupings. Moreover, their careful planning and their large number of subjects permitted sophisticated statistical analyses of data. However, the unavoidable problem of selective subject dropout, as explicated in Figure 3, remained.

Their study includes not only the five PMA test scores and totals of these, but also other procedures. However, since the central thesis is not altered appreciably if the discussion is confined to the PMA, this will be done here for the sake of simplicity.

Age Changes. Figure 5 shows the mean scores made by the subjects in the various age groups with a composite of the five PMA tests. The figure should be understood this way: Cohort I was of subjects aged approximately 25 years when they first took the test in 1956. They were aged 32 in 1963 (the time of the second testing), and 39 in 1970 (third testing). Similarly, Cohort VII was of subjects aged approximately 67, 74 and 81 years respectively. The closed circles are of traditional longitudinal data, the open circles will be discussed later. These data are the same as part of those seen in Figure 3 demonstrating the problem of selective dropout.

Schaie and Labouvie-Vief (1974) reported the study in the context of a cross-sequential analysis, i.e., a complex statistical solution in which longitudinal and cross-sectional age patterns are simultaneously examined. For now, only the longitudinal aspect of their investigation is reported (Schaie having graciously made the data available for this purpose).

It may be seen in Figure 5 (closed circles) that in the course of 14 years, no age decline at all was present in Cohorts I through IV. This is compatible with the data of Owens (1953) and of Bayley and Oden (1955) discussed earlier. However, beginning with Cohort V, i.e., beginning in the fifties, age decline continued progressively. Table 1 provides the actual mean age changes in the PMA *T*-scores. From age 53 to 67 (Cohort V), the mean decline was 3.07; from age 60 to 74, it was 3.53; and from age 67 to 81, the decline was more appreciable— 8.08 *T*-score points. (The size of these declines is best evaluated with the recognition that 10 points equal one standard deviation.) The statistical analyses by Schaie and Labouvie-Vief

indicated that the difference in age patterns among the seven cohort groups of Figure 5 was statistically significant as was the age change in the two oldest cohorts.

Age Sequence Analysis. Do these longitudinal data of Figure 5 reflect the same age patterns seen in cross-sectional data, as, for example, those of Figure 2? In the main they do. The cross-sectional data of Figure 2 indicate that to age 50 little or no change in performance is seen. Figure 5 shows this also. Figure 2 shows age decline in the second half of adulthood and so does Figure 5.

Schaie and Labouvie-Vief carried out a cross-sequential analysis and concluded that the cross-sectional age difference was greater than the longitudinal age change. Overall, this was so; it might even have been anticipated since the longitudinal age comparison was 14 years and the cross-sectional comparison was over 40 years. The basic question, however, was not asked: Do the longitudinal age sequences in Figure 5 show greater or lesser decline than do cross-sectional sequences of *the exact same age*?

An attempt was made here to answer this question by a reanalysis of their data. This may be seen in Table 1. Up to the mid-forties, the longitudinal and cross-sectional functions provided similar information—little or no age decline. The two also provided similar information for the oldest age sequence, 67 to 81

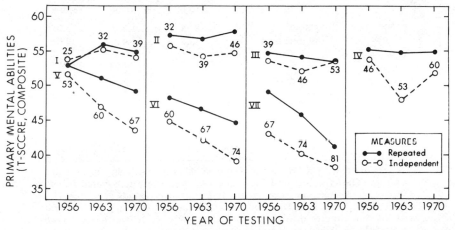

Figure 5. Age change analysis: longitudinal (repeated) measures and independent sample measures. Drawn from data provided by Schaie. (Reported in different form in Schaie and Labouvie-Vief, 1974; Schaie, Labouvie, and Buech, 1973).

years, showing age declines of between 8 and 9 *T*-score points. However, during the years represented in Cohorts IV through VI, the cross-sectional method showed greater age decline than the longitudinal.

The largest difference between cross-sectional and longitudinal age sequences was with Cohort V, between ages 53 and 67. The longitudinal age decline was 3.07, the cross-sectional was 9.03. It is possible, however, that this latter decline is unrepresentatively large. The 1956 age difference covering this period was 3.67, and the comparable age difference in 1970 was

4.11. For some reason the age difference in the 1963 testing was 8.96. (Note that 9.03 is not the mean of these three values—the cross-sectional age sequence decline scores were derived in the manner indicated in Table 1.)

The main point of Table 1 has been suggested several times previously: the difference between longitudinal and cross-sectional age patterns is more quantitative than qualitative.

Independent Groups. There is a type of age comparison which appears analogous to the longitudinal comparison, but actually it is an

TABLE 1. AGE DECLINE IN COMPOSITE PMA SCORES.
Values are the difference in age groups between means of T scores (Mean = 50; SD = 10).[a]

Cohort	Method	Age (Years)		
		25 to 32	32 to 39	25 to 39
I	Longitudinal	−2.81	1.00	−1.81
	Cross-Sectional	−4.80[b]	−3.39	−2.19[b]
		32 to 39	39 to 46	32 to 46
II	Longitudinal	0.34	−1.07	−0.73
	Cross-Sectional	−3.39	3.31	−0.08
		39 to 46	46 to 53	39 to 53
III	Longitudinal	0.66	0.38	1.04
	Cross-Sectional	3.31	−1.59	1.72
		46 to 53	53 to 60	46 to 60
IV	Longitudinal	0.37	−0.06	0.31
	Cross-Sectional	−1.59	4.62	3.03
		53 to 60	60 to 67	53 to 67
V	Longitudinal	1.54	1.53	3.07
	Cross-Sectional	4.62	4.41	9.03
		60 to 67	67 to 74	60 to 74
VI	Longitudinal	1.87	1.66	3.53
	Cross-Sectional	4.41	1.41	5.82
		67 to 74	74 to 81	67 to 81
VII	Longitudinal	3.00	5.08	8.08
	Cross-Sectional	1.41	4.07[b]	8.68[b]

[a]We are grateful to K. W. Schaie who made his data available, enabling this analysis. The cross-sectional age sequences, with exceptions noted below, were derived from the means of the three different periods of testing, i.e., 1956, 1963, and 1970. They could have been derived from any single period of the three, rather than the mean of them, with results which might have been different. The present reanalysis is not in terms of statistical tests of significance, only of observed mean differences.

[b]Cross-sectional age comparisons within a single time of measurement. All others are means of three times of measurement. Scores indicated here as negative indicate increment with age.

age comparison which is neither longitudinal nor cross-sectional, but in between. Schaie, Labouvie and Buech (1973) gave the PMA test to seven cohorts in 1956, to *different* people of the *same cohorts* in 1963, and to still *different* ones in 1970. Thus, they had independent measures (as opposed to repeated measures in longitudinal research) of subjects of the same cohort but tested in three different periods of time. It is as if they carried out a cross-sectional study, measuring the youngest age group in 1956, the next oldest in 1963, and the oldest in 1970. Schaie, Labouvie, and Buech reasoned that this type of analysis should result in the same or similar findings as the longitudinal repeated measures study. In the main, the longitudinal repeated measures and independent measures did show similar results; the two were similar in the sense that the longitudinal and cross-sectional age sequences were similar. The independent measures data may be seen in Figure 5 as the open circles.

With Cohorts I through III, no age change was seen over 14 years with either repeated or independent measures, nor was it seen cross-sectionally for this age grouping. With Cohorts IV and V, the independent measures decline scores fell in between the longitudinal and cross-sectional measures of Table 1. It was nearly identical to the cross-sectional age decline of Cohort VI (5.72 points decline) and less than both the cross-sectional and longitudinal of the oldest Cohort (VII), aged 67 to 81 years. The age decline was 5.75 points. Summarizing all these data, it would seem that where differences are found among the methods of investigation, more often than not they are in the following order in showing age declines from greater to lesser magnitude: cross-sectional, independent measures, longitudinal.

It is not surprising that the independent measures method showed greater age decline than the longitudinal repeated measures method. In the longitudinal investigation, the investigator makes every effort to retest each and every one of his subjects, but if this cannot be done, it just isn't. In the independent measurement design, if at time 2 (1963 in the case of Schaie, Labouvie and Buech) or at time 3 (1970) one subject is not available, another one may be selected—just as in cross-sectional studies. What differences were found between both methods of investigation, i.e., between longitudinal and independent measures, might be attributable to the problem of selective dropout.

Differential Performance. Each of the five PMA tests reflect their own distinctive age pattern, but in the main three show patterns not very different from that of the composite of Figure 5. The Reasoning, Space and Verbal Meaning tests show no age decline until age 53 or perhaps 60, but then decline sets in. In fact, the Verbal Meaning test shows a *rise* in the performances to this age, before the decline.

The Word Fluency and Number tests reflect different age patterns. In the cross-sectional analysis both these tests showed increased scores until the mid-forties. In the longitudinal (repeated measures) study of Schaie and Labouvie-Vief, Word Fluency scores were mainly downward beginning with Cohort II, i.e., age 32 years. This is just the opposite for the first half of the adult life span seen in the cross-sectional data. Here, if anything, the longitudinal measure showed greater decline than the cross-sectional. The Number test showed no age change at all for *any* cohort—neither rise nor decline.

ABILITY LEVELS

Do young people of relatively high intellectual ability remain so when they become old? This question cannot be answered directly by cross-sectional research but inferences may be made from some of the data. These are in the affirmative—people of high ability when young, remain so when old.

Longitudinal studies are more appropriate for answering the question. These studies suggest answers that are either just the opposite or are negative, i.e., initial ability is no indication of what will occur in time. It will be seen shortly that these two different types of results are not as incompatible as first might be suggested.

Cross-Sectional Data

Raven (1948) reported results based on a very large number of people of a wide variety of ages and occupations. The Progressive Matrices test was given to them along with the Mill Hill

Vocabulary test. The former is a nonverbal test, similar in ways to some of the subtests of the WAIS Performance scale and, perhaps, the Reasoning and Space subtests of the PMA. The Mill Hill test is very similar to the Vocabulary subtest of the Verbal scale. The Progressive Matrices involves perception, analysis, and logical thought; the Vocabulary test measures knowledge of words and their meanings.

With each of the two tests, the scores of the various age groups were divided into percentile ranks—the age groups were compared by these ranks. Thus, for example, a cross-sectional age curve for the top 5 percent of each age group (95th percentile) was available, as was a curve for the middle of each age group (50th percentile), and other percentile curves.

Two results were highlighted in this study. (1) Once again, the nonverbal test showed lower scores for the older adults than the younger, while the verbal one showed similar scores for old and young. (2) In both verbal and nonverbal functions, the cross-sectional curves suggested that intellectual ability may be maintained best by those of highest ability, and maintained least well by those of lowest ability.

In a similar study, Riegel and Riegel (1972) used four verbal achievement tests involving antonyms, synonyms, selections and classifications. Across a wide age range of subjects they selected those 15 percent who scored highest on each of the four tests and those who scored lowest. Average trends were computed for these two extreme groups. They concluded that differences in ability levels with respect to age depend on what function is measured. Tasks involving unfamiliar information seem to reflect patterns comparable to Raven's, i.e., better maintenance or slower rates of decline for the more able. On the other hand, with tasks of familiar information, such as synonyms, high ability and low ability groups become more similar as age increases.

Longitudinal Data

Owens (1959) asked the question, "Is age kinder to the initially more able?" His analysis was based on the 30-year follow-up of college students that was discussed earlier.

Owens first compared the 30-year change scores among five different groups categorized on the basis on initial level scores. No evidence was found that one initial level group changed more than another. He then compared two extreme groups, one of high gainers and one of big losers in performance scores over the 30 years. The comparison was of initial test score. Again, the conclusion was of no relationship. Thus, from 19 to 49 years age was not kinder to one ability group than another.

A more extensive analysis but with a similar conclusion was seen in the study by Baltes, Nesselroade, Schaie, and Labouvie (1972). The same PMA data reviewed earlier were the basis of this report, except that the analysis was confined to the 7-year period between 1956 and 1963.

The subjects aged 21–70 years were divided into three groups based on ability levels. By way of a variance analysis it was determined that the groups did differ in regard to change scores, but the manner in which they differed was a "regression to the mean." That is, the high ability group declined while the low ability group improved. This regression phenomenon was also reported by Eisdorfer (1963) in his 3-year WAIS retest discussed earlier (see Figure 4), and by Berkowitz and Green (1965) in an almost 9-year follow-up study of institutionalized veterans.

Baltes *et al.*, in reporting this regression phenomenon, carried out a second analysis. Instead of categorizing groups on the basis of initial scores, this time they categorized them on the basis of final (time 2) scores. It was found that those scoring highest at time 2 showed increases from time 1 to time 2, while those scoring lowest showed decreases. The regression phenomenon was thus attributed to statistical considerations, not initial ability levels.

Compatibility of Data

Two very different questions were asked above: At the start, it was asked whether people with high intellectual ability when young retain it as they age. For greater accuracy, it should have been asked whether they remained relatively high in their cohort. Owens asked another question—whether age was kinder to the initially more able. Kindness here referred to greater or lesser change. The question could have been asked whether the initially bright improve more or decrease less with age than do the less bright. In one form or another, the cross-sectional studies were concerned with relative standing within a cohort and the longitudinal studies were concerned with change scores. These two questions are not always recognized as different. A bright person can decline or regress to the mean and a dull person can improve to it, with the bright still scoring higher than the dull person. The inference of relative standing drawn from cross-sectional studies was confirmed in a longitudinal study. Berkowitz and Green (1963, p. 19) first tested institutionalized subjects of average age 56 years and then retested them 5 to 14 years later. They concluded, "The intellectually most able at the beginning of the study remained the most able at the end of the study."

SURVIVAL

It is a recurring theme that following studies of tested ability, those elderly subjects who succumb to death soonest tend to be the ones who had the lowest test scores. This is not identical with what earlier was called "terminal drop" (Kleemeier, 1962)—a *change* over time from initial test score to the last one. It may be that the initial score was low because a drop has already occurred, but this, of course, is not known to the investigator, and cannot be known. It may also be that low initial ability people tend to die sooner irrespective of a drop in scores. Perhaps poor performers, declining "normally" with age, cross a "performance threshold" which decreases their probability of survival.

Retrospective Studies

Poor Performance Scores. A variety of tests were given to 380 men and women aged 55 years and older who lived in Germany. These included a version of the WAIS, the verbal

achievement tests described before in the context of ability levels, and other tests (Riegel, Riegel, and Meyer, 1967; Riegel, 1971). Five years later a retest was given after 63 people had already died. Another 5 years passed and a second retest was made after another 100 died.

Scores made at test-time 1 by people who had died by the time of the second test were lower than those who survived and were retested. (An appreciable number of people who had not died but refused to take the test a second time were not part of the analysis. It is important to note that this group had a high death rate between the time of the second and third testings.) Riegel made an interesting observation: the relationship between retest and longevity was greater for those under 65 years than those over 65. Death, he suggested, seems to be more random at old age levels and more predictable at younger ones.

Test 1 scores were then compared between those who were tested a third time and those tested twice but who failed to survive to time 3. Again, the relationship held. Those scoring poorly initially died sooner than those retested. Riegel attributed the death between test time 2 and time 3 to terminal drop—a severe deterioration of performance.

Classic Aging Pattern Reversed? It was said several times in this chapter that, by and large, the Wechsler Verbal tests hold with age and the Performance tests do not. The latter, it was said, measure perceptual-integrative skills, often involving speed. It seems that this aging pattern may be reversed when matters of survival are assessed.

A study, unique because of the extraordinarily good health of its elderly subjects, included the WAIS and many other behavioral and physiological measurements. One subgroup of elderly men was without any apparent medical problems of any kind, and the other subgroup was composed of those men displaying mild, noninterfering difficulties. In this study the Performance test scores differentiated these two subgroups more than did the Verbal tests (Botwinick and Birren, 1963). However, 5 years later, when Birren (1968) compared survivors and nonsurvivors with respect to these test scores, it was primarily verbal information skills that distinguished them. (The concept of verbal skill approximated the WAIS categorization of Verbal but included somewhat different organizations of abilities encompassing a variety of additional procedures.) Birren concluded that "the measurements involving speed of response known to be intimately associated with age, did not show significant differences" between the nonsurvivors and the survivors. The verbal skill "likely closely reflects the presence or absence of vascular disease . . ." (p. 211).

These subjects with an approximate average age of 71 years were tested a third time when the average follow-up interval was now 11.1 years (Granick, 1971, pp. 55-57). This time, both initially low Verbal and Performance scores were associated with earlier death, with the Verbal scores somewhat more apparent in differentiation.

A similar conclusion was reached on the basis of a terminal drop notion called critical loss, i.e., change scores over time, or rate of drop (Jarvik and Falek, 1963). Over a period of as long as 10 years, an annual decrement rate of at least 2 percent on Digit Symbol, 10 percent on Similarities or any decline on the Vocabulary test was associated with death ensuing during the next 5 years. Despite the presence of Digit Symbol in this predictor battery, it was concluded that speed tests—for example, a Tapping test—"may represent a general concomitant of aging and is not a predictor of mortality" but "decline on certain tests of cognitive functioning (as the three above) is correlated with mortality" (Blum, Clark, and Jarvik, 1973, p. 19).

Others have not found one type of change (Verbal or Performance) more related to mortality than the other. For example, Reimanis and Green (1971) compared those who died within 1 year after the last test was given with those who survived, and found both Verbal and Performance change scores to have differentiated the two groups. In a similar vein, in Great Britain, both types of test scores differentiated survivor and nonsurvivor groups. Moreover, when corrections for age were taken into account, only the Performance scores were found to be differentiating (Hall, Savage, Bolton, Pidwell, and Blessed, 1972).

Thus, there is conflicting evidence regarding the classic age pattern in the prediction of survival. It is likely that the categorization of Verbal versus Performance is too gross to be useful for this purpose. Digit Symbol performance decline may be crucial in prediction, as judged by Jarvik and Falek's data, but its place in the Performance category may be incorrect as to factors of life and death.

Predictive Duration of Terminal Drop. Unlike Jarvik and Falek who found change scores predictive of death over the long run—up to 10 years—Berkowitz (1965) did not. He analyzed WAIS or WB test scores of domiciliary residents of the Veterans Administration (some of the same data of Reimanis and Green discussed previously). Berkowitz looked at change scores of people who died within 10 months of the second test, 11-20 months, 21-30 months, and those who died 31-42 months later. Only the first group, those who died within 10 months, reflected terminal drop scores greater than survivors. Berkowitz wrote: "On each subtest and on each of the three weighted scale scores, the subjects who died within 10 months after the second examination . . . show a greater mean decline and annual unit decrement between testings than do . . . survivors" (p. 4). "As the interval between the second test and death increases, the amount of decline and rate of decline decreases" (p. 10).

Critique and Questions Bearing on Studies on Survival

Altogether, it seems that survivors and nonsurvivors may be differentiated by both initial test level scores and by change scores (the former possibly reflecting change that has already occurred). Uncertain at this point are four issues: (1) How long in advance of death are indices predictive? (2) Do verbal type of scores or change scores predict mortality better than performance-speed scores? Which measures or combination of measures best make accurate predictions? (3) Many of the studies categorized people into broad age categories. In so doing, these studies failed to keep the comparisons between survivor groups and nonsurvivor groups confined to people of very similar age at the time of initial testing. Thus, age differences between survivor and nonsurvivor groups could have been the basis of the respective longevities rather than the level of the initial test scores or of the change in scores. (4) Most important, all of these studies on survival were of retrospective analyses. Would these be confirmed by the crucial test of prospective analyses? The job now is to make predictions of life and death from available longitudinal data and to allow time to test the validity of these predictions.

SUMMARY HIGHLIGHTS

1. When the limitations of the cohort effect in cross-sectional research and the selective subject dropout effect in longitudinal research are recognized, the two methods may provide similar interpretations: differences are quantitative, not qualitative. Decline with age for many functions may not be seen before ages 50 or 60, and even then the decline may be small. For other intellectual functions, however, particularly those involving speed of response of nonverbal, perceptual-manipulative skills, decline may be seen before then.

2. The problem in longitudinal research of selective subject dropout appears most severe when there are many testing occasions over a prolonged period of investigation. When this is so, decremental patterns may be obfuscated.

3. Cross-sectional and longitudinal studies suggest that people who perform relatively well when young will also perform relatively well when old. However, the performance level when young is no yardstick of whether age decline will be great, small or neither.

4. Retrospective analyses suggest that certain test performance levels or changes in these levels over time relate to closeness to death. Prospective studies are needed to confirm these results.

REFERENCES

Baltes, P. B. 1968. Longitudinal and cross-sectional sequences in the study of age and generation effects. *Hum. Develop.*, 11, 145–171.

Baltes, P. B., Nesselroade, K., Schaie, K. W., and Labouvie, E. W. 1972. On the dilemma of regression effects in examining ability-level-related differentials in ontogenetic patterns of intelligence. *Developmental Psychology*, 6, 78–84.

Baltes, P. B., Schaie, K. W., and Nardi, A. H. 1971. Age and experimental mortality in a seven-year longitudinal study of cognitive behavior. *Developmental Psychology*, 5, 18–26.

Baltes, P. B., and Schaie, K. W. 1974. Aging and IQ: The myth of the twilight years. *Psychology Today*, 7, 35–40.

Bayley, N. 1955. On the growth of intelligence. *American Psychologist*, 10, 805–823.

Bayley, N. 1970. Development of mental abilities. *In*, P. Mussen (ed.), *Carmichael's Manual of Child Psychology*, Vol. 1. pp. 1163–1209. New York: John Wiley.

Bayley, N., and Oden, M. H. 1955. The maintenance of intellectual ability in gifted adults. *J. Gerontol.*, 10, 91–107.

Berkowitz, B. 1965. Changes in intellect with age: IV. Changes in achievement and survival in older people. *Journal of Genetic Psychology*, 107, 3–14.

Berkowitz, B., and Green, R. F. 1963. Changes in intellect with age. I. Longitudinal study of Wechsler-Bellevue scores. *Journal of Genetic Psychology*, 103, 3–21.

Berkowitz, B., and Green, R. F. 1965. Changes in intellect with age: V. Differential changes as functions of time interval and original score. *Journal of Genetic Psychology*, 107, 179–192.

Birren, J.E. 1952. A factorial analysis of the Wechsler-Bellevue Scale given to an elderly population. *J. Consult. Psychol.*, 16, 399–405.

Birren, J. E. 1968. Increment and decrement in the intellectual status of the aged. *Psychiat. Res. Rep.*, 23, 207–214.

Birren, J. E. Botwinick, J., Weiss, A., and Morrison, D. F. 1963. Interrelations of mental and perceptual tests given to healthy elderly men. *In*, J. E. Birren, R. N. Butler, S. W. Greenhouse, L. Sokoloff, and M. Yarrow (eds.), *Human Aging: A Biological and Behavioral Study*, pp. 143–156. Washington, D. C.: Government Printing Office.

Birren, J. E., and Morrison, D. F. 1961. Analysis of the WAIS subtests in relation to age and education. *J. Gerontol.*, 16, 363–369.

Blum, J. E., Clark, E. T., and Jarvik, L. F. 1973. The New York State Psychiatric Institute Study of Aging Twins. *In*, L. F. Jarvik, C. Eisdorfer, and J. E. Blum (eds.), *Intellectual Functioning in Adults*, pp. 13–19. New York: Springer.

Blum, J. E., Fosshage, J. L., and Jarvik, L. F. 1972. Intellectual changes and sex differences in octogenarians: A twenty-year longitudinal study of aging. *Developmental Psychology*, 7, 178–187.

Botwinick, J. 1967. *Cognitive Processes in Maturity and Old Age.* New York: Springer.

Botwinick, J. 1973. *Aging and Behavior.* New York: Springer.

Botwinick, J., and Birren, J. E. 1963. Cognitive processes: Mental abilities and psychomotor responses in healthy aged men. *In*, J. E. Birren, R. N. Butler,

S. W. Greenhouse, L. Sokoloff, and M. Yarrow (eds.), *Human Aging: A Biological and Behavioral study*, pp. 97–108. Washington, D.C.: Government Printing Office.

Botwinick, J., and Storandt, M. 1973. Speed functions, vocabulary ability, and age. *Perceptual Motor Skills*, 36, 1123–1128.

Botwinick, J., and Storandt, M. 1974a. Vocabulary ability in later life. *Journal of Genetic Psychology*, 125, 303–308.

Botwinick, J., and Storandt, M. 1974b. *Memory, Related Functions and Age*. Springfield, Illinois: Charles C. Thomas.

Bradway, K. P., Thompson, C. W., and Cravens, R. B. 1958. Preschool IQs after twenty-five years. *J. Educ. Psych.*, 49, 278–281.

Corsini, R. J., and Fassett, K. K. 1953. Intelligence and aging. *Journal of Genetic Psychology*, 83, 249–264.

Cunningham, W. R. 1974. Age changes in human abilities. Master's thesis, University of Southern California, Los Angeles, California.

Doppelt, J. E., and Wallace, W. L. 1955. Standardization of the Wechsler Adult Intelligence Scale for older persons. *J. Abn. Soc. Psych.*, 51, 312–330.

Eisdorfer, C. 1963. The WAIS performance of the aged: A retest evaluation. *J. Gerontol.*, 18, 169–172.

Eisdorfer, C., Busse, E. W., and Cohen, L. D. 1959. The WAIS performance of an aged sample: The relationship between verbal and performance I.Q.s. *J. Gerontol.*, 14, 197–201.

Eisdorfer, C., and Wilkie, F. 1973. Intellectual changes with advancing age. *In*, L. F. Jarvik, C. Eisdorfer, and J. E. Blum (eds.), *Intellectual Functioning in Adults*, pp. 21–29. New York: Springer.

Furry, C. A., and Baltes, P. B. 1973. The effect of age differences in ability-extraneous performance variables on the assessment of intelligence in children, adults, and the elderly. *J. Gerontol.*, 28, 73–80.

Gilbert, J. G. 1973. Thirty-five year follow-up study of intellectual functioning. *J. Gerontol*, 28, 68–72.

Granick, S. 1971. Psychological test functioning. *In*, S. Granick and R. D. Patterson (eds.), *Human Aging II: An Eleven-Year Followup Biomedical and Behavioral Study*, pp. 49–62. Washington, D. C.: Government Printing Office.

Granick, S., and Friedman, A. S. 1973. Educational experience and maintenance of intellectual functioning by the aged: An overview. *In*, L. F. Jarvik, C. Eisdorfer, and J. E. Blum (eds.), *Intellectual Functioning in Adults*, pp. 59–64. New York: Springer.

Green, R. F. 1969. Age-intelligence relationship between ages sixteen and sixty-four: A rising trend. *Developmental Psychology*, 1, 618–627.

Hall, E. H., Savage, R. D., Bolton, N., Pidwell, D. M., and Blessed, G. 1972. Intellect, mental illness, and survival in the aged: A longitudinal investigation. *J. Gerontol.*, 27, 237–244.

Harwood, E., and Naylor, G. F. K. 1971. Changes in the constitution of the WAIS intelligence pattern with advancing age. *Australian J. Psychol.*, 23, 297–303.

Horn, J. L., and Cattell, R. B. 1967. Age differences in fluid and crystallized intelligence. *Acta Psychol.*, 26, 107–129.

Jarvik, L. F. 1973. Discussion: Patterns of intellectual functioning in the later years. *In*, L. F. Jarvik, C. Eisdorfer, and J. E. Blum (eds.), *Intellectual Functioning in Adults*, pp. 65–67. New York: Springer.

Jarvik, L. F., and Falek, A. 1963. Intellectual stability and survival in the aged. *J. Gerontol*, 18, 173–176.

Jarvik, L. F., Kallman, F. J., and Falek, A. 1962. Intellectual changes in aged twins. *J. Gerontol.*, 17, 289–294.

Jones, H. E. 1959. Intelligence and problem-solving. *In*, J. E. Birren (ed.), *Handbook of Aging and the Individual*, pp. 700–738. Chicago: University of Chicago Press.

Kangas, J., and Bradway, K. 1971. Intelligence at middle age: A thirty-eight-year follow-up. *Developmental Psychology*, 5, 333–337.

Kleemeier, R. W. 1962. Intellectual change in the senium. Proceedings of the Social Statistics Section of the American Statistical Association, pp. 290–295.

Klodin, V. M. 1975. Verbal facilitation of perceptual-integrative performance in relation to age. Doctoral dissertation, Washington University, St. Louis.

Lorge, I. 1936. The influence of the test upon the nature of mental decline as a function of age. *J. Educ. Psych.*, 27, 100–110.

Matarazzo, J. D. 1972. *Wechsler's Measurement and Appraisal of Adult Intelligence*. 5th Edition. Baltimore: Williams & Wilkins.

Miles, C. C. 1934. The influence of speed and age on intelligence scores of adults. *Journal of Genetic Psychology*, 10, 208–210.

Nisbet, J. D. 1957. IV.–Intelligence and age: Retesting with twenty-four years' interval. *Brit. J. Educ. Psych.*, 27, 190–198.

Owens, W. A., Jr. 1953. Age and mental abilities: A longitudinal study. *Genet. Psychol. Monogr.*, 48, 3–54.

Owens, W. A., Jr. 1959. Is age kinder to the initially more able? *J. Gerontol.*, 14, 334–337.

Owens, W. A., Jr. 1966. Age and mental abilities: A second adult follow-up. *J. Educ. Psych.*, 51, 311–325.

Raven, J. C. 1948. The comparative assessment of intellectual ability. *Brit. J. Psych.*, 39, 12–19.

Reimanis, G., and Green, R. F. 1971. Imminence of death and intellectual decrement in the aging. *Developmental Psychology*, 5, 270–272.

Rhudick, P. J., and Gordon, C. 1973. The Age Center of New England Study. *In*, L. F. Jarvik, C. Eisdorfer, and J. E. Blum (eds.), *Intellectual Functioning in Adults*, pp. 7–12. New York: Springer.

Riegel, K. F. 1971. The prediction of death and longevity in longitudinal research. *In*, E. Palmore and F. C. Jeffers (eds.), *Prediction of Life Span*, pp. 139–152. Lexington, Massachusetts: Heath.

Riegel, K. F., and Riegel, R. M. 1972. Development, drop, and death. *Developmental Psychology*, 6, 306–319.

Riegel, K. F., Riegel, R. M., and Meyer, M. 1967. A study of the dropout rate in longitudinal research on aging and the prediction of death. *J. Pers. Soc. Psychol.*, 5, 342–348.

Schaie, K. W. 1958. Rigidity-flexibility and intelligence: A cross-sectional study of the adult life-span from 20 to 70. *Psychol. Monographs*, 72 (9, Whole No. 462).

Schaie, K. W. 1959. Cross-sectional methods in the study of psychological aspects of aging. *J. Gerontol*, 14, 208–215.

Schaie, K. W. 1965. A general model for the study of developmental problems. *Psych. Bull.*, 64, 92–107.

Schaie, K. W., and Labouvie-Vief, G. 1974. Generational versus ontogenetic components of change in adult cognitive behavior: A fourteen-year cross-sequential study. *Developmental Psychology*, 10, 305–320.

Schaie, K. W., Labouvie, G. V., and Barrett, T. J. 1973. Selective attrition effects in a fourteen-year study of adult intelligence. *J. Gerontol.*, 28, 328–334.

Schaie, K. W., Labouvie, G. V., and Buech, B. U. 1973. Generational and cohort-specific differences in adult cognitive functioning: A fourteen-year study of independent samples. *Developmental Psychology*, 9, 151–166.

Schaie, K. W., Rosenthal, F., and Perlman, R. M. 1953. Differential mental deterioration of factorially "pure" functions in later maturity. *J. Gerontol.*, 8, 191–196.

Schaie, K. W., and Strother, C. R. 1968. A cross-sequential study of age changes in cognitive behavior. *Psych. Bull.*, 70, 671–680.

Schonfield, D., and Robertson, E. A. 1968. The coding and sorting of digits and symbols by an elderly sample. *J. Gerontol*, 23, 318–323.

Terman, L. M., and Oden, M. H. 1947. *The Gifted Child Grows Up: Volume IV, Genetic Studies of Genius*. Stanford, California: Stanford University Press.

Thurstone, L. L., and Thurstone, T. G. 1949. *SRA Primary Mental Abilities*. Chicago: Science Research Associates.

Tuddenham, R. D., Blumenkrantz, J., and Wilkin, W. R. 1968. Age changes on AGCT: A longitudinal study of average adults. *J. Consult. Clin. Psych.*, 32, 659–663.

Wechsler, D. 1958. *The Measurement and Appraisal of Adult Intelligence*. 4th Edition. Baltimore: Williams & Wilkins.

Weisenburg, T., Roe, A., and McBride, K. E. 1936. *Adult Intelligence*. New York: The Commonwealth Fund.

Wilkie, F., and Eisdorfer, C. 1973. Intellectual changes: A 15-year-follow-up of the Duke sample. Unpublished manuscript read at the 26th Annual Meeting of the Gerontological Society, Miami, Florida.

25
CHANGES IN PROBLEM SOLVING ABILITY IN OLD AGE

Patrick Rabbitt

The Queen's College, Oxford, University of Oxford

There is a vast literature on problem solving. It is, however, surprising that in contrast to the overwhelming literature on children, the literature on young adults and on old people is relatively scanty. One of our tasks is to explain how it comes about that people cease to be able to do complex things which they once did well. We are concerned with the relationships between the many subprocesses deployed in very complex tasks whose relationships should be orderly. By uncovering this order it is hoped that the functional relationships within the central nervous system will be exposed. In this approach we must never uncritically agree that "involution mirrors development" or that the relationships between processes mediating problem solving in young adults are *necessarily* the same as those in the old. It is possible that the evidence discovered by gerontologists on problem solving will parallel evidence in the general area of problem solving so that there will be a "unified field theory of human cognitive activity."

Another approach to the topic is to try to comment on a remarkable feature of the way in which "problem solving" has been discussed in the literature. Human experimental psychology since its inception has concentrated experimentation on the description of microsystems. Thus we have identifiable "theories of long-term memory" which are distinct from "theories of short-term memory," perhaps only because different kinds of experiments are done in each case. We have "theories of pattern perception and perceptual integration," and "theories of selective attention." "Theories of simple and choice reaction time" are distinct from almost all other theories in psychology, while "decision theory" may refer equally to psychophysics or to the evaluation of utilities in social situations.

An adequate account of problem solving must obviously involve an account of memory, of selective attention, of the rate at which information can be processed (perhaps estimated by reaction time), and of the mathematics underlying the evaluation of probabilistic evidence. Yet theories of "problem-solving" have become theories *sui genesis*, unrelated to descriptions of processes which we *know* must be components of complex activities. These descriptions are based on experiments which do not allow comment on the relative contributions of component processes.

This issue has been dodged for too long. The appearance of such theoretical overviews as that of Newell and Simon (1972) and Anderson and Bower (1973), with recent collections of theoretical papers such as that by Gregg (1974), is very welcome indeed. It may rightly be insisted that none of these, or of other recent overviews, is either comprehensive, internally consistent, or as yet precise in terms of predictions for human performance.

In this review the author will consider what little work there is on the subject of problem solving by older people and will try to cross reference the changes in performance observed in terms of the results of other experiments, particularly those designed to investigate changes in performance in memory and learning and in the rate of gain of information. If relationships between deficits in performance are apparent this may encourage others to undertake some deeper analysis. Finally it is salutory to turn from laboratory studies to a brief consideration of changes in professional efficiency in everyday life as age advances, so that we may be aware that we may have raised some simple questions, although the answers they will require are very complex indeed.

PIAGETIAN THEORIES APPLIED TO CHANGES IN PROBLEM SOLVING ABILITY IN OLD AGE

It is just to begin with applications of Piaget's theories to involution, since these evidently provide the most influential single systematic description of problem solving behavior in the literature. An interestingly dogmatic statement has been made by Storck, Looft, and Hooper (1972): " . . . with advancing age, in later life, the normal developmental pattern is a reversal of the horizontal décalage sequences (e.g. mass, weight, volume) that appear in childhood." The evidence for this strong assertion that involution indeed mirrors development is that failures by old people to solve the more complex Piagetian conservation tasks correlate highly with lower scores on conventional I.Q. tests. Specifically Hooper, Fitzgerald, and Papalia (1971) find that scores on Raven's Progressive Matrices correlate highly with measures of seriation, classification, and rigidity. Vocabulary scores correlate positively with rigidity but are unrelated to scores

on Piagetian tasks. Similarly Burnand, Richard, Tinnot, and de Ajuriaguerra (1972) find that patients with degenerative dementia perform poorly in conservation tasks and are poor at giving proofs of causality or at recognizing the implications of transitivity. It is interesting that cognitive decrements with age and with degenerative dementia should also be shown on so widely used a series of tests as the Piagetian sequence.

The nature of the measures used, however, leaves the interpretation of these decrements obscure. Much recent work on children (ably reviewed by Bryant, 1971) shows that the Piagetian concept of an hierarchy of cognitive "stages", is unrealistic. This, because the precise instructions by which the *nature of the problem* is conveyed, the apparatus used to *display the problem*, the involvement of *memory load* and the context of presentation of the problem, appears to have more to do with the probability of solution than does the chronological age of the child. It seems likely that such factors are equally critical in old people. If these factors are not considered we shall not understand the *nature* of the changes which underlie such failures. The evidence so far available does not encourage me beyond the simplistic view that Piagetian tasks offer a series of problems of graded difficulty, and that it is not surprising that old people should find the harder problems intractable and the easier soluble. I do not feel that our understanding as to what makes a hard problem difficult and a simple problem easy, either for adults or old people, has been as yet much advanced by this work.

WORK ON "CONCEPT FORMATION" TASKS

In comparison we may consider work done on "concept formation," largely stemming from experiments by Kendler and Kendler (1962). The nature of the experiments allows at least some gross quantification in terms of information transmission and so some cross-referencing with other performance measures to which the same metric is loosely applicable.

In categorization tasks subjects are usually required to deduce a classification rule in order to subdivide a population of complex displays (e.g., colored shapes in different orientations). The rule the subject is required to discover and use may be arbitrary, in the sense that it is one of several possible ways in which a population of displays may be subdivided, or it may be unique, in that it is the only rule which allows dichotomization in terms of all display features. Thus it may be simple, in that only one display feature (e.g., color) of many need be considered as relevant, all others being incidental, or it may be complex, involving the perception of several different types of relation between display features (e.g., p and q; p and/or q; p or q; p but not q; and so on). An excellent account of the logic of these and of similar kinds of experiments is given by Wason and Johnson-Laird (1972).

It thus can be seen that such tasks require the subject to retain in memory either a few or many different display features and more or fewer possible kinds of relation between these features. During such tasks, subjects typically encounter each display in turn and are told whether it represents a positive or a negative instance of the concept which they are required to deduce. It is obvious that the amount of information the subject remembers about previous displays and their classification will affect the efficiency with which he can perform the task. That is, if he faultlessly recalled all displays and their classification, we could compute the logically necessary minimum number of displays he would need to inspect in order to be certain that he had deduced the correct classification (lucky premature guesses based on inadequate evidence do not count). Obviously, the more display attributes he must consider, the greater his memory load will be and also the greater the probability of inefficient performance because of simple forgetting. Furthermore, the more complex the relationships between display attributes which define the concept, the greater will tend to be the number of displays which he logically *must* inspect before the concept is discoverable. Thus here too memory load, irrespective of other factors, is likely to set limits to performance. Finally, it is not intuitively apparent that the reduction in uncertainty as each display is presented will be different depending on whether the display is a positive or negative instance of the concept. However Arenberg (1970) has ably demonstrated that this is the case. A technique developed for equating information value of positive and negative instances has performance on a "concept function" task which is so simple that poor memory is probably the main cause of poor performance. In an experiment by Schonfield and Shooter, described by Welford (1958, pp. 209–210), subjects were shown series of dot patterns, and the task was to successively inspect patterns to determine in which pattern positions a dot occurred only once. In most cases errors increased slightly with age. More striking was a very sharp increase in the number of observations made in order to solve the problems and consequently in the times taken to do so. Equally striking was the increase with age in failures to obey an instruction incidental to the experiment (to press a key stopping a timer recording time on task). Since all patterns had to be inspected at least once, and since order of inspection within a task was not important, the reinspections made by the old (and their forgetting of the incidental instruction) suggest that this problem reduces to a simple memory task and that old people suffer from a memory deficit which forces them to make more inspections than the young.

Considered as memory tasks, concept formation tasks are those in which there is running increment in memory load and in which the iterative activity of inspecting and evaluating displays may act as an interfering task making loss of information held in memory probable. For an extended discussion of the effects of interfering tasks on memory and learning see Chapters 17 and 18 in this *Handbook*.

This general approach to problem solving tasks therefore seems to offer some diagnosis of the functional limitations of the human being (in this case memory load evidently among them), which make some problems more difficult to solve than others.

USE OF TRAINING PROCEDURES AS A METHODOLOGICAL TOOL

In attempting a diagnosis of functional limitations in problem solving, an important methodological tool is to discover how the task or the instructions may be altered to improve performance or to discover what sort of training is best to ensure easy mastery. The nature of the necessary aids, instructions, or training thus helps to define the particular handicap a given task imposes.

Sometimes age differences may be mitigated by instruction. Goulet (1972) suggests that older subjects may be taught learning strategies and that the establishment of more efficient learning sets may reduce age differences. Crovitz (1966) found that on the Wisconsin Card Sorting Test (which may be regarded as a simple concept formation task) age differences are sharply reduced by training older subjects to verbalize the sequence and the nature of their decisions. These results, even if considerably extended and replicated, would not imply that *because* age differences are mitigated by instructions, memory deficiencies play no part in problem solving failures by the aged. It is now well recognized that variations in the efficiency with which material to be recalled can be cognitively organized affect the amount recalled perhaps more than any other single factor (Kintsch, 1970, pp. 243-267). If we train old subjects to organize material they may remember more. Further, if we train them to be selective in material they commit to memory, they may *have* to remember less. The dependence of memory load on the capacity to organize efficiently and selectively encode information will be later raised in other contexts.

Let us examine one implication of the idea that a particular handicap suffered by the old is their inability to find appropriate organizational strategies in concept formation tasks. This seems likely because, as we have seen, they perform better when trained in such strategies. We may suppose that old people are poor at discovering for themselves *any* organizational strategy and so improve when a useful one is demonstrated to them. However there is another possibility. We may suppose that old people can, and do, deploy organizational strategies spontaneously and that these strategies may sometimes be quite complex. Perhaps it may be that old people persist in deploying highly unsuitable strategies and are rigid in failing to abandon them. For a full discussion of organizational strategies see Chapter 17.

EXPERIMENTS EXAMINING TRANSFER IN CONCEPT FORMATION AND IN SOME VERBAL LEARNING TASKS

The empirical technique used to examine this possibility has been to train subjects to use a particular rule or principle of organization on one task and then to examine their performance in a subsequent task where this rule or principle is no longer appropriate.

When multidimensional stimuli are used, the transfer rule may involve use of a new discrimination on the learned dimension of difference (intradimensional shift). It may involve use of a rule involving use of a new dimension of difference (extradimensional shift). Or finally it may involve a reversal of the discrimination learned on the original dimension of difference (reversal shift). On the premise that they rigidly cling to learned rules, old people should be relatively more inconvenienced than the young by extradimensional as compared to intradimensional shifts and more inconvenienced still by reversal shifts. Some data on brain damaged adults (Phelan and Gustafson, 1968) and children (Reiher, Phelan, and Kiker, 1969) suggest that this is a useful distinction to draw. However, Coppinger and Nehrke (1972) did not find that old subjects were more affected than the young by these shift changes. They draw attention to the fact that previous experience with shifts of particular kinds and differences in the salience of dimensions employed are critical variables which must be carefully controlled. Nehrke (1973), discussing an elegant experiment of this kind with some rather ambiguous results, makes a case for the assumption that older subjects regress to a more primitive "single stage" unit shift paradigm (see Spence, 1963) rather than employ a two-stage mediational strategy suggested by studies of competent performance of the young (Kendler and Kendler, 1962). It must be emphasized here that the informational complexity and the "rule demands" of tasks must be carefully unconfounded before we can make any useful statements. That is, it is pointless to compare reversal shifts in informationally simple tasks (Arenberg, 1970) with nonreversal shifts in informationally complex tasks and then draw deductions from parity of performance. More subtly, reversal shifts may become progressively more difficult than nonreversal shifts as the task becomes informationally more complex. To put the point crudely, any known strategy, even if unsuccessful, may become more appealing than none if the task is made so complex that derivation of an original strategy presents a formidable problem. So far as the present evidence goes, we can say that task *complexity* certainly handicaps the old and that *shifts* may handicap the old if they incidentally increase task complexity. However, there is as yet no clear evidence that in simple tasks the nature of the transitions between categorization rules has any effect *per se*.

In verbal paired associative learning tasks a procedure logically similar to shift transfer occurs when subjects learn a particular pairing between stimulus (A) and response (B) words (A – B list) and are then asked to learn other lists in which stimulus words, response words or both may be from the original lists or may be novel. On the premise that old people persistently cling to previously learned associations they might be expected to learn new lists less well when these involve re-ordering of previous associations than where they are entirely novel. Boyarsky and Eisdorfer (1972) failed to show that A – B/C – B transfer was relatively more difficult for old people than A – B/C – D transfer in paired associate list learning. They point out, however, that under the conditions of modified free recall they used, patterns of forgetting in older people appeared to be complicated by their greater use of contextual cues. They suggest that intelligent old subjects may be very sensitive to contextual associations, and may be distracted by them, so that the effects of transfer are blurred in their data. However, since they did not test young controls this remains but a provocative speculation.

A survey of this literature suggests that no evidence has been found that any *particular*, experimentally isolable stereotype in learning strategies interferes with the performance of old people. For example left-to-right reading habits are known to affect efficiency of paired associate learning in young people. However Monge (1971) failed to show that interference due to L-R scanning strategies was more marked in the old than in the young.

In so far as the types of experiment are re-motely comparable, the literature on aged rats is surprisingly consistent with that for old humans. Botwinick, Brinley and Robin, (1963) found that old rats were not relatively worse at reversing a learned traverse of a maze than young rats, but that maze complexity, *per se*, adversely affected the performance of older animals. Goodrick (1972) reports no age differences for learning in runways or simple (4 unit) T-mazes. However, a very difficult 14 unit T-maze was more slowly learned by old rats. In this case there was some suggestion of interference from earlier habits since the old animals appeared to make more non-random, perseverative, repetitive error sequences than the young.

It is worth emphasizing the logical difficulties in interpretation which this result raises, since they are central to problems of comparison between age-groups on problem solving or on conceptual organization on learning tasks. When mazes are very complicated, even young rats show a sharp increase in the number of non-random perseverative "repetition-error" sequences which they make while attempting to solve them. Thus this kind of behavior is evident when any task begins to stretch the animal's capacity to its limit. We have seen that the complex mazes are relatively more difficult for older animals. We cannot, therefore, say that this behavior is specifically related to *age*; it is as likely to be related to task difficulty. In an hierarchy of tasks of ascending difficulty the behavior may simply appear earlier in old animals.

In all problem solving tasks some disorganization of behavior may be evident in humans of *all* ages when task complexity is great. It is exceedingly difficult to demonstrate that older people show different *patterns* of disorganization of problem solving strategies than do the young. This is mainly because we have no clear way in which to differentiate between "patterns of organization" (see below). Until our description of problem solving strategies is precise enough to attempt a *taxonomy* of breakdown, so as to allow us to differentiate between the *kinds* of breakdown specific to old and to young people, this question will remain unsolved.

This caveat may be borne in mind in briefly considering the remaining, rather contradictory literature dealing with the question of whether preexisting habits interfere more with new learning or with the solution of novel problems by the old than by the young.

This possibility was first documented by Ruch (1934) who found that older people were particularly poor at tasks which seemed to require modification of preexisting habits (e.g., the suppression of algebraic skills when recalling nonsense equations). Korchin and Basowitz (1957) partially replicated Ruch's study in the context of verbal learning experiments and failed to confirm his findings. Gladis and Braun (1958) examined transfer and retroactive interference in paired associate learning tasks in which responses were similar in sequentially learned lists. Their results indeed suggest that interference was greater for the old than for the young. However, there was also less *positive* transfer between lists for the old than for the young in cases where this occurred at all. Thus their data suggest that old people may *benefit* less from preexisting habits even when they can profitably use them. The possible conclusion that old people are less able to use even such strategies of organization as they retain, but paradoxically suffer from more persistent interference from such strategies when these are inappropriate, would indeed be of interest and need not be discarded on simple logical grounds. However, we have seen that Boyarsky and Eisdorfer (1972) failed to show greater negative transfer in old than in young people in what was probably a simpler learning task. The rule of task complexity thus appears critical, and Gladis and Braun's data (1958) remain cryptic. Adopting a very different paradigm Canestrari (1966) trained old and young subjects on word pairs which had either high or low association value. Subjects were divided into groups who showed either high or low commonality of associations with the index of association value from which pairs were derived. Both old and young groups were found to experience the same degree of interference and facilitation as a result of differences in commonality of association. Thus in *this* case there is no evidence that existing verbal and nonverbal habits are either of less use or are more distracting to the old than to the young.

Again our lack of a *taxonomy* for "rules" or "organizational schemata" or even for "principles of association" severely limits what we can say. It seems possible that old subjects can use *simpler* "rules," "organizational schemata," etc., but that they are less able to use *complex* rules etc., even when these are familiar to them. By extension it may be that learned simpler rules interfere with the subsequent deduction of other rules, but learned complex rules will *neither* help performance in appropriate tasks nor hinder performance in inappropriate tasks. This is unsatisfactory, since some tasks may be so simple that choice between rules is evident even to old people. Thus we would have no positive or negative transfer with simple rules (because they are "too easy") and no positive or negative transfer with "difficult" rules, but we would have both positive and negative transfer with rules of "intermediate" difficulty. This would be all very well if we could quantitatively specify rule complexity. Since we cannot yet do so, our power of experimental analysis is small.

Laboratory studies are rather unrealistic and may not tap organizational strategies of the kind, or the complexity, of those encountered in everyday life. An account of an experiment by Allan, described by Welford (1958, pp. 193–198), allows a more subtle analysis. Subjects of different ages were given sets of propositions on "real-life" problems (e.g., ethical dilemmas or political economics) which they had to examine for consistency. Subjects took their own time working at home. Protocols showed that problems were either answered in terms of a set of logical deductions, more or less concisely exposing inconsistencies, or else showed little evidence at attempt at logical deduction. In the latter case, answers of *some* sort were nevertheless attempted, and subjects usually commented on each of five successive propositions in turn, on the basis of personal experience, or of presuppositions brought to the task, or of other information extraneous to that included in the propositions provided. This latter tendency appeared in some subjects of all age groups but was especially marked in older people and in those of lower educational attainment.

It seems impossible to say that older subjects were *prevented* by their personal associations of ideas from concisely making deductions. One would have to say that the same was true of the less educated (or possibly less intelligent) young people. All subjects felt compelled to give *some* sort of answer. It seems that the task of providing personal commentary is simpler for all subjects than the task of logical analysis of propositions. For our present purposes, it is important to note that to say that older people will attempt to fulfill task requirements in a way that is easier or more entertaining for them is different from saying that their perception of some kinds of relationships interferes with their potential recognition of others. Welford (1958) quotes an experiment by Speakman (1954) in the same context. Values of some British postage stamps are coded still by color. The color code had been constant for 39 years up to 1951 when it was changed. Speakman's subjects were, after the change, asked to recall the old color values. Following this they were asked to recall the new color values and if they could not completely do so, to deduce them from a "cue card" presented to them. It is interesting that the older subjects (in spite of their longer familiarity with the obsolete code) correctly recalled fewer of the old code values than did the young. They also recalled fewer of the new color values. When given the "cue card" to help them deduce the values which they had forgotten, using those which they remembered, old people thus, in most cases, had less initial information and so were faced with a harder task than were the young. But when old and young subjects were selected out for comparability, it was clear that the old tended not to attempt logical deduction but to try and recall color values as best as they could.

Here again it is not possible to say that the older people could not use logical deduction because their tendency to use a simpler strategy (recall) *inhibited* this. Among the subjects compared, 8 out of 20 people aged 20 to 40 tried a similar strategy. This would seem to be a case where a cruder strategy is attempted because a more complex strategy, for whatever reason, is not accessible to the subject, whatever his age. It is also misleading to consider this reversion to a crude strategy as adoption of a policy of despair. Speakman's (1954) analysis shows that although subjects of all ages who used logical deduction improved more than their coevals who

did not, the cruder strategy, when used, resulted in significant improvements for all age groups.

In this section we have described evidence from concept formation tasks and from other tasks which are logically similar in that they require categorization of items by principles reached by logical deduction. Old people have been shown to be less able than the young on some tasks. Considering that particular decrements in performance with age might contribute to this, we saw that all such tasks make considerable demands on the capacity to learn and recall. The ability to organize material in some logical way is known to greatly improve memory performance. The balance of evidence suggests that old people are relatively poor at such cognitive organization. (A review of evidence is omitted because it is carried out elsewhere in this *Handbook*, Chapters 17 and 18.) Nevertheless the evidence reviewed here suggests that old people can successfully detect and use simple organizational relationships in material to be remembered (e.g., concrete rather than abstract associations).

The question arose as to whether old people may fail to detect systems of relationships appropriate to a task because they rigidly cling to inappropriate systems previously learnt in other contexts. Neither data on reversal shifts, nor on negative transfer in paired associate learning, nor on other types of task discussed supports this view. As far as the evidence goes, it seems that where both simple and more complex solution procedures are available, the old will tend to use the simpler procedures. It is not possible to say, however, that the use of simpler solution procedures *inhibits* or *precludes* the use of more appropriate, complex procedures, either in old or in young people.

It seems from all this that discussions of this kind are very vague because we are forced to refer to "rules," "systems of relationships," "principles of organization," or "solution procedures" without having a satisfactory terminology to define these nebulous concepts or to rank order "rules," etc., in terms of relative difficulty or accessibility. These concepts have particular operational definitions only within the context of particular experiments. It is the greatest single failure of modern cognitive psychology that we do not yet even have the beginnings of a satisfactory taxonomy in which to discuss similarities or differences between rules, organizational procedures, etc., when these are operationally defined *across* different kinds of experiments.

For some time now, much hope has been invested in the possibility of borrowing such a taxonomy from systems analysis and computer technology, where problems of translation of sets of logical or algebraic operations into sequences of electronic transactions in particular machines are the everyday point of the art, and methods for specification of the rank order of "computability" of problems exist. We may briefly consider a line of experimentation which has proceeded in parallel with the development of electronic logic devices and computer programming techniques. In concrete terms, the logic of digital electronic devices is essentially that of combinations of parallel or serial switching circuits. It is hardly surprising that this was the first analogy to be taken up and built into experimental hardware. The resulting experiments are all concerned with what are, in essence, digital switching problems. Automatic data recording has been, perhaps, merely an incidental bonus for investigators. The logic of program construction has hardly been seriously considered.

EXPERIMENTS ON THE DEDUCTION OF PRINCIPLES UNDERLYING SWITCHING CIRCUITS

A very early experiment of this type, run by Bernadelli, using equipment derived from a design by Carpenter (1946), is described by Welford (1958, pp. 202–204). Subjects were shown schematics of resistances coupling terminals, some in series with each other and some not. They were presented with boxes with terminals mounted externally in arbitrary positions and connected by concealed wiring. The task was to identify the terminals in relation to those drawn on particular schematics, by testing resistances between them with a resistance meter. Old and young subjects succeeded in identifying very similar numbers of terminals, but the old subjects took many more readings to do so and took longer to make each individual reading. As Welford (1958, pp. 202–204) remarks, repetition of readings indicated a problem with memory for tests previously made. "The solution of a problem of the type used . . . appears to demand the bringing together of information, some of which is used at once, while the rest is being 'carried' in some form of short-term memory . . . Slowness in dealing with any part of the problem will place a strain upon the short-term memory and will cause pieces of information such as meter-readings to be forgotten so that they have to be taken again. On the other hand, any failure to carry information satisfactorily will have the effect of reducing the quantity of data that can be applied simultaneously to the part of the problem being dealt with, and at least slow down a solution if not prevent it altogether."

This puts the point very neatly. As experience with computers by investigators became more common, some similarities between man and machine were seen to be provocative. The problems faced by a programmer using a machine of limited capacity are very similar to those Welford sets out above. In this case it may be necessary to translate one possible sequence of successive operations into a series of smaller steps manageable by a limited processor. In other cases methods of accomodating sequences of operations to the limitations of a particular memory system may have to be devised. In either case economy of operations is a pragmatic rather than merely an aesthetic ideal. We may add to Welford's comments that the subject who sees in advance the *shortest*, and so *most informationally productive*, sequence of tests in advance will have to remember the results of fewer tests than a subject who tests at random. Moreover, having devised this sequence of tests in advance, he will know at any point in the testing sequence which tests he has completed and which are yet to be made. More than this, if the testing routine adopted is conditional (so that some tests are *only* necessary given particular results from others), a rigorous adherence to the sequence designed will imply that the test which is made at any moment *completely or partially specifies the outcomes of all preceding tests*. The advantages for reduction of memory load are obvious.

The appreciation that such *heuristic strategies* exist for solutions of problems of this type and that their value can be formulated in terms of the *information value* of successive tests applied and in terms of reductions in memory load led to the formulation of a particular logic-switching problem by John (1957). This difficult task is probably intractable by most human beings unless *some* heuristic procedures are deduced and used. Jerome (1959) discusses this task among others and points out that older subjects are at a disadvantage in being unable to generate appropriate heuristic rules to maximize information values of tests made and so, implicitly, reduce memory load by reducing the number of outcomes of specific tests which must be held in memory in order to reach a solution. The task requires subjects to discover sets of complicated relationships between "responses" (switch positions) and resulting events (light signals) by successive "interrogations" of switches. It can readily be seen that an interrogation is completely redundant if it has been already made, and has varying information value depending on the predictability of its outcome given the outcomes of previous interrogations. Jerome (1962) found that interrogations made by young people were relatively systematic, conforming to evident sensible heuristic strategies, whereas old people interrogated in random ways and were consequently rarely successful. Jerome (1959, 1962) suggested that education of older people in appropriate heuristic strategies might narrow or abolish the handicap of the old. Young (1966) extended Jerome's work with John's task, taking up this suggestion. Although training in heuristics was attempted, and visual aids used, age decrements were still great, and barely mitigated. A further study by Young (1971) comparing old men and old women offers essentially the same picture. The men were somewhat better than the women, but neither group was very competent and use of heuristic strategies was very poor. A longitudinal study by Arenberg (1974) raises an additional important point. Old subjects were tested and then retested after an interval of 6–7 years. On this occasion use of heuristic strategies once employed was seen to disappear with advancing age. Arenberg diagnoses distinct types of failure which become more common with advancing age. There is a failure to break down the problem into manageable units by systematically setting subgoals intermediate to a complete solution. Unsystematic interrogation resulted in *failures to recall that entire strategies had already unsuccessfully been tried*, as well as in *failures to recall the outcomes of isolated tests which had been made.*

A shortcoming of tasks as difficult as this one is that they present data which are too complex for the subjects to handle. Wetherick (1964) made this point very early, stressing that Jerome's tasks had been too difficult even for many of his young subjects. He devised a simpler task in which subjects had to set one, two, or three switches in particular positions in order for a signal lamp to light when a test was made. These switch positions were to be discovered by systematic testing.

Three problems in ascending order of difficulty were tried with matched (Raven's matrices) old and young subjects. There was, overall, no tendency for the old subjects to accumulate more redundant information. There was no difference between groups in the simplest problems nor on the most difficult. On the intermediate problem the young attempted to guess while the old did very badly. Wetherick concludes that intelligent old subjects may retain an ability to learn from experience which enables them to successfully compete with younger subjects. This partly supports Jerome's optimism. However, there seemed to be little possibility of demonstrating that the old used different *kinds* of strategies than the young. Even such elementary distinctions as that between "focusing" and "scanning" strategies suggested by Bruner, Goodnow, and Austin (1956) were quite unhelpful in interpreting age differences.

In a subsequent experiment Wetherick (1965) compared the abilities of old and young subjects to change an established concept. A possible hypothesis is that the old cling rigidly to old concepts and have consequent difficulty forming new ones. Some evidence for this point of view was found. Old subjects characteristically refused to abandon use of a display element to which their attention had first been drawn.

Difficulty in *using* negative concept instances appeared to be related to resulting increases in memory load rather than to other factors (see comments on Arenberg (1970) made earlier).

Wetherick's results therefore to some degree endorse Jerome's (1959) suggestions that failures in problem solving may be related to memory load and that old people may reduce memory load and so improve performance by the use of appropriate heuristic strategies. In the laboratory these strategies are attainable for simple but not for complex tasks. It is possible to design tasks so complicated that no subjects of any age grasp what the underlying principles may be. In such situations all subjects will fall back on random, unsystematic strategies (perceiving no relationship to guide them) or will attempt strategies appropriate to other situations. We cannot here say that they are "rigidly fixated" on these inappropriate strategies nor that their use of such strategies necessarily *inhibits* discovery of other relationships not comprehended. Further, old subjects are shown to be systematic in simple tasks. The appearance of systematic strategies is thus probably determined by the relationship of the task to the subject's abilities, more than by the *age* of the subject as an independent factor.

A further caveat is that laboratory experiments may be unrepresentative of real life situations, in which old people may retain and successfully employ complex systematic strategies built up over a number of years. Laboratory experiments have examined the ability of subjects to find strategies in *novel* tasks. Even Arenberg's (1974) longitudinal study may be taken to suggest that on re-exposure after 6–7 years subjects could not derive strategies as flexibly as before. The statement that they are shown to have *lost strategies once available* is here too strong. After 6–7 years the task might have appeared as "novel" as it did at first. We can only say that subjects could deduce more strategies at first presentation than when they were 6–7 years older.

We have discussed performance at particular types of problem-solving tasks in which information is always completely reliable and in which, if the subject persists, he can always obtain sufficient information to reach a deter-

minate solution. That is, when a solution has been attained, there is no question as to whether it is the "best" solution or not. It is usually the only one the task allows. Everyday life is not like that. Evidence may be probabilistic and each possible solution may entail different ratios of rewards to penalties (and even entail different *kinds* of rewards and penalties). Statements about problem solving by old people should include comment on their abilities to assess probabilistic evidence, their ability to compute costs and payoffs, and their preferences (if any) for particular gambling strategies when outcomes are also probabilistic.

PROBABILITY MATCHING, CALCULATIONS OF ODDS, AND WILLINGNESS TO RESPOND

At least two aspects of gambling behavior may be handled jointly by mathematical models like the theory of games (cf. Luce and Raiffa, 1957) but may be treated separately by a subject in a particular task, rendering his solutions suboptimal. First the subject must derive a list of probabilities of outcomes. Secondly, he must learn and use the costs and payoffs of these outcomes—a calculation of expected values. Knowledge of either probabilities or payoffs alone is insufficient, though a failure in optimization may reflect failure to master one or both, or failure to combine attained knowledge of both so as to derive the most desirable balance of payoffs and penalties.

The investigation of subjects' responses in "real-life" tasks has both advantages and drawbacks. The advantages are that such tasks may be more "meaningful for the old, and they may regard them as interesting, and be more motivated to consider them than to deal with more abstract problems. The disadvantage is that changes in performance are very difficult to evaluate in terms of any heuristic plan, so that some systematic trend in the data may reflect any one of a number of possible changes. For example, Botwinick (1966) presented young and old people with "life situation" scenarios, in which alternative courses of action were either described as rewarding, but risky, or unrewarding but safer. He found that young adults (18-35 years) were less cautious than older people (67-80) who showed a tendency to prefer the safer alternative. Somewhat similar results have been found by Wallach and Kogan (1961). However, in a subsequent experiment Botwinick (1969) used further sets of "scenarios" presenting life-situation problems, unique to old and unique to young people, to subjects of both age groups. There were solutions for each problem with five alternative probabilities of success. In this case the finding was that the old were *not* more cautious than the young, in the sense that they would often accept choices leading to low probabilities of success (indeed, faced with "young person" scenarios they did this significantly more often than did the young). The difference between this and the earlier study is that here old subjects were always forced to choose an alternative to which *some* risk was attached. In the earlier study when they could choose between risky and relatively certain (but unrewarding) outcomes, they selected the latter. Botwinick interprets this as a reluctance to make decisions or to take action. Perhaps it may also be seen as a tendency to prefer a completely predictable over an uncertain outcome, because the utility maximization strategy for probabilistic outcomes is felt to be too difficult to work out. When forced to select between probabilistic outcomes, old subjects may, in fact, be less able to work out appropriate solutions and so *appear* more "risky."

A number of important recent studies (e.g., Kahneman and Tversky, 1973; Tversky and Kahneman, 1973) have drawn attention to systematic misconceptions about the representativeness of subsets drawn from a population, which shape the intuitions on which highly intelligent (and statistically trained) young people may base their assessments of odds. From the point of view of age differences it would be unsurprising if these (and more elementary) misconceptions pervaded the assessment of probabilistic evidence by older people. This is an important point. Before we decide whether old people are "risky" or "cautious" we must assure ourselves that they can compute the odds at all. Odds *are* difficult to compute, as young people also know. Thus an apparent re-

luctance "to make a decision" may as easily be interpreted as a reluctance to base one's course of action upon a computation of odds which one has good reason to suspect.

A further difficulty in assessing age changes in risk taking is evident from an analysis by Birren (1969), who obtained accounts of their life situations from 100 successful older professional people. It was not only apparent from this analysis that these people had extremely long-range goals, but it was also apparent that they also had tactical insight into how these goals might be attained. However, a very striking feature was that the utilities of the middle-aged were somewhat different from those we might expect of a young sample. Such aims as "conservation of the individual," "control of affect," etc., would not be typical of a young population. Before making up our minds that old people fail to optimize in probabilistic situations, we may do well to consider whether we are sure, in real life, that old and young operate on the same system of goals, rewards, and deterrents.

We may turn to laboratory experiments in probability matching. A series of experiments by Griew (1962, 1965, 1968) suggested that when asked to predict signals in biased sequences, with a changing bias for the subject to track, old subjects did as well or better than young subjects. Rabbitt (1964) commented that, since Griew used choice reaction time (RT) tasks where RT duration was taken as an index of bias detection, such findings might well reflect the operation of a response repetition effect (Rabbitt, 1968a), since more frequent signals would be more often repeated. It seems that this explanation does not fit the case, since Sanford and Maule (1973) have shown probability matching to be equally good for young and old in situations where the repetition effect could not be invoked. Moreover, I have found (Jordan and Rabbitt, 1976) that the RT response repetition effect is, if anything, smaller in the old than in the young.

Nevertheless, a further caution occurs if we are to compare the probability guessing behavior of people tracking *changing* bias in a long sequence of signals. A man must compute the bias in a sequence by considering some finite sample of N signals (which cannot be greater than the length of the string so far experienced). The larger the sample size, N, the more reliable the estimate of bias will be at any given time in the sequence. It will thus be efficient to use a large N and perhaps tax short-term memory in the process. However, when the bias *changes* unpredictably, *tracking* of the bias will be most efficient if N is relatively small. Evidently, if N is large, many signals will have to be experienced and included in N before a change in bias is verified. It is thus paradoxical that if old subjects are indeed *better* than the young at tracking bias changes, this may well be attributable to poor short-term memory and failing powers of computation! The dependence of strategic behavior on efficiency of memory is again emphasized in a very direct way.

Sanford, Griew, and O'Donnell (1972) report that old and young subjects matched probabilities in simple two choice (0.75/0.25) and three choice (0.6/0.3/0.1) prediction tasks in about the same number of trials from the commencement of learning. This study indicated that there were no age differences in simple predictive behavior. When outcomes have also to be costed by subjects, the situation changes. Sanford and Maule (1971) required subjects to make observing responses to inspect and correct intermittent faults (of equal probability) in "machines." It is interesting that the old subjects showed learning of the probability bias but failed to maximize in their *use* of it. That is, the best optimization strategy was to test a "frequent fault" machine every time. The young but not the old did this. A similar disjunction between the accurate *assessment* of probabilities and a suboptimal *use* of probabilistic information is found by Sanford and Maule (1973). Here old people could accurately report the differences in fault likelihood between three machines. Nevertheless, their rates of *testing* for faults in machines were relatively uninfluenced by this knowledge. Young subjects had higher overall fault testing rates (machine observing response rates) than the old. At low signal rates young and old did not differ with respect to selectivity of testing, but at high signal rates the young tested more selectively than the old. Perhaps this might be interpreted as yet another example of age failure to utilize

informational redundancy in a task under paced conditions (Rabbitt, 1968a). A study of probability biased search behavior shows that old people may become more random than the young in their search patterns with extended practice (Sanford, 1973). Sanford interprets this as a failure by the old to accurately assess the odds. They fail to recognize that they cannot always guess correctly but persist in trying to do so; in this task, like the earlier ones, optimization would involve restriction of predictions to one alternative, ignoring all others.

To summarize, it seems that in real life situations old people prefer to avoid risky outcomes if possible, but if they are forced to select among a set of risky outcomes they do not behave less cautiously than the young. This may reflect an acknowledgment of their inability to compute optimization rules. This inability may also lead them to sometimes behave in an apparently "risky" way. However, where this behavior represents a computational failure the word *risky* is suspect.

In simple probability matching experiments the old apparently do as well as the young. However, they fail to optimize by concentrating predictions on a very likely alternative, as young people also sometimes do. This appears to reflect a failure to proceed from an accurate assessment of relative probability of events to a computation of odds and inference of the best betting strategy.

The age-related decrements in problem solving so far discussed have been interpreted mainly in terms of the possible contributions to them of decrements in learning and memory. This approach is certainly too limited. The difficulties experienced by old people with problem-solving tasks must eventually be related to quantitatively interpret performance in memory, learning, information processing rate, attention, perceptual integration, and so on. The difficulty is that while we have a variety of predictive models for each of these processes, we have as yet no models at all for their joint involvement in cognitive activities. Experiments designed to investigate such microsystems in human performance are possibly too elegant. By controlling out all except a very few variables, they deliberately confine the generality of their results and restrict the scope of any models which may be based on these results. We have reached a situation in which we can speculate that any one of a very large number of decrements in particular aspects of human performance will adversely affect problem-solving ability. But we cannot speak of the *relative* contributions of such performance decrements to failures in any *one* problem-solving task.

POSSIBLE EFFECTS OF CHANGES IN RATE OF INFORMATION PROCESSING WITH AGE UPON PROBLEM-SOLVING ABILITY

As we have seen, performance at concept-formation and at switching tasks may be described in terms of a sequence of successive tests. The outcomes of these tests may be described as conveying amounts of information. The tests themselves, when initiated by the subject, may thus be described as being informationally totally redundant (e.g., in a case where the same test is repeated) or as being more or less optimal, by comparing the maximum amount of information which *could* have been obtained by the *best* (i.e., informationally most productive) possible test against the amount of information which *was* obtained by a test actually made. Further inferences may also be made, e.g., that the outcome of a given test actually made *could* have conveyed X units of information to a subject, but that in the event he was only able to deduce $X-N$ units of information from it. When dealing with information measures we have the additional option of considering the rate of gain of information over time. That is, we may consider the speed with which decisions are made as a function of the complexity of these decisions, estimated as the number of units of information derived from each of them.

The work we have reviewed shows that old people are not merely inaccurate but also very slow. This is of course consistent with the bulk of evidence on simple data processing tasks in which reaction-time measures are used (for examples, reviews by Welford, 1958, 1969 and Rabbitt, 1968a). Clay (1954, 1956) presented her subjects with 3 X 3, 4 X 4, 5 X 5, and 6 X 6

matrices, in which the cells had to be filled with numbered counters to give specified row and column totals. As might be expected, errors increased with problem difficulty and with age. Solution times also increased with problem difficulty. The remarkable finding was, however, that *times* were longest for a 40-year-old group, for whom errors were as rare as for the youngest groups tested. Times actually *decreased* for the 70-year-old group who were the least accurate. Clay, and Welford in his commentary, 1958, p. 211), make the point that poor performance appeared to be related to greater memory load. In a subsequent series of experiments, Clay simplified the tasks to reduce the amount of information which had to be held in memory in order to progress through successive operations. This was done by allowing subjects to use different counters on separate matrices to arrive at the specified row and column total. In her Condition A, separate 5 X 5 matrices required solution of either 5 horizontally or 5 vertically displayed sums using 25 numbered counters provided for *each matrix*. In this condition no real age increase in either solution times or errors was observed. Clay's Condition B required the subjects to solve the same sums as in Condition A, but to use for this purpose 50 counters arrayed on a 5 X 5 matrix with diagonally split cells—counters in one half of each cell contributing to horizontal totals and counters in the other half of each cell, to vertical totals. In Condition B no errors were made by subjects younger than 40, and groups aged from 40-70 were almost equally accurate. However *times* were much longer for age 50-60, declining somewhat thereafter.

This difference between conditions appears to reflect the increased difficulty older people have in scanning and evaluating visually complex displays, also noted in visual search experiments (Rabbitt, 1968a). We thus see here a case where the complexity of a problem *per se* does not affect the accuracy or speed with which old people solve it. However the presentation of the problem differentially affects the speed and accuracy of the performance of the old. A comparison between Clay's first and second series of problems makes the further point that while old people may be able to efficiently carry out individual simple operations (in this case addition) necessary for solution of a problem, they are handicapped by increases in *memory load* necessitated by one *kind* of problem but not by the other.

In Clay's first series of experiments, the relationships between speed and accuracy with advancing age suggest that as age increased from 20+ to 50+, subjects could maintain accuracy, but only at the cost of time. This increase in time was partly due to increase in the time taken for individual decisions and partly due to an increase in the number of wrong decisions which had to be modified (i.e., to the total number of decisions made). As age advanced to 70+ subjects did not seem to be able to maintain accuracy, even by taking longer. They thus appeared to "give-up," accepting wrong solutions rather than exceeding some time which seemed to them to be "reasonable" for completion of the task.

Welford (1958, p. 211) makes the insightful point that time on such tasks interacts with memory load. The longer spent on each operation, the greater the probability that necessary information held in memory will be forgotten. We may further add that the less systematic the solution strategy employed, the more modifications to operations will be necessary, so that intervening activity as well as lapse of time will contribute to memory failure (see Chapter 17 in this *Handbook*).

It is important to recognize that a "vicious spiral" effect will here result. The greater the memory load, the greater the time for each operation. The greater the time, the greater the probability of memory inaccuracies. The greater the probability of memory inaccuracies, the greater the probability of incorrect decisions which have to be modified by extra operations. The greater the number of extra operations, the greater the elapsed time and interference by this extra activity, and the greater the probability of memory inaccuracies, etc., etc.

It seems very probable that as task complexity increases, the speed at which incidental operations may be carried on becomes an increasingly important limitation on the computing power of all human beings. The complexity of each such necessary operation will also affect

performance, not only because (as has been shown by Posner and Rossman, 1965) even when time for operations is held constant, memory errors increase with the information load of operations made between presentation of material and its subsequent recall. To put the matter simply, it is not just that hard problems take a long time to solve, it is rather also the case that there are some problems which are so complex that we may not be able to solve them at all (without recourse to artificial aides memoires), *unless* we can solve them quickly!

Clay's (1956) results are important because, as we have seen, they imply not only that difficulties with the perceptual organization of a display may affect speed and accuracy of problem solving, but further that old people find such perceptual organization more difficult than do the young. This appears to be a very promising and almost entirely neglected area of research. No further work with old people on this *specific* interaction between problem solving and display complexity is known to me. However, it may be useful to very briefly summarize evidence from a wide range of disparate tasks which suggests that old people indeed suffer particular disabilities with perceptual organization, bearing implications for problem-solving in mind.

CHANGES IN CAPACITY FOR PERCEPTUAL ORGANIZATION IN OLD AGE

Two possible hypotheses have emerged from the work reviewed above. One is that old people are less able to integrate or organize information than the young. The second, which as we have seen has less support in the memory literature, is that having adopted one scheme of organization they are unable to abandon it in favor of another.

Jalavisto's (1964) finding that in stereoscopic vision there is a fairly consistent decline in alternation between fields (retinal rivalry) with advancing age is sometimes taken as an example of perceptual rigidity. Since eye-preference may be related to quite peripheral physiological changes and is difficult to control adequately, this interpretation should not be impulsively accepted.

Other classical tests of rigidity are derived from such phenomena as reversibility of ambiguous figures. Botwinick, Robbin, and Brinley (1959) found that old subjects were less able than young to switch from one interpretation to another of Boring's "wife-and-mother-in-law" figures. Similarly Heath and Orbach (1963) report no reversal, or less frequent reversal, of Necker cubes for the old. Thus there does seem to be some evidence that where alternative schemes of organization are available old subjects may be able to use one, but not both. This may have two distinct implications. We may say that the adoption of one organizational scheme *inhibits* the subsequent adoption of any other for a given stimulus. This would again be a statement of "rigidity" or of "functional fixedness" in the aged. We may otherwise simply say that old people find *any* organization of a complex stimulus difficult. Thus where more than one organization is possible they will, in general, be able to achieve fewer possible organizations *in toto* than will the young. This would be a statement about the relative efficiencies of perceptual coding in dealing with redundant information in old and young people.

An interesting case of "reversal" of perception occurs when a single word on a tape-loop is continually repeated. Young subjects report "drifts" from one word to another as the experiment proceeds. Obusek and Warren (1973) found that such drifts or transformations were experienced less frequently by fit old people than by the young, and less frequently by seniles than by either group. The point of interest here was that the hospitalized old people experienced transformations of individual *phonemes* more frequently than either of the other groups but rarely reported transformations to a new, perceived, entire *word*. There thus appears to be some fragmentation of normal processes of perceptual integration. In the language of Gestalt psychology "the parts" are now perceived to change independently of "the whole." In a somewhat newer jargon, "chunking" for "information processing" appears to take place in terms of smaller "units." Thus the Obusek and Warren (1973) study tends to support the view that changes in perceptual flexibility relate to coding problems rather than to mutual inhibition between organizational schemata.

Much of the work on simpler tests of perceptual organization by the aged may be taken to demonstrate the same handicap. Markus (1971) and Axelrod and Cohen (1961) have shown that old people, particularly the institutionalized, are worse at the children's embedded figures test. Welsh, Laterman, and Bell (1969) have shown that old people recognize words less well than do the young when speech is presented through high or low band-pass filters. This last is a particularly interesting result, since it can be taken *either* to mean that old people require extra information which can be treated as redundant by the young *or* that old people cannot integrate information from a message distorted in an unfamiliar way. We thus come to the point that the old may possibly require *more* information (regarded by the young as redundant) before they can make a perceptual judgement. The problem of perceptual (or other, e.g., mnemonic) organization is thus twofold. The young appear to be able to optimize organization to employ the least possible number of critical variables. The old may not be able to attain such selectivity and may persist in clumsy organizational schemes incorporating variables redundant to the classification required.

In these terms the analogy with problem-solving tasks such as typical "concept formation" experiments is tempting and direct. Before enthusiastically pursuing it, however, there are caveats that elementary perceptual processes such as critical flicker fusion frequency are known to be related both to age and to intelligence (Wilson, 1963). Similarly visual acuity for moving rather than stationary targets declines sharply with age (Farrimond, 1967). The sensory-psychological changes with aging have been elegantly reviewed by Corso (1971). Thus our arguments about perceptual organization must be set against the context of gradual impairment of the *quality* and *quantity* of sensory information available to our subjects. We must further bear in mind that these changes are not simply changes in peripheral acuity, but may reflect complex central changes in the precision of sensory coding.

There is considerable evidence that the old accumulate more redundant information than the young and may so take longer to interpret their data (Bernadelli and Clay, quoted in Welford, 1958; see also Rabbitt, 1968a). Recent experiments on recognition of redundant as against nonredundant pictures and patterns are consistent with the view that the old use more information than is optimally necessary in order to make complex discriminations and so take longer to do so (Howell, 1972). There are suggestions that when sequential redundancy rather than spatial redundancy is employed (letter strings of 0, 1st, 2nd, and 4th order approximations to English orthography), short-term memory performance is enhanced equally for young and old (Kinsbourne, 1973). This experiment seems to me to belong with those on perceptual organization rather than with those reviewed under memory, since there was a suggestion that *at fast rates of presentation* old subjects made less use of redundancy than did the young. Further, it raises the points that subjects must recognize redundancy in order to *use* it and that they require *time* to recognize redundancy when it is present. Sequential redundancy is a useful paradigm case, since it involves the apprehension of abstract statistical dependencies rather than the relationship between critical and incidental features (though the latter, evidently, may be entailed by use of the former). In other words, sequential redundancies in English are highly learned and arguably more practiced by the old than the young. It seems that these familiar coding rules are equally employable by both age groups. The concept of "familiarity" or "meaningfulness" of visually presented material is relevant here. Thus it is known that with nonsense material old subjects are handicapped in tachistoscopic recognition (e.g., Rajalakshmi and Jeeves, 1963). However, this difference is mitigated if material is meaningful (Cooper-Howell, 1972). It is extremely difficult to separate the concepts of "perceptual organization" and "organization in memory." This can be shown by the following instance of (apparently) discrepant results.

Conrad (1964) showed that strings of acoustically confusable letters are poorly remembered because they are easily inadvertently transposed into the wrong order (Conrad, 1967). Rabbitt, Clancy, and Vyas (1969) tried to discover whether this was a particular handicap for old people. Subjects were presented with groups of random letters on separate cards. Old subjects showed generally poorer recall than young and were particularly bad at recalling lists of mutually confusable letters. This result was contradicted because another investigation (Baddeley, personal communication, 1968) had shown no age differences in vulnerability to acoustic confusability in immediate memory. The discrepancy has an interesting solution. It emerged that Rabbitt *et al.*'s (1969) *young* subjects, presented with *groups* of letters *simultaneously*, had learnt to mitigate acoustic confusability effects by treating them as pronounceable nonsense words or "approximations to real words." Young subjects in this experiment thus showed little effect of acoustic confusability. Baddeley (personal communication, 1968) presented letters *one at a time*, depriving his young subjects of this "trick," and forcing them to show the full confusability effect. Rabbitt *et al.*'s (1969) old subjects apparently did not encode the letter groups as "words" but as strings of individual letters. Thus, unlike their young cohorts in the same experiments, they appeared to show a greater confusability effect.

It therefore seems possible that where no coding strategies can be used old and young show very similar "immediate memory capacities." However, young subjects show ingenuity in discovering and using coding strategies where such exist—and their apparent "immediate memory capacity" may be expanded thereby. This argument is familiar as the distinction between "bits" and "chunks" and code-compression of maximum "bits per chunk" in immediate memory (Miller, 1956). For problem solving we may say that in so far as the ability to store new information in a "current" store is important, old people may be disadvantaged because their ability to *perceptually organize* and *encode* new information when *presented* makes storage (and perhaps retrieval) of current data more difficult, and successive decisions taken on the basis of such information are correspondingly less reliable.

It would be wrong to conclude this review with the suggestion that some questions raised are near solution or even with the suggestion that the complexity of human problem solving is yet understood. It is salutary therefore to briefly consider some studies which examine age changes in problem solving in everyday life.

DECLINE IN INTELLECTUAL CAPACITY WITH AGE IN EVERYDAY LIFE

Lehman (1953) was a pioneer in investigating creativity over the life span. Lehman (1966) dealt with the creativity of notable engineers and technologists and pointed out a picture familiar to most readers. Peak creative potential appears to occur in the years 35-40; the years 40-50 are comparable to the years 20-30, but the decline thereafter is both remorseless and accelerated.

Earlier comparisons between the productions of distinguished men in different professions (e.g., Lehman, 1953, 1962, 1965) shows that there is a distinction between professions such as mathematics, or chemistry, in which peaks are attained relatively early (sometimes before 30) and those such as literature and history in which they may be reached later (45 to 55). A first point is that some activities demand a stored capital of experience unattainable without considerable investment of time. Other activities which may not depend on such a capital tend to peak early in life.

A second point repeatedly made by Lehman is that this change through the life span is observed within the lives of individuals as well as on cross-sectional comparisons. This fact allows him to point out that quality and quantity of intellectual achievement are closely correlated in terms of the point in time at which they occur. Human beings produce their best work when they are producing their largest volume of work. I think this allows comment on the role of "intellectual vigor," or motivation. "Intellectual vigor," and its possible decline with age, may be important but cannot be the whole story. For otherwise those professionals reaching a peak, *both* of quantity and quality of output, at 40+ years cannot easily be distinguished on this criterion *alone* from their younger peers in other disciplines. The proposition that all historians are more "vigorous" than all chemists may rightly be resented as absurd. These points may also be extracted from more recent surveys such as Dennis (1966) on smaller samples.

A study impressive for the precision with which the possibilities of statistical comparisons are exploited is that of master chess players by Elo (1965), improving on earlier work (Rubin, 1960; Buttenweiser, 1963). Chess shares with other skills the necessity for study and discipline, with intense motivation. In chess, records are objective and unique in that one can match a given player directly against the performance of his younger and older peers. Doing this, Elo (1965) introduces the useful statistics he invented to estimate variations in a given player's strength relative to his own overall performance over his life span (weighted for the systematically varying performance of his opposition). Again we find that the performance-over-age curve approximates to Wechsler's (1958) growth and decline curves, with the peak displaced to about age 35 and performance at 63 comparable to that at age 20, Lehman's (1953) data for chess, peak at age 33 and show a somewhat more rapid decline but may be criticized in that they were not adjusted for the age, or precisely for the level, of opposition encountered.

On the involvement of motivational factors, and on factors such as the toll of restrained intellectual stress, there is little evidence. Barry (1969) presents for example, some data which suggest that the very best (and so, inferentially the most aggressive) chess players die relatively younger than their peers. The fact that many of his examples depended solely on chess for a living and tended to die poor and neglected is an example of the difficulty with this sort of demographic study.

On the larger question as to the nature of the creative process at its peak and on the nature of its decline, we are still dependent on autobiographical notes by very gifted people. Mary Cartwright, herself a talented mathematician, put the main points lucidly in an invited address at Somerville College, Oxford in 1954: "Hardy said 'No mathematician should ever allow himself to forget that mathematics, more than any other art or science, is a young man's game . . . Newton gave up mathematics at fifty, and he had lost his enthusiasm long before.' Now although one may dispute this and find counter-examples, there is some truth in it, and

I believe that one reason for it is that major advances are usually obtained by approaching a subject from a slightly different angle from that previously adopted; the ideas often come in the course of approaching, that is learning the subject. When it is fully understood interest often wanes, and ideas become fixed. . . . But I have only shifted the problem in saying that older people find it less easy to learn. Speaking for myself I feel that my brain is less persistently active than it used to be and I fear that declining mental energy is the real answer."

The question of "energy," that is, the role of motivating factors in decrement with age, has been almost totally neglected in laboratory experiments but recurs forcefully whenever real-life problems are examined by appropriate field investigations.

A research strategy too seldom used is to ask intelligent older people how they carry out activities in which they are deeply interested. Birren (1969) presents an analysis of protocols provided by 100 successful professional people, commenting on their perception of changes in their methods of coping with the demands made of them. The difficulty in dealing with such material, as well as a source of its richness, is that one is here forced to consider "strategies" in concept formation, which are, and have been, directed towards very long-term goals. A first important point that emerged is that the old probably *define* their problems differently from the young. A further interesting point is that older professionals recognized that their goals had changed, and might do so again, and allowed for this fact in deciding how to run their lives. They were thus, unexpectedly in contrast with the young, programmed for some degree of flexibility, rather than with the rigidity conventionally attributed to the elderly. They showed a recognition of the necessity for a greater discipline, and for "control of affect" towards colleagues and juniors, and this tolerance was reflected in their definitions of their goals.

Birren's (1969) study is also important in that it points out that older people become aware of inherent limitations and of those imposed on them by advancing age and consciously attempt to compensate for them in very direct ways.

For example, Birren's old subjects showed a clear recognition for the necessity for taking advice. Other compensations were recognition of the necessity for conserving time and resources of energy ("conservation of the individual"), and the ability to distinguish between critical and extraneous tasks and demands. In sum, in considering the real-life performance of older people, it is naive to regard them as passive victims of a cognitive degeneration of which they are helplessly unaware. On the contrary, older people may be said to both conserve and to exploit their intellectual resources more fully than do the young, to have a more subtle perception of points at which the complexity of decisions exceeds their capacities, and to thereby avoid unnecessary blunders. It is fitting to conclude with this reminder that the study of performance with age is not merely the study of *decrements in performance*. Unless we recognize that it is also the study of *adaptation* to decrements of performance, we shall completely miss the point.

The difficulty with the present position is not that we have too few kinds of questions to ask but too many. In view of the deterioration of memory and perceptual motor performance with advancing age, the right kind of question may well be not "why are old people so bad at cognitive tasks" but rather "how, in spite of growing disabilities, do old people preserve such relatively good performance?"

REFERENCES

Anderson, J. R., and Bower, G. H. 1973. *Human Associative Memory*. Washington, D.C.: V. H. Winston.

Arenberg, D. 1968. Concept problem solving in old and young adults. *J. Geront.*, 23, 279–282.

Arenberg, D. 1969. Concept identification and age. *Proc. 8th Intern. Cong. Geront.*, 2, 59.

Arenberg, D. 1970. Equivalence of information in concept identification. *Psych. Bull.*, 74, 355–361.

Arenberg, D. 1974. A longitudinal study of problem solving in adults. *J. Geront.*, 29, 650–658.

Axelrod, S., and Cohen, L. D. 1961. Senescence and embedded-figure performance in vision and touch. *Perceptual Motor Skills*, 12, 283–288.

Barry, H. 1969. Longevity of outstanding chess players. *Journal of Genetic Psychology*, 115, 143–148.

Birren, J. E. 1969. Age and decision strategies. *In*, A. T. Welford and J. E. Birren (eds.), *Interdispl. Topics Gerontol.*, Vol. 4, pp. 23–36. Basel: S. Karger.

Botwinick, J. 1966. Cautiousness in advanced age. *J. Geront.,* **21,** 347–353.

Botwinick, J. 1969. Disinclination to venture response versus cautiousness in responding: Age differences. *Journal of Genetic Psychology,* **115,** 55–62.

Botwinick, J., Brinley, J. F., and Robin, J. S. 1963. Learning and reversing a 4-choice multiple Y-maze by rats of three ages. *J. Geront.,* **18,** 279–282.

Botwinick, J., Robbin, J. S., and Brinley, J. F. 1959. Reorganization of perceptions with age. *J. Geront.,* **14,** 85–88.

Boyarsky, R. E., and Eisdorfer, C. 1972. Forgetting in older persons. *J. Geront.,* **27,** 254–258.

Brinley, J. F., and Sardello, R. J. 1970. Increasing the utility of negative instances in conjunctive concept classification. *Psychon. Sci.,* **18,** 101–102.

Bruner, J. G., Goodnow, J. J., and Austin, G. A. 1956. *A Study of Thinking.* New York: John Wiley.

Bryant, P. E. 1971. Cognitive development. *Brit. Med. Bull.,* **27,** 200–205.

Burnand, T., Richard, J., Tinnot, R., and de Ajuriaguerra, J. 1972. Nature of the operational deficit in the aged afflicted with degenerative dementia. *Encephale,* **61,** 5–31.

Buttenwieser, P. 1963. The relation of age to skill of expert chess-players. Unpublished Ph.D. dissertation. Stanford University.

Canestrari, R. E. 1966. The effects of commonality on paired-associate learning in two age-groups. *Journal of Genetic Psychology,* **108,** 3–7.

Carpenter, A. 1946. The effect of room temperature on the performance of the resistance box test. *M. R. C. Appl. Psych. Res. Unit Report,* 50.

Cartwright, M. 1954. Lecture at Somerville College, Oxford, Oxford University Press.

Clay, H. M. 1954. Changes of performance with age on similar tasks of varying complexity. *Brit. J. Psychol.,* **45,** 7–13.

Clay, H. M. 1956. An age difference in separating spatially contiguous data. *J. Geront.,* **11,** 318–322.

Conrad, R. 1964. Acoustic confusions in immediate memory. *Brit. J. Psychol.,* **55,** 75–84.

Conrad, R. 1967. Interference or decay over short retention intervals? *J. Verb. Lrng. Verb. Beh.,* **6,** 49–54.

Cooper-Howell, S. 1972. Familiarity and complexity in perceptual recognition. *J. Geront.,* **27,** 364–371.

Coppinger, N. W., and Nehrke, M. F. 1972. Discrimination learning and transfer of training in the aged. *Journal of Genetic Psychology,* **120,** 93–102.

Corso, J. F. 1971. Sensory processes and age effects in normal adults. *J. Geront.,* **26,** 90–105.

Crovitz, B. 1966. Recovering a learning deficit in the aged. *J. Geront.,* **21,** 236–238.

Dennis, W. 1966. Creative productivity between ages of 20 and 80 years. *J. Geront.,* **21,** 1–8.

Elo, A. E. 1965. Age changes in master chess performance. *J. Geront.,* **20,** 289–299.

Farrimond, T. 1967. Visual and auditory performance variations with age: some implications. *Austr. J. Psychol.,* **19,** 193–201.

Gladis, M., and Braun, H. W. 1958. Age differences in transfer and retroaction as a function of intertask response similarity. *J. Exp. Psych.,* **55,** 25–30.

Goodrick, C. L. 1972. Learning by mature-young and aged Wistar albino rats as a function of test complexity. *J. Geront.,* **27,** 353–357.

Goulet, L. R. 1972. New directions for research on aging and retention. *J. Geront.,* **27,** 52–60.

Gregg, L. W. 1974. *Knowledge and Cognition.* Potomac, Maryland: L. Erlbaum.

Griew, S. 1962. The learning of statistical structure: A preliminary study in relation to age. *In,* C. Tibbitts and W. Donahue (eds.), *Social and Psychological Aspects of Aging.* New York: Columbia University Press.

Griew, S. 1965. Anticipating events in an uncertain world. *In,* F. C. Jeffers (ed.), *Proceedings of Seminars 1961-1965.* Durham, North Carolina: Duke University, Research Centre for Study of Aging.

Griew, S. 1968. Age and the matching of signal frequency in a 2-channel detection task. *J. Geront.,* **23,** 93–96.

Heath, H. A., and Orbach, J. 1963. Reversibility of the Necker-cube: IV Responses of elderly people. *Perceptual Motor Skills,* **17,** 625–626.

Hooper, F. H., Fitzgerald, J., and Papalia, D. 1971. Piagetian theory and the aging process. *Aging and Human Development,* **2,** 3–20.

Howell, S. C. 1972. Age, familiarity and complexity as recognition variables. *Perceptual Motor Skills,* **34,** 732–734.

Jalavisto, E. 1964. The phenomenon of retinal rivalry in the age. *Gerontologia,* **9,** 1–8.

Jerome, E. A. 1959. Age and learning—experimental studies. *In,* J. E. Birren (ed.), *Handbook of Aging and the Individual.* Chicago: University of Chicago Press.

Jerome, E. A. 1962. Decay of heuristic processes in the aged. *In,* C. Tibbitts and W. Donahue (eds.), *Social and Psychological Aspects of Aging.* New York: Columbia University Press.

John, E. R. 1957. Contributions to the study of the problem-solving process. *Psychol. Monogr.,* **71,** 1–39.

Jordan, T. C., and Rabbitt, P. M. A. *Brit. J. Psych.,* in press.

Kahneman, D., and Tversky, A. 1973. On the psychology of prediction. *Psych. Rev.,* **80,** 237–251.

Kendler, H. H., and Kendler, T. S. 1962. Vertical and horizontal processes in human problem solving. *Psych. Rev.,* **69,** 1–18.

Kinsbourne, M. 1973. Age effects on letter span related to rate and sequential dependency. *J. Geront.,* **28,** 317–319.

Kintsch, W. 1970. *Learning, Memory and Conceptual Processes.* New York: John Wiley.

Korchin, S. J., and Basowitz, H. 1957. Age differences

in verbal learning. *J. Abnorm. Psychol.*, **54**, 64–69.

Lehman, H. C. 1953. *Age and Achievement.* Princeton, New Jersey: Princeton University Press.

Lehman, H. C. 1962. The creative production rates of present versus past generations of scientists. *J. Geront.*, **17**, 409–417.

Lehman, H. C. 1965. The production of masters' works prior to age 30. *Gerontologist*, **5**, 24–30.

Lehman, H. C. 1966. The most creative years of engineers and other technologists. *Journal of Genetic Psychology*, **108**, 263–277.

Luce, R., and Raiffa, A. 1957. *Games and Decisions.* New York: John Wiley.

Markus, E. J. 1971. Perceptual field dependence among aged persons. *Perceptual Motor Skills*, **33**, 175–178.

Miller, G. A. 1956. The magical number seven, plus or minus two. *Psych. Rev.*, **63**, 81–97.

Nehrke, M. F. 1973. Age and sex differences in discrimination learning and transfer of training. *J. Geront.*, **28**, 320–327.

Newell, A., and Simon, H. A. 1972. *Human Problem Solving.* Englewood Cliffs: New Jersey: Prentice-Hall.

Obusek, C. J., and Warren, R. M. 1973. Comparison of speech perception in senile and well-preserved aged by means of the verbal transformation effect. *J. Geront.*, **28**, 184–188.

Phelan, J. G., and Gustafson, C. W. 1968. Reversal and nonreversal shifts in acute brain injury with injury diffusely localised. *J. Psych.*, **70**, 249–258.

Posner, M., and Rossman, J. 1965. Effect of size and location of informational transforms upon short-term retention. *J. Exp. Psych.*, **70**, 496–505.

Rabbitt, P. M. A. 1964. Age and time for choice between stimuli and between responses. *J. Geront.*, **19**, 307–312.

Rabbitt, P. M. A. 1965. An age-decrement in the ability to ignore irrelevant information. *J. Geront.*, **20**, 233–238.

Rabbitt, P. M. A. 1968a. Age and the use of structure in transmitted information. *In*, G. A. Talland (ed.), *Human Aging and Behaviour: Recent Advances in Research and Theory.* New York: Academic Press.

Rabbitt, P. M. A. 1968b. Repetition effects and signal classification strategies in serial choice-response tasks. *Quart. J. Exp. Psych.*, **20**, 232–240.

Rabbitt, P. M. A., Clancy, M. C., and Vyas, S. M. 1969. Proc. of XVII International Congress of Gerontology, Washington, D.C.

Rajalakshmi, R., and Jeeves, M. A. 1963. Changes in tachistoscopic form perception as a function of age and intellectual status. *J. Geront.*, **18**, 275–278.

Reiher, R. H., Phelan, J. F., and Kiker, V. L. 1969. Reversal and non-reversal shifts in neurologically handicapped children. *J. Psych.*, **72**, 41–53.

Rubin, E. 1960. The age factor in chess. *Amer. Statstc.*, **14**, 19–21.

Ruch, F. L. 1934. The differentiative effects of age upon human learning. *Journal of Genetic Psychology*, **11**, 261–286.

Sanford, A. J. 1973. Age-related differences in strategies for locating hidden targets. *Gerontologia*, **19**, 16–21.

Sanford, A. J., Griew, S., and O'Donnell, L. 1972. Age effects in simple prediction behaviour. *J. Geront.*, **27**, 259–264.

Sanford, A. J., and Maule, A. T. 1971. Age and the distribution of observing responses. *Psychon. Sci.*, **23**, 419–420.

Sanford, A. J., and Maule, A. T. 1973. The allocation of attention in multisource monitoring behaviour: Adult age differences. *Perception*, **2**, 91–100.

Speakman, D. 1954. The effect of age on the incidental relearning of stamp values. *J. Geront.*, **9**, 162–167.

Spence, K. W. 1963. The nature of discrimination learning in animals. *Psych. Rev.*, **43**, 427–449.

Storck, P. A., Looft, W. R., and Hooper, F. H. 1972. Interrelationships among Piagetian tasks and traditional measures of cognitive abilities in the mature and aged adult. *J. Geront.*, **27**, 461–465.

Tversky, A., and Kahneman, D. 1973. Availability: A heuristic for judging frequency and probability. *Cog. Psychol.*, **5**, 207–232.

Wallach, M. A., and Kogan, N. 1961. Aspects of judgement and decision making: Interrelationships and changes with age. *Behavioral Science*, **6**, 23–36.

Wason, P. C., and Johnson-Laird, P. N. 1972. *Psychology of Reasoning.* London: Batsford.

Wechsler, D. 1958. *The Measurement and Appraisal of Adult Intelligence.* Baltimore: Williams & Wilkins.

Welford, A. T. 1958. *Aging and Human Skill.* Oxford: Oxford University Press.

Welford, A. T. 1969. Age and skill: Motor, intellectual and social. *In*, A. T. Welford and J. Birren (eds.), *Interdisciplinary Topics in Gerontology*, Vol. 4. Basel: S. Karger.

Welsh, O. L., Laterman, D. M., and Bell, B. 1969. The effects of aging on responses to filtered speech. *J. Geront.*, **24**, 189–192.

Wetherick, N. E. 1964. A comparison of the problem-solving ability of young, middle-aged and old subjects. *Gerontologia*, **9**, 164–178.

Wetherick, N. E. 1965. Changing an established concept: A comparison of the ability of young, middle-aged and old subjects. *Gerontologia*, **77**, 82–95.

Wilson, T. R. 1963. Flicker fusion frequency, age and intelligence. *Gerontologia*, **7**, 200–207.

Young, M. 1966. Problem solving performance in two age groups. *J. Geront.*, **21**, 505–509.

Young, M. 1971. Age and sex differences in problem solving. *J. Geront.*, **26**, 330–336.

26
PERSONALITY AND AGING

Bernice L. Neugarten*
University of Chicago

INTRODUCTION

For the reader who comes fresh to the topic of this review, the first questions are likely to be these: Does aging affect personality? And does personality affect aging? At a common-sense level, the answer to both questions is obviously yes. If a three-part premise is tenable—that the infant is not born old; that a mind-body dualism is to be rejected; and that personality, however otherwise defined, is a set of psychological and behavioral characteristics of the human organism—then as the biology of the organism changes over time, and as the organism is changed also by interaction with the social environment, so, too, does personality change over time. With regard to the second question, it is widely recognized that different persons, even in similar states of health and in similar social settings, show different patterns of behavior and adaptation as they grow old. Thus personality, again however defined, affects aging.

The problem is that while psychologists "know" the answers to both questions, they cannot demonstrate those answers satisfactorily.

Before elaborating these points in the sections to follow, we are reminded that for centuries

*The author is indebted to William J. McDonald for his assistance in reviewing the literature on personality and aging, and to Dail A. Neugarten for her editorial assistance in converting an unwieldy first draft of this manuscript into its present form.

philosophers, historians, dramatists and poets have pondered the ways in which man's thoughts, emotions, motives, and actions change over the life span. Different cultures have produced different views of human nature, different concepts of time, and different explanations of how the two are related. In ancient Greece, men spoke of character, but not of personality; in some cultures time is not perceived as linear, but circular; and in some cultures the self is not perceived as continuous, for individuals who undergo certain religious or mystical experiences are thought to emerge as new persons. Shweder (1975) has demonstrated that the very coding systems used to describe behavior reflect the linguistic elements and the conceptual relationships that preexist in the culture, or in short, that personality lies in the ways we think about personality.

Not only concepts of human behavior but also concepts of aging are culture-bound and history-bound. Different societies have created not only varying interpretations of the fact that persons grow up, grow old, and die, but different interpretations of the effects of biological aging upon the individual's thoughts and actions. From this broad perspective it is only recently that in modern Western societies personality has become a widely-used concept in thinking about human behavior, that with the appearance of social sciences, observers who are called psychologists have laid claim to personality as an area of inquiry, and even more recently that psychologists have begun to look systematically at issues of personality and aging.

Scope of This Review

As will become more evident in the pages to follow, both the general field of personality and the field of personality and aging are without established boundaries. We have therefore selected only certain issues for discussion here.

We shall comment briefly upon some of the problems that characterize personality as a field of inquiry and some of the conceptual problems that relate more specifically to personality and aging—in the latter category, primarily at issues regarding continuity and change, and ways of marking the passage of time. We shall then look at empirical studies in which investigators have been concerned with various dimensions of personality, or with the "structure" of personality, or with the range of individual differences, as one or all of these change over time. Next we shall deal briefly with studies of the relationship between personality and adaptation; and finally, with conceptualizations that have appeared in the past 20 years that attempt to integrate personality, adaptation, and aging as these conceptualizations have emerged from empirical research.

Aging should be seen within a life-span framework, but because of space limitations we have attended primarily to studies of the second half of the life span. We have chosen to focus on so-called normal aging and have therefore omitted consideration of psychopathology and therapy, as well as studies based on institutionalized or other atypical samples. And although the relations between biological change and personality, and between cognitive change and personality, are of major importance, these topics too have been omitted.

The reader should be alerted that, even within the boundaries set here, coherence in the field of personality and aging is not easily perceived, a point made also by earlier reviewers (Chown, 1968; Kuhlen, 1945, 1959; Riegel, 1959, Riley and Foner, 1968; Schaie and Marquette, 1972). As a consequence, we have attempted to high-light only some of the problems and some of the questions that have preoccupied investigators and to be reportorial as well as critical, in the hope that future researchers, in seeing where we have been, may see better where to go.

Is the Study of Personality a Science?

Because ours is a time in history when science has been given high priority as a means of gaining knowledge, it is understandable that psychologists have attempted to use scientific methods in studying personality. Although the eventual outcome is not foreseeable, these attempts have not yet met with notable success. While the same is true of many other areas of the behavioral sciences, the field of personality poses particularly difficult problems. For one thing, there is no consensus about the range nor the essential nature of the subject matter. Should psychologists study fantasy, religious experience, and other aspects of the inner life, or should they limit themselves to more overt forms of behavior? Is it possible to use the life-history as a meaningful unit of study, or only sequences of particularistic acts? Some hold organismic or proactive views of human nature (e.g., Allport, 1937; Murray, 1938), others hold mechanistic or reactive views (e.g., Watson, 1919; Skinner, 1953), and each group has its preferred methods of inquiry. Those who focus on such broad issues as ego identity are accused of creating constructs that cannot be operationalized; those who study small units of behavior in the quest for objectivity are accused of trivializing everything they touch.

Given the lack of consensus about the subject matter, it follows that there is no general consensus about a theory of personality or a theory of behavior. Even the most cursory examination of the field shows a diversity of theories, or more properly stated, a diversity of descriptive frameworks. (Major personality theories have been summarized and compared by Hall and Lindzey, 1970; Maddi, 1972; Norbeck, Price-Williams, and McCord, 1968; and Worchel and Byrne, 1964.) And given the wide range of descriptive frameworks and methods, it is inevitable that empirical studies will show great diversity of findings, whether or not the studies have grown out of explicit theoretical frameworks and whether or not they were aimed at discovery or confirmation.

In a recent paper Fiske (1974) states that the conventional science of personality is close to its limits. This is because the field relies on words, with different investigators using different definitions of the same word, and because the field relies on attributed qualities derived from particular observations, so that there is no "personality" residing in the person independent of the perceiver. Furthermore investigators make large inductive leaps from their observations to presumed measures of their verbal concepts, so that the ties between observations and concepts are tenuous and inadequate. Fiske argues not only that the field of personality is in a prescientific state but that the problems cannot be overcome by conventional approaches. "The study of human behavior may be awaiting a Copernicus who will show us how the behavioral courses of people fall into place when we do not take our observational perspective as the center of the behavioral universe, or an Einstein who can specify the relactivity function connecting the perceptions of diverse observers, each on his own trip through behavioral space" (Fiske, 1974, p. 4).

Others have commented that psychologists have created the metaphor of personality, and that as they have attempted to specify constructs and measures that have internal logic and consistency, they have reified their constructs and have moved farther and farther from the observable behavior of persons (e.g., Passini and Norman, 1966). Thus some investigators, like those of Skinnerian persuasion, in saying that personality does not exist, focus upon those behavioral acts that can be analyzed and altered by manipulations of the environment and thus remove themselves from the field of personality altogether.

Other critics have aimed their comments primarily but not exclusively at psychologists who rely upon personality tests, saying that the study of personality is no longer synonymous with the study of persons. One of the results has been that some psychologists have attempted to differentiate themselves from the

"testers" and to say they are studying not personality but persons or the lives of persons (e.g., Carlson, 1971, 1975; Maddi, 1972; Murray, 1938; White, 1952, 1963). In the eyes of their critics, however, this only compounds the problem since those critics believe that the person is too complex a unit to be studied scientifically.

Those researchers who are committed to building a science of personality believe that, as in any other field, investigators should restrict their objectives and specify that which *can* be scientifically approached, leaving to other forms of scholarship that which cannot. Along this line, different remedies are being put forth for specifying and redefining the field. Fiske (1974), for example, suggests that alternative sciences of personality can be delineated, among them personality viewed as the study of *perceptions*. In this case, observers would study the ways in which persons perceive, interpret, and construe themselves and other persons. Mischel (1973) offers a different solution. Instead of studying traits or dispositions as they have been formulated in psychodynamic theories, he argues for a reconceptualization whereby the variability in behavior across situations is given equal weight to the variability across persons, and in which new variables would be created that link specific patterns of behavior to the conditions in which they may be expected.

Wachtel (1973), on the other hand, defends psychodynamic theory and its potential for becoming scientific, as does Livson (1973), who recently defended the trait approach elaborated most fully by Cattell (1957), and who argues that by using assessments made by trained clinicians and by accepting the challenge of imposing genotypic order upon phenotypic disorder (i.e., distinguishing the underlying motive or disposition from the variety of "surface" behaviors that are its manifestations), a science can be produced that will be linked to dynamic theories of personality. Bowers (1973) argues that an interactionist account of personality is the alternative to both a situationist and a trait approach. Maddi (1975) has still a different perspective. He holds that the multiplicity of personality theories can themselves be analyzed and grouped by the use of new semantic techniques. Then particular issues can be identified, like whether or not defensive behavior is universal, and new scientific methods can be created to pursue these issues.

Whichever of these reconceptualizations proves most fruitful in the future (and there are others not described here), they all emerge from the recognition that a crisis of paradigms exists, that to create a science of personality means to redefine the field and to start afresh in one or another direction.

The conclusion that the study of personality, to say nothing of the study of lives, is in a pre-scientific state wins agreement from most psychologists, but that very conclusion discomfits some more than others. Many authors (e.g., Farber, 1964) have written that it is unrealistic to expect, after so short a history, that psychologists can as yet produce a nontrivial science of behavior and those authors are content to proceed slowly, seeking such regularities and such relationships between variables as they can measure. Others regard it as misguided altogether to attempt to be scientific about phenomena so complex and so elusive, and they are content to seek insights in other ways. Among the latter group, many hold the position that the study of personality has been successfully pursued by the clinicians who, because they focus at close range upon an individual's interpersonal relationships, his preoccupations, and his self-reported triumphs and failures, and because they move to interpretations in ways that may be systematic but that are relatively unfettered by problems of measurement and agreement among observers, have produced the most compelling descriptions of human behavior. Thus it is Freud whose views of personality, while not based on conventional scientific methods, have been the most influential of our time.

Aging and Personality

The student of personality cannot but carry these conceptual and methodological problems with him as he enters the field of aging, but here he becomes doubly burdened by the new complexities of his subject matter. If the general field of personality psychology stands in such disarray, if new paradigms and new approaches to personality need to be created, then it will take an even longer time before a science of aging and personality can appear. This is because in addition to all the problems already mentioned, the issues for the student of aging are so global in nature, the time units so long, consistencies or inconsistencies in behavior so difficult to measure directly, and the effects of an elongated past upon the individual's present so impossible to disentangle.

It is perhaps for these reasons that conventional personality theorists have not dealt directly with issues of aging. Riegel (1959), among others, has elaborated this latter point, and it remains true today.

In the discussion to follow, there is no attempt to resolve the various issues raised above regarding personality as a field of inquiry, for that resolution continues to elude the present author, just as it has eluded so many others. The task undertaken here is to look at what has been done by investigators concerned with aging and personality, bearing in mind that all the problems thus far mentioned apply equally to the work to be reviewed below.

ADULT PERSONALITY: A DEVELOPMENTAL PERSPECTIVE

Moving away from the conventional field of personality psychology, students of personality and aging have found it more useful to look to developmental psychology, for the latter, by definition, is concerned with issues of continuity and change. From the developmental perspective, aging should be studied within the broader context of the life span; and although middle age and old age have their unique characteristics, they should be seen within the same complex of changing biological and sociocultural contexts used in studying behavior at younger ages.

A psychology of the life span has been slow to appear, in part because the quantity of empirical research on childhood and adolescence so outweighs the research on adulthood, particularly with regard to systematic observations of individuals studied over time. Not only is there a paucity of appropriate data, but there are few agreed-upon conceptual frameworks that encompass development and aging. The three recent volumes on life span developmental psychology (Goulet and Baltes, 1970; Nesselroade and Reese, 1973; Baltes and Schaie, 1973), with the third volume devoted to socialization and personality, are useful compendia of differing conceptual approaches and methodological issues, but they make clear that there is no paradigm for dealing with changes over the life span that commands consensus. And while psychologists agree that there are observable changes in adult personality, the major problems remain: What personality processes and what personality issues are the most salient at successive periods in adulthood? How shall we isolate those changes that are developmental from those that are not?

The Concept of Development

The term *developmental* refers here not only to processes that are biologically programmed and inherent in the organism, but also to those in which the organism is changed over time by interaction with the environment. Because of the cumulative record of adaptations to both biological and social events, there is a *continually changing basis within the individual* for perceiving and responding to new events. "Developmental" usually implies movement toward a higher or more differentiated end point; and therefore it is often an awkward term when used to describe aging. Nevertheless some psychologists have written of developmental change in adulthood in terms of growth or expansion or actualization (Bühler and Massarik, 1968; Jung, 1933; Kuhlen, 1964; Maslow, 1954; Rogers, 1963). Such writing is usually directed to the enhancement of human potential or mental health. Others describe adult change as decline, adopting a biological model of decrement for conceptualizing psychological change. Still others, like the early psychoanalysts, adopt a model of stability. Unlike the study of child development, where directionality of change is clear, none of these views of directionality in adulthood rests on a compelling rationale. Is the organism biologically programmed only toward maturity, with post-

maturity changes to be regarded as haphazard or as perturbations of an otherwise steady state? Or is the organism programmed toward decline and death?

For the present, the student of adult personality will find it strategic to accept age relatedness alone as the criterion and to call developmental those changes that can be demonstrated to vary in an orderly way with age regardless of the direction of change. This does not mean that chronological age is itself a meaningful variable, a point to which we shall return shortly, for the psychologist is eventually concerned not with the passage of time alone, but with the events that give substance and meaning to time. In exploring an uncharted field, however, it is a justifiable first step to use age as a preliminary index and to determine which, if any, personality phenomena are systematically age-related.

Age and Cohort

In pursuing the latter question, however, it is difficult to pinpoint which of the differences between younger and older persons are to be attributed to the effects of aging and which to the differences between cohorts (i.e., groups of persons born at different points in history). Successive cohorts have presumably been influenced by different social events and as a consequence will presumably perform differently on personality measures. Neither cross-sectional nor longitudinal methods are free from the difficulty of disentangling aging from cohort effects. Schaie and his colleagues have developed sophisticated research designs for dealing with this problem, as well as for disentangling the effects of historical time of measurement and the effects of repeated measurements on the same group of persons (see Chapter 2 in this volume), but thus far their designs have been applied only to narrow sets of questionnaire data on personality (e.g., Woodruff and Birren, 1972; Schaie and Parham, 1976), and it remains to be seen if those designs, because they are so costly to carry out, will be feasible when it comes to more complex data.

In any case, once identified, a cohort difference, like an age difference, will need to be investigated further, perhaps by methods that lie outside the psychologist's arena, to discover which social and historical events can be said to be reflected in the observed personality differences. In other words, neither cohort nor age is itself an explanatory variable.

If investigators can succeed, nevertheless, in demonstrating age relatedness of personality change in adults who vary in social and biological characteristics, it will be an important step in weighing the relative merit of a developmental approach.

THEORIES OF ADULT CHANGE

The issues regarding continuities and discontinuities in adult personality remain persistent and thorny ones. Some of the issues have recently been restated by Bortner (1966, 1967); Looft (1973); Neugarten (1969); and Riegel (1972, 1975). Although we cannot undertake here a full discussion of various descriptive frameworks as they relate to personality change in adulthood and old age, it may be useful to consider briefly the differing perspectives of psychoanalysis and ego psychology, on the one hand, and social psychology and symbolic interactionist theory, on the other, to see how they relate to the developmental perspective.

Psychoanalysis and Ego Psychology

It is usually said that psychoanalytic theory is a developmental theory only of childhood and adolescence. This is because the theory emphasizes a biologically determined sequence in the maturation of drives; and because in most psychoanalytic writings, while the ego has been seen as becoming an increasingly important and autonomous agent of change, the essential nature of adult personality has been regarded as stable (e.g., Luborsky and Schimek, 1964). Yet there have been exceptions among psychoanalysts. One was Jung (1933), who described stages of development in adulthood, commenting in particular on an increase in introversion in middle and later life and on the reorganization of value systems.

The most important exception has been Erikson (1959, 1963), who delineated eight stages in the life cycle, each representing a choice or a crisis for the expanding ego. Following the crisis of ego identity in adolescence, the last three stages relate to the development of intimacy in early adulthood (the ability to merge one's self with the self of another); then the crisis of generativity (investment in the products of one's own creation and identification with the future); and in late adulthood, the crisis of ego integrity (the view that one's life has been the product of one's own making, that it could not have been different, and that it has been a meaningful life).

Other psychoanalysts have focused on particular psychosexual events as precipitants of personality change in adulthood. Deutsch (1944, 1945) described the changes that accompany the succession of those events in women; Bibring (1959), changes associated with pregnancy; and Benedek (1950, 1959, 1970), changes associated with parenthood in both men and women and changes associated with the climacterium in women. Recently also a group of psychoanalysts in Boston have given attention to personality patterns in old age (Berezin and Cath, 1965; Levin and Kahana, 1967); and at present, at the Institute for Psychoanalysis and its affiliated Center for Psychosocial Studies in Chicago, new studies of the second half of life are being undertaken.

Another important contributor, who proceeded from a dynamic, although not a Freudian perspective, was Bühler (1935, 1959), who was among the first to ask what general principles of change hold true over the life span and what shifts in motivations and needs are typical. In her later work, Bühler gave a central place to concepts of the self, intentionality in behavior, goal seeking, and goal restructuring.

Related to the point made earlier in this paper, that it has been clinicians whose perspectives have been most influential in the general field of personality, it has also been clinicians like Bühler, Jung, and Erikson who have ventured to describe the nature of personality change in middle and old age, and whose views may therefore be said to be the prevailing ones. At the same time, the clinicians' formulations regarding aging and personality have seldom led to systematic empirical studies, for operational definitions of psychoanalytic or ego concepts have been lacking. Other investigators have thus been unable to confirm or to elaborate those formulations.

Social-Psychological Theory

A contrasting body of theory has emerged from the social psychologists, the symbolic interactionists, and the role theorists (e.g., Ahammer, 1973; Brim, 1968; Clausen, 1968; Gordon, 1972; Mead, 1934; Riley, Foner, Hess and Toby, 1969; and Strauss, 1959), many of whom have argued that there are no personality dispositions that persist across situations and that the personality should be defined as the sum (or the residues) of socialization experiences and social roles. Becker (1964), for example, suggested that the process of adjustment to new social situations is the sufficient explanation of change. Mischel's (1973) is a related point of view insofar as it emphasizes the external or environmental versus the internal or intrapersonal consistencies. Furthermore, investigators who are concerned with cohort differences imply that we should look to social and historical contexts more than to developmental processes for explaining observable differences in personality between age groups (e.g., Schaie and Parham, 1974, 1976).

The social learning and social role theorists have carried out many empirical and experimental studies demonstrating the effects of social situations on behavior change, and those perspectives are important in suggesting interpretations of change over the life cycle that are alternatives to developmental interpretations (e.g., Sarbin, 1964). At the same time, such issues as the personal sense of continuity and the consistency of self are left unexplored, concepts that become important in studying the executive aspects of adult personality involved in goal-setting, self-regulation, and self-induced change. Furthermore, because social psychologists have usually concentrated on short-term change, whether in experimental or field settings, the value of their studies for understanding long-term personality change has not yet been demonstrated.

Cognitive Theory

Thomae (1970) has briefly described a cognitive theory of the aging personality, one which is intended to integrate various biological, sociological, and interactionist perspectives while at the same time focusing upon the psychodynamics of aging. In an approach reminiscent of the one suggested by Fiske (1974), mentioned in the first part of this paper, central concepts are those of perception, perceived situation, and perceived self. Thomae postulates, for example, that it is the perception of change rather than objective change that is related to behavioral change; and that change is perceived and evaluated in terms of the individual's dominant concerns and expectations. Thomae questions the validity of any approach which defines the aging personality in terms of stable traits and suggests that the psychodynamic processes in aging center around one dominant concern: the maintenance and restructuring of the balance between cognitive and motivational systems.

Thus far, this formulation has appeared in only one brief paper, and it remains to be seen if it will be elaborated further by Thomae and by others.

Problems for the Developmentalist

The first task for the developmental psychologist interested in adult personality is not to muster evidence for or against the importance of psychodynamic or situational factors but to investigate whether or not there are orderly and sequential changes related to age, and if so, if they are significant in accounting for differences in behavior.

Thus far we have no conclusive evidence that the personality processes we can succeed in measuring in adults follow regular changes with the passage of time, but this is because we lack the data base by which to decide. For the time being, therefore, developmentalists might do well to focus on badly needed descriptive studies of adults, particularly those in which biological and social factors can be studied in relation to each other; those in which antecedent-consequent relationships can be clarified; and those from which grounded theory can be developed—in other words, studies aimed at discovery rather than confirmation, and at theory that grows from, rather than precedes, observation (Glaser and Strauss, 1967; Willems and Raush, 1969).

We have already suggested that those who identify themselves as life-span developmental psychologists have thus far concentrated on models and model-building, on research designs that will distinguish age-relatedness from other effects, and on other methodological issues. They have been more successful, then, at telling us *how* to study the life span than at helping us decide *what* to study. It remains to be seen if they will move to greater and greater abstractions that will be increasingly difficult to relate to observable behavior, or if, instead, they will turn attention to defining the salient issues of personality change and to help define the appropriate subject matter, issues which, by and large, have been more successfully addressed by the clinicians.

In the long run, then, the field of aging and personality, like the broader field of life-span psychology, will depend on the degree to which the contributions of the clinicians, the life-span developmentalists, and the conventional personality psychologists can be maximized and on the degree to which the problems inherent in each of the three approaches can be minimized. This is a large order, and progress will probably be slow.

Meanwhile, a growing number of students of aging and personality are moving ahead in the attempt to delineate an area of inquiry and to produce observations and formulations that will add to our understandings. The remainder of this review will report the major issues that have been preoccupying these investigators. After a brief presentation of ways in which time and the life span have been treated, we shall move to various empirical studies that have been undertaken, and then to recent theoretical formulations that have arisen from empirical approaches and that are based on a developmental perspective.

TIME AND THE LIFE SPAN

What are the most meaningful ways of measuring the passage of life time? Reichenbach and Mathers (1959), Frazer (1966), and Riegel (1972) are among those who have described the place of time and aging in the natural sciences and various frameworks for the measurement of time. From a different perspective, Neugarten and Datan (1973) have discussed the relations of life time (measured by chronological age), social time (the dimension that underlies the age-grade system of a society and is used in marking the individual's passage from one age status to the next), and historical time, as all three interact in influencing the life course. They have also described how a system of age norms creates a social clock that is superimposed upon the biological clock in producing orderly and sequential changes in behavior and in self-perceptions and thus is important in comprehending personality change over the life span.

Although it is an obvious point that the flow of psychological time (subjective time) is independent of the flow of calendar time, there are relatively few empirical studies of the ways in which life time is subjectively reported. Among the few such studies, it has been demonstrated that persons of different social classes have different perceptions of the timing of adult life periods (Neugarten and Peterson, 1957); and middle-aged persons show a reversal in time perspective, when time comes to be perceived as time left to live rather than time since birth (Eissler, 1955; Neugarten, 1968). Lynch (1971) has reviewed other studies of changes in time perspectives with increasing age.

Chronological Age as an Index

With regard to appropriate indicators of life time, Baer (1970), Looft (1973), and Wohlwill (1973) are among those who have discussed conceptual and methodological issues involved in the use of chronological age; Butler (1963a) has pointed to chronological age as a facade in understanding the changes that occur in old people; and along the same lines, Lieberman and Coplan (1969) have shown that distance from death is a more significant index than chronological age in studying the psychological changes that occur in very old persons.

One obvious problem is that age itself is an empty variable, as already mentioned, for it is not merely the passage of time, but the various biological and social events that occur with the passage of time that have relevance for personality change. From the latter point of view, many investigators have commented on the need to distinguish between chronological age, biological age, social age, and psychological age. Bell and his colleagues (Nuttall, 1973) are attempting to construct various measures of functional age, but it remains to be seen if one or another such measure will prove more useful than chronological age for measuring how "old" the individual is (and it will depend upon the investigator's purpose); but because chronological age is the most widely understood and the most objectively measured, it is not likely soon to be replaced.

Perceptions of the Life Span

Investigators have also been concerned with whether the life span should be regarded as a continuum or whether there are major transition points which create meaningful units of life time and which might be the markers of personality change. Child psychologists have created *stage theories* in which successive stages are qualitatively different (the most notable are Piaget's [1950] theory of cognitive development, Kohlberg's [1964] theory of moral development, and Loevinger's [1966] theory of ego development), but with the exception of Erikson's eight stages of ego development, students of adult personality have not found stage theories useful. This is because, as Kohlberg (1973) describes it, a true stage theory is structural in the sense that stages are qualitatively different from each other, they form a clustered "whole" that crosscuts various types of behavior, they form an invariant and irreversible order, and they are hierarchically arranged—a set of characteristics that are not often transferable to adulthood, where it is difficult to perceive qualitative changes, where there is no clear biological timetable and where major life events occur in even less invariant order than in childhood. (Erikson's is not a structural theory in Kohlberg's sense, for the adult stages are not closely tied to chronological age, nor are the stages mutually exclusive.)

In this respect Levinson, Darrow, Klein, Levinson, and McKee (1974) are exceptions among psychologists of adulthood, for they have advanced a descriptive framework in which, as men move from 18 to 45, they progress through invariant stages. These stages are based largely on common social events rather than upon "inner" processes like those postulated by Piaget, Kohlberg, or Loevinger, and

other investigators have taken issue with the generalizability of these stages as well as with the particular chronological ages assigned.

Gould (1972) is another exception. He has attempted to delineate a succession of psychosocial life *phases* (or stages) from early adulthood to old age, based on self-descriptive statements of men and women aged 16 to 60. Gould's formulations, like those of other lifespan psychologists mentioned here, are to be regarded as tentative, but meriting further investigation.

Kohlberg himself (1973) has illustrated the difficulty of applying stage theory to adulthood, for in a recent attempt to extend his theory of moral development, he has found it necessary to move from his own structural theory to Erikson's theory of ego development in conceptualizing adult change.

Havighurst (1972) has elaborated the concept of *developmental tasks* as markers of change along the life span, some of the tasks precipitated mainly by biological maturation, others by social role change, but with each task seen as encompassing biological, psychological, and sociological components. Developmental tasks occur in roughly the same sequence for most persons, but the tasks do not predicate "structural" change in Kohlberg's terms, nor is the sequence invariant or necessarily hierarchical. At the same time, there is an optimum point at which each task is encountered and should be "mastered," and, as is true of Erikson's stages, failure or delay on one interferes with successful resolution of the next.

The major *life events* (marriage, parenthood, climacterium, retirement, widowhood) have also been studied as possible markers of personality change, usually in terms of the accompanying changes in social roles. (We shall return to life events in discussing personality and adaptation in a section to follow.)

As an alternative to stages or tasks, there are the more generalized and more commonly-used markers of *life periods*. In all societies the differences between infants, adults, and the aged have been recognized, and unique characteristics of behavior, thought, and emotions have been ascribed to each period. In modern Western societies life periods may be said to have become increasingly differentiated. In the seventeenth and eighteenth centuries, childhood became a discernible period of life, and children were no longer regarded as "little adults" (Aries, 1962). The concept of adolescence can be viewed as an invention of the late nineteenth century (Gillis, 1974). Within the last few decades, as the transition from childhood to adulthood has become even more prolonged, the new period of "youth" has emerged (Keniston, 1970; Panel on Youth, 1973). Also in the past few decades middle age, in being distinguished from young adulthood, has become a newly delineated stage in the life span (Neugarten and Datan, 1974). This may be due not only to increased longevity but also to the historically changing rhythm of events in the family cycle, in which children grow up and leave home earlier, creating a period in which parents have diminishing family responsibilities but continuing work roles. It seems likely that still another meaningful division is now appearing, namely one between the "young-old" and the "old-old," with the former signifying a post-retirement period in which there is continuing physical vigor, new leisure time, and new opportunities for service to the community as well as for educational and recreational opportunities for self-fulfillment (Neugarten, 1974).

As these life periods become socially defined, they also become psychologically meaningful to the individual. He perceives his own "position" as he moves from youth to old age; his perceptions of life periods and of the life cycle itself change as he grows older; he learns the types of behavior that are regarded as age-appropriate in each life period; and all these perceptions affect his behavior, his self-image, and, at least in these ways, his personality.

Perceptions of life periods vary by age, by sex, and by social class. For example, for an upper-middle class person, middle age is usually described as a period of greatest productivity and of major reward, the "prime of life," while for a blue-collar worker, middle age not only comes earlier in terms of chronological age, but it is often described in terms of decline—slowing down, physical weakening, becoming a "has-been" (Neugarten and Peterson, 1957).

By and large, personality psychologists have not often treated these life periods as possible markers of life time or age, nor used these social age divisions in studying personality change. A few investigators, however, have recently focused upon middle age as being different from old age, with the thought that to discover that which is unique about a particular life period is to indirectly elucidate the question of change over time (Henry, 1968; Lowenthal, Thurnher, and Chiriboga, 1975; Neugarten, 1968); and there have been a few studies of changing relationships between personality and adaptation in successive life periods. (We shall return to those studies in a following section of this paper.)

Baltes (1973), in a symposium entitled, "Lifespan models of psychological aging: A white elephant?", raises a number of conceptual questions, asking whether the investigator is better advised to concentrate on individual life periods, and if it is premature to attempt to bridge one life period to the next. Neugarten (1969) has also addressed this point in considering the relations between childhood and adulthood and has suggested that it is exceedingly difficult to construct such bridges across widely separated life periods and thereby create a meaningful life-span approach to the study of personality.

STUDIES OF AGE-RELATED CHANGE IN PERSONALITY

What Dimensions of Personality Show Change?

Literally hundreds of cross-sectional studies have appeared in the last 20 years in which a single trait or dimension of personality has been the focus of investigation and in which the approach has been to see if age differences exist or if age is more significant than other factors such as sex or social class in accounting for the variance. The diversity of this literature can only be suggested by the examples to follow. Because of space limitations, citations have been kept to a minimum, with preference given to those which provide useful bibliographies on the topic in question.

Among the personality dimensions of current interest are egocentrism (Looft, 1972), dependency (Kalish, 1969), introversion (Chown, 1968), dogmatism (Botwinick, 1973), rigidity

(Angleitner, 1974; Botwinick, 1973; Chown, 1961), cautiousness (Botwinick, 1973), conformity (Klein, 1972), ego strength (Sealy and Cattell, 1965), risk-taking and decision-making (Robins, 1969; Welford and Birren, 1969), need-achievement (Veroff, Atkinson, Feld and Gurin, 1960), perceived locus of control (Brim, 1974b), creativity (Kogan, 1973), and hope (Haberland, 1972).

Other closely related areas include the self-concept or self-image (Bennett and Eckman, 1973; Hess and Bradshaw, 1970; Palmore, 1974; Peters, 1971), social responsibility (Schaie and Parham, 1974), happiness, morale, or life satisfaction (Adams, 1971; Back and Bourque, 1970), the nature and role of reminiscence (Butler, 1963b; Coleman, 1974; Lieberman and Falk, 1971), attitudes toward aging (Kaplan and Pokorny, 1970; Kastenbaum, Derbin, Sabatini, and Artt, 1972), and dreams and day-dreams (Giambra, 1974; Zepelin, 1972).

In each area, the findings are notably inconsistent from one study to the next, with some but not other investigators reporting age differences. The one exception is introversion, where although the various studies are methodologically flawed, the findings nevertheless add up to the generalization that introversion increases with age in the second half of life. The inconclusive findings for other personality dimensions reflect the problems cited earlier: observers do not agree about the words they use, nor their measures; and samples have been extremely varied, often without attention to controls. Whether or not age emerges as a significant variable is often a simple artifact of the sampling frame, for if a sample is relatively homogeneous with regard to other variables such as intelligence level or socioeconomic status or health status, then age differences are more likely to emerge as significant. Although the latter is an obvious methodological point, it is one of the reasons why cross-sectional studies so often show inconsistent findings.

Other problems lie in the fact that investigators have for the most part used instruments of unknown reliability or validity for older persons. Tasks or tests have been used which are themselves not meaningful to older persons so that response set becomes an overwhelming difficulty; or instruments have been applied which were originally devised for quite different purposes and which prove insensitive to age differences.

One example will serve to underline the last problem. A group of Thematic Apperception Test (TAT) protocols gathered from a representative community sample aged 40 to 70 were analyzed by using two different scoring systems which seemed, at first examination, to be quite similar (Neugarten and Associates, 1964, Ch. 5). In the first, the scoring categories were ones that had emerged from an earlier study of age-related personality differences, and in using those categories on these TAT data, statistically significant age differences appeared. In the second analysis, the scoring categories were ones that had emerged from clinical studies and had proved useful in differentiating normals, neurotics, and psychotics. In this second analysis of the same TAT data, no age differences appeared. Thus, whether it is the TAT or a paper and pencil test or another form of observation that is used to provide the data, it may be an error to anticipate that a set of personality variables originally designed to detect pathology will also detect personality differences that are part of the normal aging process.

A yet more important problem is the comparability of personality constructs when applied to persons in different life periods. Is the concept of aggression, for instance, or ego strength the same concept when applied to young adults as when applied to old people? If we pursue the genotypic-phenotypic distinction, it is extraordinarily difficult to move from phenotypic behavior at Time 1 to a satisfactory conceptualization of the genotypic trait that underlies it and then to operationalize and measure that same trait in terms of different phenotypic behavior at Time 2.

Still another problem is that in most studies of personality and aging, the investigator has asked if change is age-related without considering also whether or not marriage has intervened, or parenthood, or job failure, or illness, or widowhood. Time has been treated as independent from the events that might be regarded as precipitants of personality change. This criticism can be made not only about cross-sectional studies but also about the few longitudinal studies thus far reported.

All this says nothing of the underlying question that, for the present, remains unanswerable: How are our personality measures related to observable behavior in everyday life? For both the psychologists who create their own variables and for those who use "standard" personality tests, there is the nagging problem that personality may turn out to be only that which the tests test. Although, as stated earlier, this is a problem endemic to the whole field of personality research, it may be even a greater problem in studies of middle-aged or older persons. Because of cohort differences in education and other socialization experiences, response sets in relation to personality tests may be greater in older than in younger persons.

Multidimensional Studies

In some of the cross-sectional studies the focus has been upon multiple rather than single dimensions of personality, and the attempt has been to differentiate those dimensions that show age-related change from those that do not. Here a new question arises: How, in assessing these studies, shall we deal with the assumption that personality traits are somehow independent of each other? While we deal with "separate" traits for purposes of analysis, a personality is essentially a whole, or a set of systems within systems, and our analytic units are usually not separable in the real world of behavior.

The studies carried out by the group of investigators at the University of Chicago (Neugarten and Associates, 1964) are illustrative of multidimensional approaches, and while they do not solve the questions just stated, they have the advantage that they were based on large and representative samples of persons aged 40 to 80; they constituted a sequence of interrelated studies carried out over a 10-year period, each study growing from the preceding one; and they included various aspects of personality observed in the same population. Working from projective tests, questionnaires, and structured and unstructured interview data of various types, rather than from single personality tests, and using an inductive approach in the creation of variables, the investigators found consistent age differences in intrapsychic dimensions: e.g., a change from active to passive mastery in relating to the environment and a change from outer-world to inner-world orientation which was described as increased interiority. (The latter is close in meaning to the term introversion). Sex differences were apparent. Older men seemed more receptive than younger men to their affiliative, nurturant, and sensual promptings; older women, to their aggressive and egocentric impulses. (These findings have been confirmed by others: e.g., Shanan and Sharon, 1965; Thurnher, 1971.)

No age-related differences were found, however, in socioadaptational dimensions: e.g., in goal-directed and purposive behavior, or coping styles, or satisfaction with life, or those processes more readily available to conscious control. (We shall return to the Chicago studies in a later section of this paper.)

A different example of a multidimensional approach is the study reported by Schaie and Parham (1976) who administered a narrow set of questionnaire items twice to a large sample aged 21-84; who used a cross-sequential design in analyzing the data (i.e., one in which age differences can be distinguished from cohort differences); and who reported stability rather than age change in most of the personality factors that emerged.

In a few instances, multidimensional studies have focused directly upon the organization or "structure" of personality and to the question, do the *relationships* between traits change over the period of adulthood? The term *structure* obviously means different things to different theoreticians. To the Freudian, for instance, the structure of personality is altered through childhood and adolescence as the ego moves into a more central position. From an Eriksonian perspective, because different ego tasks become critical at different life periods, the organization of personality must continually change. And in conventional empirical studies, investigators have reported data showing that at different points in adulthood the relationship between personality variables is not the same. Craik (1964), for example, found that emotional adjustment and sociability are differently related in men and women of different ages; Cunningham and Bengtson (1974) found different patterns of personality organization not only between the sexes, but between age groups; and Lieberman, Cohler, and Welch (1975), in a study of adults aged 40 to 80, found a different constellation of personality characteristics associated with successful coping styles, not only in persons of different ethnic backgrounds, but in persons of different ages.

The question of change in personality organization has been most formalistically addressed in those studies in which multivariate statistical procedures have been used in analyzing responses to a single personality test. To use a single test for this purpose is a questionable procedure, given that different tests elicit different response sets, and any single test is a very narrow base for studying so complex a construct as personality structure. Whatever the merits of this approach, however, the Cattell 16PF or the MMPI have been used in several such studies. The studies have produced different outcomes. Slater and Scarr (1964), for example, factor-analyzed responses to the MMPI from three age groups of adults and concluded that while scale scores vary with age, a relatively constant factor structure persists and that, in this sense, personality organization remains stable. Yet Costa (1973), factor-analyzing responses to the 16PF from some 1,000 men aged 30+, found dramatic age differences in the ways personality factors are related at successive ages. Schaie and Marquette (1972) reviewed the multivariate studies undertaken up to that year and pointed out not only that they had all been cross-sectional, thus reflecting age differences rather than age changes, but that they had produced mainly conflicting findings.

Thus studies of personality organization have been no more consistent than studies of individual personality dimensions and no more enlightening with regard to the direction of change over time.

Personality and Adaptation

Another major line of inquiry has been the relationship of personality to adaptation. In some instances, the investigator has conceptualized adaptation as being itself part of personality; in other instances, the two have been treated as independent. (A major review of the concept of adaptation from a life-course perspective is provided by Lowenthal and Chiriboga [1973]; and a framework of "intentionality" for studying adaptation in adulthood, by Lowenthal [1971].) When the two are treated separately, it has been found that personality traits are usually powerful predictors of adaptation or coping styles, although the particular predictive traits may be different at successive age periods, a point illustrated in several of the studies to be cited below. In this connection, the prediction of adaptational patterns depends also, of course, upon environmental and cultural factors, a topic that cannot be pursued in the present context.

Whether or not the relationship between personality and adaptation remains generally the same in successive periods of adulthood is a complex question, complicated by the fact that the psychological issues and the preoccupations of adults change over time. For example, in young adulthood the salient issues relate not only to meeting the expectations of the world of work, but to intimacy, to parenthood, and to the attendant investment of self into the lives of a few significant others. In middle age some of the issues relate to new family roles (e.g., the responsibilities of being the child of aging parents, and the new boundaries of authority between oneself, one's parents, and one's children). Other issues refer to the changing time perspective as time becomes restructured in terms of time-left-to-live rather than time-since-birth (Eissler, 1955) and to the personalization of death which brings with it, for women, the rehearsal for widowhood, and for men, the rehearsal for illness. In old age some of the psychological issues relate to renunciation, the loss of significant others, and the yielding up of a sense of competency and authority; other issues relate to integrity and to the importance of what one has been rather than what one is; and still other issues relate to putting one's store of memories in order, dramatizing some, striving for consistency in others, perhaps as a way of preparing an ending for one's life story (e.g., Butler, 1963b).

Because these psychological issues and pre-occupations are different at successive periods in adulthood, the personality dimensions and adaptational styles which come into play at one time may not be the same as those at another. In pursuing this general question, some investigators have focused upon a particular life period. Thus Brim (1974a), Levinson *et al.* (1974), Neugarten and Datan (1974), Soddy (1967), and Vaillant and McArthur (1972) have been concerned with adaptational patterns in middle age and have discussed the presence or absence of a midlife crisis. While there are differences of opinion regarding the crisis aspects, there is general agreement that different personalities will adapt differently to the tasks of middle age.

Others have focused upon the period of old age. Reichard, Livson, and Petersen (1962), for instance, have studied types of personalities that occur among well-adjusted and poorly adjusted older men and have outlined three types who adapt well (those they named the Mature, the Rocking-chair, and the Armoured types) and two types who adapt poorly (the Angry and the Self-haters). Neugarten, Havighurst, and Tobin (1968), in a study of 70-year-old men and women, described four major personality types and measured adaptation by an independent index of life satisfaction. Of their four types, the Integrated and the Armoured were high on life satisfaction; the Passive-dependent were either high or low; and the Unintegrated were low.

Lieberman (1971, 1975) has used a quite different measure of adaptation in very aged persons, namely, survivorship. He has described the "adaptive paranoia" of old age, and his finding that grouchiness or combativeness is a survival asset. It is of interest that Gutmann (1971) found that much the same pattern of combativeness was characteristic of the longest-lived men in various preliterate societies. Lieberman (1975) has suggested that perhaps the traditional views of psychological health do not apply to aged survivors and that different processes of coping with crisis may therefore be specific to different life-stages.

Still other investigators have looked, not at life periods, but at particular life events as precipitants of change in personality and adaptation. We have already mentioned the psychoanalysts who have described the changes associated with pregnancy in women (Bibring, 1959), with parenthood in both men and women (Benedek, 1959, 1970), and with the climacterium in women (Benedek, 1950). Ahammer (1973) has also described changes that occur with marriage and parenthood; Neugarten, Kraines, and Wood (1965), with changes in women that occur with menopause and the "empty nest"; Friedmann and Orbach (1974), the changes in adaptation at retirement; and Lopata (1973) and Parkes (1964), adaptation to widowhood.

A few investigators have broadened the focus and have looked, not at single events, but at the succession of life events in adulthood, attempting to isolate those that have the greatest effect upon adaptation. Thus, Back and Morris (1974) have reported that changes in job status are of greater significance to men than changes in the family cycle.

Lowenthal, Thurnher, and Chiriboga (1975) have described in detail the adaptational patterns of men and women at each of two incremental transitions (leaving home and starting a family) and at each of two decremental transitions (the "empty nest" and retirement). Among other findings, these authors report that overall the differences between the sexes were more significant than differences between the youngest and oldest of either sex.

In discussing adaptation over the life span, Neugarten (1970) has suggested that it is not the occurrence of the life event itself which precipitates an adaptational crisis, for most such events are anticipated and rehearsed and the transition accomplished without shattering the sense of continuity of the life cycle. Instead, it is when such events occur "off-time" rather than "on-time", for example, when grandparenthood, retirement, major illness, or widowhood occur earlier in life than expected, that crisis is experienced.

In general, in studying the relations between personality, adaptation, and major life transitions, psychologists will probably gain enormously by focusing more attention upon the issues that are of major concern to the individual—what the person selects as important in his past and his present, what he hopes to do in the future, what he predicts will occur, what strategies he elects, and what meanings he attaches to time, life, and death. In short, psychologists would do well to make greater use of the person himself as the reporting and predicting agent, and by gathering systematic and repeated self-reports along with other types of data, to combine the phenomenological and the "objective" perspectives.

LONGITUDINAL AND FOLLOW-UP STUDIES

Because the empirical studies cited in the preceding sections have been cross-sectional, yielding data on age differences (or cohort differences) rather than age changes, they bear only indirectly on the questions of consistency of personality and adaptation. More direct answers must depend on follow-up and longitudinal studies, but unfortunately, few investigations have yet appeared in which persons have been followed into the second half of life.

A few studies exist in which relatively narrow sets of personality data have been gathered in youth and again in early middle age. For example, Kelly (1955) tested men and women in their 20's and again in their 40's and found that individual consistency was high with regard to values and occupational interests but low with regard to self-ratings and other personality variables. Terman and Oden (1959), in restudying a large group of gifted children when they had reached their late 40's, reported that, with few exceptions, the superior child had become the superior adult, thus supporting, in very gross terms, the generalization of continuity over time. The study by Woodruff and Birren (1972), while based on only single sets of test responses, is one of the few in which aging can be distinguished from cohort differences, for a group originally tested in college was retested 25 years later when, at the same time, a new group of college students was tested. The findings showed that cohort differences were larger than aging differences and that consistency rather than change was typical in the follow-up group.

In a second category of studies in which more complex sets of personality data have been gathered at successive points in time, individuals have seldom been followed beyond middle age. Omitting here those longitudinal studies in which children or adolescents have been followed only into young adulthood, there are now a few studies in progress in which college men have been followed into their 40's and 50's but where the findings have not yet been fully reported. Heath (1974), for instance, is studying how college men take on more or less mature patterns of adaptation from their 20's to their 40's; and Vaillant and McArthur (1972) have reported on the movement from intimacy to career consolidation to generativity, as well as on changes in ego mechanisms of defense, for only a subgroup of the college men they have studied from age 18 to 50.

The group of investigators at the Institute of Human Development in Berkeley, in following persons from infancy and childhood, have reported on their samples when they were in their 30's (e.g., Block, 1971; Peskin, 1972) and again when they were in their 40's (Haan and Day, 1974). In comparing the group in early adolescence, late adolescence, and early adulthood, Block summarized the changes for both sexes in the direction of less narcissistic impulsivity and increase in coping capacities. For men, these changes were accompanied by what Block calls an increased obsessiveness and a "diminished" self; for women, by greater affective vulnerability and reduced assertiveness. Block then proceeded to create personality types and to trace the pattern of change or stability for each of five types of men and for each of six types of women. He reported consistency for each type and concluded that his data established not only the unity principle (personality coherence) but also proof for the principle of personality consistency.

Haan and Day added the data collected when the same group had reached middle adulthood, but these investigators moved away from a typology in favor of analyzing individual personality *items* for the sample as a whole. They reported change for some items over the four periods of early adolescence, late adolescence, early adulthood, and middle adulthood, but for more of the items, especially those that relate to manner of presentation of self and responses to socialization influences, they reported consistency.

Maas and Kuypers (1975) followed up the parents of the Berkeley sample, studying parents when they were in their 30's and again in their 70's. The study focused upon life-styles and personality types at the later age, with the Time 1 data used primarily for their predictive value for Time 2. With regard to life-styles, the authors found more continuities for the fathers than for the mothers. Because the data on personality at Time 1 were relatively sparse, especially for the fathers, this study has only limited value for answering the questions of continuity and change in personality over the adult period. Such constancies as appeared over the 40-year span were more apparent in mothers than in fathers, and for the minority of mothers who showed low adaptive capacities at Time 2. For this small group of mothers, characteristics present at both Time 1 and Time 2 were low self-esteem, depression, and other problematic traits.

Overall, while the findings from the Berkeley studies cannot be fitted together to form a coherent picture of the *direction* of personality change across periods of adulthood (partly because of limitations in the data, partly because it has been children followed into middle adulthood, but parents followed into old age, and partly because of the detailed style of reporting), they nevertheless represent the most fully analyzed longitudinal data thus far available. Their major contribution has been in demonstrating *individual differences*: that persons (or types of persons) maintain their recognizability and that, in this sense, there is continuity of personality over time.

There have been four short-term longitudinal studies reported of persons in middle or old age. The first is a study of 47 healthy men studied in their 70's and the 19 who survived 11 years later (Granick and Patterson, 1971), in which personality and psychiatric data were gathered along with data on physiological and cognitive measures. Among other findings, those men who survived had had significantly higher levels of psychological adaptation at the outset of the study.

The second is one in which a small group of men and women in their 60's and 70's residing in a small Pennsylvania community were followed for a 9-year period (Britton and Britton, 1972), and in which, in addition to various measures of personality and adjustment, information about the individual was obtained from others who knew him. The data are reported both in terms of group findings and individual patterns of change. The investigators emphasized the factor of change in old age and stressed the importance of situational variables in accounting for stability or decline in levels of adaptation.

The third is a follow-up of a group of women studied when they were 45 to 57, then studied again ten years later (Noberini and Neugarten, 1975). Measures of life satisfaction, psychological and psychosomatic symptoms, coping ability, and degree of gratification with various attributes of the self and body all showed relatively high consistency from Time 1 to Time 2.

The fourth is a longitudinal study now in progress at Bonn University, in which 220 men and women aged 60 to 79 living in different parts of West Germany have been observed since 1965. The first book-length report (Thomae, 1975) shows that the personality dimension of rigidity had stayed relatively stable for the group as a whole over a 5-year period, as was true also of attitudes toward life. Overall, the findings point to a complex pattern of variables associated with consistency and change of behavior in old age, with socioeconomic status, education, health, and perceived life situation involved to at least the same degree as calendar age. As is true with regard to the other multidimensional studies mentioned earlier in this review, whether the studies are cross-sectional or longitudinal, the investigators stress the individual differences in patterns of aging.

All the follow-up and longitudinal studies of adults thus far cited have been based on relatively small and select samples, most of them middle-class, white, and above average in education, with most of the persons living in generally supportive environments; and therefore the findings cannot be generalized to larger populations. Indeed, some investigators regard these investigations as little more than groups of case studies, although recognizing that case studies provide insights regarding continuity and change that can come only from following the same persons over time. (It is of interest, in this regard, that students of aging have otherwise given little attention to the single case. The literature of case studies—if novels, biographies, and autobiographies are excluded— is singularly lacking in studies of aging men and women.)

There are other studies now in progress in which larger samples are being followed into old age, but longitudinal findings regarding personality have not yet been reported. At Duke University a group of 260 men and women aged 60+ have been followed since 1957, and another larger group aged 45 and over have been followed since 1968. Although brief reports have appeared from the Duke investigators regarding personality variables and self-concept (Palmore, 1974), these reports have been cross-sectional, and no major report of personality based on longitudinal analysis has yet appeared. The Normative Aging Study being carried out under the Veterans Administration in Boston involves a sample of some 2,000 men of all ages and all occupational levels. A few reports of personality (e.g., Costa, 1973), again cross-sectional in nature, have appeared, but not yet any longitudinal analyses.

RECENT THEORETICAL FORMULATIONS

Given this brief overview of theoretical frameworks regarding personality and aging, most of them available 20 years ago, and this brief description of empirical work that has since been undertaken, we turn now to the question—what new theoretical formulations have appeared?

We have mentioned the cognitive theory of Thomae (1970). In the United States, it has been primarily the group of investigators who began studying social and psychological aspects of middle age and aging at the University of Chicago in the 1950's who have been concerned with theory-building and who, in moving back and forth from their empirical findings to theoretical formulations, have ventured new hypotheses regarding the trajectory of change that occurs in the second half of life.

We have already commented that in a series of multidimensional studies of personality (Neugarten and Associates, 1964) based upon a

variety of projective tests, questionnaires and interviews, the Chicago investigators found consistent age differences in intrapsychic dimensions: a change from active to passive mastery styles in relating to the environment and a change from outer-world to inner-world orientation which was described as increased interiority. Although these studies were based upon cross-sectional samples, the findings suggested developmental rather than responsive processes, largely because the age differences appeared by the late 40's and 50's, well before the social losses of aging had occurred for most respondents.

Other sets of data on the same persons related to social behavior: to the amount of each day spent in interaction with others, and to levels of performance in various life roles (worker, spouse, parent, grandparent, kin-group member, homemaker, friend, neighbor, citizen, club member, church member). Role activity was lower in successive age groups, and the degree of ego investment in current social roles was lower, with marked declines appearing by the early 70's. Over the time period from middle age to advanced old age, then, there was a shrinkage in social life-space.

These findings (i.e., age-related changes in intrapsychic aspects of personality and in social interaction) gave rise to the disengagement theory first stated by Cumming and Henry (1961), which posited that the decreased social interaction of old age is characterized by mutuality: both society and the aging person withdraw, with the individual's withdrawal accompanied by decreased emotional involvement in the activities and relationships of his middle age. The data presented by Cumming and Henry suggested that among persons over 65, those who had disengaged were higher in morale than those who had not. (It should be noted that in neither the empirical data nor in the statement of the disengagement theory is it implied that the older person disengages from the values of his society.)

Some of the Chicago team, as they continued to gather data on members of their sample, devised more complex measures of social interaction and more carefully validated measures of adaptation. Using as a measure of adaptation a multidimensional scale called Life Satisfaction, they found that life satisfaction was more often present in older persons who were socially active and engaged than in persons who were inactive or disengaged. More important, however, was the diversity. All four combinations of activity and satisfaction existed: high-high and low-low were the most frequent, but there were also high-low and low-high (Havighurst, Neugarten, and Tobin, 1968).

Given the latter findings, these investigators then moved back to studying differences in personality. Using a set of empirically derived personality types (Neugarten and Associates, 1964, Ch. 8), then assessing three kinds of data on each person—extent of social interaction, life satisfaction, and personality type—they found a high degree of order in the data. Certain personality types, as they aged, seemed to slough off various role responsibilities with relative comfort and to remain highly content with life. Others showed a drop in social interaction and a drop in life satisfaction. Still others had long shown low levels of activity accompanied by high satisfaction, and these persons showed relatively little change as they aged. For instance, in one group of 70–79-year-olds, persons who were living in the community and carrying out their usual daily rounds of activities, eight different patterns of aging emerged, which the investigators named the Reorganizers, the Focused, the Disengaged, the Holding-on, the Constricted, the Succorance-seeking, the Apathetic, and the Disorganized, each based on the three types of data just mentioned, and with each name conveying something of the style of aging common to each of the subgroups (Neugarten, Havighurst, and Tobin, 1968).

These studies led to the hypothesis that personality organization or personality type is pivotal in predicting which individuals will age successfully. While it has often been demonstrated that factors such as health, financial resources, and marital status are more significant than age in influencing adaptation in older persons, and granted also that social and ecological factors produce important variations in the ways people grow old, these investigators regard personality factors as the mediating factors. Older persons, like younger, have differing capacities for coping with life stresses and for coming to terms with their changing life situations. And given a half-way supportive environment, older persons, like younger, will choose the combinations of activities that offer them the most ego involvement and that are most consonant with their self-concepts. As Havighurst (1968) has put it: From a social psychological perspective aging is better viewed, not as a process of engagement or disengagement, but as a process of adaptation in which personality is the key element. The aging individual not only plays an active role in adapting to the biological and social changes that occur with the passage of time but in *creating* patterns of life that will give him greatest ego involvement and life satisfaction.

A Cross-Cultural Approach

Meanwhile, the indication that intrapsychic changes are developmental has received its major support from the work of Gutmann, a member of the original Chicago group. Trained in anthropology as well as in clinical and developmental psychology, Gutmann (1964, 1969, 1974) has carried out a unique set of studies of aging men in preliterate societies to see if the changes from active to passive mastery, as he had described them for American men, were also to be found in other cultures. He found the same changes in men in four other societies: the Navajo in Arizona, the Lowland Mayans and the Highland Mayans of Mexico, and the Druze of the Galilean highlands of Israel.

Gutmann has since pursued the same question across a wide range of cultures (see Chapter 14 in the present volume), using as his data the accounts written by ethnographers and using cultures rather than individuals as the units of study. He has described what he regards as the same underlying pattern of age changes common across cultures, or what he refers to as a species-specific trajectory of change, whereby men move from active to passive mastery modes, with the very oldest men moving to magical mastery (i.e., the use of ritual, magic, or meditation in coping with the perceived demands of the environment), but women move in the opposite direction, from passive mastery to active (i.e., women become more domineering, more instrumental, and more at ease with their aggressive impulses). While Gutmann explains that these underlying personalty changes lead to different adaptational outcomes, depending upon the extent to which different societies give deference and prestige to the old, and depending also upon other aspects of the culture, the implication is that the common patterns of change are related to common patterns of biological aging.

Gutmann (1975) proposes a tentative explanation for the sex difference, saying that it is the requirements of parenthood that establish sex-role distinctions in the early years of adulthood, with women needing to suppress elements of aggressivity in themselves if they are to succeed in their roles as caretakers of children, and men needing to suppress elements of affiliation if they are to succeed in their roles as economic providers. After the demands of parenthood are over, the earlier suppressed elements of personality can be expressed, with a consequent movement toward the "normal unisex of later life."

While Gutmann's findings are open to various methodological criticisms, his formulation is unique in its blending of clinical, developmental, and anthropological approaches, and it provides a bold set of hypotheses that can now be checked by more conventional research designs.

Thus the Chicago group, in studying personality, social behavior, and adaptation and in following exploratory, naturalistic, and hypothesis-building approaches, have made new theoretical contributions: in setting forth the hypothesis that increased interiority and other intrapsychic changes in personality are developmental; then in formulating the disengagement theory and subsequently modifying that theory; then in stating the hypothesis that it is personality which is the pivotal factor in adaptation to aging. And Gutmann's work, which has been one of the outgrowths, led to the hypothesis that the direction of change in men from active to passive to magical mastery, and the opposite direction of change in women, are common across cultures.

CONCLUSION

In the preceding pages we have been saying, sometimes explicitly, sometimes implicitly, that personality and aging, as a newly appearing area of research, inevitably reflects the state of disarray that presently exists in the general field of personality and that the empirical work appearing over the past 20 years in the area of personality and aging has not only been sparse, but it has been marked both by methodological flaws and conceptual impoverishment. At various points we have suggested some of the next steps that need to be taken to improve the research efforts of psychologists, and we have suggested that in these efforts the insights and the methods of the conventional personality theorists, the developmentalists, and the clinicians need somehow to be combined.

We have been suggesting, furthermore, that we need to maintain a position of modesty about our endeavors as psychologists, first, by keeping in mind that the scientific approach is only one among many approaches to the study of personality; second, by recognizing that we are culture-bound and history-bound in the very ways we approach our field of study and in the conclusions we draw. Just as new paradigms are likely to appear in the field of personality, so new perspectives can be anticipated with regard to the nature of aging, for increased longevity, changing rhythms of the life cycle, and other social and biological realities will come to characterize the society in which we live. This is one way of saying, perhaps, that whether or not an Einstein appears within the field of personality, we will have changing views of aging over the next few decades, and these will themselves influence our views of the aging personality.

REFERENCES

Adams, D. L. 1971. Correlates of satisfaction among the elderly. *Gerontologist*, **11**, No. 4, Pt. 2, 64–68.

Ahammer, I. M. 1973. Social learning theory as a framework for the study of adult personality development. *In*, P. B. Baltes and K. W. Schaie (eds.), *Life-Span Developmental Psychology: Personality and Socialization*, pp. 253–284. New York: Academic Press.

Allport, G. W. 1937. *Personality*. New York: Henry Holt.

Angleitner, A. 1974. Changes in personality of older people over a 5-year period of observation. *Gerontologia*, **20**, 179–185.

Aries, P. 1962. *Centuries of Childhood*. New York: Alfred A. Knopf.

Back, K. W., and Bourque, L. 1970. Life graphs: Aging and cohort effect. *J. Gerontol.*, **25** (3), 249–255.

Back, K. W., and Morris, J. D. 1974. Perception of self and the study of whole lives. *In*, E. Palmore (ed.), *Normal Aging II: Reports from the Duke Longitudinal Studies, 1970–1973*, pp. 216–221. Durham, North Carolina: Duke University Press.

Baer, D. M. 1970. An age-irrelevant concept of development. *Merrill Palmer Quarterly*, **16**, 230–245.

Baltes, P. B. 1973. Life-span models of psychological aging: A white elephant? *Gerontologist*, **13** (4), 457–512.

Baltes, P. B., and Schaie, K. W. (eds.) 1973. *Life-Span Developmental Psychology: Personality and Socialization*. New York: Academic Press.

Becker, H. 1964. Personal change in adult life. *Sociometry*, **27**, 40–53.

Benedek, T. 1950. Climacterium: A developmental phase. *Psychoanal. Quart.*, **19**, 1–27.

Benedek, T. 1959. Parenthood as a developmental phase. *J. Am. Psychoanal. Assoc.*, **7**, 389–417.

Benedek, T. 1970. *In*, E. J. Anthony and T. Benedek (eds.), *Parenthood*, Chap. 4, 5, 6, and 7. Boston: Little, Brown.

Bennett, R., and Eckman, J. 1973. Attitudes toward aging: A critical examination of recent literature and implications for future research. *In*, C. Eisdorfer and M. P. Lawton (eds.), *The Psychology of Adult Development and Aging*. Washington, D.C.: American Psychological Association.

Berezin, M. A. and Cath, S. H. (eds.) 1965. *Geriatric Psychiatry*. New York: International Universities Press.

Bibring, G. L. 1959. Some considerations of the psychological processes of pregnancy. *Psychoanal. Study. Child.*, **14**, 113–121.

Block, J. 1971. *Lives Through Time*. Berkeley: Bancroft Books.

Bortner, R. W. 1966. Adult development or idiosyncratic change? A plea for the developmental approach. *Gerontologist*, **6**, No. 3, Pt. 1, 159–164.

Bortner, R. W. 1967. Personality and social psychology in the study of aging. *Gerontologist*, **7**, No. 2, Pt. 2, 23–36.

Botwinick, J. 1973. *Aging and Behavior: A Comprehensive Integration of Research Findings*. New York: Springer.

Bowers, K. S. 1973. Situationism in psychology: An analysis and a critique. *Psych. Rev.*, **80** (5), 307–336.

Brim, O. G. 1968. Adult socialization. *In*, J. A. Clausen (ed.), *Socialization and Society*, pp. 182–226. Boston: Little, Brown.

Brim, O. G. 1974a. Selected theories of the male midlife crisis: A comparative analysis. Paper presented at the 82nd Annual Meeting of the American Psychological Association, New Orleans.

Brim, O. G. 1974b. The sense of personal control over one's life. Paper presented at the 82nd Annual Meeting of the American Psychological Association, New Orleans.

Britton, J. H., and Britton, J. O. 1972. *Personality Changes in Aging: A Longitudinal Study of Community Residents*. New York: Springer.

Bühler, C. 1935. The curve of life as studied in biographies. *J. Appl. Psych.*, **19**, 405–409.

Bühler, C. 1959. *Der Menschliche Lebenslauf als Psychologisches Problem*. 2nd ed. Gottingen, West Germany: Hogrefe.

Bühler, C., and Massarik, F. (eds.) 1968. *The Course of Human Life*. New York: Springer.

Butler, R. N. 1963a. The facade of chronological age: An interpretative summary. *Am. J. Psychiat.*, **119** (8), 721–728.

Butler, R. N. 1963b. The life review: An interpretation of reminiscence in the aged. *Psychiatry*, **26** (1), 65–76.

Carlson, R. 1971. Where is the person in personality research? *Psych. Bull*, **75** (3), 203–219.

Carlson, R. 1975. Personality. *Ann. Rev. Psychol.*, **26**, 393–414.

Cattell, R. B. 1957. *Personality and Motivation Structure and Measurement*. New York: World.

Chown, S. M. 1961. Age and the rigidities. *J. Gerontol.*, **16**, 353–362.

Chown, S. M. 1968. Personality and aging. *In*, K. W. Schaie (ed.), *Theory and Methods of Research on Aging*, pp. 134–157. Morgantown, West Virginia: West Virginia University Library.

Clausen, J. A. (ed.) 1968. *Socialization and Society*. Boston: Little, Brown.

Coleman, P. G. 1974. Measuring reminiscence characteristics from conversation as adaptive features of old age. *Int. J. Aging Hum. Devel.*, **5** (3), 281–294.

Costa, P. T. 1973. Age differences in the structure of 16 PF surface traits. Paper presented at the 81st Annual Meeting of the American Psychological Association, Montreal.

Craik, F. I. M. 1964. An observed age difference in responses to a personality inventory. *Brit. J. Psychol.*, **55**, 453–462.

Cumming, E., and Henry, W. E. 1961. *Growing Old*. New York: Basic Books.

Cunningham, W. R., and Bengtson, V. L. 1974. Age strata differences in factor structure of personality variables. Paper presented at the Annual Meeting of the Gerontological Society, Portland.

Deutsch, H. 1944. *The Psychology of Women, Vol. I*. New York: Grune & Stratton.

Deutsch, H. 1945. *The Psychology of Women, Vol. II*. New York: Grune & Stratton.

Eissler, K. R. 1955. *The Psychiatrist and the Dying Patient*. New York: International Universities Press.

Erikson, E. H. 1959. Identity and the life cycle. *Psychological Issues*, **1**, New York: International Universities Press.

Erikson, E. H. 1963. *Childhood and Society*. 2nd ed. New York: W. W. Norton.

Farber, I. E. 1964. A framework for the study of personality as a behavioral science. *In*, P. Worchel and D. Byrne (eds.), *Personality Change*. New York: John Wiley, pp. 3–37.

Fiske, D. W. 1974. The limits for the conventional science of personality. *J. Pers.*, **42** (1), 1–11.

Frazer, J. T. 1966. *The Voices of Time.* New York: George Braziller.

Friedmann, E. A., and Orbach, H. 1974. Adjustment to retirement. *In*, S. Arieti (ed.), *American Handbook of Psychiatry*, pp. 609–645. New York: Basic Books.

Giambra, L. M. 1974. Daydreaming across the life span: Late adolescent to senior citizen. *Aging and Human Development*, 5 (2), 115–140.

Gillis, J. R. 1974. *Youth and History.* New York: Academic Press.

Glaser, B. G., and Strauss, A. 1967. *The Discovery of Grounded Theory.* Chicago: Aldine.

Gordon, C. 1972. Role and value development across the life cycle. *In*, J. A. Jackson (ed.), *Sociological Studies IV: Role*, pp. 65–105. London: Cambridge University Press.

Gould, R. 1972. The phases of adult life: a study in developmental psychology. *Amer. J. Psychiat.*, 129, 521–531.

Goulet, L. R., and Baltes, P. B. 1970. *Life-Span Developmental Psychology: Research and Theory.* New York: Academic Press.

Granick, S., and Patterson, R. D. 1971. *Human Aging II: An Eleven Year Biomedical and Behavioral Study.* Washington, D.C.: Government Printing Office.

Gutmann, D. L. 1964. An exploration of ego configurations in middle and later life. *In*, B. L. Neugarten and Associates, *Personality in Middle and Later Life*, pp. 114–148. New York: Atherton Press.

Gutmann, D. L. 1969. The country of old men: Cross-cultural studies in the psychology of later life. *Occasional Papers in Gerontology, No. 5.* Ann Arbor: Institue of Gerontology, University of Michigan-Wayne State University.

Gutmann, D. L. 1971. Dependency, illness and survival among Navajo men. *In*, E. Palmore and F. C. Jeffers (eds.). *Prediction of Life Span*, pp. 181–198. Lexington, Massachusetts: Heath Lexington.

Gutmann, D. L. 1974. Alternatives to disengagement: The old men of the Highland Druze. *In*, R. A. LeVine (ed)., *Culture and Personality: Contemporary Readings*, pp. 232–245. Chicago: Aldine.

Gutmann, D. L. 1975. Parenthood: Key to the comparative psychology of the life cycle? *In*, N. Datan and L. Ginsberg (eds.), *Life-Span Developmental Psychology: Normative Life Crises.* New York: Academic Press.

Haan, N., and Day, D. 1974. A longitudinal study of change and sameness in personality development: Adolescence to later adulthood. *Int. J. Aging Hum. Devel.*, 5 (1), 11–39.

Haberland, H. W. 1972. Psychological dimensions of hope in the aged: Relationship to adaptation, survival and institutionalization. Unpublished Ph.D. dissertation, University of Chicago.

Hall, C. S., and Lindzey, G. 1970. *Theories of Personality.* 2nd ed. New York: John Wiley.

Havighurst, R. J. 1968. A social-psychological perspective on aging. *Gerontologist*, 8 (2), 67–71.

Havighurst, R. 1972. *Developmental Tasks and Education.* New York: David McKay.

Havighurst, R., Neugarten, B. L., and Tobin, S. S. 1968. Disengagement and patterns of aging. *In*, B. L. Neugarten (ed.), *Middle Age and Aging*, pp. 161–172. Chicago: University of Chicago Press.

Heath, D. H. 1974. Personal Communication.

Henry, W. E. 1968. Personality change in middle and old age. *In*, E. Norbeck, D. Price-Williams, and W. M. McCord (eds.), *The Study of Personality: An Interdisciplinary Appraisal*, pp. 209–217. New York: Holt, Rinehart and Winston.

Hess, A. L., and Bradshaw, H. L. 1970. Positiveness of self-concept and ideal self as a function of age. *Journal of Genetic Psychology*, 117, 57–67.

Jung, C. G. 1933. *Modern Man in Search of a Soul.* New York: Harcourt, Brace & World.

Kalish, R. A. (ed.) 1969. The dependencies of old people. *Occasional Papers in Gerontology, No. 6* Ann Arbor: Institute of Gerontology, University of Michigan-Wayne State University.

Kaplan, H. B., and Pokorny, A. D. 1970. Aging and self-attitude: A conditional relationship. *Aging and Human Development*, 1, 241–250.

Kastenbaum, R., Derbin, V., Sabatini, P., and Artt, S. 1972. "The ages of me": Toward personal and interpersonal definitions of functional aging. *Aging and Human Development*, 3 (2), 197–211.

Kelly, E. L. 1955. Consistency of the adult personality. *American Psychologist*, 10, 659–681.

Keniston, K. 1970. Youth as a stage of life. *Am. Scholar.*, 39, 631–654.

Klein, R. 1972. Age, sex, and task difficulty as predictors of social conformity. *J. Geront.*, 27 (2), 229–236.

Kogan, N. 1973. Creativity and cognitive styles: A life-span perspective. *In*, P. B. Baltes and K. W. Schaie (eds.), *Life-Span Developmental Psychology: Personality and Socialization*, pp. 146–178. New York: Academic Press.

Kohlberg, L. 1964. Development of moral character and moral ideology. *In*, M. L. Hoffman and L. W. Hoffman (eds.), *Review of Child Development Research*, Vol. I, pp. 383–432. New York: Russell Sage Foundation.

Kohlberg, L. 1973. Continuities in childhood and adult moral development revisited. *In*, P. B. Baltes and K. W. Schaie (eds.), *Life-Span Developmental Psychology: Personality and Socialization*, pp. 179–204. New York: Academic Press.

Kuhlen, R. G. 1945. Age differences in personality during adult years. *Psych. Bull.*, 42, 333–358.

Kuhlen, R. G. 1959. Aging and adjustment. *In*, J. E. Birren (ed.), *Handbook of Aging and the Individual*, pp. 852–900. Chicago: University of Chicago Press.

Kuhlen, R. G. 1964. Personality change with age. *In*, P. Worchel and D. Byrne (eds.), *Personality Change*, pp. 524–555. New York: John Wiley.

Levin, S., and Kahana, R. J. 1967. *Psychodynamic Studies on Aging: Creativity, Reminiscing, and Dying.* New York: International Universities Press.

Levinson, D. J., Darrow, C. M., Klein, E. B., Levinson, M. H., and McKee, B. 1974. The psychosocial development of men in early adulthood and the mid-life transition. *In*, D. F. Ricks, A. Thomas, and M. Roff (eds.), *Life History Research in Psychopathology*, Vol. 3, pp. 243–258. Minneapolis: University of Minnesota Press.

Lieberman, M. A. 1971. Some issues in studying psychological predictors of survival. *In*, E. Palmore and F. C. Jeffers (eds.), *Prediction of Life-Span*, pp. 167–179. Lexington, Massachusetts: D. C. Heath.

Lieberman, M. A. 1975. Adaptive processes in late life. *In*, N. Datan and L. Ginsberg (eds.), *Life-Span Developmental Psychology: Normative Life Crises*. New York: Academic Press.

Lieberman, M. A., Cohler, B., and Welch, L. 1975 Ethnicity, coping and adaptation. (tentatively entitled) (in preparation)

Lieberman, M. A., and Coplan, A. S. 1969. Distance from death as a variable in the study of aging. *Developmental Psychology*, 2 (1), 71–84.

Lieberman, M. A. and Falk, J. 1971. The remembered past as a source of data for research on the life cycle. *Hum. Develop.*, 14, 132–141.

Livson, N. 1973. Developmental dimensions of personality: A life-span formulation. *In*, P. B. Baltes and K. W. Schaie (eds.), *Life-Span Developmental Psychology: Personality and Socialization*, pp. 97–122. New York: Academic Press.

Loevinger, J. 1966. The meaning and measurement of ego development. *American Psychologist*, 21, 195–206.

Looft, W. R. 1972. Egocentrism and social interaction across the life span. *Psych. Bull.*, 78, 73–92.

Looft, W. R. 1973. Socialization and personality throughout the life-span: An examination of contemporary psychological approaches. *In*, P. B. Baltes and K. W. Schaie (eds.), *Life-Span Developmental Psychology: Personality and Socialization*, pp. 26–52. New York: Academic Press.

Lopata, H. Z. 1973. *Widowhood in an American City*. Cambridge, Massachusetts: Schenkman.

Lowenthal, M. F. 1971. Intentionality: Toward a framework for the study of adaptation in adulthood. *Aging and Human Development*, 2, 79–95.

Lowenthal, M. F., and Chiriboga, D. 1973. Social stress and adaptation: Toward a life-course perspective. *In*, C. Eisdorfer and M. P. Lawton (eds.), *The Psychology of Adult Development and Aging*, pp. 281–310. Washington, D.C.: American Psychological Association.

Lowenthal, M. F., Thurnher, M., and Chiriboga, D. 1975. *Four Stages of Life: A Psychosocial Study of Women and Men Facing Transition*. San Francisco: Jossey-Bass.

Luborsky, L., and Schimek, J. 1964. Psychoanalytic theories of therapeutic and developmental change: Implications for assessment. *In*, P. Worchel and D. Byrne (eds.), *Personality Change*, pp. 73–99. New York: John Wiley.

Lynch, D. J. 1971. Future time perspective and impulsivity in old age. *Journal of Genetic Psychology*, 118, 245–252.

Maas, H. S., and Kuypers, J. A. 1975. *From Thirty to Seventy*. San Francisco: Jossey-Bass.

Maddi, S. R. 1972. *Personality Theories: A Comparative Analysis*. 2nd ed. Homewood, Illinois: Dorsey Press.

Maddi, S. R. 1975. Personal Communication.

Maslow, A. H. 1954. *Motivation and Personality*. New York: Harper & Row.

Mead, G. H. 1934. *Mind, Self, and Society*. Chicago: University of Chicago Press.

Mischel, W. 1973. Towards a cognitive social learning reconceptualization of personality. *Psych. Rev.*, 80, 252–283.

Murray, H. A. 1938. *Explorations in Personality*. New York: Oxford University Press.

Nesselroade, J. R., and Reese, H. W. (eds.) 1973. *Life-Span Developmental Psychology*. New York: Academic Press.

Neugarten, B. L. 1968. The awareness of middle age. *In*, B. L. Neugarten (ed.), *Middle Age and Aging*, pp. 93–98. Chicago: University of Chicago Press.

Neugarten, B. L. 1969. Continuities and discontinuities of psychological issues into adult life. *Hum. Develop.*, 12, 121–130.

Neugarten, B. L. 1970. Adaptation and the life cycle. *J. Geriat. Psychol.*, 4 (1), 71–87.

Neugarten, B. L. 1974. Age groups in American society and the rise of the young old. *Ann. Amer. Acad.*, pp. 187–198 (September).

Neugarten, B. L., and Associates. 1964. *Personality in Middle and Late Life*. New York: Atherton.

Neugarten, B. L., and Datan, N. 1973. Sociological perspectives on the life cycle. *In*, P. B. Baltes and K. W. Schaie (eds.), *Life-Span Developmental Psychology: Personality and Socialization*, pp. 53–69. New York: Academic Press.

Neugarten, B. L., and Datan, N. 1974. The middle years. *In*, S. Arieti (ed.), *American Handbook of Psychiatry*, pp. 592–608. New York: Basic Books.

Neugarten, B. L., Havighurst, R. J., and Tobin, S. S. 1968. Personality and patterns of aging. *In*, B. L. Neugarten (ed.), *Middle Age and Aging*, pp. 173–177. Chicago: University of Chicago Press.

Neugarten, B. L., Kraines, R., and Wood, V. 1965. Women in the middle years. Unpublished manuscript.

Neugarten, B. L., and Peterson, W. A. 1957. A study of the American age-grade system. *Proc. Int. Assoc. Gerontology, Fourth Congress, Vol. III*, pp. 497–502.

Noberini, M., and Neugarten, B. L. 1975. A follow-up study of adaptation in middle-aged women. Paper presented at the Annual Meeting of the Gerontological Society, Louisville.

Norbeck, E., Price-Williams, D., and McCord, W. M. (eds.) 1968. *The Study of Personality: An Interdisciplinary Apprasial*. New York: Holt, Rinehart and Winston.

Nuttall, R. L. 1973. How many dimensions of functional age are there? Paper presented at the 81st Annual Meeting of the American Psychological Association, Montreal.

Palmore, E. (ed.) 1974. *Normal Aging II: Reports from the Duke Longitudinal Studies, 1970-73.* Durham, North Carolina: Duke University Press.

Panel on Youth, President's Science Advisory Council. 1973. *Youth: Transition to Adulthood.* Washington, D.C.: Government Printing Office.

Parkes, C. M. 1964. Effects of bereavement on physical and mental health: A study of the medical records of widows. *Brit. Med. J.*, 2, 274-279.

Passini, F. T., and Norman, W. T. 1966. A universal conception of personality structure? *J. Pers. Soc. Psychol.*, 4, 44-49.

Peskin, H. 1972. Multiple prediction of adult psychological health and preadolescent and adolescent behavior. *J. Consult. Psychol.*, 38, 155-160.

Peters, G. R. 1971. Self-conception of the aged, age identification and aging. *Gerontologist*, 11, No. 4, Pt. 2, 69-73.

Piaget, J. 1950. *Psychology of Intelligence.* New York: Harcourt and Brace.

Reichard, S., Livson, F., and Petersen, P. G. 1962. *Aging and Personality.* New York: John Wiley.

Reichenbach, M., and Mathers, R. A. 1959. The place of time and aging in the natural sciences and scientific philosophy. *In*, J. E. Birren (ed.), *Handbook of Aging and the Individual*, pp. 43-80. Chicago: University of Chicago Press.

Riegel, K. F. 1959. Personality theory and aging. *In*, J. E. Birren (ed.), *Handbook of Aging and the Individual*, pp. 797-851. Chicago: University of Chicago Press.

Riegel, K. F. 1972. Time and change in the development of the individual and society. *In*, H. Reese (ed.), *Advances in Child Development and Behavior*, Vol. 7, pp. 81-113. New York: Academic Press.

Riegel, K. F. 1975. Adult life crises: Toward a dialectic theory of development. *In*, N. Datan and L. H. Ginsberg (eds.), *Life-Span Developmental Psychology: Normative Life Crises.* New York: Academic Press.

Riley, M. W., and Foner, A. 1968. *Aging and Society, Vol. I.* New York: Russell Sage Foundation.

Riley, M. W., Foner, A., Hess, B., and Toby, M. L. 1969. Socialization for the middle and later years. *In*, D. A. Goslin (ed.), *Handbook of Socialization Theory and Research.*, pp. 951-982. Chicago: Rand McNally.

Robins, M. B. 1969. Risk taking as a function of age, monetary incentive, and gain or loss. (University of Houston, Psychology.) *Dissertation Abstr.*, 30, 2898B.

Rogers, C. R. 1963. Actualizing tendency in relation to "motives" and to consciousness. *In*, M. R. Jones (ed.), *Nebraska Symposium on Motivation: 1963*, pp. 1-24. Lincoln: University of Nebraska Press.

Sarbin, T. R. 1964. Role theoretical interpretation of psychological change. *In*, P. Worchel and D. Byrne (eds.), *Personality Change*, pp. 176-219. New York: John Wiley.

Schaie, K. W., and Marquette, B. 1972. Personality in maturity and old age. *In*, R. M. Dreger (ed.), *Multivariate Personality Research: Contributions to the Understanding of Personality in Honor of Raymond B. Cattell*, pp. 612-632. Baton Rouge: Claitor's Publishing.

Schaie, K. W., and Parham, I. A. 1974. Social responsibility in adulthood: Ontogenetic and socio-cultural change. *J. Pers. Soc. Psychol.*, 30, 483-492.

Schaie, K. W., and Parham I. A. 1976. Stability of adult personality: Fact or fable? *J. of Pers. Soc. Psychol.*, 34, 146-158.

Sealy, A. P., and Cattell, R. B. 1965. Standard trends in personality development in men and women of 16 to 70 years, determined by 16 PF measurements. Paper read at British Psychological Society Conference, London.

Shanan, J. and Sharon, M. 1965. Personality and cognitive functioning of Israeli males during the middle years. *Hum. Develop.*, 8, 2-15.

Shweder, R. A. 1975. How relevant is an individual difference theory of personality? *J. Pers.*, in press.

Skinner, B. F. 1953. *Science and Human Behavior.* New York: Macmillan.

Slater, P. E., and Scarr, H. A. 1964. Personality in old age. *Genet. Psychol. Monogr.*, 70, 229-269.

Soddy, K. 1967. *Men in Middle Life.* Philadelphia: J. B. Lippincott.

Strauss, A. L. 1959. *Mirrors and Masks.* New York: The Free Press.

Terman, L. M., and Oden, M. H. 1959. *The Gifted Group at Mid-Life.* Stanford: Stanford University Press.

Thomae, H. 1970. Theory of aging and cognitive theory of personality. *Hum. Develop.*, 13, 1-16.

Thomae, H. (ed.) 1975. *Patterns of Aging: Findings from the Bonn Longitudinal Study of Aging.* Basel: S. Karger.

Thurnher, M. 1971. Values and goals in later middle age. Paper presented at the Annual Meeting of the Gerontological Society, Houston, Texas.

Vaillant, G. E., and McArthur, C. C. 1972. Natural history of male psychological health: The adult life cycle from 18-50. *Sem. Psychiat.*, 4 (4), 415-427.

Veroff, J., Atkinson, J. W., Feld, S. C., and Gurin, G. 1960. The use of thematic apperception to assess motivation in a nationwide interview study. *Psychol. Monogr.*, 74, 12.

Wachtel, P. L. 1973. Psychodynamics, behavior therapy, and the implacable experimenter: An inquiry into the consistency of personality. *J. Abnorm. Psychol.*, 82 (2), 324-334.

Watson, J. B. 1919. *Psychology from the Standpoint of a Behaviorist.* Philadelphia: J. B. Lippincott.

Welford, A. T., and Birren, J. E. (eds.) 1969. *Decision-Making and Age.* New York: S. Karger.

White, R. W. 1952. *Lives in Progress.* New York: Dryden.

White, R. W. (ed.) 1963. *The Study of Lives.* New York: Atherton Press.

Willems, E. P., and Raush, H. L. (eds.) 1969. *Naturalistic Viewpoints in Psychological Research.* New York: Holt, Rinehart, and Winston.

Wohlwill, J. F. 1973. *The Study of Behavioral Development.* New York: Academic Press.

Woodruff, D. S. and Birren, J. E. 1972. Age changes and cohort differences in personality. *Developmental Psychology*, 6 (2), 252–259.

Worchel, P., and Byrne, D. 1964. *Personality Change.* New York: John Wiley.

Zepelin, H. 1972. An investigation of age differences in men's dreams and thematic apperception fantasy. Unpublished Ph.D. dissertation, University of Chicago.

27
PSYCHOPATHOLOGY AND SOCIAL PATHOLOGY

Eric Pfeiffer

Duke University

INTRODUCTION

This chapter deals with the *common forms of intrapersonal and interpersonal pathology* observed in later life. Such *pathology is the result of failure to adapt* to the various crises, problems, and losses—including physiological, psychological, and social losses—frequenting this phase of the life cycle.

Adaptation in general may be defined as the process of meeting an individual's biological, psychological, and social needs, under recurrently changing circumstances. *Failure to adapt,* or pathology, may be defined as failure to meet the individual's basic needs, or meeting them only at the expense of pain, suffering, and disorder within the individual or within the environment.

Because the circumstances to which older individuals must adapt differ materially from those faced by young and middle-aged adults, aspects of the resultant failures in adaptation also differ from those observed in earlier life. This chapter will focus specifically on adaptive tasks and adaptive failures characteristic of later life.

The material in this section, and in fact throughout this chapter, draws heavily on clinical insight and observation and less on formal, methodologically impeccable, research. This is because well-controlled research on such

complex phenomena as "adaptation to old age" is still very sparse. Yet in order to comprehend the phenomena of social and psychological pathology, complex research strategies, informed by clinical insight, are needed. The work of Lowenthal and her associates in San Francisco over the past decade and a half is exemplary of the requisite integration between sound methodology and clinical knowledge (Lowenthal, 1964; Lowenthal, Berkman, Bissette, Buehler, Pierce, Robinson, and Iner, 1967; Simon, Lowenthal, and Epstein, 1970). The difficulty in controlling more than a few of the critical variables involved, the need for a multidisciplinary approach, and the need for continuity in such work by a relatively constant group of investigators over substantial periods of time (years) makes it understandable why we have more "good" research on, let us say, sensory losses than on overall adaptation to old age. The author of this chapter, himself a clinician first and a researcher second, hopes that the material presented here will not only be of immediate value to behavioral scientists but will contribute to framing appropriate research questions for future research.

Adaptive Tasks in Later Life

Adaptation to loss is one of the principal tasks facing individuals in later life. While losses can

650

occur at any age, they are ubiquitous in old age. Common losses include loss of spouse, loss of other social relationships, especially of work associates, loss of social roles, declines in income, decreases in mobility, declines in physical health, losses of opportunity for meaningful work and for recognition, to name only the most common ones (Busse and Pfeiffer, 1969, 1973). The task for the individual is twofold: (a) to replace *some* of the losses which have occurred with new relationships (e.g., new friends, remarriage); new roles (e.g., second and third careers, volunteer work); or retraining of lost capacities (e.g., speech therapy and/or physical therapy after a stroke); and (b) making do with less.

Another important task in late life is an *identity review.* Butler (1963, 1974) has spoken of this as a life review. Erikson (1959) has examined this task under the heading of "Integrity and the Life Cycle." Clinicians have long recognized that many if not most older persons engage in an evaluative backward glance at their lives, weighing their accomplishments and failures, their satisfactions and disappointments, seeking to delineate a final identity as they approach death. The task to be accomplished here is to delineate an identity which integrates the diverse elements of an individual's life and allows him to come to a reasonably positive view of his life's worth. Failing this, overt psychopathology is likely to manifest itself.

Another major task facing aging individuals is to *remain active* in order to *retain function.* The areas of function with which we are particulary concerned are the maintenance of physical activity, of social interaction, of intellectual and emotional stimulation and of self-care capacity. The various losses and declines already referred to make it likely that without specific efforts to the contrary, function will decline. Studies of successfully aging individuals (Pfeiffer, 1974a, 1975a) indicate that such persons characteristically maintain regular and vigorous physical activities, extensive social contacts, and pursue intellectually and emotionally stimulating activities. Decrease of these functions in this age period through disuse can lead to unnecessary physical limitations, social isolation, disorientation, and apathy.

Adaptive Processes in Later Life: Preponderant Use of Simple Defense Mechanisms

As the human infant grows from birth to maturity, an increasingly complex series of adaptative or defensive mechanisms become available to him, following an age-related time schedule in a more or less regular sequence, with some obvious variation for each individual in this basic timetable. Some of these adaptive or defensive mechanisms are available during the first year of life, others become available in the third or fourth or fifth or sixth year of life, while still others have to await the full physiological development of the brain and do not make their appearance until approximately age 12 or 13.

Typical of year-one adaptations to adverse circumstances are what Engel (1962) has called the "primary affects of unpleasure," namely anxiety and depression-withdrawal. Also typical of year-one and year-two adaptive mechanisms are denial, projection, and somatization (A. Freud, 1946). Some of the mechanisms available to 4 and 5 year olds are reaction formation, identification with the aggressor, etc., while such defensive mechanisms as intellectualization and rationalization do not generally become available until about 13 (Hartmann, 1958, 1964; Rapaport, 1960; Vaillant, 1971).

While some older persons continue to use the entire range of adaptive mechanisms, many return to the use of more primitive, year-one and year-two types of defense mechanisms. Thus, unmodified anxiety, depression-withdrawal, projection, somatization, and denial are the preponderant mechanisms used in this age group. Moreover in those instances where failure of adaptation has occurred, the mechanisms just outlined are used with great regularity. In fact, the preponderant use of these mechanisms shapes and forms the specific clinical syndromes seen typically in the later years.

Viewed from the point of view of the phenomenology of the clinical syndromes, clinical manifestations rather than psychodynamics, these observations can be couched in somewhat different terms. *The psychiatric syndromes characteristic of old age* are *a mere handful of relatively simple forms of psychopathology,* including prominently among them depressive reactions, hypochondriasis, paranoid reactions, and transient situational disturbances as well as chronic anxiety states. In fact, the syndromes just outlined, making use of these relatively simple defensive mechanisms, account for the vast majority of psychopathology that is not based on brain disease or loss of brain tissue functioning (Busse, 1961; Feigenbaum, 1970; Peak, Polansky and Altholz, 1971). Other psychiatric syndromes do occur in old age, either *de novo* or as continuations of psychopathology from earlier phases of life. But the syndromes just outlined and to be described in detail below constitute the prevalent modes of maladaptation in this life period.

Epidemiology of Psychopathology in Later Life

The science of epidemiology as it relates to psychological disorders in the later years is not yet well advanced. As Redick, Kramer and Taube (1973) point out, there are important unsolved problems in regard to standardization of cases finding techniques, of differential diagnostic techniques, and of measuring the severity of disturbance with any degree of reliability. Nevertheless valuable information has been gained through a variety of epidemiological studies over the past two decades in regard to this question.

Studies in regard to the total amount of psychological disturbance in the later years fall essentially into three categories: (1) those seeking to measure the existence of any, even mild, psychiatric disorders in this age group; (2) those measuring only the prevalence of "significant" or at least "moderate" degrees of psychiatric disturbances; (3) those studies assessing only the prevalence of mental disorder where the patient is actually being seen in an appropriate diagnostic or treatment facility. It is obvious that the findings have been appropriately different for each of these three types of studies.

Representative of the first category of epidemiological study are the studies by Leighton, Harding, Macklin, Macmillan, and Leighton, (1963). Using criteria of even "mild"

emotional disturbance, a figure of from 50 percent to 60 percent emerges. This is similar to the kinds of figures found in the Midtown study by Srole, Langner, Michael, Opler, and Rennie, (1962). These studies indicate no remarkable increase with advancing age of the total number of persons with *any* degree of emotional disorder. They are essentially silent on the question of an increase of the more substantial or severe psychiatric disorders.

Among studies seeking to assess the prevalence of psychopathology of at least moderate severity are those of Pasamanick (1962) in Baltimore; of Lowenthal, Berkman *et al.*, (1967) in San Francisco, of Kay, Beamish, and Roth (1964) in New Castle, Great Britain, of Nielsen (1962) in Samso, Sweden, and of Pfeiffer (1973) in Durham County, North Carolina. Data from these studies all fall within a rather narrow range of from 12 percent to 26 percent with moderate or severe psychopathology. The present author's synthesis from these various studies in diverse geographies is that *approximately 15 percent of the elderly population in the United States suffer from significant, substantial, or at least moderate psychopathology.*

The studies of Redick, Kramer, and Taube (1973) and of Kramer, Taube, and Redick (1973) focus primarily on those elderly persons actually receiving mental health services. These figures indicate that at the time of the 1970 Census approximately 125,000 persons aged 65 and over were hospitalized in psychiatric hospitals, primarily in state and county mental hospitals, with smaller numbers in V.A. and private psychiatric hospitals. Nearly 700,000 persons aged 65 and over were at the same time residents in nursing homes. It has been estimated that fully 70 percent and 80 percent of aged nursing home residents suffer from moderately severe or severe mental disorders (Whanger, 1973). This figure includes primary mental disorders or mental disorders complicating physical illnesses. Smaller proportions (60 percent) of the some 500,000 elderly residing in old age homes and small family care homes also are significantly mentally impaired (Whanger, 1973). Thus approximately 900,000 to 1,000,000 elderly persons residing in various kinds of institutional settings suffer from significant mental disorders. It should be pointed out, however, that *active treatment programs* for mental disorders exist thus far only in some state mental hospitals, and they are actually *rare* in nursing homes and old age homes. Thus the majority of institutionalized elderly with mental disorders are not so much "receiving" mental health services as they are "receiving" institutional care, primarily social and custodial care.

Factors which relate to the prevalence of psychiatric disorder in old age have been studied by a number of investigators. Advanced age is clearly associated with a higher incidence of psychopathology. This is particularly noticeable beyond age 75 and dramatically noticeable beyond age 80 (Pfeiffer, 1973). Poor physical health is associated with a higher prevalence of psychopathology, according to many investigators including Anderson and Davidson (1975), Busse (1968), Kay and Roth (1955), and Post (1969). Among the various marital states, being married is associated with the lowest incidence of psychopathology, with increasing prevalence among the widowed, but with still higher prevalences among the separated and divorced (Pfeiffer, 1973).

Functional Psychiatric Disorders *Vs.* Organic Brain Syndromes

In the next two sections of this chapter we will focus on specific forms of psychopathology common in later life. The second part of this chapter will deal with those failures in adaptation occurring *despite intact brain functioning*. The third part will deal with those disorders occurring *because of impaired brain function*. While both types of disorder are relatively common in old age and therefore can coexist it is nevertheless profitable to discuss the two types of syndromes separately. Functional psychiatric disorders and organic brain syndromes demand differing diagnostic techniques and call for differing types of intervention.

The final part of this chapter will deal with social pathologies, resulting from interpersonal difficulties or from an impoverished social environment.

FUNCTIONAL PSYCHIATRIC DISORDERS

Depression

Affective disturbances, particularly depressions, are the most frequent *functional* psychiatric disorders in the later years (Bergman, in press; Busse, 1961; Feigenbaum, 1970; Peak, Polansky, and Altholz, 1971; Tongas and Gibson, 1969). Depressions in this age group can vary greatly in duration and in degree. Many elderly persons experience fleeting episodes of saddened affect, loss of energy, and short-lived lack of interest, oftentimes in response to some adverse life situation or loss. On the other hand more severe and more lasting depressive reactions are experienced by substantially fewer elderly persons, again in response to significant losses in their lives or, more rarely, without recognizable precipitating circumstance. Depressive reactions basically are pathological responses to loss.

The Phenomenology of Depression. Depressions of significant degree and duration have both psychological as well as physical manifestations (Beck, 1967; Grinker, Miller, Salschin, Nunn, and Nunnally, 1961; Pfeiffer, 1968). The psychological characteristics of depression include abject and painful sadness, generalized withdrawal of interest and inhibition of activity, and a pervasive pessimism, manifesting itself as diminished self-esteem and by a gloomy evaluation of one's future and present situation. In addition, depressed patients often experience difficulty in making decisions, even minor ones, and their thought processes and speech are significantly slowed down as are their physical movements. Even the dream content of depressed patients is pervaded by depressive affect. Depressed patients experience vivid dreams of being lost and lonely in isolated, frightening, desolate places. They often see themselves in their dreams as crying out for help, with no one responding.

The physical symptoms of depression are also prominent. In fact, in many elderly patients they may be the first manifestation of a depressive condition. Many older persons *prefer* to mention their physical rather than their psychological symptoms. The prominent physical signs of depression include loss of appetite, significant weight loss, severe fatigue, especially fatigue early in the morning , sleeplessness, particularly early morning awakening, constipation, or more rarely diarrhea. Obviously this group of symptoms could be associated with significant physical illnesses such as carcinoma, congestive heart failure, or a number of other somatic illnesses. Thus a thorough medical *and* psychological evaluation is indicated in someone expressing this set of symptoms. Unfortunately, oftentimes an exploration of the feeling state of the patient is not carried out until it is apparent that no clear-cut physical cause for these symptoms exists.

While the above mentioned symptoms are the *core* symptoms of depressive reactions, other associated symptoms may be even more prominent than the basic depressive symptomatology in some patients. Oftentimes a considerable amount of tension and anxiety is associated with the depressive affect. Tremulousness or even agitation may be present. There can be prominent self-accusations and feelings of guilt regarding past transgressions which, to an objective observer, would appear to be only relatively minor "offenses." Weeping may be prominent, although extremely severely depressed persons may be totally unable to cry, even though they "feel" like crying.

The most characteristic feature of all depressive disorders is that they are episodic in nature. Generally they occur in persons who have previously gotten along reasonably well, without severe degrees of pathology, other than perhaps a previous episode of depression.

An interesting variant of the basic depressive reaction is what has been called a "depressive equivalent" (Gallemore and Wilson, 1969; Kennedy and Wiesel, 1946; Pfeiffer, 1971). The typical patient manifesting this disorder is a man or a woman in late life who complains of severe pain, most commonly a backache, a headache, or neckache. The pain may have been present for weeks or months, having developed either gradually or fairly suddenly. Typically the patient has been in good health previously and generally has been quite successful in his

past activities. Such patients often give a history of self-medication with aspirin or other analgesics, and some have become addicted to more major pain-killing medication. Others begin to abuse alcohol. Such patients may *appear* depressed. However, they generally deny feeling sad or depressed. In fact they generally deny adverse circumstances or losses which might constitute a basis for depression. Such patients share with other depressed patients the basic physical signs of depression, such as low energy, loss of appetite, weight loss, sleep disturbance, and constipation. It is only in relationship to the pain which they are experiencing that they may give vent to feelings of discouragement.

It is not entirely clear why some patients develop depressive equivalents rather than overt depressive reactions. In some patients there is a past history of earlier physical illness or injury or a model of such symptomatology among relatives. In addition such patients seem to be generally unable to admit to any fault within themselves, regarding symptoms of emotional disorder as "moral weakness."

Suicide in Old Age. Suicidal ideas often accompany severe depressive illness. They may take the form of relatively passive wishes for death, or they may be the starting point for an active plan to commit suicide. They must be taken very seriously when they occur in older persons. In 1970, the last year for which complete data are available, 23,480 persons (16,629 men and 6,851 women) committed suicide in the United States. Of these 7,399 (4,171 men and 3,228 women) or *3.15 percent were 65 years of age or older.* At the time of the 1970 census the population of the entire U. S. population aged 65 and over was only 9.9 percent. Thus suicide among the elderly occurred at rates *more than triple* of those experienced in the general population (U.S. Public Health Service, 1974).

The increasing risk of suicide with advancing age, especially among men, is clearly demonstrated in Table 1. Whereas the rate of suicide for the entire U.S. population in 1970 was 11.6 percent per 100,000, it was 36.9 percent per 100,000 for persons 65 years of age and older (U.S. Public Health Service, 1974).

TABLE 1. SUICIDE RATES IN THE U.S. FOR 1970 BY AGE, SEX, AND RACE.

Age range	White males	White females	Nonwhite males	Nonwhite females
15–19	9.4	2.9	5.4	2.9
20–24	19.3	5.7	19.4	5.5
25–29	19.8	8.6	20.1	6.0
30–34	20.0	9.5	19.4	5.6
35–39	21.9	12.2	13.9	4.5
40–44	24.6	13.8	11.4	4.1
45–49	28.2	13.5	16.5	4.0
50–54	30.9	13.5	11.3	5.1
55–59	34.9	13.1	12.3	1.8
60–64	35.0	11.5	8.4	2.8
65–69	37.4	9.4	11.5	3.2
70–74	40.4	9.7	8.2	3.9
75–79	42.2	7.3	5.7	3.1
80–84	51.4	7.2	22.9	3.2
85–plus	45.8	5.8	12.6	6.4

Source: *Vital Statistics of the United States, 1970 Volume II, Mortality, Part A.* Rockville, Maryland: U.S. Public Health Service, 1974.

Evidence from research studies indicates that the majority of older persons committing suicide have been depressed (Gardner, Bahn, and Mach, 1963; Robins, Gassner, Kayes, Wilkinson, and Murphy, 1959). A smaller fraction is made up of persons who have used alcohol to excess. A still smaller fraction is made up of persons with organic brain syndrome while a few percent of those committing suicide suffer from an untreatable terminal illness.

While many more young persons attempt than commit suicide (the ratio has been estimated at about 7:1), the number of old people attempting suicide is roughly the same as the number actually committing suicide (Batchelor and Napier, 1953; Benson and Brodie, 1975; Dublin, 1963; O'Neal, Robins and Schmidt, 1965). Among younger persons suicide attempts often represent an expression of hostility toward someone or an attempt to bring someone to terms. These are rarely the motivations for attempted suicide in old age. Rather, when an old person attempts suicide, he almost always fully intends to die. Rescue from a suicide attempt in old age is often accidental or due to poor planning of the attempt. Persons attempting suicide in old age should be hospi-

talized. The psychiatric diagnoses of those attempting suicide are similar to diagnoses of those actually committing suicide, a finding which is in contrast to young attempters who are diagnosed as having neurotic personalities or transient situational reactions.

Manic Reactions

Although depressive reactions predominate among the affective disturbances in later life, as they do in younger years, manic reactions occur as well. For instance in Roth's (1955) study of 220 patients hospitalized for affective disorders, 13 percent had predominately manic symptomatology. Clinically, manic reactions are in many ways a direct mirror image of depressive reactions. The patient is elated ("I feel like a million bucks"), optimistic, and feels all-powerful. Speech is rapid. Hyperactivity may be present. In some older manic patients the generally observed joviality is replaced by a general irritability, punctuated by short outbursts of anger or even of paranoid thinking. There may also be short periods of sadness or weeping interspersed among the generally euphoric or dysphoric affect. But these will suddenly give way to flights into grandiosity or belligerency.

Until the introduction of lithium carbonate for the treatment of mania, the prognosis for mania in old age was generally regarded as poor. In the last decade, considerable experience have been gained with lithium carbonate in the treatment of manic states (Goodwin, Murphy, and Bunney, 1969; Maggs, 1963; Schou, Juel-Nielsen, and Stoomgran, 1954). Special precautions must be taken to follow the electrolyte picture and the serum level of lithium in aged patients, since fluid balance may be more easily upset in such patients with marginal cardiac or renal status (Davis, Fann, El-Yousef, and Janowsky, 1973; Bressler and Palmer, 1974). In general substantially lower doses of lithium carbonate may be needed for elderly patients than for young or middle-aged adults. If cardiac, renal, or electrolyte status contraindicates the use of lithium carbonate, the phenothiazines may be of some help in controlling the overt symptomatology of manic episodes. However they are less effective in bringing about a termination of the manic episode (Platman, 1970; Prien, Caffey, and Keltt, 1972).

Paranoid Reactions

Following depressive reactions, paranoid reactions are probably the most common psychiatric disturbance in old age. Paranoia is the attribution to other people of motivations which do not in fact exist (Fish, 1959; Post, 1966). Paranoid patients are suspicious of persons and events around them and they often construct faulty, that is, unrealistic explanations of events which happen to them.

In younger persons paranoid ideas are often indicative of severe psychiatric disturbance, particularly of schizophrenia. The paranoid reactions of old age are less serious in terms of their implications, and they can be more readily explained. While the paranoid ideas of younger persons often concern themselves with powerful, mysterious, far-away influences, such as rays from another planet, messages for God, persecution by the FBI, the CIA, or more recently the Symbionese Liberation Army, the paranoid ideas of older people are often much more "down home." This observation is related to the etiology of paranoid ideas in elderly persons. In this age period it is primarily an effort to "fill in the blank spaces" in the cognitive map of the individual regarding his environment. It is therefore not surprising to note that paranoid ideas are substantially more common in persons with various kinds of sensory deficits, particularly hearing losses, but also in persons with decreased visual capacity and in persons with decreased intellectual capacity (Eisdorfer, 1960: Houston and Royse, 1954; Retterstol, 1966). Rather typically, such an elderly person might misplace her glasses or her wallet, or some other valued or needed possession, and then accuse those around her of stealing them. Or, a woman might notice that she has been receiving less and less mail. Rather than coming up with the explanation that she was simply writing fewer letters and was involved in fewer business transactions, she instead comes to the conclusion that the postman is stealing the mail from her. One elderly lady quite regularly would call the police on washday to report that her neighbors were putting lint in her laundry. Another accusation might be that some one is trying to poison the person. Changes in taste perception occur in old age and do contribute to making foods taste different now than they did earlier in life. If some hostility has occurred recently between the older person and the provider of food, then a "logical" conclusion might be that someone is in fact trying to poison the person. The unfortunate feature of paranoid reactions, even though they are in a sense "adaptive," is that their occurrence tends to alienate other persons, particularly care providers. Thus a live-in companion or nurse will sometimes quit after she has been accused by the paranoid patient of stealing from her.

Remarkably, paranoid reactions in old age are quite responsive to appropriate treatment and intervention. While treatment in general is discussed elsewhere, the basic principles of treatment of paranoid reactions grow out of an understanding of their etiology. Such understanding dictates the correction of sensory or cognitive deficits; the provision of a relatively stable, friendly, familiar environment; and the use of the so-called major tranquilizers, generally in small doses.

Since paranoid patients are suspicious of many things, they are suspicious also of medication given to them. Perhaps 60 percent of drug dosages given to paranoid patients in pill form are never taken. For this reason the drugs mentioned above should be administered to elderly paranoid patients only in liquid or concentrate form to assure that the patient actually receives the medication prescribed. In a patient who is sufficiently suspicious or sufficiently forgetful to render him unable to take medication by himself, a family member or professional health care personnel may need to administer such medication.

Hypochondriasis

Hypochondriasis is probably the next most frequent functional psychiatric disorder in the later years, behind depressive and paranoid reactions. It is substantially more frequent among older women than men, and it seems to increase in frequency with advancing age (Earley and von Mering, 1969).

Hypochondriasis is characterized by excessive preoccupation with one's bodily functioning or by the concern that one has one or more specific diseases or diseased organ systems, in the absence of significant physical pathology. Obviously, however, any older person complaining of physical symptoms deserves a thorough physical evaluation. The diagnosis of hypochondriasis cannot be made on the basis of a psychiatric examination alone nor can it be made on the basis of a negative physical examination. It must instead be made on the basis of essentially negative physical findings *and* specific psychological observations.

Observations relevant to the diagnosis of hypochondriasis is an intensive preoccupation with bodily functioning, a symptom which tends to interfere with the individual's interpersonal interactions, within his own family as well as outside of it. This preoccupation tends to become intense in the presence of a nurse or physician who might potentially take remedial action in regard to these symptoms. The interactional world has become unrewarding and hostile for the hypochondriacal patient, and he or she has turned instead towards his or her own body as an interesting theater for observation. It is as though the hypochondriacal person were intensely listening to every skipped heart beat, every muscle twitch, every skin sensation. The result is a long list of physical symptoms and complaints, often extending to every organ.

Another major characteristic of hypochondriacal patients is their resistance to and resentment of any attempt on the part of the clinician to interpret any of their symptoms as a sign of emotional stress or psychological disorder. In fact they generally resist discussion of psychological factors in their own life situation, quickly returning to a reiteration of their physical symptomatology. They have been described as "not psychologically minded."

Psychodynamics of Hypochondriasis. The syndrome of hypochondriasis can best be understood as a psychiatric maladaptation in which the form of the maladaptation is determined by the patient's unwillingness or inability to acknowledge psychological distress. The basic message of a hypochondriacal patient is that he is in difficulty, that he is sick, and in need of medical care. Being physically ill is a highly acceptable excuse for nonperformance in our society. Nonperformance as a result of emotional difficulties is far less acceptable or not acceptable at all by some individuals. The hypochondriacal patient has made an unconscious choice to present himself as physically, not as emotionally ill. He seeks help as someone physically disabled not as someone emotionally disturbed. Efforts aimed at restructuring the symptomatology of the hypochondriacal patient from physical symptoms to psychological symptoms are consequently doomed to failure. Not even the cleverest explanations of how emotional "tensions" and "anxiety" can cause physical symptoms through causing muscular tension, etc., no matter how valid they may in fact be, will be found to be acceptable by the hypochondriacal patient. He will instead feel rejected and misunderstood. To the hypochondriacal patient, the statement by a physician, following a negative physical exam, "Mrs. Jones, I have good news for you. There is nothing wrong with you," is not in fact good, but bad news. For all practical purposes it means that the physician will not assume the care of the patient but will instead send her away, empty-handed. Again, while treatment will be discussed elsewhere a correct understanding of the patient's psychodynamics will lead the clinician to accept the patient *as ill* and *as someone in need of care.*

Psychological Testing. The one psychological test which has been found useful in the hands of clinicians in differentiating hypochondriasis from other psychiatric disorders has been the Minnesota Multiphasic Personality Inventory (MMPI). In fact, a number of authors have described a rather classical hypochondriasis pattern, showing a peaking on the *Hs* scale of the MMPI (Fowler and Athey, 1971; Welsh and Dahlstrom, 1956). However, the MMPI is a lengthy test form, consisting of 566 items and requiring approximately 2½ hours for its completion. Often elderly persons are not able to complete such lengthy forms, and a shorter version of this scale would obviously be desirable. A shortened version of the MMPI, the Mini-Mult, is offered by Kincannon (1968). This is a 71-item test in which the items chosen are representative of the content clusters tapped by the three standard validity and eight clinical MMPI scales. The ability of this item pool to predict the standard scale scores was tested, and it was found that there was an estimated 9 percent loss in reliability and a 14 percent loss in correspondence in comparison with the readministration of the standard form. Because of the considerable advantages of a shorter test with an aging population, considerable use is being made of this test in clinical programs.

Adjustment Reactions of Late Life

In response to adverse circumstances or to specific traumatic events, such as the loss of a loved one or an unforeseen change in living arrangements, some older individuals experience transient or more enduring adjustment reactions characterized by a variety of emotional and physical disturbances, the most prominent of which is anxiety, with all its psychological and physiological components. Anxiety has already been mentioned above as one of the principal affects of unpleasure, occurring in response to adverse circumstances. In fact, most of the defense mechanisms used are transformations of this primary affect of unpleasure into somewhat more tolerable affects and responses. Many of the adjustment reactions of late life are unmodified anxiety responses to traumatic events. Fear sometimes to the point of panic, perplexity, emotional lability, tearfulness, and feelings of helplessness, dominates the psychological symptomatology. Tremulousness, muscular tension, a rapid heart rate, subjective feelings of shortness of breath, epigastric discomfort, and disturbed sleep characterize the physical side of this syndrome.

There is generally considerable pressure of speech and a great need to *repeatedly* recount the disturbing events. Such recountings are often punctuated by outcries of woe and distress and by outbreaks of weeping or moaning. Ven-

tilation of these events is in fact useful, especially in the presence of an empathic listener who can not only clarify the nature and the effect of the recent events but who can also begin to look at alternative methods of coping with the recent changes. When ventilation, clarification, and examination of alternative strategies alone is not enough to restore equilibrium, then the use of the so called minor tranquilizers and sedatives *on a temporary basis* (for 24 hours up to 3 or 4 days) as well as the use of nighttime hypnotics, again *on a temporary basis*, is warranted.

These episodes, however, should not become starting points for chronic medication use, since the drugs in question have undesirable characteristics for the older patients when they are used continuously. These include tolerance and psychological and physical dependence, as they do in younger patients. But equally or more important, the undesirable effects of the minor tranquilizers, when used continuously in older patients, can include a chronic delirium, with decreased memory capacity and cognitive functioning, drowsiness and loss of equilibrium, with its attendant increase in accident rate.

Used over the short run, however, they are a powerful tool to cut short the temporary upset of many older individuals, permitting their greater participation in problem solving and preventing the development of more chronic anxiety states or the development of one of the other more enduring syndromes already discussed above.

Alcoholism

Acute and chronic alcoholism is also not uncommon in old age, both in community mental health centers, psychiatric out-patient clinics, and in psychiatric hospitals generally, but especially in state mental hospitals (Gaitz and Baer, 1971; Simon, Epstein, and Reynolds, 1968; Redick, Kramer, and Taube, 1973; Whittier and Korenyi, 1961). For the most part these are individuals who have been chronic abusers of alcohol even in their younger years and who are simply continuing to abuse the product. But they also include a few new recruits to alcohol abuse. Sometimes there are other underlying psychiatric disturbances, such as a depressive illness or chronic anxiety. In such instances the individual is essentially trying to treat his basic psychiatric disturbance, using alcohol as an antidepressant or tranquilizer. Chronic alcohol abuse can result in chronic organic brain syndromes of the Korsakoff's type.

In general the symptomatology and other characteristics including appropriate treatment for chronic alcohol abusers is not substantially different in older alcoholics than it is in younger ones, with the exception that many older alcoholics have a number of coexisting physical disorders such as congestive heart failure, hypertension, emphysema, or other disabling diseases. Alcoholic intoxication and alcohol withdrawal syndromes can have more serious life threatening effects in such elderly persons.

Sleep Disturbances

Many elderly persons complain of a variety of sleep disturbances. These include difficulty in falling asleep, insufficient total sleep, restless sleep, and early awakening. The complaint of an older person sleeping too much is also heard occasionally; usually, however, it is the concern of relatives rather than of patients. Many older patients and their relatives are concerned that poor sleep will lead to serious illness.

It is important to differentiate between changes in sleep pattern which are a concomitant of normal aging and those sleep disturbances which are a manifestation of emotional or psychiatric disturbance. Although variations and disorders of sleep and activity during sleep have always been of considerable importance to clinicians, until recently there was little information of clinical significance. Most clinicians are now aware that there are four major stages of sleep and that stage 1, REM (rapid eye movement) sleep is a stage of sleep in which dreams are most likely to occur. It is generally known that there are four to five REM episodes during a night's sleep (Dement and Kleitman, 1957; Kleitman, 1963). It is also generally known that sleep patterns and sleep requirements change throughout the life span. A newborn infant sleeps between 16 and 17 hours a day. Within the first 6 months in most infants there is a gradual decline, but at least 12 hours is still the usual pattern. By age 3, 10 hours at night is the common rule, and the necessity for daytime naps is decreasing. As one moves into young adulthood and, in particular, into the middle and the later years, there are some individuals who claim an increased need for sleep and some a decrease. It is doubtful than any elderly person in reasonably good health requires more than 8 to 9 hours of sleep per night.

In elderly subjects there are some important changes in patterns of sleeping. Stage 4 sleep, that is, deep sleep, virtually disappears, and older people require a longer period to fall asleep (Kahn and Fisher, 1969; Kales, Beall, and Berger, 1968). Their sleep is lighter, with more frequent awakenings. Feinberg has recently reported that these normal aging changes are still more pronounced in persons with significant organic brain disease (Feinberg, Braun, and Schulman, 1969). Of still greater importance, perhaps, is the fact that normal aging persons distribute their sleep somewhat differently across the 24-hour cycle, including several cat naps of 15 to 60 minutes several times during the daytime hours. Clinicians should be aware that this changed sleep pattern of more frequent awakenings, less deep sleep, and several naps during the daytime is the normal sleep pattern for aging persons and that this normal pattern should not be disturbed through the regular use of sleeping medication to keep the person asleep 8 hours throughout the night or by preventing the elderly person from taking short naps during the daytime hours.

Several psychiatric disturbances already discussed, in particular severe depressive reactions and transient situational reactions, are characterized by pronounced sleep difficulty. In such instances effective nighttime hypnotics should be employed as a temporary measure to produce adequate sleep for the disturbed elderly persons, but the principal effort should be directed at resolving the basic underlying psychiatric disturbance.

Chronic use of nighttime hypnotics can have many undesirable effects, including tolerance to the drug and physical dependence and daytime retention of some of the drug, leading to day-time delirium, drowsiness, decrease in mental alertness, and/or loss of equilibrium, similar to that seen with chronic minor tranquilizer or sedative use. Older persons do not excrete these drugs as well as younger persons, and the older brain is more easily subject to delirium from sedative and hypnotic drugs. Sleeping medications should therefore be used only on a temporary basis.

Schizophrenics Grown Old in the State Hospital

There are currently residing in state mental hospitals, and to a lesser degree in nursing homes, substantial numbers of aged persons who were diagnosed as schizophrenic earlier on in life, who have spent much of their lives in institutions and also have grown old in institutions (Redick, Kramer, and Taube, 1973). These individuals, while retaining *some* schizophrenic symptomatology, are primarily manifesting the devastating impact of long-term custodial care in institutions. These individuals are not so much manifesting "schizophrenia" in old age but rather are a documentary of an era in psychiatry which had few active treatment programs to offer to schizophrenic patients. It is likely that fewer patients will be retained in mental hospitals for such inordinately long periods of time and that active treatment programs earlier in life will restore them to good mental functioning before they reach old age.

ORGANIC BRAIN SYNDROMES

In the population 65 years of age and older approximately half of all persons with significant mental impairments have organic brain syndromes due to brain cell death or brain cell malfunction (Bergman, in press; Kramer, Taube, and Redick, 1973; Redick, Kramer and Taube, 1973). The proportion with organic brain syndromes is somewhat higher in certain settings, such as in nursing homes and some long-term care V.A. facilities, and somewhat lower than 50 percent in psychiatric outpatient clinics and private mental hospitals (Peak,

1973; Redick, Kramer, and Taube, 1973; Whanger, 1973). However, with each increasing age period beyond age 65 the proportion of the mentally impaired suffering from organic brain syndromes increases, due to a marked increase, in the prevalence *rate* of organic brain syndromes (Kramer, Taube, and Redick, 1973; Riley and Foner, 1968).

Clinical Manifestations of Organic Brain Syndromes

The specific clinical manifestations of organic brain syndromes vary little with the specific cause of brain cell death or brain cell impairment. They vary greatly, however, with the extent of brain impairment, the rapidity of onset, the personality resources of the individual and the quality of the surrounding environment.

While a great variety of psychiatric symptoms, such as anxiety, depression, visual and auditory hallucinations, delusions, emotional lability, outbursts of anger, violent behavior, withdrawal, or euphoria, *may be associated* with organic brain syndromes, *none* of the above are specifically indicative of the presence of organic brain impairment. They may occur in its presence as well as in its absence.

The constellation of symptoms pathognomonic of organic brain disease are a variety of disturbances of intellectual and cognitive function. These specifically include impairments of ability to remain oriented to one's environment, of short-and long-term memory, of visual-motor coordination, of learning and retaining spatial arrangements, of ability to abstract, to change sets, and to assimilate new information, and of ability to carry out sequential tasks (such as serial mathematical tasks or the correct sequencing of events in the individual's personal history).

When the onset is gradual and when the defect is mild, only the highest intellectual functions may be impaired; that is, only the ability to abstract, to change set, and to assimilate new information may be affected. In fact, these cognitive symptoms may not be the first to make their appearance. Rather a group of rather ill-defined emotional or behavioral changes may be first to appear such as depression, loss of interest, fatigue, listlessness, or agitation. Other signs may be irritability, social withdrawal, emotional outbursts, irregular work attendance, and a change in behavioral standards. These changes are obviously not at all specific and may result in an initial diagnosis of some form of personality change or neurotic disorder, depending on which behavioral changes predominate. At times these changes are present for months or years before anyone in the patient's surroundings notices any clear-cut memory deficit, confusion, or disorientation. Nevertheless even at this stage, careful mental status examination or formal psychological testing may reveal impairment of abstraction, attention, concentration, retention of recently learned material, and particularly retention and reproduction of geometric designs involving visual-motor coordination (Bender-Gestalt test).

As deficit increases, gross disorientation for time and place, forgetting of names and telephone numbers, and general memory gaps begin to appear. The patient may now appear confused, bewildered, and perplexed. He will begin to lose his way, especially in new surroundings, but as the deficit advances, he may also begin to get lost in familiar neighborhoods or settings.

With still greater severity not only recent memories, particularly memories for time sequences, but highly learned material from earlier life also begins to disappear. Severely demented persons may no longer be able to recall the names of their own children, their previous occupation, their previous place of residence, their birthday, or their age.

In extremely advanced dementia speech may become difficult to understand, garbled, and repetitive so that no successful communication can go on. Motor control, too, may become impaired. The patient may no longer be able to feed himself, dress himself, or go to the toilet in time. Ultimately the patient may proceed to a stage of namelessness in which he either no longer knows his own name or no longer responds to his own name. Knowledge of one's own name is one of the most highly overlearned tasks and one of the last intellectual abilities to disappear, being seen only in the most severe

forms of organic brain deficit. Obviously such individuals must now be cared for by others and can no longer function independently.

With still greater severity of brain deficit the patient will lapse into coma, if the onset is rapid. Or he will become bedridden, with loss of sphincter control, and will become subject to decubitus ulcers and local or systemic infections, if the progress of brain impairment is slow.

A Short Portable Mental Status Questionnaire for the Assessment of Organic Brain Deficits in Elderly Patients

Clinicians whose practice includes any significant number of elderly persons need a short, portable, reliable, and valid instrument to determine the presence and degree of intellectual impairment. Such an instrument is now available in the form of a 10-question mental status questionnaire, standardized on a population of some 1,000 elderly persons and validated on a clinical population of mentally impaired elderly (Pfeiffer, 1975a). Standards have been developed which take into consideration the individual's educational attainment.

The test may be reliably readministered over intervals of time. Scores on the SPMSQ have distinct implications for patient management. Individuals scoring in the intact functioning range may be presumed to be able to manage their daily affairs entirely on their own, as can most people with a score of mild intellectual impairment. For individuals with moderate intellectual impairment, however, some degree of administrative management or supervision of their activities, especially of complicated business transactions or interactions involving numbers and time sequences, is needed. Individuals with scores in the severe intellectual impairment range almost uniformly require continuous monitoring and supervision of their activities and cannot be reasonably expected to function on their own, requiring the presence of a capable care-giver in their own home, or else institutional care.

The SPMSQ is equally useful in determining the presence or absence and degree of organic impairment in reversible (delirium) as well as irreversible (dementia) organic brain syndromes. The course and progress of delirium can be monitored on a day-by-day basis through the use of this questionnaire while the progress of dementia can be followed on a month-to-month or year-to-year basis.

Some Critical Issues in Dealing with Organic Brain Disease

There are several critical issues which must be addressed in the evaluation of individual patients suspected of organic brain syndrome. These issues must be assessed separately *and* in conjunction with one another. The answer to each of these questions has important implications for understanding the nature and significance of the organic brain disorder and for treatment planning.

These critical issues are:

I. Reversibility *vs.* irreversibility (brain cell malfunction *vs.* brain cell death).
II. Severity of organic impairment.
III. Acute onset *vs.* chronic presence or organic impairment.
IV. Diffuse organic impairment throughout the cortex *vs.* localized areas of organic impairment.
V. Progressive *vs.* stable organic impairment.
VI. Associated psychopathology.

Using these dimensions of organic impairment a profile can then be constructed indicating whether an individual's organic brain syndrome is reversible or irreversible; mild, moderate, or severe; acute in onset or chronic in nature; and whether the pathology is diffuse or localized to a specific area of the brain.

A profile of a typical patient with senile brain disease (dementia) would be to characterize the disorder as essentially irreversible; mild, moderate, or severe, depending on the clinical findings; chronic in nature; and diffuse in its distribution throughout the brain.

The profile of a typical patient with an acute drug intoxication (delirium) would be that it is reversible; mild, moderate, or severe in degree, depending on clinical findings; acute in onset; and diffuse in its brain distribution.

One additional issue which needs to be considered, especially in the irreversible organic brain disorders such as in presenile, senile, and arteriosclerotic brain disease, is whether the disorder is progressive or stable, and if progressive whether it is rapidly or slowly progressive. Again, answers to this question have important implications for designing a treatment or care plan for the individual.

The final determination to be made relates to the presence of any associated psychopathology of the type previously described as *not* specific for organic brain syndromes. In attempting to treat such associated symptoms, however, the basic nature of the organic impairment must be clearly kept in mind so that proposed treatment techniques (such as the use of sedatives rather than one of the major tranquilizers) will not further compromise brain function.

A schematic presentation of this systematic approach to the defining of the nature of an organic brain syndrome in a specific patient or condition is given in Table 2, using drug delirium, electroconvulsive-therapy induced delirium, senile dementia, and an unevaluated case of organic brain syndrome as illustrations.

Reversible Organic Brain Syndromes

Based on clinical studies the best estimates are that from 10 percent to 20 percent of elderly persons with organic brain sydromes have a reversible form of organic brain syndrome. It is therefore crucial to differentiate these from organic brain syndromes which are irreversible. Reversible organic brain syndromes are essentially due to temporary malfunctioning of a significant proportion of cortical cells, in general due to metabolic malfunction or due to drug intoxication (Engel and Romano, 1959). Irreversible organic brain syndromes are due to brain cell death, and it is well known that brain cells have no capacity for regeneration. It is possible for reversible and irreversible brain syndromes to coexist in the same individual, both contributing to the observed pathology. For instance, an individual with senile brain disease may also have a metabolic intoxication or a specific durg intoxication; or a strike victim may have a central area of brain surrounded by temporarily edematous or hypoxic tissues which can regain normal functioning.

TABLE 2. A SYSTEMATIC APPROACH TO THE EVALUATION OF INDIVIDUALS WITH ORGANIC BRAIN SYNDROMES.

Issues Involved	PROFILE OF PATIENT WITH			
	Undiagnosed Organic Brain Syndrome	Drug Delirium	Post-ECT Delirium	Senile Brain Disease
I. Reversibility				
1. reversible	1		1	
2. irreversible				2
3. both				
II. Severity				
1. mild		1	1	1
2. moderate		2	2	2
3. severe		3	3	3
III. Duration				
1. acute		1	1	
2. chronic		2		2
IV. Distribution				
1. diffuse		1	1	1
2. localized				
V. Progression				
0. remitting		0	0	
1. stable		1		
2. slowly progressive		2		2
3. rapidly progressive		3		
4. unknown				
VI. Associated Psychopathology				
1. None				
2. Paranoid Ideas				
3. Hallucinations				
4. Anxiety		Any	Any	Any
5. Depression				
6. Agitation				
7. Aggressive Behavior				

Therefore the possibility of uncovering reversible organic brain syndromes should lead to diagnostic and therapeutic activism, since complete restoration of functioning is possible in reversible organic syndromes while only degrees of functional improvement are likely in the irreversible organic brain syndromes. The basic strategy of treatment in the reversible brain syndromes is the elimination of the offending metabolic deficiency or the elimination of the offending drug.

The specific metabolic intoxications which can give rise to reversible organic brain syndromes are many, and in fact they cover the entire range of internal medicine and surgical practice (Engel and Romano, 1959; Engel, 1967). They include congestive heart failure, specific metabolic diseases such as diabetes, especially diabetic acidosis, hypoglycemia, heptic toxicity, renal toxicity (the accumulation of waste products ordinarily degraded or excreted by liver and kidney), vitamin deficiencies, especially vitamin B_{12} deficiency and folic acid deficiency, hypothyroid states (myxedema), orthostatic hypotension, electrolyte imbalances, particularly electrolyte depletion, and cardiac arrhythmia, such as rapid atrial fibrillation with ineffective cardiac output, to mention only the most prominent among them. What this indicates is that the differential diagnosis of potentially reversible organic brain syndromes is not a task for a psychiatrist alone but one for either a psychiatrist trained in general internal medicine or a team of psychiatrists and internists, all of whom are well versed in the diseases, particularly diseases with metabolic effects, common in elderly persons. The treatment of the organic brain syndrome in these cases on the whole is identical with the treatment of the underlying metabolic deficit. At times other supportive measures, such as the use of one of the major tranquilizers in low dosages or supportive psychotherapeutic measures, may also be indicated.

In regard to possible drug intoxication as the cause of reversible organic brain syndromes, a high index of suspicion, a complete review of the patient's drug intake, both from patient and from other informants including family members, physicians, and medical records, and a thorough knowledge of the potential for brain function impairment of the various drugs, is required. Put another way, a psychiatrist can hardly afford to stay a psychiatric specialist alone in dealing with his elderly patients. He must bring to bear general medical knowledge in order to be alert to metabolic diseases and to the implications of a variety of medications prescribed for both psychiatric and medical disorders in his elderly patients. Among the drug categories most commonly implicated are the entire range of psychotropic drugs, cardiac drugs, diuretics, antihypertensive drugs, and steroids (Eisdorfer and Fann, 1973; Fann and Maddox, 1974). Elderly patients are remarkably sensitive to drugs, due to problems of absorption, metabolic breakdown, excretion, and drug-drug interactions (Bressler and Palmer, 1974). Appropriate treatment of drug-induced organic brain syndromes consists of the elimination of the offending drug or drugs or at least a reduction in dosage.

Irreversible Organic Brain Syndromes

Senile Dementia. The organic brain syndrome secondary to senile brain disease is a clinical syndrome characterized by gradually developing generalized intellectual and cognitive impairment. It is associated with diffuse brain cell loss of unkown etiology. The specific pathological findings associated with senile brain disease are described elsewhere in this volume. The principal focus here will be on the clinical symptomatology of senile brain disease. Simple senile dementia is said to be present

when mild, moderate, or severe intellectual and cognitive impairments are documented in the presence of an otherwise basically intact personality structure, without noticeable associated psychopathology. The severity of the clinical manifestations of senile brain disease are related to several factors. First, the severity of cognitive impairments is related within very broad limits to the amount of brain cell loss which has occurred. That is, greatest intellectual impairment will be noted in those with greatest brain tissue loss, all else (see below) being equal (Blessed, Tomlinson, and Roth, 1968; Wang, Obrist, and Busse, 1970; Wang, 1973a). Second, manifestations of senile brain disease are related to the rapidity of brain cell loss. In general, manifestations are more severe and more functional psychopathology coexists when very rapid progression of organic brain syndrome occurs. This is likely to give rise to manifestations of anxiety, depression, or psychotic ideation, since the organism has little time to adjust to the decreasing adaptational capacity of the brain (Goldstein, 1959). Third, manifestations of senile brain disease are also related to initial intellectual and personality resources. Individuals with a well-integrated personality and with good social skills manage to adapt to gradually developing organic brain deficit more adequately than do less well-educated or less well-socially-accomplished individuals, again within broad limits. Fourth, manifestations of senile dementia are related to the complexity and the friendliness or hostility of the environment. Again, within broad limits, a stable, friendly, relatively simple environment, placing few demands on the individual, will tend to minimize the likelihood of associated psychopathologies. On the other hand intellectually demanding and emotionally hostile environments tend to evoke maladaptive psychological responses, such as paranoid reactions, overt anxiety, depression, aggressive or assaultive behavior, and noncooperative behavior.

Denial is an important defense mechanism in senile brain disease. In general the intellectual and cognitive deficit itself is denied by the individual, and various evasive and defensive maneuvers are developed to avoid being confronted with one's own intellectual deficit

(Weinstein and Kahn, 1955). Responses such as "Oh, I have lost interest in what's going on in the news" or "Why is a young fellow like you asking me all those silly questions" are illustrations of some of these defense mechanisms. One lady, asked by the author to indicate how old she was, responded one time by laughingly and cheerfully saying "Why, I am 150 years old." On another occasion the same lady responded to the same question by saying "Why, I am as young as that flower over there," pointing to a bouquet of roses her daughter had brought to her room.

While the use of denial obviously protects the individual from full awareness of his own deficit, and thus may protect him from becoming depressed over his deficit, denial obviously is also a liability. The person may not remember that he does not know how to find his way back from a shopping center.

Presenile Dementia. Basically the several forms of presenile dementia, including Alzheimer's and Pick's disease, are early-onset variants of senile brain disease (Burger and Vogel, 1973; Terry, 1963; Wells, 1971). Pick's disease has a somewhat different, more localized distribution of brain lesions (Mansvelt, 1954), but the clinical manifestations of the two disorders can hardly be distinguished. In these cases intellectual impairment begins either in the late 40's or in the 50's and is generally more rapidly progressive than in senile dementia. But as with senile dementia, progress of the disease can halt at any point. Neither the causes of the senile and presenile dementias nor the factors which sometime halt the progress of these diseases are known.

The one exception to this general statement is the cause of a form of presenile dementia labeled Jakob-Creutzfeldt disease (Kirschbaum, 1968). Recent research indicates that a "slow" virus is responsible for this encephalopathy and that it can in fact be transmitted (Beck, Mathews, and Stevens, 1969; Gibbs, Gajdusek, and Asher, 1968; Lampert, Gajdusek, and Gibbs, 1971). The course of Jakob-Creutzfeldt disease is generally more rapidly progressive than of the other presenile dementias.

The discovery of a specific identifiable causative agent for one of the dementias of late life provides strong encouragement for the vigorous pursuit of research into the cause or causes of the other far more common forms of dementia, particularly of senile brain disease.

Arteriosclerotic Brain Disease. The other major type of chronic organic brain syndrome is arteriosclerotic brain disease. Here the organic brain syndrome is due to localized death of brain tissue related to occlusive arterial or arteriolar disease, with subsequent infarction of brain tissue. Although in the borderline case it may be quite difficult to distinguish between senile brain disease and arteriosclerotic brain disease, there is little difficulty in doing so in the typical case.

In the typical case there is a sudden onset of both intellectual impairment and peripheral neurological deficit, either weakness and paralysis or decreased sensation affecting the face or limbs on one side of the body. The degree of intellectual impairment in arteriosclerotic brain disease tends to be most pronounced immediately at the onset, with gradual improvement of both the peripheral neurological deficits and intellectual impairment. The initial improvement, however, may be followed by repeated episodes of infarction in other areas of the brain, with cumulative impairment occurring after several such infarctions. Obviously, a series of diffuse infarctions throughout the brain, involving relatively smaller blood vessels, can produce a clinical picture very similar to that seen in senile brain disease. In such instances it is not possible to decide in the living human patient whether organic brain deficit is due to senile or to arteriosclerotic brain disease. However in the more typical cases the two types of disorders can generally be distinguished, particulary with the use of some of the newer diagnostic techniques, such as regional measurement of brain blood flow, transaxial tomography, the electroencephalogram, and cerebral arteriography, reviewed by Wang (1973b).

Treatment approaches to these disorders are discussed elsewhere in this volume.

SOCIAL PATHOLOGY

The principal social pathologies of old age are social isolation and loneliness. They derive in part from the "natural" losses which beset aging individuals. Contacts with former work associates diminish, friends begin to make their appearance in the obituary columns, and a considerable proportion of aging persons, particularly women, experience what may be the most grievous loss of all, loss of one's spouse. Brotman's (1973) data indicate that in the group 65-74 years of age 43 percent of the women but only 10 percent of the men had become widowed, while in the group 75 years of age and older this figure has reached 70 percent for women but is still only 30 percent of men. Some of the physical illnesses of old age, even some which are not life threatening, such as arthritis, or impaired sight or hearing, can significantly impede mobility and thereby seriously limit social contact.

Social Isolation

One of the circumstances which foster social isolation but which of itself does not account for it is living alone. According to Shanas (1969), some 24 percent of persons 65 and over live alone. A recent study by Pfeiffer (1973) found this true for 28 percent of aged persons living in the community. But in that same study true social isolation, defined as little or no meaningful contact with relatives, friends, and visitors, and no one willing and available as a caretaker, occurred in 9 percent. Moreover, this same percentage obtained for the 65-74, the 75 and over, and even the 80 and over group.

But solitary living arrangements and natural loss are not enough to produce social isolation. In general there has also occurred a failure on the part of the aged individual to develop any significant *new* relationships. In fact, in some individuals vigorous resistance to such new relationships is encountered. There are many factors underlying this failure to acquire new relationships. Some are related to the individual's previous lack of social skills. Lack of social opportunity, lack of transportation, decreased physical mobility, and sensory losses also contribute. Another determinant may be a philosophical conviction that the older person "should make do" with what he has and not

seek to change his life situation. Additional factors are the generally held negative stereotypes about older persons which may make many younger or middle aged persons, or even older persons themselves, shy away from new contacts with aging individuals.

Yet intriguingly, an individual's life satisfaction is closely linked to the amount and quality of his social interaction. Intriguingly also, social isolation is an entirely remediable situation. At very low costs, in terms of professional personnel, increased social contacts can be organized among elderly persons themselves, utilizing aging persons to effect organizational stuctures for social contacts, to organize neighborhood visiting programs, and to put isolated elderly persons in contact with persons in other age groups.

Since social isolation has not been seen as a "medical" problem, the current long-term care structures in the United States have not been adequately organized to deal with such social pathology. Recent work at the Duke University Center of the Study of Aging and Human Development (OARS Program) has focused on overall functional assessment of aging individuals, including assessment of their social resources (Pfeiffer, 1975b). As is the case with physical and mental disorder, *assessment* of social isolation must precede ameliorative action.

Loneliness

Loneliness is a form of social pathology which, while clearly related to social isolation, is also distinct from it. Loneliness is not merely aloneness. In fact, many aging persons living alone are not in the least lonely. Either they have for many years lived alone and have become comfortable, perhaps even more comfortable, with this state, or despite the fact of living alone they have ample social contacts. On the other hand persons with seemingly extensive social contacts can nevertheless experience profound loneliness. Fromm-Reichman (1959) in one of her last papers poignantly described loneliness as an excruciatingly painful emotion evoked by the realization of *lack of meaningful contact* with others. Episodes of loneliness occur in many people and are perhaps most common among those who have become recently widowed, that is, individuals who previously enjoyed close and intimate contact with one other person but who have recently lost that contact.

Efforts aimed at improving the general level of social interaction make it likely that the increasing social network will include one or more individuals with whom a more in-depth, intimate new relationship can be established. Even one such intense relationship can be established. Even one such intense relationship is generally able to diminish or abolish such feelings of intense loneliness.

Family Conflicts

Up to now we have discussed some social pathologies deriving from diminished social contacts. But problems can also derive from continued contacts with relatives and friends. The vast majority of older adults still have siblings, children, and more recently even parents with whom to interact. Life long family dramas may of course continue to be played out in late life, but these will not be discussed here.

Some of the conflicts *arising* specifically in this age period relate to the changing relationship between adult parent and adult child. As disability increases adult children may need to increasingly assume a caretaking or parenting role for the older individual. Such change in role is likely to produce anxieties for both parent and child.

Conflicts also arise frequently when some change in living arrangements is contemplated for the older person due to diminishing ability for self-care. Should the older person come to live with one of the children, and if so, with whom? Bitter conflicts can arise in regard to this issue, with the older persons sometimes caught in a withering crossfire between the "You take her. I've already done my share" of one sibling and the "You've got her, she likes it there. You know my husband (wife) can't get along with Mother" of the other.

Similarly, when increasing disability requires consideration of institutional care, families are plagued with much guilt, conflict, and sometimes bitter strife, with some older persons telling their well-meaning children, "I'll never forgive you for putting me here."

While the above illustrate only some of the most common family conflicts involving older persons, they are sufficient to demonstrate the vehemence, intensity, and duration of some of these conflicts.

Skilled assessment of the interactional skills of older persons and their families, knowledge of alternatives and community resources, a thorough knowledge and anticipation of some of the common conflicts in this age, and a willingness to share this knowledge with the aging persons and family members, are all needed to diffuse explosive situations in the short-run and to work out satisfactory long-range solutions. In this regard, general family therapy principles are applicable, with special understanding of the problems and processes of old age (Altholz, 1971).

Sexual Problems

Finally, sexual problems are also not infrequent among aging individuals. These include both marital sexual difficulties as well as sexual problems encountered by the nonmarried aged individual. Research work has now established that many aging men and women continue to have an active interest in sex and that many physically healthy aged individuals continue an active sex life into their 60's, 70's, 80's and even 90's, (Pfeiffer, Verwoerdt, and Wang, 1968, 1969; Pfeiffer, Verwoerdt, and Davis, 1972; Pfeiffer and Davis, 1972).

Perhaps the first step in understanding sexual problems of older persons is accepting the fact that they may have such problems. Stereotypes of the "sexless older years" still abound, and many physicians and other health care personnel do not invite or welcome discussion of sexual matters with their patients. Yet these are of real concern to many aging individuals, and a willingness to explore and discuss such problems is a first step in seeking to resolve them.

A curious mixture of problems and concerns surfaces among elderly persons in regard to sexual matters. These include concerns over failing sexual capability, where that exists, but they also include the opposite, feelings of guilt on the part of those individuals who still have or desire an active sexual life while believing that it is morally wrong for them to participate sexually at their age. Research evidence also indicates that in old age it is generally the husband who discontinues sex in the marital relationship, either due to an intercurrent physical or emotional disorder, or due to chronic illness, from a gradual loss of potency, or of desire (Pfeiffer, Verwoerdt, and Davis, 1972). It appears that no biological limit has been set to the sexuality of aging women, except insofar as with each decade fewer and fewer women have marital partners available (Masters and Johnson, 1966; Pfeiffer, 1974b). The incidence of widowhood among aging women is vastly greater than among aging men and has been reviewed earlier on.

In regard to the sexual needs of older persons, one matter which is all too frequently overlooked is the need for privacy on the part of the older person. This is true both in congregate living arrangements, such as nursing homes, homes for the aging, and family care homes, and in living arrangements in which the older person is living with his own relatives, let us say his or her adult daughter and family. In such settings oftentimes all the physical amenities are readily available to the aging individual, but privacy is not. Adult children, for many conscious and unconscious reasons, are often extremely protective of their aging parents' behavior considering that any new social, but particularly sexual, contacts would constitute an unbearable embarrassment to them. It may well be that new generations of aging individuals, as they come along, will suffer less from such unwarranted restraints on their behavior. But the right to privacy is an important social right which should not be abridged merely with the arrival of the later years.

Under the category of sexual problems some mention should also be made not only of the sexual needs of older persons but of their need for touch and closeness in general. Many older individuals respond extremely positively to touch from children, from their adult children, and from persons of their own age. Physicians and other medical personnel have also found that a judicious amount of "laying on of hands" is an important part of their interaction with older persons. Even psychiatrists in their practice with older patients will find that some amount of touch of the patients is extremely helpful in building a therapeutic alliance.

REFERENCES

Altholz, J. 1971. The family and the older person. *In*, D. T. Peak, G. Polansky, and J. Altholz (eds.), *The Final Report of the Information and Counseling Service for Older Persons*. Durham, North Carolina: Duke University, Center for the Study of Aging and Human Development.

Anderson, W. F., and Davidson, R. 1975. Concomitant physical states. *In*, J. G. Howells (ed.), *Modern Perspectives in the Psychiatry of Old Age*, pp. 84–106. New York: Brunner/Mazel.

Batchelor, I. R., and Napier, M. B. 1953. Attempted suicide in old age. *Brit. Med. J.*, **2**, 1186–1190.

Beck, A. T. 1967. *Depression*. New York: Hoeber.

Beck, E. Mathews, W. B., and Stevens, D. L. 1969. Creutzfeldt-Jakob disease. The neuropathology of a transmission experiment. *Brain*, **92**, 699.

Benson, R. A., and Brodie, D. C. 1975. Suicide by overdoses of medicines among the aged. *J. Am. Geriat. Soc.*, **23**, 304–308.

Bergman, K. Towards successful treatment of functional disorder. *In*, E. Pfeiffer (ed.), *Successful Treatment of the Elderly Mentally Ill*. Durham, North Carolina: Center for the Study of Aging and Human Development, in press.

Blessed, G., Tomlinson, B. E., and Roth, M. 1968. The association between quantitative measures of dementia and of senile change in the cerebral grey matter of elderly subjects. *Brit. J. Psychiat.*, **114**, 797–811.

Bressler, R., and Palmer, J. 1974. Drug interactions in the aged. *In*, W. E. Fann and G. L. Maddox (eds.), *Drug Issues in Geropsychiatry*, pp. 49–57. Baltimore: Williams & Wilkins.

Brotman, H. B. 1973. Who are the aging? *In*, E. W. Busse and E. Pfeiffer (eds.), *Mental Illness in Later Life*, pp. 19–39. Washington, D.C.: American Psychiatric Association.

Burger, P. C., and Vogel, F. S. 1973. The development of the pathologic changes of Alzheimer's disease the senile dementia in patients with Down's syndrome. *Am. J. Pathol.*, **73**, 457–468.

Busse, E. W. 1961. Psychoneurotic reactions and defense mechanisms in the aged. *In*, P. H. Hoch and J. Zubin (eds.), *Psychopathology of Aging*, pp. 274–284. New York: Grune & Stratton.

Busse, E. W. 1968. The mental health of the elderly.

International Mental Health Research Newsletter, **10**, 13-16.

Busse, E. W., and Pfeiffer, E. 1969. *Behavior and Adaptation in Late Life*. Boston: Little, Brown.

Busse, E. W., and Pfeiffer, E. 1973. *Mental Illness in in Later Life*. Washington, D.C.: American Psychiatric Association.

Butler, R. N. 1963. The life review: An interpretation of reminiscence in the aged. *Psychiatry*, **26**, 65-76.

Butler, R. N. 1974. Successful aging and the role of the life review. *J. Am. Geriat. Soc.*, **22**, 529-535.

Davis, J. M., Fann, W. E., El-Yousef, M. K., and Janowsky, D. S. 1973. Clinical problems in treating the aged with psychotropic drugs. *In*, C. Eisdorfer and W. E. Fann (eds.), *Psychopharmacology and Aging*, pp. 111-125. New York: Plenum Press.

Dement, W., and Kleitman, N. 1957. The relation of eye movements during sleep to dream activity. *J. Exp. Psych.*, **53**, 539.

Dublin, L. I. 1963. *Suicide*. New York: Ronald Press.

Earley, L. W., and von Mering, O. 1969. Growing old the out-patient way. *Am. J. Psychiat.*, **125**, 963-967.

Eisdorfer, C. 1960. Developmental level and sensory impairment in the aged. *J. Projective Techniques*, **24**, 129-132.

Eisdorfer, C., and Fann, W. E. 1973. *Psychopharmacology and Aging*. New York: Plenum Press.

Engel, G. 1962. Anxiety and depression-withdrawal: The primary affects of unpleasure. *Int. J. Psychoanalysis*, **43**, 89-97.

Engel, G. L. 1967. Delirium. *In*, A. M. Freedman and H. I. Kaplan (eds.), *Comprehensive Textbook of Psychiatry*, pp. 711-716. Baltimore: Williams & Wilkins.

Engel, G. L., and Romano, J. 1959. Delirium, a syndrome of cerebral insufficiency. *J. Chronic Diseases*, **9**, 260-277.

Erikson, E. H. 1959. The problem of ego identity. *In*, Identity and the Life Cycle. *Psychological Issues*, **1**, 101-164.

Fann, W. E., and Maddox, G. L. 1974. *Drug Issues in Geropsychiatry*. Baltimore: Williams & Wilkins.

Feigenbaum, E. M. 1970. *A Geriatric Psychiatric Outpatient Project*. San Francisco, California: Langley Porter Neuropsychiatric Institute.

Feinberg, I., Braun, M., and Schulman, E. 1969. EEG sleep patterns in mental retardation. *Electroencephalog. Clin. Neurophyslo.*, **27**, 128-41.

Fish, F. J. 1959. Senile paranoid states. *Gerontol. Clin.*, **1**, 127-131.

Fowler, R. D., and Athey, E. B. 1971. A cross-validation of Gilberstadt and Ducker's 1-2-3-4 profile type. *J. Clin. Psych.*, **23**, 238-240.

Freud, A. 1946. *The Ego and the Mechanisms of Defense*. New York: International Universities Press.

Fromm-Reichman, F. 1959. Loneliness. *Psychiatry*, **22**, 1-15.

Gaitz, C. M., and Baer, P. E. 1971. Characteristics of elderly patients with alcoholism. *Arch. Gen. Psychiat.*, **24**, 372-378.

Gallemore, J. L., and Wilson, W. P. 1969. The complaint of pain in the clinical setting of affective disorder. *Southern Med. J.*, **62**, 551-555.

Gardner, E., Bahn, A. K., and Mach, M. 1963. Suicide and psychiatric care in the aging. *Arch. Gen. Psychiat.*, **10**, 547-553.

Gibbs, C. J., Gajdusek, D. C., and Asher, D. M. 1968. Creutzfeldt-Jakob disease (spongiform encephalopathy): Transmission to the chimpanzee. *Science*, **161**, 388.

Goldstein, K. 1959. Functional disturbances in brain damage. *In*, S. Arieti (ed.) *American Handbook of Psychiatry*, pp. 770-94. New York: Basic Books.

Goodwin, F. K., Murphy, D. L., and Bunny, W. E., Jr. 1969. Lithium carbonate treatment in depression and mania. *Arch. Gen. Psychiat.*, **21**, 486-496.

Grinker, R. R. Sr., Miller, J., Sabschin, M., Nunn, R., and Nunnally, J. C. 1961. *Phenomena of Depression*. New York: Hoeber.

Hartmann, H. 1958. *Ego Psychology and the Problem of Adaptation*. New York: International Universities Press.

Hartmann, H. 1964. *Essays in Ego Psychology*. New York: International Universities Press.

Houston, R., and Royse, A. B. 1954. Relationship between deafness and psychotic illness. *J. Mental Sci.*, **100**, 990-993.

Kahn, E., and Fisher, C. 1969. The sleep characteristics of the normal aged male. *J. Nervous Mental Disease*, **148**, 477-494.

Kales, A., Beall, G. N., and Berger, R. J. 1968. Sleep and dreams-recent research on clinical aspects. *Ann. Internal Med.*, **68**, 1078-1104.

Kay, D. W. K., and Roth, M. 1955. Physical accompaniments of mental disorder in old age. *Lancet*, **2**, 740.

Kay, D. W. K., Beamish, P., and Roth, M. 1964. Old age mental disorders in Newcastle-upon-Tyne: I. A study of prevalence. *Brit. J. Psychiat.*, **465**, 146.

Kennedy, F., And Wiesel, B. 1946. The clinical nature of "manic-depressive equivalents" and their treatment. *Trans. Am. Neurol. Assoc.*, **71**, 96-101.

Kincannon, J. C. 1968. Prediction of the standard MMPI scores from 71 items: The Mini-Mult. *Journal of Consulting and Clinical Psychology*, **32**, 319-325.

Kirschbaum, W. R. 1968. *Jakob-Cruetzfeldt Disease*. New York: Elsevier.

Kleitman, N. 1963. *Sleep and Wakefulness*. Chicago: University of Chicago Press.

Kramer, M., Taube, C., and Redick, R. 1973. Patterns of use of psychiatric facilities by the aged: Past, present, and future. *In*, C. Eisdorfer and M. P. Lawton (eds.), *The Psychology of Adult Development and Aging*. Washington, D.C.: American Psychological Association.

Lampert, P. W., Gajdusek, D. C., and Gibbs, C. J. 1971. Experimental spongiform encephalopathy (Creutzfeldt-Jakob disease in chimpanzees). *J. Neuropathol Exp. Neurol.*, **30**, 20.

Leighton, D. C., Harding, J. S., Macklin, D. B., Macmillan, A. M., and Leighton, A. N. 1963. *The Character of Danger: Psychiatric Symptoms in Selected Communities. The Stirling County Study of Psychiatric Disorder and Sociocultural Environment,* Vol. III. New York: Basic Books.

Lowenthal, M. R. 1964. *Lives in Distress.* New York: Basic Books.

Lowenthal, M. F., Bissette, G. G., Buehler, J. A., Pierce, R. C., Robinson, B. C., and Iner, M. L. 1967. *Aging and Mental Disorder in San Francisco.* San Francisco: Jossey-Bass.

Maggs, R. 1963. Treatment of manic illness with lithium carbonate. *Brit. J. Psychiat.*, **109**, 56–65.

Mansvelt, J. 1954. *Pick's Disease, A Syndrome of Lobar Cerebral Atrophy.* Enschede, The Netherlands: Van Der Loeff.

Masters, W. H., and Johnson, V. E. 1966. *Human Sexual Response.* Boston: Little Brown.

Nielson, J. 1962. Geronto-psychiatric period-prevalence investigation in a geographically delimited population. *Acta Psychiat. Neurol. Scand.*, **38**, 307-330.

O'Neal, P., Robins, E., and Schmidt, E. H. 1956. A psychiatric study of attempted suicide in persons over sixty years of age. *A.M.A. Arch. Neurol. Psychiat.*, **75**, 275-284.

Pasamanick, B. 1962. A survey of mental disease in an urban population: VI. An approach to total prevalence by age. *Mental Hygiene*, **46**, 567-572.

Peak, D. T., Polansky, G., and Altholz, J. 1971. *Final Report of the Information and Counseling Service for Older Persons.* Durham, North Carolina: Duke University, Center for the Study of Aging and Human Development.

Peak, D. T. 1973. Clinical operations, Older Americans Resources and Services Program (OARS). Paper presented at the Annual Meeting of the Gerontological Society, Miami Beach, Florida.

Pfeiffer, E. 1968. *Disordered Behavior.* New York: Oxford University Press.

Pfeiffer, E. 1971. Treating the patient with confirmed functional pain. *Hosp. Phy.*, June 68–71, 91–92.

Pfeiffer, E. 1973. Multidimensional quantitative assessment of three populations of elderly. Paper presented at Annual Meeting of the Gerontological Society, Miami Beach, Florida.

Pfeiffer, E. 1974a. *Successful Aging.* Durham, North Carolina: Duke University Center for the Study of Aging and Human Development.

Pfeiffer, E. 1974b. Sexuality in the aging individual. *J. Am. Geriat. Soc.*, **22** (11), 481–484.

Pfeiffer, E. 1975a. Successful aging. *In*, L. E. Brown and E. O. Ellis (eds.), *Quality of Life: The Later Years*, pp. 13–21. Acton, Massachusetts: Publishing Science Group.

Pfeiffer, E. 1975b. *Functional Assessment: the OARS Multidimensional Functional Assessment Questionnaire.* Durham, North Carolina: Duke University Center for the Study of Aging and Human Development.

Pfeiffer, E. A short portable mental status questionnaire for the assessment of organic brain deficit in elderly patients. *J. Amer. Geriat. Soc.*, in Press.

Pfeiffer, E., and Davis, G. C. 1972. Determinants of sexual behavior in middle and old age. *J. Am. Geriat. Soc.*, **20**, 4.

Pfeiffer, E., Verwoerdt, A., and Davis, G. C. 1972. Sexual behavior in middle life. *Am. J. Psychiat.*, **128**, 10.

Pfeiffer, E., Verwoerdt, A., and Wang, H. S. 1968. Sexual behavior in aged men and women. Observations on 254 community volunteers. *Arch. Gen. Psychiat.*, **19**, 641–646.

Pfeiffer, E., Verwoerdt, A., and Wang, H. S. 1969. The natural history of sexual behavior in a biologically advantaged group of aged individuals. *J. Gerontol.*, **24**, 193–198.

Platman, S. R. 1970. A comparison of lithium carbonate and chlorpromazine in mania. *Am. J. Psychiat.*, **127**, 351-353.

Post, F. 1966. *Persistent Persecutory States of the Elderly.* London: Pergamon.

Post, F. 1969. The relationship to physical health of the affective illnesses in the elderly. *Proc. 8th Intern. Congr. Geront.*, Washington, D.C., **1**, 198.

Prien, R. F., Caffey, E. M., Jr., and Keltt, C. J. 1972. Comparison of lithium carbonate and chlorpromazine in the treatment of mania. *Arch. Gen. Psychiat.*, **26**, 146-153.

Rapaport, D. 1960. *The Structure of Psychoanalytic Theory. Psychological Issues*, Vol. 2, No. 2. New York: International Universities Press.

Redick, R. W., Kramer, M., and Taube, C. A. 1973. Epidemiology of mental illness and utilization of psychiatric facilities among older persons. *In*, E. W. Busse and E. Pfeiffer (eds.), *Mental Illness in Later Life.* Washington, D.C.: American Psychiatric Association.

Retterstol, N. 1966. *Paranoid and Paranoiac Psychoses.* Oslo: Universitetsforlaget.

Riley, M. W., and Foner, A. 1968. *Aging and Society: Volume One.* New York: Russell Sage Foundation.

Robins, E. et al. 1959. The communication of suicidal intent: A study of 134 consecutive cases of successful (completed) suicides. *Am. J. Psychiat.*, **115**, 724-733.

Roth, M. 1955. The natural history of mental disorder in old age. *J. Mental Sci.*, **101**, 281-301.

Schou, M., Juel-Nielson, N., and Stoomgran, E. 1954. The treatment of manic psychoses by the administration of lithium salts. *J. Neurol. Neurosurg. Psychiat.*, **17**, 250-260.

Shanas, E. 1969. Living arrangements and housing of old people. *In*, E. W. Busse and E. Pfeiffer (eds.),

Behavior and Adaptation in Late Life, pp. 129–149. Boston: Little, Brown.

Simon, A., Epstein, L. J., and Reynolds, L. 1968. Alcoholism in the geriatric mentally ill. *Geriatrics,* 23, 125–131.

Simon, A., Lowenthal, M. F., and Epstein, L. J. 1970. *Crisis and Intervention.* San Francisco: Jossey-Bass.

Srole, L., Langner, T. S., Michael, S. T., Opler, M. K., and Rennie, T. A. C. 1962. *Mental Health in the Metropolis: The Midtown Manhattan Study.* New York: McGraw-Hill.

Terry, R. D. 1963. The fine structure of neurofibrillary tangles in Alzheimer's Disease. *J. Neuropathol. Exp. Neurol.,* 22, 629.

Tongas, P. N., and Gibson, R. W. 1969. A study of older patients admitted to the Sheppard and Enoch Pratt Hospital 1966-1968. Towson, Maryland, Research Department, Sheppard and Enoch Pratt Hospital.

U.S. Public Health Service. 1974. *Vital Statistics of the United States, 1970, Volume II, Mortality Part A.* Rockville, Maryland: U.S. Department of HEW, Public Health Serivce.

Vaillant, G. E. 1971. Theoretical hierarchy of adaptive ego mechanisms. *Arch. Gen. Psychiat.,* 24, 107–118.

Wang, H. S. 1973a. Cerebral correlates of intellectual function in senescence. *In,* L. F. Jarvik, C. Eisdorfer, and J. E. Blum, *Intellectual Functioning in Adults. Psychological and Biological Influences,* pp. 95–106. New York: Springer.

Wang, H. S. 1973b. Special diagnostic procedures—the evaluation of brain impairment. *In,* E. W. Busse and E. Pfeiffer (eds.), *Mental Illness in Later Life,* pp. 75–88. Washington, D.C.: American Psychiatric Association.

Wang, H. S., Obrist, W. D., and Busse, E. W. 1970. Neurophysiological correlates of the intellectual function of elderly persons living in the community. *Am. J. Psychiat.,* 126, 39–46.

Weinstein, E., and Kahn, R. 1955. *The Denial of Illness.* Springfield, Illinois: Charles C. Thomas.

Wells, C. 1971. *Dementia.* Philadelphia: F. A. Davis.

Welsh, G. S., and Dahlstrom, W. G. 1956. *Basic Readings on the MMPI in Psychology and Medicine.* Minneapolis: University of Minnesota Press.

Whanger, A. D. 1973. A study of institutionalized elderly of Durham County. Paper presented at Annual Meeting, Gerontological Society, Miami Beach, Florida.

Whittier, J. R., and Korenyi, C. 1961. Selected characteristics of aged patients: A study of mental hospital admissions. *Comprehensive Psychiatry,* 2, 113–120.

28
MORALE, CAREERS AND PERSONAL POTENTIALS

Sheila M. Chown
Bedford College, University of London

INTRODUCTION

Morale is the emotional component of a person's attitude toward his own life and may be defined as a reflection of his feelings about his past, present, and future. When such a broad view of morale is taken, it becomes synonymous with degree of satisfaction with life. It seems likely that morale will be related to the individual's assessment both of his own potential and of his career to date and that it will reflect the degree of concordance between his original hopes and aims and his achievements.

The story of a person's adult life is taken to constitute his career for the purposes of this chapter. This may seem a broad definition, but an individual may center his life not only upon his work but on his family or some special interest or on a combination of these; and all may influence his feelings of success or failure and hopes for the future. Within each person's career there may or may not exist an individual style of life (Adler, 1927) or some less dramatic consistencies of expression which should make careers worthy of study as sources of information about personal development.

In considering personal potentials, this chapter will be concerned with people's opinions about themselves and what they think they can do. Each person uses his ability and aptitudes in his everyday life and through his successes and failures builds up his own picture of himself. His self-assessment no doubt in turn affects his aims and hopes. By this interactive process a person's view of himself may change over time and so may his goals for the future (Bortner, 1967).

This chapter will first examine work on the description and evaluation of morale, then studies on self-assessment of potential, and then work designed to describe careers. The intention is, then, to briefly review work describing reactions to some of the frustrations which occur in the later part of life, with a view toward noting their impact on self-assessment and morale. While a great deal of work has been done on the separate topics of the chapter, not many people have deliberately set out to look at the relationships among all of them. There is also very little work which is concerned wholly with only one of the topics. This has made the task of ordering what is known an awkward one, and the solution adopted has been to include in each section the work which seems most appropriate to its theme.

MORALE

Acquiring and maintaining high morale is one of the more enduring of life's tasks: assessing it has proved almost as long-term a problem. Morale scales attempt to tap mood tone, whether this be limited to satisfaction with the status quo (Cumming and McCaffrey, 1961) or be extended to cover past, present, and future (Kutner, 1956).

Havighurst (1963), after numerous approaches to the assessment of successful aging, concluded that life satisfaction could best be evaluated by asking how a person felt about himself, and he proposed that five aspects of reactions to life should be taken into account. These were zest for present life, resolution and fortitude, congruence of goals and achievements, positive self-concept, and positive mood tone. Neugarten, Havighurst, and Tobin (1961) rated interview protocols for these five, and there were two main clusters among the intercorrelations. One was between resolution, congruence, and self-concept, most probably representing the relation of past to present; and the other was between zest, mood tone, and self-concept, clearly representing current approach to life. Havighurst (1963) went on to devise two Life Satisfaction questionnaires (LSI A and LSI B) incorporating the five aspects.

There has been a suggestion that satisfaction with life may be a stable personality characteristic. Lieberman (1970) found that students and old people obtained similar mean scores on LSI A but that the old scored on items concerning the past and the students on items referring to the present and future. More work is needed on this topic, however, for it is clear that life satisfaction scores certainly may change with circumstances; for example, Wylie (1970) showed that scores increased among older people who had participated in a program of work to help young people.

A variety of other measures have been used to assess morale and satisfaction with life. Meltzer and Ludwig (1967) took the relative number of pleasant incidents remembered and found a decrease among the over-40's. The Barron Ego Strength scale was used by Cameron (1967a,b) who found that those over 70 had lower morale scores and less felt competency than 30 years olds although the groups did not differ in immediate feelings of unhappiness. In Cantril's (1965) study an 11-point scale referring to the present was used to get a measure of current satisfaction with life. This was correlated with 20 personal and 7 demographic ratings by Bortner and Hultsch (1970). A significant multiple correlation for current satisfaction with life was obtained in which the social and psychological measures emerged as more important than age and economic level.

Outlook on the future, little emphasized in the life satisfaction indices, has been investigated by Lehr (1967) and by Spence (1968), who found that interest in and plans for the future went with well-being and happiness except in the extremely old.

To measure dissatisfaction, Srole (1956) concentrated on anomie, and Zung (1970) on depression, but their scales have a clinical flavor and cannot be regarded as the opposite end of the life satisfaction/morale dimension.

Job Satisfaction

Overall satisfaction with life is presumably based on views about satisfaction with the constituent aspects of life, but as yet little is known about the process of integration. Satisfaction with one aspect of life, work, has received attention from industrial psychologists and has been found to alter with age. Saleh and Otis (1964) found that remembered job satisfaction increased up to the 50–59 year-old decade but decreased during the last 5 years of the working life. Quality of satisfaction also appeared to change from intrinsic (factors concerned with achievement and responsibility) to extrinsic (factors such as income, interpersonal relationships, and company policy). Saleh suggests that intrinsic rewards are irrelevant to people approaching retirement, and so they turn to the extrinsic factors. For example, a decline with age in interest in promotion opportunities was noted long ago by Strong (1931), and this is realistic since the chances of promotion diminish after middle age. Using cross-sectional results, Meltzer (1965b) reported that 45 was the key age for job satisfaction; thereafter, it was less.

Laurence (1961) found some age differences in job satisfaction among women; older ones saw health and keeping busy as future problems and were less worried than the younger ones about recognition of merits and possibility of future achievement. It seems likely that further work on sex differences in job satisfaction changes with age would be worthwhile.

There is more than a hint in these data that the changes in job satisfaction are due to job circumstances and retirement practices rather than to aging *per se*. Little is known as yet of the relation between satisfaction with work and general satisfaction with life, to what extent the two vary concomitantly, or to what extent other satisfactions substitute if job satisfaction is low.

ASSESSMENT OF PERSONAL POTENTIALS

Studies relating to assessment of personal potentials have been grouped into those which look at stereotypes and expectations, and those which examine data on current outlook, whether with respect to personality and emotion or to attitudes toward performance of tasks.

Stereotypes and Expectations

Cameron (1969) inquired where people placed the limits of young adulthood, middle age, old age, and aged and got the answers 18 to 25, 40 to 55, 65 to 80, and over 80. Some ages were, therefore, indeterminate. Wertheimer (1960) found that age boundaries depended upon the age of the respondent. When asked to identify people's age, it is physical cues which are most used (Davies and Chown, 1969; Nash, 1958), though mention of negative cues may be avoided by emphasizing the good points of exceptional people "young for their age."

There are stereotyped expectations about the behavior of old people which are held by the old themselves as well as by the young. Power, activity, and effectiveness are rated lower for the old (Eisdorfer and Altrocchi, 1961). The older person is seen as set in his ways, rooted in the past, having fewer interests, more physical ailments, and as sorry for himself (Axelrod and Eisdorfer, 1961; Jones, 1961; Laurence, 1964). People tended to project their own symptoms onto the elderly (Tuckman and Lorge, 1958b). When ranking age decades for happiness, freedom from worry, and for ambi-

tion, all age groups put young adults first, then childhood, then middle age, and last, old age (Meltzer, 1960; Tuckman and Lorge, 1954), and a similar order emerged for stability (Cameron, 1971). Negative views about old age were found among students in six countries (Arnhoff, Leon, and Lorge, 1964), but people with direct experience with the elderly seem somewhat less willing to endorse negative views (Rosencranz and McNevin, 1969; Tuckman and Lorge, 1958a), and the old themselves may be slightly less negative about old age than are the young (Kogan, 1961).

In order to try to tap people's expectations about themselves, Back and Bourque (1970) asked adults to draw graphs of certain behaviors and personal characteristics projected up to the age of 80. Most graphs peaked at 55. Other studies have also shown that the self is seen as most fully developed at that age (Bloom, 1961; Hess and Bradshaw, 1970).

Neugarten collected views on appropriate behaviors from people aged 20 to 60 and found that as their own ages went up, the upper "permitted limits" for behaviors came down while limits for "own behavior" went up. The two estimates converged at 60, suggesting that older people have greater constraints in their age-norm systems (Neugarten, Moore, and Lowe, 1965).

It is clear that the old are seen as having few advantages over younger people, and that the old themselves concur in this view, yet that late middle age is seen as a time of fulfilment. In building up subjective feelings of age, lack of mobility and cognitive deficit have been found important but so have the feedbacks obtained from the reactions of other people towards the individual (Dodge, 1961; Lehr and Puschner, 1964; Phillips, 1961; Werner, Perlin, Butler, and Pollin, 1961). The young looking, mobile, and alert person is better placed for presenting a "youthful image" both to other people and to himself.

Current Outlook

Erikson (1959) considered that socialization continues through life, and he postulated eight sequential challenges, three of which relate to adulthood. The sixth challenge is to become close to at least one other person, the seventh is to produce and nurture (in terms of ideas or offspring), and the eighth is to formulate a philosophy of life allowing full self-acceptance. These three bear upon such topics as emotional relationships, performance on tasks, and assessment of careers.

Emotional Relationships. These could be expected to be most important in early adulthood, and in fact older people seem to be slightly more introverted than younger people on conventional questionnaires, though social responsibility holds up into the fifties (Chown, 1968; Kuhlen, 1964b). Questionnaire contents are often ill-adapted for older people (Livson, 1973), and results from them therefore need careful scrutiny. However, other studies do show similar age effects. Phillips (1969) noted that people over 50 mentioned fewer positive feelings about friends, neighbors, and organizations; the nature of personal worries has been shown by several workers to change from emphasis on social interaction to concern with personal well-being (Carp 1967a,b; Dykman, Heimann, and Kerr, 1952; Pressey and Jones, 1955); and fewer expressions of anger have been reported by older people (Cason, 1930; Friedman and Granick, 1963).

Results from projective tests also show some qualitative differences in emotional responses. Rosen and Neugarten (1960) found that TAT stories by older people were less intense and described fewer conflicts. Shanan and Sharon (1965), working in Israel, agreed that older men used fewer conflicts. They also found more pessimistic themes, fewer achievement themes, and more negative endings, but in aggregate there were no age differences in the number and intensity of emotions. Lakin and Eisdorfer (1960) analyzed responses to stick figures (thus controlling for possible age differences in ease of identification with the figures). They found fewer emotional responses in old people but no differences in emotional intensity. Neugarten and Gutman (1958) found from story themes that 40-year-old subjects saw the world as a place they could control, but 60-year-olds saw it as requiring them to adapt. Thus most studies show older people as more concerned with themselves and having less outgoing or less pleasant emotions.

Attitudes to Performance on Tasks. From Erikson's seventh challenge, people could be expected to be more interested in doing well at tasks in middle age than in old age. Reactions by those of different ages to success and failure have been studied in two level of aspiration experiments. Krugman (1959) compared the performance on a Rotter board of residents and nursing staff in an old age home. The residents in the home changed their aspiration level less to both success and failure than did the nursing staff.

Davis (1967) used a similar task with ordinary people aged 20 to 85. He found that false norms to suggest failure resulted in lowered aspirations for both young and old. However, when false norms suggested success, the young increased their aspiration level, but the old *lowered* theirs. This seems important. Davis suggested that the old were more ready to conform to a group norm and did not try to beat their own performance, but another interpretation is possible. In Atkinson's (1958) model of achievement motivation, estimated ability interacts with preponderance of either need to achieve or fearfulness of failure to determine the next task or aspiration level. Lack of responsiveness suggests a person motivated by fear of failure (which would not be surprising in an old age home) or a person so weak in the need to achieve that success and failure do not act as reinforcers. The response of lowering aspiration to both "failure" and "success" suggests the need achiever who continues to believe both tasks were too difficult for him to have an even chance of success, although he has happened to succeed on one of them.

There is certainly some evidence that need to achieve is somewhat weaker in older people, but the age differences are not great. Veroff, Atkinson, Feld, and Gurin (1960) found fewer high scores on need achievement among the older subjects in their large-scale TAT study in the United States, and Smith (1970) noted slightly lower average need achievement scores among older British subjects.

The findings on caution and rigidity are, however, consistent with the explanation that tasks are seen as too difficult. There is considerable evidence from questionnaires that caution increases with age (Wallach and Kogan, 1961). The elderly are more confident about their cautious statements than are young people about their less cautious ones (suggesting that a different criterion for decision has been chosen), and caution may disappear if old people are forced to make decisions (Botwinick, 1969, 1970; Craik, 1962). Older people see themselves as less willing to experience change (Chown, 1960; Schaie, 1958) and an increase in dogmatism has also been noted (Riegel and Riegel, 1960; Weir, 1961). Such age differences should be considered in the light of changes in psychomotor skills, and Chown (1961) for one regards the increase in rigidity as due to, and commensurate with, decrease in intelligence. It seems possible that the decrease in achievement motivation and the lower flexibility of level of aspiration may also be outcomes of reactions to poorer performance in older people.

There is no satisfactory way to ensure that all age groups are equally "involved" in a given task. Ganzler (1964) tried to tackle this by looking at the effects of neutral and motivating instructions on two age groups of VA residents. The instructions were effective, but no age differences occurred. However, such experiments do not tell the full story since physiological records suggest that older people may show increased heart rate and take longer to return to normal under test conditions (Thiesen, Brown, Forgus, Evans, Williams, and Taylor, 1965). The older group in that study had an average age of 60, so even greater differences might have been found with still older people.

Assessment of Careers. Reminiscence has been suggested as a function of Erikson's eighth challenge (Butler, 1963, 1968), furthering resolution of past conflicts and self-integration. Gorney (1968) expected reminiscence to be a phase, ending once integration was achieved, but Revere (1971) noted that some people reminisced a great deal without moving toward self-acceptance and McMahon and Rhudick (1964) found that reminiscence ceased in depression.

Lack of reminiscence and compulsive reminiscence can both be signs of disturbance (Coleman, 1972), and pleasant reminiscence a sign of adjustment (Coleman, 1972; Havighurst and Glasser, 1972). In short, reminiscence may or may not serve an adaptive function (Lieberman and Falk, 1971).

Reminiscence relates to the later years of adulthood, but there is some evidence that Erikson's eighth challenge emerges much earlier, in the forties. Jacques (1966) has referred to the mid-life crisis when people become conscious of limitations on their future opportunities. Neugarten, Birren, and Kraines (1966) found that successful managers of about age 45 thought themselves at the height of their powers but were beginning to reflect that this would not last, and to look on discrepancies between their original hopes and current achievements as likely to continue. Leblanc (1969) found TAT stories from people aged 10 to 90 changed at about age 45 to a greater emphasis on the past. Fink (1957) found a similar increase in past themes after age 50. Linden and Courtney (1953) tried to relate the mid-life change in outlook to a biological base—failure of reproductive capacity—but in an interview study with women, Neugarten (1966) was unable to find such a link. It seems more likely that it is the thoughts of impending changes which cause self-appraisal to occur.

Bühler (1959) believed a person's life was aimed at reaching goals set in youth, and that assessment of progress was most marked in the forties. (Kuhlen (1959) discusses Bühler's ideas fully.) Slotkin (1954) pointed out that the dissatisfied 40 year old must either change these goals, become resigned to failure, or cling unrealistically to hope of future success. It is also possible that a person may achieve his goals only to find them unsatisfying. Such a person also faces the alternatives of resignation or change of goals. In spite of the possibilities raised by this theory, there have been few studies of changes of goals, probably because longitudinal work is needed. Kuhlen and Johnson's study (1952) of school teachers' aims was cross-sectional. The unmarried women under 30 wanted marriage; those over 30 mentioned career ambitions, having apparently come to see marriage as unlikely. Haug and Sussman (1970) did carry out a retrospective study by questioning late entrant trainees for social work; but found that the change of career usually sprang from situational rather than motivational causes. Kuhlen (1964a) suggests that sources of gratification change with time both between fields of life (that is, family, occupation and social relationships), and within each field. This area calls for a great deal more research, for remarkably little is known of the ongoing processes of personal assessment in middle life.

CAREERS

Most people play many roles in their lives, and many researchers have concentrated on one area of life rather than attempting a global picture.

Family Roles

In the area of family life, there is agreement that people expect the family to help older members but younger people expect some help with the task, and also want some independent life (Britton, Mather and Lansing, 1961; Smith, 1954). While many older people prefer independent living, some elderly parents expect a continuing close relationship with their children and when disappointed have subjective feelings of being neglected (Brown, 1960; Kerckhoff, 1966; Smith, 1961). Clearly, differences between generations in role expectations may lead to unhappiness. In an investigation of family relationships some 20 years ago, Albrecht (1954) found that elderly parents were not neglected although in 15 percent of the sample relationships between parents and children were not close. In a more recent study, it was noted that family ties were usually based on memories of affection (Simos, 1970). Townsend (1957), writing about old people in Britain, presented a picture of family loyalty which nevertheless often covered difficulties and conflicts. Shanas and Streib's (1965) collection of papers about intergenerational family relationships reflected the inevitability of many such conflicts because of the different aims of the different generations. Such differences may extend to the

interpretation of emotional roles. In a TAT study, Neugarten and Gutman (1958) found that middle-aged people saw a young woman as loving, a young man as ambitious, an old woman as nurturant and an old man as authoritative. However, elderly people saw the young woman as dutiful, the young man as achievement oriented, the old woman as assertive and the old man as passive. If such discrepancies exist then hurtful misunderstandings must arise between generations. For example, in the case of women, younger women will feel, correctly, that their love is not appreciated, and the older women will feel, also correctly, that their authority is not accepted. More work is urgently needed on this topic, through some other means than the use of projective material. Should the findings turn out to be substantiated by other work, then a primary need will be for some re-education to build up more tolerance between generations.

Within the nuclear family in old age, the roles of husbands and wives alter, becoming more alike (Kerckhoff, 1964; Lipman, 1961). This can be a serious threat to a family where the wife has just been "a good housewife" and the husband "a good provider." Activities may be assigned rather than shared, with certain jobs such as laundering and bedmaking remaining firmly "women's work" (Ballweg, 1967), although Kerckhoff (1966) found this pattern indicated a less close relationship between the couple.

Wider family relationships may strengthen in old age (Cumming and Schneider, 1961) though contacts outside the family are usually with other retired people (Bultena, 1968; Rose, 1965). Closeness to at least one other person may greatly aid resilience when disasters threaten (Lowenthal and Haven, 1968).

Leisure Roles

Leisure roles do not appear to be age-related and (contrary to the stereotype) individual interests seem to be remarkably stable over time (Palmore, 1968; Stone and Norris, 1966), although activities may become slightly fewer with age (Cowgill and Baulch, 1962; Cunningham, Montoye, Metzner, and Keller, 1968; Havighurst, 1957a; Zborowski, 1962).

Opportunity and health are important for the continuation of activities. Chalfen (1956) found that old people attending a day center had more activities than those in residential homes, and Desroches, Kaiman, and Carman (1965) found that during a 4-year period men in a VA domiciliary unit changed their interests and activities only when forced to do so by environmental changes.

Vocational interests as measured by the Strong test (1931) also remain stable. Campbell (1966) retested retired bankers after 30 years and found little longitudinal change. Vogel and Schell (1968) looked at the pattern of occupational interests of retired men attending a day center. Those older than 72 had higher scores on social interaction occupations whereas those younger than 72 scored higher on liking for individual responsibility. This finding may reflect a change with long retirement or self-selection with age in day center attendance, with its opportunities for social interaction.

Work Roles

For many people work occupies a central position in their lives, both with respect to time and to importance. Meltzer (1965b) noted that work took up a more significant part of the life of people over 45, and cross-sectional studies suggest that workers nearing retirement may have higher attachment to their jobs than do younger men (Indik, Seashore, and Slesinger, 1964; Meltzer, 1965a). Managerial staff expect older men to be more dependable and better timekeepers, but also to be less quick to learn and slower in their actions than young men (Bowers, 1952; Heron and Chown, 1961; Kirchner and Dunnette, 1954). On training and speed there is much experimental and observational evidence to back up these beliefs (see Chapter 19, this volume). The evidence on work skills is, however, largely laboratory based, since industrial records show little or no change with age, probably because people leave industrial work if they can no longer cope with it (Breen and Spaeth, 1960; Greenberg, 1961).

Creative work is a separate issue, and a controversy about it was sparked off by Lehman (1953) who attempted to show that the crowning achievements of creative men came early in life, in science before the age of 40 and in the arts and literature before the age of 45 (Lehman, 1960a,b, 1963, 1964, 1965, 1966a,b). He clearly demonstrated that great innovators begin early, but he included short-lived persons, thus cutting down the possibility of achievements at older ages—this may have pulled down the average age of greatest achievement. Backing for Lehman's view was provided by Manniche and Falk's (1957) analysis of Nobel prize winners; the prizewinning work was usually carried out in the thirties (Physics and Chemistry) or the forties (Biology and Medicine). However, Lehman's own investigations did produce many examples of older great achievers whose later researches were worthwhile.

Dennis (1954a,b, 1956a,b, 1966) took a different approach. He concentrated on counting total creative output and was careful to study only people who lived to old age. He found that age declines usually began only in the decade before death although there was some decrement in production in late middle age for those working in art, music and literature. He believed this occurred because the artist works as an individual, whereas scientists can work in teams. Stewart and Sparks (1966) would probably dispute that explanation. They looked at the individual patent registrations of 89 chemists and chemical engineers from one division of one firm and found that no fall in the registrations occurred with age; indeed, if anything a slight rise was apparent. However, no check was made on the history of moves to other work, and presumably the group studied was self-selected for creative ability.

Tests of originality and fluency of ideas do show age declines after middle age but improvement up to then (Bromley, 1967; Chown, 1961). The relation of these scores to age is quite different from that of nonverbal intelligence scores which decline from the mid-twenties.

On the whole, the data suggest that individual creativity tends to decline after the forties though other capacities such as leadership and experience can become substitutes for completely fresh ideas so that creative output may in the end suffer little (Lyons, 1968).

Life Structure

So far the work discussed has focused on separate areas of a career, but to provide knowledge of a person's life structure some wider view is necessary. Havighurst (1954, 1957b, 1959) has looked at profiles of activity counts for the many different roles each person plays. He demonstrated that the roles played by women varied little with age, whereas men as they aged experienced fewer roles and less activity in the roles they had. Sussman (1960) showed that some changes in the time devoted to various roles occurred when the last child left home. Havighurst (1954, 1959) thought that the successful experience of many roles in middle age and an attempt to keep the range of roles open would probably aid the adaptation to old age. He looked at patterns of roles among people aged 40 to 70, and found that they could be grouped into home centered, home and community centered, and uninvolved. Besides differing in the range of roles in which they were involved, people also differed in the level of activity in their roles. Some appeared to be highly active in all of them, some in some of them, and others showed low activity even in their most prominent role. Work on roles provides a useful starting point for assessing changes in pattern of life with age, and in considering the extent of the relationship between activity and adjustment.

Activity and Disengagement

For many years it was accepted that activity represented adjustment (Havighurst and Albrecht, 1953). Many investigators have indeed found that continued activity and high morale are correlated (Anderson, 1967; Kutner, 1956; Lipman and Smith, 1968; Maddox, 1965; Phillips, 1969; Tobin and Neugarten, 1961; Zborowski and Eyde 1962), although Maddox (1965) did find that over a 7-year period there was some decrease in activity for most elderly people.

In contrast, disengagement theory suggests that aging people like to become less involved with the world and with social norms, and to be more interested and preoccupied with their own standards and philosophy of life (Cumming, Dean, Newell, and McCaffrey, 1960; Cumming and Henry, 1961). In a study with 50 to 90 year olds, they found that older people played fewer roles and had fewer and less intimate interactions with others.

However, disengagement is neither simple nor an all or none affair. Carp (1968a,b) found that disengagement took place separately for work, volunteer services and leisure pastimes. She also looked closely at involvements with family, with other people and with outside activities, and showed that whereas disengagement from other people and outside activities occurred together, disengagement from family members was a quite separate issue. The findings could be thought to suggest two groups of activities to which people had quite different attitudes. Lemon, Bengtson, and Peterson (1972) drew attention to the fact that morale was only affected by loss of activity salient to the individual and moreover that there was often an element of choice in what was given up.

Disengagement may not be entirely voluntary, however. In many instances the environment plays a considerable part in determining social withdrawal. Barker and Barker (1961) compared the Midwest United States with Yoredale, England. The Midwest elderly occupied a greater range of behavior settings, played more roles and showed more activity patterns than the Yoredale elderly. The absolute loss for the elderly was greater in Yoredale; they had in fact less choice about whether to disengage. Similarly, physical limitations often play a part in forcing withdrawal (Britton and Britton, 1966; Youmans, 1967). When there are no such constraints, disengagement may be minimal. This was the case with two groups of professional people who did not have to disengage unless they wished (Atchley, 1971; Roman and Taietz, 1967).

There is now good evidence that voluntary disengagement is not harmful to morale, but that forced disengagement whether due to poor health, disability, widowhood, retirement, or low income, does affect not only social interaction but also morale (Lowenthal and Boler, 1965; Tallmer and Kutner, 1969). Tobin (1965) commented that some people disengage voluntarily, but others wish to retain a high level of activity. In other words, as in most aspects of life there are individual differences in the style of life which people seem to desire and in the extent to which they alter their preferences as they age. A study by Lowenthal (1965) suggested that people relatively isolated all their lives did not suffer when they were isolated in old age; presumably they were continuing a long-held pattern of life.

Out of the work on voluntary and forced disengagement has come the concept of readiness for disengagement or disengagement potential. Cumming and McCaffrey (1961) found that satisfaction with present life varied according to readiness for disengagement and amount of social responsibilities. Congruence was required for high morale. Work by Tissue (1968, 1971) illustrates this also. His Guttman scale of disengagement potential asks questions about predisposition towards passivity, ability to tolerate solitude and inactivity, acceptance of one's own mortality and lessening of emotional intensity. Age, sex, and current social interaction were not related to disengagement potential, but morale was high only where current social activity matched that indicated as correct by the disengagment potential scores. This relationship between disengagement potential and amount of social interaction, with congruence leading to high morale, needs further investigation. People from a wider range of backgrounds than those included in Tissue's study, and people who have and have not experienced forced withdrawal should be tested before too many generalizations are made.

Life Styles

As discussed already, individual differences have been shown to exist in role profiles and in levels of social interaction in middle age. Many attempts have been made to try to categorize people according to their patterns of response to social interaction; the earlier ones based on feel for the data, and later ones on analyses of intercorrelations of ratings.

Williams and Wirths (1965) looked for the central characteristics of people's lives and diagnosed six types. These were "living alone," "work," and "easing through life," which were all concerned with acts rather than people; and "family," "couplehood," and "living fully," which were all concerned with human relationships. The latter played more roles, had greater life satisfaction, less anomie and isolation, and more leisure interests. The classification of people into task-orientated and people-oriented seems an important one and fits in with certain studies in social psychology (Bales, 1950) but it has so far not been followed further in work on aging.

Hamlin (1967) suggested a two-fold classification into task-oriented and non-task-oriented people. He thought that task-oriented people require positive satisfactions, are energetic, and like dealing with uncertainty and change; non-task-oriented people seek to avoid dissatisfaction, like to be placid and quiet, dislike uncertainty and prefer continuity to change. He based his ideas on those of Herzberg relating to job satisfaction, but does not seem to have followed them up as yet. The notion of an active-passive dichotomy has appeared in other suggested classifications, including those based on correlational analyses.

Bühler (1961a,b) classified approaches to life into four groups. These were active, passive, resigned, and frustrated/guilty/regretful. She illustrated these from a large number of life history records, making it clear that it was reactions to events rather than type of events which interested her.

Reichard, Livson, and Petersen (1962) attempted a more objective approach. They correlated ratings based on interviews for "attitude to aging" with those for 114 other variables. As a result of cluster analysis they found three favorable attitude clusters, and two negative ones. The favorable clusters were "Mature" (philosophic, integrated people), "Rocking Chair" (passive, liking an easy life), and "Armored" (keeping active as a defense). The unfavorable clusters were "Aggressive" (projecting anger onto the world), and "Self-hating" (projecting anger onto themselves). Unfortunately, the original ratings were unreliable, and the clusters accounted for only half the subjects, but the results were encouragingly similar to Bühler's intuitive analysis.

As a result of this work, Neugarten, Crotty, and Tobin (1964) reanalyzed the Kansas City data used by Williams and Wirths. They rated the interview protocols for 45 personality characteristics. In spite of obscure definitions, the raters knew what they meant, for there were high inter-rater reliabilities. Factor analysis of the intercorrelations between the characteristics produced four main groups. These were the Integrated, the Armored, the Passive-Dependent, and the Unintegrated. These terms begin to look familiar. The life-styles all appeared in each age group over the range 50 to 90 years. Role counts revealed that each of the first three styles included people with high, medium, and low role counts, whereas the last one consisted of people with low role counts only. The ratings for life satisfaction were high for Integrated people, whether they had high role counts (active individuals) or low ones (disengaged people). Within each of the other groups, higher life satisfaction appeared to go with higher role counts. This study seems to demonstrate in a most safisfactory way the notion that a personal style of life is followed using the opportunities available, and that the two interact together to provide life satisfaction or dissatisfaction.

So far, no attempt has been made to look for life-style change in individuals, but only (without success) to look for differences between age groups. It may be suspected, for example, that few people would alter so drastically as to warrant reclassification from active to passive in the course of their lives. In normal people, changes in personality seem, from the few studies available, to be minor when compared with the differences between people (Kelly, 1955; Woodruff and Birren, 1972). However, an important gap in the work on life-styles exists. Nothing is yet known of the reaction of people whose style of life is seriously threatened by chronic illness or disablement. It would be interesting to know how people of different basic styles meet and adjust to such interference.

REACTIONS TO FRUSTRATION

The rest of this chapter will be devoted to attempts to look at interactions between morale, careers, and personal potentials in the context of reactions to change in career circumstances. That lack of change preserves self-concepts is well illustrated by Kaplan and Pokorny (1970). They found that there were a few people who, at the age of 65 or older, expressed less self-derogation than young people did. They investigated the circumstances of these exceptional older people and found that they were in good health, comfortably off, living with their spouses, and that, in short, their long established way of life had never been threatened.

Older people can be expected to react to frustration in a variety of ways, just as do younger ones. Some may deny frustration; Shrut (1958a,b) found that his subjects denied their ill health. Some may become aggressive, and although this may be a less usual reaction in old age (Dean, 1962; Friedman and Granick, 1963), it is interesting to note that Preston (1966) found that retired men thought themselves more hostile and aggressive than did nonretired men of the same age. Another reaction might be regression, possibly through illness or hypochondria (Kral, Grad, and Berenson, 1968; Miller and Lieberman, 1965), although Desroches, Kaiman, and Ballard (1967) thought hypochondria more likely to be a long established habit. Yet another possible reaction is to retreat into fantasy. Lewis (1971) suggested that reminiscers use remembrance of the past as a defense against present threat to self-esteem. One other reaction is possible, to look ahead "beyond the grave." Those in good health and with wide interests are often evasive about death (Swenson, 1961); those facing it appear to come to accept it (Kastenbaum, 1967); but neurotic, hypochondriac or depressed people are often greatly concerned with the topic (Rhudick and Dibner, 1961; Templer, 1971). Pressey and Kuhlen (1957) suggested that interest in religion would be greater when personal crises occur; no direct test of this has been carried out, but the religious old appear to face the future with more sense of purpose (Acuff and Allen, 1970; Cavan, 1949; Jeffers, Nichols, and Eisdorfer, 1961). Whether older people display any more religious involvement than younger people is uncertain, for cohort differences may affect the issue (Moberg, 1953, 1965).

People say they fear facing economic want and loss of health with age (Carp, 1967a,b; Neugarten and Garron, 1959). Pressey (1957) lists good health, adequate income, feeling useful, having opportunities for social interaction and having lively interests as the main determinants of a happy old age. These may be threatened by a number of conditions or events outside the control of the older person, such as retirement, relocation, and bereavement, illness and loneliness.

Retirement

Retirement has long been considered a crisis (Mack, 1958; Maddox, 1970), because work occupies so much time and provides such varied rewards including income, opportunities for social interaction and a basis for self-esteem. People who continue to work into old age nearly always score highly on inventories inquiring into morale, happiness and adjustment (Carp 1968a,b). A number of studies have looked for personal and social characteristics making for ease or difficulty of adjustment. Longitudinal work has been done by Emerson (1959) in a 1-year follow-up, Stokes and Maddox (1967) over 10 years, and Streib and Schneider (1971) over 6 years, and these largely confirm retrospective studies. From all the work, there seem to be five particularly influential factors which will now be discussed.

Type of Job. People deeply involved in their work continue working as long as they possibly can (Atchley, 1971; Fillenbaum, 1971; Friedman and Havighurst, 1954; Havighurst and Shanas, 1953; Johnson and Strother, 1962; Roman and Taietz 1967). It is interesting that Simpson and McKinney (1966) found that if work which had engrossed a person was missed after retirement, morale tended to be high, suggesting that the feeling of loss was being accepted as a justification of the engrossment.

Streib and Schneider (1971) found that white-collar workers were most willing to retire, then skilled workers, then managers, then unskilled workers, and least of all professional people. Stokes and Maddox (1967) found that white-collar workers were initially more dis-

satisfied with retirement than blue-collar workers, but after 10 years the positions were reversed and the white-collar retirees were more satisfied than the blue-collar retirees.

Health. Poor health is the main cause of voluntary and early retirement (Lloyd, 1955; Osborn, 1971; Pollman, 1971; Steiner and Dorfman, 1957; Townsend, 1957). Tuckman (1956) found that voluntary retirement was in fact forced on people by loss of health, and was resented as much as compulsory retirement. The old notion of retirement impact causing ill health or even death, because of its threat to self-esteem, has been disproved by Emerson (1959) and Streib and Schneider (1971), for both noted that in many instances health actually improved after the stress of work was removed. Feelings of poor health invariably correlate with low current satisfaction (Payne, 1953; Streib and Schneider, 1971).

Income. Income falls upon retirement for most people and low income is associated with low morale among the retired (Osborn, 1971; Payne, 1953; Pollman, 1971; Preston and Gudiksen, 1966; Streib and Schneider, 1971). Simpson and McKinney (1966) found that income loss was influential only among the initially badly off; moreover, as Streib and Schneider (1971) noted, people with low economic resources did not wish to retire, and even found work after retirement if they were fit enough to do so.

Family. Emotional support and acceptance of a person's retirement by the immediate family is an important element in adjustment to retirement (Heyman and Jeffers, 1968; Payne, 1953; Townsend, 1957). Through the family the retired can obtain status, feelings of usefulness and high morale.

Purpose in Life. Feelings of usefulness and involvement help adjustment to retirement, whereas feeling useless leads to low morale. Emerson (1959) found that blue-collar workers experienced both boredom and depression upon retirement. The depression passed, but the boredom remained. A quarter of Streib and

Schneider's (1971) sample reported feeling useless.

Morale often seems lower among the retired than among those still working (Carp, 1968a; Kutner, 1956) though not all have found this (Preston, 1967); furthermore, Streib and Schneider (1971) discovered in their longitudinal study that low morale was a long-term condition and was not due to the effects of retirement after all. Simpson and McKinney (1966) reported that having a number of interests helped to maintain involvement to some extent, but these interests were similarly of long standing and not acquired after retirement.

Looking forward to retirement was related to adjustment to it, but only in those cases where the plans made were both realistic and put into operation (Streib and Schneider, 1971). Havighurst, Munnichs, Neugarten, and Thomae (1969) showed that differences existed in retirement activities between professional and skilled people, and between nationalities in the western world, but all stressed the need for some meaningful activity and opportunities for social interaction.

Thus, in summary, it seems that retirement does constitute a serious threat to the way of life of most people, and some reorganization of the way they satisfy their needs has to ensue. Moreover, the situation is for most exacerbated to some extent by a drop in income, and for many by poor health. However, retirement is not in itself a lethal crisis, and it is greatly ameliorated if the family can provide substitute satisfactions for those which have been lost. More work is needed on the way in which people do manage to substitute the rewards which they obtained from their jobs. Simpson and McKinney (1966) looked at style of work (dealing with symbols, people or things) and found that continuity of style into retirement activities could be detrimental if it emphasized some missing social context, but was usually helpful in other situations.

Relocation

Moving into a retirement community is usually a matter of free personal choice which it is possible to reverse later. It is the opportunities which such communities offer for informal contact and friendship which seem to be valued (Burgess, 1954; Messer, 1968; Michelon, 1954). Health and social interaction provide status in such communities (Rose and Peterson, 1965), with occupational status playing a secondary part (Bultena, 1969). Carp's (1966) study of the Victoria Plaza apartments shows that adjustment to a desired change of location was an easy one. For the new inhabitants of the building, activities and happiness increased, although they had less money after the move than before.

Results are very different when people are relocated against their own preferences. Death and illness rates rise in the first months after change (Aldrich and Mendkoff, 1963; Kral, Grad, and Berenson, 1968; Markus , Blenkner, Bloom, and Downs, 1971, 1972; Miller and Lieberman, 1965). Lieberman, Prock, and Tobin (1968), reviewing work on first institutionalization, thought that behavior often improved, but that there were deficits to set against this such as decreases in feelings of power.

Institution residents seem to have lower self-esteem than people living independently (Pollack, Karp, Kahn, and Goldfarb, 1962; Shrut, 1958b) and people waiting to enter old age homes are unhappy and low on self-esteem (Lieberman, Prock, and Tobin 1968; Rose and Peterson, 1965). It may be that the decision to enter such a home, entailing as it does, the threat of loss of functional independence and admission of helplessness, is the critical point. Gordon and Vinacke (1971) found that within an institution, highly dependent men had poor current self-concepts, whereas highly dependent women had good current self-concepts. A post hoc explanation in terms of different cultural expectations for the two sexes is attractive here. Institution residents develop a social hierarchy partly based on length of stay in the institution (Friedman, 1967). Self-esteem and feelings of belonging depend upon status in the home, maintaining informal social relationships, and seeing the point of any rules (Anderson, 1967; Bell, 1967; Kahana and Coe, 1969).

The key point in predicting the effect of relocation appears to be whether or not it threatens self-esteem. From existing studies, friendships within the institution appear to offer the best hope of amelioration, but from the practical point of view, much more information is needed on ways to preserve and rebuild self-esteem.

Bereavement, Illness and Loneliness

Reactions to bereavement in the elderly have rarely been studied in their own right, but some of the effects of the loss of a spouse have been noted in general studies of role change (Acuff and Allen, 1970; Lowenthal and Boler, 1965; Phillips, 1957). Low morale, low current life satisfaction, and lack of purpose have all been found; however, the impact of bereavement may be similar at any age, as Chown (1969) showed in an age analysis of Gorer's cases (1965).

Although health estimates given by people themselves usually agree quite well with those given by their physicians, cultural expectations and traditions such as complaining or being stoical may affect a person's view of himself (Shanas, Townsend, Wedderburn, Friis, Milhøj, and Stehouwer, 1968), as may habitual mode of reaction to life, whether optimistic, pessimistic or realistic (Friedsam and Martin, 1963). Feelings of ill health seem to make people feel older, and hamper adjustment (Lehr and Puschner, 1964); they prevent happiness (Lebo, 1953; Mack, 1953), promote pessimism (Ludwig and Eichorn, 1967) and weaken the self-image (Schwartz and Kleemeier, 1965). The elderly are prone to depression (Busse, Barnes, Silverman, Shy, Thaler, and Frost, 1954; Zung, 1970) and this lessens self-esteem.

Subjective loneliness increases in old age and this is understandable, as friends and relatives die, mobility and level of activity decrease, and fewer new contacts are made (Dean, 1962; Munnichs, 1964, 1966). Only the individual can say what level of interaction, and what type, he would prefer; but older people are often prevented by circumstances from altering levels of interaction to suit themselves. Other people cannot be sure whether more or less interaction is desired. Tissue's (1971) work on

disengagement potential may find application here.

This brief review of some of the crises of old age makes it clear that people's opinions about themselves are likely to alter as a result of such crises, and that morale is closely related to the experience of these crises also. However, there have been few longitudinal studies, and those that exist have not explored fully the nature of the links between morale, careers and personal potentials.

In studying reactions to all late-life crises, "replaceability," linked to the notion of relative deprivation, would seem to be a useful concept (Friedsam, 1961). If a relationship, activity, or object can be replaced, then the impact of the loss is likely to be less. It would be difficult to quantify the parameters of loss, such as degree of involvement, centrality, and opportunity for replacement, sufficiently well to carry out a test of the replacement hypothesis, but the task presents a worthwhile challenge.

Another way of looking at the problem of reactions to crises leads to the suggestion that threats to careers may well be most disruptive to morale when a person's freedom of choice becomes restricted as a result of them (Goldman, 1971; Smith and Lipman, 1972). Such constriction is so common that it is often taken for granted as typical of old age; it is worth noting that when it occurs among the young it also affects morale (Goffman, 1961). Phillips (1957) held the view that lack of concordance between needs and fulfillment represents lack of adjustment, though as Lawton (1970) points out, perfect congruence between demand and capacity would rule out challenge and challenge is good for people. However, challenge is not the same as insuperable difficulty, and ill health and low income may prevent old people from overcoming other difficulties which, were they to be present, would not so greatly hamper younger people. Schwartz and Poppe (1970) suggest the provision of as many aids as possible to the aged so as to cut down the number of constraints on their freedom of choice. It would seem likely, from what is already known, that any such moves would aid the preservation of morale rather than lead to its deterioration.

FUTURE RESEARCH

It would be useful to see some increase in the number of studies specifically directed to the problems of the relationship between career events, self-assessment and morale, and in particular to the way in which people adapt to crises and handicaps imposed upon them.

General studies of life satisfaction in relation to original goals and to actual accomplishment would also be welcome, as would work on the extent to which goals change throughout life. Generational effects and differences between the sexes in reactions to events require further investigation.

On the applied side, an urgent attack is needed on the problems of providing ways for the elderly to control their own levels of social interaction and activity, both to overcome physical and environmental barriers and also those of social isolation.

REFERENCES

Acuff, G., and Allen, D. 1970. Hiatus in "meaning"; disengagement for retired professors. *J. Gerontol.*, 25, 126-128.

Adler, A. 1927. *Practice and Theory of Individual Psychology*. New York: Harcourt Brace.

Albrecht, R. 1954. Relationship of older parents with their children. *Marr. Fam. Living*, 16, 32-35.

Aldrich, C. K., and Mendkoff, E. 1963. Relocation of the aged and disabled: a mortality study. *J. Am. Geriat. Soc.*, 11, 185-194.

Anderson, N. E. 1967. Effects of institutionalization on self esteem. *J. Gerontol.*, 22, 313-317.

Arnhoff, F. N., Leon, H. V., and Lorge, I. 1964. Cross cultural acceptance of stereotypes towards aging. *Journal of Social Psychology*, 63, 41-58.

Atchley, R. C. 1971. Disengagement among professors. *J. Gerontol.*, 26, 476-480.

Atkinson, J. W. (ed.), 1958. *The Achievement Motive in Fantasy, Action and Society*. Princeton: Van Nostrand.

Axelrod, S., and Eisdorfer, C. 1961. Attitudes towards old people: an empirical analysis of the stimulus. *J. Gerontol.*, 16, 75-83.

Back, K. W. and Bourque, L. B. 1970. Life graphs: aging and cohort effect. *J. Gerontol.*, 25, 249-255.

Bales, R. F. 1950. *Interaction Process Analysis*. Cambridge: Addison-Wesley.

Ballweg, J. A. 1967. Resolution of conjugal role adjustment after retirement. *Marr. Fam. Living*, 29, 277-281.

Barker, R. G., and Barker, L. S. 1961. The psychologi-

cal ecology of old people in Midwest, Kansas, and Yoredale, Yorkshire. *J. Gerontol.*, 16, 144-149.

Bell, T. 1967. The relationship between social involvement and feeling old among residents in homes for the aged. *J. Gerontol.*, 22, 17-22.

Bloom, K. L. 1961. Age and the self concept. *Am. J. Psychiat.*, 118, 534-538.

Bortner, R. W. 1967. Personality and social psychology in the study of aging. *Gerontologist*, 7, 23.

Bortner, R. W., and Hultsch, D. F. 1970. A multivariate analysis of correlates of life satisfaction in adulthood. *J. Gerontol.*, 25, 41-47.

Botwinick, J. 1969. Disinclination to venture response versus cautiousness in responding: age differences *Journal of Genetic Psychology*, 115, 55-62.

Botwinick, J. 1970. Age differences in self ratings of confidence. *Psych. Rep.*, 27, 865-866.

Bowers, W. H. 1952. An appraisal of worker characteristics related to age. *J. Appl. Psych.*, 36, 296-300.

Breen, L. Z., and Spaeth, J. L. 1960. Age and productivity among workers in four Chicago companies. *J. Gerontol.*, 15, 68-70.

Britton, J. H., and Britton, J. O. 1966. Continuity of personality in the aged. *Proceedings, 7th Intern. Congr. Geront.*, Vienna.

Britton, J. H., Mather, W. G., and Lansing, A. K. 1961. Expectations for older persons in a rural community: living arrangements and family relationships. *J. Gerontol.*, 16, 156-162.

Bromley, D. B. 1967. Age and sex differences in the serial productions of creative conceptual responses. *J. Gerontol.*, 22, 32-42.

Brown, R. G. 1960. Family structure and social isolation of older persons. *J. Gerontol.*, 15, 170-172.

Bühler, C. 1959. Theoretical observations about life's basic tendencies. *Amer. J. Psychother.* 13, 561-581.

Bühler, C. 1961a. Meaningful life in the mature years. *In*, R. W. Kleemeier (ed.), *Aging and Leisure*, pp. 345-387. New York: Oxford University Press.

Bühler, C. 1961b. Old age and fulfillment of life with considerations of the use of time in old age. *Acta Psychol.*, 19, 126-148.

Bultena, G. L. 1968. Age grading in the social interaction of an elderly male population. *J. Gerontol.*, 23, 539-543.

Bultena, G. L. 1969. The relationship of occupational status to friendship ties in three planned retirement communities. *J. Gerontol.*, 24, 461-464.

Burgess, E. W. 1954. Social relations, activities and personal adjustment. *Am. J. Sociol.*, 59, 352-360.

Busse, E. W., Barnes, R. H., Silverman, A. J., Shy, G. M., Thaler, M., and Frost, L. L. 1954. Studies of the process of aging: factors that influence the psyche of elderly persons. *Am. J. Psychiat.*, 110, 897-903.

Butler, R. N. 1963. The life review: an interpretation of reminiscence in the aged. *Psychiat.*, 26, 65-76.

Butler, R. N. 1968. Toward a psychiatry of the life cycle. *Amer. Psychiat. Assoc: Psychiat. Res. Rep.*, 23, 233-248.

Cameron, P. 1967a. Ego strength and happiness of the aged. *J. Gerontol.*, **22**, 199.

Cameron, P. 1967b. Introversion and egocentricity among the aged. *J. Gerontol.*, **22**, 465.

Cameron, P. 1969. Age parameters of young, adult, middle aged, old, and aged. *J. Gerontol.*, **24**, 201–202.

Cameron, P. 1971. The generation gap: beliefs about stability of life. *J. Gerontol.*, **26**, 81.

Campbell, D. P. 1966. Stability of interests within an occupation over 30 years. *J. Appl. Psych.*, **50**, 51–56.

Cantril, H. 1965. *The Pattern of Human Careers.* New Jersey: Rutgers University Press.

Carp, F. M. 1966. *A Future for The Aged: Victoria Plaza and its Residents.* Austin: University of Texas Press.

Carp, F. M. 1967a. Attitudes of old persons towards themselves and towards others. *J. Gerontol.*, **22**, 308.

Carp, F. M. 1967b. The applicability of an empirical scoring standard for a sentence completion test administered to two age groups. *J. Gerontol.*, **22**, 301.

Carp, F. M. 1968a. Person situation congruence in engagement. *Gerontologist*, **8**, 184–188.

Carp, F. M. 1968b. Some components of disengagement. *J. Gerontol.*, **23**, 382–386.

Cason, H. 1930. Common annoyances. *Psychol. Monogr.*, **40**(2).

Cavan, R. 1949. *Personal Adjustment in Old Age.* Chicago: Science Research Associates.

Chalfen, L. 1956. Leisure time and adjustment of the aged; activities and interests and some factors influencing choice. *Journal of Genetic Psychology*, **88**, 261–276.

Chown, S. M. 1960. A factor analysis of the Wesley rigidity inventory. *J. Abn. Soc. Psych.* **61**, 491–494.

Chown, S. M. 1961. Age and the rigidities. *J. Gerontol.*, **16**, 353–362.

Chown, S. M. 1968. Personality and aging. *In*, K. W. Schaie (ed.), *Theory and Methods of Research in Aging.* pp. 134–137. Morgantown: West Virginia Press.

Chown, S. M. 1969. Cybernetics applied to the study of personality. *Proceedings, 8th Intern. Congr. Geront.*, Washington, D.C.

Coleman, P. G. 1972. *The role of the past in adaptation to old age.* Ph.D. thesis. University of London, England.

Cowgill, D. O., and Baulch, N. 1962. The use of leisure time by older people. *Gerontolgist*, **2**, 47–50.

Craik, F. I. M. 1962. The effects of age and the experimental situation in confidence behaviour. *Bull. Brit. Psychol. Soc.*, **A21** (Abstr).

Cumming, E., Dean, L. R., Newell, D. S., and McCaffrey, I. 1960. Disengagement: a tentative theory of aging. *Sociometry*, **23**, 23–35.

Cumming, E., and Henry, W. E. 1961. *Growing Old.* New York: Basic Books.

Cumming, E., and McCaffrey, I., 1961. Some condi-

tions associated with morale among the aging. *In*, P. H. Hock and J. Zubin (eds.), *Psychopathology of Aging.* New York: Grune & Stratton.

Cumming, E., and Schneider, D. M. 1961. Sibling solidarity; a property of American kinship. *Am. Anthropologist*, **63**, 498–507.

Cunningham, D. A., Montoye, H. J., Metzner, H. L., and Keller, J. B. 1968. Active leisure time activities as related to age among males in a total population. *J. Gerontol.*, **23**, 551–556.

Davies, A. D. M., and Chown, S. M. 1969. The perception of another's age. *Proceedings, 8th Intern. Congr. Geront.*, Washington, D.C.

Davis, R. W. 1967. Social influences on the aspiration tendency of older people. *J. Gerontol.*, **22**, 510–516.

Dean, L. R. 1962. Aging and the decline of affect. *J. Gerontol.*, **17**, 440–446.

Dennis, W. 1954a. Productivity among American psychologists. *American Psychologist*, **9**, 191–194.

Dennis, W. 1954b. Predicting scientific productivity in later maturity from records of earlier decades. *J. Gerontol.*, **9**, 465–467.

Dennis, W. 1956a. Age and achievement: a critique. *J. Gerontol.*, **11**, 331–333.

Dennis, W. 1956b. Age and productivity among scientists. *Science*, **123**, 724–725.

Dennis, W. 1966. Creative productivity between the ages of 20 and 80 years. *J. Gerontol.*, **21**, 1–8.

Desroches, H. F., Kaiman, B. D., and Ballard, A. T. 1967. Factors influencing reporting of physical symptoms by the aged patient. *Geriatrics*, **22**, 169–175.

Desroches, H. F., Kaiman, B. D., and Carman, P. M. 1965. Age and leisure time activities in a VA domiciliary. *Geriatrics*, **20**, 1065–1069.

Dodge, J. S. 1961. Changes in the self percept with age. *Perceptual Motor Skills*, **13**, 88.

Dykman, R. A., Heimann, E. K., and Kerr, W. E. 1952. Life-time worry patterns of three diverse adult cultural groups. *Journal of Social Psychology*, **35**, 91–100.

Eisdorfer, C., and Altrocchi, J. 1961. A comparison of attitudes toward old age and mental illness. *J. Gerontol.*, **16**, 340–343.

Emerson, A. R. 1959. The first year of retirement. *Occupational Psychology*, **33**, 197–208.

Erikson, E. H. 1959. Identity and the life cycle. *Psychological Issues, Monograph* 1.

Fillenbaum, G., 1971. The working retired. *J. Gerontol.*, **26**, 82–89.

Fink, H. F. 1957. The relationship of time perspective to age, institutionalization and activity. *J. Gerontol.*, **12**, 414–417.

Friedman, A. S., and Granick, S. 1963. A note on anger and aggression in old age. *J. Gerontol.*, **18**, 283–285.

Friedman, E. A., and Havighurst, R. J. 1954. *The meaning of Work and Retirement.* Chicago: University of Chicago Press.

Friedman, E. P. 1967. Age, length of institutionalization and social status in a home for the aged. *J. Gerontol.*, **22**, 474–477.

Friedsam, H. J. 1961. Reactions of older persons to disaster caused losses: an hypothesis of relative deprivation. *Gerontologist*, **1**, 34–37.

Friedsam, H. J., and Martin, H. W. A. 1963. Comparison of self and physician's health ratings in an older population. *J. Health Hum. Behav.*, **4**, 179–183.

Ganzler, H. 1964. Motivation as a factor in the psychological deficit of aging. *J. Gerontol*, **19**, 425–429.

Goffman, E. 1961. *Asylums*. New York: Doubleday Anchor.

Goldman, S. 1971. Social aging, disorganization and loss of choice. *Gerontologist*, **11**, 158–162.

Gordon, S., and Vinacke, W. E. 1971. Self and ideal self concepts and dependency in aged persons residing in institutions. *J. Gerontol*, **26**, 337–343.

Gorer, G. 1965. *Death, Grief and Mourning*. London: Cresset.

Gorney, J. E. 1968. *Experiencing and age: patterns of reminiscence among the elderly*. Ph.D. thesis. University of Chicago.

Greenberg, L. 1961. Productivity of older workers. *Gerontologist*, **1**, 38–41.

Hamlin, R. M. 1967. A utility theory of old age. *Gerontologist*, **7**, 37–45.

Haug, M., and Sussman, M. B. 1970. The second career: variant of a sociological concept. *In*, H. L. Sheppard (ed.), *Towards an Industrial Gerontology*, pp. 123–131. New York: Schenkman.

Havighurst, R. J. 1954. Flexibility and the social roles of the retired. *Am. J. Sociol.*, **59**, 309–311.

Havighurst, R. J. 1957a. The leisure activities of the middle aged. *Am. J. Sociol.*, **63**, 152–162.

Havighurst, R. J. 1957b. The social competence of middle aged people. *Genetic Psychol. Monogr.*, **56**, 297–375.

Havighurst, R. J. 1959. Life styles of middle aged people. *Vita Humana*, **2**, 23–34.

Havighurst, R. J. 1963. Successful aging, pp. 299–320. *In*, R. J. Williams, C. Tibbitts, and W. Donahue, (eds.), *Processes of Aging*. New York: Atherton Press.

Havighurst, R. J., and Albrecht, R. 1953. *Older People*. New York: Longmans.

Havighurst, R. J., and Glasser, R. 1972. An exploratory study of reminiscence. *J. Gerontol.*, **27**, 245–253.

Havighurst, R. J., Munnicho, J. M. A., Neugarten, B. L., and Thomae, H. 1969. *Adjustment to Retirement, a Cross National Study*. Assen: Van Gorkum.

Havighurst, R. J., and Shanas, E. 1953. Retirement and the professional worker. *J. Gerontol.*, **8**, 81–85.

Heron, A., and Chown, S. M. 1961. Aging and the semi-skilled. *Med. Res. Council Memo No. 40*. London: HMSO.

Hess, A. L., and Bradshaw, H. L. 1970. Positiveness of self concept and ideal self as a function of age. *Journal of Genetic Psychology*, **117**, 57–67.

Heyman, D. K., and Jeffers, F. 1968. Wives and retirement: a pilot study. *J. Gerontol.*, **23**, 488–496.

Indik, B., Seashore, S. E., and Slesinger, J. 1964. Demographic correlates of psychological strain. *J. Abn. Soc. Psych.*, **69**, 26–38.

Jacques, E. 1966. Death and the mid-life crisis. *Rev. Psicoanal.*, **23**, 401–423.

Jeffers, F., Nichols, C. R., and Eisdorfer, C. 1961. Attitudes of older persons towards death; a preliminary study. *J. Gerontol.*, **16**, 53–56.

Johnson, L., and Strother, G. B. 1962. Job expectations and retirement planning. *J. Gerontol*, **17**, 418–423.

Jones, H. E. 1961. The age-relative study of personality. *Acta Psychol.*, **19**, 140–142.

Kahana, E., and Coe, R. M. 1969. Dimensions of conformity: a multidisciplinary view. *J. Gerontol.*, **24**, 76–81.

Kaplan, H. B., and Pokorny, A. D. 1970. Aging and self attitude, a conditional relationship. *Aging and Human Development*, **1**, 241–250.

Kastenbaum, R. 1967. The mental life of dying geriatric patients. *Gerontologist*, **7**, 97–100.

Kelly, E. L. 1955. Consistency of the adult personality. *American Psychologist*, **10**, 659–681.

Kerckhoff, A. C. 1964. Husband-wife expectations and reactions to retirement. *J. Gerontol.*, **19**, 510–516.

Kerckhoff, A. C. 1966. Family patterns and morale in retirement. *In*, I. H. Simpson and J. C. McKinney (eds.), *Social Aspects of Aging*. Durham: Duke University Press.

Kirchner, W. K., and Dunnette, M. D. 1954. Attitudes towards older workers. *Personnel Psychol.*, **7**, 257–265.

Kogan, N. 1961. Attitude toward old people in an older sample. *J. Abn. Soc. Psych.*, **62**, 616–622.

Kral, V. A., Grad, B., and Berenson, J. 1968. Stress reactions resulting from the relocation of an aged population. *Canadian Psychiatric Association Journal.*, **13**, 201–209.

Krugman, A. D. 1959. A note on level of aspiration behavior and aging. *J. Gerontol.*, **14**, 222–225.

Kuhlen, R. G. 1959. Aging and life adjustment. *In*, J. E. Birren (ed.), *Handbook of Aging and the Individual*, pp. 852–897. Chicago: University of Chicago Press.

Kuhlen, R. G. 1964a. Developmental changes in motivation during the adult years. *In*, J. E. Birren (ed.), *Relation of Development and Aging*, pp. 209–246. Springfield, Illinois: Charles C. Thomas.

Kuhlen, R. G. 1964b. Personality change with age. *In*, P. Worchel and D. Byrne (eds.) *Personality Change*, pp. 524–525. New York: John Wiley.

Kuhlen, R. G. and Johnson, G. H. 1952. Changes in goals with adult increasing age. *J. Consult. Psych.*, **16**, 1–4.

Kutner, B. 1956. Index of morale: In Kutner, B., Fanshel, D., Togo, A. M. & Langner, T. S. *Five Hundred over 60*. New York: Russell Sage.

Lakin, M., and Eisdorfer, C. 1960. Affective expression among the aged. *J. Proj. Tech.*, 24, 403–408.

Laurence, M. 1961. Sources of satisfaction in the lives of working women. *J. Gerontol.*, 16, 163–167.

Laurence, M. 1964. Sex differences in the perception of men and women at four different ages. *J. Gerontol.*, 19, 343–348.

Lawton, M. P. 1970. Assessment integration and environments for older people. *Gerontologist*, 10, 38–46.

Le Blanc, A. F. 1969. Time orientation and time estimation, a function of age. *Journal of Genetic Psychology.*, 115, 187–194.

Lebo, D. 1953. Some factors said to make for happiness in old age. *J. Clin. Psych.*, 9, 385–387.

Lehman, H. C. 1953. *Age and Achievement.* Princeton: Princeton University Press.

Lehman, H. C. 1960a. Age and outstanding achievement in creative chemistry. *Geriatrics*, 5, 19–37.

Lehman, H. C. 1960b. The age decrement in outstanding scientific creativity. *American Psychologist*, 15, 128–134.

Lehman, H. C. 1963. Chronological age versus present day contributions to medical progress. *Gerontologist*, 3, 71–75.

Lehman, H. C. 1964. The relationship between chronological age and high level research output in Physics and Chemistry. *J. Gerontol.*, 19, 157–164.

Lehman, H. C. 1965. The production of master works prior to age 30. *Gerontologist*, 5, 24–30.

Lehman, H. C. 1966a. The most creative years of engineers and other technologists. *Journal of Genetic Psychology*, 108, 263–277.

Lehman, H. C. 1966b. The psychologists most creative years. *American Psychologist*, 21, 363–369.

Lehr, U. 1967. Attitudes towards the future in old age. *Hum. Develop.*, 10, 230–238.

Lehr, U., and Puschner, I. 1964. Studies in the awareness of aging, pp. 425–427. *In*, P. Hansen (ed.), *Age with a Future.* Copenhagen: Munksgaard.

Lemon, B. W., Bengtson, V. L., and Peterson, J. A. 1972. An exploration of the activity theory of aging activity types and life satisfaction among inmovers to a retirement community. *J. Gerontol.*, 27, 511–523.

Lewis, C. N. 1971. Reminiscing and self concept in old age. *J. Gerontol.*, 26, 240–243.

Liberman, L. R. 1970. Life satisfaction in young and the old. *Psych. Reports*, 27, 75–79.

Lieberman, M. A., and Falk, J. M. 1971. The remembered past as a source of data for research on the life cycle. *Hum. Develop.*, 14, 132–141.

Lieberman, M. A., Prock, V., and Tobin, S. 1968. Psychological effects of institutionalization. *J. Gerontol.*, 23, 343–353.

Linden, M. E., and Courtney, D. 1953. The human life cycle and its interruptions. *Am. J. Psychiat.*, 109, 906–915.

Lipman, A. 1961. Role conceptions and morale of couples in retirement. *J. Gerontol.*, 16, 267–271.

Lipman, A., and Smith, K. J. 1968. Functionality of disengagement in old age. *J. Gerontol.*, 23, 517–521.

Livson, N. 1973. Developmental dimensions of personality: a life span formulation. *In*, P. B. Baltes and K. W. Schaie (eds.), *Life-Span Developmental Psychology*, pp. 97–122. New York: Academic Press.

Lloyd, R. G. 1955. Social and personal adjustment of retired persons. *Sociol. & Soc. Res.*, 39, 312–316.

Lowenthal, M. F. 1965. Antecedents of isolation and mental illness in old age. *Arch. Gen. Psychiat.*, 12, 245–254.

Lowentahl, M. F., and Boler, D. 1965. Voluntary vs involuntary social withdrawal. *J. Gerontol.*, 20, 363–371.

Lowenthal, M. F., and Haven, C. 1968. Interaction and adaptation: intimacy as a critical variable. *Am. Soc. Rev.*, 33, 20–30.

Ludwig, E., and Eichorn, R. L. 1967. Age and disillusionment; a study of value changes associated with aging. *J. Gerontol.*, 22, 59.

Lyons, J. 1968. Chronological age, professional age and eminence in Psychology. *American Psychologist*, 23, 371–374.

Mack, M. J. 1953. Personal adjustment of chronically ill old people under home care. *Geriatrics*, 8, 407–416.

Mack, M. J. 1958. An evaluation of a retirement planning program. *J. Gerontol.*, 13, 198–202.

Maddox, G. 1965. Fact and artifact: evidence bearing on disengagement theory from the Duke geriatric project. *Hum. Develop.*, 8, 117–130.

Maddox, G. 1970. Adaptation to retirement. *Gerontologist*, 10, 14–18.

Manniche, E., and Falk, G. 1957. Age and the Nobel prize. *Behavioral Science*, 2, 301–307.

Markus, E., Blenkner, M., Bloom, M., and Downs, T. 1971. The impact of relocation upon mortality rates of institutionalized aged persons. *J. Gerontol.*, 26, 537–541.

Markus, E., Blenkner, M., Bloom, M., and Downs, T. 1972. Some factors and their association with post-relocation mortality among institutionalized aged persons. *J. Gerontol.*, 27, 376–382.

McMahon, A. W., and Rhudick, P. J. 1964. Reminiscing: adaptational significance in the aged. *Arch. Gen. Psychiat.*, 10, 292–298.

Meltzer, H. 1960. Workers' perceptual stereotypes of age differences. *Perceptual Motor Skills*, 11, 89.

Meltzer, H. 1965a. Attitudes of workers before and after 40. *Geriatrics*, 20, 425–443.

Meltzer, H. 1965b. Mental health implications of aging in industry. *Journal of Genetic Psychology*, 107, 193–203.

Meltzer, H., and Ludwig, D. 1967. Age differences in memory, optimism and pessimism in workers. *Journal of Genetic Psychology*, 110, 17–30.

Messer, M. 1968. Race differences in selected attitude dimensions of the elderly. *Gerontologist*, 8, 245–249.

Michelon, L. C. 1954. The new leisure class. *Am. J. Sociol.*, 59, 371–378.

Miller, D., and Lieberman, M. 1965. The relationship of affect state and adaptive capacity to reactions to stress. *J. Gerontol.*, **20**, 492–497.

Moberg, D. O. 1953. Church membership and personal adjustment in old age. *J. Gerontol.*, **8**, 207–211.

Moberg, D. O. 1965. Religiosity in old age. *Gerontologist*, **5**, 78.

Munnichs, J. 1964. Loneliness, isolation and social relations in old age: a pilot survey. *Vita Humana*, **7**, 228–238.

Munnichs, J. 1966. Old age and finitude. *Hum. Develop.*, Suppl. 4.

Nash, F. A. 1958. Observation of real age and apparent age. *J. Am. Geriat. Soc.*, **6**, 515–521.

Neugarten, B., 1966. Adult personality: a developmental view. *Hum. Develop.*, **9**, 1–2.

Neugarten, B., Birren, J. E., and Kraines, P. J. 1966. Psychological issues of middle age. *Proceedings*, *7th Intern. Congr. Geront.*, Vienna.

Neugarten, B., Crotty, V. J., and Tobin, S. 1964. Personality types in an aged population. *In*, B. L. Neugarten (ed.), *Personality in Middle and Later Life*. pp. 158–187. New York: Atherton Press.

Neugarten, B., and Datan, N. 1973. Sociological perspectives on the life cycle. *In*, P. B. Baltes and K. W. Schaie (eds.), *Life-Span Developmental Psychology*, pp. 53–69. New York: Academic Press.

Neugarten, B., and Garron, D. C. 1959. Attitudes of middle aged persons toward growing older. *Geriatrics*, **14**, 21–24.

Neugarten, B., and Gutman, D. L. 1958. Age and sex roles in personality in middle age; a TAT study. *Psychol. Monogr.*, **72** (71) Whole No. 470).

Neugarten, B., Havighurst, R. J., and Tobin, S. 1961. The measurement of life satisfaction. *J. Gerontol.*, **16**, 134–143.

Neugarten, B., Moore, J. W., and Lowe, J. C. 1965. Age norms, age constraints, and adult socialization. *Am. J. Sociol.*, **70**, 710–717.

Osborn, R. W. 1971. Social and economic factors in reported chronic morbidity. *J. Gerontol.*, **26**, 217–223.

Palmore, E. 1968. The effects of aging on activities and attitudes. *Gerontologist*, **8**, 259–263.

Payne, S. L. 1953. The Cleveland survey of retired men. *Personnel Psychol.*, **6**, 81–110.

Phillips, B. S. 1957. A role theory approach to adjustment in old age. *Am. Soc. Rev.*, **22**, 212–217.

Phillips, B. S. 1961. Role change, subjective age and adjustment, a correlational analysis. *J. Gerontol.*, **16**, 347–352.

Phillips, D. L. 1969. Social class, social participation and happiness, a consideration of interaction opportunities and investment. *Sociol. Quart.*, **10**, 3–21.

Pollack, M., Karp, E., Kahn, R. L., and Goldfarb, A. I. 1962. Perception of self in institutionalized aged. *J. Gerontol.*, **17**, 405–408.

Pollman, A. W. 1971. Early retirement: a comparison of poor health to other retirement factors. *J. Gerontol.*, **26**, 41–45.

Pressey, S. L. 1957. Potentials of age: an exploratory field study. *Genet. Psychol. Monogr.*, **56**, 159–205.

Pressey, S. L., and Jones, A. W. 1955. Age changes in moral codes, anxieties and interests as shown by the cross-out tests. *J. Psych.*, **39**, 485–502.

Pressey, S. L., and Kuhlen R. G. 1957. *Psychological Development Through the Life Span*. New York: Harper Row.

Preston, C. E. 1966. Traits endorsed by older non-retired and retired subjects. *J. Gerontol.*, **21**, 261–264.

Preston, C. E. 1967. Self reporting among older retired and nonretired subjects. *J. Gerontol.*, **22**, 415–420.

Preston, C. E., & Gudiksen, K. S. 1966. A measure of self perception among older people. *J. Gerontol.*, **21**, 63–71.

Reichard, S., Livson, F., and Petersen, P. G. 1962. *Aging and Personality*. New York: John Wiley.

Revere, V. 1971. *The remembered past: its reconstruction at different life stages*. Ph.D. thesis. University of Chicago.

Rhudick, P. J., and Dibner, A. S. 1961. Age, personality and health correlates of death concerns in normal aged individuals. *J. Gerontol.*, **16**, 44–49.

Riegel, K. F., and Riegel, R. M. 1960. A study on changes of attitudes and interests during later years of life. *Vita Humana*, **3**, 177–206.

Roman, P., and Taietz, P. 1967. Organizational structure and disengagement; the emeritus professor. *Gerontologist*, **7**, 147–152.

Rose, A. M. 1965. The subculture of the aging; a framework for research in social gerontology. *In*, A. M. Rose and W. A. Peterson (eds.), *Older Persons and Their Social World*. Philadelphia: F. A. Davis.

Rose, A. M., and Peterson, W. A. 1965. *Older People and Their Social World*. Philadelphia: F. A. Davis.

Rosen, J., and Neugarten, B. 1960. Ego functions in the middle and later years: a TAT study of normal adults. *J. Gerontol.*, **15**, 62–67.

Rosencranz, H., and McNevin, T. 1969. A factor analysis of attitudes towards the aged. *Gerontologist*, **9**, 55–59.

Saleh, S. D., and Otis, J. L. 1964. Age and level of job satisfaction. *Personnel Psychol.*, **17**, 425–430.

Schaie, K. W. 1958. Rigidity-flexibility and intelligence: a cross sectional study of the adult life span from 20 to 70 years. *Psychol. Monogr.*, **72** (9).

Schwartz, A. N., and Kleemeier, R. W. 1965. The effects of illness and age upon some aspects of personality. *J. Gerontol.*, **20**, 85–91.

Schwartz, A. N., and Poppe, H. G. 1970. Toward person/environment transactional research in aging. *Gerontologist*, **10**, 228–232.

Shanan, J., and Sharon, M. 1965. Personality and cognitive functioning of Israeli males during the middle years. *Hum. Develop.*, **8**, 2–15.

Shanas, E., and Streib, G. F. (eds.) 1965. *Social Structure and the Family: Generational relations*. Englewood Cliffs: Prentice-Hall.

Shanas, E., Townsend, P., Wedderburn, D., Friis, H., Milhøj, P., and Stehouwer, J. 1968. The psychology of health. *In,* E. Shanas (ed.), *Old People in Three Industrial Societies.* New York: Atherton Press. pp. 18-70.

Shrut, S. D. 1958a. Attitudes towards old age and death. *Mental Hygiene,* 42, 259-266.

Shrut, S. D. 1958b. Evaluation of two aged populations living under two modes of institutional residence within the same institution. *J. Am. Geriat. Soc.,* 6, 44-59.

Simos, B. G. 1970. Relations of adults with aging parents. *Gerontologist,* 10, 135-139.

Simpson, I. H., and McKinney, J. C. 1966. *Social Aspects of Aging.* Durham: Duke University Press.

Slotkin, J. S. 1954. Life course in middle age. *J. Soc. Forces,* 33, 171-177.

Smith, J. M. 1970. Age differences in achievement motivation. *Brit. J. Soc. Clin. Psychol.,* 9, 175-176.

Smith, K. J., and Lipman, A. 1972. Constraint and life satisfaction. *J. Gerontol.,* 27, 77-82.

Smith, W. E. 1961. Housing preferences of elderly people. *J. Gerontol.,* 16, 261-266.

Smith, W. M. 1954. Family plans for later years. *Marr. Fam. Living,* 16, 36-40.

Spence, D. L. 1968. The role of futurity in aging adaptation. *Gerontologist,* 8, 180-183.

Srole, L. 1956. Social integration and certain corollaries. *Am. Soc. Rev.,* 21, 709-716.

Steiner, P. O., and Dorfman, R. 1957. *The Economic Status of the Elderly.* Berkeley: University of California Press.

Stewart, N., and Sparks, W. J. 1966. Patent productivity of research chemists as related to age and experience. *Personnel & Guidance J.,* 4, 28-36.

Stokes, R. G., and Maddox, G. L. 1967. Some social factors in retirement adaptation. *J. Gerontol.,* 22, 329-333.

Stone, J., and Norris, A. H. 1966. Activities and attitudes of participants in the Baltimore longitudinal study. *J. Gerontol.,* 21, 575.

Streib, G. F., and Schneider, C. J. 1971. *Retirement in American Society, Impact and Process.* Ithaca: Cornell University Press.

Strong, E. L. 1931. *Change of Interests with Age.* Stanford: Stanford University Press.

Sussman, M. B. 1960. Intergenerational family relationships and social role changes in middle age. *J. Gerontol.,* 15, 71-75.

Swenson, W. M. 1961. Attitudes toward death in an aged population. *J. Gerontol.,* 16, 49-52.

Tallmer, M., and Kutner, B. 1969. Disengagement and the stresses of aging. *J. Gerontol.,* 24, 70-75.

Templer, D. I. 1971. Death anxiety as related to depression and health of retired persons. *J. Gerontol.,* 26, 521-523.

Thiesen, J. W., Brown, K. D., Forgus, P. H., Evans, S. M., Williams, C. M., and Taylor, J. 1965. Further data on a stress syndrome related to achievement motivation: relationship with age and basal serum cholesterol level. *Perceptual Motor Skills,* 20, 1277-1292.

Tissue, T. 1968. A Guttman scale of disengagement potential. *J. Gerontol.,* 23, 513-516.

Tissue, T. 1971. Disengagement potential: replication and use as an explanatory variable. *J. Gerontol.,* 26, 76-80.

Tobin, S. 1965. Basic needs of all older people. *In,* U.S. Department of Health, Education and Welfare: *Planning Welfare Services for Older People.* Washington, D.C.: U.S. Government Printing Office.

Tobin, S., and Neugarten, B. 1961. Life satisfaction and social interaction in the aging. *J. Gerontol.,* 16, 344-346.

Townsend, P. 1957. *The Family Life of Old People.* London: Routledge & Kegan Paul.

Tuckman, J. 1956. Retirement attitudes of compulsory and noncompulsory retired workers. *Geriatrics,* 11, 569-572.

Tuckman, J., and Lorge, I. 1954. Old people's appraisal of adjustment over the life span. *J. Pers.,* 22, 417-422.

Tuckman, J., and Lorge, I. 1958a. Attitude toward aging of individuals with experiences with the aged. *Journal of Genetic Psychology,* 92, 199-204.

Tuckman, J., and Lorge, I. 1958b. The projection of personal symptoms into stereotypes about aging. *J. Gerontol.,* 13, 70-73.

Veroff, J., Atkinson, J. W., Feld, S. C., and Gurin, G. 1960. The use of the TAT to assess motivation in a nationwide interview study. *Psychol. Monogr.,* 74 (12) Whole No. 499.

Vogel, B. S., and Schell, R. E. 1968. Vocational interest patterns in late maturity and retirement. *J. Gerontol.,* 23, 66-70.

Wallach, M. A., and Kogan, N. 1961. Aspects of judgement and decision making: interrelationships and changes with age. *Behavioral Science,* 6, 23-26.

Weir, A. 1961. Value judgements and personality in old age. *Acta Psychol.,* 19, 148-149.

Werner, M., Perlin, S., Butler, R. N., and Pollin, W. 1961. Self perceived changes in community resident aged: "aging image" and adaptation. *Arch. Gen. Psychiat.,* 4, 501-508.

Wertheimer, M. 1960. Conception of chronological age as a function of chronological age. *Psych. Reports,* 7, 450.

Williams, R. H., and Wirths, C. G. 1965. *Lives Through the Years.* New York: Atherton Press.

Woodruff, D., and Birren, J. E. 1972. Age changes and

cohort differences in personality. *Developmental Psychology*, **6**, 252–259.

Wylie, M., 1970. Life satisfaction as a program impact criterion. *J. Gerontol.*, **25**, 36–40.

Youmans, E. G. 1967. Family disengagement among older urban and rural women. *J. Gerontol.*, **22**, 209.

Zborowski, M. 1962. Aging and recreation. *J. Gerontol.*, **17**, 302–309.

Zborowski, M., and Eyde, L. E. 1962. Aging and social participation. *J. Gerontol.*, **17**, 424–430.

Zung, W. W. 1970. Mood disturbances in the elderly. *Gerontologist*, **10**, 2–4.

29
CLINICAL ASSESSMENT AND AGING

K. Warner Schaie
University of Southern California
and
Joyce P. Schaie
University of California at Los Angeles

INTRODUCTION

Although for the first few decades in the history of clinical psychology, psychometrics and psychological assessment ruled supreme, in the fifties, disenchantment set in. As in the fairy tale we suddenly discovered that the emperor had no clothes, we found that our elaborate techniques lacked validity or were simply irrelevant to the kind of questions mental health professionals wanted answered.

In retrospect, it seems today that the techniques may have been sounder than we suspected, but that our error was to put the cart before the horse. That is, we developed elegant techniques before we knew what questions should be asked. Practitioners of clinical assessment in psychology today have become a good bit more sophisticated. In particular, it has been recognized that the clinical assessment process must conform to the general strictures of the scientific method by utilizing the model of the hypothetico-deductive experiment with an N of 1, the client. In modern clinical assessment, we do not give a test battery and then try to figure out what the results mean. Rather, the assessment goals are first defined and expressed in

the form of hypotheses about the client's behavior. Appropriate methods including tests and interview procedures are then selected which are relevant to test these hypotheses. If new "hunches" are discovered, their interpretation must then conform to the limitations of all post-hoc analyses. More properly, such "hunches" are operationalized via alternate assessment procedures so that they too can be formally tested before the clinician proceeds to draw formal conclusions. (Also see Sarbin, Taft, and Bailey, 1960).

As part of the general neglect by mental health professionals of the needs of the elderly (Lawton and Gottesman, 1974), relatively little attention has been paid to the role of clinical assessment in dealing with the psychological problems of the aged. There is, nevertheless, a voluminous amount of material which is relevant to problems of clinical assessment in the elderly and twice the space allotted could have been used easily if all had been considered, if we had elected to organize the material by diagnostic categories, or if we had covered every popular psychological assessment tool. Instead we have limited our discussion to four major aspects. First, we address the question as to why one should assess old people. Next, we examine the specific methodological problems raised when assessment tools developed for young adults are applied to the aged. We then consider the evidence on the utility of specific assessment techniques with the elderly, and finally try to indicate how assessment data might be related to the life prospects of the aged client.

Why Should One Assess Old People

Assessment is inevitably related to the intent to do something for or to the individual being assessed. What is to be done depends upon the value judgements of the agent seeking action. If the agent is the older person, then assessment may be sought in self-defense, i.e., to establish remaining competence, to seek remediation of disabling psychological symptoms or to obtain counseling in regard to changing self-concept, circumstances and social role. Where the agent is another, the objective is frequently to obtain evidence which will permit the institutionalization or obtaining of guardianship for a troublesome older relative, or in more positive instances to seek remediation of the symptoms which may make difficult the maintenance of the older person in a family or community situation.

For functional purposes we can group all these assessment questions into three rubrics: First, the *diagnosis* of psychopathology, or the differentiation of psychopathology from "normal aging." Second, the determination of base line behaviors to permit comparison following behavioral *intervention* (whether by milieu change, psychotherapy, conditioning methods, or drug treatment). And, thirdly, a review of the prevailing level of adjustment to changed life roles needed for *counseling* the older individual to help achieve better adjustment in the later years.

Diagnosis of Behavior Disorders. The major issue in the study of behavior disturbances in the elderly seems to be the need to establish criteria for what level or range of functioning is "characteristic" for an age group or what

might be termed "normal" age decrement rather than pathology. A serious complication arises from the observation that in the elderly many of the physical and psychological systems may be operating near the edge of their reserve capacity. Thus multiple system interactions (Pfeiffer, 1973) may be elicited by stress-induced pathology in either physical or psychological systems.

It is necessary to consider what is meant by successful as opposed to unsuccessful aging (cf. Mensh, 1973) since it is only the latter which will distinguish the behavior disorders of later life from those disorders which prevail at all adult age levels. This is not to say that the latter do not deserve attention, nor that their occurrence in the older organism may not create special problems. Nevertheless, it is the definition of unsuccessful aging which is of special concern to the clinical psychologist in his work with the elderly client.

The identification of behavior reflecting unsuccessful aging necessarily depends upon one's model of adaptation in old age (Lissitz, 1970; Maddox, 1970). Such models are frequently established by the middle-aged *for* older persons (Schaie, 1973) rather than reflecting the needs and goals the older person sets for himself. Moreover, disengagement, an example of a frequently discussed model (Cumming and Henry, 1961) may be optimal for some, while maintenance of activity (Havighurst, 1973) may reflect the normative behavior of other old people. In either case, the level of adaptive functioning in older people is not necessarily identical with that for young adults. (Also see Birren, Butler, Greenhouse, Sokoloff and Yarrow, 1963.) Dispositional questions will therefore be addressed to the presence, relative importance, or level of severity of disabling symptoms (Gaitz, 1969; Schaie, Chatham, and Weiss, 1961; Schaie, Rommel, and Weiss, 1959).

The issue of competence to handle one's own affairs will often predominate and require the evaluation of questions such as level of reality contact, intactness of judgement and problem solving ability, distortion of affect and the ability to maintain adaptive interpersonal relations.

Base Line Determination for Behavior Intervention. When considering behavioral intervention, we must first determine whether the behavior repertory of the client is such that the proposed intervention technique is appropriate and can reasonably be expected to achieve some success (Hulicka, 1967). It is also clearly necessary to know the level of behavior from which we start if progress of any psychological, physiological or sociological behavior modification program is to be evaluated.

Base line determinations in the elderly are fraught with the difficulties always encountered when we deal with an organism which is functioning close to its marginal limits. Extensive behavior samples, including "testing limits" (Schmidt, 1970), may be required to reduce unreliability attributable to the greater variability of the older organism. A multiple sampling may also be required because older subjects tend to gain more from practice than do the young (Lehman and Kral, 1968; Murrell, 1970). Similar concerns are raised when personality assessment tools are administered to clients who are unfamiliar with such techniques, and whose behavior may reflect response to the techniques rather than revealing information about the traits being investigated. In addition, we need to be concerned that the behavior sample obtained in the assessment situation may not accurately reflect the aged client's capability in a naturalistic setting (Gaitz, 1973).

It is imperative to demand precise specification of the goal of the intervention procedures and to insist upon the delineation of the precise behaviors which are to be modified. The more global characteristics of the individual which are thought to be altered or affected by the specific intervention procedure should also be indicated. Any less specific assessment procedure would of necessity be superficial and wasteful rather than addressing itself to those questions which can indeed be answered.

Review of Adjustment to Changed Life Roles. Perhaps the most important role of clinical assessment is related to questions posed by the older person who seeks assistance in handling experienced or anticipated changed life circumstances. At least six different types of questions can be identified: (1) The client may ask whether he should or should not retire. Counseling here may require assessment of intellectual ability and personality variables as they relate to the client's job and the social situation within which his occupational role is embedded. (2) Job-related ability levels may require study in the context of determining eligibility for various support programs, such as social security and disability. (3) Assessment may be directed toward the client's need for reacculturation, to determine his degree of cultural and technological obsolescence and to suggest areas where re-training for the exercise of new roles may be called for. (4) The maintenance or proposed abandonment of role independence may involve assessment of both psychological and physical factors. (5) Clients may seek more specific residence counseling related to their values and psychological needs. (6) Involvement in new life roles may finally require definition of interests and skills, not unlike the assessments conducted by the counseling psychologist in work with adolescents.

Applicability of Conventional Clinical Assessment Techniques to The Aged

With a few exceptions (e.g., Demming and Pressey, 1957) most tests, questionnaires and other procedures now used with the elderly were devised either in a nondevelopmental, pathology-oriented context (e.g., MMPI, Rorschach, Bender-Gestalt) or based upon what was known about children and young adults (e.g., Stanford-Binet, Army Alpha, and the Guilford and Cattell type personality inventories). Only as an afterthought were norms for older groups collected for some of these procedures. Even where special procedures for aged subjects have been developed in recent years for research purposes, thought has rarely been given to their extension for clinical purposes (Birren *et al.*, 1963).

Therefore, before we can apply most standard clinical procedures with any feeling of confidence, we must consider some general issues of validity and reliability which affect such procedures when they are applied to an aged population (cf. Oberleder, 1967), which may have different test-taking motivation than young adults (Botwinick, 1969; Salzman, Shader, Kochansky, and Cronin, 1972a, 1972b), and in which there may be a high incidence of sensory and motor problems.

Special Problems of Nomothetic Data Applied to the Aged. It is often taken for granted by gerontologically unsophisticated clinicians that normative data for adults can be applied meaningfully to aging subjects, even though such norms would frequently misclassify well functioning older people as brain damaged or neurotic (cf. Swenson, 1961). Some gerontologists on the other hand, assume that all behavior changes as a function of age so that virtually no young adult norms may be applied to the aged, and that the validity of all techniques not developed on the aged is automatically suspect (cf. Oberleder, 1964). For critiques of the latter position see Baltes and Schaie (1974) and Schaie and Parham (1976).

Construct and predictive validity of assessment techniques used for the elderly need to be considered separately. In the case of construct validity we must conclude for the areas of intellectual functioning that it simply is not safe to assume that a given test measures the same construct in the old as in the young (see also Botwinick, Chapter 24 in this volume). But with respect to personality traits the matter may be much more equivocal (Schaie and Marquette, 1972; Neugarten, Chapter 26 in this volume).

A less obvious aspect of the issue of construct validity of tests for the elderly is the fact that tests age as well as do individuals. Tests which have been constructed for a given cohort at young adulthood may conceivably remain valid for that cohort throughout adulthood, but may not be valid for successive cohorts (Andres, 1969; Schaie, 1970). As a consequence, it is likely that, for example, the Wechsler-Bellevue would have greater construct validity for today's aged than does the WAIS, and even greater validity than the most recent WAIS revision.

The criterion goal for most assessment instruments has been the determination of optimal function in young adulthood. Such techniques

may retain high concurrent and construct validity for the purpose of determining whether or not an elderly client maintains adequate levels of function when comparison with younger individuals is an essential assessment goal. At the same time, construct validity may be quite low when the objective is to assess change of function within the individual. Moreover, if the assessment goal is clearly defined, suitable techniques are then available to improve the validity of one's instrument (Schaie, 1963).

The issue of predictive validity is tied directly to the availability of appropriate age-corrected norms, as well as to the availability of realistic criterion variables. To predict whether the individual is on a decrement trajectory or is developing age-related psychopathology, we must have accurate information on how he compares with other normally-functioning persons of similar age.

Since all age-corrected norms found in the literature have been developed from cross-sectional studies they are in these writers' opinion strictly cohort specific. The practicing clinician would therefore be well-advised to substitute the range of birth years for the age range given as of the year the norms were established, to obtain a more accurate reading. Test constructors are urged to publish their age-corrected norms in this form unless they are prepared to present data from sequential studies and then publish estimates of expected changes in norms at given ages (e.g., Schaie and Parham, 1975, for the Test of Behavioral Rigidity).

Where comparison with young adult norms is involved older clients will have had less education, be at a lower socioeconomic status, and be in poorer health. Normative data can rarely take into account the multiple-classifications required to adjust for such factors but the gero-clinician will need to be sensitive to these issues in his diagnostic enterprise.

Motivational Factors in Assessment. The underuse of mental health facilities by the elderly (Lawton and Gottesman, 1974) may well be related to fears that the services provided may lead to loss of independence and other negative status changes. Self-referral may therefore be subject to much more serious selection problems than among the young (Atchley, 1969).

Most clinical assessment of younger adults is based on the interaction between a client and a clinician both of whom are highly motivated to elicit information which will be helpful to the client. A similar situation might be thought to prevail with the aged self-referred client, but we must take into account the greater cautiousness of the elderly, their not-unrealistic expectation of receiving negative feedback, and the extension of risk-avoiding behavior in the context of the assessment situation (Botwinick, 1969; Furry and Baltes, 1973). Such behavior, however, is readily modifiable when suitable incentives are introduced into the assessment situation (Hoyer, Labouvie, and Baltes, 1973; Birkhill and Schaie, 1975). On the other hand, older persons may at times over-report symptoms by describing complaints which are relevant to earlier discomforts even though they are no longer relevant (Denney, Kole, and Matarazzo, 1965).

Of greater concern is the tendency of the young observer to attend to stereotypes about the old rather than to the characteristics of the client he is working with (cf. Ahammer and Baltes, 1972). Such stereotypes are reduced, however, with respect to observers who have substantial familiarity with the behaviors to be described. Thus information on apparent senile changes reported by family members were found to correlate highly with clinical findings (Blessed, Tomlinson, and Roth, 1968).

Sensory and Motor Problems in Psychological Assessment of the Aged. Apparent decremental findings on intelligence tests, suspected confusion or reality distortion on projective techniques, random-appearing questionnaire response, as well as apparent perceptual distortions on visual motor tasks in the aged may all be a function of deficit in peripheral sensory and motor function rather than being diagnostic of organic or functional pathology.

Visual defects common in old age include decreased transparency of the lens, reduction in pupil size, changes in the vitreous humor and retinal changes (Comalli, 1970; Corso, 1971 and Chapter 21 in this volume). The clinician ought to satisfy himself that visual acuity is corrected to the point that the client can handle test materials without significant interference. Furthermore, alternate forms of traditional questionnaires in larger typefaces are urgently needed for use with the elderly.

Auditory changes (see Chapter 21 in this volume) may also effect even the otherwise well-functioning older adult (Schaie, Strother, and Baltes, 1964), and the tendency of many older people to attempt pleasing the professional examiner (Hurwitz and Allison, 1965) may make it very likely that auditory deficit may be overlooked.

Finally, the more subtle changes in motor coordination and muscular control (see also Welford, Chapter 19 in this volume) will tend to influence test behavior, both in terms of the greater response time required in speeded tasks, and the tendency to produce motoric behaviors which, in younger individuals, might provide diagnostic clues of cortical pathology, but which in the aged may have much more diffuse origins and therefore lack diagnostic utility.

TECHNIQUES OF ASSESSMENT

While the introductory section of this chapter dealt with reasons for and problems peculiar to assessing the aged, the following section is organized into rather traditional categories of content. The intent here is to discuss techniques which are available for selection depending upon the purposes guiding the clinician and the specific assessment questions. In addition, modifications are suggested for existing techniques and areas lacking adequate instruments for work with the elderly are identified. This material is organized into six problem areas: interview techniques; the application of neuropsychological approaches to issues of nervous system functioning; the potential of psychophysiological techniques for clinical purposes; intellectual competence; assessment of learning, memory and problem solving abilities; and the description of personality parameters.

Interview Techniques

Interviews vary from a brief screening-type encounter to extensive systematic questioning.

They also vary in the degree of structuring from a general encouragement such as "Tell me about yourself" to quite specific questions or tasks. Interviews have been used to elicit content such as demographic information, or attitudes, or to obtain samples of behavior such as memory function. They have also provided means to observe a respondent's manner of approaching the task or of interacting with the interviewer.

Various precautions have been suggested as particularly relevant to interviewing elderly persons. Gurland (1973) insists that sessions should be brief to avoid fatigue. But others report no difficulty in conducting interviews of several hours duration (Birren *et al.*, 1963; Jarvik, Bennett, and Blumner, 1973; Schaie and Gribbin, 1975; Thurnher, 1973). Because of the particular vulnerability of many older persons, questions which might be stressful or which might make a respondent particularly aware of his/her disabilities should be spaced throughout the interview rather than massed (Gurland, 1973).

There is a particular need to be sensitive to personality and cultural differences in older persons' willingness to report feelings and behaviors (Clausen, 1968; Gergen and Back, 1966). A particular response bias may be individual or age or cohort related. For example, Gergen and Back (1966) noted that their more highly educated respondents were less reactive in an opinion eliciting situation regardless of the behavior of the interviewer. Technically well-trained persons can be totally ineffective in communicating with elderly clinic patients (Fletcher, 1972). But Pihlblad, Rosencranz, and McNevin (1967) demonstrated that in spite of measurable differences among their interviewers in attitudes toward the aged, they were able to train them to rate their older respondents reliably.

The Psychiatric Status Interview. The psychiatric status interview is intended to evaluate orientation, memory, judgment and cognitive abilities. The tendency in recent years has been toward a use of fairly structured schedules. These include the Mental Status Test (Perlin and Butler, 1963), and a mental status schedule based on factor analytically derived scales (Spitzer, Fleiss, Endicott, and Cohen, 1967) with a special geriatric supplement (Spitzer, Endicott, Cohen, Bennett, and Weinstock, 1969), as well as three brief 10-item questionnaires (Kahn, Goldfarb, Pollack, and Peck, 1966; Miller and Lieberman, 1965; Pfeiffer, Chapter 27 in this volume).

The Geriatric Mental Status Schedule was developed and its usefulness demonstrated as part of the recent major effort of the Cross-national Study of Diagnosis of Mental Disorders in the United States and the United Kingdom (Copeland, *et al.*, 1976; Gurland, *et al.*, 1976).

Psychodynamic Interviews. A number of interview approaches have been developed for the clinical assessment of the elderly which stress intrapsychic processes.

Psychoanalytically-Oriented Approaches. A study of elderly San Franciscans (Lowenthal, Berkman, and associates, 1967; Brissette, 1967) employed a psychoanalytic approach in which intensive interviews were used to reconstruct life histories and to elicit respondents' feelings regarding the problems of aging. Rating check lists included items from life goal data and from the works of Fromm, Riesman, Erikson, Murray, Neugarten, Kroeber, and Brissette (1967). Psychoanalytic approaches emphasize changes in coping strategies that are necessary as a person ages and Goldfarb (1962) has stressed the importance of assessing the intrapsychic processes of elderly persons. Werner, Perlin, Butler, and Pollin (1961) provide a discussion of mechanisms which may be used by persons in response to experienced deterioration.

In psychoanalytic assessment, defensive distortion of self-report data may become a problem (Lowenthal *et al.*, 1967). Tobin and Etigson (1968) suggest caution in interpreting themes of earliest memory from a traditional Freudian or Adlerian framework. Using a five-point ordinal scale of introduced loss, they reported that the stress of institutionalization resulted in a greater increase in the severity of loss themes reported in first memories than in a control group.

Phenomenological-existential approaches. The manner in which persons view themselves in relationship to time, their experiences and other persons has spawned a number of interview-derived measurement techniques for use with the elderly. Although primarily used for research purposes, they would seem to hold promise for clinical application.

Kastenbaum (1965) applied developmental field theory to determine where a person is located in his/her "temporal life space." He also developed VIRO (vigor, intactness, relationship, and orientation), a scale designed expressly to assess the interview behavior of the elderly (Kastenbaum and Sherwood, 1967), and a "social space" interview procedure (Kastenbaum and Cameron, 1969) used to distinguish between cognitive and emotional dependency in later life.

Spence (1968) has derived a morale (adjustment) scale via cluster analysis which identifies four types of persons: unsettled planners, composed planners, disgruntled and complacent.

Thurnher (1973) described use of a "Life Evaluation Chart," a phenomenological evaluation by rating yearly satisfaction/dissatisfaction over the past and projected life span. In a follow-up interview, respondents are provided with a review of their ratings and are asked to describe the circumstances prevailing at the time.

Riegel (1972) has suggested a return to a phenomenlogical approach "as a means of supplementing existential theoretical and experimental approaches." If this is to happen and if it is to become a useful way of thinking about persons in a clinical setting, considerably more work will be needed to provide assessment tools.

Techniques for Life-Review and/or Assessment of Life-Styles. Several examples are available of structured interview schedules developed to elicit comprehensive views of life history or life-style.

Lieberman and Falk (1971) questioned the assumption which underlies all interview life-history approaches and then proceeded to inquire whether reminiscence data held up under systematic analysis and whether they can provide psychological insight into human development. Three sources of data were used: an interview in which an individual recounted the story of his life; questions requiring reflective life evaluation; and questions about the role of reminiscence. Indices were developed which provided measures of reminiscence including the importance of reminiscence to aged persons, the restructuring of memories, the selection processes used by the individual in reporting his life history and content measures. The authors concluded that reminiscence is an important source of data for developing a psychology of the life cycle.

A recent book edited by Jarvik, Eisdorfer, and Blum (1973) reports several life review instruments not fully described elsewhere. The Life History Interview Schedule was intended to identify characteristics of successful aging. This schedule, requiring about 5 hours to administer, includes items related to nutrition, health and medication, activities, social relations, including isolation and stress, personal history and psychological data.

Thurnher's (1973) life history interview schedule requires 6 to 8 hours to administer. Her schedule was developed for high school seniors but was subsequently modified for a pre-retirement group. It provides phenomenological emphasis including open-ended questions but also sufficient structure to make the data quantifiable and amenable to statistical analysis.

Butler and Lewis (1973) have reported the use of a Life Review Form—a personal mental health data form for older people. Data elicited included personal and family status and history, interests and community involvements, friendship patterns and prejudice, medical information including sleep, drug and sexual habits, and psychiatric information including attitudes toward death and self views.

Schaie and Gribbin (1975) developed a Life Complexity Interview Schedule for use in their sequential studies of changes in cognitive functioning. In addition to the usual sorts of demographic family, personal and health items, the schedule also focuses on work and travel experiences, mobility and social interaction with one goal being to determine the complexity of persons' environment and history. A group of questions specifically applicable to the housewife are also included.

Owens (1971) has proposed a conceptual scheme for assessment which provides both actuarial and descriptive information. He has developed a technique for computer sorting of biographical data and arrived at factored dimensions and scale loadings.

Techniques for the Assessment of Perceived Status. Instruments mentioned here are less inclusive than those designed to construct a picture of an entire life span. The essential goal here is a description of a respondent's self-concept with regard to personal situation, adjustment or mental health.

Lowenthal *et al.* (1967) described a Baseline Community Questionnaire which includes extensive questions regarding characteristics of socioeconomic status, demography, social supports and activity, capacity for self-maintenance and physical health. Other techniques of this kind have been reported by Gubrium (1971), Langner and Michael (1963) and by Miller and Lieberman (1965).

Neuropsychological Assessment

There are two main reasons for trying to assess neuropsychological function in the elderly. One is to identify pathological function which might be reversed or slowed with appropriate intervention. The other is to help elderly clients develop realistic self-concepts and establish satisfactory living arrangements and life goals. Requirements for assessment techniques which could fulfill these demands are that they be able to differentiate between normal and pathological function among aged persons and/or to differentiate among normal age range groups.

The Measurement of Central Nervous System Decrement via Psychological Tests. Psychological tests may not always correlate with functional levels. For example, Granick (1971b) and Oberleder (1967) report that "many brain damaged elderly persons live out their lives in competent fashion without any recognition of their condition until it may happen to show up in autopsy," and Benton and Van Allen (1972)

reported "a lack of concordance between the test measures (which may indicate only slight impairment) and the quite obvious behavioral incompetence."

Davison (1974) discussed a number of variables which influence the behavioral characteristics which are observed to result from brain damage. These include laterality; location within the hemisphere; agent(s) causing lesion; age of person when the lesion occurred; time between onset of the lesion and testing; other conditions at time of testing, e.g., drugs; lateral motor and higher cortical function dominance; premorbid condition of patient; and severity and extent of lesion.

Two of the factors discussed by Davison need specific mention here. One is the age of the person, and unfortunately very little information is available regarding behavioral indications of brain damage in the elderly. The second is the time between the onset of the lesion and the testing. Processes of compensation are known to be initiated where physical loss has occurred. The extent and nature of compensation possible or likely for persons of various age groups is, however, not clearly understood. Further, where physical loss is gradual, as is true in normal aging and several forms of pathology frequently seen in the elderly, compensatory processes are likely to occur gradually and continuously.

Tests that differentiate between normal and pathological functions among young groups cannot be assumed to do so with older persons as well. Validation of existing techniques with older groups is needed. But, quite different procedures from those useful in assessing pathological functioning may also be required to differentiate between stages of normal or expected aging and neuropathology.

Measures of Intellectual Functions and Neuropathology. Score patterns on the Wechsler tests have been studied both to examine age differences for normative purposes and to derive clinical indices of decrement in specific functions. In his chapter on "Brain Damage," Matarazzo (1972) curiously makes no mention of the peculiar problems of assessment of brain damage in the elderly. This is not to say, however, that Matarazzo ignored a host of available studies. The chapter largely reflects the state of clinical ignorance regarding diagnosis among the elderly.

Davies (1968b) points up the problem of using tests which have been validated with younger persons to assess brain function in older persons. In comparing groups of young normals, old normals, and young brain damaged on a variety of tests (not including the WAIS) she concluded that "the intellectual deterioration of the brain damaged group was equivalent to that of about 35 years of aging." Davies further reported that the Raven Progressive Matrices were more sensitive to aging than to brain damage and that the Mill Hill Vocabulary Test was more sensitive to brain damage than to aging.

Overall and Gorham (1972), testing the hypothesis that increasingly poor performance of older persons was due to developing organic brain syndrome, found to the contrary, that the pattern of change associated with normal old age is different from the pattern associated with brain syndrome in the elderly. Scores on the WAIS and the Holtzman Inkblot Techniques both confirmed the differential patterns.

Reitan and his associates (Reitan and Davison, 1974) have done considerable work in the assessment of specific loss via psychological, neurological and post-mortem examinations. By and large, however, they have not systematically looked at groups of elderly patients, but instead report data for groups of multi-age adults with a mean age of around 50 years.

A reasonable approach would seem to be to compare Botwinick's (Chapter 24 in this volume) summary data on Wechsler subtest scores of "normal" elderly persons with those of persons with independently assessed brain damage of at least the categories of right lateralized, left lateralized and diffuse, with subgroups within each of chronic and acute patients. It is also evident, however, that the best comparisons would include age breakdowns for normal and pathological subjects in the above categories of ages 50–59, 60–69, 70–79 and 80 and above. But, adequate data permitting such complete comparisons simply do not exist to the authors' knowledge.

If normal age changes reflect loss similar to that seen in brain damaged patients, one would hypothesize that the test performance of the elderly should look like the performance characteristic of a group of chronic diffuse brain damaged patients. A comparison of Botwinick's summary data on Wechsler's subtests with Fitzhugh, Fitzhugh, and Reitan's (1962) adult data, however, show that the aging pattern differs from both the chronic and acute diffuse groups. In fact, the verbal-performance discrepancy is reversed from what would have been expected. Figure 1 represents a conversion of the brain damage data into rank order scores for purposes of comparison with Botwinick's Figure 9. On the other hand, the aging pattern is indistinguishable from both the chronic and acute right lateralization patients. See Figure 2.

These comparisons suggest that investigators who have thought old persons looked like brain damaged persons may have had many right lateralization patients in their comparison groups. Otherwise one would need to conclude that "normal" aging involves greater right than left hemispheric loss. Reference to work attempting to verify lateralized change in brain function with age follows in the next section. In any case, general adult norms for chronic diffuse loss simply cannot be used to assess brain damage in the elderly. Whatever is characteristic of brain damaged elderly must therefore be assessed against normal elderly patterns.

Other Tests with Some Demonstrated Usefulness. A task analysis of the block design performance of older normal and right and left hemispheric brain injured persons did not reveal any aspects which were unique to the brain damaged. However, brain injured subjects were inferior to normals on a measure of "competence" and right and left hemiplegic patients differed on several parameters of "style of performance" while not differing on "competence" level (Ben-Yishay, Diller, Mandleberg, Gordon, and Gerstman, 1971).

McDonald (1969) administered six tests of memory, six of parietal lobe function, six of aphasia and the Weigl-Goldstein-Scheerer Color Form sorting test to a group of institutionalized female patients with a mean age of 80.3, all of

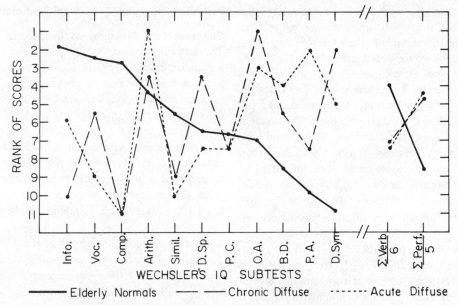

Figure 1. Wechsler Intelligence Scale pattern of elderly normals compared with chronic and acute diffuse brain damaged patients.

whom were diagnosed as senile dementia. The parietal function tests identified a group which, while older in age showed a much lower 6-month mortality, and a younger group whose prognosis was less good.

Bettner, Jarvik, and Blum (1971) report a positive relationship for women between organic brain syndrome and a derived color difficulty score on the Stroop Color-Word Test (Comalli, Wapner, and Werner, 1962). They

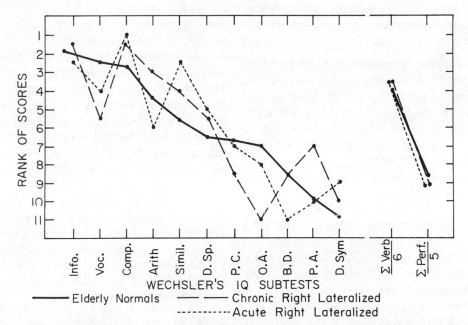

Figure 2. Wechsler Intelligence Scale pattern of elderly normals compared with chronic and acute right lateralization patients.

also found, however, that the age-related decline in Stroop performance was more pronounced for the men in their sample.

The Background Interference Procedure (BIP) (Canter and Straumanis, 1969) used with the Bender-Gestalt Test, proved useful in discriminating between chronic brain syndrome patients and healthy elderly subjects. The conventional use of Bender error scores and the discrepancy between WAIS Vocabulary and Block Design scores would have identified at least one-fourth of their healthy elderly as having organic brain damage. The use of the BIP, however, permitted a discrimination between normal decline and degree of pathology in the brain syndrome patients.

Lehman and Ban (1970) tried a series of seven tests as discriminators among several groups of elderly persons: noninstitutionalized normals, non-psychiatric residents of old peoples homes and hospitalized chronically functional and organic brain syndrome patients. The test which best matched the rank of pathological severity was digit span backward. The worst test was word association time. Tapping speed discriminated well in the mild to moderate range of organic pathology and critical flicker fusion discriminated well among seriously affected organic patients. Simple auditory reaction time proved to be a fair measure over the whole range.

Tests without Demonstrated Usefulness with the Elderly. A number of widely used tests for the psychological diagnosis of brain damage which are effective with the young, fail to discriminate in older populations and should be avoided by the practicing clinician. These include the *Trail Making Test* (Reitan, 1955) for which the percentage of misclassification of normal subjects increases with age; 50 percent for patients in the fifties and 70 percent for patients in the seventies (Davies, 1968a; Goul and Brown, 1970). Evidence questioning the construct validity of the Trail Making Test for older clients has also been reported (Lindsey and Coppinger, 1969).

Serious misclassification problems have also been reported by Alexander (1970) for the *Memory For Designs Test* (Graham and Kendall, 1960) and by Irving (1971) for the *Arrow Drawing Test* (Goodly and Reinhold, 1964).

Psychophysiological Assessment Techniques

Electrocortical Measures as Diagnostic Tools. The current state of knowledge does not allow a clinician to use a specific biological characteristic or function as a diagnostic index. Yet a number of psychophysiological studies indicate some promise for the development of assessment techniques.

Cortical measures have been looked at both as indicators of intellectual functions and as clues to altered cognitive styles in behavior disorders. With few exceptions, when age has been reported or treated as a variable, elderly groups have not been included in the samples taken. Thus, the potential usefulness of most psychophysiological assessment techniques awaits the demonstration of their significance for elderly persons and the availability of norms.

Marsh and Thompson (Chapter 11 in this volume) provide an extensive discussion of available information regarding cortical changes with age and their behavioral significance. Selected findings are discussed here in terms of their potential for clinical assessment.

Diffuse Slowing. The clearest and most consistent finding of clinical significance is the diffuse slowing in the EEG. Up to age 75, healthy community volunteer old persons showed no more diffuse slowing than did healthy young persons. Above age 75 about 20 percent showed sufficient slowing to be classed as abnormal (Obrist and Busse, 1965). Marsh and Thompson (Chapter 11 in this volume) suggest that marked EEG slowing, even among elderly persons, indicates organic deterioration and correlates highly with a variety of behavioral indices. They also note that older functional patients typically show little diffuse slowing.

Muller and Grad (1974) conversely found that sharp diffuse activity correlated positively with good performance on a variety of tasks; although persons with sharp activity also give indications of greater irritability and anxiety. The authors hypothesize that sharp diffuse activity reflects a "mechanism which delays the decay of higher mental functions."

Alpha Slowing. Alpha slowing has been observed with intellectual impairment in the elderly (see Marsh and Thompson, Chapter 11 in this volume). Surwillo's (1966) hypothesis, which related the timing of alpha cycles to the timing of behavioral processes, may eventually result in the development of an assessment tool. The correlations he has observed, however, while significant, are too low to be of practical value in prediction.

Shagass (1972), in considering some of Surwillo's work, notes that "the reaction time-alpha frequency correlation is greater than the correlation of either variable alone with age." This finding implies that brain wave frequency may have similar behavioral significance whether a person is a young adult or elderly.

Evoked Potentials and Intelligence. Callaway (1973) provides the most thorough recent review of studies relating evoked potential measures to intelligence. He mentions the need to take known age-related changes in cortical measures into account when evaluating the behavioral significance of evoked potentials but warns against simply comparing evoked potentials with conventional tests of IQ.

Shucard and Horn (1972) related visual evoked potentials to measures of fluid and crystalized intelligence, but did not find support for Cattell's theory. Marsh and Thompson (Chapter 11 in this volume) suggest that cognitive processing may be the critical factor in performance tests of intelligence while memory functions may be critical for verbal tests in the elderly. They suggest therefore looking at evoked potential measures such as the LPC (late positive component) or P300 which is thought to reflect a processing component.

Evoked Potentials and Personality. Shagass and Schwartz (1966) report alterations in the recovery of somatosensory responses following stimulation in psychiatric patients. Previously reported findings of increased amplitudes, however, were discounted as having been due to insufficient control for age.

Shagass and Schwartz (1965) found that age interacted with scores on the Maudsley extraversion (E) measure in terms of amplitudes of somatosensory responses. Younger high E subjects showed greater amplitudes than younger low E subjects whereas older high E subjects showed lower amplitudes than older low E subjects.

The contingent negative variation (CNV) is another evoked potential measure which may eventually have diagnostic value with the elderly. The behavioral significance of various components of this measure is not yet clear, but a number of studies have shown correlations of CNV amplitude with psychiatric diagnosis (McCallum, 1973; Shagass, 1972; Small and Small, 1971; Timsit-Berthier, Delauncy, Konick, and Rousseau, 1973).

Syndulko, Parker, Maltzman, Jens, and Ziskind (1975) report a study in which diagnosis (sociopaths *vs.* controls) and age (15-26 years and 30-43 years) in four groups of adults were treated as variables. The older sociopaths showed CNV amplitude deviations when compared with older controls, a difference which did not appear between the younger groups. The LPC or P300 amplitude was smaller for the sociopath group but the statistical significance was due largely to the fact that the older sociopath group showed a much smaller P300 (Syndulko, Parker, Maltzman, Jens and Ziskind, 1974).

Other relationships found between evoked potential and personality measures which might be fruitful for work with the elderly include the observations that high field-dependent psychiatric patients had larger evoked potential amplitudes than low scorers (Shagass and Canter, 1966); that auditory evoked potential differences between schizophrenic and normal subjects lessened as the schizophrenics improved (Callaway, Jones and Layne, 1965; Jones, Blacker, Callaway, and Layne, 1965); that the Disinhibition Factor score from the Sensation Seeking Scale differentiates rather well between cortical augmenters and reducers (Zuckerman, Murtaugh and Siegel, 1974) and that Rotter's I-E scores and P300 amplitudes were related (Poon, Thompson, Williams, and Marsh, 1974).

Autonomic Assessment. Obrist (1971) reviewed studies that related measures of intelligence to cardiovascular insufficiency as measured by cerebral blood flow. A lengthy history of any one of a number of cardiovascular diseases correlated negatively with intelligence test scores. On the other hand, there is indication that within normal ranges, slightly elevated blood pressure helps to maintain most efficient cognitive function (Wilkie and Eisdorfer, 1971).

Autonomic measures of altered orienting responses, habituation patterns and conditionability have been implicated in various behavioral disorders. The potential usefulness of such autonomic indices of behavioral pathology with elderly persons, however, will depend on a systematic working out of the confounds which cloud the present state of knowledge. For example, sociopaths (Hare, 1970) and hospitalized depressed patients (Dawson, Schell, and Catania, 1974) have shown weak heart rate and skin conductance indices of orienting. Furthermore, some investigators have argued that the sociopath is over-aroused (Eysenck, 1964; Schacter and Latane, 1964) while others have concluded that such persons are under-aroused. Similar conflicting data on lessened reactivity as well as over an under-arousal have been reported for the elderly (Thompson and Marsh, 1973; Marsh and Thompson, Chapter 11 in this volume).

Many investigators have considered changes in autonomic measures as indicators of the presence of anxiety or defensiveness. While extreme caution must be used with such a procedure in any study, its use with elderly persons produces further complications. Busse and Pfeiffer (1969) report "the psychophysiological manifestations of anxiety undoubtedly change with advancing age." It appears that responses to an anxiety-producing stimulus in the elderly is often delayed and may be increased or decreased, depending on which manifestation of anxiety is being measured. Furthermore, the same stimuli which produce anxiety in younger persons may not produce the same reaction in the elderly and vice versa.

In any case, before autonomic measures can be useful as clinical indices, normal age norms and cutting scores appropriate to identify pathology in an aged population are necessary. Such are lacking at the present time for most autonomic measures.

Capability to Utilize Biofeedback Training. The use of training to assist persons to learn to control visceral and/or cortical functions to enhance sensorimotor and cognitive functioning in the elderly has been suggested (Marsh and Thompson, Chapter 11 in this volume; Thompson and Marsh, 1973). Many questions remain,

however, regarding the most efficient procedures for initial training as well as for maintenance of changes in biofeedback (Blanchard and Young, 1973; Shapiro and Schwartz, 1972). More specific questions as to who is most likely to benefit from which kinds of training and what might be done to make a person more amenable to training need to be asked and answered by the clinician. Studies either fit into the category of bodily awareness or into the topic of more traditional personality variables.

Shapiro (1974) hypothesizes that subjects may need to be able to see a relationship between their responses on a physiological variable and the stimulus situation in which the response occurs. In the same vein, Brener (1974) proposes a general model of voluntary behavior applicable to learned cardiovascular control. In this model, "the development of instructional control over an activity is seen to depend on the subject learning the association between the words employed in the instruction, and on the sensory consequences of the acts to which those words refer."

One technique for measuring bodily awareness is Mandler's Autonomic Perception Questionnaire (Mandler, Mandler, and Uviller, 1958). Persons with low to middle scores on the APQ have shown more ability to control heart rate than high scorers (Bergman and Johnson, 1971; Blanchard, Young, and McLeod, 1972).

Engstrom (in press) compares hypnosis and biofeedback and suggests that the successful subject in both processes develops a cognitive set (reflected and observable alpha functioning) which focuses attention on a specific body response, and eliminates distracting stimuli. Techniques for measuring ability to develop such a cognitive set therefore become critical.

A personality measure which has shown some ability to differentiate among persons' ability to change as a function of biofeedback is Rotter's Internalizer-Externalizer (I-E) Scale. Ray and Lamb (1974) found that Internalizers were better able to increase their heart rate while Externalizers were better able to decrease their heart rate.

Unfortunately, none of the above studies have involved work with elderly persons; yet, their findings suggest some directions which could be explored as beginning points.

The Definition of Intellectual Functioning

One of the most important contributions to be made in clinical assessment of the aged may well be the determination of whether intellectual competence is maintained or has declined as compared with the previous level of functioning. The controversy surrounding the issue of whether or not intellectual decrement is a normal accompaniment of the aging process is reviewed in detail elsewhere in this volume (Botwinick, Chapter 24 in this volume). Here we shall merely consider the implications of this problem for clinical assessment.

Problems in Distinguishing Between Decrement and Obsolescence. For the clinician the issues can be simplified to the question of whether the behavior of his client is to be measured with instruments developed for assessing criteria relevant to the old or to the young and whether we are to detect changes in function within the individual by comparing him with his aged peers, or with members of a younger generation. In sum, we are concerned both with the validity for older persons of tests developed for young adults such as the Wechsler series and others, and with the issue of norms (cf. Schaie, 1974).

Matarazzo (1972) provides an extensive review of problems related to developing norms for older persons. He notes, for example, that the means for various age groups on the same test of intelligence have consistently increased over the last 20 years or so. He gives the hypothetical example of an executive who had been tested first at age 35 and then again at age 55 following brain injury in an accident. Matarazzo notes that it would be inappropriate to use the norms for 55 year olds from 20 years earlier in estimating the loss. This is one instance in which the degree of loss would be underestimated. Instances are usually cited in discussions of tests for the elderly in which deficit is likely to be overestimated because the tests are speeded or contain generationally inappropriate content. But, in this instance, the 55-year-old norms from 20-year-old tests should be lower

than appropriate for a person who is only now 55 years old.

Obviously, age-corrected norms based on cross-sectional data have very transient value, but such are the only currently available even for the widely used Wechsler tests. Moreover, norms for the older age groups have typically been obtained from special studies with non-representative samples. Such norms, therefore, may be questionable even for comparison with the performance of younger subjects at the time the norms have been published (cf. Green, 1969).

Unfortunately, there are as yet no data-bases from which to project changes in norms which would be useful to the clinician. However, our experience with data from the Primary Mental Abilities Test (PMA) (Schaie and Labouvie-Vief, 1974) may be suggestive. For tests where speed is not significantly involved it appears that there are few within individual changes until the sixties, with limited decline thereafter, but with substantial differences between generations. It would seem therefore, that a measure such as Wechsler's efficiency quotient (EQ) (Wechsler, 1939) may have renewed utility in terms of assessing the individual's obsolescence as compared with younger contemporaries. On the other hand, proper age-corrected norms would be useful in detecting a drop in competence from previous levels of functioning as compared to individuals of the same age.

Changes in the factor structure of the WAIS across the adult age span (see Reinert, 1970, for full discussion) suggest that the meaning, at least of the performance part of the test shifts too much to permit valid use for internal consistency analysis as detailed in the next section.

Once again, we need to call attention to the fact that all presently used intelligence tests assess the intellectual competence of the aged with respect to constructs defined for the young (also see Schaie, 1974). Thus, intelligence tests designed to estimate criteria relevant to the lives of old people remain to be developed and clinically validated.

Estimation of Intellectual Deficit. Barring the availability of longitudinal data on changes in intellectual function in the individual studied, it may still be possible to obtain estimates by careful analysis of within-test variation or other indirect sources of information. The use of intra-test variability was first suggested by Babcock (1930) who suggested that vocabulary could be used as a measure of previous function, while speed and learning tests would be indicative of current intellectual efficiency. Constrasting measures would then lead to a deterioration index (Gilbert, 1935).

Wechsler (1939, 1941, 1944, 1958) applied the principle of contrasting measures presumed to deteriorate with those that do not to develop a variety of deterioration measures. One kind of "hold/don't hold" measure was based specifically on the notion that some subtests hold up with age while others do not. Other hold/don't hold patterns were developed in the attempts to describe the test characteristics of various functional disorders (Matarazzo, 1972).

Norman (1966) compared the deterioration loss (DL) from Wechsler's first edition (1939) with the deterioration quotient (DQ) from the fourth edition (Wechsler, 1958) in regard to their usefulness for looking at age changes. He expressed preference for the earlier formula for women based on the differential number of hold/don't hold tests on which men/women tend to perform better. One longitudinal study (Gilbert, 1973) supports the construct validity of the efficiency index from the Babcock test. Unfortunately, it is based on only 14 subjects.

On the whole, deterioration measures do not seem to receive wide attention in the aging research literature. The most thorough evaluation of the use of Wechsler-based deterioration measures with elderly individuals is found in Savage, Britton, Bolton, and Hall (1973). Botwinick's chapter in this volume does not mention them and it is not known to what extent they are currently used in clinical practice with elderly patients. A more frequently appearing comparison seems to be that of contrasting overall verbal versus performance scores on the WAIS, but Bolton, Britton, and Savage (1966) and Savage, Britton, George, O'Connor, and Hall, (1972) raise serious questions regarding its clinical utility.

The extent to which this comparison will be useful to distinguish between "normal" and clinical syndromes, either functional or organic, will depend again on whether reliable norms become available for older groups such that validity checks can be made. (See also the earlier discussion regarding brain damage.)

Another source of information often neglected by the clinician, is the contrast of what is known about characteristic levels of ability and performance associated with various professional and role functions previously carried on with success by the individual under study. Because of the high correlation of general intelligence with social status, achievement and occupation (cf. Burt, 1943; Schaie and Gribbin, 1975), knowledge of the client's demographic status may help in hypothesizing previous level of intellectual functioning which can be contrasted with present performance.

Measures Used to Assess Intelligence in the Aged. Most extensive norms and other data on work with the aged are currently available for the Wechsler Adult Intelligence Scale (WAIS). This work has been extensively summarized recently by Matarazzo (1972) and is further reviewed in Botwinick's chapter in this volume. Also reviewed there is the extensive work on the Primary Mental Abilities. Unfortunately the latter has not been systematically applied to clinical populations even though extensive age and cohort corrected norms could readily be provided from the various studies conducted by the senior author and his associates.

Brief Tests. The question of finding good but short instruments which can minimize fatigue in the elderly has been raised for intellectual as well as personality testing. Britton and Savage (1966) and Savage, Britton, Bolton, and Hall (1973) proposed a short form of the WAIS for use with the aged. Granick (1971a) reviewed several techniques including the use of selected Wechsler subtests. The brief test most studied for use with the elderly persons is the Quick Test (Ammons and Ammons, 1962). Levine (1971) found high correlations of Quick Test Scores with the WAIS in four groups of elderly volunteers. Gendreau, Roach, and Gendreau (1973) provided some normative data for a sample averaging 80.7 years of age. They reported that scores did not vary with socioeconomic status or years of institutionalization but did discriminate among degrees of special care or assistance needed. They further discussed Ammons and Ammons' (1962) original suggested age corrections but, based on their data, recommended a somewhat different correction.

Other Tests. Fozard and Nuttall (1971) reported a main effect for age as a result of analyzing *General Aptitude Test Scores* (GATB). They pointed out the fact that no attempts had been made to adjust for age in deriving Occupational Aptitude Patterns (OAP) on the basis of the GATB scores. They further questioned the assumption that OAP's should be used regardless of age because they are based on an evaluation of skills needed for a particular occupation. They reported that the validity of OAP's in terms of job performance have not been established and conclude that age adjustments or different test procedures need to be explored in the attempt to assess the abilities of older workers.

The factoring out of the intellectual components named fluid (Gf) and crystallized (Gc) by Cattell (1963), and the ensuing theory generated considerable interest in these measures for investigating age changes. Horn (1970) reviews some of this work. The basic hypothesis predicted age-related decline in fluid intelligence in advanced years and gradual continual increment in crystallized intelligence. Oversimplified, crystallized intelligence is thought to be dependent more on experiential input while fluid intelligence is thought to be tied more closely to biological functioning competencies.

Savage and Britton (1968) and Savage, Britton, Bolton, and Hall (1973) reported finding support for the hypothesis that fluid components assume a greater importance in the structure of abilities in the aged than in the young. They argue that the influence of experiential factors remains almost stable while biologically-influenced fluid characteristics assume greater importance. They suggest a need for further research into fluid and crystallized aspects in "normal and pathological intellectual deterioration and deficit in the elderly." The fact remains, however, that research findings of this sort are not yet available for clinical usage.

Hall, Savage, Bolton, Pidwell, and Blessed (1972) called on the concept of fluid intelligence to explain why the WAIS performance IQ was the best predictor of non-survival. Also using a factor analytic approach, Nesselroade, Schaie, and Baltes (1972) in a longitudinal study found changes in two factors to be age-related: crystallized intelligence increased and visuomotor flexibility decreased. On the other hand, cognitive flexibility and visualization showed no significant age-related change. Marked decrements in cognitive flexibility and/or visualization may well signal pathological functioning, and further refined measures and derived factors may consequently be found useful for assessment of the elderly.

Assessment of Memory, Learning and Problem Solving Abilities

The ability of older persons to acquire new information or concepts, to alter behavior as a result of experience, and to develop new skills are characteristics of considerable interest to the clinician in assessing the competence and potential of older persons.

Some of the behaviors sampled are closely related to measures of intelligence and personality. Certainly the issues of learning and memory are intertwined. Relevant chapters in this volume (Craik, Chapter 17 on memory; Arenberg and Robertson, Chapter 18 on learning) inevitably point to similar hypothesized processes in the attempt to understand age differences and changes. In most test procedures, learning and memory are completely confounded, but so are they in everyday experience. This chapter therefore focuses on the possible utility of available techniques for assessing the competence and potential of older adults.

Memory Tests. Assessment of specific memory functions may play an important role in assessing intellectual abilities in older persons. Botwinick (1973) summarized a body of findings by reporting that memory does not significantly differentiate among younger persons but that it does in older persons. Botwinick and Storandt (1974) compared scores on a variety of measures of long and short term memory with age, sex, mental health status and performance on other kinds of clinical tests. The persons tested were community volunteers and no comparisons were made with clinical populations. Nevertheless, several findings illustrate the problem of developing appropriate "normal" old age norms against which to compare clinical groups. Not all tests of memory were affected equally by age. Highly significant sex differences were found. Further, a strong case for the importance of meaningfulness of the material to be remembered by different cohorts was made. For example, the data suggested that the age at which an item was learned may be more important than the age at which it is recalled.

Savage and Britton (1968) reported factor analytic evidence for the importance of the memory component in the intelligence test scores of an aged sample. They noted that in spite of differences in findings by various investigators regarding the factor structure of the WAIS for older persons, there has been consistency in reporting a tendency for the memory factor to lose its independence in the aged and to load on other factors. They reported that a memory component had permeated both the verbal and space performance factors in their aged sample. If memory plays a significant role in tests purporting to measure other variables, the use of an independent measure of memory function would seem to be called for. Savage, Britton, Bolton, and Hall (1973) suggested that for clinical purposes, in addition to the verbal and performance sub-tests (short form of the WAIS) the Vocabulary test be used to provide the "new" words for the Modified Word Learning Test (MWLT) (Walton and Black, 1957) and that the Block Design items be used as a performance learning test (BDLT).

Schaie and Strother (1968) used the Wechsler Memory Scale with an elderly sample. This test, providing seven subtest scores which combine to yield a memory quotient (MQ), seems worthy of further investigation for usefulness with older groups. Several of the subtests entail both learning and memory components. Dujoune and Levy (1971) factor analyzed Wechsler Memory Scale items for a group of normals aged 16–71 years and a group of psychiatric patients aged 16–72 years. They did not investigate differences in structure for age groups but did find differences for the two groups investigated. They concluded that items could be grouped according to factorial composition resulting in three scores rather than one composite MQ. The names of the factors for the normal group indicate the kinds of functions measured: general retentiveness, simple learning, and associational flexibility. While Walton (1958) reported a high percentage of misclassification using a single administration of the Wechsler Memory Scale, he found that four repetitions of the tests produced different responses in functional and organic patients.

Other investigators have looked at digit span tasks as indicators of immediate memory function. Arenberg (1973) summarized the literature as indicating little, if any, age deficit on this task, thus implying that large decrements could be clinically significant. Taub (1972) has found relative superiority of performance with presentation in the auditory as compared to the visual mode, and cautions clinicians to be sensitive to presentation differences when using tests of memory.

Verbal Learning and Information Processing. Elderly persons make less effective use of information presented or available to them, and the experimental work being done to separate out various steps used in dealing with information may eventually permit the clinician to make rather fine discriminations where performance decrement is observed. Techniques used to distinguish among such sub-processes are still experimental and lack normative data sufficient for diagnostic purposes. Several verbal learning tests have found some use with elderly groups. The Modified Word Learning Test has been found useful in identifying generalized brain damage (Walton and Black, 1957; Bolton, Savage, and Roth, 1967; Savage, Britton, Bolton, and Hall, 1973). Drop in a verbal learning score based on the Modified Word Learning Test was found by Hall *et al.* (1972) in a longitudinal study to discriminate between survivors and non-survivors, though not as well as WAIS Performance IQ's. It also differentiated between normals and psychiatric patients among the survivors.

Paired associate learning tasks have been found useful in differentiating among groups of elderly normals and patients (Caird, Sanderson, and Inglis, 1962; Irving, Robinson, and McAdam, 1970). Fowler (1969) provides normative data for the Non-Language Object Paired-Associate Learning Test which he developed for use with persons having language deficits.

Lieberman and Coplan (1970) found that the Paired-Associate Learning Test discriminated between near and far from death persons. Kendrick (1967) suggested changing certain cut-off points in scores from the Synonym Learning Test (Kendrick, Parboosingh, and Post, 1965) in order to assess brain pathology in the aged. Hemsi, Whitehead, and Post (1968) found elderly demented patients scored significantly lower than elderly depressives.

The findings by Ross (1968), that working under supportive (*vs.* challenging) conditions decreased the difference between young and old subjects' performance in verbal learning tasks, raises the question of standardization of conditions for assessment purposes. In that study, challenging instructions did not have as disruptive an effect on relearning the difficult material as it had on the acquisition phase. This raises additional questions of motivational influences on performance.

Problem Solving. Arenberg (1973) reviewed the limited experimental literature available on problem solving abilities in elderly persons. One study (Wetherick, 1966) suggested an intriguing application to problems frequently of interest in the clinical assessment of older persons. He hypothesized that problems of prejudice and rigidity may result from an inability to handle disconfirming information. Such a hypothesis suggests both an assessment approach and a possible explanatory mechanism through which understanding might permit development of alleviation techniques. Studies by Crovitz (1966) and Meichenbaum (1972) have demonstrated that training techniques can assist older persons in improving their performance in concept formation and problem solving. The

assessment question remains completely open, however, as to whether any measurement procedures available provide clinically useful information.

Rabbitt (Chapter 25 in this volume) reviews the literature regarding such aspects as task complexity, strategies used, and advantages and disadvantages to the elderly of preexisting "heuristics" or "rules."

Ability to Benefit from Behavior Modification Programs. Gottesman, Quarterman, and Cohn (1973) have reviewed the use of behavior modification procedures with the elderly. Lawton and Gottesman (1974) mention optimism for the further use of such techniques in mental health settings. Hoyer, Labouvie, and Baltes (1973) reported success in modifying presumably age-related decline in cognitive functioning via operant procedures. Labouvie-Vief, Hoyer, Baltes, and Baltes (1974) reviewed the assumptions related to the use of such techniques and discussed alternative controls and designs which might optimize constructive changes in behavior in the elderly. Not much has been done, however, to investigate individual differences among older adults which might require different approaches to modification. Cautela and Kastenbaum (1967) reported one study of responses of institutionalized and noninstitutionalized elderly to two assessment procedures, the Fear Survey and the Reinforcement Survey Schedule. Further efforts at developing and validating tests which would assist in appropriate linking of persons and programs seem in order.

Personality Assessment

This section will not consider the theoretical question whether personality does or does not change with age (Schaie and Parham, 1976; Neugarten, Chapter 26 in this volume), but instead, addresses the issue of whether specific personality assessment techniques are appropriate for use with elderly persons. Chown (1968) and Schaie and Marquette (1972) provide reviews regarding the usefulness of personality tests as measures of age differences but only one review has been addressed to clinical usage with the elderly (Salzman *et al.* 1972a). The latter furthermore confines evaluation of validity to whether tests have demonstrated drug sensitivity among elderly patients and to questions of content validity and mechanisms of administration.

After reviewing both multiple symptom and individual mood scales, Salzman *et al.* (1972a) concluded that the individual scales offered little advantage over brief, well-constructed multidimensional scales. General considerations related to assessment of personality variables in the elderly raised by Salzman *et al.* included the fact that very few scales have been designed for geriatric use, that cognitive and neurological deficits may make ratings difficult, and that scales that contain items of little relevance to the geriatric patient may bias the response to the remaining items. The length of most multiple mood scales limits their usefulness with geriatric groups, and differentiation into as many as four response alternatives may be difficult unless clearly defined. They further concluded that no rating scale is useful unless the respondent is cooperative; that the scale is relatively brief with clear distinctions between response choices; that questions are clearly stated and relevant to the older persons' current life situation; and that mechanical obstacles to completing a scale are avoided.

Use of Structured Questionnaires with the Aged. Probably the most commonly used scale of this sort is the Minnesota Multiphasic Personality Inventory (MMPI). In spite of many attempts reported in the literature, no consistent findings have emerged with regard to scale score changes with advancing age (Chown, 1968; Schaie and Marquette, 1972). Some studies, however, do raise hope for separating out score effects due to age *vs.* pathological functioning. For example, Swenson (1961) found significant differences between institutionalized and non-institutionalized older persons, and, Aaronson (1960) developed an aging index of MMPI items which is relatively independent of psychopathology.

Practitioners and institutions continue the clinical use of the MMPI with elderly persons as if young adult norms were appropriate.

There seems, however, to be an increasing concern over age and cohort effects on item responses and scale scores.

Pfeiffer (Chapter 27 in this volume) reports extensive use of the Mini-Mult, a shortened version of the MMPI (Kincannon, 1968). This 71-item test produces estimates of the three validity and eight clinical scale scores and is reported by Pfeiffer as being quite useful for diagnostic purposes with the elderly. The use of the Mini-Mult meets Salzman's criterion of providing a brief, multidimensional instrument. The questions of what is being measured and for what purposes scores are valid for the elderly remain open for future research.

One study (Uecker, 1969) specifically advises against the use of the MMPI for personality assessment of elderly brain damaged patients because of lack of retest reliability. This caution is not limited to the MMPI, as Salzman *et al.* (1972b) note. Pfeiffer (Chapter 27 in this volume) however, specifically proposes the use of the Mini-Mult for assessing associated pathology in organic brain syndrome patients.

Only the MMPI (Slater and Scarr, 1964) and the Guilford-Zimmerman Temperament Survey (Bendig, 1960) have been studied for comparison of factor structure over age groups extending into the elderly range. Cattell, Eber, and Tatsuoka, (1970) provided age corrections for the 16 Personality Factors Questionnaire (16 P-F), but they admit the need for additional work in this regard. The California Test of Personality can claim one study which investigated cohort effects on scores (Woodruff and Birren, 1972).

There are a few brighter spots when it comes to single scale instruments. Gough's Adjective Check List can claim one clinical validity study (Apfeldorf and Hunley, 1971) with an aged institutionalized sample. Conte (1970) reported on the construct validity for several tests of body image with older samples. Preston and Gudiksen (1966) report concurrent validity for an aged sample of a 110-item true-false measure of self-perception. Rotter's I-E Scales scores have been found to correlate in predicted ways with other clinical assessment measures and with stress and situational characteristics which realistically affect a person's ability to be in control (Kuypers, 1972; Levinson, 1974). The scale which thus far provides the most complete background of information regarding age, cohort and time of measurement effects as well as providing age norms and validity studies is the Social Responsibility Scale, a revision of the Gough, McCloskey, and Meehl (1952) instrument adapted by Schaie (1959) for greater appropriateness with older adults (see also Schaie and Strother, 1968; Schaie and Parham, 1974).

Several Q sort techniques have been used with some effectiveness with older persons. Block's California Q sort (Block, 1962; Livson and Peskin, 1967) has been used extensively for research purposes at the Institute of Human Development at the University of California at Berkeley, but studies of use for clinical purposes are lacking.

The Psychiatric Evaluation Index (Weiss, Schaie, and Rommel, 1959; Weiss and Schaie, 1964) and the Self-Concept Q sort (Butler and Haigh, 1954; Lewis, 1971) both provide some limited validity evidence for assessing personality change due to situational factors. A different kind of self sort based on the eight octant category system of Leary (1957) was found useful by Lieberman and Coplan (1970) in distinguishing persons near and far from death.

Special Techniques for the Assessment of "Disengagement." Disengagement has been one of the most widely discussed notions in the aging literature of the past 15 years. Related concepts such as altered relationships with other persons, increased self-preoccupation, decreased response to normative controls, decline in ego energy, decreased optimism and decreased morale, have encouraged many attempts at measurement, some of which may have utility for clinical assessment. Of interest here are a morale measure developed by Kutner, Fanshel, Togo, and Langner (1956), an index of interaction describing contacts and relationships with friends and neighbors (Messer, 1967), and a five-item scale of psychological readiness for withdrawal or disengagement potential which meets the formal requirements for Guttman scaling (Tissue, 1971).

Shanas (1968) used five items from Cumming

and Henry's (1961) life space measure which dealt with self-perception or psychological restriction in life space, three of her own items to measure optimism (life satisfaction, feelings of usefulness and belief in afterlife) and two statements from Srole's (1956) anomie scale. She reported an increase in self-preoccupation, continued optimism and no evidence of decreased response to normative controls.

The disengagement concept is important to clinicians trying to assess aspects of successful/ unsuccessful aging. It would appear at this point however, that neither the concept nor the measurement techniques available to date provide very clear diagnostic or status indicators.

Structured Behavior Observation. A number of scales are available for behavior observation which are specifically intended for use with older adults (Salzman et al., 1972b). The large majority of these are designed for management use with institutionalized patients, an observation which reflects the fact that services to the elderly have historically been primarily of that sort. Further, behavior observation requires a period of contact time which institutionalization provides. Scales, in this context, are typically used by nurses and aides.

One advantage of the strict behavior rating scale is that it does not require the cooperation of a person as does a self-administered or interview procedure. Behavior ratings which can be made by ward attendants, if well done, provide an obvious time advantage for the professional staff. Meer and Baker (1966) also discussed a positive side effect in that nurses and technicians became more sensitive to and aware of patients' behaviors as they made ratings.

In addition to the extensive listing of available instruments, Salzman et al. (1972b) listed some studies attesting to the validity and usefulness of the scales. Taylor and Bloom (1974) provide a more recent report and discussion of the validity of the Stockton Geriatric Rating Scale. Examples of other validity studies not mentioned by Salzman are Katz, Downs, Cash, and Grotz, (1970) and Finch, Welsh, Haney, and Dinoff (1970) for the Minimal Social Behavior Scale. Gurel, Linn, and Linn (1972) reported the development of a new scale, the

Physical and Mental Impairment of Function Evaluation (PAMIE). A brief discussion of techniques designed for behavior modification programs is included earlier in this chapter.

Performance Tests of Personality. The possibility of studying personality via performance on structured tasks has barely been explored. The Embedded Figures Test (Witkin, Dyk, Paterson, Goodenough, and Karp, 1962) is one such possibility but has not been systematically explored with older adults.

Schaie and Heiss (1964) developed the Color Pyramid Test as a means of using color preferences as an indicant of personality. But again, exploration of possible use with older persons is just beginning.

Performance on the Test of Behavioral Rigidity (Schaie, 1955; Schaie and Parham, 1975) has been studied across a wide age range (20–84 years) and the test manual provides cohort-corrected age norms. Behaviors measured yield three scores: psychomotor speed, personality-perceptual rigidity and motor-cognitive rigidity.

Projective Techniques. The status of projective techniques is much like that for more structured instruments in that reports (largely cross-sectional) are available on age differences but few studies have examined validity criteria for older persons. In contrast to structured instruments, where scoring is straightforward but questions remain regarding the appropriateness of norms, in projective techniques the problem would seem to be more whether or not scoring standards should be altered for older persons. Further, the question of what a test measures is not as dependent upon the test's factor structure as on the criteria for deciding whether a response qualifies to be categorized or called by a specific name.

Except when cut-off scores have been determined for a diagnosis of brain damage, norms for projective techniques are not used in the same way as structured tests. Instead, the summaries of scores or profiles have typically been used to provide a "rich" description of how a person "characteristically" views, handles or interacts with the world. Exactly the same problem remains as to whether the descriptions are useful in analyzing how effectively a person is functioning or in making predictions of future behavior.

The Rorschach. Ames, Metraux, Rodell, and Walker (1973) have suggested that the Rorschach is particularly appropriate for use with the elderly because it is well-accepted by them, does not unduly penalize them if they have problems of memory or coordination, and speed is not a critical factor. It should be noted, however, that Eisdorfer (1970) reported that hearing loss, though not defective vision, was related to poorer Rorschach scores.

Oberleder (1967) confirms the non-threatening nature of the Rorschach and for that reason suggests it be given first in a battery to old persons. She raises a caution regarding interpretation because of a lack of "meaningful norms and external correlates," and further suggests that predictions should be applied only to situations which involve the same degree of risk and uncertainty as the test. For very constricted persons, she suggests that a more structured projective may be higher in stimulus potency.

Ames and her associates have provided the most thorough description and discussion of Rorschach responses in old age. The most recent volume (1973) reports very few consistent findings dependent on age, either when comparing younger normals with samples in their seventies, eighties, and nineties or when looking for trends within these later years. Chown (1968) provides a brief review of the earlier references. Ames *et al.* (1973) continue to find it useful to categorize Rorschach performances into normal, presenile and senile. These categories are clearly defined on the basis of score profiles, and distinguishing signs and tables useful for categorizing profiles are provided. Validity data in the sense of correlations of these categories with external criteria are not reported except for an indication of institutionalized *vs.* non-institutionalized, and socioeconomic status differences, and Oberleder (1967) has criticized the use of the categories as dangerous "test-bound" reasoning.

One study (Weinlander, 1967) in using the Structured-Objective Rorschach Test (SORT) with groups of younger and older alcoholics confirmed few age differences in performance and hence implied its usefulness across age groups. Another inkblot technique, the Holtzman, has been suggested as an alternative by Oberleder (1967) for assessing hostility, anxiety, reality testing and impulse control in the elderly.

Thematic Apperception Test and Related Techniques. The TAT has probably been the most frequently used projective technique in connection with research into age differences. In addition to Murray's original cards and scoring procedures, several variations have been recently developed specifically for use with the elderly. Chown (1968) reviewed TAT type instruments and their use with elderly persons.

A TAT-like picture of a family scene which includes middle-aged adults has been developed and used by Neugarten and Gutmann (1958) to study role image differences with age. The Senior Apperception Technique (SAT) has recently been published (Bellak and Bellak, 1973) but little further information is yet available. The Gerontological Apperception Test (GAT) (Wolk and Wolk, 1971) similarly has not yet appeared frequently enough in the literature to assess its usefulness. Wolk (1972) states that the GAT "relates to specific problems with which the aged person's defense system may not be able to cope, such as isolation, loss of physical mobility and virility and the lessening of vocational, social and familial abilities."

In terms of validity studies, Miller and Lieberman (1965) did not find analysis of the TAT useful in predicting which persons would "negatively" adapt in a group of women who were forced to move because the home for the aged in which they had resided was closed. Lieberman and Coplan (1970) did find the Old Age TAT sensitive to the disintegrative process taking place in those close to death.

Figure Drawings. Chown (1968) reviewed the conflicting findings of draw-a-person techniques regarding age differences in the later years. Gravitz (1966) reported an age and sex interaction for the sex of the figure drawn among normals. The upper age limit in his sample, however, was 59 years and the numbers were quite small in his older groups. This sort of interaction must be verified in older persons

before interpretations for clinical significance can be suggested.

Wolk (1972) reports that the House-Tree-Person Test has been applied to the diagnostic evaluation of older people (Wolk and Goldfarb, 1967; Wolk, 1968) but that "frequently, errors in evaluation result, because aspects of drawings by the older person do not mean the same thing as drawings by younger people." He cautions that poor form may be the result of limited psychomotor coordination, eyesight, or lack of having used a crayon for many years.

Jones and Rich (1965) suggest that the height of a drawing was as good a measure of intelligence as more conventional intelligence tests, and Lakin (1960) reported that the height, area, and centeredness of figure drawings differentiated between institutionalized and noninstitutionalized aged. Apfeldorf, Randolph, and Whiteman (1966) furthermore, found that centeredness correlated with furlough usage in an aged institutionalized population. The authors suggested that additional studies are needed regarding the validity of centeredness as an indicant of anxiety or regression.

Butler and Lewis (1973) have been exploring the use of self drawings without or in front of a mirror with aged persons. They also have used the instruction to "Draw your insides." Although they do not report systematic studies, they propose that inner body parts protruding out or located completely outside may suggest confusion or organicity.

Sentence Completion Test. Carp (1967) reported the development of an objective scoring system for a sentence completion test which was applicable across ages including an older group. She demonstrated high interrater agreement and reliability for retest. No validity data for the instrument were reported except to note that the concerns expressed in responses reflected the different life circumstances of younger and older persons.

RELATING ASSESSMENT DATA TO THE LIFE PROSPECTS OF THE AGED CLIENT

The final section of this chapter is concerned with the utilization of assessment data on behalf of the aged client. Here the literature is of little help, since in this context most treatments of psychological functioning in the aged are typically addressed to professionals other than psychologists (e.g., Burr, 1971; Gaitz, 1970). Rather than searching through the diffuse hints scattered here and there, we have elected to present the reader with our own brief formulation as to what might represent reasonably constructive usage of psychological assessment data in work with the aged client.

Definition of Status

Little or no purpose is served by a descriptive analysis of psychometric findings, but it may be most useful to analyze assessment data with regard to determining whether or not actual behavior change from a previous point in time can be inferred. Such inference demands that present level of function be compared with an actual measure or an estimate of previous level. Further, it is often useful to relate present level of competence to the role requirements demanded from the client in his present or proposed life situation. For counseling purposes, it is also useful to contrast the client's perception of his level of function with the objectively determined data.

Comparison with Assumed Prior Level of Functioning. This issue is of paramount importance whenever assessment procedures are used to determine whether an individual remains competent to manage his affairs or whether institutional care is essential for the protection of the client or his family. It is indeed rare that the clinician has available past psychometric data, but a routine effort should be made to obtain such information whenever possible. In their absence, age-corrected nomothetic data may need to be relied upon. Here, particular emphasis should be placed on indices involving intra-individual discrepancies in function and for this purpose some of the Wechsler hold/don't hold indices may be quite useful (see earlier discussion). But assessment data should also be scrutinized to determine whether test findings are compatible or not with the known educational and professional activities previously accomplished by the client.

Adequacy of Capabilities and Adaptive Response to Role Requirements. Even if strong evidence is presented by the data that present

performance or adjustment is below previous levels, it must be recognized that changes in role requirements may require lesser levels of competence still well within reach of the client. Alternately, new roles may make more severe demands upon the client's adjustment, particularly in the absence of previously available environmental support systems (such as work or family). The clinician's major task therefore is not simply to define the change in the client's psychological status, but to determine its adequacy to his current life demands. The latter must be clearly delineated as part of the assessment process, and where normative data on performance requirements are not readily available, intensive individual exploration may be required.

Client's Satisfaction with Current Status. When status determination serves as the basis of counseling procedures, it may be particularly important to determine to what extent the client himself perceives alterations in function, and whether or not such alterations are seen to be disabling. Certain clients will need to be shown precise instances of apparent deleterious behavioral change in order to permit them to accept the need for status or behavior change. More frequently, however, clients infer problems attributed to aging which cannot be objectively verified. For example, frequently reported memory loss may often be parsimoniously explained by changes in the individual's support system which are unrelated to age. Thus, the retired executive who has lost his secretary may now complain of memory loss because he is no longer being cued by an outside source. Reassurance may be possible on the basis of objective test evidence showing substantially maintained levels of function. Important also is the identification of possible alternatives for the client, since the older person's retention of life choices may be critical for successful role adaptation (Goldman, 1971).

Recommendations Regarding Status Change

Determinations of the individual's capability to maintain independent role function, the alternate need to institutionalize, as well as assignment to rehabilitation programs fall into this class of inferences to be drawn from assessment data. Evaluation of specific procedures is sadly lacking and again the clinician has little alternative but to develop his own rules of thumb to help him determine the minimal levels of function and pathology which require recommendations for status change for his client.

Assessment of Psychological Capacity to Maintain an Independent Role. Assessment here will not be dissimilar in principle from that conducted with individuals of borderline competence at any life stage. It is necessary to determine whether enough intellectual competence remains so that the client can be expected to engage in reasonably prudent management of his daily affairs and the problem solving efforts required for this purpose. In addition, however, it will be necessary to consider general questions of personal adjustment. That is, does the client have enough self-confidence to maintain himself in an environment which may be full of objective and subjective hazards? Will the client fail to utilize available support systems due to interfering needs related to his personality traits? Does he appear to be functioning at a stable, albeit reduced, level of function? The clinician here will frequently have to consider factors which might enable him to project the "trajectory" of behavior change. More often than not the inference will be drawn that while status change is not yet mandatory, conditions can be specified under which such change will become inevitable.

Evaluation of Psychopathology in Relation to Requirements for Custodial Care. The determination of need for custodial care is not simply the opposite side of the coin of the evaluation of capability for independent role function. Here data must be more closely scrutinized to determine whether custodial care or treatment programs are indicated. Specifically, attention must be given to the question of whether there is acute or chronic psychopathology, or whether we are simply dealing with behavior deemed "peculiar" by the middle-aged observer, but quite characteristic of the ethno-cohort to which the client belongs. Unfortunately, decisions for shifts between inpatient mental health facilities and custodial care units have in the past been made without regard for assessing diagnostic characteristics of

the individuals transferred (cf. Markson and Cumming, 1975). But, determination of the stability of treatment-amenability of the client's syndrome as well as his needs and expectations may be a fertile field for systematic assessment and subsequent well-considered professional recommendations.

Assessment of Capability to Benefit from Treatment Programs. Although it is now taken for granted that aged clients can benefit from psychotherapeutic intervention, it does not follow that the same rules used by clinicians for assigning younger clients retain validity. Certainly, techniques assessing residual learning capability, as well as assessment of cognitive styles which relate to openness to behavior change should be useful. Further, a delineation of the hierarchy of behaviors to be modified would be important. In contrast to a similar analysis with younger clients, it is important to recognize that what is required is not a description of basic personality patterns as such, since no profound personality reorganization is likely to be attempted. Thus, much more emphasis will likely be given to state than to trait variables. Several conceptually divergent types of treatment efforts may be recommended as a function of the assessment effort.

Rehabilitation or Retraining. A detailed investigation of competencies and interests will be required to suggest how previously acquired skills and interests will fit into the development of new role functions (also see Chapter 30 in this volume for further discussion). Assessment efforts here will focus on the detection of the remaining areas of strength.

Modification of Attitudes and Self-Concept. The assumption is made that the aged individual's function could be enhanced if negative feelings about his adequacy and perceived value were modified. In this context, useful information may be obtained from a number of conventional self-description techniques, as well as instruments specifically developed for an aged clientele (e.g., Schaie, Chatham, and Weiss, 1961). Again, it may be useful to distinguish between attitudes which refer to present situational problems from those relating to the individual's stable personality style.

Modification of Interpersonal Behavior and Roles. If questions have been appropriately focused it should also be possible to specify some of the particular interpersonal behaviors of the individual which interfere with his optimal functioning. With the aged client, attention might well be focused on issues such as inter-generational conflict (including problems of parent-child role reversal), the regaining of independence and the need to engage in courtship behavior to replace a deceased spouse. Such situationally determined themes can be readily determined upon proper assessment and have greater utility than general personality themes.

SOME CONCLUDING THOUGHTS ON THE STATUS OF CLINICAL PSYCHOLOGICAL ASSESSMENT

Our scrutiny of the state of the art in clinical psychological assessment suggests that there are many good reasons why assessment should be particularly important with the aged. But many of the assessment efforts reviewed in this chapter suffer because (a) very few psychologists have been trained to work with the aged, (b) with some few exceptions adequate norms are not yet available for most of the techniques found useful with young adults, and (c) new techniques specifically constructed for clinical work with the aged are sparse and, where available, lack clear-cut demonstration of acceptable psychometric characteristics.

It is also clear that in the future, clinical assessment with the aged will need to emphasize psychophysiological indices of both autonomic and cortical functions. The technology is now available but as yet has to be applied to elderly populations. Base line assessment with both traditional and innovative techniques, and new techniques suggested by some of the lines of relevant experimental inquiry discussed here will be particularly important in the study of psychological factors in many of the chronic diseases so prevalent in the aged. Work in this area, as well as the development of new definitions of competence and role appropriate behavior in the aged should mark much of the activities of the next decade.

Given the literature to date, several additional directions seem fruitful for the future development of assessment techniques. We must begin not only to describe the present status of functioning but also to determine possible and/or optimal levels. Most current tests do only the first, if at all. To this end, learning-type tasks will likely become more important as will trials to criterion or relearning measures.

Further, in the attempt to determine the specific components of cognitive functioning which are particularly critical for the elderly, more focused tasks must be used, such as those for specific memory functions and for constructs like cognitive flexibility. Psychophysiological measures will become more important as the interrelationships between physiological functioning and behavior are better understood.

The above directions imply that the effective clinician should have available the best information from all of the experimental fields investigating the underlying mechanisms of specific behaviors. Only then could one be certain that the most appropriate behaviors were being sampled and measured. That, however, is an overwhelming task and one to which most clinicians do not even aspire.

Even with experimental knowledge, the validity of measures of specific functions for predicting important real life behaviors would still not be demonstrated. Good assessment cannot occur without checks on the validity of specific test measures for criteria of relevance for older adults. This must be done by clinically-minded persons. The pure experimentalists are not likely to do it for them.

REFERENCES

Aaronson, B. S. 1960. A dimension of personality change with aging. *J. Clin. Psychol.,* **16**, 63–65.

Ahammer, I. M., and Baltes, P. B. 1972. Objective versus perceived age differences in personality: How do adolescents, adults, and older people view themselves and each other. *J. Gerontol.,* **27**, 46–51.

Alexander, D. A. 1970. The application of the Graham-Kendall Memory-for-Designs Test to elderly normal and psychiatric groups. *Brit. J. Soc. Clin. Psychol.,* **9**, 85–86.

Ames, L. B., Metraux, R. W., Rodell, J. L., and Walker, R. N. 1973. *Rorschach Responses in Old Age.* New York: Brunner-Mazel.

Ammons, R. B., and Ammons, C. H. 1962. The Quick Test: Provisional manual. *Psych. Reports,* **11,** 111-161.

Andres, R. 1969. Physiological factors of aging significant to the clinician: Summary of remarks. *J. Am. Geriat. Soc.,* **17,** 274-277.

Apfeldorf, M., and Hunley, P. J. 1971. The adjective check list applied to older institutionalized men. *J. Proj. Tech. Person. Assessm.,* **35,** 457-462.

Apfeldorf, M., Randolph, J. J., and Whiteman, G. L. 1966. Figure drawing correlates of furlough utilization in an aged institutionalized population. *J. Proj. Tech. Person. Assessm.,* **30,** 467-470.

Arenberg, D. 1973. Cognition and aging: Verbal learning, memory, problem solving and aging. In, C. Eisdorfer and M. P. Lawton (eds.), *The Psychology of Adult Development and Aging,* pp. 74-97. Washington, D.C.: American Psychological Association.

Atchley, R. C. 1969. Respondents vs. refusers in an interview study of retired women: An analysis of selected characteristics. *J. Gerontol.,* **24,** 27-42.

Babcock, H. 1930. An experiment in the measurement of mental deterioration. *Arch. Psych.,* No. 117.

Baltes, P. B., and Schaie, K. W. 1974. Aging and IQ: The myth of the Twilight Years. *Psychology Today,* **7** (10), 35-40.

Bellak, L., and Bellak, S. S. 1973. *Senior Apperception Technique.* Larchmont, New York: C.P.S.

Bendig, A. W. 1960. Age differences in the interscale factor structure of the Guilford-Zimmerman Temperament Survey. *J. Consult. Psychol.,* **24,** 134-138.

Benton, A. L., and Van Allen, M. W. 1972. Neuropsychological assessment of cerebal disease. *In,* C. M. Gaitz (ed.), *Aging and the Brain,* pp. 29-41. New York: Plenum Press.

Ben-Yishay, Y., Diller, L., Mandleberg, I., Gordon, W., and Gerstman, L. J. 1971. Similarities and differences in block design performance between older normal and brain-injured persons: a task analysis. *J. Abnorm. Psychol.,* **78,** 17-25.

Bergman, J. S., and Johnson, H. J. 1971. The effects of instructional set and autonomic perception on cardiac control. *Psychophysiology,* **8,** 180-190.

Bettner, L. G., Jarvick, L. F., and Blum, J. E. 1971. Stroop Color-Word Test, non-psychotic organic brain syndrome and chromosome loss in aged twins. *J. Geronotol.,* **26,** 458-468.

Birkhill, W. R., and Schaie, K. W. 1975. The effect of differential reinforcement and intellectual performance of the elderly. *J. Gerontol.,* **30,** 578-583.

Birren, J. E., Butler, R. N., Greenhouse, S. W., Sokoloff, L., and Yarrow, M. R. (eds.) 1963. *Human Aging I: A Biological and Behaviorial Study* (USPHS Publ. No. 986). Washington, D.C.: U.S. Government Printing Office.

Blanchard, E. B., and Young, L. B. 1973. Self-control of cardiac functioning: A promise as yet unfulfilled. *Psych. Bull.,* **79,** 145-163.

Blanchard, E. B., Young, L. B., and McLeod, P. 1972.

Awareness of heart activity and self-control of heart rate. *Psychophysiology,* **9,** 63-68.

Blessed, G., Tomlinson, B. E., and Roth, M. 1968. The association between quantitative measures of dementia and of senile change in the cerebral gray matter of elderly subjects. *Brit. J. Psychiat.,* **114,** 797.

Block, J. 1962. *The Q Sort Method in Personality Assessment and Psychological Research.* Springfield, Illinois: Charles C. Thomas.

Bolton, N., Britton, P. G., and Savage, R. D. 1966. Some normative data on the WAIS and its indices in an aged population. *J. Clin. Psych.,* **22,** 184-188.

Bolton, N., Savage, R. D., and Roth, M. 1967. The modified Word Learning Test and the aged psychiatric patient. *Brit. J. Psychiat.,* **113,** 1139-1140.

Botwinick, J. 1969. Disinclination to venture response versus cautiousness in responding: age differences. *Journal of Genetic Psychology,* **115,** 55-62.

Botwinick, J. 1973. *Aging and Behavior.* New York: Springer.

Botwinick, J., and Storandt, M. 1974. *Memory, related functions and age.* Springfield, Ill.: Charles C. Thomas.

Brener, J. 1974. A general model of voluntary control applied to the phenomena of learned cardiovascular change. *In,* P. A. Obrist, A. H. Black, J. Brener, and L. V. DiCara (eds.), *Cardiovascular Psychophysiology,* pp. 365-391. Chicago: Aldine.

Brissette, G. G. 1967. The significance of life goals in aging adjustment: a pilot study. *California Mental Health Research Monograph,* No. 9.

Britton, P. G., and Savage, R. D. 1966. A short form of WAIS for use with the aged. *Brit. J. Psychiat.,* **112,** 417-418.

Burr, H. T. (ed.) 1971. *Psychological Functioning of Older People.* Springfield, Illinois: Charles C. Thomas.

Burt, C. 1943. Ability and income. *Brit. J. Educ. Psych.,* **13,** 83-98.

Busse, E. W., and Pfeiffer, E. 1969. Functional psychiatric disorders in old age. *In,* E. W. Busse and E. Pfeiffer (eds.), *Behavior and Adaptation in Late Life,* pp. 183-236. Boston: Little Brown.

Butler, J., and Haigh, G. 1954. Changes in the relationship between self-concepts and ideal concepts consequent upon client centered counseling. *In,* C. Rogers and R. Dymond (eds.), *Psychotherapy and Personality Change,* pp. 55-75, Chicago: University of Chicago Press.

Butler, R. N., and Lewis, M. I. 1973. *Aging and Mental Health: Positive Psychosocial Approaches.* St. Louis: C. V. Mosby.

Caird, W. K., Sanderson, R. E., and Inglis, J. 1962. Cross-validation of a learning test for use with elderly psychiatric patients. *J. Mental Sci.,* **108,** 368-370.

Callaway, E. 1973. Correlations between averaged evoked potentials and measures of intelligence. *Arch. Gen. Psychiat.,* **29,** 553-558.

Callaway, E., Jones, R. T., and Layne, R. S. 1965. Evoked responses and segmental set of schizophrenia. *Arch. Gen. Psychiat.*, 12, 83–89.

Canter, A., and Straumanis, J. J. 1969. Performance of senile and healthy aged persons on the BIP Bender Test. *Perceptual Motor Skills*, 28, 695–698.

Carp, F. M. 1967. The applicability of an empirical scoring standard for a sentence completion test administration to two age groups. *J. Gerontol.*, 22, 301–307.

Cattell, R. B. 1963. Theory of fluid and crystallized intelligence: An initial experiment. *J. Educ. Psych.*, 105, 105–111.

Cattell, R. B., Eber, H. W., and Tatsuoka, M. M. 1970. *Handbook for the Sixteen Personality Factor Questionnaire* (16 P-F). Champaign, Illinois: Institute for Personality and Ability Testing.

Cautela, J. R., and Kastenbaum, R. 1967. Assessment procedures for behavior modification with the aged. *Proc. 20th Ann. Meet. Gerontol. Soc.*, p. 38.

Chown, S. M. 1968. Personality and aging. *In*, K. W. Schaie (ed.), *Theory and Methods of Research on Aging*, pp. 134–157. Morgantown, West Virginia University Library.

Clausen, J. A. 1968. Conceptual and methodologic issues in the assessment of mental health in the aged. *Psychiat. Res. Rep.*, 23, 151–160.

Comalli, P. E., Jr. 1970. Life-span changes in visual perception. *In*, L. P. Goulet and P. B. Baltes (eds.), *Life-Span Developmental Psychology: Research and Theory*, pp. 211–227. New York: Academic Press.

Comalli, P. E., Wapner, S., and Werner, H. 1962. Interference effects of the Stroop Color-Word Test in childhood, adulthood and aging. *Journal of Genetic Psychology*, 100, 47–53.

Conte, H. R. 1970. Studies of body image: body worries and body discomforts. *Proc. Ann. Conv. Am. Psychol. Assoc.*, 6, Part 2, 595–596.

Copeland, J. R. M., Kelleher, M. J., Kellett, J. M., Gourlay, A. J., Gurland, B. J., Fleiss, J. L., and Sharpe, L. 1976. A semi-structured clinical interview for the assessment of diagnosis and mental state in the elderly: The Geriatric Mental Status Schedule. I. Development and reliability. *Psychological Medicine*, 6, in press.

Corso, J. F. 1971. Sensory processes and age effects in normal adults. *J. Gerontol.*, 26, 90–105.

Crovitz, E. 1966. Reversing a learning deficit in the aged. *J. Gerontol.*, 21, 236–238.

Cumming, E., and Henry, W. E. 1961. *Growing Old: The Process of Disengagement*. New York: Basic Books.

Davies, A. D. M. 1968a. The influence of age on Trail-Making Test performance. *J. Clin. Psych.*, 24, 96–98.

Davies, A. D. M. 1968b. Measures of mental deterioration in aging and brain damage. *In*, S. Chown and K. Riegel (eds.), *Interdisciplinary Topics in Gerontology*, Vol. 1, pp. 78–90. Basel: Karger.

Davison, L. A. 1974. Introduction. *In*, R. M. Reitan and L. A. Davison (eds.), *Clinical Neuropsychology: Current Status and Application*, pp. 1–18. Washington, D.C.: Winston.

Dawson, M., Schell, A. M., and Catania, J. 1974. Autonomic activity in depressive illness. Paper read at the *14th Ann. Meet. Soc. Psychophysiol. Res.*, Salt Lake City, Utah.

Demming, J. A., and Pressey, S. L. 1957. Tests indigenous to the adult and older years. *J. Consult. Psychol.*, 4, 144–148.

Denney, D., Kole, D. M., and Matarazzo, R. G. 1965. The number of symptoms reported by patients. *J. Gerontol.*, 20, 50–54.

Dujoune, B. E., and Levy, B. I. 1971. The psychometric structure of the Wechsler Memory Scale. *J. Clin. Psych.*, 27, 351–354.

Eisdorfer, C. 1970. Rorschach rigidity and sensory decrement in a senescent population. *In*, E. Palmore (ed.), *Normal Aging*, pp. 232–237. Durham, North Carolina: Duke University Press.

Engstrom, D. R. In press. Hypnotic susceptibility and the EEG. *In*, G. E. Schwartz and D. Shapiro (eds.), *Consciousness and Self-regulation*. New York: Plenum Press.

Eysenck, H. J. 1964. *Crime and Personality*. London: Methuen.

Finch, A. J., Welsh, D. K., Haney, J. R., and Dinoff, M. 1970. Comparison of two versions of a Minimal Social Behavior Scale. *Psychol. Reports*, 26, 985–986.

Fitzhugh, K. B., Fitzhugh, L. C., and Reitan, R. M. 1962. Wechsler-Bellevue comparisons in groups with "chronic" and "current" lateralized and diffuse brain lesions. *J. Consult. Psychol.*, 26, 306–310.

Fletcher, C. R. 1972. How not to interview an elderly clinic patient: A case illustration and the interviewer's explanation. *Gerontologist*, 12, 398–402.

Fowler, R. S. 1969. A simple non-language test of new learning. *Perceptual Motor Skills*, 29, 895–901.

Fozard, J. L., and Nuttall, R. L. 1971. General aptitude test battery scores for men differing in age and socioeconomic status. *J. Appl. Psych.*, 55, 372–379.

Furry, C. A., and Baltes, P. B. 1973. The effect of age differences in ability on extraneous variables on the assessment of intelligence in children, adults, and the elderly. *J. Gerontol.*, 28, 73–80.

Gaitz, C. M. 1969. Functional assessment of the suspected mentally ill aged. *J. Am. Geriat. Soc.*, 17, 541–548.

Gaitz, C. M. 1970. Diagnostic assessment of the elderly: a multifunctional model. *Gerontologist*, 10, 47–52.

Gaitz, C. M. 1973. Mental disorders: Diagnosis and treatment. *In*, E. Busse (ed.), *Theory and Therapeutics of Aging*. New York: Medcom Press.

Gendreau, L., Roach, T., and Gendreau, P. 1973. Assessing the intelligence of aged persons: report on the Quick Test. *Psych. Reports*, 32, 475–480.

Gergen, J., and Back, W. 1966. Communication in the interview and the disengaged respondent. *Public Opinion Quarterly*, 30, 385–398.

Gilbert, J. G. 1935. Mental efficiency in senescence. *Arch. Psych.* **188**, 1–60.

Gilbert, J. G. 1973. Thirty-five-year follow-up study of intellectual functioning. *J. Gerontol.*, **28**, 68–72.

Goldfarb, A. I. 1962. The psychotherapy of elderly patients. *In*, H. Blumenthal (ed.), *Aging Around the World: Medical and Clinical Aspects of Aging.* New York: Columbia University Press.

Goldman, S. 1971. Social aging, disorganization and loss of choice. *Gerontologist*, **11**, 158–162.

Goodly, W., and Reinhold, M. 1964. The sense of direction and the Arrow form. *In*, L. Halpern (ed.), *Problems of Dynamic Neurology.* Jerusalem: Hebrew University, Hadassah Medical School.

Gottesman, L. E., Quarterman, C. E., and Cohn, G. M. 1973. Psychosocial treatment of the aged. *In*, C. Eisdorfer and M. P. Lawton (eds.), *The Psychology of Adult Development and Aging,* pp. 378–427. Washington, D.C.: American Psychological Association.

Gough, H. G., McCloskey, H., and Meehl, P. E. 1952. A personality scale for social responsibility. *J. Abn. Soc. Psych.*, **47**, 73–80.

Goul, W. R., and Brown, M. 1970. Effects of age and intelligence on Trail Making Tests performance and validity. *Perceptual Motor Skills*, **30**, 319–326.

Graham, F. K, and Kendall, B. S. 1960. Memory for Designs Test: revised general manual. *Perceptual Motor Skills*, **11**, 147–188.

Granick, S. 1971a. Brief tests and their interrelations as intelligence measures of aged subjects. *Proc. Ann. Conv. Am. Psychol. Assoc.*, **6**, Part 2, 599–600.

Granick, S. 1971b. Psychological test functioning. *In*, S. Granick and R. D. Patterson (eds.), *Human Aging II* (DHEW Publ. No. (HSM) 71-91037). Washington, D.C.: U.S. Government Printing Office.

Gravitz, M. A. 1966. Normal adult differentiation patterns on the figure drawing test. *J. Proj. Tech. Person. Assess.*, **30**, 471–473.

Green, R. F. 1969. Age-intelligence relationship between ages sixteen and sixty-four: a rising trend. *Developmental Psychology*, **1**, 618–627.

Gubrium, J. F. 1971. Self-conceptions of mental health among the aged. *Mental Hygiene*, **55**, 398–403.

Gurel, L., Linn, M. W., and Linn, B. S. 1972. Physical and mental impairment-of-function evaluation in the aged: The PAMIE Scale. *J. Gerontol.*, **27**, 83–90.

Gurland, B J. 1973. A broad clinical assessment of psychopathology in the aged. *In*, C. Eisdorfer and M. P. Lawton (eds.), *The Psychology of Adult Development and Aging,* pp. 343–377. Washington, D.C.: American Psychological Association.

Gurland, B. J., Fleiss, J. L., Goldberg, K., Sharpe, L., Copeland, J. R. M., Kelleher, M. J., and Kellett, J. M. 1976. The Geriatric Mental Status Schedule. II. Factor analysis. *Psychological Medicine*, **6**, in press.

Hall, E. H., Savage, R. D., Bolton, N., Pidwell, D. M., and Blessed, G. 1972. Intellect, mental illness and survival in the aged: A longitudinal investigation. *J. Gerontol.*, **27**, 237–244.

Hare, R. D. 1970. *Psychopathy: Theory and Research.* New York: John Wiley.

Havighurst, R. J. 1973. Social roles, work, leisure, and education. *In*. C. Eisdorfer and M. P. Lawton (eds.), *The Psychology of Adult Development and Aging,* pp. 598–618. Washington, D. C.: American Psychological Association.

Hemsi, L. K., Whitehead, A., and Post, F. 1968. Cognitive functioning and cerebral arousal in elderly depressives and dements. *J. Psychosomatic Res.*, **12**, 145–156.

Horn, J. L. 1970. Organization of data on life span development of human abilities. *In*, L. R. Goulet and P. B. Baltes (eds.), *Life-Span Developmental Psychology: Research and Theory,* pp. 424–467. New York: Academic Press.

Hoyer, W. J., Labouvie, G. V., and Baltes, P. B. 1973. Modification of response speed and intellectual performance in the elderly. *Hum. Develop.*, **16**, 233–242.

Hulicka, I. M. 1967. Research problems with reference to treatment programs for the elderly. *Gerontologist*, **7** (2), Part II, 3–12.

Hurwitz, L. J., and Allison, R. S. 1965. Factors influencing performance in psychological testing of the aged. *In*, A. T. Welford and J. E. Birren (eds.), *Behavior Aging and the Nervous System,* pp. 461–475. Springfield, Illinois: Charles C. Thomas.

Irving, G. 1971. The performance of elderly subjects on Goodly's Arrow Drawing Test. *Brit. J. Soc. Clin. Psychol.*, **10**, 360–361.

Irving, G., Robinson, R. A., and McAdam, W. 1970. The validity of some cognitive tests in the diagnosis of dementia. *Brit. J. Psychiat.*, **117**, 149.

Jarvick, L. F., Bennett, R., and Blumner, B. 1973. Design of a comprehensive life history interview schedule. *In*, L. F. Jarvik, C. Eisdorfer, and J. E. Blum (eds.), *Intellectual Functioning in Adults,* pp. 127–136. New York: Springer.

Jarvik, L. F., Eisdorfer, C., and Blum, J. E. (eds.) 1973. *Intellectual Functioning in Adults.* New York: Springer.

Jones, R. T., Blacker, K. H., Callaway, E., and Layne, R. S. 1965. The auditory evoked response as a diagnostic and prognostic measure in schizophrenia. *Am. J. Psychiat.*, **122**, 33–41.

Jones, W., and Rich, R. A. 1965. The Goodenough Draw-a-man Test as a measure of intelligence in aged adults. *J. Consult. Psychol.*, **21**, 235–238.

Kahn, R. L., Goldfarb, A. I., Pollack, M., and Peck, A. 1966. A brief objective measure for the determination of mental status of the aged. *Am. J. Psychiat.*, **117**, 326–328.

Kastenbaum, R. 1965. Engrossment and perspective in later life: a developmental - field approach. *In*, R. Kastenbaum (ed.), *Contributions to the Psychobiology of Aging,* pp. 3–18. New York: Springer.

Kastenbaum, R., and Cameron, P. 1969. Cognitive

and emotional dependencies in later life. *In*, R. A. Kalish (ed.), *The Dependencies of Older People*, pp. 39–58. Ann Arbor: University of Michigan, Institute of Gerontology.

Kastenbaum, R., and Sherwood, S. 1967. A new scale for assessing the interview behavior of elderly people. *Gerontologist*, 7 (Part II), 41.

Katz, S., Downs, T. D., Cash, H., and Grotz, R. C. 1970. Progress in development of the index of ADL. *Gerontologist*, 10, Part 1, 20–30.

Kendrick, D. C. 1967. A cross-validation of the use of the SLT and DCT in screening for diffuse brain pathology in elderly subjects. *Brit. J. Med. Psychol.*, 40, 173–177.

Kendrick, D. C., Parboosingh, R. C., and Post, F. 1965. A synonym learning test for use with elderly psychiatric subjects: A validation study. *Brit. J. Soc. Clin. Psychol.*, 4, 63–71.

Kincannon, J. G. 1968. Prediction of the Standard MMPI Scale Scores from 71 Items: The Mini-mult. *J. Consult. Psychol.*, 32, 319–325.

Kutner, B., Fanshel, D., Togo, A. M., and Langner, T. S. 1956. *Five Hundred over Sixty*. New York: Russell Sage Foundation.

Kuypers, J. A. 1972. Internal-external locus of control, ego functioning and personality characteristics in old age. *Gerontologist*, 12, 168–173.

Labouvie-Vief, G., Hoyer, W. J., Baltes, M. M., and Baltes, P. B. 1974. Operant analysis of intellectual behavior in old age. *Hum. Develop.*, 17, 259–272.

Lakin, M. 1960. Formal characteristics of human figure drawings by institutionalized and non-institutionalized aged. *J. Gerontol.*, 15, 76–78.

Langner, T. S., and Michael, S. T. 1963. *Life Stress and Mental Health*. New York: The Free Press.

Lawton, M. P., and Gottesman, L. E. 1974. Psychological services to the elderly. *American Psychologist*, 29, 689–693.

Leary, T. 1957. *Interpersonal Diagnosis of Personality*. New York: Ronald.

Lehman, H. E., and Ban, T. 1970. Psychometric tests in evaluation of brain pathology response to drugs. *Geriatrics*, 25, 142–147.

Lehman, H. E., and Kral, V. A. 1968. Psychological Tests: Practice effect in geriatric patients. *Geriatrics*, 2, 160–163.

Levine, N. R. 1971. Validation of the Quick Test of intelligence screening of the elderly. *Psych. Reports*, 29, 167–172.

Levinson, E. J. 1974. Correlates of the internal-external locus of control scale and effects of social roles in any aging population. Paper read at the 82nd Annual Meeting of the American Psychological Association, New Orleans.

Lewis, C. N. 1971. Reminiscing and self-concept in old age. *J. Gerontol.*, 26, 240–243.

Lieberman, M. A., and Coplan, A. S. 1970. Distance from death as a variable in the study of aging. *Developmental Psychology*, 2, 71–84.

Lieberman, M. A., and Falk, J. M. 1971. The remembered past as a source of data for research on the life cycle. *Hum. Develop.*, 14, 132–141.

Lindsey, B. A., and Coppinger, N. W. 1969. Age-related deficits in simple capabilities and their consequences for trail making performance. *J. Clin. Psych.*, 25, 156–159.

Lissitz, S. 1970. Theoretical conceptions of institutional and community care of the aged. *Gerontologist*, 10, 298–304.

Livson, N., and Peskin, H. 1967. Predictions of adult psychological health in a longitudinal study. *J. Abnorm. Psychol.*, 72, 509–518.

Lowenthal, M., Berkman, P. L., and associates. 1967. *Aging and Mental Disorder in San Francisco*. San Francisco: Jossey-Bass.

Maddox, G. L. 1970. Themes and issues in sociological theories of human aging. *Hum. Develop.*, 13, 17–27.

Mandler, G., Mandler, O., and Uviller, O. 1958. Autonomic feedback: The perception of autonomic activity. *J. Abn. Soc. Psych.*, 56, 367–373.

Markson, E. W., and Cumming, J. H. 1975. The post-transfer fate of relocated mental patients in New York. *Gerontologist*, 15, 104–108.

Matarazzo, J. D. 1972. *Wechsler's Measurement and Appraisal of Adult Intelligence*. Baltimore: Williams & Wilkins.

McCallum, C. 1973. The CNV and conditionability in psychopaths. *Electroencephalo. Clin. Neurophysiol. Suppl.*, 33, 337–343.

McDonald, C. 1969. Clinical heterogeneity in senile dementia. *Brit. J. Psychiat.*, 115, 267–271.

Meer, B., and Baker, J. A. 1966. The Stockton Geriatric Rating Scale. *J. Gerontol.*, 21, 392–403.

Meichenbaum, D. H. 1972. Training the aged in the verbal control of behavior. *Proc. 9th Int. Congr. Gerontol.*, Kiev.

Mensh, I. N. 1973. Community mental health and other health services for the Aged. *In*, C. Eisdorfer and M. P. Lawton (eds.), *The Psychology of Adult Development and Aging*, pp. 529–571. Washington, D.C.: American Psychological Association.

Messer, M. 1967. The possibility of an age-concentrated environment becoming a normative system. *Gerontologist*, 7, 247–251.

Miller, D., and Lieberman, M. 1965. The relationship of affect state and adaptive capacity to reaction to stress. *J. Gerontol.*, 20, 492–497.

Muller, H. F., and Grad, B. G. 1974. Clinical psychological, electroencephalographic and adrenocortical relationships in elderly psychiatric patients. *J. Gerontol.*, 29, 28–38.

Murrell, K. F. H. 1970. The effect of extensive practice on age differences in reaction time. *J. Gerontol.*, 25, 268–274.

Nesselroade, J. R., Schaie, K. W., and Baltes, P. B. 1972. Ontogenetic and generational components of structural and quantitative change in adult cognitive behavior. *J. Gerontol.*, 27, 222–228.

Neugarten, B. L., and Gutmann, D. L. 1958. Age-sex roles and personality in middle age: A thematic apperception study. *Psychol. Monographs*, **72**, 1–33.

Norman, R. D. 1966. A revised deterioration formula for the Wechsler Adult Intelligence Scale. *J. Clin. Psych.*, **22**, 287–294.

Oberleder, M. 1964. Aging: It's importance for clinical psychology. *In*, L. E. Abt and B. F. Riess (eds.), *Progress in Clinical Psychology*. New York: Grune & Stratton.

Oberleder, M. 1967. Adapting current psychological techniques for use in testing the aged. *Gerontologist*, **7**, 188–191.

Obrist, W. D. 1971. Cerebral physiology of the aged: influence of circulatory disorders. *In*, C. M. Gaitz (ed.), *Aging and the Brain*, pp. 117–133. New York: Plenum Press.

Obrist, W. D., and Busse, E. S. 1965. The electroencephalogram in old age. *In*, W. P. Wilson (ed.), *Application of Electroencephalography in Psychiatry*. Durham, North Carolina: Duke University Press.

Overall, J. E., and Gorham, D. R. 1972. Organicity versus old age in objective and projective test performance. *J. Consult. Clin. Psych.*, **39**, 98–105.

Owens, W. A. 1971. A quasi-actuarial basis for individual assessment. *American Psychologist*, **26**, 992–999.

Perlin, S., and Butler, R. N. 1963. Psychiatric aspects of adaptation to the aging experience. *In*, J. E. Birren, R. N. Butler, S. W. Greenhouse, L. Sokoloff, and M. R. Yarrow (eds.), *Human Aging: A Biological and Behavioral Study* (USPHS Publ. No. 986). Washington, D.C.: U. S. Government Printing Office.

Pfeiffer, E. A. 1973. Multiple System Interaction and high bodily concern as problems in the management of aging patients. *In*, C. Eisdorfer and W. E. Fann (eds.), *Psychopharmacology and Aging*, pp. 151–158. Durham, North Carolina: Duke University Press.

Pihlblad, C. T., Rosencranz, H. A., and McNevin, T. E. 1967. An examination of the effects of perceptual frames of reference in interviewing older respondent. *Gerontologist*, **7**, 125–127.

Poon, L. W., Thompson, L. W., Williams, R. B., and Marsh, G. R. 1974. Changes of antero-posterior distribution of CNV and later positive component as a function of information processing demands. *Psychophysiology*, **11**, 660–673.

Preston, C. E., and Gudiksen, K. S. 1966. A measure of self perception among older people. *J. Gerontol.*, **21**, 63–71.

Ray, W. J., and Lamb, S. 1974. Locus of control and the voluntary control of heart rate. *Psychosomat. Med.*, **36**, 180–182.

Reinert, G. 1970. Comparative factor analytic studies of intelligence throughout the human life-span. *In*, L. R. Goulet and P. B. Baltes (eds.), *Life-Span Developmental Psychology: Research and Theory*, pp. 468–485. New York: Academic Press.

Reitan, R. M. 1955. The relationship of the Trail Making Test to organic brain damage. *J. Consult. Psychol.*, **19**, 393–395.

Reitan, R. M., and Davison, L. A. (eds.) 1974. *Clinical Neuropsychology: Current Status and Application*. Washington, D.C.: Winston.

Riegel, K. F. 1972. Time and change in the development of the individual and society. *In*, H. W. Reese (ed.), *Advances in Child Development and Behavior*, Vol. 7, pp. 81–113. New York: Academic Press.

Ross, E. 1968. Effects of challenging and supportive instructions on verbal learning in older persons. *J. Educ. Psych.*, **59**, 261–266.

Salzman, C., Kochansky, G. E., Shader, R. T., and Cronin, D. M. 1972a. Rating scales for psychotropic drug research with geriatric patients. II. Mood ratings. *J. Am. Geriat. Soc.*, **20**, 215–221.

Salzman, C., Shader, R. T., Kochansky, G. E., and Cronin, D. M. 1972b. Rating scales for psychotropic drug research with geriatric patients: I. Behavior ratings. *J. Am. Geriat. Soc.*, **20**, 209–214.

Sarbin, T. R., Taft, R., and Bailey, D. E. 1960. *Clinical Inference and Cognitive Theory*. New York: Holt.

Savage, R. D., and Britton, P. G. 1968. The factorial structure of the WAIS in an aged sample. *J. Gerontol.*, **23**, 183–186.

Savage, R. D., Britton, P. G., Bolton, N., and Hall, E. H. 1973. *Intellectual functioning in the aged*. New York: Harper and Row.

Savage, R. D., Britton, P. G., George, S., O'Connor, D., and Hall, E. H. 1972. A developmental investigation of intellectual functioning in the community aged. *Journal of Genetic Psychology*, **121**, 163–167.

Schacter, S., and Latane, B. 1964. Crime, cognition and the autonomic nervous system. *In*, M. R. Jones (ed.), *Nebraska Symposium on Motivation*. Lincoln: University of Nebraska Press.

Schaie, K. W. 1955. A test of behavioral rigidity. *J. Abn. Soc. Psych.*, **51**, 604–610.

Schaie, K. W. 1959. The effect of age on a scale of social responsibility. *Journal of Social Psychology*, **50**, 221–224.

Schaie, K. W. 1963. Scaling the scales: use of expert judgment in improving the validity of questionnaire scales. *J. Consult. Psychol.*, **27**, 257–350.

Schaie, K. W. 1970. A reinterpretation of age-related changes in cognitive structure and functioning. *In*, L. R. Goulet and P. B. Baltes (eds.), *Life-Span Developmental Psychology: Research and Theory*, pp. 485–507. New York: Academic Press.

Schaie, K. W. 1973. Reflections on papers by Looft, Peterson and Sparks: Towards an ageless society. *Gerontologist*, **13**, 31–35.

Schaie, K. W. 1974. Translations in gerontology—from lab to life: intellectual functioning. *American Psychologist*, **29**, 802–807.

Schaie, K. W., Chatham, L. R., and Weiss, J. M. A. 1961. The multiprofessional intake assessment of older psychiatric patients. *J. Psychiat. Res.*, **1**, 92–100.

Schaie, K. W., and Gribbin, K. 1975. The impact of

environmental complexity upon adult cognitive development. *Proc. 3rd Bienn. Meet. Int. Soc. Stud. Behav. Develop.*, Guildford, England.

Schaie, K. W., and Heiss, R. 1964. *Color and Personality.* New York: Grune & Stratton.

Schaie, K. W., and Labouvie-Vief, G. V. 1974. Generational versus ontogenetic components of change in adult cognitive behavior: a fourteen year cross-sectional study. *Developmental Psychology*, **10**, 305–320.

Schaie, K. W., and Marquette, B. W. 1972. Personality in maturity and old age. *In*, R. M. Dreger (ed.), *Multivariate Contributions to the Understanding of Personality in Honor of Raymond B. Cattell*, pp. 612–632. Baton Rouge, Louisiana: Claitor's Publishing.

Schaie, K. W., and Parham, I. A. 1974. Social responsibility in adulthood: Ontogenetic and sociocultural change. *J. Pers. Soc. Psychol.*, **30**, 483–492.

Schaie, K. W., and Parham, I. A. 1975. *Manual for the Test of Behavioral Rigidity.* 2nd Edition. Palo Alto, California: Consulting Psychologists Press.

Schaie, K. W., and Parham, I. A. 1976. Stability of adult personality traits: fact or fable. *J. Pers. Soc. Psychol.*, **34**, 146–158.

Schaie, K. W., Rommel, L. A., and Weiss, J. M. A. 1959. Judging the relative severity of psychiatric out-patient complaints. *J. Clin. Psychol.*, **15**, 380–388.

Schaie, K. W., and Strother, C. R. 1968. Cognitive and personality variables in college graduates of advanced age. *In*, G. A. Talland (ed.). *Human Aging and Behavior*, pp. 281–308. New York: Academic Press.

Schaie, K. W., Strother, C. R., and Baltes, P. B. 1964. A study of auditory sensitivity in advanced age. *J. Gerontol.*, **19**, 453–457.

Schmidt, L. R. 1970. Testing the limits im Leistungsverhalten: Möglichkeiten und Grenzen. *In*, Duhm (ed.), *Praxis der Klinischen Psychologie*, Vol. 2. Göttingen: Hogrefe.

Shagass, C. 1972. Electrical activity of the brain. *In*, N. S. Greenfield and R. A. Sternback (eds.), *Handbook of Psychophysiology*, pp. 263–328. New York: Holt, Rinehart and Winston.

Shagass, C., and Canter, A. 1966. Some personality correlates of cerebral evoked response characteristics. *Proc. 18th Int. Congr. Psychol.*, Symposium No. 6.

Shagass, C., and Schwartz, M. 1965. Age, personality and somatosensory cerebral evoked responses. *Science*, **148**, 1359–1361.

Shagass, C., and Schwartz, M. 1966. Somatosensory cerebral evoked responses in psychotic depression. *Brit. J. Psychiat.*, **112**, 799–807.

Shanas, E. 1968. A note on restriction of life space: attitudes of age cohorts. *J. of Health Soc. Behavior*, **9**, 86–90.

Shapiro, D. 1974. Operant-feedback control of human blood pressure: Some clinical issues. *In*, P. A. Obrist,

A. H. Black, J. Brener and L. V. DiCara (eds.), *Cardiovascular Psychophysiology*, pp. 441–455. Chicago: Aldine.

Shapiro, D., and Schwartz, G. E. 1972. Biofeedback and visual learning: Clinical applications. *Semin. Psychiat.*, **4**, 171–184.

Shucard, D. W., and Horn, J. F. 1972. Evoked cortical potentials and measurement of human abilities. *J. Comp. Physiol. Psychol.*, **78**, 59–68.

Slater, P. E., and Scarr, H. A. 1964. Personality in old age. *Genet. Psychol. Monogr.*, **70**, 229–269.

Small, J. G., and Small, I. F. 1971. Contingent negative variation (CNV) correlations with psychiatric diagnosis. *Arch. Gen. Psychiat.*, **25**, 550–554.

Spence, D. L. 1968. The role of futurity in aging adaptation. *Gerontol.*, **8**, 180–183.

Spitzer, R. L., Endicott, J., Cohen, J., Bennett, R., and Weinstock, C. 1969. *Mental Status Schedule-Geriatric Supplement.* Biometrics Research, New York State Department of Mental Hygiene.

Spitzer, R. L., Fleiss, J. L., Endicott, J., and Cohen, J. 1967. Mental Status Schedule: Properties of factor-analytically derived scales. *Arch. Gen. Psychiat.*, **16**, 479–493.

Srole, L. 1956. Social integration and certain corollaries: an exploratory study. *Am. Soc. Rev.*, **21**, 709–716.

Surwillo, W. W. 1966. On the relation of latency of alpha attenuation to alpha rhythm frequency and the influence of age. *Electroencephalo. Clin. Neurophysiol.*, **20**, 129–132.

Swenson, W. M. 1961. Structured personality testing in the aged: a MMPI study of the gerontic population. *J. Clin. Psych.*, **17**, 302–304.

Syndulko, K., Parker, D., Maltzman, I., Jens, R., and Ziskind, E. 1974. An electrocortical measure of orienting in sociopaths. Paper read at *14th Ann. Meet. Soc. Psychophysiol. Res.*, Salt Lake City, Utah.

Syndulko, K., Parker, D., Maltzman, I., Jens, R., and Ziskind, E. 1975. Psychophysiology of sociopathy: electrocortical measures. *Biol. Psych.*, **3**, 185–200.

Taub, H. A. 1972. A comparison of young adult and old age groups on various digit span tasks. *Developmental Psychology*, **6**, 60–65.

Taylor, H. G., and Bloom, L. M. 1974. Cross-validation and methodological extension of the Stockton Geriatric Rating Scale. *J. Gerontol.*, **29**, 190–193.

Thompson, L. W., and Marsh, G. 1973. Psychophysiological studies of aging. *In*, C. Eisdorfer and M. P. Lawton (eds.), *The Psychology of Adult Development*, pp. 112–150. Washington, D. C.: American Psychological Association.

Thurnher, M. 1973. Adaptability of life history interviews to the study of adult development. *In*, L. F. Jarvik, C. Eisdorfer and J. E. Blum (eds.), *Intellectual Functioning in Adults*, pp. 137–142. New York: Springer.

Timsit-Berthier, M., Delauncy, J., Konick, N., and

Rousseau, J. C. 1973. Slow potential changes in psychiatry. I. Contingent negative variation. *Electroencephalo. Clin. Neurophysiol.*, 35, 355–362.

Tissue, T. 1971. Disengagement potential: replication and use as an exploratory variable. *J. Gerontol.*, 26, 76–80.

Tobin, S. S., and Etigson, E. 1968. Effect of stress on earliest memory. *Arch. Gen. Psychiat.*, 19, 435–444.

Uecker, A. E. 1969. Comparability of two methods of administering the MMPI to brain damaged geriatric patients. *J. Clin. Psych.*, 25, 196–198.

Walton, D. 1958. The diagnostic and predictive accuracy of the Wechsler Memory Scale in psychiatric patients over 65. *J. Ment. Sci.*, 104, 1111–1118.

Walton, D., and Black, D. A. 1957. The validity of a psychological test of brain damage. *Brit. J. Med. Psychol.*, 30, 270–271.

Walton, D., and Black, D. A. 1959. The predictive validity of a psychological test of brain damage. *J. Ment. Sci.*, 105, 807–810.

Wechsler, D. 1939. *The Measurement of Adult Intelligence*. Williams & Wilkins.

Wechsler, D. 1941. *The Measurement of Adult Intelligence*. 2nd Edition. Baltimore: Williams & Wilkins.

Wechsler, D. 1944. *The Measurement of Adult Intelligence*. 3rd Edition. Baltimore: Williams & Wilkins.

Wechsler, D. 1945. A standardized memory scale for clinical use. *Journal of Psychology*, 19, 87–95.

Wechsler, D. 1958. *The Measurement and Appraisal of Adult Intelligence*. 4th Edition. Baltimore: Williams & Wilkins.

Weinlander, M. M. 1967. Alcoholics and the influence of age on the variables of the structured-objective Rorschach Test (SORT). *J. Psych.*, 65, 57–58.

Weiss, J. M. A., and Schaie, K. W. 1964. The Psychiatric Evaluation Index: potential use in assessment of the results of psychotherapy. *Amer. J. Psychother.*, Suppl. I, 18, 3–14, 61–63.

Weiss, J. M. A., Schaie, K. W., and Rommel, L. A. 1959. The presenting problems of older patients referred to a psychiatric clinic. *J. Gerontol.*, 14, 477–481.

Werner, M., Perlin, S., Butler, R. M., and Pollin, W. 1961. Self-perceived changes in community-resident aged: "aging image" and adaptation. *Arch. Gen. Psychiat.*, 4, 501–508.

Wetherick, N. E. 1966. The inferential basis of concept attainment. *Brit. J. Psychol.*, 57, 61–69.

Wilkie, F., and Eisdorfer, C. 1971. Intelligence and blood pressure in the aged. *Science*, 172, 959–962.

Witkin, H. A., Dyk, R. B., Paterson, H. F., Goodenough, D. R., and Karp, S. A. 1962. *Psychological Differentiation: Studies of Development*. New York: John Wiley.

Wolk, R. L. 1968. Projective drawings of aged people. *In*, J. Buch and E. F. Hammer (eds.), *Advances in the H-T-P: Variations and Applications*. Los Angeles: Western Psychological Services.

Wolk, R. L. 1972. Refined projective techniques with the aged. *In*, D. P. Kent, R. Kastenbaum, and S. Sherwood (eds.), *Research Planning and Action for the Elderly: The Power and Potential of Social Science*, pp. 218–251. New York: Behavioral Publications.

Wolk, R. L., and Goldfarb, A. I., 1967. The response to group psychotherapy of aged recent admissions compared with long-term mental hospital patients. *Am. J. Psychiat.*, 123, 1251–1257.

Wolk, R. L., and Wolk, R. B. 1971. *The Gerontological Apperception Test*. New York: Behavioral Publications.

Woodruff, D. S., and Birren, J. E. 1972. Age changes and cohort difference in personality. *Developmental Psychology*, 6, 252–259.

Zuckerman, M., Murtaugh, T., and Siegel, J. 1974. Sensation-seeking and cortical augmenting-reducing. *Psychophysiology*, 11, 535–542.

30
INTERVENTION, TREATMENT, AND REHABILITATION OF PSYCHIATRIC DISORDERS

Carl Eisdorfer
and
Bernard A. Stotsky
University of Washington

INTRODUCTION

Reactions to deviant behavior or psychiatric illness in older persons are subject to a number of significant cultural variables beyond those usually associated with such disorders. Lowenthal, Berkman and Associates (1967) have demonstrated that in the absence of behavior which is physically harmful to self or others, the deviance of older persons in the community may be ignored for long periods of time. Among "normal" older male volunteers, diagnosable psychopathology is seen in significant numbers, with depression as the most common symptom (Birren, Butler, Greenhouse *et al.*, 1963; Granick and Patterson, 1971). The prevalence of behavioral or emotional disorders significant enough to be labeled psychiatric disease ranges from 20 to 45 percent among aged persons (Busse, 1973).

If we are to develop rational and effective strategies for the treatment of psychological and psychiatric disorders in the aged, it is essential that we be able to describe systematically and with some insight the nature of such disorders. This applies not only to description but to etiology as well.

Intervention and treatment refer to socially sanctioned practices and procedures for preventing, modifying, or eliminating disordered or undesirable behavior. Rehabilitation refers to the restoration of the patient to the maximum possible level of psychological, physical, and vocational function and self-sufficiency. We shall focus on three approaches to this material: (a) physical: the use of medications and other physical agents, (b) psychological: individual, group, and family psychotherapy, behavior modification, and counseling, (c) social, institutional, and environmental manipulation: special treatment programs in hospitals and in the community which include evaluative screening and "crisis intervention" as well as long-term services.

Rehabilitation overlaps with intervention and therapy in so many ways that any distinction between them must be artificial. Our review will be selective rather than comprehensive, illustrative rather than exhaustive.

ISSUES IN TREATMENT

Diagnosis

The diagnosis of much of geriatric psychiatric illness is open to question. Diagnosis implies careful evaluation of signs and symptoms as well as an appreciation of etiologic issues in the disorder being evaluated. For a variety of reasons, older individuals do not always receive such care (Lowenthal, Berkman, and Associates 1967; Kramer, Taube, and Redick, 1973). Even when they do, the etiology of these disorders typically represents a mixture of psychosocial and medical problems (see Eisdorfer and Wilkie in this volume), often including disorders of unknown etiology.

Expectancy and Outcome

The expectation of the therapist is a salient issue in treatment. While it is clear that therapeutic nihilism is unwarranted from an objective viewpoint, the stereotypic postures toward the elderly such as ambiguous expectations and a posture of "you can't cure aging" are often noted. Poor normative data for psychodiagnostic instruments (see Schaie in this volume) add to this problem of inappropriate outcome measures.

The Model of Disorder

The nature of deviance or disorder is a complex socioscientific issue and a variety of conceptual patterns have been and are being used to approach the problem. The "medical" model—probably the most frequently used by physicians—is based upon the assumption of a dichotomy between health and disease and assumes that diseases may be classified into groups by common etiology. This approach, probably more appropriately called the "medical-pathology" model, employs the skills of a cadre of pathologists who define (often retrospectively) the disordered state of the tissue or organ and, consequently, of the patient. The tissue (or metabolic) disturbance is in turn related to the patient's complaints and other indices of deviance (i.e., symptoms and signs), and this defines a disease. In many instances, the consistency of

this complex of signs, symptoms, and pathologic findings is such that we can make a clinical diagnosis based upon only partial data and predict outcome and/or initiate intervention to ameliorate the situation.

In describing behavior, however, this approach may not be appropriate. Whether a specific act is deviant or not is often contextual, and its evaluation is based upon social definitions of appropriateness or effectiveness which may vary from one subculture to another. The data which may lead to an act may or may not be available to those evaluating the act, and the behavioral pattern may be based upon antecedent events of longer or shorter time frames. Thus adaptational models emerge which do not relate to disease, and treatment is designed to overcome barriers to effectiveness. The criteria for effectiveness, however, may be personal or social and as, in the case of the aged, may relate to cohort differences and socially mitigated expectancies. Compounding these developments is a social welfare model of care which posits that all individuals in a culture should be supplied with minimal resources. This assumes that lack of effectiveness or pathology may be offset by increasing one's resource capacity. Since each of these strategies (and there are more) has some merit (and a data base) to support it, the problem of defining appropriate interventions is not uncomplicated. Evaluation is typically based upon one or another model and deals with physical, psychological, or social adaptation—thus compounding the confusion.

PHYSICAL INTERVENTIONS

The use of pharmacological and other physical agents for the treatment of the psychiatric disorders of later years is rapidly expanding, but not without hazards. The management of medication for the older patient is complicated by changes in the metabolism of drugs with age. With the decrease of mucosal cells, enzymes for transport, and arterial blood flow, absorption of orally administered medication may be diminished. On the other hand, in older individuals protein is replaced by fatty tissue so that lipid-soluble drugs may remain in the system longer. Metabolic activity in older persons is diminished. As a result, increased tissue and plasma levels of drugs may develop with concomitant prolongation of action. In addition, with a decrease in renal blood flow and a drop in glomerular filtration rate with aging, elimination of drugs is delayed (Salzman, Shader, and Pearlman, 1970; Stotsky, 1969, 1970b).

Three of the four factors in the metabolism of drugs mentioned above clearly promote retention of active drugs in the system, although there is much variability in the aged with respect to the operation of these mechanisms. The physical activity of the person, the sensitivity of the target organ (Eisdorfer, 1972), the rate of cell depletion, nutritional status, and other variables figure prominently as issues in the understanding of drug action among the aged. The ultimate effect of these changes is to decrease tolerance and increase sensitivity to drugs so that older patients require a lower therapeutic dosage of psychoactive drugs (over 50 percent less in many cases) and are more prone to side effects and adverse reactions to medications than are younger patients (Stotsky, 1970c). The absence of good data on pharmacokinetics in the elderly is a serious issue (Raskind and Eisdorfer, 1975), and available data on effectiveness are still lacking in many instances (Prien, Caffey, and Klett, 1974).

Apart from the biological action of drugs, a number of issues are involved with medications. Health problems of older persons may result in an increased dependency on the physician for the maintenance of well-being. Transference reactions develop, manifested in admiration, antagonism, and/or envy on the part of older persons (Berezin and Stotsky, 1970). Paranoid reactions to the physician are not rare, particularly when the side effects of medication are experienced. In extreme forms, accusations of poisoning and assault may be leveled (Goldfarb, 1970, 1967; Safirstein, 1972). The ambivalent attitude of our culture to drugs further complicates this issue (Eisdorfer, 1973).

An informal group therapy may take place in the doctor's waiting room. For some who resist psychotherapy, visits for maintenance medication serve as a basis for becoming participants in this interpersonal process (Stotsky, 1969, 1970a, 1972), and even after therapeutic gains

are achieved, some patients may feel the need for continued medication as a justification for their illness and the social experiences associated with it. Gains to physicians should not be overlooked insofar as the administration of medication increases feelings of competence and control and protects them from pessimism and hopelessness (Stotsky, 1967d).

Salzman, Kochansky, and Shader (1972) have reviewed available scales, tests, and psychometric techniques. Although deficiencies are noted in all instruments, it is possible to obtain measures of the symptoms and disturbed behaviors for which physicians prescribe drugs. Such measures include cognitive functions, emotional disturbance, motivational changes, competence in performance of self-care functions, and psychophysiological symptoms. The frequency with which such measures are used by physicians is not known.

Problems arise in determining indications for drugs. Behavioral disorders may be manifestations of physical events in the older person, or the reverse may be true. For example, depressions may or may not suggest the presence of an organic brain syndrome (Post, 1968). Neurotic depressions are sometimes hard to differentiate from psychotic depressions, yet the treatments may vary greatly. Overt paranoid or schizophrenic disorders in the presence of an organic brain syndrome have a different course, prognosis, and response to pharmacotherapy from that of "functional" disorders. Acute psychotic reactions reflective of a transient situational disturbance demand a different mode of management, and the presense of concomitant physical disease complicates the management of mental disorders by pharmacological means (Stotsky, 1970b, 1972). Thus a key issue in evaluation of therapeutic outcome is the elucidation of the basis for the diagnosis as well as a statement of the hypothetical state (i.e., diagnosis) being treated.

Drug-induced confusion, disorientation, and sensory defects are not rare (Dawson-Butterworth, 1970; Simon, 1970; Stotsky, 1970a,c), nor are changes in vital signs, bowel and urinary function, or in blood and liver indices (Davis, Fann, El-Yousef, and Janowsky, 1973). The major side effects to the central nervous system include the dyskinesias (acute, reactive, and tardive) (Dynes, 1970), dystonias, oculogyric crises, akathisia, Parkinson-like reactions, seizures, and coma. Cardiovascular-cerebrovascular system effects including vascular insufficiency, myocardial infarction, arrhythmias, and congestive failure, have also been noted; as have hypersensitivity reactions including jaundice; autonomic effects ranging from dryness of nose and mouth to blurring of vision, urinary retention, and bowel difficulties; and a variety of paradoxical behavioral reactions.

Many terms are used to describe different classes of psychotropic drugs. We propose a strategy similar to that of Hollister (1973) involving a simple approach to classifying psychotropic medication by identifying these drugs according to their areas of effectiveness as follows: (1) antipsychotic, (2) antidepressive, (3) antimanic, (4) antianxiety, and (5) cognitive acting.

Antipsychotic Medications

The antipsychotic drugs comprise six basic classes of agents based upon chemical structure. These include rauwolfia, phenothiazines, thioxanthenes, butyrophenones, tricyclic derivatives, and indole compounds. The most frequently used drugs have been in the phenothiazine group (which includes three subgroups: aliphatic, piperidyl, and piperazine). Rauwolfia is primarily an antihypertensive medication and not in current use as a psychotropic drug, although it has historic interest in this regard. The phenothiazines and the more recently developed butyrophenones, thioxanthenes, tricyclic derivatives, and indole compounds are effective for the treatment of patients manifesting psychotic behavior, except for retarded depressions (Birkett, Hirschfield, and Simpson, 1972; Hollister, 1973; May, 1968; Stotsky, 1973). The most popular drugs reportedly employed for geriatric patients are thioridazine (Altman, Melita, Evenson, and Sletten, 1973), chlorpromazine (Birkett and Boltuch, 1972), and haloperidol (Tsuang, Lu, Stotsky, and Cole, 1971).

The principal value of antipsychotic agents lies in their ability to relieve the symptoms of agitation, violent and irrational behavior, and the perceptual disturbances typically accompanying psychoses. As a secondary consequence, they are involved in the production of undesirable extra-pyramidal side effects. This is not surprising in view of their mechanism of action. These drugs probably provide a postsynaptic block of noradrenaline or dopamine receptors and simultaneously decrease membrane excitbility. In addition, they also have an anticholinergic action. The side effects of the antipsychotic drugs are thus somewhat predictable and, apart from the anticholinergic effects, appear under three general categories. The most frequent of these takes the form of extrapyramidal motor signs including tremors.

A second side effect associated with long-term use of antipsychotic medication is tardive dyskinesia. This disorder which appears to occur particularly in older female patients is associated with involuntary bucco-facio-mandibular and bucco-lingual movements, occasionally involving the limbs and trunk. Tardive dyskinesia may persist for years, indeed indefinitely. There is a strong suggestion that permanent central nervous system change in either dopaminergic fibers or their receptors is the basis for these signs. Paradoxically, increasing the dosage of medication does appear to reverse the signs, but only temporarily. The pattern reappears, thus forcing the physician to use ever-increasing dosages. The emergence of tardive dyskinesia after long-term use of antipsychotic medication has led most authorities to recommend drug holidays, reduced dosages, and programmed withdrawal of the drug in the expectation that reducing the total quantity of drug given through the years might reduce the probability of occurrence of these events (Raskind and Eisdorfer, 1975).

A third neurologic side effect of antipsychotic drugs is that of akathisia. This appears after relatively brief periods on the drug and takes the form of uncontrolled restlessness and agitation not usually associated with the psychotic state. This responds surprisingly well to medication.

Hypotension is a chronic problem, as are side effects which appear secondary to anticholinergic action, including constipation, urinary retention, and increased potential for glaucoma.

Electrocardiographic changes may also appear with long-term use in some patients, as may a reduction in drive, initiative, and libido. Since the clinical trials of most psychopharmacologic agents are performed with younger patients in better physical condition, the consequences of long-term use among the elderly are only now beginning to be appreciated. Newer strategies of treatment including routine determinations of serum levels of drugs are rare.

Antidepressant Medication

Pharmacological treatment for depression is neither simple nor consistently successful (Prange, 1973; Salzman and Shader, 1973) in part, because the admixture of symptoms and physical problems complicates this diagnosis in the elderly. Antidepressants are no more effective against agitated depressions or schizoaffective disorders than antianxiety or antipsychotic drugs alone. They are, however, effective for the treatment of retarded and mixed depressions. The most commonly used (and most efficacious) are the tricyclic drugs (Prien, Caffey, and Klett, 1974). Monoamine oxidase inhibitors and stimulants have also been used.

The current basis for the use of antidepressant medication is the "catecholamine hypothesis," which proposes that deprivation of physiologically available norephinephrine and/or serotonin at CNS receptor sites leads to the symptoms of depression, while an increase in the uptake of these neurotransmitters yields a reversal of the depressive symptoms. The early use of monoamine oxidase inhibitors as antidepressants was a rational therapy based on the demonstration that monoamine oxidase metabolized biological amines. The action of tricyclic antidepressants is less clear, but presumably they act to make more neurotransmitter substance available at the appropriate sites.

The monoamine oxidase inhibitors have been generally used for reactive depressions, phobias and hysterical depression, but seem least appropriate for the aged (Prange, 1973; Stotsky, 1975). Their use is limited by their tendency to produce severe hypotension, hepatic insufficiency, and, in interaction with foods containing tyramine, hypertensive crises. Controlled studies do not endorse the combination of phenothiazines and tricyclics for the treatment of depressive disorders in which anxiety or agitation is present. The tendency to use many drugs to treat one syndrome has been termed "polypharmacy" and may be hazardous for the aged patient (Merlis, Sheppard, Collins, and Fiorentino, 1970).

The use of stimulants in the treatment of depression was studied by Jacobson (1958), who reported that methylphenidate as an adjunct to psychotherapy was superior to placebo. The ratings in his study were not blind; however, Kastenbaum, Slater, and Aisenberg (1964) showed that dextroamphetamine produced deterioration in affect. Kaplitz (1975) reported significant improvement. Prange (1973) reported that following an initial improvement in mood, patients on stimulants become dysphoric with continued treatment. The predictable side effects of stimulants include anorexia and, in a few cases, heightened response to other medications.

Electroconvulsant Treatment

More severe refractory depressions, characterized by suicidal preoccupation or attempts, muteness, stupor, or marked retardation and withdrawal, frequently respond to electroconvulsant treatment (ECT). Although current practice typically involves a failure of outpatient drug treatment before ECT is selected as the treatment of choice, many psychiatrists believe in its use early during illness (Wilson and Major, 1973). ECT may also be employed in preference to tricyclic medication because of the possible cardiac side effects of the latter (Raskind and Eisdorfer, 1975; Stotsky, 1975). Unilateral (nondominant side) ECT has been found superior to bilateral ECT in reducing posttreatment confusion and amnesia.

ECT is most useful for unipolar depressions, refractory bipolar disorders, and involutional depressions. Patients with mild to moderate organic syndromes must be given ECT with care. If they show increased impairment, treatment should be discontinued.

Antimanic Medication

Lithium carbonate, an antimanic drug, deserves special mention for its therapeutic efficacy in manic states (Baastrup and Schon, 1967; Prien, Caffey, and Klett, 1972), considering its proven prophylactic ability to prevent relapses if medication is taken regularly and the blood level is carefully titrated between 0.6 and 0.8 mEq/L for aged patients. Dosage has to be adjusted individually but is usually within the range of 600 to 1,200 mg per day. The aged are particularly prone to side effects, especially patients with active renal, hepatic, or cardiac disease (Van der Velde, 1971).

Antianxiety Medication

In spite of the widespread use of antianxiety drugs, surprisingly little research has been reported on their efficacy in the aged. Four classes of antianxiety drugs are in common use, although the first, the barbiturates, are being used less frequently because of their side effects and abuse potential. Stotsky and Borozne (1972) found a barbiturate (butabarbital) to be equal or superior to a benzodiazepine (chlordiazepoxide) in an outpatient sample with mixed neurotic symptoms. This was in contrast to the findings of Wheatley (1968) and the Rickels' group (Rickels, Clark, Etezady Sachs, Sapra, and Yee, 1970).

Barbiturates are effective and safe if employed in moderate dosage according to Stotsky and Borozne (1972). Unfortunately, this class of medications includes agents which produce habituation and addiction and lend themselves to abuse in overdose for suicide attempts. They also interact with other agents by activating hepatic enzymes which accelerate the degradation and inactivation of other medications. In the aged, they also produce untoward central nervous system side effects and paradoxical behavioral reactions. Barbiturates are felt by some (Dawson-Butterworth, 1970) to be absolutely contraindicated in the aged.

In younger patients, the benzodiazepines have been found to be equally or more effective than barbiturates (Rickels et al., 1970; Wheatley, 1968; Greenblatt and Shader, 1974). Withdrawal does not result in a physical abstinence syndrome, and the low level of toxicity makes it most difficult to commit suicide through overdose. Habituation and central nervous system side effects are not uncommon, and the dangers of psychological dependence can be very great for these drugs. Withdrawal symptoms have been reported in chronic users. The most commonly prescribed drugs in this group are chlordiazepoxide, diazepam (DeLamos, Clements, and Nickels, 1965), oxazepam (Chesrow, Kaplitz, Sabatini et al., 1965; Chesrow and Kaplitz, 1970; Sanders, 1965), and clorazepate. Older patients generally require about half of the average adult dose and seem to be most susceptible to cerebellar side effects (ataxia and other difficulties with gait, intention tremor, etc.).

A third family of drugs commonly prescribed for anxiety is the alcohol-glycol group. Their action is similar to that of barbiturates, and most of the problems associated with the latter are also associated with the former. They have generally been found to be less effective than benzodiazepines. The most commonly prescribed are meprobamate and tybamate (Goldstein, 1967; Stern, 1964).

A fourth group consists of the diphenylmethanes, typified by hydroxyzine, diphenylhydramine, and benactyzine. They are effective but require high dosages which often result in marked sedation and increased incidence of central nervous system side effects. As a result, their use for daytime sedation has been limited. Among patients with organic brain syndromes, these drugs should be used cautiously for daytime sedation (Gershon, 1973).

Alcohol has been successfully used to facilitate social interaction, and in carefully controlled doses has psychotherapeutic properties (Chien, 1971; Chien, Stotsky, and Cole, 1973). Unfortunately the hazards of uncontrolled alcohol ingestion are severe in susceptible individuals (Simon, Epstein, and Reynolds, 1968). Kastenbaum (1965) has demonstrated its effectiveness in institutional settings, although the effect seems more socially than physiologically mediated.

Cognitive Acting Drugs

Intellectual impairment has always been regarded as an inevitable concomitant of normal aging. Recent studies (Eisdorfer and Wilkie, 1973) suggest that the deficit is not as large as was thought, and for certain abilities may not occur at all or until shortly before death. The intellectual decline, when it is present, may result from response interference or restrictions on retrieval. It may also be a function of the speed of presentation of stimuli and of autonomic dysfunction (Eisdorfer, Nowlin, and Wilkie, 1970; Granville-Grossman and Turner, 1966).

Cognitive impairment is one of the hallmarks of organic brain syndrome, regardless of etiology. For this reason, the search for drugs which may reverse or retard such impairment and the behavioral regression due to such impairment is intense. A wide range of medications has been investigated for their properties in this regard (Jarvik, 1973).

Stimulants and analeptics such as amphetamines, methylphenidate, deanol, pipradrol, (Turek, Kurland, Ota, and Hanlon, 1969) pentylenetetrazol, and magnesium pemoline have been reported to increase activity level, alertness, and attention to stimuli, to improve recall and recognition, to counteract lethargy, and to stimulate circulation and respiration. Early positive findings have not been supported by later controlled research (Gilbert, Donnelly, Zimmer, and Kubis, 1973).

The drug most widely used in geriatric studies is pentylenetetrazol. Equivocal or negative findings in recent controlled studies (Leckman, Ananth, Ban, and Lehmann, 1971; Lu, Stotsky, and Cole, 1971; Stotsky, Cole, Lu, and Sniffin, 1972) suggest that it is limited in effectiveness. The mode of action is thought to be: increased synaptic transmission in the central nervous system, stimulation of psychomotor areas, vasomotor and respiratory centers, and decreased lactic acid concentration.

Magnesium pemoline (Cylert) was hailed as a possible breakthrough following positive findings in improving learning and memory in animal studies and in uncontrolled studies on humans. Follow-up studies were unable to confirm the initial encouraging reports, though it was found to have mild stimulant properties (Eisdorfer, Conner, and Wilkie, 1968; Gilbert et al., 1973; Greenblatt, DiMascio, Messier, and Stotsky, 1969.)

Vasodilator medications (nicotinyl alcohol, papaverine, cyclandelate, isoxsuprine, hexobendine) relax the smooth muscle of blood vessel walls in the peripheral circulation and possibly in the cerebral vessels. If this effect is not counterbalanced by compensatory mechanisms, the major effect is to increase cerebral blood flow and, therefore, oxygenation of brain tissue. The presumed effect has not yet been convincingly demonstrated, however. Moreover, mental changes may not necessarily accompany increased cerebral blood flow and improved metabolism of glucose in hypoxic areas.

Papaverine, an alkaloid derivative of opium, has been studied. General improvement in behavior and in the performance of activities of daily living, as well as increased cerebral blood flow and decreased arterial resistance have been reported. Unfortunately, significant intellectual improvement has not been consistently demonstrated (Jayne, Scheinber, Rich, 1952: Lu, Stotsky, and Cole, 1971).

Cyclandelate is similar in its action to papaverine. Positive findings have been reported (Birkett, 1971; Hall, 1976; Smith, Lowrey, and Davis, 1968) in which patients improved on long-term memory, verbal expansiveness, reasoning, and orientation.

Ergot alkaloid (Hydergine), consisting of three hydrogenated alkaloids of ergot, has been reported to increase cerebral blood flow and oxygen uptake by direct action on ganglion cell metabolism without producing hypotension (Emmenegger and Meier-Ruge, 1968). The vast majority of controlled studies against placebo have been positive (Banen, 1972; Ditch, Kelley, and Resnick, 1971; Gerin, 1969; Roubicek, Geiger, and Abt, 1972; Rao and Norris, 1972). Four studies comparing it to papaverine, found Hydergine to be clearly superior (Bazo, 1973, Nelson, 1975, Rosen, 1975, Einspruch, 1976). Improvements have been reported in attitude, ward behavior, activities of daily living, and somatic complaints, but have not been demonstrated quantitatively in cognitive functions. Its mechanism of action is still unclear.

Walsh (1969a,b; Walsh and Walsh, 1972), using bishydroxycoumarin, an anticoagulant, claimed remarkable improvements in intellectual function, apparently confirming earlier clinical reports of such changes. The action is presumed to be due to decreased sludging and a decreased tendency to thrombus formation in the circulatory system. These pilot findings have not been widely pursued due to the high risk of adverse reactions attendant to the use of anticoagulants in the aged which necessitate close supervision and the exclusion of patients with certain physical disorders.

With respect to RNA-like compounds, piracetam, tricyanoaminopropene, RNA-stimulating agents such as magnesium pemoline, and both RNA and DNA have been administered to patients with conflicting and as yet equivocal reports of significantly positive intellectual changes (Cameron and Solyom, 1961; Cameron, Sved, and Solyom, 1963; Kral, Solyom, and Enesco, 1967).

For years a buffered form of procaine amide has been promoted enthusiastically as an anti-aging medication (usually given intramuscularly three times a week for 12 weeks). Many uncontrolled studies, for the most part in Europe, found it effective in the treatment of a broad spectrum of physical and mental disorders associated with aging. Procaine amide was studied intensively in England, Canada, and in the United States by controlled studies which were mostly negative (Kral, Cahn, Deutsch, 1962). For a time Gerovital ("European" procaine) was discredited. Recently interest has been revived after it was found to be a reversible inhibitor of monoamine oxidase and thought to be more stable in solution than procaine amide (Hrachovec, 1973).

A series of open and controlled studies have been conducted to evaluate its efficacy in the treatment of psychiatric disorders of aging (Cohen and Ditman, 1974; Zung, Gianturco, Pfeiffer, et al., 1974; Sakalis, Oh, Gershon, et al., 1974, Zwerling, Plutchik, Hotz, et al. 1975.) Two controlled and one open study report an antidepressant effect of varying magnitude. The Zwerling, Plutchik, Hotz et al. (1975) study reported no significant ameliorative effect. Jarvik and Milne (1975) have reviewed the literature as have Ostfeld, Smith, and Stotsky (1976, in press). Its efficacy for depression or organic brain syndromes has not been established.

Following remarkably positive findings by Jacobs and her associates (Jacobs, Winter, Alvis, and Small, 1969) on the effectiveness of pure oxygen administered under high pressure (hyperbaric oxygenation, 100 percent at 2.5 atmospheres absolute for 3 hours a day for 15 days) in improving memory and other cognitive functions, other investigators undertook to replicate their findings. Neither Goldfarb, Hochstadt, Jacobson, and Weinstein (1972) nor Thompson (1975) have been able to confirm these findings. Systematic studies are now underway to further evaluate this phenomenon. One serious problem is the transiency of any improvements and the elaborate procedures required for relatively few patients.

Other cognitive-acting drugs such as antidepressants, vitamin preparations, antioxidants, hormones, antipsychotic, and antianxiety drugs have all been investigated, but no consistent findings have been obtained with respect to changes in cognitive functioning. Obviously, in cases of depression with symptoms comparable to "senile dementia," antidepressive medication appears to improve cognitive functioning (Caserta and Mazzola, 1970; Cretallaz, 1968; Currier, Smith, and Steinninger, 1961; Jarvik, Gritz, and Schneider, 1972; Jarvik, 1973; Kral, Solyom, Enesco, and Ledwidge, 1970; Salzman and Shader, 1973; Turek, Kurland, Ota, and Hanlon, 1969).

Eisdorfer, Nowlin, and Wilkie (1970) administered propranolol, a beta-adrenergic receptor blocking agent, to normal older men and found that performance on serial rote learning improved while heart rate decreased and the level of serum free fatty acids dropped. This suggests that decreasing heightened autonomic nervous system arousal in aged adults may have an ameliorative effect on cognitive function. This early finding warrants further investigation. Diphenylhydantoin and other anticonvulsants have not usually produced significant intellectual improvement although one study reported significant improvement in Wechsler adult intelligent scores for patients on diphenylhydantoin (Smith and Lowrey, 1975).

In overview, none of the cognitive acting drugs has demonstrated significant long-term reversal of intellectual impairment. The ergot alkyloids, some of the vasodilators, and for some patients limited amounts of alcohol in social settings have yielded at least temporary improvement in attitudes, moods, and performance of activities of daily living. The treatment of disorders leading to or associated with cognitive change (e.g., grief, depression, nutritional disorder, metabolic crisis, etc.) remains the most significant clinical strategy currently utilized. Since cognitive loss may be the result of a wide variety of etiologic events, the accurate assessment of the individual is crucial to treatment.

Sedatives and Hypnotics

Sleep disturbances are common in the aged. Sleep is not as deep, with stage 4 markedly reduced. Awakening often occurs during the night. Terminal (early morning) sleep is often fitful, and insomnia during the early morning hours is a frequent complaint. While older persons may need considerably less sleep, many become concerned at diminishing sleep and request medication. Exercise during the day and the employment of nocturnal waking periods for reading or work supplemented by daytime naps is emerging as a clinical procedure to avoid medication. The result of such alternatives has not been evaluated to date. The problems with the use of sleep-inducing medications, referred to as hypnotics include: increase in nocturnal confusion should the patient awaken, night terrors, hallucinatory phenomena, agitation, difficulties with gait and balance, morning "hangover," and depression.

Barbiturates, while initially effective, produce all of the adverse effects listed above, as well as tolerance and habituation. Antihistamines have been employed as hypnotics but seem to lose their potency with time. Antianxiety medications and sedative antidepressants have been prescribed as bedtime medications and may produce sleep with few side effects.

Of unique concern for aged patients is determination of the source of sleep disturbance. It may not be associated with the usual causes; for example, frequent naps during the day, boredom, depression, rising tension at night, etc.

Electrosleep (low doses of electricity applied to the head) has been tried (Hearst, Cloninger, Crews *et al.*, 1974), but there is some question with respect to its efficacy for the entire night at an acceptable level of risk.

PSYCHOLOGICAL THERAPIES

For much of the first half of the twentieth century, psychologically oriented therapies were dominated by psychoanalytic concepts. These included the formulation that psychoanalytic treatment techniques would have little impact upon the aged, who were too rigid and had insufficient energy resources to effect change in their lives.

Psychotherapy and counseling for the aged, once frowned upon, are now practiced in many forms. The duration may vary from a few visits, as in crisis-oriented therapy, to long-term insight-oriented and reconstructive treatment (Brody, Kleban, Lawton, and Silverman, 1971; Butler, 1968; Goldfarb, 1970; Gottesman, Quarterman, and Cohn, 1973). The aged are still not seen in significant numbers in outpatient psychiatric clinics and mental health centers (Kramer, Taube, and Redick, 1973), and therapists remain resistant to dealing with aged patients. The present cohort of older persons is reported to be unsophisticated with respect to and suspicious of mental health professionals (Lowenthal, Berkman, and Associates, 1967).

During the past decade, many modalities of psychotherapeutic intervention have been found to be feasible for the aged. Obviously, the mode of treatment should be determined by the needs, abilities, and emotional problems of the patient, as well as the patient's accessibility to treatment. Since many programs of treatment are oriented to one or another theory or methodology, the fit between patient and intervention may be inexact or limited in scope.

Gottesman, Quarterman, and Cohn (1973) have conceptualized four levels of treatment: (a) self-treatment which focuses on the lifestyle of the individual in adjusting to the changes in self and the environment; (b) individual psychological treatments; (c) small group therapy; and (d) societal treatment (the last will be considered under a separate heading).

Individual Approaches

As noted earlier, relatively few of the aged are seen in outpatient psychiatric settings. Although they comprise 10 percent of the population in the United States and are a population at heightened risk for psychiatric institutionalization, they comprise only 2 percent of the cases in outpatient clinics and 4 percent in community mental health centers (Kramer, Taube, and Redick, 1973).

It took many years to overcome the attitude that the aged were unacceptable as candidates for psychoanalytic psychotherapy. Modified psychoanalytic approaches have been employed, particularly as recommended by Goldfarb (1962, 1967), who has encouraged the acceptance of certain dependency needs of the aged to help them cope with their difficulties. Meerloo (1971) describes other modifications with aged patients which include no analysis of resistance, carefully selected interpretations, the use of screen memories to make contact, stimulation of initiative, increasing sexual activity, evaluation of the patient's "pact with death," and consideration of the traumatic nature of being old. Hiatt (1971) discusses unusual features of the transference and the countertransference with older patients. Safirstein (1972) illustrates both dynamic and cognitive approaches with ten illustrative cases, seven with short-term crisis intervention and three requiring extended treatment. Shapiro (1969) reports the treatment of grief in an elderly woman at the death of her youngest child. Dodgen and Arthur (1967) describe the psychotherapy of a sexagenarian which he illustrates with the vividness of recall of significant childhood conflicts as well as aspects of transference, dream analysis, and termination. Gruen (1957) considers old age as a positive factor in motivation for treatment.

Butler (1968) concerns himself with some of the issues in old age, particularly fear of death and the need to counteract fear of obsolescence. He also considers some of the noxious effects of public attitudes and public policy (Butler, 1972) in influencing older persons.

Up to this time, however, controlled studies of the efficacy of dynamic psychoanalytically oriented treatment for the aged have been largely absent. In view of the widespread and growing interest in such treatment, outcome studies would appear to be warranted.

The cognitive approach is often combined with other techniques (Hedri, 1967; Buckley, 1972). Its focus may be on understanding and sharing to foster growth, reality counseling

geared to facilitating orientation (Folsom, 1968), or building friendships and making adjustments to increased dependency on persons and institutions through role training (Pressey and Pressey, 1972). In this technique, the therapist plays an active role and uses expression of feelings and interpretation to increase the patient's insight (Wolff, 1971b). As one reviews the literature, the differences between psychodynamic and cognitive approaches are smaller than might be supposed. Both techniques are modified in light of the status and needs of the patient and the requirements and limitations of the situation. Of particular concern in both are morale (Schooler, 1969) and self-esteem (Anderson, 1967; Maxwell and Silverman, 1970). Outcome studies again are in short supply.

Gottesman, Quarterman, and Cohn (1973) have summarized developments in behavioral modification therapy and, citing the review of Gendlin and Rychlak (1970), Krasner (1971), and Ullman and Krasner (1969) have identified four major techniques used with aged patients: positive reinforcement, desensitization, aversive procedures, and modeling.

Cautela (1966, 1969) has related the classical conditioning approach to modification of the behavior of aged patients, while Hoyer (1973) has employed operant conditioning. Ankus and Quarrington (1972), through the use of both primary and secondary reinforcement, were able to obtain normal fixed-ratio behavior in memory disordered subjects between the ages of 55 and 80. Weinman, Gelbart, Wallace, and Post (1972), however, found that socioenvironmental therapy was more effective than systematic desensitization or relaxation in older male schizophrenics. Wanderer (1972), on the other hand, successfully used systematic desensitization to treat a 60-year-old man with chronic, severe depression and aerophobia. In this instance, positive self-evaluative thoughts were reinforced. Grosicki (1968) attempted to extend operant conditioning to modify incontinence in psychogeriatric patients. Experimental subjects did less well than controls with respect to incontinence, though they showed significant behavioral changes in response to social reinforcement. Patterson and Teigen (1973) attempted to apply behavioral techniques to delusional responses of a chronic psychotic patient through the conditioning of nondelusional responses. The experimental analysis of behavior technique is becoming more and more popular, particularly as it can yield behavioral changes in the more chronic demented patients who become severe nursing problems.

Group Therapies

The goals of group therapeutic techniques in homes for the aged have been isolated by Feil (1967) into two primary categories; first, to stimulate verbalization and interaction between group members, and second, to promote a sense of self-worth so that the individual can move toward some degree of independent action which will make him feel part of the community life of the home. Again the implicit goal appears to be improved management through better adjustment to residence in the long-term care situation. Yalom and Terrazas (1968) have discussed some of the virtues of group therapy for the psychotic elderly patient: (1) setting realistic goals, (2) increasing patient interaction, (3) focusing on patient strengths, and (4) building group cohesiveness. The establishment of appropriate outcome variables is a salient issue. Is independence (*vs.* accepting dependence) valued; is personal freedom an asset or a liability; is criticism of the program appropriate or a problem?

Linden (1953) and Wolff (1957, 1971a) among others, have been strong supporters of group psychotherapy for the aged. Liederman, Green, and Liederman (1967) reported the results of group therapy combined with psychotropic drugs for 11 patients designed to prevent or postpone confinement in nursing homes or hospitals and to improve the patient's patterns of living. Only one patient was hospitalized.

Wolk and Goldfarb (1967) studied the effects of 1 year of group therapy upon two types of geriatric patients in state mental hospitals; long-term patients who had aged in the hospital, mostly schizophrenics, and recently admitted patients, mostly with chronic brain syndromes. Improvement in long-term patients was greater than in recently admitted patients, but group therapy helped both groups.

Burnside (1970a, b, c, 1971), in a series of papers, described experiences with a variety of group techniques ranging from book discussion groups to psychoanalytic groups. Key variables were reported to be flexibility, warmth, perseverance, patience, and the ability to listen. Process was emphasized rather than outcome. Loss was a persistent theme emerging from group work with the aged in nursing homes. Topics for discussion centered upon deceased loved ones, disabilities, and loss of independence. It is believed that group work helps by allowing the patients to discuss and share losses. Long-term group work (2 years) with the aged in a convalescent hospital was reportedly successful in facilitating communication and resocialization of members of the group (Burnside, 1971), although such outcome is self-fulfilling from the nature of the process.

McNiel and Verwoerdt (1972) combined group therapy with a work project using a buddy system in which 33 inpatients ranging from 15 to 67 years of age worked with patients in the geriatric unit of a state hospital. Improved care for elderly patients and improvement in staff morale were reported. The most successful patient-therapists were middle-aged neurotic females.

Manaster (1972) found changes in attitude, improved behavior, greater expression of feelings, and an increased sense of personal identity in a group of senile, deteriorated patients who met for 40-minute sessions. Gunn (1967), in 12 months of weekly intermittent group therapy sessions, noted increased use of antidepressants but less behavioral disturbance on the ward. The behavioral change was from behavioral disturbance to verbalization of depressive ideas.

In summary, group techniques combining verbal and nonverbal modalities have achieved wide acceptance, but there is still a lack of carefully controlled studies to determine the efficacy of various approaches. It is hard to sort out the more from the less successful programs and to determine the importance of therapist skill and type and mix of patients in achieving successful group experiences. Patient selection factors, the enthusiasm of the therapist, anxiety reduction in staff because someone is "treating" the patient, and the confusion between process and outcome (particularly when no outcome measure is employed at the start) do little to clarify this picture and only emphasize the problems of separating any main effect of treatment from the placebo effect.

Conjoint Family Therapy

Conjoint family therapy has been found useful in mental health centers (Kilpatrick, 1968), in day centers (Grauer, Betts, and Birnbom, 1973), and in outpatient as well as inpatient settings. It often includes role playing as well as environmental manipulation. Kilpatrick (1968) described two cases in which conjoint treatment lessened the need for continuing relationships with the mental health center after the initial crisis had been resolved.

The need for family services is illustrated by a study (Hoenig and Hamilton, 1966) in which a follow-up of extramural services to elderly patients after 4 years revealed an increase in the burden on families both objectively and subjectively, even though patients were kept out of the hospital. Savitsky, Sharkey, Sulesky, and Taishoff (1969) combined family services with an interdisciplinary team approach to family therapy in which separation of hostile family members is achieved through placement in a day hospital. Gray (1973) describes an interesting approach in which problems encountered and suggested solutions are demonstrated in dramatics programs in New York senior citizen centers and residential care facilities.

Interest in family therapy as an approach particularly suitable for aged patients and their families has quickened, and we can expect many new starts involving this approach to treatment. The effects of such treatment are reportedly potentially explosive, and a high degree of therapeutic skill is necessary to maintain control and positive movement (Berezin and Stotsky, 1970). Again the data are largely conjectural.

The importance of assessment of degree and depth of psychopathology would seem to be so obvious as to need no restatement. It should be noted, however, that most reports in the literature do not define this parameter of patient status. In general, it would appear that the more intact the patient, the earlier he or she

would be discharged from an institutional facility in good health (Anderson, 1968).

Post (1968, 1972) describes a wide range of problems managed successfully through early diagnosis and cooperation between the family physician, local health authorities, social service personnel, psychiatrists, and geriatricians. These included sexual problems, alcoholism, hypochondriasis, affective disorders, suicidal ideas, persecutory states, and organic mental disorders.

The positive impact of early intervention in a crisis situation and the provision of emergency services (Borton and Whitehead, 1968; Simon, 1970) have been assessed, and the findings underline the importance of early detection and treatment (Burnside, 1970a; MacMillan, 1967; Oberleder, 1970; Simon, 1970; Stotsky, 1970a). Baker (1968) differentiates between two types of facilities: one for assessment and short-term treatment, the other for long-term care for patients unlikely to respond or recover.

SOCIAL, INSTITUTIONAL, ENVIRONMENTAL

Since the early 1950s, the patient population of federal mental hospitals has declined in response to the impact of new forms of treatment. As the total population of state mental hospitals declined by more than 50 percent, the number of older inpatients shrank dramatically, particularly since the enactment of the Kerr-Mills Act (Medical Assistance to the Aged) which eventuated in Medicaid, Title XIX of Public Law 89-97. From 1955 to 1968, the absolute number of inpatients 65+ years of age declined from 158,285 to 120,140, a 24 percent decrease (Kramer, Taube, and Redick, 1973) despite an increase in the absolute and relative number of aged in the population.

This trend modified the tendency to assign elderly patients with psychiatric disorders to state mental hospitals, where they often received less attention and treatment than younger patients. Now many of these patients are kept "in the community" and are placed in nursing homes (Pinchak, 1967). For elderly in minority groups where private facilities are often lacking, problems of treatment and placement arose which required special management

(Zimberg, 1971). Many facilities were simply incapable of providing adequate treatment. However, another problem arose—massive transfers of patients to these "community" facilities (nursing homes, homes for the aged, boarding homes) were undertaken without adequate follow-up and care because of failure to allocate adequate funds and personnel for this purpose, i.e., the lack of commitment of state and community mental health centers to treating the aged and the economic disincentive of psychiatric "labels" (Kramer, Taube, and Starr, 1968; Kramer, Taube, and Redick, 1973, Stotsky, 1970a).

Thus, Kistin and Morris (1972) reported that many elderly patients in nursing homes did not need sheltered care but were placed there because of the lack of basic supportive services at affordable costs. This aspect of isolation was seen by Spitzer (1969) as slow spiritual suicide, the end result of social rejection. Lieberman (1969) noted the detrimental effects of institutionalization on elderly patients' behavior.

In Great Britain, where coordination between geriatric and psychiatric units within the same area was programmed, misplacements were noted for up to 8.4 percent of the patients. Fortunately there is no evidence of a detrimental effect on outcome (Mezey, Hodgkinson, and Evans, 1968).

This shift of geriatric patients from state hospitals to nursing homes has received some publicity, but no definitive answer has been obtained as to the adequacy of the nursing home environment for patients leaving mental hospitals (Stotsky, 1970 a,b, 1972). Positive elements (Levey, Stotsky and Kinloch et al., 1973; Pincus, 1968; Savitz, 1967; Stotsky, 1966, 1967c, 1968, 1970 a,b) as well as negative effects (Epstein and Simon, 1968) have been noted. Clearly, the extended care facility has become an important resource for the treatment of chronically ill patients (Krauss and Goldstein, 1967, Libow, Viola, and Stein, 1968; Mishara, 1971; Nice, 1969) including those aged with mental illness. Intermittent readmission to hospitals has been helpful (MacDonnell, McKenzie, and Cheetham, 1968). Kramer, Taube, and Redick (1973) pointed to the increased need for trained persons to work with the aged in the right place, and Linn and her collaborators (1966; Linn and Gurel 1969) conducted a series of studies on veterans to determine the characteristics of patients who go to nursing homes, their initial reactions, and the attitudes of wives regarding the facilities (Greenwald and Linn, 1970). Since public policy is turning against the institution, another shift to the "community" may be underway, and alternatives to institutional care are being avidly proposed. The value of such an alternative has, as yet, not been assessed (i.e., for whom would it be valuable under what circumstances), but the economic incentives to reducing the cost of care are quite imperative.

The term "milieu therapy" was introduced to describe the techniques for remotivation, resocialization, and reorientation of patients through involving the entire staff (and patients themselves) as therapeutic personnel. Gottesman and coworkers in a large mental hospital and in other institutional settings, (Gottesman 1973; Gottesman, Quarterman and Cohn, 1973) and Stotsky and his colleagues (McGinity and Stotsky, 1967; Stotsky, 1967b,c,d, 1970b) working in nursing homes, demonstrated the feasibility and effectiveness of such programs. Cohen and Kraft (1968a,b) pointed out the revitalizing effect on 700 geriatric patients of transfer to a geriatric center from a state hospital.

In one hospital, the integration of young and old patients appeared to serve as a spur to mutual stimulation and interaction. This led to a decline of maladaptive behavior and some improvement of intellectual functioning (Kahana and Kahana, 1970a,b) among the aged.

Day hospitals and day care centers have been organized to serve older patients with outreach programs developed to provide direct services to persons in the areas served by community mental health centers (Coons, 1973; Sperlinga, Andrus, Andrus, Stotsky et al., 1972).

Mensch (1973) and Millard (1968) have reviewed the vicissitudes of intervention programs in the community, and Taylor and Gaitz (1968) have called attention to deviations in practice from plan. Studies by Blenkner and her associates (Blenkner, 1967; Bloom and Blenkner, 1970) have also demonstrated the potential hazards of intensive, direct social service in encouraging dependency. Those of her subjects who received the most services had higher rates of institutionalization after 1 and 5 years, a higher rate of mortality after 1 year and after 4 years for those institutionalized than did those who received less services.

Rosenblatt (1972) focused on the resistance by isolated, elderly persons to participation in social activities in a community mental health program, even when these were readily available. The assumption was that they were depressed, withdrawn, "disengaged," and unable to use leisure. Another possibility was prejudice against a mental health facility and fear of stigmatization. However, even minimal levels of activity may be effective (Kaiman, Desroches, and Ballard, 1966), although the issue of self-selection of patients is necessarily a factor in evaluating such results.

Nurses based in senior centers or similar places have appraised behavior indicative of resistance to social activity and attempted to counteract these patterns by home visits, referrals to community agencies and mental health education groups, as well as the use of resource persons to extend assistance to isolated and resistant elderly persons (Brown, 1969; Davis, 1968).

Geriatric evaluation and screening services based on the model of the Langley Porter unit (Epstein and Simon, 1968) have been replicated and, in some instances, provide psychiatric services to patients in their own homes (Raskind, Alvarez, Pietrzyk, Westerlund, and Herlin, 1974), including occupational therapy in addition to the traditional mental health services (Goldberg, Latif, and Abrams, 1970). MacMillan (1967) argues for careful preadmission assessment at home and short-term admissions. The effectiveness of such services is usually measured in patients "kept out" of institutions or overt adaptation to the community.

The roles of social workers in planning (Kaplan, 1970), in social casework (Bloom and Monro, 1972; Heyman and Polansky, 1969), and in developing modifications to deal with special problems of the aged (Burnside, 1970a, b,c; Lowy, 1967; Wasser, 1966) have been described. Relationships between social adjust-

ment and visiting patterns (Gelfand, 1968; Jonas, Oberdalhoff, and Schulze, 1969), patient morale and supervised visiting programs (Holzman and Sabel, 1968), as well as the success of foster care (Handy, 1968a) and the foster grandparent program (Rybak, Sadnavitch, and Mason, 1968) have also been described.

Donabedian and Rosenfeld (1964) and Justice and Bender (1968a,b) have made the disturbing statement that elderly patients are a mixed group, many of whom are placed in mental hospitals or nursing homes for convenience rather than as a treatment of choice. Also meriting attention is the finding of the remarkably small number of black patients in nursing homes. Many of the minority aged are reported to have specific problems as a result of their group membership in relation to mental health care (Carter, 1972), but without adequate care given to this problem. Oberleder (1970) and Burnside (1970a, 1971) describe programs of crisis intervention which appeared to be effective.

A closer relationship between the community and institutions resulted in decreased barriers to the transfer of patients from one facility to another (Stotsky and Levey, 1967). MacDonell, McKenzie, and Cheetham (1968) were able to demonstrate benefits for the patient and his family by intermittent readmissions. This pattern led to improved interpersonal relationships, better hospital bed use, decreased length of stay, and reduced frequency of permanent institutionalization. This approach may prevent the adaptation of the patient to a "sick role," which is a frequent retardant to rehabilitation (Starkey, 1968).

This of course raises the issue of the social utility of the sick role for the patient and the definition of being "cured." The significance of this variable in intervention programs is not well documented.

More flexible approaches would appear to result in improvement in behavior as the environment is restructured to meet individual needs as contrasted with institutional needs (Cain, 1969; Weinberg, 1969, 1970; Wolff, 1966a,b, 1971a).

A number of papers have examined the problems of treatment and aftercare for chronically ill patients in the community (Bidwell, Berner, and Meier, 1972; Justice and Bender, 1968b; Rosenstock, Goldman, and Rothenberg, 1969; Susser, Stein, Mountney, and Freeman, 1970; Weinberg, 1970; Williams, Kraiuciunas, and Rodriques, 1970).

In the past, the issue of efficacy of environmental therapy was posed in adversary fashion, i.e., environmental therapy versus psychotherapy or pharmacotherapy (May, 1968). Perhaps the most significant point which emerges from this review is the necessity for interdigitation of various therapies with community programs and the other modalities of therapeutic intervention. Treatment programs should maximize the patient's (client's) potential with the different disciplines bringing skills to bear on behalf of the patient for this purpose (Anderson, 1968; Bidwell, Berner, and Meier, 1972; Cain, 1969; Peffer, Margolin, Stotsky, and Mason, 1956; Rudd and Feingold, 1957; Rudd and Margolin, 1968; Stotsky, 1967b,d, 1968). Goals should be made explicit in advance of treatment and outcome assessed in relation to the objectives. Assessment should be part of any treatment plan. Included should be medical as well as psychiatric, psychological, and social status screening.

Psychosocial assessment programs may lead to appropriate intervention activities to serve the needs of patients (Arie, 1971; Beber, 1965; Beck and Stangle, 1968; Bernstein, 1966; Putter, 1967). Nowhere is this more important than in nursing homes, where so little endeavor is oriented to rehabilitative treatment (Hefferin, 1968; Oppenheim, Levey, and Stotsky, 1972).

Gottesman (1973) noted that many persons in nursing homes were continuing a marginal pattern of adjustment which long antedated placement, again highlighting the importance of including a historical overview of the patient's life-style.

The setting is of major significance. Despite rehabilitation and therapy, state mental hospital patients remain more impaired than patients who remained in the community (Lowenthal and Trier, 1967). Cohen and Kraft (1968 a,b) refer to the experience at South Mountain Geriatric Center in rediscovering the restorative potential of elderly long-term residents of state mental hospitals. The hospital-based rehabilitation programs apparently did not enable patients to realize their potential so long as they resided within the institution. The expectancies and attitudes of institutional staff toward the possibility of successful treatment requires further study. Brody et al. (1971) report on the effectiveness of short-term geriatric evaluation and treatment centers geared to match patient needs with appropriate staff and program resources. Rapid diagnosis and treatment resulted in a decreased rate of entry into state hospitals, and in the first 8 months, 70 percent of patients were able to go home.

Rehabilitation as part of a larger program of intervention was very successful and well received in nursing homes (Stotsky, 1967b). In each instance, it was imperative to adjust the program to the facility and to develop programs which could be continued after the intervention team left. Staying attuned to the patient's routine daily concerns and immediate needs was a key factor.

Cost of treatment and systems of reimbursement markedly influence the extent of commitment to rehabilitative therapies and size of program (Levey, Stotsky, Kinloch, et al., 1973; Oppenheim, Levey, and Stotsky, 1972).

In a study by Bidwell, Berner, and Meier (1972), discharged patients with physical disabilities reported an array of financial, marital, vocational, and family problems for which counseling was needed but not received. Perpetuation of disability is often a function of the staff's reluctance to encourage the patient's participation (Becker, Zucker, Parsonnet, and Gilbert, 1967; Bonner, 1969; Brusis, 1968) and of the presence of psychological problems independent of the physical disability (Archibald and Gelfter, 1970; Harris, 1970). To some extent, the same is true of patients with sensory impairment (Carolan, 1973; Richman, 1969).

The importance of psychological factors can be seen in the successful management of a wide range of physical disorders including stroke (Gordon and Kohn, 1966; Newman, 1967; Policoff, 1970), diabetes (Hadley, 1968), and other neurological disorders (Gordon and Kohn, 1966).

In a highly successful program for rehabilitation of chronic geriatric patients with physical infirmities, Williams, Kriauciunas, and Rodriquez (1970) used team screening procedures for selection of candidates and an appropriate rehabilitation program for each patient. Of the 67 patients, 63 were discharged. Most showed increased mobility, improved speech, and more independence, sociability, and mental efficiency.

Hefferin (1968) reviewed rehabilitation in nursing homes and found success to be related to the patient's mental and physical status, social situation, the experience, training, and rehabilitative orientation of personnel, the availability of rehabilitative resources in the community, and the home's ability to afford the cost of the program. The last point deserves more attention since Oppenheim, Levey, and Stotsky (1972) found that in the state of Massachusetts, the allocation of funds available for rehabilitation was wholly inadequate. Moreover, the costs of rehabilitation were not reimbursable despite emphasis on rehabilitation in classifying level of care. This was cited as an example of the "schizoid" character of state regulatory policies toward community facilities—a condition by no means limited to one state.

Rehabilitation programs with older patients enable the staff to shift from physical care to interpersonal interaction and thus to improve the patient's daily behavior (Foreyt and Felton, 1970). Wolff (1971a) argues the primary importance of conveying hope, reestablishing confidence, and overcoming undue fear of death as necessary ingredients in rehabilitation. Gottesman (1970) emphasizes the critical role of the administrator in setting the tone for rehabilitation programs in community facilities. Stotsky and Dominick (1970) include the nursing supervisor, and the team approach is favored by some (Handy, 1968b).

A recurrent theme in the literature is the need for total mobilization of resources (Remmerswaal, 1972) including an activity program (Davis, 1967; Herman, 1968), occupational and/or recreational (Srour, Finnegan, and Delcioppo, 1966), physical (Morrison, 1969), and other forms of therapy to stimulate patients to respond (Loew and Silverstone, 1971). Dubey

(1968) found an increased discharge rate for patients after 12 months in a rehabilitation program. Saul, Turner, and Goldfarb (1967) stress the importance of social interaction among staff and residents. In the Soviet Union, restorative therapy is felt to markedly affect the social and biologic adaptation of chronic patients (Kabanov, 1967).

A controversy has existed among rehabilitation professionals. Some favor the view that the application of specific professional skills is most useful to the patient; others place emphasis on attainment of goals while cutting across disciplinary lines, through remotivation (Larue, 1973; Metzelaar, 1973; Wallen, 1970) and resocialization (Gottesman, 1973; Gottesman, et al. 1973). There are no compelling data supporting one position over the other.

A 14-week physical therapy program produced significant physiological and psychological changes in aged persons (Morrison, 1969). Recreational therapy elicited improvement in 50 percent of the patients studied by making use of competitive spirit, closer patient-therapist relationships, awarding prizes of personal value, and recognizing efforts by peers and hospital employees (Srour, Finnegan, and Delcioppo, 1966). Of interest here is that 10 percent of those studied showed a negative response. Giordano and Giordano (1969) discussed activities programs in a home for the aged in the Virgin Islands in which the dehumanizing aspects of institutional life were offset by social workers acting as change agents to revitalize the program. Even pets have been used therapeutically in nursing homes (Levinson, 1970).

Intensive remotivation techniques for geriatric patients in state mental hospitals have emphasized changes in social competence, interest, and personal neatness (Bovey, 1972). Group process has been used for resocialization purposes (Brudno and Seltzer, 1968), and even minimal involvement (1 hour per week) on a regular basis was reported to reduce anxiety (Kaiman, Desroches, and Ballard, 1966).

The successful use of music as therapy for patients (Shapiro, 1969; Shatin, Kotter, and Langmore, 1967) has focused attention on a modality which has been utilized extensively since the mid-forties (Liederman, 1967). Wagner and Lerner (1968) describe two cases for whom art therapy as an outlet for self-expression was useful. Activity therapy, employing techniques to create a vivid and stimulating environment and utilizing challenge as a motivational tool to encourage independence and self-assertiveness, has been successful in patients (Loew and Silverstone, 1971).

Another approach to improving morale is by a supervised visiting program (Holzman and Sabel, 1968). Jonas, Oberdalhoff, and Schulze (1969) describe some of the perils and advantages of such programs.

The foster grandparent program has been beneficial both for the foster grandparents and the children served by them (Rybak, Sadnavitch, and Mason, 1968). Companionship therapy has also been successful (Arthur, 1971).

Rehabilitation therapy is difficult to execute and errors are often made (Taylor and Gaitz, 1968). Overcoming staff resistance in custodial institutions as well as other obstacles is often a complex process requiring much time and energy (Giordano and Giordano, 1972). High morale is crucial and improving unorthodox approaches such as that reported by Holzman and Sabel (1968) utilizing a supervised visiting program.

Education of key institutional personnel in mental health concepts may be effective as an approach (Goldman and Woog, 1973). Clearly, interdisciplinary coordination is a necessity to maximize the impact of treatment.

CONCLUSION

The initial step in intervention and rehabilitation of aged persons with psychiatric disorders should be the accurate diagnosis and evaluation of resources. This has not always been accomplished for various intervention techniques and/or for a wide variety of rehabilitative techniques. Techniques have been employed which vary in complexity and in the actual application of methods. Success, where measured, typically depends upon the therapist's technical skills, degree of commitment, utilization of pragmatic strategies, and recognition of environmental influences. In evaluating a program's effectiveness, naturalistic observation and case analysis are employed, and occasionally quantified clinical judgements are available.

The second step involves, we hope, controlled experimental studies using reliable, standardized measures to evaluate the efficacy of a particular modality against a standard procedure or the relative efficacy of one modality versus another.

Psychotherapeutic techniques, including behavior modification, have not routinely been submitted to controlled experimental study except in a few instances. One of the major objectives for the future should be the evaluation, under controlled conditions, of the efficacy of single methods as well as of combinations of treatment methods (a) to sharpen the specificity of our diagnoses and techniques of intervention, (b) to quantify the dosages or optimal quanta required for specific disorders, and (c) to select appropriate combinations of techniques for particular disorders. Revision of expectancies for treatment should follow such evaluation. The next step will be to develop an effective delivery system of treatments available on a wide enough scale and at a cost which the patients and the insurers of their health (public and private) can afford.

REFERENCES

Altman, H., Melita, D., Evenson, R. C., and Sletten, I. W. 1973. Behavioral effects of drug therapy on psychogeriatric inpatients. *J. Am. Geriat. Soc.*, **21**, 241–248.

Anderson, C. J. 1968. A multidisciplinary study of psychogeriatric patients. *Geriatrics*, **23**, 105–113.

Anderson, N. N. 1967. Effects of institutionalization on self-esteem. *J. Gerontol.*, **22**, 313–317.

Ankus, M., and Quarrington, B. 1972. Operant behavior in the memory-disordered. *J. Gerontol.*, **27**, 500–510.

Archibald, K. C., and Gelfter, W. I. 1970. Rehabilitation of the elderly cardiac patient. *Geriatrics*, **25**, 133–141.

Arie, T. 1971. Morale and the planning of psychogeriatric services. *Brit. Med. J.*, **3**, 166–170.

Arthur, G. L. 1971. Companionship therapy with the aged in a nursing home. *Dissertation Abstracts International*, **32**, 3614.

Baastrup, P. C., and Schon, M. 1967. Lithium as a prophylactic agent. Its effect against recurrent depressions and manic-depressive psychosis. *Arch. Gen. Psychiat.*, **16**, 162-172.

Baker, G. H. 1968. Community psychiatric care of elderly patients. *Hosp. Comm. Psychiatry*, **19**, 81-83.

Banen, D. M. 1972. An ergot preparation (Hydergine) for relief of symptoms of cerebrovascular insufficiency. *J. Am. Geriat. Soc.*, **20**, 22-24.

Bazo, A. J. 1973. An ergot preparation (hydergine) vs. papaverine in treating common complaints of the aged: Double-blind study. *J. Am. Geriat. Soc.*, **21**, 63-71.

Beber, C. R. 1965. Management of behavior in the institutionalized aged. *Diseases of the Nervous System*, **26**, 591-595.

Beck, L. D., and Stangle, E. K. 1968. Geriatric rehabilitation. *Geriatrics*, **23**, 118-126.

Becker, M. C., Zucker, I. R., Parsonnet, V., and Gilbert, L. 1967. Rehabilitation of the patient with permanent pacemaker. *Geriatrics*, **22**, 106-111.

Berezin, M. A., and Stotsky, B. A. 1970. The geriatric patient. *In*, H. Grunebaum (ed.), *The Practice of Community Mental Health*, pp. 219-244. Boston: Little, Brown.

Berstein, L. 1966. Patterns of geriatric rehabilitation care: Patients and institutions. *Dissertation Abstracts International*, **27**, 1205.

Bidwell, G., Berner, B., and Meier, R. D. 1972. Chronic disability post-hospital survey: A focus on ancillary service needs. *Rehabilitation Psychology*, **19**, 80-84.

Birkett, D. P. 1971. Vasodilators in geriatric psychiatry. *M. Med. Soc. New Jersey*, **68**, 619-623.

Birkett, D. P., and Boltuch, B. 1972. Chlorpromazine in geriatric psychiatry. *J. Am. Geriat. Soc.*, **20**, 403-406.

Birkett, D. P., Hirschfield, R. S., and Simpson, C. 1972. Thiothixene in the treatment of disease of the senium. *Curr. Ther. Res.*, **14**, 775-779.

Birren, J. E., Butler, R. N., Greenhouse, S. W., Sokoloff, S. W., and Yarrow, M. R. (eds.) 1963. *Human Aging: A Biological and Behavioral Study* (USPHS Publ. No. 986.). Washington, D.C.: U.S. Government Printing Office.

Blenkner, M. 1967. Environmental change and the aging individual. *Gerontologist*, **7**, 101-105.

Bloom, M., and Blenkner, M. 1970. Assessing functioning of older persons living in the community. *Gerontologist*, **10**, 31-37.

Bloom, N., and Monro, A. 1972. Social work and the aging family. *Family Coordinator*, **21**, 103-115.

Bonner, C. D. 1969. Rehabilitation instead of bed rest? *Geriatrics*, **24**, 109-118.

Borton, R., and Whitehead, J. A. 1968. A psychogeriatric domiciliary emergency service. *Brit. J. Psychiat.*, **114**, 107-108.

Bovey, J. A. 1972. The effect of intensive remotivation techniques on institutionalized geriatric mental patients in a state mental hospital. *Dissertation Abstracts International*, **32**, 4201-4202.

Brody, E. M., Kleban, M. H., Lawton, M. P., and Silverman, H. A. 1971. Excess disabilities of mentally impaired aged: Impact of individualized treatment. *Gerontologist*, **11**, 124-133.

Brown, M. I. 1969. Nursing care of the aged. *In*, F. C. Jeffers (ed.), *Duke University Council on Aging and Human Development. Proceedings of Seminar, 1965-69*, pp. 121-137. Center for Study of Aging and Human Development, Duke University, Durham.

Brudno, J. J., and Seltzer, H. 1968. Re-socialization therapy through group process with senile patients in a geriatric hospital. *Gerontologist*, **8**, 211-214.

Brusis, O. A. 1968. Rehabilitating coronary patients through exercise. *Postgrad. Med.*, **44**, 131-135.

Buckley, M. 1972. Counseling the aging. *Pers. Guid. Journal*, **59**, 755-758.

Burnside, I. M. 1970a. Crisis intervention with geriatric hospitalized patients. *Journal of Psychiatric Nursing and Mental Health Services*, **8**, 17-20.

Burnside, I. M. 1970b. Group work with the aged: Selected literature. *Gerontologist*, **10**, 241-246.

Burnside, I. M. 1970c. Loss: A constant theme in group work with the aged. *Hosp. Comm. Psychiatry*, **21**, 173-177.

Burnside, I. M. 1971. Long-term group work with hospitalized aged. *Gerontologist*, **11**, 213-218.

Busse, E. W. 1973. Mental disorders in later life-organic brain syndromes. *In*, E. W. Busse and E. Pfeiffer (eds.), *Mental Illness in Later Life*, pp. 89-106. Washington, D.C.: American Psychiatric Association.

Butler, R. N. 1968. Toward a psychiatry of the life-cycle: Implications of sociopsychological studies of the aging process of the psychotherapeutic situation. *Psychiat. Res. Rep.*, **23**, 233-248.

Butler, R. N. 1972. Mental health care in old age: Conflicts in public policy. *Psychiatric Annals*, **2**, 28-44.

Cain, L. S. 1969. Determining the factors that affect rehabilitation. *J. Am. Geriat. Soc.*, **17**, 595-604.

Cameron, D. E., and Solyom, L. 1961. Effects of ribonucleic acid on memory. *Geriatrics*, **16**, 74-81.

Cameron, D. E., Sved, S., and Solyom, L. 1963. Effects of ribonucleic acid on memory defects in the aged. *Am. J. Psychiat.*, **120**, 320-325.

Carolan, R. H. 1973. Sensory stimulation in the nursing home. *New Outlook for the Blind*, **67**, 126-130.

Carter, J. H. 1972. Psychiatry, racism, and aging. *J. Am. Geriat. Soc.*, **20**, 343-346.

Caserta, F., and Mazzola, G. S. 1970. Effect of pyridoxine upon mental efficiency. *Acta Neurologica*, **25**, 731-739.

Cautela, J. R. 1966. Behavior therapy and geriatrics. *Journal of Genetic Psychology*, **108**, 9-17.

Cautela, J. R. 1969. A classical conditioning approach to the development and modification of behavior in the aged. *Gerontologist*, **9**, 109-113.

Chesrow, E. J., and Kaplitz, S. E. 1970. Sustained-release tranquilizer therapy in hospitalized geriatric patients. *J. Am. Geriat. Soc.*, **18**, 72-80.

Chesrow, E. J., Kaplitz, S. E., Sabatini, R. *et al.* 1965. A new psychotherapeutic agent effective in the management of geriatric anxiety, depression, and behavioral reactions. *J. Am. Geriat. Soc.*, **13**, 449–454.

Chien, C. P. 1971. Psychiatric treatment for geriatric patients: "pub" or drug? *Am. J. Psychiat.*, **127**, 1070–1075.

Chien, C. P., Stotsky, B. A., and Cole, J. O. 1973. Psychiatric treatment for nursing home patients: Drug, alcohol, and milieu. *Am. J. Psychiat.*, **130**, 543–548.

Cohen, E. S., and Kraft, A. C. 1968a. The restorative potential of elderly long-term residents of mental hospitals. *Gerontologist*, **8**, 264–268.

Cohen, E. S., and Kraft, A. C. 1968b. The restorative potential of elderly long-term patients of mental hospitals. *Penn. Psychiat. Quart.*, **8**, 63–69.

Cohen, S., and Ditman, K. S. 1974. Gerovital-H3 in the treatment of depressed aging patient. *Psychosomatics*, **15**, 15–19.

Coons, D. H. 1973. The process of changes. Ann Arbor: Institute of Gerontology.

Cretallaz, G. 1968. Therapeutic possibilities of cerebral phospholipids in senile mental enfeeblement and traumatic cranial sequelae. *Annales Medico-Psychologiques*, **1**, 619.

Currier, R. D., Smith, C. M., and Steinninger, M. 1961. A study of L-Glutavite as compared to a Ritalin combination in the chronic brain syndrome. *Geriatrics*, **16**, 311–316.

Davis, J. M., Fann, W. E. El-Yousef, M. K., and Janowsky, D. 1973. Clinical problems in treating the aged with psychotropic drugs. *In*, C. Eisdorfer and W. E. Fann (eds.), *Psychopharmacology and Aging*, pp. 111–125. New York: Plenum Press.

Davis, R. M. 1967. Activity therapy in a geriatric setting. *J. Am. Geriat. Soc.*, **15**, 1144–1152.

Davis, R. W. 1968. Psychologic aspects of geriatric nursing. *Amer. J. Nursing*, **68**, 802–804.

Dawson-Butterworth, K. 1970. The chemotherapeutics of geriatric sedation. *J. Am. Geriat. Soc.*, **18**, 97–114.

DeLamos, G. P., Clements, W. R., and Nickels, E. 1965. Effects of diazepam suspension in geriatric patients hospitalized for psychiatric illness. *J. Am. Geriat. Soc.*, **13**, 355–359.

Ditch, M., Kelley, R. J., and Resnick, O. 1971. An ergot preparation (Hydergine) in the treatment of cerebrovascular disorders in the geriatric patient: Double blind study. *J. Am. Geriat. Soc.*, **19**, 208–217.

Dodgen, J. S., and Arthur, R. J. 1967. Psychotherapy of a sexagenarian. *Diseases of the Nervous System*, **28**, 680–683.

Donabedian, A., and Rosenfeld, L. S. 1964. Follow-up study of chronically ill patients discharged from the hospital. *J. Chronic Diseases*, **17**, 847–862.

Dubey, E. 1968. Intensive treatment of the institutionalized, ambulatory geriatric patient. *Geriatrics*, **23**, 170–178.

Dynes, J. B. 1970. Oral Dyskinesias: Occurrence and treatment. *Diseases of the Nervous System*, **31**, 854–859.

Einspruch, H. C. 1976. Helping to make the final years meaningful for the elderly residents of nursing homes. *Diseases of The Nervous System*, **37**, 439–442.

Eisdorfer, C. 1972. Autonomic changes in aging. *In*, C. M. Gaitz (ed.), *Aging and the Brain*, pp. 145–151. New York: Plenum Press.

Eisdorfer, C., Conner, J. F., and Wilkie, F. L. 1968. Effect of magnesium pemoline on cognition and behavior. *J. Gerontol.*, **23**, 283–288.

Eisdorfer, C., Nowlin, J., and Wilkie, F. 1970. Improvement of learning in the aged by modification of autonomic nervous system activity. *Science*, **170**, 1327–1329.

Eisdorfer, C., and Wilkie, F. 1973. Intellectual changes with advancing age. *In*, L. F. Jarvik, C. Eisdorfer and J. E. Blum (eds.), *Intellectual Functioning in Adults*, pp. 21–29. New York: Springer.

Emmenegger, H., and Meier-Ruge, W. 1968. The actions of Hydergine on the brain. *Pharmacology*, **1**, 65–78.

Epstein, L. J., and Simon, A. 1968. Alternatives to state hospitalization for the geriatric mentally ill. *Am. J. Psychiat.*, **124**, 955–961.

Feil, N. W. 1967. Group therapy in a home for the aged. *Gerontologist*, **7**, 192–195.

Folsom, J. C. 1968. Reality orientation for the elderly mental patient. *Journal of Geriatric Psychiatry*, **1**, 291–307.

Foreyt, J. P., and Felton, G. S. 1970. Change in behavior of hospitalized psychiatric patients in a milieu therapy setting. *Psychotherapy: Theory, research and practice*, **7**, 139–141.

Gelfand, D. E. 1968. Visiting patterns and social adjustment in an old age home. *Gerontologist*, **8**, 272–275.

Gendlin, E., and Rychlak, J. F. 1970. Psychotherapeutic processes. *In*, P. H. Mussen and M. R. Rosenzqeig (eds.), *Annual Review of Psychology*, **21**, 155–190.

Gerin, J. 1969. Symptomatic treatment of cerebrovascular insufficiency with Hydergine. *Curr. Ther. Res.*, **11**, 539–546.

Gershon, S. 1973. Antianxiety agents. *In*, C. Eisdorfer and W. E. Fann (eds.), *Psychopharmacology and Aging*, pp. 183–188. New York: Plenum.

Gilbert, J., Donnelly, K. J., Zimmer, L. E., and Kubis, J. F. 1973. Effect of magnesium pemoline and methylphenidate on memory improvement and mood in normal aging subjects. *Aging and Human Development*, **4**, 35–51.

Giordano, J., and Giordano, G. 1969. An activities program in a home for the aged in the Virgin Islands. *Social Work*, **14**, 61–66.

Giordano, J., and Giordano, G. 1972. Overcoming resistance to change in custodial institutions. *Hosp. Comm. Psychiatry*, **23**, 183–185.

Goldberg, H. L., Latif, J., and Abrams, S. 1970. Psychiatric consultation: A strategic service to nursing home staffs. *Gerontologist*, **10**. 221-224.

Goldfarb, A. I. 1962. The psychotherapy of elderly patients. *In*, H. T. Blumenthal (ed.), *Medical and Clinical Aspects of Aging*, pp. 106-114. New York: Columbia University Press.

Goldfarb, A. I. 1967. Psychiatry in geriatrics. *Med. Clin. N. Am.*, **51**, 1515-1527.

Goldfarb, A. I. 1970. The physician and the chronic care institution. *Gerontologist*, **10**, 45-49.

Goldfarb, A. I., Hochstadt, N. J., Jacobson, J. H., and Weinstein, E. A. 1972. Hyperbaric oxygen treatment of organic mental syndrome in aged person. *J. Gerontol.*, **27**, 212-217.

Goldman, E. B., and Woog, P. 1973. Mental health in nursing homes training project 1972-1973. Paper presented at meeting of the Gerontological Society, Miami Beach, Florida, November 6, 1973.

Goldstein, B. J. 1967. Double blind comparison of Tybamate and Chlordiazepoxide in geriatric patients. *Psychosomatics*, **8**, 334-337.

Gordon, E. E., and Kohn, K. H. 1966. Evaluation of rehabilitation methods in the hemiplegic patient. *J. Chronic Diseases*, **19**, 3-16.

Gottesman, L. E. 1970. Organizing rehabilitation services for the elderly. *Gerontologist*, **10**, 287-293.

Gottesman, L. E. 1973. Milieu treatment of the aged in institutions. *Gerontologist*, **13**, 23-26.

Gottesman, L. E., Quarterman, C. E., and Cohn, G. M. 1973. Psychosocial treatment of the aged. *In*, C. Eisdorfer and M. P. Lawton (eds.), *The Psychology of Adult Development and Aging*, pp. 378-427. Washington, D.C.: American Psychological Association.

Granick, S., and Patterson, R. D. (eds.) 1971. *Human Aging II: An Eleven-Year Followup Biomedical and Behavioral Study*. Washington, D.C.: U.S. Government Printing Office.

Granville-Grossman, K. L. and Turner, P. 1966. The effect of propranolol on anxiety. *Lancet*, **1**, 788-790.

Grauer, H., Betts, D., and Birnbom, F. 1973. Welfare emotions and family therapy in geriatrics. *J. Am. Geriat. Soc.*, **21**, 21-24.

Gray, P. E. 1973. Dramatics for the elderly: A survey of characteristics, problems encountered, and solutions suggested in dramatics programs in New York senior centers and residential care settings. *Dissertation Abstracts International*, **33**, 4-192.

Greenblatt, D. J., DiMascio, A., Messier, M., and Stotsky, B. A. 1969. Magnesium pemoline and job performance in mentally handicapped workers. *Clin. Pharmacol. Therap.*, **10**, 530-533.

Greenblatt, D. J., and Shader, R. I. 1974. *Benzodiazepines in Clinical Practice*. New York: Raven Press.

Greenwald, S., and Linn, M. W. 1970. What wives say about nursing homes. *J. Am. Geriat. Soc.*, **18**, 166-171.

Grosicki, J. P. 1968. Effect of operant conditioning on modification of incontinence in neuropsychiatric geriatric patients. *Nursing Res.*, **17**, 304-311.

Gruen, A. 1957. Old age as a factor in motivation for therapy. *Int. J. Soc. Psychiat.*, **3**, 61-66.

Gunn, J. C. 1967. Group psychotherapy on a geriatric ward. *Psychotherapy and Psychosomatics*, **15**, 26.

Hadley, W. 1968. Maintenance therapy with diabetic patients. *In*, J. L. Rudd and R. J. Margolin (eds.), *Maintenance Therapy for the Geriatric Patient*, pp. 158-173. Springfield, Illinois: Charles C. Thomas.

Hall, P. 1976. Cyclandelate in the treatment of cerebral arteriosclerosis. *J. Am. Geriat. Soc.*, **24**: 41-45.

Handy, I. A. 1968a. Foster care as a therapeutic program for geriatric psychiatric patients. *J. Am. Geriat. Soc.*, **16**, 350-358.

Handy, I. A. 1968b. The team approach in the rehabilitation of psychiatric patients. *J. Am. Geriat. Soc.*, **16**, 1058-1065.

Harris, R. 1970. The management of geriatric cardiovascular disease. Philadelphia: J. B. Lippincott.

Hearst, E. D., Cloninger, C. R., Crews, E. L. *et al.* 1974. Electrosleep therapy. *Arch. Gen. Psychiat.*, **30**, 463-466.

Hedri, A. 1967. Psychotherapy in old age. *Psychotherapy and Psychosomatics*, **15**, 28.

Hefferin, E. A. 1968. Rehabilitation in nursing home situations: A survey of the literature. *J. Am. Geriat. Soc.*, **16**, 296-313.

Herman, M. 1968. Activity programs in personal care homes. *Canad. J. Occup. Ther.*, **35**, 98-100.

Heyman, D. K., and Polansky, G. H. 1969. Social casework and community services for the aged. *In*, E. W. Busse and E. Pfeiffer (eds.), *Behavior and Adaptation in Late Life*, pp. 323-343. Boston: Little, Brown.

Hiatt, H. 1971. Dynamic psychotherapy with the aging patient. *Amer. J. Psychother.*, **25**, 591-600.

Hoenig, J., and Hamilton, M. W. 1966. Elderly psychiatric patients and the burden on the household. *Psychiat. Neurol.*, **152**, 281-293.

Hollister, L. E. 1973. *Clinical use of Psychotherapeutic drugs*. Springfield, Illinois: Charles C. Thomas.

Holzman, S., and Sabel, N. E. 1968. Improving the morale of the patients and the staff in a geriatric institution by a supervised visiting program. *Gerontologist*, **8**, 29-33.

Hoyer, W. J. 1973. Application of operant techniques to the modification of elderly behavior. *Gerontologist*, **13**, 18-22.

Hrachovec, J. P. 1973. Inhibitory effect of Gerovital H_3 and Procaine on monoamine oxidase in rat brain, liver, heart, and platelets. Paper presented at 26th annual meeting of the Gerontological Society, Miami Beach, Florida, November 9, 1973.

Jacobs, E. A., Winter, P. M., Alvis, H. J., and Small, H. M. 1969. Hyperoxygenation effect on cognitive function in the aged. *New Engl. J. Med.*, **281**, 753.

Jacobson, A. 1958. The use of Ritalin in psychotherapy of depression of the aged. *Psychiat. Quart.*, **32**, 475-483.

Jarvik, L., and Milne, J. F. 1975. Gerovital-H3: A review of the literature. *In* S. Gershon and A. Raskin (eds.) *Aging Vol. 2: Genesis and Treatment of Psy-*

chologic Disorders in the Elderly. pp. 203–227, New York: Raven Press.

Jarvik, M. E. 1973. A survey of drug effects upon cognitive activities of the aged. *In,* C. Eisdorfer and W. E. Fann (eds.), *Psychopharmacology and Aging,* pp. 129–144. New York: Plenum Press.

Jarvik, M. E., Gritz, E. R., and Schneider, N. G. 1972. Drugs and memory disorders in human aging. *Behavioral Biology,* 7, 643–668.

Jayne, H. W., Scheinber, P., Rich, M. *et al.* 1952. The effect of intravenous papaverine hydrochloride on the cerebral circulation. *J. Clin. Invest.,* **31,** 111–114.

Jonas, R., Oberdalhoff, H. E., and Schulze, H. H. 1969. Visitor attendance at psychiatric and nonpsychiatric hospitals. *Social Psychiat.,* **4,** 69–75.

Justice, V. O., and Bender, D. 1968a. Community placement of elderly patients. *Hosp. Comm. Psychiatry,* **19,** 144–145.

Justice, V. O., and Bender, D. 1968b. Returning the geriatric veteran to the community from a neuropsychiatric hospital. *J. Am. Geriat. Soc.,* **16,** 359–362.

Kabanov, M. M. 1967. An experience with restoratory therapy and social readaptation of the mentally ill. *Zh. Nevropatol. I Psikhiatr.,* **67,** 1072–1077.

Kahana, B., and Kahana, E. 1970a. Changes in mental status of elderly patients in age-integrated and age-segregated hospital milieus. *J. Abnorm. Psychol.,* **75,** 177–181.

Kahana, E., and Kahana, B. 1970b. Therapeutic potential of age integration: Effects of age-integrated hospital environments on elderly psychiatric patients. *Arch. Gen. Psychiat.,* **23,** 20–29.

Kaiman, B. D., Desroches, H. F., and Ballard, H. T. 1966. Therapeutic effectiveness of minimal activity in an aged population. *Psychol. Reports,* **19,** 439–433.

Kaplan, J. 1970. Social planning: A continuing challenge. *Gerontologist,* **10,** 189–213.

Kaplitz, S. E. 1975. Withdrawn, apathetic geriatric patients responsive to methylphenidate. *J. Am. Geriat. Soc.,* **23,** 271–276.

Kastenbaum, R. 1965. Wine and fellowship in aging: An exploratory action program. *J. Hum. Rela.,* **13:** 266–275.

Kastenbaum, R., Slater, P. E., and Aisenberg, R. 1964. Toward a conceptual model of geriatric psychopharmacology: An experiment with thioridazine and dextroamphetamine. *Gerontologist,* **4,** 68–71.

Kilpatrick, A. C. 1968. Conjoint family therapy with geriatric patients. *J. Fort Logan Mental Health Center,* **5,** 29–35.

Kistin, H., and Morris, R. 1972. Alternatives to institutional care for the elderly and disabled. *Gerontologist,* **12,** 139–142.

Kral, V. A., Cahn, C., Deutsch, M. 1962. Procaine (Novacain) treatment of patients with senile and arteriosclerotic brain disease. *Can. Med. Assoc. J.,* **87,** 1109–1113.

Kral, V. A., Solyom, L., and Enesco, H. E. 1967. Effect of short-term oral RNA therapy on the serum uric acid level and memory function in senile versus senescent subjects. *J. Am. Geriat. Soc.,* **15,** 364–372.

Kral, V. A., Solyom, L., Enesco, H., and Ledwidge, B. 1970. Relationship of vitamin B_{12} and folic acid to memory function. *Biol. Psych.,* **2,** 19–26.

Kramer, M., Taube, C. A., and Redick, R. W. 1973. Patterns of use of psychiatric facilities by the aged: Past, present and future. *In,* C. Eisdorfer and M. P. Lawton (eds.), *The Psychology of Adult Development and Aging,* pp. 428–528. Washington, D.C.: American Psychological Association.

Kramer, M., Taube, C. and Starr, S. 1968. Patterns of use of psychiatric facilities by the aged: Current status trends and implications. *In: Aging in Modern Society.* Washington, D.C.: American Psychiatric Association.

Krasner, L. 1971. Behavior therapy. *Annual Review of Psychology,* **22,** 483–532.

Krauss, T. C., and Goldstein, H. N. 1967. Medical management of mentally impaired patients in long-term care facilities. *Gerontologist,* 7, 278–282.

Larue, V. 1973. *Two Years with Eighty Patients.* Ann Arbor: Institute of Gerontology.

Leckman, J., Ananth, J. W., Ban, T. A., and Lehmann, H. E. 1971. Pentylenetetrazol in the treatment of geriatric patients with disturbed memory function. *J. Clin. Pharmacol. New Drugs,* **11,** 301–303.

Levey, S., Stotsky, B. A., Kinloch, D. R. *et al.* 1973. Study reveals increases in costs, in per diem rates, and in per diem expenditures. *Modern Nurs. Home,* **31,** 52–54.

Levinson, B. M., 1970. The pet in the nursing home: A psychological adventure for the patient. *Silver Threads,* 3–7.

Libow, L. A., Viola, R. M., and Stein, M. F. 1968. The extended care facility at Mount Sinai City Hospital Center, Elmhurst, New York: Three-year experience. *J. Am. Geriat. Soc.,* **16,** 1164–1172.

Lieberman, M. A. 1969. Institutionalization of the aged: effects on behavior. *J. Gerontol.,* **24,** 330–340.

Liederman, P. C. 1967. Music and rhythm group therapy for geriatric patients. *J. Music Ther.,* **4,** 126–127.

Liederman, P. C., Green, R., and Liederman, V. R. 1967. Outpatient group therapy with geriatric patients. *Geriatrics,* **22,** 148–153.

Linden, M. 1953. Group psychotherapy with institutionalized senile women: Study in gerontologic human relations. *Intern. J. Gp. Psychother.,* 150–170.

Linn, M. W. 1966. Who goes to nursing homes? *J. Am. Geriat. Soc.,* **14,** 647–650.

Linn, M. W., and Gurel, L. 1969. Initial reactions to nursing home placement. *J. Am. Geriat. Soc.,* **17,** 219–223.

Loew, C. A., and Silverstone, B. M. 1971. A program of intensified stimulation and response facilitation for the senile aged. *Gerontologist,* **11,** 341–347.

Lowenthal, M. F., Berkman, P. L. and Associates. 1967. *Aging and Mental Disorder in San Francisco: A Social Psychiatric Study*. San Francisco: Jossey-Bass.

Lowenthal, M. F., and Trier, M. 1967. The elderly ex-mental patient. *Int. J. Soc. Psychiat.*, 13, 101–114.

Lowy, L. 1967. Roadbloacks in groupwork practice with older people: A framework for analysis. *Gerontologist*, 7, 109–113.

Lu, L. M., Stotsky, B. A., and Cole, J. O. 1971. A controlled study of drugs in long-term geriatric psychiatric patients. *Arch. Gen. Psychiat.*, 25, 284–288.

MacDonnell, J. A. McKenzie, D. A., and Cheetham, E. 1968. Social effects of intermittent readmission. *Gerontologist*, 8, 38–42.

McGinity, P. J., and Stotsky, B. A. 1967. The patient in the nursing home. *Nurs. Forum*, 6, 238–261.

MacMillan, D. 1967. Problems of a geriatric mental health service. *Brit. J. Psychiat.*, 113, 175–181.

McNeil, J. N., and Verwoerdt, A. 1972. A group treatment program combined with a work project on the geriatric unit of a state hospital. *J. Am. Geriat. Soc.*, 20, 259–264.

Manaster, A. 1972. Therapy with the "senile" geriatric patient. *Intern. J. Gp. Psychother.*, 22, 250–257.

Maxwell, R. J., and Silverman, P. 1970. Information and esteem: Cultural considerations in the treatment of the aged. *Aging and Human Development*, 1, 361–392.

May, P. R. A. 1968. *Treatment of Schizophrenia. A Comparative Study of Five Treatment Methods*. New York: Science House.

Meerloo, J. A. 1971. Psychotherapy with the aged. *Nederlands Tijdschrift Voor Gerontologie*, 2, 160–169.

Mensch, I. N. 1973. Community mental health and other health services for the aged. *In*, C. Eisdorfer and M. P. Lawton (eds.), *The Psychology of Adult Development and Aging*, pp. 529–571. Washington, D.C: American Psychological Association.

Merlis, S., Sheppard, C., Collins, L., and Fiorentino, D. 1970. Polypharmacy in psychiatry: Patterns of differential treatment. *Am. J. Psychiat.*, 126, 1647–1651.

Metzelaar, L. 1973. *Social Interaction Groups in a Therapeutic Community*. Ann Arbor: Institute of Gerontology.

Mezey, A. G. Hodgkinson, H. M., and Evans, G. J. 1968. The elderly in the wrong unit. *Brit. Med. J.*, 3, 16–18.

Millard, D. W. 1968. The clinician in the community. *Brit. J. Psychiat. Soc. Wk.*, 9, 124–129.

Mishara, B. L. 1971. Effects of a rehabilitation program for chronic elderly "mental" patients: Changes in care needed. *Proceedings of the Annual Convention of the American Psychological Association*, 6, 645–646.

Morrison, M. 1969. Rehabilitation of the elderly patient. *Physiotherapy*, 55, 190–197.

Nelson, J. J. 1975. Relieving select symptoms of the elderly. *Geriatrics*, 30, 133–142.

Newman, L. B. 1967. Physical medicine and rehabilitation for stroke patients. *J. Am. Geriat. Soc.*, 15, 111–128.

Nice, R. M. 1969. Psychology, extended care facility, and the community. *Journal of Psychiatric Nursing and Mental Health Services*, 7, 136–139.

Oberleder, M. 1970. Crisis therapy in mental breakdown of the aging. *Gerontologist*, 10, 111–114.

Oppenheim, W., Levey, S., and Stotsky, B. A. 1972. Nursing home expenditures for recreation and rehabilitation services: Some implications of neglect. *Amer. Arch. Rehabilit. Ther.*, 20, 45–51.

Ostfeld, A., Smith, C. M., and Stotsky, B. A. 1976. A review of the systemic use of procaine in the treatment of the elderly. *J. Am. Geriat. Soc.*, in press.

Patterson, R. L., and Teigen, J. R. 1973. Conditioning and post-hospital generalization of nondelusional responses in a chronic psychotic patient. *J. Appl. Behav. Anal.*, 6, 65–70.

Peffer, P. A., Margolin, R. J., Stotsky, B. A., and Mason, A. S. 1956. *Member-Employee Program*. Brockton: Veterans Administration Hospital.

Pinchak, L. 1967. Procedures for placing patients in nursing homes. *Hosp. Comm. Psychiatry*, 18, 365–367.

Pincus, A. 1968. The definition and measurement of the institutional environment in homes for the aged. *Gerontologist*, 8, 207–210.

Policoff, L. D. 1970. The philosophy of stroke rehabilitation. *Geriatrics*, 25, 99–107.

Post, F. 1968. Management of senile psychiatric disorders. *Brit. Med. J.*, 4, 627–630.

Post, F. 1972. The management and nature of depressive illness in late life: A follow-through study, *Brit. J. Psychiat.*, 121, 393–404.

Prange, A. J., Jr. 1973. Use of antidepressant drugs in the elderly patient. *In*, C. Eisdorfer and W. E. Fann (eds.), *Psychopharmacology and Aging*, pp. 225–237. New York: Plenum Press.

Pressey, S. L., and Pressey, A. D. 1972. Major neglected need opportunity: Old-age counseling. *J. Counsel. Psychol.*, 19, 362–366.

Prien, R. F., Caffey, E. M., Jr., and Klett, C. J. 1972. A comparison of lithium carbonate and chlorpromazine in the treatment of mania. *Arch. Gen. Psychiat.*, 26, 146–153.

Prien, R. F., Caffey, E. M., Jr., and Klett, C. J. 1974. Factors associated with treatment success in lithium carbonate prophylaxis. *Arch. Gen. Psychiat.*, 31, 189–192.

Putter, Z. H. 1967. Group approaches in the care of the chronically ill. *J. Jewish Communal Service*, 44, 177–183.

Raskind, M. A., Alvarez, C., Pietrzyk, M., Westerlund, K., and Herlin, S. 1976. Helping the elderly psychiatric patient in crisis. *Geriatrics*, June, 51–56.

Raskind, M. A., and Eisdorfer, C. 1975. Psychopharmacology of the aged. *In*, L. L. Simpson (ed.), *The*

Use of Psychotherapeutic Drugs in the Treatment of Mental Illness. New York: Raven Press. In press.

Remmerswaal, P. W. 1972. Twelve and a half years development of "Niewv Toutenburg." *Nederlands Tijdschrift voor Gerontologie*, 3, 16–27.

Richman, L. 1969. Sensory training for geriatric patients. *Amer. J. Occup. Ther.*, 23, 254–257.

Rickels, K., Clark, E. L., Etezady, M. H. *et al.* 1970. Butabarbital sodium and chlordiazepoxide in anxious neurotic outpatients: A collaborative controlled study. *Clin. Pharmacol. Therap.*, 11, 538–550.

Rosen, J. H. 1975. Mental decline in the elderly: Pharmacotherapy (ergot alkaloids versus papaverine). *J. Am. Geriat. Soc.*, 23, 169–174.

Rosenblatt, C. 1972. Isolation and resistance in the elderly: A community mental health program. *Journal of Psychiatric Nursing and Mental Health Services*, 10, 22–25.

Rosenstock, F. W., Goldman, M., and Rothenberg, R. 1969. Rehabilitation of the long-term patient. An action research program in milieu therapy. *J. Chronic Diseases*, 22, 493–503.

Roubicek, J., Geiger, C. H., and Abt, K. 1972. An ergot alkaloid preparation (Hydergine) in geriatric therapy. *J. Am. Geriat. Soc.*, 20, 222–229.

Rudd, J. L., and Feingold, S. N. 1957. Medical and vocational cooperation for the aging. *J. Am. Geriat. Soc.*, 5, 263–270.

Rudd, J. L., and Margolin, R. J. 1968. The role of physical medicine and rehabilitation in maintenance therapy. *In*, J. L. Rudd and R. J. Margolin (eds.), *Maintenance Therapy for the Geriatric Patient*, pp. 28–47. Springfield, Illinois: Charles C. Thomas.

Rybak, W. S., Sadnavitch, J. M., and Mason, B. J. 1968. A foster grandparent program. *Hosp. Comm. Psychiatry*, 19, 47.

Safirstein, S. L. 1972. Psychotherapy for geriatric patients. *N. Y. State J. Med.*, 72, 2743–2748.

Sakalis, G., Oh, D., Gershon, S., *et al.* 1974. A trial of gerovital in depression during senility. *Curr. Therap. Res.*, 16, 59–63.

Salzman, C., Kochansky, G. E., and Shader, R. I. 1972. Rating scales for geriatric pscyhopharmacology: A review. *Psychopharmacology Bull.*, 8, 3–50.

Salzman, C., and Shader, R. I. 1973. Responses to psychotropic drugs in the normal elderly. *In*, C. Eisdorfer and W. E. Fann (eds.), *Psychopharmacology and Aging*, pp. 159–168. New York: Plenum Press.

Salzman, C., Shader, R. I., and Pearlman, M. 1970. Psychopharmacology and the elderly. *In*, R. I, Shader and A. Di Mascio (eds.), *Psychotropic Drug Side Effects*, pp. 261–279. Baltimore: Williams & Wilkins.

Sanders, J. F. 1965. Evaluation of oxazepam and placebo in emotionally disturbed aged patients. *Geriatrics*, 20, 739–746.

Saul, S. R., Turner, H. R., and Goldfarb, A. I. 1967. Social interaction and program for the mentally impaired in homes for the aged. *Proceedings of the 20th Annual Meeting of the Gerontological Society*, 45.

Savitsky, E., Sharkey, H., Sulesky, F., and Taishoff, B. 1969. Clinical services to the aged with special reference to family study. *Am. J. Orthopsychiat.*, 39, 498–503.

Savitz, H. A. 1967. Humanizing institutional care for the aged. *J. Amer. Geriat. Soc.*, 15, 203–210.

Schooler, K. K. 1969. The relationship between social interaction and morale of the elderly as a function of environmental characteristics. *Gerontologist*, 9, 25–29.

Shapiro, A. 1969. A pilot program in music therapy with residents of a home for the aged. *Gerontologist*, 9, 128–133.

Shatin, L. Kotter, W., and Langmore, G. 1967. Psychosocial prescription for music therapy in hospitals. *Diseases of the Nervous System*, 28, 231–233.

Simon, A. 1970. Screening of the aged mentally ill. *Journal of Geriatric Psychiatry*, 4, 5–17.

Simon, A., Epstein, L., and Reynolds, L. 1968. Alcoholism in the geriatric mentally ill. *Geriatrics*, 23, 125–131.

Smith, W. L., and Lowrey, J. B. 1975. Effects of diphenylhydantoin on mental abilities in the elderly. *J. Am. Geriat. Soc.*, 23, 207–211.

Smith, W. L., Lowrey, J. B., and Davis, J. A. 1968. The effects of cyclandelate on psychological test performance in patients with cerebrovascular insufficienty. *Curr. Ther. Res.*, 10, 613–618.

Sperlinga, J., Andrus, B. Andrus, Q., Stotsky, B. *et al.* 1972. A demonstration project in geriatric day care. *Amer. Arch. Rehabilit. Ther.*, 20, 39–44.

Spitzer, E. P. 1969. Disengagement: Self-preservation or self-defense? *Voices: The Art and Science of Psychotherapy*, 5, 28–32.

Srour, G. M., Finnegan, R. J., and Delcioppo, C. A. 1966. A new approach to recreational therapy with older chronically hospitalized patients. *Psychiat. Quart. Suppl.*, 40, 10–16.

Starkey, P. D. 1968. Sick-role retention as a factor in non-rehabilitation. *J. Counsel. Psychol.*, 15, 75–79.

Stern, F. H. 1964. A new drug (Tybamate) effective in the management of chronic brain syndrome. *J. Am. Geriat. Soc.*, 12, 1066.

Stotsky, B. A. 1966. Nursing homes: a review. *Am. J. Psychiat.*, 123, 249–258.

Stotsky, B. A. 1967a. Allegedly nonpsychiatric patients in nursing homes. *J. Am. Geriat. Soc.*, 15, 535–544.

Stotsky, B. A. 1967b. A systematic study of therapeutic interventions in nursing homes. *Genet. Psychol. Monogr.*, 76, 257–320.

Stotsky, B. A. 1967c. Nursing home or mental hospital: Which is better for the geriatric mental patient? *Journal of Genetic Psychology*, 111, 113–117.

Stotsky, B. A. 1967d. The physician's responsibility in rehabilitation of the aging. *In*, R. J. Margolin and G. J. Goldin (eds.), *Dynamic Programming in the*

Rehabilitation of the Aging, pp. 43–58. Boston: Northeastern University.

Stotsky, B. A. 1968. Psychiatric aspects of maintenance care of the aged patient. *In*, J. L Rudd and R. J. Margolin (eds.), *Maintenance Care of the Aged Patient*, pp. 126–157. Springfield, Illinois: Charles C. Thomas.

Stotsky, B. A. 1969. Pharmacologic treatment of emotional disturbances in the aged. *Geriatrics Digest*, 6, 20–27.

Stotsky, B. A. 1970a. Discussion of: The screening of the mentally ill. *Journal of Geriatric Psychiatry*, 4, 18–22.

Stotsky, B. A. 1970b. *The Nursing Home and the aged Psychiatric Patient*. New York: Appleton-Century-Crofts.

Stotsky, B. A. 1970c. Use of psychopharmacologic agents for geriatric patients. *In*, A. DiMascio and R. I. Shader (eds.), *Clinical Handbook of Psychopharmacology*, pp. 265–278. New York: Science House.

Stotsky, B. A. 1972. Social and clinical issues in geriatric psychiatry, *Am. J. Psychiat.*, 129, 117–126.

Stotsky, B. A. 1973. Psychoses in the elderly. *In*, C. Eisdorfer and W. E. Fann (eds.), *Psychopharmacology and Aging*, pp. 193–202. New York: Plenum Press.

Stotsky, B. A. 1975. Psychoactive drugs for geriatric patients with psychiatric disorders. *In* S. Gershon and A. Raskin (eds.) *Aging Vol. 2: Genesis and Treatment of Psychologic Disorders in the Elderly*, pp. 229–258. New York: Raven Press.

Stotsky, B. A., and Borozne, J. 1972. Butisol sodium vs. Librium among geriatric and younger outpatients and nursing home patients. *Diseases of the Nervous System*, 33, 254–267.

Stotsky, B. A., Cole, J. O., Lu, L. M., and Sniffin, C. 1972. A controlled study of the efficacy of pentylenetetrazol in hard-core hospitalized psychogeriatric patients. *Am. J. Psychiat.*, 129, 387–391.

Stotsky, B. A., and Dominick, J. P. 1970. The physician's role in the nursing and retirement home. *Gerontologist*, 10, 38–44.

Stotsky, B. A., and Levey, S. 1967. The interdisciplinary responsibilities of public health and mental health in nursing homes. *Prof. Nurs. Home*, 9, 49–55.

Susser, M. W., Stein, Z., Mountney, G. H., and Freeman, H. L. 1970. Chronic disability following mental illness in an English City: I. Total prevalence in and out of mental hospital. *Social Psychiat.*, 5, 63–69.

Taylor, J., and Gaitz, C. N. 1968. An obstacle in rehabilitation of geriatric patients: Errors in following regimen. *Gerontologist*, 8, 24 (abstract).

Thompson, L. W. 1975. Effects of hyperbaric oxygen on behavioral functioning in elderly persons with intellectual impairment. *In* S. Gershon and A. Raskin (eds.) *Aging Vol. 2: Genesis and Treatment of Psychologic Disorders in the Elderly*, pp. 169–177, New York: Raven Press.

Tsuang, M. M., Lu, L. M., Stotsky, B. A., and Cole, J. O. 1971. Haloperidol versus thioridazine for hospitalized psychogeriatric patients: double-blind study. *J. Am. Geriat. Soc.*, 19, 593–600.

Turek, I., Kurland, A. A., Ota, K. Y., and Hanlon, T. E. 1969. Effects of pipradrol hydrochloride on geriatric patients. *J. Am. Geriat. Soc.*, 17, 408–413.

Ullman, L. P., and Krasner, L. 1969. *A Psychological Approach to Abnormal Behavior*. Englewood Cliffs, New Jersey: Prentice-Hall.

Van der Velde, C. D. 1971. Toxicity of lithium carbonate in elderly patients. *Am. J. Psychiat.*, 127, 1075–1077.

Wagner, A., and Lerner, J. 1968. Art therapy in the psychiatric hospital. *J. Am. Geriat. Soc.*, 16, 867–873.

Wallen, V. 1970. Motivation therapy with the aging geriatric veteran patient. *Military Med.*, 135, 1007–1010.

Walsh, A. C. 1969a. Arterial insufficiency of the brain: Progression prevented by long-term anticoagulant therapy in eleven patients. *J. Am. Geriat. Soc.*, 17, 93–104.

Walsh, A. C. 1969b. Prevention of senile and presenile dementia by bishydroxy-coumarin therapy. *J. Am. Geriat. Soc.*, 17, 447–487.

Walsh, A. C., and Walsh, B. H. 1972. Senile and presenile dementia: Further observations on the benefits of dicumarol-psychotherapy regimen. *J. Am. Geriat. Soc.*, 20, 127–131.

Wanderer, Z. W. 1972. Existential depression treated by desensitization of phobias: Strategy and transcript. *J. Behav. Ther. Exper. Ther.*, 3, 111–116.

Wasser, E. 1966. *Creative Approaches in Casework with the Aging*. New York: Family Service Association of America.

Weinberg, J. 1969. Rehabilitation of geriatric patients. *Illinois Med. J.*, 163, 63–66.

Weinberg, J. 1970. Environment, its language and the aging. *J. Am. Geriat. Soc.*, 18, 681–686.

Weinman, B., Gelbart, P., Wallace, M., and Post, M. 1972. Inducing assertive behavior in chronic schizophrenics: A comparison of socioenvironmental, desensitization, and relaxation therapies. *J. Consult. Clin. Psych.*, 30, 246–252.

Wheatley, D. 1968. Drug insufficiencies in the treatment of neurotic illness. *Excerpta Medica International Congress Series No. 180*, 556–558.

Williams, J. R., Kriauciunas, R., and Rodriquez, A. 1970. Physical, mental, and social rehabilitation for elderly and infirm patients. *Hosp. Comm. Psychiatry*, 21, 130–132.

Wilson, W. P., and Major, L. F. 1973. Electroshock and the aged patient. *In*, C. Eisdorfer and W. E. Fann (eds.), *Psychopharmacology and Aging*, pp. 239–244. New York: Plenum Press.

Wolff, K. 1957. Group psychotherapy with geriatric patients in a mental hospital. *J. Am. Geriat. Soc.*, 5, 13–19.

Wolff, K. 1966a. The emotional rehabilitation of the

geriatric patient. I. Theoretical considerations. *J. Am. Geriat. Soc.*, **14**, 75–79.

Wolff, K. 1966b. The emotional rehabilitation of the geriatric patient. II. Therapeutic principles. *J. Am. Geriat. Soc.*, **14**, 1150–1152.

Wolff, K. 1971a. Rehabilitating geriatric patients. *Hosp. Comm. Psychiatry*, **22**, 8–11.

Wolff, K. 1971b. Individual psychotherapy with geriatric patients. *Psychosomatics*, **12**, 89–93.

Wolk, R. L., and Goldfarb, A. I. 1967. The response to group psychotherapy of aged recent admissions compared with long-term mental hospital patients. *Am. J. Psychiat.*, **123**, 1251–1257.

Yalom, I. D., and Terrazas, F. 1968. Group therapy for psychiatric elderly patients. *Amer. J. Nursing*, **68**, 1690–1694.

Zimberg, S. 1971. The psychiatrist and medical home care: Geriatric psychiatry in the Harlem community. *Am. J. Psychiat.*, **127**, 1062–1066.

Zung, W. W. K., Gianturco, D., Pfeiffer, E., *et al.* 1974. Pharmacology of depression in the aged: Evaluation of gerovital-H3 as an antidepressant drug. *Psychosomatics*, **15**: 127–131.

Zwerling, I., Plutchik, R., Hotz, M., *et al.* 1975. Effects of a procaine preparation (gerovital H₃) in hospitalized geriatric patients: A double-blind study. *J. Am. Geriat. Soc.*, **24**, 355–359.

INDEXES

AUTHOR INDEX

SUBJECT INDEX

and motor performance, 458; studies on, 84, 622; vocational testing, 678
See also Retirement
Oligodendrocytes
See Neuroglial cells
Open field activity: environment and, 363, 364; feedback effect, 367, 368; genotype and, 363, 364; testing of, 363, 364
See also Activity; Behavior; Exploration; Mice; Rats
Operant conditioning, 22, 24, 85
Osteoporosis, 191, 210
Otis Test, 74, 89, 198
Ovary, 7
Oxidative phosphorylation, 183
Oxygen, 106, 107; in brain disorders, 220; cerebral consumption, 220; and EEG, 220; in senile dementia, 220

Pain: age changes, 575, 576; cutaneous, 569; deep, 569, 572; motivational aspects, 569, 570, 576; placebo effect, 572, 576; response threshold, 563, 564, 569-571; sex differences, 570; tolerance to, 569-571
Paired associate paradigm: in learning, 422-427, 429, 432; tasks in assessment, 709; verbal tasks, 610
Paramecia, 195
Paranoia: in aged, 656, 726; and schizophrenia, 656, 726; treatment, 656, 726, 735
Parental longevity factor, 13, 14, 17, 25, 26, 104
Parenthood: effect on sex roles, 312, 346
Parkinson's disease, 547
Pathology: as adaptive failure, 650; in aging models, 40, 41; in sample selection, 51; screening studies, 55; and stress, 270, 693
See also Pharmacology; Psychopathology
Perceived neighborhood concept, 278
Perception: age changes, 27, 207; changes in aneuploids, 213; genetic basis for, 207; testing of, 79, 89, 207-ambiguous figures, 79, 522, 620; forms, 79, 207; illusions, 79, 524-528; Raven progressive matrices, 207
Perception, visual: acuity, 513, 514; aftereffects, 522-524; age changes, 497, 517-529; in behavior, 497; binocular rivalry, 523; convergence, 514, 515; defined, 497; depth, 514-517; environmental engineering, 497; expectation effects, 497, 498, 521, 522; and fatigue, 520; and memory, 520-522; and perceptual closure, 527, 528; and perceptual motor tasks, 517-521; and perceptual regression, 526, 528; practice effects on, 519; scanning process, 514; search time, 519; target identification, 513; target presentation rate, 519; testing methods for, 513-521; verticality judgments, 527
Perceptual tests: Mueller-Lyer Illusion, 524-526; Poggendorf Illusion, 525, 526; Ponzo Illusion, 525, 526; Stroop Color-Word Test, 524, 701; Titchner Circle Illusion, 525, 526
Performance: age changes in, 374, 375; blood pressure and, 453; free fatty acid levels, 374; GSR, 374; and meaningfulness, 374, 375, 379, 428; and memory span, 374, 375; motivation, 374, 375, 675, 676; pulse rate, 453
Personality: and adaptation, 627, 638-640, 642; age changes, 629, 631-633, 635-644; and aging, successful, 642; assessment of, 626-628, 635-644, 709, 710; and behavior, 626, 637, 639-643; change with time, 626, 630, 636-644; cohort differences, 630-

632, 637, 640; coronary-prone behavior, 262, 264- Type A, 264, 265, 269, 270; Type B, 264, 265, 269, 270-; cultural considerations, 626, 627, 638, 643, 644; defined, 626, 632; and developmental psychology, 629, 630, 632, 633; developmental theories, 81, 82, 84; and ego, 627, 631, 632, 635-637, 643; environmental influences, 141; intrapsychic changes, 642, 643; and life events, 634-639; and life periods, 634, 635, 638; measurement of, 89, 198, 636-641, 692-715; psychosexual determinants, 631, 637; research designs, 630, 636, 637; role theorists, 632; as a science, 627-629, 644; self-concept of, 631, 635, 640; stability of, 631, 637, 638, 640-642; stress effects, 262; structure of, 627, 637, 638; studies on, 40, 81, 82-constitutional types, 81; descriptive, need for, 632, 636, 639-641, 644; role theory, 81, 84; stability model, 40; trait-state distinction, 62, 64-; theories of, 627-631, 634, 637, 638, 642-cognitive, 632, 634, 642; psychoanalytic, 631; psychodynamic, 628, 629; social-psychological, 632, 642-; trait approach, 628, 629, 632, 635-637
Personality tests: and age, 15; controlling factors, 636, 638; on twins, 198
See specific names
Personal style: concept of, 277, 672; environmental transactions, 277; life approaches, 680; orientations in, 680
Pharmacology: for aged, 187, 725-732; antianxiety drugs, 729, 731; antidepressants, 728, 731; antimanics, 728, 729; antipsychotics, 727, 728; cognitive-acting, 729-732; dose considerations, 726; hypnotics, 732; metabolic changes, 725, 726; sedatives, 732
Phenylketonuria, 191, 205
Pheromones, 203
Phototaxis, 203
Pick's disease, 212, 665
Pineal gland, 7
Pituitary, 7, 110, 258-260
Placebo effect, 572, 576-in learning, 428
Play, animal studies, 364
Popoyan, studies on, 306
Population: age-sex pyramids, 345; change implications, 344-346; heterogeneity of aged, 347, 348; projections for, 344, 345
See also Demographics
Pregnancy, and immunity, 202
Presbycusis
See Ear
Primary mental abilities, 521, 584, 586, 587, 590, 596, 599, 600, 705
Primates, 195, 200, 206; learning studies, 436, 437, 445; maturational studies, 364; sexual behavior, 364, 372; social behavior, 364
Problem solving: age changes, 607-623, 709; as assessment tool, 606-609, 693, 715; and caution, 615-617; concept formation tasks, 607-613, 618, 620; and discrimination, 609; factors involved in, 606; gambling behavior, 615-617; and information processing rate, 618, 619; meaningfulness, 611, 612, 615-617; memory and, 425, 606, 608, 609, 615, 617-623; perceptual organization, 609-613, 619-622; principle deduction tests, 613-615; -and heuristic strategies, 613-615-; probability judgments, 616, 617; rigidity in, 610, 611, 614, 615, 619, 620, 623; strategy patterns in, 610, 617, 618, 623; testing of, 608, 609, 707; theories of, 606
Progeria, 9, 211